THE HEATH INTRODUCTION TO DRAMA

The Heath
Introduction to
Drama

*with
a Preface
on Drama and
Introductory Notes*

by Jordan Y. Miller
University of Rhode Island

D. C. Heath and Company

Lexington, Massachusetts   Toronto   London

ACKNOWLEDGMENTS

Oedipus Rex: An English Version by Dudley Fitts and Robert Fitzgerald, copyright, 1949, by Harcourt Brace Jovanovich, Inc. and reprinted with their permission. CAUTION: All rights, including professional, amateur, motion picture, recitation, lecturing, public reading, radio broadcasting, and television are strictly reserved. Inquiries on all rights should be addressed to Harcourt Brace Jovanovich, Inc., 757 Third Avenue, New York, N. Y. 10017.

Lysistrata: An English Version by Dudley Fitts, copyright, 1954, by Harcourt Brace Jovanovich, Inc. and reprinted with their permission. CAUTION: All rights, including professional, amateur, motion picture, recitation, lecturing, public reading, radio broadcasting, and television are strictly reserved. Inquiries on all rights should be addressed to Harcourt Brace Jovanovich, Inc., 757 Third Avenue, New York, N. Y. 10017.

The Second Shepherds' Play, a modernized version by John Gassner, copyright © 1935, 1940, 1951 by Simon & Schuster, Inc. Reprinted by permission of the publisher.

Hamlet, by William Shakespeare, edited by Willard Farnham, in "The Pelican Shakespeare," General Editor: Alfred Harbage (rev. ed.; New York and Baltimore: Penguin Books Inc., 1970). Copyright © Penguin Books Inc., 1957, 1970. Reprinted by permission of Penguin Books Inc.

The Misanthrope, by Molière, translated by Richard Wilbur, Copyright © 1954, 1955, by Richard Wilbur. Reprinted by permission of Harcourt Brace Jovanovich, Inc. CAUTION: Professionals and amateurs are hereby warned that this translation, being fully protected under the copyright laws of the United States, the British Empire, including the Dominion of Canada, and all other countries which are signatories to the Universal Copyright Convention, is subject to royalty. All rights, including professional, amateur, motion picture, recitation, lecturing, public reading, radio broadcasting, and television, are strictly reserved. Particular emphasis is laid on the question of readings, permission for which must be secured from the author's agent in writing. Inquiries on professional rights (except for amateur rights) should be addressed to Mr. Gilbert Parker, Curtis Brown, Ltd., 60 East 56th Street, New York, N. Y. 10022. The amateur acting rights are controlled exclusively by the Dramatists Play Service, Inc., 440 Park Avenue South, New York, N. Y. 10016. No amateur performance of the play may be given without obtaining in advance the written permission of the Dramatists Play Service, Inc. and paying the requisite fee.

Miss Julie, by August Strindberg, translated by Elizabeth Sprigge. Reprinted by permission of Collins-Knowlton-Wing. Copyright © 1955 by Elizabeth Sprigge.

Hedda Gabler, by Henrik Ibsen, Copyright © 1962 by Chandler Publishing Co. from *Hedda Gabler* by Henrik Ibsen, translated by Otto Reinert, with permission of Chandler Publishing Co., a Dun-Donnelly Publisher.

The Cherry Orchard, by Anton Chekhov, translated by Stark Young. Copyright, 1939, 1941, 1947 and 1950 by Stark Young. Copyright © 1956 by Stark Young. Reprinted by permission of Leah Salisbury, Inc.

CONTENTS

Foreword   ix

PREFACE—ON DRAMA   1

    Concerning the Drama, the Theatre, and the Play   1
    Concerning the Form, the Type, and the Style   12

THE DRAMAS

    OEDIPUS REX (c. 430 B.C.)—Sophocles   31
    Translated by Dudley Fitts and Robert Fitzgerald

    LYSISTRATA (411 B.C.)—Aristophanes   77
    English version by Dudley Fitts

    THE SECOND SHEPHERDS' PLAY (c. 1420)—Anonymous   125
    A modernized version by John Gassner

    HAMLET (1600)—William Shakespeare   153
    Edited by Willard Farnham

    THE MISANTHROPE (1666)—Molière   275
    English version by Richard Wilbur

    MISS JULIE (1888)—August Strindberg   327
    Translated by Elizabeth Sprigge

HEDDA GABLER (1890)—Henrik Ibsen   361
Translated by Otto Reinert

THE CHERRY ORCHARD (1904)—Anton Chekhov   435
Translated by Stark Young

MAJOR BARBARA (1905)—Bernard Shaw   485

SIX CHARACTERS IN SEARCH OF AN AUTHOR (1921)—
    Luigi Pirandello   567
English version by Edward Storer

DESIRE UNDER THE ELMS (1924)—Eugene O'Neill   617

MOTHER COURAGE (1939)—Bertolt Brecht   671
English version by Eric Bentley

THE GLASS MENAGERIE (1944)—Tennessee Williams   727

DEATH OF A SALESMAN (1949)—Arthur Miller   785

THE DUMB WAITER (1957)—Harold Pinter   871

Select Bibliography   903

Index   905

FOREWORD

The *Preface—On Drama,* the *Introductory Notes,* and the *Select Bibliography* are the work of Jordan Y. Miller, University of Rhode Island; the balance of the volume is our responsibility. We are grateful to many teachers of drama at colleges throughout the country for their suggestions concerning dramas to be included in this collection. The fifteen dramas chosen reflect, to a large degree, those that were most often mentioned, though we also sought to avoid a near duplication of anthologies already available.

"And now to patient judgments we appeal"

H. HOLTON JOHNSON, EDITOR

D. C. Heath and Company

PREFACE—ON DRAMA

PREFACE—ON DRAMA

Concerning the Drama, the Theatre, and the Play

To Perform Is to Entertain

Ever since Og returned to the cave and, for the benefit of Zog and his friends, elaborated on the size of the saber-tooth tiger that got away, the human animal has delighted in putting on a show. While we may not possess Og's complete script, we do know from such surviving evidence as Europe's cave paintings and various artifacts of primitive masks, wigs, and costumes that men and women since prehistory have possessed a keen sense of the beauties and emotional stimulation of man and beast in motion. The essence of theatre has been with us in tribal dance or religious ecstasy from far back in human time, whether we have shaken the rattle and sung the songs ourselves, or have witnessed the proceedings in awed fear or happy delight in the give and take which is the fundamental nature of the art.

Everything that follows in this volume is a direct descendant of the show that Og probably put on for Zog. The fact that, in a comparative instant of history, we have developed the ability to put it all down in the scratchings we call written language and have come to possess thereby what we call a "body of dramatic literature" does

1

not alter the basic primitive formula. Every major culture has, at one time or another, possessed a highly developed tradition of theatre. The survival of this tradition in the form of the written word, in considerable quantity in Western culture, less so in others, has provided unique insights into those cultures available in no other form of art.

The reading of "dramatic literature" is a dismally poor alternative to the theatrical experience itself. There is no way to substitute for the interrelationship that exists between those who *do* and those who *watch*. The only reason Og told Zog about that tiger was to create a reaction in his listener that he hoped would approach his own emotion. The drama, that is, the story, be it literal truth or fantastic embellishment as Og may have related it, simultaneously demands that the interpreter bring it to life as theatre and that the audience react appreciatively. In that manner the full impact of the art has been manifested. But for all practical purposes we have no alternative to reading the written words, strictly second best as that choice may be. Doing so can be made most rewarding by a constant awareness of the Og-Zog relationship. Every written piece in this book was designed first and foremost for *performance*.

Furthermore, every work contained here is a great piece of *entertainment*. Whatever sophisticated social or religious theme, whatever erudite subject, propagandistic motive, or moral didacticism that may be apparent in any single play does not alter the fact that to witness a theatrical performance in a Greek amphitheatre holding 15,000 spectators or in a tiny converted night club with room for fewer than 200 is to be entertained. This does not imply mere passing amusement, an aspect of theatre valid enough in its own right. It does, however, imply that we who watch expect to experience some form of emotional pleasure. We can be excited, mystified, intrigued, challenged, frightened, or horrified, and we can be driven to tears or laughter, concurrently, consecutively, or entirely independently, but one thing is sure: we will have enjoyed the experience that has been offered to us, for we have, in short, been entertained.

How It Is Said

The drama, the theatre, and the play are so closely related in their broad connotations as to be, on occasion, interchangeable. For our purposes here, however, they will be separately identified in order to establish a sharper distinction among their meanings. Each element demands a different appreciation, and each performs a distinct function. We shall restrict the term *drama* to the written form, the creation of the *dramatist*,[1] who starts on square one with a clean sheet of paper and pen or typewriter at the ready. But unlike the creative artistry of other writers, it does not end on the paper. Once the pages are filled, the novelist, the poet, or the essayist has, to all intents and purposes, concluded his effort. The dramatist, on the other hand, has just begun his ordeal. Before it's all over there looms ahead the intervention of all elements of *theatre* and the transformation of the entire effort into the production of the *play*. The trip will not be smooth.

Regardless of the eventual metamorphosis in the theatre, what appears in performance is essentially the artistic creation of the dramatist, who comes up with the *idea* in the first place. The source of the idea may be religion and its faith and morals, whence all Western drama originated, or it may be a sociological problem, a philosophical question, a political viewpoint, or, indeed, almost anything that strikes the artist's fancy. Closely related to idea is *theme*, the fabric that holds the idea together. Idea and theme can sometimes be very close to the same thing, but generally speaking the development of an idea is planned along specific thematic lines such as the family, the state, and various human relationships, or the more abstract concepts of cowardice and heroism, good and evil, right and wrong.

The *type* of the drama remains the prerogative of the dramatist, and this choice now begins to place him in a somewhat different creative area from other writers. For the novelist or short story writer there are choices as well, whether to be serious or comic, to create pure fiction, re-create history, and so on. The poet, too, chooses whether to write a lyric, a sonnet, a narrative epic, or something in between. But the dramatist is creating for that special medium, the theatre, and while he is not necessarily prevented from developing along any lines he may wish, he is restrained by certain limitations of the medium and its long traditions which, as we shall see, convey specialized artistic meaning to such terms as tragedy or comedy and which, of course, assume a number of physical restrictions. Then, when the dramatist makes his choice of *style*, the manner in which his creation is to be staged, he finds himself with far more problems than his other literary colleagues. While they, of course, may ma-

---

[1] If you prefer the term *playwright*—maker of plays—well and good, although we're going to regard the *play* as the entire finished product put on before an audience.

nipulate their language to suggest anything from literal transcription of contemporary speech to the most imaginative stream-of-consciousness, or may choose to describe the most vivid photographic detail or expand into the realms of utter fantasy, the dramatist must conceive of his style far beyond the printed page and into the live and visible arena of the stage where not only what is said but how it is delivered to and visualized by the audience in both sight and sound become primary considerations. As in the choice of *type*, so in the choice of *style* the dramatist must face the realities of his medium and be prepared to function within the strict limitations it presents.

What Is to Be Said

As Aristotle pointed out some 2300 years ago in writing that first great piece of dramatic criticism, *The Poetics*, in the fourth century B.C., the most important element of tragedy (to him all serious drama was tragedy) is the *fable*, or more colloquially, the *story*. Some people call it plot, but whatever you want to call it there can be little argument with Aristotle that what goes on and the way it happens is the single most important consideration for the dramatist in putting across his idea and his theme. This fable, says Aristotle, has to have a beginning, a middle, and an end. Ridiculously self-evident as this statement may seem, Aristotle is emphasizing a basic dramatic tenet which insists that the dramatist begin his creation at a clearly defined point, proceed in a logical fashion to develop it, and arrive at a conclusion which follows equally logically upon what has happened. The many convolutions into which a novelist may enter in the course of telling his tale in whatever length he pleases are not the privilege of the dramatist, upon whom is imposed an absolute limit that other literary artists never have to worry about: *time*.

The conventional Western dramatist, following the traditions that have existed since the ancient Greeks, must hold the telling of his story to the constraints of a very few hours of time upon the stage. Further, within that time, he must do it all at once. Those who watch cannot put his story down, pick it up tomorrow, and go back to Chapter One to remind themselves of what has happened. Moreover, there is a limit to the physical endurance of the audience who must sit or stand, or even crouch, within that entire length of time. The dramatist places heavy demands of concentration upon his audience, but it, in turn, puts strict demands on him. If he must repeat too much to make a point, he will quickly bore and lose the audience. If he leaps too many gaps and assumes an ability to comprehend beyond normal capacity, he will leave his audience muddled, confused, and disappointed. Within the strict confines of time the dramatist must arrive at what he has to say in a linear progression that keeps his audience constantly with him, and that's all that Aristotle was really saying.

Who Says It

The consideration which comes next, regarded as second in importance by Aristotle as well, is *character*. It is interesting that a more literal translation of the word is *indicant*—the one who indicates what is going on. Who relates the story? Who goes through the action? The limitations placed upon the dramatist continue to be unique in literature, for he must carefully consider not only the restrictions of physical space in which his characters move but also that ever-present space: time. The dramatist must be careful not to clutter the stage with crowds and complicated action which can become an impossible logistics problem. The alarums and excursions of Shakespeare's battle scenes, properly handled, are far more effective with a handful of participants than any try at verisimilitude could ever be. But probably more important to the dramatist is how many principal characters, the ones on whom the audience's interest centers, can be accommodated within the time allotted for proper identification and establishment of relationships.

Unlike the novelist, who can take any amount of time to inform his solitary reader about who is who (plus that constant advantage of checking Chapter One), the dramatist must do everything relatively quickly, and he must do it clearly. The audience left at final curtain trying to figure out who all those people were and what they were doing will depart unsatisfied, and the play will fail. Everyone knows from reading Shakespeare how closely one must keep track of the many dukes, lords, and ladies who come and go with such rapidity, but one also notices that it doesn't take Shakespeare long to make clear who's getting the focus of attention. The dramatist does have one distinct advantage over the novelist, for he has the privilege of instant visibility. Once a character has made his entrance and established who or what he is, he is going to be recognized promptly the next time around.

Because of the visual element and the fact that his story is being told by live bodies, moving and speaking, the dramatist must maintain a constant awareness of the physical appearance and capabilities of his characters. How will they look together? What variations are desirable and possible? Is there need for some kind of characteristic that costume or makeup can't convey, such as a dwarf or a very young child? Will the character need to fly, like Peter Pan? Will there perhaps be an animal, like Harvey, the giant rabbit, who *never* appears,[2] or like the birds in Aristophanes' ancient Greek comedy of that name, who do? Within the closely limited time will the characters age? or get younger? or become something else, in the frog-into-prince or Beauty-and-the-Beast tradition? Will the audience accept it, or be turned off? The novelist can do anything he wants in this regard, but the dramatist must plan with extreme care what every single character, living and breathing on a stage, will be, whether human, divine, supernatural, or four-legged.

The Method of Saying It

Everything now comes down to the end-all and be-all of what we are pursuing in the study of dramatic literature, the *dialogue*. Aristotle says that what is said (*thought*) and how it is said (*diction*) are next in importance after character, and they obviously combine in what we call dialogue. Without it, we would have nothing, and dramatic literature would not exist.

Dialogue isn't, literally, everything, for there are exceedingly fine plays in our literature in which the importance of theme, plot, or character transcend pedestrian writing. The total artistic creation, however, does rely ultimately on the strength of the dialogue which, even when less than grand, must carry everything along. The dramatist who creates it must have that innate, undefinable consciousness of what will work on stage; he must have a *sense of thetre* or he will be in trouble. This sense is virtually impossible to define, and many a writer of successful fiction has found he does not have it. Such was the case of the American writer, Henry James, one of the great novelists of all time, who was fascinated by the theatre and tried play after play, only to fail so badly as to be hooted off the stage. He did not realize that he possessed no sense of theatre in relating his story through dialogue alone. Instead of holding his audience, as he held his readers, he succeeded only in being boring, turgid, and deadly dull. Ironically, many of the stories he wrote, placed in the hands of good dramatists, became critical successes and popular theatre pieces.

---

[2] In the very early tryout days of Mary Chase's phenomenally successful farce in 1944 Harvey, who gave the play its title, was fully visible, but an actor in a six-foot rabbit suit could not make the fantasy work and the idea was dropped.

The dramatist must be aware of what he is doing and how he is doing it through the single medium of making his characters speak all the time. From opening curtain to final exit everything that goes on must be revealed through what people say to each other. During some periods of theatre history audiences relied on dialogue to convey almost everything, including the scenery and the time of day, as when Horatio in the opening of *Hamlet* tells the spectators, standing in broad daylight, that dawn is breaking. But more importantly, dialogue exists as the only means by which characters may develop and establish relationships. In all manner of speeches from long poetic soliloquies to contemporary gutter language, the only way we can learn what characters think of themselves and each other is the way they talk.

Dialogue presents a paradox in the theatre. Because it keeps up incessantly throughout the drama, it becomes essentially unreal. On the other hand, even in blank verse or heroic couplets, the dialogue must still *appear* real. The fact that nobody really talks that way is totally irrelevant. It must *seem* that they talk that way, no matter how they say it. The quality of the dialogue, the words that the dramatist puts on paper for his characters to say and for us to read, is what makes the difference between the merely *literate* drama and true *dramatic literature*. All drama is, of course, literate, but it is the exceptional drama that survives as great literature. The Greeks and the Elizabethans wrote mostly in verse, and today we write almost entirely in prose (which at times can be highly poetic), but however it is written, effective dialogue must have a sense of the rhythms and patterns of speech that are appropriate to the speaker and the particular dramatic situation in which he is placed. Characters in the great dramas do not just talk; they speak a highly literate dramatic dialogue. It holds the audience, it tells the story, it reveals the character, and it exposes the theme and idea. The quality of what everybody says to everybody else is what finally comes through as the essence of great literature.

Where It Is Said

Unless, in the manner of Browning or Shelley or one or two others, the dramatist wants to end it all here and publish a "closet" drama, meant only to be read, there is still a long road before him. The drama, as written, contains within it the dramatic situations conceived by the dramatist, including everything we've talked about so far, but however brilliant the concept it will go nowhere until it is put in motion. What happens from here on out is *theatre,* the visual and the audible within the three-dimension physical structure that holds the performance. Now the time arrives when the dramatist needs every bit of faith in himself, because he will witness the awful truth of what takes place when his vision comes to life. Although it may please and delight, the far greater chance is for shock and dismay, and there is probably no dramatist who ever lived who at one time or another has not suffered the horrifying trauma of one who witnesses the sacrificial slaughter of a loved one. There were, at one time, those who wrote, produced, and acted, and even owned the theatre together with the company that played in it, so they could hold the drama they created reasonably close to their initial concepts. In the contemporary theatre this kind of impresario has all but disappeared, and a great army of individuals charged with putting on the production subject the dramatist's work to their wills and their skills in order to place it in front of the audience for which it was originally designed.

We are now in the realm of *spectacle,* the theatrical consideration which Aristotle places far down the list, for he was correctly aware, even in his time, that the dramatist who focussed primarily on the showy aspects was bound to write inferior pieces. Moreover, the decor, including setting and costumes, the whole picture which we lump together with lighting under the term *mise-en-scène,* is meant not to dominate the drama but to serve it.

The prime mover among the many who will eventually place their stamp upon the drama in the playhouse, producing that "spectacle," is the *director.* He alone has the final say on what appears. Unheard of until this century, the director has achieved such prominence in the modern theatre that he may receive billing and pay equal to, and perhaps even above, the dramatist or the star. The final production is his. He may succeed in driving the audience out of the theatre, the play out the window, and the dramatist off the roof by the time it is all over, but what he says goes. Under his guidance all others function. In order to provide the appropriate area in which the characters move, he approves the setting, conceived by the scene designer, who can be a highly accomplished professional artist in his own right, and built by the stage technician and his crew. So that everybody is fully visible (or invisible, if so demanded), the director must approve the lighting, designed and supervised by another skilled artist whose conceptions are carried out by the electrician and *his* crew. Costumes, created by yet another artist (who can be and frequently is the scene designer as well), and constructed by still another crew, must also receive the director's approval. And so with sound or any other special effects. Everybody and everything must function flawlessly together, all under the eye and ear of the director.

In addition to all those aspects of the spectacle, there happens to be a very important element that remains the director's primary responsibility and *raison d'être*. He must choose the actors, and he must move them around the stage to project as best he can everything that the dramatist has to say. If the writer is living and available, the director may consult him or even have him present from day one to opening night. More than one dramatist has been forced to watch the characters he created, interpreted by the actors chosen by and under the guidance of the director, become something quite apart from his first conception. Lighting, setting, sound, even costumes, are one thing, but the living and thinking actors, under a living and thinking director, observed by the living and thinking dramatist who thought everything up can be quite another. If the writer witnesses precisely what he had in mind, he's lucky. If he runs screaming into the street, denying all, he isn't. It's all a part of the game of theatre, and the dramatist knows, whatever the pleasures and pains, that he must play it if he is to survive at all.

Who Hears It Said

Unlike all other art forms, the drama demands a very special participant for its full effect and enjoyment: the *audience*. It is the group of people out front which finally turns everything that has been accomplished up to now into the mutual experience of the *play*. No artist outside the theatre is concerned with pleasing numbers of people simultaneously. Outside of the theatre the admiration of a work of art is a very personal thing, experienced on a one-to-one basis. The painter, the composer, or almost any artist you can name, other than the dramatist, conceives of his audience, broad-based and numerous as he may hope for, as encountering and reacting to his work as a single individual, unrelated to the crowd around him. To enjoy a great symphony or to admire the beauties of the graceful intricacies of ballet does not depend upon whether or not others are watching at the same time. In no other art form is there anything comparable to the instantaneous and continuing action and reaction between the performers and the spectators who form a unit, a living entity, that reacts entirely independently from the separate psyches which make up the individual human components. The sense of mass participation in spectator sports, where the individual identity becomes melded into and altered by the "mob" psychology, is well known, but in art only the theatre expects and receives that same participation.

The psychology of the theatre, functioning on this basis of simultaneous mass experience, does not differentiate among the sizes of the audiences so much as it does the capacity of the area that holds them. The proper response comes best when the house, however large or small, is full, or at least seems to be. The spark that flies all the way between stage and gallery will ignite effectively only if everyone's there. The play, to work, needs audience response. If there's nobody there, the actors know it; the spark doesn't fly back, and the house turns into an echo chamber. Besides, if you're sitting out there alone, with rows of empty seats between you and the rest of the crowd, it's not easy to catch the spark and throw it back.

The poet Samuel Taylor Coleridge was a drama and theatre critic who explained in very simple terms what actually happens in the theatre. Watching a play, he said, involves a tacit agreement between actors and audience to enter into a *willing suspension of disbelief*. It works in both directions. On the part of the actor it involves a sincere belief in the role, a belief that must be conveyed to the audience. Mary Smith believes in Hedda, but she knows, all the same, that she herself is *not* Hedda. But she does not disbelieve that she is Hedda, either, knowing that the belief in the role is a vital part of the illusion that she, Mary Smith, really is Hedda after all. The audience, while it must believe in what is going on in front of it, knows full well, on the other hand, that Hedda is, in reality, merely Mary Smith. Still, it puts that reality aside and *refuses to disbelieve* that it is watching Hedda and not Mary Smith. The audience knows that Mary Smith will get up and walk away after the curtain comes down; it also knows that Hedda won't. In Coleridge's terms one neither denies what is happening nor truly believes what is happening. One remains suspended, accepting as truth neither illusion nor reality. In the enjoyment of the performance, it's just a matter of agreeing not *not* to believe.

In order for the suspension of disbelief to function properly, a balance must exist between performer and spectator in a kind of two-way stretch. Pulling one way is *empathy;* pulling the other is the maintenance of *aesthetic distance.*

Empathy means emotional identification, a "going out to" the characters by the audience. Although none of us will have met a fraction of the problems of an Oedipus or a Hamlet, we know that each is suffering physical and emotional pain in the same manner as all humankind. Thus we identify as fellow human beings, regardless of the circumstances, so long as our sympathies and understanding, our ultimate belief in the characters and the incidents portrayed, are kept within reasonable bounds. Failure of empathy can be the fault of the dramatist, whose characters appear too gross, too repulsive, extravagant, or ridiculous. It can be the fault of the director, whose control over what is said and done may be so unimaginative, exaggerated, or dull that the audience refuses to accept the theatrical validity of what it sees. Or it can be the fault of the actors who just don't "come across" and who fail to convince. The audience must constantly believe in what it sees. The whole thing must be convincingly plausible, even if it's set on Mars. The audience, in short, must be kept interested and sympathetic.

Against this force is the equal and opposite reaction, *aesthetic distance*. While moving constantly toward the stage in emotional, that is, empathic belief, the audience must simultaneously pull back in the realization that what it witnesses is art, not life. However vivid the stage picture, the audience must never lose that sense of remaining outside, at a distance. Excessive violence, for instance, can alter the balance very quickly. If the audience feels that the actor— not the character, but the actor—is really suffering so that the difference between illusion and reality is indistinguishable, aesthetic distance can be lost. If the situation on stage is unclear and the audience cannot distinguish between a planned event, something written into the play, or an accidental event, resulting, say, from an actor's lapsed memory, empathy and aesthetic distance both suffer. Children and animals are notorious destroyers of the empathy-aesthetic distance balance. Will they behave? Does the child know its lines? Or, on the other side: How well-trained they are! How brilliantly they perform! The animal is judged against its human counterpart, and the child against the adult. The illusion, laboriously established, can easily disintegrate.

It's relatively easy to put on a show. It's not all that difficult to mount a good play, but it's very nearly impossible to write, stage, and perform a piece of dramatic and theatrical art that will survive as genuinely great literature. The hurdles are nigh insurmountable, but when they are successfully leaped, there emerges an *Oedipus Rex* or a *Hamlet*. There's an irony behind many of the greatest works of dramatic art. We read them and we go to see them performed, and we praise them for their durability, their insights, their poetry, their stories, their universality. It's hard, sometimes, to remember how many were originally written and performed only for the moment, with survival in an enduring body of dramatic literature very likely never considered. The ancient Greeks staged their plays as part of a religious festival and, once performed, the dramas were normally never revived. Shakespeare was in the business for the money, and he had to keep hopping to help provide his acting company with good playable scripts. If somebody had not safely stored that manuscript of Sophocles in some ancient vault, we might never have known of Oedipus. If Ben Jonson, seeing the First Folio through the press, had not been determined to keep the memory of his friend Shakespeare alive, we would have missed about half of that marvelous collection. Instantaneous, ephemeral, existing only for the time it takes to watch, a hybrid of all the arts, a bastard art claimed as nobody's child but everybody's responsibility, the greatest *drama* survives through its language on a printed page, but it must not be permanently entombed there. Somewhat like the butterfly, encased within its cocoon, the drama is ready for the performer's art, for the *theatre,* emerging from its chrysalis to display its fragile beauty in that single exciting moment of becoming a *play,* before it once more disappears.

Concerning the Form, the Type, and the Style

Literature other than that created for the stage has no particular bounds imposed upon it with regard to the way it is put together or the way it treats its subject matter. The dramatist, however, even beyond the matters of time and space, has further restrictions imposed upon him to a far greater degree than other writers. Dramatic art by no means lays exclusive claim to what we are going to discuss in the next several pages, but if one hears of a piece of literature that is an "expressionistic comedy," a "naturalistic tragedy," or a "romantic melodrama" it is almost certain that reference is being made only to a play. Furthermore, the drama is constructed and shaped within fairly close limits controlled by factors relating almost wholly to drama and theatre alone.

The Way It's Put Together

If the fable, or the story, is the soul of drama as Aristotle maintains, the heart is the *agon,* or *argument.* Aristotle defines a tragedy as the imitation of an action, and he meant just that—action. A tragedy was not mere narration, which he assigned to the epic poem. Further, recognizing the element of time, he set forth a number of conditions that should be met in the development of that action as it involved the incidents and the character relationships. To sum it up, though he may not have said it in precisely these words, it is the *conflict* surrounding the argument which becomes the very pulse of drama. The two sides of the conflict, the pros and cons of the agon, center around the *protagonistic* forces and the *antagonistic* forces. The *protagonist* may be one person or many, and the *antagonist* may be a person, a group, a thing, or a force—supernatural, natural, or divine.

The manner by which the argument is developed becomes the structure or the *form* of the play, involving how the beginning, middle, and end of which Aristotle speaks are put together. First of all there has to be a starting point, known as the *point of attack,* at which moment the dramatist leads his audience into the picture. He can start at the beginning of things, in an *accretive plot,* with the essentials cumulatively revealed as they actually occur, thus permitting both the audience and the characters to discover what's going on at the same time. This is the method Shakespeare uses in *Hamlet.* Or he can start at the middle of things, or even very near the end, in a *climactic plot,* with the forward progress of the story gradually revealing the essentials that have already transpired. This is the method Sophocles uses in *Oedipus.*

No matter where the point of attack takes place, the first thing the dramatist has to do is to establish what is going on and who is involved, which he does through the technique of *exposition,* the exposing of the facts. This can involve a variety of approaches, from the maid and visitor routine of characters telling each other, and thus telling the audience, what the basic situation is, such as Ibsen uses in *Hedda Gabler,* to the direct and immediate involvement in fast developing action that Shakespeare employs in the opening of *Hamlet.* Exposition must be revealed clearly and slowly enough for the audience to retain the necessary information in order to relate it to subsequent scenes, and dramatic exposition can continue well into the play, through several scenes, as the past is revealed, the present explained, and characters introduced and assimilated. Then, once everything is sufficiently established, the conflict heads toward its climax and eventual resolution, and the dramatist cannot return to any further exposition without confusing the audience and muddying up what he has already said.

Almost at once, having established where things stand, the dramatist proceeds with the *complications* that provide the conflict with its depth and breadth. These proceed through the *rising action,* a literal building of interest through suspense, emotional reaction, deepening mystery, and so on. It is the time for plottings and counterplottings, intrigues and conspiracies, accumulation of incidents and development of character. Revelations from the past, forebodings and foreshadowings of the future begin carrying the conflict toward the play's high point, its *climax.* Here everything is pulled together. The protagonist and antagonist have established their sides of the agon and have, in one way or another, met head on. This is the point toward which everything has aimed, and the confrontation of protagonist and antagonist results in a climactic showdown, serious or comic, which is termed the *obligatory scene,* the one that everybody knows must happen. It is, in other words, a turning point, after which nothing new can be added. Any high point in the story hereafter becomes *anticlimactic,* and is in serious danger of losing any dramatic effect it may have. There may be a lot of the play left, or it may all terminate very quickly, but once reached, the climax is a point of no return. It can be but a moment, as when Oedipus finally learns the truth of who and what he is, very late in the play, or it can be a series of events, as in *Hamlet,* somewhat past the middle, from the mousetrap play scene to the killing of Polonius.

Following the climax everything heads downward in *falling action,* the period when the action unravels. Now we can see how it all comes out, for there is no more building toward a suspenseful moment in the manner of the rising action. Things fall into place, and the play heads toward the conclusion, or *denouement,* or, as the Greeks put it, particularly as it pertains to tragedy, the *catastrophe.* Then it's all over, the bodies are removed, the lovers embrace, and everybody goes home.

A great number of plays follow the exposition-to-denouement routine in almost perfect balance, capable of being graphically illustrated, scene by scene, act by act, in a uniformly parabolic curve. Such plays have been given the label "well-made," and because the structure rather than the theme or idea or character became the most important aspect, emphasizing mass popular entertainment rather than good dramatic literature, the term "well-made" has long been one of critical disfavor. But all great plays are essentially "well-made," as you will discover in the brilliant structure of plays as diverse as *Oedipus, Hamlet* or *Hedda Gabler.* It is what the dramatist does with his story, how he develops the conflict of that fable, how well defined his protagonist and antagonist, that make the real difference. That parabola may be perfectly formed or completely erratic in its rise and fall. That is not what really matters. Mix everything up, change things around, invent new ways of displaying them, be as "well-made" or experimental as you please, but by the time the last curtain comes down, the dramatist must have established his conflict, developed both sides of his argument, and reached a reasonable conclusion—all involving the elements we have discussed here, for the basic structure, the form of the play, whatever else, remains a whole made out of these very fundamental parts.

What Kind of Play It Is

Polonius gives Hamlet a pretty good catalogue of the variety of entertainment provided by the strolling players who happen by Elsinore:

> The best actors in the world, either for tragedy, comedy, history, pastoral, pastoral-comical, historical-pastoral, tragical-historical, tragical-comical-historical-pastoral, scene individable, or poem unlimited. Seneca cannot be too heavy, nor Plautus too light. For the law of writ and the liberty, these are the only men.

Apparently the performers of that day could, upon occasion, do just about everything.

What Polonius was describing, of course, was a variety of dramatic *types*, or individual kinds of plays. Whether or not all the multiple combinations he cites would be recognizable definitions today remains a question, but Polonius touched upon the full spectrum of his own time from the most serious classical to the lightest contemporary approach. He well knew that there could be extensive intermingling of the serious and comic and he recognized the difficulty of pigeonholing any single play, but he was equally aware that what he said conveyed meaning to the Prince in terms of the dramatic types that lay within the players' repertoire.

Tragedy and *comedy* were common terms in fifth-century Greece, as we know from Aristotle. They remain today as the most all-inclusive identifications of type, though there are important variations. The Elizabethans, as Polonius states, were familiar with *historical* plays as in the Richard and Henry sequences of Shakespeare, but the term "tragedy" was used almost universally to mean a serious treatment of the subject. Throughout the Renaissance the *pastoral* was a major form, dealing, as in Shakespeare's *As You Like It* with shepherds, shepherdesses, and the pure country life. But pastorals are essentially comedies and, as a distinct type, have not survived.

On the serious side in today's definitions of type are the three broadly general terms of *tragedy, melodrama,* and *drama,* sometimes called a *"straight play,"* or, in more precise critical terms, the *"middle genre"* or *drame.* On the lighter side are *comedy* and *farce.* Recognizing, like Polonius, that nothing falls easily into one place, we can still fairly easily put the bulk of dramatic art into one of these five broad definitions.[3]

Dramatic tragedy is not what nearly everybody will say it is—a sad play with an unhappy ending. The root of tragedy has nothing at all to do with death or sadness, for it comes down to us from the Greek *tragos,* or goat, plus *aeidein,* to sing, or, simply put, "song of the goat." The goat was sacred to Dionysus, god of wine and fertility in whose name were held the early festivals of song and dance out of which the drama grew. The whole concept of tragedy as we shall now define it is a product of Greek civilization and remains virtually unknown outside the West, for it is founded upon a very special view which the Greeks held concerning mankind and its relationship to the gods. The Greek gods were not animals or freakish creatures. They were human beings in perfect form, immortal to be sure, but subject to every passion of love, hate, jealousy, rage, and sensual delight endured by men and women on earth. The Greeks admired the human body, male and female, and in the great classic age which concerns us here painted and sculpted it undraped, to be revealed, not hidden. Not only did they marvel at its physical beauty, but at the accomplishments it could achieve. There was, in fact, such admiration for the human creature that the Greeks created their gods in the image of themselves, beautiful, handsome, radiant, powerful. Developing naturally from this concept was the realization that Zeus, the king of gods, could be stricken with helpless infatuation for a nubile earthling, and that Hera, his wife, the goddess queen, could be violently jealous. The gods did not necessarily act with common sense and good judgment, any more than their human counterparts, but when they did act, it was along human lines which could be readily understood if not entirely appreciated by ordinary mortals. And the gods were not completely independent, for they were subject to the final act of the Fates, the three sisters who spun out the thread of life, drew it to its full length, and cut it, an event the gods could not alter.

Bearing this in mind, we can fairly easily see how the idea of tragedy developed. It is an assertion of the fundamental greatness of man. It demonstrates the individual's ability to rise to heights of human dignity in the face of an antagonistic force which he himself knows will finally destroy him. The protagonist of the tragedy may commit the most heinous deeds, knowingly or unknowingly, but because the gods are as they are, capable of carrying grudges and

---

[3] The *tragi-comedy,* a serious play approaching tragedy but with a "happy" ending, is sometimes identified as a sixth type.

taking offense in the same manner as their mortal counterparts, he may suffer from outrageous curses upon himself and his family unto several generations. The point of tragedy is that the protagonist, male or female, when faced with the inevitability of the fact that the forces arrayed against him are to cause his literal or figurative death, can rise to the occasion and assert his magnificence as a human being, defying those forces and, in the end, bringing them to bay or destroying them with himself. For the tragic protagonist there is no possibility of escape. He is doomed, and we watch in awe as, finally, in full recognition of his inevitable fate, he proceeds toward that doom. Thereafter comes a balance of forces, a tranquility, a laying to rest, and an absolute finality. Nothing comes afterwards. The end is complete. What the protagonist has done in the process of the struggle and in facing the actual or symbolic death is what counts. Without hope of rescue or relief, absolutely alone against the forces that he knows will destroy him, the tragic protagonist, whatever foul deeds he may have committed or whatever human foolishness he may have displayed, rises to the ultimate in strength, courage, and defiance, demonstrating the potential godlike quality that lies within mankind, but which only legendary figures in tragedy can ever approach.

Tragedy is not saddening and depressing in the ordinary sense of a fatal accident or some destructive human or natural catastrophe. Tragedy is positive and optimistic in its view of the heights the human being can reach. There is considerable distinction, as well, between the tragic protagonist and the martyr. The martyr suffers and dies for a particular cause, but the death of a martyr, unlike that of the tragic protagonist, implies that something comes after, making the suffering and death worth the pain. Those who survive are expected to carry on in the name of whatever cause may have driven the martyr to his fate. Things begin, they do not end, as in tragedy, with the death of the central figure. A martyr, asserting his cause, may consciously seek death. The tragic protagonist, on the contrary, has every reason to live, and he makes a heroic struggle to survive in the face of the overwhelming odds against him. So long as he survives, there is no tragedy. Only in death does the tragic grandeur emerge. The death of the tragic protagonist is, however, a kind of passion, not necessarily religious, for that would enter into the area of martyrdom, but there is a certain kinship in the great sacrifice involved. At the moment of his destruction the tragic protagonist has proven the best there is in mankind, far beyond what's in most of us, but still very very human, and his death is a profound loss to humanity. If the protagonist could accomplish that much in death, what might he have accomplished in life? But that's the irony of tragedy. Proof of human greatness, in the tragic sense, comes only in death, and mankind has sacrificed something he can ill afford to lose. A genuine sacrifice is the offering of a highly valued, even priceless, possession for the benefit of the gods and the demonstration of one's faith. In the case of tragedy, however, this sacrifice is not offered in the usual sense. The protagonist, displaying his greatness, actually approaches the god-like, and his sacrifice is a kind of reverse act, an offering not for the benefit of the gods but for the benefit of mankind—a proof of ultimate human worthiness.

Such tears as may be shed at the final catastrophe are not tears of sadness, but of compassion. There can be profound emotional involvement, but there remains the fundamental optimism that must be present at the end of the best of tragedy. We have witnessed how near the gods a man can be. Aristotle gets involved in this whole matter of emotion when he speaks briefly of the *catharsis,* or *purgation* as sometimes translated, and the arousal in the audience of *pity* and *terror,* or *fear.* What he seems to be saying is that when one views a tragedy he is moved by a compassionate pity toward the protagonist for what he endures, and it is not a sentimental pity, nor merely a "pitiful" reaction. Similarly, one experiences an emotional reaction akin to terror from a realization of the magnitude of the forces and their power in bringing down the struggling protagonist. By the end, when tranquility has been restored, the audience has gone through a kind of cleansing, a kind of spiritual purgation, in the realization of how great the human creature can be upon occasion.

What kind of person is the "ideal" tragic protagonist? Aristotle goes into some detail, and his general description applies amazingly well even now. Certainly the protagonist is human and cannot be a god. He must also be of a certain noble stature. Originally this meant royalty or similar "nobility," whose deaths could make empires tremble and kingdoms crumble. The ordinary man in the street held virtually no interest. Today, of course, if we are to assert that tragedy can exist there must still be contained within the protagonist that element of human greatness involving stature beyond the ordinary. The tragic protagonist may, in today's drama, be a little man, but he is not in any sense a little person.

The tragic protagonist cannot be evil or villainous by nature, a person whose death the audience welcomes as justified. Neither can the protagonist be all good, for then his death becomes truly pitiable and shocking, displeasing to those who watch. What makes him consistently and recognizably human is the fact that he suffers, as Hamlet says, from "some vicious mole of nature" in him which can and will destroy. In other words, for all his potential, the protagonist must have within him the *tragic flaw,* the making of his own destruction. To the Greeks *hubris,* or excessive pride, more often than not could drive the tragic protagonist to his fate. But whether you call it pride, arrogance, vanity, or whatever, within the human psyche must rest the seeds of doom. In the end, the protagonist must finally recognize what he is and what is happening. He neither cringes nor flees. He turns and shouts his defiance, much as Macbeth in his final moments, who welcomes his advancing adversary with, "Lay on, Macduff/ And damn'd be him that first cries, 'Hold, enough!' "

Throughout tragedy runs the constant thread of *irony.* The variations are almost endless, but the force of tragic irony contributes substantially to the final impact of the tragic experience. Irony can involve the audience, aware of what is going to happen, or aware of why it is happening from a knowledge of the past, while the protagonist remains in ignorance. It can involve the twists and turns of fate when the harder the protagonist seeks to avoid the catastrophe, the faster it arrives. It can involve human procrastination or unthinking impulsiveness, as in the refusal of Hamlet to kill the king when he has the chance, or in his killing Polonius whom he takes to be the king while knowing full well it cannot possibly be the king.

The dramatist who thinks he has created tragedy, but ends up with merely a "sad" play with an "unhappy" ending, is not writing tragedy at all. If the catastrophe brings only sorrow, lacking awe; if it brings pathos instead of majesty, depression instead of elevation; or if the dramatist moralizes upon the fate of his protagonist and speaks of "justice," he is not entertaining the tragic view.

Melodrama, like tragedy, has come to mean something quite different from its original semantic roots. A combination of *melo,* music, plus *drama,* it means "a play with music." The term originated some time during the eighteenth century when the popular theatre of the day, offering entertainment outside the limited number of duly licensed theatres in London or the aristocratic, more "classical" theatres in Paris, made extensive use of background and incidental music. The subject matter of these theatrical diversions was full of blood and thunder with lots of broad and exciting action. By the end of the eighteenth century, when melodrama as a theatrical type emerged both in England and France, a great many of these characteristics were inherited, together with the most significant tradition of innocent maidens persecuted by villains and saved by handsome heroes.

The difference between a tragedy which, like *Oedipus* or *Hamlet,* may rely upon the sensational events and excitement of what we now call melodrama, and a true melodrama lies in the degree of emphasis. Action in a tragedy is an integral part of the progression toward a final catastrophe, while melodrama creates action for its own sake. Characters in tragedy are well developed, more "rounded out"; those in melodrama are flat and instantly recognizable so that the action and the fast developing plot can move along unencumbered. The end of a tragedy is unrelated to justice and retribution as such; melodrama punishes the bad and rewards the good. Melodrama anticipates that things will all work out in the end, thus creating hope. Tragedy, as we know, provides its central figure with no hope and no way out.

The non-tragic, non-melodramatic, non-comic play known as the *middle genre*, the *"straight" drama*, or the *drame*, is a product of literary realism. It achieves its hold on its audience by means of its treatment of men and women who may be king or commoner, rich or poor, in terms of their essential everyday humanity, encountering neither Hamlet's slings and arrows of outrageous fortune nor the arbitrary sensations of a contrived melodrama, but facing the challenges of daily existence in the milieu of a familiar and easily recognizable society, reasonably contemporary to that in which the audience itself exists. It avoids the extravagances of tragedy or melodrama at either end, and can present its protagonist as one who may, upon occasion, refuse to shout and who may, if he feels like it, run, hide, whimper, or beg. Such characters and the action that they encounter are no less attractive as dramatic figures than their tragic or melodramatic counterparts. In fact, the logic and the rationale of what they are and what they experience may win audiences far more easily and send them home far more satisfied, for they will have seen before them individuals far closer to what they are themselves.

Aristotle had little to say about *comedy*, at least in *The Poetics*, and if he said much at all it has been lost. His main observation holds true, for he said that tragedy shows men as greater than they are, while comedy shows them as less than they are. One thing is certain, Aristotle or not: comedy keeps reminding us how unlike the gods we are, all of our noblest urges notwithstanding.

The popular idea is that comedy is "funny," and that it has a "happy ending." In general, yes. But a comedy can have death and suffering of all kinds. The main thing that distinguishes it from serious drama is the *detached point of view*. Any comic situation carried through to its logical conclusion would probably end in disaster, but comedy forces us to keep our distance, compelling us to recognize that the pain is not damaging nor the disaster permanent. Comedy does not let those who watch become emotionally involved. The moment that we do so, the comedy has ended.

Comedy continually emphasizes the inferior, second-rate nature of most of us, pulling us down from the heights with a reminder of our vulnerability and the foolishness of our posturing. It does this by tripping us up with the sudden reversal, the unexpected twist, the ludicrous juxtaposition and gross exaggeration. Comedy makes us fall flat on our face, and although we who hit the ground with a thud may not like it and may fail to see the joke, those watching see it as ridiculous, and they refuse to feel the pain. It is in this action-reaction combination that comedy treads a very narrow emotional line. Things that have made people laugh may not have changed through history, but artistic taste in dramatic comedy has altered. Physical defects, race, or mental instability no longer work as comic devices among sophisticated audiences in the manner they once did. We do not hire hunchbacks to be our jesters any more, nor go to the insane asylum of a Sunday afternoon to watch the inmates perform, as the Elizabethans would do at Bethlehem (Bedlam) Hospital. Still with us, however, basically unaltered and effective as ever, is the sex joke in its infinity of variations, along with the pratfall, the pie-in-the-face routine, the wisecrack and the witty epigram.

The extremes of comedy are generally identified as "high" and "low." *High comedy* in its best form, defined from time to time as *social comedy, comedy of manners,* or *drawing room comedy,* is intellectual in its appeal, relying heavily upon sex, sophistication, and brilliant wit. High comedy is mostly dramatic, rather than theatrical, with very little action. It is static, given to words more than deeds. Most of the characters are fairly well rounded, and they are aware of the fact that they are playing an elaborate game in a comic world. The game, however, is taken very seriously, and the rules by which it operates bring laughter through the reversal of normally expected values. At the other end is *farce,* which includes many of the same qualities of melodrama, but the result is meant for fun and laughter, in toto and without exception. Farce is considered "low" comedy, but that does not mean inferiority. High comedy has a fairly narrow intellectual appeal, while low comedy, in farce, has a broad and anti-intellectual appeal. Incident piles on incident; the jokes, the sight gags and wisecracks come thick and fast. Farce is theatrical, and its premise is that of a wacky world without much sense, inhabited by a lot of zany people, where logic and reason have no known function. The more a sane rationale is sought by characters within a farce, the more it is likely to escape and, hence, the more the laughter. Farce, like melodrama, is visceral. The "belly laugh" means just that.

The large in-between area, neither "high" nor "low" is inhabited by "straight" comedy or, as much of it can also be defined, the *comedy of sensibility.* Those who inhabit this middle genre of comedy are, like their counterparts in the "straight" drama or *drame,* comparatively unsophisticated people who can, in the course of events, experience death and suffering as well as fun and games. Plot development depends mostly on its emphasis on character behavior and attitude, avoiding the vulgarities of farce as well as the intellectual appeal of high comedy. This broad range of the comic shows the fundamental charm of average, plodding, ordinary people, but the characters maintain their comic character, permitting the audience no opportunity for lingering sentimentality, even if the pain and suffering get a little close to home. As Henri Bergson has said in his famous essay on laughter, when we laugh, especially in this type of comedy, we put affection aside and silence our pity. The heart, he said, must undergo "a momentary anesthesia."

The Manner in Which It's Done

Style was not much of a concern in drama and theatre until well within the last hundred years. In fact, the meaning of the term as we use it today would have conveyed little sense to a dramatist or an actor of ancient Greece or Elizabethan England. *Style* refers to the *manner* and *method* in which a drama is originally conceived and written and in which it is produced on stage. There are dramatic as well as theatrical styles, each typical of a given period in history, each complementing the other. The drama of one era, such as the Greek, or the Elizabethan, or the Restoration, was designed for production in a specific kind of theatre building, and the building itself was designed to accommodate the drama it received. Until roughly the last century, the style of drama and the style of theatre worked in harmony to present the audience with a style of play relatively unaltered in form for periods of 75 to 100 years or more. Regardless of subject, theme, character, or incident, the general style of what we call Shakespearean (or Elizabethan), for instance, remained consistent in costuming, staging, theatre structure and dramaturgy from the opening of the first commercial theatre, the familiar open-air Globe-like structure patterned after Elizabethan innyards, in 1576 until all theatres were closed by the Puritans in 1642. Likewise, from the time of the reopening of the theatres by Charles II in 1660, the style that we have come to call Restoration and Eighteenth Century remained relatively constant in dramatic form and structure, in subject matter and theme, and, of course, in the increasingly large indoor opera-house type of theatre with its horseshoe galleries and sloping stage. Today all this has changed, as style is no longer so rigidly associated with a particular time and place but involves an almost limitless variety of methods of writing and staging, unrestricted by custom or theatre structure.

It would, of course, be possible to spend a considerable amount of time in discussing this stylistic evolution through a couple of thousand years, but for our purposes we will restrict ourselves to four fairly broad basic styles which are now associated with the writing of drama and its production in the theatre. While these are clearly arbitrary, they have significant meanings and connotations in today's theatre, even though the variations, combinations, and overlappings are everywhere apparent.

Classic

The *classic style* is carefully structured in its dramaturgy in the manner of Greek tragedy which, like all ancient Greek art, followed clean structural lines conceived, like the Parthenon and other classic temples, primarily for the aesthetic effect. In keeping with the traditions of classic Greek drama, the classic style restricts its subject matter to a single story, avoiding side issues and sub-plots, devoted mainly to heroic legendary or historical myths and tales. Behavior on stage is decorous and lacks overt physical violence, nearly all of which takes place offstage, though to be sure the physical and mental agonies, such as suffered by an Oedipus, are in full view. Action is held in the main to a single place and a single time. Dialogue is elevated in tone, highly poetic, carefully planned in long set speeches alternating with passages of quick exchange of lines between the major characters. Staging itself is uncluttered, with the whole production, writing included, suggesting the smoothness of polished marble, the grace of fluted columns, the dignity of the Acropolis, the magnificence of a sculptured god or goddess. The dramatist who entertains the *classic* view is interested in the relationship of his larger-than-life characters to the gods (or God, or Fate, or Nature, or the Universe) as well as to each other, and he frequently raises profound philosophical questions about human behavior and the forces that control it. Though not necessarily synonymous, the classic and tragic views work very closely together.

Romantic

The *romantic style* chooses its emphasis quite differently. Because the romanticist sees man as essentially good, unaffected by curses from malevolent gods and untainted by original sin, he finds that the rigid uniformity of subject matter, theme, and decor of the classic style is overly restrictive and innovatively stifling. Instead of the artificialities and the stately decorum of the classic view, the romantic outlook calls for originality, freedom to innovate and to move about in time and space, and to entertain high adventure and multiple plotlines. This means, especially in staging, a lot of color, spectacle, exciting adventure, and derring-do. It means the free appeal directly to the emotions, so apparent in melodrama, the dramatic style most obviously an exponent of the romantic.

Central to the philosophy of the romantic is the idea that many of man's problems are caused by the veneer imposed upon him by "civilization," thus hiding his true nature. Strip it away and underneath will be revealed not the horrors of a soul doomed by primal curse or original sin to eternal damnation but the source of human kindness and goodness. "Natural man" to the romanticist is pure and uncontaminated. Hence, the romanticist looks to nature itself, to the woods, fields, streams, to the winds, rains, storms and sunshine for the understanding of mankind. In addition, because, in retrospect, the past invariably seems to have been a time of "better days," the romanticist is historically oriented, recalling the times when men were men and challenges were met with honor and dignity.[4] The romantic attitude involves delight in playing upon the senses, emphasizing sentiment, nostalgia, and the emotionalism of undying love and eternal devotion. At heart, there is eternal optimism.

At the opposite extreme, in a kind of contradiction, obsessed as he is with the goodness of things, the romanticist maintains an equal fascination with the powers of evil and the mysteries of death. The hold upon the mind of evil deeds and Satanic acts is ever gripping; there is far more dramatic appeal in the Hellish than in the Heavenly. What is death? Whence comes it? Can it be overcome? What exists on the other side of the grave? The romantic seeks to know, and he revels in the fantastic, the supernatural, the magical, and the exotic, setting his tales in secluded vales, on treacherous shores, atop craggy mountains, or in far distant and mysterious lands.

---

[4] The romanticist often cannot resist altering history, preferring as he does the ideal of what ought to have been, rather than what actually happened. The German romanticist Friedrich Schiller wrote a version of the Joan of Arc story in 1801 and sent his heroine to her death in battle. His 1800 version of Mary of Scotland brings Mary and Elizabeth together in a key confrontation that never took place. We are still affected in the same manner today. The 1970 movie version of the same story brought the two queens together twice.

Realism and Naturalism

The classicist writes of royalty and nobility, viewing them with awe and a certain fearful respect. The romanticist becomes involved with his sentiments and his emotions in his treatment of men and nature, preferring the ideal, trusting in nature and natural goodness. The literary artist drawn to the realities of life and death, in the ordinary individual man and woman as part and product of their surroundings, their civilization, their society, quite apart from moral aspects of sin and retribution and punishing gods, displays interest in one of the stylistic Siamese twins of *realism* and *naturalism*. The metaphorical joining of these two terms is not without good reason. Trying to separate them reveals so many overlappings and duplications that contemporary critics use them almost interchangeably. They are, however, separate entities in enough ways to make them exist individually, if not entirely independently.

Realism, then, as we apply it to the drama, takes mankind pretty much as it is in the society in which it operates, with that society in turn presented as a product of the men and women in it. The subject matter thus becomes a transcription of reality, placing on stage individuals and their surroundings through language and action as they would be found in real life, performing against the background of a fully articulated illusionistic stage setting. Within the theatre the characters become isolated from the audience behind the proscenium arch where, through the brilliance of electric lighting, the one great invention which forever changed the basic concepts of staging and provided controlled illumination never before available to the theatrical producer, they address each other as if in complete privacy. Asides, soliloquies, and declamatory speeches, the hallmarks of nearly all drama of the past, disappear. The characters become those with whom the audience has a close personal identity. The realist, writing of what transpires in the actual world, presents his characters for what they are as the product of their own society, unromanticized and unsentimentalized. The realist strips nothing away, presenting what he sees as in the eye of the camera. The characters he creates are made into rounded, three-dimensional individuals, neither wholly good nor wholly evil, but wholly human, appearing strong or fragile, heroic or fearful as the situation demands.

The dialogue of realism is keyed to the idiom of the time. Poetry gives way to the cadences of ordinary speech. Action flows naturally upon previous action, avoiding all arbitrary twists of plot merely for the effect they may create. Realistic drama recognizes that the events portrayed did not begin with the rise, nor do they end with the fall of the curtain. Of course the realist must be selective about what he places upon the stage, for he is creating art, however "real" the illusion he creates. This presents one of the major challenges for the realistic dramatist, for he must learn how to balance the illusion of reality with the creativity of art. Recognizing the impossibility of placing reality literally on stage, the dramatist must determine how to convey the sense of reality, through art, while still keeping it "artless." How does one contrive "reality"? The coincidences and accidents which make up reality will appear as contrivances artificially introduced for effect if the dramatist is not careful. Life may lead an individual up one blind alley after another, but too many of them in a realistic play will make an audience restless, dissatisfied at having been fooled too many times. The dramatic realist knows that art is art and life is life. Each can only suggest, not become, the other. What the dramatist writes and places on the stage must remain reasonably real, for it is only realis*tic*; it cannot be *reality*. It must be, in fact, a highly contrived art which consistently must mask its contrivances. It must eliminate the imaginative play of the mind, while compelling the audience to imagine that the illusion is real. It is art that is not art; it is reality that is not reality.

The emphasis of *naturalism* is somewhat different. It makes use of the same subject matter, but regards the characters it treats in a more objective or even scientific sense. To the naturalistic writer characters are subjects for close analysis, a kind of artistic dissection. The naturalist is interested in the fundamental nature of man, what makes him function not so much as a character in society but as a creature in the natural world. According to the naturalist's perspective, society has imposed upon the individual a certain pattern of behavior made up of the customs and taboos of civilized behavior. If that veneer is removed, man stands revealed in his animalistic primitiveness, interested primarily in the three urges of natural gratification: eating, evacuation, and sex. Because the naturalist dwells upon these things and, unlike the realist, is not particularly selective, preferring to reveal all, he has often been accused of being a mere sensationalist, a seeker of horrors. His defense rests upon the need to remove society's veneer in order to get to the analysis itself and to probe the forces of nature that have made man what he is. As a result, life, as seen by the naturalist, tends to become a jungle. Sex becomes an animal battle, often to the death. The naturalistic writer avoids the subjective emotional involvement of the romanticist, sees little to be gained from lessons of the past. He regards the future with pessimism, as opposed to his realist counterpart who is really neither a pessimist nor an optimist. The eternal "progress" toward a better world seen by the romanticist is not a part of man's nature to the naturalist, who sees very little possibility of becoming better.

Recognizing that the forces of nature which work on mankind, making him a direct product of his natural environment, can be devastating, the naturalist can offer no particular solutions. He is uncertain as to whether or not there are any. The realist, in treating the social problems of his day, often takes a stand, advocates a cause, perhaps even offers a solution. Still, a lot of the difference between the artistic realist and the artistic naturalist comes down to a degree of emphasis. Henrik Ibsen, regarded as the first great dramatic realist, once explained the difference between himself and Emile Zola, widely recognized as one of the greatest naturalists at the end of the nineteenth century. In words to this effect Ibsen is supposed to have said, "When I go down into the sewer I go to clean it out. When Zola goes down, he takes a bath."

Stylization—Expressionism, Impressionism, Absurdism

Realism (we shall use the single term from now on) has become the commonly accepted definition of the style of "modern" drama, which means from the time of Ibsen in the 1870s and 1880s until the present, and any departure in writing or staging has come to be known as *stylization*. Stylization works in two directions, involving the staging of contemporary plays and revivals of plays from the past. A contemporary subject treated dramatically or theatrically in non-realistic fashion, as discussed below, is regarded as "stylized." On the other hand, the staging of a Shakespearean play in nineteenth-century Edwardian costume and setting, as was recently done with *Much Ado About Nothing,* or the portrayal of a Hamlet or Macbeth in strictly modern costume is also "stylized." Our interest here, however, is in the departures from realism which modern theatre techniques in sound and lighting have made possible, opening up a wide variety of inventive possibilities for the dramatist.

Foremost among the forms of stylization is *expressionism*. First acknowledged in a 1902 drama by the Swedish ultra-realist, August Strindberg, entitled *The Dream Play,* this style placed upon the stage a graphic picture of a nightmare in which time, place, and characters interchanged, blended, and disappeared in the fashion of a long dream. It was the theatrical *expression* of a very subjective viewpoint of life. That is what the expressionist does. He takes reality and expresses it as he sees it, not as life is, but as it seems. If the artist finds man to be a cipher in the monolith of big business he can call him, as Elmer Rice did in his expressionistic play *The Adding*

Machine of 1924, Mr. Zero, and his friends Mr. and Mrs. One, Two, and Three. If a man or woman seems indistinguishable from the machines he or she operates, make them speak and move as mechanical automatons. If they seem to make no sense in what they say and do in daily living, make their voices monotonous, sing-song, metallic, or staccato. Give them gibberish to say. Display them in a world that is being closed in, if escape is hopeless, by constricting scenery. If you are an expressionist, *express* your views and display them with the fullest extent of dramatic and theatrical distortion, exaggeration, or caricature.

Expressionism is socially oriented in its philosophy, critical in serious as well as comic vein, concerned with the present that man has created for himself, and fearful of the future which may or may not arrive. It is a thoroughly pessimistic view in one perspective, but realizing that mankind has done all this to himself, expressionism has an air of hope that things might be corrected before it is too late. Like the naturalist, however, the expressionist doesn't have much faith in what the past can teach, and the present bodes ill for the questionable future.

Expressionism as an independent style was popular for only two or three decades at the beginning of this century, but its effects have remained a permanent legacy in the theatre. Today, the "style" of a play can range from the starkest literal realism in setting, characters, and dialogue, to the most highly imaginative expression of the author's innermost thoughts and attitudes. The expressionist opened up the use of the stage, including even the theatre auditorium itself as an acting area, and imposed no limits whatever on dramatic or theatrical technique. The result is that the "offshoots" (or, at least, the parallel developments) of styles like *impressionism* and *absurdism* are equally at home in the modern theatre. The *impressionist* with his view of life from a particular vantage point, through the haze of physical or psychical distance, can make use of sights and sounds, dialogue and actions not wholly real, not wholly unreal, to create not a distorted "expression," but a highly personal "impression," and he can find an audience. The *absurdist* can view his world as a ridiculous dark joke, with life as a pointless existentialist exercise, a baffling endurance contest with unknown disinterested forces, an absurdity on the face of it, and he can send his characters through a thoroughly stylized world to make his point. And all because the expressionist, making use of the miracle controls of electric lighting and eventually of mobile stages—revolving, elevator, or what not—and electronic sound, went on his own independent and imaginative way while the realist sought to present life as it really is. But both were doing the same thing. Each created a style, each based that style on the same premises about humanity and its place in society. The outward, literal, objective presentation is *realism*. The inward, imaginative, subjective presentation is *expressionism*. Independently and collectively they have brought the contemporary drama and the contemporary theatre a lot of excitement and intellectual stimulation.

The retelling of Og's exploits before the cave fire was a type of dramatic experience which had its own form and style, created in the mind, presented with embellishments of sight and sound, ending in a presentation before an audience. There was a *drama,* there was *theatre,* and there was a *play.* Things haven't changed much since. They've just become more complicated.

Everything you will read in this volume has proven its worth, deserving by one means or another to be known as great literature—a special literature for a special kind of experience. Each drama that you read will affect you differently, as it did every man or woman who came to watch or the critic who came to judge since the first one was displayed two and a half thousand years ago. These dramas represent artistic accomplishments that rank among the finest creations of the human mind. But they were meant first and foremost to entertain. They must be approached as sources of aesthetic pleasure, for which reason they were created in the first place.

So read.

Enjoy.

Jordan Y. Miller

OEDIPUS REX (c. 430 B.C.)

SOPHOCLES (496–406 B.C.)

The tale of the House of Thebes is one of the two great Greek myths of families cursed by the gods. The other, the House of Atreus, forms the subject of three plays by Aeschylus (c. 513–c. 456 B.C.) written in 458. Known collectively as *The Oresteia,* this only surviving trilogy involves the blood feud within the family of King Agamemnon, hero of the Trojan War, his wife and murderer, Clytemnestra, and their avenging children, Electra and Orestes. The cycle of plays by Sophocles concerning King Oedipus and his family exists in three separate works, the *Oedipus Rex,* first in sequence but second to be written, *Oedipus at Colonus* (c. 406) his last play, and *Antigone* (c. 446). Together with Aeschylus' *Seven Against Thebes* (467) they provide the full story of this tremendously exciting and powerfully moving legend.

The Greek gods seldom acted without provocation, but when they brought their wrath upon a mortal it could be devastating through several generations. So it is with the House of Thebes. Somewhere in the dim past the founder of the city, King Kadmos, somehow offended the gods; the reason remains obscure. A curse fell upon his seed, bringing its greatest destruction to the family of the fourth generation, King Oedipus. This play is the story of his tragic final hours.

Oedipus Rex, favored by critics ever since Aristotle, is probably the greatest tragedy ever written. The central figure of the King, powerful, respected, impetuous, given to emotional extravagances and violent outbursts, subject to the fatal flaw of pride, emerges as

31

the finest example of the classic tragic protagonist. Doomed even before his birth to commit the most heinous and repulsive of crimes, this giant figure still arouses the emotions. His terrifying experiences demand compassionate understanding from the audience as he struggles to make the discoveries that will tell him the truth while rushing him headlong into his frightful destruction. Of exceeding noble stature, but fatefully human, he rises in his final symbolic death to the heights which give tragedy its deepest meaning.

As a play the *Oedipus* is brilliantly structured, one of the enduringly great examples of effective dramatic art. From the opening exchange between the King and the suppliants to the horrifying climax, the dramatist has complete control of his action and the development of his characters. Each central figure is fully realized, prompted by recognizable human motives. Each scene rises successively toward the inevitable catastrophe, piling up the evidence, compelling the participants, even the frightened Jocasta on whom the truth dawns early, to reject its terrible implications, arriving at the almost unbearable but inevitable revelation. In the true classic sense the play proceeds relentlessly in uncluttered fashion, its lines as severe and orderly as a Greek temple. The ironies multiply; the trap around the doomed protagonist steadily closes. Knowing all the while the fate that must come, still we cringe, hold our breath, and find ourselves gripped by the mounting tensions. The powerful effect of the poetic language, even in translation, is moving as it carries the dialogue along with dignity and steady pace.

Sophocles survives in but seven plays as the "middle" of the three great Greek tragedians with Aeschylus and Euripides (c. 485–c. 407 B.C.). The plays of Aeschylus frequently sought out the deeper meanings behind men's struggles with primal forces and their search for reason and rational behavior. Euripides often reduced his legendary figures to realistic, almost everyday proportions. Sophocles expressed his great concern for men and women struggling to find their individual identities and to establish an understandable relationship with impersonal gods and disinterested fate. His major protagonists are worthy heroic figures, and his tragedy is the best we have.

Oedipus Rex

SOPHOCLES

Translated by Dudley Fitts and Robert Fitzgerald

CHARACTERS

OEDIPUS, *King of Thebes, supposed son of Polybos and Meropê,*
  King and Queen of Corinth
IOKASTÊ, *wife of Oedipus and widow of the late King Laïos*
KREON, *brother of Iokastê, a prince of Thebes*
TEIRESIAS, *a blind seer who serves Apollo*
PRIEST
MESSENGER, *from Corinth*
SHEPHERD, *former servant of Laïos*
SECOND MESSENGER, *from the palace*
CHORUS OF THEBAN ELDERS
CHORAGOS, *leader of the Chorus*
ANTIGONE *and* ISMENE, *young daughters of Oedipus and*
  Iokastê. They appear in the Éxodos but do not speak.
SUPPLIANTS, GUARDS, SERVANTS

THE SCENE. *Before the palace of* OEDIPUS, *King of Thebes. A central door and two lateral doors open onto a platform which runs the length of the façade. On the platform, right and left, are altars; and three steps lead down into the* orchêstra *or chorus-ground. At the beginning of the action these steps are crowded by suppliants who have brought branches and chaplets of olive leaves and who sit in various attitudes of despair.* OEDIPUS *enters.*

PROLOGUE

OEDIPUS My children, generations of the living
  In the line of Kadmos,[1] nursed at his ancient hearth:
  Why have you strewn yourselves before these altars
  In supplication, with your boughs and garlands?

---

[1] *Kadmos* founder of Thebes

33

The breath of incense rises from the city
With a sound of prayer and lamentation.
>   Children,
I would not have you speak through messengers,
And therefore I have come myself to hear you—
I, Oedipus, who bear the famous name.
(*To a* PRIEST) You, there, since you are eldest in the company,
Speak for them all, tell me what preys upon you,
Whether you come in dread, or crave some blessing:
Tell me, and never doubt that I will help you
In every way I can; I should be heartless
Were I not moved to find you suppliant here.

PRIEST   Great Oedipus, O powerful king of Thebes!
You see how all the ages of our people
Cling to your altar steps: here are boys
Who can barely stand alone, and here are priests
By weight of age, as I am a priest of God,
And young men chosen from those yet unmarried;
As for the others, all that multitude,
They wait with olive chaplets in the squares,
At the two shrines of Pallas, and where Apollo
Speaks in the glowing embers.
>   Your own eyes
Must tell you: Thebes is tossed on a murdering sea
And can not lift her head from the death surge.
A rust consumes the buds and fruits of the earth;
The herds are sick; children die unborn,
And labor is vain. The god of plague and pyre
Raids like detestable lightning through the city,
And all the house of Kadmos is laid waste,
All emptied, and all darkened: Death alone
Battens upon the misery of Thebes.

You are not one of the immortal gods, we know;
Yet we have come to you to make our prayer
As to the man surest in mortal ways
And wisest in the ways of God. You saved us
From the Sphinx, that flinty singer, and the tribute
We paid to her so long; yet you were never
Better informed than we, nor could we teach you:
A god's touch, it seems, enabled you to help us.

Therefore, O mighty power, we turn to you:
Find us our safety, find us a remedy,

Whether by counsel of the gods or of men.
A king of wisdom tested in the past
Can act in a time of troubles, and act well.
Noblest of men, restore
Life to your city! Think how all men call you
Liberator for your boldness long ago;
Ah, when your years of kingship are remembered,
Let them not say *We rose, but later fell*—
Keep the State from going down in the storm!
Once, years ago, with happy augury,
You brought us fortune; be the same again!
No man questions your power to rule the land:
But rule over men, not over a dead city!
Ships are only hulls, high walls are nothing,
When no life moves in the empty passageways.

OEDIPUS   Poor children! You may be sure I know
All that you longed for in your coming here.
I know that you are deathly sick; and yet,
Sick as you are, not one is as sick as I.
Each of you suffers in himself alone
His anguish, not another's; but my spirit
Groans for the city, for myself, for you.

I was not sleeping, you are not waking me.
No, I have been in tears for a long while
And in my restless thought walked many ways.
In all my search I found one remedy,
And I have adopted it: I have sent Kreon,
Son of Menoikeus, brother of the queen,
To Delphi, Apollo's place of revelation,
To learn there, if he can,
What act or pledge of mine may save the city.
I have counted the days, and now, this very day,
I am troubled, for he has overstayed his time.
What is he doing? He has been gone too long.
Yet whenever he comes back, I should do ill
Not to take any action the god orders.

PRIEST   It is a timely promise. At this instant
They tell me Kreon is here.

OEDIPUS   O Lord Apollo!
May his news be fair as his face is radiant!

PRIEST   Good news, I gather! he is crowned with bay,
The chaplet is thick with berries.

OEDIPUS   We shall soon know;
  He is near enough to hear us now.

(*Enter* KREON.)

                      O prince:
  Brother: son of Menoikeus:
  What answer do you bring us from the god?
KREON   A strong one. I can tell you, great afflictions
  Will turn out well, if they are taken well.
OEDIPUS   What was the oracle? These vague words
  Leave me still hanging between hope and fear.
KREON   Is it your pleasure to hear me with all these
  Gathered around us? I am prepared to speak,
  But should we not go in?
OEDIPUS   Speak to them all,
  It is for them I suffer, more than for myself.
KREON   Then I will tell you what I heard at Delphi.
  In plain words
  The god commands us to expel from the land of Thebes
  An old defilement we are sheltering.
  It is a deathly thing, beyond cure;
  We must not let it feed upon us longer.
OEDIPUS   What defilement? How shall we rid ourselves of it?
KREON   By exile or death, blood for blood. It was
  Murder that brought the plague-wind on the city.
OEDIPUS   Murder of whom? Surely the god has named him?
KREON   My lord: Laïos once ruled this land,
  Before you came to govern us.
OEDIPUS   I know;
  I learned of him from others; I never saw him.
KREON   He was murdered; and Apollo commands us now
  To take revenge upon whoever killed him.
OEDIPUS   Upon whom? Where are they? Where shall we find a clue
  To solve that crime, after so many years?
KREON   Here in this land, he said. Search reveals
  Things that escape an inattentive man.
OEDIPUS   Tell me: Was Laïos murdered in his house,
  Or in the fields, or in some foreign country?
KREON   He said he planned to make a pilgrimage.
  He did not come home again.
OEDIPUS   And was there no one,
  No witness, no companion, to tell what happened?
KREON   They were all killed but one, and he got away

So frightened that he could remember one thing only.

OEDIPUS   What was the one thing? One may be the key
To everything, if we resolve to use it.

KREON   He said that a band of highwaymen attacked them,
Outnumbered them, and overwhelmed the king.

OEDIPUS   Strange, that a highwayman should be so daring—
Unless some faction here bribed him to do it.

KREON   We thought of that. But after Laïos' death
New troubles arose and we had no avenger.

OEDIPUS   What troubles could prevent your hunting down
the killers?

KREON   The riddling Sphinx's song
Made us deaf to all mysteries but her own.

OEDIPUS   Then once more I must bring what is dark to light.
It is most fitting that Apollo shows,
As you do, this compunction for the dead.
You shall see how I stand by you, as I should,
Avenging this country and the god as well,
And not as though it were for some distant friend,
But for my own sake, to be rid of evil.
Whoever killed King Laïos might—who knows?—
Lay violent hands even on me—and soon.
I act for the murdered king in my own interest.

Come, then, my children: leave the altar steps,
Lift up your olive boughs!
                              One of you go
And summon the people of Kadmos to gather here.
I will do all that I can; you may tell them that.

(*Exit a* PAGE.)

So, with the help of God,
We shall be saved—or else indeed we are lost.

PRIEST   Let us rise, children. It was for this we came,
And now the king has promised it.
Phoibos[1] has sent us an oracle; may he descend
Himself to save us and drive out the plague.

(*Exeunt* OEDIPUS *and* KREON *into the palace by the central door. The*
PRIEST *and the* SUPPLIANTS *disperse R and L. After a short pause the*
CHORUS *enters the* orchêstra.)

---

[1] *Phoibos* Apollo

PARODOS [1]

Strophe 1

CHORUS   What is God singing in his profound
  Delphi of gold and shadow?
What oracle for Thebes, the sunwhipped city?
Fear unjoints me, the roots of my heart tremble.
Now I remember, O Healer, your power, and wonder:
Will you send doom like a sudden cloud, or weave it
Like nightfall of the past?
Speak to me, tell me, O
Child of golden Hope, immortal Voice.

Antistrophe 1

Let me pray to Athenê, the immortal daughter of Zeus,
And to Artemis her sister
Who keeps her famous throne in the market ring,
And to Apollo, archer from distant heaven—
O gods, descend! Like three streams leap against
The fires of our grief, the fires of darkness;
Be swift to bring us rest!
As in the old time from the brilliant house
Of air you stepped to save us, come again!

Strophe 2

Now our afflictions have no end,
Now all our stricken host lies down
And no man fights off death with his mind;
The noble plowland bears no grain,
And groaning mothers can not bear—
See, how our lives like birds take wing,

---

1 *Parados* the song or ode chanted by the chorus on their entry. It is accompanied by dancing and music played on a flute. The chorus, in this play, represents elders of the city of Thebes. They remain on stage (on a level lower than the principal actors) for the remainder of the play. The choral odes and dances serve to separate one scene from another (there was no curtain in Greek theatre) as well as to comment on the action, reinforce the emotion, and interpret the situation. The chorus also performs dance movements during certain portions of the scenes themselves. *Strophe* and *antistrophe* are terms denoting the movement and counter-movement of the chorus from one side of their playing area to the other. When the chorus participates in dialogue with the other characters, their lines are spoken by the Choragos, their leader.

Like sparks that fly when a fire soars,
To the shore of the god of evening.

Antistrophe 2

The plague burns on, it is pitiless,
Though pallid children laden with death
Lie unwept in the stony ways,
And old gray women by every path
Flock to the strand about the altars
There to strike their breasts and cry
Worship of Phoibos in wailing prayers:
Be kind, God's golden child!

Strophe 3

There are no swords in this attack by fire,
No shields, but we are ringed with cries.
Send the besieger plunging from our homes
Into the vast sea-room of the Atlantic
Or into the waves that foam eastward of Thrace—
For the day ravages what the night spares—
Destroy our enemy, lord of the thunder!
Let him be riven by lightning from heaven!

Antistrophe 3

Phoibos Apollo, stretch the sun's bowstring,
That golden cord, until it sing for us,
Flashing arrows in heaven!
                              Artemis, Huntress,
Race with flaring lights upon our mountains!
O scarlet god, O golden-banded brow,
O Theban Bacchos in a storm of Maenads,

(*Enter* OEDIPUS, *C.*)

Whirl upon Death, that all the Undying hate!
Come with blinding torches, come in joy!

SCENE I

OEDIPUS Is this your prayer? It may be answered. Come,
Listen to me, act as the crisis demands,
And you shall have relief from all these evils.

Until now I was a stranger to this tale,
As I had been a stranger to the crime.

Could I track down the murderer without a clue?
But now, friends,
As one who became a citizen after the murder,
I make this proclamation to all Thebans:
If any man knows by whose hand Laïos, son of Labdakos,
Met his death, I direct that man to tell me everything,
No matter what he fears for having so long withheld it.
Let it stand as promised that no further trouble
Will come to him, but he may leave the land in safety.

Moreover: If anyone knows the murderer to be foreign,
Let him not keep silent: he shall have his reward from me.
However, if he does conceal it; if any man
Fearing for his friend or for himself disobeys this edict,
Hear what I propose to do:

I solemnly forbid the people of this country,
Where power and throne are mine, ever to receive that man
Or speak to him, no matter who he is, or let him
Join in sacrifice, lustration, or in prayer.
I decree that he be driven from every house,
Being, as he is, corruption itself to us: the Delphic
Voice of Apollo has pronounced this revelation.
Thus I associate myself with the oracle
And take the side of the murdered king.

As for the criminal, I pray to God—
Whether it be a lurking thief, or one of a number—
I pray that that man's life be consumed in evil and wretchedness.
And as for me, this curse applies no less
If it should turn out that the culprit is my guest here,
Sharing my hearth.
                              You have heard the penalty.
I lay it on you now to attend to this
For my sake, for Apollo's, for the sick
Sterile city that heaven has abandoned.
Suppose the oracle had given you no command:
Should this defilement go uncleansed for ever?
You should have found the murderer: your king,
A noble king, had been destroyed!
                              Now I,
Having the power that he held before me,
Having his bed, begetting children there
Upon his wife, as he would have, had he lived—
Their son would have been my children's brother,

If Laïos had had luck in fatherhood!
(And now his bad fortune has struck him down)—
I say I take the son's part, just as though
I were his son, to press the fight for him
And see it won! I'll find the hand that brought
Death to Labdakos' and Polydoros' child,
Heir of Kadmos' and Agenor's line.[1]
And as for those who fail me,
May the gods deny them the fruit of the earth,
Fruit of the womb, and may they rot utterly!
Let them be wretched as we are wretched, and worse!

For you, for loyal Thebans, and for all
Who find my actions right, I pray the favor
Of justice, and of all the immortal gods.
CHORAGOS   Since I am under oath, my lord, I swear
I did not do the murder, I can not name
The murderer. Phoibos ordained the search;
Why did he not say who the culprit was?
OEDIPUS   An honest question. But no man in the world
Can make the gods do more than the gods will.
CHORAGOS   There is an alternative, I think—
OEDIPUS   Tell me.
Any or all, you must not fail to tell me.
CHORAGOS   A lord clairvoyant to the lord Apollo,
As we all know, is the skilled Teiresias.
One might learn much about this from him, Oedipus.
OEDIPUS   I am not wasting time:
Kreon spoke of this, and I have sent for him—
Twice, in fact; it is strange that he is not here.
CHORAGOS   The other matter—that old report—seems useless.
OEDIPUS   What was that? I am interested in all reports.
CHORAGOS   The king was said to have been killed by highwaymen.
OEDIPUS   I know. But we have no witnesses to that.
CHORAGOS   If the killer can feel a particle of dread,
Your curse will bring him out of hiding!
OEDIPUS   No.
The man who dared that act will fear no curse.

(*Enter the blind seer* TEIRESIAS, *led by a* PAGE.)

CHORAGOS   But there is one man who may detect the criminal.

---

[1] *Labdakos, Polydoros, Kadmos,* and *Agenor* father, grandfather, great-grandfather, and great-great-grandfather of Laïos

This is Teiresias, this is the holy prophet
In whom, alone of all men, truth was born.
OEDIPUS   Teiresias: seer: student of mysteries,
Of all that's taught and all that no man tells,
Secrets of Heaven and secrets of the earth:
Blind though you are, you know the city lies
Sick with plague; and from this plague, my lord,
We find that you alone can guard or save us.

Possibly you did not hear the messengers?
Apollo, when we sent to him,
Sent us back word that this great pestilence
Would lift, but only if we established clearly
The identity of those who murdered Laïos.
They must be killed or exiled.
                                        Can you use
Birdflight[1] or any art of divination
To purify yourself, and Thebes, and me
From this contagion? We are in your hands.
There is no fairer duty
Than that of helping others in distress.
TEIRESIAS   How dreadful knowledge of the truth can be
When there's no help in truth! I knew this well,
But did not act on it: else I should not have come.
OEDIPUS   What is troubling you? Why are your eyes so cold?
TEIRESIAS   Let me go home. Bear your own fate, and I'll
Bear mine. It is better so: trust what I say.
OEDIPUS   What you say is ungracious and unhelpful
To your native country. Do not refuse to speak.
TEIRESIAS   When it comes to speech, your own is neither temperate
Nor opportune. I wish to be more prudent.
OEDIPUS   In God's name, we all beg you—
TEIRESIAS   You are all ignorant.
No; I will never tell you what I know.
Now it is my misery; then, it would be yours.
OEDIPUS   What! You do know something, and will not tell us?
You would betray us all and wreck the State?
TEIRESIAS   I do not intend to torture myself, or you.
Why persist in asking? You will not persuade me.
OEDIPUS   What a wicked old man you are! You'd try a stone's
Patience! Out with it! Have you no feeling at all?

---

[1] *Birdflight* Prophets predicted the future or divined the unknown by observing the flight of birds.

TEIRESIAS   You call me unfeeling. If you could only see
  The nature of your own feelings . . .
OEDIPUS   Why,
  Who would not feel as I do? Who could endure
  Your arrogance toward the city?
TEIRESIAS   What does it matter?
  Whether I speak or not, it is bound to come.
OEDIPUS   Then, if "it" is bound to come, you are bound to tell me.
TEIRESIAS   No, I will not go on. Rage as you please.
OEDIPUS   Rage? Why not!
                          And I'll tell you what I think:
  You planned it, you had it done, you all but
  Killed him with your own hands: if you had eyes,
  I'd say the crime was yours, and yours alone.
TEIRESIAS   So? I charge you, then,
  Abide by the proclamation you have made:
  From this day forth
  Never speak again to these men or to me;
  You yourself are the pollution of this country.
OEDIPUS   You dare say that! Can you possibly think you have
  Some way of going free, after such insolence?
TEIRESIAS   I have gone free. It is the truth sustains me.
OEDIPUS   Who taught you shamelessness? It was not your craft.
TEIRESIAS   You did. You made me speak. I did not want to.
OEDIPUS   Speak what? Let me hear it again more clearly.
TEIRESIAS   Was it not clear before? Are you tempting me?
OEDIPUS   I did not understand it. Say it again.
TEIRESIAS   I say that you are the murderer whom you seek.
OEDIPUS   Now twice you have spat out infamy. You'll pay for it!
TEIRESIAS   Would you care for more? Do you wish to be
  really angry?
OEDIPUS   Say what you will. Whatever you say is worthless.
TEIRESIAS   I say you live in hideous shame with those
  Most dear to you. You can not see the evil.
OEDIPUS   Can you go on babbling like this for ever?
TEIRESIAS   I can, if there is power in truth.
OEDIPUS   There is:
  But not for you, not for you,
  You sightless, witless, senseless, mad old man!
TEIRESIAS   You are the madman. There is no one here
  Who will not curse you soon, as you curse me.
OEDIPUS   You child of total night! I would not touch you;
  Neither would any man who sees the sun.
TEIRESIAS   True: it is not from you my fate will come.

    That lies within Apollo's competence,
    As it is his concern.
OEDIPUS   Tell me, who made
    These fine discoveries? Kreon? or someone else?
TEIRESIAS   Kreon is no threat. You weave your own doom.
OEDIPUS   Wealth, power, craft of statesmanship!
    Kingly position, everywhere admired!
    What savage envy is stored up against these,
    If Kreon, whom I trusted, Kreon my friend,
    For this great office which the city once
    Put in my hands unsought—if for this power
    Kreon desires in secret to destroy me!

    He has bought this decrepit fortune-teller, this
    Collector of dirty pennies, this prophet fraud—
    Why, he is no more clairvoyant than I am!
                           Tell us:
    Has your mystic mummery ever approached the truth?
    When that hellcat the Sphinx was performing here,
    What help were you to these people?
    Her magic was not for the first man who came along:
    It demanded a real exorcist. Your birds—
    What good were they? or the gods, for the matter of that?
    But I came by,
    Oedipus, the simple man, who knows nothing—
    I thought it out for myself, no birds helped me!
    And this is the man you think you can destroy,
    That you may be close to Kreon when he's king!
    Well, you and your friend Kreon, it seems to me,
    Will suffer most. If you were not an old man,
    You would have paid already for your plot.
CHORAGOS   We can not see that his words or yours
    Have been spoken except in anger, Oedipus,
    And of anger we have no need. How to accomplish
    The god's will best: that is what most concerns us.
TEIRESIAS   You are a king. But where argument's concerned
    I am your man, as much a king as you.
    I am not your servant, but Apollo's.
    I have no need of Kreon or Kreon's name.

    Listen to me. You mock my blindness, do you?
    But I say that you, with both your eyes, are blind:
    You can not see the wretchedness of your life,
    Nor in whose house you live, no, nor with whom.
    Who are your father and mother? Can you tell me?

You do not even know the blind wrongs
That you have done them, on earth and in the world below.
But the double lash of your parents' curse will whip you
Out of this land some day, with only night
Upon your precious eyes.
Your cries then—where will they not be heard?
What fastness of Kithairon[1] will not echo them?
And that bridal-descant of yours—you'll know it then,
The song they sang when you came here to Thebes
And found your misguided berthing.
All this, and more, that you can not guess at now,
Will bring you to yourself among your children.

Be angry, then. Curse Kreon. Curse my words.
I tell you, no man that walks upon the earth
Shall be rooted out more horribly than you.
OEDIPUS Am I to bear this from him?—Damnation
   Take you! Out of this place! Out of my sight!
TEIRESIAS I would not have come at all if you had not asked me.
OEDIPUS Could I have told that you'd talk nonsense, that
   You'd come here to make a fool of yourself, and of me?
TEIRESIAS A fool? Your parents thought me sane enough.
OEDIPUS My parents again!—Wait: who were my parents?
TEIRESIAS This day will give you a father, and break your heart.
OEDIPUS Your infantile riddles! Your damned abracadabra!
TEIRESIAS You were a great man once at solving riddles.
OEDIPUS Mock me with that if you like; you will find it true.
TEIRESIAS It was true enough. It brought about your ruin.
OEDIPUS But if it saved this town?
TEIRESIAS (*to the* PAGE)   Boy, give me your hand.
OEDIPUS Yes, boy; lead him away.

                                          —While you are here
   We can do nothing. Go; leave us in peace.
TEIRESIAS I will go when I have said what I have to say.
   How can you hurt me? And I tell you again:
   The man you have been looking for all this time,
   The damned man, the murderer of Laïos,
   That man is in Thebes. To your mind he is foreign-born,
   But it will soon be shown that he is a Theban,
   A revelation that will fail to please.

                                 A blind man,

---

[1] *Kithairon* the mountain where Oedipus was taken to be exposed as an infant

Who has his eyes now; a penniless man, who is rich now;
And he will go tapping the strange earth with his staff.
To the children with whom he lives now he will be
Brother and father—the very same; to her
Who bore him, son and husband—the very same
Who came to his father's bed, wet with his father's blood.

Enough. Go think that over.
If later you find error in what I have said,
You may say that I have no skill in prophecy.

(*Exit* TEIRESIAS, *led by his* PAGE. OEDIPUS *goes into the palace.*)

ODE I

Strophe 1

CHORUS   The Delphic stone of prophecies
Remembers ancient regicide
And a still bloody hand.
That killer's hour of flight has come.
He must be stronger than riderless
Coursers of untiring wind,
For the son[1] of Zeus armed with his father's thunder
Leaps in lightning after him;
And the Furies hold his track, the sad Furies.

Antistrophe 1

Holy Parnassos'[2] peak of snow
Flashes and blinds that secret man,
That all shall hunt him down:
Though he may roam the forest shade
Like a bull gone wild from pasture
To rage through glooms of stone.
Doom comes down on him; flight will not avail him;
For the world's heart calls him desolate,
And the immortal voices follow, for ever follow.

Strophe 2

But now a wilder thing is heard
From the old man skilled at hearing Fate in the wing-beat
    of a bird.

---

[1] *son* Apollo
[2] *Parnassos* mountain sacred to Apollo

Bewildered as a blown bird, my soul hovers and can not find
Foothold in this debate, or any reason or rest of mind.
But no man ever brought—none can bring
Proof of strife between Thebes' royal house,
Labdakos' line, and the son of Polybos;
And never until now has any man brought word
Of Laïos' dark death staining Oedipus the King.

Antistrophe 2

Divine Zeus and Apollo hold
Perfect intelligence alone of all tales ever told;
And well though this diviner works, he works in his own night;
No man can judge that rough unknown or trust in second sight,
For wisdom changes hands among the wise.
Shall I believe my great lord criminal
At a raging word that a blind old man let fall?
I saw him, when the carrion woman[1] faced him of old,
Prove his heroic mind. These evil words are lies.

SCENE II

KREON   Men of Thebes:
I am told that heavy accusations
Have been brought against me by King Oedipus.

I am not the kind of man to bear this tamely.

If in these present difficulties
He holds me accountable for any harm to him
Through anything I have said or done—why, then,
I do not value life in this dishonor.
It is not as though this rumor touched upon
Some private indiscretion. The matter is grave.
The fact is that I am being called disloyal
To the State, to my fellow citizens, to my friends.
CHORAGOS   He may have spoken in anger, not from his mind.
KREON   But did you not hear him say I was the one
Who seduced the old prophet into lying?
CHORAGOS   The thing was said; I do not know how seriously.
KREON   But you were watching him! Were his eyes steady?
Did he look like a man in his right mind?
CHORAGOS   I do not know.

---

[1] *woman* the Sphinx

I can not judge the behavior of great men.
But here is the king himself.

(*Enter* OEDIPUS.)

OEDIPUS   So you dared come back.
Why? How brazen of you to come to my house,
You murderer!
                    Do you think I do not know
That you plotted to kill me, plotted to steal my throne?
Tell me, in God's name: am I coward, a fool,
That you should dream you could accomplish this?
A fool who could not see your slippery game?
A coward, not to fight back when I saw it?
You are the fool, Kreon, are you not? hoping
Without support or friends to get a throne?
Thrones may be won or bought: you could do neither.

KREON   Now listen to me. You have talked; let me talk, too.
You can not judge unless you know the facts.

OEDIPUS   You speak well: there is one fact; but I find it hard
To learn from the deadliest enemy I have.

KREON   That above all I must dispute with you.

OEDIPUS   That above all I will not hear you deny.

KREON   If you think there is anything good in being stubborn
Against all reason, then I say you are wrong.

OEDIPUS   If you think a man can sin against his own kind
And not be punished for it, I say you are mad.

KREON   I agree. But tell me: What have I done to you?

OEDIPUS   You advised me to send for that wizard, did you not?

KREON   I did. I should do it again.

OEDIPUS   Very well. Now tell me:
How long has it been since Laïos—

KREON   What of Laïos?

OEDIPUS   Since he vanished in that onset by the road?

KREON   It was long ago, a long time.

OEDIPUS   And this prophet,
Was he practicing here then?

KREON   He was; and with honor, as now.

OEDIPUS   Did he speak of me at that time?

KREON   He never did,
At least, not when I was present.

OEDIPUS   But . . . the enquiry?
I suppose you held one?

KREON   We did, but we learned nothing.

OEDIPUS   Why did the prophet not speak against me then?
KREON   I do not know; and I am the kind of man
  Who holds his tongue when he has no facts to go on.
OEDIPUS   There's one fact that you know, and you could tell it.
KREON   What fact is that? If I know it, you shall have it.
OEDIPUS   If he were not involved with you, he could not say
  That it was I who murdered Laïos.
KREON   If he says that, you are the one that knows it!—
  But now it is my turn to question you.
OEDIPUS   Put your questions. I am no murderer.
KREON   First, then: You married my sister?
OEDIPUS   I married your sister.
KREON   And you rule the kingdom equally with her?
OEDIPUS   Everything that she wants she has from me.
KREON   And I am the third, equal to both of you?
OEDIPUS   That is why I call you a bad friend.
KREON   No. Reason it out, as I have done.
  Think of this first: Would any sane man prefer
  Power, with all a king's anxieties,
  To that same power and the grace of sleep?
  Certainly not I.
  I have never longed for the king's power—only his rights.
  Would any wise man differ from me in this?
  As matters stand, I have my way in everything
  With your consent, and no responsibilities.
  If I were king, I should be a slave to policy.

  How could I desire a scepter more
  Than what is now mine—untroubled influence?
  No, I have not gone mad; I need no honors,
  Except those with the perquisites I have now.
  I am welcome everywhere; every man salutes me,
  And those who want your favor seek my ear,
  Since I know how to manage what they ask.
  Should I exchange this ease for that anxiety?
  Besides, no sober mind is treasonable.
  I hate anarchy
  And never would deal with any man who likes it.
  Test what I have said. Go to the priestess
  At Delphi, ask if I quoted her correctly.
  And as for this other thing: if I am found
  Guilty of treason with Teiresias,
  Then sentence me to death. You have my word

It is a sentence I should cast my vote for—
But not without evidence!
                              You do wrong
When you take good men for bad, bad men for good.
A true friend thrown aside—why, life itself
Is not more precious!
                              In time you will know this well:
For time, and time alone, will show the just man,
Though scoundrels are discovered in a day.

CHORAGOS   This is well said, and a prudent man would ponder it.
    Judgments too quickly formed are dangerous.

OEDIPUS   But is he not quick in his duplicity?
    And shall I not be quick to parry him?
    Would you have me stand still, hold my peace, and let
    This man win everything, through my inaction?

KREON   And you want—what is it, then? To banish me?

OEDIPUS   No, not exile. It is your death I want,
    So that all the world may see what treason means.

KREON   You will persist, then? You will not believe me?

OEDIPUS   How can I believe you?

KREON   Then you are a fool.

OEDIPUS   To save myself?

KREON   In justice, think of me.

OEDIPUS   You are evil incarnate.

KREON   But suppose that you are wrong?

OEDIPUS   Still I must rule.

KREON   But not if you rule badly.

OEDIPUS   O city, city!

KREON   It is my city, too!

CHORAGOS   Now, my lords, be still. I see the queen,
    Iokastê, coming from her palace chambers;
    And it is time she came, for the sake of you both.
    This dreadful quarrel can be resolved through her.

(*Enter* IOKASTÊ.)

IOKASTÊ   Poor foolish men, what wicked din is this?
    With Thebes sick to death, is it not shameful
    That you should rake some private quarrel up?
    (*To* OEDIPUS) Come into the house.
                              —And you, Kreon, go now:
    Let us have no more of this tumult over nothing.

KREON   Nothing? No, sister: what your husband plans for me
    Is one of two great evils: exile or death.

OEDIPUS   He is right.
Why, woman I have caught him squarely
Plotting against my life.
KREON   No! Let me die
Accurst if ever I have wished you harm!
IOKASTÊ   Ah, believe it, Oedipus!
In the name of the gods, respect this oath of his
For my sake, for the sake of these people here!

Strophe 1

CHORAGOS   Open your mind to her, my lord. Be ruled by her, I beg
you!
OEDIPUS   What would you have me do?
CHORAGOS   Respect Kreon's word. He has never spoken like a fool,
And now he has sworn an oath.
OEDIPUS   You know what you ask?
CHORAGOS   I do.
OEDIPUS   Speak on, then.
CHORAGOS   A friend so sworn should not be baited so,
In blind malice, and without final proof.
OEDIPUS   You are aware, I hope, that what you say
Means death for me, or exile at the least.

Strophe 2

CHORAGOS   No, I swear by Helios, first in Heaven!
May I die friendless and accurst,
The worst of deaths, if ever I meant that!
It is the withering fields
That hurt my sick heart:
Must we bear all these ills,
And now your bad blood as well?
OEDIPUS   Then let him go. And let me die, if I must,
Or be driven by him in shame from the land of Thebes.
It is your unhappiness, and not his talk,
That touches me.
As for him—
Wherever he goes, hatred will follow him.
KREON   Ugly in yielding, as you were ugly in rage!
Natures like yours chiefly torment themselves.
OEDIPUS   Can you not go? Can you not leave me?
KREON   I can.
You do not know me; but the city knows me,
And in its eyes I am just, if not in yours.

(*Exit* KREON.)

Antistrophe 1

CHORAGOS   Lady Iokastê, did you not ask the King to go to
his chambers?

IOKASTÊ   First tell me what has happened.

CHORAGOS   There was suspicion without evidence; yet it rankled
As even false charges will.

IOKASTÊ   On both sides?

CHORAGOS   On both.

IOKASTÊ   But what was said?

CHORAGOS.   Oh let it rest, let it be done with!
Have we not suffered enough?

OEDIPUS   You see to what your decency has brought you:
You have made difficulties where my heart saw none.

Antistrophe 2

CHORAGOS   Oedipus, it is not once only I have told you—
You must know I should count myself unwise
To the point of madness, should I now forsake you—
                    You, under whose hand,
                         In the storm of another time,
                    Our dear land sailed out free.
                         But now stand fast at the helm!

IOKASTÊ   In God's name, Oedipus, inform your wife as well:
Why are you so set in this hard anger?

OEDIPUS   I will tell you, for none of these men deserves
My confidence as you do. It is Kreon's work,
His treachery, his plotting against me.

IOKASTÊ   Go on, if you can make this clear to me.

OEDIPUS   He charges me with the murder of Laïos.

IOKASTÊ   Has he some knowledge? Or does he speak from hearsay?

OEDIPUS   He would not commit himself to such a charge,
But he has brought in that damnable soothsayer
To tell his story.

IOKASTÊ   Set your mind at rest.
If it is a question of soothsayers, I tell you
That you will find no man whose craft gives knowledge
Of the unknowable.
                    Here is my proof:
An oracle was reported to Laïos once
(I will not say from Phoibos himself, but from
His appointed ministers, at any rate)

That his doom would be death at the hands of his own son—
His son, born of his flesh and of mine!

Now, you remember the story: Laïos was killed
By marauding strangers where three highways meet;
But his child had not been three days in this world
Before the king had pierced the baby's ankles
And left him to die on a lonely mountainside.

Thus, Apollo never caused that child
To kill his father, and it was not Laïos' fate
To die at the hands of his son, as he had feared.
This is what prophets and prophecies are worth!
Have no dread of them.
                                        It is God himself
Who can show us what he wills, in his own way.

OEDIPUS   How strange a shadowy memory crossed my mind,
Just now while you were speaking; it chilled my heart.

IOKASTÊ   What do you mean? What memory do you speak of?

OEDIPUS   If I understand you, Laïos was killed
At a place where three roads meet.

IOKASTÊ   So it was said;
We have no later story.

OEDIPUS   Where did it happen?

IOKASTÊ   Phokis, it is called: at a place where the Theban Way
Divides into the roads toward Delphi and Daulia.

OEDIPUS   When?

IOKASTÊ   We had the news not long before you came
And proved the right to your succession here.

OEDIPUS   Ah, what net has God been weaving for me?

IOKASTÊ   Oedipus! Why does this trouble you?

OEDIPUS   Do not ask me yet.
First, tell me how Laïos looked, and tell me
How old he was.

IOKASTÊ   He was tall, his hair just touched
With white; his form was not unlike your own.

OEDIPUS   I think that I myself may be accurst
By my own ignorant edict.

IOKASTÊ   You speak strangely.
It makes me tremble to look at you, my king.

OEDIPUS   I am not sure that the blind man can not see.
But I should know better if you were to tell me—

IOKASTÊ   Anything—though I dread to hear you ask it.

OEDIPUS   Was the king lightly escorted, or did he ride
With a large company, as a ruler should?
IOKASTÊ   There were five men with him in all: one was a herald.
And a single chariot, which he was driving.
OEDIPUS   Alas, that makes it plain enough!
                                                But who—
Who told you how it happened?
IOKASTÊ   A household servant,
The only one to escape.
OEDIPUS   And is he still
A servant of ours?
IOKASTÊ   No; for when he came back at last
And found you enthroned in the place of the dead king,
He came to me, touched my hand with his, and begged
That I would send him away to the frontier district
Where only the shepherds go—
As far away from the city as I could send him.
I granted his prayer; for although the man was a slave,
He had earned more than this favor at my hands.
OEDIPUS   Can he be called back quickly?
IOKASTÊ   Easily.
But why?
OEDIPUS   I have taken too much upon myself
Without enquiry; therefore I wish to consult him.
IOKASTÊ   Then he shall come.
                                    But am I not one also
To whom you might confide these fears of yours?
OEDIPUS   That is your right; it will not be denied you,
Now least of all; for I have reached a pitch
Of wild foreboding. Is there anyone
To whom I should sooner speak?

Polybos of Corinth is my father.
My mother is a Dorian: Meropê.
I grew up chief among the men of Corinth
Until a strange thing happened—
Not worth my passion, it may be, but strange.
At a feast, a drunken man maundering in his cups
Cries out that I am not my father's son! [1]

---

[1] *not my father's son* Oedipus perhaps interprets this as an allegation that
he is a bastard, the son of Meropê but not of Polybos. The implication, at
any rate, is that he is not of royal birth, not the legitimate heir to the
throne of Corinth.

I contained myself that night, though I felt anger
And a sinking heart. The next day I visited
My father and mother, and questioned them. They stormed,
Calling it all the slanderous rant of a fool;
And this relieved me. Yet the suspicion
Remained always aching in my mind;
I knew there was talk; I could not rest;
And finally, saying nothing to my parents,
I went to the shrine at Delphi.

The god dismissed my question without reply;
He spoke of other things.
                                        Some were clear,
Full of wretchedness, dreadful, unbearable:
As, that I should lie with my own mother, breed
Children from whom all men would turn their eyes;
And that I should be my father's murderer.

I heard all this, and fled. And from that day
Corinth to me was only in the stars
Descending in that quarter of the sky,
As I wandered farther and farther on my way
To a land where I should never see the evil
Sung by the oracle. And I came to this country
Where, so you say, King Laïos was killed.

I will tell you all that happened there, my lady.

There were three highways
Coming together at a place I passed;
And there a herald came towards me, and a chariot
Drawn by horses, with a man such as you describe
Seated in it. The groom leading the horses
Forced me off the road at his lord's command;
But as this charioteer lurched over towards me
I struck him in my rage. The old man saw me
And brought his double goad down upon my head
As I came abreast.
                              He was paid back, and more!
Swinging my club in this right hand I knocked him
Out of his car, and he rolled on the ground.
                                                        I killed him.

I killed them all.
Now if that stranger and Laïos were—kin,
Where is a man more miserable than I?
More hated by the gods? Citizen and alien alike

Must never shelter me or speak to me—
I must be shunned by all.

                   And I myself
Pronounced this malediction upon myself!

Think of it: I have touched you with these hands,
These hands that killed your husband. What defilement!

Am I all evil, then? It must be so,
Since I must flee from Thebes, yet never again
See my own countrymen, my own country,
For fear of joining my mother in marriage
And killing Polybos, my father.

                      Ah,
If I was created so, born to this fate,
Who could deny the savagery of God?

O holy majesty of heavenly powers!
May I never see that day! Never!
Rather let me vanish from the race of men
Than know the abomination destined me!

CHORAGOS We too, my lord, have felt dismay at this.
  But there is hope: you have yet to hear the shepherd.
OEDIPUS Indeed, I fear no other hope is left me.
IOKASTÊ What do you hope from him when he comes?
OEDIPUS   This much:
  If his account of the murder tallies with yours,
  Then I am cleared.
IOKASTÊ   What was it that I said
  Of such importance?
OEDIPUS   Why, "marauders," you said,
  Killed the king, according to this man's story.
  If he maintains that still, if there were several,
  Clearly the guilt is not mine: I was alone.
  But if he says one man, singlehanded, did it,
  Then the evidence all points to me.
IOKASTÊ You may be sure that he said there were several;
  And can he call back that story now? He can not.
  The whole city heard it as plainly as I.
  But suppose he alters some detail of it:
  He can not ever show that Laïos' death
  Fulfilled the oracle: for Apollo said
  My child was doomed to kill him; and my child—
  Poor baby!—it was my child that died first.

No. From now on, where oracles are concerned,
I would not waste a second thought on any.
OEDIPUS   You may be right.

But come: let someone go
For the shepherd at once. This matter must be settled.
IOKASTÊ   I will send for him.
I would not wish to cross you in anything,
And surely not in this.—Let us go in.

(*Exeunt into the palace.*)

ODE II

Strophe 1

CHORUS   Let me be reverent in the ways of right,
Lowly the paths I journey on;
Let all my words and actions keep
The laws of the pure universe
From highest Heaven handed down.
For Heaven is their bright nurse,
Those generations of the realms of light;
Ah, never of mortal kind were they begot,
Nor are they slaves of memory, lost in sleep:
Their Father is greater than Time, and ages not.

Antistrophe 1

The tyrant is a child of Pride
Who drinks from his great sickening cup
Recklessness and vanity,
Until from his high crest headlong
He plummets to the dust of hope.
That strong man is not strong.
But let no fair ambition be denied;
May God protect the wrestler for the State
In government, in comely policy,
Who will fear God, and on His ordinance wait.

Strophe 2

Haughtiness and the high hand of disdain
Tempt and outrage God's holy law;
And any mortal who dares hold
No immortal Power in awe
Will be caught up in a net of pain:

The price for which his levity is sold.
Let each man take due earnings, then,
And keep his hands from holy things,
And from blasphemy stand apart—
Else the crackling blast of heaven
Blows on his head, and on his desperate heart.
Though fools will honor impious men,
In their cities no tragic poet sings.

Antistrophe 2

Shall we lose faith in Delphi's obscurities,
We who have heard the world's core
Discredited, and the sacred wood
Of Zeus at Elis praised no more?
The deeds and the strange prophecies
Must make a pattern yet to be understood.
Zeus, if indeed you are lord of all,
Throned in light over night and day,
Mirror this in your endless mind:
Our masters call the oracle
Words on the wind, and the Delphic vision blind!
Their hearts no longer know Apollo,
And reverence for the gods has died away.

SCENE III

Enter IOKASTÊ.

IOKASTÊ   Princes of Thebes, it has occurred to me
To visit the altars of the gods, bearing
These branches as a suppliant, and this incense.
Our king is not himself: his noble soul
Is overwrought with fantasies of dread,
Else he would consider
The new prophecies in the light of the old.
He will listen to any voice that speaks disaster,
And my advice goes for nothing.

(*She approaches the altar, R.*)

                              To you, then, Apollo,
Lycéan lord, since you are nearest, I turn in prayer.
Receive these offerings, and grant us deliverance
From defilement. Our hearts are heavy with fear

When we see our leader distracted, as helpless sailors
Are terrified by the confusion of their helmsman.

(*Enter* MESSENGER.)

MESSENGER   Friends, no doubt you can direct me:
Where shall I find the house of Oedipus,
Or, better still, where is the king himself?
CHORAGOS   It is this very place, stranger; he is inside.
This is his wife and mother of his children.
MESSENGER   I wish her happiness in a happy house,
Blest in all the fulfillment of her marriage.
IOKASTÊ   I wish as much for you: your courtesy
Deserves a like good fortune. But now, tell me:
Why have you come? What have you to say to us?
MESSENGER   Good news, my lady, for your house and your husband.
IOKASTÊ   What news? Who sent you here?
MESSENGER   I am from Corinth.
The news I bring ought to mean joy for you,
Though it may be you will find some grief in it.
IOKASTÊ   What is it? How can it touch us in both ways?
MESSENGER   The word is that the people of the Isthmus
Intend to call Oedipus to be their king.
IOKASTÊ   But old King Polybos—is he not reigning still?
MESSENGER   No. Death holds him in his sepulchre.
IOKASTÊ   What are you saying? Polybos is dead?
MESSENGER   If I am not telling the truth, may I die myself.
IOKASTÊ (*to a* MAIDSERVANT)   Go in, go quickly; tell this to
your master.

O riddlers of God's will, where are you now!
This was the man whom Oedipus, long ago,
Feared so, fled so, in dread of destroying him—
But it was another fate by which he died.

(*Enter* OEDIPUS, *C.*)

OEDIPUS   Dearest Iokasté, why have you sent for me?
IOKASTÊ   Listen to what this man says, and then tell me
What has become of the solemn prophecies.
OEDIPUS   Who is this man? What is his news for me?
IOKASTÊ   He has come from Corinth to announce your
father's death!
OEDIPUS   Is it true, stranger? Tell me in your own words.
MESSENGER   I can not say it more clearly: the king is dead.

OEDIPUS   Was it by treason? Or by an attack of illness?

MESSENGER   A little thing brings old men to their rest.

OEDIPUS   It was sickness, then?

MESSENGER   Yes, and his many years.

OEDIPUS   Ah!

Why should a man respect the Pythian hearth,[1] or
Give heed to the birds that jangle above his head?
They prophesied that I should kill Polybos,
Kill my own father; but he is dead and buried,
And I am here—I never touched him, never,
Unless he died of grief for my departure,
And thus, in a sense, through me. No. Polybos
Has packed the oracles off with him underground.
They are empty words.

IOKASTÊ   Had I not told you so?

OEDIPUS   You had; it was my faint heart that betrayed me.

IOKASTÊ   From now on never think of those things again.

OEDIPUS   And yet—must I not fear my mother's bed?

IOKASTÊ   Why should anyone in this world be afraid,
Since Fate rules us and nothing can be foreseen?
A man should live only for the present day.

Have no more fear of sleeping with your mother:
How many men, in dreams, have lain with their mothers!
No reasonable man is troubled by such things.

OEDIPUS   That is true; only—
If only my mother were not still alive!
But she is alive. I can not help my dread.

IOKASTÊ   Yet this news of your father's death is wonderful.

OEDIPUS   Wonderful. But I fear the living woman.

MESSENGER   Tell me, who is this woman that you fear?

OEDIPUS   It is Meropê, man; the wife of King Polybos.

MESSENGER   Meropê? Why should you be afraid of her?

OEDIPUS   An oracle of the gods, a dreadful saying.

MESSENGER   Can you tell me about it or are you sworn to silence?

OEDIPUS   I can tell you, and I will.
Apollo said through his prophet that I was the man
Who should marry his own mother, shed his father's blood
With his own hands. And so, for all these years
I have kept clear of Corinth, and no harm has come—
Though it would have been sweet to see my parents again.

---

[1] *Pythian hearth* Delphi

MESSENGER   And is this the fear that drove you out of Corinth?

OEDIPUS   Would you have me kill my father?

MESSENGER   As for that
You must be reassured by the news I gave you.

OEDIPUS   If you could reassure me, I would reward you.

MESSENGER   I had that in mind, I will confess: I thought
I could count on you when you returned to Corinth.

OEDIPUS   No: I will never go near my parents again.

MESSENGER   Ah, son, you still do not know what you are doing—

OEDIPUS   What do you mean? In the name of God tell me!

MESSENGER   —if these are your reasons for not going home.

OEDIPUS   I tell you, I fear the oracle may come true.

MESSENGER   And guilt may come upon you through your parents?

OEDIPUS   That is the dread that is always in my heart.

MESSENGER   Can you not see that all your fears are groundless?

OEDIPUS   Groundless? Am I not my parents' son?

MESSENGER   Polybos was not your father.

OEDIPUS   Not my father?

MESSENGER   No more your father than the man speaking to you.

OEDIPUS   But you are nothing to me!

MESSENGER   Neither was he.

OEDIPUS   Then why did he call me son?

MESSENGER   I will tell you:
Long ago he had you from my hands, as a gift.

OEDIPUS   Then how could he love me so, if I was not his?

MESSENGER   He had no children, and his heart turned to you.

OEDIPUS   What of you? Did you buy me? Did you find me by
chance?

MESSENGER   I came upon you in the woody vales of Kithairon.

OEDIPUS   And what were you doing there?

MESSENGER   Tending my flocks.

OEDIPUS   A wandering shepherd?

MESSENGER   But your savior, son, that day.

OEDIPUS   From what did you save me?

MESSENGER   Your ankles should tell you that.

OEDIPUS   Ah, stranger, why do you speak of that childhood pain?

MESSENGER   I pulled the skewer that pinned your feet together.

OEDIPUS   I have had the mark as long as I can remember.

MESSENGER   That was why you were given the name you bear.

OEDIPUS   God! Was it my father or my mother who did it?
Tell me!

MESSENGER   I do not know. The man who gave you to me
Can tell you better than I.

OEDIPUS   It was not you that found me, but another?

MESSENGER It was another shepherd gave you to me.

OEDIPUS Who was he? Can you tell me who he was?

MESSENGER I think he was said to be one of Laïos' people.

OEDIPUS You mean the Laïos who was king here years ago?

MESSENGER Yes; King Laïos; and the man was one of his
    herdsmen.

OEDIPUS Is he still alive? Can I see him?

MESSENGER   These men here
    Know best about such things.

OEDIPUS   Does anyone here
    Know this shepherd that he is talking about?
    Have you seen him in the fields, or in the town?
    If you have, tell me. It is time things were made plain.

CHORAGOS I think the man he means is that same shepherd
    You have already asked to see. Iokastê perhaps
    Could tell you something.

OEDIPUS   Do you know anything
    About him, Lady? Is he the man we have summoned?
    Is that the man this shepherd means?

IOKASTÊ   Why think of him?
    Forget this herdsman. Forget it all.
    This talk is a waste of time.

OEDIPUS   How can you say that,
    When the clues to my true birth are in my hands?

IOKASTÊ For God's love, let us have no more questioning!
    Is your life nothing to you?
    My own is pain enough for me to bear.

OEDIPUS You need not worry. Suppose my mother a slave,
    And born of slaves: no baseness can touch you.

IOKASTÊ Listen to me, I beg you: do not do this thing!

OEDIPUS I will not listen; the truth must be made known.

IOKASTÊ Everything that I say is for your own good!

OEDIPUS   My own good
    Snaps my patience, then! I want none of it.

IOKASTÊ You are fatally wrong! May you never learn who you are!

OEDIPUS Go, one of you, and bring the shepherd here.
    Let us leave this woman to brag of her royal name.

IOKASTÊ Ah, miserable!
    That is the only word I have for you now.
    That is the only word I can ever have.

(Exit into the palace.)

CHORAGOS Why has she left us, Oedipus? Why has she gone

In such a passion of sorrow? I fear this silence:
Something dreadful may come of it.
OEDIPUS   Let it come!
However base my birth, I must know about it.
The Queen, like a woman, is perhaps ashamed
To think of my low origin. But I
Am a child of Luck; I can not be dishonered.
Luck is my mother; the passing months, my brothers,
Have seen me rich and poor.
                                        If this is so,
How could I wish that I were someone else?
How could I not be glad to know my birth?

ODE III

Strophe

CHORUS   If ever the coming time were known
    To my heart's pondering,
    Kithairon, now by Heaven I see the torches
    At the festival of the next full moon,
    And see the dance, and hear the choir sing
    A grace to your gentle shade:
    Mountain where Oedipus was found,
    O mountain guard of a noble race!
    May the god [1] who heals us lend his aid,
    And let that glory come to pass
    For our king's cradling-ground.

Antistrophe

    Of the nymphs that flower beyond the years,
    Who bore you,[2] royal child,
    To Pan of the hills or the timberline Apollo,
    Cold in delight where the upland clears,
    Or Hermês for whom Kyllenê's heights are piled?
    Or flushed as evening cloud,
    Great Dionysos, roamer of mountains,
    He—was it he who found you there,

---

[1] *god* Apollo
[2] *Who bore you* The chorus is suggesting that perhaps Oedipus is the son of one of the immortal nymphs and of a god—Pan, Apollo, Hermes, or Dionysos. The "sweet god-ravisher" (below) is the presumed mother.

And caught you up in his own proud
Arms from the sweet god-ravisher
Who laughed by the Muses' fountains?

SCENE IV

OEDIPUS Sirs: though I do not know the man,
I think I see him coming, this shepherd we want:
He is old, like our friend here, and the men
Bringing him seem to be servants of my house.
But you can tell, if you have ever seen him.

(*Enter* SHEPHERD *escorted by* SERVANTS.)

CHORAGOS I know him, he was Laïos' man. You can trust him.
OEDIPUS Tell me first, you from Corinth: is this the shepherd
We were discussing?
MESSENGER This is the very man.
OEDIPUS (*to* SHEPHERD) Come here. No, look at me. You
must answer
Everything I ask.—You belonged to Laïos?
SHEPHERD Yes: born his slave, brought up in his house.
OEDIPUS Tell me: what kind of work did you do for him?
SHEPHERD I was a shepherd of his, most of my life.
OEDIPUS Where mainly did you go for pasturage?
SHEPHERD Sometimes Kithairon, sometimes the hills near-by.
OEDIPUS Do you remember ever seeing this man out there?
SHEPHERD What would he be doing there? This man?
OEDIPUS This man standing here. Have you ever seen him before?
SHEPHERD No. At least, not to my recollection.
MESSENGER And that is not strange, my lord. But I'll refresh
His memory: he must remember when we two
Spent three whole seasons together, March to September,
On Kithairon or thereabouts. He had two flocks;
I had one. Each autumn I'd drive mine home
And he would go back with his to Laïos' sheepfold.—
Is this not true, just as I have described it?
SHEPHERD True, yes; but it was all so long ago.
MESSENGER Well, then: do you remember, back in those days,
That you gave me a baby boy to bring up as my own?
SHEPHERD What if I did? What are you trying to say?
MESSENGER King Oedipus was once that little child.
SHEPHERD Damn you, hold your tongue!
OEDIPUS   No more of that!
It is your tongue needs watching, not this man's.

SHEPHERD   My king, my master, what is it I have done wrong?
OEDIPUS   You have not answered his question about the boy.
SHEPHERD   He does not know ... He is only making trouble ...
OEDIPUS   Come, speak plainly, or it will go hard with you.
SHEPHERD   In God's name, do not torture an old man!
OEDIPUS   Come here, one of you; bind his arms behind him.
SHEPHERD   Unhappy king! What more do you wish to learn?
OEDIPUS   Did you give this man the child he speaks of?
SHEPHERD   I did.

   And I would to God I had died that very day.
OEDIPUS   You will die now unless you speak the truth.
SHEPHERD   Yet if I speak the truth, I am worse than dead.
OEDIPUS (*to* ATTENDANT)   He intends to draw it out, apparently—
SHEPHERD   No! I have told you already that I gave him the boy.
OEDIPUS   Where did you get him? From your house? From
    somewhere else?
SHEPHERD   Not from mine, no. A man gave him to me.
OEDIPUS   Is that man here? Whose house did he belong to?
SHEPHERD   For God's love, my king, do not ask me any more!
OEDIPUS   You are a dead man if I have to ask you again.
SHEPHERD   Then ... Then the child was from the palace of Laïos.
OEDIPUS   A slave child? or a child of his own line?
SHEPHERD   Ah, I am on the brink of dreadful speech!
OEDIPUS   And I of dreadful hearing. Yet I must hear.
SHEPHERD   If you must be told, then ...

                      They said it was Laïos' child;
   But it is your wife who can tell you about that.
OEDIPUS   My wife!—Did she give it to you?
SHEPHERD   My lord, she did.
OEDIPUS   Do you know why?
SHEPHERD   I was told to get rid of it.
OEDIPUS   Oh heartless mother!
SHEPHERD   But in dread of prophecies ...
OEDIPUS   Tell me.
SHEPHERD   It was said that the boy would kill his own father.
OEDIPUS   Then why did you give him over to this old man?
SHEPHERD   I pitied the baby, my king,
   And I thought that this man would take him far away
   To his own country.
                He saved him—but for what a fate!
   For if you are what this man says you are,
   No man living is more wretched than Oedipus.
OEDIPUS   Ah God!
   It was true!

All the prophecies!
                    —Now,
O Light, may I look on you for the last time!
I, Oedipus,
Oedipus, damned in his birth, in his marriage damned,
Damned in the blood he shed with his own hand!

(*He rushes into the palace.*)

ODE IV

Strophe 1

CHORUS   Alas for the seed of men.
    What measure shall I give these generations
    That breathe on the void and are void
    And exist and do not exist?
    Who bears more weight of joy
    Than mass of sunlight shifting in images,
    Or who shall make his thought stay on
    That down time drifts away?
    Your splendor is all fallen.
    O naked brow of wrath and tears,
    O change of Oedipus!
    I who saw your days call no man blest—
    Your great days like ghosts gone.

Antistrophe 1

    That mind was a strong bow.
    Deep, how deep you drew it then, hard archer,
    At a dim fearful range,
    And brought dear glory down!
    You overcame the stranger[1]—
    The virgin with her hooking lion claws—
    And though death sang, stood like a tower
    To make pale Thebes take heart.
    Fortress against our sorrow!
    True king, giver of laws,
    Majestic Oedipus!
    No prince in Thebes had ever such renown,
    No prince won such grace of power.

---

[1] *stranger* the Sphinx

Strophe 2

And now of all men ever known
Most pitiful is this man's story:
His fortunes are most changed, his state
Fallen to a low slave's
Ground under bitter fate.
O Oedipus, most royal one!
The great door[1] that expelled you to the light
Gave at night—ah, gave night to your glory:
As to the father, to the fathering son.
All understood too late.
How could that queen whom Laïos won,
The garden that he harrowed at his height,
Be silent when that act was done?

Antistrophe 2

But all eyes fail before time's eye,
All actions come to justice there.
Though never willed, though far down the deep past,
Your bed, your dread sirings,
Are brought to book at last.
Child by Laïos doomed to die,
Then doomed to lose that fortunate little death,
Would God you never took breath in this air
That with my wailing lips I take to cry:
For I weep the world's outcast.
I was blind, and now I can tell why:
Asleep, for you had given ease of breath
To Thebes, while the false years went by.

EXODOS [2]

Enter, from the palace, SECOND MESSENGER.

SECOND MESSENGER   Elders of Thebes, most honored in this land,
What horrors are yours to see and hear, what weight
Of sorrow to be endured, if, true to your birth,
You venerate the line of Labdakos!
I think neither Istros nor Phasis, those great rivers,
Could purify this place of all the evil

---

[1] *door* Iokastê's womb
[2] *Exodos* final scene

It shelters now, or soon must bring to light—
Evil not done unconsciously, but willed.

The greatest griefs are those we cause ourselves.
CHORAGOS   Surely, friend, we have grief enough already;
   What new sorrow do you mean?
SECOND MESSENGER   The queen is dead.
CHORAGOS   O miserable queen! But at whose hand?
SECOND MESSENGER   Her own.
   The full horror of what happened you can not know,
   For you did not see it; but I, who did, will tell you
   As clearly as I can how she met her death.

When she had left us,
In passionate silence, passing through the court,
She ran to her apartment in the house,
Her hair clutched by the fingers of both hands.
She closed the doors behind her; then, by that bed
Where long ago the fatal son was conceived—
That son who should bring about his father's death—
We heard her call upon Laïos, dead so many years,
And heard her wail for the double fruit of her marriage,
A husband by her husband, children by her child.

Exactly how she died I do not know:
For Oedipus burst in moaning and would not let us
Keep vigil to the end: it was by him
As he stormed about the room that our eyes were caught.
From one to another of us he went, begging a sword,
Hunting the wife who was not his wife, the mother
Whose womb had carried his own children and himself.
I do not know: it was none of us aided him,
But surely one of the gods was in control!
For with a dreadful cry
He hurled his weight, as though wrenched out of himself,
At the twin doors: the bolts gave, and he rushed in.
And there we saw her hanging, her body swaying
From the cruel cord she had noosed about her neck.
A great sob broke from him, heartbreaking to hear,
As he loosed the rope and lowered her to the ground.

I would blot out from my mind what happened next!
For the king ripped from her gown the golden brooches
That were her ornament, and raised them, and plunged
   them down

Straight into his own eyeballs, crying, "No more,
No more shall you look on the misery about me,
The horrors of my own doing! Too long you have known
The faces of those whom I should never have seen,
Too long been blind to those for whom I was searching!
From this hour, go in darkness!" And as he spoke,
He struck at his eyes—not once, but many times;
And the blood spattered his beard,
Bursting from his ruined sockets like red hail.

So from the unhappiness of two this evil has sprung,
A curse on the man and woman alike. The old
Happiness of the house of Labdakos
Was happiness enough: where is it today?
It is all wailing and ruin, disgrace, death—all
The misery of mankind that has a name—
And it is wholly and for ever theirs.

CHORAGOS Is he in agony still? Is there no rest for him?
SECOND MESSENGER He is calling for someone to open the
        doors wide
So that all the children of Kadmos may look upon
His father's murderer, his mother's—no,
I can not say it!
                    And then he will leave Thebes,
Self-exiled, in order that the curse
Which he himself pronounced may depart from the house.
He is weak, and there is none to lead him,
So terrible is his suffering.
                        But you will see:
Look, the doors are opening; in a moment
You will see a thing that would crush a heart of stone.

(*The central door is opened;* OEDIPUS, *blinded, is led in.*)

CHORAGOS Dreadful indeed for men to see.
    Never have my own eyes
    Looked on a sight so full of fear.

    Oedipus!
    What madness came upon you, what daemon
    Leaped on your life with heavier
    Punishment than a mortal man can bear?
    No: I can not even
    Look at you, poor ruined one.
    And I would speak, question, ponder,

If I were able. No.
You make me shudder.
OEDIPUS   God. God.
   Is there a sorrow greater?
   Where shall I find harbor in this world?
   My voice is hurled far on a dark wind.
   What has God done to me?
CHORAGOS   Too terrible to think of, or to see.

Strophe 1

OEDIPUS   O cloud of night,
   Never to be turned away: night coming on,
   I can not tell how: night like a shroud!
   My fair winds brought me here.
                              O God. Again
   The pain of the spikes where I had sight,
   The flooding pain
   Of memory, never to be gouged out.
CHORAGOS   This is not strange.
   You suffer it all twice over, remorse in pain,
   Pain in remorse.

Antistrophe 1

OEDIPUS   Ah dear friend
   Are you faithful even yet, you alone?
   Are you still standing near me, will you stay here,
   Patient, to care for the blind?
                           The blind man!
   Yet even blind I know who it is attends me,
   By the voice's tone—
   Though my new darkness hide the comforter.
CHORAGOS   Oh fearful act!
   What god was it drove you to rake black
   Night across your eyes?

Strophe 2

OEDIPUS   Apollo. Apollo. Dear
   Children, the god was Apollo.
   He brought my sick, sick fate upon me.
   But the blinding hand was my own!
   How could I bear to see
   When all my sight was horror everywhere?
CHORAGOS   Everywhere; that is true.

OEDIPUS   And now what is left?
  Images? Love? A greeting even,
  Sweet to the senses? Is there anything?
  Ah, no, friends: lead me away.
  Lead me away from Thebes.
                          Lead the great wreck
  And hell of Oedipus, whom the gods hate.
CHORAGOS   Your misery, you are not blind to that.
  Would God you had never found it out!

Antistrophe 2

OEDIPUS   Death take the man who unbound
  My feet on that hillside
  And delivered me from death to life! What life?
  If only I had died,
  This weight of monstrous doom
  Could not have dragged me and my darlings down.
CHORAGOS   I would have wished the same.
OEDIPUS   Oh never to have come here
  With my father's blood upon me! Never
  To have been the man they call his mother's husband!
  Oh accurst! Oh child of evil,
  To have entered that wretched bed—
                          the selfsame one!
  More primal than sin itself, this fell to me.
CHORAGOS   I do not know what words to offer you.
  You were better dead than alive and blind.

OEDIPUS   Do not counsel me any more. This punishment
  That I have laid upon myself is just.
  If I had eyes,
  I do not know how I could bear the sight
  Of my father, when I came to the house of Death,
  Or my mother: for I have sinned against them both
  So vilely that I could not make my peace
  By strangling my own life.
                          Or do you think my children,
  Born as they were born, would be sweet to my eyes?
  Ah never, never! Nor this town with its high walls,
  Nor the holy images of the gods.
                          For I,
  Thrice miserable!—Oedipus, noblest of all the line
  Of Kadmos, have condemned myself to enjoy

These things no more, by my own malediction
Expelling that man whom the gods declared
To be a defilement in the house of Laïos.
After exposing the rankness of my own guilt,
How could I look men frankly in the eyes?
No, I swear it,
If I could have stifled my hearing at its source,
I would have done it and made all this body
A tight cell of misery, blank to light and sound:
So I should have been safe in my dark mind
Beyond external evil.
Ah Kithairon!
Why did you shelter me? When I was cast upon you,
Why did I not die? Then I should never
Have shown the world my execrable birth.

Ah Polybos! Corinth, city that I believed
The ancient seat of my ancestors: how fair
I seemed, your child! And all the while this evil
Was cancerous within me!
For I am sick
In my own being, sick in my origin.

O three roads, dark ravine, woodland and way
Where three roads met: you, drinking my father's blood,
My own blood, spilled by my own hand: can you remember
The unspeakable things I did there, and the things
I went on from there to do?
O marriage, marriage!
That act that engendered me, and again the act
Performed by the son in the same bed—
Ah, the net
Of incest, mingling fathers, brothers, sons,
With brides, wives, mothers: the last evil
That can be known by men: no tongue can say
How evil!
No. For the love of God, conceal me
Somewhere far from Thebes; or kill me; or hurl me
Into the sea, away from men's eyes for ever.

Come, lead me. You need not fear to touch me.
Of all men, I alone can bear this guilt.

(*Enter* KREON.)

CHORAGOS   Kreon is here now. As to what you ask,
   He may decide the course to take. He only
   Is left to protect the city in your place.
OEDIPUS   Alas, how can I speak to him? What right have I
   To beg his courtesy whom I have deeply wronged?
KREON   I have not come to mock you, Oedipus,
   Or to reproach you, either. (*To* ATTENDANTS)
                              —You, standing there:
   If you have lost all respect for man's dignity,
   At least respect the flame of Lord Helios:
   Do not allow this pollution to show itself
   Openly here, an affront to the earth
   And Heaven's rain and the light of day. No, take him
   Into the house as quickly as you can.
   For it is proper
   That only the close kindred see his grief.
OEDIPUS   I pray you in God's name, since your courtesy
   Ignores my dark expectation, visiting
   With mercy this man of all men most execrable:
   Give me what I ask—for your good, not for mine.
KREON   And what is it that you turn to me begging for?
OEDIPUS   Drive me out of this country as quickly as may be
   To a place where no human voice can ever greet me.
KREON   I should have done that before now—only,
   God's will had not been wholly revealed to me.
OEDIPUS   But his command is plain: the parricide
   Must be destroyed. I am that evil man.
KREON   That is the sense of it, yes; but as things are,
   We had best discover clearly what is to be done.
OEDIPUS   You would learn more about a man like me?
KREON   You are ready now to listen to the god.
OEDIPUS   I will listen. But it is to you
   That I must turn for help. I beg you, hear me.

   The woman in there—
   Give her whatever funeral you think proper:
   She is your sister.
                    —But let me go, Kreon!
   Let me purge my father's Thebes of the pollution
   Of my living here, and go out to the wild hills,
   To Kithairon, that has won such fame with me,
   The tomb my mother and father appointed for me,
   And let me die there, as they willed I should.

And yet I know
Death will not ever come to me through sickness
Or in any natural way: I have been preserved
For some unthinkable fate. But let that be.

As for my sons, you need not care for them.
They are men, they will find some way to live.
But my poor daughters, who have shared my table,
Who never before have been parted from their father—
Take care of them, Kreon; do this for me.

And will you let me touch them with my hands
A last time, and let us weep together?
Be kind, my lord,
Great prince, be kind!
                    Could I but touch them,
They would be mine again, as when I had my eyes.

(*Enter* ANTIGONE *and* ISMENE, *attended.*)

Ah, God!
Is it my dearest children I hear weeping?
Has Kreon pitied me and sent my daughters?
KREON   Yes, Oedipus: I knew that they were dear to you
In the old days, and know you must love them still.
OEDIPUS   May God bless you for this—and be a friendlier
Guardian to you than he has been to me!

Children, where are you?
Come quickly to my hands: they are your brother's—
Hands that have brought your father's once clear eyes
To this way of seeing—
                    Ah dearest ones,
I had neither sight nor knowledge then, your father
By the woman who was the source of his own life!
And I weep for you—having no strength to see you—,
I weep for you when I think of the bitterness
That men will visit upon you all your lives.
What homes, what festivals can you attend
Without being forced to depart again in tears?
And when you come to marriageable age,
Where is the man, my daughters, who would dare
Risk the bane that lies on all my children?
Is there any evil wanting? Your father killed
His father; sowed the womb of her who bore him;
Engendered you at the fount of his own existence!

That is what they will say of you.

Then, whom

Can you ever marry? There are no bridegrooms for you,
And your lives must wither away in sterile dreaming.

O Kreon, son of Menoikeus!
You are the only father my daughters have,
Since we, their parents, are both of us gone for ever.
They are your own blood: you will not let them
Fall into beggary and loneliness;
You will keep them from the miseries that are mine!
Take pity on them; see, they are only children,
Friendless except for you. Promise me this,
Great prince, and give me your hand in token of it.

(KREON *clasps his right hand.*)

Children:
I could say much, if you could understand me,
But as it is, I have only this prayer for you:
Live where you can, be as happy as you can—
Happier, please God, than God has made your father.

KREON   Enough. You have wept enough. Now go within.

OEDIPUS   I must; but it is hard.

KREON   Time eases all things.

OEDIPUS   You know my mind, then?

KREON   Say what you desire.

OEDIPUS   Send me from Thebes!

KREON   God grant that I may!

OEDIPUS   But since God hates me . . .

KREON   No, he will grant your wish.

OEDIPUS   You promise?

KREON   I can not speak beyond my knowledge.

OEDIPUS   Then lead me in.

KREON   Come now, and leave your children.

OEDIPUS   No! Do not take them from me!

KREON   Think no longer

That you are in command here, but rather think
How, when you were, you served your own destruction.

(*Exeunt into the house all but the* CHORUS; *the* CHORAGOS *chants directly to the audience.*)

CHORAGOS   Men of Thebes: look upon Oedipus.

This is the king who solved the famous riddle
And towered up, most powerful of men.

No mortal eyes but looked on him with envy,
Yet in the end ruin swept over him.

Let every man in mankind's frailty
Consider his last day; and let none
Presume on his good fortune until he find
Life, at his death, a memory without pain.

LYSISTRATA (411 B.C.)

ARISTOPHANES (c. 450–387 B.C.)

"Old" Greek comedy, represented only by the eleven surviving plays of Aristophanes, is a combination of farce, strip-tease burlesque, music hall routine, fantasy, and serious literary and political satire. It is, in fact, a unique form which did not extend beyond its brief era in history, but it is one of the most delightfully original and entertaining of all comic drama. The *Lysistrata* is the most eminently producible and the most easily appreciated today, with a plot line and variety of characters that appeal to contemporary audiences. Furthermore, its satire on the idiocies of war and the incompetent bumblers who conduct it is universal and immediately comprehensible.

Tragedies were presented in the mornings at the Festival of Dionysus, while afternoons were apparently reserved for comedy. They, too, followed a fairly rigid structural form, including set choral passages and dancing, and a unique section known as the *parabasis* during which the author presented directly to the audience his own personal views about a variety of things. The most characteristic aspect of Old Comedy, however, was its broadly licentious nature, evident, as in the Lysistrata, in the overt sexual and scatalogical passages and in the traditional costume. The uniform characteristic of male figures (all characters were taken by men, as in tragedy) was the huge leather sex organ, the *phallus,* worn just beneath the extremely short tunic and in full view at all times.

We should not associate the phallic aspect of Greek comedy with decadence or debilitating immoral social behavior. The Dionysiac Festival was a time of revelry, and Dionysus was god not only of the vine, hence wine, but also of fertility and, by extension, plain ordinary sex. The ancient Greek, who accepted the performance of athletic events by nude participants (though witnessed only by men) and admired the beauties of the male and female undraped body, entertained a healthy respect for sex as a perfectly natural function, susceptible, as in all civilizations, to a lot of very funny dirty jokes. Once a year the performance of these comedies at the Dionysiac was regarded as an appropriate outlet for a very natural urge. The Greek husband may have kept his wife virtually secluded in his house as an individual with few civil rights, but he was not above thoroughly enjoying in public the rambunctious obscenities of Aristophanic comedy.

The *Lysistrata* is emphatically not in itself a "dirty" play. It is, even more than fairly liberal modern translations indicate, a hilariously obscene play, but it is certainly not pornographic. True, the central theme of the sex strike extends the jokes longer and more fully than in any other of Aristophanes' plays, but the wide-open nature of his exploration of the women's use of their ultimate weapon is tremendously funny and wholly free from any sniggering peep-show quality. It is not, as in most contemporary X-rated "adult" entertainment, sex reduced to a mechanical act displayed by bored participants for its own sake. This play presents sex as a source for pointed social and political comment, but there is no gainsaying that Aristophanes is also providing, fully intentionally, some of the best comic sex sequences in Western drama.

Lysistrata should be read and experienced in production as what it is meant to be: a brilliant satire on sex itself and on the relative position of supposedly dominating men and submissive women turned topsy-turvy in a society gone mad, and as a superb condemnation of the stupidities of the politicians and bureaucrats who have lived in every historical age and who don't know how to stop the troubles they have let themselves in for. Athens experienced its Vietnam in the Pelopponesian war against which Aristophanes rages in many of his plays. When it ended, Athens of the Golden Age had been permanently destroyed. If he couldn't stop the foolishness in any other way, Aristophanes must have hoped that, through the *Lysistrata*, he could at least laugh it to death.

Lysistrata

ARISTOPHANES

English version by Dudley Fitts

CHARACTERS

LYSISTRATA ⎫
KALONIKE ⎬ *Athenian women*
MYRRHINE ⎭
LAMPITO, *a Spartan woman*
CHORUS
MAGISTRATE
KINESIAS, *husband of Myrrhine*
SPARTAN HERALD
SPARTAN AMBASSADOR
A SENTRY
ATHENIAN DRUNKARD

The supernumeraries include the BABY SON *of Kinesias;* STRATYLLIS, *a member of the hemichorus of Old Women; various individual speakers, both Spartan and Athenian.*
Until the exodos, *the* CHORUS *is divided into two hemichori: the first, of Old Men; the second, of Old Women. Each of these has its* CHORAGOS. *In the exodos, the hemichori return as Athenians and Spartans.*

Athens. First, a public square; later, beneath the walls of the Acropolis; later, a courtyard within the Acropolis. Time: early in 411 B.C.

Athens; a public square; early morning; LYSISTRATA *sola.*

LYSISTRATA   If someone had invited them to a festival—
Bacchus's, say, or Pan's, or Aphrodite's, or
that Genetyllis business[1]—, you couldn't get through the streets,
what with the drums and the dancing. But now,
not a woman in sight!
                        Except—oh, yes!

---

[1] *Bacchus, Pan, Aphrodite, Genetyllis* references to cults of love and wine

(*Enter* KALONIKE)

Here's one, at last. Good
morning, Kalonike.

KALONIKE   Good morning, Lysistrata.

Darling,
don't frown so! You'll ruin your face!

LYSISTRATA   Never mind my face.
Kalonike,
the way we women behave! Really, I don't blame the men
for what they say about us.

KALONIKE   No; I imagine they're right.

LYSISTRATA   For example: I call a meeting
to think out a most important matter—and what happens?
The women all stay in bed!

KALONIKE   Oh, they'll be along.
It's hard to get away, you know: a husband, a cook,
a child . . . Home life can be *so* demanding!

LYSISTRATA   What I have in mind is even more demanding.

KALONIKE   Tell me: what is it?

LYSISTRATA   Something big.

KALONIKE   Goodness! *How* big?

LYSISTRATA   Big enough for all of us.

KALONIKE   But we're not all here!

LYSISTRATA   We would be, if *that's* what was up!

No, Kalonike,
this is something I've been turning over for nights;
and, I may say, sleepless nights.

KALONIKE   Can't be so hard, then,
if you've spent so much time on it.

LYSISTRATA   Hard or not,
it comes to this: Only we women can save Greece!

KALONIKE   Only we women? Poor Greece!

LYSISTRATA   Just the same,
it's up to us. First, we must liquidate
the Peloponnesians—

KALONIKE   Fun, fun!

LYSISTRATA   —and then the Boeotians.

KALONIKE   Oh! But not those heavenly eels! [1]

LYSISTRATA   You needn't worry.
Athens shall have her sea food. —But here's the point:
If we can get the women from those places

---

[1] *eels* Boeotia was famous for its sea food, especially its eels.

to join us women here, why, we can save
all Greece!

KALONIKE   But dearest Lysistrata!
How can women do a thing so austere, so
political? We belong at home. Our only armor's
our transparent saffron dresses and
our pretty little shoes!

LYSISTRATA   That's it exactly.
Those transparent saffron dresses, those little shoes—
well, there we are!

KALONIKE   Oh?

LYSISTRATA   Not a single man would lift
his spear—

KALONIKE   I'll get my dress from the dyer's tomorrow!

LYSISTRATA   —or need a shield—

KALONIKE   The sweetest little negligée—

LYSISTRATA   —or bring out his sword.

KALONIKE   I know where I can buy
the dreamiest sandals!

LYSISTRATA   Well, so you see. Now, shouldn't
the women have come?

KALONIKE   Come? they should have *flown*!

LYSISTRATA   Athenians are always late.

                                But imagine!
There's no one here from the South Shore.

KALONIKE   They go to work early,
I can swear to that.

LYSISTRATA   And nobody from Acharnai.
They should have been here hours ago!

KALONIKE   Well, you'll get
that awful Theagenes woman: she's been having
her fortune told at Hecate's shrine.[1]

                                But look!
Someone at last! Can you see who they are?

(*Enter* MYRRHINE *and other women*)

LYSISTRATA   People from the suburbs.

KALONIKE   Yes! The entire
membership of the Suburban League!

---

[1] *Hecate's shrine* Theagenes was notoriously superstitious; his practice of
never leaving home without consulting Hecate is here transferred to his
wife.

MYRRHINE   Sorry to be late, Lysistrata.

Oh, come,

don't scowl so! Say something!

LYSISTRATA   My dear Myrrhine,
what is there to say? After all,
you've been pretty casual about the whole thing.

MYRRHINE   Couldn't find
my girdle in the dark, that's all.

But what *is*

"the whole thing"?

LYSISTRATA   Wait for the rest of them.

KALONIKE   I suppose so. But, look!
Here's Lampito!

(*Enter* LAMPITO *with women from Sparta*)

LYSISTRATA   Darling Lampito,
how pretty you are today! What a nice color!
Goodness, you look as though you could strangle a bull!

LAMPITO   Ah think Ah could! It's the work-out
in the gym every day; and, of co'se that dance of ahs
where y' kick yo' own tail.[1]

LYSISTRATA   What lovely breasts!

LAMPITO   Lawdy, when y' touch me lahk that,
Ah feel lahk a heifer at the altar!

LYSISTRATA   And this young lady?
Where is she from?

LAMPITO   Boeotia. Social-Register type.

LYSISTRATA   Good morning, Boeotian. You're as pretty as
green grass.

KALONIKE   And if you look,
you'll find that the lawn has just been cut.

LYSISTRATA   And this lady?

LAMPITO   From Corinth. But a good woman.

LYSISTRATA   Well, in Corinth
anything's possible.

LAMPITO   But let's get to work. Which one of you
called this meeting, and why?

LYSISTRATA   *I* did.

LAMPITO   Well, then:
what's up?

---

[1] *tail* Among the physical exercises practised by Greek girls was the strenuous
bibasis, a dance in which the dancer kicked her buttocks with her heels.

MYRRHINE   Yes, what *is* "the whole thing," after all?

LYSISTRATA   I'll tell you. —But first, one question.

MYRRHINE   Ask away!

LYSISTRATA   It's your husbands. Fathers of your children. Doesn't it bother you
that they're always off with the Army? I'll stake my life,
not one of you has a man in the house this minute!

KALONIKE   Mine's been in Thrace the last five months, keeping an eye
on that General.[1]

MYRRHINE   Mine's been in Pylos for seven.

LAMPITO   And mahn,
whenever he gets a *dis*charge, he goes raht back
with that li'l ole speah of his, and enlists again!

LYSISTRATA   And not the ghost of a lover to be found!
From the very day the war began—
                                    those Milesians!
I could skin them alive!
                            —I've not seen so much, even,
as one of those devices they call Widow's Delight.
But there! What's important is: I've found a way
to end the war, are you with me?

MYRRHINE   I should *say* so!
Even if I have to pawn my best dress and
drink up the proceeds.[2]

KALONIKE   Me, too! Even if they split me
right up the middle, like a flounder.

LAMPITO   Ah'm shorely with you.
Ah'd crawl up Taygetos[3] on mah knees
if that'd bring peace.

LYSISTRATA   Then here it is.
Women! Sisters!
If we really want our men to make an armistice,
we must be ready to give up—

MYRRHINE   Give up what?
Quick, tell us!

LYSISTRATA   But *will* you?

MYRRHINE   We will, even if it kills us.

---

[1] *General* a certain Eukrates about whom nothing is known

[2] *drink up the proceeds* Athenian women were frequently satirized for heavy drinking.

[3] *Taygetos* a rugged mountain range in the Peloponnesus

LYSISTRATA   Then we must give up sleeping with our men. (*Long
    silence*)
    Oh? So now you're sorry? Won't look at me?
    Doubtful? Pale? All teary-eyed?
                                        But come: be frank with me,
    as I've certainly been with you. Will you do it?
MYRRHINE   I couldn't. No.
    Let the war go on.
KALONIKE   Nor I. Let the war go on.
LYSISTRATA   You, you little flounder,
    ready to be split up the middle?
KALONIKE   Lysistrata, no!
    I'd walk through fire for you—you *know* I would!—, but don't
    ask us to give up *that*! Why, there's nothing like it!
LYSISTRATA   And you?
BOEOTIAN   No. I must say *I'd* rather walk through fire.
LYSISTRATA   You little salamanders!
    No wonder poets write tragedies about women.
    All we want's a quick tumble!
                                        But you from Sparta:
    if you stand by me, we may win yet! Will you?
    It means so much!
LAMPITO   Ah sweah, it means *too* much!
    By the Two Goddesses,[1] it does! Asking a girl
    to sleep—Heaven knows how long!—in a great big bed
    with nobody there but herself! But Ah'll stay with you!
    Peace comes first!
LYSISTRATA   Spoken like a true Spartan!
KALONIKE   But, if—
                  oh dear!
                                —if we give up what you tell us to,
    will there *be* any peace?
LYSISTRATA   Why, mercy, of course there will!
    We'll just sit snug in our very thinnest gowns,
    perfumed and powdered from top to bottom, and those men
    simply won't stand still! And when we say No,
    they'll go out of their minds! And there's your peace.
    You can take my word for it.
LAMPITO   Ah seem to remember
    that Colonel Menelaus threw his sword away
    when he saw Helen's breast all bare.

---

[1] *Two Goddesses* Demeter and Persephone; a woman's oath

KALONIKE   But, goodness me!
What if they just get up and leave us?
LYSISTRATA   Well,
we'd have to fall back on ourselves, of course.
But they won't.
KALONIKE   What if they drag us into the bedroom?
LYSISTRATA   Hang on to the door.
KALONIKE   What if they slap us?
LYSISTRATA   If they do, you'd better give in.
But be sulky about it. Do I have to teach you how?
You know there's no fun for men when they have to force you.
There are millions of ways of getting them to see reason.
Don't you worry: a man
doesn't like it unless the girl co-operates.
KALONIKE   I suppose so. Oh, all right! We'll go along!
LAMPITO   Ah imagine us Spahtans can arrange a peace. But you
Athenians! Why, you're just war-mongerers!
LYSISTRATA   Leave that to me.
I know how to make them listen.
LAMPITO   Ah don't see how.
After all, they've got their boats; and there's lots of money
piled up in the Acropolis.
LYSISTRATA   The Acropolis? Darling,
we're taking over the Acropolis today!
That's the older women's job. All the rest of us
are going to the Citadel to sacrifice—you understand me?
And once there, we're in for good!
LAMPITO   Whee! Up the rebels!
Ah can see you're a good strat*ee*gist.
LYSISTRATA   Well, then, Lampito,
let's take the oath.
LAMPITO   Say it. We'll sweah.
LYSISTRATA   This is it.
—But Lord! Where's our Inner Guard? Never mind.
                                        —You see this
shield? Put it down there. Now bring me the victim's entrails.
KALONIKE   But the oath?
LYSISTRATA   You remember how in Aeschylus' *Seven*[1]
they killed a sheep and swore on a shield? Well, then?
KALONIKE   But I don't see how you can swear for peace on a shield.
LYSISTRATA   What else do you suggest?

---

[1] *Seven Seven Against Thebes*

KALONIKE   Why not a white horse?
We could swear by that.

LYSISTRATA   And where will you get a white horse?

KALONIKE   I never thought of that. *What* can we do?

MYRRHINE   I have it!
Let's set this big black wine-bowl on the ground
and pour in a gallon or so of Thasian,[1] and swear
not to add one drop of water.

LAMPITO   Ah lahk *that* oath!

LYSISTRATA   Bring the bowl and the wine-jug.

KALONIKE   Oh, what a simply *huge* one!

LYSISTRATA   Set it down; and, women, place your hands on the gift-
offering.

O Goddess of Persuasion! And thou, O Loving-cup!
Look upon this our sacrifice, and
be gracious!

KALONIKE   It spills out like blood. How red and pretty it is!

LAMPITO   And Ah must say it smells good.

MYRRHINE   Let me swear first!

KALONIKE   No, by Aphrodite, let's toss for it!

LYSISTRATA   Lampito: all of you women: come, touch the bowl,
and repeat after me:
I WILL HAVE NOTHING TO DO WITH MY HUSBAND
OR MY LOVER

KALONIKE   *I will have nothing to do with my husband or my lover*

LYSISTRATA   THOUGH HE COME TO ME IN PITIABLE
CONDITION

KALONIKE   *Though he come to me in pitiable condition*
(Oh, Lysistrata! This is killing me!)

LYSISTRATA   I WILL STAY IN MY HOUSE UNTOUCHABLE

KALONIKE   *I will stay in my house untouchable*

LYSISTRATA   IN MY THINNEST SAFFRON SILK

KALONIKE   *In my thinnest saffron silk*

LYSISTRATA   AND MAKE HIM LONG FOR ME.

KALONIKE   *And make him long for me.*

LYSISTRATA   I WILL NOT GIVE MYSELF

KALONIKE   *I will not give myself*

LYSISTRATA   AND IF HE CONSTRAINS ME

---

[1] *Thasian* a popular wine from Thasos

KALONIKE   *And if he constrains me*
LYSISTRATA   I WILL BE AS COLD AS ICE AND NEVER
     MOVE
KALONIKE   *I will be as cold as ice and never move*
LYSISTRATA   I WILL NOT LIFT MY SLIPPERS TOWARD
     THE CEILING
KALONIKE   *I will not lift my slippers toward the ceiling*
LYSISTRATA   OR CROUCH ON ALL FOURS LIKE THE
     LIONESS IN THE CARVING
KALONIKE   *Or crouch on all fours like the lioness in the carving*
LYSISTRATA   AND IF I KEEP THIS OATH LET ME DRINK
     FROM THIS BOWL
KALONIKE   *And if I keep this oath let me drink from this bowl*
LYSISTRATA   IF NOT, LET MY OWN BOWL BE FILLED
     WITH WATER.
KALONIKE   *If not, let my own bowl be filled with water.*
LYSISTRATA   You have all sworn?
MYRRHINE   We have.
LYSISTRATA   Then thus
     I sacrifice the victim. (*Drinks largely*)
KALONIKE   Save some for us!
     Here's to you, darling, and to you, and to you! It's all
     for us women. (*Loud cries off-stage*)
LAMPITO   What's all *that* whoozy-goozy?
LYSISTRATA   Just what I told you.
     The older women have taken the Acropolis. Now you, Lampito,
     rush back to Sparta. We'll take care of things here. And
     be sure you get organized!
                           The rest of you girls,
     up to the Citadel: and mind you push in the bolts.
KALONIKE   But the men? Won't they be after us?
LYSISTRATA   Just you leave
     the men to me. There's not fire enough in the world
     to make me open *my* door.
KALONIKE   I hope so, by Aphrodite!
     At any rate,
     let's remember the League's reputation for hanging on!

(*Exeunt*)

The hillside just under the Acropolis

(*Enter* CHORUS OF OLD MEN *with burning torches and braziers; much puffing and coughing*)

MALE CHORAGOS   Easy, Drakes, old friend! Don't skin your shoulders
with those damnable big olive-branches. What a job!

Strophe 1

OLD MEN   Forward, forward, comrades! Whew!
The things that old age does to you!
Neighbor Strymodoros, would you have thought it?
    We've caught it—
                And from women, too!
Women that used to board with us, bed with us—
Now, by the gods, they've got ahead of us,
Taken the Acropolis (Heaven knows why!),
Profaned the sacred statuar-y,
                And barred the doors,
                The aggravating whores!
MALE CHORAGOS   Come, Philourgos, quick, pile your brushwood
next to the wall there.
                These traitors to Athens and to us,
we'll fry each last one of them! And the very first
will be old Lykon's wife.[1]

Antistrophe 1

OLD MEN   By Demeter I swear it—(ouch!),
I'll not perform the Kleomenes-crouch!
How he looked—and a good soldier, too—
    When out he flew,
                that filthy pouch
Of a body of his all stinking and shaggy,
Bare as an eel, except for the bag he
Covered his rear with. Lord, what a mess!
Never a bath in six years, I'd guess!
                Unhappy Sparta,
                With such a martyr! [2]
MALE CHORAGOS   What a siege, friends! Seventeen ranks strong
we stood at the Gate, and never a chance for a nap.
And all because of women, whom the gods hate
(and so does Euripides).
                It's enough to make a veteran
turn in his medals from Marathon!

---

[1] *Lykon's wife* Rhodia, a famous belle of the day
[2] *martyr* Kleomenes, a King of Sparta, had captured the Acropolis but had
been forced to give it up.

Strophe 2

OLD MEN   Forward, men! Just up the hillside,
  And we're there!
 Keep to the path! A yoke of oxen
  Wouldn't care
   To haul this lumber. Mind the fire,
   Or it'll die before we're higher!
    Puff! Puff!
   This smoke will strangle me, sure enough!

Antistrophe 2

 Holy Heracles, I'm blinded,
  Sure as fate!
 It's Lemnos-fire[1] we've been toting;
  And isn't it great
   To be singed by this infernal flame?
   (Laches, remember the Goddess: for shame!)
    Woof! Woof!
  A few steps more, and we're under the roof!
MALE CHORAGOS   It catches! It's blazing!
 Down with your loads!
 We'll sizzle 'em now,
 By all the gods!
 Vine-branches here, quick!
 Light 'em up,
 And in through the gate with 'em!
 If that doesn't stop
 Their nonsense—well,
 We'll smoke 'em to Hell.
 Ker*shoo*!
 (What we really need
 Is a grad-u-ate,
 Top of his class,
 From Samos Military State.[2]
 Achoo!)
 Come, do
 Your duty, you!
 Pour out your braziers,

---

[1] *Lemnos-fire* volcanic; Mount Moschylus on the island of Lemnos was the site of Vulcan's forge.

[2] *Samos Military State* At this time Samos was the headquarters of Athenian military activities.

Embers ablaze!
But first, Gentlemen, allow me to raise
The paean:
                    Lady
Victory, now
Assist thine adherents
Here below!
Down with women!
Up with men!
Io triumphe! [1]

OLD MEN   Amen!

(*Enter* CHORUS OF OLD WOMEN *on the walls of the Acropolis, carrying jars of water to extinguish the fire set by the* CHORUS OF OLD MEN.)

FEMALE CHORAGOS   Fire, fire!
   Quickly, quickly, women, if we're to save ourselves!

Strophe

OLD WOMEN   Nikodike, run!
        Or Kalyke's done
        To a turn, and poor Kratylla's
        Smoked like a ham.
                            Damn
        These men and their wars,
        Their hateful ways!
        I nearly died before I got to the place
        Where we fill our jars:
            Slaves pushing and jostling—
            Such a hustling
        I never saw in all my days!

Antistrophe

        But here's water at last.
        Sisters, make haste
        And slosh it down on them,
        The silly old wrecks!
                            Sex
        Almighty! What they want's
        A hot bath? Send it down!
        And thou, Athena of Athens town,
        Assist us in drowning their wheezy taunts!

---

[1] *Io triumphe* a ritual cry of triumph

O Trito-born! [1] Helmet of Gold!
Help us to cripple their backs, the old
Fools with their semi-incendiary brawn!

(*The* OLD MEN *capture a woman,* STRATYLLIS)

STRATYLLIS   Let me go! Let me go!
FEMALE CHORAGOS   You walking corpses,
have you no shame?
MALE CHORAGOS   I wouldn't have believed it!
An army of women in the Acropolis!
FEMALE CHORAGOS   So we scare you, do we? Grandpa, you've seen
only our pickets yet!
MALE CHORAGOS   Hey, Phaidrias!
Help me with the necks of these jabbering hens!
FEMALE CHORAGOS   Down with your pots, girls! We'll need
both hands
if these antiques attack us.
MALE CHORAGOS   Want your face kicked in?
FEMALE CHORAGOS   Want to try my teeth?
MALE CHORAGOS   Look out! I've got a stick!
FEMALE CHORAGOS   You lay a half-inch of your stick on Stratyllis,
and you'll never stick again!
MALE CHORAGOS   Fall apart!
FEMALE CHORAGOS   I'll chew your guts!
MALE CHORAGOS   Euripides! Master!
How well you knew women!
FEMALE CHORAGOS   Listen to him! Rhodippe,
up with the pots!
MALE CHORAGOS   Demolition of God,
what good are your pots?
FEMALE CHORAGOS   You refugee from the tomb,
what good is your fire?
MALE CHORAGOS   Good enough to make a pyre
to barbecue you!
FEMALE CHORAGOS   We'll squizzle your kindling!
MALE CHORAGOS   You think so?
FEMALE CHORAGOS   Yah! Just hang around a while!
MALE CHORAGOS   Want a touch of my torch?
FEMALE CHORAGOS   Your torch needs a bath.
MALE CHORAGOS   How about you?

---

[1] *Trito-born* Athena; according to some versions of her story, she was born
at Lake Tritonis in Libya.

FEMALE CHORAGOS   Soap for a senile bridegroom!
MALE CHORAGOS   Senile? Hold your trap!
FEMALE CHORAGOS   Just *you* try to hold it!
MALE CHORAGOS   The yammer of women!
FEMALE CHORAGOS   The yatter of men!
   But you'll never sit in the jury-box again.
MALE CHORAGOS   Gentlemen, I beg you, burn off that woman's hair!
FEMALE CHORAGOS   Let it come down! (*They empty their pots on
   the men*)
MALE CHORAGOS   What a way to drown!
FEMALE CHORAGOS   Hot, hey?
MALE CHORAGOS   Say,
   enough!
FEMALE CHORAGOS   Dandruff
   needs watering. I'll make you
   nice and fresh.
MALE CHORAGOS   For God's sake, you
   sluts, hold off!

(*Enter a* MAGISTRATE *accompanied by four constables*)

MAGISTRATE   These degenerate women! What a racket of little
   drums,
what a yapping for Adonis on every house-top!
It's like the time in the Assembly when I was listening
to a speech—out of order, as usual—by that fool
Demostratos,[1] all about troops for Sicily,
that kind of nonsense—
               and there was his wife
trotting around in circles howling
Alas for Adonis!—
          and Demostratos insisting
we must draft every last Zakynthian that can walk—
and his wife up there on the roof,
drunk as an owl, yowling
Oh weep for Adonis!—
          and that damned ox Demostratos
mooing away through the rumpus. That's what we get
for putting up with this wretched woman-business!

---

[1] *Demostratos* a well known demagogue; the speech alludes to the festival in
honor of Adonis which four years earlier had coincided with the decision
to undertake the disastrous Sicilian expedition. It was believed that the
women's madness in lamenting Adonis had influenced the decision.

MALE CHORAGOS   Sir, you haven't heard the half of it. They laughed
at us!
Insulted us! They took pitchers of water
and nearly drowned us! We're still wringing out our clothes,
for all the world like unhousebroken brats.
MAGISTRATE   And a good thing, by Poseidon!
Whose fault is it if these women-folk of ours
get out of hand? We coddle them,
we teach them to be wasteful and loose. You'll see a husband
go into a jeweler's. "Look," he'll say,
"jeweler," he'll say, "you remember that gold choker
"you made for my wife? Well, she went to a dance last night
"and broke the clasp. Now, I've got to go to Salamis,
"and can't be bothered. Run over to my house tonight,
"will you, and see if you can put it together for her."
Or another one
goes to a cobbler—a good strong workman, too,
with an awl that was never meant for child's play. "Here,"
he'll tell him, "one of my wife's shoes is pinching
"her little toe. Could you come up about noon
"and stretch it out for her?"
                                            Well, what do you expect?
Look at me, for example. I'm a Public Officer,
and it's one of my duties to pay off the sailors.
And where's the money? Up there in the Acropolis!
And those blasted women slam the door in my face!
But what are we waiting for?
                                            —Look here, constable,
stop sniffing around for a tavern, and get us
some crowbars. We'll force their gates! As a matter of fact,
I'll do a little forcing myself.

(*Enter* LYSISTRATA, *above, with* MYRRHINE, KALONIKE, *and the*
BOEOTIAN)

LYSISTRATA   No need of forcing.
Here I am, of my own accord. And all this talk
about locked doors—! We don't need locked doors,
but just the least bit of common sense.
MAGISTRATE   Is that so, ma'am!
                                            —Where's my constable?
                                                        —Constable,
arrest that woman, and tie her hands behind her.
LYSISTRATA   If he touches me, I swear by Artemis
there'll be one scamp dropped from the public pay-roll tomorrow!

MAGISTRATE   Well, constable? You're not afraid, I suppose? Grab
her,
two of you, around the middle!
KALONIKE   No, by Pandrosos! [1]
Lay a hand on her, and I'll jump on you so hard
your guts will come out the back door!
MAGISTRATE   That's what *you* think!
Where's the sergeant?—Here, you: tie up that trollop first,
the one with the pretty talk!
MYRRHINE   By the Moon-Goddess! [2]
Just you try it, and you'd better call a surgeon!
MAGISTRATE   Another one!
                               Officer, seize that woman!
                                                       I swear
I'll put an end to this riot!
BOEOTIAN   By the Taurian, [3]
one inch closer and you won't have a hair on your head!
MAGISTRATE   Lord, what a mess! And my constables seem to have
left me.
But—women get the best of us? By God, no!
                                       —Scythians! [4]
Close ranks and forward march!
LYSISTRATA   "Forward," indeed!
By the Two Goddesses, what's the sense in *that*?
They're up against four companies of women
armed from top to bottom.
MAGISTRATE   Forward, my Scythians!
LYSISTRATA   Forward, yourselves, dear comrades!
You grainlettucebeanseedmarket girls!
You garlicandonionbreadbakery girls!
Give it to 'em! Knock 'em down! Scratch 'em!
Tell 'em what you think of 'em! (*General mêlée; the Scythians
yield*)
                                       —Ah, that's enough!
Sound a retreat; good soldiers don't rob the dead!
MAGISTRATE   A nice day *this* has been for the police!
LYSISTRATA   Well, there you are.—Did you really think we women

---

[1] *Pandrosos* one of the daughters of the founder of Athens; a woman's oath
[2] *Moon-Goddess* Artemis
[3] *Taurian* again Artemis, who was worshipped at Taurica Chersonesos
[4] *Scythians* Athens' finest archers

would be driven like slaves? Maybe now you'll admit
that a woman knows something about glory.

MAGISTRATE   Glory enough.
especially glory in bottles! Dear Lord Apollo!

MALE CHORAGOS   Your Honor, there's no use talking to them. Words
mean nothing whatever to wild animals like these.
Think of the sousing they gave us! and the water
was not, I believe, of the purest.

FEMALE CHORAGOS   You shouldn't have come after us. And if you
try it again,
you'll be one eye short!—Although, as a matter of fact,
what I like best is just to stay at home and read,
like a sweet little bride: never hurting a soul, no,
never going out. But if you *must* shake hornets' nests,
look out for the hornets!

Strophe

OLD MEN   Good God, what can we do?
What are we coming to?
These women! Who could bear it? But, for that matter, who
Will find
What they had in mind
When they seized Cranaos' city
And held it (more's the pity!)
Against us men of Athens, and our police force, too?

MALE CHORAGOS   We might question them, I suppose. But I warn
you, sir,
don't believe anything you hear! It would be un-Athenian
not to get to the bottom of this plot.

MAGISTRATE   Very well.
My first question is this: Why, so help you God,
did you bar the gates of the Acropolis?

LYSISTRATA   Why?
To keep the money, of course. No money, no war.

MAGISTRATE   You think that money's the cause of war?

LYSISTRATA   I do.
Money brought about the Peisandros business[1]

---

[1] *Peisandros* a politician who, even as Aristophanes was completing this play,
was bringing about the revolution of the Four Hundred, which overthrew
Athenian democracy

and all the other attacks on the State. Well and good!
They'll not get another cent here!

MAGISTRATE   And what will you do?

LYSISTRATA   What a question! From now on, we intend
to control the Treasury.

MAGISTRATE   Control the Treasury!

LYSISTRATA   Why not? Does that seem strange? After all,
we control our household budgets.

MAGISTRATE   But that's different!

LYSISTRATA   "Different"? What do you mean?

MAGISTRATE   I mean simply this:
it's the Treasury that pays for National Defense.

LYSISTRATA   Unnecessary. We propose to abolish war!

MAGISTRATE   Good God.—And National Security?

LYSISTRATA   Leave that to us.

MAGISTRATE   You?

LYSISTRATA   Us.

MAGISTRATE   We're done for, then!

LYSISTRATA   Never mind.
We women will save you in spite of yourselves.

MAGISTRATE   What nonsense!

LYSISTRATA   If you like. But you must accept it, like it or not.

MAGISTRATE   Why, this is downright subversion!

LYSISTRATA   Maybe it is.
But we're going to save you, Judge.

MAGISTRATE   I don't *want* to be saved!

LYSISTRATA   Tut. The death-wish. All the more reason.

MAGISTRATE   But the idea
of women bothering themselves about peace and war!

LYSISTRATA   Will you listen to me?

MAGISTRATE   Yes. But be brief, or I'll—

LYSISTRATA   This is no time for stupid threats.

MAGISTRATE   By the gods,
I'm losing my mind!

AN OLD WOMAN   That's nice. If you do, remember
you've less to lose than *we* have.

MAGISTRATE   Quiet, you old buzzard!
Now, Lysistrata: tell me what you're thinking.

LYSISTRATA   Glad to.
                 Ever since this war began
we women have been watching you men, agreeing with you,
keeping our thoughts to ourselves. That doesn't mean
we were happy: we weren't, for we saw how things were going;

but we'd listen to you at dinner
arguing this way and that.
                              —Oh you, and your big
Top Secrets!—
                    And then we'd grin like little patriots
(though goodness knows we didn't feel like grinning) and ask you:
"Dear, did the Armistice come up in Assembly today?"
And you'd say, "None of your business! Pipe down!," you'd say.
And so we would.
AN OLD WOMAN   *I* wouldn't have, by God!
MAGISTRATE   You'd have taken a beating, then!
                                                    —Please go on.
LYSISTRATA   Well, we'd be quiet. But then, you know, all at once
you men would think up something worse than ever.
Even *I* could see it was fatal. And, "Darling," I'd say,
"have you gone completely mad?" And my husband would look at
    me
and say, "Wife, you've got your weaving to attend to.
"Mind your tongue, if you don't want a slap. 'War's
" 'a man's affair!' " [1]
MAGISTRATE   Good words, and well pronounced!
LYSISTRATA   You're a fool if you think so.
                                        It was hard enough
to put up with all this banquet-hall strategy.
But then we'd hear you out in the public square:
"Nobody left for the draft-quota here in Athens?"
you'd say; and, "No," someone else would say, "not a man!"
And so we women decided to rescue Greece.
You might as well listen to us now: you'll have to, later.
MAGISTRATE   *You* rescue Greece? Absurd!
LYSISTRATA   You're the absurd one!
MAGISTRATE   You expect me to take orders from a woman?
LYSISTRATA   Heavens, if that's what's bothering you, take my veil,
here, and my girdle, and my market-basket. Go home
to your weaving and your cooking! I tell you, "War's
a woman's affair!"
FEMALE CHORAGOS   Down with your pitchers, comrades,
but keep them close at hand. It's time for a rally!

---

[1] *War's a man's affair* quoted from Hector's farewell to Andromache, *Iliad,*
VI, 492

Antistrophe

OLD WOMEN   Dance, girls, dance for peace!
>   Who cares if our knees
> Wobble and creak? Shall we not dance for such allies as these?
>   Their wit! their grace! their beauty!
>   It's a municipal duty
> To dance them luck and happiness who risk their all for Greece!

FEMALE CHORAGOS   Women, remember your grandmothers! Remember, you were born
among brambles and nettles! Dance for victory!

LYSISTRATA   O Eros, god of delight! O Aphrodite! Cyprian!
Drench us now with the savor of love!
Let these men, getting wind of us, dream such joy
that they'll tail us through all the provinces of Hellas!

MAGISTRATE   And if we do?

LYSISTRATA   Well, for one thing, we shan't have to watch you
going to market, a spear in one hand, and heavens knows
what in the other.

FEMALE CHORAGOS   Nicely said, by Aphrodite!

LYSISTRATA   As things stand now, you're neither men nor women.
Armor clanking with kitchen pans and pots—
you sound like a pack of Corybantes! [1]

MAGISTRATE   A man must do what a man must do.

LYSISTRATA   So I'm told.
But to see a General, complete with Gorgon-shield,
jingling along the dock to buy a couple of herrings!

FEMALE CHORAGOS   *I* saw a Captain the other day—lovely fellow he was,
nice curly hair—sitting on his horse; and—can you believe it?—
he'd just bought some soup, and was pouring it into his helmet!
And there was a soldier from Thrace
swishing his lance like something out of Euripides,
and the poor fruit-store woman got so scared
that she ran away and let him have his figs free!

MAGISTRATE   All this is beside the point.
                                        Will you be so kind
as to tell me how you mean to save Greece?

LYSISTRATA   Of course!
Nothing could be simpler.

---

[1] *Corybantes* wild and frenzied dancers; attendants of the goddess Cybele

MAGISTRATE   I assure you, I'm all ears.

LYSISTRATA   Do you know anything about weaving?
Say the yarn gets tangled: we thread it
this way and that through the skein, up and down,
until it's free. And it's like that with war.
We'll send our envoys
up and down, this way and that, all over Greece,
until it's finished.

MAGISTRATE   Yarn? Thread? Skein?
Are you out of your mind? I tell you,
war is a serious business.

LYSISTRATA   So serious
that I'd like to go on talking about weaving.

MAGISTRATE   All right. Go ahead.

LYSISTRATA   The first thing we have to do
is to wash our yarn, get the dirt out of it.
You see? Isn't there too much dirt here in Athens?
You must wash those men away.

                    Then our spoiled wool—
that's like your job-hunters, out for a life
of no work and big pay. Back to the basket,
citizens or not, allies or not,
or friendly immigrants!

                    And your colonies?
Hanks of wool lost in various places. Pull them
together, weave them into one great whole,
and our voters are clothed for ever.

MAGISTRATE   It would take a woman
to reduce state questions to a matter of carding and weaving!

LYSISTRATA   You fool! Who were the mothers whose sons sailed off
to fight for Athens in Sicily?

MAGISTRATE   Enough!
I beg you, do not call back those memories.

LYSISTRATA   And then,
instead of the love that every woman needs,
we have only our single beds, where we can dream
of our husbands off with the Army.

                          Bad enough for wives!
But what about our girls, getting older every day,
and older, and no kisses?

MAGISTRATE   Men get older, too.

LYSISTRATA   Not in the same sense.

                    A soldier's discharged,
and he may be bald and toothless, yet he'll find

a pretty young thing to go to bed with.
                                        But a woman!
Her beauty is gone with the first grey hair.
She can spend her time
consulting the oracles and the fortune-tellers,
but they'll never send her a husband.

MAGISTRATE   Still, if a man can rise to the occasion—

LYSISTRATA (*Furiously*)   Rise? Rise, yourself!
Go invest in a coffin!
                        You've money enough.
                                        I'll bake you
a cake for the Underworld.[1]
                        And here's your funeral
wreath! (*She pours water upon him*)

MYRRHINE   And here's another! (*More water*)

KALONIKE   And here's
my contribution! (*More water*)

LYSISTRATA   What are you waiting for?
All aboard Styx Ferry! [2]
                        Charon's calling for you!
It's sailing-time: don't disrupt the schedule!

MAGISTRATE   The insolence of women! And to me!
No, by God, I'll go back to court and show
the rest of the Bench the things that might happen to them!

(*Exit* MAGISTRATE)

LYSISTRATA   Really, I suppose we should have laid out his corpse
on the doorstep, in the usual way.
                        But never mind!
We'll give him the rites of the dead tomorrow morning!

(*Exit* LYSISTRATA *with* MYRRHINE *and* KALONIKE)

Strophe 1

OLD MEN   Sons of Liberty, strip off your clothes for action! Men
     arise!
Shall we stand here limp and useless while old Cleisthenes' [3] allies

---

[1] *Underworld* a honey cake was usually placed in the hand of the dead to
be given to Cerberus, the three-headed dog guarding the gates of Hades

[2] *Styx Ferry* the Styx was the river over which Charon ferried the souls of
the dead

[3] *Cleisthenes* an Athenian of notorious bisexual tendencies

Prod a herd of furious grandmas to attempt to bring to pass
A female restoration of the Reign of Hippias? [1]
      Forbid it, gods misogynist!
      Return our Treasury, at least!
We must clothe ourselves and feed ourselves to face these civic
    rages,
And who can do a single thing if they cut off our wages?

MALE CHORAGOS   Gentlemen, we are disgraced forever if we allow
   these madwomen to jabber about spears and shields
   and make friends with the Spartans. What's a Spartan? a wild
   wolf's a safer companion any day! No; their plan's
   to bring back Dictatorship; and we won't stand for that!
   From now on, let's go armed, each one of us
   a new Aristogeiton!
              And to begin with,
   I propose to poke a number of teeth
   down the gullet of that harridan over there.

Antistrophe 1

OLD WOMEN   Hold your tongues, you senile bravoes, or I swear,
   when you get home
   Your own mothers wouldn't know you! Strip for action, ladies,
   come!
   I bore the holy vessels in my eighth year,[2] and at ten
   I was pounding out the barley for Athena Goddess,[3] then
              They elected me Little Bear
              For Artemis at Brauron Fair,[4]
   I'd been made a Basket-Carrier[5] by the time I came of age:
   So trust me to advise you in this feminist rampage!

FEMALE CHORAGOS   As a woman, I pay my taxes to the State,
   though I pay them in baby boys. What do you contribute,
   you impotent horrors? Nothing but waste:

---

[1] *Hippias* last of the Athenian tyrants. He had ruled with his brother Hipparchos until the latter's death at the hands of the patriots Aristogeiton and Harmonius; Hippias was killed later at Marathon

[2] *eighth year* four girls of high birth between the ages of seven and eleven were appointed to service in the Temple of Athena on the Acropolis

[3] *Athena Goddess* at ten a girl of aristocratic family was eligible to be Millmaid and to grind the sacred grain of Athena

[4] *Brauron Fair* Brauron was a town on the coast of Attica where a ceremony to Artemis was celebrated in which a little girl impersonated a bear

[5] *Basket-Carrier* girls carried baskets containing precious objects sacred to Athena

our treasury, the so-called Glory of the Persian Wars,
gone! rifled! parceled out for privilege! And you
have the insolence to control public policy,
leading us all to disaster!

> No, don't answer back
unless you want the heel of my slipper
slap against that ugly jaw of yours!

Strophe 2

OLD MEN What impudence!
What malevolence!
Comrades, make haste,
All those of you who still are sensitive below the waist!
Off with your clothes, men!
Nobody knows when
We'll put them back on.
Remember Leipsydrion! [1]
We may be old,
But let's be bold!

MALE CHORAGOS Give them an inch, and we're done for! We'll have
them
launching boats next and planning naval strategy.
Or perhaps they fancy themselves as cavalry!
That's fair enough: women know how to ride,
they're good in the saddle. Just think of Mikon's paintings,[2]
all those Amazons wrestling with men! No, it's time
to bridle these wild mares!

Antistrophe 2

OLD WOMEN Hold on, or
You *are* done for,
By the Two Goddesses above!
Strip, strip, my women: we've got the veterans on the move!
Tangle with me, Gramps,
And you'll have cramps
For the rest of your days!
No more beans! No more cheese!

---

[1] *Leipsydrion* after the patriots had killed Hipparchos, they fled and fortified
themselves in Leipsydrion; after a heroic defense they were forced to surrender

[2] *Mikon's paintings* Mikon was one of the many painters who dealt with the
invasion of Attica by the Amazons, a fabulous race of warrior-women

My two legs
Will scramble your eggs!
FEMALE CHORAGOS   If Lampito stands by me, and that elegant
   Theban girl, Ismenia—what good are *you*?

                                          Pass your laws!
   Laws upon laws, you decrepit legislators!
   At the worst you're just a nuisance, rationing Boeotian eels
   on the Feast of Hecate, making our girls go without!
   That was statesmanship! And we'll have to put up with it
   until some patriot slits your silly old gizzards!

(Exeunt omnes)

The scene shifts to a court within the Acropolis

(Re-enter LYSISTRATA*)*

FEMALE CHORAGOS   But Lysistrata! Leader! Why such a grim face?
LYSISTRATA   Oh the behavior of these idiotic women!
   There's something about the female temperament
   that I can't bear!
FEMALE CHORAGOS   What in the world do you mean?
LYSISTRATA   Exactly what I say.
FEMALE CHORAGOS   What dreadful thing has happened?
   Come, tell us: we're all your friends.
LYSISTRATA   It isn't easy
   to say it; yet, God knows, we can't hush it up.
FEMALE CHORAGOS   Well, then? Out with it!
LYSISTRATA   To put it bluntly,
   we're desperate for men.
FEMALE CHORAGOS   Almighty God!
LYSISTRATA   Why bring God into it?—No, it's just as I say.
   I can't manage them any longer: they've gone man-crazy,
   they're all trying to get out.
                          Why, look:
   one of them was sneaking out the back door
   over there by Pan's cave,[1] another
   was sliding down the walls with rope and tackle;
   another was climbing aboard a sparrow,[2] ready to take off
   for the nearest brothel—I dragged *her* back by the hair!
   They're all finding some reason to leave.
                          Look there!

---

[1] *Pan's cave* a grotto on the north side of the Acropolis
[2] *sparrow* a bird sacred to Aphrodite; it had been harnessed to the chariot
of the goddess

There goes another one.

                        —Just a minute, you!
Where are you off to so fast?

FIRST WOMAN   I've got to get home!
I've a lot of Milesian wool, and the worms are spoiling it.

LYSISTRATA   Oh bother you and your worms! Get back inside!

FIRST WOMAN   I'll be back right away, I swear I will!
I just want to get it stretched out on my bed.

LYSISTRATA   You'll do no such thing. You'll stay right here.

FIRST WOMAN   And my wool?
You want it ruined?

LYSISTRATA   Yes, for all I care.

SECOND WOMAN   Oh dear! My lovely new flax from Amorgos—[1]
I left it at home, all uncarded!

LYSISTRATA   Another one!
And all she wants is someone to card her flax.
Get back in there!

SECOND WOMAN   But I swear by the Moon-Goddess,
the minute I get it done, I'll be back!

LYSISTRATA   I say No!
If you, why not all the other women as well?

THIRD WOMAN   O Lady Eileithyia![2] Radiant goddess! Thou
intercessor for women in childbirth! Stay, I pray thee,
oh stay this parturition! Shall I pollute
a sacred spot?

LYSISTRATA   And what's the matter with *you*?

THIRD WOMAN   I'm having a baby—any minute now!

LYSISTRATA   But you weren't pregnant yesterday.

THIRD WOMAN   Well, I am today!
Let me go home for a midwife, Lysistrata:
there's not much time.

LYSISTRATA   I never heard such nonsense.
What's that bulging under your cloak?

THIRD WOMAN   A little baby boy.

LYSISTRATA   It certainly isn't. But it's something hollow,
like a basin or— Why, it's the helmet of Athena!
And you said you were having a baby!

THIRD WOMAN   Well, I am! So there!

LYSISTRATA   Then why the helmet?

---

[1] *Amorgos* an island in the Aegean famed for its flax

[2] *Lady Eileithyia* the goddess invoked by women at childbirth; it was un
lawful to bear children on the Acropolis because it was holy ground

THIRD WOMAN   I was afraid that my pains
  might begin here in the Acropolis; and I wanted
  to drop my chick into it, just as the dear doves do.
LYSISTRATA   Lies! Evasions!—But at least one thing's clear:
  you can't leave the place before your purification.
THIRD WOMAN   But I can't stay here in the Acropolis! Last night I
      dreamed
  of a snake.[1]
FIRST WOMAN   And those horrible owls,[2] the noise they make!
  I can't get a bit of sleep; I'm just about dead.
LYSISTRATA   You useless girls, that's enough: Let's have no more
      lying.
  Of course you want your men. But don't you imagine
  that they want you just as much? I'll give you my word,
  their nights must be pretty hard.
                          Just stick it out!
  A little patience, that's all, and our battle's won.
  I have heard an Oracle. Should you like to hear it?
FIRST WOMAN   An Oracle? Yes, tell us!
LYSISTRATA   Quiet, then.—Here
  is what it said:
  IF EVER THE SWALLOWS, ESCHEWING HOOPOE-BIRDS,
  SHALL CONSPIRE TOGETHER TO DENY THEM ALL
      ACCESS,
  THEIR GRIEF IS FOREVER OVER.
                          These are the words
  from the Shrine itself.
                          AYE, AND ZEUS WILL REDRESS
  THEIR WRONGS, AND SET THE LOWER ABOVE THE
      HIGHER.
FIRST WOMAN   Does that mean we'll be on top?
LYSISTRATA   BUT IF THEY RETIRE,
  EACH SWALLOW HER OWN WAY, FROM THIS HOLY
      PLACE,
  LET THE WORLD PROCLAIM NO BIRD OF SORRIER
      GRACE
  THAN THE SWALLOW.
FIRST WOMAN   I swear, *that* Oracle makes sense!
LYSISTRATA   Now, then, by all the gods,

---

[1] *snake* the sacred snake of the Acropolis; it was never seen but was believed
  to guard the holy ground
[2] *owls* birds sacred to Athena

let's show that we're bigger than these annoyances.
Back to your places! Let's not disgrace the Oracle.

(*Exeunt* LYSISTRATA *and the dissident women; the* CHORUSES *renew their conflict*)

Strophe

OLD MEN   I know a little story that I learned way back in school
Goes like this:
Once upon a time there was a young man—and no fool—
Named Melanion;[1] and his
One aversi-on was marriage. He loathed the very thought!
So he ran off to the hills, and in a special grot
Raised a dog, and spent his days
Hunting rabbits. And it says
That he never never never did come home.
It might be called a refuge *from* the womb.
All right,
      all right,
           all right!
We're as pure as young Melanion, and we hate the very sight
Of you sluts!
A MAN   How about a kiss, old woman?
A WOMAN   Here's an onion in your eye!
A MAN   A kick in the guts, then?
A WOMAN   Try, old bristle-tail, just try!
A MAN   Yet they say Myronides[2]
On hands and knees
Looked just as shaggy fore and aft as I!

Antistrophe

OLD WOMEN   Well, *I* know a little story, and it's just as good as yours.
Goes like this:
Once there was a man named Timon[3]—a rough diamond, of
   course,
And that whiskery face of his
Looked like murder in the shrubbery. By God, he was a son
Of the Furies, let me tell you! And what did he do but run
From the world and all its ways,

---

[1] *Melanion* the suitor of Atalanta, who hated men. The Chorus of Old Men have made him a hater of women
[2] *Myronides* a famous Athenenian general
[3] *Timon* a famous Athenian misanthrope

Cursing mankind! And it says
That his choicest execrations as of then
Were leveled almost wholly at *old* men.
All right,
      all right,
            all right!
But there's one thing about Timon: he could always stand the sight
Of us "sluts"!

A WOMAN   How about a crack in the jaw, Pop?

A MAN   I can take it, Ma—no fear!

A WOMAN   How about a kick in the face?

A MAN   You'd show your venerable rear.

A WOMAN   I may be old;
But I've been told
That I've nothing to worry about down there!

(Re-enter LYSISTRATA*)*

LYSISTRATA   Oh, quick, girls, quick! Come here!

FEMALE CHORAGOS   What is it?

LYSISTRATA   A man!
A man simply bulging with love!
                    O Cyprian Queen,
O Paphian, O Cythereian! Hear us and aid us!

FEMALE CHORAGOS   Where is this enemy?

LYSISTRATA   Over there, by Demeter's shrine.

FEMALE CHORAGOS   Damned if he isn't. But who *is* he?

MYRRHINE   My husband.
Kinesias.

LYSISTRATA   Oh then, get busy! Tease him! Undermine him!
Wreck him! Give him everything—kissing, tickling, nudging,
whatever you generally torture him with—: give him everything
except what we swore on the wine we would not give.

MYRRHINE   Trust me!

LYSISTRATA   I do. But I'll help you get him started.
The rest of you women, stay back.

(Enter KINESIAS*)*

KINESIAS   Oh God! Oh my God!
I'm stiff for lack of exercise. All I can do to stand up!

LYSISTRATA   Halt! Who are you, approaching our lines?

KINESIAS   Me? I.

LYSISTRATA   A man?

KINESIAS   You have eyes, haven't you?

LYSISTRATA   Go away.

KINESIAS   Who says so?

LYSISTRATA   Officer of the Day.

KINESIAS   Officer, I beg you,
by all the gods at once, bring Myrrhine out!

LYSISTRATA   Myrrhine? And who, my good sir, are you?

KINESIAS   Kinesias. Last name's Pennison. Her husband.

LYSISTRATA   Oh, of course. I beg your pardon. We're glad to see
you.
We've heard so much about you. Dearest Myrrhine
is always talking about "Kinesias"—never nibbles an egg
or an apple without saying
"Here's to Kinesias!"

KINESIAS   Do you really mean it?

LYSISTRATA   I do.
When we're discussing men, she always says,
"Well, after all, there's nobody like Kinesias!"

KINESIAS   Good God.—Well, then, please send her down here.

LYSISTRATA   And what do *I* get out of it?

KINESIAS   A standing promise.

LYSISTRATA   I'll take it up with her.

(*Exit* LYSISTRATA)

KINESIAS   But be quick about it!
Lord, what's life without a wife? Can't eat. Can't sleep.
Every time I go home, the place is so empty, so
insufferably sad! Love's killing me! Oh,
hurry!

(*Enter* MANES, *a slave, with Kinesias' baby; the voice of* MYRRHINE *is
heard off-stage*)

MYRRHINE   But of course I love him! Adore him!—but no,
he hates love. No. I won't go down.

(*Enter* MYRRHINE, *above*)

KINESIAS   Myrrhine!
Darlingest little Myrrhine! Come down quick!

MYRRHINE   Certainly not.

KINESIAS   Not? But why, Myrrhine?

MYRRHINE   Why? You don't need me.

KINESIAS   Need you? My God, *look* at me!

MYRRHINE   So long! (*Turns to go*)

KINESIAS   Myrrhine, Myrrhine, Myrrhine!
If not for my sake, for our child! (*Pinches* BABY)
                    —All right, you: pipe up!

BABY Mummie! Mummie! Mummie!

KINESIAS   You hear that?
Pitiful, I call it. Six days now
with never a bath; no food; enough to break your heart!

MYRRHINE My darlingest child! What a father *you* acquired!

KINESIAS At least come down for his sake!

MYRRHINE   I suppose I must.
Oh, this mother business! [1]

(*Exit*)

KINESIAS   How pretty she is! And younger!
She's so much nicer when she's bothered!

(MYRRHINE *enters, below*)

MYRRHINE   Dearest child,
you're as sweet as your father's horrid. Give me a kiss.

KINESIAS Now you see how wrong it was to get involved
in this scheming League of women. All this agony
for nothing!

MYRRHINE   Keep your hands to yourself!

KINESIAS   But our house
going to rack and ruin?

MYRRHINE   *I* don't care.

KINESIAS   And your knitting
all torn to pieces by the chickens? Don't you care?

MYRRHINE Not at all.

KINESIAS   And our vows to Aphrodite?
Oh, *won't* you come back?

MYRRHINE   No.—At least, not until you men
make a treaty to end the war.

KINESIAS   Why, if that's all you want,
by God, we'll make your treaty!

MYRRHINE   Oh? Very well.
When you've done that, I'll come home. But meanwhile,
I've sworn an oath.

KINESIAS   Don't worry.—Now, let's have fun.

MYRRHINE No! Stop it! I said no!
                                        —Although, of course,
I *do* love you.

---

[1] *Oh, this mother business!* a line that parodies Euripides' *Iphigenia at Aulis,* 917

KINESIAS   I know you do. Darling Myrrhine:
   come, shall we?
MYRRHINE   Are you out of your mind? In front of the child?
KINESIAS   Take him home, Manes.

(*Exit* MANES *with baby*)

                                        There. He's gone.

                                                Come on!
There's nothing to stop us now.
MYRRHINE   You devil! But where?
KINESIAS   In Pan's cave. What could be snugger than that?
MYRRHINE   But my purification before I go back to the Citadel?
KINESIAS   There's always the Klepsydra.[1]
MYRRHINE   And my oath?
KINESIAS   Leave the oath to me.
   After all, I'm the man.
MYRRHINE   Well . . . if you say so!

                                        I'll go find a bed.
KINESIAS   Oh, bother a bed! The ground's good enough for me!
MYRRHINE   No. You're a bad man, but you deserve something
   better than dirt.

(*Exit* MYRRHINE)

KINESIAS   What a love she is! And how thoughtful!

(*Re-enter* MYRRHINE)

MYRRHINE   Here's your bed.
   Now let me get my clothes off.

                              But, good horrors!
   We haven't a mattress!
KINESIAS   Oh, forget the mattress!
MYRRHINE   No.
   Just lying on blankets? Too sordid!
KINESIAS   Give me a kiss.
MYRRHINE   Just a second.

(*Exit* MYRRHINE)

KINESIAS   I swear, I'll explode!

(*Re-enter* MYRRHINE)

---

[1] *Klepsydra* a sacred spring near Pan's cave

MYRRHINE   Here's your mattress.
Go to bed now. I'll just take my dress off.
                                        But look—
where's our pillow?
KINESIAS   I don't need a pillow!
MYRRHINE   Well, *I* do.

(*Exit* MYRRHINE)

KINESIAS   I don't suppose even Heracles
would stand for this!

(*Re-enter* MYRRHINE)

MYRRHINE   There we are. Ups-a-daisy!
KINESIAS   So we are. Well, come to bed.
MYRRHINE   But I wonder:
is everything ready now?
KINESIAS   I can swear to that. Come, darling!
MYRRHINE   Just getting out of my girdle.
                                        But remember, now,
what you promised about the treaty!
KINESIAS   I'll remember.
MYRRHINE   But no coverlet!
KINESIAS   Damn it, I'll be
your coverlet!
MYRRHINE   Be right back.

(*Exit* MYRRHINE)

KINESIAS   This girl and her coverlets
will be the death of me.

(*Re-enter* MYRRHINE)

MYRRHINE   Here we are. Up you go!
KINESIAS   Up? I've been up for ages!
MYRRHINE   Some perfume?
KINESIAS   No, by Apollo!
MYRRHINE   Yes, by Aphrodite!
I don't care whether you want it or not.

(*Exit* MYRRHINE)

KINESIAS   For love's sake, hurry!

(*Re-enter* MYRRHINE)

MYRRHINE   Here, in your hand. Rub it right in.

KINESIAS   Never cared for perfume.
And this is particularly strong. Still, here goes!
MYRRHINE   What a nitwit I am! I brought you the Rhodian bottle! [1]
KINESIAS   Forget it.
MYRRHINE   No trouble at all. You just wait here.

(*Exit* MYRRHINE)

KINESIAS   God damn the man who invented perfume!

(*Re-enter* MYRRHINE)

MYRRHINE   At last! The right bottle!
KINESIAS   I've got the rightest
bottle of all, and it's right here waiting for you.
Darling, forget everything else. Do come to bed!
MYRRHINE   Just let me get my shoes off.

                                      —And, by the way,
you'll vote for the treaty?
KINESIAS   I'll think about it.

(MYRRHINE *runs away*)

There! That's done it! Off she runs,
with never a thought for the way I'm feeling. I must
have *some*one, or I'll go mad! Myrrhine
has just about ruined me.

                           And you, strutting little soldier:
what about you? There's nothing for it, I guess,
but an expedition to old Dog-fox's[2] bordello.
OLD MEN   She's left you in a sorry state:
                 You have my sympathy.
             What upright citizen could bear
                 Your pain? I swear, not I!
Just the look of you, with never a woman
To come to your aid! It isn't human!
KINESIAS   The agony!
MALE CHORAGOS   Well, why not?
             She has you on the spot!
FEMALE CHORAGOS   A lovelier girl never breathed, you old sot!
KINESIAS   A lovelier girl? Zeus! Zeus!
             Produce a hurricane

---

[1] *Rhodian bottle* i.e. from Rhodes
[2] *Dog-fox* nickname for a famous procurer

> To hoist these lovely girls aloft
> And drop them down again
> Bump on our lances! Then they'd know
> What they do that makes men suffer so.

(*Exit* KINESIAS)

(*Enter a* SPARTAN HERALD)

HERALD   Gentlemen, Ah beg you will be so kind
as to direct me to the Central Committee.
Ah have a communication.

(*Re-enter* MAGISTRATE)

MAGISTRATE   Are you a man,
or a fertility symbol?
HERALD   Ah refuse to answer that question!
Ah'm a certified herald from Spahta, and Ah've come
to talk about an ahmistice.
MAGISTRATE   Then why
that spear under your cloak?
HERALD   Ah have no speah!
MAGISTRATE   You don't walk naturally, with your tunic
poked out so. You have a tumor, maybe,
or a hernia?
HERALD   No, by Castor! [1]
MAGISTRATE   Well,
something's wrong, I can see that. And I don't like it.
HERALD   Colonel, Ah resent this.
MAGISTRATE   So I see. But what *is* it?
HERALD   A scroll
with a message from Spahta.
MAGISTRATE   Oh. I've heard about these scrolls.
Well, then, man, speak out: How are things in Sparta?
HERALD   Hard, Colonel, hard! We're at a standstill.
Can't seem to think of anything but women.
MAGISTRATE   How curious! Tell me, do you Spartans think
that maybe Pan's to blame?
HERALD   Pan? No. Lampito and her little naked friends.
They won't let a man come near them.
MAGISTRATE   How are you handling it?

---

[1] *Castor* one of Sparta's protective spirits

HERALD   Losing our minds,
   if you want to know, and walking around hunched over
   like men carrying candles in a gale.
   The women have sworn they'll have nothing to do with us
   until we get a treaty.
MAGISTRATE   Yes, I know.
   It's a general uprising, sir, in all parts of Greece.
   But as for the answer—
                          Sir: go back to Sparta
   and have them send us your Armistice Commission.
   I'll arrange things in Athens.
                          And I may say
   that my standing is good enough to make them listen.
HERALD   A man after mah own heart! Sir, Ah thank you!

(*Exit* HERALD)

Strophe

OLD MEN   Oh these women! Where will you find
        A slavering beast that's more unkind?
          Where a hotter fire?
        Give me a panther, any day!
        He's not so merciless as they,
          And panthers don't conspire!

Antistrophe

OLD WOMEN   We may be hard, you silly old ass,
        But who brought you to this stupid pass?
          You're the ones to blame.
        Fighting with us, your oldest friends,
        Simply to serve your selfish ends—
          Really, you have no shame!
MALE CHORAGOS   No, I'm through with women for ever! [1]
FEMALE CHORAGOS   If you say so.
   Still, you might put some clothes on. You look too absurd
   standing around naked. Come, get into this cloak.
MALE CHORAGOS   Thank you; you're right. I merely took it off
   because I was in such a temper.
FEMALE CHORAGOS   That's much better
   Now you resemble a man again.
                          Why have you been so horrid?

---

[1] Parodies lines in Euripides' *Hippolytus*

And look: there's some sort of insect in your eye!
Shall I take it out?

MALE CHORAGOS   An insect, is it? So that's
what's been bothering me! Lord, yes: take it out!

FEMALE CHORAGOS   You might be more polite.

                                                                  —But, heavens!

What an enormous gnat!

MALE CHORAGOS   You've saved my life.
That gnat was drilling an artesian well
in my left eye.

FEMALE CHORAGOS   Let me wipe
those tears away!—And now: one little kiss?

MALE CHORAGOS   Over my dead body!

FEMALE CHORAGOS   You're so difficult!

MALE CHORAGOS   These impossible women! How they do get around
us!
The poet was right: Can't live with them, or without them!
But let's be friends.
And to celebrate, you might lead off with an Ode.

Strophe

OLD WOMEN   Let it never be said
                        That my tongue is malicious:
                        Both by word and by deed
I would set an example that's noble and gracious.
                        We've had sorrow and care
                        Till we're sick of the tune.
                        Is there anyone here
                        Who would like a small loan?
                              My purse is crammed,
                              As you'll soon find;
And you needn't pay me back if the Peace gets signed!
                        I've invited to lunch
                        Some Karystian rips—[1]
                        An esurient bunch,
But I've ordered a menu to water their lips!
                        I can still make soup
                        And slaughter a pig.
                        You're all coming, I hope?
                        But a bath first, I beg!

---

[1] *Karystian rips* the Karystians were allies of Athens at this time, but were
disdained for their primitive manners and loose morals

Walk right up
As though you owned the place,
And you'll get the front door slammed to in your face!

(*Enter* SPARTAN AMBASSADOR, *with entourage*)

MALE CHORAGOS The Commission has arrived from Sparta.

How oddly
they're walking!

Gentlemen, welcome to Athens!
How is life in Laconia?

AMBASSADOR Need we discuss that?
Simply use your eyes.

OLD MEN The poor man's right:
What a sight!

AMBASSADOR Words fail me.
But come, gentlemen, call in your Commissioners,
and let's get down to a Peace.

MALE CHORAGOS The state we're in! Can't bear
a stitch below the waist. It's a kind of pelvic
paralysis.

AN ATHENIAN Won't somebody call Lysistrata?
She has the answer.

A SPARTAN Yes, there, look at him.
Same thing.

Seh, do y'all feel a certain strain
early in the morning?

ATHENIAN I do, sir. It's worse than a strain.
A few more days, and there's nothing for us but Cleisthenes,
that broken blossom!

MALE CHORAGOS But you'd better get dressed again.
You know these prudes who go around Athens with chisels,
looking for prominent statues.[1]

ATHENIAN Sir, you are right.

SPARTAN He certainly is! Ah'll put mah own clothes back on.

(*Enter* ATHENIAN COMMISSIONERS)

AN ATHENIAN They're no better off than we are!

—Greetings, Laconians!

SPARTAN (*To one of his own group*) Colonel, we got dressed just
in time.

---

[1] *prominent statues* i.e. statues with prominent male sexual organs, or *phalloi*

                    Ah sweah,
if they'd seen us the way we were, there'd have been a new war
between the states.
ATHENIAN   Call the meeting to order.
                                    Now, Laconians,
what's your proposal?
AMBASSADOR   We'd lahk to consider peace.
ATHENIAN   Good. That's on our minds, too.
                                    —Summon Lysistrata.
We'll never get anywhere without her.
AMBASSADOR   Lysistrata?
Summon Lysis-*any*body! [1] Only, summon!
MALE CHORAGOS   No need to summon:
here she is, herself.

(*Enter* LYSISTRATA)

                        Lysistrata! Lion of women!
This is your hour to be
hard and yielding, outspoken and sly, austere and
gentle. You see here
the best brains of Hellas (confused, I admit,
by your devious charming) met as one man
to turn the future over to you.
LYSISTRATA   That's fair enough,
unless you men take it into your heads
to turn to each other instead of to me. But I'd know
soon enough if you did!
                        —Where is that goddess of Peace?
Go, some of you: bring her here.

(*Exeunt two* SERVANTS)

                            And now,
summon the Spartan Commission. Treat them courteously:
our husbands have been lax in that respect.
Take them by the hand, women,
or by anything else, if they seem unwilling.
                                    —Spartans:
you stand here. Athenians: on this side. Now listen to me.

(*Re-enter* SERVANTS, *staggering under the weight of a more than life-size statue of a naked woman: this is* PEACE)

---

[1] *Lysis-anybody* Lysistrata's name means "dissolver of armies"

I'm only a woman, I know; but I've a mind,
and I can distinguish between sense and foolishness.
I owe the first to my father; the rest
to the local politicians.[1] So much for that.
Now, then.
What I have to say concerns both sides in this war.
We are all Greeks.
Must I remind you of Thermopylae? of Olympia?
of Delphi? names deep in all our hearts?
And yet you men go raiding through the country,
Greek killing Greek, storming down Greek cities—
and all the time the Barbarian across the sea
is waiting for his chance.—That's my first point.

AN ATHENIAN   Lord! I can hardly contain myself!

LYSISTRATA   And you Spartans:
Was it so long ago that Pericleides
came here to beg our help?[2] I can see him still,
his white face, his sombre gown. And what did he want?
An army from Athens! Messenia
was at your heels, and the sea-god splitting your shores.
Well, Kimon and his men,
four thousand infantry, marched out of here to save you.
What thanks do we get? You come back to murder us.

ATHENIAN   Can't trust a Spartan, Lysistrata!

A SPARTAN   Ah admit it.
When Ah look at those legs, Ah sweah Ah can't trust mahself!

LYSISTRATA   And you, men of Athens:
you might remember that bad time when we were down,
and an army came from Sparta
and sent Hippias and the Thessalians
whimpering back to the hills. That was Sparta,
and only Sparta; without Sparta, we'd now be
cringing helots, not walking about like free men!

(*From this point, the male responses are less to* LYSISTRATA *than to the
statue of* PEACE)

A SPARTAN   An eloquent speech!

AN ATHENIAN   An elegant construction!

---

[1] The preceding four lines are probably quoted from Euripides' *Melanippe
the Wise*

[2] *help* in 464 B.C. during a revolt in Sparta, when an earthquake had just
severely damaged the city

LYSISTRATA   Why are we fighting each other? Why not make peace?
AMBASSADOR   Spahta is ready, ma'am,
  so long as we get that place back.
LYSISTRATA   Place? What place?
AMBASSADOR   Ah refer to Pylos.[1]
MAGISTRATE   Not while I'm alive, by God!
LYSISTRATA   You'd better give in.
MAGISTRATE   But—what were we fighting about?
LYSISTRATA   Lots of places left.
MAGISTRATE   All right. Well, then:
  Hog Island first, and that gulf behind there, and the land between
  the Legs of Megara.
AMBASSADOR   Mah government objects.
LYSISTRATA   Over-ruled. Why fuss about a pair of legs?

(*General assent; the statue of* PEACE *is removed*)

AN ATHENIAN   Let's take off our clothes and plow our fields.
A SPARTAN   Ah'll fertilize mahn first, by the Heavenly Twins!
LYSISTRATA   And so you shall,
  once we have peace. If you are serious,
  go, both of you, and talk with your allies.
ATHENIAN   Too much talk already. We'll stand together!
  We've only one end in view. All that we want
  is our women: and I speak for our allies.
AMBASSADOR   Mah government concurs.
ATHENIAN   So does Karystos.
LYSISTRATA   Good.—But before you come inside
  to join your wives at supper, you must perform
  the usual lustration. Then we'll open
  our baskets for you, and all that we have is yours.
  But you must promise upright good behavior
  from this day on. Then each man home with his woman!
ATHENIAN   Let's get it over with!
SPARTAN   Lead on: Ah follow!
ATHENIAN   Quick as a cat can wink!

(*Exeunt all but the* CHORUSES)

Antistrophe

OLD WOMEN   Embroideries and
              Twinkling ornaments and

---

[1] *Pylos* A lost Spartan possession; for the moment political and sexual desires
become confused

Pretty dresses—I hand
Them all over to you, and with never a qualm.
They'll be nice for your daughters
On festival days
When the girls bring the Goddess
The ritual prize.
Come in, one and all:
Take what you will.
I've nothing here so tightly corked that you can't make it spill!
You may search my house,
But you'll not find
The least thing of use,
Unless your two eyes are keener than mine.
Your numberless brats
Are half starved? and your slaves?
Courage, grandpa! I've lots
Of grain left, and big loaves.
I'll fill your guts,
I'll go the whole hog;
But if you come too close to me, remember: 'ware the dog!

(*Exeunt* CHORUSES)

(*An* ATHENIAN DRUNKARD *approaches the gate and is halted by a* SENTRY)

DRUNKARD   Open. The. Door.

SENTRY   Now, friend, just shove along!
So you want to sit down! If it weren't such an old joke,
I'd tickle your tail with this torch. Just the sort of thing
that this kind of audience appreciates.

DRUNKARD   I. Stay. Right. Here.

SENTRY   Oh, all right. But you'll see some funny sights!

DRUNKARD   Bring. Them. On.

SENTRY   No, what am I thinking of?
The gentlemen from Sparta are just coming back from supper.
Get out of here, or I'll scalp you!

(*Exit* DRUNKARD)

(*The general company re-enters; the two* CHORUSES *now represent* SPARTANS *and* ATHENIANS)

MAGISTRATE   I must say,
I've never tasted a better meal. And those Laconians!
They're gentlemen, by the Lord! Just goes to show:
a drink to the wise is sufficient. And why not?

A sober man's an ass.
Men of Athens, mark my words: the only efficient
Ambassador's a drunk Ambassador. Is that clear?
Look: we go to Sparta,
and when we get there we're dead sober. The result?
Everyone cackling at everyone else. They make speeches;
and even if we understand, we get it all wrong
when we file our reports in Athens. But today—!
Everybody's happy. Couldn't tell the difference
between *Drink to Me Only* and
the *Star Spangled Athens.*
                         What's a few lies,
washed down in good strong drink?

(*Re-enter* DRUNKARD)

SENTRY   God almighty,
   he's back again!
DRUNKARD   I. Resume. My. Place.
A SPARTAN (*To an* ATHENIAN)   I beg you, seh,
   take your instrument in your hand and play for us.
   Ah'm told
   you understand the in*tri*cacies of the floot?
   Ah'd lahk to execute a song and dance
   in honor of Athens,
                       and, of course, of Spahta.

(*The following song is a solo—an aria—accompanied by the flute. The* CHORUS OF SPARTANS *begins a slow dance*)

DRUNKARD   Toot. On. Your. Flute.
SPARTAN CHORAGOS   Mnemosyne,[1]
   Inspire once more the Grecian Muse
   To sing of glory glory glory without end.
   Sing Artemesion's shore,[2]
Where Athens fluttered the Persian fleet—
   Alalai,[3] that great
   Victory! Sing Leonidas and his men,
   Those wild boars, sweat and blood

---

[1] *Mnemosyne* goddess of memory and mother of the Muses
[2] *Artemesion's shore* where in 480 B.C. the Athenian fleet successfully engaged the Persians, while Leonidas and his Spartans were making their famous stand at Thermopylae
[3] *Alalai* a war cry

Down in a red drench. Then, then
The barbarians broke, though they had stood
A myriad strong before!

                  O Artemis,
Virgin Goddess, whose darts
Flash in our forests: approve
This pact of peace, and join our hearts,
From this day on, in love.
Huntress, descend!

LYSISTRATA   All that will come in time.

                         But now, Laconians,
take home your wives. Athenians, take yours.
Each man be kind to his woman; and you, women,
be equally kind. Never again, pray God,
shall we lose our way in such madness.

                         —And now
let's dance our joy! (*From this point the dance becomes general*)

CHORUS OF ATHENIANS   Dance!

                Dance!

                      Dance, you Graces!
Artemis, dance!

                Dance, Phoebus, Lord of dancing!
Dance, Dionysus, in a scurry of Maenads!

                Dance, Zeus Thunderer!
        Dance, Lady Hera,
Queen of the sky!

                Dance, dance, all you gods!
Dance for the dearest, the bringer of peace,
Deathless Aphrodite!

LYSISTRATA   Now let us have another song from Sparta.

CHORUS OF SPARTANS   From Taygetos' skyey summit,
           Laconian Muse, come down!
    Sing the glories of Apollo,
        Regent of Amyclae Town.
          Sing of Leda's Twins,
          Those gallant sons,
          On the banks of Eurotas—
          Alalai Evohe! [1]
    Here's to our girls
        With their tangling curls,
         Legs a-wriggle,

---

[1] *Alalai Evohe!* now an orgiastic war cry

Bellies a-jiggle,
A riot of hair,
A fury of feet,
Evohe! Evohai! Evohe!
as they pass
Dancing,
dancing,
dancing,
to greet
Athena of the House of Brass! [1]

---

[1] *House of Brass* a famous temple on the acropolis of Sparta

THE SECOND SHEPHERDS' PLAY (c. 1420)

ANONYMOUS

During the Dark Ages of Western Europe, roughly from the fall of Rome in 410 A.D. to the end of the first millennium, the drama had disappeared as a literature as well as a form of public entertainment. As in Greece, however, it would find its new origins in the religion of the time, with Christian myth and legend forming its source material.

At some time in the tenth century A.D., particularly at Easter and Christmas, the churches began to attempt to make the stories from the Bible more graphic, and hence more comprehensible to their mostly illiterate parishioners, through short exchanges of dialogue called *tropes* inserted into the regular liturgy. These expanded within the churches to become what is known as *liturgical drama,* and when they became too elaborate and too secular, they went out into the squares and streets and grew into the great body of Medieval drama which flourished as the *mysteries* and *miracles* of the thirteenth through fifteenth centuries. Both in England and on the Continent these series of playlets, called "cycles" because of the sequence of their presentation, told the stories from Creation to Revelation, appearing on complex platforms in public squares or carried from place to place on large scenic wagons, with elaborate costumes and theatrical effects. Often taking days to perform, they were major aspects of public holiday entertainment.

Large numbers of these cycle plays have survived. *The Second Shepherds' Play* is part of what is known as the Wakefield Cycle, and it derives its title as the second Nativity play within a large series. It is widely regarded as a nearly perfect example of popular humor of its age, with its farce among the best within the scores of existing cycle plays. The characters are well articulated and the fast action conveys an amazing sense of realism. Even today it can command extensive laughter with its earthy fun and slapstick routines.

To appreciate what the play is and to understand the sudden shift from hilarity to solemnity one must understand the conditions of its presentation. It is not a disrespectful play in any sense. It is devoutly religious. In the same manner that the Greeks regarded sex in Aristophanes' comedy, the Middle Ages treated religion as a very immediate and human part of existence. The Bible stories were not only accepted as literal truths but were regarded with a familiarity that enabled worshippers to visualize the characters in scripture in terms of ordinary individuals like themselves.

Therefore, instead of seeing the shepherds as the stilted unreal figures of the standard Sunday school pageant, the writer of *The Second Shepherds' Play* saw them for what they most likely really were: crude, unlettered, ignorant, perpetually overworked, poverty-stricken peasants, bent on satisfying their bellies and getting a warm night's sleep. The shepherds on this hillside are thoroughly comic, and thoroughly human, characters. Among them arrives a thief and con man as slick as any nineteenth-century riverboat cardsharp. Through the shenanigans of Mak, Gill, and the shepherds we go through a marvellously funny parody of the Nativity, replete with anachronistic oaths "by Our Lady" and "by Christ's cross," none of which worried the audiences a whit.

At the end, however, once the angels have arrived, the play switches to a touchingly human Nativity scene, seriously religious, but still retaining the basic humanity of the rest of the play. It is a brilliant concept. Whatever one's faith, *The Second Shepherds' Play* can be enjoyed as the telling of a very ancient religious story in a thoroughly delightful and naively inoffensive manner.

The Second Shepherds' Play

A modernized version by John Gassner

CHARACTERS

FIRST SHEPHERD, *Coll*
SECOND SHEPHERD, *Gib*
THIRD SHEPHERD, *Daw*
MAK
MAK'S WIFE, *Gill*
AN ANGEL
THE VIRGIN MARY
THE INFANT CHRIST

One unchanged setting, consisting of two huts—one representing MAK'S
*cottage and the other the manger or stable of the Nativity. The space
between the two huts represents the moors or fields. The action occurs in
Palestine, but only in name; actually the local color of the play is drawn
from the countryside of Wakefield, England.*
*The action is continuous; although scene divisions have been added to
the original text, there is no need to drop curtains to indicate a lapse of
time.*

SCENE I

The moors.

1ST SHEPHERD Lord, but these weathers are cold, and I am ill-
   wrapped!
   Nearly numb of hand, so long have I napped;
   My legs, they fold; my fingers are chapped.
   It is not as I would, for I am all lapped
         In sorrow.
   In storms and tempest,
   Now in the east, now in the west,

Woe is him has never rest,
    Mid-day or morrow!

But we poor shepherds that walk on the moor,
In faith, we are near-hands out of the door.
No wonder, as it stands, if we be poor,
For the tilth of our lands lies as fallow as a floor,
    As ye ken.[1]
We are so lamed,
Overtaxed and blamed,[2]
We are made hand-tamed
    By these gentlery-men.

Thus they rob us of our rest, Our Lady them harry!
These men that are tied fast, their plough must tarry.
What men say is for the best, we find it contrary!
Thus are farming-men oppressed, in point to miscarry
    Alive:
Thus the lords hold us under,
Thus they bring us in blunder—
It were great wonder,
    If ever we should thrive.

Let man but get a painted sleeve or brooch nowadays,
Woe to one that grieves him or once gainsays;
No man dare reprove him that mastery has,
And yet may no man believe one word that he says—
    No letter!
He can make purveyance
With boast and braggance,
And all is through maintenance
    By men that are better.

There shall come a swain as proud as a po;[3]
And he must borrow my wain, my plow also
That I am full glad to grant before he go:
Thus live we in pain, anger, and woe,
    By night and day.
He must have if he wants it
Though I must do without it;
I were better off hanged
    Than once say him Nay!

---

[1] *ken* know
[2] *blamed* literally "crushed"
[3] *po* peacock

It does me good as I walk thus by my own
Of this world for to talk in manner of moan.
To my sheep I will stalk and listen anon,
There abide on a ridge or sit on a stone
      Full soon.
For I think, pardie!
True men if they be,
We shall get more company
      Ere it be noon.

(*A* Second Shepherd *appears on the moor, without at first noticing
the* First Shepherd, *so absorbed is he in his own thoughts*)

2ND SHEPHERD   *Benedicite*[1] and *Dominus!* what may this mean?
Why fares this world thus? Oft have we not seen:
Lord, these weathers are spiteful, and the winds are keen,
And the frosts so hideous they water my een:[2]
      No lie it be!
Now in dry, now in wet,
Now in snow, now in sleet,
When my shoes freeze to my feet,
      It is not at all easy.

But as far as I know, or yet as I go,
We poor wed men suffer much, we do;
We have sorrow then and then, it falls often so.
Poor Cappel, our hen, both to and fro
      She cackles,
But begin she to rock,
To groan or to cluck,
Woe is to him, our cock,
      For he is then in shackles!

These men that are wed have not all their will;
When they are set upon, they sigh full still.
God knows they are led full hard and full ill,
In bower or in bed they have their fill
      Beside.
My part have I found,
Know my lesson sound:
Woe is him that is bound,
      For he must abide.

---

[1] *Benedicite* he pronounces this, by contraction of the Latin for "Bless you,"
as "Bencité"
[2] *een* eyes

But now late in our lives—marvel to me!
That I think my heart breaks such wonder to see:
That, as destiny drives, it should so be
That some men will have two wives, and some have three
     In store.
To some is woe that have any,
But so far as I see, I tell ye,
Woe is him that has many,
       For he feels sore.

(*Addressing the audience*)

But young men awooing, by God that you bought,
Beware of a wedding and mind in your thought
"Had I known" is a thing that serves you nought.
So much still mourning has wedding home brought
     And grief,
With many a sharp shower;
For ye may catch in an hour
What shall savor full sour
      As long as you live.

For, as ever read I scripture, I have *her* I keep near:
As sharp as a thistle, as rough as a briar;
She is browed like a bristle with sour-looking cheer.
Had she once wet her whistle, she could sing full clear
     Her Pater-Noster.
She is as great as a whale,
She has a gallon of gall;
By Him that died for us all,
      I would I had run till I lost her!

(*By now he has been observed by the* First Shepherd, *who rouses him from his meditations roughly*)

1st shepherd   God look over the row, you there, that deafly stand!
2nd shepherd (*Startled*)   Yea, the devil in thy maw!
  —In tarrying, friend,
Saw you Daw about?
1st shepherd   Yes, on fallow land
  I heard him blow. He comes here at hand
     Not far.
  Stand still!
2nd shepherd   Why?
1st shepherd   For he comes on, hope I.

1ST SHEPHERD   He will din us both a lie
          Unless we beware.

(*A* THIRD SHEPHERD, *a boy called* DAW, *employed by the* FIRST SHEP-
HERD, *appears. The weather has put him out of humor*)

3RD SHEPHERD   Christ's cross me speed, and Saint Nicholas!
    Thereof had I need: it is worse than it was!
    Whoso could, take heed! and let the world pass;
    It is ever in dread and brittle as glass,
          And slides.
    This world fared never so,
    With marvels more and more,
    Now in weal, now in woe;
          And everything rides!

    Was never since Noah's flood such floods seen,
    Winds and rains so rude, and storms so keen;
    Some stammered, some stood in doubt, as I ween.
    Now God turn all to good! I say as I mean
          And ponder.
    These floods, so they drown
    Both fields and town
    And bear all down—
          That it is a wonder.

    We that walk in the nights our cattle to keep,
    We see sudden sights when other men sleep—

(*Noticing that he is being observed by the other* SHEPHERDS)

    But methinks my heart lightens, I see them peep.
    Yea, you tall fellows!—I think I'll give my sheep
          A turn.

(*He is about to turn away, but changes his mind*)

    But this is ill intent,
    For as I walk on this bent
    I may lightly repent
          And stub my toes.

(*Pretending to have just seen them*)

    Ah, sir, God you save, and you, master mine!

(*Coming up to them*)

    A drink fain would I have and somewhat to dine.

1ST SHEPHERD Christ's curse, my knave, thou art a lazy swine!
2ND SHEPHERD What, the boy pleases to rave? You'll wait on line
    When we have made it.
I'll drum on thy pate!
Though the knave comes late,
Yet is he in state
    To dine, if he had it.

3RD SHEPHERD (*Grumbling*) Such servants as I, that sweats and
    swinks,[1]
Eats our bread dry, and that is ill, I thinks!
We are oft wet and weary when master-men winks,
Yet come full lately the dinners and the drinks.
    But neatly,
Both our dame and our sire,
When we have run in the mire,
They can nip us of our hire
    And pay us full lately.

But hear my oath: For the food that you serve, I say,
I shall do hereafter—work as you pay:
I shall work a little and a little play,
For yet my supper never on my stomach lay
    In the fields.
I won't complain, but a heap
With my staff I shall leap;
For a thing bought too cheap
    Nothing yields.

1ST SHEPHERD Yea, thou wert a fool, lad, a-wooing to ride
With one that had but little for spending by his side.
2ND SHEPHERD Peace, boy! And no more jangling I'll bide,
Or I shall make thee full sad, by heaven's King, beside,
    For thy gauds.[2]
Where are our sheep? Thy japes we scorn.
3RD SHEPHERD Sir, this same day at morn
I left them in the corn
    When the bells rang Lauds.

They have pasture good, they cannot go wrong.
1ST SHEPHERD That is right. By the rood, these nights are long!
Yet I would, ere we went, one gave us a song.

---

[1] *swinks* works; his speech is ungrammatical
[2] *gauds* tricks or jests

2ND SHEPHERD   So *I* thought as I stood—to cheer us along.

3RD SHEPHERD   I grant!

1ST SHEPHERD   Let me sing the tenory.

2ND SHEPHERD   And I the treble so high.

3RD SHEPHERD   Then the mean falls to me.
    Let's start the chant.

(*At this point,* MAK *appears, his cloak thrown over his tunic*)

MAK (*To himself*)   Lord, for Thy names seven, that made the moon
    and stars on high
  Well more than I reckon: Thy will, Lord, leaves me dry
  And lacking, so that of my wits I am shy:
  Now would God I were in heaven, for there no children cry
      So still.[1]

1ST SHEPHERD (*Looking around*)   Who is that pipes so poor?

MAK (*Still grumbling to himself*)   Would God knew how I endure:
  A man that walks on the moor
      Without his will.

(*The* SHEPHERDS *now recognize him as the thief they know.* MAK *is
startled, but pretends he does not know them*)

2ND SHEPHERD   Mak, where have you been? Tell us tidings.

3RD SHEPHERD   Is *he* come, then let each one take heed to his
    things.

(*He takes* MAK's *cloak from him and shakes it, to see whether* MAK
has stolen anything)

MAK (*Spluttering*)   What! I be a yeoman, I tell ye, of the king's.
  The self and same, sent from a great lording's
      And such.
  Fie on you! Go hence
  Out of my presence;
  I must have reverence—
      You grieve me much!

1ST SHEPHERD   Why make ye it so quaint, Mak? You do wrong.

2ND SHEPHERD   Mak, play ye the saint? For this do ye long?

3RD SHEPHERD   I know the knave can deceive, the devil him hang!

MAK   I shall make complaint and get ye many a thwang
      At a word
  When I tell my lord how ye do.

---

1 *so still* so continuously

1ST SHEPHERD (*Sarcastically*)   But, Mak, is that true
Come, that southern tooth[1] unscrew
  And set it in a turd.

2ND SHEPHERD   Mak, the devil in your eye, a stroke will I lend you.
 (*He strikes him*)

3RD SHEPHERD   Mak, know ye not me? By God, I could beat ye too.
 (*As he too is about to strike him,* MAK *draws back and pretends to
have just recognized the* SHEPHERDS)

MAK   God, look—you all three? Methought—how do you do?
Ye are a fair company.
1ST SHEPHERD   May we now recognize you?
2ND SHEPHERD   Blast your jest-dealing!
When a man so lately goes
What will good men suppose?
Ye have an ill name one knows
  For sheep-stealing.

MAK   And true as steel I am, know ye not?
But a sickness I feel that holds me full hot:
My belly fares not well, for it is out of estate.
3RD SHEPHERD (*Unsympathetically*)   Seldom lies the devil dead by
 the gate!
MAK (*Ignoring the thrust*)   Therefore,
Full sore am I and ill;
I stand stone-still,
I ate not a tittle
  This month and more.

1ST SHEPHERD   How fares thy wife? By my hood, tell us true.
MAK   She lies lolling by the road, by the fire too,
And a house full of brew she drinks well too.
Ill speed other things that she will shift
  To do.
Eats as fast as she can,
And each year that comes to man
She brings forth a brat—an'
  Some years, two.

But were I yet more gracious, and richer at will,
Eaten out of house and home I would be still.

---

[1] *southern tooth* in pretending to be in the king's service, the actor playing
Mak may have affected a Southern—that is, London—accent

Yet she is a foul dear, if ye come at her close;
None there is looks worse, as none knows
>Better than I.
Now will ye see what I proffer:
To give all in my coffer
And tomorrow next, to offer
>Mass-pence, should she die.

(*The* SHEPHERDS *have begun to feel drowsy during this recital*)

2ND SHEPHERD   So weary with watching is none in this shire:
I would sleep if it cost me a part of my hire.
3RD SHEPHERD   And I am cold and naked, and would have a fire.
1ST SHEPHERD   I am weary of walking, and I have run in the mire.

(*To the* SECOND SHEPHERD)

>Keep the watch, you!
2ND SHEPHERD   Nay, I will lie down by,
For I must sleep or die.
3RD SHEPHERD   For sleep as good a man's son am I;
>It is my due.

(*They begin to lie down to sleep. But the* THIRD SHEPHERD *eyes* MAK *suspiciously*)

3RD SHEPHERD   But, Mak, come hither; between us you shall lie down.
MAK (*Unhappily*)   But I may hinder your sleep and make you frown.

(*The* SHEPHERDS *force him down and compel him to stretch out among them, in order to prevent him from robbing them*)

>Ah well, no dread I heed:
From my head to my toe,

(*Crossing himself*)

Manus tuas commendo,
Pontio Pilato.[1]
>Christ's cross me speed.

(*Before long the* THREE SHEPHERDS *are in a deep sleep, and* MAK *disentangles himself and rises*)

MAK   Now were time for a man that lacks what he would

---

[1] "Into your hands I commend myself, Pontius Pilate." The humor lies, of course, in the misquotation.

To stalk privily then into the fold
And nimbly to work, though not to be too bold,
For he might regret the bargain if it were told
    At the ending.
Now time for to work in the dell,
For he needs good counsel
That fain would fare well
    And has but little spending.

(*He begins to work a spell on the sleepers, drawing a circle around them*)

But about you a circle round as the moon,
Till I have done what I will, till that it be noon—
That ye lie stone-still, until I am done;
And now I shall say thereto of good words a rune
    Anon:
Over your heads my hand I light;
Out go your eyes, blind be your sight!
And now that it may come out right
    I must shift on.

(*He starts to leave in the direction of the sheep further down the field while the* SHEPHERDS *snore*)

Lord, but they sleep hard—that may one hear . . .
Was I never shepherd, but now I will shear;
Though the flock be scared, yet shall I nip near;
I must draw hitherward and mend our cheer
    From sorrow.

(*He spies a sheep that attracts him*)

A fat sheep, I daresay,
A good fleece, I dare lay;
Repay when I may—

(*Seizing the animal*)

But this will I *borrow*.

SCENE II

MAK'S *cottage: the exterior and the interior.*
At first MAK *stands outside and knocks at the door. Later he enters and the action transpires inside.*

MAK (*Knocking*)   How, Gill, art thou in? Get us some light.

WIFE   Who makes such din this time of the night?
  I am set for to spin: I think not I might
  Rise a penny to win—a curse on him alight.
      So fares she,
  A housewife, I ween,
  To be raced thus between.
  In house may no work be seen
      Because of such small chores that be.

MAK   Good wife, open the door. Do ye not see what I bring?
WIFE   Then let thou draw the latch.

(As he enters)

                       Ah! come in, my sweeting!
MAK *(Grumpily)*   Yea, and no thought for my long standing!
WIFE *(Observing the sheep)*   By the naked neck thou art like to
  get thy hanging.

MAK   Get away!
  I am worthy my meat,
  For in a pinch can I get
  More than they that swink and sweat
      All day.

Thus if fell to my lot, Gill, I had such grace.
WIFE   It were a foul blot to be hanged for the case.
MAK   I have escaped oft from as narrow place.
WIFE   But so long goes the pot to the water, one says,
      At last
Comes it home broken.
MAK   Well I know the token;
  But let it never be spoken!—
      But come and help fast.

(Gill helps to take the sheep in)

I would it were slain and I sat down to eat:
This twelvemonth was I not so fain for sheep-meat.
WIFE   Come they ere it be slain and hear the sheep bleat—
MAK   Then might I be taken; cold's the sweat I am in, my sweet—
      Go, make fast
The outer door.
WIFE *(Going to the door)*   Yes, Mak,
  If they came at thy back—
MAK   Then got I from that pack
      The devil's own cast.

WIFE (*Coming back*)   A good jest I have spied, since thou
    hast none:

(*Pointing to the cradle*)

Here shall we hide it till they be gone;
In the cradle may it abide. Let me alone,
And I shall lie beside in childbed and groan.

MAK   Well said!
And I shall say you are light
Of a man-child this night.
WIFE   How well it is, day bright,
      That ever I bred.

This is a good guise and a far cast:
A woman's advice, it helps at the last.
I shall care never who spies, so go thou fast!
MAK (*Outside, walking in the fields toward the sleeping* SHEPHERDS)
    If I do not come ere they rise, a cold blast
      Will blow; back to sleep
I go. Yet sleeps this company,
And I shall slip in privily
As it had never been me
      That carried their sheep.

SCENE III

The moors.
MAK *slips in among the sleepers. The* SHEPHERDS *begin to stir.*

1ST SHEPHERD (*Rising*)   *Resurrex a mortruis:*[1] reach me a hand!
Judas carnas dominus! I may not well stand.
My foot sleeps, by Jesus, and I thirst—and
I thought that we laid us full near England.
2ND SHEPHERD (*Rising*)
    Ah-ye!
Lord, I have slept well!
I am fresh as an eel,
As light I feel
    As leaf on tree.

3RD SHEPHERD (*Awaking but dazed*)   *Ben'cite* be herein; so my
    body quakes,

---

[1] *Resurrex a mortruis* The unlettered shepherd is babbling Latin words he
has picked up imperfectly and makes no particular sense.

My heart is out of my skin with the noise it makes.
Who makes all this din, so my brow aches?
To the door will I win. Hark, fellows, who wakes?
>We were four:
See ye anywhere Mak now?
1ST SHEPHERD   We were up ere thou.
2ND SHEPHERD   Man, I give God a vow
>That he went nowhere.

3RD SHEPHERD (*Troubled*)   Methought he lay wrapped up in a
>wolf-skin.
1ST SHEPHERD   Many are thus wrapped now—that is, within!
2ND SHEPHERD   When we had long napped, methought with a gin[1]
A fat sheep he trapped without making a din.
3RD SHEPHERD (*Pointing toward* Mak, *who pretends to be asleep*)
>Be still:
This dream makes thee wild,
>It is but phantom, by the Holy Child! [2]
1ST SHEPHERD   Now God turn all things mild,
>If it be His will.

(*The* SHEPHERDS *rouse* MAK)

2ND SHEPHERD   Rise, Mak, for shame! Ye lie right long.
MAK (*Stirring*)   Now Christ's Holy Name, be it among
Us! What's this? By Saint James, I am not strong!
I hope I am the same—my neck has lain wrong
>All night!

(*As they help him up*)

Many thanks! Since yester-even,
I swear by Saint Steven,
I was flayed by a dream, so driven
>That my heart was not right.

Methought my Gill began to croak, full sad
To labor well nigh at first cock—a lad
To add to our flock; and I never glad
To have more to provide, more than ever I had.
>Ah, my head!

---

[1] *gin* trick
[2] *Holy Child* An anachronism characteristic of naïve folk literature, since the
Holy Child has not yet been born. In the next few lines there are other
anachronisms: "Christ's Holy Name," "By Saint James," and "by Saint
Steven"—or Stephen.

A house full of young mouths—banes!
The devil knock out their brains!
Woe him that so many brats gains
        And so little bread.

I must go home, by your leave; to Gill, I thought.
But first look in my sleeve that I have stolen naught:
I am loth to grieve you or to take from you aught.
3RD SHEPHERD   Go forth, and ill may you thrive!

(MAK *leaves*)

                        Still I would we sought
        This morn
Whether we have all our store.
1ST SHEPHERD   Good! I will go before.
   Let us meet.
2ND SHEPHERD   Where?
3RD SHEPHERD   At the crooked thorn.

SCENE IV

MAK's *cottage.*

MAK (*At his door*)   Undo this door! Who is here? How long shall
   I stand?
WIFE   Who makes such a stir, to walk in the moon-waning?
MAK   Ah, Gill, what cheer? It is I, Mak, your husband.
WIFE (*Grumpily*)   Then see we here the devil himself in a band,
        Sir Guile!
   Lo, he comes with a noise about
   As if he were held by the snout,
   I may not do my work for that lout
        A hand-long while.

MAK   Will ye hear what noise she makes for an excuse
   And does nothing but play about and stroke her toes!
WIFE   Why, who wanders, who wakes, who comes, who goes?
   Who brews, who bakes—now who do you suppose?
        And more then
   That it is pity to behold—
   Now in hot, now in cold.
   Full woefull is the household
        That lacks women.

But what end have ye made with the shepherds, Mak?

MAK   The last word that they said when I turned my back,
They would look that they had of their sheep all the pack;
I fear they will not be well pleased when they their sheep lack,
        Pardie!
But howso the sport goes
I'm the thief they'll suppose
And come with a full nose
        To cry out on me.

But thou must do as thou planned.
WIFE   They'll find me able!
I shall swaddle it right in my cradle.
When I sup with the Devil I use the long ladle!
I will lie down straightway. Come wrap me.
MAK (*Doing so*)   I will.
WIFE (*Sharply*)
        Behind!—
If Coll and his mate come, to our sorrow,
They will nip us full narrow.
MAK   But I may run and cry "Harrow"
        If the sheep they find.

WIFE   Listen close when they call—they will come anon.
Come and make ready all, and sing thou alone:
Sing "Lullay" you shall, for I must groan
And cry out by the wall on Mary and John
        As if sore.
Sing "Lullay" on fast
When you hear them at last,
And if I play a false cast
        Trust me no more!

SCENE V

The moors, as the SHEPHERDS *meet.*

3RD SHEPHERD   Ah, Coll, good morn: why sleep ye not?
1ST SHEPHERD   Alas, that ever was I born! We have a foul blot—
A fat wether have we lost.
3RD SHEPHERD   God forbid; say it not!
2ND SHEPHERD   Who should have done that harm? That were a
        foul spot.
1ST SHEPHERD
        Some knave—beshrew!
I have sought with my dogs

All Horbury shrogs,[1]
And of fifteen hogs[2]
    I lack one ewe.

3RD SHEPHERD   Now trust me if ye will—by Saint Thomas of Kent!,
Either Mak or Gill a hand to it lent.
1ST SHEPHERD   Peace, man, be still: I watched when he went;
You slander him ill, you ought to repent
    With speed.
2ND SHEPHERD   Yet as ever I thrive or be,
Though the good Lord slay me,
I would say it were he
    That did the same deed.

3RD SHEPHERD   Go we thither then, I say, and let us run fleet;
Till I know the truth, may I never bread eat.
1ST SHEPHERD   Nor take drink in my head till with him I meet.
2ND SHEPHERD   I will take to no bed until I him greet,
    My brother!
One promise I will plight:
Till I get him in sight
I will never sleep one night
    Where I sleep another.

SCENE VI

MAK's *cottage*.
MAK *is heard singing within, while* GILL *is heard groaning as though she were delivering a child.*

3RD SHEPHERD   Will you hear how they hack away; our sir likes to
    croon.
1ST SHEPHERD   Heard I never none crack so clear out of tune.
    Call on him!
2ND SHEPHERD   Mak, undo your door—soon!
MAK   Who is that spoke, as if it were noon
    Aloft?
  Who is that, I say?

(*He opens the door*)

3RD SHEPHERD   Good fellows you'd see, were it day.

---

[1] *Horbury shrogs* By this is meant the thickets of Horbury, about four miles
from Wakefield, where the play was given.
[2] *hogs* young sheep

MAK   As far as ye may,
          Friends, speak soft
    Over a sick woman's head that is at malease;
    I had sooner be dead than cause her dis-ease.
WIFE   Go to another place—I cannot breathe; please!
    Each foot ye tread goes through my nose with a squeeze,
          Woe is me.
1ST SHEPHERD   Tell us, Mak, if ye may:
    How fare ye, I say?
MAK   But are ye in this town today?—
          How fare *ye?*
    Ye have run in the mire and are wet a bit;
    I shall make you a fire, if ye will sit.

    (*Pointing at his* WIFE)

    A nurse I would hire; think ye on it.
    Well paid is my hire—my dream this is it,
          In season.
    I have brats if ye knew
    Many more than will do;

    (*With resignation*)

    But, then, we must drink as we brew,
          And that is but reason!

    I would ye dined ere you go; methinks that ye sweat.
2ND SHEPHERD   Nay, neither drink nor meat will mend us yet.
MAK   (*Innocently*)   Why, sirs, what ails ye?
3RD SHEPHERD   Our sheep we must get
    That was stolen. It is great loss that we met.

    (MAK *offers a drink*)

MAK   Sirs, drink!
    Had I been near,
    Someone should have bought it full dear.
1ST SHEPHERD   Marry, some men think that ye were.
          And that makes us think!

2ND SHEPHERD   Mak, some men think that it should be ye.
3RD SHEPHERD   Either you or your spouse, so say we.
MAK   Now if ye have suspicion against my Gill or me,
    Come and search our house, and then may ye see
          Who had her,
    Or if any sheep I got,

Either cow or stot.[1]
And Gill, my wife, rose not
  Here since she laid her.

If I am not true and loyal, to God I pray

 (*Pointing to the cradle, where the sheep—the alleged child—is hidden*)

That *this* be the first meal I shall eat this day.
1st shepherd Mak, as I may fare well, take heed, I say!
"He learned early to steal that could not say nay."

 (*The* Shepherds *start to search the room, but* Gill *waves them away when they approach the cradle near her*)

wife I faint!
 Out, thieves, from my dwelling!
 Ye come to rob while I am swelling—
mak Your hearts should melt now she's yelling
  In plaint.

wife Away, thieves, from my child; over him don't pore.
mak Knew ye how much she has borne, your hearts would be sore.
 Ye do wrong, I warn you, thus to rummage before
 A woman that has suffered—but I say no more!
wife (*Yelling*)
  Ah, my middle!
 I pray to God so mild,
 If I ever you beguiled,
 That I *eat* this child
  That lies in this cradle.
mak (*Pretending concern for her*) Peace, woman, for God's pain,
 and cry not so:
Thou spill'st thy brain and fill'st me with woe.
2nd shepherd (*To the other* Two Shepherds) I think our
 sheep be slain; what find ye two?
3rd shepherd All this is in vain: we may as well go:

 (*Finding only rags of clothing as he searches*)

  Only tatters!
 I can find no flesh,
 Hard nor soft,
 Salt nor fresh,
  But two bare platters.

---

[1] *stot* bullock

(*But as he approaches the cradle and sniffs the air, he makes a grimace*)

Yet live cattle, as I may have bliss, nor tame nor wild,
None has smelled so strong as this—this child!
WIFE (*Protesting*)   Ah no, so God bless and give me joy, this child
smells mild.
1ST SHEPHERD   We have aimed amiss: We were elsewhere beguiled.

(*He is about to leave*)

2ND SHEPHERD (*Also giving up the search*)
Sir, we are done!
But sir—Our Lady him save!—
Is your child a lad?
MAK (*Proudly*)   Any lord might him have
This child to his son.

When he wakens he has a grip that is a joy to see.
3RD SHEPHERD   Blessings on his hips, and happiness may he see.
But who were his godparents, will ye tell me?
MAK (*Floundering*)   Blessed be their lips!—
1ST SHEPHERD (*Aside*)   Now, what will the lie be?
MAK   So God them thank,—
Parkin and Gibbon Waller, be it said,
And gentle John Horne in good stead—
He that made the great riot spread,
He with the big shank.

2ND SHEPHERD   (*Preparing to leave*)   Mak, friends will we be, for
we are all one.
MAK (*Pretending to have been hurt by their suspicions*)   *We?* Now
I must hold back, for amends is there none.
Farewell, all three, and very glad to see you gone!

(*The* SHEPHERDS *leave the house, and we see them outside*)

3RD SHEPHERD   "Fair words may there be, but love is there none
This year."
1ST SHEPHERD (*To the 2nd*)   Gave ye the child anything?
2ND SHEPHERD   No, not a farthing.
3RD SHEPHERD   Fast back will I fling:
Await ye me here.

(*He goes back to* MAK's *cottage, the others following him*)

Mak, take it to no grief if I come to thy lad.
MAK   Nay, ye have grieved me much and made me sad.

3RD SHEPHERD   The child it will not grieve, thy little day-star
    so glad;
  Mak, with your leave, let me give the child you have had
        But sixpence.
MAK   Nay, go away; he sleeps!
3RD SHEPHERD   Methinks, it peeps.[1]
MAK   When he wakens, he weeps;
        I pray you go hence.

(*The other* SHEPHERDS *enter*)

3RD SHEPHERD (*Coming closer*)   Give me leave him to kiss and to
  lift up the clout.

(*He lifts the cover a little*)

What the devil is this? He has a long snout!
1ST SHEPHERD   He is birth-marked amiss; let us not waste time
  hereabout.
2ND SHEPHERD   "From an ill-spun woof ever comes foul out."

(*As he looks closer*)

      Ay—so!
  He is like our sheep.
3RD SHEPHERD   How, Gib? May I peep?
1ST SHEPHERD   "Nature will still creep
    Where it may not go."
2ND SHEPHERD   This was a quaint trick and a far cast;
  It was a high fraud!
3RD SHEPHERD   Yea, sirs, I am aghast!
  Let's burn this bawd and bind her fast;
  A false scold hangs at the last—
      So shalt thou.

(*He has pulled the covers off*)

Will ye see how they swaddle
His four feet in the middle?
Saw I never in a cradle
    A hornèd lad ere now.

MAK (*Who stands behind them and does not see the sheep uncovered; still attempting to brazen it out*)

---

[1] *peeps* whimpers

Peace, bid I! And let be your fare;
I am he that him gat and yon woman him bare.[1]

1ST SHEPHERD (*Mocking him*)   What devil shall he be called, Mak?
Lo, God! Mak's heir!

2ND SHEPHERD   An end to all jesting; now God give thee care
I say!

(*As she is lying in bed, the* WIFE *does not see that they have completely uncovered the sheep*)

WIFE   As pretty child is he
As sits on woman's knee;
A dilly-down, perdie,
To make one gay.

3RD SHEPHERD   I know my sheep by the ear-mark—this good token.

MAK   I tell you, sirs, hear me: his nose was broken,
Since, as the priest told me, he was by witchcraft bespoken.

1ST SHEPHERD   This is false work and must be avenged; I have
spoken:
Get weapon!

WIFE   The child was taken by an elf—
I saw it myself.
When the clock struck twelve,
Was he mis-shapen.

2ND SHEPHERD   Ye two are right deft, and belong in the same bed.

3RD SHEPHERD   Since they maintain their theft, let us do them dead.

(*They seize* MAK)

MAK (*Seeing the game is up*)   If I trespass again, strike off my
head.
I'll let you be the judge!

3RD SHEPHERD (*To the others*)   Sirs, instead:
For this trespass
We need neither curse nor spite,
Nor chide nor fight,
But take him forthright
And toss him in canvas.

(*They drag* MAK *outside and toss him lustily in a sheet while he yells with pain*)

---

[1] *bare* bore

SCENE VII

The fields near Bethlehem in Judea.
We see the three SHEPHERDS *again, weary after their sport with* MAK
and tired with walking.

1ST SHEPHERD   Lord, how I am sore and like to burst in the breast!
In faith, I can stand no more, therefore will I rest.
2ND SHEPHERD   As a sheep of seven score Mak weighed in my fist;
To sleep anywhere methink I would list.
3RD SHEPHERD   Then I pray you,
Lie down on this green.
1ST SHEPHERD (*Hesitating*)   On these thefts to think I yet mean.
3RD SHEPHERD   Whereto should ye be worried lean?
Do as I tell you.

They lie down to sleep; but they have barely done so when an Angel
*appears above. He first sings the hymn "Gloria in Excelsis," then ad-
dresses the* SHEPHERDS

ANGEL   Rise, herdsmen gentle, for now is He born
That shall take from the Fiend what Adam had lorn;[1]
That fiend to overthrow this night is He born;
God is made your Friend. Now at this morn.
He commands,
To Bedlem[2] you go see:
There lies that divine He
In a crib that full poorly
Betwixt two beasts stands.

(*The* ANGEL *disappears*)

1ST SHEPHERD   This was a quaint voice that ever yet I heard.
It is a marvel to relate thus to be stirred.
2ND SHEPHERD   Of God's son of heaven, he spoke from above,
All the wood was in lightning as he spoke of love:
I thought it fair.
3RD SHEPHERD   Of a child heard I tell
In Bedlem; I heard it well.

(*Pointing to a star that has begun to blaze*)

Yonder star, above the dell:
Let us follow him there.

---

[1] *lorn* lost or forfeited
[2] *Bedlem* Bethlehem

2ND SHEPHERD   Say, what was his song? Heard ye how he sang it?
  Three breves[1] to a long.
3RD SHEPHERD   Yes, marry, he thwacked it;
  Was no crotchet wrong, nor nothing lacked it.
1ST SHEPHERD   For to sing it again right as he trilled it.
          I can, if I may.
2ND SHEPHERD   Let me see how ye croon,
  Or do ye but bark at the moon?
3RD SHEPHERD   Hold your tongues! Have done!
1ST SHEPHERD
          Hark after me, I say!

(*They try to sing the hymn as best they can*)

2ND SHEPHERD   To Bedlem he bade that we should go;
  I am troubled that we tarry too slow.
3RD SHEPHERD   Be merry and not sad: of mirth is our song, lo!
  Everlasting glad in the rewards that will flow,
          No plaint may we make.
1ST SHEPHERD   Hie we thither, cheery,
  Though we be wet and weary;
  To that Child and that Lady
          Let us our way take.

2ND SHEPHERD   We find by the prophecy—let be your din!—
  Of David and Isaiah, and more therein,
  As prophesied by clergy, that on a virgin
  Should He light and lie, to redeem our sin
          And slake it.
  Our kind from woe
  To save—Isaiah said so.—
          "*Ecce virgo
          Concipict* a child that is naked." [2]
3RD SHEPHERD   Full glad may we be, and await that day
  That lovely day that He shall with His might sway.
  Lord, well for me for once and for aye!
  Might I but kneel on my knee some word for to say
          To that child.
  But the angel said
  In a crib is He laid,

---

[1] *breves* A *breve* is equal to two whole notes; a *long* is equal to six whole
  notes; a *crotchet* is a quarter note.
[2] "Behold, a virgin shall conceive." (Isaiah, 7:14)

He is poorly arrayed,
    So meek and mild.

1ST SHEPHERD   Patriarchs that have been, and prophets beforne,
  They desired to have seen this Child that is born;
  But *they* are gone full clean, from life forlorn—
  It is *we* shall see him, ere it be morn
      By token.
  When I see Him and feel,
  Then shall I know full well
  It is true as steel
      What prophets have spoken:

  To so poor as we are that he would appear,
  We the first to find and be his messenger!
2ND SHEPHERD   Go we now, let us fare: the place must be near.
3RD SHEPHERD   I am ready and eager: go we together
      To that Light!
  Lord! If Thy will it be,
  Though we are lowly all three,
  Grant us of Thy glee,
      To comfort Thy wight.[1]

(*They move on, following the star, to Bethlehem*)

SCENE VIII

The stable or manger in Bethlehem.
The SHEPHERDS *enter and kneel before the* VIRGIN *and* CHILD.

1ST SHEPHERD   Hail, comely and clean; hail, young child!
  Hail, Maker, as I mean, born of maiden so mild!
  Thou hast banned, I deem, the devil so wild;
  The evil beguiler now goes beguiled.

(*Pointing to the* CHILD)

      Lo, merry He is!
  Lo, he laughs, my sweeting,
  A welcome greeting!
  I have had my meeting—

(*Offering the* CHILD *some cherries*)

      Have a bob of cherries?

---

[1] *wight* creature

2ND SHEPHERD   Hail, sovereign Saviour, for Thou hast us sought!
Hail, Nursling, leaf and flower, that all things hath wrought!
Hail, full of favor, that made all of nought!

(*Offering a bird*)

Hail, I kneel and I cower.—A bird have I brought
Without mar.
Hail, little, tiny mop,
Of our creed thou art the crop;
I would drink from thy cup,
Little day-star.

3RD SHEPHERD   Hail, darling dear, full of godhead!
I pray Thee be near when that I have need.
Hail! Sweet is Thy cheer! And my heart would bleed
To see Thee sit here clothed so poor indeed,
With no pennies.
Hail! Thy hand put forth to us all—
I bring thee but a ball;
Take and play with it withall,
And go to the tennis.

THE VIRGIN MARY   The Father of heaven, God omnipotent,
That set all aright, His son has He sent.
My name He chose forth, and on me His light spent;
And I conceived Him forthwith through His might as God meant:
And now is the Child born.
May He keep you from woe!
I shall pray Him so.
Tell the glad news as ye go,
And remember this morn.

1ST SHEPHERD   Farewell, Lady, so fair to behold
With thy child on thy knee.
2ND SHEPHERD   —But he lies full cold.—
Lord, it is well with me! Now we go, ye may behold.
3RD SHEPHERD   In truth, already it seems to be told
Full oft
1ST SHEPHERD   What grace we have found.
2ND SHEPHERD   Come forth! Now are we won!
3RD SHEPHERD   To sing of it we're bound:
Let us sing aloft!

(*They leave the stable, singing*)

Explicit Pagina Pastorum
(*Here ends The Shepherds' Pageant*)

HAMLET (1600)

WILLIAM SHAKESPEARE (1564–1616)

The hyperbole may be too strong in defining *Hamlet* as the greatest play ever written, but it is a superlative drama and a magnificent piece of theatre. It is virtually impossible to perform a thoroughly bad *Hamlet*. The play has so much to offer, is so "actor proof," that no matter how ineffective a particular interpretation may be or however inept the staging, so much comes through that the magnificence of its artistry transcends even the most botched and bowdlerized version.

There has probably been more serious scholarship and more pompous blather written about who, what, and why Hamlet is what he is than about any other person, living, dead, or imagined. Millions of words in thousands of documents have explained, analyzed, and dissected this most fascinating of dramatic characters. That a dramatist like William Shakespeare, who may or may not have been educated beyond the most elementary schooling, who was basically a theatre producer and actor grinding out pieces for his company's repertoire, could have created within the framework of some few hours upon the stage an individual so alive in the consciences and minds of generations ever since is one of the great tributes to human artistic genius.

At the heart of things, *Hamlet* is a rip-roaring Elizabethan revenge melodrama. Dark doings behind dismal castle walls, conspiracies, bloody ghosts crying vengeance, an innocent maiden, a faithless wife, a usurping king, treacherous friends, swordplay and derring-do.

They are all here in profusion, and the play moves from first to last through a series of events that scarcely permit one to catch his breath. More than that, the story, Aristotle's soul, is perfectly plotted. The opening sequences on the parapets slam the audience into the thick of things from the first lines. Scenes of fervent activity followed by calm; then quick and exciting action, then sober introspection. Brutality and tenderness, a seamy court intrigue, a deadly cat-and-mouse game, a gentle family caught helplessly in the middle—all this and more combine in a totally absorbing tale of noble acts and infamous skulduggery. The characters are revealed in thoroughly convincing depth and breadth, their actions humanly reasonable and comprehensible. And all told in some of the most magnificent dramatic poetry ever written.

More than that, of course, *Hamlet* is a superb psychological study. Into the unfathomable and increasingly horrible affairs in Elsinore is thrown the young prince, still at the university, unprepared for the deeds he must do, aware of his unquestioned obligation to do them. The tax upon his strength, his mind, his personal philosophy of life is tremendous and eventually overwhelming. The constant peaks and valleys of the trauma through which he moves are fascinating to observe.

But finally, *Hamlet* is a tragedy. The prince is doomed, driven by forces beyond his control into the ultimate catastrophe. He wishes to avoid it, seeks to postpone it, becomes increasingly aware that it must come and that he must himself bring it about. Hamlet is no coward, but he blames himself for being one. He is not a procrastinator by nature, yet he fatally procrastinates. He is a thinker who weighs his thoughts and deeds, yet he acts with foolish impetuosity and unthinking cruelty. He commands our passion and our understanding. He is a potentially great man, capable of being a great king, but he must face the task the fates have ordained for him, ultimately realizing that escape is impossible, disaster inevitable. Who cannot weep, not for sentiment, but for the tremendous loss, the sacrifice endured, when, as Horatio tells us, "Now cracks a noble heart." As old Hamlet's perturbed spirit has been laid to rest, so we wish, with Horatio, for young Hamlet, that flights of angels sing him to his rest.

Hamlet, Prince of Denmark

CHARACTERS

CLAUDIUS, *King of Denmark*
HAMLET, *son to the late, and nephew to the present, King*
POLONIUS, *Lord Chamberlain*
HORATIO, *friend to Hamlet*
LAERTES, *son to Polonius*
VOLTEMAND ⎤
CORNELIUS ⎟
ROSENCRANTZ ⎟
GUILDENSTERN ⎬ *courtiers*
OSRIC ⎟
A GENTLEMAN ⎦
A PRIEST
MARCELLUS ⎤ *officers*
BERNARDO ⎦
FRANCISCO, *a soldier*
REYNALDO, *servant to Polonius*
PLAYERS
TWO CLOWNS, *gravediggers*
FORTINBRAS, *Prince of Norway*
A NORWEGIAN CAPTAIN
ENGLISH AMBASSADORS
GERTRUDE, *Queen of Denmark, mother to Hamlet*
OPHELIA, *daughter to Polonius*
GHOST OF HAMLET'S FATHER
LORDS, LADIES, OFFICERS, SOLDIERS, SAILORS, MESSENGERS,
    ATTENDANTS

155

ACT I

Scene I

Elsinore Castle: a sentry-post

(*Enter* BERNARDO *and* FRANCISCO, *two sentinels*)

BERNARDO   Who's there?
FRANCISCO   Nay, answer me. Stand and unfold yourself.
BERNARDO   Long live the king!
FRANCISCO   Bernardo?
BERNARDO   He.
FRANCISCO   You come most carefully upon your hour.
BERNARDO   'Tis now struck twelve. Get thee to bed, Francisco.
FRANCISCO   For this relief much thanks. 'Tis bitter cold,
  And I am sick at heart.
BERNARDO   Have you had quiet guard?
FRANCISCO   Not a mouse stirring.
BERNARDO   Well, good night.
  If you do meet Horatio and Marcellus,
  The rivals[1] of my watch, bid them make haste.

(*Enter* HORATIO *and* MARCELLUS)

FRANCISCO   I think I hear them. Stand, ho! Who is there?
HORATIO   Friends to this ground.
MARCELLUS   And liegemen to the Dane.[2]
FRANCISCO   Give you good night.
MARCELLUS   O, farewell, honest soldier.
  Who hath relieved you?
FRANCISCO   Bernardo hath my place.
  Give you good night.

(*Exit* FRANCISCO)

MARCELLUS   Holla, Bernardo!
BERNARDO   Say—
  What, is Horatio there?
HORATIO   A piece of him.
BERNARDO   Welcome, Horatio. Welcome, good Marcellus.
HORATIO   What, has this thing appeared again to-night?
BERNARDO   I have seen nothing.
MARCELLUS   Horatio says 'tis but our fantasy,
  And will not let belief take hold of him

---

[1] *rivals* sharers   [2] *Dane* King of Denmark

Touching this dreaded sight twice seen of us.
Therefore I have entreated him along
With us to watch the minutes of this night,
That, if again this apparition come,
He may approve[3] our eyes and speak to it.
HORATIO   Tush, tush, 'twill not appear.
BERNARDO   Sit down awhile,
  And let us once again assail your ears,
  That are so fortified against our story,
  What we two nights have seen.
HORATIO   Well, sit we down,
  And let us hear Bernardo speak of this.
BERNARDO   Last night of all,
  When yond same star that's westward from the pole[4]
  Had made his course t' illume that part of heaven
  Where now it burns, Marcellus and myself,
  The bell then beating one——

  (*Enter* GHOST)

MARCELLUS   Peace, break thee off. Look where it comes again.
BERNARDO   In the same figure like the king that's dead.
MARCELLUS   Thou art a scholar; speak to it, Horatio.
BERNARDO   Looks 'a not like the king? Mark it, Horatio.
HORATIO   Most like. It harrows me with fear and wonder.
BERNARDO   It would be spoke to.
MARCELLUS   Speak to it, Horatio.
HORATIO   What art thou that usurp'st this time of night
  Together with that fair and warlike form
  In which the majesty of buried Denmark[5]
  Did sometimes[6] march? By heaven I charge thee, speak.
MARCELLUS   It is offended.
BERNARDO   See, it stalks away.
HORATIO   Stay. Speak, speak. I charge thee, speak.

  (*Exit* GHOST)

MARCELLUS   'Tis gone and will not answer.
BERNARDO   How now, Horatio? You tremble and look pale.
  Is not this something more than fantasy?
  What think you on't?
HORATIO   Before my God, I might not this believe

---

[3] *approve* confirm   [4] *pole* polestar   [5] *buried Denmark* the buried King of
Denmark   [6] *sometimes* formerly

Without the sensible and true avouch
Of mine own eyes.

MARCELLUS   Is it not like the king?

HORATIO   As thou art to thyself.
Such was the very armor he had on
When he th' ambitious Norway[7] combated.
So frowned he once when, in an angry parle,[8]
He smote the sledded Polacks on the ice.
'Tis strange.

MARCELLUS   Thus twice before, and jump[9] at this dead hour,
With martial stalk hath he gone by our watch.

HORATIO   In what particular thought to work I know not;
But, in the gross and scope[10] of my opinion,
This bodes some strange eruption to our state.

MARCELLUS   Good now, sit down, and tell me he that knows,
Why this same strict and most observant watch
So nightly toils the subject[11] of the land,
And why such daily cast of brazen cannon
And foreign mart[12] for implements of war,
Why such impress[13] of shipwrights, whose sore task
Does not divide the Sunday from the week.
What might be toward [14] that this sweaty haste
Doth make the night joint-laborer with the day?
Who is't that can inform me?

HORATIO   That can I.
At least the whisper goes so. Our last king,
Whose image even but now appeared to us,
Was as you know by Fortinbras of Norway,
Thereto pricked on by a most emulate[15] pride,
Dared to the combat; in which our valiant Hamlet
(For so this side of our known world esteemed him)
Did slay this Fortinbras; who, by a sealed compact
Well ratified by law and heraldry,[16]
Did forfeit, with his life, all those his lands
Which he stood seized [17] of to the conqueror;
Against the which a moiety competent[18]
Was gagèd [19] by our king, which had returned
To the inheritance of Fortinbras

---

[7] *Norway* King of Norway   [8] *parle* parley   [9] *jump* just, exactly   [10] *gross and scope* gross scope, general view   [11] *toils* makes toil; *subject* subjects   [12] *mart* trading   [13] *impress* conscription   [14] *toward* in preparation   [15] *emulate* jealously rivalling   [16] *law and heraldry* law of heralds regulating combat   [17] *seized* possessed   [18] *moiety competent* sufficient portion   [19] *gagèd* engaged, staked

Had he been vanquisher, as, by the same comart[20]
And carriage[21] of the article designed,
His fell to Hamlet. Now, sir, young Fortinbras,
Of unimprovèd [22] mettle hot and full,
Hath in the skirts of Norway here and there
Sharked [23] up a list of lawless resolutes[24]
For food and diet to some enterprise
That hath a stomach[25] in't; which is no other,
As it doth well appear unto our state,
But to recover of us by strong hand
And terms compulsatory those foresaid lands
So by his father lost; and this, I take it,
Is the main motive of our preparations,
The source of this our watch, and the chief head [26]
Of this posthaste and romage[27] in the land.

BERNARDO   I think it be no other but e'en so.
Well may it sort[28] that this portentous figure
Comes armèd through our watch so like the king
That was and is the question of these wars.

HORATIO   A mote[29] it is to trouble the mind's eye.
In the most high and palmy state of Rome,
A little ere the mightiest Julius fell,
The graves stood tenantless and the sheeted [30] dead
Did squeak and gibber in the Roman streets;
As stars with trains of fire and dews of blood,
Disasters[31] in the sun; and the moist star[32]
Upon whose influence Neptune's empire stands
Was sick almost to doomsday with eclipse.
And even the like precurse[33] of feared events,
As harbingers[34] preceding still [35] the fates
And prologue to the omen[36] coming on,
Have heaven and earth together demonstrated
Unto our climatures[37] and countrymen.

(*Enter* GHOST)

But soft, behold, lo where it comes again!

---

[20] *comart* joint bargain   [21] *carriage* purport   [22] *unimprovèd* unused
[23] *Sharked* snatched indiscriminately as the shark takes prey [24] *resolutes*
desperadoes [25] *stomach* show of venturesomeness [26] *head* fountainhead,
source [27] *romage* intense activity [28] *sort* suit [29] *mote* speck of dust
[30] *sheeted* in shrouds [31] *Disasters* ominous signs [32] *moist star* moon [33] *precurse* foreshadowing [34] *harbingers* forerunners [35] *still* constantly [36] *omen* calamity [37] *climatures* regions

I'll cross it,[38] though it blast me.—Stay, illusion.

(*He spreads his arms*)

If thou hast any sound or use of voice,
Speak to me.
If there be any good thing to be done
That may to thee do ease and grace to me,
Speak to me.
If thou art privy to thy country's fate,
Which happily[39] foreknowing may avoid,
O, speak!
Or if thou hast uphoarded in thy life
Extorted treasure in the womb of earth,
For which, they say, you spirits oft walk in death,

(*The cock crows*)

Speak of it. Stay and speak. Stop it, Marcellus.
MARCELLUS   Shall I strike at it with my partisan? [40]
HORATIO   Do, if it will not stand.
BERNARDO   'Tis here.
HORATIO   'Tis here.

(*Exit* GHOST)

MARCELLUS   'Tis gone.
We do it wrong, being so majestical,
To offer it the show of violence,
For it is as the air invulnerable,
And our vain blows malicious mockery.
BERNARDO   It was about to speak when the cock crew.
HORATIO   And then it started, like a guilty thing
Upon a fearful summons. I have heard
The cock, that is the trumpet to the morn,
Doth with his lofty and shrill-sounding throat
Awake the god of day, and at his warning,
Whether in sea or fire, in earth or air,
Th' extravagant[41] and erring[42] spirit hies
To his confine; and of the truth herein
This present object made probation.[43]

---

[38] *cross it* cross its path   [39] *happily* haply, perchance   [40] *partisan* pike   [41] *extravagant* wandering beyond bounds   [42] *erring* wandering   [43] *probation* proof

MARCELLUS   It faded on the crowing of the cock.
  Some say that ever 'gainst[44] that season comes
  Wherein our Saviour's birth is celebrated,
  This bird of dawning singeth all night long,
  And then, they say, no spirit dare stir abroad,
  The nights are wholesome, then no planets strike,[45]
  No fairy takes,[46] nor witch hath power to charm.
  So hallowed and so gracious is that time.
HORATIO   So have I heard and do in part believe it.
  But look, the morn in russet mantle clad
  Walks o'er the dew of yon high eastward hill.
  Break we our watch up, and by my advice
  Let us impart what we have seen to-night
  Unto young Hamlet, for upon my life
  This spirit, dumb to us, will speak to him.
  Do you consent we shall acquaint him with it,
  As needful in our loves, fitting our duty?
MARCELLUS   Let's do't, I pray, and I this morning know
  Where we shall find him most conveniently.

  (*Exeunt*)

Act I, Scene II

Elsinore Castle: a room of state

Flourish. Enter CLAUDIUS, *King of Denmark*, GERTRUDE *the Queen*, COUN-
CILLORS, POLONIUS *and his son* LAERTES, HAMLET, *cum aliis*[1] [*including*
VOLTEMAND *and* CORNELIUS]

KING   Though yet of Hamlet our dear brother's death
  The memory be green, and that it us befitted
  To bear our hearts in grief, and our whole kingdom
  To be contracted in one brow of woe,
  Yet so far hath discretion fought with nature
  That we with wisest sorrow think on him
  Together with remembrance of ourselves.
  Therefore our sometime sister, now our queen,
  Th' imperial jointress[2] to this warlike state,
  Have we, as 'twere with a defeated joy,
  With an auspicious and a dropping eye,

---

[44] *'gainst* just before   [45] *strike* work evil by influence   [46] *takes* bewitches
[1] *cum aliis* with others   [2] *jointress* a woman who has a jointure, or joint ten-
ancy of an estate

With mirth in funeral and with dirge in marriage,
In equal scale weighing delight and dole,
Taken to wife. Nor have we herein barred [3]
Your better wisdoms, which have freely gone
With this affair along. For all, our thanks.
Now follows, that you know, young Fortinbras,
Holding a weak supposal of our worth,
Or thinking by our late dear brother's death
Our state to be disjoint and out of frame,
Colleaguèd [4] with this dream of his advantage,
He hath not failed to pester us with message
Importing the surrender of those lands
Lost by his father, with all bands of law,
To our most valiant brother. So much for him.
Now for ourself and for this time of meeting.
Thus much the business is: we have here writ
To Norway, uncle of young Fortinbras—
Who, impotent and bedrid, scarcely hears
Of this his nephew's purpose—to suppress
His further gait[5] herein, in that the levies,
The lists, and full proportions[6] are all made
Out of his subject; and we here dispatch
You, good Cornelius, and you, Voltemand,
For bearers of this greeting to old Norway,
Giving to you no further personal power
To business with the king, more than the scope
Of these delated [7] articles allow.
Farewell, and let your haste commend your duty.

CORNELIUS, VOLTEMAND   In that, and all things, will we show our
    duty.

KING   We doubt it nothing. Heartily farewell.

(*Exeunt* VOLTEMAND *and* CORNELIUS)

And now, Laertes, what's the news with you?
You told us of some suit. What is't, Laertes?
You cannot speak of reason to the Dane[8]
And lose your voice.[9] What wouldst thou beg, Laertes,
That shall not be my offer, not thy asking?
The head is not more native[10] to the heart,

---

[3] *barred* excluded   [4] *Colleaguèd* united   [5] *gait* going   [6] *proportions* amounts
of forces and supplies   [7] *delated* detailed   [8] *Dane* King of Denmark   [9] *lose
your voice* speak in vain   [10] *native* joined by nature

The hand more instrumental [11] to the mouth,
Than is the throne of Denmark to thy father.
What wouldst thou have, Laertes?
LAERTES   My dread lord,
Your leave and favor to return to France,
From whence though willingly I came to Denmark
To show my duty in your coronation,
Yet now I must confess, that duty done,
My thoughts and wishes bend again toward France
And bow them to your gracious leave and pardon.
KING   Have you your father's leave? What says Polonius?
POLONIUS   He hath, my lord, wrung from me my slow leave
By laborsome petition, and at last
Upon his will I sealed my hard consent.
I do beseech you give him leave to go.
KING   Take thy fair hour, Laertes. Time be thine,
And thy best graces spend it at thy will.
But now, my cousin [12] Hamlet, and my son—
HAMLET (*aside*)   A little more than kin, [13] and less than kind! [14]
KING   How is it that the clouds still hang on you?
HAMLET   Not so, my lord. I am too much in the sun. [15]
QUEEN   Good Hamlet, cast thy nighted color off,
And let thine eye look like a friend on Denmark.
Do not for ever with thy vailèd [16] lids
Seek for thy noble father in the dust.
Thou know'st 'tis common. All that lives must die,
Passing through nature to eternity.
HAMLET   Ay, madam, it is common.
QUEEN   If it be,
Why seems it so particular with thee?
HAMLET   Seems, madam? Nay, it is. I know not "seems."
'Tis not alone my inky cloak, good mother,
Nor customary suits of solemn black,
Nor windy suspiration of forced breath,
No, nor the fruitful [17] river in the eye,
Nor the dejected havior of the visage,
Together with all forms, moods, shapes of grief,

---

11 *instrumental* serviceable   12 *cousin* kinsman more distant than parent,
child, brother, or sister   13 *kin* related as nephew   14 *kind* kindly in feeling,
as by kind, or nature, a son would be to his father   15 *sun* sunshine of the
king's undesired favor (with the punning additional meaning of "place of a
son")   16 *vailèd* downcast   17 *fruitful* copious

That can denote me truly. These indeed seem,
For they are actions that a man might play,
But I have that within which passeth show—
These but the trappings and the suits of woe.
KING   'Tis sweet and commendable in your nature, Hamlet,
To give these mourning duties to your father,
But you must know your father lost a father,
That father lost, lost his, and the survivor bound
In filial obligation for some term
To do obsequious[18] sorrow. But to persever[19]
In obstinate condolement is a course
Of impious stubbornness. 'Tis unmanly grief.
It shows a will most incorrect to heaven,
A heart unfortified, a mind impatient,
An understanding simple and unschooled.
For what we know must be and is as common
As any the most vulgar thing to sense,
Why should we in our peevish opposition
Take it to heart? Fie, 'tis a fault to heaven,
A fault against the dead, a fault to nature,
To reason most absurd, whose common theme
Is death of fathers, and who still hath cried,
From the first corse till he that died to-day,
"This must be so." We pray you throw to earth
This unprevailing woe, and think of us
As a father, for let the world take note
You are the most immediate to our throne,
And with no less nobility of love
Than that which dearest father bears his son
Do I impart toward you. For your intent
In going back to school in Wittenberg,
It is most retrograde[20] to our desire,
And we beseech you, bend you to remain
Here in the cheer and comfort of our eye,
Our chiefest courtier, cousin, and our son.
QUEEN   Let not thy mother lose her prayers, Hamlet.
I pray thee stay with us, go not to Wittenberg.
HAMLET   I shall in all my best obey you, madam.
KING   Why, 'tis a loving and a fair reply.
Be as ourself in Denmark. Madam, come.

---

[18] *obsequious* proper to obsequies or funerals   [19] *persever* persevere (accented
on the second syllable, as always in Shakespeare)   [20] *retrograde* contrary

This gentle and unforced accord of Hamlet
Sits smiling to my heart, in grace whereof
No jocund health that Denmark drinks to-day
But the great cannon to the clouds shall tell,
And the king's rouse[21] the heaven shall bruit[22] again,
Respeaking earthly thunder. Come away.

(Flourish. Exeunt all but HAMLET*)*

HAMLET   O that this too too sullied flesh would melt,
Thaw, and resolve itself into a dew,
Or that the Everlasting had not fixed
His canon[23] gainst self-slaughter. O God, God,
How weary, stale, flat, and unprofitable
Seem to me all the uses of this world!
Fie on't, ah, fie, 'tis an unweeded garden
That grows to seed. Things rank and gross in nature
Possess it merely.[24] That it should come to this,
But two months dead, nay, not so much, not two,
So excellent a king, that was to this
Hyperion[25] to a satyr, so loving to my mother
That he might not beteem[26] the winds of heaven
Visit her face too roughly. Heaven and earth,
Must I remember? Why, she would hang on him
As if increase of appetite had grown
By what it fed on, and yet within a month—
Let me not think on't; frailty, thy name is woman—
A little month, or ere those shoes were old
With which she followed my poor father's body
Like Niobe,[27] all tears, why she, even she—
O God, a beast that wants discourse[28] of reason
Would have mourned longer—married with my uncle,
My father's brother, but no more like my father
Than I to Hercules. Within a month,
Ere yet the salt of most unrighteous tears
Had left the flushing in her gallèd [29] eyes,
She married. O, most wicked speed, to post
With such dexterity to incestuous sheets!

(important soliloquy)

---

[21] *rouse* toast drunk in wine   [22] *bruit* echo   [23] *canon* law   [24] *merely* completely   [25] *Hyperion* the sun god   [26] *beteem* allow   [27] *Niobe* the proud
mother who boasted of having more children than Leto and was punished
when they were slain by Apollo and Artemis, children of Leto; the grieving
Niobe was changed by Zeus into a stone, which continually dropped tears
[28] *discourse* logical power or process   [29] *gallèd* irritated

It is not nor it cannot come to good.
But break my heart, for I must hold my tongue.

(*Enter* HORATIO, MARCELLUS, *and* BERNARDO)

HORATIO   Hail to your lordship!
HAMLET   I am glad to see you well.
   Horatio—or I do forget myself.
HORATIO   The same, my lord, and your poor servant ever.
HAMLET   Sir, my good friend, I'll change[30] that name with you.
   And what make[31] you from Wittenberg, Horatio?
   Marcellus?
MARCELLUS   My good lord!
HAMLET   I am very glad to see you. (*to* BERNARDO) Good even, sir.
   But what, in faith, make you from Wittenberg?
HORATIO   A truant disposition, good my lord.
HAMLET   I would not hear your enemy say so,
   Nor shall you do my ear that violence
   To make it truster of your own report
   Against yourself. I know you are no truant.
   But what is your affair in Elsinore?
   We'll teach you to drink deep ere you depart.
HORATIO   My lord, I came to see your father's funeral.
HAMLET   I prithee do not mock me, fellow student.
   I think it was to see my mother's wedding.
HORATIO   Indeed, my lord, it followed hard upon.
HAMLET   Thrift, thrift, Horatio. The funeral baked meats
   Did coldly furnish forth the marriage tables.
   Would I had met my dearest[32] foe in heaven
   Or ever I had seen that day, Horatio!
   My father—methinks I see my father.
HORATIO   Where, my lord?
HAMLET   In my mind's eye, Horatio.
HORATIO   I saw him once. 'A was a goodly king.
HAMLET   'A was a man, take him for all in all,
   I shall not look upon his like again.
HORATIO   My lord, I think I saw him yesternight.
HAMLET   Saw? who?
HORATIO   My lord, the king your father.
HAMLET   The king my father?
HORATIO   Season your admiration[33] for a while

---

[30] *change* exchange   [31] *make* do   [32] *dearest* direst, bitterest   [33] *Season your admiration* control your wonder

With an attent ear till I may deliver
Upon the witness of these gentlemen
This marvel to you.
HAMLET   For God's love let me hear!
HORATIO   Two nights together had these gentlemen,
   Marcellus and Bernardo, on their watch
   In the dead waste and middle of the night
   Been thus encountered. A figure like your father,
   Armèd at point[34] exactly, cap-a-pe,[35]
   Appears before them and with solemn march
   Goes slow and stately by them. Thrice he walked
   By their oppressed and fear-surprisèd eyes
   Within his truncheon's[36] length, whilst they, distilled
   Almost to jelly with the act of fear,
   Stand dumb and speak not to him. This to me
   In dreadful secrecy impart they did,
   And I with them the third night kept the watch,
   Where, as they had delivered, both in time,
   Form of the thing, each word made true and good,
   The apparition comes. I knew your father.
   These hands are not more like.
HAMLET   But where was this?
MARCELLUS   My lord, upon the platform where we watched.
HAMLET   Did you not speak to it?
HORATIO   My lord, I did,
   But answer made it none. Yet once methought
   It lifted up it[37] head and did address
   Itself to motion like as it would speak.
   But even then the morning cock crew loud,
   And at the sound it shrunk in haste away
   And vanished from our sight.
HAMLET   'Tis very strange.
HORATIO   As I do live, my honored lord, 'tis true,
   And we did think it writ down in our duty
   To let you know of it.
HAMLET   Indeed, indeed, sirs, but this troubles me.
   Hold you the watch to-night?
ALL   We do, my lord.
HAMLET   Armed, say you?
ALL   Armed, my lord.

---

[34] *at point* completely   [35] *cap-a pe* from head to foot   [36] *truncheon* military
commander's baton   [37] *it* its

HAMLET	From top to toe?
ALL	My lord, from head to foot.
HAMLET	Then saw you not his face?
HORATIO	O, yes, my lord. He wore his beaver[38] up.
HAMLET	What, looked he frowningly?
HORATIO	A countenance more in sorrow than in anger.
HAMLET	Pale or red?
HORATIO	Nay, very pale.
HAMLET	And fixed his eyes upon you?
HORATIO	Most constantly.
HAMLET	I would I had been there.
HORATIO	It would have much amazed you.
HAMLET	Very like, very like. Stayed it long?
HORATIO	While one with moderate haste might tell [39] a hundred.
BOTH	Longer, longer.
HORATIO	Not when I saw't.
HAMLET	His beard was grizzled,[40] no?
HORATIO	It was as I have seen it in his life,

A sable silvered.[41]

HAMLET   I will watch to-night.
Perchance 'twill walk again.

HORATIO   I warr'nt it will.

HAMLET   If it assume my noble father's person,
I'll speak to it though hell itself should gape
And bid me hold my peace. I pray you all,
If you have hitherto concealed this sight,
Let it be tenable[42] in your silence still,
And whatsomever else shall hap to-night,
Give it an understanding but no tongue.
I will requite your loves. So fare you well.
Upon the platform, 'twixt eleven and twelve
I'll visit you.

ALL   Our duty to your honor.

HAMLET   Your loves, as mine to you. Farewell.

(*Exeunt all but* HAMLET)

My father's spirit—in arms? All is not well.
I doubt[43] some foul play. Would the night were come!

---

[38] *beaver* visor or movable faceguard of the helmet   [39] *tell* count   [40] *grizzled* grey   [41] *sable silvered* black mixed with white   [42] *tenable* held firmly   [43] *doubt* suspect, fear

Till then sit still, my soul. Foul deeds will rise,
Though all the earth o'erwhelm them, to men's eyes.

(*Exit*)

Act I, Scene III

Elsinore Castle: the chambers of POLONIUS

(*Enter* LAERTES *and* OPHELIA, *his sister*)

LAERTES   My necessaries are embarked. Farewell.
And, sister, as the winds give benefit
And convoy[1] is assistant, do not sleep,
But let me hear from you.
OPHELIA   Do you doubt that?
LAERTES   For Hamlet, and the trifling of his favor,
Hold it a fashion and a toy in blood,
A violet in the youth of primy[2] nature,
Forward, not permanent, sweet, not lasting,
The perfume and suppliance[3] of a minute,
No more.
OPHELIA   No more but so?
LAERTES   Think it no more.
For nature crescent[4] does not grow alone
In thews and bulk, but as this temple[5] waxes
The inward service of the mind and soul
Grows wide withal. Perhaps he loves you now,
And now no soil nor cautel[6] doth besmirch
The virtue of his will,[7] but you must fear,
His greatness weighed,[8] his will is not his own.
(For he himself is subject to his birth.)
He may not, as unvalued persons do,
Carve for himself, for on his choice depends
The safety and health of this whole state,
And therefore must his choice be circumscribed
Unto the voice and yielding[9] of that body
Whereof he is the head. Then if he says he loves you,
It fits your wisdom so far to believe it
As he in his particular act and place

---

[1] *convoy* means of transport   [2] *primy* of the springtime   [3] *perfume and suppliance* filling sweetness   [4] *crescent* growing   [5] *this temple* the body   [6] *cautel* deceit   [7] *will* desire   [8] *greatness weighed* high position considered   [9] *yielding* assent

May give his saying deed, which is no further
Than the main voice of Denmark goes withal.
Then weigh what loss your honor may sustain
If with too credent[10] ear you list his songs,
Or lose your heart, or your chaste treasure open
To his unmastered importunity.
Fear it, Ophelia, fear it, my dear sister,
And keep you in the rear of your affection,[11]
Out of the shot and danger of desire.
The chariest maid is prodigal enough
If she unmask her beauty to the moon.
Virtue itself scapes not calumnious strokes.
The canker[12] galls[13] the infants of the spring
Too oft before their buttons[14] be disclosed,
And in the morn and liquid dew of youth
Contagious blastments[15] are most imminent.
Be wary then; best safety lies in fear.
Youth to itself rebels, though none else near.

OPHELIA   I shall the effect of this good lesson keep
As watchman to my heart, but, good my brother,
Do not as some ungracious pastors do,
Show me the steep and thorny way to heaven,
Whiles like a puffed and reckless libertine
Himself the primrose path of dalliance treads
And recks[16] not his own rede.[17]

(*Enter* POLONIUS)

LAERTES   O, fear me not.
I stay too long. But here my father comes.
A double blessing is a double grace;
Occasion smiles upon a second leave.

POLONIUS   Yet here, Laertes? Aboard, aboard, for shame!
The wind sits in the shoulder of your sail,
And you are stayed for. There—my blessing with thee,
And these few precepts in thy memory
Look thou character.[18] Give thy thoughts no tongue,
Nor any unproportioned[19] thought his act.

---

[10] *credent* credulous   [11] *affection* feelings, which rashly lead forward into dangers   [12] *canker* rose worm   [13] *galls* injures   [14] *buttons* buds   [15] *blastments* blights   [16] *recks* regards   [17]*rede* counsel   [18] *character* inscribe   [19] *unproportioned* unadjusted to what is right

Be thou familiar, but by no means vulgar.
Those friends thou hast, and their adoption tried,
Grapple them unto thy soul with hoops of steel,
But do not dull thy palm with entertainment
Of each new-hatched, unfledged courage.[20] Beware
Of entrance to a quarrel; but being in,
Bear't that th' opposèd may beware of thee.
Give every man thine ear, but few thy voice;
Take each man's censure,[21] but reserve thy judgment.
Costly thy habit as thy purse can buy,
But not expressed in fancy; rich, not gaudy,
For the apparel oft proclaims the man,
And they in France of the best rank and station
Are of a most select and generous chief [22] in that.
Neither a borrower nor a lender be,
For loan oft loses both itself and friend,
And borrowing dulleth edge of husbandry.[23]
This above all, to thine own self be true,
And it must follow as the night the day
Thou canst not then be false to any man.
Farewell. My blessing season[24] this in thee!

LAERTES   Most humbly do I take my leave, my lord.
POLONIUS   The time invites you. Go, your servants tend.[25]
LAERTES   Farewell, Ophelia, and remember well
What I have said to you.
OPHELIA   'Tis in my memory locked,
And you yourself shall keep the key of it.
LAERTES   Farewell.

(*Exit* LAERTES)

POLONIUS   What is't, Ophelia, he hath said to you?
OPHELIA   So please you, something touching the Lord Hamlet.
POLONIUS   Marry,[26] well bethought.
'Tis told me he hath very oft of late
Given private time to you, and you yourself
Have of your audience been most free and bounteous.
If it be so—as so 'tis put on me,
And that in way of caution—I must tell you

---

[20] *courage* man of spirit, young blood   [21] *censure* judgment   [22] *chief* eminence   [23] *husbandry* thriftiness   [24] *season* ripen and make fruitful   [25] *tend* wait   [26] *Marry* by Mary

You do not understand yourself so clearly
As it behooves my daughter and your honor.
What is between you? Give me up the truth.

OPHELIA He hath, my lord, of late made many tenders[27]
Of his affection to me.

POLONIUS Affection? Pooh! You speak like a green girl,
Unsifted [28] in such perilous circumstance.
Do you believe his tenders, as you call them?

OPHELIA I do not know, my lord, what I should think.

POLONIUS Marry, I will teach you. Think yourself a baby
That you have ta'en these tenders[29] for true pay
Which are not sterling. Tender yourself more dearly,
Or (not to crack the wind of [30] the poor phrase,
Running it thus) you'll tender me a fool.

OPHELIA My lord, he hath importuned me with love
In honorable fashion.

POLONIUS Ay, fashion you may call it. Go to, go to.[31]

OPHELIA And hath given countenance to his speech, my lord,
With almost all the holy vows of heaven.

POLONIUS Ay, springes[32] to catch woodcocks.[33] I do know,
When the blood burns, how prodigal the soul
Lends the tongue vows. These blazes, daughter,
Giving more light than heat, extinct in both
Even in their promise, as it is a-making,
You must not take for fire. From this time
Be something scanter of your maiden presence.
Set your entreatments[34] at a higher rate
Than a command to parley.[35] For Lord Hamlet,
Believe so much in him that he is young,
And with a larger tether may he walk
Than may be given you. In few, Ophelia,
Do not believe his vows, for they are brokers,[36]
Not of that dye which their investments[37] show,

---

[27] *tenders* offers [28] *Unsifted* untested [29] *tenders ... Tender ... tender* offers ... hold in regard ... present (a word play going through three meanings, the last use of the word yielding further complexity with its valid implications that she will show herself to him as a fool, will show him to the world as a fool, and may go so far as to present him with a baby, which would be a fool because "fool" was an Elizabethan term of endearment especially applicable to an infant as a "little innocent") [30] *crack ... of* make wheeze like a horse driven too hard [31] *Go to* go away, go on (expressing impatience) [32] *springes* snares [33] *woodcocks* birds believed foolish [34] *entreatments* military negotiations for surrender [35] *parley* confer with a besieger [36] *brokers* middlemen, panders [37] *investments* clothes

But mere implorators of unholy suits,
Breathing like sanctified and pious bawds,
The better to beguile. This is for all:
I would not, in plain terms, from this time forth
Have you so slander[38] any moment[39] leisure
As to give words or talk with the Lord Hamlet.
Look to't, I charge you. Come your ways.

OPHELIA   I shall obey, my lord.

(*Exeunt*)

Act I, Scene IV

The sentry-post

(*Enter* HAMLET, HORATIO, *and* MARCELLUS)

HAMLET   The air bites shrewdly[1]; it is very cold.
HORATIO   It is a nipping and an eager[2] air.
HAMLET   What hour now?
HORATIO   I think it lacks of twelve.
MARCELLUS   No, it is struck.
HORATIO   Indeed? I heard it not. It then draws near the season
Wherein the spirit held his wont to walk.

(*A flourish of trumpets, and two pieces goes off*)

What does this mean, my lord?
HAMLET   The king doth wake to-night and takes his rouse,[3]
Keeps wassail, and the swaggering upspring[4] reels,
And as he drains his draughts of Rhenish[5] down
The kettledrum and trumpet thus bray out
The triumph[6] of his pledge.
HORATIO   Is it a custom?
HAMLET   Ay, marry, is't,
But to my mind, though I am native here
And to the manner born, it is a custom
More honored in the breach than the observance.[7]
This heavy-headed revel east and west
Makes us traduced and taxed of [8] other nations.
They clepe[9] us drunkards and with swinish phrase

---

[38] *slander* use disgracefully   [39] *moment* momentary
[1] *shrewdly* wickedly   [2] *eager* sharp   [3] *rouse* carousal   [4] *upspring* a German dance   [5] *Rhenish* Rhine wine   [6] *triumph* achievement, feat (in downing a cup of wine at one draught)   [7] *More ... observance* better broken than observed   [8] *taxed of* censured by   [9] *clepe* call

Soil our addition,[10] and indeed it takes
From our achievements, though performed at height,
The pith and marrow of our attribute.[11]
So oft it chances in particular men
That (for some vicious mole[12] of nature in them,
As in their birth, wherein they are not guilty,
Since nature cannot choose his[13] origin)
By the o'ergrowth of some complexion,[14]
Oft breaking down the pales[15] and forts of reason,
Or by some habit that too much o'erleavens[16]
The form of plausive[17] manners—that (these men
Carrying, I say, the stamp of one defect,
Being nature's livery,[18] or fortune's star)[19]
Their virtues else, be they as pure as grace,
As infinite as man may undergo,
Shall in the general censure take corruption
From that particular fault. The dram of evil
Doth all the noble substance of a doubt,
To his own scandal.

(*Enter* GHOST)

HORATIO   Look, my lord, it comes.
HAMLET   Angels and ministers of grace defend us!
Be thou a spirit of health[20] or goblin[21] damned,
Bring with thee airs from heaven or blasts from hell,
Be thy intents wicked or charitable,
Thou com'st in such a questionable shape
That I will speak to thee. I'll call thee Hamlet,
King, father, royal Dane. O, answer me!
Let me not burst in ignorance, but tell
Why thy canonized [22] bones, hearsèd in death,
Have burst their cerements,[23] why the sepulchre
Wherein we saw thee quietly interred
Hath oped his ponderous and marble jaws
To cast thee up again. What may this mean

---

[10] *addition* reputation, title added as a distinction   [11] *attribute* reputation, what is attributed   [12] *mole* blemish, flaw   [13] *his* its   [14] *complexion* part of the make-up, combination of humors   [15] *pales* barriers, fences   [16] *o'erleavens* works change throughout, as yeast ferments dough   [17] *plausive* pleasing   [18] *livery* characteristic equipment or provision   [19] *star* make-up as formed by stellar influence   [20] *of health* sound, good   [21] *goblin* fiend   [22] *canonized* buried with the established rites of the Church   [23] *cerements* waxed gravecloths

That thou, dead corse, again in complete steel,
Revisits thus the glimpses of the moon,
Making night hideous, and we fools of nature[24]
So horridly to shake our disposition
With thoughts beyond the reaches of our souls?
Say, why is this? wherefore? what should we do?

(GHOST *beckons*)

HORATIO   It beckons you to go away with it,
As if it some impartment did desire
To you alone.
MARCELLUS   Look with what courteous action
It waves you to a more removèd ground.
But do not go with it.
HORATIO   No, by no means.
HAMLET   It will not speak. Then will I follow it.
HORATIO   Do not, my lord.
HAMLET   Why, what should be the fear?
I do not set my life at a pin's fee,
And for my soul, what can it do to that,
Being a thing immortal as itself?
It waves me forth again. I'll follow it.
HORATIO   What if it tempt you toward the flood, my lord,
Or to the dreadful summit of the cliff
That beetles[25] o'er his base into the sea,
And there assume some other horrible form,
Which might deprive[26] your sovereignty of reason[27]
And draw you into madness? Think of it.
The very place puts toys[28] of desperation,
Without more motive, into every brain
That looks so many fathoms to the sea
And hears it roar beneath.
HAMLET   It waves me still.
Go on. I'll follow thee.
MARCELLUS   You shall not go, my lord.
HAMLET   Hold off your hands.
HORATIO   Be ruled. You shall not go.
HAMLET   My fate cries out
And makes each petty artere[29] in this body

---

[24] *fools of nature* men made conscious of natural limitations by a supernatural
manifestation   [25] *beetles* juts out   [26] *deprive* take away   [27] *sovereignty of
reason* state of being ruled by reason   [28] *toys* fancies   [29] *artere* artery

As hardy as the Nemean lion's [30] nerve.[31]
Still am I called. Unhand me, gentlemen.
By heaven, I'll make a ghost of him that lets[32] me!
I say, away! Go on. I'll follow thee.

(*Exit* GHOST, *and* HAMLET)

HORATIO   He waxes desperate with imagination.
MARCELLUS   Let's follow. 'Tis not fit thus to obey him.
HORATIO   Have after. To what issue will this come?
MARCELLUS   Something is rotten in the state of Denmark.
HORATIO   Heaven will direct it.
MARCELLUS   Nay, let's follow him.

(*Exeunt*)

Act I, Scene V

Another part of the fortifications

(*Enter* GHOST *and* HAMLET)

HAMLET   Whither wilt thou lead me? Speak. I'll go no further.
GHOST   Mark me.
HAMLET   I will.
GHOST   My hour is almost come,
   When I to sulph'rous and tormenting flames[1]
   Must render up myself.
HAMLET   Alas, poor ghost!
GHOST   Pity me not, but lend thy serious hearing
   To what I shall unfold.
HAMLET   Speak. I am bound to hear.
GHOST   So art thou to revenge, when thou shalt hear.
HAMLET   What?
GHOST   I am thy father's spirit,
   Doomed for a certain term to walk the night,
   And for the day confined to fast[2] in fires,
   Till the foul crimes done in my days of nature
   Are burnt and purged away. But that I am forbid
   To tell the secrets of my prison house,
   I could a tale unfold whose lightest word
   Would harrow up thy soul, freeze thy young blood,

---

[30] *Nemean lion* a lion slain by Hercules in the performance of one of his
twelve labors   [31] *nerve* sinew   [32] *lets* hinders
[1] *flames* sufferings in purgatory (not hell)   [2] *fast* do penance

Make thy two eyes like stars start from their spheres,[3]
Thy knotted and combinèd locks to part,
And each particular hair to stand an[4] end
Like quills upon the fretful porpentine.[5]
But this eternal blazon[6] must not be
To ears of flesh and blood. List, list, O, list!
If thou didst ever thy dear father love—

HAMLET   O God!

GHOST   Revenge his foul and most unnatural murder.

HAMLET   Murder?

GHOST   Murder most foul, as in the best it is,
But this most foul, strange, and unnatural.

HAMLET   Haste me to know't, that I, with wings as swift
As meditation[7] or the thoughts of love,
May sweep to my revenge.

GHOST   I find thee apt,
And duller shouldst thou be than the fat weed
That roots itself in ease on Lethe[8] wharf,
Wouldst thou not stir in this. Now, Hamlet, hear.
'Tis given out that, sleeping in my orchard,
A serpent stung me. So the whole ear of Denmark
Is by a forgèd process[9] of my death
Rankly abused. But know, thou noble youth,
The serpent that did sting thy father's life
Now wears his crown.

HAMLET   O my prophetic soul!
My uncle?

GHOST   Ay, that incestuous, that adulterate[10] beast,
With witchcraft of his wit, with traitorous gifts—
O wicked wit and gifts, that have the power
So to seduce!—won to this shameful lust
The will of my most seeming-virtuous queen.
O Hamlet, what a falling-off was there,
From me, whose love was of that dignity
That it went hand in hand even with the vow
I made to her in marriage, and to decline

---

[3] *spheres* transparent revolving shells in each of which, according to the Ptolemaic astronomy, a planet or other heavenly body was placed   [4] *an* on   [5] *porpentine* porcupine   [6] *eternal blazon* revelation of eternity   [7] *meditation* thought   [8] *Lethe* the river in Hades which brings forgetfulness of past life to a spirit who drinks of it   [9] *forgèd process* falsified official report   [10] *adulterate* adulterous

Upon a wretch whose natural gifts were poor
To those of mine!
But virtue, as it never will be moved,
Though lewdness court it in a shape of heaven,[11]
So lust, though to a radiant angel linked,
Will sate itself in a celestial bed
And prey on garbage.
But soft, methinks I scent the morning air.
Brief let me be. Sleeping within my orchard,
My custom always of the afternoon,
Upon my secure[12] hour thy uncle stole
With juice of cursed hebona[13] in a vial,
And in the porches of my ears did pour
The leperous distilment, whose effect
Holds such an enmity with blood of man
That swift as quicksilver it courses through
The natural gates and alleys of the body,
And with a sudden vigor it doth posset[14]
And curd, like eager[15] droppings into milk,
The thin and wholesome blood. So did it mine,
And a most instant tetter[16] barked [17] about
Most lazar-like[18] with vile and loathsome crust
All my smooth body.
Thus was I sleeping by a brother's hand
Of life, of crown, of queen at once dispatched,
Cut off even in the blossoms of my sin,
Unhouseled,[19] disappointed,[20] unaneled,[21]
No reck'ning made, but sent to my account
With all my imperfections on my head.
O, horrible! O, horrible! most horrible!
If thou hast nature in thee, bear it not.
Let not the royal bed of Denmark be
A couch for luxury[22] and damnèd incest.
But howsomever thou pursues this act,
Taint not thy mind, nor let thy soul contrive
Against thy mother aught. Leave her to heaven
And to those thorns that in her bosom lodge

---

[11] *shape of heaven* angelic disguise [12] *secure* carefree, unsuspecting [13] *hebona* some poisonous plant [14] *posset* curdle [15] *eager* sour [16] *tetter* eruption [17] *barked* covered as with a bark [18] *lazar-like* leper-like [19] *Unhouseled* without the Sacrament [20] *disappointed* unprepared spiritually [21] *unaneled* without extreme unction [22] *luxury* lust

To prick and sting her. Fare thee well at once.
The glowworm shows the matin[23] to be near
And gins to pale his uneffectual fire.
Adieu, adieu, adieu. Remember me.

(*Exit*)

HAMLET   O all you host of heaven! O earth! What else?
And shall I couple hell? O fie! Hold, hold, my heart,
And you, my sinews, grow not instant old,
But bear me stiffly up. Remember thee?
Ay, thou poor ghost, while memory holds a seat
In this distracted globe.[24] Remember thee?
Yea, from the table[25] of my memory
I'll wipe away all trivial fond records,
All saws[26] of books, all forms,[27] all pressures[28] past
That youth and observation copied there,
And thy commandment all alone shall live
Within the book and volume of my brain,
Unmixed with baser matter. Yes, by heaven!
O most pernicious woman!
O villain, villain, smiling, damnèd villain!
My tables—meet it is I set it down
That one may smile, and smile, and be a villain.
At least I am sure it may be so in Denmark.

(*Writes*)

So, uncle, there you are. Now to my word:
It is "Adieu, adieu, remember me."
I have sworn't.

(*Enter* HORATIO *and* MARCELLUS)

HORATIO   My lord, my lord!
MARCELLUS   Lord Hamlet!
HORATIO   Heavens secure him!
HAMLET   So be it!
MARCELLUS   Illo, ho, ho,[29] my lord!
HAMLET   Hillo, ho, ho, boy! Come, bird, come.
MARCELLUS   How is't, my noble lord?
HORATIO   What news, my lord?

---

[23] *matin* morning   [24] *globe* head   [25] *table* writing tablet, record book
[26] *saws* wise sayings   [27] *forms* mental images, concepts   [28] *pressures* impressions   [29] *Illo, ho, ho* cry of the falconer to summon his hawk

HAMLET   O, wonderful!

HORATIO   Good my lord, tell it.

HAMLET   No, you will reveal it.

HORATIO   Not I, my lord, by heaven.

MARCELLUS   Nor I, my lord.

HAMLET   How say you then? Would heart of man once think it?
But you'll be secret?

BOTH   Ay, by heaven, my lord.

HAMLET   There's never a villain dwelling in all Denmark
But he's an arrant knave.

HORATIO   There needs no ghost, my lord, come from the grave
To tell us this.

HAMLET   Why, right, you are in the right,
And so, without more circumstance[30] at all,
I hold it fit that we shake hands and part:
You, as your business and desires shall point you,
For every man hath business and desire
Such as it is, and for my own poor part,
Look you, I'll go pray.

HORATIO   These are but wild and whirling words, my lord.

HAMLET   I am sorry they offend you, heartily;
Yes, faith, heartily.

HORATIO   There's no offense, my lord.

HAMLET   Yes, by Saint Patrick, but there is, Horatio,
And much offense too. Touching this vision here,
It is an honest[31] ghost, that let me tell you.
For your desire to know what is between us,
O'ermaster't as you may. And now, good friends,
As you are friends, scholars, and soldiers,
Give me one poor request.

HORATIO   What is't, my lord? We will.

HAMLET   Never make known what you have seen to-night.

BOTH   My lord, we will not.

HAMLET   Nay, but swear't.

HORATIO   In faith,
My lord, not I.

MARCELLUS   Nor I, my lord—in faith.

HAMLET   Upon my sword.[32]

MARCELLUS   We have sworn, my lord, already.

---

[30] *circumstance* ceremony   [31] *honest* genuine (not a disguised demon)
[32] *sword* i.e. upon the cross formed by the sword hilt

HAMLET   Indeed, upon my sword, indeed.

(GHOST *cries under the stage*)

GHOST   Swear.
HAMLET   Ha, ha, boy, say'st thou so? Art thou there, truepenny? [33]'
Come on. You hear this fellow in the cellarage.
Consent to swear.
HORATIO   Propose the oath, my lord.
HAMLET   Never to speak of this that you have seen,
Swear by my sword.
GHOST (*beneath*)   Swear.
HAMLET   Hic et ubique? [34] Then we'll shift our ground.
Come hither, gentlemen,
And lay your hands again upon my sword.
Swear by my sword
Never to speak of this that you have heard.
GHOST (*beneath*)   Swear by his sword.
HAMLET   Well said, old mole! Canst work i' th' earth so fast?
A worthy pioner! [35] Once more remove, good friends.
HORATIO   O day and night, but this is wondrous strange!
HAMLET   And therefore as a stranger give it welcome.
There are more things in heaven and earth, Horatio,
Than are dreamt of in your philosophy.[36]
But come:
Here as before, never, so help you mercy,
How strange or odd some'er I bear myself
(As I perchance hereafter shall think meet
To put an antic[37] disposition on),
That you, at such times seeing me, never shall,
With arms encumb'red [38] thus, or this head-shake,
Or by pronouncing of some doubtful phrase,
As "Well, well, we know," or "We could, an if [39] we would,"
Or "If we list to speak," or "There be, an if they might,"
Or such ambiguous giving out, to note
That you know aught of me—this do swear,
So grace and mercy at your most need help you.
GHOST (*beneath*)   Swear.

(*They swear*)

---

[33] *truepenny* honest old fellow   [34] *Hic et ubique* here and everywhere   [35] *pi-oner* pioneer, miner   [36] *your philosophy* this philosophy one hears about   [37] *antic* grotesque, mad   [38] *encumb'red* folded   [39] *an if* if

HAMLET Rest, rest, perturbèd spirit! So, gentlemen,
With all my love I do commend [40] me to you,
And what so poor a man as Hamlet is
May do t' express his love and friending to you,
God willing, shall not lack. Let us go in together,
And still [41] your fingers on your lips, I pray.
The time is out of joint. O cursèd spite
That ever I was born to set it right!
Nay, come, let's go together.

(*Exeunt*)

ACT II

Scene I

The chambers of POLONIUS

(*Enter old* POLONIUS, *with his man* [REYNALDO])

POLONIUS Give him this money and these notes, Reynaldo.
REYNALDO I will, my lord.
POLONIUS You shall do marvellous wisely, good Reynaldo,
Before you visit him, to make inquire
Of his behavior.
REYNALDO My lord, I did intend it.
POLONIUS Marry, well said, very well said. Look you, sir,
Enquire me first what Danskers[1] are in Paris,
And how, and who, what means,[2] and where they keep,[3]
What company, at what expense; and finding
By this encompassment[4] and drift of question
That they do know my son, come you more nearer
Than your particular demands[5] will touch it.
Take you as 'twere some distant knowledge of him,
As thus, "I know his father and his friends,
And in part him"—do you mark this, Reynaldo?
REYNALDO Ay, very well, my lord.
POLONIUS "And in part him, but," you may say, "not well,
But if't be he I mean, he's very wild
Addicted so and so." And there put on him
What forgeries[6] you please; marry, none so rank

---

[40] *commend* entrust [41] *still* always
[1] *Danskers* Danes [2] *what means* what their wealth [3] *keep* dwell [4] *encompassment* circling about [5] *particular demands* definite questions [6] *forgeries* invented wrongdoings

As may dishonor him—take heed of that—
But, sir, such wanton, wild, and usual slips
As are companions noted and most known
To youth and liberty.
REYNALDO   As gaming, my lord.
POLONIUS   Ay, or drinking, fencing, swearing, quarrelling,
Drabbing.[7] You may go so far.
REYNALDO   My lord, that would dishonor him.
POLONIUS   Faith, no, as you may season[8] it in the charge.
You must not put another scandal on him,
That he is open to incontinency.[9]
That's not my meaning. But breathe his faults so quaintly[10]
That they may seem the taints of liberty,
The flash and outbreak of a fiery mind,
A savageness in unreclaimèd [11] blood,
Of general assault.[12]
REYNALDO   But, my good lord—
POLONIUS   Wherefore should you do this?
REYNALDO   Ay, my lord,
I would know that.
POLONIUS   Marry, sir, here's my drift,
And I believe it is a fetch of warrant.[13]
You laying these slight sullies on my son
As 'twere a thing a little soiled i' th' working,
Mark you,
Your party in converse, him you would sound,
Having ever[14] seen in the prenominate[15] crimes
The youth you breathe of guilty, be assured
He closes with you[16] in this consequence:[17]
"Good sir," or so, or "friend," or "gentleman"—
According to the phrase or the addition[18]
Of man and country—
REYNALDO   Very good, my lord.
POLONIUS   And then, sir, does 'a this—'a does—
What was I about to say? By the mass, I was about to say something! Where did I leave?

---

[7] *Drabbing* whoring   [8] *season* soften   [9] *incontinency* extreme sensuality   [10] *quaintly* expertly, gracefully   [11] *unreclaimèd* untamed   [12] *Of general assault* assailing all young men   [13] *fetch of warrant* allowable trick   [14] *Having ever* if he has ever   [15] *prenominate* aforementioned   [16] *closes with you* follows your lead to a conclusion   [17] *consequence* following way   [18] *addition* title

REYNALDO   At "closes in the consequence," at "friend or so," and
  "gentleman."
POLONIUS   At "closes in the consequence"—Ay, marry!
  He closes thus: "I know the gentleman;
  I saw him yesterday, or t' other day,
  Or then, or then, with such or such, and, as you say,
  There was 'a gaming, there o'ertook[19] in's rouse,[20]
  There falling[21] out at tennis"; or perchance,
  "I saw him enter such a house of sale,"
  Videlicet,[22] a brothel, or so forth.
  See you now—
  Your bait of falsehood takes this carp of truth,
  And thus do we of wisdom and of reach,[23]
  With windlasses[24] and with assays of bias,[25]
  By indirections find directions[26] out.
  So, by my former lecture and advice,
  Shall you my son. You have me, have you not?
REYNALDO   My lord, I have.
POLONIUS   God bye ye,[27] fare ye well.
REYNALDO   Good my lord.
POLONIUS   Observe his inclination in yourself.
REYNALDO   I shall, my lord.
POLONIUS   And let him ply his music.
REYNALDO   Well, my lord.
POLONIUS   Farewell.

  (*Exit* REYNALDO)

  (*Enter* OPHELIA)

                          How now, Ophelia, what's the matter?
OPHELIA   O my lord, my lord, I have been so affrighted!
POLONIUS   With what, i' th' name of God?
OPHELIA   My lord, as I was sewing in my closet,[28]
  Lord Hamlet, with his doublet[29] all unbraced,[30]
  No hat upon his head, his stockings fouled,
  Ungartered, and down-gyvèd [31] to his ankle,
  Pale as his shirt, his knees knocking each other,

---

[19] *o'ertook* overcome with drunkenness   [20] *rouse* carousal   [21] *falling out* quarrelling   [22] *Videlicet* namely   [23] *reach* far-reaching comprehension   [24] *windlasses* roundabout courses   [25] *assays of bias* devious attacks   [26] *directions* ways of procedure   [27] *God bye ye* God be with you, good-bye   [28] *closet* private living-room   [29] *doublet* jacket   [30] *unbraced* unlaced   [31] *down-gyvèd* fallen down like gyves or fetters on a prisoner's legs

And with a look so piteous in purport
As if he had been loosèd out of hell
To speak of horrors—he comes before me.
POLONIUS   Mad for thy love?
OPHELIA   My lord, I do not know,
But truly I do fear it.
POLONIUS   What said he?
OPHELIA   He took me by the wrist and held me hard.
Then goes he to the length of all his arm,
And with his other hand thus o'er his brow
He falls to such perusal of my face
As 'a would draw it. Long stayed he so.
At last, a little shaking of mine arm
And thrice his head thus waving up and down,
He raised a sigh so piteous and profound
As it did seem to shatter all his bulk
And end his being. That done, he lets me go,
And with his head over his shoulder turned
He seemed to find his way without his eyes,
For out o' doors he went without their helps
And to the last bended their light on me.
POLONIUS   Come, go with me. I will go seek the king.
This is the very ecstasy[32] of love,
Whose violent property[33] fordoes[34] itself
And leads the will to desperate undertakings
As oft as any passion under heaven
That does afflict our natures. I am sorry.
What, have you given him any hard words of late?
OPHELIA   No, my good lord; but as you did command
I did repel his letters and denied
His access to me.
POLONIUS   That hath made him mad.
I am sorry that with better heed and judgment
I had not quoted[35] him. I feared he did but trifle
And meant to wrack thee; but beshrew[36] my jealousy.
By heaven, it is as proper to our age
To cast beyond ourselves[37] in our opinions
As it is common for the younger sort
To lack discretion. Come, go we to the king.

---

[32] *ecstasy* madness   [33] *property* quality   [34] *fordoes* destroys   [35] *quoted* observed   [36] *beshrew* curse   [37] *cast beyond ourselves* find by calculation more significance in something than we ought to

This must be known, which, being kept close,[38] might move[39]
More grief to hide than hate to utter love.[40]
Come.

(*Exeunt*)

Act II, Scene II

A chamber in the castle

(*Flourish. Enter* KING *and* QUEEN, ROSENCRANTZ, *and* GUILDENSTERN
[*with others*])

KING   Welcome, dear Rosencrantz and Guildenstern.
Moreover that[1] we much did long to see you,
. The need we have to use you did provoke
Our hasty sending. Something have you heard
Of Hamlet's transformation—so call it,
Sith[2] nor th' exterior nor the inward man
Resembles that it was. What it should be,
More than his father's death, that thus hath put him
So much from th' understanding of himself,
I cannot dream of. I entreat you both
That, being of so young days brought up with him,
And sith so neighbored to his youth and havior,[3]
That you vouchsafe your rest here in our court
Some little time, so by your companies
To draw him on to pleasures, and to gather
So much as from occasion you may glean,
Whether aught to us unknown afflicts him thus,
That opened [4] lies within our remedy.
QUEEN   Good gentlemen, he hath much talked of you,
And sure I am two men there are not living
To whom he more adheres.[5] If it will please you
To show us so much gentry[6] and good will
As to expend your time with us awhile
For the supply and profit of our hope,
Your visitation shall receive such thanks
As fits a king's remembrance.

---

[38] *close* secret   [39] *move* cause   [40] *to hide . . . love* by such hiding of love than there would be hate moved by a revelation of it (a violently condensed putting of the case which is a triumph of special statement for Polonius) [1] *Moreover that* besides the fact that   [2] *Sith* since   [3] *youth and havior* youthful ways of life   [4] *opened* revealed   [5] *more adheres* is more attached [6] *gentry* courtesy

ROSENCRANTZ   Both your majesties
  Might, by the sovereign power you have of us,
  Put your dread pleasures more into command
  Than to entreaty.
GUILDENSTERN   But we both obey,
  And here give up ourselves in the full bent[7]
  To lay our service freely at your feet,
  To be commanded.
KING   Thanks, Rosencrantz and gentle Guildenstern.
QUEEN   Thanks, Guildenstern and gentle Rosencrantz.
  And I beseech you instantly to visit
  My too much changèd son.—Go, some of you,
  And bring these gentlemen where Hamlet is.
GUILDENSTERN   Heavens make our presence and our practices
  Pleasant and helpful to him!
QUEEN   Ay, amen!

  (*Exeunt* ROSENCRANTZ *and* GUILDENSTERN [*with some* ATTENDANTS])

  (*Enter* POLONIUS)

POLONIUS   Th' ambassadors from Norway, my good lord,
  Are joyfully returned.
KING   Thou still [8] hast been the father of good news.
POLONIUS   Have I, my lord? Assure you, my good liege,
  I hold my duty as I hold my soul,
  Both to my God and to my gracious king,
  And I do think—or else this brain of mine
  Hunts not the trail of policy so sure
  As it hath used to do—that I have found
  The very cause of Hamlet's lunacy.
KING   O, speak of that! That do I long to hear.
POLONIUS   Give first admittance to th' ambassadors.
  My news shall be the fruit[9] to that great feast.
KING   Thyself do grace[10] to them and bring them in.

  (*Exit* POLONIUS)

  He tells me, my dear Gertrude, he hath found
  The head and source of all your son's distemper.
QUEEN   I doubt[11] it is no other but the main,
  His father's death and our o'erhasty marriage.

---

[7] *in the full bent* at the limit of bending (of a bow), to full capacity   [8] *still*
always   [9] *fruit* dessert   [10] *grace* honor   [11] *doubt* suspect

KING Well, we shall sift him.

(*Enter* AMBASSADORS [VOLTEMAND *and* CORNELIUS, *with* POLONIUS])

Welcome, my good friends.
Say, Voltemand, what from our brother Norway?

VOLTEMAND Most fair return of greetings and desires.
Upon our first,[12] he sent out to suppress
His nephew's levies, which to him appeared
To be a preparation 'gainst the Polack,
But better looked into, he truly found
It was against your highness, whereat grieved,
That so his sickness, age, and impotence
Was falsely borne in hand,[13] sends out arrests
On Fortinbras; which he in brief obeys,
Receives rebuke from Norway, and in fine[14]
Makes vow before his uncle never more
To give th' assay[15] of arms against your majesty.
Whereon old Norway, overcome with joy,
Gives him threescore thousand crowns in annual fee
And his commission to employ those soldiers,
So levied as before, against the Polack,
With an entreaty, herein further shown,

(*Gives a paper*)

That it might please you to give quiet pass
Through your dominions for this enterprise,
On such regards[16] of safety and allowance
As therein are set down.

KING   It likes us well;
And at our more considered time[17] we'll read,
Answer, and think upon this business.
Meantime we thank you for your well-took labor.
Go to your rest; at night we'll feast together.
Most welcome home!

(*Exeunt* AMBASSADORS)

POLONIUS   This business is well ended.
My liege and madam, to expostulate[18]
What majesty should be, what duty is,

---

[12] *our first* our first words about the matter [13] *borne in hand* deceived [14] *in fine* in the end [15] *assay* trial [16] *regards* terms [17] *considered time* convenient time for consideration [18] *expostulate* discuss

Why day is day, night night, and time is time,
Were nothing but to waste night, day, and time.
Therefore, since brevity is the soul of wit,[19]
And tediousness the limbs and outward flourishes,
I will be brief. Your noble son is mad.
Mad call I it, for, to define true madness,
What is't but to be nothing else but mad?
But let that go.

QUEEN   More matter, with less art.

POLONIUS   Madam, I swear I use no art at all.
That he is mad, 'tis true: 'tis true 'tis pity,
And pity 'tis 'tis true—a foolish figure.[20]
But farewell it, for I will use no art.
Mad let us grant him then, and now remains
That we find out the cause of this effect—
Or rather say, the cause of this defect,
For this effect defective comes by cause.
Thus it remains, and the remainder thus.
Perpend.[21]
I have a daughter (have while she is mine),
Who in her duty and obedience, mark,
Hath given me this. Now gather, and surmise.

(Reads the letter)

"To the celestial, and my soul's idol, the most beautified
Ophelia,"—
That's an ill phrase, a vile phrase; "beautified" is a vile phrase.
 But you shall hear. Thus:

(Reads)

"In her excellent white bosom, these, &c."

QUEEN   Came this from Hamlet to her?

POLONIUS   Good madam, stay awhile. I will be faithful.

(Reads)

          "Doubt thou the stars are fire;
             Doubt that the sun doth move;
          Doubt[22] truth to be a liar;
             But never doubt I love.
O dear Ophelia, I am ill at these numbers.[23] I have not art to

---

[19] *wit* understanding   [20] *figure* figure in rhetoric   [21] *Perpend* ponder
[22] *Doubt* suspect   [23] *numbers* verses

reckon my groans, but that I love thee best, O most best, believe it. Adieu.

> Thine evermore, most dear lady,
>> whilst this machine[24] is to[25] him, Hamlet."

This in obedience hath my daughter shown me,
And more above[26] hath his solicitings,
As they fell out by time, by means, and place,
All given to mine ear.
KING   But how hath she
Received his love?
POLONIUS   What do you think of me?
KING   As of a man faithful and honorable.
POLONIUS   I would fain prove so. But what might you think,
When I had seen this hot love on the wing
(As I perceived it, I must tell you that,
Before my daughter told me), what might you,
Or my dear majesty your queen here, think,
If I had played the desk or table book,[27]
Or given my heart a winking,[28] mute and dumb,
Or looked upon this love with idle sight?
What might you think? No, I went round [29] to work
And my young mistress thus I did bespeak:
"Lord Hamlet is a prince, out of thy star.[30]
This must not be." And then I prescripts[31] gave her,
That she should lock herself from his resort,
Admit no messengers, receive no tokens.
Which done, she took the fruits of my advice,
And he, repellèd, a short tale to make,
Fell into a sadness, then into a fast,
Thence to a watch,[32] thence into a weakness,
Thence to a lightness,[33] and, by this declension,
Into the madness wherein now he raves,
And all we mourn for.
KING   Do you think 'tis this?
QUEEN   It may be, very like.
POLONIUS   Hath there been such a time—I would fain know that—

---

24 *machine* body   25 *to* attached to   26 *above* besides   27 *desk or table book*
i.e. silent receiver   28 *winking* closing of the eyes   29 *round* roundly, plainly
30 *star* condition determined by stellar influence   31 *prescripts* instructions
32 *watch* sleepless state   33 *lightness* lightheadedness

That I have positively said " 'Tis so,"
When it proved otherwise?
KING   Not that I know.
POLONIUS (*pointing to his head and shoulder*)
    Take this from this, if this be otherwise.
    If circumstances lead me, I will find
    Where truth is hid, though it were hid indeed
    Within the center.[34]
KING   How may we try it further?
POLONIUS You know sometimes he walks four hours together
    Here in the lobby.
QUEEN   So he does indeed.
POLONIUS At such a time I'll loose my daughter to him.
    Be you and I behind an arras[35] then.
    Mark the encounter. If he love her not,
    And be not from his reason fallen thereon,[36]
    Let me be no assistant for a state
    But keep a farm and carters.
KING   We will try it.

(*Enter* HAMLET [*reading on a book*])

QUEEN But look where sadly the poor wretch comes reading.
POLONIUS Away, I do beseech you both, away.

(*Exit* KING *and* QUEEN [*with* ATTENDANTS])

    I'll board [37] him presently.[38] O, give me leave.
    How does my good Lord Hamlet?
HAMLET Well, God-a-mercy.[39]
POLONIUS Do you know me, my lord?
HAMLET Excellent well. You are a fishmonger.[40]
POLONIUS Not I, my lord.
HAMLET Then I would you were so honest a man.
POLONIUS Honest, my lord?
HAMLET Ay, sir. To be honest, as this world goes, is to be one man
    picked out of ten thousand.
POLONIUS That's very true, my lord.

---

[34] *center* center of the earth and also of the Ptolemaic universe [35] *arras*
hanging tapestry [36] *thereon* on that account [37] *board* accost [38] *presently*
at once [39] *God-a-mercy* thank you (literally, "God have mercy!") [40] *fishmonger* seller of harlots, procurer (a cant term used here with a glance at
the fishing Polonius is doing when he offers Ophelia as bait)

HAMLET   For if the sun breed maggots in a dead dog, being a good kissing carrion[41]—Have you a daughter?

POLONIUS   I have, my lord.

HAMLET   Let her not walk i' th' sun. Conception is a blessing, but as your daughter may conceive, friend, look to't.

POLONIUS (*aside*)   How say you by that? Still harping on my daughter. Yet he knew me not at first. 'A said I was a fishmonger. 'A is far gone, far gone. And truly in my youth I suffered much extremity for love, very near this. I'll speak to him again.—What do you read, my lord?

HAMLET   Words, words, words.

POLONIUS   What is the matter, my lord?

HAMLET   Between who? [42]

POLONIUS   I mean the matter that you read, my lord.

HAMLET   Slanders, sir, for the satirical rogue says here that old men have grey beards, that their faces are wrinkled, their eyes purging thick amber and plum-tree gum, and that they have a plentiful lack of wit, together with most weak hams. All which, sir, though I most powerfully and potently believe, yet I hold it not honesty to have it thus set down, for you yourself, sir, should be old as I am if, like a crab, you could go backward.

POLONIUS (*aside*)   Though this be madness, yet there is method in't. —Will you walk out of the air, my lord?

HAMLET   Into my grave?

POLONIUS   Indeed, that's out of the air. (*aside*) How pregnant[43] sometimes his replies are! a happiness[44] that often madness hits on, which reason and sanity could not so prosperously be delivered of. I will leave him and suddenly contrive the means of meeting between him and my daughter.—My honorable lord, I will most humbly take my leave of you.

HAMLET   You cannot, sir, take from me anything that I will more willingly part withal[45]—except my life, except my life, except my life.

(*Enter* GUILDENSTERN *and* ROSENCRANTZ)

POLONIUS   Fare you well, my lord.

HAMLET   These tedious old fools!

POLONIUS   You go to seek the Lord Hamlet. There he is.

---

[41] *good kissing carrion* good bit of flesh for kissing   [42] *Between who* matter for a quarrel between what persons (Hamlet's willful misunderstanding)   [43] *pregnant* full of meaning   [44] *happiness* aptness of expression   [45] *withal* with

ROSENCRANTZ (*to* POLONIUS) God save you, sir!

(*Exit* POLONIUS)

GUILDENSTERN My honored lord!

ROSENCRANTZ My most dear lord!

HAMLET My excellent good friends! How dost thou, Guildenstern?
Ah, Rosencrantz! Good lads, how do ye both?

ROSENCRANTZ As the indifferent[46] children of the earth.

GUILDENSTERN Happy in that we are not over-happy.
On Fortune's cap we are not the very button.

HAMLET Nor the soles of her shoe?

ROSENCRANTZ Neither, my lord.

HAMLET Then you live about her waist, or in the middle of her
favors?

GUILDENSTERN Faith, her privates[47] we.

HAMLET In the secret parts of Fortune? O, most true! she is a
strumpet. What news?

ROSENCRANTZ None, my lord, but that the world's grown honest.

HAMLET Then is doomsday near. But your news is not true. (Let
me question more in particular.) What have you, my good friends,
deserved at the hands of Fortune that she sends you to prison
hither?

GUILDENSTERN Prison, my lord?

HAMLET Denmark 's a prison.

ROSENCRANTZ Then is the world one.

HAMLET A goodly one; in which there are many confines,[48]
wards,[49] and dungeons, Denmark being one o' th' worst.

ROSENCRANTZ We think not so, my lord.

HAMLET Why, then 'tis none to you, for there is nothing either
good or bad but thinking makes it so. To me it is a prison.

ROSENCRANTZ Why, then your ambition makes it one. 'Tis too narrow for your mind.

HAMLET O God, I could be hounded in a nutshell and count myself
a king of infinite space, were it not that I have bad dreams.

GUILDENSTERN Which dreams indeed are ambition, for the very
substance of the ambitious is merely the shadow of a dream.

HAMLET A dream itself is but a shadow.

ROSENCRANTZ Truly, and I hold ambition of so airy and light a
quality that it is but a shadow's shadow.

---

[46] *indifferent* average [47] *privates* ordinary men in private, not public, life
(with obvious play upon the sexual term "private parts") [48] *confines* places
of imprisonment [49] *wards* cells

HAMLET   Then are our beggars bodies,[50] and our monarchs and outstretched [51] heroes the beggars' shadows. Shall we to th' court?
for, by my fay,[52] I cannot reason.

BOTH   We'll wait upon[53] you.

HAMLET   No such matter. I will not sort you with the rest of my
servants, for, to speak to you like an honest man, I am most dreadfully attended. But in the beaten way of friendship, what make[54]
you at Elsinore?

ROSENCRANTZ   To visit you, my lord; no other occasion.

HAMLET   Beggar that I am, I am even poor in thanks, but I thank
you; and sure, dear friends, my thanks are too dear a halfpenny.[55]
Were you not sent for? Is it your own inclining? Is it a free visitation? Come, come, deal justly with me. Come, come. Nay, speak.

GUILDENSTERN   What should we say, my lord?

HAMLET   Why, anything—but to th' purpose. You were sent for,
and there is a kind of confession in your looks, which your modes-
ties have not craft enough to color. I know the good king and
queen have sent for you.

ROSENCRANTZ   To what end, my lord?

HAMLET   That you must teach me. But let me conjure you by the
rights of our fellowship, by the consonancy[56] of our youth, by the
obligation of our ever-preserved love, and by what more dear a
better proposer[57] can charge you withal,[58] be even[59] and direct
with me whether you were sent for or no.

ROSENCRANTZ (*aside to* GUILDENSTERN)   What say you?

HAMLET (*aside*)   Nay then, I have an eye of you.—If you love me,
hold not off.

GUILDENSTERN   My lord, we were sent for.

HAMLET   I will tell you why. So shall my anticipation prevent[60]
your discovery,[61] and your secrecy to the king and queen moult no
feather.[62] I have of late—but wherefore I know not—lost all my
mirth, forgone all custom of exercises; and indeed, it goes so heavily with my disposition that this goodly frame the earth seems to
me a sterile promontory; this most excellent canopy, the air, look
you, this brave o'erhanging firmament,[63] this majestical roof

---

[50] *bodies* solid substances, not shadows (because beggars lack ambition)
[51] *outstretched* elongated as shadows (with a corollary implication of far-
reaching with respect to the ambitions that make both heroes and monarchs
into shadows)   [52] *fay* faith   [53] *wait upon* attend   [54] *make* do   [55] *a halfpenny* at a halfpenny   [56] *consonancy* accord (in sameness of age)   [57] *proposer* propounder   [58] *withal* with   [59] *even* straight   [60] *prevent* forestall
[61] *discovery* disclosure   [62] *moult no feather* be left whole   [63] *firmament* sky

fretted [64] with golden fire—why, it appeareth nothing to me but a foul and pestilent congregation of vapors. What a piece of work is a man, how noble in reason, how infinite in faculties; in form and moving how express[65] and admirable, in action how like an angel, in apprehension how like a god: the beauty of the world, the paragon of animals! And yet to me what is this quintessence[66] of dust? Man delights not me—nor woman neither, though by your smiling you seem to say so.

ROSENCRANTZ My lord, there was no such stuff in my thoughts.

HAMLET Why did ye laugh then, when I said "Man delights not me"?

ROSENCRANTZ To think, my lord, if you delight not in man, what lenten[67] entertainment the players shall receive from you. We coted [68] them on the way, and hither are they coming to offer you service.

HAMLET He that plays the king shall be welcome—his majesty shall have tribute of me—, the adventurous knight shall use his foil and target,[69] the lover shall not sigh gratis, the humorous man[70] shall end his part in peace, the clown shall make those laugh whose lungs are tickle o' th' sere,[71] and the lady shall say her mind freely, or the blank verse shall halt[72] for't. What players are they?

ROSENCRANTZ Even those you were wont to take such delight in, the tragedians of the city.

HAMLET How chances it they travel? Their residence,[73] both in reputation and profit, was better both ways.

ROSENCRANTZ I think their inhibition[74] comes by the means of the late innovation.[75]

HAMLET Do they hold the same estimation they did when I was in the city? Are they so followed?

ROSENCRANTZ No indeed, are they not.

HAMLET How comes it? Do they grow rusty?

ROSENCRANTZ Nay, their endeavor keeps in the wonted pace, but there is, sir, an eyrie[76] of children, little eyases,[77] that cry out on

---

[64] *fretted* decorated with fretwork [65] *express* well framed [66] *quintessence* fifth or last and finest essence (an alchemical term) [67] *lenten* scanty [68] *coted* overtook [69] *foil and target* sword and shield [70] *humorous man* eccentric character dominated by one of the humours [71] *tickle o' th' sere* hair-triggered for the discharge of laughter ("sere": part of a gunlock) [72] *halt* go lame [73] *residence* residing at the capital [74] *inhibition* impediment to acting in residence (formal prohibition?) [75] *innovation* new fashion of having companies of boy actors play on the "private" stage (?), political upheaval (?) [76] *eyrie* nest [77] *eyases* nestling hawks

the top of question[78] and are most tyranically clapped for't. These are now the fashion, and so berattle[79] the common stages[80] (so they call them) that many wearing rapiers are afraid of goose-quills[81] and dare scarce come thither.

HAMLET   What, are they children? Who maintains 'em? How are they escoted? [82] Will they pursue the quality[83] no longer than they can sing? [84] Will they not say afterwards, if they should grow themselves to common players (as it is most like, if their means are no better), their writers do them wrong to make them exclaim against their own succession?

ROSENCRANTZ   Faith, there has been much to do on both sides, and the nation holds it no sin to tarre[85] them to controversy. There was, for a while, no money bid for argument[86] unless the poet and the player went to cuffs in the question.

HAMLET   Is't possible?

GUILDENSTERN   O, there has been much throwing about of brains.

HAMLET   Do the boys carry it away?

ROSENCRANTZ   Ay, that they do, my lord—Hercules and his load [87] too.

HAMLET   It is not very strange, for my uncle is King of Denmark, and those that would make mows[88] at him while my father lived give twenty, forty, fifty, a hundred ducats apiece for his picture in little. 'Sblood,[89] there is something in this more than natural, if philosophy could find it out.

A flourish

GUILDENSTERN   There are the players.

HAMLET   Gentlemen, you are welcome to Elsinore. Your hands, come then. Th' appurtenance of welcome is fashion and ceremony. Let me comply with you in this garb,[90] lest my extent[91] to the players (which I tell you must show fairly outwards) should more appear like entertainment than yours. You are welcome. But my uncle-father and aunt-mother are deceived.

---

[78] *on the top of question* above others on matter of dispute   [79] *berattle* berate   [80] *common stages* "public" theatres of the "common" players, who were organized in companies mainly composed of adult actors (allusion being made to the "War of the Theatres" in Shakespeare's London)   [81] *goosequills* pens (of satirists who made out that the London public stage showed low taste)   [82] *escoted* supported   [83] *quality* profession of acting   [84] *sing* i.e. with unchanged voices   [85] *tarre* incite   [86] *argument* matter of a play   [87] *load* i.e. the whole word (with a topical reference to the sign of the Globe Theatre, a representation of Hercules bearing the world on his shoulders)   [88] *mows* grimaces   [89] *'Sblood* by God's blood   [90] *garb* fashion   [91] *extent* showing of welcome

GUILDENSTERN   In what, my dear lord?

HAMLET   I am but mad north-north-west. When the wind is southerly I know a hawk from a handsaw.[92]

(*Enter* POLONIUS)

POLONIUS   Well be with you, gentlemen.

HAMLET   Hark you, Guildenstern—and you too—at each ear a hearer. That great baby you see there is not yet out of his swaddling clouts.[93]

ROSENCRANTZ   Happily[94] he is the second time come to them, for they say an old man is twice a child.

HAMLET   I will prophesy he comes to tell me of the players. Mark it.—You say right, sir; a Monday morning, 'twas then indeed.

POLONIUS   My lord, I have news to tell you.

HAMLET   My lord, I have news to tell you. When Roscius[95] was an actor in Rome—

POLONIUS   The actors are come hither, my lord.

HAMLET   Buzz, buzz.

POLONIUS   Upon my honor—

HAMLET   Then came each actor on his ass—

POLONIUS   The best actors in the world, either for tragedy, comedy, history, pastoral, pastoral-comical, historical-pastoral, tragical-historical, tragical-comical-historical-pastoral; scene individable,[96] or poem unlimited.[97] Seneca[98] cannot be too heavy, nor Plautus[99] too light. For the law of writ[100] and the liberty,[101] these are the only men.

HAMLET   O Jephthah,[102] judge of Israel, what a treasure hadst thou!

POLONIUS   What treasure had he, my lord?

HAMLET   Why,

> "One fair daughter, and no more,
> The which he lovèd passing[103] well."

---

[92] *hawk* mattock or pickaxe (also called "hack"; here used apparently with a play on "hawk": a bird); *handsaw* carpenter's tool (apparently with a play on some corrupt form of "hernshaw"; heron, a bird often hunted with the hawk)   [93] *clouts* clothes   [94] *Happily* haply, perhaps   [95] *Roscius* the greatest of Roman comic actors   [96] *scene individable* drama observing the unities   [97] *poem unlimited* drama not observing the unities   [98] *Seneca* Roman writer of tragedies   [99] *Plautus* Roman writer of comedies   [100] *law of writ* orthodoxy determined by critical rules of the drama   [101] *liberty* freedom from such orthodoxy   [102] *Jephthah* the compelled sacrificer of a dearly beloved daughter (Judges xi)   [103] *passing* surpassingly (verses are from a ballad on Jephthah)

POLONIUS *(aside)* Still on my daughter.

HAMLET Am I not i' th' right, old Jephthah?

POLONIUS If you call me Jephthah, my lord, I have a daughter that I love passing well.

HAMLET Nay, that follows not.

POLONIUS What follows then, my lord?

HAMLET Why,

"As by lot, God wot,"

and then, you know,

"It came to pass, as most like it was."

The first row[104] of the pious chanson[105] will show you more, for look where my abridgment[106] comes.

(Enter the PLAYERS*)*

You are welcome, masters, welcome, all.—I am glad to see thee well.—Welcome, good friends.—O, old friend, why, thy face is valanced [107] since I saw thee last. Com'st thou to beard me in Denmark?—What, my young lady[108] and mistress? By'r Lady, your ladyship is nearer to heaven than when I saw you last by the altitude of a chopine.[109] Pray God your voice, like a piece of uncurrent[110] gold, be not cracked within the ring.[111]—Masters, you are all welcome. We'll e'en to't like French falconers, fly at anything we see. We'll have a speech straight. Come, give us a taste of your quality. Come, a passionate speech.

PLAYER What speech, my good lord?

HAMLET I heard thee speak me a speech once, but it was never acted, or if it was, not above once, for the play, I remember, pleased not the million; 'twas caviary[112] to the general,[113] but it was (as I received it, and others, whose judgments in such matters cried in the top of [114] mine) an excellent play, well digested in the scenes, set down with as much modesty as cunning. I remember one said there were no sallets[115] in the lines to make the matter savory, nor no matter in the phrase that might indict the author of affectation, but called it an honest method, as wholesome as sweet, and by very much more handsome than fine. One speech

---

104 *row* stanza   105 *chanson* song   106 *my abridgment* that which shortens my talk   107 *valanced* fringed (with a beard)   108 *young lady* boy who plays women's parts   109 *chopine* women's thick-soled shoe   110 *uncurrent* not legal tender   111 *within the ring* from the edge through the line circling the design on the coin (with a play on "ring": a sound)   112 *caviary* caviare   113 *general* multitude   114 *in the top of* more authoritatively than   115 *sallets* salads, highly seasoned passages

in't I chiefly loved. 'Twas Aeneas' tale to Dido, and thereabout of it especially where he speaks of Priam's[116] slaughter. If it live in your memory, begin at this line—let me see, let me see:

"The rugged Pyrrhus, like th' Hyrcanian beast[117]—"

'Tis not so; it begins with Pyrrhus:

"The rugged Pyrrhus, he whose sable[118] arms,
 Black as his purpose, did the night resemble
 When he lay couchèd in the ominous[119] horse,[120]
 Hath now this dread and black complexion smeared
 With heraldry more dismal.[121] Head to foot
 Now is he total gules,[122] horridly tricked [123]
 With blood of fathers, mothers, daughters, sons,
 Baked and impasted with the parching[124] streets,
 That lend a tyrannous and a damnèd light
 To their lord's murder. Roasted in wrath and fire,
 And thus o'ersizèd [125] with coagulate[126] gore,
 With eyes like carbuncles, the hellish Pyrrhus
 Old grandsire Priam seeks."

So, proceed you.

POLONIUS   Fore God, my lord, well spoken, with good accent and good discretion.

PLAYER   "Anon he finds him,
 Striking too short at Greeks. His antique sword,
 Rebellious to his arms, lies where it falls,
 Repugnant to command. Unequal matched,
 Pyrrhus at Priam drives, in rage strikes wide,
 But with the whiff and wind of his fell [127] sword
 Th' unnervèd father falls. Then senseless[128] Ilium,
 Seeming to feel this blow, with flaming top
 Stoops to his[129] base, and with a hideous crash
 Takes prisoner Pyrrhus' ear. For lo! his sword,
 Which was declining on the milky head
 Of reverend Priam, seemed i' th' air to stick.
 So as a painted [130] tyrant Pyrrhus stood,

---

116 *Priam's slaughter* i.e. at the fall of Troy (Aeneid II, 506 ff.)   117 *Hyrcanian beast* tiger   118 *sable* black   119 *ominous* fateful   120 *horse* the wooden horse by which the Greeks gained entrance to Troy   121 *dismal* ill-omened   122 *gules* red (heraldic term)   123 *tricked* decorated in color (heraldic term)   124 *parching* i.e. because Troy was burning   125 *o'ersizèd* covered as with size, a glutinous material used for filling pores of plaster, etc.   126 *coagulate* clotted   127 *fell* cruel   128 *senseless* without feeling   129 *his* its   130 *painted* pictured

And like a neutral to his will and matter[131]
Did nothing.
But as we often see, against[132] some storm,
A silence in the heavens, the rack[133] stand still,
The bold winds speechless, and the orb below
As hush as death, anon the dreadful thunder
Doth rend the region,[134] so after Pyrrhus' pause,
A013 vengeance sets him new awork,
And never did the Cyclops' [135] hammers fall
On Mars' armor, forged for proof eterne,[136]
With less remorse than Pyrrhus' bleeding sword
Now falls on Priam.
Out, out, thou strumpet Fortune! All you gods,
In general synod take away her power,
Break all the spokes and fellies[137] from her wheel,
And bowl the round nave[138] down the hill of heaven,
As low as to the fiends."

POLONIUS   This is too long.

HAMLET   It shall to the barber's, with your beard.—Prithee say on.
He's for a jig[139] or a tale of bawdry, or he sleeps. Say on; come to
Hecuba.

PLAYER   "But who (ah woe!) had seen the mobled [140] queen—"

HAMLET   "The mobled queen"?

POLONIUS   That's good. "Mobled queen" is good.

PLAYER   "Run barefoot up and down, threat'ning the flames
With bisson rheum;[141] a clout[142] upon that head
Where late the diadem stood, and for a robe,
About her lank and all o'erteemèd [143] loins,
A blanket in the alarm of fear caught up—
Who this had seen, with tongue in venom steeped
'Gainst Fortune's state[144] would treason have pronounced.
But if the gods themselves did see her then,
When she saw Pyrrhus make malicious sport
In mincing with his sword her husband's limbs,
The instant burst of clamor that she made

---

[131] *will and matter* purpose and its realization (between which he stands motionless)   [132] *against* just before   [133] *rack* clouds   [134] *region* sky   [135] *Cyclops* giant workmen who made armor in the smithy of Vulcan   [136] *proof eterne* eternal protection   [137] *fellies* segments of the rim   [138] *nave* hub   [139] *jig* short comic piece with singing and dancing often presented after a play   [140] *mobled* muffled   [141] *bisson rheum* blinding tears   [142] *clout* cloth   [143] *o'erteemèd* overproductive of children   [144] *state* government of worldly events

(Unless things mortal move them not at all)
Would have made milch[145] the burning eyes[146] of heaven
And passion in the gods."

POLONIUS   Look, whe'r[147] he has not turned his color, and has tears in's eyes. Prithee no more.

HAMLET   'Tis well. I'll have thee speak out the rest of this soon.— Good my lord, will you see the players well bestowed?[148] Do you hear? Let them be well used, for they are the abstract and brief chronicles of the time. After your death you were better have a bad epitaph than their ill report while you live.

POLONIUS   My lord, I will use them according to their desert.

HAMLET   God's bodkin,[149] man, much better! Use every man after his desert, and who shall scape whipping? Use them after your own honor and dignity. The less they deserve, the more merit is in your bounty. Take them in.

POLONIUS   Come, sirs.

HAMLET   Follow him, friends. We'll hear a play tomorrow. (*aside to* PLAYER) Dost thou hear me, old friend? Can you play "The Murder of Gonzago"?

PLAYER   Ay, my lord.

HAMLET   We'll ha't to-morrow night. You could for a need study a speech of some dozen or sixteen lines which I would set down and insert in't, could you not?

PLAYER   Ay, my lord.

HAMLET   Very well. Follow that lord, and look you mock him not. —My good friends, I'll leave you till night. You are welcome to Elsinore.

(*Exeunt* POLONIUS *and* PLAYERS)

ROSENCRANTZ   Good my lord.

(*Exeunt* ROSENCRANTZ *and* GUILDENSTERN)

HAMLET   Ay, so, God bye to you.—Now I am alone.
O, what a rogue and peasant slave am I!
Is it not monstrous that this player here,
But in a fiction, in a dream of passion,
Could force his soul so to his own conceit[150]
That from her working all his visage wanned,
Tears in his eyes, distraction in his aspect.

---

[145] *milch* tearful (milk-giving)   [146] *eyes* i.e. stars   [147] *whe'r* whether   [148] *bestowed* lodged   [149] *God's bodkin* by God's little body   [150] *conceit* conception, idea

A broken voice, and his whole function[151] suiting
With forms to his conceit? And all for nothing,
For Hecuba!
What's Hecuba to him, or he to Hecuba,
That he should weep for her? What would he do
Had he the motive and the cue for passion
That I have? He would drown the stage with tears
And cleave the general ear with horrid speech,
Make mad the guilty and appal the free,
Confound the ignorant, and amaze indeed
The very faculties of eyes and ears.
Yet I,
A dull and muddy-mettled [152] rascal, peak[153]
Like John-a-dreams,[154] unpregnant[155] of my cause,
And can say nothing. No, not for a king,
Upon whose property and most dear life
A damned defeat was made. Am I a coward?
Who calls me villain? breaks my pate across?
Plucks off my beard and blows it in my face?
Tweaks me by the nose? gives me the lie i' th' throat
As deep as to the lungs? Who does me this?
Ha, 'swounds,[156] I should take it, for it cannot be
But I am pigeon-livered [157] and lack gall
To make oppression bitter, or ere this
I should ha' fatted all the region kites[158]
With this slave's offal.[159] Bloody, bawdy villain!
Remorseless, treacherous, lecherous, kindless[160] villain!
O, vengeance!
Why, what an ass am I! This is most brave,
That I, the son of a dear father murdered,
Prompted to my revenge by heaven and hell,
Must like a whore unpack my heart with words
And fall a-cursing like a very drab,
A stallion! [161] Fie upon't, foh! About, my brains.
Hum—
I have heard that guilty creatures sitting at a play
Have by the very cunning of the scene

---

[151] *function* action of bodily powers   [152] *muddy-mettled* dull-spirited
[153] *peak* mope   [154] *John-a-dreams* a sleepy dawdler   [155] *unpregnant* barren
of realization   [156] *'swounds* by God's wounds   [157] *pigeon-livered* of dove-like
gentleness   [158] *region kites* kites of the air   [159] *offal* guts   [160] *kindless* unnatural   [161] *stallion* prostitute (male or female)

Been struck so to the soul that presently[162]
They have proclaimed their malefactions.
For murder, though it have no tongue, will speak
With most miraculous organ. I'll have these players
Play something like the murder of my father
Before mine uncle. I'll observe his looks.
I'll tent[163] him to the quick. If 'a do blench,[164]
I know my course. The spirit that I have seen
May be a devil, and the devil hath power
T' assume a pleasing shape, yea, and perhaps
Out of my weakness and my melancholy,
As he is very potent with such spirits,
Abuses[165] me to damn me. I'll have grounds
More relative[166] than this. The play 's the thing
Wherein I'll catch the conscience of the king.

(*Exit*)

ACT III

Scene I

A chamber in the castle

(*Enter* KING, QUEEN, POLONIUS, OPHELIA, ROSENCRANTZ, GUILDEN-
STERN, LORDS)

KING   And can you by no drift of conference[1]
Get from him why he puts on this confusion,
Grating so harshly all his days of quiet
With turbulent and dangerous lunacy?
ROSENCRANTZ   He does confess he feels himself distracted,
But from what cause 'a will by no means speak.
GUILDENSTERN   Nor do we find him forward to be sounded,
But with a crafty madness keeps aloof
When we would bring him on to some confession
Of his true state.
QUEEN   Did he receive you well?
ROSENCRANTZ   Most like a gentleman.
GUILDENSTERN   But with much forcing of his disposition.
ROSENCRANTZ   Niggard of question, but of our demands
Most free in his reply.

---

162 *presently* immediately   163 *tent* probe   164 *blench* flinch   165 *Abuses* de-
ludes   166 *relative* pertinent
1 *drift of conference* direction of conversation

QUEEN   Did you assay[2] him
    To any pastime?
ROSENCRANTZ   Madam, it so fell out that certain players
    We o'erraught[3] on the way. Of these we told him,
    And there did seem in him a kind of joy
    To hear of it. They are here about the court,
    And, as I think, they have already order
    This night to play before him.
POLONIUS   'Tis most true,
    And he beseeched me to entreat your majesties
    To hear and see the matter.
KING   With all my heart, and it doth much content me
    To hear him so inclined.
    Good gentlemen, give him a further edge[4]
    And drive his purpose into these delights.
ROSENCRANTZ   We shall, my lord.

    (*Exeunt* ROSENCRANTZ *and* GUILDENSTERN)

KING   Sweet Gertrude, leave us too,
    For we have closely[5] sent for Hamlet hither,
    That he, as 'twere by accident, may here
    Affront[6] Ophelia.
    Her father and myself (lawful espials[7])
    Will so bestow ourselves that, seeing unseen,
    We may of their encounter frankly judge
    And gather by him, as he is behaved,
    If't be th' affliction of his love or no
    That thus he suffers for.
QUEEN   I shall obey you.—
    And for your part, Ophelia, I do wish
    That your good beauties be the happy cause
    Of Hamlet's wildness. So shall I hope your virtues
    Will bring him to his wonted way again,
    To both your honors.
OPHELIA   Madam, I wish it may.

    (*Exit* QUEEN)

POLONIUS   Ophelia, walk you here.—Gracious, so please you,
    We will bestow ourselves.—

---

[2] *assay* try to win   [3] *o'erraught* overtook   [4] *edge* keenness of desire   [5] *closely* privately   [6] *Affront* come face to face with   [7] *espials* spies

(*To* OPHELIA)

Read on this book,
That show of such an exercise[8] may color[9]
Your loneliness. We are oft to blame in this,
'Tis too much proved, that with devotion's visage
And pious action we do sugar o'er
The devil himself.

KING (*aside*)   O, 'tis too true.
How smart a lash that speech doth give my conscience!
The harlot's cheek, beautied with plast'ring art,
Is not more ugly to[10] the thing that helps it
Than is my deed to my most painted word.
O heavy burthen!

POLONIUS   I hear him coming. Let's withdraw, my lord.

(*Exeunt* KING *and* POLONIUS)

(*Enter* HAMLET)

HAMLET   To be, or not to be—that is the question:
Whether 'tis nobler in the mind to suffer
The slings and arrows of outrageous fortune
Or to take arms against a sea of troubles
And by opposing end them. To die, to sleep—
No more—and by a sleep to say we end
The heartache, and the thousand natural shocks
That flesh is heir to. 'Tis a consummation
Devoutly to be wished. To die, to sleep—
To sleep—perchance to dream: ay, there's the rub,[11]
For in that sleep of death what dreams may come
When we have shuffled off [12] this mortal coil,[13]
Must give us pause. There's the respect[14]
That makes calamity of so long life.[15]
For who would bear the whips and scorns of time,
Th' oppressor's wrong, the proud man's contumely
The pangs of despised love, the law's delay,
The insolence of office, and the spurns
That patient merit of th' unworthy takes,
When he himself might his quietus[16] make

---

[8] *exercise* religious exercise (the book being obviously one of devotion
[9] *color* give an appearance of naturalness to   [10] *to* compared to   [11] *rub* obstacle (literally, obstruction encountered by a bowler's ball)   [12] *shuffled off* cast off as an encumbrance   [13] *coil* to-do, turmoil   [14] *respect* consideration
[15] *of so long life* so long-lived   [16] *quietus* settlement (literally, release from debt)

With a bare bodkin? [17] Who would fardels[18] bear,
To grunt and sweat under a weary life,
But that the dread of something after death,
The undiscovered country, from whose bourn[19]
No traveller returns, puzzles the will,
And makes us rather bear those ills we have
Than fly to others that we know not of?
Thus conscience does make cowards of us all,
And thus the native hue of resolution
Is sicklied o'er with the pale cast of thought,
And enterprises of great pitch[20] and moment
With this regard [21] their currents turn awry
And lose the name of action.—Soft you now,
The fair Ophelia!—Nymph, in thy orisons[22]
Be all my sins remembered.

OPHELIA   Good my lord,
How does your honor for this many a day?

HAMLET   I humbly thank you, well, well, well.

OPHELIA   My lord, I have remembrances of yours
That I have longèd long to re-deliver.
I pray you, now receive them.

HAMLET   No, not I,
I never gave you aught.

OPHELIA   My honored lord, you know right well you did,
And with them words of so sweet breath composed
As made the things more rich. Their perfume lost,
Take these again, for to the noble mind
Rich gifts wax poor when givers prove unkind.
There, my lord.

HAMLET   Ha, ha! Are you honest? [23]

OPHELIA   My lord?

HAMLET   Are you fair?

OPHELIA   What means your lordship?

HAMLET   That if you be honest and fair, your honesty should admit
no discourse to your beauty.

OPHELIA   Could beauty, my lord, have better commerce[24] than
with honesty?

HAMLET   Ay, truly; for the power of beauty will sooner transform

---

[17] *bodkin* dagger   [18] *fardels* burdens   [19] *bourn* confine, region   [20] *pitch*
height (of a soaring falcon's flight)   [21] *regard* consideration   [22] *orisons*
prayers (because of the book of devotion she reads)   [23] *honest* chaste
[24] *commerce* intercourse

honesty from what it is to a bawd than the force of honesty can translate beauty into his likeness. This was sometime a paradox,[25] but now the time gives it proof. I did love you once.

OPHELIA Indeed, my lord, you made me believe so.

HAMLET You should not have believed me, for virtue cannot so inoculate[26] our old stock but we shall relish[27] of it. I loved you not.

OPHELIA I was the more deceived.

HAMLET Get thee to a nunnery. Why wouldst thou be a breeder of sinners? I am myself indifferent honest,[28] but yet I could accuse me of such things that it were better my mother had not borne me: I am very proud, revengeful, ambitious, with more offenses at my beck than I have thoughts to put them in, imagination to give them shape, or time to act them in. What should such fellows as I do crawling between earth and heaven? We are arrant knaves all; believe none of us. Go thy ways to a nunnery. Where's your father?

OPHELIA At home, my lord.

HAMLET Let the doors be shut upon him, that he may play the fool nowhere but in's own house. Farewell.

OPHELIA O, help him, you sweet heavens!

HAMLET If thou dost marry, I'll give thee this plague for thy dowry: be thou as chaste as ice, as pure as snow, thou shalt not escape calumny. Get thee to a nunnery. Go, farewell. Or if thou wilt needs marry, marry a fool, for wise men know well enough what monsters[29] you make of them. To a nunnery, go, and quickly too. Farewell.

OPHELIA O heavenly powers, restore him!

HAMLET I have heard of your paintings too, well enough. God hath given you one face, and you make yourselves another. You jig, you amble, and you lisp; you nickname God's creatures and make your wantonness[30] your ignorance.[31] Go to, I'll no more on't; it hath made me mad. I say we will have no more marriage. Those that are married already—all but one—shall live. The rest shall keep as they are. To a nunnery, go.

(*Exit*)

OPHELIA O, what a noble mind is here o'erthrown!

---

[25] *paradox* idea contrary to common opinion   [26] *inoculate* graft   [27] *relish* have a flavor (because of original sin)   [28] *indifferent honest* moderately respectable   [29] *monsters* i.e. unnatural combinations of wisdom and uxorious folly   [30] *wantonness* affectation   [31] *your ignorance* a matter for which you offer the excuse that you don't know any better

The courtier's, soldier's, scholar's, eye, tongue, sword,
Th' expectancy and rose[32] of the fair state,
The glass[33] of fashion and the mould of form,
Th' observed of all observers, quite, quite down!
And I, of ladies most deject and wretched,
That sucked the honey of his music vows,
Now see that noble and most sovereign reason
Like sweet bells jangled, out of time and harsh,
That unmatched form and feature of blown youth
Blasted with ecstasy.[34] O, woe is me
T' have seen what I have seen, see what I see!

(*Enter* KING *and* POLONIUS)

KING   Love? his affections[35] do not that way tend,
Nor what he spake, though it lacked form a little,
Was not like madness. There's something in his soul
O'er which his melancholy sits on brood,
And I do doubt[36] the hatch and the disclose
Will be some danger; which for to prevent,
I have in quick determination
Thus set it down: he shall with speed to England
For the demand of our neglected tribute.
Haply the seas, and countries different,
With variable objects, shall expel
This something-settled [37] matter in his heart,
Whereon his brains still beating puts him thus
From fashion of himself. What think you on't?
POLONIUS   It shall do well. But yet do I believe
The origin and commencement of his grief
Sprung from neglected love.—How now, Ophelia?
You need not tell us what Lord Hamlet said.
We heard it all.—My lord, do as you please,
But if you hold it fit, after the play
Let his queen mother all alone entreat him
To show his grief. Let her be round [38] with him,
And I'll be placed, so please you, in the ear
Of all their conference. If she find him not,
To England send him, or confine him where
Your wisdom best shall think.

---

[32] *expectancy and rose* fair hope   [33] *glass* mirror   [34] *ecstasy* madness   [35] *affections* emotions   [36] *doubt* fear   [37] *something-settled* somewhat settled   [38] *round* plain-spoken

KING " " It shall be so.
Madness in great ones must not unwatched go.

(*Exeunt*)

Act III, Scene II

The hall of the castle

(*Enter* HAMLET *and three of the* PLAYERS)

HAMLET Speak the speech, I pray you, as I pronounced it to you,
trippingly[1] on the tongue. But if you mouth it, as many of our
players do, I had as lief the town crier spoke my lines. Nor do
not saw the air too much with your hand, thus, but use all gently,
for in the very torrent, tempest, and (as I may say) whirlwind of
your passion, you must acquire and beget a temperance that may
give it smoothness. O, it offends me to the soul to hear a robustious[2] periwig-pated [3] fellow tear a passion to tatters, to very rags,
to split the ears of the groundlings,[4] who for the most part are
capable of nothing but inexplicable dumb shows[5] and noise. I
would have such a fellow whipped for o'erdoing Termagant.[6] It
out-herods Herod.[7] Pray you avoid it.

PLAYER I warrant your honor.

HAMLET Be not too tame neither, but let your own discretion be
your tutor. Suit the action to the word, the word to the action,
with this special observance, that you o'erstep not the modesty of
nature. For anything so overdone is from[8] the purpose of playing,
whose end, both at the first and now, was and is, to hold, as
'twere, the mirror up to nature, to show virtue her own feature,
scorn her own image, and the very age and body of the time his
form and pressure.[9] Now this overdone, or come tardy off,[10]
though it make the unskillful laugh, cannot but make the judi-
cious grieve, the censure of the which one[11] must in your allowance o'erweigh a whole theatre of others. O, there be players that
I have seen play, and heard others praise, and that highly (not to

---

[1] *trippingly* easily [2] *robustious* boisterous [3] *periwig-pated* wig-wearing (after the custom of actors) [4] *groundlings* spectators who paid least and stood on
the ground in the pit or yard of the theatre [5] *dumb shows* brief actions
without words, forecasting dramatic matter to follow (the play presented
later in this scene giving an old-fashioned example) [6] *Termagant* a Saracen
"god" in medieval romance and drama [7] *Herod* the raging tyrant of old
Biblical plays [8] *from* apart from [9] *pressure* impressed or printed character
[10] *come tardy off* brought off slowly and badly [11] *the censure of the which
one* the judgment of even one of whom

speak it profanely), that neither having th' accent of Christians, nor the gait of Christian, pagan, nor man, have so strutted and bellowed that I have thought some of Nature's journeymen[12] had made men, and not made them well, they imitated humanity so abominably.

PLAYER   I hope we have reformed that indifferently[13] with us, sir.

HAMLET   O, reform it altogether! And let those that play your clowns speak no more than is set down for them, for there be of them[14] that will themselves laugh, to set on some quantity of barren spectators to laugh too, though in the mean time some necessary question of the play be then to be considered. That's villainous and shows a most pitiful ambition in the fool that uses it. Go make you ready.

(*Exeunt* PLAYERS)

(*Enter* POLONIUS, GUILDENSTERN, *and* ROSENCRANTZ)

How now, my lord? Will the king hear this piece of work?

POLONIUS   And the queen too, and that presently.[15]

HAMLET   Bid the players make haste.

(*Exit* POLONIUS)

Will you two help to hasten them?

ROSENCRANTZ   Ay, my lord.

(*Exeunt they two*)

HAMLET   What, ho, Horatio!

(*Enter* HORATIO)

HORATIO   Here, sweet lord, at your service.

HAMLET   Horatio, thou art e'en as just a man
As e'er my conversation coped withal.[16]

HORATIO   O, my dear lord—

HAMLET   Nay, do not think I flatter.
For what advancement may I hope from thee,
That no revenue hast but thy good spirits
To feed and clothe thee? Why should the poor be flattered?
No, let the candied tongue lick absurd pomp,
And crook the pregnant[17] hinges of the knee

---

12 *journeymen* workmen not yet masters of their trade   13 *indifferently* fairly well   14 *of them* some of them   15 *presently* at once   16 *conversation coped withal* intercourse with men encountered   17 *pregnant* quick to move

Where thrift[18] may follow fawning. Dost thou hear?
Since my dear soul was mistress of her choice
And could of men distinguish her election,
S' hath sealed [19] thee for herself, for thou hast been
As one in suff'ring all that suffers nothing,
A man that Fortune's buffets and rewards
Hast ta'en with equal thanks; and blest are those
Whose blood [20] and judgment are so well commeddled [21]
That they are not a pipe for Fortune's finger
To sound what stop she please. Give me that man
That is not passion's slave, and I will wear him
In my heart's core, ay, in my heart of heart,
As I do thee. Something too much of this—
There is a play to-night before the king.
One scene of it comes near the circumstance
Which I have told thee, of my father's death.
I prithee, when thou seest that act afoot,
Even with the very comment of thy soul [22]
Observe my uncle. If his occulted [23] guilt
Do not itself unkennel in one speech,
It is a damnèd ghost[24] that we have seen,
And my imaginations are as foul
As Vulcan's stithy.[25] Give him heedful note,
For I mine eyes will rivet to his face,
And after we will both our judgments join
In censure of [26] his seeming.

HORATIO   Well, my lord.
If 'a steal aught the while this play is playing,
And scape detecting, I will pay the theft.

(*Enter* TRUMPETS *and* KETTLEDRUMS, KING, QUEEN, POLONIUS, OPHE-
LIA, [ROSENCRANTZ, GUILDENSTERN, *and other* LORDS *attendant*])

HAMLET   They are coming to the play. I must be idle.[27]
   Get you a place.
KING   How fares our cousin[28] Hamlet?
HAMLET   Excellent, i' faith, of the chameleon's dish.[29] I eat the air,
   promise-crammed. You cannot feed capons so.

---

[18] *thrift* profit   [19] *sealed* marked   [20] *blood* passion   [21] *commeddled* mixed
together   [22] *the very ... soul* thy deepest sagacity   [23] *occulted* hidden
[24] *damnèd ghost* evil spirit, devil   [25] *stithy* smithy   [26] *censure of* sentence
upon   [27] *be idle* be foolish, act the madman   [28] *cousin* nephew   [29] *chameleon's dish* i.e. air (which was believed the chameleon's food; Hamlet willfully takes *fares* in the sense of "feeds")

KING I have nothing with this answer, Hamlet. These words are not mine.[30]

HAMLET No, nor mine now. (*to Polonius*) My lord, you played once i' th' university, you say?

POLONIUS That did I, my lord, and was accounted a good actor.

HAMLET What did you enact?

POLONIUS I did enact Julius Caesar. I was killed i' th' Capitol; Brutus killed me.

HAMLET It was a brute part of him to kill so capital a calf there. Be the players ready?

ROSENCRANTZ Ay, my lord. They stay upon your patience.[31]

QUEEN Come hither, my dear Hamlet, sit by me.

HAMLET No, good mother. Here's metal more attractive.

POLONIUS (*to the King*) O ho! do you mark that?

HAMLET Lady, shall I lie in your lap?

He lies at OPHELIA's *feet*

OPHELIA No, my lord.

HAMLET I mean, my head upon your lap?

OPHELIA Ay, my lord.

HAMLET Do you think I meant country matters?[32]

OPHELIA I think nothing, my lord.

HAMLET That's a fair thought to lie between maids' legs.

OPHELIA What is, my lord?

HAMLET Nothing.

OPHELIA You are merry, my lord.

HAMLET Who, I?

OPHELIA Ay, my lord.

HAMLET O God, your only jig-maker![33] What should a man do but be merry? For look you how cheerfully my mother looks, and my father died within's two hours.

OPHELIA Nay, 'tis twice two months, my lord.

HAMLET So long? Nay then, let the devil wear black, for I'll have a suit of sables.[34] O heavens! die two months ago, and not forgotten yet? Then there's hope a great man's memory may outlive his life half a year. But, by'r Lady, 'a must build churches then, or else shall 'a suffer not thinking on, with the hobby-

---

[30] *not mine* not for me as the asker of my question [31] *stay upon your patience* await your indulgence [32] *country matters* rustic goings-on, barnyard mating (with a play upon a sexual term) [33] *jig-maker* writer of jigs [34] *sables* black furs (luxurious garb, not for mourning)

horse,[35] whose epitaph is "For O, for O, the hobby-horse is forgot!"

The trumpets sound. Dumb show follows:
Enter a KING *and a* QUEEN [*very lovingly*], *the* QUEEN *embracing him, and he her.* [*She kneels; and makes show of protestation unto him.*] *He takes her up, and declines his head upon her neck. He lies him down upon a bank of flowers. She, seeing him asleep, leaves him. Anon come in another man: takes off his crown, kisses it, pours poison in the sleeper's ears, and leaves him. The* QUEEN *returns, finds the* KING *dead, makes passionate action. The poisoner, with some three or four, come in again, seem to condole with her. The dead body is carried away. The poisoner woos the* QUEEN *with gifts; she seems harsh awhile, but in the end accepts love.*

(*Exeunt*)

OPHELIA   What means this, my lord?
HAMLET   Marry, this is miching mallecho;[36] it means mischief.
OPHELIA   Belike this show imports the argument of the play.

(*Enter* PROLOGUE)

HAMLET   We shall know by this fellow. The players cannot keep counsel; they'll tell all.
OPHELIA   Will 'a tell us what this show meant?
HAMLET   Ay, or any show that you'll show him. Be not you ashamed to show, he'll not shame to tell you what it means.
OPHELIA   You are naught, you are naught.[37] I'll mark the play.
PROLOGUE   For us and for our tragedy,
                Here stooping to your clemency,
                We beg your hearing patiently.

(*Exit*)

HAMLET   Is this a prologue, or the posy[38] of a ring? [39]
OPHELIA   'Tis brief, my lord.
HAMLET   As woman's love.

(*Enter* [*two* PLAYERS *as*] KING *and* QUEEN)

[P.] KING   Full thirty times hath Phoebus' cart[40] gone round
                Neptune's salt wash and Tellus' [41] orbèd ground,
                And thirty dozen moons with borrowed [42] sheen

---

[35] *hobby-horse* traditional figure strapped round the waist of a performer in May games and morris dances   [36] *miching mallecho* sneaking iniquity   [37] *naught* indecent   [38] *posy* brief motto in rhyme ("poesy")   [39] *ring* finger ring   [40] *Phoebus' cart* the sun's chariot   [41] *Tellus* Roman goddess of the earth   [42] *borrowed* i.e. taken from the sun

About the world have times twelve thirties been,
Since love our hearts, and Hymen[43] did our hands,
Unite commutual [44] in most sacred bands.
[P.] QUEEN   So many journeys may the sun and moon
Make us again count o'er ere love be done!
But woe is me, you are so sick of late,
So far from cheer and from your former state,
That I distrust you.[45] Yet, though I distrust,
Discomfort you, my lord, it nothing must.
For women fear too much, even as they love,
And women's fear and love hold quantity,[46]
In neither aught, or in extremity.
Now what my love is, proof hath made you know,
And as my love is sized, my fear is so.
Where love is great, the littlest doubts are fear;
Where little fears grow great, great love grows there.
[P.] KING   Faith, I must leave thee, love, and shortly too;
My operant powers[47] their functions leave to do.
And thou shalt live in this fair world behind,
Honored, beloved, and haply one as kind
For husband shalt thou—
[P.] QUEEN   O, confound the rest!
Such love must needs be treason in my breast.
In second husband let me be accurst!
None wed the second but who killed the first.
HAMLET *(aside)*   That's wormwood.[48]
[P.] QUEEN   The instances[49] that second marriage move
Are base respects of thrift, but none of love.
A second time I kill my husband dead
When second husband kisses me in bed.
[P.] KING   I do believe you think what now you speak,
But what we do determine oft we break.
Purpose is but the slave to[50] memory,
Of violent birth, but poor validity,[51]
Which now like fruit unripe sticks on the tree,
But fall unshaken when they mellow be.
Most necessary 'tis that we forget
To pay ourselves what to ourselves is debt.

---

[43] *Hymen* Greek god of marriage   [44] *commutual* mutually   [45] *distrust you* fear for you   [46] *quantity* proportion   [47] *operant powers* active bodily forces   [48] *wormwood* a bitter herb   [49] *instances* motives   [50] *slave to* i.e. dependent upon for life   [51] *validity* strength

What to ourselves in passion we propose,
The passion ending, doth the purpose lose.
The violence of either grief or joy
Their own enactures[52] with themselves destroy.
Where joy most revels, grief doth most lament;
Grief joys, joy grieves, on slender accident.
This world is not for aye, nor 'tis not strange
That even our loves should with our fortunes change,
For 'tis a question left us yet to prove,
Whether love lead fortune, or else fortune love.
The great man down, you mark his favorite flies,
The poor advanced makes friends of enemies;
And hitherto doth love on fortune tend,
For who not needs shall never lack a friend,
And who in want a hollow friend doth try,
Directly seasons him[53] his enemy.
But, orderly to end where I begun,
Our wills and fates do so contrary run
That our devices still [54] are overthrown;
Our thoughts are ours, their ends none of our own.
So think thou wilt no second husband wed,
But die thy thoughts when thy first lord is dead.

[P.] QUEEN   Nor earth to me give food, nor heaven light,
Sport and repose lock from me day and night,
To desperation turn my trust and hope,
An anchor's[55] cheer in prison be my scope,
Each opposite that blanks[56] the face of joy
Meet what I would have well, and it destroy,
Both here and hence[57] pursue me lasting strife,
If, once a widow, ever I be wife!

HAMLET   If she should break it now!

[P.] KING   'Tis deeply sworn. Sweet, leave me here awhile.
My spirits grow dull, and fain I would beguile
The tedious day with sleep.

[P.] QUEEN   Sleep rock thy brain,

(*He sleeps*)

And never come mischance between us twain!

(*Exit*)

---

[52] *enactures* fulfillments   [53] *seasons him* ripens him into   [54] *still* always
[55] *anchor's* hermit's   [56] *blanks* blanches, makes pale   [57] *hence* in the next
world.

HAMLET   Madam, how like you this play?

QUEEN   The lady doth protest too much, methinks.

HAMLET   O, but she'll keep her word.

KING   Have you heard the argument?[58] Is there no offense in't?

HAMLET   No, no, they do but jest, poison in jest; no offense i' th' world.

KING   What do you call the play?

HAMLET   "The Mousetrap." Marry, how? Tropically.[59] This play is the image of a murder done in Vienna. Gonzago is the duke's name; his wife, Baptista. You shall see anon. 'Tis a knavish piece of work, but what o' that? Your majesty, and we that have free[60] souls, it touches us not. Let the galled [61] jade[62] winch;[63] our withers[64] are unwrung.

(*Enter* LUCIANUS)

This is one Lucianus, nephew to the king.

OPHELIA   You are as good as a chorus,[65] my lord.

HAMLET   I could interpret between you and your love, if I could see the puppets[66] dallying.

OPHELIA   You are keen, my lord, you are keen.

HAMLET   It would cost you a groaning to take off my edge.

OPHELIA   Still better, and worse.

HAMLET   So you must take your husbands.—Begin, murderer. Leave thy damnable faces and begin. Come, the croaking raven doth bellow for revenge.

LUCIANUS   Thoughts black, hands apt, drugs fit, and time agreeing,
Confederate season,[67] else no creature seeing,
Thou mixture rank, of midnight weeds collected,
With Hecate's[68] ban[69] thrice blasted, thrice infected,
Thy natural magic and dire property
On wholesome life usurps immediately.

(*Pours the poison in his ears*)

HAMLET   'A poisons him i' th' garden for his estate. His name's Gonzago. The story is extant, and written in very choice Italian. You shall see anon how the murderer gets the love of Gonzago's wife.

---

[58] *argument* plot summary   [59] *Tropically* in the way of a trope or figure (with a play on "trapically")   [60] *free* guiltless   [61] *galled* sore-backed   [62] *jade* horse   [63] *winch* wince   [64] *withers* shoulders   [65] *chorus* one in a play who explains the action   [66] *puppets* i.e. you and your lover as in a puppet show   [67] *Confederate season* the occasion being my ally   [68] *Hecate* goddess of witchcraft and black magic   [69] *ban* curse

OPHELIA   The king rises.

HAMLET   What, frighted with false fire? [70]

QUEEN   How fares my lord?

POLONIUS   Give o'er the play.

KING   Give me some light. Away!

POLONIUS   Lights, lights, lights!

(*Exeunt all but* HAMLET *and* HORATIO)

HAMLET   Why, let the strucken deer go weep,
          The hart ungallèd play.
      For some must watch, while some must sleep;
          Thus runs the world away.
   Would not this, sir, and a forest of feathers[71]—if the rest of my
   fortunes turn Turk[72] with me—with two Provincial roses[73] on my
   razed [74] shoes, get me a fellowship in a cry[75] of players, sir?

HORATIO   Half a share.

HAMLET   A whole one, I.
          For thou dost know, O Damon dear,
            This realm dismantled was
          Of Jove himself; and now reigns here
            A very, very—peacock.

HORATIO   You might have rhymed.

HAMLET   O good Horatio, I'll take the ghost's word for a thousand
   pound. Didst perceive?

HORATIO   Very well, my lord.

HAMLET   Upon the talk of the poisoning?

HORATIO   I did very well note him.

HAMLET   Aha! Come, some music! Come, the recorders! [76]
          For if the king like not the comedy,
          Why then, belike he likes it not, perdy.[77]
   Come, some music!

(*Enter* ROSENCRANTZ *and* GUILDENSTERN)

GUILDENSTERN   Good my lord, vouchsafe me a word with you.

HAMLET   Sir, a whole history.

GUILDENSTERN   The king, sir—

HAMLET   Ay, sir, what of him?

---

[70] *false fire* a firing of a gun charged with powder but no shot, a blank-discharge   [71] *feathers* plumes for actors' costumes   [72] *turn Turk* turn renegade, like a Christian turning Mohammedan   [73] *Provincial roses* ribbon rosettes   [74] *razed* decorated with cut patterns   [75] *cry* pack   [76] *recorders* musical instruments of the flute class   [77] *perdy* by God ("*par dieu*")

GUILDENSTERN　Is in his retirement marvellous distempered.[78]

HAMLET　With drink, sir?

GUILDENSTERN　No, my lord, with choler.[79]

HAMLET　Your wisdom should show itself more richer to signify this to the doctor, for for me to put him to his purgation would perhaps plunge him into more choler.

GUILDENSTERN　Good my lord, put your discourse into some frame,[80] and start not so wildly from my affair.

HAMLET　I am tame, sir; pronounce.

GUILDENSTERN　The queen, your mother, in most great affliction of spirit hath sent me to you.

HAMLET　You are welcome.

GUILDENSTERN　Nay, good my lord, this courtesy is not of the right breed. If it shall please you to make me a wholesome answer, I will do your mother's commandment. If not, your pardon and my return shall be the end of my business.

HAMLET　Sir, I cannot.

ROSENCRANTZ　What, my lord?

HAMLET　Make you a wholesome answer; my wit's diseased. But, sir, such answer as I can make, you shall command, or rather, as you say, my mother. Therefore no more, but to the matter. My mother, you say—

ROSENCRANTZ　Then thus she says: your behavior hath struck her into amazement and admiration.[81]

HAMLET　O wonderful son, that can so stonish a mother! But is there no sequel at the heels of this mother's admiration? Impart.

ROSENCRANTZ　She desires to speak with you in her closet[82] ere you go to bed.

HAMLET　We shall obey, were she ten times our mother. Have you any further trade with us?

ROSENCRANTZ　My lord, you once did love me.

HAMLET　And do still, by these pickers and stealers.[83]

ROSENCRANTZ　Good my lord, what is your cause of distemper? You do surely bar the door upon your own liberty, if you deny your griefs to your friend.

HAMLET　Sir, I lack advancement.

ROSENCRANTZ　How can that be, when you have the voice of the king himself for your succession in Denmark?

---

[78] *distempered* out of temper, vexed (twisted by Hamlet into "deranged")
[79] *choler* anger (twisted by Hamlet into "biliousness")　[80] *frame* logical order
[81] *admiration* wonder　[82] *closet* private room　[83] *pickers and stealers* i.e. hands

HAMLET Ay, sir, but "while the grass grows" [84] the proverb is something musty.

(*Enter the* PLAYER *with recorders*)

O, the recorders. Let me see one. To withdraw[85] with you—why do you go about to recover the wind [86] of me, as if you would drive me into a toil? [87]

GUILDENSTERN O my lord, if my duty be too bold, my love is too unmannerly.[88]

HAMLET I do not well understand that. Will you play upon this pipe?

GUILDENSTERN My lord, I cannot.

HAMLET I pray you.

GUILDENSTERN Believe me, I cannot.

HAMLET I do beseech you.

GUILDENSTERN I know no touch of it, my lord.

HAMLET It is as easy as lying. Govern these ventages[89] with your fingers and thumb, give it breath with your mouth, and it will discourse most eloquent music. Look you, these are the stops.

GUILDENSTERN But these cannot I command to any utt'rance of harmony. I have not the skill.

HAMLET Why, look you now, how unworthy a thing you make of me! You would play upon me, you would seem to know my stops, you would pluck out the heart of my mystery, you would sound me from my lowest note to the top of my compass; and there is much music, excellent voice, in this little organ, yet cannot you make it speak. 'Sblood, do you think I am easier to be played on than a pipe? Call me what instrument you will, though you can fret[90] me, you cannot play upon me.

(*Enter* POLONIUS)

God bless you, sir!

POLONIUS My lord, the queen would speak with you, and presently.[91]

HAMLET Do you see yonder cloud that's almost in shape of a camel?

POLONIUS By th' mass and 'tis, like a camel indeed.

---

[84] *while the grass grows* (a proverb, ending: "the horse starves") [85] *withdraw* step aside [86] *recover the wind* come up to windward like a hunter [87] *toil* snare [88] *is too unmannerly* leads me beyond the restraint of good manners [89] *ventages* holes, vents [90] *fret* irritate (with a play on the fret-fingering of certain stringed musical instruments) [91] *presently* at once

HAMLET   Methinks it is like a weasel.

POLONIUS   It is backed like a weasel.

HAMLET   Or like a whale.

POLONIUS   Very like a whale.

HAMLET   Then I will come to my mother by and by.[92] (*aside*)
They fool me to the top of my bent.—I will come by and by.

POLONIUS   I will say so.

(*Exit*)

HAMLET   "By and by" is easily said. Leave me, friends.

(*Exeunt all but* HAMLET)

'Tis now the very witching time of night,
When churchyards yawn, and hell itself breathes out
Contagion to this world. Now could I drink hot blood
And do such bitter business as the day
Would quake to look on. Soft, now to my mother.
O heart, lose not thy nature; let not ever
The soul of Nero[93] enter this firm bosom.
Let me be cruel, not unnatural;
I will speak daggers to her, but use none.
My tongue and soul in this be hypocrites:
How in my words somever she be shent,[94]
To give them seals[95] never, my soul, consent!

(*Exit*)

Act III, Scene III

A chamber in the castle

(*Enter* KING, ROSENCRANTZ, *and* GUILDENSTERN)

KING   I like him not, nor stands it safe with us
To let his madness range. Therefore prepare you.
I your commission will forthwith dispatch,
And he to England shall along with you.
The terms[1] of our estate[2] may not endure
Hazard so near's as doth hourly grow
Out of his brows.[3]

---

[92] *by and by* immediately   [93] *Nero* murderer of his mother   [94] *shent* reproved
[95] *seals* authentications in actions
[1] *terms* circumstances   [2] *estate* royal position   [3] *brows* effronteries (apparently with an implication of knitted brows)

GUILDENSTERN   We will ourselves provide.
  Most holy and religious fear it is
  To keep those many many bodies safe
  That live and feed upon your majesty.
ROSENCRANTZ   The single and peculiar[4] life is bound
  With all the strength and armor of the mind
  To keep itself from noyance,[5] but much more
  That spirit upon whose weal depends and rests
  The lives of many. The cess[6] of majesty
  Dies not alone, but like a gulf [7]doth draw
  What's near it with it; or 'tis a massy wheel
  Fixed on the summit of the highest mount,
  To whose huge spokes ten thousand lesser things
  Are mortised and adjoined, which when it falls,
  Each small annexment, petty consequence,
  Attends[8] the boist'rous ruin. Never alone
  Did the king sigh, but with a general groan.
KING   Arm[9] you, I pray you, to this speedy voyage,
  For we will fetters put upon this fear,
  Which now goes too free-footed.
ROSENCRANTZ   We will haste us.

(*Exeunt* GENTLEMEN)

(*Enter* POLONIUS)

POLONIUS   My lord, he's going to his mother's closet.
  Behind the arras I'll convey myself
  To hear the process.[10] I'll warrant she'll tax him home,[11]
  And, as you said, and wisely was it said,
  'Tis meet that some more audience than a mother,
  Since nature makes them partial, should o'erhear
  The speech, of vantage.[12] Fare you well, my liege.
  I'll call upon you ere you go to bed
  And tell you what I know.
KING   Thanks, dear my lord.

(*Exit* POLONIUS)

  O, my offense is rank, it smells to heaven;
  It hath the primal eldest curse[13] upon't,

---

[4] *peculiar* individual   [5] *noyance* harm   [6] *cess* cessation, decease   [7] *gulf* whirlpool   [8] *Attends* joins in (like a royal attendant)   [9] *Arm* prepare   [10] *process* proceedings   [11] *tax him home* thrust home in reprimanding him   [12] *of vantage* from an advantageous position   [13] *primal eldest curse* that of Cain, who also murdered a brother

A brother's murder. Pray can I not,
Though inclination be as sharp as will.
My stronger guilt defeats my strong intent,
And like a man to double business bound
I stand in pause where I shall first begin,
And both neglect. What if this cursèd hand
Were thicker than itself with brother's blood,
Is there not rain enough in the sweet heavens
To wash it white as snow? Whereto serves mercy
But to confront the visage of offense? [14]
And what's in prayer but this twofold force,
To be forestallèd ere we come to fall,
Or pardoned being down? Then I'll look up.
My fault is past. But, O, what form of prayer
Can serve my turn? "Forgive me my foul murder"?
That cannot be, since I am still possessed
Of those effects[15] for which I did the murder,
My crown, mine own ambition, and my queen.
May one be pardoned and retain th' offense?
In the corrupted currents of this world
Offense's gilded [16] hand may shove by justice,
And oft 'tis seen the wicked prize itself
Buys out the law. But 'tis not so above.
There is no shuffling;[17] there the action[18] lies
In his true nature, and we ourselves compelled,
Even to the teeth and forehead [19] of our faults,
To give in evidence. What then? What rests?
Try what repentance can. What can it not?
Yet what can it when one cannot repent?
O wretched state! O bosom black as death!
O limèd [20] soul, that struggling to be free
Art more engaged! [21] Help, angels! Make assay.[22]
Bow, stubborn knees, and, heart with strings of steel,
Be soft as sinews of the new-born babe.
All may be well.

He kneels

    (*Enter* HAMLET)

---

[14] *offense* sin   [15] *effects* things acquired   [16] *gilded* gold-laden   [17] *shuffling* sharp practice, double-dealing   [18] *action* legal proceeding (in heaven's court) [19] *teeth and forehead* face-to-face recognition   [20] *limèd* caught in birdlime, a gluey material spread as a bird-snare   [21] *engaged* embedded   [22] *assay* an attempt

HAMLET   Now might I do it pat,[23] now 'a is a-praying,
  And now I'll do't. And so 'a goes to heaven,
  And so am I revenged. That would be scanned.
  A villain kills my father, and for that
  I, his sole son, do this same villain send
  To heaven.
  Why, this is hire and salary, not revenge.
  'A took my father grossly,[24] full of bread,[25]
  With all his crimes broad blown,[26] as flush[27] as May;
  And how his audit[28] stands, who knows save heaven?
  But in our circumstance and course of thought,
  'Tis heavy with him; and am I then revenged,
  To take him in the purging of his soul,
  When he is fit and seasoned for his passage?
  No.
  Up, sword, and know thou a more horrid hent.[29]
  When he is drunk asleep, or in his rage,
  Or in th' incestuous pleasure of his bed,
  At game a-swearing, or about some act
  That has no relish[30] of salvation in't—
  Then trip him, that his heels may kick at heaven,
  And that his soul may be as damned and black
  As hell, whereto it goes. My mother stays.
  This physic but prolongs thy sickly days.

  (*Exit*)

KING (*rises*)   My words fly up, my thoughts remain below.
  Words without thoughts never to heaven go.

  (*Exit*)

Act III, Scene IV

The private chamber of the QUEEN

  (*Enter* [QUEEN] GERTRUDE *and* POLONIUS)

POLONIUS   'A will come straight. Look you lay[1] home to him.
  Tell him his pranks have been too broad [2] to bear with,
  And that your grace hath screened and stood between

---

[23] *pat* opportunely   [24] *grossly* in a state of gross unpreparedness   [25] *bread*
i.e. worldly sense gratification   [26] *broad blown* fully blossomed   [27] *flush* vigorous   [28] *audit* account   [29] *more horrid hent* grasping by me on a more
horrid occasion   [30] *relish* flavor
[1] *lay* thrust   [2] *broad* unrestrained

Much heat and him. I'll silence me even here.
Pray you be round ³ with him.

[HAMLET (*within*)   Mother, mother, mother!]

QUEEN   I'll warrant you; fear me not. Withdraw; I hear him
coming.

(POLONIUS *hides behind the arras*)

(*Enter* HAMLET)

HAMLET   Now, mother, what's the matter?

QUEEN   Hamlet, thou hast thy father much offended.

HAMLET   Mother, you have my father much offended.

QUEEN   Come, come, you answer with an idle⁴ tongue.

HAMLET   Go, go, you question with a wicked tongue.

QUEEN   Why, how now, Hamlet?

HAMLET   What's the matter now?

QUEEN   Have you forgot me?

HAMLET   No, by the rood,⁵ not so!
You are the queen, your husband's brother's wife,
And (would it were not so) you are my mother.

QUEEN   Nay, then I'll set those to you that can speak.

HAMLET   Come, come, and sit you down. You shall not budge.
You go not till I set you up a glass
Where you may see the inmost part of you.

QUEEN   What wilt thou do? Thou wilt not murder me?
Help, ho!

POLONIUS (*behind*)   What, ho! help!

HAMLET (*draws*)   How now? a rat? Dead for a ducat, dead!

(*Makes a pass through the arras and kills* POLONIUS)

POLONIUS (*behind*)   O, I am slain!

QUEEN   O me, what hast thou done?

HAMLET   Nay, I know not. Is it the king?

QUEEN   O, what a rash and bloody deed is this!

HAMLET   A bloody deed—almost as bad, good mother,
As kill a king, and marry with his brother.

QUEEN   As kill a king?

HAMLET   Ay, lady, it was my word.

(*Lifts up the arras and sees* POLONIUS)

Thou wretched, rash, intruding fool, farewell!

---

³ *round* plain-spoken   ⁴ *idle* foolish   ⁵ *rood* cross

I took thee for thy better. Take thy fortune.
Thou find'st to be too busy is some danger.—
Leave wringing of your hands. Peace, sit you down
And let me wring your heart, for so I shall
If it be made of penetrable stuff,
If damnèd custom[6] have not brazed [7] it so
That it is proof [8] and bulwark against sense.[9]

QUEEN   What have I done that thou dar'st wag thy tongue
In noise so rude against me?

HAMLET   Such an act
That blurs the grace and blush of modesty,
Calls virtue hypocrite, takes off the rose
From the fair forehead of an innocent love,
And sets a blister[10] there, makes marriage vows
As false as dicers' oaths. O, such a deed
As from the body of contraction[11] plucks
The very soul, and sweet religion[12] makes
A rhapsody of words! Heaven's face does glow,
And this solidity and compound mass,[13]
With heated visage, as against[14] the doom,[15]
Is thought-sick at the act.

QUEEN   Ay me, what act,
That roars so loud and thunders in the index? [16]

HAMLET   Look here upon this picture, and on this,
The counterfeit presentment[17] of two brothers.
See what a grace was seated on this brow:
Hyperion's[18] curls, the front[19] of Jove himself,
An eye like Mars, to threaten and command,
A station[20] like the herald Mercury
New lighted on a heaven-kissing hill—
A combination and a form indeed
Where every god did seem to set his seal
To give the world assurance of a man.
This was your husband. Look you now what follows.
Here is your husband, like a mildewed ear
Blasting his wholesome brother. Have you eyes?

---

6 *custom* habit   7 *brazed* hardened like brass   8 *proof* armor   9 *sense* feeling   10 *blister* brand (of degradation)   11 *contraction* the marriage contract
12 *religion* i.e. sacred marriage vows   13 *compound mass* the earth as compounded of the four elements   14 *against* in expectation of   15 *doom* Day
of Judgment   16 *index* table of contents preceding the body of a book
17 *counterfeit presentment* portrayed representation   18 *Hyperion* the sun god
19 *front* forehead   20 *station* attitude in standing

Could you on this fair mountain leave to feed,
And batten[21] on this moor? Ha! have you eyes?
You cannot call it love, for at your age
The heyday[22] in the blood is tame, it's humble,
And waits upon[23] the judgment, and what judgment
Would step from this to this? Sense[24] sure you have,
Else could you not have motion,[25] but sure that sense
Is apoplexed,[26] for madness would not err,
Nor sense to ecstasy[27] was ne'er so thralled
But it reserved some quantity of choice
To serve in such a difference. What devil was't
That thus hath cozened [28] you at hoodman-blind? [29]
Eyes without feeling, feeling without sight,
Ears without hands or eyes, smelling sans[30] all,
Or but a sickly part of one true sense
Could not so mope.[31]
O shame, where is thy blush? Rebellious hell,
If thou canst mutine[32] in a matron's bones,
To flaming youth let virtue be as wax
And melt in her own fire. Proclaim no shame
When the compulsive[33] ardor gives the charge,[34]
Since frost itself as actively doth burn,
And reason panders will.[35]

QUEEN   O Hamlet, speak no more.
   Thou turn'st mine eyes into my very soul,
   And there I see such black and grainèd [36] spots
   As will not leave their tinct.[37]

HAMLET   Nay, but to live
   In the rank sweat of an enseamèd [38] bed,
   Stewed in corruption, honeying and making love
   Over the nasty sty—

QUEEN   O, speak to me no more.
   These words like daggers enter in mine ears.
   No more, sweet Hamlet.

HAMLET   A murderer and a villain,
   A slave that is not twentieth part the tithe[39]

---

[21] *batten* feed greedily   [22] *heyday* excitement of passion   [23] *waits upon* yields to   [24] *Sense* feeling   [25] *motion* desire, impulse   [26] *apoplexed* paralyzed   [27] *ecstasy* madness   [28] *cozened* cheated   [29] *hoodman-blind* blindman's buff   [30] *sans* without   [31] *mope* be stupid   [32] *mutine* mutiny   [33] *compulsive* compelling   [34] *gives the charge* delivers the attack   [35] *panders will* acts as procurer for desire   [36] *grainèd* dyed in grain   [37] *tinct* color   [38] *enseamèd* grease-laden   [39] *tithe* tenth part

Of your precedent lord, a vice[40] of kings,
A cutpurse[41] of the empire and the rule,
That from a shelf the precious diadem stole
And put it in his pocket—

QUEEN   No more.

(*Enter [the]* GHOST [*in his nightgown*[42]])

HAMLET   A king of shreds and patches—
  Save me and hover o'er me with your wings,
  You heavenly guards? What would your gracious figure?
QUEEN   Alas, he's mad.
HAMLET   Do you not come your tardy son to chide,
  That, lapsed in time and passion,[43] lets go by
  Th' important acting of your dread command?
  O, say!
GHOST   Do not forget. This visitation
  Is but to whet thy almost blunted purpose.
  But look, amazement on thy mother sits.
  O, step between her and her fighting soul!
  Conceit[44] in weakest bodies strongest works.
  Speak to her, Hamlet.
HAMLET   How is it with you, lady?
QUEEN   Alas, how is't with you,
  That you do bend your eye on vacancy,
  And with th' incorporal [45] air do hold discourse?
  Forth at your eyes your spirits wildly peep,
  And as the sleeping soldiers in th' alarm
  Your bedded hairs like life in excrements[46]
  Start up and stand an[47] end. O gentle son,
  Upon the heat and flame of thy distemper[48]
  Sprinkle cool patience. Whereon do you look?
HAMLET   On him, on him! Look you, how pale he glares!
  His form and cause conjoined, preaching to stones,
  Would make them capable.[49]—Do not look upon me,
  Lest with his piteous action you convert
  My stern effects.[50] Then what I have to do
  Will want true color—tears perchance for blood.

---

40 *vice* clownish rogue (like the Vice of the morality plays)   41 *cutpurse*
skulking thief   42 *nightgown* dressing gown   43 *lapsed ... passion* having let
the moment slip and passion cool   44 *Conceit* imagination   45 *incorporal*
bodiless   46 *excrements* outgrowths   47 *an* on   48 *distemper* mental disorder
49 *capable* susceptible   50 *effects* manifestations of emotion and purpose

QUEEN   To whom do you speak this?

HAMLET   Do you see nothing there?

QUEEN   Nothing at all; yet all that is I see.

HAMLET   Nor did you nothing hear?

QUEEN   No, nothing but ourselves.

HAMLET   Why, look you there! Look how it steals away!
My father, in his habit as he lived!
Look where he goes even now out at the portal!

(*Exit* GHOST)

QUEEN   This is the very coinage of your brain.
This bodiless creation ecstasy[51]
Is very cunning in.

HAMLET   Ecstasy?
My pulse as yours doth temperately keep time
And makes as healthful music. It is not madness
That I have uttered. Bring me to the test,
And I the matter will reword, which madness
Would gambol [52] from. Mother, for love of grace,
Lay not that flattering unction[53] to your soul,
That not your trespass but my madness speaks.
It will but skin and film the ulcerous place
Whiles rank corruption, mining[54] all within,
Infects unseen. Confess yourself to heaven,
Repent what's past, avoid what is to come,
And do not spread the compost[55] on the weeds
To make them ranker. Forgive me this my virtue.
For in the fatness[56] of these pursy[57] times
Virtue itself of vice must pardon beg,
Yea, curb[58] and woo for leave to do him good.

QUEEN   O Hamlet, thou hast cleft my heart in twain.

HAMLET   O, throw away the worser part of it,
And live the purer with the other half.
Good night—but go not to my uncle's bed.
Assume a virtue, if you have it not.
That monster custom, who all sense doth eat,
Of habits devil, is angel yet in this,
That to the use of actions fair and good

---

[51] *ecstasy* madness   [52] *gambol* shy (like a startled horse)   [53] *unction* ointment   [54] *mining* undermining   [55] *compost* fertilizing mixture   [56] *fatness*
gross slackness   [57] *pursy* corpulent   [58] *curb* bow to

He likewise gives a frock or livery[59]
That aptly is put on. Refrain to-night,
And that shall lend a kind of easiness
To the next abstinence; the next more easy;
For use[60] almost can change the stamp[61] of nature,
And either [. . .] [62] the devil, or throw him out
With wondrous potency. Once more, good night,
And when you are desirous to be blest,
I'll blessing beg of you.—For this same lord,
I do repent; but heaven hath pleased it so,
To punish me with this, and this with me,
That I must be their scourge and minister.
I will bestow[63] him and will answer well
The death I gave him. So again, good night.
I must be cruel only to be kind.
Thus bad begins, and worse remains behind.[64]
One word more, good lady.

QUEEN   What shall I do?

HAMLET   Not this, by no means, that I bid you do:
Let the bloat[65] king tempt you again to bed,
Pinch wanton on your cheek, call you his mouse,
And let him, for a pair of reechy[66] kisses,
Or paddling in your neck with his damned fingers,
Make you to ravel all this matter out,[67]
That I essentially am not in madness,
But mad in craft. 'Twere good you let him know,
For who that's but a queen, fair, sober, wise,
Would from a paddock,[68] from a bat, a gib,[69]
Such dear concernings[70] hide? Who would do so?
No, in despite of sense and secrecy,
Unpeg the basket on the house's top,
Let the birds fly, and like the famous ape,[71]
To try conclusions,[72] in the basket creep
And break your own neck down.

QUEEN   Be thou assured, if words be made of breath,
And breath of life, I have no life to breathe

---

[59] *livery* characteristic dress (accompanying the suggestion of "garb" in *habits*)   [60] *use* habit   [61] *stamp* impression, form   [62] A word is apparently omitted here   [63] *bestow* stow, hide   [64] *behind* to come   [65] *bloat* bloated with sense gratification   [66] *reechy* filthy   [67] *ravel . . . out* disentangle   [68] *paddock* toad   [69] *gib* tomcat   [70] *dear concernings* matters of great personal significance   [71] *famous ape* (one in a story now unknown)   [72] *conclusions* experiments

What thou hast said to me.

HAMLET   I must to England; you know that?

QUEEN   Alack,
I had forgot. 'Tis so concluded on.

HAMLET   There's letters sealed, and my two schoolfellows,
Whom I will trust as I will adders fanged,
They bear the mandate;[73] they must sweep my way
And marshal me to knavery. Let it work.
For 'tis the sport to have the enginer[74]
Hoist[75] with his own petar,[76] and 't shall go hard
But I will delve one yard below their mines
And blow them at the moon. O, 'tis most sweet
When in one line two crafts directly meet.
This man shall set me packing.[77]
I'll lug the guts into the neighbor room.
Mother, good night. Indeed, this counsellor
Is now most still, most secret, and most grave,
Who was in life a foolish prating knave.
Come, sir, to draw toward an end with you.
Good night, mother.

(*Exit the* QUEEN. *Then exit* HAMLET, *tugging in* POLONIUS)

ACT IV

Scene I

A chamber in the castle

(*Enter* KING *and* QUEEN, *with* ROSENCRANTZ *and* GUILDENSTERN)

KING   There's matter in these sighs. These profound heaves
You must translate; 'tis fit we understand them.
Where is your son?

QUEEN   Bestow this place on us a little while.

(*Exeunt* ROSENCRANTZ *and* GUILDENSTERN)

Ah, mine own lord, what have I seen to-night!

KING   What, Gertrude? How does Hamlet?

---

[73] *mandate* order   [74] *enginer* engineer, constructor of military engines or
works   [75] *Hoist* blown up   [76] *petar* petard, bomb or mine   [77] *packing* travelling in a hurry (with a play upon his "packing" or shouldering of Polonius'
body and also upon his "packing" in the sense of "plotting" or "contriving")

QUEEN   Mad as the sea and wind when both contend
  Which is the mightier. In his lawless fit,
  Behind the arras hearing something stir,
  Whips out his rapier, cries, "A rat, a rat!"
  And in this brainish apprehension[1] kills
  The unseen good old man.
KING   O heavy deed!
  It had been so with us, had we been there.
  His liberty is full of threats to all,
  To you yourself, to us, to every one.
  Alas, how shall this bloody deed be answered?
  It will be laid to us, whose providence[2]
  Should have kept short, restrained, and out of haunt[3]
  This mad young man. But so much was our love
  We would not understand what was most fit,
  But, like the owner of a foul disease,
  To keep it from divulging,[4] let it feed
  Even on the pith of life. Where is he gone?
QUEEN   To draw apart the body he hath killed;
  O'er whom his very madness, like some ore[5]
  Among a mineral[6] of metals base,
  Shows itself pure. 'A weeps for what is done.
KING   O Gertrude, come away!
  The sun no sooner shall the mountains touch
  But we will ship him hence, and this vile deed
  We must with all our majesty and skill
  Both countenance and excuse. Ho, Guildenstern!

(*Enter* ROSENCRANTZ *and* GUILDENSTERN)

  Friends both, go join you with some further aid.
  Hamlet in madness hath Polonius slain,
  And from his mother's closet hath he dragged him.
  Go seek him out; speak fair, and bring the body
  Into the chapel. I pray you haste in this.

(*Exeunt* ROSENCRANTZ *and* GUILDENSTERN)

  Come, Gertrude, we'll call up our wisest friends
  And let them know both what we mean to do
  And what's untimely done [. . .][7]

---

[1] *brainish apprehension* headstrong conception   [2] *providence* foresight
[3] *haunt* association with others   [4] *divulging* becoming known   [5] *ore* vein of
gold   [6] *mineral* mine   [7] Incomplete line; Capell suggests "So, haply, slander"

Whose whisper o'er the world's diameter,
As level [8] as the cannon to his blank[9]
Transports his poisoned shot, may miss our name
And hit the woundless air. O, come away!
My soul is full of discord and dismay.

(*Exeunt*)

Act IV, Scene II

A passage in the castle

(*Enter* HAMLET)

HAMLET   Safely stowed.
GENTLEMEN (*within*)   Hamlet! Lord Hamlet!
HAMLET   But soft, what noise? Who calls on Hamlet? O, here they come.

(*Enter* ROSENCRANTZ, GUILDENSTERN, *and others*)

ROSENCRANTZ   What have you done, my lord, with the dead body?
HAMLET   Compounded it with dust, whereto 'tis kin.
ROSENCRANTZ   Tell us where 'tis, that we may take it thence
And bear it to the chapel.
HAMLET   Do not believe it.
ROSENCRANTZ   Believe what?
HAMLET   That I can keep your counsel and not mine own. Besides, to be demanded of a sponge, what replication[1] should be made by the son of a king?
ROSENCRANTZ   Take you me for a sponge, my lord?
HAMLET   Ay, sir, that soaks up the king's countenance,[2] his rewards, his authorities. But such officers do the king best service in the end. He keeps them, like an ape, in the corner of his jaw, first mouthed, to be last swallowed. When he needs what you have gleaned, it is but squeezing you and, sponge, you shall be dry again.
ROSENCRANTZ   I understand you not, my lord.
HAMLET   I am glad of it. A knavish speech sleeps in[3] a foolish ear.
ROSENCRANTZ   My lord, you must tell us where the body is and go with us to the king.
HAMLET   The body is with the king, but the king is not with the body. The king is a thing—

---

[8] *As level* with as direct aim   [9] *blank* mark, central white spot on a target
[1] *replication* reply   [2] *countenance* favor   [3] *sleeps in* means nothing to

GUILDENSTERN   A thing, my lord?
HAMLET   Of nothing.[4] Bring me to him. Hide fox, and all after.[5]

(*Exeunt*)

Act IV, Scene III

A chamber in the castle

(*Enter* KING, *and two or three*)

KING   I have sent to seek him and to find the body.
How dangerous is it that this man goes loose!
Yet must not we put the strong law on him;
He's loved of the distracted [1] multitude,
Who like not in their judgment, but their eyes,
And where 'tis so, th' offender's scourge[2] is weighed,
But never the offense. To bear all smooth and even,
This sudden sending him away must seem
Deliberate pause.[3] Diseases desperate grown
By desperate appliance are relieved,
Or not at all.

(*Enter* ROSENCRANTZ, GUILDENSTERN, *and all the rest*)

How now? What hath befallen?
ROSENCRANTZ   Where the dead body is bestowed, my lord,
We cannot get from him.
KING   But where is he?
ROSENCRANTZ   Without, my lord; guarded, to know your pleasure.
KING   Bring him before us.
ROSENCRANTZ   Ho! Bring in the lord.

(*They enter* [*with* HAMLET])

KING   Now, Hamlet, where's Polonius?
HAMLET   At supper.
KING   At supper? Where?
HAMLET   Not where he eats, but where 'a is eaten. A certain con-
vocation of politic worms[4] are e'en at him. Your worm is your

---

[4] *Of nothing* (cf. Prayer Book, Psalm cxliv, 4, "Man is like a thing of naught:
his time passeth away like a shadow")   [5] *Hide . . . after* (apparently well-
known words from some game of hide-and-seek)
[1] *distracted* confused   [2] *scourge* punishment   [3] *Deliberate pause* something
done with much deliberation   [4] *politic worms* political and craftily scheming
worms (such as Polonius might well attract)

only emperor for diet.[5] We fat all creatures else to fat us, and we fat ourselves for maggots. Your fat king and your lean beggar is but variable service[6]—two dishes, but to one table. That's the end.

KING Alas, alas!

HAMLET A man may fish with the worm that hath eat of a king, and eat of the fish that hath fed of that worm.

KING What dost thou mean by this?

HAMLET Nothing but to show you how a king may go a progress[7] through the guts of a beggar.

KING Where is Polonius?

HAMLET In heaven. Send thither to see. If your messenger find him not there, seek him i' th' other place yourself. But if indeed you find him not within this month, you shall nose him as you go up the stairs into the lobby.

KING (*to* ATTENDANTS) Go seek him there.

HAMLET 'A will stay till you come.

(*Exeunt* ATTENDANTS)

KING Hamlet, this deed, for thine especial safety,
Which we do tender[8] as we dearly[9] grieve
For that which thou hast done, must send thee hence
With fiery quickness. Therefore prepare thyself.
The bark is ready and the wind at help,
Th' associates tend,[10] and everything is bent[11]
For England.

HAMLET For England?

KING Ay, Hamlet.

HAMLET Good.

KING So is it, if thou knew'st our purposes.

HAMLET I see a cherub[12] that sees them. But come, for England! Farewell, dear mother.

KING Thy loving father, Hamlet.

HAMLET My mother—father and mother is man and wife, man and wife is one flesh, and so, my mother. Come, for England!

(*Exit*)

---

[5] *diet* food and drink (perhaps with a play upon a famous "convocation," the Diet of Worms opened by the Emperor Charles V on January 28, 1521, before which Luther appeared) [6] *variable service* different servings of one food [7] *progress* royal journey of state [8] *tender* hold dear [9] *dearly* intensely [10] *tend* wait [11] *bent* set in readiness (like a bent bow) [12] *cherub* one of the cherubim (angels with a distinctive quality of knowledge)

KING Follow him at foot;[13] tempt him with speed aboard.
Delay it not; I'll have him hence to-night.
Away! for everything is sealed and done
That else leans on[14] th' affair. Pray you make haste.

(*Exeunt all but the* KING)

And, England,[15] if my love thou hold'st at aught—
As my great power thereof may give thee sense,
Since yet thy cicatrice looks raw and red
After the Danish sword, and thy free awe[16]
Pays homage to us—thou mayst not coldly set[17]
Our sovereign process,[18] which imports at full
By letters congruing[19] to that effect
The present[20] death of Hamlet. Do it, England,
For like the hectic[21] in my blood he rages,
And thou must cure me. Till I know 'tis done,
Howe'er my haps,[22] my joys were ne'er begun.

(*Exit*)

Act IV, Scene IV

A coastal highway

(*Enter* FORTINBRAS *with his* ARMY *over the stage*)

FORTINBRAS Go, captain, from me greet the Danish king.
Tell him that by his license Fortinbras
Craves the conveyance[1] of a promised march
Over his kingdom. You know the rendezvous.
If that his majesty would aught with us,
We shall express our duty in his eye;[2]
And let him know so.
CAPTAIN   I will do't, my lord.
FORTINBRAS Go softly[3] on.

(*Exeunt all but the* CAPTAIN)

(*Enter* HAMLET, ROSENCRANTZ, GUILDENSTERN, *and others*)

HAMLET Good sir, whose powers[4] are these?

---

[13] *at foot* at heel, close [14] *leans on* is connected with [15] *England* King of England [16] *free awe* voluntary show of respect [17] *set* esteem [18] *process* formal command [19] *congruing* agreeing [20] *present* instant [21] *hectic* a continuous fever [22] *haps* fortunes
[1] *conveyance* escort [2] *eye* presence [3] *softly* slowly [4] *powers* forces

CAPTAIN   They are of Norway, sir.

HAMLET   How purposed, sir, I pray you?

CAPTAIN   Against some part of Poland.

HAMLET   Who commands them, sir?

CAPTAIN   The nephew to old Norway, Fortinbras.

HAMLET   Goes it against the main[5] of Poland, sir,
Or for some frontier?

CAPTAIN   Truly to speak, and with no addition,[6]
We go to gain a little patch of ground
That hath in it no profit but the name.
To pay[7] five ducats, five, I would not farm it,
Nor will it yield to Norway or the Pole
A ranker[8] rate, should it be sold in fee.[9]

HAMLET   Why, then the Polack never will defend it.

CAPTAIN   Yes, it is already garrisoned.

HAMLET   Two thousand souls and twenty thousand ducats
Will not debate the question of this straw.
This is th' imposthume[10] of much wealth and peace,
That inward breaks, and shows no cause without
Why the man dies. I humbly thank you, sir.

CAPTAIN   God bye you, sir.

(*Exit*)

ROSENCRANTZ   Will't please you go, my lord?

HAMLET   I'll be with you straight. Go a little before.

(*Exeunt all but* HAMLET)

How all occasions do inform[11] against me
And spur my dull revenge! What is a man,
If his chief good and market of [12] his time
Be but to sleep and feed? A beast, no more.
Sure he that made us with such large discourse,[13]
Looking before and after, gave us not
That capability and godlike reason
To fust[14] in us unused. Now, whether it be
Bestial oblivion,[15] or some craven scruple
Of thinking too precisely on th' event—[16]

---

[5] *main* main body   [6] *addition* exaggeration   [7] *To pay* i.e. for a yearly rental
of   [8] *ranker* more abundant   [9] *in fee* outright   [10] *imposthume* abscess   [11] *inform* take shape   [12] *market of* compensation for   [13] *discourse* power of
thought   [14] *fust* grow mouldy   [15] *oblivion* forgetfulness   [16] *event* outcome

A thought which, quartered, hath but one part wisdom *[handwritten: questioning his own ability]*
And ever three parts coward—I do not know
Why yet I live to say, "This thing 's to do,"
Sith I have cause, and will, and strength, and means
To do't. Examples gross[17] as earth exhort me.
Witness this army of such mass and charge,[18]
Led by a delicate and tender prince,
Whose spirit, with divine ambition puffed,
Makes mouths[19] at the invisible event,
Exposing what is mortal and unsure
To all that fortune, death, and danger dare,
Even for an eggshell. Rightly to be great
Is not to stir without great argument,
But greatly to find quarrel in a straw[20]
When honor 's at the stake. How stand I then, *[handwritten: firm resolution to fight back since Fort.'s army is ready to fight for a mere plot of land.]*
That have a father killed, a mother stained,
Excitements of my reason and my blood,
And let all sleep, while to my shame I see
The imminent death of twenty thousand men
That for a fantasy[21] and trick[22] of fame
Go to their graves like beds, fight for a plot
Whereon the numbers cannot try the cause,[23]
Which is not tomb enough and continent[24]
To hide the slain? O, from this time forth,
My thoughts be bloody, or be nothing worth!

(*Exit*)

Act IV, Scene V

A chamber in the castle

(*Enter* Horatio, [Queen] Gertrude, *and a* Gentleman)

QUEEN   I will not speak with her.
GENTLEMAN   She is importunate, indeed distract.[1]
    Her mood will needs be pitied.
QUEEN   What would she have?
GENTLEMAN   She speaks much of her father, says she hears

---

[17] *gross* large and evident   [18] *charge* expense   [19] *Makes mouths* makes faces
scornfully   [20] *greatly . . . straw* to recognize the great argument even in some
small matter   [21] *fantasy* fanciful image   [22] *trick* toy   [23] *try the cause* find
space in which to settle the issue by battle   [24] *continent* receptacle
[1] *distract* insane

There's tricks[2] i' th' world, and hems, and beats her heart,
Spurns enviously[3] at straws,[4] speaks things in doubt
That carry but half sense. Her speech is nothing,
Yet the unshapèd use[5] of it doth move
The hearers to collection;[6] they aim[7] at it,
And botch[8] the words up fit to their own thoughts,
Which, as her winks and nods and gestures yield them,
Indeed would make one think there might be thought,
Though nothing sure, yet much unhappily.
HORATIO   'Twere good she were spoken with, for she may strew
Dangerous conjectures in ill-breeding minds.
QUEEN   Let her come in.

(*Exit* GENTLEMAN)

(*Aside*)

To my sick soul (as sin's true nature is)
Each toy[9] seems prologue to some great amiss.[10]
So full of artless[11] jealousy[12] is guilt
It spills[13] itself in fearing to be spilt.

(*Enter* OPHELIA [*distracted*])

OPHELIA   Where is the beauteous majesty of Denmark?
QUEEN   How now, Ophelia?
OPHELIA (*She sings.*)
　　How should I your true-love know
　　　　From another one?
　　By his cockle hat[14] and staff
　　　　And his sandal shoon.[15]
QUEEN   Alas, sweet lady, what imports this song?
OPHELIA   Say you? Nay, pray you mark.

Song

　　He is dead and gone, lady,
　　　　He is dead and gone;
　　At his head a grass-green turf,
　　　　At his heels a stone.
　　O, ho!

---

[2] *tricks* deceits [3] *Spurns enviously* kicks spitefully, takes offense [4] *straws* trifles [5] *unshapèd use* disordered manner [6] *collection* attempts at shaping meaning [7] *aim* guess [8] *botch* patch [9] *toy* trifle [10] *amiss* calamity [11] *artless* unskillfully managed [12] *jealousy* suspicion [13] *spills* destroys [14] *cockle hat* hat bearing a cockle shell, worn by a pilgrim who had been to the shrine of St James of Compostela [15] *shoon* shoes

QUEEN Nay, but Ophelia—
OPHELIA Pray you mark.
  (*Sings*) White his shroud as the mountain snow—

  (*Enter* KING)

QUEEN Alas, look here, my lord.
OPHELIA

Song

>   Larded [16] all with sweet flowers;
>   Which bewept to the grave did not go
>   With true-love showers.

KING How do you, pretty lady?
OPHELIA Well, God dild [17] you! They say the owl [18] was a baker's daughter. Lord, we know what we are, but know not what we may be. God be at your table!
KING Conceit[19] upon her father.
OPHELIA Pray let's have no words of this, but when they ask you what it means, say you this:

Song

>   To-morrow is Saint Valentine's day.
>   All in the morning betime,[20]
>   And I a maid at your window,
>   To be your Valentine.
>   Then up he rose and donned his clo'es
>   And dupped [21] the chamber door,
>   Let in the maid, that out a maid
>   Never departed more.

KING Pretty Ophelia!
OPHELIA Indeed, la, without an oath, I'll make an end on't:
  (*Sings*) By Gis[22] and by Saint Charity,
        Alack, and fie for shame!
      Young men will do't if they come to't.
        By Cock,[23] they are to blame.
      Quoth she, "Before you tumbled me,
        You promised me to wed."

---

[16] *Larded* garnished [17] *dild* yield, repay [18] *the owl* an owl into which, according to a folk-tale, a baker's daughter was transformed because of her failure to show whole-hearted generosity when Christ asked for bread in the baker's shop [19] *Conceit* thought [20] *betime* early [21] *dupped* opened [22] *Gis* Jesus [23] *Cock* God (with a perversion of the name not uncommon in oaths)

He answers:
>"So would I 'a' done, by yonder sun,
>   And thou hadst not come to my bed."

KING   How long hath she been thus?

OPHELIA   I hope all will be well. We must be patient, but I cannot choose but weep to think they would lay him i' th' cold ground. My brother shall know of it; and so I thank you for your good counsel. Come, my coach! Good night, ladies, good night. Sweet ladies, good night, good night.

(*Exit*)

KING   Follow her close; give her good watch, I pray you.

(*Exit* HORATIO)

O, this is the poison of deep grief; it springs
All from her father's death—and now behold!
O Gertrude, Gertrude,
When sorrows come, they come not single spies,
But in battalions: first, her father slain;
Next, your son gone, and he most violent author
Of his own just remove; the people muddied,[24]
Thick and unwholesome in their thoughts and whispers
For good Polonius' death, and we have done but greenly[25]
In hugger-mugger[26] to inter him; poor Ophelia
Divided from herself and her fair judgment,
Without the which we are pictures or mere beasts;
Last, and as much containing as all these,
Her brother is in secret come from France,
Feeds on his wonder, keeps himself in clouds,[27]
And wants[28] not buzzers[29] to infect his ear
With pestilent speeches of his father's death,
Wherein necessity, of matter beggared,[30]
Will nothing stick[31] our person to arraign[32]
In ear and ear. O my dear Gertrude, this,
Like to a murd'ring piece,[33] in many places
Gives me superfluous death.

A noise within

---

[24] *muddied* stirred up and confused   [25] *greenly* foolishly   [26] *hugger-mugger* secrecy and disorder   [27] *clouds* obscurity   [28] *wants* lacks   [29] *buzzers* whispering tale-bearers   [30] *of matter beggared* unprovided with facts   [31] *nothing stick* in no way hesitate   [32] *arraign* accuse   [33] *murd'ring piece* cannon loaded with shot meant to scatter

(Enter a MESSENGER*)*

QUEEN   Alack, what noise is this?
KING   Attend, where are my Switzers? [34] Let them guard the door.
   What is the matter?
MESSENGER   Save yourself, my lord.
   The ocean, overpeering of [35] his list,[36]
   Eats not the flats with more impiteous[37] haste
   Than young Laertes, in a riotous head,[38]
   O'erbears your officers. The rabble call him lord,
   And, as the world were now but to begin,
   Antiquity forgot, custom not known,
   The ratifiers and props of every word,[39]
   They cry, "Choose we! Laertes shall be king!"
   Caps, hands, and tongues applaud it to the clouds,
   "Laertes shall be king! Laertes king!"

A noise within

QUEEN   How cheerfully on the false trail they cry!
   O, this is counter,[40] you false Danish dogs!
KING   The doors are broke.

(Enter LAERTES *with others)*

LAERTES   Where is this king?—Sirs, stand you all without.
ALL   No, let's come in.
LAERTES   I pray you give me leave.
ALL   We will, we will.
LAERTES   I thank you. Keep the door.

(Exeunt his FOLLOWERS*)*

                                         O thou vile king,
   Give me my father.
QUEEN   Calmly, good Laertes.
LAERTES   That drop of blood that's calm proclaims me bastard,
   Cries cuckold to my father, brands the harlot
   Even here between the chaste unsmirchèd brows
   Of my true mother.
KING   What is the cause, Laertes,
   That thy rebellion looks so giant-like?
   Let him go, Gertrude. Do not fear[41] our person.

---

[34] *Switzers* hired Swiss guards   [35] *overpeering of* rising to look over and pass
beyond   [36] *list* boundary   [37] *impiteous* pitiless   [38] *head* armed force   [39] *word*
promise   [40] *counter* hunting backward on the trail   [41] *fear* fear for

There's such divinity doth hedge a king
That treason can but peep to[42] what it would,
Acts little of his will. Tell me, Laertes,
Why thou art thus incensed. Let him go, Gertrude.
Speak, man.

LAERTES   Where is my father?

KING   Dead.

QUEEN   But not by him.

KING   Let him demand his fill.

LAERTES   How came he dead? I'll not be juggled with.
To hell allegiance, vows to the blackest devil,
Conscience and grace to the profoundest pit!
I dare damnation. To this point I stand,
That both the worlds[43] I give to negligence,[44]
Let come what comes, only I'll be revenged
Most throughly[45] for my father.

KING   Who shall stay you?

LAERTES   My will, not all the world's.
And for my means, I'll husband them so well
They shall go far with little.

KING   Good Laertes,
If you desire to know the certainty
Of your dear father, is't writ in your revenge
That swoopstake[46] you will draw both friend and foe,
Winner and loser?

LAERTES   None but his enemies.

KING   Will you know them then?

LAERTES   To his good friends thus wide I'll ope my arms
And like the kind life-rend'ring[47] pelican
Repast them with my blood.

KING   Why, now you speak
Like a good child and a true gentleman.
That I am guiltless of your father's death,
And am most sensibly[48] in grief for it,
It shall as level [49] to your judgment 'pear
As day does to your eye.
     A noise within: "Let her come in!"

---

[42] *peep to* i.e. through the barrier   [43] *both the worlds* whatever may result in this world or the next   [44] *give to negligence* disregard   [45] *throughly* thoroughly   [46] *swoopstake* sweepstake, taking all stakes on the gambling table   [47] *life-rend'ring* life-yielding (because the mother pelican supposedly took blood from her breast with her bill to feed her young)   [48] *sensibly* feelingly   [49] *level* plain

LAERTES   How now? What noise is that?

(*Enter* OPHELIA)

O heat, dry up my brains; tears seven times salt
Burn out the sense and virtue of mine eye!
By heaven, thy madness shall be paid by weight
Till our scale turn the beam.[50] O rose of May,
Dear maid, kind sister, sweet Ophelia!
O heavens, is't possible a young maid's wits
Should be as mortal as an old man's life?
Nature is fine[51] in love, and where 'tis fine,
It sends some precious instance[52] of itself
After the thing it loves.

OPHELIA

Song

   They bore him barefaced on the bier
      Hey non nony, nony, hey nony
   And in his grave rained many a tear—
Fare you well, my dove!

LAERTES   Hadst thou thy wits, and didst persuade revenge,
It could not move thus.

OPHELIA   You must sing "A-down a-down, and you call him
a-down-a." O, how the wheel[53] becomes it! It is the false stew-
ard, that stole his master's daughter.

LAERTES   This nothing 's more than matter.[54]

OPHELIA   There's rosemary, that's for remembrance. Pray you, love,
remember. And there is pansies, that's for thoughts.

LAERTES   A document[55] in madness, thoughts and remembrance
fitted.

OPHELIA   There's fennel[56] for you, and columbines.[57] There's rue[58]
for you, and here's some for me. We may call it herb of grace o'
Sundays. O, you must wear your rue with a difference. There's
a daisy.[59] I would give you some violets,[60] but they withered all
when my father died. They say 'a made a good end.
   (*Sings*)   For bonny sweet Robin is all my joy.

LAERTES   Thought and affliction, passion, hell itself,
She turns to favor[61] and to prettiness.

---

[50] *beam* bar of a balance   [51] *fine* refined to purity   [52] *instance* token   [53] *wheel*
burden, refrain   [54] *more than matter* more meaningful than sane speech
[55] *document* lesson   [56] *fennel* symbol of flattery   [57] *columbines* symbol of
thanklessness   [58] *rue* symbol of repentance   [59] *daisy* symbol of dissembling
[60] *violets* symbol of faithfulness   [61] *favor* charm

OPHELIA

Song

> And will 'a not come again?
> And will 'a not come again?
>   No, no, he is dead;
>   Go to thy deathbed;
> He never will come again.
> His beard was as white as snow,
> All flaxen was his poll.[62]
>   He is gone, he is gone,
>   And we cast away moan.
>   God 'a' mercy on his soul!
> And of [63] all Christian souls, I pray God. God bye you.

(*Exit*)

LAERTES   Do you see this, O God?

KING   Laertes, I must commune with your grief,
Or you deny me right. Go but apart,
Make choice of whom your wisest friends you will,
And they shall hear and judge 'twixt you and me.
If by direct or by collateral [64] hand
They find us touched,[65] we will our kingdom give,
Our crown, our life, and all that we call ours,
To you in satisfaction; but if not,
Be you content to lend your patience to us,
And we shall jointly labor with your soul
To give it due content.

LAERTES   Let this be so.
His means of death, his obscure funeral—
No trophy,[66] sword, nor hatchment[67] o'er his bones,
No noble rite nor formal ostentation[68]—
Cry to be heard, as 'twere from heaven to earth,
That[69] I must call't in question.

KING   So you shall;
And where th' offense is, let the great axe fall.
I pray you go with me.

(*Exeunt*)

---

[62] *poll* head   [63] *of* on   [64] *collateral* indirect   [65] *touched* i.e. with the crime
[66] *trophy* memorial   [67] *hatchment* coat of arms   [68] *ostentation* ceremony
[69] *That* so that

Act IV, Scene VI

A chamber in the castle

(*Enter* HORATIO *and others*)

HORATIO   What are they that would speak with me?
GENTLEMAN   Seafaring men, sir. They say they have letters for you.
HORATIO   Let them come in.

(*Exit* ATTENDANT)

I do not know from what part of the world
I should be greeted, if not from Lord Hamlet.

(*Enter* SAILORS)

SAILOR   God bless you, sir.
HORATIO   Let him bless thee too.
SAILOR   'A shall, sir, an't please him. There's a letter for you, sir—
it came from th' ambassador that was bound for England—if
your name be Horatio, as I am let to know it is.
HORATIO   (*reads the letter*)   "Horatio, when thou shalt have overlooked [1] this, give these fellows some means[2] to the king. They
have letters for him. Ere we were two days old at sea, a pirate of
very warlike appointment[3] gave us chase. Finding ourselves too
slow of sail, we put on a compelled valor, and in the grapple I
boarded them. On the instant they got clear of our ship; so I
alone became their prisoner. They have dealt with me like thieves
of mercy,[4] but they knew what they did: I am to do a good turn
for them. Let the king have the letters I have sent, and repair
thou to me with as much speed as thou wouldest fly death. I have
words to speak in thine ear will make thee dumb; yet are they
much too light for the bore[5] of the matter. These good fellows
will bring thee where I am. Rosencrantz and Guildenstern hold
their course for England. Of them I have much to tell thee.
Farewell.
                              He that thou knowest thine, Hamlet."
Come, I will give you way for these your letters,
And do't the speedier that you may direct me
To him from whom you brought them.

(*Exeunt*)

---

[1] *overlooked* surveyed, scanned   [2] *means* i.e. of access   [3] *appointment* equipment   [4] *thieves of mercy* merciful thieves   [5] *bore* caliber (as of a gun)

Act IV, Scene VII

A chamber in the castle

(*Enter* KING *and* LAERTES)

KING   Now must your conscience my acquittance seal,
And you must put me in your heart for friend,
Sith you have heard, and with a knowing ear,
That he which hath your noble father slain
Pursued my life.

LAERTES   It well appears. But tell me
Why you proceeded not against these feats[1]
So crimeful and so capital[2] in nature,
As by your safety, wisdom, all things else,
You mainly[3] were stirred up.

KING   O, for two special reasons,
Which may to you perhaps seem much unsinewed,
But yet to me they're strong. The queen his mother
Lives almost by his looks, and for myself—
My virtue or my plague, be it either which—
She is so conjunctive[4] to my life and soul
That, as the star moves not but in his sphere,
I could not but by her. The other motive
Why to a public count[5] I might not go
Is the great love the general gender[6] bear him,
Who, dipping all his faults in their affection,
Would, like the spring that turneth wood to stone,
Convert his gyves[7] to graces; so that my arrows,
Too slightly timbered for so loud a wind,
Would have reverted to my bow again,
And not where I had aimed them.

LAERTES   And so have I a noble father lost,
A sister driven into desp'rate terms,[8]
Whose worth, if praises may go back again,[9]
Stood challenger on mount[10] of all the age
For her perfections. But my revenge will come.

KING   Break not your sleeps for that. You must not think
That we are made of stuff so flat and dull
That we can let our beard be shook with danger,

---

[1] *feats* deeds   [2] *capital* punishable by death   [3] *mainly* powerfully   [4] *conjunctive* closely united   [5] *count* trial, accounting   [6] *general gender* common people   [7] *gyves* fetters   [8] *terms* circumstances   [9] *back again* i.e. to her better circumstances   [10] *on mount* on a height

And think it pastime. You shortly shall hear more.
I loved your father, and we love ourself,
And that, I hope, will teach you to imagine—

(*Enter a* MESSENGER *with letters*)

How now? What news?
MESSENGER   Letters, my lord, from Hamlet:
These to your majesty, this to the queen.
KING   From Hamlet? Who brought them?
MESSENGER   Sailors, my lord, they say; I saw them not.
They were given me by Claudio; he received them
Of him that brought them.
KING   Laertes, you shall hear them.—
Leave us.

(*Exit* MESSENGER)

(*Reads*)   "High and mighty, you shall know I am set naked [11]
on your kingdom. To-morrow shall I beg leave to see your kingly
eyes; when I shall (first asking your pardon thereunto) recount
the occasion of my sudden and more strange return.   Hamlet."
What should this mean? Are all the rest come back?
Or is it some abuse,[12] and no such thing?
LAERTES   Know you the hand?
KING   'Tis Hamlet's character.[13] "Naked"!
And in a postscript here, he says "alone."
Can you devise[14] me?
LAERTES   I am lost in it, my lord. But let him come.
It warms the very sickness in my heart
That I shall live and tell him to his teeth,
"Thus diddest thou."
KING   If it be so, Laertes,
(As how should it be so? how otherwise?)
Will you be ruled by me?
LAERTES   Ay, my lord,
So you will not o'errule me to a peace.
KING   To thine own peace. If he be now returned,
As checking at[15] his voyage, and that he means
No more to undertake it, I will work him

---

[11] *naked* destitute   [12] *abuse* imposture   [13] *character* handwriting   [14] *devise*
explain to   [15] *checking at* turning aside from (like a falcon turning from its
quarry for other prey)

To an exploit now ripe in my device,
Under the which he shall not choose but fall;
And for his death no wind of blame shall breathe,
But even his mother shall uncharge the practice[16]
And call it accident.

LAERTES   My lord, I will be ruled;
The rather if you could devise it so
That I might be the organ.[17]

KING   It falls right.
You have been talked of since your travel much,
And that in Hamlet's hearing, for a quality
Wherein they say you shine. Your sum of parts
Did not together pluck such envy from him
As did that one, and that, in my regard,
Of the unworthiest siege.[18]

LAERTES   What part is that, my lord?

KING   A very riband [19] in the cap of youth,
Yet needful too, for youth no less becomes
The light and careless livery[20] that it wears
Than settled age his sables[21] and his weeds,[22]
Importing health[23] and graveness. Two months since
Here was a gentleman of Normandy.
I have seen myself, and served against, the French,
And they can well [24] on horseback, but this gallant
Had witchcraft in't. He grew unto his seat,
And to such wondrous doing brought his horse
As had he been incorpsed [25] and demi-natured [26]
With the brave beast. So far he topped [27] my thought[28]
That I, in forgery[29] of shapes and tricks,
Come short of what he did.

LAERTES   A Norman was't?

KING   A Norman.

LAERTES   Upon my life, Lamord.

KING   The very same.

LAERTES   I know him well. He is the brooch[30] indeed

---

16 *uncharge the practice* acquit the stratagem of being a plot   17 *organ* instrument   18 *siege* seat, rank   19 *riband* decoration   20 *livery* distinctive attire   21 *sables* dignified robes richly furred with sable   22 *weeds* distinctive garments   23 *health* welfare, prosperity   24 *can well* can perform well   25 *incorpsed* made one body   26 *demi-natured* made sharer of nature half and half (as man shares with horse in the centaur)   27 *topped* excelled   28 *thought* imagination of possibilities   29 *forgery* invention   30 *brooch* ornament

And gem of all the nation.

KING   He made confession[31] of you,
And gave you such a masterly report
For art and exercise in your defense,
And for your rapier most especial,
That he cried out 'twould be a sight indeed
If one could match you. The scrimers[32] of their nation
He swore had neither motion, guard, nor eye,
If you opposed them. Sir, this report of his
Did Hamlet so envenom with his envy
That he could nothing do but wish and beg
Your sudden coming o'er to play with you.
Now, out of this—

LAERTES   What out of this, my lord?

KING   Laertes, was your father dear to you?
Or are you like the painting of a sorrow,
A face without a heart?

LAERTES   Why ask you this?

KING   Not that I think you did not love your father,
But that I know love is begun by time,
And that I see, in passages of proof,[33]
Time qualifies[34] the spark and fire of it.
There lives within the very flame of love
A kind of wick or snuff [35] that will abate it,
And nothing is at a like goodness still,[36]
For goodness, growing to a plurisy,[37]
Dies in his own too-much. That we would do
We should do when we would, for this "would" changes,
And hath abatements and delays as many
As there are tongues, are hands, are accidents,
And then this "should" is like a spendthrift sigh,
That hurts[38] by easing. But to the quick[39] o' th' ulcer—
Hamlet comes back; what would you undertake
To show yourself your father's son in deed
More than in words?

LAERTES   To cut his throat i' th' church!

---

31 *made confession* admitted the rival accomplishments   32 *scrimers* fencers
33 *passages of proof* incidents of experience   34 *qualifies* weakens   35 *snuff*
unconsumed portion of the burned wick   36 *still* always   37 *plurisy* excess
38 *hurts* i.e. shortens life by drawing blood from the heart (as was believed)
39 *quick* sensitive flesh

KING　No place indeed should murder sanctuarize;[40]
　　Revenge should have no bounds. But, good Laertes,
　　Will you do this? Keep close within your chamber.
　　Hamlet returned shall know you are come home.
　　We'll put on[41] those shall praise your excellence
　　And set a double varnish on the fame
　　The Frenchman gave you, bring you in fine[42] together
　　And wager on your heads. He, being remiss,[43]
　　Most generous, and free from all contriving,
　　Will not peruse[44] the foils, so that with ease,
　　Or with a little shuffling, you may choose
　　A sword unbated,[45] and, in a pass of practice,[46]
　　Requite him for your father.

LAERTES　　　　　　　　　　I will do't,
　　And for that purpose I'll anoint my sword.
　　I bought an unction[47] of a mountebank,[48]
　　So mortal that, but dip a knife in it,
　　Where it draws blood no cataplasm[49] so rare,
　　Collected from all simples[50] that have virtue
　　Under the moon, can save the thing from death
　　That is but scratched withal.[51] I'll touch my point
　　With this contagion, that, if I gall [52] him slightly,
　　It may be death.

KING　　　　　　　Let's further think of this,
　　Weigh what convenience both of time and means
　　May fit us to our shape.[53] If this should fail,
　　And that our drift[54] look[55] through our bad performance,
　　'Twere better not assayed. Therefore this project
　　Should have a back or second, that might hold
　　If this did blast in proof.[56] Soft, let me see.
　　We'll make a solemn wager on your cunnings—
　　I ha't!
　　When in your motion you are hot and dry—
　　As make your bouts more violent to that end—
　　And that he calls for drink, I'll have preferred [57] him
　　A chalice for the nonce,[58] whereon but sipping,

---

[40] *sanctuarize* protect from punishment, give sanctuary to　　[41] *put on* instigate
[42] *in fine* finally　　[43] *remiss* negligent　　[44] *peruse* scan　　[45] *unbated* not blunted
[46] *pass of practice* thrust made effective by trickery　　[47] *unction* ointment
[48] *mountebank* quack-doctor　　[49] *cataplasm* poultice　　[50] *simples* herbs　　[51] *withal*
with it　　[52] *gall* scratch　　[53] *shape* plan　　[54] *drift* intention　　[55] *look* show
[56] *blast in proof* burst during trial (like a faulty cannon)　　[57] *preferred* offered
[58] *nonce* occasion

If he by chance escape your venomed stuck,[59]
Our purpose may hold there.—But stay, what noise?

(*Enter* QUEEN)

QUEEN   One woe doth tread upon another's heel,
So fast they follow. Your sister 's drowned, Laertes.
LAERTES   Drowned! O, where?
QUEEN   There is a willow grows askant[60] the brook,
That shows his hoar[61] leaves in the glassy stream.
Therewith fantastic garlands did she make
Of crowflowers, nettles, daisies, and long purples,
That liberal [62] shepherds give a grosser name,
But our cold maids do dead men's fingers call them.
There on the pendent boughs her crownet[63] weeds
Clamb'ring to hang, an envious sliver broke,
When down her weedy trophies and herself
Fell in the weeping brook. Her clothes spread wide,
And mermaid-like awhile they bore her up,
Which time she chanted snatches of old lauds,[64]
As one incapable of [65] her own distress,
Or like a creature native and indued [66]
Unto that element. But long it could not be
Till that her garments, heavy with their drink,
Pulled the poor wretch from her melodious lay
To muddy death.
LAERTES   Alas, then she is drowned?
QUEEN   Drowned, drowned.
LAERTES   Too much of water hast thou, poor Ophelia,
And therefore I forbid my tears; but yet
It is our trick;[67] nature her custom holds,
Let shame say what it will. When these are gone,
The woman[68] will be out. Adieu, my lord.
I have a speech o' fire, that fain would blaze
But that this folly drowns it.

(*Exit*)

KING   Let's follow, Gertrude.
How much I had to do to calm his rage!

---

[59] *stuck* thrust   [60] *askant* alongside   [61] *hoar* grey   [62] *liberal* free-spoken, licentious   [63] *crownet* coronet   [64] *lauds* hymns   [65] *incapable of* insensible to   [66] *indued* endowed   [67] *trick* way (i.e. to shed tears when sorrowful) [68] *woman* unmanly part of nature.

Now fear I this will give it start again;
Therefore let's follow.

(*Exeunt*)

ACT V

Scene I

A churchyard

(*Enter two* CLOWNS[1])

CLOWN   Is she to be buried in Christian burial [2] when she willfully seeks her own salvation?

OTHER   I tell thee she is. Therefore make her grave straight.[3] The crowner[4] hath sate on her, and finds it Christian burial.

CLOWN   How can that be, unless she drowned herself in her own defense?

OTHER   Why, 'tis found so.

CLOWN   It must be *se offendendo*;[5] it cannot be else. For here lies the point: if I drown myself wittingly, it argues an act, and an act hath three branches—it is to act, to do, and to perform. Argal,[6] she drowned herself wittingly.

OTHER   Nay, but hear you, Goodman Delver.[7]

CLOWN   Give me leave. Here lies the water—good. Here stands the man—good. If the man go to this water and drown himself, it is, will he nill he,[8] he goes, mark you that. But if the water come to him and drown him, he drowns not himself. Argal, he that is not guilty of his own death shortens not his own life.

OTHER   But is this law?

CLOWN   Ay marry, is't—crowner's quest[9] law.

OTHER   Will you ha' the truth on't? If this had not been a gentlewoman, she should have been buried out o' Christian burial.

CLOWN   Why, there thou say'st.[10] And the more pity that great folk should have count'nance[11] in this world to drown or hang themselves more than their even-Christen.[12] Come, my spade. There

---

[1] *Clowns* rustics   [2] *in Christian burial* in consecrated ground with the prescribed service of the Church (a burial denied to suicides)   [3] *straight* straightway, at once   [4] *crowner* coroner   [5] *se offendendo* a clownish transformation of *"se defendendo,"* "in self-defense"   [6] *Argal* for *"ergo,"* "therefore"   [7] *Delver* Digger   [8] *will he nill he* willy-nilly   [9] *quest* inquest   [10] *thou say'st* you have it right   [11] *count'nance* privilege   [12] *even-Christen* fellow Christian

is no ancient gentlemen but gard'ners, ditchers, and grave-makers. They hold up Adam's profession.

OTHER   Was he a gentleman?

CLOWN   'A was the first that ever bore arms.

OTHER   Why, he had none.[13]

CLOWN   What, art a heathen? How dost thou understand the Scripture? The Scripture says Adam digged. Could he dig without arms? I'll put another question to thee. If thou answerest me not to the purpose, confess thyself—

OTHER   Go to.

CLOWN   What is he that builds stronger than either the mason, the shipwright, or the carpenter?

OTHER   The gallows-maker, for that frame outlives a thousand tenants.

CLOWN   I like thy wit well, in good faith. The gallows does well. But how does it well? It does well to those that do ill. Now thou dost ill to say the gallows is built stronger than the church. Argal, the gallows may do well to thee. To't again, come.

OTHER   Who builds stronger than a mason, a shipwright, or a carpenter?

CLOWN   Ay, tell me that, and unyoke.[14]

OTHER   Marry, now I can tell.

CLOWN   To't.

OTHER   Mass,[15] I cannot tell.

CLOWN   Cudgel thy brains no more about it, for your dull ass will not mend his pace with beating. And when you are asked this question next, say "a grave-maker." The houses he makes last till doomsday. Go, get thee in, and fetch me a stoup[16] of liquor.

(*Exit* OTHER CLOWN)

(*Enter* HAMLET *and* HORATIO [*as* CLOWN *digs and sings*])

Song

> In youth when I did love, did love,
>   Methought it was very sweet
> To contract—O—the time for—a—my behove,[17]
>   O, methought there—a—was nothing—a—meet.

HAMLET   Has this fellow no feeling of his business, that 'a sings at grave-making?

---

[13] *had none* i.e. had no gentleman's coat of arms   [14] *unyoke* i.e. unharness your powers of thought after a good day's work   [15] *Mass* by the Mass   [16] *stoup* large mug   [17] *behove* behoof, benefit

HORATIO   Custom hath made it in him a property[18] of easiness.[19]

HAMLET   'Tis e'en so. The hand of little employment hath the daintier sense.[20]

CLOWN

Song

> But age with his stealing steps
>   Hath clawed me in his clutch,
> And hath shipped me intil [21] the land,
>   As if I had never been such.

(Throws up a skull)

HAMLET   That skull had a tongue in it, and could sing once. How the knave jowls[22] it to the ground, as if 'twere Cain's jawbone, that did the first murder! This might be the pate of a politician,[23] which this ass now o'erreaches;[24] one that would circumvent God, might it not?

HORATIO   It might, my lord.

HAMLET   Or of a courtier, which could say "Good morrow, sweet lord! How dost thou, sweet lord?" This might be my Lord Such-a-one, that praised my Lord Such-a-one's horse when 'a meant to beg it, might it not?

HORATIO   Ay, my lord.

HAMLET   Why, e'en so, and now my Lady Worm's, chapless,[25] and knocked about the mazzard [26] with a sexton's spade. Here's fine revolution, an we had the trick to see't. Did these bones cost no more the breeding but to play at loggets[27] with 'em? Mine ache to think on't.

CLOWN

Song

> A pickaxe and a spade, a spade,
>   For and [28] a shrouding sheet;
> O, a pit of clay for to be made
>   For such a guest is meet.

(Throws up another skull)

---

[18] *property* peculiarity   [19] *easiness* easy acceptability   [20] *daintier sense* more delicate feeling (because the hand is less calloused)   [21] *intil* into   [22] *jowls* hurls   [23] *politician* crafty schemer   [24] *o'erreaches* gets the better of (with a play upon the literal meaning)   [25] *chapless* lacking the lower chap or jaw   [26] *mazzard* head   [27] *loggets* small pieces of wood thrown in a game   [28] *For and* and

HAMLET   There's another. Why may not that be the skull of a lawyer? Where be his quiddities[29] now, his quillities,[30] his cases, his
tenures,[31] and his tricks? Why does he suffer this mad knave now
to knock him about the sconce[32] with a dirty shovel, and will not
tell him of his action of battery? Hum! This fellow might be in's
time a great buyer of land, with his statutes, his recognizances,[33]
his fines,[34] his double vouchers,[35] his recoveries. Is this the fine[36]
of his fines, and the recovery of his recoveries, to have his fine
pate full of fine dirt? Will his vouchers vouch him no more of his
purchases, and double ones too, than the length and breadth of
a pair of indentures? [37] The very conveyances[38] of his lands will
scarcely lie in this box, and must th' inheritor himself have no
more, ha?

HORATIO   Not a jot more, my lord.

HAMLET   Is not parchment made of sheepskins?

HORATIO   Ay, my lord, and of calveskins too.

HAMLET   They are sheep and calves which seek out assurance in
that. I will speak to this fellow. Whose grave 's this, sirrah?

CLOWN   Mine, sir.

   (*Sings*)   O, a pit of clay for to be made
               For such a guest is meet.

HAMLET   I think it be thine indeed, for thou liest in't.

CLOWN   You lie out on't, sir, and therefore 'tis not yours. For my
part, I do not lie in't, yet it is mine.

HAMLET   Thou dost lie in't, to be in't and say it is thine. 'Tis for
the dead, not for the quick;[39] therefore thou liest.

CLOWN   'Tis a quick lie, sir; 'twill away again from me to you.

HAMLET   What man dost thou dig it for?

CLOWN   For no man, sir.

HAMLET   What woman then?

CLOWN   For none neither.

HAMLET   Who is to be buried in't?

CLOWN   One that was a woman, sir; but, rest her soul, she's dead.

HAMLET   How absolute[40] the knave is! We must speak by the

---

[29] *quiddities* subtleties (from scholastic *"quidditas,"* meaning the distinctive
nature of anything)   [30] *quillities* nice distinctions   [31] *tenures* holdings of
property   [32] *sconce* head   [33] *statutes, recognizances* legal documents or bonds
acknowledging debt   [34] *fines, recoveries* modes of converting estate tail into
fee simple   [35] *vouchers* persons vouched or called on to warrant a title
[36] *fine* end (introducing a word play involving four meanings of "fine")
[37] *pair of indentures* deed or legal agreement in duplicate   [38] *conveyances*
deeds   [39] *quick* living   [40] *absolute* positive

card,[41] or equivocation[42] will undo us. By the Lord, Horatio, this three years I have taken note of it, the age is grown so picked [43] that the toe of the peasant comes so near the heel of the courtier he galls[44] his kibe.[45]—How long hast thou been a grave-maker?

CLOWN   Of all the days i' th' year, I came to't that day that our last king Hamlet overcame Fortinbras.

HAMLET   How long is that since?

CLOWN   Cannot you tell that? Every fool can tell that. It was the very day that young Hamlet was born—he that is mad, and sent into England.

HAMLET   Ay, marry, why was he sent into England?

CLOWN   Why, because 'a was mad. 'A shall recover his wits there; or, if 'a do not, 'tis no great matter there.

HAMLET   Why?

CLOWN   'Twill not be seen in him there. There the men are as mad as he.

HAMLET   How came he mad?

CLOWN   Very strangely, they say.

HAMLET   How strangely?

CLOWN   Faith, e'en with losing his wits.

HAMLET   Upon what ground?

CLOWN   Why, here in Denmark. I have been sexton here, man and boy, thirty years.

HAMLET   How long will a man lie i' th' earth ere he rot?

CLOWN   Faith, if 'a be not rotten before 'a die (as we have many pocky[46] corses now-a-days that will scarce hold the laying in), 'a will last you some eight year or nine year. A tanner will last you nine year.

HAMLET   Why he more than another?

CLOWN   Why, sir, his hide is so tanned with his trade that 'a will keep out water a great while, and your water is a sore decayer of your whoreson dead body. Here's a skull now hath lien you i' th' earth three-and-twenty years.

HAMLET   Whose was it?

CLOWN   A whoreson mad fellow's it was. Whose do you think it was?

HAMLET   Nay, I know not.

---

[41] *by the card* by the card on which the points of the mariner's compass are marked, absolutely to the point   [42] *equivocation* ambiguity   [43] *picked* refined, spruce   [44] *galls* chafes   [45] *kibe* chilblain   [46] *pocky* rotten (literally, corrupted by pox, or syphilis)

CLOWN   A pestilence on him for a mad rogue! 'A poured a flagon of Rhenish[47] on my head once. This same skull, sir, was—sir— Yorick's skull, the king's jester.

HAMLET   This?

CLOWN   E'en that.

HAMLET   Let me see. (*Takes the skull.*) Alas, poor Yorick! I knew him, Horatio, a fellow of infinite jest, of most excellent fancy. He hath borne me on his back a thousand times. And now how abhorred in my imagination it is! My gorge rises at it. Here hung those lips that I have kissed I know not how oft. Where be your gibes now? Your gambols, your songs, your flashes of merriment that were wont to set the table on a roar? Not one now to mock your own grinning? Quite chapfall'n?[48] Now get you to my lady's chamber, and tell her, let her paint an inch thick, to this favor[49] she must come. Make her laugh at that. Prithee, Horatio, tell me one thing.

HORATIO   What's that, my lord?

HAMLET   Dost thou think Alexander looked o' this fashion i' th' earth?

HORATIO   E'en so.

HAMLET   And smelt so? Pah!

(*Puts down the skull*)

HORATIO   E'en so, my lord.

HAMLET   To what base uses we may return, Horatio! Why may not imagination trace the noble dust of Alexander till 'a find it stopping a bunghole?

HORATIO   'Twere to consider too curiously,[50] to consider so.

HAMLET   No, faith, not a jot, but to follow him thither with modesty[51] enough, and likelihood to lead it; as thus: Alexander died, Alexander was buried, Alexander returneth to dust; the dust is earth; of earth we make loam; and why of that loam whereto he was converted might they not stop a beer barrel?
Imperious[52] Caesar, dead and turned to clay,
Might stop a hole to keep the wind away.
O, that that earth which kept the world in awe
Should patch a wall t' expel the winter's flaw![53]

---

[47] *Rhenish* Rhine wine   [48] *chapfall'n* lacking the lower chap, or jaw (with a play on the sense "down in the mouth," "dejected")   [49] *favor* countenance, aspect   [50] *curiously* minutely   [51] *modesty* moderation   [52] *Imperious* imperial   [53] *flaw* gust of wind

But soft, but soft awhile! Here comes the king—

(*Enter* KING, QUEEN, LAERTES, *and the* CORSE [*with* LORDS *attendant and a* DOCTOR OF DIVINITY *as* PRIEST])

The queen, the courtiers. Who is this they follow?
And with such maimèd rites? This doth betoken
The corse they follow did with desp'rate hand
Fordo[54] it[55] own life. 'Twas of some estate.[56]
Couch[57] we awhile, and mark.

(*Retires with* HORATIO)

LAERTES   What ceremony else?
HAMLET   That is Laertes,
  A very noble youth. Mark.
LAERTES   What ceremony else?
DOCTOR   Her obsequies have been as far enlarged
  As we have warranty. Her death was doubtful,
  And, but that great command o'ersways the order,
  She should in ground unsanctified have lodged
  Till the last trumpet. For charitable prayers,
  Shards,[58] flints, and pebbles should be thrown on her.
  Yet here she is allowed her virgin crants,[59]
  Her maiden strewments,[60] and the bringing home[61]
  Of bell and burial.
LAERTES   Must there no more be done?
DOCTOR   No more be done.
  We should profane the service of the dead
  To sing a requiem and such rest to her
  As to peace-parted souls.
LAERTES   Lay her i' th' earth,
  And from her fair and unpolluted flesh
  May violets spring! I tell thee, churlish priest,
  A minist'ring angel shall my sister be
  When thou liest howling.
HAMLET   What, the fair Ophelia?
QUEEN   Sweets to the sweet! Farewell.

(*Scatters flowers*)

I hoped thou shouldst have been my Hamlet's wife.

---

[54] *Fordo* destroy   [55] *it* its   [56] *estate* rank   [57] *Couch* hide   [58] *Shards* broken pieces of pottery   [59] *crants* garland   [60] *strewments* strewings of the grave with flowers   [61] *bringing home* laying to rest

I thought thy bride-bed to have decked, sweet maid,
And not have strewed thy grave.

LAERTES   O, treble woe
Fall ten times treble on that cursèd head
Whose wicked deed thy most ingenious[62] sense
Deprived thee of! Hold off the earth awhile,
Till I have caught her once more in mine arms.

(Leaps in the grave)

Now pile your dust upon the quick and dead
Till of this flat a mountain you have made
T' o'ertop old Pelion[63] or the skyish head
Of blue Olympus.

HAMLET *(coming forward)*   What is he whose grief
Bears such an emphasis? whose phrase of sorrow
Conjures[64] the wand'ring stars,[65] and makes them stand
Like wonder-wounded hearers? This is I,
Hamlet the Dane.

(Leaps in after LAERTES)

LAERTES   The devil take thy soul!

(Grapples with him)

HAMLET   Thou pray'st not well.
I prithee take thy fingers from my throat,
For, though I am not splenitive[66] and rash,
Yet have I in me something dangerous,
Which let thy wisdom fear. Hold off thy hand.

KING   Pluck them asunder.

QUEEN   Hamlet, Hamlet!

ALL   Gentlemen!

HORATIO   Good my lord, be quiet.

(ATTENDANTS part them, and they come out of the grave)

HAMLET   Why, I will fight with him upon this theme
Until my eyelids will no longer wag.

QUEEN   O my son, what theme?

---

[62] *most ingenious* of quickest apprehension   [63] *Pelion* a mountain in Thessaly,
like Olympus and also Ossa (the allusion being to the war in which the Titans
fought the gods and attempted to heap Ossa and Olympus on Pelion, or
Pelion and Ossa on Olympus, in order to scale heaven)   [64] *Conjures* charms,
puts a spell upon   [65] *wand'ring stars* planets   [66] *splenitive* of fiery temper
(the spleen being considered the seat of anger)

HAMLET   I loved Ophelia. Forty thousand brothers
   Could not with all their quantity of love
   Make up my sum. What wilt thou do for her?
KING   O, he is mad, Laertes.
QUEEN   For love of God, forbear him.
HAMLET   'Swounds, show me what thou't do.
   Woo't [67] weep? woo't fight? woo't fast? woo't tear thyself?
   Woo't drink up esill? [68] eat a crocodile?
   I'll do't. Dost thou come here to whine?
   To outface me with leaping in her grave?
   Be buried quick[69] with her, and so will I.
   And if thou prate of mountains, let them throw
   Millions of acres on us, till our ground,
   Singeing his pate against the burning zone,
   Make Ossa like a wart! Nay, an thou'lt mouth,
   I'll rant as well as thou.
QUEEN   This is mere[70] madness;
   And thus a while the fit will work on him.
   Anon, as patient as the female dove
   When that her golden couplets[71] are disclosed,[72]
   His silence will sit drooping.
HAMLET   Hear you, sir.
   What is the reason that you use me thus?
   I loved you ever. But it is no matter.
   Let Hercules himself do what he may,
   The cat will mew, and dog will have his day.
KING   I pray thee, good Horatio, wait upon him.

(*Exit* HAMLET *and* HORATIO)

(*To* LAERTES)

Strengthen your patience in[73] our last night's speech.
We'll put the matter to the present push.[74]
Good Gertrude, set some watch over your son.—
This grave shall have a living monument.
An hour of quiet shortly shall we see;
Till then in patience our proceeding be.

(*Exeunt*)

---

[67] *Woo't* wilt (thou)   [68] *esill* vinegar   [69] *quick* alive   [70] *mere* absolute
[71] *couplets* pair of fledglings   [72] *disclosed* hatched   [73] *in* by calling to mind
[74] *present push* immediate trial

Act V, Scene II

The hall of the castle

(*Enter* HAMLET *and* HORATIO)

HAMLET   So much for this, sir; now shall you see the other.
    You do remember all the circumstance?
HORATIO   Remember it, my lord!
HAMLET   Sir, in my heart there was a kind of fighting
    That would not let me sleep. Methought I lay
    Worse than the mutines[1] in the bilboes.[2] Rashly,
    And praised be rashness for it—let us know,
    Our indiscretion sometime serves us well
    When our deep plots do pall,[3] and that should learn us
    There's a divinity that shapes our ends,
    Rough-hew[4] them how we will—
HORATIO   That is most certain.
HAMLET   Up from my cabin,
    My sea-gown scarfed about me, in the dark
    Groped I to find out them, had my desire,
    Fingered [5] their packet, and in fine[6] withdrew
    To mine own room again, making so bold,
    My fears forgetting manners, to unseal
    Their grand commission; where I found, Horatio—
    Ah, royal knavery!—an exact command,
    Larded [7] with many several sorts of reasons,
    Importing[8] Denmark's health, and England's too,
    With, ho! such bugs[9] and goblins in my life,[10]
    That on the supervise,[11] no leisure bated,[12]
    No, not to stay the grinding of the axe,
    My head should be struck off.
HORATIO   Is't possible?
HAMLET   Here's the commission; read it at more leisure.
    But wilt thou hear me how I did proceed?
HORATIO   I beseech you.
HAMLET   Being thus benetted round with villainies,
    Or[13] I could make a prologue to my brains,
    They had begun the play. I sat me down,

---

[1] *mutines* mutineers [2] *bilboes* fetters [3] *pall* fail [4] *Rough-hew* shape roughly in trial form [5] *Fingered* filched [6] *in fine* finally [7] *Larded* enriched [8] *Importing* relating to [9] *bugs* bugbears [10] *in my life* to be encountered as dangers if I should be allowed to live [11] *supervise* perusal [12] *bated* deducted, allowed [13] *Or* ere

Devised a new commission, wrote it fair.
I once did hold it, as our statists[14] do,
A baseness to write fair,[15] and labored much
How to forget that learning, but, sir, now
It did me yeoman's service.[16] Wilt thou know
Th' effect[17] of what I wrote?

HORATIO   Ay, good my lord.

HAMLET   An earnest conjuration from the king,
As England was his faithful tributary,
As love between them like the palm might flourish,
As peace should still her wheaten garland [18] wear
And stand a comma[19] 'tween their amities,
And many such-like as's of great charge,[20]
That on the view and knowing of these contents,
Without debatement further, more or less,
He should the bearers put to sudden death,
Not shriving time[21] allowed.

HORATIO   How was this sealed?

HAMLET   Why, even in that was heaven ordinant.[22]
I had my father's signet in my purse,
Which was the model [23] of that Danish seal,
Folded the writ up in the form of th' other,
Subscribed it, gave't th' impression,[24] placed it safely,
The changeling never known. Now, the next day
Was our sea-fight, and what to this was sequent[25]
Thou know'st already.

HORATIO   So Guildenstern and Rosencrantz go to't.

HAMLET   Why, man, they did make love to this employment.
They are not near my conscience; their defeat
Does by their own insinuation[26] grow.
'Tis dangerous when the baser nature comes
Between the pass[27] and fell [28] incensèd points
Of mighty opposites.

---

[14] *statists* statesmen   [15] *fair* with professional clarity (like a clerk or a scrivener, not like a gentleman)   [16] *yeoman's service* stout service such as yeomen footsoldiers gave as archers   [17] *effect* purport   [18] *wheaten garland* adornment of fruitful agriculture   [19] *comma* connective (because it indicates continuity of thought in a sentence)   [20] *charge* burden (with a double meaning to fit a play that makes *as's* into "asses"   [21] *shriving time* time for confession and absolution   [22] *ordinant* controlling   [23] *model* counterpart   [24] *impression* i.e. of the signet   [25] *sequent* subsequent   [26] *insinuation* intrusion   [27] *pass* thrust   [28] *fell* fierce

HORATIO   Why, what a king is this!

HAMLET   Does it not, think thee, stand [29] me now upon—
He that hath killed my king, and whored my mother,
Popped in between th' election[30] and my hopes,
Thrown out his angle[31] for my proper[32] life,
And with such coz'nage[33]—is't not perfect conscience
To quit[34] him with this arm? And is't not to be damned
To let this canker[35] of our nature come
In further evil?

HORATIO   It must be shortly known to him from England
What is the issue of the business there.

HAMLET   It will be short; the interim is mine,
And a man's life 's no more than to say "one."
But I am very sorry, good Horatio,
That to Laertes I forgot myself,
For by the image of my cause I see
The portraiture of his. I'll court his favors.
But sure the bravery[36] of his grief did put me
Into a tow'ring passion.

HORATIO   Peace, who comes here?

(*Enter* OSRIC, *a courtier*)

OSRIC   Your lordship is right welcome back to Denmark.

HAMLET   I humbly thank you, sir. (*aside to* HORATIO) Dost know
this waterfly?

HORATIO (*aside to* HAMLET)   No, my good lord.

HAMLET (*aside to* HORATIO)   Thy state is the more gracious, for
'tis a vice to know him. He hath much land, and fertile. Let a
beast be lord of beasts, and his crib shall stand at the king's
mess.[37] 'Tis a chough,[38] but, as I say, spacious in the possession
of dirt.

OSRIC   Sweet lord, if your lordship were at leisure, I should impart
a thing to you from his majesty.

HAMLET   I will receive it, sir, with all diligence of spirit. Put your
bonnet to his right use. 'Tis for the head.

OSRIC   I thank your lordship, it is very hot.

HAMLET   No, believe me, 'tis very cold; the wind is northerly.

OSRIC   It is indifferent[39] cold, my lord, indeed.

---

[29] *stand* rest incumbent   [30] *election* i.e. to the kingship (the Danish kingship
being elective)   [31] *angle* fishing line   [32] *proper* own   [33] *coz'nage* cozenage,
trickery   [34] *quit* repay   [35] *canker* cancer, ulcer   [36] *bravery* ostentatious display   [37] *mess* table   [38] *chough* jackdaw, chatterer   [39] *indifferent* somewhat

HAMLET   But yet methinks it is very sultry and hot for my complexion.[40]

OSRIC   Exceedingly, my lord; it is very sultry, as 'twere—I cannot tell how. But, my lord, his majesty bade me signify to you that 'a has laid a great wager on your head. Sir, this is the matter—

HAMLET   I beseech you remember.[41]

(HAMLET *moves him to put on his hat*)

OSRIC   Nay, good my lord; for mine ease,[42] in good faith. Sir, here is newly come to court Laertes—believe me, an absolute gentleman, full of most excellent differences,[43] of very soft society[44] and great showing.[45] Indeed, to speak feelingly[46] of him, he is the card [47] or calendar[48] of gentry,[49] for you shall find in him the continent[50] of what part a gentleman would see.

HAMLET   Sir, his definement[51] suffers no perdition[52] in you, though, I know, to divide him inventorially would dozy[53] th' arithmetic of memory, and yet but yaw[54] neither[55] in respect of [56] his quick sail. But, in the verity of extolment, I take him to be a soul of great article,[57] and his infusion[58] of such dearth[59] and rareness as, to make true diction of him, his semblable[60] is his mirror, and who else would trace[61] him, his umbrage,[62] nothing more.

OSRIC   Your lordship speaks most infallibly of him.

HAMLET   The concernancy,[63] sir? Why do we wrap the gentleman in our more rawer[64] breath?

OSRIC   Sir?

HORATIO   Is't not possible to understand in another tongue? You will to't,[65] sir, really.

HAMLET   What imports the nomination[66] of this gentleman?

OSRIC   Of Laertes?

---

[40] *complexion* temperament   [41] *remember* i.e. remember you have done all that courtesy demands   [42] *for mine ease* i.e. I keep my hat off just for comfort (a conventional polite phrase)   [43] *differences* differentiating characteristics, special qualities   [44] *soft society* gentle manners   [45] *great showing* noble appearance   [46] *feelingly* appropriately   [47] *card* map   [48] *calendar* guide   [49] *gentry* gentlemanliness   [50] *continent* all-containing embodiment (with an implication of geographical continent to go with *card*)   [51] *definement* definition   [52] *perdition* loss   [53] *dozy* dizzy, stagger   [54] *yaw* hold to a course unsteadily like a ship that steers wild   [55] *neither* for all that   [56] *in respect of* in comparison with   [57] *article* scope, importance   [58] *infusion* essence   [59] *dearth* scarcity   [60] *semblable* likeness (i.e. only true likeness)   [61] *trace* follow   [62] *umbrage* shadow   [63] *concernancy* relevance   [64] *rawer breath* cruder speech   [65] *to't* i.e. get to an understanding   [66] *nomination* mention

HORATIO (*aside to* HAMLET) His purse is empty already. All's golden words are spent.

HAMLET Of him, sir.

OSRIC I know you are not ignorant—

HAMLET I would you did, sir; yet, in faith, if you did, it would not much approve me.[67] Well, sir?

OSRIC You are not ignorant of what excellence Laertes is—

HAMLET I dare not confess that, lest I should compare[68] with him in excellence; but to know a man well were to know himself.

OSRIC I mean, sir, for his weapon; but in the imputation laid on him by them, in his meed [69] he's unfellowed.

HAMLET What's his weapon?

OSRIC Rapier and dagger.

HAMLET That's two of his weapons—but well.

OSRIC The king, sir, hath wagered with him six Barbary horses, against the which he has impawned,[70] as I take it, six French rapiers and poniards, with their assigns,[71] as girdle, hangers,[72] and so. Three of the carriages, in faith, are very dear to fancy,[73] very responsive[74] to the hilts, most delicate carriages, and of very liberal conceit.[75]

HAMLET What call you the carriages?

HORATIO (*aside to* HAMLET) I knew you must be edified by the margent[76] ere you had done.

OSRIC The carriages, sir, are the hangers.

HAMLET The phrase would be more germane to the matter if we could carry a cannon by our sides. I would it might be hangers till then. But on! Six Barbary horses against six French swords, their assigns, and three liberal-conceited carriages—that's the French bet against the Danish. Why is this all impawned, as you call it?

OSRIC The king, sir, hath laid, sir, that in a dozen passes between yourself and him he shall not exceed you three hits; he hath laid on twelve for nine, and it would come to immediate trial if your lordship would vouchsafe the answer.

HAMLET How if I answer no?

OSRIC I mean, my lord, the opposition of your person in trial.

---

[67] *approve me* be to my credit   [68] *compare* compete   [69] *meed* worth   [70] *impawned* staked   [71] *assigns* appurtenances   [72] *hangers* straps by which the sword hangs from the belt   [73] *dear to fancy* finely designed   [74] *responsive* corresponding closely   [75] *liberal conceit* tasteful design, refined conception   [76] *margent* margin (i.e. explanatory notes there printed)

HAMLET   Sir, I will walk here in the hall. If it please his majesty, it is the breathing time[77] of day with me. Let the foils be brought, the gentleman willing, and the king hold his purpose, I will win for him an[78] I can; if not, I will gain nothing but my shame and the odd hits.

OSRIC   Shall I redeliver you e'en so?

HAMLET   To this effect, sir, after what flourish your nature will.

OSRIC   I commend my duty to your lordship.

HAMLET   Your, yours. (*Exit* OSRIC) He does well to commend it himself; there are no tongues else for's turn.

HORATIO   This lapwing[79] runs away with the shell on his head.

HAMLET   'A did comply,[80] sir, with his dug[81] before 'a sucked it. Thus has he, and many more of the same bevy[82] that I know the drossy[83] age dotes on, only got the tune of the time and, out of an habit of encounter, a kind of yeasty collection, which carries them through and through the most fanned and winnowed [84] opinions; and do but blow them to their trial, the bubbles are out.

(*Enter a* LORD)

LORD   My lord, his majesty commended him to you by young Osric, who brings back to him that you attend him in the hall. He sends to know if your pleasure hold to play with Laertes, or that you will take longer time.

HAMLET   I am constant to my purposes; they follow the king's pleasure. If his fitness speaks, mine is ready; now or whensoever, provided I be so able as now.

LORD   The king and queen and all are coming down.

HAMLET   In happy time.[85]

LORD   The queen desires you to use some gentle entertainment[86] to Laertes before you fall to play.

HAMLET   She well instructs me.

(*Exit* LORD)

HORATIO   You will lose this wager, my lord.

HAMLET   I do not think so. Since he went into France I have been in continual practice. I shall win at the odds. But thou wouldst not think how ill all's here about my heart. But it is no matter.

---

[77] *breathing time* exercise hour   [78] *an* if   [79] *lapwing* a bird reputed to be so precocious as to run as soon as hatched   [80] *comply* observe formalities of courtesy   [81] *dug* mother's nipple   [82] *bevy* company   [83] *drossy* frivolous   [84] *fanned and winnowed* select and refined   [85] *In happy time* I am happy (a polite response)   [86] *entertainment* words of reception or greeting

HORATIO Nay, good my lord—

HAMLET It is but foolery, but it is such a kind of gaingiving[87] as would perhaps trouble a woman.

HORATIO If your mind dislike anything, obey it. I will forestall their repair hither and say you are not fit.

HAMLET Not a whit, we defy augury. There is special providence in the fall of a sparrow. If it be now, 'tis not to come; if it be not to come, it will be now; if it be not now, yet it will come. The readiness is all.[88] Since no man of aught he leaves knows, what is't to leave betimes? Let be.

A table prepared. Enter TRUMPETS, DRUMS, *and* OFFICERS *with cushions;* KING, QUEEN, OSRIC, *and all the* STATE, *with foils, daggers, and stoups of wine borne in; and* LAERTES

KING Come, Hamlet, come, and take this hand from me.

(*The* KING *puts* LAERTES' *hand into* HAMLET'S)

HAMLET Give me your pardon, sir. I have done you wrong,
But pardon't, as you are a gentleman.
This presence[89] knows, and you must needs have heard,
How I am punished with a sore distraction.
What I have done
That might your nature, honor, and exception[90]
Roughly awake, I here proclaim was madness.
Was't Hamlet wronged Laertes? Never Hamlet.
If Hamlet from himself be ta'en away,
And when he's not himself does wrong Laertes,
Then Hamlet does it not, Hamlet denies it.
Who does it then? His madness. If't be so,
Hamlet is of the faction[91] that is wronged;
His madness is poor Hamlet's enemy.
Sir, in this audience,
Let my disclaiming from a purposed evil
Free me so far in your most generous thoughts
That I have shot my arrow o'er the house
And hurt my brother.

LAERTES   I am satisfied in nature,[92]
Whose motive in this case should stir me most
To my revenge. But in my terms of honor[93]

---

[87] *gaingiving* misgiving   [88] *all* all that matters   [89] *presence* assembly   [90] *exception* disapproval   [91] *faction* body of persons taking a side in a contention   [92] *nature* natural feeling as a person   [93] *terms of honor* position as a man of honor

I stand aloof, and will no reconcilement
Till by some elder masters of known honor
I have a voice[94] and precedent of peace
To keep my name ungored.[95] But till that time
I do receive your offered love like love,
And will not wrong it.

HAMLET   I embrace it freely,
And will this brother's wager frankly play.
Give us the foils. Come on.

LAERTES   Come, one for me.

HAMLET   I'll be your foil,[96] Laertes. In mine ignorance
Your skill shall, like a star i' th' darkest night,
Stick fiery off [97] indeed.

LAERTES   You mock me, sir.

HAMLET   No, by this hand.

KING   Give them the foils, young Osric. Cousin Hamlet,
You know the wager?

HAMLET   Very well, my lord.
Your grace has laid the odds o' the' weaker side.

KING   I do not fear it, I have seen you both;
But since he is bettered, we have therefore odds.

LAERTES   This is too heavy; let me see another.

HAMLET   This likes me well. These foils have all a length?

Prepare to play

OSRIC   Ay, my good lord.

KING   Set me the stoups of wine upon that table.
If Hamlet give the first or second hit,
Or quit[98] in answer of the third exchange,
Let all the battlements their ordnance fire.
The king shall drink to Hamlet's better breath,
And in the cup an union[99] shall he throw
Richer than that which four successive kings
In Denmark's crown have worn. Give me the cups,
And let the kettle[100] to the trumpet speak,
The trumpet to the cannoneer without,
The cannons to the heavens, the heaven to earth,

---

[94] *voice* authoritative statement   [95] *ungored* uninjured   [96] *foil* setting that displays a jewel advantageously (with a play upon the meaning "weapon") [97] *Stick fiery off* show in brilliant relief   [98] *quit* repay by a hit   [99] *union* pearl   [100] *kettle* kettledrum

"Now the king drinks to Hamlet." Come, begin.

Trumpets the while

And you, the judges, bear a wary eye.
HAMLET   Come on, sir.
LAERTES   Come, my lord.

They play

HAMLET   One.
LAERTES   No.
HAMLET   Judgment?
OSRIC   A hit, a very palpable hit.

DRUM, TRUMPETS, *and* SHOT. *Flourish; a piece goes off*

LAERTES   Well, again.
KING   Stay, give me drink. Hamlet, this pearl is thine.
   Here's to thy health. Give him the cup.
HAMLET   I'll play this bout first; set it by awhile.
   Come. (*They play*) Another hit. What say you?
LAERTES   A touch, a touch; I do confess't.
KING   Our son shall win.
QUEEN   He's fat,[101] and scant of breath.
   Here, Hamlet, take my napkin,[102] rub thy brows.
   The queen carouses[103] to thy fortune, Hamlet.
HAMLET   Good madam!
KING   Gertrude, do not drink.
QUEEN   I will, my lord; I pray you pardon me.

Drinks

KING (*aside*)   It is the poisoned cup; it is too late.
HAMLET   I dare not drink yet, madam—by and by.
QUEEN   Come, let me wipe thy face.
LAERTES   My lord, I'll hit him now.
KING   I do not think't.
LAERTES (*aside*)   And yet it is almost against my conscience.
HAMLET   Come for the third, Laertes. You but dally.
   I pray you pass with your best violence;
   I am afeard you make a wanton[104] of me.

---

[101] *fat* not physically fit, out of training   [102] *napkin* handkerchief   [103] *carouses* drinks a toast   [104] *wanton* pampered child

LAERTES   Say you so? Come on.

They play

OSRIC   Nothing neither way.
LAERTES   Have at you now!

In scuffling they change rapiers, and both are wounded with the poisoned weapon

KING   Part them. They are incensed.
HAMLET   Nay, come—again!

The QUEEN *falls*

OSRIC   Look to the queen there, ho!
HORATIO   They bleed on both sides. How is it, my lord?
OSRIC   How is't, Laertes?
LAERTES   Why, as a woodcock[105] to mine own springe,[106] Osric.
  I am justly killed with mine own treachery.
HAMLET   How does the queen?
KING   She sounds[107] to see them bleed.
QUEEN   No, no, the drink, the drink! O my dear Hamlet!
  The drink, the drink! I am poisoned.

Dies

HAMLET   O villainy! Ho! let the door be locked.
  Treachery! Seek it out.

LAERTES *falls*

LAERTES   It is here, Hamlet. Hamlet, thou art slain;
  No med'cine in the world can do thee good.
  In thee there is not half an hour's life.
  The treacherous instrument is in thy hand,
  Unbated [108] and envenomed. The foul practice[109]
  Hath turned itself on me. Lo, here I lie,
  Never to rise again. Thy mother 's poisoned.
  I can no more. The king, the king 's to blame.
HAMLET   The point envenomed too?
  Then venom, to thy work.

Hurts the KING

ALL   Treason! treason!

---

[105] *woodcock* a bird reputed to be stupid and easily trapped   [106] *springe* trap
[107] *sounds* swoons   [108] *Unbated* unblunted   [109] *practice* stratagem

KING   O, yet defend me, friends. I am but hurt.

HAMLET   Here, thou incestuous, murd'rous, damnèd Dane,
Drink off this potion. Is thy union here?
Follow my mother.

KING *dies*

LAERTES   He is justly served.
It is a poison tempered [110] by himself.
Exchange forgiveness with me, noble Hamlet.
Mine and my father's death come not upon thee,
Nor thine on me!

Dies

HAMLET   Heaven make thee free of it! I follow thee.
I am dead, Horatio. Wretched queen, adieu!
You that look pale and tremble at this chance,
That are but mutes[111] or audience to this act,
Had I but time—as this fell sergeant,[112] Death,
Is strict in his arrest—O, I could tell you—
But let it be. Horatio, I am dead;
Thou livest; report me and my cause aright
To the unsatisfied.

HORATIO   Never believe it.
I am more an antique Roman than a Dane.
Here's yet some liquor left.

HAMLET   As th' art a man,
Give me the cup. Let go. By heaven, I'll ha't!
O God, Horatio, what a wounded name,
Things standing thus unknown, shall live behind me!
If thou didst ever hold me in thy heart,
Absent thee from felicity awhile,
And in this harsh world draw thy breath in pain,
To tell my story.

A march afar off

                    What warlike noise is this?

OSRIC   Young Fortinbras, with conquest come from Poland,
To the ambassadors of England gives
This warlike volley.

HAMLET   O, I die, Horatio!

---

[110] *tempered* mixed   [111] *mutes* actors in a play who speak no lines   [112] *sergeant* sheriff's officer

The potent poison quite o'ercrows[113] my spirit.
I cannot live to hear the news from England,
But I do prophesy th' election[114] lights
On Fortinbras. He has my dying voice.[115]
So tell him, with th' occurrents,[116] more and less,
Which have solicited [117]—the rest is silence.

Dies *displaying superior moral qualities* *dignity, worthy*

HORATIO   Now cracks a noble heart. Good night, sweet prince,
And flights of angels sing thee to thy rest!

March within

Why does the drum come hither?

(*Enter* FORTINBRAS, *with the* AMBASSADORS [*and with his train of* DRUM, COLORS, *and* ATTENDANTS])

FORTINBRAS   Where is this sight?
HORATIO   What is it you would see?
If aught of woe or wonder, cease your search.
FORTINBRAS   This quarry[118] cries on[119] havoc.[120] O proud Death,
What feast is toward [121] in thine eternal cell
That thou so many princes at a shot
So bloodily hast struck?
AMBASSADOR   The sight is dismal;
And our affairs from England come too late.
The ears are senseless that should give us hearing
To tell him his commandment is fulfilled,
That Rosencrantz and Guildenstern are dead.
Where should we have our thanks?
HORATIO   Not from his mouth,
Had it th' ability of life to thank you.
He never gave commandment for their death.
But since, so jump[122] upon this bloody question,
You from the Polack wars, and you from England,
Are here arrived, give order that these bodies
High on a stage[123] be placèd to the view,

---

113 *o'ercrows* triumphs over (like a victor in a cockfight)   114 *election* i.e. to the throne   115 *voice* vote   116 *occurrents* occurrences   117 *solicited* incited, provoked   118 *quarry* pile of dead (literally, of dead deer gathered after the hunt)   119 *cries on* proclaims loudly   120 *havoc* indiscriminate killing and destruction such as would follow the order "havoc," or "pillage," given to an army   121 *toward* forthcoming   122 *jump* precisely   123 *stage* platform

And let me speak to th' yet unknowing world
How these things came about. So shall you hear
Of carnal, bloody, and unnatural acts,
Of accidental judgments,[124] casual [125] slaughters,
Of deaths put on[126] by cunning and forced cause,
And, in this upshot, purposes mistook
Fall'n on th' inventors' heads. All this can I
Truly deliver.

FORTINBRAS   Let us haste to hear it,
And call the noblest to the audience.
For me, with sorrow I embrace my fortune.
I have some rights of memory[127] in this kingdom,
Which now to claim my vantage[128] doth invite me.

HORATIO   Of that I shall have also cause to speak,
And from his mouth whose voice will draw on more.[129]
But let this same be presently[130] performed,
Even while men's minds are wild, lest more mischance
On[131] plots and errors happen.

FORTINBRAS   Let four captains
Bear Hamlet like a soldier to the stage,
For he was likely, had he been put on,[132]
To have proved most royal; and for his passage[133]
The soldiers' music and the rites of war
Speak loudly for him.
Take up the bodies. Such a sight as this
Becomes the field, but here shows much amiss.
Go, bid the soldiers shoot.

(*Exeunt* [*marching; after the which a peal of ordinance are shot off*])

---

[124] *judgments* retributions   [125] *casual* not humanly planned (reinforcing *accidental*)   [126] *put on* instigated   [127] *of memory* traditional and kept in mind   [128] *vantage* advantageous opportunity   [129] *more* i.e. more voices, or votes, for the kingship   [130] *presently* immediately   [131] *On* on the basis of   [132] *put on* set to perform in office   [133] *passage* death

THE MISANTHROPE (1666)

MOLIÈRE (1622–1673)

Jean Baptiste Poquelin, better known as Molière, lived right in the middle of the century which saw the greatest achievements of the French neo-classic (new classic) revival. Molière, together with Pierre Corneille (1606–1684) and Jean Racine (1639–1699), created the greatest of the tragedies and comedies written during the French Renaissance. Although the modern appeal of the tragedies has never been strong outside France, the comedies of Molière seem to go on and on, as fresh and amusing as the day they were written. We have been fortunate in this country to have had the talents of Richard Wilbur as translator, for his rhymed couplet versions have retained the lilt of the original poetry and the spontaneous freshness and spirit which Molière injected into his very funny plays.

The structure, form, and style of the classics were regarded by the Renaissance as works of perfection, the imitation of which was obligatory if one were to create a "proper" tragedy. This included the application of the three "Unities," broadly adapted from Aristotle's *Poetics* as absolutes of dramatic law. The Unity of Time limited a play to one day; the Unity of Place, something Aristotle never mentions, held it to a single spot; the Unity of Action permitted a single story only, with no sub-plots of any kind. Subject matter was restricted to myths and legends, including the Bible. The overwhelming majority of French and Italian Renaissance tragedies, except for a few like Corneille's *The Cid* (1637) and Racine's *Phaedra* (1677), which present some effective and memorable dramatic characters, were insufferably boring and now rest in history's musty storerooms. Not so Molière.

The comedies of Molière may not at first seem "classic" in the sense of the tragedies, but as a comic dramatist he is in the best tradition of the "new" Greek comedies of Menander (343–291 B.C.), who gave the world the basic formula for the situation comedy as we know it today. The Renaissance became acquainted with the form through imitations of the Roman Plautus (254?–184? B.C.) and Terence (c. 190–159 B.C.). The endless struggles of young lovers to overcome the stupidities of ancient parents, particularly fathers, or husbands or guardians, the farcical intrigues, plots and counterplots and the impossibly happy endings are "classic" comedy situations. Molière knew how to handle them with great skill.

Molière, a highly versatile man of the theatre as actor, producer, and dramatist, was continually running into trouble with the church and the secular authorities for his frequently stinging satirical attacks against the "establishment" of seventeenth century France. His *Tartuffe,* concerning religious hypocrisy, was banned until King Louis XIV ordered it for presentation at court. But in *The Misanthrope* Molière is on comparatively safe ground as he presents the dilettantism and affected meaninglessness of the lives of those who occupy the higher levels of an indolent aristocratic society, dependent for diversion upon scandal, petty lawsuits, and seductive intrigues to revive flagging interests. *The Misanthrope* is fine high comedy, full of wit and sophisticated banter in its portrayal of a glittering human society without humanity, one which the straightforward Alceste insists on treating as it deserves. Opposed to him in their not altogether ineffective defense of their way of life are the more practical Philinte and the beautiful, talented, and intellectual Célimène. She is the personification of the kind of brittle brilliance the society of Molière's day could foster, living on her charm and her wit, aware of the artificial hothouse world in which she functions, but preferring it to the arid austerities of Alceste's desert island. *The Misanthrope* is a sparkling comedy of manners which can be performed today with considerable success.

The Misanthrope

MOLIÈRE

English version by Richard Wilbur

CHARACTERS

ALCESTE, *in love with Célimène*
PHILINTE, *Alceste's friend*
ORONTE, *in love with Célimène*
CÉLIMÈNE, *Alceste's beloved*
ÉLIANTE, *Célimène's cousin*
ARSINOÉ, *a friend of Célimène's*
ACASTE $\Big\}$ *Marquesses*
CLITANDRE
BASQUE, *Célimène's servant*
A GUARD *of the Marshalsea*
DUBOIS, *Alceste's valet*

The Scene throughout is in CÉLIMÈNE's *house at Paris*

ACT I

Scene I (PHILINTE, ALCESTE)

PHILINTE   Now, what's got into you?
ALCESTE (*seated*)   Kindly leave me alone.
PHILINTE   Come, come, what is it? This lugubrious tone . . .
ALCESTE   Leave me, I said; you spoil my solitude.
PHILINTE   Oh, listen to me, now, and don't be rude.
ALCESTE   I choose to be rude, Sir, and to be hard of hearing.
PHILINTE   These ugly moods of yours are not endearing;
    Friends though we are, I really must insist . . .
ALCESTE (*abruptly rising*)   Friends? Friends, you say? Well, cross
    me off your list.
    I've been your friend till now, as you well know;
    But after what I saw a moment ago
    I tell you flatly that our ways must part.
    I wish no place in a dishonest heart.

PHILINTE   Why, what have I done, Alceste? Is this quite just?
ALCESTE   My God, you ought to die of self-disgust.
   I call your conduct inexcusable, Sir,
   And every man of honor will concur.
   I see you almost hug a man to death,
   Exclaim for joy until you're out of breath,
   And supplement these loving demonstrations
   With endless offers, vows, and protestations;
   Then when I ask you "Who was that?" I find
   That you can barely bring his name to mind!
   Once the man's back is turned, you cease to love him,
   And speak with absolute indifference of him!
   By God, I say it's base and scandalous
   To falsify the heart's affections thus;
   If I caught myself behaving in such a way,
   I'd hang myself for shame, without delay.
PHILINTE   It hardly seems a hanging matter to me;
   I hope that you will take it graciously
   If I extend myself a slight reprieve,
   And live a little longer, by your leave.
ALCESTE   How dare you joke about a crime so grave?
PHILINTE   What crime? How else are people to behave?
ALCESTE   I'd have them be sincere, and never part
   With any word that isn't from the heart.
PHILINTE   When someone greets us with a show of pleasure,
   It's but polite to give him equal measure,
   Return his love the best that we know how,
   And trade him offer for offer, vow for vow.
ALCESTE   No, no, this formula you'd have me follow,
   However fashionable, is false and hollow,
   And I despise the frenzied operations
   Of all these barterers of protestations,
   These lavishers of meaningless embraces,
   These utterers of obliging commonplaces,
   Who court and flatter everyone on earth
   And praise the fool no less than the man of worth.
   Should you rejoice that someone fondles you,
   Offers his love and service, swears to be true,
   And fills your ears with praises of your name,
   When to the first damned fop he'll say the same?
   No, no: no self-respecting heart would dream
   Of prizing so promiscuous an esteem;
   However high the praise, there's nothing worse
   Than sharing honors with the universe.

Esteem is founded on comparison:
To honor all men is to honor none.
Since you embrace this indiscriminate vice,
Your friendship comes at far too cheap a price;
I spurn the easy tribute of a heart
Which will not set the worthy man apart:
I choose, Sir, to be chosen; and in fine,
The friend of mankind is no friend of mine.

PHILINTE   But in polite society, custom decrees
That we show certain outward courtesies. . . .

ALCESTE   Ah, no! we should condemn with all our force
Such false and artificial intercourse.
Let man behave like men; let them display
Their inmost hearts in everything they say;
Let the heart speak, and let our sentiments
Not mask themselves in silly compliments.

PHILINTE   In certain cases it would be uncouth
And most absurd to speak the naked truth;
With all respect for your exalted notions,
It's often best to veil one's true emotions.
Wouldn't the social fabric come undone
If we were wholly frank with everyone?
Suppose you met with someone you couldn't bear;
Would you inform him of it then and there?

ALCESTE   Yes.

PHILINTE   Then you'd tell old Emilie it's pathetic
The way she daubs her features with cosmetic
And plays the gay coquette at sixty-four?

ALCESTE   I would.

PHILINTE   And you'd call Dorilas a bore,
And tell him every ear at court is lame
From hearing him brag about his noble name?

ALCESTE   Precisely.

PHILINTE   Ah, you're joking.

ALCESTE   *Au contraire:*
In this regard there's none I'd choose to spare.
All are corrupt; there's nothing to be seen
In court or town but aggravates my spleen.
I fall into deep gloom and melancholy
When I survey the scene of human folly,
Finding on every hand base flattery,
Injustice, fraud, self-interest, treachery. . . .
Ah, it's too much; mankind has grown so base,
I mean to break with the whole human race.

PHILINTE   This philosophic rage is a bit extreme;
  You've no idea how comical you seem;
  Indeed, we're like those brothers in the play
  Called *School for Husbands,* one of whom was prey . . .
ALCESTE   Enough, now! None of your stupid similes.
PHILINTE   Then let's have no more tirades, if you please.
  The world won't change, whatever you say or do;
  And since plain speaking means so much to you,
  I'll tell you plainly that by being frank
  You've earned the reputation of a crank,
  And that you're thought ridiculous when you rage
  And rant against the manners of the age.
ALCESTE   So much the better; just what I wish to hear.
  No news could be more grateful to my ear.
  All men are so detestable in my eyes,
  I should be sorry if they thought me wise.
PHILINTE   Your hatred's very sweeping, is it not?
ALCESTE   Quite right: I hate the whole degraded lot.
PHILINTE   Must all poor human creatures be embraced,
  Without distinction, by your vast distaste?
  Even in these bad times, there are surely a few . . .
ALCESTE   No, I include all men in one dim view:
  Some men I hate for being rogues: the others
  I hate because they treat the rogues like brothers,
  And, lacking a virtuous scorn for what is vile,
  Receive the villain with a complaisant smile.
  Notice how tolerant people choose to be
  Toward that bold rascal who's at law with me.
  His social polish can't conceal his nature;
  One sees at once that he's a treacherous creature;
  No one could possibly be taken in
  By those soft speeches and that sugary grin.
  The whole world knows the shady means by which
  The low-brow's grown so powerful and rich,
  And risen to a rank so bright and high
  That virtue can but blush, and merit sigh.
  Whenever his name comes up in conversation,
  None will defend his wretched reputation;
  Call him knave, liar, scoundrel, and all the rest,
  Each head will nod, and no one will protest.
  And yet his smirk is seen in every house,
  He's greeted everywhere with smiles and bows,
  And when there's any honor that can be got

By pulling strings, he'll get it, like as not.
My God! It chills my heart to see the ways
Men come to terms with evil nowadays;
Sometimes, I swear, I'm moved to flee and find
Some desert land unfouled by humankind.

PHILINTE   Come, let's forget the follies of the times
And pardon mankind for its petty crimes;
Let's have an end of rantings and of railings,
And show some leniency toward human failings.
This world requires a pliant rectitude;
Too stern a virtue makes one stiff and rude;
Good sense views all extremes with detestation,
And bids us to be noble in moderation.
The rigid virtues of the ancient days
Are not for us; they jar with all our ways
And ask of us too lofty a perfection.
Wise men accept their times without objection,
And there's no greater folly, if you ask me,
Than trying to reform society.
Like you, I see each day a hundred and one
Unhandsome deeds that might be better done,
But still, for all the faults that meet my view,
I'm never known to storm and rave like you.
I take men as they are, or let them be,
And teach my soul to bear their frailty;
And whether in court or town, whatever the scene,
My phlegm's as philosophic as your spleen.

ALCESTE   This phlegm which you so eloquently commend,
Does nothing ever rile it up, my friend?
Suppose some man you trust should treacherously
Conspire to rob you of your property,
And do his best to wreck your reputation?
Wouldn't you feel a certain indignation?

PHILINTE   Why, no. These faults of which you so complain
Are part of human nature, I maintain,
And it's no more a matter for disgust
That men are knavish, selfish and unjust,
That that the vulture dines upon the dead,
And wolves are furious, and apes ill-bred.

ALCESTE   Shall I see myself betrayed, robbed, torn to bits,
And not . . . Oh, let's be still and rest our wits.
Enough of reasoning, now. I've had my fill.

PHILINTE   Indeed, you would do well, Sir, to be still.

Rage less at your opponent, and give some thought
To how you'll win this lawsuit that he's brought.
ALCESTE   I assure you I'll do nothing of the sort.
PHILINTE   Then who will plead your case before the court?
ALCESTE   Reason and right and justice will plead for me.
PHILINTE   Oh, Lord. What judges do you plan to see?
ALCESTE   Why, none. The justice of my cause is clear.
PHILINTE   Of course, man; but there's politics to fear. . . .
ALCESTE   No, I refuse to lift a hand. That's flat.
I'm either right, or wrong.
PHILINTE   Don't count on that.
ALCESTE   No, I'll do nothing.
PHILINTE   Your enemy's influence
Is great, you know . . .
ALCESTE   That makes no difference.
PHILINTE   It will; you'll see.
ALCESTE   Must honor bow to guile?
If so, I shall be proud to lose the trial.
PHILINTE   Oh, really . . .
ALCESTE   I'll discover by this case
Whether or not men are sufficiently base
And impudent and villainous and perverse
To do me wrong before the universe.
PHILINTE   What a man!
ALCESTE   Oh, I could wish, whatever the cost,
Just for the beauty of it, that my trial were lost.
PHILINTE   If people heard you talking so, Alceste,
They'd split their sides. Your name would be a jest.
ALCESTE   So much the worse for jesters.
PHILINTE   May I enquire
Whether this rectitude you so admire,
And these hard virtues you're enamored of
Are qualities of the lady whom you love?
It much surprises me that you, who seem
To view mankind with furious disesteem,
Have yet found something to enchant your eyes
Amidst a species which you so despise.
And what is more amazing, I'm afraid,
Is the most curious choice your heart has made.
The honest Éliante is fond of you,
Arsinoé, the prude, admires you too;
And yet your spirit's been perversely led
To choose the flighty Célimène instead,

Whose brittle malice and coquettish ways
So typify the manners of our days.
How is it that the traits you most abhor
Are bearable in this lady you adore?
Are you so blind with love that you can't find them?
Or do you contrive, in her case, not to mind them?

ALCESTE   My love for that young widow's not the kind
That can't perceive defects; no, I'm not blind.
I see her faults, despite my ardent love,
And all I see I fervently reprove.
And yet I'm weak; for all her falsity,
That woman knows the art of pleasing me,
And though I never cease complaining of her,
I swear I cannot manage not to love her.
Her charm outweighs her faults; I can but aim
To cleanse her spirit in my love's pure flame.

PHILINTE   That's no small task; I wish you all success.
You think then that she loves you?

ALCESTE   Heavens, yes!
I wouldn't love her did she not love me.

PHILINTE   Well, if her taste for you is plain to see,
Why do these rivals cause you such despair?

ALCESTE   True love, Sir, is possessive, and cannot bear
To share with all the world. I'm here today
To tell her she must send that mob away.

PHILINTE   If I were you, and had your choice to make,
Éliante, her cousin, would be the one I'd take;
That honest heart, which cares for you alone,
Would harmonize far better with your own.

ALCESTE   True, true: each day my reason tells me so;
But reason doesn't rule in love, you know.

PHILINTE   I fear some bitter sorrow is in store;
This love . . .

Scene II (ORONTE, ALCESTE, PHILINTE)

ORONTE (*to* ALCESTE)   The servants told me at the door
That Éliante and Célimène were out,
But when I heard, dear Sir, that you were about,
I came to say, without exaggeration,
That I hold you in the vastest admiration,
And that it's always been my dearest desire
To be the friend of one I so admire.
I hope to see my love of merit requited,

And you and I in friendship's bond united.
I'm sure you won't refuse—if I may be frank—
A friend of my devotedness—and rank.

During this speech of ORONTE'S, ALCESTE *is abstracted, and seems unaware that he is being spoken to. He only breaks off his reverie when* ORONTE *says:*

It was for you, if you please, that my words were intended.
ALCESTE   For me, Sir?
ORONTE   Yes, for you. You're not offended?
ALCESTE   By no means. But this much surprises me. . . .
The honor comes most unexpectedly. . . .
ORONTE   My high regard should not astonish you;
The whole world feels the same. It is your due.
ALCESTE   Sir . . .
ORONTE   Why, in all the State there isn't one
Can match your merits; they shine, Sir, like the sun.
ALCESTE   Sir . . .
ORONTE   You are higher in my estimation
Than all that's most illustrious in the nation.
ALCESTE   Sir . . .
ORONTE   If I lie, may heaven strike me dead!
To show you that I mean what I have said,
Permit me, Sir, to embrace you most sincerely,
And swear that I will prize our friendship dearly.
Give me your hand. And now, Sir, if you choose,
We'll make our vows.
ALCESTE   Sir . . .
ORONTE   What! You refuse?
ALCESTE   Sir, it's a very great honor you extend:
But friendship is a sacred thing, my friend;
It would be profanation to bestow
The name of friend on one you hardly know.
All parts are better played when well-rehearsed;
Let's put off friendship, and get acquainted first.
We may discover it would be unwise
To try to make our natures harmonize.
ORONTE   By heaven! You're sagacious to the core;
This speech has made me admire you even more.
Let time, then, bring us closer day by day;
Meanwhile, I shall be yours in every way.
If, for example, there should be anything
You wish at court, I'll mention it to the King.

I have his ear, of course; it's quite well known
That I am much in favor with the throne.
In short, I am your servant. And now, dear friend,
Since you have such fine judgment, I intend
To please you, if I can, with a small sonnet
I wrote not long ago. Please comment on it,
And tell me whether I ought to publish it.

ALCESTE   You must excuse me, Sir; I'm hardly fit
To judge such matters.

ORONTE   Why not?

ALCESTE   I am, I fear,
Inclined to be unfashionably sincere.

ORONTE   Just what I ask; I'd take no satisfaction
In anything but your sincere reaction.
I beg you not to dream of being kind.

ALCESTE   Since you desire it, Sir, I'll speak my mind.

ORONTE   *Sonnet.* It's a sonnet. . . . *Hope* . . . The poem's addressed
To a lady who wakened hopes within my breast.
Hope . . . this is not the pompous sort of thing,
Just modest little verses, with a tender ring.

ALCESTE   Well, we shall see.

ORONTE   *Hope* . . . I'm anxious to hear
Whether the style seems properly smooth and clear,
And whether the choice of words is good or bad.

ALCESTE   We'll see, we'll see.

ORONTE   Perhaps I ought to add
That it took me only a quarter-hour to write it.

ALCESTE   The time's irrelevant, Sir: kindly recite it.

ORONTE (*reading*)
> *Hope comforts us awhile, 'tis true,*
> *Lulling our cares with careless laughter,*
> *And yet such joy is full of rue,*
> *My Phyllis, if nothing follows after.*

PHILINTE   I'm charmed by this already; the style's delightful.

ALCESTE (*sotto voce, to* PHILINTE)   How can you say that?
Why, the thing is frightful.

ORONTE   *Your fair face smiled on me awhile,*
> *But was it kindness so to enchant me?*
> *'Twould have been fairer not to smile,*
> *If hope was all you meant to grant me.*

PHILINTE   What a clever thought! How handsomely you phrase it!

ALCESTE (*sotto voce, to* PHILINTE)   You know the thing is trash.
How dare you praise it?

ORONTE   *If it's to be my passion's fate*
            Thus everlastingly to wait,
            Then death will come to set me free:
            For death is fairer than the fair;
            Phyllis, to hope is to despair
            When one must hope eternally.

PHILINTE   The close is exquisite—full of feeling and grace.

ALCESTE (*sotto voce, aside*)   Oh, blast the close; you'd better close your face
    Before you send your lying soul to hell.

PHILINTE   I can't remember a poem I've liked so well.

ALCESTE (*sotto voce, aside*)   Good Lord!

ORONTE (*to* PHILINTE)   I fear you're flattering me a bit.

PHILINTE   Oh, no!

ALCESTE (*sotto voce, aside*)   What else d'you call it, you hypocrite?

ORONTE (*to* ALCESTE)   But you, Sir, keep your promise now: don't shrink
    From telling me sincerely what you think.

ALCESTE   Sir, these are delicate matters; we all desire
    To be told that we've the true poetic fire.
    But once, to one whose name I shall not mention,
    I said, regarding some verse of his invention,
    That gentlemen should rigorously control
    That itch to write which often afflicts the soul;
    That one should curb the heady inclination
    To publicize one's little avocation;
    And that in showing off one's works of art
    One often plays a very clownish part.

ORONTE   Are you suggesting in a devious way
    That I ought not . . .

ALCESTE   Oh, that I do not say.
    Further, I told him that no fault is worse
    Than that of writing frigid, lifeless verse,
    And that the merest whisper of such a shame
    Suffices to destroy a man's good name.

ORONTE   D'you mean to say my sonnet's dull and trite?

ALCESTE   I don't say that. But I went on to cite
    Numerous cases of once-respected men
    Who came to grief by taking up the pen.

ORONTE   And am I like them? Do I write so poorly?

ALCESTE   I don't say that. But I told this person, "Surely
    You're under no necessity to compose;
    Why you should wish to publish, heaven knows.

There's no excuse for printing tedious rot
Unless one writes for bread, as you do not.
Resist temptation, then, I beg of you;
Conceal your pastimes from the public view;
And don't give up, on any provocation,
Your present high and courtly reputation,
To purchase at a greedy printer's shop
The name of silly author and scribbling fop."
These were the points I tried to make him see.

ORONTE   I sense that they are also aimed at me;
But now—about my sonnet—I'd like to be told . . .

ALCESTE   Frankly, that sonnet should be pigeonholed.
You've chosen the worst models to imitate.
The style's unnatural. Let me illustrate:
For example, *Your fair face smiled on me awhile,*
Followed by, *'Twould have been fairer not to smile!*
Or this: *such joy is full of rue;*
Or this: *For death is fairer than the fair;*
Or, *Phyllis, to hope is to despair*
   When one must hope eternally!
This artificial style, that's all the fashion,
Has neither taste, nor honesty, nor passion;
It's nothing but a sort of wordy play,
And nature never spoke in such a way.
What, in this shallow age, is not debased?
Our fathers, though less refined, had better taste;
I'd barter all that men admire today
For one old love song I shall try to say:

>   *If the King had given me for my own*
>   *Paris, his citadel,*
>   *And I for that must leave alone*
>   *Her whom I love so well,*
>   *I'd say then to the Crown,*
>   *Take back your glittering town;*
>   *My darling is more fair, I swear,*
>   *My darling is more fair.*

The rhyme's not rich, the style is rough and old,
But don't you see that it's the purest gold
Beside the tinsel nonsense now preferred,
And that there's passion in its every word?

>   *If the King had given me for my own*
>   *Paris, his citadel,*
>   *And I for that must leave alone*

> *Her whom I love so well,*
> *I'd say then to the Crown,*
> *Take back your glittering town;*
> *My darling is more fair, I swear,*
> *My darling is more fair.*

There speaks a loving heart. (*To* PHILINTE.) You're laughing, eh?
Laugh on, my precious wit. Whatever you say,
I hold that song's worth all the bibelots
That people hail today with ah's and oh's.

ORONTE   And I maintain my sonnet's very good.

ALCESTE   It's not at all surprising that you should.
You have your reasons; permit me to have mine
For thinking that you cannot write a line.

ORONTE   Others have praised my sonnet to the skies.

ALCESTE   I lack their art of telling pleasant lies.

ORONTE   You seem to think you've got no end of wit.

ALCESTE   To praise your verse, I'd need still more of it.

ORONTE   I'm not in need of your approval, Sir.

ALCESTE   That's good; you couldn't have it if you were.

ORONTE   Come now, I'll lend you the subject of my sonnet;
I'd like to see you try to improve upon it.

ALCESTE   I might, by chance, write something just as shoddy;
But then I wouldn't show it to everybody.

ORONTE   You're most opinionated and conceited.

ALCESTE   Go find your flatterers, and be better treated.

ORONTE   Look here, my little fellow, pray watch your tone.

ALCESTE   My great big fellow, you'd better watch your own.

PHILINTE (*stepping between them*)   Oh, please, please, gentlemen!
This will never do.

ORONTE   The fault is mine, and I leave the field to you.
I am your servant, Sir, in every way.

ALCESTE   And I, Sir, am your most abject valet.

Scene III (PHILINTE, ALCESTE)

PHILINTE   Well, as you see, sincerity in excess
Can get you into a very pretty mess;
Oronte was hungry for appreciation. . . .

ALCESTE   Don't speak to me.

PHILINTE   What?

ALCESTE   No more conversation.

PHILINTE   Really, now . . .

ALCESTE   Leave me alone.

PHILINTE   If I . . .

ALCESTE   Out of my sight!

PHILINTE But what . . .
ALCESTE   I won't listen.
PHILINTE   But . . .
ALCESTE   Silence!
PHILINTE   Now, is it polite . . .
ALCESTE By heaven, I've had enough. Don't follow me.
PHILINTE Ah, you're just joking. I'll keep you company.

ACT II

Scene I (ALCESTE, CÉLIMÈNE)

ALCESTE Shall I speak plainly, Madam? I confess
　　Your conduct gives me infinite distress,
　　And my resentment's grown too hot to smother.
　　Soon, I foresee, we'll break with one another.
　　If I said otherwise, I should deceive you;
　　Sooner or later, I shall be forced to leave you,
　　And if I swore that we shall never part,
　　I should misread the omens of my heart.
CÉLIMÈNE You kindly saw me home, it would appear,
　　So as to pour invectives in my ear.
ALCESTE I've no desire to quarrel. But I deplore
　　Your inability to shut the door
　　On all these suitors who beset you so.
　　There's what annoys me, if you care to know.
CÉLIMÈNE Is it my fault that all these men pursue me?
　　Am I to blame if they're attracted to me?
　　And when they gently beg an audience,
　　Ought I to take a stick and drive them hence?
ALCESTE Madam, there's no necessity for a stick;
　　A less responsive heart would do the trick.
　　Of your attractiveness I don't complain;
　　But those your charms attract, you then detain
　　By a most melting and receptive manner,
　　And so enlist their hearts beneath your banner.
　　It's the agreeable hopes which you excite
　　That keep these lovers round you day and night;
　　Were they less liberally smiled upon,
　　That sighing troop would very soon be gone.
　　But tell me, Madam, why it is that lately
　　This man Clitandre interests you so greatly?
　　Because of what high merits do you deem
　　Him worthy of the honor of your esteem?

Is it that your admiring glances linger
On the splendidly long nail of his little finger?
Or do you share the general deep respect
For the blond wig he chooses to affect?
Are you in love with his embroidered hose?
Do you adore his ribbons and his bows?
Or is it that this paragon bewitches
Your tasteful eye with his vast German breeches?
Perhaps his giggle, or his falsetto voice,
Makes him the latest gallant of your choice?

CÉLIMÈNE You're much mistaken to resent him so.
Why I put up with him you surely know:
My lawsuit's very shortly to be tried,
And I must have his influence on my side.

ALCESTE Then lose your lawsuit, Madam, or let it drop;
Don't torture me by humoring such a fop.

CÉLIMÈNE You're jealous of the whole world, Sir.

ALCESTE   That's true,
Since the whole world is well-received by you.

CÉLIMÈNE That my good nature is so unconfined
Should serve to pacify your jealous mind;
Were I to smile on one, and scorn the rest,
Then you might have some cause to be distressed.

ALCESTE Well, if I mustn't be jealous, tell me, then,
Just how I'm better treated than other men.

CÉLIMÈNE You know you have my love. Will that not do?

ALCESTE What proof have I that what you say is true?

CÉLIMÈNE I would expect, Sir, that my having said it
Might give the statement a sufficient credit.

ALCESTE But how can I be sure that you don't tell
The selfsame thing to other men as well?

CÉLIMÈNE What a gallant speech! How flattering to me!
What a sweet creature you make me out to be!
Well then, to save you from the pangs of doubt,
All that I've said I hereby cancel out;
Now, none but yourself shall make a monkey of you:
Are you content?

ALCESTE   Why, why am I doomed to love you?
I swear that I shall bless the blissful hour
When this poor heart's no longer in your power!
I make no secret of it: I've done my best
To exorcise this passion from my breast;
But thus far all in vain; it will not go;
It's for my sins that I must love you so.

CÉLIMÈNE   Your love for me is matchless, Sir; that's clear.

ALCESTE   Indeed, in all the world it has no peer;
  Words can't describe the nature of my passion,
  And no man ever loved in such a fashion.

CÉLIMÈNE   Yes, it's a brand-new fashion, I agree:
  You show your love by castigating me,
  And all your speeches are enraged and rude.
  I've never been so furiously wooed.

ALCESTE   Yet you could calm that fury, if you chose.
  Come, shall we bring our quarrels to a close?
  Let's speak with open hearts, then, and begin . . .

Scene II (CÉLIMÈNE, ALCESTE, BASQUE)

CÉLIMÈNE   What is it?

BASQUE   Acaste is here.

CÉLIMÈNE   Well, send him in.

Scene III (CÉLIMÈNE, ALCESTE)

ALCESTE   What! Shall we never be alone at all?
  You're always ready to receive a call,
  And you can't bear, for ten ticks of the clock,
  Not to keep open house for all who knock.

CÉLIMÈNE   I couldn't refuse him: he'd be most put out.

ALCESTE   Surely that's not worth worrying about.

CÉLIMÈNE   Acaste would never forgive me if he guessed
  That I consider him a dreadful pest.

ALCESTE   If he's a pest, why bother with him then?

CÉLIMÈNE   Heavens! One can't antagonize such men;
  Why, they're the chartered gossips of the court,
  And have a say in things of every sort.
  One must receive them, and be full of charm;
  They're no great help, but they can do you harm,
  And though your influence be ever so great,
  They're hardly the best people to alienate.

ALCESTE   I see, dear lady, that you could make a case
  For putting up with the whole human race;
  These friendships that you calculate so nicely . . .

Scene IV (ALCESTE, CÉLIMÈNE, BASQUE)

BASQUE   Madam, Clitandre is here as well.

ALCESTE   Precisely.

CÉLIMÈNE   Where are you going?

ALCESTE   Elsewhere.

CÉLIMÈNE   Stay.

ALCESTE   No, no.

CÉLIMÈNE   Stay, Sir.

ALCESTE   I can't.

CÉLIMÈNE   I wish it.

ALCESTE   No, I must go.
  I beg you, Madam, not to press the matter;
  You know I have no taste for idle chatter.

CÉLIMÈNE   Stay. I command you.

ALCESTE   No, I cannot stay.

CÉLIMÈNE   Very well; you have my leave to go away.

Scene V (ÉLIANTE, PHILINTE, ACASTE, CLITANDRE, ALCESTE, CÉLIMÈNE, BASQUE)

ÉLIANTE (*to* CÉLIMÈNE)   The Marquesses have kindly come to call.
  Were they announced?

CÉLIMÈNE   Yes. Basque, bring chairs for all.

BASQUE *provides the chairs, and exits.*

  (*To* ALCESTE.) You haven't gone?

ALCESTE   No; and I shan't depart
  Till you decide who's foremost in your heart.

CÉLIMÈNE   Oh, hush.

ALCESTE   It's time to choose; take them, or me.

CÉLIMÈNE   You're mad.

ALCESTE   I'm not, as you shall shortly see.

CÉLIMÈNE   Oh?

ALCESTE   You'll decide.

CÉLIMÈNE   You're joking now, dear friend.

ALCESTE   No, no; you'll choose; my patience is at an end.

CLITANDRE   Madam, I come from court, where poor Cléonte
  Behaved like a perfect fool, as is his wont.
  Has he no friend to counsel him, I wonder,
  And teach him less unerringly to blunder?

CÉLIMÈNE   It's true, the man's a most accomplished dunce;
  His gauche behavior charms the eye at once;
  And every time one sees him, on my word,
  His manner's grown a trifle more asburd.

ACASTE   Speaking of dunces, I've just now conversed
  With old Damon, who's one of the very worst;
  I stood a lifetime in the broiling sun.
  Before his dreary monologue was done.

CÉLIMÈNE   Oh, he's a wondrous talker, and has the power
  To tell you nothing hour after hour:

If, by mistake, he ever came to the point,
The shock would put his jawbone out of joint.
ÉLIANTE (*to* PHILINTE) The conversation takes its usual turn,
And all our dear friends' ears will shortly burn.
CLINTANDRE Timante's a character, Madam.
CÉLIMÈNE   Isn't he, though?
A man of mystery from top to toe,
Who moves about in a romantic mist
On secret missions which do not exist.
His talk is full of eyebrows and grimaces;
How tired one gets of his momentous faces;
He's always whispering something confidential
Which turns out to be quite inconsequential;
Nothing's too slight for him to mystify;
He even whispers when he says "good-by."
ACASTE Tell us about Géralde.
CÉLIMÈNE   That tiresome ass.
He mixes only with the titled class,
And fawns on dukes and princes, and is bored
With anyone who's not at least a lord.
The man's obsessed with rank, and his discourses
Are all of hounds and carriages and horses;
He uses Christian names with all the great,
And the word Milord, with him, is out of date.
CLITANDRE He's very taken with Bélise, I hear.
CÉLIMÈNE She is the dreariest company, poor dear.
Whenever she comes to call, I grope about
To find some topic which will draw her out,
But, owing to her dry and faint replies,
The conversation wilts, and droops, and dies.
In vain one hopes to animate her face
By mentioning the ultimate commonplace;
But sun or shower, even hail or frost
Are matters she can instantly exhaust.
Meanwhile her visit, painful though it is,
Drags on and on through mute eternities,
And though you ask the time, and yawn, and yawn,
She sits there like a stone and won't be gone.
ACASTE Now for Adraste.
CÉLIMÉNE   Oh, that conceited elf
Has a gigantic passion for himself;
He rails against the court, and cannot bear it
That none will recognize his hidden merit;

All honors given to others give offense
To his imaginary excellence.

CLITANDRE   What about young Cléon? His house, they say,
Is full of the best society, night and day.

CÉLIMÈNE   His cook has made him popular, not he:
It's Cléon's table that people come to see.

ÉLIANTE   He gives a splendid dinner, you must admit.

CÉLIMÈNE   But must he serve himself along with it?
For my taste, he's a most insipid dish
Whose presence sours the wine and spoils the fish.

PHILINTE   Damis, his uncle, is admired no end.
What's your opinion, Madam?

CÉLIMÈNE   Why, he's my friend.

PHILINTE   He seems a decent fellow, and rather clever.

CÉLIMÈNE   He works too hard at cleverness, however.
I hate to see him sweat and struggle so
To fill his conversation with bons mots.
Since he's decided to become a wit
His taste's so pure that nothing pleases it;
He scolds at all the latest books and plays,
Thinking that wit must never stoop to praise,
That finding fault's a sign of intellect,
That all appreciation is abject,
And that by damning everything in sight
One shows oneself in a distinguished light.
He's scornful even of our conversations:
Their trivial nature sorely tries his patience;
He folds his arms, and stands above the battle,
And listens sadly to our childish prattle.

ACASTE   Wonderful, Madam! You've hit him off precisely.

CLITANDRE   No one can sketch a character so nicely.

ALCESTE   How bravely, Sirs, you cut and thrust at all
These absent fools, till one by one they fall:
But let one come in sight, and you'll at once
Embrace the man you lately called a dunce,
Telling him in a tone sincere and fervent
How proud you are to be his humble servant.

CLITANDRE   Why pick on us? *Madame's* been speaking, Sir.
And you should quarrel, if you must, with her.

ALCESTE   No, no, by God, the fault is yours, because
You lead her on with laughter and applause,
And make her think that she's the more delightful
The more her talk is scandalous and spiteful.
Oh, she would stoop to malice far, far less

If no such claque approved her cleverness.
It's flatterers like you whose foolish praise
Nourishes all the vices of these days.
PHILINTE   But why protest when someone ridicules
Those you'd condemn, yourself, as knaves or fools?
CÉLIMÈNE   Why, Sir? Because he loves to make a fuss.
You don't expect him to agree with us,
When there's an opportunity to express
His heaven-sent spirit of contrariness?
What other people think, he can't abide;
Whatever they say, he's on the other side;
He lives in deadly terror of agreeing;
'Twould make him seem an ordinary being.
Indeed, he's so in love with contradiction,
He'll turn against his most profound conviction
And with a furious eloquence deplore it,
If only someone else is speaking for it.
ALCESTE   Go on, dear lady, mock me as you please;
You have your audience in ecstasies.
PHILINTE   But what she says is true: you have a way
Of bridling at whatever people say;
Whether they praise or blame, your angry spirit
Is equally unsatisfied to hear it.
ALCESTE   Men, Sir, are always wrong, and that's the reason
That righteous anger's never out of season;
All that I hear in all their conversation
Is flattering praise or reckless condemnation.
CÉLIMÈNE   But . . .
ALCESTE   No, no, Madam, I am forced to state
That you have pleasures which I deprecate,
And that these others, here, are much to blame
For nourishing the faults which are your shame.
CLITANDRE   I shan't defend myself, Sir; but I vow
I'd thought this lady faultless until now.
ACASTE   I see her charms and graces, which are many;
But as for faults, I've never noticed any.
ALCESTE   I see them, Sir; and rather than ignore them,
I strenuously criticize her for them.
The more one loves, the more one should object
To every blemish, every least defect.
Were I this lady, I would soon get rid
Of lovers who approved of all I did,
And by their slack indulgence and applause
Endorsed my follies and excused my flaws.

CÉLIMÈNE   If all hearts beat according to your measure,
  The dawn of love would be the end of pleasure;
  And love would find its perfect consummation
  In ecstasies of rage and reprobation.
ÉLIANTE   Love, as a rule, affects men otherwise,
  And lovers rarely love to criticize.
  They see their lady as a charming blur,
  And find all things commendable in her.
  If she has any blemish, fault, or shame,
  They will redeem it by a pleasing name.
  The pale-faced lady's lily-white, perforce;
  The swarthy one's a sweet brunette, of course;
  The spindly lady has a slender grace;
  The fat one has a most majestic pace;
  The plain one, with her dress in disarray,
  They classify as *beauté négligée*;
  The hulking one's a goddess in their eyes,
  The dwarf, a concentrate of Paradise;
  The haughty lady has a noble mind;
  The mean one's witty, and the dull one's kind;
  The chatterbox has liveliness and verve,
  The mute one has a virtuous reserve.
  So lovers manage, in their passion's cause,
  To love their ladies even for their flaws.
ALCESTE   But I still say . . .
CÉLIMÈNE   I think it would be nice
  To stroll around the gallery once or twice.
  What! You're not going, Sirs?
CLITANDRE AND ACASTE   No, Madam, no.
ALCESTE   You seem to be in terror lest they go.
  Do what you will, Sirs; leave, or linger on,
  But I shan't go till after you are gone.
ACASTE   I'm free to linger, unless I should perceive
  Madame is tired, and wishes me to leave.
CLITANDRE   And as for me, I needn't go today
  Until the hour of the King's *coucher*.
CÉLIMÈNE (*to* ALCESTE)   You're joking, surely?
ALCESTE   Not in the least; we'll see
  Whether you'd rather part with them, or me.

Scene VI (ALCESTE, CÉLIMÈNE, ÉLIANTE, ACASTE, PHILINTE, CLITANDRE, BASQUE)

BASQUE (*to* ALCESTE)   Sir, there's a fellow here who bids me state
  That he must see you, and that it can't wait.

ALCESTE Tell him that I have no such pressing affairs.

BASQUE It's a long tailcoat that this fellow wears,
  With gold all over.

CÉLIMÈNE (*to* ALCESTE) You'd best go down and see.
  Or—have him enter.

Scene VII (ALCESTE, CÉLIMÈNE, ÉLIANTE, ACASTE, PHILINTE,
  CLITANDRE, GUARD)

ALCESTE (*confronting the* GUARD) Well, what do you want with
    me?
  Come in, Sir.

GUARD   I've a word, Sir, for your ear.

ALCESTE Speak it aloud, Sir; I shall strive to hear.

GUARD The Marshals have instructed me to say
  You must report to them without delay.

ALCESTE Who? Me, Sir?

GUARD   Yes, Sir; you.

ALCESTE   But what do they want?

PHILINTE (*to* ALCESTE) To scotch your silly quarrel with Oronte.

CÉLIMÈNE (*to* PHILINTE) What quarrel?

PHILINTE   Oronte and he have fallen out
  Over some verse he spoke his mind about;
  The Marshals wish to arbitrate the matter.

ALCESTE Never shall I equivocate or flatter!

PHILINTE You'd best obey their summons; come, let's go.

ALCESTE How can they mend our quarrel, I'd like to know?
  Am I to make a cowardly retraction,
  And praise those jingles to his satisfaction?
  I'll not recant; I've judged that sonnet rightly.
  It's bad.

PHILINTE   But you might say so more politely. . . .

ALCESTE I'll not back down; his verses make me sick.

PHILINTE If only you could be more politic!
  But come, let's go.

ALCESTE   I'll go, but I won't unsay
  A single word.

PHILINTE   Well, let's be on our way.

ALCESTE Till I am ordered by my lord the King
  To praise that poem, I shall say the thing
  Is scandalous, by God, and that the poet
  Ought to be hanged for having the nerve to show it.
  (*To* CLITANDRE *and* ACASTE, *who are laughing.*) By heaven, Sirs,
    I really didn't know
  That I was being humorous.

CÉLIMÈNE   Go, Sir, go;
  Settle your business.
ALCESTE   I shall, and when I'm through,
  I shall return to settle things with you.

ACT III

Scene I (CLITANDRE, ACASTE)

CLITANDRE   Dear Marquess, how contented you appear;
  All things delight you, nothing mars your cheer.
  Can you, in perfect honesty, declare
  That you've a right to be so debonair?
ACASTE   By Jove, when I survey myself, I find
  No cause whatever for distress of mind.
  I'm young and rich; I can in modesty
  Lay claim to an exalted pedigree;
  And owing to my name and my condition
  I shall not want for honors and position.
  Then as to courage, that most precious trait,
  I seem to have it, as was proved of late
  Upon the field of honor, where my bearing,
  They say, was very cool and rather daring.
  I've wit, of course; and taste in such perfection
  That I can judge without the least reflection,
  And at the theater, which is my delight,
  Can make or break a play on opening night,
  And lead the crowd in hisses or bravos,
  And generally be known as one who knows.
  I'm clever, handsome, gracefully polite;
  My waist is small, my teeth are strong and white;
  As for my dress, the world's astonished eyes
  Assure me that I bear away the prize.
  I find myself in favor everywhere,
  Honored by men, and worshiped by the fair;
  And since these things are so, it seems to me
  I'm justified in my complacency.
CLITANDRE   Well, if so many ladies hold you dear,
  Why do you press a hopeless courtship here?
ACASTE   Hopeless, you say? I'm not the sort of fool
  That likes his ladies difficult and cool.
  Men who are awkward, shy, and peasantish

May pine for heartless beauties, if they wish,
Grovel before them, bear their cruelties,
Woo them with tears and sighs and bended knees,
And hope by dogged faithfulness to gain
What their poor merits never could obtain.
For men like me, however, it makes no sense
To love on trust, and foot the whole expense.
Whatever any lady's merits be,
I think, thank God, that I'm as choice as she;
That if my heart is kind enough to burn
For her, she owes me something in return;
And that in any proper love affair
The partners must invest an equal share.

CLITANDRE   You think, then, that our hostess favors you?

ACASTE   I've reason to believe that that is true.

CLITANDRE   How did you come to such a mad conclusion?
You're blind, dear fellow. This is sheer delusion.

ACASTE   All right, then: I'm deluded and I'm blind.

CLITANDRE   Whatever put the notion in your mind?

ACASTE   Delusion.

CLITANDRE   What persuades you that you're right?

ACASTE   I'm blind.

CLITANDRE   But have you any proofs to cite?

ACASTE   I tell you I'm deluded.

CLITANDRE   Have you, then,
Received some secret pledge from Célimène?

ACASTE   Oh, no: she scorns me.

CLITANDRE   Tell me the truth, I beg.

ACASTE   She just can't bear me.

CLITANDRE   Ah, don't pull my leg.
Tell me what hope she's given you, I pray.

ACASTE   I'm hopeless, and it's you who win the day.
She hates me thoroughly, and I'm so vexed
I mean to hang myself on Tuesday next.

CLITANDRE   Dear Marquess, let us have an armistice
And make a treaty. What do you say to this?
If ever one of us can plainly prove
That Célimène encourages his love,
The other must abandon hope, and yield,
And leave him in possession of the field.

ACASTE   Now, there's a bargain that appeals to me;
With all my heart, dear Marquess, I agree.
But hush.

Scene II (CÉLIMÈNE, ACASTE, CLITANDRE)

CÉLIMÈNE   Still here?

CLITANDRE   'Twas love that stayed our feet.

CÉLIMÈNE   I think I heard a carriage in the street.
Whose is it? D'you know?

Scene III (CÉLIMÈNE, ACASTE, CLITANDRE, BASQUE)

BASQUE   Arsinoé is here,
Madame.

CÉLIMÈNE   Arsinoé, you say? Oh, dear.

BASQUE   Éliante is entertaining her below.

CÉLIMÈNE   What brings the creature here, I'd like to know?

ACASTE   They say she's dreadfully prudish, but in fact
I think her piety . . .

CÉLIMÈNE   It's all an act.
At heart she's worldly, and her poor success
In snaring men explains her prudishness.
It breaks her heart to see the beaux and gallants
Engrossed by other women's charms and talents,
And so she's always in a jealous rage
Against the faulty standards of the age.
She lets the world believe that she's a prude
To justify her loveless solitude,
And strives to put a brand of moral shame
On all the graces that she cannot claim.
But still she'd love a lover; and Alceste
Appears to be the one she'd love the best.
His visits here are poison to her pride;
She seems to think I've lured him from her side;
And everywhere, at court or in the town,
The spiteful, envious woman runs me down.
In short, she's just as stupid as can be,
Vicious and arrogant in the last degree,
And . . .

Scene IV (ARSINOÉ, CÉLIMÈNE, CLITANDRE, ACASTE)

CÉLIMÈNE   Ah! What happy chance has brought you here?
I've thought about you ever so much, my dear.

ARSINOÉ   I've come to tell you something you should know.

CÉLIMÈNE   How good of you to think of doing so!

CLITANDRE *and* ACASTE *go out, laughing.*

Scene V (ARSINOÉ, CÉLIMÈNE)

ARSINOÉ   It's just as well those gentlemen didn't tarry.
CÉLIMÈNE   Shall we sit down?
ARSINOÉ   That won't be necessary.
   Madam, the flame of friendship ought to burn
   Brightest in matters of the most concern,
   And as there's nothing which concerns us more
   Than honor, I have hastened to your door
   To bring you, as your friend, some information
   About the status of your reputation.
   I visited, last night, some virtuous folk,
   And, quite by chance, it was of you they spoke;
   There was, I fear, no tendency to praise
   Your light behavior and your dashing ways.
   The quantity of gentlemen you see
   And your by now notorious coquetry
   Were both so vehemently criticized
   By everyone, that I was much surprised.
   Of course, I needn't tell you where I stood;
   I came to your defense as best I could,
   Assured them you were harmless, and declared
   Your soul was absolutely unimpaired.
   But there are some things, you must realize,
   One can't excuse, however hard one tries,
   And I was forced at last into conceding
   That your behavior, Madam, is misleading,
   That it makes a bad impression, giving rise
   To ugly gossip and obscene surmise,
   And that if you were more *overtly* good,
   You wouldn't be so much misunderstood.
   Not that I think you've been unchaste—no! no!
   The saints preserve me from a thought so low!
   But mere good conscience never did suffice:
   One must avoid the outward show of vice.
   Madam, you're too intelligent, I'm sure,
   To think my motives anything but pure
   In offering you this counsel—which I do
   Out of a zealous interest in you.
CÉLIMÈNE   Madam, I haven't taken you amiss;
   I'm very much obliged to you for this;
   And I'll at once discharge the obligation
   By telling you about *your* reputation.
   You've been so friendly as to let me know

What certain people say of me, and so
I mean to follow your benign example
By offering you a somewhat similar sample.
The other day, I went to an affair
And found some most distinguished people there
Discussing piety, both false and true.
The conversation soon came round to you.
Alas! Your prudery and bustling zeal
Appeared to have a very slight appeal.
Your affectation of a grave demeanor,
Your endless talk of virtue and of honor,
The aptitude of your suspicious mind
For finding sin where there is none to find,
Your towering self-esteem, that pitying face
With which you contemplate the human race,
Your sermonizings and your sharp aspersions
On people's pure and innocent diversions—
All these were mentioned, Madam, and, in fact,
Were roundly and concertedly attacked.
"What good," they said, "are all these outward shows,
When everything belies her pious pose?
She prays incessantly; but then, they say,
She beats her maids and cheats them of their pay;
She shows her zeal in every holy place,
But still she's vain enough to paint her face;
She holds that naked statues are immoral,
But with a naked *man* she'd have no quarrel."
Of course, I said to everybody there
That they were being viciously unfair;
But still they were disposed to criticize you,
And all agreed that someone should advise you
To leave the morals of the world alone,
And worry rather more about your own.
They felt that one's self-knowledge should be great
Before one thinks of setting others straight;
That one should learn the art of living well
Before one threatens other men with hell,
And that the Church is best equipped, no doubt,
To guide our souls and root our vices out.
Madam, you're too intelligent, I'm sure,
To think my motives anything but pure
In offering you this counsel—which I do
Out of a zealous interest in you.

ARSINOÉ I dared not hope for gratitude, but I
  Did not expect so acid a reply;
  I judge, since you've been so extremely tart,
  That my good counsel pierced you to the heart.
CÉLIMÈNE Far from it, Madam. Indeed, it seems to me
  We ought to trade advice more frequently.
  One's vision of oneself is so defective
  That it would be an excellent corrective.
  If you are willing, Madam, let's arrange
  Shortly to have another frank exchange
  In which we'll tell each other, *entre nous,*
  What you've heard tell of me, and I of you.
ARSINOÉ Oh, people never censure you, my dear;
  It's me they criticize. Or so I hear.
CÉLIMÈNE Madam, I think we either blame or praise
  According to our taste and length of days.
  There is a time of life for coquetry,
  And there's a season, too, for prudery.
  When all one's charms are gone, it is, I'm sure,
  Good strategy to be devout and pure:
  It makes one seem a little less forsaken.
  Some day, perhaps, I'll take the road you've taken:
  Time brings all things. But I have time aplenty,
  And see no cause to be a prude at twenty.
ARSINOÉ You give your age in such a gloating tone
  That one would think I was an ancient crone;
  We're not so far apart, in sober truth,
  That you can mock me with a boast of youth!
  Madam, you baffle me. I wish I knew
  What moves you to provoke me as you do.
CÉLIMÈNE For my part, Madam, I should like to know
  Why you abuse me everywhere you go.
  Is it my fault, dear lady, that your hand
  Is not, alas, in very great demand?
  If men admire me, if they pay me court
  And daily make me offers of the sort
  You'd dearly love to have them make to you,
  How can I help it? What would you have me do?
  If what you want is lovers, please feel free
  To take as many as you can from me.
ARSINOÉ Oh, come. D'you think the world is losing sleep
  Over the flock of lovers which you keep,
  Or that we find it difficult to guess

What price you pay for their devotedness?
Surely you don't expect us to suppose
Mere merit could attract so many beaux?
It's not your virtue that they're dazzled by;
Nor is it virtuous love for which they sigh.
You're fooling no one, Madam; the world's not blind;
There's many a lady heaven has designed
To call men's noblest, tenderest feelings out,
Who has no lovers dogging her about;
From which it's plain that lovers nowadays
Must be acquired in bold and shameless ways,
And only pay one court for such reward
As modesty and virtue can't afford.
Then don't be quite so puffed up, if you please,
About your tawdry little victories;
Try, if you can, to be a shade less vain,
And treat the world with somewhat less disdain.
If one were envious of your amours,
One soon could have a following like yours;
Lovers are no great trouble to collect
If one prefers them to one's self-respect.

CÉLIMÈNE   Collect them then, my dear; I'd love to see
You demonstrate that charming theory;
Who knows, you might . . .

ARSINOÉ   Now, Madam, that will do;
It's time to end this trying interview.
My coach is late in coming to your door.
Or I'd have taken leave of you before.

CÉLIMÈNE   Oh, please don't feel that you must rush away;
I'd be delighted, Madam, if you'd stay.
However, lest my conversation bore you,
Let me provide some better company for you;
This gentleman, who comes most apropos,
Will please you more than I could do, I know.

Scene VI (ALCESTE, CÉLIMÈNE, ARSINOÉ)

CÉLIMÈNE   Alceste, I have a little note to write
Which simply must go out before tonight;
Please entertain *Madame;* I'm sure that she
Will overlook my incivility.

Scene VII (ALCESTE, ARSINOÉ)

ARSINOÉ   Well, Sir, our hostess graciously contrives
For us to chat until my coach arrives;

And I shall be forever in her debt
For granting me this little tête-à-tête.
We women very rightly give our hearts
To men of noble character and parts,
And your especial merits, dear Alceste,
Have roused the deepest sympathy in my breast.
Oh, how I wish they had sufficient sense
At court, to recognize your excellence!
They wrong you greatly, Sir. How it must hurt you
Never to be rewarded for your virtue!

ALCESTE   Why, Madam, what cause have I to feel aggrieved?
What great and brilliant thing have I achieved?
What service have I rendered to the King
That I should look to him for anything?

ARSINOÉ   Not everyone who's honored by the State
Has done great services. A man must wait
Till time and fortune offer him the chance.
Your merit, Sir, is obvious at a glance,
And . . .

ALCESTE   Ah, forgot my merit; I am not neglected.
The court, I think, can hardly be expected
To mine men's souls for merit, and unearth
Our hidden virtues and our secret worth.

ARSINOÉ   *Some* virtues, though, are far too bright to hide;
Yours are acknowledged, Sir, on every side.
Indeed, I've heard you warmly praised of late
By persons of considerable weight.

ALCESTE   This fawning age has praise for everyone,
And all distinctions, Madam, are undone.
All things have equal honor nowadays,
And no one should be gratified by praise.
To be admired, one only need exist,
And every lackey's on the honors list.

ARSINOÉ.   I only wish, Sir, that you had your eye
On some position at court, however high;
You'd only have to hint at such a notion
For me to set the proper wheels in motion;
I've certain friendships I'd be glad to use
To get you any office you might choose.

ALCESTE   Madam, I fear that any such ambition
Is wholly foreign to my disposition.
The soul God gave me isn't of the sort
That prospers in the weather of a court.
It's all too obvious that I don't possess

The virtues necessary for success.
My only great talent is for speaking plain;
I've never learned to flatter or to feign;
And anyone so stupidly sincere
Had best not seek a courtier's career.
Outside the court, I know, one must dispense
With honors, privilege, and influence;
But still one gains the right, foregoing these,
Not to be tortured by the wish to please.
One needn't live in dread of snubs and slights,
Nor praise the verse that every idiot writes,
Nor humor silly Marquesses, nor bestow
Politic sighs on Madam So-and-So.

ARSINOÉ   Forget the court, then; let the matter rest.
But I've another cause to be distressed
About your present situation, Sir.
It's to your love affair that I refer.
She whom you love, and who pretends to love you,
Is, I regret to say, unworthy of you.

ALCESTE   Why, Madam? Can you seriously intend
To make so grave a charge against your friend?

ARSINOÉ   Alas, I must. I've stood aside too long
And let that lady do you grievous wrong;
But now my debt to conscience shall be paid:
I tell you that your love has been betrayed.

ALCESTE   I thank you, Madam; you're extremely kind.
Such words are soothing to a lover's mind.

ARSINOÉ   Yes, though she *is* my friend, I say again
You're very much too good for Célimène.
She's wantonly misled you from the start.

ALCESTE   You may be right; who knows another's heart?
But ask yourself if it's the part of charity
To shake my soul with doubts of her sincerity.

ARSINOÉ   Well, if you'd rather be a dupe than doubt her,
That's your affair. I'll say no more about her.

ALCESTE   Madam, you know that doubt and vague suspicion
Are painful to a man in my position;
It's most unkind to worry me this way
Unless you've some real proof of what you say.

ARSINOÉ   Sir, say no more: all doubts shall be removed,
And all that I've been saying shall be proved.
You've only to escort me home, and there
We'll look into the heart of this affair.
I've ocular evidence which will persuade you

Beyond a doubt, that Célimène's betrayed you.
Then, if you're saddened by that revelation,
Perhaps I can provide some consolation.

ACT IV

Scene I (ÉLIANTE, PHILINTE)

PHILINTE   Madam, he acted like a stubborn child;
  I thought they never would be reconciled;
  In vain we reasoned, threatened, and appealed;
  He stood his ground and simply would not yield.
  The Marshals, I feel sure, have never heard
  An argument so splendidly absurd.
  "No, gentlemen," said he, "I'll not retract.
  His verse is bad: extremely bad, in fact.
  Surely it does the man no harm to know it.
  Does it disgrace him, not to be a poet?
  A gentleman may be respected still,
  Whether he writes a sonnet well or ill.
  That I dislike his verse should not offend him;
  In all that touches honor, I commend him;
  He's noble, brave, and virtuous—but I fear
  He can't in truth be called a sonneteer.
  I'll gladly praise his wardrobe; I'll endorse
  His dancing, or the way he sits a horse;
  But, gentlemen, I cannot praise his rhyme.
  In fact, it ought to be a capital crime
  For anyone so sadly unendowed
  To write a sonnet and read the thing aloud."
  At length he fell into a gentler mood
  And, striking a concessive attitude,
  He paid Oronte the following courtesies:
  "Sir, I regret that I'm so hard to please,
  And I'm profoundly sorry that your lyric
  Failed to provoke me to a panegyric."
  After these curious words, the two embraced,
  And then the hearing was adjourned—in haste.
ÉLIANTE   His conduct has been very singular lately;
  Still, I confess that I respect him greatly.
  The honesty in which he takes such pride
  Has—to my mind—its noble, heroic side.
  In this false age, such candor seems outrageous;
  But I could wish that it were more contagious.

PHILINTE   What most intrigues me in our friend Alceste
Is the grand passion that rages in his breast.
The sullen humors he's compounded of
Should not, I think, dispose his heart to love;
But since they do, it puzzles me still more
That he should choose your cousin to adore.

ÉLIANTE   It does, indeed, belie the theory
That love is born of gentle sympathy,
And that the tender passion must be based
On sweet accords of temper and of taste.

PHILINTE   Does she return his love, do you suppose?

ÉLIANTE   Ah, that's a difficult question, Sir. Who knows?
How can we judge the truth of her devotion?
Her heart's a stranger to its own emotion.
Sometimes it thinks it loves, when no love's there;
At other times it loves quite unaware.

PHILINTE   I rather think Alceste is in for more
Distress and sorrow than he's bargained for;
Were he of my mind, Madam, his affection
Would turn in quite a different direction,
And we would see him more responsive to
The kind regard which he receives from you.

ÉLIANTE   Sir, I believe in frankness, and I'm inclined,
In matters of the heart, to speak my mind.
I don't oppose his love for her; indeed,
I hope with all my heart that he'll succeed,
And were it in my power, I'd rejoice
In giving him the lady of his choice.
But if, as happens frequently enough
In love affairs, he meets with a rebuff—
If Célimène should grant some rival's suit—
I'd gladly play the role of substitute;
Nor would his tender speeches please me less
Because they'd once been made without success.

PHILINTE   Well, Madam, as for me, I don't oppose
Your hopes in this affair; and heaven knows
That in my conversations with the man
I plead your cause as often as I can.
But if those two should marry, and so remove
All chance that he will offer you his love,
Then I'll declare my own, and hope to see
Your gracious favor pass from him to me.
In short, should you be cheated of Alceste,
I'd be most happy to be second best.

ÉLIANTE Philinte, you're teasing.

PHILINTE   Ah, Madam, never fear;
  No words of mine were ever so sincere,
  And I shall live in fretful expectation
  Till I can make a fuller declaration.

Scene II (ALCESTE, ÉLIANTE, PHILINTE)

ALCESTE Avenge me, Madam! I must have satisfaction,
  Or this great wrong will drive me to distraction!

ÉLIANTE Why, what's the matter? What's upset you so?

ALCESTE Madam, I've had a mortal, mortal blow.
  If Chaos repossessed the universe,
  I swear I'd not be shaken any worse.
  I'm ruined. . . . I can say no more. . . . My soul . . .

ÉLIANTE Do try, Sir, to regain your self-control.

ALCESTE Just heaven! Why were so much beauty and grace
  Bestowed on one so vicious and so base?

ÉLIANTE Once more, Sir, tell us. . . .

ALCESTE   My world has gone to wrack;
  I'm—I'm betrayed; she's stabbed me in the back:
  Yes, Célimène (who would have thought it of her?)
  Is false to me, and has another lover.

ÉLIANTE Are you quite certain? Can you prove these things?

PHILINTE Lovers are prey to wild imaginings
  And jealous fancies. No doubt there's some mistake. . . .

ALCESTE Mind your own business, Sir, for heaven's sake.
  (*To* ÉLIANTE.) Madam, I have the proof that you demand
  Here in my pocket, penned by her own hand.
  Yes, all the shameful evidence one could want
  Lies in this letter written to Oronte—
  Oronte! whom I felt sure she couldn't love,
  And hardly bothered to be jealous of.

PHILINTE Still, in a letter, appearances may deceive;
  This may not be so bad as you believe.

ALCESTE Once more I beg you, Sir, to let me be;
  Tend to your own affairs; leave mine to me.

ÉLIANTE Compose yourself; this anguish that you feel . . .

ALCESTE Is something, Madam, you alone can heal.
  My outraged heart, beside itself with grief,
  Appeals to you for comfort and relief.
  Avenge me on your cousin, whose unjust
  And faithless nature has deceived my trust;
  Avenge a crime your pure soul must detest.

ÉLIANTE But how, Sir?

ALCESTE   Madam, this heart within my breast
   Is yours; pray take it; redeem my heart from her,
   And so avenge me on my torturer.
   Let her be punished by the fond emotion,
   The ardent love, the bottomless devotion,
   The faithful worship which this heart of mine
   Will offer up to yours as to a shrine.
ÉLIANTE You have my sympathy, Sir, in all you suffer;
   Nor do I scorn the noble heart you offer;
   But I suspect you'll soon be mollified,
   And this desire for vengeance will subside.
   When some belovèd hand has done us wrong
   We thirst for retribution—but not for long;
   However dark the deed that she's committed,
   A lovely culprit's very soon acquitted.
   Nothing's so stormy as an injured lover,
   And yet no storm so quickly passes over.
ALCESTE No, Madam, no—this is no lovers' spat;
   I'll not forgive her; it's gone too far for that;
   My mind's made up; I'll kill myself before
   I waste my hopes upon her any more.
   Ah, here she is. My wrath intensifies.
   I shall confront her with her tricks and lies,
   And crush her utterly, and bring you then
   A heart no longer slave to Célimène.

Scene III (CÉLIMÈNE, ALCESTE)

ALCESTE (*aside*) Sweet heaven, help me to control my passion.
CÉLIMÈNE (*aside*) Oh, Lord.
   (*To* ALCESTE.)   Why stand there staring in that fashion?
   And what d'you mean by those dramatic sighs,
   And that malignant glitter in your eyes?
ALCESTE I mean that sins which cause the blood to freeze
   Look innocent beside your treacheries;
   That nothing Hell's or Heaven's wrath could do
   Ever produced so bad a thing as you.
CÉLIMÈNE Your compliments were always sweet and pretty.
ALCESTE Madam, it's not the moment to be witty.
   No, blush and hang your head; you've ample reason,
   Since I've the fullest evidence of your treason.
   Ah, this is what my sad heart prophesied;
   Now all my anxious fears are verified;
   My dark suspicion and my gloomy doubt

Divined the truth, and now the truth is out.
For all your trickery, I was not deceived;
It was my bitter stars that I believed.
But don't imagine that you'll go scot-free;
You shan't misuse me with impunity.
I know that love's irrational and blind;
I know the heart's not subject to the mind,
And can't be reasoned into beating faster;
I know each soul is free to choose its master;
Therefore had you but spoken from the heart,
Rejecting my attentions from the start,
I'd have no grievance, or at any rate
I could complain of nothing but my fate.
Ah, but so falsely to encourage me—
That was a treason and a treachery
For which you cannot suffer too severely,
And you shall pay for that behavior dearly.
Yes, now I have no pity, not a shred;
My temper's out of hand; I've lost my head;
Shocked by the knowledge of your double-dealings,
My reason can't restrain my savage feelings;
A righteous wrath deprives me of my senses,
And I won't answer for the consequences.

CÉLIMÈNE   What does this outburst mean? Will you please explain?
Have you, by any chance, gone quite insane?

ALCESTE   Yes, yes, I went insane the day I fell
A victim to your black and fatal spell,
Thinking to meet with some sincerity
Among the treacherous charms that beckoned me.

CÉLIMÈNE   Pooh. Of what treachery can you complain?

ALCESTE   How sly you are, how cleverly you feign!
But you'll not victimize me any more.
Look: here's a document you've seen before.
This evidence, which I acquired today,
Leaves you, I think, without a thing to say.

CÉLIMÈNE   Is this what sent you into such a fit?

ALCESTE   You should be blushing at the sight of it.

CÉLIMÈNE   Ought I to blush? I truly don't see why.

ALCESTE   Ah, now you're being bold as well as sly;
Since there's no signature, perhaps you'll claim . . .

CÉLIMÈNE   I wrote it, whether or not it bears my name.

ALCESTE   And you can view with equanimity
This proof of your disloyalty to me!

CÉLIMÈNE   Oh, don't be so outrageous and extreme.

ALCESTE   You take this matter lightly, it would seem.
Was it no wrong to me, no shame to you,
That you should send Oronte this billet-doux?

CÉLIMÈNTE   Oronte! Who said it was for him?

ALCESTE   Why, those
Who brought me this example of your prose.
But what's the difference? If you wrote the letter
To someone else, it pleases me no better.
My grievance and your guilt remain the same.

CÉLIMÈNE   But need you rage, and need I blush for shame,
If this was written to a *woman* friend?

ALCESTE   Ah! Most ingenious. I'm impressed no end;
And after that incredible evasion
Your guilt is clear. I need no more persuasion.
How dare you try so clumsy a deception?
D'you think I'm wholly wanting in perception?
Come, come, let's see how brazenly you'll try
To bolster up so palpable a lie:
Kindly construe this ardent closing section
As nothing more than sisterly affection!
Here, let me read it. Tell me, if you dare to,
That this is for a woman . . .

CÉLIMÈNE   I don't care to.
What right have you to badger and berate me,
And so highhandedly interrogate me?

ALCESTE   Now, don't be angry; all I ask of you
Is that you justify a phrase or two . . .

CÉLIMÈNE   No, I shall not. I utterly refuse,
And you may take those phrases as you choose.

ALCESTE   Just show me how this letter could be meant
For a woman's eyes, and I shall be content.

CÉLIMÈNE   No, no, it's for Oronte; you're perfectly right.
I welcome his attentions with delight,
I prize his character and his intellect,
And everything is just as you suspect.
Come, do your worst now; give your rage free rein;
But kindly cease to bicker and complain.

ALCESTE *(aside)*   Good God! Could anything be more inhuman?
Was ever a heart so mangled by a woman?
When I complain of how she has betrayed me,
She bridles, and commences to upbraid me!
She tries my tortured patience to the limit;
She won't deny her guilt; she glories in it!

And yet my heart's too faint and cowardly
To break these chains of passion, and be free,
To scorn her as it should, and rise above
This unrewarded, mad, and bitter love.
(*To* CÉLIMÈNE.)   Ah, traitress, in how confident a fashion
You take advantage of my helpless passion,
And use my weakness for your faithless charms
To make me once again throw down my arms!
But do at least deny this black transgression;
Take back that mocking and perverse confession;
Defend this letter and your innocence,
And I, poor fool, will aid in your defense.
Pretend, pretend, that you are just and true,
And I shall make myself believe in you.

CÉLIMÈNE   Oh, stop it. Don't be such a jealous dunce,
Or I shall leave off loving you at once.
Just why should I *pretend?* What could impel me
To stoop so low as that? And kindly tell me
Why, if I loved another, I shouldn't merely
Inform you of it, simply and sincerely!
I've told you where you stand, and that admission
Should altogether clear me of suspicion;
After so generous a guarantee,
What right have you to harbor doubts of me?
Since women are (from natural reticence)
Reluctant to declare their sentiments,
And since the honor of our sex requires
That we conceal our amorous desires,
Ought any man for whom such laws are broken
To question what the oracle has spoken?
Should he not rather feel an obligation
To trust that most obliging declaration?
Enough, now. Your suspicions quite disgust me;
Why should I love a man who doesn't trust me?
I cannot understand why I continue,
Fool that I am, to take an interest in you.
I ought to choose a man less prone to doubt,
And give you something to be vexed about.

ALCESTE   Ah, what a poor enchanted fool I am;
These gentle words, no doubt, were all a sham,
But destiny requires me to entrust
My happiness to you, and so I must.
I'll love you to the bitter end, and see
How false and treacherous you dare to be.

CÉLIMÈNE   No, you don't really love me as you ought.
ALCESTE   I love you more than can be said or thought;
   Indeed, I wish you were in such distress
   That I might show my deep devotedness.
   Yes, I could wish that you were wretchedly poor,
   Unloved, uncherished, utterly obscure;
   That fate had set you down upon the earth
   Without possessions, rank, or gentle birth;
   Then, by the offer of my heart, I might
   Repair the great injustice of your plight;
   I'd raise you from the dust, and proudly prove
   The purity and vastness of my love.
CÉLIMÈNE   This is a strange benevolence indeed!
   God grant that I may never be in need. . . .
   Ah, here's Monsieur Dubois, in quaint disguise.

Scene IV (CÉLIMÈNE, ALCESTE, DUBOIS)

ALCESTE   Well, why this costume? Why those frightened eyes?
   What ails you?
DUBOIS   Well, Sir, things are most mysterious.
ALCESTE   What do you mean?
DUBOIS   I fear they're very serious.
ALCESTE   What?
DUBOIS   Shall I speak more loudly?
ALCESTE   Yes; speak out.
DUBOIS   Isn't there someone here, Sir?
ALCESTE   Speak, you lout!
   Stop wasting time.
DUBOIS   Sir, we must slip away.
ALCESTE   How's that?
DUBOIS   We must decamp without delay.
ALCESTE   Explain yourself.
DUBOIS   I tell you we must fly.
ALCESTE   What for?
DUBOIS   We mustn't pause to say good-by.
ALCESTE   Now what d'you mean by all of this, you clown?
DUBOIS   I mean, Sir, that we've got to leave this town.
ALCESTE   I'll tear you limb from limb and joint from joint
   If you don't come more quickly to the point.
DUBOIS   Well, Sir, today a man in a black suit,
   Who wore a black and ugly scowl to boot,
   Left us a document scrawled in such a hand
   As even Satan couldn't understand.

It bears upon your lawsuit, I don't doubt;
But all hell's devils couldn't make it out.

ALCESTE Well, well, go on. What then? I fail to see
How this event obliges us to flee.

DUBOIS Well, Sir, an hour later, hardly more,
A gentleman who's often called before
Came looking for you in an anxious way.
Not finding you, he asked me to convey
(Knowing I could be trusted with the same)
The following message. . . . Now, what *was* his name?

ALCESTE Forget his name, you idiot. What did he say?

DUBOIS Well, it was one of your friends, Sir, anyway.
He warned you to begone, and he suggested
That if you stay, you may well be arrested.

ALCESTE What? Nothing more specific? Think, man, think!

DUBOIS No, Sir. He had me bring him pen and ink,
And dashed you off a letter which, I'm sure,
Will render things distinctly less obscure.

ALCESTE Well—let me have it!

CÉLIMÈNE   What *is* this all about?

ALCESTE God knows; but I have hopes of finding out.
How long am I to wait, you blitherer?

DUBOIS (*after a protracted search for the letter*) I must have left
it on your table, Sir.

ALCESTE I ought to . . .

CÉLIMÉNE   No, no, keep your self-control;
Go find out what's behind his rigmarole.

ALCESTE It seems that fate, no matter what I do,
Has sworn that I may not converse with you;
But, Madam, pray permit your faithful lover
To try once more before the day is over.

ACT V

Scene I (ALCESTE, PHILINTE)

ALCESTE No, it's too much. My mind's made up, I tell you.

PHILINTE Why should this blow, however hard, compel you . . .

ALCESTE No, no, don't waste your breath in argument;
Nothing you say will alter my intent;
This age is vile, and I've made up my mind
To have no further commerce with mankind.
Did not truth, honor, decency, and the laws

Oppose my enemy and approve my cause?
My claims were justified in all men's sight;
I put my trust in equity and right;
Yet, to my horror and the world's disgrace,
Justice is mocked, and I have lost my case!
A scoundrel whose dishonesty is notorious
Emerges from another lie victorious!
Honor and right condone his brazen fraud,
While rectitude and decency applaud!
Before his smirking face, the truth stands charmed,
And virtue conquered, and the law disarmed!
His crime is sanctioned by a court decree!
And not content with what he's done to me,
The dog now seeks to ruin me by stating
That I composed a book now circulating,
A book so wholly criminal and vicious
That even to speak its title is seditious!
Meanwhile Oronte, my rival, lends his credit
To the same libelous tale, and helps to spread it!
Oronte! a man of honor and of rank,
With whom I've been entirely fair and frank;
Who sought me out and forced me, willy nilly,
To judge some verse I found extremely silly;
And who, because I properly refused
To flatter him, or see the truth abused,
Abets my enemy in a rotten slander!
There's the reward of honesty and candor!
The man will hate me to the end of time
For failing to commend his wretched rhyme!
And not this man alone, but all humanity
Do what they do from interest and vanity;
They prate of honor, truth, and righteousness,
But lie, betray, and swindle nonetheless.
Come then: man's villainy is too much to bear;
Let's leave this jungle and this jackal's lair.
Yes! treacherous and savage race of men,
You shall not look upon my face again.

PHILINTE   Oh, don't rush into exile prematurely;
Things aren't as dreadful as you make them, surely.
It's rather obvious, since you're still at large,
That people don't believe your enemy's charge.
Indeed, his tale's so patently untrue
That it may do more harm to him than you.

ALCESTE   Nothing could do that scoundrel any harm:
   His frank corruption is his greatest charm,
   And, far from hurting him, a further shame
   Would only serve to magnify his name.
PHILINTE   In any case, his bald prevarication
   Has done no injury to your reputation,
   And you may feel secure in that regard.
   As for your lawsuit, it should not be hard
   To have the case reopened, and contest
   This judgment . . .
ALCESTE   No, no, let the verdict rest.
   Whatever cruel penalty it may bring,
   I wouldn't have it changed for anything.
   It shows the times' injustice with such clarity
   That I shall pass it down to our posterity
   As a great proof and signal demonstration
   Of the black wickedness of this generation.
   It may cost twenty thousand francs; but I
   Shall pay their twenty thousand, and gain thereby
   The right to storm and rage at human evil,
   And send the race of mankind to the devil.
PHILINTE   Listen to me . . .
ALCESTE   Why? What can you possibly say?
   Don't argue, Sir; your labor's thrown away.
   Do you propose to offer lame excuses
   For men's behavior and the times' abuses?
PHILINTE   No, all you say I'll readily concede:
   This is a low, conniving age indeed;
   Nothing but trickery prospers nowadays,
   And people ought to mend their shabby ways.
   Yes, man's a beastly creature; but must we then
   Abandon the society of men?
   Here in the world, each human frailty
   Provides occasion for philosophy,
   And that is virtue's noblest exercise;
   If honesty shone forth from all men's eyes,
   If every heart were frank and kind and just.
   What could our virtues do but gather dust
   (Since their employment is to help us bear
   The villainies of men without despair)?
   A heart well-armed with virtue can endure. . . .
ALCESTE   Sir, you're a matchless reasoner, to be sure;
   Your words are fine and full of cogency;

But don't waste time and eloquence on me.
My reason bids me go, for my own good.
My tongue won't lie and flatter as it should;
God knows what frankness it might next commit,
And what I'd suffer on account of it.
Pray let me wait for Célimène's return
In peace and quiet. I shall shortly learn,
By her response to what I have in view,
Whether her love for me is feigned or true.

PHILINTE   Till then, let's visit Éliante upstairs.

ALCESTE   No, I am too weighed down with somber cares.
Go to her, do; and leave me with my gloom
Here in the darkened corner of this room.

PHILINTE   Why, that's no sort of company, my friend;
I'll see if Éliante will not descend.

Scene II (CÉLIMÈNE, ORONTE, ALCESTE)

ORONTE   Yes, Madam, if you wish me to remain
Your true and ardent lover, you must deign
To give me some more positive assurance.
All this suspense is quite beyond endurance.
If your heart shares the sweet desires of mine,
Show me as much by some convincing sign;
And here's the sign I urgently suggest:
That you no longer tolerate Alceste,
But sacrifice him to my love, and sever
All your relations with the man forever.

CÉLIMÈNE   Why do you suddenly dislike him so?
You praised him to the skies not long ago.

ORONTE   Madam, that's not the point. I'm here to find
Which way your tender feelings are inclined.
Choose, if you please, between Alceste and me,
And I shall stay or go accordingly.

ALCESTE (*emerging from the corner*)   Yes, Madam, choose; this
gentleman's demand
Is wholly just, and I support his stand.
I too am true and ardent; I too am here
To ask you that you make your feelings clear.
No more delays, now; no equivocation;
The time has come to make your declaration.

ORONTE   Sir, I've no wish in any way to be
An obstacle to your felicity.

ALCESTE Sir, I've no wish to share her heart with you;
  That may sound jealous, but at least it's true.
ORONTE If, weighing us, she leans in your direction . . .
ALCESTE If she regards you with the least affection . . .
ORONTE I swear I'll yield her to you there and then.
ALCESTE I swear I'll never see her face again.
ORONTE Now, Madam, tell us what we've come to hear.
ALCESTE Madam, speak openly and have no fear.
ORONTE Just say which one is to remain your lover.
ALCESTE Just name one name, and it will all be over.
ORONTE What! Is it possible that you're undecided?
ALCESTE What! Can your feelings possibly be divided?
CÉLIMÈNE Enough: this inquisition's gone too far:
  How utterly unreasonable you are!
  Not that I couldn't make the choice with ease;
  My heart has no conflicting sympathies;
  I know full well which one of you I favor,
  And you'd not see me hesitate or waver.
  But how can you expect me to reveal
  So cruelly and bluntly what I feel?
  I think it altogether too unpleasant
  To choose between two men when both are present;
  One's heart has means more subtle and more kind
  Of letting its affections be divined,
  Nor need one be uncharitably plain
  To let a lover know he loves in vain.
ORONTE No, no, speak plainly; I for one can stand it.
  I beg you to be frank.
ALCESTE   And I demand it.
  The simple truth is what I wish to know,
  And there's no need for softening the blow.
  You've made an art of pleasing everyone,
  But now your days of coquetry are done:
  You have no choice now, Madam, but to choose,
  For I'll know what to think if you refuse;
  I'll take your silence for a clear admission
  That I'm entitled to my worst suspicion.
ORONTE I thank you for this ultimatum, Sir,
  And I may say I heartily concur.
CÉLIMÈNE Really, this foolishness is very wearing:
  Must you be so unjust and overbearing?
  Haven't I told you why I must demur?
  Ah, here's Éliante; I'll put the case to her.

Scene III (Éliante, Philinte, Célimène, Oronte, Alceste)

CÉLIMÈNE   Cousin, I'm being persecuted here
By these two persons, who, it would appear,
Will not be satisfied till I confess
Which one I love the more, and which the less,
And tell the latter to his face that he
Is henceforth banished from my company.
Tell me, has ever such a thing been done?

ÉLIANTE   You'd best not turn to me; I'm not the one
To back you in a matter of this kind:
I'm all for those who frankly speak their mind.

ORONTE   Madam, you'll search in vain for a defender.

ALCESTE   You're beaten, Madam, and may as well surrender.

ORONTE   Speak, speak, you must; and end this awful strain.

ALCESTE   Or don't, and your position will be plain.

ORONTE   A single word will close this painful scene.

ALCESTE   But if you're silent, I'll know what you mean.

Scene IV (Arsinoé, Célimène, Éliante, Alceste, Philinte, Acaste, Clitandre, Oronte)

ACASTE (*to* CÉLIMÈNE)   Madam, with all due deference, we two
Have come to pick a little bone with you.

CLITANDRE (*to* ORONTE *and* ALCESTE)   I'm glad you're present,
Sirs, as you'll soon learn,
Our business here is also your concern.

ARSINOÉ (*to* CÉLIMÈNE)   Madam, I visit you so soon again
Only because of these two gentlemen,
Who came to me indignant and aggrieved
About a crime too base to be believed.
Knowing your virtue, having such confidence in it,
I couldn't think you guilty for a minute,
In spite of all their telling evidence;
And, rising above our little difference,
I've hastened here in friendship's name to see
You clear yourself of this great calumny.

ACASTE   Yes, Madam, let us see with what composure
You'll manage to respond to this disclosure.
You lately sent Clitandre this tender note.

CLITANDRE   And this one, for Acaste, you also wrote.

ACASTE (*to* ORONTE *and* ALCESTE)   You'll recognize this writing,
Sirs, I think;
The lady is so free with pen and ink

That you must know it all too well, I fear.
But listen: this is something you should hear.

> "How absurd you are to condemn my lightheartedness in so-
> ciety, and to accuse me of being happiest in the company of
> others. Nothing could be more unjust; and if you do not come
> to me instantly and beg pardon for saying such a thing, I
> shall never forgive you as long as I live. Our big bumbling
> friend the Viscount . . ."

What a shame that he's not here.

> "Our big bumbling friend the Viscount, whose name stands
> first in your complaint, is hardly a man to my taste; and ever
> since the day I watched him spend three-quarters of an hour
> spitting into a well, so as to make circles in the water, I have
> been unable to think highly of him. As for the little Mar-
> quess . . ."

In all modesty, gentlemen, that is I.

> "As for the little Marquess, who sat squeezing my hand for
> such a long while yesterday, I find him in all respects the most
> trifling creature alive; and the only things of value about him
> are his cape and his sword. As for the man with the green
> ribbons . . ."

(*To* ALCESTE.)   It's your turn now, Sir.

> "As for the man with the green ribbons, he amuses me now
> and then with his bluntness and his bearish ill-humor; but
> there are many times indeed when I think him the greatest
> bore in the world. And as for the sonneteer . . ."

(*To* ORONTE.)   Here's your helping.

> "And as for the sonneteer, who has taken it into his head to
> be witty, and insists on being an author in the teeth of opin-
> ion, I simply cannot be bothered to listen to him, and his
> prose wearies me quite as much as his poetry. Be assured that
> I am not always so well-entertained as you suppose; that I
> long for your company, more than I dare to say, at all these
> entertainments to which people drag me; and that the pres-
> ence of those one loves is the true and perfect seasoning to all
> one's pleasures."

CLITANDRE   And now for me.

"Clitandre, whom you mention, and who so pesters me with his
saccharine speeches, is the last man on earth for whom I
could feel any affection. He is quite mad to suppose that I
love him, and so are you, to doubt that you are loved. Do
come to your senses; exchange your suppositions for his; and
visit me as often as possible, to help me bear the annoyance
of his unwelcome attentions."

It's sweet character that these letters show,
And what to call it, Madam, you well know.
Enough. We're off to make the world acquainted
With this sublime self-portrait that you've painted.
ACASTE   Madam, I'll make you no farewell oration;
No, you're not worthy of my indignation.
Far choicer hearts than yours, as you'll discover,
Would like this little Marquess for a lover.

Scene V (CÉLIMÈNE, ÉLIANTE, ARSINOÉ, ALCESTE, ORONTE,
PHILINTE)

ORONTE   So! After all those loving letters you wrote,
You turn on me like this, and cut my throat!
And your dissembling, faithless heart, I find,
Has pledged itself by turns to all mankind!
How blind I've been! But now I clearly see;
I thank you, Madam, for enlightening me.
My heart is mine once more, and I'm content;
The loss of it shall be your punishment.
(*To* ALCESTE)   Sir, she is yours; I'll seek no more to stand
Between your wishes and this lady's hand.

Scene VI (CÉLIMÈNE, ÉLIANTE, ARSINOÉ, ALCESTE, PHILINTE)

ARSINOÉ (*to* CÉLIMÈNE)   Madam, I'm forced to speak. I'm
far too stirred
To keep my counsel, after what I've heard.
I'm shocked and staggered by your want of morals.
It's not my way to mix in others' quarrels;
But really, when this fine and noble spirit,
This man of honor and surpassing merit,
Laid down the offering of his heart before you,
How *could* you . . .
ALCESTE   Madam, permit me, I implore you,
To represent myself in this debate.
Don't bother, please, to be my advocate.
My heart, in any case, could not afford
To give your services their due reward;

And if I chose, for consolation's sake,
Some other lady, 'twould not be you I'd take.
ARSINOÉ   What makes you think you could, Sir? And how dare you
Imply that I've been trying to ensnare you?
If you can for a moment entertain
Such flattering fancies, you're extremely vain.
I'm not so interested as you suppose
In Célimène's discarded gigolos.
Get rid of that absurd illusion, do.
Women like me are not for such as you.
Stay with this creature, to whom you're so attached;
I've never seen two people better matched.

Scene VII (CÉLIMÈNE, ÉLIANTE, ALCESTE, PHILINTE)

ALCESTE (*to* CÉLIMÈNE)   Well, I've been still throughout this
    exposé,
Till everyone but me has said his say.
Come, have I shown sufficient self-restraint?
And may I now . . .
CÉLIMÈNE   Yes, make your just complaint.
Reproach me freely, call me what you will;
You've every right to say I've used you ill.
I've wronged you, I confess it; and in my shame
I'll make no effort to escape the blame.
The anger of those others I could despise;
My guilt toward you I sadly recognize.
Your wrath is wholly justified, I fear;
I know how culpable I must appear,
I know all things bespeak my treachery,
And that, in short, you've grounds for hating me.
Do so; I give you leave.
ALCESTE   Ah, traitress—how,
How should I cease to love you, even now?
Though mind and will were passionately bent
On hating you, my heart would not consent.
(*To* ÉLIANTE *and* PHILINTE.)   Be witness to my madness, both of
    you;
See what infatuation drives one to;
But wait; my folly's only just begun,
And I shall prove to you before I'm done
How strange the human heart is, and how far
From rational we sorry creatures are.
(*To* CÉLIMÈNE.)   Woman, I'm willing to forget your shame,
And clothe your treacheries in a sweeter name;

I'll call them youthful errors, instead of crimes,
And lay the blame on these corrupting times.
My one condition is that you agree
To share my chosen fate, and fly with me
To that wild, trackless, solitary place
In which I shall forget the human race.
Only by such a course can you atone
For those atrocious letters; by that alone
Can you remove my present horror of you,
And make it possible for me to love you.

CÉLIMÈNE What! *I* renounce the world at my young age,
And die of boredom in some hermitage?

ALCESTE Ah, if you really loved me as you ought,
You wouldn't give the world a moment's thought;
Must you have me, and all the world beside?

CÉLIMÈNE Alas, at twenty one is terrified
Of solitude. I fear I lack the force
And depth of soul to take so stern a course.
But if my hand in marriage will content you,
Why, there's a plan which I might well consent to,
And . . .

ALCESTE No, I detest you now. I could excuse
Everything else, but since you thus refuse
To love me wholly, as a wife should do,
And see the world in me, as I in you,
Go! I reject your hand, and disenthrall
My heart from your enchantments, once for all.

Scene VIII (ÉLIANTE, ALCESTE, PHILINTE)

ALCESTE (*to* ÉLIANTE) Madam, your virtuous beauty has no peer;
Of all this world you only are sincere;
I've long esteemed you highly, as you know;
Permit me ever to esteem you so,
And if I do not now request your hand,
Forgive me, Madam, and try to understand.
I feel unworthy of it; I sense that fate
Does not intend me for the married state,
That I should do you wrong by offering you
My shattered heart's unhappy residue,
And that in short . . .

ÉLIANTE   Your argument's well taken:
Nor need you fear that I shall feel forsaken.
Were I to offer him this hand of mine,
Your friend Philinte, I think, would not decline.

PHILINTE   Ah, Madam, that's my heart's most cherished goal,
For which I'd gladly give my life and soul.
ALCESTE (*to* ÉLIANTE *and* PHILINTE)   May you be true to all
you now profess,
And so deserve unending happiness.
Meanwhile, betrayed and wronged in everything,
I'll flee this bitter world where vice is king,
And seek some spot unpeopled and apart
Where I'll be free to have an honest heart.
PHILINTE   Come, Madam, let's do everything we can
To change the mind of this unhappy man.

MISS JULIE (1888)

AUGUST STRINDBERG (1849–1912)

In 1887 Strindberg wrote one of the great naturalistic plays, *The Father*. In this jungle battle of the sexes, husband and wife are pitted against each other in a death struggle, the winner of which is the predatory emasculating female. Belittled by his spouse, the father, a retired cavalry officer, finds his scientific experiments degraded and his paternity questioned so that in the end there is total victory for the exultant wife and a straightjacket for her raving husband.

One of the earliest exponents of expressionism in his *Dream Play* (1902) and *The Spook* (or *Ghost*) *Sonata* (1907), Strindberg created highly stylized interpretations of the nightmare world of life in extremely complex and difficult plays almost impossible to produce. But of equal, if not greater, importance is Strindberg's portrayal of one of the great emotional struggles of his own life—sex and marriage—in at least three almost unbearably intense dramas, *The Father*, *The Dance of Death* (1901) and *Miss Julie*. The young Eugene O'Neill in the United States was fascinated by Strindberg and publicly acknowledged the strong influence which the Swedish dramatist had on his own development. The detailed dissection of the human soul, the baring of raw flesh and the animal snarling and tearing that goes on in Strindberg's marital battlefield, and which the young O'Neill often closely copied, are among the best examples that we have of the techniques of the dramatic naturalist.

Miss Julie is in many ways a terrifying play as it exhibits the conscious degradation of the protagonist who seeks to destroy what she cannot have and is simultaneously destroyed in turn in a kind of reversal from the usual Strindbergian female triumphant. Amidst the eroticisms of the festivities of Midsummer Eve, the long day-night of the Scandinavian summer season, the nightmare of Julie's own depravity takes place. She is out of her element, which is "above stairs," but she must lower herself, having been rejected by her more "proper" lover's refusal to leap at her command, to establish her own female prowess. This time she orders her social inferior, her father's valet, to perform as she bids. The risks are great; the ultimate destruction complete.

Miss Julie is an excellent example of the spine-chilling effect which the naturalistic writer can weave when he chooses to delve into the elements of the inner soul and expose them piece by piece before an audience. The bloody execution of the bird, for no really legitimate reason, parallels the execution of the grovelling Julie, butchered first symbolically by the violation of her body in the self-induced seduction, and then by the knife-blade in the barn, again self-administered, paralleling the sexual "violation" of her aristocratic purity. The natural strength of the more earthy sexual prowess of Jean has triumphed, but only at the "order" of the victim; the artificial strength of Julie's snobbery and spoiled rottenness, the result of her "higher" birth, has been conquered. There is nothing left but death.

Julie almost becomes in the inevitability of her catastrophe a tragic protagonist. She is a product of what nature and society have made her, a kind of hybrid monster, unable to control her fundamental natural sensuous urges. Ready to lower herself to become the wife of an innkeeper, obviously incapable of surviving under such conditions, she finally recognizes what she is and she sees the doom from which there is no escape. She must encounter it alone. Whether or not she rises to sufficient stature as a tragic protagonist may be a question, but there is a size, a certain larger-than-life quality about her, which makes her one of modern drama's most hypnotically fascinating naturalistic heroines.

Miss Julie
STRINDBERG

Translated by Elizabeth Sprigge

CHARACTERS

MISS JULIE, *aged 25*
JEAN, *the valet, aged 30*
KRISTIN, *the cook, aged 35*

SCENE: *The large kitchen of a Swedish manor house in a country district in the eighties.*
  Midsummer eve.
  The kitchen has three doors, two small ones into JEAN'S *and* KRISTIN'S *bedrooms, and a large, glass-fronted double one, opening on to a courtyard. This is the only way to the rest of the house.*
  Through these glass doors can be seen part of a fountain with a cupid, lilac bushes in flower and the tops of some Lombardy poplars. On one wall are shelves edged with scalloped paper on which are kitchen utensils of copper, iron and tin.
  To the left is the corner of a large tiled range and part of its chimney-hood, to the right the end of the servants' dinner table with chairs beside it.
  The stove is decorated with birch boughs, the floor strewn with twigs of juniper. On the end of the table is a large Japanese spice jar full of lilac.
  There are also an ice-box, a scullery table and a sink. Above the double door hangs a big old-fashioned bell; near it is a speaking-tube.
  A fiddle can be heard from the dance in the barn near-by. KRISTIN *is standing at the stove, frying something in a pan. She wears a light-coloured cotton dress and a big apron.*
  JEAN *enters, wearing livery and carrying a pair of large riding-boots with spurs, which he puts in a conspicuous place.*

JEAN   Miss Julie's crazy again to-night, absolutely crazy.
KRISTIN   Oh, so you're back, are you?
JEAN   When I'd taken the Count to the station, I came back and dropped in at the Barn for a dance. And who did I see there but our young lady leading off with the gamekeeper. But the moment she sets eyes on me, up she rushes and invites me to waltz with

329

her. And how she waltzed—I've never seen anything like it! She's crazy.

KRISTIN   Always has been, but never so bad as this last fortnight since the engagement was broken off.

JEAN   Yes, that was a pretty business, to be sure. He's a decent enough chap, too, even if he isn't rich. Oh, but they're choosy! (*Sits down at the end of the table.*) In any case, it's a bit odd that our young—er—lady would rather stay at home with the yokels than go with her father to visit her relations.

KRISTIN   Perhaps she feels a bit awkward, after that bust-up with her fiancé.

JEAN   Maybe. That chap had some guts, though. Do you know the sort of thing that was going on, Kristin? I saw it with my own eyes, though I didn't let on I had.

KRISTIN   You saw them . . . ?

JEAN   Didn't I just! Came across the pair of them one evening in the stableyard. Miss Julie was doing what she called "training" him. Know what that was? Making him jump over her riding-whip—the way you teach a dog. He did it twice and got a cut each time for his pains, but when it came to the third go, he snatched the whip out of her hand and broke it into simthereens. And then he cleared off.

KRISTIN   What goings on! I never did!

JEAN   Well, that's how it was with that little affair . . . Now, what have you got for me, Kristin? Something tasty?

KRISTIN   (*serving from the pan to his plate*)   Well, it's just a little bit of kidney I cut off their joint.

JEAN   (*smelling it*)   Fine! That's my special delice. (*Feels the plate.*) But you might have warmed the plate.

KRISTIN   When you choose to be finicky you're worse than the Count himself. (*Pulls his hair affectionately.*)

JEAN   (*crossly*)   Stop pulling my hair. You know how sensitive I am.

KRISTIN   There, there! It's only love, you know.

(JEAN *eats.* KRISTIN *brings a bottle of beer.*)

JEAN   Beer on Midsummer Eve? No thanks! I've got something better than that. (*From a drawer in the table brings out a bottle of red wine with a yellow seal.*) Yellow seal, see! Now get me a glass. You use a glass with a stem, of course, when you're drinking it straight.

KRISTIN   (*giving him a wine-glass*)   Lord help the woman who gets you for a husband, you old fusser! (*She puts the beer in the ice-box and sets a small sauce-pan on the stove.*)

JEAN   Nonsense!   You'll be glad enough to get a fellow as smart as me. And I don't think it's done you any harm people calling me your fiancé. (*Tastes the wine.*) Good. Very good indeed. But not quite warmed enough. (*Warms the glass in his hand.*)   We bought this in Dijon. Four francs the litre without the bottle, and duty on top of that. What are you cooking now? It stinks.

KRISTIN   Some bloody muck Miss Julie wants for Diana.

JEAN   You should be more refined in your speech, Kristin. But why should you spend a holiday cooking for that bitch? Is she sick or what?

KRISTIN   Yes, she's sick. She sneaked out with the pug at the lodge and got in the usual mess. And that, you know, Miss Julie won't have.

JEAN   Miss Julie's too high-and-mighty in some respects, and not enough in others, just like her mother before her. The Countess was more at home in the kitchen and cowsheds than anywhere else, but would she ever go driving with only one horse? She went round with her cuffs filthy, but she had to have the coronet on the cuff-links. Our young lady—to come back to her—hasn't any proper respect for herself or her position. I mean she isn't refined. In the Barn just now she dragged the gamekeeper away from Anna and made him dance with her—no waiting to be asked. We wouldn't do a thing like that. But that's what happens when the gentry try to behave like the common people—they become common . . . Still, she's a fine girl. Smashing! What shoulders! And what—er etcetera!

KRISTIN   Oh come off it! I know what Clara says, and she dresses her.

JEAN   Clara? Pooh, you're all jealous! But I've been out riding with her . . . and as for her dancing!

KRISTIN   Listen, Jean. You will dance with me, won't you, as soon as I'm through?

JEAN   Of course I will.

KRISTIN   Promise?

JEAN   Promise? When I say I'll do a thing I do it. Well, thanks for the supper. It was a real treat. (*Corks the bottle.*)

(JULIE *appears in the doorway, speaking to someone outside.*)

JULIE   I'll be back in a moment. Don't wait.

(JEAN *slips the bottle into the drawer and rises respectfully.* JULIE *enters and joins* KRISTIN *at the stove.*)

Well, have you made it? (KRISTIN *signs that* JEAN *is near them.*)

JEAN (*gallantly*)   Have you ladies got some secret?

JULIE (*flipping his face with her handkerchief*) You're very inquisitive.

JEAN What a delicious smell! Violets.

JULIE (*coquettishly*) Impertinence! Are you an expert of scent too? I must say you know how to dance. Now don't look. Go away. (*The music of a schottische begins.*)

JEAN (*with impudent politeness*) Is it some witches' brew you're cooking on Midsummer Eve? Something to tell your stars by, so you can see your future?

JULIE (*sharply*) If you could see that you'd have good eyes. (*To* KRISTIN.) Put it in a bottle and cork it tight. Come and dance this schottische with me, Jean.

JEAN (*hesitating*) I don't want to be rude, but I've promised to dance this one with Kristin.

JULIE Well, she can have another, can't you, Kristin? You'll lend me Jean, won't you?

KRISTIN (*bottling*) It's nothing to do with me. When you're so condescending, Miss, it's not his place to say no. Go on, Jean, and thank Miss Julie for the honour.

JEAN Frankly speaking, Miss, and no offence meant, I wonder if it's wise for you to dance twice running with the same partner, specially as those people are so ready to jump to conclusions.

JULIE (*flaring up*) What did you say? What sort of conclusions? What do you mean?

JEAN (*meekly*) As you choose not to understand, Miss Julie, I'll have to speak more plainly. It looks bad to show a preference for one of your retainers when they're all hoping for the same unusual favour.

JULIE Show a preference! The very idea! I'm surprised at you. I'm doing the people an honour by attending their ball when I'm mistress of the house, but if I'm really going to dance, I mean to have a partner who can lead and doesn't make me look ridiculous.

JEAN If those are your orders, Miss, I'm at your service.

JULIE (*gently*) Don't take it as an order. To-night we're all just people enjoying a party. There's no question of class. So now give me your arm. Don't worry, Kristin. I shan't steal your sweetheart.

(JEAN *gives* JULIE *his arm and leads her out.*)

Left alone, KRISTIN *plays her scene in an unhurried, natural way, humming to the tune of the schottische, played on a distant violin. She clears* JEAN's *place, washes up and puts things away, then takes off her apron, brings out a small mirror from a drawer, props it against the jar of lilac, lights a candle, warms a small pair of tongs and curls her fringe. She*

goes to the door and listens, then turning back to the table finds Miss
Julie's *forgotten handkerchief. She smells it, then meditatively smooths
it out and folds it.*

(*Enter* Jean.)

JEAN   She really *is* crazy. What a way to dance! With people standing grinning at her too from behind the doors. What's got into
her, Kristin?

KRISTIN   Oh, it's just her time coming on. She's always queer then.
Are you going to dance with me now?

JEAN   Then you're not wild with me for cutting that one?

KRISTIN   You know I'm not—for a little thing like that. Besides, I
know my place.

JEAN   (*putting his arm around her waist*)   You're a sensible girl,
Kristin, and you'll make a very good wife . . .

(*Enter* Julie, *unpleasantly surprised.*)

JULIE   (*with forced gaiety*)   You're a fine beau—running away
from your partner.

JEAN   Not away, Miss Julie, but as you see, back to the one I
deserted.

JULIE   (*changing her tone*)   You really can dance, you know. But
why are you wearing your livery on a holiday? Take it off at
once.

JEAN   Then I must ask you to go away for a moment, Miss. My
black coat's here. (*Indicates it hanging on the door to his room.*)

JULIE   Are you so shy of me—just over changing a coat? Go into
your room then—or stay here and I'll turn my back.

JEAN   Excuse me then, Miss. (*He goes to his room and is partly
visible as he changes his coat.*)

JULIE   Tell me, Kristin, is Jean your fiancé? You seem very intimate.

KRISTIN   My fiancé? Yes, if you like. We call it that.

JULIE   Call it?

KRISTIN   Well, you've had a fiancé yourself, Miss, and . . .

JULIE   But we really were engaged.

KRISTIN   All the same it didn't come to anything.

(Jean *returns in his black coat.*)

JULIE   Très gentil, Monsieur Jean. Très gentil.

JEAN   Vous voulez plaisanter, Madame.

JULIE   Et vous voulez parler français. Where did you learn it?

JEAN   In Switzerland, when I was sommelier at one of the biggest
hotels in Lucerne.

JULIE   You look quite the gentleman in that get-up. Charming. (*Sits at the table.*)

JEAN   Oh, you're just flattering me!

JULIE (*annoyed*)   Flattering you?

JEAN   I'm too modest to believe you would pay real compliments to a man like me, so I must take it you are exaggerating—that this is what's known as flattery.

JULIE   Where on earth did you learn to make speeches like that? Perhaps you've been to the theatre a lot.

JEAN   That's right. And travelled a lot too.

JULIE   But you come from this neighbourhood, don't you?

JEAN   Yes, my father was a labourer on the next estate—the District Attorney's place. I often used to see you, Miss Julie, when you were little, though you never noticed me.

JULIE   Did you really?

JEAN   Yes. One time specially I remember . . . but I can't tell you about that.

JULIE   Oh do! Why not? This is just the time.

JEAN   No, I really can't now. Another time, perhaps.

JULIE   Another time means never. What harm in now?

JEAN   No harm, but I'd rather not.

(*Points to* KRISTIN, *now fast asleep.*)

Look at her.

JULIE   She'll make a charming wife, won't she? I wonder if she snores.

JEAN   No, she doesn't, but she talks in her sleep.

JULIE (*cynically*)   How do you know she talks in her sleep?

JEAN (*brazenly*)   I've heard her.

(*Pause. They look at one another.*)

JULIE   Why don't you sit down?

JEAN   I can't take such a liberty in your presence.

JULIE   Supposing I order you to.

JEAN   I'll obey.

JULIE   Then sit down. No, wait a minute. Will you get me a drink first?

JEAN   I don't know what's in the ice-box. Only beer, I expect.

JULIE   There's no only about it. My taste is so simple I prefer it to wine.

(JEAN *takes a bottle from the ice-box, fetches a glass and plate and serves the beer.*)

JEAN   At your service.

JULIE   Thank you. Won't you have some yourself?

JEAN   I'm not really a beer-drinker, but if it's an order . .

JULIE   Order? I should have thought it was ordinary manners keep your partner company.

JEAN   That's a good way of putting it.

(*He opens another bottle and fetches a glass.*)

JULIE   Now, drink my health. (*He hesitates.*) I believe the ma really is shy.

(JEAN *kneels and raises his glass with mock ceremony.*)

JEAN   To the health of my lady!

JULIE   Bravo! Now kiss my shoe and everything will be perfect. (*He hesitates, then boldly takes hold of her foot and lightly kisses it.*) Splendid. You ought to have been an actor.

JEAN   (*rising*)   We can't go on like this, Miss Julie. Someone might come in and see us.

JULIE   Why would that matter?

JEAN   For the simple reason that they'd talk, And if you knew the way their tongues were wagging out there just now, you . . .

JULIE   What were they saying? Tell me. Sit down.

JEAN   (*sitting*)   No offence meant, Miss, but . . . well, their language wasn't nice, and they were hinting . . . oh, you know quite well what. You're not a child, and if a lady's seen drinking alone at night with a man—and a servant at that—then . . .

JULIE   Then what? Besides, we're not alone. Kristin's here.

JEAN   Yes, asleep.

JULIE   I'll wake her up. (*Rises.*) Kristin, are you asleep? (KRISTIN *mumbles in her sleep.*) Kristin! Goodness, how she sleeps!

KRISTIN   (*in her sleep*)   The Count's boots are cleaned—put the coffee on—yes, yes, at once . . . (*Mumbles incoherently.*)

JULIE   (*tweaking her nose*)   Wake up, can't you!

JEAN   (*sharply*)   Let her sleep.

JULIE   What?

JEAN   When you've been standing at the stove all day you're likely to be tired at night. And sleep should be respected.

JULIE   (*changing her tone*)   What a nice idea. It does you credit. Thank you for it. (*Holds out her hand to him.*) Now come out and pick some lilac for me.

(*During the following,* KRISTIN *goes sleepily into her bedroom.*)

JEAN   Out with you, Miss Julie?

JULIE   Yes.

JEAN   It wouldn't do. It really wouldn't.

JULIE   I don't know what you mean. You can't possibly imagine that . . .

JEAN   I don't, but others do.

JULIE   What? That I'm in love with the valet?

JEAN   I'm not a conceited man, but such a thing's been known to happen, and to these rustics nothing's sacred.

JULIE   You, I take it, are an aristocrat.

JEAN   Yes, I am.

JULIE   And I am coming down in the world.

JEAN   Don't come down, Miss Julie. Take my advice. No one will believe you came down of your own accord. They'll all say you fell.

JULIE   I have a higher opinion of our people than you. Come and put it to the test. Come on. (*Gazes into his eyes.*)

JEAN   You're very strange, you know.

JULIE   Perhaps I am, but so are you. For that matter everything is strange. Life, human beings, everything, just scum drifting about on the water until it sinks—down and down. That reminds me of a dream I sometimes have, in which I'm on top of a pillar and can't see any way of getting down. When I look down I'm dizzy; I have to get down but I haven't the courage to jump. I can't stay there and I long to fall, but I don't fall. There's no respite. There can't be any peace at all for me until I'm down, right down on the ground. And if I did get to the ground I'd want to be under the ground . . . Have you ever felt like that?

JEAN   No. In my dream I'm lying under a great tree in a dark wood. I want to get up, up to the top of it, and look out over the bright landscape where the sun is shining and rob that high nest of its golden eggs. And I climb and climb, but the trunk is so thick and smooth and it's so far to the first branch. But I know if I can once reach that first branch I'll go to the top just as if I'm on a ladder. I haven't reached it yet, but I shall get there, even if only in my dreams.

JULIE   Here I am chattering about dreams with you. Come on. Only into the park. (*She takes his arm and they go towards the door.*)

JEAN   We must sleep on nine midsummer flowers tonight; then our dreams will come true, Miss Julie.

(*They turn at the door. He has a hand to his eye.*)

JULIE   Have you got something in your eye? Let me see.

JEAN   Oh, it's nothing. Just a speck of dust. It'll be gone in a minute.

JULIE   My sleeve must have rubbed against you. Sit down and let me see to it. (*Takes him by the arm and makes him sit down, bends his head back and tries to get the speck out with the corner of her handkerchief.*) Keep still now, quite still. (*Slaps his hand.*) Do as I tell you. Why, I believe you're trembling, big, strong man though you are! (*Feels his biceps.*) What muscles!

JEAN (*warning*)   Miss Julie!

JULIE   Yes, Monsieur Jean?

JEAN   Attention. Je ne suis qu'un homme.

JULIE   Will you stay still! There now. It's out. Kiss my hand and say thank you.

JEAN (*rising*)   Miss Julie, listen. Kristin's gone to bed now. Will you listen?

JULIE   Kiss my hand first.

JEAN   Very well, but you'll have only yourself to blame.

JULIE   For what?

JEAN   For what! Are you still a child at twenty-five? Don't you know it's dangerous to play with fire?

JULIE   Not for me. I'm insured.

JEAN (*bluntly*)   No, you're not. And even if you are, there's still stuff here to kindle a flame.

JULIE   Meaning yourself?

JEAN   Yes. Not because I'm me, but because I'm a man and young and . . .

JULIE   And good-looking? What incredible conceit! A Don Juan perhaps? Or a Joseph? Good Lord, I do believe you are a Joseph!

JEAN   Do you?

JULIE   I'm rather afraid so.

(JEAN *goes boldly up and tries to put his arms round her and kiss her. She boxes his ears.*)

How dare you!

JEAN   Was that in earnest or a joke?

JULIE   In earnest.

JEAN   Then what went before was in earnest too. You take your games too seriously and that's dangerous. Anyhow, I'm tired of playing now and beg leave to return to my work. The Count will want his boots first thing and it's past midnight now.

JULIE   Put those boots down.

JEAN   No. This is my work, which it's my duty to do. But I never undertook to be your playfellow and I never will be. I consider myself too good for that.

JULIE   You're proud.

JEAN   In some ways—not all.

JULIE   Have you ever been in love?

JEAN   We don't put it that way, but I've been gone on quite a few girls. And once I went sick because I couldn't have the one I wanted. Sick, I mean, like those princes in the Arabian Nights who couldn't eat or drink for love.

JULIE   Who was she? (*No answer.*) Who was she?

JEAN   You can't force me to tell you that.

JULIE   If I ask as an equal, ask as a—friend? Who was she?

JEAN   You.

JULIE (*sitting*)   How absurd!

JEAN   Yes, ludicrous, if you like. That's the story I wouldn't tell you before, see, but now I will . . . Do you know what the world looks like from below? No, you don't. No more than the hawks and falcons do whose backs one hardly ever sees because they're always soaring up aloft. I lived in a labourer's hovel with seven other children and a pig, out in the grey fields where there isn't a single tree. But from the window I could see the wall round the Count's park with apple-trees above it. That was the Garden of Eden, guarded by many terrible angels with flaming swords. All the same I and the other boys managed to get to the tree of life. Does all this make you despise me?

JULIE   Goodness, all boys steal apples!

JEAN   You say that now, but all the same you do despise me. However, one time I went into the Garden of Eden with my mother to weed the onion beds. Close to the kitchen garden there was a Turkish pavilion hung all over with jasmine and honeysuckle. I hadn't any idea what it was used for, but I'd never seen such a beautiful building. People used to go in and then come out again, and one day the door was left open. I crept up and saw the walls covered with pictures of kings and emperors, and the windows had red curtains with fringes—you know now what the place was, don't you? I . . . (*Breaks off a piece of lilac and holds it for* JULIE *to smell. As he talks, she takes it from him.*) I had never been inside the manor, never seen anything but the church, and this was more beautiful. No matter where my thoughts went, they always came back—to that place. The longing went on growing in me to enjoy it fully, just once. Enfin, I sneaked in, gazed and admired. Then I heard someone coming. There was only one way out for the gentry, but for me there was another and I had no choice but to take it. (JULIE *drops the lilac on the table.*) Then I took to my heels, plunged through the raspberry canes, dashed across the strawberry beds and found myself on the rose terrace. There I saw a pink dress and a pair of white stockings—it was you. I crawled into a weed pile and lay there right under it among prickly thistles and damp rank earth. I watched you walking among the roses and said to myself: "If its true that a thief can get to heaven and be with the angels, it's pretty strange that a labourer's child here on God's earth mayn't come in the park and play with the Count's daughter."

JULIE (*sentimentally*) Do you think all poor children feel the way you did?

JEAN (*taken aback, then rallying*) *All* poor children?...Yes, of course they do. Of course.

JULIE It must be terrible to be poor.

JEAN (*with exaggerated distress*) Oh yes, Miss Julie, yes. A dog may lie on the Countess's sofa, a horse may have his nose stroked by a young lady, but a servant... (*change of tone*) well, yes, now and then you meet one with guts enough to rise in the world, but how often? Anyhow, do you know what I did? Jumped in the millstream with my clothes on, was pulled out and got a hiding. But the next Sunday, when Father and all the rest went to Granny's, I managed to get left behind. Then I washed with soap and hot water, put my best clothes on and went to church so as to see you. I did see you and went home determined to die. But I wanted to die beautifully and peacefully, without any pain. Then I remembered it was dangerous to sleep under an elder bush. We had a big one in full bloom, so I stripped it and climbed into the oats-bin with the flowers. Have you ever noticed how smooth oats are? Soft to touch as human skin... Well, I closed the lid and shut my eyes, fell asleep, and when they woke me I was very ill. But I didn't die, as you see. What I meant by all that, I don't know. There was no hope of winning you—you were simply a symbol of the hopelessness of ever getting out of the class I was born in.

JULIE You put things very well, you know. Did you go to school?

JEAN For a while. But I've read a lot of novels and been to the theatre. Besides, I've heard educated folk talking—that's what's taught me most.

JULIE Do you stand round listening to what we're saying?

JEAN Yes, of course. And I've heard quite a bit too! On the carriage box or rowing the boat. Once I heard you, Miss Julie, and one of your young lady friends...

JULIE Oh! Whatever did you hear?

JEAN Well, it wouldn't be nice to repeat it. And I must say I was pretty startled. I couldn't think where you had learnt such words. Perhaps, at bottom, there isn't as much difference between people as one's led to believe.

JULIE   How dare you! We don't behave as you do when we're engaged.

JEAN   (*looking hard at her*)   Are you sure? It's no use making out so innocent to me.

JULIE   The man I gave my love to was a rotter.

JEAN   That's what you always say—afterwards.

JULIE   Always?

JEAN   I think it must be always. I've heard the expression several times in similar circumstances.

JULIE   What circumstances?

JEAN   Like those in question. The last time . . .

JULIE   (*rising*)   Stop. I don't want to hear any more.

JEAN   Nor did *she*—curiously enough. May I go to bed now, please?

JULIE   (*gently*)   Go to bed on Midsummer Eve?

JEAN   Yes. Dancing with that crowd doesn't really amuse me.

JULIE   Get the key of the boathouse and row me out on the lake. I want to see the sun rise.

JEAN   Would that be wise?

JULIE   You sound as though you're frightened for your reputation.

JEAN   Why not? I don't want to be made a fool of, nor to be sent packing without a character when I'm trying to better myself. Besides, I have Kristin to consider.

JULIE   So now it's Kristin.

JEAN   Yes, but it's you I'm thinking about too. Take my advice and go to bed.

JULIE   Am I to take orders from you?

JEAN   Just this once, for your own sake. Please. It's very late and sleepiness goes to one's head and makes one rash. Go to bed. What's more, if my ears don't deceive me, I hear people coming this way. They'll be looking for me, and if they find us here, you're done for.

(*The* CHORUS *approaches, singing. During the following dialogue the song is heard in snatches, and in full when the peasants enter.*)

Out of the wood two women came,
Tridiri-ralla, tridiri-ra.
The feet of one were bare and cold,
Tridiri-ralla-la.

The other talked of bags of gold,
Tridiri-ralla, tridiri-ra.
But neither had a sou to her name,
Tridiri-ralla-la.

The bridal wreath I give to you,
Tridiri-ralla, tridiri-ra.
But to another I'll be true,
Tridiri-ralla-la.

JULIE   I know our people and I love them, just as they do me. Let them come. You'll see.

JEAN   No, Miss Julie, they don't love you. They take your food, then spit at it. You must believe me. Listen to them, just listen to what they're singing . . . No, don't listen.

JULIE (*listening*)   What are they singing?

JEAN   They're mocking—you and me.

JULIE   Oh no! How horrible! What cowards!

JEAN   A pack like that's always cowardly. But against such odds there's nothing we can do but run away.

JULIE   Run away? Where to? We can't get out and we can't go into Kristin's room.

JEAN   Into mine, then. Necessity knows no rules. And you can trust me. I really am your true and devoted friend.

JULIE   But supposing . . . supposing they were to look for you in there?

JEAN   I'll bolt the door, and if they try to break in I'll shoot. Come on. (*Pleading.*) Please come.

JULIE (*tensely*)   Do you promise . . . ?

JEAN   I swear!

(JULIE *goes quickly into his room and he excitedly follows her.*)

Led by the fiddler, the peasants enter in the festive attire with flowers in their hats. They put a barrel of beer and a keg of spirits, garlanded with leaves, on the table, fetch glasses and begin to carouse. The scene becomes a ballet. They form a ring and dance and sing and mime: "Out of the wood two women came." Finally they go out, still singing.

(JULIE *comes in alone. She looks at the havoc in the kitchen, wrings her hands, then takes out her powder puff and powders her face.*)

(JEAN *enters in high spirits.*)

JEAN   Now you see! And you heard, didn't you? Do you still think it's possible for us to stay here?

JULIE   No, I don't. But what can we do?

JEAN   Run away. Far away. Take a journey.

JULIE   Journey? But where to?

JEAN   Switzerland. The Italian lakes. Ever been there?

JULIE   No. Is it nice?

JEAN   Ah! Eternal summer, oranges, evergreens . . . ah!

JULIE But what would we do there?

JEAN I'll start a hotel. First-class accommodation and first-class customers.

JULIE Hotel?

JEAN There's life for you. New faces all the time, new languages —no time for nerves or worries, no need to look for something to do—work rolling up of its own accord. Bells ringing night and day, trains whistling, buses coming and going, and all the time gold pieces rolling on to the counter. There's life for you!

JULIE For *you*. And I?

JEAN Mistress of the house, ornament of the firm. With your looks, and your style ... oh, it's bound to be a success! Terrific! You'll sit like a queen in the office and set your slaves in motion by pressing an electric button. The guests will file past your throne and nervously lay their treasure on your table. You've no idea the way people tremble when they get their bills. I'll salt the bills and you'll sugar them with your sweetest smiles. Ah, let's get away from here! (*Produces a time-table.*) At once, by the next train. We shall be at Malmö at six-thirty, Hamburg eight-forty next morning, Frankfurt-Basle the following day, and Como by the St. Gothard pass in—let's see—three days. Three days!

JULIE That's all very well. But Jean, you must give me courage. Tell me you love me. Come and take me in your arms.

JEAN (*reluctantly*) I'd like to, but I daren't. Not again in this house. I love you—that goes without saying. You can't doubt that, Miss Julie, can you?

JULIE (*shyly, very feminine*) Miss? Call me Julie. There aren't any barriers between us now. Call me Julie.

JEAN (*uneasily*) I can't. As long as we're in this house, there *are* barriers between us. There's the past and there's the Count. I've never been so servile to anyone as I am to him. I've only got to see his gloves on a chair to feel small. I've only to hear his bell and I shy like a horse. Even now, when I look at his boots, standing there so proud and stiff, I feel my back beginning to bend. (*Kicks the boots.*) It's those old, narrow-minded notions drummed into us as children ... but they can soon be forgotten. You've only got to get to another country, a republic, and people will bend themselves double before my porter's livery. Yes, double they'll bend themselves, but I shan't. I wasn't born to bend. I've got guts, I've got character, and one I reach that first branch, you'll watch me climb. Today I'm valet, next year I'll be pro-prietor, in ten years I'll have made a fortune, and then I'll go to Roumania, get myself decorated and I may, I only say *may*, mind you, end up as a Count.

JULIE (*sadly*) That would be very nice.

JEAN You see in Roumania one can buy a title, and then you'll be a Countess after all. My Countess.

JULIE What do I care about all that? I'm putting those things behind me. Tell me you love me, because if you don't . . . if you don't, what am I?

JEAN I'll tell you a thousand times over—later. But not here. No sentimentality now or everything will be lost. We must consider this thing calmly like reasonable people. (*Takes a cigar, cuts and lights it.*) You sit down there and I'll sit here and we'll talk as if nothing has happened.

JULIE My God, have you no feelings at all?

JEAN Nobody has more. But I know how to control them.

JULIE A short time ago you were kissing my shoe. And now . . .

JEAN (*harshly*) Yes, that was then. Now, we have something else to think about.

JULIE Don't speak to me so brutally.

JEAN I'm not. Just sensibly. One folly's been committed, don't let's have more. The Count will be back at any moment and we've got to settle our future before that. Now, what do you think of my plans? Do you approve?

JULIE It seems a very good idea—but just one thing. Such a big undertaking would need a lot of capital. Have you got any?

JEAN (*chewing his cigar*) I certainly have. I've got my professional skill, my wide experience and my knowledge of foreign languages. That's capital worth having, it seems to me.

JULIE But it won't buy even one railway ticket.

JEAN Quite true. That's why I need a backer to advance some ready cash.

JULIE How could you get that at a moment's notice?

JEAN You must get it, if you want to be my partner.

JULIE I can't. I haven't any money of my own. (*Pause.*)

JEAN Then the whole thing's off.

JULIE And . . . ?

JEAN We go on as we are.

JULIE Do you think I'm going to stay under this roof as your mistress? With everyone pointing at me? Do you think I can face my father after this? No. Take me away from here, away from this shame, this humiliation. Oh my God, what have I done? My God, my God! (*Weeps.*)

JEAN So that's the tune now, is it? What have you done? Same as many before you.

JULIE (*hysterically*) And now you despise me. I'm falling, I'm falling.

JEAN   Fall as far as me and I'll lift you up again.

JULIE   Why was I so terribly attracted to you? The weak to the strong, the falling to the rising? Or was it love? Is that love? Do you know what love is?

JEAN   Do I? You bet I do. Do you think I never had a girl before?

JULIE   The things you say, the things you think!

JEAN   That's what life's taught me, and that's what I am. It's no good getting hysterical or giving yourself airs. We're both in the same boat now. Here, my dear girl, let me give you a glass of something special.

(*Opens the drawer, takes out the bottle of wine and fills two used glasses.*)

JULIE   Where did you get that wine?

JEAN   From the cellar.

JULIE   My father's burgundy.

JEAN   Why not, for his son-in-law?

JULIE   And I drink beer.

JEAN   That only shows your taste's not so good as mine.

JULIE   Thief!

JEAN   Are you going to tell on me?

JULIE   Oh God! The accomplice of a petty thief! Was I blind drunk? Have I dreamt this whole night? Midsummer Eve, the night for innocent merrymaking.

JEAN   Innocent, eh?

JULIE   Is anyone on earth as wretched as I am now?

JEAN   Why should *you* be? After such a conquest. What about Kristin in there? Don't you think she has any feelings?

JULIE   I did think so, but I don't any longer. No. A menial is a menial . . .

JEAN   And a whore is a whore.

JULIE   (*falling to her knees, her hands clasped*)   O God in heaven, put an end to my miserable life! Lift me out of this filth in which I'm sinking. Save me! Save me!

JEAN   I must admit I'm sorry for you. When I was in the onion bed and saw you up there among the roses, I . . . yes, I'll tell you now . . . I had the same dirty thoughts as all boys.

JULIE   You, who wanted to die because of me?

JEAN   In the oats-bin? That was just talk.

JULIE   Lies, you mean.

JEAN   (*getting sleepy*)   More or less. I think I read a story in some paper about a chimney-sweep who shut himself up in a chest full of lilac because he'd been summonsed for not supporting some brat . . .

JULIE   So this is what you're like.

JEAN   I had to think up something. It's always the fancy stuff that catches the women.

JULIE   Beast!

JEAN   Merde!

JULIE   Now you have seen the falcon's back.

JEAN   Not exactly its *back*.

JULIE   I was to be the first branch.

JEAN   But the branch was rotten.

JULIE   I was to be a hotel sign.

JEAN   And I the hotel.

JULIE   Sit at your counter, attract your clients and cook their accounts.

JEAN   I'd have done that myself.

JULIE   That any human being can be so steeped in filth!

JEAN   Clean it up, then.

JULIE   Menial! Lackey! Stand up when I speak to you.

JEAN   Menial's whore, lackey's harlot, shut your mouth and get out of here! Are you the one to lecture me for being coarse? Nobody of my kind would ever be as coarse as you were tonight. Do you think any servant girl would throw herself at a man that way? Have you ever seen a girl of my class asking for it like that? I haven't. Only animals and prostitutes.

JULIE   (*broken*)   Go on. Hit me, trample on me—it's all I deserve. I'm rotten. But help me! If there's any way out at all, help me.

JEAN   (*more gently*)   I'm not denying myself a share in the honour of seducing you, but do you think anybody in my place would have dared look in your direction if you yourself hadn't asked for it? I'm still amazed . . .

JULIE   And proud.

JEAN   Why not? Though I must admit the victory was too easy to make me lose my head.

JULIE   Go on hitting me.

JEAN   (*rising*)   No. On the contrary, I apologise for what I've said. I don't hit a person who's down—least of all a woman. I can't deny there's a certain satisfaction in finding that what dazzled one below was just moonshine, that that falcon's back is grey after all, that there's powder on the lovely cheek, that polished nails can have black tips, that the handkerchief is dirty although it smells of scent. On the other hand, it hurts to find that what I was struggling to reach wasn't high and isn't real. It hurts to see you fallen so low you're far lower than your own cook. Hurts like when you see the last flowers of summer lashed to pieces by rain and turned to mud.

JULIE You're talking as if you're already my superior.

JEAN I am. I might make you a Countess, but you could never make me a Count, you know.

JULIE But I am the child of a Count, and you could never be that.

JEAN True, but I might be the father of Counts if . . .

JULIE You're a thief. I'm not.

JEAN There are worse things than being a thief—much lower. Besides, when I'm in a place I regard myself as a member of the family to some extent, as one of the children. You don't call it stealing when children pinch a berry from overladen bushes. (*His passion is roused again.*) Miss Julie, you're a glorious woman, far too good for a man like me. You were carried away by some kind of madness, and now you're trying to cover up your mistake by persuading yourself you're in love with me. You're not, although you may find me physically attractive, which means your love's no better than mine. But I wouldn't be satisfied with being nothing but an animal for you, and I could never make you love me.

JULIE Are you sure?

JEAN You think there's a chance? Of my loving you, yes, of course. You're beautiful, refined (*takes her hand*) educated, and you can be nice when you want to be. The fire you kindle in a man isn't likely to go out. (*Puts his arm round her.*) You're like mulled wine, full of spices, and your kisses . . . (*He tries to pull her to him, but she breaks away.*)

JULIE Let go of me! You won't win me that way.

JEAN Not that way, how then? Not by kisses and fine speeches, not by planning the future and saving you from shame? How then?

JULIE How? I don't know. There isn't any way. I loathe you—loathe you as I loathe rats, but I can't escape from you.

JEAN Escape with me.

JULIE (*pulling herself together*) Escape? Yes, we must escape. But I'm so tired. Give me a glass of wine. (*He pours it out. She looks at her watch.*) First we must talk. We still have a little time. (*Empties the glass and holds it out for more.*)

JEAN Don't drink like that. You'll get tipsy.

JULIE What's that matter?

JEAN What's it matter? It's vulgar to get drunk. Well, what have you got to say?

JULIE We've got to run away, but we must talk first—or rather, I must, for so far you've done all the talking. You've told me about your life, now I want to tell you about mine, so that we really know each other before we begin this journey together.

JEAN   Wait. Excuse my saying so, but don't you think you may be sorry afterwards if you give away your secrets to me?

JULIE   Aren't you my friend?

JEAN   On the whole. But don't rely on me.

JULIE   You can't mean that. But anyway, everyone knows my secrets. Listen. My mother wasn't well-born; she came of quite humble people, and was brought up with all those new ideas of sex-equality and women's rights and so on. She thought marriage was quite wrong. So when my father proposed to her, she said she would never become his *wife* . . . but in the end she did. I came into the world, as far as I can make out, against my mother's will, and I was left to run wild, but I had to do all the things a boy does—to prove women are as good as men. I had to wear boys' clothes; I was taught to handle horses—and I wasn't allowed in the dairy. She made me groom and harness and go out hunting; I even had to try to plough. All the men on the estate were given the women's jobs, and the women the men's, until the whole place went to rack and ruin and we were the laughing-stock of the neighbourhood. At last my father seems to have come to his senses and rebelled. He changed everything and ran the place his own way. My mother got ill—I don't know what was the matter with her, but she used to have strange attacks and hide herself in the attic or the garden. Sometimes she stayed out all night. Then came the great fire which you have heard people talking about. The house and the stables and the barns—the whole place burnt to the ground. In very suspicious circumstances. Because the accident happened the very day the insurance had to be renewed, and my father had sent the new premium, but through some carelessness of the messenger it arrived too late.

(*Refills her glass and drinks.*)

JEAN   Don't drink any more.

JULIE   Oh, what does it matter? We were destitute and had to sleep in the carriages. My father didn't know how to get money to rebuild, and then my mother suggested he should borrow from an old friend of hers, a local brick manufacturer. My father got the loan and, to his surprise, without having to pay interest. So the place was rebuilt. (*Drinks.*) Do you know who set fire to it?

JEAN   Your lady mother.

JULIE   Do you know who the brick manufacturer was?

JEAN   Your mother's lover?

JULIE   Do you know whose the money was?

JEAN   Wait . . . no, I don't know that.

JULIE   It was my mother's.

JEAN   In other words, the Count's, unless there was a settlement.

JULIE   There wasn't any settlement. My mother had a little money of her own which she didn't want my father to control, so she invested it with her—friend.

JEAN   Who grabbed it.

JULIE   Exactly. He appropriated it. My father came to know all this. He couldn't bring an action, couldn't pay his wife's lover, nor prove it was his wife's money. That was my mother's revenge because he made himself master in his own house. He nearly shot himself then—at least there's a rumour he tried and didn't bring it off. So he went on living, and my mother had to pay dearly for what she'd done. Imagine what those five years were like for me. My natural sympathies were with my father, yet I took my mother's side, because I didn't know the facts. I'd learnt from her to hate and distrust men—you know how she loathed the whole male sex. And I swore to her I'd never become the slave of any man.

JEAN   And so you got engaged to that attorney.

JULIE   So that he should be my slave.

JEAN   But he wouldn't be.

JULIE   Oh yes, he wanted to be, but he didn't have the chance. I got bored with him.

JEAN   Is that what I saw—in the stable-yard?

JULIE   What did you see?

JEAN   What I saw was him breaking off the engagement.

JULIE   That's a lie. It was I who broke it off. Did he sày it was him? The cad.

JEAN   He's not a cad. Do you hate men, Miss Julie?

JULIE   Yes ... most of the time. But when that weakness comes, oh ... the shame!

JEAN   Then, do you hate me?

JULIE   Beyond words. I'd gladly have you killed like an animal.

JEAN   Quick as you'd shoot a mad dog, eh?

JULIE   Yes.

JEAN   But there's nothing here to shoot with—and there isn't a dog. So what do we do now?

JULIE   Go abroad.

JEAN   To make each other miserable for the rest of our lives?

JULIE   No, to enjoy ourselves for a day or two, for a week, for as long as enjoyment lasts, and then—to die ...

JEAN   Die? How silly! I think it would be far better to start a hotel.

JULIE   (*without listening*)   ... die on the shores of Lake Como, where the sun always shines and at Christmas time there are green trees and glowing oranges.

JEAN   Lake Como's a rainy hole and I didn't see any oranges outside the shops. But it's a good place for tourists. Plenty of villas to be rented by—er—honeymoon couples. Profitable business, that. Know why? Because they all sign a lease for six months and all leave after three weeks.

JULIE (*naïvely*)   After three weeks? Why?

JEAN   They quarrel, of course. But the rent has to be paid just the same. And then it's let again. So it goes on and on, for there's plenty of love although it doesn't last long.

JULIE   You don't want to die with me?

JEAN   I don't want to die at all. For one thing I like living and for another I consider suicide's a sin against the Creator who gave us life.

JULIE   You believe in God—*you?*

JEAN   Yes, of course. And I go to church every Sunday. Look here, I'm tired of all this. I'm going to bed.

JULIE   Indeed! And do you think I'm going to leave things like this? Don't you know what you owe the woman you've ruined?

JEAN   (*taking out his purse and throwing a silver coin on the table*) There you are. I don't want to be in anybody's debt.

JULIE (*pretending not to notice the insult*)   Don't you know what the law is?

JEAN   There's no law unfortunately that punishes a woman for seducing a man.

JULIE   But can you see anything for it but to go abroad, get married and then divorce?

JEAN   What if I refuse this mésalliance?

JULIE   Mésalliance?

JEAN   Yes, for me. I'm better bred than you, see! Nobody in my family committed arson.

JULIE   How do you know?

JEAN   Well, you can't prove otherwise, because we haven't any family records outside the Registrar's office. But I've seen your family tree in that book on the drawing-room table. Do you know who the founder of your family was? A miller who let his wife sleep with the King one night during the Danish war. I haven't any ancestors at all, but I might become one.

JULIE   This is what I get for confiding in someone so low, for sacrificing my family honour . . .

JEAN   Dishonour! Well, I told you so. One shouldn't drink, because then one talks. And one shouldn't talk.

JULIE Oh, how ashamed I am, how bitterly ashamed! If at least you loved me!

JEAN Look here—for the last time—what do you want? Am I to burst into tears? Am I to jump over your riding whip? Shall I kiss you and carry you off to Lake Como for three weeks, after which . . . What am I to do? What do you want? This is getting unbearable, but that's what comes of playing around with women. Miss Julie, I can see how miserable you are; I know you're going through hell, but I don't understand you. We don't have scenes like this; we don't go in for hating each other. We make love for fun in our spare time, but we haven't all day and all night for it like you. I think you must be ill. I'm sure you're ill.

JULIE Then you must be kind to me. You sound almost human now.

JEAN Well, be human yourself. You spit at me, then won't let me wipe it off—on you.

JULIE Help me, help me! Tell me what to do, where to go.

JEAN Jesus, as if I knew!

JULIE I've been mad, raving mad, but there must be a way out.

JEAN Stay here and keep quiet. Nobody knows anything.

JULIE I can't. People do know. Kristin knows.

JEAN They don't know and they wouldn't believe such a thing.

JULIE (*hesitating*) But—it might happen again.

JEAN That's true.

JULIE And there might be—consequences.

JEAN (*in panic*) Consequences! Fool that I am I never thought of that. Yes, there's nothing for it but to go. At once. I can't come with you. That would be a complete giveaway. You must go alone—abroad—anywhere.

JULIE Alone? Where to? I can't.

JEAN You must. And before the Count gets back. If you stay, we know what will happen. Once you've sinned you feel you might as well go on, as the harm's done. Then you get more and more reckless and in the end you're found out. No. You must go abroad. Then write to the Count and tell him everything, except that it was me. He'll never guess that—and I don't think he'll want to.

JULIE I'll go if you come with me.

JEAN Are you crazy, woman? "Miss Julie elopes with valet." Next day it would be in the headlines, and the Count would never live it down.

JULIE I can't go. I can't stay. I'm so tired, so completely worn out. Give me orders. Set me going. I can't think any more, can't act . . .

JEAN You see what weaklings you are. Why do you give yourselves airs and turn up your noses as if you're the lords of creation? Very well, I'll give you your orders. Go upstairs and dress. Get money for the journey and come down here again.

JULIE (*softly*) Come up with me.

JEAN To your room? Now you've gone crazy again. (*Hesitates a moment.*) No! Go along at once. (*Takes her hand and pulls her to the door.*)

JULIE (*as she goes*) Speak kindly to me, Jean.

JEAN Orders always sound unkind. Now you know. Now you know.

(*Left alone,* JEAN *sighs with relief, sits down at the table, takes out a note-book and pencil and adds up figures, now and then aloud. Dawn begins to break.* KRISTIN *enters dressed for church, carrying his white dickey and tie.*)

KRISTIN Lord Jesus, look at the state the place is in! What have you been up to?

(*Turns out the lamp.*)

JEAN Oh, Miss Julie invited the crowd in. Did you sleep through it? Didn't you hear anything?

KRISTIN I slept like a log.

JEAN And dressed for church already.

KRISTIN Yes, you promised to come to Communion with me today.

JEAN Why, so I did. And you've got my bib and tucker, I see. Come on then. (*Sits.* KRISTIN *begins to put his things on. Pause. Sleepily.*) What's the lesson today?

KRISTIN It's about the beheading of John the Baptist, I think.

JEAN That's sure to be horribly long. Hi, you're choking me! Oh Lord, I'm so sleepy, so sleepy!

KRISTIN Yes, what have you been doing up all night? You look absolutely green.

JEAN Just sitting here talking with Miss Julie.

KRISTIN She doesn't know what's proper, that one. (*Pause.*)

JEAN I say, Kristin.

KRISTIN What?

JEAN It's queer really, isn't it, when you come to think of it? Her.

KRISTIN What's queer?

JEAN The whole thing. (*Pause.*)

KRISTIN (*looking at the half-filled glasses on the table*) Have you been drinking together too?

JEAN Yes.

KRISTIN More shame you. Look me straight in the face.

JEAN   Yes.

KRISTIN   Is it possible? Is it possible?

JEAN (*after a moment*)   Yes, it is.

KRISTIN   Oh! This I would never have believed. How low!

JEAN   You're not jealous of her, surely?

KRISTIN   No, I'm not. If it had been Clara or Sophie I'd have scratched your eyes out. But not of her. I don't know why; that's how it is, though. But it's disgusting.

JEAN   You're angry with her, then.

KRISTIN   No. With you. It was wicked of you, very very wicked. Poor girl. And, mark my words, I won't stay here any longer now —in a place where one can't respect one's employers.

JEAN   Why should one respect them?

KRISTIN   You should know since you're so smart. But you don't want to stay in the service of people who aren't respectable, do you? I wouldn't demean myself.

JEAN   But it's rather a comfort to find out they're no better than us.

KRISTIN   I don't think so. If they're no better there's nothing for us to live up to. Oh and think of the Count! Think of him. He's been through so much already. No, I won't stay in the place any longer. A fellow like you too! If it had been that attorney, now, or somebody of her own class . . .

JEAN   Why, what's wrong with . . .

KRISTIN   Oh, you're all right in your own way, but when all's said and done there is a difference between one class and another. No, this is something I'll never be able to stomach. That our young lady who was so proud and so down on men you'd never believe she'd let one come near her should go and give herself to one like you. She who wanted to have poor Diana shot for running after the lodge-keeper's pug. No, I must say . . . ! Well, I won't stay here any longer. On the twenty-fourth of October I quit.

JEAN   And then?

KRISTIN   Well, since you mention it, it's about time you began to look around, if we're ever going to get married.

JEAN   But what am I to look for? I shan't get a place like this when I'm married.

KRISTIN   I know you won't. But you might get a job as porter or caretaker in some public institution. Government rations are small but sure, and there's a pension for the widow and children.

JEAN   That's all very fine, but it's not in my line to start thinking at once about dying for my wife and children. I must say I had rather bigger ideas.

KRISTIN   You and your ideas! You've got obligations too, and you'd better start thinking about them.

JEAN   Don't *you* start pestering me about obligations. I've had enough of that. (*Listens to a sound upstairs.*) Anyway, we've plenty of time to work things out. Go and get ready, now, and we'll be off to church.

KRISTIN   Who's that walking about upstairs?

JEAN   Don't know—unless it's Clara.

KRISTIN (*going*)   You don't think the Count could have come back without our hearing him?

JEAN (*scared*)   The Count? No, he can't have. He'd have rung for me.

KRISTIN   God help us! I've never known such goings on

(*Exit.*)

(*The sun has now risen and is shining on the treetops. The light gradually changes until it slants in through the windows. JEAN goes to the door and beckons. JULIE enters in travelling clothes, carrying a small bird-cage covered with a cloth which she puts on a chair.*)

JULIE   I'm ready.

JEAN   Hush! Kristin's up.

JULIE (*in a very nervous state*)   Does she suspect anything?

JEAN   Not a thing. But, my God, what a sight you are!

JULIE   Sight? What do you mean?

JEAN   You're white as a corpse and—pardon me—your face is dirty.

JULIE   Let me wash, then. (*Goes to the sink and washes her face and hands.*) There. Give me a towel. Oh! The sun is rising!

JEAN   And that breaks the spell.

JULIE   Yes. The spell of Midsummer Eve . . . But listen, Jean. Come with me. I've got the money.

JEAN (*skeptically*)   Enough?

JULIE   Enough to start with. Come with me. I can't travel alone today. It's Midsummer Day, remember. I'd be packed into a suffocating train among crowds of people who'd all stare at me. And it would stop at every station while I yearned for wings. No, I can't do that, I simply can't. There will be memories too; memories of Midsummer Days when I was little. The leafy church—birch and lilac—the gaily spread dinner table, relatives, friends—evening in the park—dancing and music and flowers and fun. Oh, however far you run away—there'll always be memories in the baggage car—and remorse and guilt.

JEAN   I will come with you, but quickly now then, before it's too late. At once.

JULIE   Put on your things. (*Picks up the cage.*)

JEAN   No luggage, mind. That would give us away.

JULIE   No, only what we can take with us in the carriage.

JEAN (*fetching his hat*)   What on earth have you got there? What is it?

JULIE   Only my greenfinch. I don't want to leave it behind.

JEAN   Well, I'll be damned! We're to take a bird-cage along, are we? You're crazy. Put that cage down.

JULIE   It's the only thing I'm taking from my home. The only living creature who cares for me since Diana went off like that. Don't be cruel. Let me take it.

JEAN   Put that cage down, I tell you—and don't talk so loud. Kristin will hear.

JULIE   No, I won't leave it in strange hands. I'd rather you killed it.

JEAN   Give the little beast here, then, and I'll wring its neck.

JULIE   But don't hurt it, don't . . . no, I can't.

JEAN   Give it here. I *can*.

JULIE (*taking the bird out of the cage and kissing it*)   Dear little Serena, must you die and leave your mistress?

JEAN   Please don't make a scene. It's *your* life and future we're worrying about. Come on, quick now!

(*He snatches the bird from her, puts it on a board and picks up a chopper.* JULIE *turns away.*)

You should have learnt how to kill chickens instead of target-shooting. Then you wouldn't faint at a drop of blood.

JULIE (*screaming*)   Kill me too! Kill me! You who can butcher an innocent creature without a quiver. Oh, how I hate you, how I loathe you! There is blood between us now. I curse the hour I first saw you. I curse the hour I was conceived in my mother's womb.

JEAN   What's the use of cursing? Let's go.

JULIE (*going to the chopping-block as if drawn against her will*)   No, I won't go yet. I can't . . . I must look. Listen! There's a carriage. (*Listens without taking her eyes off the board and chopper.*) You don't think I can bear the sight of blood. You think I'm so weak. Oh, how I should like to see your blood and your brains on a chopping-block! I'd like to see the whole of your sex swimming like that in a sea of blood. I think I could drink out of your skull, bathe my feet in your broken breast and eat your heart roasted whole. You think I'm weak. You think I love you, that my womb yearned for your seed and I want to carry your off-spring under my heart and nourish it with my blood. You think I want to bear your child and take your name. By the way, what is your name? I've never heard your surname. I don't suppose you've got one. I should be "Mrs. Hovel" or "Madam Dunghill." You dog wearing my collar, you lackey with my crest on your buttons! I share you with my cook; I'm my own servant's rival! Oh! Oh! Oh! . . . You think I'm a coward and will run away. No, now I'm going to stay—and let the storm break. My father will come back . . . find his desk broken open . . . his money gone. Then he'll ring that bell—twice for the valet—and then he'll send for the police . . . and I shall tell everything. Everything. Oh how wonderful to make an end of it all—a real end! He has a stroke and dies and that's the end of all of us. Just peace and quietness . . . eternal rest. The coat of arms broken on the coffin and the Count's line extinct . . . But the valet's line goes on in an orphanage, wins laurels in the gutter and ends in jail.

JEAN   There speaks the noble blood! Bravo, Miss Julie. But now, don't let the cat out of the bag.

(KRISTIN *enters dressed for church, carrying a prayer-book.* JULIE *rushes to her and flings herself into her arms for protection.*)

JULIE   Help me, Kristin! Protect me from this man!

KRISTIN   (*unmoved and cold*)   What goings-on for a feast day morning! (*Sees the board.*) And what a filthy mess. What's it all about? Why are you screaming and carrying on so?

JULIE   Kristin, you're a woman and my friend. Beware of that scoundrel!

JEAN   (*embarrassed*)   While you ladies are talking things over, I'll go and shave. (*Slips into his room.*)

JULIE   You must understand. You must listen to me.

KRISTIN   I certainly don't understand such loose ways. Where are you off to in those travelling clothes? And he had his hat on, didn't he, eh?

JULIE   Listen, Kristin. Listen, I'll tell you everything.

KRISTIN   I don't wan't to know anything.

JULIE   You must listen.

KRISTIN   What to? Your nonsense with Jean? I don't care a rap about that; it's nothing to do with me. But if you're thinking of getting him to run off with you, we'll soon put a stop to that.

JULIE   (*very nervously*)   Please try to be calm, Kristin, and listen. I can't stay here, nor can Jean—so we must go abroad.

KRISTIN   Hm, hm!

JULIE   (*brightening*)   But you see, I've had an idea. Supposing we all three go—abroad—to Switzerland and start a hotel together ... I've got some money, you see ... and Jean and I could run the whole thing—and I thought you would take charge of the kitchen. Wouldn't that be splendid? Say yes, do. If you come with us everything will be fine. Oh do say yes! (*Puts her arms round* KRISTIN.)

KRISTIN (*coolly thinking*)   Hm, hm.

JULIE (*presto tempo*).   You've never travelled, Kristin. You should go abroad and see the world. You've no idea how nice it is travelling by train—new faces all the time and new countries. On our way through Hamburg well go to the zoo—you'll love that—and we'll go to the theatre and the opera too ... and when we get to Munich there'll be the museums, dear, and pictures by Rubens and Raphael—the great painters, you know ... You've heard of Munich, haven't you? Where King Ludwig lived—you know, the king who went mad. ... We'll see his castles—some of his castles are still just like in fairy-tales ... and from there it's not far to Switzerland—and the Alps. Think of the Alps, Kristin dear, covered with snow in the middle of summer ... and there are oranges there and trees that are green the whole year round ...

(JEAN *is seen in the door of his room, sharpening his razor on a strop which he holds with his teeth and his left hand. He listens to the talk with satisfaction and now and then nods approval.* JULIE *continues, tempo prestissimo.*)

And then we'll get a hotel ... and I'll sit at the desk, while Jean receives the guests and goes out marketing and writes letters ... There's life for you! Trains whistling, buses driving up, bells ringing upstairs and downstairs ... and I shall make out the bills—and I shall cook them too ... you've no idea how nervous travellers are when it comes to paying their bills. And you—you'll sit like a queen in the kitchen ... of course there won't be any standing at the stove for you. You'll always have to be nicely dressed and ready to be seen, and with your looks—no, I'm not flattering you—one fine day you'll catch yourself a husband ... some rich Englishman, I shouldn't wonder—they're the ones who are easy (*slowing down*) to catch ... and then we'll get rich and build ourselves a villa on Lake Como ... of course it rains there a little now and then—but—(*dully*)—the sun must shine there too sometimes—even though it seems gloomy—and if not—then we can come home again—come back—(*pause*)—here—or somewhere else ...

KRISTIN   Look here, Miss Julie, do you believe all that yourself?

JULIE (*exhausted*)   Do I believe it?

KRISTIN Yes.

JULIE (*wearily*) I don't know. I don't believe anything any more. (*Sinks down on the bench; her head in her arms on the table.*) Nothing. Nothing at all.

KRISTIN (*turning to* JEAN) So you meant to beat it, did you?

JEAN (*disconcerted, putting the razor on the table*) Beat it? What are you talking about? You've heard Miss Julie's plan, and though she's tired now with being up all night, it's a perfectly sound plan.

KRISTIN Oh, is it? If you thought I'd work for that . . .

JEAN (*interrupting*) Kindly use decent language in front of your mistress. Do you hear?

KRISTIN Mistress?

JEAN Yes.

KRISTIN Well, well, just listen to that!

JEAN Yes, it would be a good thing if you did listen and talked less. Miss Julie is your mistress and what's made you lose your respect for her now ought to make you feel the same about yourself.

KRISTIN I've always had enough self-respect——

JEAN To despise other people.

KRISTIN —not to go below my own station. Has the Count's cook ever gone with the groom or the swineherd? Tell me that.

JEAN No, you were lucky enough to have a high-class chap for your beau.

KRISTIN High-class all right—selling the oats out of the Count's stable.

JEAN You're a fine one to talk—taking a commission on the groceries and bribes from the butcher.

KRISTIN What the devil . . . ?

JEAN And now you can't feel any respect for your employers. You, you!

KRISTIN Are you coming to church with me? I should think you need a good sermon after your fine deeds.

JEAN No, I'm not going to church today. You can go alone and confess your own sins.

KRISTIN Yes, I'll do that and bring back enough forgiveness to cover yours too. The Saviour suffered and died on the cross for all our sins, and if we go to Him with faith and a penitent heart, He takes all our sins upon Himself.

JEAN Even grocery thefts?

JULIE Do you believe that, Kristin?

KRISTIN That is my living faith, as sure as I stand here. The faith I learnt as a child and have kept ever since, Miss Julie. "But where sin abounded, grace did much more abound."

JULIE Oh, if I had your faith! Oh, if . . .

KRISTIN   But you see you can't have it without God's special grace, and it's not given to all to have that.

JULIE   Who is it given to then?

KRISTIN   That's the great secret of the workings of grace, Miss Julie. God is no respecter of persons, and with Him the last shall be first . . .

JULIE   Then I suppose He does respect the last.

KRISTIN   (*continuing*)   . . . and it is easier for a camel to go through the eye of a needle than for a rich man to enter into the kingdom of God. That's how it is, Miss Julie. Now I'm going—alone, and on my way I shall tell the groom not to let any of the horses out, in case anyone should want to leave before the Count gets back. Goodbye.

(*Exit.*)

JEAN   What a devil! And all on account of a greenfinch.

JULIE   (*wearily*)   Never mind the greenfinch. Do you see any way out of this, any end to it?

JEAN   (*pondering*)   No.

JULIE   If you were in my place, what would you do?

JEAN   In your place? Wait a bit. If I was a woman—a lady of rank who had—fallen. I don't know. Yes, I do know now.

JULIE   (*picking up the razor and making a gesture*)   This?

JEAN   Yes. But *I* wouldn't do it, you know. There's a difference between us.

JULIE   Because you're a man and I'm a woman? What is the difference?

JEAN   The usual difference—between man and woman.

JULIE   (*holding the razor*)   I'd like to. But I can't. My father couldn't either, that time he wanted to.

JEAN   No, he didn't want to. He had to be revenged first.

JULIE   And now my mother is revenged again, through me.

JEAN   Didn't you ever love your father, Miss Julie?

JULIE   Deeply, but I must have hated him too—unconsciously. And he let me be brought up to despise my own sex, to be half woman, half man. Whose fault is what's happened? My father's, my mother's or my own? My own? I haven't anything that's my own. I haven't one single thought that I didn't get from my father, one emotion that didn't come from my mother, and as for this last idea—about all people being equal—I got that from him, my fiancé—that's why I call him a cad. How can it be my fault? Push the responsibility on to Jesus, like Kristin does? No, I'm too proud and—thanks to my father's teaching—too intelligent. As for all that about a rich person not being able to get into heaven, it's just a lie, but Kristin, who has money in the savings-bank, will certainly not get in. Whose fault is it? What does it matter whose fault it is? In any case I must take the blame and bear the consequences.

JEAN   Yes, but... (*There are two sharp rings on the bell.* JULIE *jumps to her feet.* JEAN *changes into his livery.*) The Count is back. Supposing Kristin... (*Goes to the speaking-tube, presses it and listens.*)

JULIE   Has he been to his desk yet?

JEAN   This is Jean, sir. (*Listens.*) Yes, sir. (*Listens.*) Yes, sir, very good, sir. (*Listens.*) At once, sir? (*Listens.*) Very good, sir. In half an hour.

JULIE (*in panic*)   What did he say? My God, what did he say?

JEAN   He ordered his boots and his coffee in half an hour.

JULIE   Then there's half an hour... Oh, I'm so tired! I can't do anything. Can't be sorry, can't run away, can't stay, can't live— can't die. Help me. Order me, and I'll obey like a dog. Do me this last service—save my honour, save his name. You know what I ought to do, but haven't the strength to do. Use your strength and order me to do it.

JEAN   I don't know why—I can't now—I don't understand... It's just as if this coat made me—I can't give you orders—and now that the Count has spoken to me—I can't quite explain, but... well, that devil of a lackey is bending my back again. I believe if the Count came down now and ordered me to cut my throat, I'd do it on the spot.

JULIE   Then pretend you're him and I'm you. You did some fine acting before, when you knelt to me and played the aristocrat. Or... Have you ever seen a hypnotist at the theatre? (*He nods.*) He says to the person "Take the broom," and he takes it. He says "Sweep," and he sweeps...

JEAN   But the person has to be asleep.

JULIE (*as if in a trance*)   I am asleep already... the whole room has turned to smoke—and you look like a stove—a stove like a man in black with a tall hat—your eyes are glowing like coals when the fire is low—and your face is a white patch like ashes. (*The sunlight has now reached the floor and lights up* JEAN.) How nice and warm it is! (*She holds out her hands as though warming them at a fire.*) And so light—and so peaceful.

JEAN (*putting the razor in her hand*)   Here is the broom. Go now while its light—out to the barn—and... (*Whispers in her ear.*)

JULIE (*waking*)   Thank you. I am going now—to rest. But just tell me that even the first can receive the gift of grace.

JEAN   The first? No, I can't tell you that. But wait... Miss Julie,

I've got it! You aren't one of the first any longer. You're one of the last.

JULIE That's true. I'm one of the very last. I *am* the last. Oh! . . . But now I can't go. Tell me again to go.

JEAN No, I can't now, either. I can't.

JULIE And the first shall be last.

JEAN Don't think, don't think. You're taking my strength away too and making me a coward. What's that? I thought I saw the bell move . . . To be so frightened of a bell! Yes, but it's not just a bell. There's somebody behind it—a hand moving it—and something else moving the hand—and if you stop your ears—if you stop your ears—yes, then it rings louder than ever. Rings and rings until you answer—and then its too late. Then the police come and . . . and . . . (*The bell rings twice loudly.* JEAN *flinches, then straightens himself up.*) It's horrible. But there's no other way to end it . . . Go!

(JULIE *walks firmly out through the door.*)

Curtain

HEDDA GABLER (1890)

HENRIK IBSEN (1828–1906)

Henrik Ibsen is widely regarded as the "father" of modern drama because of his highly realistic plays devoted to the contemporary political and social problems of the 1870s and 1880s. He produced the dramatic shot heard round the world in *A Doll's House* (1870) in which he sent the young wife, Nora, out into the Norwegian cold, slamming the door on home and children as she broke with the social forces that had kept her a plaything in her husband's house.

Ibsen has frequently been regarded as the first writer seriously to espouse the "liberation" of women. Both *A Doll's House* and *Hedda Gabler* could be so interpreted, as could certain others such as *Rosmersholm* (1886) and *The Master Builder* (1892), in which Ibsen presents fairly "liberated" feminine characters. He was not so much an advocate of "women's lib" in the general sense of the term today as he was a strong advocate of the right of individuals, irrespective of sex, to assert their own human dignity and integrity as persons, regardless of the forces that society brought to bear on them to hold their lives to the established patterns of morality.

Thus it would probably be a misinterpretation of *Hedda Gabler* to regard it as a polemic that advocates freeing a woman as potentially attractive and capable as Hedda from the bonds of social deprivation and injustice. It is, however, a near-tragedy of what can occur in the society which really has no place for the Heddas among it, who have been raised to money and privilege and who have been denied the opportunity to develop their personal talents to the degree necessary to establish some kind of individual identity. It is true that Hedda is selfish, at times rude, sexually frigid, in many ways unattractive. But she is handsome if not beautiful, physically appealing, a genuine "catch" for the right man, who happens not to be the man she finally marries.

Has Hedda been trapped because of her upbringing, her spoiled nature, her ability to ride and shoot like a man, while being expected to behave as a woman? Is her marriage with Tesman the only thing left for her because nobody else will have her, or is not afraid of her? As General Gabler's daughter she had status and social position; as a woman she is in many ways frightening. Only a Tesman, insensitive, pedantic, a bore, would seem to be left for her. Socially he is certainly appropriate, but emotionally he could not be worse. This is a pity. Frustrated by having spent a honeymoon visiting musty libraries, her sexual drive sublimated even more within her psyche by this totally unbelievable wedding trip with the virtually sexless Tesman, yet faced with the imminent possibility of motherhood, Hedda is driven to displaying her strong self-centeredness and her distorted emotionalism by literally destroying the father/lover in Løvborg as well as his symbolic child, the manuscript. Unable to offer the sexual and emotional attractiveness of a Thora Elvsted, and also faced with sexual blackmail from the unscrupulous Judge Brack, Hedda is driven to her own destruction both as a positive assertion of her own control over herself, and as a display of her own weakness and this personal control gone wrong.

Hedda Gabler, as a woman, is probably Ibsen's best character portrayal, and although he surrenders to much of the artificiality of nineteenth-century "well-made play" construction, he is able to paint a fascinating portrait of a woman whom society doesn't really seem to know what to do with.

Hedda Gabler (1890)

IBSEN

Translated by Otto Reinert

CHARACTERS

JØRGEN TESMAN, *University Research Fellow in the History of Civilization*
HEDDA, *his wife*
MISS JULIANE TESMAN, *his aunt*
MRS. ELVSTED
JUDGE BRACK
EILERT LØVBORG
BERTE, *the Tesmans' maid*

SCENE. *The* TESMANS' *villa in a fashionable residential section of the town.*

A NOTE ON PRONUNCIATION. *The approximate Norwegian pronunciation of names likely to be difficult to a speaker of English is suggested below (the syllable in capitals is accented; the unaccented* e *is close to English* e *in* quiet).

Jørgen   *YUR-gen* (g *as in* bargain)
Julle   *YOOL-le* (*short* oo)
Eilert Løvborg   *AY-lert LUV-borg*[1]
Berte   *BAIR-te*

ACT I

A spacious, handsome, tastefully furnished room. Dark décor. In the rear, a wide doorway with open portieres. Beyond is a smaller room, furnished in the same style as the front room. A door, right, leads to the front hall. Left, French doors, with portieres drawn aside, through which can be seen a part of a roofed verandah and trees with autumn foliage. Front center, an oval table covered with a cloth. Chairs around it. Front right, a wide, dark, porcelain stove, a high-backed easy chair, a footstool with a pillow,

---

[1] *Løvborg* means, literally, "leaf-castle"—a fact of possible bearing on the play's symbolism. [Reinert's note.]

and two ottomans. In the corner far right, a sofa and a small, round table. Front left, a sofa, set out from the wall. Far left, beyond the French doors, an upright piano. On both sides of the doorway, rear center, whatnots with knickknacks. Against the rear wall of the inner room, a sofa, and in front of it a table and two chairs. Above the sofa, a portrait of a handsome, elderly man in general's uniform. Over the table hangs a lamp with milky, white glass. There are several bouquets of flowers, in vases and glasses, in various places in the front room. Others are lying on the tables. Thick carpets on the floors of both rooms. The morning sun is shining through the French doors.

Miss Juliane Tesman, *with hat and parasol, enters right, followed by* Berte, *who carries a bouquet of flowers wrapped in paper.* Miss Tesman *is a nice-looking woman of 65, of pleasant mien, neatly but not expensively dressed in a gray suit.* Berte *is a middle-aged servant girl, of rather plain and countrified appearance.*

MISS TESMAN (*stops inside the door, listens, says in a low voice*) On my word—I don't think they are even up yet!

BERTE (*also softly*) That's what I told you, miss. When you think how late the steamer got in last night. And afterwards—! Goodness!—all the stuff she wanted unpacked before she turned in.

MISS TESMAN Well—just let them sleep. But fresh morning air— *that* we can give them when they come in here. (*Goes and opens the French doors wide.*)

BERTE (*by the table, lost, still holding the flowers*) Please, miss—I just don't see a bit of space anywhere! I think I'd better put these over here. (*Puts the flowers down on the piano.*)

MISS TESMAN Well, well, my dear Berte. So you've got yourself a new mistress now. The good Lord knows it was hard for me to let you go.

BERTE (*near tears*) What about me, then, miss! What shall *I* say? I who have served you and Miss Rina all these blessed years.

MISS TESMAN We shall just have to make the best of it, Berte. That's all. Jørgen can't do without you, you know. He just can't. You've looked after him ever since he was a little boy.

BERTE Yes, but miss—I'm ever so worried about leaving Miss Rina. The poor dear lying there all helpless. With that new girl and all! She'll never learn how to make things nice and comfortable for an invalid.

MISS TESMAN Oh yes, you'll see. I'll teach her. And of course, you know, I'll do most of it myself. So don't you worry yourself about my poor sister, Berte.

BERTE Yes, but there's another thing, too, miss. I'm scared I won't be able to suit young Mrs. Tesman.

MISS TESMAN   Oh, well. Good heavens. So there is a thing or two—
Right at first—

BERTE   For I believe she's ever so particular.

MISS TESMAN   Can you wonder? General Gabler's daughter? Just
think of the kind of life she was used to when the General was
alive. Do you remember when she rode by with her father? That
long black riding habit she wore? And the feather in her hat?

BERTE   Oh, I remember, all right. But I'll be blessed if I ever
thought she and the young master would make a pair of it.

MISS TESMAN   Nor did I. By the way, while I think of it, Berte.
Jørgen has a new title now. From now on you should call him
"the Doctor."

BERTE   Yes, the young mistress said something about that, too, last
night. Soon as they were inside the door. Then it's really so, miss?

MISS TESMAN   It certainly is. Just think, Berte—they have made
him a doctor abroad. During the trip, you know. I hadn't heard
a thing about it till last night on the pier.

BERTE   Well, I daresay he could be anything he put his mind to, *he*
could—smart as *he* is. But I must say I'd never thought he'd
turn to doctoring people, too.

MISS TESMAN   Oh, that's not the kind of doctor he is. (*Nods sig-
nificantly.*) And as far as that is concerned, there is no telling
but pretty soon you may have to call him something grander yet.

BERTE   You don't say! What might that be, miss?

MISS TESMAN (*smiles*)   Wouldn't you like to know! (*Moved.*) Ah
yes, indeed—! If only dear Jochum could see from his grave what
has become of his little boy! (*Looking around.*) But look, Berte
—what's this for? Why have you taken off all the slip covers?

BERTE   She told me to. Said she can't stand slip covers on chairs.

MISS TESMAN   Do you think they mean to make this their everyday
living room, then?

BERTE   It sure sounded that way. Mrs. Tesman did, I mean. For
he—the doctor—he didn't say anything.

(JØRGEN TESMAN *enters from the right side of the inner room. He is
humming to himself. He carries an open, empty suitcase. He is of
medium height, youthful-looking, thirty-three years old; somewhat stoutish. Round, open, cheerful face. Blond hair and beard. He wears glasses
and is dressed in a comfortable, rather casual suit.*)

MISS TESMAN   Good morning, good morning, Jørgen!

TESMAN (*in the doorway*)   Auntie! Dearest Aunt Julle! (*Comes
forward and shakes her hand.*) All the way out here—as early as
this! Hm?

MISS TESMAN   Well—I just had to drop in for a moment. To see how you are getting along, you know.

TESMAN   Even though you haven't had a good night's sleep.

MISS TESMAN   Oh, that doesn't matter at all.

TESMAN   But you did get home from the pier all right, I hope. Hm?

MISS TESMAN   Oh yes, I certainly did, thank you. The Judge was kind enough to see me all the way to my door.

TESMAN   We were so sorry we couldn't give you a ride in our carriage. But you saw for yourself—all the boxes Hedda had.

MISS TESMAN   Yes, she certainly brought quite a collection.

BERTE (*to* TESMAN)   Should I go and ask Mrs. Tesman if there's anything I can help her with?

TESMAN   No, thank you, Berte—you'd better not. She said she'll ring if she wants you.

BERTE (*going right*)   Well, all right.

TESMAN   But, look—you might take this suitcase with you.

BERTE (*takes it*)   I'll put it in the attic.

(*Exits right*)

TESMAN   Just think, Auntie—that whole suitcase was brimful of copies of old documents. You wouldn't believe me if I told you all the things I have collected from libraries and archives all over. Quaint old items nobody has known anything about.

MISS TESMAN   Well, no, Jørgen. I'm sure you haven't wasted your time on your honeymoon.

TESMAN   No, I think I may say I have not. But take your hat off, Auntie—for goodness' sake. Here! Let me untie the ribbon for you. Hm?

MISS TESMAN (*while he does so*)   Ah, God forgive me, if this isn't just as if you were still at home with us!

TESMAN (*inspecting the hat*)   My, what a fine-looking hat you've got yourself!

MISS TESMAN   I bought it for Hedda's sake.

TESMAN   For Hedda's sake? Hm?

MISS TESMAN   So she won't need to feel ashamed of me if we ever go out together.

TESMAN (*patting her cheek*)   If you don't think of everything, Auntie! (*Puts the hat down on a chair by the table.*)   And now —over here to the sofa—we'll just sit and chat for a while till Hedda comes.

They seat themselves. She places her parasol in the corner by the sofa.

MISS TESMAN (*takes both his hands in hers and gazes at him*) What a blessing it is to have you back again, Jørgen, big as life! You—Jochum's little boy!

TESMAN   For me, too, Aunt Julle. Seeing you again. For you have been both father and mother to me.

MISS TESMAN   Ah, yes—don't you think I know you'll always keep a spot in your heart for these two old aunts of yours!

TESMAN   So Aunt Rina isn't any better, hm?

MISS TESMAN   Oh no. We mustn't look for improvement in her case, poor dear. She is lying there just as she has been all these years. Just the same, may the good Lord keep her for me a long time yet! For else I just wouldn't know what to do with myself, Jørgen. Especially now, when I don't have you to look after any more.

TESMAN (*pats her back*)   There, there, now!

MISS TESMAN (*changing tone*)   And to think that you are a married man, Jørgen! And that you were the one to walk off with Hedda Gabler. The lovely Hedda Gabler. Just think! As many admirers as she had!

TESMAN (*hums a little, smiles complacently*)   Yes, I daresay I have quite a few good friends here in town who'd gladly be in my shoes, hm?

MISS TESMAN   And such a long and lovely honeymoon you had! More than five—almost six months!

TESMAN   Well, you know—for me it has been a kind of study tour as well. All the collections I had to go through. And the books I had to read!

MISS TESMAN   Yes, I suppose. (*More confidentially, her voice lowered a little.*) But listen, Jørgen—haven't you got something—something special to tell me?

TESMAN   About the trip?

MISS TESMAN   Yes.

TESMAN   No—I don't know of anything besides what I wrote in my letters. They gave me a doctor's degree down there—but I told you that last night; I'm sure I did.

MISS TESMAN   Well, yes, that sort of thing—What I mean is—don't you have certain—certain—expectations?

TESMAN   Expectations?

MISS TESMAN   Ah for goodness' sake, Jørgen! I am your old Auntie, after all!

TESMAN   Certainly I have expectations.

MISS TESMAN   Well!!

TESMAN   I fully expect to be made a professor one of these days.

MISS TESMAN   Professor—oh yes—

TESMAN   I may even say I am quite certain of it. But dear Aunt Julle—you know this just as well as I do!

MISS TESMAN (*laughing a little*)   Of course I do. You're quite right. (*Changing topic.*) But about the trip. It must have cost a great deal of money—hm, Jørgen?

TESMAN   Well, now; you know that large stipend went quite a long way.

MISS TESMAN   I just don't see how you made it do for both of you, though.

TESMAN   No, I suppose that's not so easy to understand, hm?

MISS TESMAN   Particularly with a lady along. For I have always heard that is ever so much more expensive.

TESMAN   Well, yes, naturally. That *is* rather more expensive. But Hedda had to have this trip, Auntie! She really had to. Nothing less would do.

MISS TESMAN   No, I daresay. For a wedding journey is quite the thing these days. But now tell me—have you had a chance to look around here yet?

TESMAN   I certainly have. I have been up and about ever since dawn.

MISS TESMAN   And what do you think of it all?

TESMAN   Delightful! Perfectly delightful! The only thing is I don't see what we are going to do with the two empty rooms between the second sitting room in there and Hedda's bedroom.

MISS TESMAN (*with a chuckle*)   Oh my dear Jørgen—you may find them useful enough—when the time comes!

TESMAN   Of course, you're right, Auntie! As my library expands, hm?

MISS TESMAN   Quite so, my dear boy. It was your library I was thinking of.

TESMAN   But I'm really most happy on Hedda's behalf. For you know, before we were engaged she used to say she wouldn't care to live anywhere but in Secretary Falk's house.

MISS TESMAN   Yes, just think—wasn't that a lucky coincidence, that it was up for sale right after you had left?

TESMAN   Yes, Aunt Julle. We've certainly been lucky. Hm?

MISS TESMAN   But it will be expensive, my dear Jørgen. Terribly expensive—all this.

TESMAN (*looks at her, a bit crestfallen*)   Yes, I daresay it will, Auntie.

MISS TESMAN   Heavens, yes!

TESMAN   How much, do you think? Roughly. Hm?

MISS TESMAN   No, I couldn't possibly say till all the bills arrive.

TESMAN Well, anyway, Judge Brack managed to get very reasonable terms for us. He said so himself in a letter to Hedda.

MISS TESMAN Yes, and I won't have you uneasy on that account, Jørgen. Besides, I have given security for the furniture and the carpets.

TESMAN Security? You? But dear Aunt Julle—what kind of security could you give?

MISS TESMAN The annuity.

TESMAN (*jumps up*) What! Your and Aunt Rina's annuity?

MISS TESMAN Yes. I didn't know what else to do, you see.

TESMAN (*standing before her*) But are you clear out of your mind, Auntie! That annuity—that's all the two of you have to live on!

MISS TESMAN Oh well, there's nothing to get so excited about, I'm sure. It's all just a matter of form, you know. That's what the Judge said, too. For he was kind enough to arrange the whole thing for me. Just a matter of form—those were his words.

TESMAN That's all very well. Still—

MISS TESMAN For now you'll have your own salary, you know. And, goodness—what if we do have a few expenses—Help out a bit right at first—? That would only be a joy for us—

TESMAN Oh, Auntie! When will you ever stop making sacrifices for my sake!

MISS TESMAN (*gets up, puts her hands on his shoulders*) But what other happiness do I have in this world than being able to smooth your way a little, my own dear boy? Orphan as you were, with no one to lean on but us? And now the goal is in sight, Jørgen. Things may have looked black at times. But heaven be praised; now you've arrived!

TESMAN Yes, it's really quite remarkable the way things have worked out.

MISS TESMAN Yes—and those who were against you—who tried to block your way—now they are tasting defeat. They are down, Jørgen! He, the most dangerous of them all, his fall was the greatest! He made his bed, and now he is lying in it—poor, lost wretch that he is!

TESMAN Have you had any news about Eilert? Since I went away, I mean?

MISS TESMAN Just that he is supposed to have published a new book.

TESMAN What? Eilert Løvborg? Recently? Hm?

MISS TESMAN That's what they say. But I wonder if there can be much to it. What do you think? Ah—but when *your* new book comes, that will be something quite different, Jørgen! What is it going to be about?

TESMAN   It deals with the domestic industries of Brabant during the Middle Ages.

MISS TESMAN   Just think—being able to write about something like that!

TESMAN   But as far as that is concerned, it may be quite some time before it is ready. I have all these collections to put in order first, you see.

MISS TESMAN   Yes, collecting and putting things in order—you certainly know how to do that. In that you are your father's own son.

TESMAN   Well, I must say I am looking forward to getting started. Particularly now, that I've got my own delightful home to work in.

MISS TESMAN   And most of all now that you have the one your heart desired, dear Jørgen.

TESMAN (*embracing her*)   Oh yes, yes, Aunt Julle! Hedda—she is the most wonderful part of it all! (*Look toward the doorway.*) There—I think she is coming now, hm?

(HEDDA *enters from the left side of the inner room. She is twenty-nine years old. Both features and figure are noble and elegant. Pale, ivory complexion. Steel-gray eyes, expressive of cold, clear calm. Beautiful brown hair, though not particularly ample. She is dressed in a tasteful, rather loose-fitting morning costume.*)

MISS TESMAN (*going toward her*)   Good morning, my dear Hedda! A very happy morning to you!

HEDDA (*giving her hand*)   Good morning, dear Miss Tesman! So early a call? That is most kind.

MISS TESMAN (*seems slightly embarrassed*)   And—has the little lady of the house slept well the first night in her new home?

HEDDA   Passably, thank you.

TESMAN (*laughs*)   Passably! You are a good one, Hedda! You were sleeping like a log when I got up.

HEDDA   Fortunately. And then, of course, Miss Tesman, it always takes time to get used to new surroundings. That has to come gradually. (*Looks left.*) Oh dear. The maid has left the verandah doors wide open. There's a veritable flood of sunlight in here.

MISS TESMAN (*toward the doors*)   Well, then, we'll just close them.

HEDDA   No, no, not that. Tesman, dear, please pull the curtains. That will give a softer light.

TESMAN (*over by the French doors*)   Yes, dear. There, now! Now you have both shade and fresh air, Hedda.

HEDDA   We certainly can use some air in here. Such loads of flow-ers—but, Miss Tesman, please—won't you be seated?

MISS TESMAN   No thanks. I just wanted to see if everything was all right—and so it is, thank goodness. I had better get back to Rina. I know she is waiting for me, poor thing.

TESMAN   Be sure to give her my love, Auntie. And tell her I'll be around to see her later today.

MISS TESMAN   I'll certainly do that!—Oh my! I almost forgot! (*Searches the pocket of her dress.*) I have something for you, Jørgen. Here.

TESMAN   What's that, Auntie? Hm?

MISS TESMAN (*pulls out a flat parcel wrapped in newspaper and gives it to him*). Here you are, dear.

TESMAN (*opens the parcel*)   Well, well, well! So you took care of them for me, Aunt Julle! Hedda! Now, isn't that sweet, hm?

HEDDA (*by the whatnot, right*)   If you'd tell me what it is—

TESMAN   My old slippers! *You* know!

HEDDA   Oh really? I remember you often talked about them on the trip.

TESMAN   Yes, for I missed them so. (*Walks over to her.*) Here—now you can see what they're like, Hedda.

HEDDA (*crosses toward stove*)   Thanks. I don't know that I really care.

TESMAN (*following*)   Just think—Aunt Rina embroidered these slippers for me. Ill as she was. You can't imagine how many mem-ories they hold for me!

HEDDA (*by the table*)   Hardly for me.

MISS TESMAN   That's true, you know, Jørgen.

TESMAN   Yes, but—I just thought that now that she's one of the family—

HEDDA (*interrupting*)   I don't think we'll get on with that maid, Tesman.

MISS TESMAN   Not get on with Berte?

TESMAN   Whatever makes you say that, dear? Hm?

HEDDA (*points*)   Look—she has left her old hat on the chair over there.

TESMAN (*appalled, drops the slippers*)   But Hedda—!

HEDDA   What if somebody were to come and see it!

TESMAN   No, no, Hedda—that's Aunt Julle's hat!

HEDDA   Oh?

MISS TESMAN (*picking up the hat*)   Yes, indeed it is. And it isn't old either, my dear young lady.

HEDDA   I really didn't look that closely—

MISS TESMAN (*tying the ribbons*)   I want you to know that this is the first time I have had it on my head. On my word it is!

TESMAN   And very handsome it is, too. Really a splendid-looking hat!

MISS TESMAN   Oh, I don't know that it is anything so special, Jørgen. (*Looks around.*) My parasol—? Ah, here it is. (*Picks it up.*) For that is mine, too. (*Mutters.*) Not Berte's.

TESMAN   New hat and new parasol! What do you think of that, Hedda!

HEDDA   Very nice indeed.

TESMAN   Yes, don't you think so? Hm? But, Auntie, take a good look at Hedda before you leave. See how pretty and blooming she looks.

MISS TESMAN   Dear me, Jørgen; that's nothing new. Hedda has been lovely all her days. (*She nods and walks right.*)

TESMAN (*following*)   Yes, but have you noticed how full-figured and healthy she looks after the trip? How she has filled out?

HEDDA (*crossing*)   Oh—stop it!

MISS TESMAN (*halts, turns around*)   Filled out?

TESMAN   Yes, Aunt Julle. You can't see it so well now when she wears that dress. But I, who have the opportunity—

HEDDA (*by the French doors, impatiently*)   Oh, you haven't any opportunities at all!

TESMAN   It must be the mountain air in Tyrol.

HEDDA (*curtly interrupting*)   I am just as I was when I left.

TESMAN   Yes, so you say. I just don't think you're right. What do you think, Auntie?

MISS TESMAN (*has folded her hands, gazes at* HEDDA)   Lovely— lovely—lovely; that is what Hedda is. (*Goes over to her, inclines her head forward with both her hands, and kisses her hair.*) God bless and keep Hedda Tesman. For Jørgen's sake.

HEDDA (*gently freeing herself*)   There, there. Now let me go.

MISS TESMAN (*in quiet emotion*)   Every single day I'll be over and see you two.

TESMAN   Yes, please do, Auntie. Hm?

MISS TESMAN   Goodbye, goodbye!

(*She leaves through door, right.* TESMAN *sees her out. The door remains ajar.* TESMAN *is heard repeating his greetings for* AUNT RINA *and his thanks for the slippers. In the meantime,* HEDDA *paces up and down, raises her arms, clenching her fist, as in quiet rage. Opens the curtains by the French doors and stands looking out. In a few moments,* TESMAN *re-enters and closes the door behind him.*)

TESMAN (*picking up the slippers*)   What are you looking at, Hedda?

HEDDA (*once again calm and controlled*)   Just the leaves. They are so yellow. And withered.

TESMAN (*wrapping the slippers in their paper, putting the parcel down on the table*)   Well, you know—we're in September now.

HEDDA (*again restless*)   Yes—just think. It's already—September.

TESMAN   Don't you think Aunt Julle acted strange, Hedda? Almost solemn. I wonder why. Hm?

HEDDA   I hardly know her, you see. Isn't she often like that?

TESMAN   Not the way she was today.

HEDDA (*turning away from the French doors*)   Do you think she minded that business with the hat?

TESMAN   Oh, I don't think so. Not much. Perhaps a little bit right at the moment—

HEDDA   Well, I'm sorry, but I must say it strikes me as very odd— putting her hat down here in the living room. One just doesn't do that.

TESMAN   Well, you may be sure Aunt Julle won't ever do it again.

HEDDA   Anyway, I'll make it up to her, somehow.

TESMAN   Oh yes, Hedda; if only you would!

HEDDA   When you go over there today, why don't you ask her over for tonight?

TESMAN   I'll certainly do that. And then there is one other thing you could do that she'd appreciate ever so much.

HEDDA   What?

TESMAN   If you could just bring yourself to call her Auntie. For my sake, Hedda, hm?

HEDDA   No, Tesman, no. You really mustn't ask me to do that. I have already told you I can't. I'll try to call her Aunt Juliane. That will have to do.

TESMAN   All right, if you say so. I just thought that now that you're in the family—

HEDDA   Hmmm—I don't know about that—(*She walks toward the doorway.*)

TESMAN (*after a brief pause*)   Anything the matter, Hedda? Hm?

HEDDA   I'm just looking at my old piano. It doesn't quite go with the other furniture in here.

TESMAN   As soon as I get my first pay check we'll have it traded in.

HEDDA   No—I don't want to do that. I want to keep it. But let's put it in this inner room and get another one for out here. Whenever it's convenient. I mean.

TESMAN (*a little taken back*)   Well—yes—we could do that—

HEDDA (*picks up the bouquet from the piano*)   These flowers weren't here last night.

TESMAN   I suppose Aunt Julle brought them for you.

HEDDA   (*looking at the flowers*)   There's a card here. (*Takes it out and reads.*) "Will be back later." Can you guess who it's from?

TESMAN   No. Who? Hm?

HEDDA   Thea Elvsted.

TESMAN   No, really? Mrs. Elvsted! Miss Rysing that was.

HEDDA   That's right. The one with that irritating head of hair she used to show off with. An old flame of yours, I understand.

TESMAN   (*laughs*)   Well, now—that didn't last long! Anyway, that was before I knew you, Hedda. Just think—her being in town.

HEDDA   Strange, that she'd call on us. I have hardly seen her since we went to school together.

TESMAN   As far as that goes, I haven't seen her either for—God knows how long. I don't see how she can stand living in that out-of-the-way place. Hm?

HEDDA   (*suddenly struck by a thought*)   Listen, Tesman—isn't it some place near there that he lives—what's his name—Eilert Løvborg?

TESMAN   Yes, that's right. He is up there, too.

(BERTE *enters right.*)

BERTE   Ma'am, she's here again, that lady who brought those flowers a while back. (*Pointing.*) The flowers you're holding in your hand, ma'am.

HEDDA   Ah, she is? Well, show her in, please.

(BERTE *opens the door for* MRS. ELVSTED *and exits.* MRS. ELVSTED *is of slight build, with a pretty, soft face. Her eyes are light blue, large, round, rather prominent, of a timid and querying expression. Her hair is strikingly light in color, almost whitish, and unusually rich and wavy. She is a couple of years younger than* HEDDA. *She is dressed in a dark visiting dress, tasteful, but not quite in the most recent fashion.*)

HEDDA   (*walks toward her. Friendly*)   Good morning, my dear Mrs. Elvsted. How very nice to see you again.

MRS. ELVSTED   (*nervous, trying not to show it*)   Well, yes, it is quite some time since we met.

TESMAN   (*shaking hands*)   And we, too. Hm?

HEDDA   Thank you for your lovely flowers—

MRS. ELVSTED   Please, don't—I would have come here yesterday afternoon. But I was told you were still traveling—

TESMAN   You've just arrived in town, hm?

MRS. ELVSTED   I got here yesterday, at noon. Oh, I was quite desperate when I learned you weren't home.

HEDDA   Desperate? But why?

TESMAN But my dear Mrs. Rysing—I mean Mrs. Elvsted—

HEDDA There is nothing wrong, I hope?

MRS. ELVSTED Yes there is. And I don't know a single soul other than you that I can turn to here.

HEDDA (*putting the flowers down on the table*) Come—let's sit down here on the sofa.

MRS. ELVSTED Oh, I'm in no mood to sit!

HEDDA Of course you are. Come on. (*She pulls* MRS. ELVSTED *over to the sofa and sits down next to her.*)

TESMAN Well, now, Mrs.—? Exactly what—?

HEDDA Has something—special happened at home?

MRS. ELVSTED Well, yes—and no. Oh, but I am so afraid you won't understand!

HEDDA In that case, it seems to me you ought to tell us exactly what has happened, Mrs. Elvsted.

TESMAN After all, that's why you are here. Hm?

MRS. ELVSTED Yes, yes, of course. Well, then, maybe you already know—Eilert Løvborg is in town.

HEDDA Is Løvborg—!

TESMAN No! You don't say! Just think, Hedda—Løvborg's back!

HEDDA All right. I can hear.

MRS. ELVSTED He has been here a week already. Imagine—a whole week! In this dangerous place. Alone! With all that bad company around.

HEDDA But my dear Mrs. Elvsted—why is he a concern of yours?

MRS. ELVSTED (*with an apprehensive look at her, says quickly*) He tutored the children.

HEDDA Your children?

MRS. ELVSTED My husband's. I don't have any.

HEDDA In other words, your stepchildren.

MRS. ELVSTED Yes.

TESMAN (*with some hesitation*) But was he—I don't quite know how to put this—was he sufficiently—regular—in his way of life to be thus employed? Hm?

MRS. ELVSTED For the last two years, there hasn't been a thing to object to in his conduct.

TESMAN No, really? Just think, Hedda!

HEDDA I hear.

MRS. ELVSTED Not the least little bit, I assure you! Not in any respect. And yet—knowing he's here—in the big city—And with all that money, too! I'm scared to death!

TESMAN But in that case, why didn't he remain with you and your husband? Hm?

MRS. ELVSTED After his book came out, he was too restless to stay.

TESMAN Ah yes, that's right. Aunt Julle said he has published a new book.

MRS. ELVSTED Yes, a big new book, about the course of civilization in general. It came out about two weeks ago. And since it has had such big sales and been discussed so much and made such a big splash—

TESMAN It has, has it? I suppose this is something he has had lying around from better days?

MRS. ELVSTED You mean from earlier?

TESMAN Yes.

MRS. ELVSTED No; it's all been written since he came to stay with us. During this last year.

TESMAN Well, now! That's very good news, Hedda! Just think!

MRS. ELVSTED Yes, if it only would last!

HEDDA Have you seen him since you came to town?

MRS. ELVSTED No, not yet. I had a great deal of trouble finding his address. But this morning I finally tracked him down.

HEDDA (*looks searchingly at her*) Isn't it rather odd that your husband—hm—

MRS. ELVSTED (*with a nervous start*) My husband! What about him?

HEDDA That he sends you to town on such an errand? That he doesn't go and look after his friend himself?

MRS. ELVSTED Oh, no, no—my husband doesn't have time for things like that. Besides, I have some—some shopping to do, anyway.

HEDDA (*with a slight smile*) Well, in that case, of course—

MRS. ELVSTED (*getting up, restlessly*) And now I beg of you, Mr. Tesman—won't you please receive Eilert Løvborg nicely if he calls on you? And I am sure he will. After all—Such good friends as you two used to be. And then you both do the same kind of work—the same field of study, as far as I know.

TESMAN We used to, at any rate.

MRS. ELVSTED Yes. And that's why I implore you to please, please, try to keep an eye on him—you too. You'll do that, Mr. Tesman, won't you? Promise?

TESMAN With the greatest pleasure, Mrs. Rysing.

HEDDA Elvsted.

TESMAN I'll gladly do as much for Eilert as I possibly can. You may certainly count on that.

MRS. ELVSTED Oh, how good and kind you are! (*Clasps his hands.*) Thank you, thank you, thank you! (*Nervously.*) You see, my husband is so very fond of him.

HEDDA (*getting up*) You ought to write him a note, Tesman. Maybe he won't come without an invitation.

TESMAN Yes, I suppose that would be the right thing to do, Hedda. Hm?

HEDDA The sooner the better. Right away, *I* think.

MRS. ELVSTED (*pleadingly*) If only you would!

TESMAN I'll write this minute. Do you have his address, Mrs.— Mrs. Elvsted?

MRS. ELVSTED Yes. (*Pulls a slip of paper from her bag and gives it to him*). Here it is.

TESMAN Very good. Well, then, if you'll excuse me—(*Looks around.*) By the way—the slippers? Ah, here we are. (*Leaving with the parcel.*)

HEDDA Be sure you write a nice, warm, friendly letter, Tesman. And a long one, too.

TESMAN Certainly, certainly.

MRS. ELVSTED But not a word that it is I who—!

TESMAN No, that goes without saying, I should think. Hm?

(*Goes out right through inner room.*)

HEDDA (*goes over to* MRS. ELVSTED, *smiles, says in a low voice*) There! We just killed two birds with one stone.

MRS. ELVSTED What do you mean?

HEDDA Didn't you see I wanted him out of the room?

MRS. ELVSTED Yes, to write that letter—

HEDDA And to speak to you alone.

MRS. ELVSTED (*flustered*) About this same thing?

HEDDA Exactly.

MRS. ELVSTED (*anxious*) But there *is* nothing more, Mrs. Tesman! Really, there isn't!

HEDDA Oh yes, there is. There is considerably more. I can see that much. Over here—We are going to have a real, nice, confidential talk, you and I. (*She forces* MRS. ELVSTED *down in the easy chair and seats herself on one of the ottomans.*)

MRS. ELVSTED (*worried, looks at her watch*) But my dear Mrs. Tesman—I had really thought I would be on my way now.

HEDDA Oh I am sure there is no rush. Now, then. Tell me about yourself. How are things at home?

MRS. ELVSTED That is just what I don't want to talk about.

HEDDA But to me—! After all, we are old schoolmates.

MRS. ELVSTED But you were a year ahead of me. And I used to be so scared of you!

HEDDA Scared of me?

MRS. ELVSTED   Terribly. For when we met on the stairs, you always ruffled my hair.

HEDDA   Did I really?

MRS. ELVSTED   Yes. And once you said you were going to burn it off.

HEDDA   Oh, but you know—I wasn't serious!

MRS. ELVSTED   No, but I was such a silly, then. Anyway, afterwards we drifted far apart. Our circles are so very different, you know.

HEDDA   All the more reason for getting close again. Listen. In school we called each other by our first names.

MRS. ELVSTED   Oh I'm sure you're wrong—

HEDDA   I'm sure I'm not! I remember it quite clearly. And now we want to be open with one another, just the way we used to. (*Moves the ottoman closer.*) There, now! (*Kisses her cheek.*) You call me Hedda.

MRS. ELVSTED (*seizes her hands*)   Oh you are so good and kind! I'm not used to that.

HEDDA   There, there! And I'll call you my dear Thora, just as in the old days.

MRS. ELVSTED   My name is Thea.

HEDDA   So it is. Of course. I meant Thea. (*Looks at her with compassion.*) So you're not much used to goodness and kindness, Thea? Not in your own home?

MRS. ELVSTED   If I even had a home! But I don't. I never have had one.

HEDDA (*looks at her for a moment*)   I thought there might be something like this.

MRS. ELVSTED (*helplessly, looking straight ahead*)   Yes—yes—yes—

HEDDA   I am not sure if I quite remember—Didn't you first come to your husband as his housekeeper?

MRS. ELVSTED   I was really hired as governess. But his wife—his first wife—was ailing already then and practically bedridden. So I had to take charge of the household as well.

HEDDA   But in the end you become his wife.

MRS. ELVSTED (*dully*)   So I did.

HEDDA   Let's see. How long ago is that?

MRS. ELVSTED   Since my marriage?

HEDDA   Yes.

MRS. ELVSTED   About five years.

HEDDA   Right. It must be that long.

MRS. ELVSTED   Oh, those five years! Or mostly the last two or three! Oh, Mrs. Tesman—if you could just imagine!

HEDDA (*slaps her hand lightly*)   Mrs. Tesman? Shame on you!

MRS. ELVSTED Oh yes; all right, I'll try. Yes—if you could just—conceive—understand—

HEDDA (*casually*) And Eilert Løvborg has been living near you for some three years or so, hasn't he?

MRS. ELVSTED (*looks at her uncertainly*) Eilert Løvborg? Yes—he has.

HEDDA Did you know him before? Here in town?

MRS. ELVSTED Hardly at all. That is, of course I did in a way. I mean, I knew *of* him.

HEDDA But up there—You saw a good deal of him; did you?

MRS. ELVSTED Yes, he came over to us every day. He was supposed to tutor the children, you see. For I just couldn't do it all by myself.

HEDDA Of course not. And your husband—? I suppose he travels quite a bit.

MRS. ELVSTED Well, yes, Mrs. Tes—Hedda—as a public magistrate, you know, he very often has to travel all over his district.

HEDDA (*leaning against the armrest on the easy chair*) Thea—poor, sweet Thea—now you have to tell me everything—just as it is.

MRS. ELVSTED You'd better ask me, then.

HEDDA How *is* your husband, Thea? I mean—you know—*really*? To be with. What kind of person is he? Is he good to you?

MRS. ELVSTED (*evasively*) I believe he thinks he does everything for the best.

HEDDA But isn't he altogether too old for you? He is more than twenty years older, isn't he?

MRS. ELVSTED (*with irritation*) Yes, there is that, too. But there isn't just one thing. Every single little thing about him repels me! We don't have a thought in common, he and I. Not a thing in the world!

HEDDA But isn't he fond of you all the same? I mean in his own way?

MRS. ELVSTED I don't know. I think I am just useful to him. And I don't use much money. I am inexpensive.

HEDDA That is foolish of you.

MRS. ELVSTED (*shakes her head*) Can't be changed. Not with him. I don't think he cares for anybody much except himself. Perhaps the children a little.

HEDDA And Eilert Løvborg, Thea.

MRS. ELVSTED (*looks at her*). Eilert Løvborg? What makes you think that?

HEDDA Well, it seems to me that when he sends you all the way to town to look after him—(*With an almost imperceptible smile.*) Besides, you said so yourself. To Tesman.

MRS. ELVSTED (*with a nervous twitch*) Did I? I suppose I did. (*With a muted outburst.*) No! I might as well tell you now as later. For it's bound to come out, anyway.

HEDDA But my dear Thea—?

MRS. ELVSTED All right. My husband doesn't know I've gone!

HEDDA What! He doesn't know?

MRS. ELVSTED He wasn't even home. He's away again. Oh, I just couldn't take it any longer, Hedda! It had become utterly impossible. All alone as I was.

HEDDA So what did you do?

MRS. ELVSTED I packed some of my things. Just the most necessary. Without telling anybody. And left.

HEDDA Just like that?

MRS. ELVSTED Yes. And took the next train to town.

HEDDA But dearest Thea—how did you dare to do a thing like that!

MRS. ELVSTED (*rises, walks*) What else could I do?

HEDDA But what do you think your husband will say when you go back?

MRS. ELVSTED (*by the table; looks at her*) Go back to him?

HEDDA Yes!

MRS. ELVSTED I'll never go back.

HEDDA (*rises, approaches her slowly*) So you have really, seriously —left everything?

MRS. ELVSTED Yes. It seemed to me there was nothing else I could do.

HEDDA And quite openly, too.

MRS. ELVSTED You can't keep a thing like that secret, anyway.

HEDDA But what do you think people will say, Thea?

MRS. ELVSTED In God's name, let them say whatever they like. (*Sits down on the sofa, dully, tired.*) For I have only done what I had to do.

HEDDA (*after a brief silence*) And what do you plan to do with yourself? What sort of work will you do?

MRS. ELVSTED I don't know yet. I only know I have to live where Eilert Løvborg is. If I am to live at all.

HEDDA (*moves a chair from the table closer to* MRS. ELVSTED, *sits down, strokes her hands*) Thea—tell me. How did this—this friendship between you and Eilert—how did it begin?

MRS. ELVSTED Oh, it grew little by little. I got some sort of power over him.

HEDDA Oh?

MRS. ELVSTED He dropped his old ways. Not because I asked him to. I never dared to do that. But I think he must have noticed how I felt about that kind of life. So he changed.

HEDDA (*quickly suppresses a cynical smile*) So you have—rehabilitated him, as they say. Haven't you, Thea?

MRS. ELVSTED At least, that's what *he* says. On the other hand, he has turned me into a real human being. Taught me to think— and understand—all sorts of things.

HEDDA Maybe he tutored you, too?

MRS. ELVSTED No, not tutored exactly. But he talked to me. About so many, many things. And then came that lovely, lovely time when I could share his work with him. He let me help him!

HEDDA He did?

MRS. ELVSTED Yes! Whatever he wrote, he wanted us to be together about it.

HEDDA Just like two good comrades.

MRS. ELVSTED (*with animation*) Comrades!—that's it! Imagine, Hedda—that's just what he called it, too. Oh, I really ought to feel so happy. But I can't. For you see, I don't know if it will last.

HEDDA You don't trust him any more than that?

MRS. ELVSTED (*heavily*) The shadow of a woman stands between Eilert Løvborg and me.

HEDDA (*tensely, looks at her*) Who?

MRS. ELVSTED I don't know. Somebody or other from—his past. I don't think he has ever really forgotten her.

HEDDA What has he told you about it?

MRS. ELVSTED He has mentioned it only once—just casually.

HEDDA And what did he say?

MRS. ELVSTED He said that when they parted she was going to kill him with a gun.

HEDDA (*cold, controlled*) Oh, nonsense. People don't do that sort of thing here.

MRS. ELVSTED No, I know. And that is why I think it must be that red-headed singer he used to—

HEDDA Yes, I suppose so.

MRS. ELVSTED For I remember people said she carried a loaded gun.

HEDDA Well, then I'm sure it's she.

MRS. ELVSTED (*wringing her hands*) Yes, but just think, Hedda— now I hear that she—that singer—that she's here in town again, too! Oh, I'm just desperate—!

HEDDA (*with a glance toward the inner room*) Shhh! Here's Tesman. (*Rises and whispers.*) Not a word about all this to anybody, Thea!

MRS. ELVSTED (*jumps up*) No, no. For God's sake—!

(TESMAN, *carrying a letter, enters from the right side of the inner room.*)

TESMAN There now—here's the missive, all ready to go!

HEDDA Good. But I believe Mrs. Elvsted wants to be on her way. Wait a moment. I'll see you to the garden gate.

TESMAN Say, Hedda—do you think Berte could take care of this?

HEDDA (*takes the letter*) I'll tell her.

(BERTE *enters right.*)

BERTE Judge Brack is here and wants to know if you're receiving.

HEDDA Yes, ask the Judge please to come in. And—here—drop this in a mailbox, will you?

BERTE (*takes the letter*) Yes, ma'am.

(*She opens the door for* JUDGE BRACK *and exits. The* JUDGE *is forty-five years of age. Rather thickset, but well-built and with brisk athletic movements. Roundish face, aristocratic profile. His hair is short, still almost completely black, very neatly dressed. Lively, sparkling eyes. Thick eyebrows and mustache with cut-off points. He is dressed in an elegant suit, a trifle youthful for his age. He wears pince-nez glasses, attached to a string, and lets them drop from time to time.*)

JUDGE BRACK (*hat in hand, salutes*) May one pay one's respects as early as this?

HEDDA One certainly may.

TESMAN (*shaking his hand*) You are always welcome. (*Introducing.*) Judge Brack—Miss Rysing—

HEDDA *groans.*

BRACK (*bowing*) Delighted!

HEDDA (*looks at him, laughs*) How nice it is to see you in daylight, Judge!

BRACK You find me changed, perhaps?

HEDDA A bit younger, I think.

BRACK Much obliged.

TESMAN But what do you think of Hedda? Hm? Did you ever see her in such bloom? She positively—

HEDDA Will you please leave me out of this? You had better thank the Judge for all the trouble he has taken.

BRACK Oh, nonsense. It's been a pleasure.

HEDDA Yes, you are indeed a faithful soul. But my friend here is dying to be off. Don't leave, Judge. I'll be back in a minute.

(*Mutual goodbyes.* MRS. ELVSTED *and* HEDDA *exit, right.*)

BRACK Well, now—your wife—is she tolerably satisfied?

TESMAN Yes, indeed, and we really can't thank you enough. That is, I understand there will have to be some slight changes made here and there. And there are still a few things—just a few trifles —we'll have to get.

BRACK Oh? Really?

TESMAN But we certainly don't want to bother you with that. Hedda said she's going to take care of it herself. But do sit down, hm?

BRACK Thanks. Maybe just for a moment—(*Sits down by the table.*) There's one thing I'd like to talk to you about, my dear Tesman.

TESMAN Oh? Ah, I see! (*Sits down.*) I suppose it's the serious part of the festivities that's beginning now. Hm?

BRACK Oh—there's no great rush as far as the money is concerned. Though I must say I wish we could have established ourselves a trifle more economically.

TESMAN Out of the question, my dear fellow! Remember, it's all for Hedda! You, who know her so well—! After all, I couldn't put her up like any little middle-class housewife—

BRACK No, I suppose—That's just it.

TESMAN Besides—fortunately—it can't be long now before I receive my appointment.

BRACK Well, you know—things like that have a way of hanging fire.

TESMAN Perhaps you have heard something? Something definite? Hm?

BRACK No, nothing certain—(*Interrupting himself.*) But that reminds me. I have some news for you.

TESMAN Oh?

BRACK Your old friend Eilert Løvborg is back in town.

TESMAN I know that already.

BRACK So? Who told you?

TESMAN The lady who just left.

BRACK I see. What did you say her name was again? I didn't quite catch—

TESMAN Mrs. Elvsted.

BRACK Ah yes—the Commissioner's wife. Yes, it's up in her part of the country that Løvborg has been staying, too.

TESMAN And just think. I am so glad to hear it. He is quite respectable again.

BRACK Yes, so they say.

TESMAN And he has published a new book, hm?

BRACK Oh yes.

TESMAN Which is making quite a stir.

BRACK Quite an unusual stir.

TESMAN Just think! Isn't that just wonderful! He—with his remarkable gifts. And I was so sure he'd gone under for good.

BRACK That seems to have been the general opinion.

TESMAN What I don't understand, though, is what he is going to do with himself. What sort of living can he make? Hm?

(During the last remark HEDDA *re-enters, right.)*

HEDDA *(to* BRACK, *with a scornful little laugh)* Tesman is forever worrying about how people are going to make a living.

TESMAN Well, you see, we are talking about poor Eilert Løvborg, Hedda.

HEDDA *(with a quick look at him)* You are? *(Sits down in the easy chair by the stove and asks casually.)* What is the matter with him?

TESMAN Well, you see, I believe he's run through his inheritance a long time ago. And I don't suppose he can write a new book every year. Hm? So I really must ask how he is going to make out.

BRACK Maybe I could help you answer that.

TESMAN Yes?

BRACK Remember, he has relatives with considerable influence.

TESMAN Ah—unfortunately, those relatives have washed their hands of him long ago.

BRACK Just the same, they used to call him the hope of the family.

TESMAN Yes, before! But he has ruined all that.

HEDDA Who knows? *(With a little smile.)* I hear the Elvsteds have rehabilitated him.

BRACK And then this book—

TESMAN Well, I certainly hope they will help him to find something or other. I just wrote him a letter. Hedda, dear, I asked him to come out here tonight.

BRACK Oh dear, I am sorry. Don't you remember—you're supposed to come to my little stag dinner tonight? You accepted last night on the pier, you know.

HEDDA Had you forgotten, Tesman?

TESMAN So I had.

BRACK Oh well, I'm sure he won't come, so it doesn't really make any difference.

TESMAN Why is that? Hm?

BRACK *(gets up somewhat hesitantly, rests his hands on the back of the chair)* Dear Tesman—and you, too, Mrs. Tesman—I cannot in good conscience let you remain in ignorance of something, which—which—

TESMAN   Something to do with Eilert?

BRACK   With both you and him.

TESMAN   But my dear Judge, do speak!

BRACK   You must be prepared to find that your appointment will not come through as soon as you hope and expect.

TESMAN   (*jumps up, nervously*)   Something's happened? Hm?

BRACK   It may conceivably be made contingent upon the result of a competition.

TESMAN   Competition! Just think, Hedda!

HEDDA   (*leaning farther back in her chair*)   Ah—I see, I see—!

TESMAN   But with whom? Don't tell me with—?

BRACK   Precisely. With Eilert Løvborg.

TESMAN   (*claps his hands together*)   No, no! This can't be! It is unthinkable! Quite impossible! Hm?

BRACK   All the same, that's the way it may turn out.

TESMAN   No, but Judge, this would amount to the most incredible callousness toward me! (*Waving his arms.*) For just think—I'm a married man! We married on the strength of these prospects, Hedda and I. Got ourselves deep in debt. Borrowed money from Aunt Julle, too. After all, I had practically been promised the post, you know. Hm?

BRACK   Well, well. I daresay you'll get it in the end. If only after a competition.

HEDDA   (*motionless in her chair*)   Just think, Tesman. It will be like a kind of contest.

TESMAN   But dearest Hedda, how can you be so unconcerned!

HEDDA   (*still without moving*)   I'm not at all unconcerned. I'm dying to see who wins.

BRACK   In any case, Mrs. Tesman, I'm glad you know the situation as it is. I mean—before you proceed to make the little additional purchases I understand you threaten us with.

HEDDA   This makes no difference as far as that is concerned.

BRACK   Really? Well, in that case, of course—Goodbye! (*To* TESMAN.) I'll pick you up on my afternoon walk.

TESMAN   What? Oh yes, yes, of course. I'm sorry; I'm just all flustered.

HEDDA   (*without getting up, gives her hand*)   Goodbye, Judge. Come back soon.

BRACK   Thanks. Goodbye, goodbye.

TESMAN   (*sees him to the door*)   Goodbye, my dear Judge. You really must excuse me—

(JUDGE BRACK *exits, right.*)

TESMAN (*pacing the floor*)   Oh, Hedda, Hedda! One should never venture into fairyland. Hm?

HEDDA (*looks at him, smiles*)   Do *you* do that?

TESMAN   Well, yes—it can't be denied—it was most venturesome of me to rush into marriage and set up a home on the strength of mere prospects.

HEDDA   Well, maybe you're right.

TESMAN   Anyway—we do have our own nice, comfortable home, now. Just think, Hedda—the very home both of us dreamed about. Set our hearts on, I may almost say. Hm?

HEDDA (*rises, slowly, tired*)   The agreement was that we were to maintain a certain position—entertain—

TESMAN   Don't I know it! Dearest Hedda—I have been so looking forward to seeing you as hostess in a select circle! Hm? Well, well, well! In the meantime, we'll just have to be content with one another. See Aunt Julle once in a while. Nothing more. And you were meant for such a different kind of life, altogether!

HEDDA   I suppose a footman is completely out of the question.

TESMAN   I'm afraid so. Under the circumstances, you see—we couldn't possibly—

HEDDA   And as for getting my own riding horse—

TESMAN (*aghast*)   Riding horse!

HEDDA   I suppose I mustn't even think of that.

TESMAN   Good heavens, no! That goes without saying, I hope!

HEDDA (*walking*)   Well—at least I have one thing to amuse myself with in the meantime.

TESMAN (*overjoyed*)   Oh thank goodness for that! And what *is* that, Hedda, hm?

HEDDA (*in the doorway, looks at him with suppressed scorn*)   My guns—Jørgen!

TESMAN (*in fear*)   Your guns!

HEDDA (*with cold eyes*)   General Gabler's guns.

(*She exits left, through the inner room.*)

TESMAN (*runs up to the doorway, calls after her*)   But Hedda! Good gracious! Hedda, dear! Please don't touch those dangerous things! For my sake, Hedda! Hm?

ACT II

The same room at the TESMANS'. *The piano has been moved out and re-placed by an elegant little writing desk. A small table has been placed near the sofa, left. Most of the flowers have been removed.* MRS. ELVSTED's *bou-quet is on the big table front center. Afternoon.*

HEDDA, *dressed to receive callers, is alone. She is standing near the open*

French doors, loading a revolver. Its mate is lying in an open case on the desk.

HEDDA (*looking down into the garden, calls*)   Hello there, Judge! Welcome back!

JUDGE BRACK (*off stage*)   Thanks, Mrs. Tesman!

HEDDA (*raises the gun, sights*)   I am going to shoot you, Judge Brack!

BRACK (*calls off stage*)   No—no—no! Don't point the gun at me like that!

HEDDA   That's what you get for sneaking in the back door! (*Fires.*)

BRACK (*closer*)   Are you out of your mind—!

HEDDA   Oh dear—did I hit you?

BRACK (*still off stage*)   Stop that nonsense!

HEDDA   Come on in, then.

(JUDGE BRACK, *dressed for dinner, enters, left. He carries a light over-coat over his arm.*)

BRACK   Dammit! Do you still fool around with that thing? What are you shooting at, anyway?

HEDDA   Oh—just firing off into blue air.

BRACK (*gently but firmly taking the gun away from her*)   With your permission, Mrs. Tesman. (*Looks at it.*) Ah yes, I remember this gun very well. (*Looks around.*) Where is the case? Ah, here we are. (*Puts the gun in the case and closes it.*) That's enough of that silliness for today.

HEDDA   But in the name of heaven, what do you expect me to do with myself?

BRACK   No callers?

HEDDA (*closing the French doors*)   Not a soul. All my close friends are still out of town, it seems.

BRACK   And Tesman is out, too, perhaps?

HEDDA (*by the desk, puts the gun case in a drawer*)   Yes. He took off for the aunts' right after lunch. He didn't expect you so early.

BRACK   I should have thought of that. That was stupid of me.

HEDDA (*turns her head, looks at him*)   Why stupid?

BRACK   I would have come a little—sooner.

HEDDA (*crossing*)   If you had, you wouldn't have found anybody home. For I have been in my room ever since lunch, changing my clothes.

BRACK   And isn't there the tiniest little opening in the door for negotiations?

HEDDA   You forgot to provide one.

BRACK   Another stupidity.

HEDDA   So we'll have to stay in here. And wait. For I don't think Tesman will be back for some time.

BRACK   By all means. I'll be very patient.

HEDDA *sits on the sofa in the corner.* BRACK *puts his overcoat over the back of the nearest chair and sits down, keeping his hat in his hand. Brief silence. They look at one another.*

HEDDA   Well?

BRACK   (*in the same tone*)   Well?

HEDDA   I said it first.

BRACK   (*leans forward a little*)   All right. Let's have a nice little chat, Mrs. Tesman.

HEDDA   (*leans back*)   Don't you think it's an eternity since last time we talked! I don't count last night and this morning. That was nothing.

BRACK   You mean—just the two of us?

HEDDA   Mmm. If you like.

BRACK   There hasn't been a day I haven't wished you were back again.

HEDDA   My feelings, exactly.

BRACK   Yours? Really, Mrs. Tesman? And I have been assuming you were having such a wonderful time.

HEDDA   I'd say!

BRACK   All Tesman's letters said so.

HEDDA   Oh yes, he! He's happy just poking through old collections of books. And copying old parchments—or whatever they are.

BRACK   (*with a touch of malice*)   Well, that's his calling, you know. Partly, anyway.

HEDDA   Yes, so it is. And in that case I suppose—But I! Oh, Judge! You've no idea how bored I've been.

BRACK   (*with sympathy*)   Really? You're serious?

HEDDA   Surely you can understand that? For a whole half year never to see anyone who knows even a little bit about our circle? And talks our language?

BRACK   Yes, I think I would find that trying, too.

HEDDA   And then the most unbearable thing of all—

BRACK   Well?

HEDDA   —everlastingly to be in the company of the same person—

BRACK   (*nods in agreement*)   Both early and late—yes. I can imagine—at all possible times—

HEDDA   I said everlastingly.

BRACK   All right. Still, it seems to me that with as excellent a person as our Tesman, it ought to be possible—

HEDDA My dear Judge—Tesman is a specialist.

BRACK Granted.

HEDDA And specialists are not at all entertaining travel companions. Not in the long run, at any rate.

BRACK Not even—the specialist—one happens to love?

HEDDA Bah! That nauseating word!

BRACK (*puzzled*) Really, now, Mrs. Tesman—?

HEDDA (*half laughing, half annoyed*) *You* ought to try it some time! Listening to talk about the history of civilization, early and late—

BRACK Everlastingly—

HEDDA All right. And then this business about the domestic industry in the Middle Ages—! That's the ghastliest part of it all!

BRACK (*looking searchingly at her*) But in that case—tell me—how am I to explain—?

HEDDA That Jørgen Tesman and I made a pair of it, you mean?

BRACK If you want to put it that way—yes.

HEDDA Come now. Do you really find that so strange?

BRACK Both yes and no—Mrs. Tesman.

HEDDA I had danced myself tired, my dear Judge. My season was over—(*Gives a slight start.*) No, no—I don't really mean that. Won't think it, either!

BRACK Nor do you have the slightest reason to, I am sure.

HEDDA Oh—as far as reasons are concerned—(*Looks at him as if trying to read his mind.*) And, after all, Jørgen Tesman must be said to be a most proper young man in all respects.

BRACK Both proper and substantial. Most certainly.

HEDDA And one can't say there is anything exactly comical about him. Do you think there is?

BRACK Comical? No—o. I wouldn't say that—

HEDDA All right, then. And he is a most assiduous collector. Nobody can deny that. I think it is perfectly possible he may go quite far, after all.

BRACK (*looks at her rather uncertainly*) I assumed that you, like everybody else, thought he'll in time become an exceptionally eminent man?

HEDDA (*with a weary expression*) Yes, I did. And then, you see—there he was, wanting so desperately to be allowed to provide for me—I don't know why I shouldn't have accepted?

BRACK No, certainly. From that point of view—

HEDDA For you know, Judge, that was considerably more than my other admirers were willing to do.

BRACK (*laughs*) Well! Of course I can't answer for all the others.

But as far as I am concerned, I have always had a certain degree of—respect for the bonds of matrimony. You know—as a general proposition, Mrs. Tesman.

HEDDA (*lightly*) Well, I never really counted very heavily on *you*—

BRACK All I want is a nice, confidential circle, in which I can be of service, both in deed and in counsel. Be allowed to come and go like a true and trusted friend—

HEDDA You mean, of the master of the house—?

BRACK (*with a slight bow*) To be perfectly frank—rather of the mistress. But by all means—the master, too, of course. Do you know, that kind of—shall I say, triangular?—relationship can really be a great comfort to all parties involved.

HEDDA Yes, many were the times I missed a second travel companion. To be twosome in the compartment—brrr!

BRACK Fortunately, the wedding trip is over.

HEDDA (*shakes her head*) There's a long journey ahead. I've just arrived at a station on the way.

BRACK Well, at the station one gets out and moves around a bit, Mrs. Tesman.

HEDDA I never get out.

BRACK Really?

HEDDA No. For there's always someone around, who—

BRACK (*laughs*) —looks at one's legs; is that it?

HEDDA Exactly.

BRACK Oh well, really now—

HEDDA (*with a silencing gesture*) I won't have it! Rather stay in my seat—once I'm seated. Twosome and all.

BRACK I see. But what if a third party were to join the couple?

HEDDA Well, now—*that* would be something altogether different!

BRACK A proven, understanding friend—

HEDDA —entertaining in all sorts of lively ways—

BRACK —and not at all a specialist!

HEDDA (*with audible breath*) Yes, that would indeed be a comfort.

BRACK (*hearing the front door open, looking at her*) The triangle is complete.

HEDDA (*half aloud*) And the train goes on.

(TESMAN, *in gray walking suit and soft hat, enters, right. He carries a pile of paperbound books under his arm. Others are stuffed in his pockets.*)

TESMAN (*as he walks up to the table in front of the corner sofa*). Puuhh—! Quite some load to carry, all this—and in this heat, too. (*Puts the books down.*) I am positively perspiring, Hedda. Well, well. So you're here already, my dear Judge. Hm? And Berte didn't tell me.

BRACK (*rises*)   I came through the garden.

HEDDA   What are all those books?

TESMAN (*leafing through some of them*)   Just some new publications in my special field.

HEDDA   Special field, hm?

BRACK   Ah yes—professional publications, Mrs. Tesman.

BRACK *and* HEDDA *exchange knowing smiles.*

HEDDA   Do you still need more books?

TESMAN   Yes, my dear. There is no such thing as having too many books in one's special field. One has to keep up with what is being written and published, you know.

HEDDA   I suppose.

TESMAN (*searching among the books*)   And look. Here is Eilert Løvborg's new book, too. (*Offers it to her.*) Want to take a look at it, Hedda? Hm?

HEDDA   No—thanks just the same. Or perhaps later.

TESMAN   I glanced at it on my way home.

BRACK   And what do you think of it? As a specialist yourself?

TESMAN   It is remarkable for its sobriety. He never wrote like that before. (*Gathers up all the books.*) I just want to take these into my study. I am so much looking forward to cutting them open! And then I'll change. (*To* BRACK.) I assume there's no rush to be off, is there?

BRACK   Not at all. We have plenty of time.

TESMAN   In that case, I think I'll indulge myself a little. (*On his way out with the books he halts in the doorway and turns.*) By the way, Hedda—Aunt Julle won't be out to see you tonight, after all.

HEDDA   No? Is it that business with the hat, do you think?

TESMAN   Oh, no—not at all. How can you believe a thing like that about Aunt Julle! Just think! No, it's Aunt Rina. She's feeling very poorly.

HEDDA   Isn't she always?

TESMAN   Yes, but it's especially bad today, poor thing.

HEDDA   Well, in that case I suppose she ought to stay home. I shall have to put up with it; that's all.

TESMAN   And you have no idea how perfectly delighted Aunt Julle was, even so. Because of how splendid you look after the trip, Hedda!

HEDDA (*half aloud, rising*)   Oh, these everlasting aunts!

TESMAN   Hm?

HEDDA   (*walks over to the French doors*)   Nothing.

TESMAN   No? All right. Well, excuse me.

(*Exits right, through inner room.*)

BRACK   What is this about a hat?

HEDDA   Oh, something with Miss Tesman this morning. She had put her hat down on the chair over there. (*Looks at him, smiles.*) So I pretended to think it was the maid's.

BRACK   (*shakes his head*)   But my dear Mrs. Tesman—how could you do a thing like that! And to that excellent old lady, too!

HEDDA   (*nervously pacing the floor*)   Well, you see—something just takes hold of me at times. And then I can't help myself— (*Throws herself down in the easy chair near the stove.*) Oh I can't explain it even to myself.

BRACK   (*behind her chair*)   You aren't really happy—that's the trouble.

HEDDA   (*staring into space*)   I don't know any reason why I should be. Do you?

BRACK   Well, yes—partly because you've got the home you've always wanted.

HEDDA   (*looks up at him and laughs*)   So you too believe that story about my great wish?

BRACK   You mean, there is nothing to it?

HEDDA   Well, yes; there is *something* to it.

BRACK   Well?

HEDDA   There is this much to it, that last summer I used Tesman to see me home from evening parties.

BRACK   Unfortunately—my route was in quite a different direction.

HEDDA   True. You walked on other roads last summer.

BRACK   (*laughs*)   Shame on you, Mrs. Tesman! So, all right—you and Tesman—?

HEDDA   One evening we passed by here. And Tesman, poor thing, was practically turning himself into knots trying to find something to talk about. So I felt sorry for all that erudition—

BRACK   (*with a doubting smile*)   You did? Hm—

HEDDA   I really did. So, just to help him out of his misery, I happened to say that I'd like to live in this house.

BRACK   Just that?

HEDDA   That was all—*that* evening.

BRACK   But afterwards—?

HEDDA   Yes, my frivolity had consequences, Judge.

BRACK   Unfortunately—that's often the way with frivolities. It happens to all of us, Mrs. Tesman.

HEDDA Thanks! So in our common enthusiasm for Mr. Secretary Falk's villa Tesman and I found each other, you see! The result was engagement and wedding and honeymoon abroad and all the rest of it. Well, yes, my dear Judge—I've made my bed—I almost said.

BRACK But this is priceless! And you didn't really care for the house at all?

HEDDA Certainly not.

BRACK Not even now? After all, we've set up quite a comfortable home for you here, haven't we?

HEDDA Oh—it seems to me I smell lavender and rose sachets in all the rooms. But maybe that's a smell Aunt Julle brought with her.

BRACK (*laughs*) My guess is rather the late lamented Secretary's wife.

HEDDA It smells of mortality, whoever it is. Like corsages—the next day. (*Clasps her hands behind her neck, leans back, looks at him.*) Judge, you have no idea how dreadfully bored I'll be—out here.

BRACK But don't you think life may hold some task for you, too, Mrs. Tesman?

HEDDA A task? With any kind of appeal?

BRACK Preferably that, of course.

HEDDA Heaven knows what kind of task that might be. There are times when I wonder if—(*Interrupts herself.*) No; I'm sure that wouldn't work, either.

BRACK Who knows? Tell me.

HEDDA It has occurred to me that maybe I could get Tesman to enter politics.

BRACK (*laughs*) Tesman! No, really—I must confess that—politics doesn't strike me as being exactly Tesman's line.

HEDDA I agree. But suppose I were to prevail on him, all the same?

BRACK What satisfaction could you possibly find in that? If he can't succeed—why do you want him even to try?

HEDDA Because I am bored, I tell you! (*After a brief pause.*) So you think it's quite out of the question that Tesman could ever become prime minister?

BRACK Well, you see, Mrs. Tesman—to do that he'd first of all have to be a fairly wealthy man.

HEDDA (*getting up, impatiently*) Yes! There we are! These shabby circumstances I've married into! (*Crosses the floor.*) That's what makes life so mean. So—so—ridiculous! For that's what it is, you know.

BRACK Personally I believe something else is to blame.

HEDDA What?

BRACK   You've never been through anything that's really stirred you.

HEDDA   Something serious, you mean?

BRACK   If you like. But maybe it's coming now.

HEDDA (*with a toss of her head*)   You are thinking of that silly old professorship! That's Tesman's business. I refuse to give it a thought.

BRACK   As you wish. But now—to put it in the grand style—now when a solemn challenge of responsibility is being posed? Demands made on you? (*Smiles.*) New demands, Mrs. Tesman.

HEDDA (*angry*)   Quiet! You'll never see anything of the kind.

BRACK (*cautiously*)   We'll talk about this a year from now—on the outside.

HEDDA (*curtly*)   I'm not made for that sort of thing, Judge! No demands for me!

BRACK   But surely you, like most women, are made for a duty, which—

HEDDA (*over by the French doors*)   Oh, do be quiet! Often it seems to me there's only one thing in the world that I am made for.

BRACK (*coming close*)   And may I ask what that is?

HEDDA (*looking out*)   To be bored to death. Now you know. (*Turns, looks toward the inner room, laughs.*) Just as I thought. Here comes the professor.

BRACK (*warningly, in a low voice*)   Steady, now, Mrs. Tesman!

(TESMAN, *dressed for a party, carrying his hat and gloves, enters from the right side of the inner room.*)

TESMAN   Hedda, any word yet from Eilert Løvborg that he isn't coming, hm?

HEDDA   No.

TESMAN   In that case, I wouldn't be a bit surprised if we have him here in a few minutes.

BRACK   You really think he'll come?

TESMAN   I am almost certain he will. For I'm sure it's only idle gossip that you told me this morning.

BRACK   Oh?

TESMAN   Anyway, that's what Aunt Julle said. She doesn't for a moment believe he'll stand in my way. Just think!

BRACK   I'm very glad to hear that.

TESMAN (*puts his hat and his gloves down on a chair, right*)   But you must let me wait for him as long as possible.

BRACK   By all means. We have plenty of time. Nobody will arrive at my place before seven—seven-thirty, or so.

TESMAN   And in the meantime we can keep Hedda company. Take our time. Hm?

HEDDA   (*carrying* BRACK's *hat and coat over to the sofa in the corner*) And if worst comes to worst, Mr. Løvborg can stay here with me.

BRACK   (*trying to take the things away from her*) Let me, Mrs. Tesman—What do you mean—"if worst comes to worst?"

HEDDA   If he doesn't want to go with you and Tesman.

TESMAN   (*looks dubiously at her*) But, dearest Hedda—do you think that will quite do? He staying here with you? Hm? Remember, Aunt Julle won't be here.

HEDDA   No, but Mrs. Elvsted will. The three of us will have a cup of tea together.

TESMAN   Oh yes; *that* will be perfectly all right!

BRACK   (*with a smile*) And perhaps the wiser course of action for him.

HEDDA   What do you mean?

BRACK   Begging your pardon, Mrs. Tesman—you've often enough looked askance at my little stag dinners. It's been your opinion that only men of the firmest principles ought to attend.

HEDDA   I should think Mr. Løvborg is firm-principled enough now. A reformed sinner—

(BERTE *appears in door, right.*)

BERTE   Ma'am—there's a gentleman here who asks if—

HEDDA   Show him in, please.

TESMAN   (*softly*) I'm sure it's he! Just think!

(EILERT LØVBORG *enters, right. He is slim, gaunt. Of* TESMAN's *age, but he looks older and somewhat dissipated. Brown hair and beard. Pale, longish face, reddish spots on the cheekbones. Dressed for visiting in elegant, black, brand-new suit. He carries a silk hat and dark gloves in his hand. He remains near the door, makes a quick bow. He appears a little embarrassed.*)

TESMAN   (*goes over to him, shakes his hand*) My dear Eilert—at last we meet again!

EILERT LØVBORG   (*subdued voice*) Thanks for your note, Jørgen! (*Approaching* HEDDA.) Am I allowed to shake your hand, too, Mrs. Tesman?

HEDDA   (*accepting his proffered hand*) I am very glad to see you, Mr. Løvborg. (*With a gesture.*) I don't know if you two gentlemen—

LØVBORG   (*with a slight bow*) Judge Brack, I believe.

BRACK (*also bowing lightly*) Certainly. Some years ago—

TESMAN (*to* LØVBORG, *both hands on his shoulders*) And now I want you to feel quite at home here, Eilert! Isn't that right, Hedda? For you plan to stay here in town, I understand. Hm?

LØVBORG Yes, I do.

TESMAN Perfectly reasonable. Listen—I just got hold of your new book, but I haven't had a chance to read it yet.

LØVBORG You may save yourself the trouble.

TESMAN Why do you say that?

LØVBORG There's not much to it.

TESMAN Just think—you saying that!

BRACK Nevertheless, people seem to have very good things to say about it.

LØVBORG That's exactly why I wrote it—so everybody would like it.

BRACK Very wise of you.

TESMAN Yes, but Eilert—!

LØVBORG For I am trying to rebuild my position. Start all over again.

TESMAN (*with some embarrassment*) Yes, I suppose you are, aren't you? Hm?

LØVBORG (*smiles, puts his hat down, pulls a parcel out of his pocket*) When *this* appears—Jørgen Tesman—this you must read. For this is the real thing. This is me.

TESMAN Oh really? And what is it?

LØVBORG The continuation.

TESMAN Continuation? Of what?

LØVBORG Of the book.

TESMAN Of the new book?

LØVBORG Of course.

TESMAN But Eilert—you've carried the story all the way up to the present!

LØVBORG So I have. And this is about the future.

TESMAN The future! But, heavens—we don't know a thing about the future!

LØVBORG No, we don't. But there are a couple of things to be said about it all the same. (*Unwraps the parcel.*) Here, let me show you—

TESMAN But that's not your handwriting.

LØVBORG I have dictated it (*Leafs through portions of the manuscript.*) It's in two parts. The first is about the forces that will shape the civilization of the future. And the second (*riffling through more pages*)—about the course which that future civilization will take.

TESMAN How remarkable! It would never occur to me to write anything like that.

HEDDA (*over by the French doors, her fingers drumming the pane*) Hmm—I daresay—

LØVBORG (*replacing the manuscript in its wrappings and putting it down on the table*) I brought it along, for I thought maybe I'd read parts of it aloud to you this evening.

TESMAN That's very good of you, Eilert. But this evening—? (*Looks at* BRACK.) I'm not quite sure how to arrange that—

LØVBORG Some other time, then. There's no hurry.

BRACK You see, Mr. Løvborg, there's a little get-together over at my house tonight. Mainly for Tesman, you know—

LØVBORG (*looking for his hat*) In that case, I certainly won't—

BRACK No, listen. Won't you do me the pleasure to join us?

LØVBORG (*firmly*) No, I won't. But thanks all the same.

BRACK Oh come on! Why don't you do that? We'll be a small, select circle. And I think I can promise you a fairly lively evening, as Hed—as Mrs. Tesman would say.

LØVBORG I don't doubt that. Nevertheless—

BRACK And you may bring your manuscript along and read aloud to Tesman over at my house. I have plenty of room.

TESMAN Just think, Eilert! Wouldn't that be nice, hm?

HEDDA (*intervening*) But can't you see that Mr. Løvborg doesn't want to? I'm sure he would rather stay here and have supper with me.

LØVBORG (*looks at her*) With you, Mrs. Tesman?

HEDDA And with Mrs. Elvsted.

LØVBORG Ah—! (*Casually.*) I ran into her at noon today.

HEDDA Oh? Well, she'll be here tonight. So you see your presence is really required, Mr. Løvborg. Otherwise she won't have anybody to see her home.

LØVBORG True. All right, then, Mrs. Tesman—I'll stay, thank you.

HEDDA Good. I'll just tell the maid. (*She rings for* BERTE *over by the door, right.*)

(BERTE *appears just off stage.* HEDDA *talks with her in a low voice, points toward the inner room.* BERTE *nods and exits.*)

TESMAN (*while* HEDDA *and* BERTE *are talking, to* LØVBORG) Tell me, Eilert—is it this new subject—about the future—is that what you plan to lecture on?

LØVBORG Yes.

TESMAN For the bookseller told me you have announced a lecture series for this fall.

LØVBORG   Yes, I have. I hope you won't mind too much.

TESMAN   Of course not! But—

LØVBORG   For of course I realize it is rather awkward for you.

TESMAN   (*unhappily*)   Oh well—I certainly can't expect—that just for my sake—

LØVBORG   But I will wait till you receive your appointment.

TESMAN   Wait? But—but—but—you mean you aren't going to compete with me? Hm?

LØVBORG   No. Just triumph over you. In people's opinion.

TESMAN   Oh, for goodness' sake! Then Aunt Julle was right, after all! I knew it all the time. Hedda! Do you hear that! Just think— Eilert Løvborg isn't going to stand in our way after all.

HEDDA   (*tersely*)   *Our?* I have nothing to do with this.

HEDDA walks into the inner room, where BERTE is bringing in a tray with decanters and glasses. HEDDA nods her approval and comes forward again.

TESMAN   (*during the foregoing business*)   How about that, Judge? What do you say to this? Hm?

BRACK   I say that moral victory and all that—hm—may be glorious enough and beautiful enough—

TESMAN   Oh, I agree. All the same—

HEDDA   (*looks at* TESMAN *with a cold smile*)   You look thunderstruck.

TESMAN   Well, I am—pretty much—I really believe—

BRACK   After all, Mrs. Tesman, that was quite a thunderstorm that just passed over.

HEDDA   (*points to the inner room*)   How about a glass of cold punch, gentlemen?

BRACK   (*looks at his watch*)   A stirrup cup. Not a bad idea.

TESMAN   Splendid, Hedda. Perfectly splendid. In such a lighthearted mood as I am now—

HEDDA   Please. You, too, Mr. Løvborg.

LØVBORG   (*with a gesture of refusal*)   No, thanks. Really. Nothing for me.

BRACK   Good heavens, man! Cold punch isn't poison, you know!

LØVBORG   Perhaps not for everybody.

HEDDA   I'll keep Mr. Løvborg company in the meantime.

TESMAN   All right, Hedda. You do that.

He and BRACK go into the inner room, sit down, drink punch, smoke cigarettes, and engage in lively conversation during the next scene. EILERT LØVBORG remains standing near the stove. HEDDA walks over to the desk.

HEDDA   (*her voice a little louder than usual*)   I'll show you some pictures, if you like. You see—Tesman and I, we took a trip through Tyrol on our way back.

She brings an album over to the table by the sofa. She sits down in the far corner of the sofa. Løvborg approaches, stops, looks at her. He takes a chair and sits down at her left, his back toward the inner room.

HEDDA (*opens the album*) Do you see these mountains, Mr. Løvborg? They are the Ortler group. Tesman has written their name below. Here it is: "The Ortler group near Meran."

LØVBORG (*has looked steadily at her all this time. Says slowly*) Hedda—Gabler!

HEDDA (*with a quick glance sideways*) Not that! Shhh!

LØVBORG (*again*) Hedda Gabler!

HEDDA (*looking at the album*) Yes, that used to be my name. When—when we two knew each other.

LØVBORG And so from now on—for the whole rest of my life—I must get used to never again saying Hedda Gabler.

HEDDA (*still occupied with the album*) Yes, you must. And you might as well start right now. The sooner the better, I think.

LØVBORG (*with indignation*) Hedda Gabler married? And married to—Jørgen Tesman!

HEDDA Yes—that's the way it goes.

LØVBORG Oh, Hedda, Hedda—how could you throw yourself away like that!

HEDDA (*with a fierce glance at him*) What's this? I won't have any of that!

LØVBORG What do you mean?

(TESMAN *enters from the inner room.*)

HEDDA (*hears him coming and remarks casually*) And this here, Mr. Løvborg, this is from somewhere in the Ampezzo valley. Just look at those peaks over there. (*With a kindly look at* TESMAN.) What did you say those peaks were called, dear?

TESMAN Let me see. Oh, they—they are the Dolomites.

HEDDA Right. Those are the Dolomites, Mr. Løvborg.

TESMAN Hedda, I thought I'd just ask you if you don't want me to bring you some punch, after all? For you, anyway? Hm?

HEDDA Well, yes; thanks. And a couple of cookies, maybe.

TESMAN No cigarettes?

HEDDA No.

TESMAN All right.

He returns to the inner room, then turns right. BRACK is in there, keeping an eye on HEDDA and LØVBORG from time to time.

LØVBORG (*still in a low voice*) Answer me, Hedda. How could you do a thing like that?

HEDDA (*apparently engrossed in the album*) If you keep on using my first name I won't talk to you.

LØVBORG Not even when we're alone?

HEDDA No. You may think it, but you must not say it.

LØVBORG I see. It offends your love for—Jørgen Tesman.

HEDDA (*glances at him, smiles*) Love? That's a good one!

LØVBORG Not love, then.

HEDDA But no infidelities, either! I won't have it.

LØVBORG Hedda—answer me just one thing—

HEDDA Shhh!

(TESMAN *enters with a tray from the inner room.*)

TESMAN Here! Here are the goodies (*Puts the tray down.*)

HEDDA Why don't you get Berte to do it?

TESMAN (*pouring punch*) Because I think it's so much fun waiting on you, Hedda.

HEDDA But you've filled both glasses. And Mr. Løvborg didn't want any—

TESMAN I know, but Mrs. Elvsted will soon be here, won't she?

HEDDA That's right. So she will.

TESMAN Had you forgotten about her? Hm?

HEDDA We've been so busy looking at this. (*Shows him a picture.*) Remember that little village?

TESMAN That's the one just below the Brenner Pass, isn't it? We spent the night there—

HEDDA —and ran into that lively crowd of summer guests.

TESMAN Right! Just think—if we only could have had you with us, Eilert! Oh well.

Returns to the inner room, sits down, and resumes his conversation with BRACK.

LØVBORG Just tell me this, Hedda—

HEDDA What?

LØVBORG Wasn't there love in your feelings for me, either? Not a touch—not a shimmer of love? Wasn't there?

HEDDA I wonder. To me, we seemed to be simply two good comrades. Two close friends. (*Smiles.*) You, particularly, were very frank.

LØVBORG You wanted it that way.

HEDDA And yet—when I look back upon it now, there was something beautiful, something thrilling, something brave, I think, about the secret frankness—that comradeship that not a single soul so much as suspected.

LØVBORG Yes, wasn't there, Hedda? Wasn't there? When I called on your father in the afternoons—And the General sat by the window with his newspapers—his back turned—

HEDDA And we two in the sofa in the corner—

LØVBORG —always with the same illustrated magazine—

HEDDA —for want of an album, yes—

LØVBORG Yes, Hedda—and then when I confessed to you—! Told you all about myself, things the others didn't know. Sat and told you about my orgies by day and night. Dissipation day in and day out! Oh, Hedda—what sort of power in you was it that forced me to tell you things like that?

HEDDA You think there was some power in me?

LØVBORG How else can I explain it? And all those veiled questions you asked—

HEDDA —which you understood so perfectly well—

LØVBORG That you could ask such questions! With such complete frankness!

HEDDA *Veiled,* if you please.

LØVBORG But frankly all the same. All about—that!

HEDDA And to think that you answered, Mr. Løvborg!

LØVBORG Yes, that's just what I can't understand—now, afterwards. But tell me, Hedda; wasn't love at the bottom of our whole relationship? Didn't you feel some kind of urge to—purify me—when I came to you in confession? Wasn't that it?

HEDDA No, not quite.

LØVBORG Then what made you do it?

HEDDA Do you find it so very strange that a young girl—when she can do so, without anyone knowing—

LØVBORG Yes—?

HEDDA —that she wants to take a peek into a world which—

LØVBORG —which—?

HEDDA —she is not supposed to know anything about?

LØVBORG So that was it!

HEDDA That, too. That, too—I think—

LØVBORG Companionship in the lust for life. But why couldn't *that* at least have continued?

HEDDA That was your own fault.

LØVBORG You were the one who broke off.

HEDDA Yes, when reality threatened to enter our relationship. Shame on you, Eilert Løvborg! How could you want to do a thing like that to your frank and trusting comrade!

LØVBORG (*clenching his hands*) Oh, why didn't you do it! Why didn't you shoot me down, as you said you would!

HEDDA Because I'm scared of scandal.

LØVBORG Yes, Hedda. You are really a coward.

HEDDA A terrible coward. (*Changing her tone.*) But that was your good luck, wasn't it? And now the Elvsteds have healed your broken heart very nicely.

LØVBORG I know what Thea has told you.

HEDDA Perhaps you have told her about us?

LØVBORG Not a word. She is too stupid to understand.

HEDDA Stupid?

LØVBORG In things like that.

HEDDA And I'm a coward. (*Leans forward, without looking in his eyes, whispers.*) But now *I* am going to confess something to *you*.

LØVBORG (*tense*) What?

HEDDA That I didn't dare to shoot—

LØVBORG Yes—?

HEDDA —that was not the worst of my cowardice that night.

LØVBORG (*looks at her a moment, understands, whispers passionately*) Oh, Hedda! Hedda Gabler! Now I begin to see what was behind the companionship! You and I! So it *was* your lust for life—!

HEDDA (*in a low voice, with an angry glance*) Take care! Don't you believe it!

(*Darkness is falling. The door, right, is opened, and* BERTE *enters.*)

HEDDA (*closing the album, calls out, smiling*) At last! So there you are, dearest Thea! Come in!

(MRS. ELVSTED *enters. She is dressed for a party.* BERTE *exits, closing the door behind her.*)

HEDDA (*on the sofa, reaching out for* MRS. ELVSTED) Sweetest Thea, you have no idea how I've waited for you.

In passing, MRS. ELVSTED *exchanges quick greetings with* TESMAN *and* BRACK *in the inner room. She walks up to the table and shakes* HEDDA'S *hand.* EILERT LØVBORG *rises. He and* MRS. ELVSTED *greet one another with a silent nod.*

MRS. ELVSTED Shouldn't I go in and say hello to your husband?

HEDDA No, never mind that. Leave them alone. They're soon leaving, anyway.

MRS. ELVSTED Leaving?

HEDDA They're going out to drink.

MRS. ELVSTED (*quickly, to* LØVBORG) Not you?

LØVBORG   No.

HEDDA   Mr. Løvborg stays here with us.

MRS. ELVSTED   (*pulls up a chair, is about to sit down next to* LØV-
BORG)   Oh, how wonderful it is to be here!

HEDDA   Oh no, little Thea. Not that. Not there. Over here by me,
please. *I* want to be in the middle.

MRS. ELVSTED   Just as you like. (*She walks in front of the table and
seats herself on the sofa, on* HEDDA's *right.* LØVBORG *sits down
again on his chair.*)

LØVBORG   (*after a brief pause, to* HEDDA)   Isn't she lovely to look
at?

HEDDA   (*gently stroking her hair*)   Just to look at?

LØVBORG   Yes. For you see—she and I—we are real comrades. We
have absolute faith in one another. And we can talk together in
full freedom.

HEDDA   Unveiled, Mr. Løvborg?

LØVBORG   Well—

MRS. ELVSTED   (*in a low voice, clinging to* HEDDA)   Oh, I am so
happy, Hedda! For just think—he also says I have inspired him!

HEDDA   (*looks at her with a smile*)   No, really! He says that?

LØVBORG   And she has such courage, Mrs. Tesman! Such courage
of action.

MRS. ELVSTED   Oh, my God—courage—! I!

LØVBORG   Infinite courage—when it concerns the comrade.

HEDDA   Yes, courage—if one only had that.

LØVBORG   What then?

HEDDA   Then maybe life would be tolerable, after all. (*Changing
her tone.*) But now, dearest Thea, you want a glass of nice, cold
punch.

MRS. ELVSTED   No, thanks. I never drink things like that.

HEDDA   Then what about you, Mr. Løvborg?

LØVBORG   Thanks. Nothing for me, either.

MRS. ELVSTED   No, nothing for him, either.

HEDDA   (*looks firmly at him*)   If I say so?

LØVBORG   Makes no difference.

HEDDA   (*laughs*)   Oh dear! So I have no power over you at all. Is
that it?

LØVBORG   Not in that respect.

HEDDA   Seriously, though; I really think you should. For your own
sake.

MRS. ELVSTED   No, but Hedda—!

LØVBORG   Why so?

HEDDA   Or rather for people's sake.

LØVBORG   Oh?

HEDDA   For else they might think you don't really trust yourself—
That you lack self-confidence—

MRS. ELVSTED (*softly*)   Don't, Hedda!

LØVBORG   People may think whatever they like for all I care—for
the time being.

MRS. ELVSTED (*happy*)   Exactly!

HEDDA   I could easily tell from watching Judge Brack just now.

LØVBORG   Tell what?

HEDDA   He smiled so contemptuously when you didn't dare to join
them in there.

LØVBORG   Didn't I dare to! It's just that I'd much rather stay here
and talk with you!

MRS. ELVSTED   But that's only natural, Hedda.

HEDDA   The Judge had no way of knowing that. And I also noticed
he smiled and looked at Tesman when you didn't dare to go to
his silly old party.

LØVBORG   Didn't dare! Are you saying I didn't dare?

HEDDA   *I* am not. But that's how Judge Brack understood it.

LØVBORG   Let him.

HEDDA   So you're not going?

LØVBORG   I'm staying here with you and Thea.

MRS. ELVSTED   Of course, he is, Hedda!

HEDDA (*smiles, nods approvingly*)   That's what I call firm founda-
tions. Principled forever; that's the way a man ought to be!
(*Turning to* MRS. ELVSTED, *stroking her cheek.*) What did I tell
you this morning—when you came here, quite beside yourself—?

LØVBORG (*puzzled*)   Beside herself?

MRS. ELVSTED (*in terror*)   Hedda—Hedda—don't!

HEDDA   Now do you see? There was no need at all for that mortal
fear of yours—(*Interrupting herself.*) There, now! Now we can
all three relax and enjoy ourselves.

LØVBORG (*startled*)   What's all this, Mrs. Tesman?

MRS. ELVSTED   Oh, God, Hedda—what are you saying? What are
you doing?

HEDDA   Please be quiet. That horrible Judge is looking at you.

LØVBORG   In mortal fear? So that's it. For my sake.

MRS. ELVSTED (*softly, wailing*)   Oh, Hedda—if you only knew how
utterly miserable you have made me!

LØVBORG (*stares at her for a moment. His face is distorted.*)   So
that was the comrade's happy confidence in me!

MRS. ELVSTED   Oh, my dearest friend—listen to me first—!

LØVBORG (*picks up one of the glasses of punch, raises it, says
hoarsely*)   Here's to you, Thea! (*Empties the glass, puts it down,
picks up the other one.*)

MRS. ELVSTED (*softly*) Hedda, Hedda—why did you want to do this?

HEDDA Want to! I! Are you mad?

LØVBORG And here's to you, too, Mrs. Tesman! Thanks for telling me the truth. Long live the truth! (*He drains the glass and is about to fill it again.*)

HEDDA (*restrains him*) That's enough for now. Remember you are going to a party.

MRS. ELVSTED No, no, no!

HEDDA Shhh! They are looking at you.

LØVBORG (*puts his glass down*) Listen, Thea—tell me the truth—

MRS. ELVSTED I will, I will!

LØVBORG Did your husband know you were coming after me?

MRS. ELVSTED (*wringing her hands*) Oh, Hedda—do you hear what he's asking?

LØVBORG Did the two of you agree that you were to come here and look after me? Maybe it was his idea, even? Did he send you? Ah, I know what it was—he missed me in the office, didn't he? Or was it at the card table?

MRS. ELVSTED (*softly, in agony*) Oh, Løvborg, Løvborg!

LØVBORG (*grabs a glass and is about to fill it*) Here's to the old Commissioner, too!

HEDDA (*stops him*) No more now. You're supposed to read aloud for Tesman tonight—remember?

LØVBORG (*calm again, puts the glass down*) This was silly of me, Thea. I'm sorry. Taking it this way. Please, don't be angry with me. You'll see—both you and all those others—that even if I have been down—! With your help, Thea—dear comrade.

MRS. ELVSTED (*beaming*) Oh, thank God—!

In the meantime, BRACK *has looked at his watch. He and* TESMAN *get up and come forward.*

BRACK (*picking up his coat and hat*) Well, Mrs. Tesman; our time is up.

HEDDA I suppose it is.

LØVBORG (*rising*) Mine, too, Judge.

MRS. ELVSTED (*softly, pleadingly*) Oh, Løvborg—don't do it!

HEDDA (*pinches her arm*) They can hear you!

MRS. ELVSTED (*with a soft exclamation*) Ouch!

LØVBORG (*to* BRACK) You were good enough to ask me—

BRACK So you're coming, after all?

LØVBORG If I may.

BRACK I'm delighted.

LØVBORG (*picks up his manuscript and says to* TESMAN) For there are a couple of things here I'd like to show you before I send it off.

TESMAN   Just think! Isn't that nice! But—dearest Hedda—? In that case, how are you going to get Mrs. Elvsted home? Hm?

HEDDA   We'll manage somehow.

LØVBORG (*looking at the two women*)   Mrs. Elvsted? I'll be back to pick her up, of course. (*Coming closer.*) About ten o'clock, Mrs. Tesman? Is that convenient?

HEDDA   Certainly. That will be fine.

TESMAN   Then everything is nice and settled. But don't expect me that early, Hedda.

HEDDA   You just stay as long as—as long as you want to, dear.

MRS. ELVSTED (*in secret fear*)   I'll be waiting for you here, then, Mr. Løvborg.

LØVBORG (*hat in hand*)   Of course, Mrs. Elvsted.

BRACK   All aboard the pleasure train, gentlemen! I hope we'll have a lively evening—as a certain fair lady would say.

HEDDA   Ah—if only the fair lady could be present. Invisibly.

BRACK   Why invisibly?

HEDDA   To listen to some of your unadulterated liveliness, Judge.

BRACK (*laughs*)   I shouldn't advise the fair lady to do that!

TESMAN (*also laughing*)   You're a good one, Hedda! Just think!

BRACK   Well—good night, ladies!

LØVBORG (*with a bow*)   Till about ten, then.

(BRACK, LØVBORG, *and* TESMAN *go out, right. At the same time* BERTE *enters from the inner room with a lighted lamp, which she places on the table, front center. She goes out the same way.*)

MRS. ELVSTED (*has risen and paces restlessly up and down*)   Hedda, Hedda—how do you think all this will end?

HEDDA   At ten o'clock he'll be here. I see him already. With vine leaves in his hair. Flushed and confident.

MRS. ELVSTED   I only hope you're right.

HEDDA   For then, you see, he'll have mastered himself. And be a free man for all the days of his life.

MRS. ELVSTED   Dear God—how I hope you are right! That he'll come back like that.

HEDDA   That is the way he will come. No other way. (*She rises and goes closer to* MRS. ELVSTED.) *You* may doubt as long as you like. I believe in him. And now we'll see—

MRS. ELVSTED   There is something behind all this, Hedda. Some hidden purpose.

HEDDA   Yes, there is! For once in my life I want to have power over a human destiny.

MRS. ELVSTED   But don't you already?

HEDDA   I don't and I never have.

MRS. ELVSTED   But your husband—?

HEDDA   You think that's worth the trouble? Oh, if you knew how poor I am! And you got to be so rich! (*Embraces her passionately.*) I think I'll have to burn your hair off, after all!

MRS. ELVSTED   Let me go! Let me go! You scare me, Hedda!

BERTE (*in the doorway*)   Supper is served, ma'am.

HEDDA   Good. We're coming.

MRS. ELVSTED   No, no, no! I'd rather go home by myself! Right now!

HEDDA   Nonsense! You'll have your cup of tea first, you little silly. And then—at ten o'clock—Eilert Løvborg comes—with vine leaves in his hair! (*She almost pulls* MRS. ELVSTED *toward the doorway.*)

ACT III

The same room at the TESMANS'. *The doorway and the French windows both have their portieres closed. The lamp, turned half down, is still on the table. The stove is open. Some dying embers can be seen.* MRS. ELVSTED, *wrapped in a big shawl, is in the easy chair near the stove, her feet on a footstool.* HEDDA, *also dressed, is lying on the sofa, covered by a blanket.*

MRS. ELVSTED (*after a while suddenly sits up, listens anxiously; then she wearily sinks back in her chair, whimpers softly*)   Oh my God, my God—not yet!

(BERTE *enters cautiously, right, carrying a letter.*)

MRS. ELVSTED (*turns and whispers tensely*)   Well—has anybody been here?

BERTE (*in a low voice*)   Yes. Just now there was a girl with this letter.

MRS. ELVSTED (*quickly, reaches for it*)   A letter! Give it to me.

BERTE   No, ma'am. It's for the Doctor.

MRS. ELVSTED   I see.

BERTE   Miss Tesman's maid brought it. I'll leave it here on the table.

MRS. ELVSTED   All right.

BERTE (*puts the letter down*)   I'd better put out the lamp. It just reeks.

MRS. ELVSTED   Yes, do that. It must be daylight soon, anyway.

BERTE (*putting out the lamp*)   It's light already, ma'am.

MRS. ELVSTED   Light already! And still not back!

BERTE   No, so help us. Not that I didn't expect as much—

MRS. ELVSTED   You did?

BERTE   Yes, when I saw a certain character was back in town. Taking them off with him. We sure heard enough about him in the old days!

MRS. ELVSTED   Not so loud. You are waking up Mrs. Tesman.

BERTE   (*looks toward the sofa, sighs*)   God forbid—! Let her sleep, poor thing. Do you want me to get the fire going again?

MRS. ELVSTED   Not on my account, thank you.

BERTE—All right.

(*Exits quietly, right.*)

HEDDA   (*awakened by the closing door*)   What's that?

MRS. ELVSTED   Just the maid.

HEDDA   (*looks around*)   Why in here—? Oh, I remember! (*Sits up, rubs her eyes, stretches.*) What time is it, Thea?

MRS. ELVSTED   (*looks at her watch*)   Past seven.

HEDDA   When did Tesman get home?

MRS. ELVSTED   He didn't.

HEDDA   Not home yet!

MRS. ELVSTED   (*getting up*)   Nobody's come.

HEDDA   And we waited till four!

MRS. ELVSTED   (*wringing her hands*)   And *how* we waited!

HEDDA   (*her hand covering a yawn*)   We—ll. We could have saved ourselves that trouble.

MRS. ELVSTED   Did you get any sleep at all?

HEDDA   Yes, I slept pretty well, I think. Didn't you?

MRS. ELVSTED   Not a wink. I just couldn't, Hedda! It was just impossible.

HEDDA   (*rises, walks over to her*)   Well, now! There's nothing to worry about, for heaven's sake. I know exactly what's happened.

MRS. ELVSTED   Then tell me please. Where do you think they are?

HEDDA   Well, first of all, I'm sure they were terribly late leaving the Judge's—

MRS. ELVSTED   Dear, yes. I'm sure you're right. Still—

HEDDA   —and so Tesman didn't want to wake us up in the middle of the night. (*Laughs.*) Maybe he didn't want us to see him, either—after a party like that.

MRS. ELVSTED   But where do you think he has gone?

HEDDA   To the aunts', of course. His old room is still there, all ready for him.

MRS. ELVSTED   No, he can't be there. Just a few minutes ago there came a letter for him from Miss Tesman. It's over there.

HEDDA   Oh? (*Looks at the envelope.*) So it is—Auntie Julle herself. In that case. I suppose he's still at Brack's. And there's Eilert Løvborg, too—reading aloud, with vine leaves in his hair.

MRS. ELVSTED   Oh Hedda—you're only saying things you don't believe yourself.

HEDDA   My, what a little imbecile you really are, Thea!

MRS. ELVSTED   Yes, I suppose I am.

HEDDA   And you look dead tired, too.

MRS. ELVSTED   I *am* dead tired.

HEDDA   Why don't you do as I say. Go into my room and lie down.

MRS. ELVSTED   No, no—I wouldn't be able to go to sleep, anyway.

HEDDA   Of course, you would.

MRS. ELVSTED   And your husband is bound to be home any minute now. And I have to know right away.

HEDDA   I'll let you know as soon as he gets here.

MRS. ELVSTED   You promise me that, Hedda?

HEDDA   I do. You just go to sleep.

MRS. ELVSTED   Thanks. At least I'll try.

(*Exits through inner room.*)

HEDDA *goes to the French doors, opens the portieres. The room is now in full daylight. She picks up a little hand mirror from the desk, looks at herself, smooths her hair. Walks over to door, right, rings the bell for the maid.* BERTE *presently appears.*

BERTE   You want something, ma'am?

HEDDA   Yes. You'll have to start the fire again. I'm cold.

BFRTE   Yes, ma'am! I'll get it warm in no time. (*Rakes the embers together and puts in another piece of wood. Then she suddenly listens.*) There's the doorbell, ma'am.

HEDDA   All right. See who it is. I'll take care of the stove myself.

BERTE   You'll have a nice blaze going in a minute.

(*Exits right.*)

HEDDA *kneels on the footstool and puts in more pieces of wood. Presently* TESMAN *enters, right. He looks tired and somber. He tiptoes toward the doorway and is about to disappear between the portieres.*

HEDDA (*by the stove, without looking up*)   Good morning.

TESMAN (*turning*)   Hedda! (*Comes closer.*) For heaven's sake—you up already! Hm?

HEDDA   Yes, I got up very early this morning.

TESMAN   And I was sure you'd still be sound asleep! Just think!

HEDDA   Not so loud. Mrs. Elvsted is asleep in my room.

TESMAN   Mrs. Elvsted stayed here all night?

HEDDA   Yes. Nobody came for her, you know.

TESMAN No, I suppose—

HEDDA (*closes the stove, rises*) Well, did you have a good time at the Judge's?

TESMAN Were you worried about me? Hm?

HEDDA I'd never dream of worrying about you. I asked if you had a good time.

TESMAN Yes, indeed. Nice for a change anyway. But I think I liked it best early in the evening. For then Eilert read to me. Just think—we were more than an hour early! And Brack, of course, had things to see to. So Eilert read.

HEDDA (*sits down at the right side of the table*) So? Tell me all about it.

TESMAN (*sits down on an ottoman near the stove*) Oh Hedda, you'll never believe what a book that will be! It must be just the most remarkable thing ever written! Just think!

HEDDA Yes, but I don't really care about that—

TESMAN I must tell you, Hedda—I have a confession to make. As he was reading—something ugly came over me—

HEDDA Ugly?

TESMAN I sat there envying Eilert for being able to write like that! Just think, Hedda!

HEDDA All right. I'm thinking!

TESMAN And yet, with all his gifts—he's incorrigible, after all.

HEDDA I suppose you mean he has more courage for life than the rest of you?

TESMAN No, no—I don't mean that. I mean that he's incapable of exercising moderation in his pleasures.

HEDDA What happened—in the end?

TESMAN Well—*I* would call it a bacchanal, Hedda.

HEDDA Did he have vine leaves in his hair?

TESMAN Vine leaves? No, I didn't notice any vine leaves. But he gave a long, muddled speech in honor of the woman who had inspired him in his work. Those were his words.

HEDDA Did he mention her name?

TESMAN No, he didn't. But I'm sure it must be Mrs. Elvsted. You just wait and see if I'm not right!

HEDDA And where did you and he part company?

TESMAN On the way back to town. We left—the last of us did—at the same time. And Brack came along, too, to get some fresh air. Then we decided we'd better see Eilert home. You see, he had had altogether too much to drink!

HEDDA I can imagine.

TESMAN But then the strangest thing of all happened, Hedda! Or maybe I should say the saddest. I'm almost ashamed—on Eilert's behalf—even talking about it.

HEDDA   Well—?

TESMAN   You see, on the way back I happened to be behind the others a little. Just for a minute or two—you know—

HEDDA   All right, all right—!

TESMAN   And when I hurried to catch up with them, can you guess what I found by the roadside? Hm?

HEDDA   How can I possibly—?

TESMAN   You mustn't tell this to a living soul, Hedda! Do you hear! Promise me that, for Eilert's sake. (*Pulls a parcel out of his coat pocket.*) Just think—I found this!

HEDDA   Isn't that what he had with him here yesterday?

TESMAN   Yes! It's his whole, precious, irreplaceable manuscript! And he had dropped it—just like that! Without even noticing! Just think, Hedda! Isn't that awfully sad?

HEDDA   But why didn't you give it back to him?

TESMAN   In the condition he was in! Dear—I just didn't dare to.

HEDDA   And you didn't tell any of the others that you had found it, either?

TESMAN   Of course not. I didn't want to, for Eilert's sake—don't you see?

HEDDA   So nobody knows that you have Eilert Løvborg's papers?

TESMAN   Nobody. And nobody must know, either.

HEDDA   And what did you and he talk about afterwards?

TESMAN   I didn't have a chance to talk to him at all after that. For when we came into town, he and a couple of the others simply vanished. Just think!

HEDDA   Oh? I expect they took him home.

TESMAN   I suppose that must be it. And Brack took off on his own, too.

HEDDA   And what have you been doing with yourself since then?

TESMAN   Well, you see, I and some of the others went home with one of the younger fellows and had a cup of early morning coffee. Or night coffee maybe, rather. Hm? And now, after I've rested a bit and poor Eilert's had some sleep, I'll take this back to him.

HEDDA   (*reaches for the parcel*)   No—don't do that! Not right away, I mean. Let me look at it first.

TESMAN   Dearest Hedda—honestly, I just don't dare to.

HEDDA   Don't you dare to?

TESMAN   No, for I'm sure you realize how utterly desperate he'll be when he wakes up and finds that the manuscript is gone. For he hasn't a copy, you know. He said so himself.

HEDDA (*looks searchingly at him*)   But can't a thing like that be written over again?

TESMAN   Hardly. I really don't think so. For, you see—the inspiration—

HEDDA   Yes, I daresay that's the main thing. (*Casually.*) By the way, here's a letter for you.

TESMAN   Imagine!

HEDDA (*gives it to him*)   It came early this morning.

TESMAN   It's from Aunt Julle, Hedda! I wonder what it can be. (*Puts the manuscript down on the other ottoman, opens the letter, skims the content, jumps up.*) Oh Hedda! She says here that poor Aunt Rina is dying!

HEDDA   You know we had to expect that.

TESMAN   And if I want to see her again I had better hurry. I'll rush over right away.

HEDDA (*suppressing a smile*)   You'll rush?

TESMAN   Dearest Hedda of mine—if only you could bring yourself to come along! Hm?

HEDDA (*rises, weary, with an air of refusal*)   No, no. You mustn't ask me that. I don't want to look at death and disease. I don't want anything to do with ugliness.

TESMAN   Well, all right—(*Rushing around.*) My hat? My coat? Oh—out here in the hall. I just hope I won't be too late, Hedda. Hm?

HEDDA   Oh I'm sure that if you rush—

(BERTE *appears in the door, right.*)

BERTE   Judge Brack is here and wants to know if he may see you.

TESMAN   At this hour! No, no. I can't possibly see him now!

HEDDA   But *I* can. (*To* BERTE.) Tell the Judge please to come in.

(BERTE *exits.*)

HEDDA (*with a quick whisper*)   Tesman! The package! (*She grabs it from the ottoman.*)

TESMAN   Yes! Give it to me!

HEDDA   No, no. I'll hide it for you till later.

She walks over to the desk and sticks the parcel in among the books on the shelf. In his hurry TESMAN *is having difficulties getting his gloves on.* JUDGE BRACK *enters, right.*

HEDDA (*nods to him*)   If *you* aren't an early bird—

BRACK   Yes, don't you think so? (*To* TESMAN.) You're going out, too?

TESMAN Yes, I must go and see the aunts. Just think, the invalid —she's dying!

BRACK Oh, I'm terribly sorry! In that case, don't let me keep you. At such a moment—

TESMAN Yes, I really must run. Goodbye, goodbye!

(*Hurries out, right.*)

HEDDA (*approaching* BRACK) It appears that things were quite lively last night over at your house.

BRACK Indeed, Mrs. Tesman—I didn't get to bed at all.

HEDDA You didn't either?

BRACK As you see. But tell me—what has Tesman told you about the night's adventures?

HEDDA Just some tiresome story about having coffee with somebody someplace—

BRACK I believe I know all about that coffee. Eilert Løvborg wasn't one of them, was he?

HEDDA No, they had taken him home first.

BRACK Tesman, too?

HEDDA No. Some of the others, he said.

BRACK (*smiles*) Jørgen Tesman is really an ingenuous soul, you know.

HEDDA He certainly is. But why do you say that? Is there something more to all this?

BRACK Yes, there is.

HEDDA Well! In that case, why don't we make ourselves comfortable, Judge. You'll tell your story better, too.

She sits down at the left side of the table, BRACK *near her at the adjacent side.*

HEDDA All right?

BRACK For reasons of my own I wanted to keep track of my guests' movements last night. Or, rather—some of my guests.

HEDDA Eilert Løvborg was one of them, perhaps?

BRACK As a matter of fact—he was.

HEDDA Now you are really making me curious.

BRACK Do you know where he and a couple of the others spent the rest of the night, Mrs. Tesman?

HEDDA No—tell me. If it can be told.

BRACK Oh, certainly. They turned up at an exceptionally gay early morning gathering.

HEDDA Of the lively kind?

BRACK Of the liveliest.

HEDDA   A little more about this, Judge.

BRACK   Løvborg had been invited beforehand. I knew about that. But he had declined. He is a reformed character, you know.

HEDDA   As of his stay with the Elvsteds—yes. But he went after all?

BRACK   Well, yes, you see, Mrs. Tesman—unfortunately, the spirit moved him over at my house last evening.

HEDDA   Yes, I understand he became inspired.

BRACK   Quite violently inspired. And that, I gather, must have changed his mind. You know, we men don't always have as much integrity as we ought to have.

HEDDA   Oh, I'm sure you're an exception, Judge Brack. But about Løvborg—?

BRACK   To make a long story short—he ended up at Miss Diana's establishment.

HEDDA   Miss Diana's?

BRACK   She was the hostess at this gathering—a select circle of intimate friends, male and female.

HEDDA   Is she a redhead, by any chance?

BRACK   That's correct.

HEDDA   And a singer—of sorts?

BRACK   Yes—that, too. And a mighty huntress—of men, Mrs. Tesman. You seem to have heard of her. Eilert Løvborg used to be one of her most devoted protectors in his more affluent days.

HEDDA   And how did it all end?

BRACK   Not in a very friendly fashion, apparently. It seems that after the tenderest reception Miss Diana resorted to brute force—

HEDDA   Against Løvborg?

BRACK   Yes. He accused her or her women friends of having stolen something of his. Said his wallet was gone. And other things, too. In brief, he's supposed to have started a pretty wicked row.

HEDDA   And—?

BRACK   Well—there was a general free-for-all—men and women both. Fortunately, the police stepped in—

HEDDA   The police—!

BRACK   Yes. But I'm afraid this will be an expensive escapade for Eilert Løvborg, crazy fool that he is.

HEDDA   Well!

BRACK   It appears that he made quite violent objection—struck an officer in the car and tore his coat. So they had to take him along.

HEDDA   How do you know all this?

BRACK   From the police.

HEDDA   (*staring straight ahead*)   So that's how it was. No vine leaves in his hair.

BRACK   Vine leaves, Mrs. Tesman?

HEDDA   (*changing her tone*)   But tell me, Judge Brack—why did you keep such a close watch on Eilert Løvborg?

BRACK   Well—for one thing, it is obviously of some concern to me if he testifies that he came straight from my party.

HEDDA   So you think there will be an investigation?

BRACK   Naturally. But I suppose that doesn't really matter too much. However, as a friend of the house I considered it my duty to give you and Tesman a full account of his night-time exploits.

HEDDA   Yes, but why?

BRACK   Because I very strongly suspect that he intends to use you as a kind of screen.

HEDDA   Really! Why do you think that?

BRACK   Oh, come now, Mrs. Tesman! We can use our eyes, can't we? This Mrs. Elvsted—she isn't leaving town right away you know.

HEDDA   Well, even if there should be something going on between those two, I'd think there would be plenty of other places they could meet.

BRACK   But no home. After last night, every respectable house will once again be closed to Eilert Løvborg.

HEDDA   And so should mine, you mean?

BRACK   Yes. I admit I would find it more than embarrassing if the gentleman were to become a daily guest here, Mrs. Tesman. If he, as an outsider—a highly dispensable outsider—if he were to intrude himself—

HEDDA   —into the triangle?

BRACK   Precisely. It would amount to homelessness for me.

HEDDA   (*smiling*)   Sole cock-o'-the-walk—so, that's your goal, is it, Judge?

BRACK   (*nods slowly, lowers his voice*)   Yes. That is my goal. And for that I will fight with every means at my disposal.

HEDDA   (*her smile fading*)   You're really a dangerous person, you know—when you come right down to it.

BRACK   You think so?

HEDDA   Yes, I am beginning to think so now. And I must say I am exceedingly glad you don't have any kind of hold on me.

BRACK   (*with a noncommittal laugh*)   Well, well, Mrs. Tesman! Maybe there is something to what you are saying, at that. Who knows what I might do if I did.

HEDDA   Really, now, Judge Brack! Are you threatening me?

BRACK   (*rising*)   —Nonsense! For the triangle, you see—is best maintained on a voluntary basis.

HEDDA   My sentiments, exactly.

BRACK Well, I have said what I came to say. And now I should get back to town. Goodbye, Mrs. Tesman! (*Walks toward the French doors.*)

HEDDA (*rises*) You're going through the garden?

BRACK Yes. For me that's a short cut.

HEDDA Yes, and then it's a back way.

BRACK Quite true. I have nothing against back ways. There are times when they are most intriguing.

HEDDA You mean when real ammunition is used?

BRACK (*in the doorway, laughs back at her*) Oh good heavens! I don't suppose one shoots one's tame roosters!

HEDDA (*laughs also*) No—not if one has only one—!

They nod to each other, both still laughing. He leaves. She closes the door behind him. For a few moments she remains by the door, quite serious now, looking into the garden. Then she walks over to the doorway and opens the portieres wide enough to look into the inner room. Goes to the desk, pulls LØVBORG's *manuscript from the bookshelf and is about to read it when* BERTE's *voice, very loud, is heard from the hall, right.* HEDDA *turns around, listens. She hurriedly puts the manuscript into the drawer of the desk and puts the key down on its top.* EILERT LØVBORG, *wearing his coat and with his hat in his hand, flings open the door, right. He looks somewhat confused and excited.*

LØVBORG (*turned toward the invisible* BERTE *in the hall*) —And I say I must! You can't stop me! (*He closes the door, turns, sees* HEDDA, *immediately controls himself, greets her.*)

HEDDA (*by the desk*) Well, well, Mr. Løvborg—aren't you a trifle late coming for Thea?

LØVBORG Or a trifle early for calling on you. I apologize.

HEDDA How do you know she is still here?

LØVBORG The people she is staying with told me she's been gone all night.

HEDDA (*walks over to the table*) Did they seem—strange—when they said it?

LØVBORG (*puzzled*) Strange?

HEDDA I mean, did they seem to find it a little—unusual?

LØVBORG (*suddenly understands*) Ah, I see what you mean! Of course! I'm dragging her down with me. No, as a matter of fact, I didn't notice anything. I suppose Tesman isn't up yet?

HEDDA I—I don't think so—

LØVBORG When did he get home?

HEDDA Very late.

LØVBORG Did he tell you anything?

HEDDA Yes, he said you'd all had quite a time over at Brack's.

LØVBORG   Just that?

HEDDA   I think so. But I was so awfully sleepy—

(MRS. ELVSTED *enters through portieres in the rear.*)

MRS. ELVSTED (*toward him*)   Oh, Løvborg! At last!

LØVBORG   Yes, at last. And too late.

MRS. ELVSTED (*in fear*)   What is too late?

LØVBORG   Everything is too late now. It's all over with me.

MRS. ELVSTED   Oh no, no! Don't say things like that!

LØVBORG   You'll say the same yourself when you hear—

MRS. ELVSTED   I don't want to hear—!

HEDDA   Maybe you'd rather talk with her alone? I'll leave.

LØVBORG   No stay—you, too. I beg you to.

MRS. ELVSTED   But I don't want to listen, do you hear?

LØVBORG   It isn't last night I want to talk about.

MRS. ELVSTED   What about, then?

LØVBORG   We'll have to part, Thea.

MRS. ELVSTED   Part!

HEDDA (*involuntarily*)   I knew it!

LØVBORG   For I don't need you any more.

MRS. ELVSTED   And you can stand there and tell me a thing like that! Don't need me! Why can't I help you the way I did before? Aren't we going to keep on working together?

LØVBORG   I don't intend to work any more.

MRS. ELVSTED (*desperately*)   What am I going to do with my life, then?

LØVBORG   You'll have to try to live your life as if you'd never known me.

MRS. ELVSTED   But I can't do that!

LØVBORG   Try, Thea. Go back home.

MRS. ELVSTED (*agitated*)   Never again! Where you are I want to be! And you can't chase me away just like that! I want to stay right here! Be with you when the book appears.

HEDDA (*in a tense whisper*)   Ah—yes—the book!

LØVBORG (*looks at her*)   My book—and Thea's. For that's what it is.

MRS. ELVSTED   That's what I feel, too. And that's why I have the right to be with you when it comes out. I want to see all the honor and all the fame you'll get. And the joy—I want to share the joy, too.

LØVBORG   Thea, our book is never going to come out.

HEDDA   Ah!

MRS. ELVSTED   It won't!

LØVBORG *Can't* ever appear.

MRS. ELVSTED (*with fearful suspicion*) Løvborg, what have you done with the manuscript?

HEDDA (*watching him tensely*) Yes—what about the manuscript?

MRS. ELVSTED Where is it?

LØVBORG Oh Thea—please, don't ask me about that!

MRS. ELVSTED Yes, yes—I want to be told! I have the right to know—right now!

LØVBORG All right. I've torn it to pieces.

MRS. ELVSTED (*screams*) Oh, no! No!

HEDDA (*involuntarily*) But that's not—!

LØVBORG (*looks at her*) Not true, you think?

HEDDA (*composing herself*) Well, of course, if you say so. You should know. It just sounds so—so unbelievable.

LØVBORG All the same, it's true.

MRS. ELVSTED (*hands clenched*) Oh God—oh God, Hedda. He has torn his own work to pieces!

LØVBORG I have torn my whole life to pieces, so why not my life's work as well?

MRS. ELVSTED And that's what you did last night?

LØVBORG Yes, I tell you! In a thousand pieces. And scattered them in the fjord. Far out—where the water is clean and salty. Let them drift there, with wind and current. Then they'll sink. Deep, deep down. Like me, Thea.

MRS. ELVSTED Do you know, Løvborg—this thing you've done to the book—all the rest of my life I'll think of it as killing a little child.

LØVBORG You are right. It is like murdering a child.

MRS. ELVSTED But then, how could you? For the child was mine, too!

HEDDA (*almost soundlessly*) The child—

MRS. ELVSTED (*with a deep sigh*) So it's all over. I'll go now, Hedda.

HEDDA But you aren't leaving town?

MRS. ELVSTED Oh, I don't know myself what I'll do. There's only darkness before me.

(*Exits, right.*)

HEDDA (*waits for a moment*) Arent' you going to see her home, Mr. Løvborg?

LØVBORG I? Through the streets? Letting people see her with me?

HEDDA Of course, I don't know what else may have happened last night. But is it really so absolutely irreparable—?

LØVBORG   Last night is not the end of it. That I know. And yet, I don't really care for that kind of life any more. Not again. She has broken all the courage for life and all the defiance that was in me.

HEDDA   (*staring ahead*)   So that sweet little goose has had her hand in a human destiny. (*Looks at him*)   But that you could be so heartless, even so!

LØVBORG   Don't tell me I was heartless!

HEDDA   To ruin everything that's filled her soul for such a long time! You don't call that heartless!

LØVBORG   Hedda—to you I can tell the truth.

HEDDA   The truth?

LØVBORG   But first promise me—give me your word you'll never let Thea know what I'm going to tell you now.

HEDDA   You have it.

LØVBORG   All right. It isn't true, what I just told her.

HEDDA   About the manuscript?

LØVBORG   Yes. I have not torn it up. Not thrown it in the sea, either.

HEDDA   But then—where is it?

LØVBORG   I've destroyed it just the same. Really, I have, Hedda!

HEDDA   I don't understand.

LØVBORG   Thea said that what I had done seemed to her like murdering a child.

HEDDA   Yes—she did.

LØVBORG   But killing a child, that's not the worst thing a father can do to it.

HEDDA   No?

LØVBORG   No. And the worst is what I don't want Thea to know.

HEDDA   What *is* the worst?

LØVBORG   Hedda—suppose a man, say, early in the morning, after a stupid, drunken night—suppose he comes home to his child's mother and says: Listen, I've been in such and such a place. I've been here—and I've been there. And I had our child with me. In all those places. And the child is lost. Gone. Vanished. I'll be damned if I know where it is. Who's got hold of it—

HEDDA   Yes—but when all is said and done—it is only a book, you know.

LØVBORG   Thea's pure soul was in that book.

HEDDA   I realize that.

LØVBORG   Then you surely also realize that she and I can have no future together.

HEDDA   Where do you go from here?

LØVBORG   Nowhere. Just finish everything off. The sooner the better.

HEDDA (*a step closer*)   Listen—Eilert Løvborg—Couldn't you make sure it's done beautifully?

LØVBORG   Beautifully? (*Smiles.*) With vine leaves in the hair, as you used to say.

HEDDA   Oh no. I don't believe in vine leaves any more. But still beautifully! For once. Goodbye. Go now. And don't come back.

LØVBORG   Goodbye, Mrs. Tesman. Give my regards to Jørgen Tesman. (*He is about to leave.*)

HEDDA   Wait! I want to give you something—a remembrance. (*Goes to the desk, opens the drawer, takes out the gun case. Returns to LØVBORG with one of the revolvers.*)

LØVBORG   The gun? That's the remembrance?

HEDDA (*nods slowly*)   Do you recognize it? It was pointed at you once.

LØVBORG   You should have used it then.

HEDDA   Take it! *You* use it.

LØVBORG (*pockets the gun*)   Thanks!

HEDDA   And beautifully, Eilert Løvborg! That's all I ask!

LØVBORG   Goodbye, Hedda Gabler.

(*Exits, right.*)

HEDDA *listens by the door for a moment. Then she crosses to the desk, takes out the manuscript, glances inside the cover, pulls some of the pages halfway out and looks at them. Carries the whole manuscript over to the chair by the stove. She sits down with the parcel in her lap. After a moment she opens the stove and then the manuscript.*

HEDDA (*throws a bundle of sheets into the fire, whispers*)   Now I'm burning your child, Thea. You—curlyhead! (*Throws more sheets in.*) Your and Eilert Løvborg's child. (*Throws all the rest of the manuscript into the stove.*)   I am burning—I am burning your child.

ACT IV

The same rooms at the TESMANS'. *Evening. The front room is dark. The inner room is lighted by the ceiling lamp over the table. Portieres cover the French doors.*

HEDDA, *in black, is walking up and down in the dark of the front room. She goes into the inner room, turning left in the doorway. She is heard playing a few bars on the piano. She reappears and comes forward again.* BERTE *enters from the right side of the inner room. She carries a lighted lamp, which she puts down on the table in front of the corner sofa. Her eyes show signs of weeping; she wears black ribbons on her uniform. She exits quietly, right.* HEDDA *goes over to the French windows, looks between the portieres into the dark. Presently* MISS TESMAN, *in mourning, with hat and veil, enters, right.* HEDDA *walks over to meet her, gives her her hand.*

MISS TESMAN   Yes, my dearest Hedda—here you see me in my garb of grief. For now at last my poor sister has fought her fight to the end.

HEDDA   I already know—as you see. Tesman sent word.

MISS TESMAN   Yes, he promised he'd do that. But I thought that to you, Hedda—here in the house of life—I really ought to bring you the tidings of death myself.

HEDDA   That is very kind of you.

MISS TESMAN   Ah, but Rina shouldn't have died just now. There should be no mourning in Hedda's house at this time.

HEDDA   (*changing the topic*)   I understand she had a very quiet end.

MISS TESMAN   Oh so beautiful, so peaceful! She left us so quietly! And then the unspeakable happiness of seeing Jørgen one more time! To say goodbye to him to her heart's content! Isn't he back yet?

HEDDA   No. He wrote I mustn't expect him back very soon. But do sit down.

MISS TESMAN   No—no, thanks, my dear, blessed Hedda. Not that I wouldn't like to. But I don't have much time. I must go back and prepare her as best I can. I want her to look right pretty when she goes into her grave.

HEDDA   Is there anything I can help you with?

MISS TESMAN   I won't have you as much as think of it! That's not for Hedda Tesman to lend a hand to. Or lend thoughts to either. Not now, of all times!

HEDDA   Oh—thoughts! We can't always control our thoughts—

MISS TESMAN   (*still preoccupied*)   Ah yes—such is life. At home we're making a shroud for Rina. And here, too, there'll be sewing to do soon, I expect. But of quite a different kind, thank God!

(TESMAN *enters, right.*)

HEDDA.   Finally!

TESMAN   You here, Aunt Julle? With Hedda? Just think!

MISS TESMAN   I am just about to leave, Jørgen dear. Well—did you do all the things you promised me you'd do?

TESMAN   No, I'm afraid I forgot half of them, Auntie. I'd better run in again tomorrow. I'm all confused today. I can't seem to keep my thoughts together.

MISS TESMAN   But dearest Jørgen—you mustn't take it this way!

TESMAN   Oh, I mustn't? How do you mean?

MISS TESMAN   You ought to be joyful in the midst of your sorrow. Glad for what's happened. The way I am.

TESMAN   Oh yes, of course. You're thinking of Aunt Rina.

HEDDA   You're going to feel lonely now, Miss Tesman.

MISS TESMAN   The first few days, yes. But I hope that won't last long. Dear Rina's little parlor won't be empty for long, if I can help it!

TESMAN   Oh? And who do you want to move in there. Hm?

MISS TESMAN   Ah—it's not very hard to find some poor soul who needs nursing and comfort.

HEDDA   And you really want to take on such a burden all over again?

MISS TESMAN   Heavens! God forgive you, child—burden? It has not been a burden to me.

HEDDA   Still—a stranger, who—

MISS TESMAN   Oh, it's easy to make friends with sick people. And I need somebody to live for, too. Well, the Lord be praised, maybe soon there'll be a thing or two an old aunt can turn her hand to here.

HEDDA   Oh, never mind us—

TESMAN   Yes, just think—how lovely it would be for the three of us, if only—

HEDDA   If only—?

TESMAN (*uneasy*)   Oh, nothing. I daresay it will all work out. Let's hope it will, hm?

MISS TESMAN   Well, well. I can see that you two have something to talk about. (*With a smile.*) And perhaps Hedda has something to tell you, Jørgen! Goodbye! I'm going home to Rina, now. (*Turns round in the door.*) Dear, dear—how strange to think— Now Rina is both with me and with Jochum!

TESMAN   Yes, just think, Aunt Julle! Hm?

(MISS TESMAN *exits, right.*)

HEDDA (*coldly scrutinizing* TESMAN)   I wouldn't be at all surprised if you aren't more affected by this death than she is.

TESMAN   Oh, it isn't just Aunt Rina's death, Hedda. It's Eilert I worry about.

HEDDA (*quickly*)   Any news about him?

TESMAN   I went over to his room this afternoon to tell him the manuscript is safe.

HEDDA   Well? And didn't you see him?

TESMAN   No. He wasn't home. But I ran into Mrs. Elvsted and she told me he'd been here early this morning.

HEDDA   Yes, right after you'd left.

TESMAN   And he said he'd torn up the manuscript? Did he really say that?

HEDDA   Yes. So he claimed.

TESMAN   But dear God—in that case he really must have been out of his mind! So I assume you didn't give it to him either, hm, Hedda?

HEDDA   No. He didn't get it.

TESMAN   But you told him we had it, of course?

HEDDA   No. (*Quickly.*) Did you tell Mrs. Elvsted?

TESMAN   No, I didn't want to. But you ought to have told him, Hedda. Just think—what if he does something rash—something to hurt himself! Give me the manuscript, Hedda! I want to rush down to him with it right this minute. Where is it?

HEDDA   (*cold motionless, one arm resting on the chair*)   I haven't got it any more.

TESMAN   You haven't got it! What do you mean by that?

HEDDA   I burned it—the whole thing.

TESMAN   (*jumps up*)   Burned it! Burned Eilert's book!

HEDDA   Don't shout. The maid might hear you.

TESMAN   Burned it? But good God—no, no, no—! This can't be—!

HEDDA   It is, all the same.

TESMAN   But do you realize what you've done, Hedda? It's illegal! Willful destruction of lost property! You just ask Judge Brack! He'll tell you!

HEDDA   You'd better not talk about this to anyone—the Judge or anybody else.

TESMAN   But how could you do a thing like that! I never heard anything like it! What came over you? What can possibly have been going on in your head? Answer me! Hm?

HEDDA   (*suppresses an almost imperceptible smile*)   I did it for your sake, Jørgen.

TESMAN   For my sake!

HEDDA   When you came back this morning and told me he had read aloud to you—

TESMAN   Yes, yes! What then?

HEDDA   You admitted you were jealous of him for having written such a book.

TESMAN   But good gracious—! I didn't mean it as seriously as all that!

HEDDA   All the same. I couldn't stand the thought that somebody else was to overshadow you.

TESMAN   (*in an outburst of mingled doubt and joy*)   Hedda—oh Hedda! Is it true what you're saying. But—but—but—I never knew you loved me like that! Just think!

HEDDA   In that case, I might as well tell you—that—just at this time—(*Breaks off, vehemently.*) No, no! You can ask Aunt Julle. She'll tell you.

TESMAN   I almost think I know what you mean, Hedda! (*Claps his hands.*) For goodness sake! Can that really be so! Hm?

HEDDA   Don't shout so! The maid can hear you.

TESMAN   (*laughing with exuberant joy*)   The maid! Well, if you don't take the prize, Hedda! The maid—but that's Berte! I'm going to tell Berte myself this very minute!

HEDDA   (*her hands clenched in despair*)   Oh I'll die—I'll die, in all this!

TESMAN   In what, Hedda? Hm?

HEDDA   (*cold and composed*)   In all this—ludicrousness, Jørgen.

TESMAN   Ludicrous? That I'm so happy? Still—maybe I oughtn't to tell Berte, after all.

HEDDA   Oh, go ahead. What difference does it make?

TESMAN   No, not yet. But on my word—Aunt Julle must be told. And that you've started to call me "Jørgen," too! Just think! She'll be ever so happy—Aunt Julle will!

HEDDA   Even when you tell her that I have burned Eilert Løvborg's papers?

TESMAN   No, oh no! That's true! That about the manuscript—nobody must know about that. But to think that you'd burn for me, Hedda—I certainly want to tell *that* to Aunt Julle! I wonder now—is that sort of thing usual with young wives, hm?

HEDDA   Why don't you ask Aunt Julle about that, too?

TESMAN   I shall—I certainly shall, when I get the chance. (*Looks uneasy and disturbed again.*) But the manuscript! Good God— I don't dare to think what this is going to do to poor Eilert!

(MRS. ELVSTED, *dressed as on her first visit, wearing hat and coat, enters, right.*)

MRS. ELVSTED   (*gives a hurried greeting, is obviously upset*)   Oh Hedda, you must forgive me for coming here again!

HEDDA   What has happened, Thea?

TESMAN   Something to do with Eilert Løvborg again? Hm?

MRS. ELVSTED   Yes, yes—I'm so terribly afraid something's happened to him.

HEDDA   (*seizing her arm*)   Ah—you think so?

TESMAN   Oh dear—why do you think that, Mrs. Elvsted?

MRS. ELVSTED   I heard them talking about him in the boarding house, just as I came in. And people are saying the most incredible things about him today.

TESMAN   Yes, imagine! I heard that, too! And I can testify that he went straight home to bed! Just think!

HEDDA   And what did they say in the boarding house?

MRS. ELVSTED   Oh, I didn't find out anything. Either they didn't know any details or—They all became silent when they saw me. And I didn't dare to ask.

TESMAN (*pacing the floor uneasily*)   We'll just have to hope—to hope that you heard wrong, Mrs. Elvsted!

MRS. ELVSTED   No, no. I'm sure it was he they were talking about. And somebody said something about the hospital or—

TESMAN   The hospital—!

HEDDA   Surely, that can't be so!

MRS. ELVSTED   I got so terribly frightened! So I went up to his room and asked for him there.

HEDDA   Could you bring yourself to do that, Thea?

MRS. ELVSTED   What else could I do? For I felt I just couldn't stand the uncertainty any longer.

TESMAN   But I suppose you didn't find him in, either, did you? Hm?

MRS. ELVSTED   No. And the people there didn't know anything about him. He hadn't been home since yesterday afternoon, they said.

TESMAN   Yesterday! Just think! How could they say that!

MRS. ELVSTED   I don't know what else *to* think—something bad must have happened to him!

TESMAN   Hedda, dear—? What if I were to walk downtown and ask around for him—?

HEDDA   No, no—don't you go get mixed up in all this.

(JUDGE BRACK, *hat in hand, enters through the door, right, which* BERTE *opens and closes for him. He looks serious and greets the others in silence.*)

TESMAN   So here you are, Judge, hm?

BRACK   Yes. I had to see you this evening.

TESMAN   I can see you have got Aunt Julle's message.

BRACK   That, too—yes.

TESMAN   Isn't it sad, though?

BRACK   Well, my dear Tesman—that depends on how you look at it.

TESMAN (*looks at him uncertainly*)   Has something else happened?

BRACK   Yes.

HEDDA (*tense*)   Something sad, Judge Brack?

BRACK   That, too, depends on how you look at it, Mrs. Tesman.

MRS. ELVSTED (*bursting out*)   Oh, I'm sure it has something to do with Eilert Løvborg!

BRACK (*looks at her for a moment*)   Why do you think that, Mrs. Elvsted? Maybe you already know something—?

MRS. ELVSTED (*confused*)   No, no; not at all. It's just—

TESMAN   For heaven's sake, Brack, out with it!

BRACK (*shrugging his shoulders*)   Well—unfortunately, Eilert Løvborg's in the hospital. Dying.

MRS. ELVSTED (*screams*)   Oh God, oh God!

TESMAN   In the hospital! And dying!

HEDDA (*without thinking*)   So soon—!

MRS. ELVSTED (*wailing*)   And we didn't even part as friends, Hedda!

HEDDA (*whispers*)   Thea, Thea—for heaven's sake—!

MRS. ELVSTED (*paying no attention to her*)   I want to see him! I want to see him alive!

BRACK   Won't do you any good, Mrs. Elvsted. Nobody can see him.

MRS. ELVSTED   Then tell me what's happened to him! What?

TESMAN   For, surely, he hasn't himself—!

HEDDA   I'm sure he has.

TESMAN   Hedda! How can you—!

BRACK (*observing her all this time*)   I am sorry to say that your guess is absolutely correct, Mrs. Tesman.

MRS. ELVSTED   Oh, how awful!

TESMAN   Did it himself! Just think!

HEDDA   Shot himself!

BRACK   Right again, Mrs. Tesman.

MRS. ELVSTED (*trying to pull herself together*)   When did this happen, Judge?

BRACK   This afternoon. Between three and four.

TESMAN   But dear me—where can he have done a thing like that? Hm?

BRACK (*a little uncertain*)   Where? Well—I suppose in his room. I don't really know—

MRS. ELVSTED   No, it can't have been there. For I was up there sometime between six and seven.

BRACK   Well, then, some other place. I really can't say. All I know is that he was found. He had shot himself—in the chest.

MRS. ELVSTED   Oh, how horrible to think! That he was to end like that!

HEDDA (*to* BRACK)   In the chest?

BRACK   Yes—as I just told you.

HEDDA   Not the temple?

BRACK   In the chest, Mrs. Tesman.

HEDDA   Well, well—the chest is a good place, too.

BRACK   How is that, Mrs. Tesman?

HEDDA   (*turning him aside*)   Oh—nothing.

TESMAN   And you say the wound is fatal? Hm?

BRACK   No doubt about it—absolutely fatal. He's probably dead already.

MRS. ELVSTED   Yes, yes! I feel you're right! It's over! It's all over! Oh, Hedda!

TESMAN   But tell me—how do *you* know all this?

BRACK   (*tersely*)   A man on the force told me. One I had some business with.

HEDDA   (*loudly*)   At last a deed!

TESMAN   (*appalled*)   Oh dear—what are you saying, Hedda!

HEDDA   I am saying there is beauty in this.

BRACK   Well, now—Mrs. Tesman—

TESMAN   Beauty—! Just think!

MRS. ELVSTED   Oh, Hedda—how can you talk about beauty in a thing like this!

HEDDA   Eilert Løvborg has settled his account with himself. He has had the courage to do—what had to be done.

MRS. ELVSTED   But you mustn't believe it happened that way! He did it when he was not himself!

TESMAN   In despair! That's how!

HEDDA   He did not. I am certain of that.

MRS. ELVSTED   Yes he did! He was not himself! That's the way he tore up the book, too!

BRACK   (*puzzled*)   The book? You mean the manuscript? Has he torn it up?

MRS. ELVSTED   Yes, last night.

TESMAN   (*whispers*)   Oh, Hedda—we'll never get clear of all this!

BRACK   That is strange.

TESMAN   (*walking the floor*)   To think that this was to be the end of Eilert! Not to leave behind him anything that would have preserved his name—

MRS. ELVSTED   Oh, if only it could be put together again!

TESMAN   Yes, if only it could. I don't know what I wouldn't give—

MRS. ELVSTED   Maybe it can, Mr. Tesman.

TESMAN   What do you mean?

MRS. ELVSTED   (*searching her dress pocket*)   Look. I have kept these little slips he dictated from.

HEDDA   (*a step closer*)   Ah—!

TESMAN   You've kept them, Mrs. Elvsted? Hm?

MRS. ELVSTED   Yes. Here they are. I took them with me when I left. And I've had them in my pocket ever since—

TESMAN   Please, let me see—

MRS. ELVSTED (*gives him a pile of small paper slips*)   But it's such a mess. Without any kind of system or order—!

TESMAN   But just think if we could make sense out of them, all the same! Perhaps if we helped each other—

MRS. ELVSTED   Oh yes! Let's try, anyway!

TESMAN   It will work! It *has* to work! I'll stake my whole life on this!

HEDDA   You, Jørgen? Your life?

TESMAN   Yes, or at any rate all the time I can set aside. My own collections can wait. Hedda, you understand—don't you? Hm? This is something I owe Eilert's memory.

HEDDA   Maybe so.

TESMAN   And now, my dear Mrs. Elvsted, we want to get to work. Good heavens, there's no point brooding over what's happened. Hm? We'll just have to acquire sufficient peace of mind to—

MRS. ELVSTED   All right, Mr. Tesman. I'll try to do my best.

TESMAN   Very well, then. Come over here. Let's look at these slips right away. Where can we sit? Here? No, it's better in the other room. If you'll excuse us, Judge! Come along, Mrs. Elvsted.

MRS. ELVSTED   Oh dear God—if only it were possible—!

TESMAN *and* MRS. ELVSTED *go into the inner room. She takes off her hat and coat. Both sit down at the table under the hanging lamp and absorb themselves in the slips.* HEDDA *walks over toward the stove and sits down in the easy chair. After a while,* BRACK *walks over to her.*

HEDDA (*in a low voice*)   Ah, Judge—what a liberation there is in this thing with Eilert Løvborg!

BRACK   Liberation, Mrs. Tesman? Well, yes, for him perhaps one may say there was liberation of a kind—

HEDDA   I mean for me. There is liberation in knowing that there is such a thing in the world as an act of free courage. Something which becomes beautiful by its very nature.

BRACK (*smiles*)   Well—dear Mrs. Tesman—

HEDDA   Oh I know what you're going to say! For you see—you really are a kind of specialist, too!

BRACK (*looks at her fixedly*)   Eilert Løvborg has meant more to you than perhaps you're willing to admit, even to yourself. Or am I wrong?

HEDDA   I won't answer such questions. All I know is that Eilert Løvborg had the courage to live his own life. And then now— this—magnificence! The beauty of it! Having the strength and the will to get up and leave life's feast—so early—

BRACK Believe me, Mrs. Tesman, this pains me, but I see it is necessary that I destroy a pretty illusion—

HEDDA An illusion?

BRACK Which could not have been maintained for very long, anyway.

HEDDA And what is that?

BRACK He didn't shoot himself—of his own free will.

HEDDA Not of his own—!

BRACK No. To tell the truth, the circumstances of Eilert Løvborg's death aren't exactly what I said they were.

HEDDA (*tense*) You've held something back? What?

BRACK For the sake of poor Mrs. Elvsted I used a few euphemisms.

HEDDA What?

BRACK First—he is already dead.

HEDDA In the hospital.

BRACK Yes. And without regaining consciousness.

HEDDA What else haven't you told?

BRACK That fact that it didn't happen in his room.

HEDDA Well, does that really make much difference?

BRACK Some. You see—Eilert Løvborg was found shot in Miss Diana's bedroom.

HEDDA (*is about to jump up, but sinks back*) That's impossible, Judge Brack! He can't have been there again today!

BRACK He was there this afternoon. He came to claim something he said they had taken from him. Spoke some gibberish about a lost child—

HEDDA So that's why—!

BRACK I thought maybe he meant his manuscript. But now I hear he has destroyed that himself. So I suppose it must have been something else.

HEDDA I suppose. So it was there—so they found him there?

BRACK Yes. With a fired gun in his pocket. Mortally wounded.

HEDDA Yes—in the chest.

BRACK No—in the guts.

HEDDA (*looks at him with an expression of disgust*) That, too! What is this curse that turns everything I touch into something ludicrous and low!

BRACK There is something else, Mrs. Tesman. Something I'd call —nasty.

HEDDA And what is that.

BRACK The gun they found—

HEDDA (*breathless*) What about it?

BRACK   He must have stolen it.

HEDDA   (*jumps up*)   Stolen! That's not true! He didn't!

BRACK   Anything else is impossible. He *must* have stolen it.—Shhh!

TESMAN and MRS. ELVSTED have risen from the table and come forward into the front room.

TESMAN   (*with papers in both hands*)   D'you know, Hedda—you can hardly see in there with that lamp! Just think!

HEDDA   I am thinking.

TESMAN   I wonder if you'd let us use your desk, hm?

HEDDA   Certainly, if you like. (*Adds quickly.*) Wait a minute, though! Let me clear it off a bit first.

TESMAN   Ah, there's no need for that, Hedda. There's plenty of room.

HEDDA   No, no. I want to straighten it up. I'll carry all this in here. I'll put it on top of the piano for the time being.

She has pulled an object, covered by note paper, out of the bookcase. She puts several other sheets of paper on top of it and carries the whole pile into the left part of the inner room. TESMAN puts the papers down on the desk and moves the lamp from the corner table over to the desk. He and MRS. ELVSTED sit down and resume their work. HEDDA returns.

HEDDA   (*behind MRS. ELVSTED's chair, softly ruffling her hair*)   Well, little Thea—how is Eilert Løvborg's memorial coming along?

MRS. ELVSTED   (*looks up at her, discouraged*)   Oh God—I'm sure it's going to be terribly hard to make anything out of all this.

TESMAN   But we have to. We just don't have a choice. And putting other people's papers in order—that's just the thing for me.

HEDDA walks over to the stove and sits down on one of the ottomans. BRACK stands over her, leaning on the easy chair.

HEDDA   (*whispers*)   What were you saying about the gun?

BRACK   (*also softly*)   That he must have stolen it.

HEDDA   Why, necessarily?

BRACK   Because any other explanation ought to be out of the question, Mrs. Tesman.

HEDDA   Oh?

BRACK   (*looks at her for a moment*)   Eilert Løvborg was here this morning, of course. Isn't that so?

HEDDA   Yes.

BRACK   Were you alone with him?

HEDDA   Yes, for a while.

BRACK You didn't leave the room while he was here?

HEDDA No.

BRACK Think. Not at all? Not even for a moment?

HEDDA Well—maybe just for a moment—out in the hall.

BRACK And where was the gun case?

HEDDA In the—

BRACK Mrs. Tesman?

HEDDA On the desk.

BRACK Have you looked to see if both guns are still there?

HEDDA No.

BRACK You needn't bother. I saw the gun they found on Løvborg, and I knew it immediately. From yesterday—and from earlier occasions, too.

HEDDA Perhaps you have it?

BRACK No, the police do.

HEDDA What are the police going to do with it?

BRACK Try to find the owner.

HEDDA Do you think they will?

BRACK (*leans over her, whispers*) No, Hedda Gabler—not as long as I keep quiet.

HEDDA (*with a hunted look*) And if you don't?

BRACK (*shrugs his shoulders*) Of course, there's always the chance that the gun was stolen.

HEDDA (*firmly*) Rather die!

BRACK (*smiles*) People *say* things like that. They don't *do* them.

HEDDA (*without answering*) And if the gun was not stolen—and if they find the owner—then what happens?

BRACK Well, Hedda—then comes the scandal!

HEDDA The scandal!

BRACK Yes—the scandal. That you are so afraid of. You will of course be required to testify. Both you and Miss Diana. Obviously, she'll have to explain how the whole thing happened. Whether it was accidental or homicide. Did he try to pull the gun out of his pocket to threaten her? And did it fire accidentally? Or did she grab the gun away from him, shoot him, and put it back in his pocket? She might just possibly have done that. She's a pretty tough girl—Miss Diana.

HEDDA But this whole disgusting mess has nothing to do with me.

BRACK Quite so. But you'll have to answer the question: Why did you give Eilert Løvborg the gun? And what inferences will be drawn from the fact that you did?

HEDDA (*lowers her head*) That's true. I hadn't thought of that.

BRACK Well—luckily, there's nothing to worry about as long as I don't say anything.

HEDDA (*looks up at him*) So then I'm in your power, Judge. From now on you can do anything you like with me.

BRACK (*in an even softer whisper*) Dearest Hedda—believe me, I'll not misuse my position.

HEDDA In your power, all the same. Dependent on your will. Servant to your demands. Not free. Not free! (*Rises suddenly.*) No —I can't stand that thought! Never!

BRACK (*looks at her, half mockingly*) Most people submit to the inevitable.

HEDDA (*returning his glance*) Perhaps. (*Walks over to the desk. Suppresses a smile and mimics* TESMAN's *way of speaking.*) Well? Do you think you can do it, Jørgen? Hm?

TESMAN Lord knows, Hedda. Anyway, I can already see it will take months.

HEDDA (*still mimicking*) Just think! (*Runs her hands lightly through* MRS. ELVSTED's *hair.*) Doesn't this seem strange to you, Thea? Sitting here with Tesman—just the way you used to with Eilert Løvborg?

MRS. ELVSTED Oh dear—if only I could inspire your husband, too!

HEDDA Oh, I'm sure that will come—in time.

TESMAN Well, yes—do you know, Hedda? I really think I begin to feel something of the kind. But why don't you go and talk to the Judge again.

HEDDA Isn't there anything you two can use me for?

TESMAN No, not a thing, dear. (*Turns around.*) From now on, you must be good enough to keep Hedda company, my dear Judge!

BRACK (*glancing at* HEDDA) I'll be only too delighted.

HEDDA Thank you. But I'm tired tonight. I think I'll go and lie down for a while.

TESMAN Yes, you do that, dear; why don't you? Hm?

HEDDA *goes into the inner room, closes the portieres behind her. Brief pause. Suddenly, she is heard playing a frenzied dance tune on the piano.*

MRS. ELVSTED (*jumps up*) Oh God! What's that!

TESMAN (*running to the doorway*) But dearest Hedda—you mustn't play dance music tonight, for goodness' sake! Think of Aunt Rina! And Eilert, too!

HEDDA (*peeks in from between the portieres*) And Aunt Julle. And everybody. I'll be quiet. (*She pulls the portieres shut again.*)

TESMAN (*back at the desk*) I don't think it's good for her to see us at such a melancholy task. I'll tell you what, Mrs. Elvsted. You move in with Aunt Julle, and then I'll come over in the evenings. Then we can sit and work over there. Hm?

MRS. ELVSTED   Maybe that would be better—

HEDDA (*from inner room*)   I hear every word you're saying, Tesman. And how am I going to spend my evenings?

TESMAN (*busy with the papers*)   Oh, I'm sure Judge Brack will be good enough to come out and see you, anyway.

BRACK (*in the easy chair, calls out gaily*)   Every single night, as far as I'm concerned, Mrs. Tesman! I'm sure we're going to have a lovely time, you and I!

HEDDA (*loud and clear*)   Yes, don't you think that would be nice, Judge Brack? You—sole cock-o'-the walk—

A shot is heard from the inner room. TESMAN, MRS. ELVSTED, *and* JUDGE BRACK *all jump up.*

TESMAN   There she is, fooling with those guns again.

He pulls the portieres apart and runs inside. MRS. ELVSTED *also.* HEDDA, *lifeless, is lying on the sofa. Cries and confusion.* BERTE, *flustered, enters, right.*

TESMAN (*shouts to* BRACK)   She's shot herself! In the temple! Just think!

BRACK (*half stunned in the easy chair*)   But, merciful God—! One just doesn't *do* that!

THE CHERRY ORCHARD (1904)

ANTON CHEKHOV (1860–1904)

The good, gentle physician, Dr. Chekhov, doomed to die of consumption at a distressingly early age, wrote four plays, *The Seagull* (1896), *Uncle Vanya* (1899), *The Three Sisters* (1901), and *The Cherry Orchard,* uniformly regarded as among our finest pieces of dramatic realism. It is a very special kind of realism, and it makes unusual demands upon the actors who perform and the audience who watches. At first encounter, these dramas strike one as virtually plotless discussions of unrequited love and frustrated careers among a group of self-centered directionless human beings existing in genteel poverty who do nothing but sit around decaying country estates, attempting, mostly without success, to entertain or make love to each other, and drinking endless glasses of tea. Their creator regarded them as comedies.

What Chekhov has written, in fact, *are* some of the best examples of the realistic comedy of sensibility. With great sensitivity and sympathy, he portrays a modestly high level of Russian society whose members are caught amidst rapid social change that will soon see the end of their calm and indolent world. They are pitiful people, distressed in their inability to figure out what is happening while remaining resentfully incapable of adjusting. They are ultimately doomed, but they are charming refined people whose mundane daily existences the dramatist transforms into effective and highly literate drama. Their encounters may be far removed from our own, but their emotional reactions are not, and Chekhov is able to convey their humdrum, surfacy, existence through a downbeat but universally appealing portrayal of the human experience. He shows us his characters for what they are, mostly ordinary and second-rate, essentially comic, but very human personalities.

The task that is put upon the actor in Chekhov, plainly evident in *The Cherry Orchard,* is the ability to rise above the almost total lack of action in the story itself and to demonstrate the surging force of the drama that exists beneath each individual surface. The actor in Chekhov must portray, for instance, a Madame Ranevsky who is not actually a simpleton in her wasteful extravagances and her inability to recognize that her fortune is gone, but one who is a thoroughly sympathetic woman whose foolishness we may not condone but we at least comprehend. Gayeff and his incessant billiards must come across as confused, charmingly absentminded, but certainly not crazy. Lopahin, confused as all the rest, must evoke sympathy, not antagonism, for he is far from being a villain. He may lack taste and "good breeding" but his search for security and social status as the son of a serf is legitimate. All of the characters are a touching lot, intrinsically comic, without being particularly funny. Yet it is impossible not to laugh at them. We are both amused and bemused. Emotionally we identify, while we seeth in frustration at their disturbing reality. And that's the problem in watching Chekhov. As an audience we yearn for action, for something to happen. If we remain disciplined in our observance, however, we recognize the storm and stress that make for genuinely effective drama.

Chekhov's plays support no stars. They demand something entirely new to the theatre of their time: carefully controlled *ensemble* acting. There is no leading part, no single major character. The group is the collective protagonist, and the actor who performs Chekhov must surrender any artistic ego to that group. At the same time, he must maintain the individual characterization needed to set himself apart from all the others. The performer must recognize how Chekhov loves the people he has created, refusing to criticize, but realizing their quiet desperation. He offers them for what they are, ordinary people, unimportant to the world around them, desperately important to themselves, while those among whom they exist continually look the other way.

The Cherry Orchard

CHEKHOV

Translated by Stark Young

CHARACTERS

YERMOLAY ALEXEEVICH LOPAHIN, *a merchant*
DUNYASHA, *a maid*
SEMYON PANTELEEVICH EPIHODOFF, *a clerk*
FIERS, *a valet, an old man of eighty-seven*
LYUBOFF ANDREEVNA RANEVSKAYA, *a landowner*
ANYA, *her daughter, seventeen years old*
CHARLOTTA IVANOVNA, *a governess*
VARYA, *Madam Ranevskaya's adopted daughter, twenty-four
    years old*
LEONID ANDREEVICH GAYEFF, *brother of Madam Ranevskaya*
BORIS BORISOVICH SEMYONOFF-PISHTCHIK, *a landowner*
YASHA, *a young valet*
PYOTR SERGEEVICH TROFIMOFF, *a student*
A STRANGER WHO PASSES BY
THE STATION-MASTER
A POST-OFFICE CLERK
VISITORS
SERVANTS

ACT I

A room that is still called the nursery. One of the doors leads into ANYA'S
*room. Dawn, the sun will soon be rising. It is May, the cherry trees are in
blossom but in the orchard it is cold, with a morning frost. The windows
in the room are closed.* DUNYASHA *enters with a candle and* LOPAHIN *with
a book in his hand.*

LOPAHIN   The train got in, thank God! What time is it?
DUNYASHA   It's nearly two. (*Blows out his candle.*) It's already
    daylight.
LOPAHIN   But how late was the train? Two hours at least. (*Yawn-
    ing and stretching.*) I'm a fine one, I am, look what a fool thing

I did! I drove here on purpose just to meet them at the station, and then all of a sudden I'd overslept myself! Fell asleep in my chair. How provoking!—You could have waked me up.

DUNYASHA   I thought you had gone. (*Listening.*) Listen, I think they are coming now.

LOPAHIN (*listening*)   No—No, there's the luggage and one thing and another. (*A pause.*) Lyuboff Andreevna has been living abroad five years. I don't know what she is like now—She is a good woman. An easy-going, simple woman. I remember when I was a boy about fifteen, my father, who is at rest—in those days he ran a shop here in the village—hit me in the face with his fist, my nose was bleeding—We'd come to the yard together for something or other, and he was a little drunk. Lyuboff Andreevna, I can see her now, still so young, so slim, led me to the washbasin here in this very room, in the nursery. "Don't cry," she says, "little peasant, it will be well in time for your wedding"— (*A pause.*) Yes, little peasant—My father was a peasant truly, and here I am in a white waistcoat and yellow shoes. Like a pig rooting in a pastry shop—I've got this rich, lots of money, but if you really stop and think of it, I'm just a peasant— (*Turning the pages of a book.*) Here I was reading a book and didn't get a thing out of it. Reading and went to sleep. (*A pause.*)

DUNYASHA   And all night long the dogs were not asleep, they know their masters are coming.

LOPAHIN   What is it, Dunyasha, you're so—

DUNYASHA   My hands are shaking. I'm going to faint.

LOPAHIN   You're just so delicate, Dunyasha. And all dressed up like a lady, and your hair all done up! Mustn't do that. Must know your place.

(EPIHODOFF *enters, with a bouquet: he wears a jacket and highly polished boots with a loud squeak. As he enters he drops the bouquet.*)

EPIHODOFF (*picking up the bouquet*)   Look, the gardener sent these, he says to put them in the dining room.

(*Giving the bouquet to* DUNYASHA.)

LOPAHIN   And bring me some kvass.

DUNYASHA   Yes, sir.

(*Goes out.*)

EPIHODOFF   There is a morning frost now, three degrees of frost (*sighing*) and the cherries all in bloom. I cannot approve of our climate—I cannot. Our climate can never quite rise to the occasion. Listen, Yermolay Alexeevich, allow me to subtend, I bought myself, day before yesterday, some boots and they, I venture to assure you, squeak so that it is impossible. What could I grease them with?

LOPAHIN   Go on. You annoy me.

EPIHODOFF   Every day some misfortune happens to me. But I don't complain, I am used to it and I even smile.

(DUNYASHA *enters, serves* LOPAHIN *the kvass.*)

EPIHODOFF   I'm going. (*Stumbling over a chair and upsetting it.*) There (*as if triumphant*), there, you see, pardon the expression, a circumstance like that, among others—It is simply quite remarkable.

(*Goes out.*)

DUNYASHA   And I must tell you, Yermolay Alexeevich, that Epihodoff has proposed to me.

LOPAHIN   Ah!

DUNYASHA   I don't know really what to—He is a quiet man but sometimes when he starts talking, you can't understand a thing he means. It's all very nice, and full of feeling, but just doesn't make any sense. I sort of like him. He loves me madly. He's a man that's unfortunate, every day there's something or other. They tease him around here, call him twenty-two misfortunes—

LOPAHIN (*cocking his ear*)   Listen, I think they are coming—

DUNYASHA   They are coming! But what's the matter with me— I'm cold all over.

LOPAHIN   They're really coming. Let's go meet them. Will she recognize me? It's five years we haven't seen each other.

DUNYASHA (*excitedly*)   I'm going to faint this very minute. Ah, I'm going to faint!

Two carriages can be heard driving up to the house. LOPAHIN *and* DUNYASHA *hurry out. The stage is empty. In the adjoining rooms a noise begins.* FIERS *hurries across the stage, leaning on a stick; he has been to meet* LYUBOFF ANDREEVNA, *and wears an old-fashioned livery and a high hat; he mutters something to himself, but you cannot understand a word of it. The noise offstage gets louder and louder. A voice: "Look! Let's go through here—"* LYUBOFF ANDREEVNA, ANYA *and* CHARLOTTA IVANOVNA, *with a little dog on a chain, all of them dressed for traveling,* VARYA, *in a coat and kerchief,* GAYEFF, SEMYONOFF-PISHTCHIK, LOPAHIN, DUNYASHA, *with a bundle and an umbrella, servants with pieces of luggage—all pass through the room.*

ANYA   Let's go through here. Mama, do you remember what room this is?

LYUBOFF ANDREEVNA (*happily, through her tears*)   The nursery!

VARYA How cold it is, my hands are stiff. (*To* LYUBOFF ANDRE-
EVNA.) Your rooms, the white one and the violet, are just the
same as ever, Mama.

LYUBOFF ANDREEVNA The nursery, my dear beautiful room—I
slept here when I was little—(*Crying.*) And now I am like a
child— (*Kisses her brother and* VARYA, *then her brother again.*)
And Varya is just the same as ever, looks like a nun. And I knew
Dunyasha— (*Kisses* DUNYASHA.)

GAYEFF The train was two hours late. How's that? How's that for
good management?

CHARLOTTA (*to* PISHTCHIK) My dog he eats nuts too.

PISHTCHIK (*astonished*) Think of that!

(*Everybody goes out except* ANYA *and* DUNYASHA.)

DUNYASHA We waited so long—(*Taking off* ANYA's *coat and hat.*)

ANYA I didn't sleep all four nights on the way. And now I feel so
chilly.

DUNYASHA It was Lent when you left, there was some snow then,
there was frost, and now? My darling (*laughing and kissing her*),
I waited so long for you, my joy, my life—I'm telling you now,
I can't keep from it another minute.

ANYA (*wearily*) There we go again—

DUNYASHA The clerk Epihodoff, proposed to me after Holy Week.

ANYA You're always talking about the same thing— (*Arranging
her hair.*) I've lost all my hairpins— (*She is tired to the point of
staggering.*)

DUNYASHA I just don't know what to think. He loves me, loves
me so!

ANYA (*looks in through her door, tenderly*) My room, my windows, its just as if I had never been away. I'm home! Tomorrow
morning I'll get up, I'll run into the orchard—Oh, if I only could
go to sleep! I haven't slept all the way, I was tormented by
anxiety.

DUNYASHA Day before yesterday, Pyotr Sergeevich arrived.

ANYA (*joyfully*) Petya!

DUNYASHA He's asleep in the bathhouse, he lives there. I am
afraid, he says, of being in the way. (*Taking her watch from her
pocket and looking at it.*) Somebody ought to wake him up. It's
only that Varvara Mikhailovna told us not to. Don't you wake
him up, she said.

(VARYA *enters with a bunch of keys at her belt.*)

VARYA Dunyasha, coffee, quick—Mama is asking for coffee.

DUNYASHA   This minute.

(*Goes out.*)

VARYA   Well, thank goodness, you've come back. You are home again. (*Caressingly.*) My darling is back! My precious is back!

ANYA   I've had such a time.

VARYA   I can imagine!

ANYA   I left during Holy Week, it was cold then. Charlotta talked all the way and did her tricks. Why did you fasten Charlotta on to me—?

VARYA   But you couldn't have traveled alone, darling; not at seventeen!

ANYA   We arrived in Paris, it was cold there and snowing. I speak terrible French. Mama lived on the fifth floor; I went to see her; there were some French people in her room, ladies, an old priest with his prayer book, and the place was full of tobacco smoke— very dreary. Suddenly I began to feel sorry for Mama, so sorry, I drew her to me, held her close and couldn't let her go. Then Mama kept hugging me, crying—yes—

VARYA (*tearfully*)   Don't—oh, don't—

ANYA   Her villa near Mentone she had already sold, she had nothing left, nothing. And I didn't have a kopeck left. It was all we could do to get here. And Mama doesn't understand! We sit down to dinner at a station and she orders, insists on the most expensive things and gives the waiters rouble tips. Charlotta does the same. Yasha too demands his share; it's simply dreadful. Mama has her butler, Yasha, we've brought him here—

VARYA   I saw the wretch.

ANYA   Well, how are things? Has the interest on the mortgage been paid?

VARYA   How could we?

ANYA   Oh, my God, my God—!

VARYA   In August the estate is to be sold—

ANYA   My God—!

LOPAHIN (*looking in through the door and mooing like a cow*)   Moo-o-o— (*Goes away.*)

VARYA (*tearfully*)   I'd land him one like that— (*Shaking her fist.*)

ANYA (*embracing* VARYA *gently*)   Varya, has he proposed? (VARYA *shakes her head.*) But he loves you—Why don't you have it out with him, what are you waiting for?

VARYA   I don't think anything will come of it for us. He is very busy, he hasn't any time for me—And doesn't notice me. God knows, it's painful for me to see him—Everybody talks about our marriage, everybody congratulates us, and the truth is, there's nothing to it—it's all like a dream— (*In a different tone.*) You have a brooch looks like a bee.

ANYA (*sadly*) Mama bought it. (*Going toward her room, speaking gaily, like a child.*) And in Paris I went up in a balloon!

VARYA My darling is back! My precious is back! (DUNYASHA *has returned with the coffee pot and is making coffee.* VARYA *is standing by the door.*) Darling, I'm busy all day long with the house and I go around thinking things. If only you could be married to a rich man, I'd be more at peace too, I would go all by myself to a hermitage—then to Kiev—to Moscow, and I'd keep going like that from one holy place to another—I would go on and on. Heavenly!

ANYA The birds are singing in the orchard. What time is it now?

VARYA It must be after two. It's time you were asleep, darling. (*Going into* ANYA's *room.*) Heavenly!

(YASHA *enters with a lap robe and a traveling bag.*)

YASHA (*crossing the stage airily*) May I go through here?

DUNYASHA We'd hardly recognize you, Yasha; you've changed so abroad!

YASHA Hm—And who are you?

DUNYASHA When you left here, I was like that— (*Her hand so high from the floor.*) I'm Dunyasha, Fyodor Kozoyedoff's daughter. You don't remember!

YASHA Hm—You little peach!

Looking around before he embraces her; she shrieks and drops a saucer; YASHA *hurries out.*

VARYA (*at the door, in a vexed tone*) And what's going on here?

DUNYASHA (*tearfully*) I broke a saucer—

VARYA That's good luck.

ANYA (*emerging from her room*) We ought to tell Mama beforehand: Petya is here—

VARYA I told them not to wake him up.

ANYA (*pensively*) Six years ago our father died, a month later our brother Grisha was drowned in the river, such a pretty little boy, just seven. Mama couldn't bear it, she went away, went away without ever looking back— (*Shuddering.*) How I understand her, if she only knew I did. (*A pause.*) And Petya Trofimoff was Grisha's tutor, he might remind—

(FIERS *enters; he is in a jacket and white waistcoat.*)

FIERS (*going to the coffee urn, busy with it*) The mistress will have her breakfast here— (*Putting on white gloves.*) Is the coffee ready? (*To* DUNYASHA, *sternly.*) You! What about the cream?

DUNYASHA   Oh, my God—

(*Hurrying out.*)

FIERS (*busy at the coffee urn*)   Oh, you good-for-nothing—! (*Muttering to himself.*) Come back from Paris—And the master used to go to Paris by coach— (*Laughing.*)

VARYA   Fiers, what are you—?

FIERS   At your service. (*Joyfully.*) My mistress is back! It's what I've been waiting for! Now I'm ready to die— (*Crying for joy.*)

(LYUBOFF ANDREEVNA, GAYEFF *and* SEMYONOFF-PISHTCHIK *enter;* SEMYONOFF-PISHTCHIK *is in a podyovka[1] of fine cloth and sharovary.[2]* GAYEFF *enters; he makes gestures with his hands and body as if he were playing billiards.*)

LYUBOFF ANDREEVNA   How is it? Let me remember—Yellow into the corner! Duplicate in the middle!

GAYEFF   I cut into the corner. Sister, you and I slept here in this very room once, and now I am fifty-one years old, strange as that may seem—

LOPAHIN   Yes, time passes.

GAYEFF   What?

LOPAHIN   Time, I say, passes.

GAYEFF   And it smells like patchouli here.

ANYA   I'm going to bed. Good night, Mama. (*Kissing her mother.*)

LYUBOFF ANDREEVNA   My sweet little child. (*Kissing her hands.*) You're glad you are home? I still can't get myself together.

ANYA   Good-by, Uncle.

GAYEFF (*kissing her face and hands*)   God be with you. How like your mother you are! (*To his sister.*) Lyuba, at her age you were exactly like her.

(ANYA *shakes hands with* LOPAHIN *and* PISHTCHIK, *goes out and closes the door behind her.*)

LYUBOFF ANDREEVNA   She's very tired.

PISHTCHIK   It is a long trip, I imagine.

VARYA (*to* LOPAHIN *and* PISHTCHIK)   Well, then, sirs? It's going on three o'clock, time for gentlemen to be going.

LYUBOFF ANDREEVNA (*laughing*)   The same old Varya. (*Drawing*

---

[1] *podyovka* short tunic worn under a coat or jacket
[2] *sharovary* loose, bloused trousers, the legs of which are tied at the ankle or tucked into the boots

her to her and kissing her.) There, I'll drink my coffee, then we'll all go. (FIERS *puts a small cushion under her feet.*) Thank you, my dear. I am used to coffee. Drink it day and night. Thank you, my dear old soul. (*Kissing* FIERS.)

VARYA   I'll go see if all the things have come.

(*Goes out.*)

LYUBOFF ANDREEVNA   Is it really me sitting here? (*Laughing.*) I'd like to jump around and wave my arms. (*Covering her face with her hands.*) But I may be dreaming! God knows I love my country, love it deeply, I couldn't look out of the car window, I just kept crying. (*Tearfully.*) However, I must drink my coffee. Thank you, Fiers, thank you, my dear old friend. I'm so glad you're still alive.

FIERS   Day before yesterday.

GAYEFF   He doesn't hear well.

LOPAHIN   And I must leave right now. It's nearly five o'clock in the morning, for Kharkov. What a nuisance! I wanted to look at you—talk—You are as beautiful as ever.

PISHTCHIK (*breathing heavily*)   Even more beautiful—In your Paris clothes—It's a feast for the eyes—

LOPAHIN   Your brother, Leonid Andreevich here, says I'm a boor, a peasant money grubber, but that's all the same to me, absolutely. Let him say it. All I wish is you'd trust me as you used to, and your wonderful, touching eyes would look at me as they did. Merciful God! My father was a serf; belonged to your grandfather and your father; but you, your own self, you did so much for me once that I've forgotten all that and love you like my own kin— more than my kin.

LYUBOFF ANDREEVNA   I can't sit still—I can't. (*Jumping up and walking about in great excitement.*) I'll never live through this happiness—Laugh at me, I'm silly—My own little bookcase—! (*Kissing the bookcase.*) My little table!

GAYEFF   And in your absence the nurse here died.

LYUBOFF ANDREEVNA (*sitting down and drinking coffee*)   Yes, may she rest in Heaven! They wrote me.

GAYEFF   And Anastasy died. Cross-eyed Petrushka left me and lives in town now at the police officer's. (*Taking out of his pocket a box of hard candy and sucking a piece.*)

PISHTCHIK   My daughter, Dashenka—sends you her greetings—

LOPAHIN   I want to tell you something very pleasant, cheerful. (*Glancing at his watch.*) I'm going right away. There's no time for talking. Well, I'll make it two or three words. As you know, your cherry orchard is to be sold for your debts; the auction is set for August 22nd, but don't you worry, my dear, you just sleep in peace, there's a way out of it. Here's my plan. Please listen to me. Your estate is only thirteen miles from town. They've run the railroad by it. Now if the cherry orchard and the land along the river were cut up into building lots and leased for summer cottages, you'd have at the very lowest twenty-five thousand roubles per year income.

GAYEFF   Excuse me, what rot!

LYUBOFF ANDREEVNA   I don't quite understand you, Yermolay Alexeevich.

LOPAHIN   At the very least you will get from the summer residents twenty-five roubles per year for a two-and-a-half acre lot and if you post a notice right off, I'll bet you anything that by autumn you won't have a single patch of land free, everything will be taken. In a word, my congratulations, you are saved. The location is wonderful, the river's so deep. Except, of course, it all needs to be tidied up, cleared—For instance, let's say, tear all the old buildings down and this house, which is no good any more, and cut down the old cherry orchard—

LYUBOFF ANDREEVNA   Cut down? My dear, forgive me, you don't understand at all. If there's one thing in the whole province that's interesting—not to say remarkable—it's our cherry orchard.

LOPAHIN   The only remarkable thing about this cherry orchard is that it's very big. There's a crop of cherries once every two years and even that's hard to get rid of. Nobody buys them.

GAYEFF   This orchard is even mentioned in the encyclopedia.

LOPAHIN   (*glancing at his watch*)   If we don't cook up something and don't get somewhere, the cherry orchard and the entire estate will be sold at auction on the twenty-second of August. Do get it settled then! I swear there is no other way out. Not a one!

FIERS   There was a time, forty-fifty years ago when the cherries were dried, soaked, pickled, cooked into jam and it used to be—

GAYEFF   Keep quiet, Fiers.

FIERS   And it used to be that the dried cherries were shipped by the wagon-load to Moscow and to Kharkov. And the money there was! And the dried cherries were soft then, juicy, sweet, fragrant—They had a way of treating them then—

LYUBOFF ANDREEVNA   And where is that way now?

FIERS   They have forgotten it. Nobody remembers it.

PISHTCHIK   (*to* LYUBOFF ANDREEVNA)   What's happening in Paris? How is everything? Did you eat frogs?

LYUBOFF ANDREEVNA   I ate crocodiles.

PISHTCHIK   Think of it—!

LOPAHIN   Up to now in the country there have been only the gentry and the peasants, but now in summer the villa people too are coming in. All the towns, even the least big ones, are surrounded with cottages. In about twenty years very likely the summer resident will multiply enormously. He merely drinks tea on the porch now, but it might well happen that on this two-and-a-half acre lot of his, he'll go in for farming, and then your cherry orchard would be happy, rich, splendid—

GAYEFF (*getting hot*) What rot!

(VARYA *and* YASHA *enter.*)

VARYA Here, Mama. Two telegrams for you. (*Choosing a key and opening the old bookcase noisily.*) Here they are.

LYUBOFF ANDREEVNA From Paris. (*Tearing up the telegrams without reading them.*) Paris, that's all over—

GAYEFF Do you know how old this bookcase is, Lyuba? A week ago I pulled out the bottom drawer and looked, and there the figures were burned on it. The bookcase was made exactly a hundred years ago. How's that? Eh? You might celebrate its jubilee. It's an inanimate object, but all the same, be that as it may, it's a bookcase.

PISHTCHIK (*in astonishment*) A hundred years—! Think of it—!

GAYEFF Yes—quite something— (*Shaking the bookcase.*) Dear, honored bookcase! I saluted your existence, which for more than a hundred years has been directed toward the clear ideals of goodness and justice; your silent appeal to fruitful endeavor has not flagged in all the course of a hundred years, sustaining (*tearfully.*) through the generations of our family, our courage and our faith in a better future and nurturing in us ideals of goodness and of a social consciousness.

(*A pause.*)

LOPAHIN Yes.

LYUBOFF ANDREEVNA You're the same as ever, Lenya.

GAYEFF (*slightly embarrassed*) Carom to the right into the corner pocket. I cut into the side pocket!

LOPAHIN (*glancing at his watch*) Well, it's time for me to go.

YASHA (*handing medicine to* LYUBOFF ANDREEVNA) Perhaps you'll take the pills now—

PISHTCHIK You should never take medicaments, dear madam— They do neither harm nor good—Hand them here, dearest lady. (*He takes the pillbox, shakes the pills out into his palm, blows on them, puts them in his mouth and washes them down with kvass.*) There! Now!

LYUBOFF ANDREEVNA (*startled*) Why, you've lost your mind!

PISHTCHIK   I took all the pills.

LOPAHIN   Such a glutton! (*Everyone laughs.*)

FIERS   The gentleman stayed with us during Holy Week, he ate half a bucket of pickles— (*Muttering.*)

LYUBOFF ANDREEVNA   What is he muttering about?

VARYA   He's been muttering like that for three years. We're used to it.

YASHA   In his dotage.

(CHARLOTTA IVANOVNA *in a white dress—she is very thin, her corset laced very tight—with a lorgnette at her belt, crosses the stage.*)

LOPAHIN   Excuse me, Charlotta Ivanovna, I haven't had a chance yet to welcome you. (*Trying to kiss her hand.*)

CHARLOTTA (*drawing her hand away*)   If I let you kiss my hand, 'twould be my elbow next, then my shoulder—

LOPAHIN   No luck for me today. (*Everyone laughs.*) Charlotta Ivanovna, show us a trick!

CHARLOTTA   No. I want to go to bed.

(*She goes out.*)

LOPAHIN   In three weeks we shall see each other. (*Kissing* LYUBOFF ANDREEVNA's *hand.*) Till then, good-by. It's time. (*To* GAYEFF.) See you soon. (*Kissing* PISHTCHIK.) See you soon. (*Shaking* VARYA's *hand, then* FIER's *and* YASHA's.) I don't feel like going. (*To* LYUBOFF ANDREEVNA.) If you think it over and make up your mind about the summer cottages, let me know and I'll arrange a loan of something like fifty thousand roubles. Think it over seriously.

VARYA (*angrily*)   Do go on, anyhow, will you!

LOPAHIN   I'm going, I'm going—

(*He goes out.*)

GAYEFF   Boor. However, pardon—Varya is going to marry him, it's Varya's little fiancé.

VARYA   Don't talk too much, Uncle.

LYUBOFF ANDREEVNA   Well, Varya, I should be very glad. He's a good man.

PISHTCHIK   A man, one must say truthfully—A most worthy— And my Dashenka—says also that—she says all sorts of things— (*Snoring but immediately waking up.*) Nevertheless, dearest lady, oblige me—With a loan of two hundred and forty roubles—To-morrow the interest on my mortgage has got to be paid—

VARYA (*startled*)   There's not any money, none at all.

LYUBOFF ANDREEVNA   Really, I haven't got anything.

PISHTCHIK I'll find it, somehow. (*Laughing.*) I never give up hope. There, I think to myself, all is lost, I am ruined and lo and behold—a railroad is put through my land and—they paid me. And then, just watch, something else will turn up—if not today, then tomorrow—Dashenka will win two hundred thousand—She has a ticket.

LYUBOFF ANDREEVNA We've finished the coffee, now we can go to bed.

FIERS (*brushing* GAYEFF's *clothes, reprovingly*) You put on the wrong trousers again. What am I going to do with you!

VARYA (*softly*) Anya is asleep. (*Opening the window softly.*) Already the sun's rising—it's not cold. Look, Mama! What beautiful trees! My Lord, what air! The starlings are singing!

GAYEFF (*opening another window*) The orchard is all white. You haven't forgotten, Lyuba? That long lane there runs straight— as a strap stretched out. It glistens on moonlight nights. Do you remember? You haven't forgotten it?

LYUBOFF ANDREEVNA (*looking out of the window on to the orchard*) Oh, my childhood, my innocence! I slept in this nursery and looked out on the orchard from here, every morning happiness awoke with me, it was just as it is now, then, nothing has changed. (*Laughing with joy.*) All, all white! Oh, my orchard! After a dark, rainy autumn and cold winter, you are young again and full of happiness. The heavenly angels have not deserted you—If I only could lift the weight from my breast, from my shoulders, if I could only forget my past!

GAYEFF Yes, and the orchard will be sold for debt, strange as that may seem.

LYUBOFF ANDREEVNA Look, our dear mother is walking through the orchard—In a white dress! (*Laughing happily.*) It's she.

GAYEFF Where?

VARYA God be with you, Mama!

LYUBOFF ANDREEVNA There's not anybody, it only seemed so. To the right, as you turn to the summerhouse, a little white tree is leaning there, looks like a woman— (TROFIMOFF *enters, in a student's uniform, well worn, and glasses.*) What a wonderful orchard! The white masses of blossoms, the sky all blue.

TROFIMOFF Lyuboff Andreevna! (*She looks around at him.*) I will just greet you and go immediately. (*Kissing her hand warmly.*) I was told to wait until morning, but I hadn't the patience—

(LYUBOFF ANDREEVNA *looks at him puzzled.*)

VARYA (*tearfully*) This is Petya Trofimoff—

TROFIMOFF   Petya Trofimoff, the former tutor of your Grisha—
Have I really changed so?

(LYUBOFF ANDREEVNA *embraces him, crying quietly.*)

GAYEFF   (*embarrassed*)   There, there, Lyuba.

VARYA   (*crying*)   I told you, Petya, to wait till tomorrow.

LYUBOFF ANDREEVNA   My Grisha—My boy—Grisha—Son—

VARYA   What can we do, Mama? It's God's will.

TROFIMOFF   (*in a low voice tearfully*)   There, there—

LYUBOFF ANDREEVNA   (*weeping softly*)   My boy was lost, drowned—
Why? Why, my friend? (*More quietly.*) Anya is asleep there, and
I am talking so loud—Making so much noise—But why, Petya?
Why have you lost your looks? Why do you look so much older?

TROFIMOFF   A peasant woman on the train called me a mangy-
looking gentleman.

LYUBOFF ANDREEVNA   You were a mere boy then, a charming
young student, and now your hair's not very thick any more and
you wear glasses. Are you really a student still? (*Going to the
door.*)

TROFIMOFF   Very likely I'll be a perennial student.

LYUBOFF ANDREEVNA   (*kissing her brother, then* VARYA)   Well, go
to bed—You've grown older too, Leonid.

PISHTCHIK   (*following her*)   So that's it, we are going to bed now.
Oh, my gout! I'm staying here—I'd like, Lyuboff Andreevna, my
soul, tomorrow morning—Two hundred and forty roubles—

GAYEFF   He's still at it.

PISHTCHIK   Two hundred and forty roubles—To pay interest on
the mortgage.

LYUBOFF ANDREEVNA   I haven't any money, my dove.

PISHTCHIK   I'll pay it back, my dear—It's a trifling sum—

LYUBOFF ANDREEVNA   Oh, very well, Leonid will give—You give it
to him, Leonid.

GAYEFF   Oh, certainly, I'll give it to him. Hold out your pockets.

LYUBOFF ANDREEVNA   What can we do, give it, he needs it—He'll
pay it back.

(LYUBOFF ANDREEVNA, TROFIMOFF, PISHTCHIK *and* FIERS *go out.*
GAYEFF, VARYA *and* YASHA *remain.*)

GAYEFF   My sister hasn't yet lost her habit of throwing money away.
(*To* YASHA.) Get away, my good fellow, you smell like hens.

YASHA   (*with a grin*)   And you are just the same as you used to be,
Leonid Andreevich.

GAYEFF   What? (*To* VARYA.) What did he say?

VARYA (*to* YASHA) Your mother has come from the village, she's been sitting in the servants' hall ever since yesterday, she wants to see you—

YASHA The devil take her!

VARYA Ach, shameless creature!

YASHA A lot I need her! She might have come tomorrow.

(*Goes out.*)

VARYA Mama is just the same as she was, she hasn't changed at all. If she could, she'd give away everything she has.

GAYEFF Yes—If many remedies are prescribed for an illness, you may know the illness is incurable. I keep thinking, I wrack my brains, I have many remedies, a great many, and that means, really, I haven't any at all. It would be fine to inherit a fortune from somebody, it would be fine to marry off our Anya to a very rich man, it would be fine to go to Yaroslavl and try our luck with our old aunt, the Countess. Auntie is very, very rich.

VARYA (*crying*) If God would only help us!

GAYEFF Don't bawl! Auntie is very rich but she doesn't like us. To begin with, Sister married a lawyer, not a nobleman— (ANYA *appears at the door.*) Married not a nobleman and behaved herself, you could say, not very virtuously. She is good, kind, nice, I love her very much, but no matter how much you allow for the extenuating circumstances, you must admit she's a depraved woman. You feel it in her slightest movement.

VARYA (*whispering*) Anya is standing in the door there.

GAYEFF What? (*A pause.*) It's amazing, something got in my right eye. I am beginning to see poorly. And on Thursday, when I was in the District Court—

(ANYA *enters.*)

VARYA But why aren't you asleep, Anya?

ANYA I don't feel like sleeping. I can't.

GAYEFF My little girl— (*Kissing* ANYA's *face and hands.*) My child— (*Tearfully.*) You are not my niece, you are my angel, you are everything to me. Believe me, believe—

ANYA I believe you, Uncle. Everybody loves you, respects you— But dear Uncle, you must keep quiet, just keep quiet—What were you saying, just now, about my mother, about your own sister? What did you say that for?

GAYEFF Yes, yes— (*Putting her hand up over his face.*) Really, it's terrible! My God! Oh, God, save me! And today I made a speech to the bookcase—So silly! And it was only when I finished it that I could see it was silly.

VARYA   It's true, Uncle, you ought to keep quiet. Just keep quiet. That's all.

ANYA   If you kept quiet, you'd have more peace.

GAYEFF   I'll keep quiet. (*Kissing* ANYA's *and* VARYA's *hands.*) I'll keep quiet. Only this, it's about business. On Thursday I was in the District Court; well, a few of us gathered around and a conversation began about this and that, about lots of things; apparently it will be possible to arrange a loan on a promissory note to pay the bank the interest due.

VARYA   If the Lord would only help us!

GAYEFF   Tuesday I shall go and talk it over again. (*To* VARYA.) Don't bawl! (*To* ANYA.) Your mother will talk to Lopahin; of course, he won't refuse her ... And as soon as you rest up, you will go to Yaroslavl to your great-aunt, the Countess. There, that's how we will move from three directions, and the business is in the bag. We'll pay the interest. I am convinced of that— (*Putting a hard candy in his mouth.*) On my honor I'll swear, by anything you like, that the estate shall not be sold! (*Excitedly.*) By my happiness, I swear! Here's my hand, call me a worthless, dishonorable man, if I allow it to come up for auction! With all my soul I swear it!

ANYA   (*A quieter mood returns to her; she is happy*)   How good you are, Uncle, how clever! (*Embracing her uncle.*) I feel easy now! I feel easy! I'm happy!

FIERS   (*enters, reproachfully*)   Leonid Andreevich, have you no fear of God! When are you going to bed?

GAYEFF   Right away, right away. You may go, Fiers. For this once I'll undress myself. Well, children, beddy bye—More details tomorrow, and now, go to bed (*kissing* ANYA *and* VARYA). I am a man of the eighties—It is a period that's not admired, but I can say, nevertheless, that I've suffered no little for my convictions in the course of my life. It is not for nothing that the peasant loves me. One must know the peasant! One must know from what—

ANYA   Again, Uncle!

VARYA   You, Uncle dear, keep quiet.

FIERS   (*angrily*)   Leonid Andreevich!

GAYEFF   I'm coming, I'm coming—Go to bed. A double bank into the side pocket! A clean shot—

(*Goes out,* FIERS *hobbling after him.*)

ANYA   I feel easy now. I don't feel like going to Yaroslavl; I don't like Great-aunt, but still I feel easy. Thanks to Uncle. (*Sits down.*)

VARYA   I must get to sleep. I'm going. And there was unpleasantness here during your absence. In the old servants' quarters, as you know, live only the old servants: Yephemushka, Polya, Yevstignay, well, and Karp. They began to let every sort of creature spend the night with them—I didn't say anything. But then I hear they've spread the rumor that I'd given orders to feed them nothing but beans. Out of stinginess, you see—And all that from Yevstignay—Very well, I think to myself. If that's the way it is, I think to myself, then you just wait. I call in Yevstignay— (*Yawning.*) He comes—How is it, I say, that you, Yevstignay— You're such a fool— (*Glancing at* ANYA.) Anitchka!— (*A pause.*) Asleep! (*Takes* ANYA *by her arm.*) Let's go to bed—Come on!— (*Leading her.*) My little darling fell asleep! Come on— (*They go. Far away beyond the orchard a shepherd is playing on a pipe.* TROFIMOFF *walks across the stage and, seeing* VARYA *and* ANYA, *stops.*) Shh—She is asleep—asleep—Let's go, dear.

ANYA (*softly, half dreaming*) I'm so tired—All the bells!—Uncle —dear—And Mama and Uncle—Varya.

VARYA Come on, my dear, come on. (*They go into* ANYA's *room.*)

TROFIMOFF (*tenderly*) My little sun! My spring!

ACT II

A field. An old chapel, long abandoned, with crooked walls, near it a well, big stones that apparently were once tombstones, and an old bench. A road to the estate of GAYEFF *can be seen. On one side poplars rise, casting their shadows, the cherry orchard begins there. In the distance a row of telegraph poles; and far, far away, faintly traced on the horizon, is a large town, visible only in the clearest weather. The sun will soon be down.* CHARLOTTA, YASHA *and* DUNYASHA *are sitting on the bench;* EPIHODOFF *is standing near and playing the guitar; everyone sits lost in thought.* CHARLOTTA *wears an old peak cap [fourrage];[1] she has taken a rifle from off her shoulders and is adjusting the buckle on the strap.*

CHARLOTTA (*pensively*) I have no proper passport, I don't know how old I am—it always seems to me I'm very young. When I was a little girl, my father and mother traveled from fair to fair and gave performances, very good ones. And I did *salto mortale*[2] and different tricks. And when Papa and Mama died, a German lady took me to live with her and began teaching me. Good. I grew up. And became a governess. But where I came from and who I am I don't know—Who my parents were, perhaps they weren't even married—I don't know. (*Taking a cucumber out of her pocket and beginning to eat it.*) I don't know a thing. (*A*

---

[1] *fourrage* for hunting
[2] *salto mortale* leap of death

pause.) I'd like so much to talk but there's not anybody. I haven't anybody.

EPIHODOFF (*playing the guitar and singing*) "What care I for the noisy world, what care I for friends and foes."—How pleasant it is to play the mandolin!

DUNYASHA That's a guitar, not a mandolin. (*Looking into a little mirror and powdering her face.*)

EPIHODOFF For a madman who is in love this is a mandolin— (*Singing.*) "If only my heart were warm with the fire of requited love." (*Yasha sings with him.*)

CHARLOTTA How dreadfully these people sing—Phooey! Like jack-als.

DUNYASHA (*to* YASHA) All the same what happiness to have been abroad.

YASHA Yes, of course. I cannot disagree with you. (*Yawning and then lighting a cigar.*)

EPIHODOFF That's easily understood. Abroad everything long since attained its complete development.

YASHA That's obvious.

EPIHODOFF I am a cultured man. I read all kinds of remarkable books, but the trouble is I cannot discover my own inclinations, whether to live or to shoot myself, but nevertheless, I always carry a revolver on me. Here it is— (*Showing a revolver.*)

CHARLOTTA That's done. Now I am going. (*Slinging the rifle over her shoulder.*) You are a very clever man, Epihodoff, and a very terrible one; the women must love you madly. Brrrr-r-r-r! (*Going.*) These clever people are all so silly, I haven't anybody to talk with. I'm always alone, alone, I have nobody and—Who I am, why I am, is unknown—

(*Goes out without hurrying.*)

EPIHODOFF Strictly speaking, not touching on other subjects, I must state about myself, in passing, that fate treats me merci-lessly, as a storm does a small ship. If, let us suppose, I am mis-taken, then why, to mention one instance, do I wake up this morning, look and there on my chest is a spider of terrific size— There, like that. (*Showing the size with both hands.*) And also I take some kvass to drink and in it I find something in the high-est degree indecent, such as a cockroach. (*A pause.*) Have you read Buckle? [1] (*A pause.*) I desire to trouble you, Avdotya Feo-dorovna, with a couple of words.

---

[1] *Buckle* Henry Thomas Buckle (1821–1862), English historian who pro-posed a scientific method for writing history

DUNYASHA   Speak.

EPIHODOFF   I have a desire to speak with you alone— (*Sighing.*)

DUNYASHA (*embarrassed*)   Very well—But bring me my cape first —by the cupboard—It's rather damp here—

EPIHODOFF   Very well—I'll fetch it—Now I know what I should do with my revolver— (*Takes the guitar and goes out playing.*)

YASHA   Twenty-two misfortunes! Between us he's a stupid man, it must be said. (*Yawning.*)

DUNYASHA   God forbid he should shoot himself. (*A pause.*) I've grown so uneasy, I'm always fretting. I was only a girl when I was taken into the master's house, and now I've lost the habit of simple living—and here are my hands white, white as a lady's. I've become so delicate, fragile, ladylike, afraid of everything— Frightfully so. And, Yasha, if you deceive me, I don't know what will happen to my nerves.

YASHA (*kissing her*)   You little cucumber! Of course every girl must behave properly. What I dislike above everything is for a girl to conduct herself badly.

DUNYASHA   I have come to love you passionately, you are educated, you can discuss anything. (*A pause.*)

YASHA (*yawning*)   Yes, sir—To my mind it is like this: If a girl loves someone, it means she is immoral. (*A pause.*) It is pleasant to smoke a cigar in the clear air— (*Listening.*) They are coming here—It is the ladies and gentlemen— (DUNYASHA *impulsively embraces him.*)

YASHA   Go to the house, as though you had been to bathe in the river, go by this path, otherwise, they might meet you and suspect me of making a rendezvous with you. That I cannot tolerate.

DUNYASHA (*with a little cough*)   Your cigar has given me the headache.

(*Goes out.*)

(YASHA *remains, sitting near the chapel.* LYUBOFF ANDREEVNA, GAYEFF *and* LOPAHIN *enter.*)

LOPAHIN   We must decide definitely, time doesn't wait. Why, the matter's quite simple. Are you willing to lease your land for summer cottages or are you not? Answer in one word, yes or no? Just one word!

LYUBOFF ANDREEVNA   Who is it smokes those disgusting cigars out here—? (*Sitting down.*)

GAYEFF   The railroad running so near is a great convenience. (*Sitting down.*) We made a trip to town and lunched there—Yellow in the side pocket! Perhaps I should go in the house first and play one game—

LYUBOFF ANDREEVNA You'll have time.

LOPAHIN Just one word! (*Imploringly.*) Do give me your answer!

GAYEFF (*yawning*) What?

LYUBOFF ANDREEVNA (*looking in her purse*) Yesterday there was lots of money in it. Today there's very little. My poor Varya! For the sake of economy she feeds everybody milk soup, and in the kitchen the old people get nothing but beans, and here I spend money—senselessly— (*Dropping her purse and scattering gold coins.*) There they go scattering! (*She is vexed.*)

YASHA Allow me, I'll pick them up in a second. (*Picking up the coins.*)

LYUBOFF ANDREEVNA If you will, Yasha. And why did I go in town for lunch—? Your restaurant with its music is trashy, the tablecloths smell of soap—Why drink so much, Lyonya? Why eat so much? Why talk so much? Today in the restaurant you were talking a lot again, and all of it beside the point. About the seventies, about the decadents. And to whom? Talking to waiters about the decadents!

LOPAHIN Yes.

GAYEFF (*waving his hand*) I am incorrigible, that's evident— (*To* YASHA *irritably.*) What is it?—You are forever swirling around in front of us!

YASHA (*laughing*) I cannot hear your voice without laughing.

GAYEFF (*to his sister*) Either I or he—

LYUBOFF ANDREEVNA Go away, Yasha. Go on—

YASHA (*giving* LYUBOFF ANDREEVNA *her purse*) I am going right away. (*Barely suppressing his laughter.*) This minute.

(*Goes out.*)

LOPAHIN The rich Deriganoff intends to buy your estate. They say he is coming personally to the auction.

LYUBOFF ANDREEVNA And where did you hear that?

LOPAHIN In town they are saying it.

GAYEFF Our Yaroslavl aunt promised to send us something, but when and how much she will send, nobody knows—

LOPAHIN How much will she send? A hundred thousand? Two hundred?

LYUBOFF ANDREEVNA Well—maybe ten, fifteen thousand—we'd be thankful for that.

LOPAHIN Excuse me, but such light-minded people as you are, such odd, unbusinesslike people, I never saw. You are told in plain Russian that your estate is being sold up and you just don't seem to take it in.

LYUBOFF ANDREEVNA But what are we to do? Tell us what?

LOPAHIN   I tell you every day. Every day I tell you the same thing. Both the cherry orchard and the land have got to be leased for summer cottages, it has to be done right now, quick—The auction is right under your noses. Do understand! Once you finally decide that there are to be summer cottages, you will get all the money you want, and then you'll be saved.

LYUBOFF ANDREEVNA   Summer cottages and summer residents—it is so trivial, excuse me.

GAYEFF   I absolutely agree with you.

LOPAHIN   I'll either burst out crying, or scream, or faint. I can't bear it! You are torturing me! (*To* GAYEFF.) You're a perfect old woman!

GAYEFF   What?

LOPAHIN   A perfect old woman! (*About to go.*)

LYUBOFF ANDREEVNA (*alarmed*)   No, don't go, stay, my lamb, I beg you. Perhaps we will think of something!

LOPAHIN   What is there to think about?

LYUBOFF ANDREEVNA   Don't go, I beg you. With you here it is more cheerful anyhow— (*A pause.*) I keep waiting for something, as if the house were about to tumble down on our heads.

GAYEFF (*deep in thought*)   Double into the corner pocket—Bank into the wide pocket—

LYUBOFF ANDREEVNA   We have sinned so much—

LOPAHIN   What sins have you—?

GAYEFF (*puts a hard candy into his mouth*)   They say I've eaten my fortune up in hard candies— (*Laughing.*)

LYUBOFF ANDREEVNA   Oh, my sins—I've always thrown money around like mad, recklessly, and I married a man who accumulated nothing but debts. My husband died from champagne—he drank fearfully—and to my misfortune I fell in love with another man. I lived with him, and just at that time—it was my first punishment—a blow over the head: right here in the river my boy was drowned and I went abroad—went away for good, never to return, never to see this river again—I shut my eyes, ran away, beside myself, and he after me—mercilessly, brutally. I bought a villa near Mentone, because he fell ill there, and for three years I knew no rest day or night, the sick man exhausted me, my soul dried up. And last year when the villa was sold for debts, I went to Paris and there he robbed me of everything, threw me over, took up with another woman; I tried to poison myself—so stupid, so shameful—And suddenly I was seized with longing for Russia, for my own country, for my little girl— (*Wiping away her tears.*) Lord, Lord, have mercy, forgive me my sins! Don't punish me any more! (*Getting a telegram out of her pocket.*) I got this to-day from Paris, he asks forgiveness, begs me to return— (*Tears up the telegram.*) That sounds like music somewhere.

(*Listening.*)

GAYEFF   It is our famous Jewish orchestra. You remember, four violins, a flute and double bass.

LYUBOFF ANDREEVNA   Does it still exist? We ought to get hold of it sometime and give a party.

LOPAHIN (*listening*)   Can't hear it— (*Singing softly.*) "And for money the Germans will frenchify a Russian." (*Laughing.*) What a play I saw yesterday at the theatre, very funny!

LYUBOFF ANDREEVNA   And most likely there was nothing funny about it. You shouldn't look at plays, but look oftener at your-selves. How gray all your lives are, what a lot of idle things you say!

LOPAHIN   That's true. It must be said frankly this life of ours is idiotic— (*A pause.*) My father was a peasant, an idiot, he under-stood nothing, he taught me nothing, he just beat me in his drunken fits and always with a stick. At bottom I am just as big a dolt and idiot as he was. I wasn't taught anything, my hand-writing is vile, I write like a pig—I am ashamed for people to see it.

LYUBOFF ANDREEVNA   You ought to get married, my friend.

LOPAHIN   Yes—That's true.

LYUBOFF ANDREEVNA   To our Varya, perhaps. She is a good girl.

LOPAHIN   Yes.

LYUBOFF ANDREEVNA   She comes from simple people, and she works all day long, but the main thing is she loves you. And you, too, have liked her a long time.

LOPAHIN   Why not? I am not against it—She's a good girl. (*A pause.*)

GAYEFF   They are offering me a position in a bank. Six thousand a year—Have you heard that?

LYUBOFF ANDREEVNA   Not you! You stay where you are—

(FIERS *enters, bringing an overcoat.*)

FIERS (*to* GAYEFF)   Pray, Sir, put this on, it's damp.

GAYEFF (*putting on the overcoat*)   You're a pest, old man.

FIERS   That's all right—This morning you went off without letting me know. (*Looking him over.*)

LYUBOFF ANDREEVNA   How old you've grown, Fiers!

FIERS   At your service.

LOPAHIN   She says you've grown very old!

FIERS   I've lived a long time. They were planning to marry me off before your papa was born. (*Laughing.*) And at the time the serfs were freed I was already the head footman. I didn't want to be freed then, I stayed with the masters— (*A pause.*) And I remember, everybody was happy, but what they were happy about they didn't know themselves.

LOPAHIN   In the old days it was fine. At least they flogged.

FIERS (*not hearing*)   But, of course. The peasants stuck to the masters, the masters stuck to the peasants, and now everything is all smashed up, you can't tell about anything.

GAYEFF   Keep still, Fiers. Tomorrow I must go to town. They have promised to introduce me to a certain general who might make us a loan.

LOPAHIN   Nothing will come of it. And you can rest assured you won't pay the interest.

LYUBOFF ANDREEVNA   He's just raving on. There aren't any such generals.

(TROFIMOFF, ANYA *and* VARYA *enter.*)

GAYEFF   Here they come.

ANYA   There is Mama sitting there.

LYUBOFF ANDREEVNA (*tenderly*)   Come, come—My darlings— (*Embracing* ANYA *and* VARYA.) If you only knew how I love you both! Come sit by me—there—like that.

(*Everybody sits down.*)

LOPAHIN   Our perennial student is always strolling with the young ladies.

TROFIMOFF   It's none of your business.

LOPAHIN   He will soon be fifty and he's still a student.

TROFIMOFF   Stop your stupid jokes.

LOPAHIN   But why are you so peevish, you queer duck?

TROFIMOFF   Don't you pester me.

LOPAHIN (*laughing*)   Permit me to ask you, what do you make of me?

TROFIMOFF   Yermolay Alexeevich, I make this of you: you are a rich man, you'll soon be a millionaire. Just as it is in the metabolism of nature, a wild beast is needed to eat up everything that comes his way; so you, too, are needed.

(*Everyone laughs.*)

VARYA   Petya, you'd better tell us about the planets.

LYUBOFF ANDREEVNA   No, let's go on with yesterday's conversation.

TROFIMOFF   What was it about?

GAYEFF   About the proud man.

TROFIMOFF   We talked a long time yesterday, but didn't get anywhere. In a proud man, in your sense of the word, there is something mystical. Maybe you are right, from your standpoint, but
if we are to discuss it in simple terms, without whimsy, then what
pride can there be, is there any sense in it, if man physiologically
is poorly constructed, if in the great majority he is crude, unintel-
ligent, profoundly miserable. One must stop admiring oneself.
One must only work.

GAYEFF   All the same, you will die.

TROFIMOFF   Who knows? And what does it mean—you will die?
Man may have a hundred senses, and when he dies only the five
that are known to us may perish, and the remaining ninety-five
go on living.

LYUBOFF ANDREEVNA   How clever you are, Petya!

LOPAHIN (*ironically*)   Terribly!

TROFIMOFF   Humanity goes forward, perfecting its powers. Everything that's unattainable now will some day become familiar, understandable; it is only that one must work and must help with
all one's might those who seek the truth. With us in Russia so far
only a very few work. The great majority of the intelligentsia that
I know are looking for nothing, doing nothing, and as yet have
no capacity for work. They call themselves intelligentsia, are free
and easy with the servants, treat the peasants like animals, edu-
cate themselves poorly, read nothing seriously, do absolutely nothing; about science they just talk and about art they understand
very little. Every one of them is serious, all have stern faces; they
all talk of nothing but important things, philosophize, and all the
time everybody can see that the workmen eat abominably, sleep
without any pillows, thirty or forty to a room, and everywhere
there are bedbugs, stench, dampness, moral uncleanness—And
apparently with us, all the fine talk is only to divert the attention
of ourselves and of others. Show me where we have the day
nurseries they are always talking so much about, where are the
reading rooms? They only write of these in novels, for the truth
is there are not any at all. There is only filth, vulgarity, orien-
talism—I am afraid of very serious faces and dislike them. I'm
afraid of serious conversations. Rather than that let's just keep
still.

LOPAHIN   You know I get up before five o'clock in the morning
and work from morning till night. Well, I always have money,
my own and other people's, on hand, and I see what the people
around me are. One has only to start doing something to find

out how few honest and decent people there are. At times when I can't go to sleep, I think: Lord, thou gavest us immense forests, unbounded fields and the widest horizons, and living in the midst of them we should indeed be giants—

LYUBOFF ANDREEVNA   You feel the need for giants—They are good only in fairly tales, anywhere else they only frighten us.

(*At the back of the stage* EPIHODOFF *passes by, playing the guitar.*)

LYUBOFF ANDREEVNA (*lost in thought*)   Epihodoff is coming—
ANYA (*lost in thought*)   Epihodoff is coming.
GAYEFF   The sun has set, ladies and gentlemen.
TROFIMOFF   Yes.
GAYEFF (*not loud and as if he were declaiming*)   Oh, Nature, wonderful, you gleam with eternal radiance, beautiful and indifferent, you, whom we call Mother, combine in yourself both life and death, you give life and you take it away.
VARYA (*beseechingly*)   Uncle!
ANYA   Uncle, you're doing it again!
TROFIMOFF   You'd better bank the yellow into the side pocket.
GAYEFF   I'll be quiet, quiet.

(*All sit absorbed in their thoughts. There is only the silence.* FIERS *is heard muttering to himself softly. Suddenly a distant sound is heard, as if from the sky, like the sound of a snapped string, dying away, mournful.*)

LYUBOFF ANDREEVNA   What's that?
LOPAHIN   I don't know. Somewhere far off in a mine shaft a bucket fell. But somewhere very far off.
GAYEFF   And it may be some bird—like a heron.
TROFIMOFF   Or an owl—
LYUBOFF ANDREEVNA (*shivering*)   It's unpleasant, somehow. (*A pause.*)
FIERS   Before the disaster it was like that. The owl hooted and the samovar hummed without stopping, both.
GAYEFF   Before what disaster?
FIERS   Before the emancipation.

(*A pause.*)

LYUBOFF ANDREEVNA   You know, my friends, let's go. Twilight is falling. (*To* ANYA.) You have tears in your eyes—What is it, my dear little girl? (*Embracing her.*)
ANYA   It's just that, Mama. It's nothing.
TROFIMOFF   Somebody is coming.

(A stranger appears in a shabby white cap, and an overcoat; he is a little drunk.)

THE STRANGER Allow me to ask you, can I go straight through here to the station?

GAYEFF You can. Go by that road.

THE STRANGER I am heartily grateful to you. *(Coughing.)* The weather is splendid— *(Declaiming.)* Brother of mine, suffering brother—Go out to the Volga, whose moans— *(To* VARYA.*)* Mademoiselle, grant a hungry Russian man some thirty kopecks— *(*VARYA *is frightened and gives a shriek.)*

LOPAHIN *(angrily)* There's a limit to everything.

LYUBOFF ANDREEVNA *(flustered)* Take this—Here's this for you— *(Searching in her purse.)* No silver—It's all the same, here's a gold piece for you—

THE STRANGER I am heartily grateful to you.

(Goes out.)

(Laughter.)

VARYA *(frightened)* I'm going—I'm going—Oh, Mama, you poor little Mama! There's nothing in the house for people to eat, and you gave him a gold piece.

LYUBOFF ANDREEVNA What is to be done with me, so silly? I shall give you all I have in the house. Yermolay Alexeevich, you will lend me some this once more!—

LOPAHIN Agreed.

LYUBOFF ANDREEVNA Let's go, ladies and gentlemen, it's time. And here, Varya, we have definitely made a match for you, I congratulate you.

VARYA *(through her tears)* Mama, that's not something to joke about.

LOPAHIN Achmelia, get thee to a nunnery.[1]

GAYEFF And my hands are trembling; it is a long time since I have played billiards.

LOPAHIN Achmelia, Oh nymph, in thine orisons be all my sins remember'd—[2]

LYUBOFF ANDREEVNA Let's go, my dear friends, it will soon be suppertime.

VARYA He frightened me. My heart is thumping so!

---

[1] *Achmelia . . . nunnery* Shakespeare, *Hamlet,* III.i.139 ff.
[2] *Achmelia . . . remember'd Hamlet,* III.i.88 ff.

LOPAHIN   I remind you, ladies and gentlemen: August 22nd the cherry orchard will be auctioned off. Think about that!— Think!—

(*All go out except* TROFIMOFF *and* ANYA.)

ANYA (*laughing*)   My thanks to the stranger, he frightened Varya, now we are alone.

TROFIMOFF   Varya is afraid we might begin to love each other and all day long she won't leave us to ourselves. With her narrow mind she cannot understand that we are above love. To sidestep the petty and illusory, which prevent our being free and happy, that is the aim and meaning of our life. Forward! We march on irresistibly toward the bright star that burns there in the distance. Forward! Do not fall behind, friends!

ANYA (*extending her arms upward*)   How well you talk! (*A pause.*) It's wonderful here today!

TROFIMOFF   Yes, the weather is marvelous.

ANYA   What have you done to me, Petya, why don't I love the cherry orchard any longer the way I used to? I loved it so tenderly, it seemed to me there was not a better place on earth than our orchard.

TROFIMOFF   All Russia is our orchard. The earth is immense and beautiful, and on it are many wonderful places. (*A pause.*) Just think, Anya: your grandfather, great-grandfather and all your ancestors were slave owners, in possession of living souls, and can you doubt that from every cherry in the orchard, from every leaf, from every trunk, human beings are looking at you, can it be that you don't hear their voices? To possess living souls, well, that depraved all of you who lived before and who are living now, so that your mother and you, and your uncle no longer notice that you live by debt, at somebody else's expense, at the expense of those very people whom you wouldn't let past your front door— We are at least two hundred years behind the times, we have as yet absolutely nothing, we have no definite attitude toward the past, we only philosophize, complain of our sadness or drink vodka. Why, it is quite clear that to begin to live in the present we must first atone for our past, must be done with it; and we can atone for it only through suffering, only through uncommon, incessant labor. Understand that, Anya.

ANYA   The house we live in ceased to be ours long ago, and I'll go away, I give you my word.

TROFIMOFF   If you have the household keys, throw them in the well and go away. Be free as the wind.

ANYA (*transported*)   How well you said that!

TROFIMOFF   Believe me, Anya, believe me! I am not thirty yet, I am young, I am still a student, but I have already borne so much! Every winter I am hungry, sick, anxious, poor as a beggar, and— where has destiny not chased me, where haven't I been! And yet, my soul has always, every minute, day and night, been full of inexplicable premonitions. I have a premonition of happiness, Anya, I see it already—

ANYA (*pensively*)   The moon is rising.

(EPIHODOFF *is heard playing on the guitar, always the same sad song. The moon rises. Somewhere near the poplars* VARYA *is looking for* ANYA *and calling:* "ANYA! *Where are you?"*)

TROFIMOFF   Yes, the moon is rising. (*A pause.*) Here is happiness, here it comes, comes always nearer and nearer, I hear its footsteps now. And if we shall not see it, shall not come to know it, what does that matter? Others will see it!

VARYA (*off*)   Anya! Where are you?

TROFIMOFF   Again, that Varya! (*Angrily.*) It's scandalous!

ANYA   Well, let's go to the river. It's lovely there.

TROFIMOFF   Let's go. (*They go out.*)

VARYA (*off*)   Anya! Anya!

ACT III

The drawing room, separated by an arch from the ballroom. A chandelier is lighted. A Jewish orchestra is playing—the same that was mentioned in Act II. Evening. In the ballroom they are dancing grand rond.[1] The voice of SEMYONOFF-PISHTCHIK: "*Promenade à une paire!*"[2] *They enter the drawing room; in the first couple are* PISHTCHIK *and* CHARLOTTA IVA-NOVNA; *in the second,* TROFIMOFF *and* LYUBOFF ANDREEVNA; *in the third,* ANYA *with the* POST-OFFICE CLERK; *in the fourth,* VARYA *with the* STA-TION-MASTER, *et cetera—*VARYA *is crying softly and wipes away her tears while she is dancing.* DUNYASHA *is in the last couple through the drawing room.* PISHTCHIK *shouts:* "*Grand rond, balancez!*"[3] *and* "*Les Cavaliers à genoux et remerciez vos dames!*"[4]

(FIERS *in a frock coat goes by with seltzer water on a tray.* PISHTCHIK *and* TROFIMOFF *come into the drawing room.*)

PISHTCHIK   I am full-blooded, I have had two strokes already, and dancing is hard for me, but as they say, if you are in a pack

---

[1] *grand rond* great circle, a dance
[2] *promenade . . . paire* promenade by single couple
[3] *balancez* a technical dance movement
[4] *Les . . . dames* "Gentlemen, kneel and thank your ladies"

of dogs, you may bark and bark, but you must still wag your tail. At that, I have the health of a horse. My dear father—he was a great joker—may he dwell in Heaven—used to talk as if our ancient line, the Semyonoff-Pishtchiks, were descended from the very horse that Caligula made a Senator— (*Sitting down.*) But here's my trouble: I haven't any money. A hungry dog believes in nothing but meat— (*Snoring but waking at once.*) And the same way with me—I can't talk about anything but money.

TROFIMOFF   Well, to tell you the truth, there is something of a horse about your figure.

PISHTCHIK   Well—a horse is a fine animal—You can sell a horse—

(*The sound of playing billiards comes from the next room.* VARYA *appears under the arch to the ballroom.*)

TROFIMOFF (*teasing*)   Madam Lopahin! Madam Lopahin!

VARYA (*angrily*)   A mangy-looking gentleman!

TROFIMOFF   Yes, I am a mangy-looking gentleman, and proud of it!

VARYA (*in bitter thought*)   Here we have gone and hired musicians and what are we going to pay them with?

(*Goes out.*)

TROFIMOFF (*to* PISHTCHIK)   If the energy you have wasted in the course of your life trying to find money to pay the interest had gone into something else, you could very likely have turned the world upside down before you were done with it.

PISHTCHIK   Nietzsche—the philosopher—the greatest—the most celebrated—a man of tremendous mind—says in his works that one may make counterfeit money.

TROFIMOFF   And have you read Nietzsche?

PISHTCHIK   Well—Dashenka told me. And I'm in such a state now that I could make counterfeit money myself— Day after tomorrow three hundred and ten roubles must be paid—one hundred and thirty I've on hand— (*Feeling in his pockets, alarmed.*) The money is gone! I have lost the money! (*Tearfully.*) Where is the money? (*Joyfully.*) Here it is, inside the lining—I was in quite a sweat—

(LYUBOFF ANDREEVNA *and* CHARLOTTA IVANOVNA *come in.*)

LYUBOFF ANDREEVNA (*humming lazginka, a Georgian dance*)   Why does Leonid take so long? What's he doing in town? (*To* DUNYASHA.) Dunyasha, offer the musicians some tea—

TROFIMOFF   In all probability the auction did not take place.

LYUBOFF ANDREEVNA   And the musicians came at an unfortunate moment and we planned the ball at an unfortunate moment— Well, it doesn't matter. (*Sitting down and singing softly.*)

CHARLOTTA (*gives* PISHTCHIK *a deck of cards*) Here is a deck of cards for you, think of some one card.

PISHTCHIK I have thought of one.

CHARLOTTA Now, shuffle the deck. Very good. Hand it here; oh, my dear Monsieur Pishtchik. *Ein, zwei, drei!* Now look for it, it's in your coat pocket—

PISHTCHIK (*getting a card out of his coat pocket*) The eight of spades, that's absolutely right! (*Amazed.*) Fancy that!

CHARLOTTA (*holding a deck of cards in her palm; to* TROFIMOFF) Tell me quick now, which card is on top?

TROFIMOFF What is it? Well—the Queen of Spades.

CHARLOTTA Right! (*To* PISHTCHIK.) Well? Which card's on top?

PISHTCHIK The Ace of Hearts.

CHARLOTTA Right! (*Strikes the deck against her palm; the deck of cards disappears.*) And what beautiful weather we are having to-day!

(*A mysterious feminine voice answers her, as if from under the floor: "Oh, yes. The weather is splendid, madame." "You are so nice, you're my ideal—" The voice: "Madame, you too please me greatly."*)

THE STATIONMASTER (*applauding*) Madam Ventriloquist, bravo!

PISHTCHIK (*amazed*) Fancy that! Most charming Charlotta Ivanovna—I am simply in love with you.

CHARLOTTA In love? (*Shrugging her shoulders.*) Is it possible that you can love? *Guter Mensch aber schlechter Musikant.*[1]

TROFIMOFF (*slapping* PISHTCHIK *on the shoulder*) You horse, you—

CHARLOTTA I beg your attention, one more trick. (*Taking a lap robe from the chair.*) Here is a very fine lap robe—I want to sell it— (*Shaking it out.*) Wouldn't somebody like to buy it?

PISHTCHIK (*amazed*) Fancy that!

CHARLOTTA *Ein, zwei, drei!*

(*She quickly raises the lowered robe, behind it stands* ANYA, *who curtseys, runs to her mother, embraces her and runs back into the ballroom amid the general delight.*)

LYUBOFF ANDREEVNA (*applauding*) Bravo, bravo—!

CHARLOTTA Now again! *Ein, zwei, drei!*

(*Lifting the robe: behind it stands* VARYA, *she bows.*)

---

[1] *Guter . . . Musikant* "A good man, but a sloppy musician"

PISHTCHIK (*amazed*) Fancy that!

CHARLOTTA That's all. (*Throwing the robe at* PISHTCHIK, *curtseying and running into the ballroom.*)

PISHTCHIK (*hurrying after her*) You little rascal—What a girl! What a girl!

(*Goes out.*)

LYUBOFF ANDREEVNA And Leonid is not here yet. What he's doing in town so long, I don't understand! Everything is finished there, either the estate is sold by now, or the auction didn't take place. Why keep it from us so long?

VARYA (*trying to comfort her*) Uncle has bought it, I am sure of that.

TROFIMOFF (*mockingly*) Yes.

VARYA Great-aunt sent him power of attorney to buy it in her name and transfer the debt. She did this for Anya. And I feel certain, God willing, that Uncle will buy it.

LYUBOFF ANDREEVNA Our Yaroslavl great-aunt has sent fifteen thousand to buy the estate in her name—She doesn't trust us, but that wouldn't be enough to pay the interest even— (*Covering her face with her hands.*) Today my fate will be decided, my fate—

TROFIMOFF (*teasing* VARYA) Madam Lopahin!

VARYA (*angrily*) Perennial student! You have already been expelled from the University twice.

LYUBOFF ANDREEVNA But why are you angry, Varya? He teases you about Lopahin, what of it? Marry Lopahin if you want to, he is a good man, interesting. If you don't want to, don't marry him; darling, nobody is making you do it.

VARYA I look at this matter seriously, Mama, one must speak straight out. He's a good man, I like him.

LYUBOFF ANDREEVNA Then marry him. What there is to wait for I don't understand!

VARYA But I can't propose to him myself, Mama. It's two years now; everyone has been talking to me about him, everyone talks, and he either remains silent or jokes. I understand. He's getting rich, he's busy with his own affairs, and has no time for me. If there were money, ever so little, even a hundred roubles, I would drop everything, and go far away. I'd go to a nunnery.

TROFIMOFF How saintly!

VARYA (*to* TROFIMOFF) A student should be intelligent! (*In a low voice, tearfully.*) How homely you have grown, Petya, how old you've got. (*To* LYUBOFF ANDREEVNA, *no longer crying.*) It is just that I can't live without working, Mama. I must be doing something every minute.

YASHA (*enters, barely restraining his laughter*)   Epihodoff has broken a billiard cue!—

(*Goes out.*)

VARYA   But why is Epihodoff here? Who allowed him to play billiards? I don't understand these people—

(*Goes out.*)

LYUBOFF ANDREEVNA   Don't tease her, Petya; you can see she has troubles enough without that.

TROFIMOFF   She is just too zealous. Sticking her nose into things that are none of her business. All summer she gave us no peace, neither me nor Anya; she was afraid a romance would spring up between us. What business is that of hers? And besides I haven't shown any signs of it. I am so remote from triviality. We are above love!

LYUBOFF ANDREEVNA   Well, then, I must be beneath love. (*Very anxiously.*) Why isn't Leonid here? Just to tell us whether the estate is sold or not? Calamity seems to me so incredible that I don't know what to think, I'm lost—I could scream this minute— I could do something insane. Save me, Petya. Say something, do say. . . .

TROFIMOFF   Whether the estate is sold today or is not sold—is it not the same? There is no turning back, the path is all grown over. Calm yourself, my dear, all that was over long ago. One mustn't deceive oneself, one must for once at least in one's life look truth straight in the eye.

LYUBOFF ANDREEVNA   What truth? You see where the truth is and where the untruth is, but as for me, it's as if I had lost my sight, I see nothing. You boldly decide all important questions, but tell me, my dear boy, isn't that because you are young and haven't had time yet to suffer through any one of your problems? You look boldly ahead, and isn't that because you don't see and don't expect anything terrible, since life is still hidden from your young eyes? You are braver, more honest, more profound than we are, but stop and think, be magnanimous, have a little mercy on me, just a little. Why, I was born here. My father and mother lived here and my grandfather. I love this house, I can't imagine my life without the cherry orchard and if it is very necessary to sell it, then sell me along with the orchard— (*Embracing* TROFIMOFF *and kissing him on the forehead.*) Why, my son was drowned here— (*Crying.*) Have mercy on me, good, kind man.

TROFIMOFF   You know I sympathize with you from the bottom of my heart.

LYUBOFF ANDREEVNA But that should be said differently, differently— (*Taking out her handkerchief; a telegram falls on the
floor.*) My heart is heavy today, you can't imagine how heavy. It
is too noisy for me here, my soul trembles at every sound, I tremble all over and yet I can't go off to myself, when I am alone the
silence frightens me. Don't blame me, Petya—I love you as one
of my own. I should gladly have given you Anya's hand, I assure
you, only, my dear, you must study and finish your course. You
do nothing. Fate simply flings you about from place to place, and
that's so strange—Isn't that so? Yes? And you must do something
about your beard, to make it grow somehow— (*Laughing.*) You
look funny!

TROFIMOFF (*picking up the telegram*) I do not desire to be beautiful.

LYUBOFF ANDREEVNA This telegram is from Paris. I get one every
day. Yesterday and today too. That wild man has fallen ill again,
something is wrong again with him—He asks forgiveness, begs me
to come, and really I ought to make a trip to Paris and stay
awhile near him. Your face looks stern, Petya, but what is there
to do, my dear, what am I to do, he is ill, he is alone, unhappy,
and who will look after him there, who will keep him from doing
the wrong thing, who will give him his medicine on time? And
what is there to hide or keep still about? I love him, that's plain.
I love him, love him—It's a stone about my neck, I'm sinking to
the bottom with it, but I love that stone and live without it I
cannot. (*Pressing* TROFIMOFF's *hand.*) Don't think harshly of me,
Petya, don't say anything to me, don't—

TROFIMOFF (*tearfully*) Forgive my frankness, for God's sake! Why,
he picked your bones.

LYUBOFF ANDREEVNA No, no, no, you must not talk like that.
(*Stopping her ears.*)

TROFIMOFF But he is a scoundrel, only you, you are the only one
that doesn't know it. He is a petty scoundrel, a nonentity—

LYUBOFF ANDREEVNA (*angry but controlling herself*) You are
twenty-six years old or twenty-seven, but you are still a schoolboy
in the second grade!

TROFIMOFF Very well!

LYUBOFF ANDREEVNA You should be a man—at your age you
should understand people who love. And you yourself should love
someone—you should fall in love! (*Angrily.*) Yes, yes! And there
is no purity in you; you are simply smug, a ridiculous crank, a
freak—

TROFIMOFF (*horrified*) What is she saying!

LYUBOFF ANDREEVNA   "I am above love!" You are not above love,
Petya, you are, as our Fiers would say, just a good-for-nothing.
Imagine, at your age, not having a mistress—!

TROFIMOFF (*horrified*)   This is terrible! What is she saying! (*Goes
quickly into the ballroom, clutching his head.*) This is horrible—
I can't bear it, I am going— (*Goes out but immediately returns.*)
All is over between us. (*Goes out into the hall.*)

LYUBOFF ANDREEVNA (*shouting after him*)   Petya, wait! You funny
creature, I was joking! Petya! (*In the hall someone can be heard
running up the stairs and suddenly falling back down with a
crash. ANYA and VARYA scream but immediately begin laughing.*)
What's that?

ANYA (*runs in, laughing*)   Petya fell down the stairs! (*Runs out.*)

LYUBOFF ANDREEVNA   What a funny boy that Petya is—! (*The
STATION-MASTER stops in the center of the ballroom and begins
to recite "The Sinner" by A. Tolstoi. They listen to him but he
has recited only a few lines when the strains of a waltz are heard
from the hall and the recitation is broken off. They all dance.
TROFIMOFF, ANYA, VARYA and LYUBOFF ANDREEVNA come in
from the hall.*) But, Petya—but, dear soul—I beg your forgiveness—Let's go dance.

(*She dances with TROFIMOFF. ANYA and VARYA dance. FIERS enters,
leaving his stick by the side door. YASHA also comes into the drawing
room and watches the dancers.*)

YASHA   What is it, Grandpa?

FIERS   I don't feel very well. In the old days there were generals,
barons, admirals dancing at our parties, and now we send for the
post-office clerk and the stationmaster, and even they are none
too anxious to come. Somehow I've grown feeble. The old master,
the grandfather, treated everybody with sealing-wax for all sick-
nesses. I take sealing-wax every day, have done so for twenty-odd
years or more; it may be due to that that I'm alive.

YASHA   You are tiresome, Grandpa. (*Yawning.*) Why don't you go
off and die?

FIERS   Aw, you—good-for-nothing!— (*Muttering.*)

(*TROFIMOFF and LYUBOFF ANDREEVNA dance in the ballroom and then
in the drawing room.*)

LYUBOFF ANDREEVNA   *Merci.* I'll sit down awhile— (*Sitting down.*)
I'm tired.

ANYA (*enters, agitated*)   And just now in the kitchen some man
was saying that the cherry orchard had been sold today.

LYUBOFF ANDREEVNA Sold to whom?

ANYA He didn't say who to. He's gone.

(*Dancing with* TROFIMOFF, *they pass into the ballroom.*)

YASHA It was some old man babbling there. A stranger.

FIERS And Leonid Andreevich is still not here, he has not arrived. The overcoat he has on is light, mid-season—let's hope he won't catch cold. Ach, these young things!

LYUBOFF ANDREEVNA I shall die this minute. Go, Yasha, find out who it was sold to.

YASHA But he's been gone a long time, the old fellow. (*Laughing.*)

LYUBOFF ANDREEVNA (*with some annoyance*) Well, what are you laughing at? What are you so amused at?

YASHA Epihodoff is just too funny. An empty-headed man. Twenty-two misfortunes!

LYUBOFF ANDREEVNA Fiers, if the estate is sold, where will you go?

FIERS Wherever you say, there I'll go.

LYUBOFF ANDREEVNA Why do you look like that? Aren't you well? You know you ought to go to bed—

FIERS Yes— (*With a sneer.*) I go to bed and without me who's going to serve, who'll take care of things? I'm the only one in the whole house.

YASHA (*to* LYUBOFF ANDREEVNA) Lyuboff Andreevna, let me ask a favor of you, do be so kind! If you ever go back to Paris, take me with you, please do! It's impossible for me to stay here. (*Looking around him, and speaking in a low voice.*) Why talk about it? You can see for yourself it's an uncivilized country, an immoral people and not only that, there's the boredom of it. The food they give us in that kitchen is abominable and there's that Fiers, too, walking about and muttering all kinds of words that are out of place. Take me with you, be so kind!

PISHTCHIK (*enters*) Allow me to ask you—for a little waltz, most beautiful lady— (LYUBOFF ANDREEVNA *goes with him.*) Charming lady, I must borrow a hundred and eighty roubles from you —will borrow— (*dancing*) a hundred and eighty roubles— (*They pass into the ballroom.*)

YASHA (*singing low*) "Wilt thou know the unrest in my soul!"

(*In the ballroom a figure in a gray top hat and checked trousers waves both hands and jumps about; there are shouts of "Bravo,* CHARLOTTA IVANOVNA!*"*)

DUNYASHA (*stopping to powder her face*) The young lady orders me to dance—there are a lot of gentlemen and very few ladies— but dancing makes my head swim and my heart thump. Fiers

Nikolaevich, the post-office clerk said something to me just now that took my breath away.

(*The music plays more softly.*)

FIERS What did he say to you?

DUNYASHA You are like a flower, he says.

YASHA (*yawning*) What ignorance—!

(*Goes out.*)

DUNYASHA Like a flower—I am such a sensitive girl, I love tender words awfully.

FIERS You'll be getting your head turned.

(EPIHODOFF *enters.*)

EPIHODOFF Avdotya Feodorovna, you don't want to see me—It's as if I were some sort of insect. (*Sighing.*) Ach, life!

DUNYASHA What do you want?

EPIHODOFF Undoubtedly you may be right. (*Sighing.*) But of course, if one considers it from a given point of view, then you, I will allow myself so to express it, forgive my frankness, absolutely led me into a state of mind. I know my fate, every day some misfortune happens to me, but I have long since become accustomed to that, and so I look on my misfortunes with a smile. You gave me your word and, although I—

DUNYASHA I beg you, we'll talk later on, but leave me now in peace. I'm in a dream now. (*Playing with her fan.*)

EPIHODOFF I have something wrong happen every day—I will allow myself so to express it—I just smile, I even laugh.

VARYA (*enters from the ballroom*) You are not gone yet, Semyon? What a really disrespectful man you are! (*To* DUNYASHA.) Get out of here, Dunyasha. (*To* EPIHODOFF.) You either play billiards and break a cue or you walk about the drawing room like a guest.

EPIHODOFF Allow me to tell you, you cannot make any demands on me.

VARYA I'm not making any demands on you, I'm talking to you. All you know is to walk from place to place but not do any work. We keep a clerk, but what for, nobody knows.

EPIHODOFF (*offended*) Whether I work, whether I walk, whether I eat, or whether I play billiards are matters to be discussed only by people of understanding and my seniors.

VARYA You dare to say that to me! (*Flying into a temper.*) You dare? So I don't understand anything? Get out of here! This minute!

EPIHODOFF (*alarmed*) I beg you to express yourself in a delicate manner.

VARYA (*beside herself*) This very minute, get out of here! Get out! (*He goes to the door; she follows him.*) Twenty-two misfortunes! Don't you dare breathe in here! Don't let me set eyes on you! (EPIHODOFF *has gone out, but his voice comes from outside the door: "I shall complain about you."*) Ah, you are coming back? (*Grabbing the stick that* FIERS *put by the door.*) Come on, come —come on, I'll show you—Ah, you are coming? You are coming? Take that then—!

She swings the stick, at the very moment when LOPAHIN *is coming in.*

LOPAHIN Most humbly, I thank you.

VARYA (*angrily and ironically*) I beg your pardon!

LOPAHIN It's nothing at all. I humbly thank you for the pleasant treat.

VARYA It isn't worth your thanks. (*Moving away, then looking back and asking gently.*) I haven't hurt you?

LOPAHIN No, it's nothing. There's a great bump coming though.

*Voices in the ballroom: "*LOPAHIN *has come back." "*YERMOLAY ALEXEE-VICH!"*

PISHTCHIK (*enters*) See what we see, hear what we hear—! (*He and* LOPAHIN *kiss one another.*) You smell slightly of cognac, my dear, my good old chap. And we are amusing ourselves here too.

LYUBOFF ANDREEVNA (*enters*) Is that you, Yermolay Alexeevich? Why were you so long? Where is Leonid?

LOPAHIN Leonid Andreevich got back when I did, he's coming.

LYUBOFF ANDREEVNA (*agitated*) Well, what? Was there an auction? Do speak!

LOPAHIN (*embarrassed, afraid of showing the joy he feels*) The auction was over by four o'clock—We were late for the train, had to wait till half-past nine. (*Sighing heavily.*) Ugh, my head's swimming a bit!

(GAYEFF *enters; with his right hand he carries his purchases, with his left he wipes away his tears.*)

LYUBOFF ANDREEVNA Lyona, what? Lyona, eh? (*Impatiently, with tears in her eyes.*) Quick, for God's sake—

GAYEFF (*not answering her, merely waving his hand; to* FIERS, *crying*) Here, take it—There are anchovies, some Kertch herrings —I haven't eaten anything all day—What I have suffered! (*The door into the billiard room is open; you hear the balls clicking and* YASHA's *voice: "Seven and eighteen!"* GAYEFF's *expression changes, he is no longer crying.*) I'm terribly tired. You help me change, Fiers.

(*Goes to his room through the ballroom,* FIERS *behind him.*)

PISHTCHIK   What happened at the auction? Go on, tell us!

LYUBOFF ANDREEVNA   Is the cherry orchard sold?

LOPAHIN   It's sold.

LYUBOFF ANDREEVNA   Who bought it?

LOPAHIN   I bought it. (*A pause.* LYUBOFF ANDREEVNA *is overcome. She would have fallen had she not been standing near the chair and table.* VARYA *takes the keys from her belt, throws them on the floor in the middle of the drawing room and goes out.*) I bought it. Kindly wait a moment, ladies and gentlemen, everything is muddled up in my head, I can't speak— (*Laughing.*) We arrived at the auction, Deriganoff was already there. Leonid Andreevich had only fifteen thousand and Deriganoff right off bids thirty over and above indebtedness. I see how things are, I match him with forty thousand. He forty-five. I fifty-five. That is to say he raises it by fives, I by tens.—So it ended. Over and above the indebtedness, I bid up to ninety thousand, it was knocked down to me. The cherry orchard is mine now. Mine! (*Guffawing.*) My God, Lord, the cherry orchard is mine! Tell me I'm drunk, out of my head, that I'm imagining all this— (*Stamps his feet.*) Don't laugh at me! If only my father and grandfather could rise from their graves and see this whole business, see how their Yermolay, beaten, half-illiterate Yermolay, who used to run around barefoot in winter, how that very Yermolay has bought an estate that nothing in the world can beat. I bought the estate where grandfather and father were slaves, where you wouldn't even let me in the kitchen. I am asleep, it's only some dream of mine, it only seems so to me—That's nothing but the fruit of your imagination, covered with the darkness of the unknown— (*Picking up the keys, with a gentle smile.*) She threw down the keys, wants to show she is not mistress any more— (*Jingling the keys.*) Well, it's all the same. (*The orchestra is heard tuning up.*) Hey, musicians, play, I want to hear you! Come on, everybody, and see how Yermolay Lopahin will swing the ax in the cherry orchard, how the trees will fall to the ground! We are going to build villas and our grandsons and great-grandsons will see a new life here— Music, play! (*The music is playing.* LYUBOFF ANDREEVNA *has sunk into a chair, crying bitterly.* LOPAHIN *reproachfully.*) Why, then, didn't you listen to me? My poor dear, it can't be undone now. (*With tears.*) Oh, if this could all be over soon, if somehow our awkward, unhappy life would be changed!

PISHTCHIK (*taking him by the arm, in a low voice*) She is crying. Come on in the ballroom, let her be by herself—Come on—

(*Taking him by the arm and leading him into the ballroom.*)

LOPAHIN What's the matter? Music, there, play up! (*Sarcastically.*) Everything is to be as I want it! Here comes the new squire, the owner of the cherry orchard. (*Quite accidentally, he bumps into the little table, and very nearly upsets the candelabra.*) I can pay for everything!

(*Goes out with* PISHTCHIK. *There is nobody left either in the ballroom or the drawing room but* LYUBOFF ANDREEVNA, *who sits all huddled up and crying bitterly. The music plays softly.* ANYA *and* TROFIMOFF *enter hurriedly.* ANYA *comes up to her mother and kneels in front of her.* TROFIMOFF *remains at the ballroom door.*)

ANYA Mama—! Mama, you are crying? My dear, kind, good Mama, my beautiful, I love you—I bless you. The cherry orchard is sold, it's not ours any more, that's true, true; but don't cry, Mama, you've your life still left you, you've your good, pure heart ahead of you—Come with me, come on, darling, away from here, come on—We will plant a new orchard, finer than this one, you'll see it, you'll understand; and joy, quiet, deep joy will sink into your heart, like the sun at evening, and you'll smile, Mama! Come, darling, come on!

ACT IV

The same setting as in Act I. There are neither curtains on the windows nor are there any pictures on the walls. Only a little furniture remains piled up in one corner as if for sale. A sense of emptiness is felt. Near the outer door, at the rear of the stage, is a pile of suitcases, traveling bags, and so on. The door on the left is open, and through it VARYA's *and* ANYA's *voices are heard.* LOPAHIN *is standing waiting.* YASHA *is holding a tray with glasses of champagne. In the hall* EPIHODOFF *is tying up a box. Offstage at the rear there is a hum. It is the peasants who have come to say good-by.* GAYEFF's *voice: "Thanks, brothers, thank you."*

YASHA The simple folk have come to say good-by. I am of the opinion, Yermolay Alexeevich, that the people are kind enough but don't understand anything.

(*The hum subsides.* LYUBOFF ANDREEVNA *enters through the hall with* GAYEFF; *she is not crying, but is pale, her face quivers, she is not able to speak.*)

GAYEFF You gave them your purse, Lyuba. Mustn't do that! Mustn't do that!

LYUBOFF ANDREEVNA I couldn't help it! I couldn't help it!

(*Both go out.*)

LOPAHIN (*calling through the door after them*) Please, I humbly beg you! A little glass at parting. I didn't think to bring some from town, and at the station I found just one bottle. Please! (*A pause.*) Well, then, ladies and gentlemen! You don't want it? (*Moving away from the door.*) If I'd known that, I wouldn't have bought it. Well, then I won't drink any either. (YASHA *carefully sets the tray down on a chair.*) At least, you have some, Yasha.

YASHA To those who are departing! Pleasant days to those who stay behind! (*Drinking.*) This champagne is not the real stuff, I can assure you.

LOPAHIN Eight roubles a bottle. (*A pause.*) It's devilish cold in here.

YASHA They didn't heat up today, we are leaving anyway. (*Laughing.*)

LOPAHIN What are you laughing about?

YASHA For joy.

LOPAHIN Outside it's October, but it's sunny and still, like summer. Good for building. (*Looking at his watch, then through the door.*) Ladies and gentlemen, bear in mind we have forty-six minutes in all till train time! Which means you have to go to the station in twenty minutes. Hurry up a little.

TROFIMOFF (*in an overcoat, entering from outside*) Seems to me it is time to go. The carriages are ready. The devil knows where my rubbers are. They've disappeared. (*In the door.*) Anya, my rubbers are not here! I can't find them.

LOPAHIN And I have to go to Kharkov. I'm going on the same train with you. I'm going to live in Kharkov all winter. I've been dilly-dallying along with you, I'm tired of doing nothing. I can't be without work, look, I don't know what to do with my hands here, see, they are dangling somehow, as if they didn't belong to me.

TROFIMOFF We are leaving right away, and you'll set about your useful labors again.

LOPAHIN Here, drink a glass.

TROFIMOFF I shan't.

LOPAHIN It's to Moscow now?

TROFIMOFF Yes. I'll see them off to town, and tomorrow to Moscow.

LOPAHIN Yes—Maybe the professors are not giving their lectures. I imagine they are waiting till you arrive.

TROFIMOFF   That's none of your business.

LOPAHIN   How many years is it you've been studying at the University?

TROFIMOFF   Think of something newer. This is old and flat. (*Looking for his rubbers.*) You know, perhaps, we shall not see each other again; therefore, permit me to give you one piece of advice at parting! Don't wave your arms! Cure yourself of that habit— of arm waving. And also of building summer cottages, figuring that the summer residents will in time become individual land-owners; figuring like that is arm waving too—Just the same, however, I like you. You have delicate soft fingers like an artist, you have a delicate soft heart—

LOPAHIN   (*embracing him*) Good-by, my dear boy. Thanks for everything. If you need it, take some money from me for the trip.

TROFIMOFF   Why should I? There's no need for it.

LOPAHIN   But you haven't any!

TROFIMOFF   I have. Thank you. I got some for a translation. Here it is in my pocket. (*Anxiously.*) But my rubbers are gone.

VARYA   (*from another room*) Take your nasty things!

(*Throws a pair of rubbers on to the stage.*)

TROFIMOFF   But what are you angry about, Varya? Hm—Why, these are not my rubbers.

LOPAHIN   In the spring I planted twenty-seven hundred acres of poppies and now I've made forty thousand clear. And when my poppies were in bloom, what a picture it was! So look, as I say, I've made forty thousand, which means I'm offering you a loan because I can afford to. Why turn up your nose? I'm a peasant— I speak straight out.

TROFIMOFF   Your father was a peasant, mine—an apothecary— and from that absolutely nothing follows. (LOPAHIN *takes out his wallet.*) Leave it alone, leave it alone—If you gave me two hundred thousand even, I wouldn't take it. I am a free man. And everything that you all value so highly and dearly, both rich man and beggars, has not the slightest power over me, it's like a mere feather floating in the air. I can get along without you, I can pass you by, I am strong and proud. Humanity is moving toward the loftiest truth, toward the loftiest happiness that is possible on earth and I am in the front ranks.

LOPAHIN   Will you get there?

TROFIMOFF   I'll get there. (*A pause.*) I'll get there, or I'll show the others the way to get there.

(*In the distance is heard the sound of an ax on a tree.*)

LOPAHIN   Well, good-by, my dear boy. It's time to go. We turn up our noses at one another, but life keeps on passing. When I work a long time without stopping, my thoughts are clearer, and it seems as if I, too, know what I exist for, and, brother, how many people are there in Russia who exist, nobody knows for what! Well, all the same, it's not that that keeps things circulating. Leonid Andreevich, they say, has accepted a position—he'll be in a bank, six thousand a year—the only thing is he won't stay there, he's very lazy—

ANYA   (*in the doorway*)   Mama begs of you until she's gone, not to cut down the orchard.

TROFIMOFF   Honestly, haven't you enough tact to—

(*Goes out through the hall.*)

LOPAHIN   Right away, right away—What people, really!

(*Goes out after him.*)

ANYA   Has Fiers been sent to the hospital?

YASHA   I told them to this morning. They must have sent him.

ANYA   (*to* EPIHODOFF, *who is passing through the room*)   Semyon Panteleevich, please inquire whether or not they have taken Fiers to the hospital.

YASHA   (*huffily*)   This morning, I told Igor. Why ask ten times over!

EPIHODOFF   The venerable Fiers, according to my conclusive opinion, is not worth mending, he ought to join his forefathers. And I can only envy him. (*Putting a suitcase on a hatbox and crushing it.*) Well, there you are, of course. I knew it.

(*Goes out.*)

YASHA   (*mockingly*)   Twenty-two misfortunes—

VARYA   (*on the other side of the door*)   Have they taken Fiers to the hospital?

ANYA   They have.

VARYA   Then why didn't they take the letter to the doctor?

ANYA   We must send it on after them—

(*Goes out.*)

VARYA   (*from the next room*)   Where is Yasha? Tell him his mother has come, she wants to say good-by to him.

YASHA   (*waving his hand*)   They merely try my patience.

(DUNYASHA *has been busying herself with the luggage; now when* YASHA *is left alone, she goes up to him.*)

DUNYASHA If you'd only look at me once, Yasha. You are going away—leaving me— (*Crying and throwing herself on his neck.*)

YASHA Why are you crying? (*Drinking champagne.*) In six days I'll be in Paris again. Tomorrow we will board the express train and dash off out of sight; somehow, I can't believe it. *Vive la France!* It doesn't suit me here—I can't live here—Can't help that. I've seen enough ignorance—enough for me. (*Drinking champagne.*) Why do you cry? Behave yourself properly, then you won't be crying.

DUNYASHA (*powdering her face, looking into a small mirror*) Send me a letter from Paris. I loved you, Yasha, you know, loved you so! I am a tender creature, Yasha!

YASHA They are coming here. (*Bustling about near the suitcases, humming low.*)

(LYUBOFF ANDREEVNA, GAYEFF, ANYA *and* CHARLOTTA IVANOVNA *enter.*)

GAYEFF We should be going. There is very little time left. (*Looking at* YASHA.) Who is it smells like herring!

LYUBOFF ANDREEVNA In about ten minutes let's be in the carriage— (*Glancing around the room.*) Good-by, dear house, old Grandfather. Winter will pass; spring will be here, but you won't be here any longer, they'll tear you down. How much these walls have seen! (*Kissing her daughter warmly.*) My treasure, you are beaming, your eyes are dancing like two diamonds. Are you happy? Very?

ANYA Very! It's the beginning of a new life, Mama!

GAYEFF (*gaily*) Yes, indeed, everything is fine now. Before the sale of the cherry orchard, we all were troubled, distressed, and then when the question was settled definitely, irrevocably, we all calmed down and were even cheerful—I'm a bank official. I am a financier now—Yellow ball into the side pocket, anyway, Lyuba, you look better, no doubt about that.

LYUBOFF ANDREEVNA Yes. My nerves are better, that's true. (*They hand her her hat and coat.*) I sleep well. Carry out my things, Yasha. It's time. (*To* ANYA.) My little girl, we shall see each other again soon—I am going to Paris, I shall live there on the money your Yaroslavl great-aunt sent for the purchase of the estate— long live Great-aunt! But that money won't last long.

ANYA Mama, you'll come back soon, soon—Isn't that so? I'll prepare myself, pass the examination at high school, and then I'll work, I will help you. We'll read all sorts of books together. Mama, isn't that so? (*Kissing her mother's hands.*) We'll read in the autumn evenings, read lots of books, and a new, wonderful world will open up before us— (*daydreaming*) Mama, do come—

LYUBOFF ANDREEVNA I'll come, my precious. (*Embracing her daughter.*)

(LOPAHIN *enters with* CHARLOTTA *who is softly humming a song.*)

GAYEFF Lucky Charlotta: she's singing!

CHARLOTTA (*taking a bundle that looks like a baby wrapped up*) My baby, bye, bye— (*A baby's cry is heard: Ooah, ooah—!*) Hush, my darling, my dear little boy. (*Ooah, ooah—!*) I am so sorry for you! (*Throwing the bundle back.*) Will you please find me a position? I cannot go on like this.

LOPAHIN We will find something, Charlotta Ivanovna, don't worry.

GAYEFF Everybody is dropping us, Varya is going away.—All of a sudden we are not needed.

CHARLOTTA I have no place in town to live. I must go away. (*Humming.*) It's all the same—

(PISHTCHIK *enters.*)

LOPAHIN The freak of nature—!

PISHTCHIK (*out of breath*) Ugh, let me catch my breath—I'm exhausted—My honored friends—Give me some water—

GAYEFF After money, I suppose? This humble servant will flee from sin!

(*Goes out.*)

PISHTCHIK It's a long time since I was here—Most beautiful lady— (*To* LOPAHIN) You here—? Glad to see you—a man of the greatest intellect—Here—Take it— (*Giving* LOPAHIN *some money.*) Four hundred roubles—That leaves eight hundred and forty I still owe you—

LOPAHIN (*with astonishment, shrugging his shoulders*) I must be dreaming. But where did you get it?

PISHTCHIK Wait—I'm hot—Most extraordinary event. Some Englishmen came and found on my land some kind of white clay— (*To* LYUBOFF ANDREEVNA.) And four hundred for you—Beautiful lady—Wonderful lady— (*Handing over the money.*) The rest later. (*Taking a drink of water.*) Just now a young man was saying on the train that some great philosopher recommends jumping off roofs—"Jump!" he says, and "therein lies the whole problem." (*With astonishment.*) You don't say! Water!

LOPAHIN And what Englishmen were they?

PISHTCHIK I leased them the parcel of land with the clay for twenty-four years—And now, excuse me, I haven't time—I must run along—I'm going to Znoykoff's—To Kardamonoff's—I owe everybody— (*Drinking.*) I wish you well—I'll drop in on Thursday—

LYUBOFF ANDREEVNA   We are moving to town right away, and to-morrow I'm going abroad—

PISHTCHIK   What? (*Alarmed.*) Why to town? That's why I see furniture—Suitcases—Well, no matter— (*Tearfully.*) No matter —Men of the greatest minds—those Englishmen—No matter— Good luck! God will help you—No matter—Everything in this world comes to an end— (*Kissing* LYUBOFF ANDREEVNA's *hand.*) And should the report reach you that my end has come, think of that well-known horse and say: "There was once on earth a so and so—Semyonoff Pishtchik—The kingdom of Heaven be his." Most remarkable weather—yes— (*Going out greatly disconcerted, but immediately returning and speaking from the door.*) Dashenka sends her greetings!

(*Goes out.*)

LYUBOFF ANDREEVNA   And now we can go. I am leaving with two worries. First, that Fiers is sick. (*Glancing at her watch.*) We still have five minutes—

ANYA   Mama, Fiers has already been sent to the hospital. Yasha sent him off this morning.

LYUBOFF ANDREEVNA   My second worry—is Varya. She is used to getting up early and working, and now without any work she is like a fish out of water. She has grown thin, pale and cries all the time, poor thing— (*A pause.*) You know this, Yermolay Alexeevich: I dreamed—of marrying her to you. And there was every sign of your getting married. (*Whispering to* ANYA, *who beckons to* CHARLOTTA; *both go out.*) She loves you, you are fond of her, and I don't know, don't know why it is you seem to avoid each other—I don't understand it!

LOPAHIN   I don't understand it either, I must confess. It's all strange somehow—If there's still time, I am ready right now even—Let's finish it up—and *basta*,[1] but without you I feel I won't propose.

LYUBOFF ANDREEVNA   But that's excellent. Surely it takes only a minute. I'll call her at once.

LOPAHIN   And to fit the occasion there's the champagne. (*Looking at the glasses.*) Empty, somebody has already drunk them. (YASHA *coughs.*) That's what's called lapping it up—

---

[1] *basta* be done with it

LYUBOFF ANDREEVNA (*vivaciously*) Splendid! We'll go out—
Yasha, *allez!* [1] I'll call her— (*Through the door.*) Varya, drop
everything and come here. Come on! (*Goes out with* YASHA.)
LOPAHIN (*looking at his watch*) Yes—

(*A pause. Behind the door you hear smothered laughter, whispering,
finally* VARYA *enters.*)

VARYA (*looking at the luggage a long time*) That's strange, I just
can't find it—
LOPAHIN What are you looking for?
VARYA I packed it myself and don't remember where.

(*A pause.*)

LOPAHIN Where do you expect to go now, Varvara Mikhailovna?
VARYA I? To Regulin's. I agreed to go there to look after the house
—As a sort of housekeeper.
LOPAHIN That's in Yashnevo? It's nigh on to seventy miles. (*A
pause.*) And here ends life in this house—
VARYA (*examining the luggage*) But where is it? Either I put it in
the trunk, perhaps—Yes, life in this house is ended—it won't be
any more—
LOPAHIN And I am going to Kharkov now—By the next train.
I've a lot to do. And I am leaving Epihodoff—on the ground
here—I've hired him.
VARYA Well!
LOPAHIN Last year at this time it had already been snowing, if you
remember, and now it's quiet, it's sunny. It's only that it's cold,
about three degrees of frost.
VARYA I haven't noticed. (*A pause.*) And besides our thermometer
is broken— (*A pause. A voice from the yard through the door.*)
Yermolay Alexeevich—
LOPAHIN (*as if he had been expecting this call for a long time*)
This minute!

(*Goes out quickly.*)

(VARYA, *sitting on the floor, putting her head on a bundle of clothes,
sobs quietly. The door opens,* LYUBOFF ANDREEVNA *enters cautiously.*)

VARYA (*She is not crying any longer, and has wiped her eyes.*) Yes,
it's time, Mama. I can get to Regulin's today, if we are just not
too late for the train— (*Through the door.*) Anya, put your

---

[1] *allez* go

things on! (ANYA, *then* GAYEFF *and* CHARLOTTA IVANOVNA *enter.* GAYEFF *has on a warm overcoat, with a hood. The servants gather, also the drivers.* EPIHODOFF *busies himself with the luggage.*) Now we can be on our way.

ANYA (*joyfully*) On our way!

GAYEFF My friends, my dear, kind friends! Leaving this house forever, can I remain silent, can I restrain myself from expressing, as we say, farewell, those feelings that fill now my whole being—

ANYA (*beseechingly*) Uncle!

VARYA Dear Uncle, don't!

GAYEFF (*dejectedly*) Bank the yellow into the side pocket—I am silent—

(TROFIMOFF *and then* LOPAHIN *enter.*)

TROFIMOFF Well, ladies and gentlemen, it's time to go!

LOPAHIN Epihodoff, my coat!

LYUBOFF ANDREEVNA I'll sit here just a minute more. It's as if I had never seen before what the walls in this house are like, what kind of ceilings, and now I look at them greedily, with such tender love—

GAYEFF I remember when I was six years old, on Trinity Day, I sat in this window and watched my father going to Church—

LYUBOFF ANDREEVNA Are all the things taken out?

LOPAHIN Everything, I think. (*Putting on his overcoat. To* EPIHODOFF.) Epihodoff, you see that everything is in order.

EPIHODOFF (*talking in a hoarse voice*) Don't worry, Yermolay Alexeevich!

LOPAHIN Why is your voice like that?

EPIHODOFF Just drank some water, swallowed something.

YASHA (*with contempt*) The ignorance—

LYUBOFF ANDREEVNA We are going and there won't be a soul left here—

LOPAHIN Till spring.

VARYA (*pulls an umbrella out from a bundle, it looks as if she were going to hit someone;* LOPAHIN *pretends to be frightened*) What do you, what do you—I never thought of it.

TROFIMOFF Ladies and gentlemen, let's get in the carriages—It's time! The train is coming any minute.

VARYA Petya, here they are, your rubbers, by the suitcase. (*Tearfully.*) And how dirty yours are, how old—!

TROFIMOFF (*putting on the rubbers*) Let's go, ladies and gentlemen!

GAYEFF (*greatly embarrassed, afraid he will cry*) The train—The station—Cross into the side, combination off the white into the corner—

LYUBOFF ANDREEVNA Let's go!

LOPAHIN Everybody here? Nobody there? (*Locking the side door on the left.*) Things are stored here, it must be locked up, let's go!

ANYA Good-by, house! Good-by, the old life!

TROFIMOFF Long live the new life!

(*Goes out with* ANYA. VARYA *casts a glance around the room and, without hurrying, goes out.* YASHA *and* CHARLOTTA, *with her dog, go out.*)

LOPAHIN And so, till spring. Out, ladies and gentlemen—Till we meet.

(*Goes out.*)

(LYUBOFF ANDREEVNA *and* GAYEFF *are left alone. As if they had been waiting for this, they throw themselves on one another's necks sobbing, but smothering their sobs as if afraid of being heard.*)

GAYEFF (*in despair*) Oh, Sister, Sister—

LYUBOFF ANDREEVNA Oh, my dear, my lovely, beautiful orchard! My life, my youth, my happiness, good-by!

ANYA (ANYA's *voice, gaily, appealingly*) Mama—!

TROFIMOFF (*gaily, excitedly*) Aaooch!

LYUBOFF ANDREEVNA For the last time, just to look at the walls, at the window—My dear mother used to love to walk around in this room—

GAYEFF Oh, Sister, Sister—!

ANYA (*from outside*) Mama—!

TROFIMOFF (*from outside*) Aaooch—!

LYUBOFF ANDREEVNA We are coming!

(*They go out.*)

(*The stage is empty. One hears the keys locking all the doors, then the carriages driving off. It grows quiet. In the silence the dull thud of an ax on a tree, a lonely, mournful sound. Footsteps are heard. From the door on the right* FIERS *appears. He is dressed as usual, in a jacket and a white waistcoat, slippers on his feet. He is sick.*)

FIERS (*going to the door and trying the knob*) Locked. They've gone. (*Sitting down on the sofa.*) They forgot about me—No matter—I'll sit here awhile—And Leonid Andreevich, for sure, didn't put on his fur coat, he went off with his topcoat— (*Sighing anxiously.*) And I didn't see to it—The young saplings! (*He mutters something that cannot be understood.*) Life has gone by, as if I hadn't lived at all— (*Lying down.*) I'll lie down awhile— You haven't got any strength, nothing is left, nothing—Ach, you —good-for-nothing— (*He lies still.*)

(*There is a far-off sound as if out of the sky, the sound of a snapped string, dying away, sad. A stillness falls, and there is only the thud of an ax on a tree, far away in the orchard.*)

MAJOR BARBARA (1905)

BERNARD SHAW (1856–1950)

It once appeared that George Bernard Shaw would live forever. He had begun his career as a music and drama critic and as a sometime writer of fiction. He was a staunch supporter of the works of Ibsen, and his *The Quintessence of Ibsenism,* first published in 1891, is one of the earliest significant endorsements of the Norwegian dramatist's realism. Shaw was 36 before his own first play, *Widower's Houses,* was written in 1892, and his greatest plays were done between his forties and seventies. He was still writing acceptable works into his eighties. Opinionated, garrulous, supremely egotistical, he was, as well, a true theatrical genius. He wrote some of the most superb comedies in the English language, introduced in published versions by prefatory essays expounding widely on politics, economics, and philosophy, often exceeding in length the plays themselves. As a public figure he was a born performer. It was next to impossible to determine the "real" Shaw, if, indeed, there ever was one, since he acted continually as if he were on stage. He could command actors, directors, and audiences to do his bidding, even across oceans. He could at one moment be the bearded English pixie and the next the goading, irascible, devilish socialist.

Early in his life Shaw joined the Fabian Society in England and was a longtime advocate of state socialism, even, at times when it was dangerously unpopular to do so, supporting Russian Communism. He strongly espoused Ibsen's abandonment of the conventional attitude toward the "womanly woman," *i.e.,* the traditional female who performed at the command of her husband and male-oriented society, imprisoned by the strictures of an unbending and arbitrary morality. He saw strength in the "life force," that of natural sexuality, as a positive, driving element in the world, while assigning his romantic couples to virtually passionless, albeit thoroughly charming, affairs. Shaw himself advocated celibacy to the point of having endured, so far as is known, a totally abstinent marriage, while carrying on a kind of public, if Platonic, love affair of his own with the beautiful actress Mrs. Patrick Campbell, for whom he created *Pygmalion* in 1913, forever with us in *My Fair Lady*. One of the most "liberated" of women appears in his high comedy masterpiece, *Candida,* in 1895. His most magnificent feminine creation, at once a near-tragic and delightfully comic figure, is in *Saint Joan* of 1923, Shaw's own personal view of one of history's freest and most captive women.

Above all, Shaw regarded poverty as an out-and-out crime. In *Major Barbara* he has written an effective exposé of human hypocrisy in the way society insists on handling its poor, and he has devised his Utopian state, the perfect benevolent society, in a tongue-in-cheek manner by assigning it to the supercapitalist munitions lord. Against the diabolic reasoning of Undershaft, though it is based on the powderkeg of a cannon foundry, the classical scholarly mind of Adolphus ultimately loses, or at least seems to lose, in order to win the hand of the thoroughly do-good Barbara. She, disillusioned, surrenders as well to the powers of darkness as she sadly discovers that anyone in the world can be bought if the right amount of hard cash comes along. The fortuitous discovery of Adolphus's illegitimacy as a foundling, eligible for the Undershaft fortune, is not without its ironies.

Shaw is at his best in stringing us along, as he does so well in *Major Barbara,* but what fun there is in following him! Who has really been "had" in all of this? the Army? Bill? Barbara and Dolly? All of us and none of us? Whatever the socialist "thinker" that Shaw makes himself out to be, beneath everything is a dramatist who knows his theatre, for which he creates incident and action at their keenest levels, with thoroughly attractive characters and brilliantly sophisticated comedy.

Major Barbara

ACT I

It is after dinner in January 1906, in the library in LADY BRITOMART
UNDERSHAFT's *house in Wilton Crescent. A large and comfortable settee
is in the middle of the room, upholstered in dark leather. A person sitting
on it (it is vacant at present) would have, on his right,* LADY BRITOMART's
*writing table, with the lady herself busy at it; a smaller writing table
behind him on his left; the door behind him on* LADY BRITOMART's *side;
and a window with a window seat directly on his left. Near the window
is an armchair.*

LADY BRITOMART *is a woman of fifty or thereabouts, well dressed and
yet careless of her dress, well bred and quite reckless of her breeding,
well mannered and yet appallingly outspoken and indifferent to the opinion of her interlocutors, amiable and yet peremptory, arbitrary, and high-
tempered to the last bearable degree, and withal a very typical managing
matron of the upper class, treated as a naughty child until she grew into
a scolding mother, and finally settling down with plenty of practical ability
and worldly experience, limited in the oddest way with domestic and class
limitations, conceiving the universe exactly as if it were a large house in
Wilton Crescent, though handling her corner of it very effectively on that
assumption, and being quite enlightened and liberal as to the books in the
library, the pictures on the walls, the music in the portfolios, and the
articles in the papers.*

Her son, STEPHEN, *comes in. He is a gravely correct young man under
25, taking himself very seriously, but still in some awe of his mother, from
childish habit and bachelor shyness rather than from any weakness of
character.*

STEPHEN   Whats the matter?

LADY BRITOMART   Presently, Stephen.

STEPHEN *submissively walks to the settee and sits down. He takes up a
Liberal weekly called The Speaker.*

LADY BRITOMART   Dont begin to read, Stephen. I shall require all
your attention.

STEPHEN   It was only while I was waiting—

LADY BRITOMART   Dont make excuses, Stephen. (*He puts down The
Speaker.*) Now! (*She finishes her writing; rises; and comes to the
settee.*) I have not kept you waiting very long, I think.

STEPHEN   Not at all, mother.

LADY BRITOMART   Bring me my cushion. (*He takes the cushion from the chair at the desk and arranges it for her as she sits down on the settee.*) Sit down. (*He sits down and fingers his tie nervously.*) Dont fiddle with your tie, Stephen: there is nothing the matter with it.

STEPHEN   I beg your pardon. (*He fiddles with his watch chain instead.*)

LADY BRITOMART   Now are you attending to me, Stephen?

STEPHEN   Of course, mother.

LADY BRITOMART   No: it's not of course. I want something much more than your everyday matter-of-course attention. I am going to speak to you very seriously, Stephen. I wish you would let that chain alone.

STEPHEN   (*hastily relinquishing the chain*)   Have I done anything to annoy you, mother? If so, it was quite unintentional.

LADY BRITOMART   (*astonished*)   Nonsense! (*With some remorse.*) My poor boy, did you think I was angry with you?

STEPHEN   What is it, then, mother? You are making me very uneasy.

LADY BRITOMART   (*squaring herself at him rather aggressively*)   Stephen: may I ask how soon you intend to realize that you are a grown-up man, and that I am only a woman?

STEPHEN   (*amazed*)   Only a—

LADY BRITOMART   Dont repeat my words, please: it is a most aggravating habit. You must learn to face life seriously, Stephen. I really cannot bear the whole burden of our family affairs any longer. You must advise me: you must assume the responsibility.

STEPHEN   I!

LADY BRITOMART   Yes, you, of course. You were 24 last June. Youve been at Harrow and Cambridge. Youve been to India and Japan. You must know a lot of things, now; unless you have wasted your time most scandalously. Well, advise me.

STEPHEN   (*much perplexed*)   You know I have never interfered in the household—

LADY BRITOMART   No: I should think not. I dont want you to order the dinner.

STEPHEN   I mean in our family affairs.

LADY BRITOMART   Well, you must interfere now for they are getting quite beyond me.

STEPHEN   (*troubled*)   I have thought sometimes that perhaps I ought; but really, mother, I know so little about them; and what I do know is so painful! it is so impossible to mention some things to you—(*he stops, ashamed*).

LADY BRITOMART   I suppose you mean your father.

STEPHEN   (*almost inaudibly*)   Yes.

LADY BRITOMART   My dear: we cant go on all our lives not mentioning him. Of course you were quite right not to open the subject until I asked you to; but you are old enough now to be taken into my confidence, and to help me to deal with him about the girls.

STEPHEN   But the girls are all right. They are engaged.

LADY BRITOMART   (*complacently*)   Yes: I have made a very good match for Sarah. Charles Lomax will be a millionaire at 35. But that is ten years ahead; and in the meantime his trustees cannot under the terms of his father's will allow him more than £800 a year.

STEPHEN   But the will says also that if he increases his income by his own exertions, they may double the increase.

LADY BRITOMART   Charles Lomax's exertions are much more likely to decrease his income than to increase it. Sarah will have to find at least another £800 a year for the next ten years; and even then they will be as poor as church mice. And what about Barbara? I thought Barbara was going to make the most brilliant career of all of you. And what does she do? Joins the Salvation Army; discharges her maid; lives on a pound a week and walks in one evening with a professor of Greek whom she has picked up in the street, and who pretends to be a Salvationist, and actually plays the big drum for her in public because he has fallen head over ears in love with her.

STEPHEN   I was certainly rather taken aback when I heard they were engaged. Cusins is a very nice fellow, certainly: nobody would ever guess that he was born in Australia; but—

LADY BRITOMART   Oh, Adolphus Cusins will make a very good husband. After all, nobody can say a word against Greek: it stamps a man at once as an educated gentleman. And my family, thank Heaven, is not a pig-headed Tory one. We are Whigs, and believe in liberty. Let snobbish people say what they please: Barbara shall marry, not the man they like, but the man *I* like.

STEPHEN   Of course I was thinking only of his income. However, he is not likely to be extravagant.

LADY BRITOMART   Dont be too sure of that, Stephen. I know your quiet, simple, refined, poetic people like Adolphus: quite content with the best of everything! They cost more than your extravagant people, who are always as mean as they are second rate. No: Barbara will need at least £2000 a year. You see it means two additional households. Besides, my dear, you must marry soon. I dont approve of the present fashion of philandering bachelors and late marriages; and I am trying to arrange something for you.

STEPHEN It's very good of you, mother; but perhaps I had better arrange that for myself.

LADY BRITOMART Nonsense! you are much too young to begin matchmaking: you would be taken in by some pretty little nobody. Of course I dont mean that you are not to be consulted: you know that as well as I do. (STEPHEN *closes his lips and is silent.*) Now dont sulk, Stephen.

STEPHEN I am not sulking, mother. What has all this got to do with—with—with my father?

LADY BRITOMART My dear Stephen: where is the money to come from? It is easy enough for you and the other children to live on my income as long as we are in the same house; but I cant keep four families in four separate houses. You know how poor my father is: he has barely seven thousand a year now; and really, if he were not the Earl of Stevenage, he would have to give up society. He can do nothing for us. He says, naturally enough, that it is absurd that he should be asked to provide for the children of a man who is rolling in money. You see, Stephen, your father must be fabulously wealthy, because there is always a war going on somewhere.

STEPHEN You need not remind me of that, mother. I have hardly ever opened a newspaper in my life without seeing our name in it. The Undershaft torpedo! The Undershaft quick firers! The Undershaft ten inch! the Undershaft disappearing rampart gun! the Undershaft submarine! and now the Undershaft aerial battleship! At Harrow they called me the Woolwich Infant. At Cambridge it was the same. A little brute at King's who was always trying to get up revivals, spoilt my Bible—your first birthday present to me—by writing under my name, "Son and heir to Undershaft and Lazarus, Death and Destruction Dealers: address Christendom and Judea." But that was not so bad as the way I was kowtowed to everywhere because my father was making millions by selling cannons.

LADY BRITOMART It is not only the cannons, but the war loans that Lazarus arranges under cover of giving credit for the cannons. You know, Stephen, it's perfectly scandalous. Those two men, Andrew Undershaft and Lazarus, positively have Europe under their thumbs. That is why your father is able to behave as he does. He is above the law. Do you think Bismarck or Gladstone or Disraeli could have openly defied every social and moral obligation all their lives as your father has? They simply wouldnt have dared. I asked Gladstone to take it up. I asked The Times to take it up. I asked the Lord Chamberlain to take it up. But it was just like asking them to declare war on the Sultan. They wouldnt. They said they couldnt touch him. I believe they were afraid.

STEPHEN   What could they do? He does not actually break the law.

LADY BRITOMART   Not break the law! He is always breaking the law. He broke the law when he was born: his parents were not married.

STEPHEN   Mother! Is that true?

LADY BRITOMART   Of course it's true: that was why we separated.

STEPHEN   He married without letting you know that!

LADY BRITOMART (*rather taken aback by this inference*)   Oh no. To do Andrew justice, that was not the sort of thing he did. Besides, you know the Undershaft motto: Unashamed. Everybody knew.

STEPHEN   But you said that was why you separated.

LADY BRITOMART   Yes, because he was not content with being a foundling himself: he wanted to disinherit you for another foundling. That was what I couldnt stand.

STEPHEN (*ashamed*)   Do you mean for—for—for—

LADY BRITOMART   Dont stammer, Stephen. Speak distinctly.

STEPHEN   But this is so frightful to me, mother. To have to speak to you about such things!

LADY BRITOMART   It's not pleasant for me, either, especially if you are still so childish that you must make it worse by a display of embarrassment. It is only in the middle classes, Stephen, that people get into a state of dumb helpless horror when they find that there are wicked people in the world. In our class, we have to decide what is to be done with wicked people; and nothing should disturb our self-possession. Now ask your question properly.

STEPHEN   Mother: have you no consideration for me? For Heaven's sake either treat me as a child, as you always do, and tell me nothing at all or tell me everything and let me take it as best I can.

LADY BRITOMART   Treat you as a child! What do you mean? It is most unkind and ungrateful of you to say such a thing. You know I have never treated any of you as children. I have always made you my companions and friends, and allowed you perfect freedom to do and say whatever you like, so long as you liked what I could approve of.

STEPHEN (*desperately*)   I daresay we have been the very imperfect children of a very perfect mother; but I do beg you to let me alone for once, and tell me about this horrible business of my father wanting to set me aside for another son.

LADY BRITOMART (*amazed*)   Another son! I never said anything of the kind. I never dreamt of such a thing. This is what comes of interrupting me.

STEPHEN   But you said—

LADY BRITOMART (*cutting him short*)   Now be a good boy, Stephen, and listen to me patiently. The Undershafts are descended from a foundling in the parish of St Andrew Undershaft in the city. That was long ago, in the reign of James the First. Well, this foundling was adopted by an armorer and gun-maker. In the course of time the foundling succeeded to the business; and from some notion of gratitude, or some vow or something, he adopted another foundling, and left the business to him. And that foundling did the same. Ever since that, the cannon business has always been left to an adopted foundling named Andrew Undershaft.

STEPHEN   But did they never marry? Were there no legitimate sons?

LADY BRITOMART   Oh yes: they married just as your father did; and they were rich enough to buy land for their own children and leave them well provided for. But they always adopted and trained some foundling to succeed them in the business; and of course they always quarrelled with their wives furiously over it. Your father was adopted in that way and he pretends to consider himself bound to keep up the tradition and adopt somebody to leave the business to. Of course I was not going to stand that. There may have been some reason for it when the Undershafts could only marry women in their own class, whose sons were not fit to govern great estates. But there could be no excuse for passing over my son.

STEPHEN (*dubiously*)   I am afraid I should make a poor hand of managing a cannon foundry.

LADY BRITOMART   Nonsense! you could easily get a manager and pay him a salary.

STEPHEN   My father evidently had no great opinion of my capacity.

LADY BRITOMART   Stuff, child! you were only a baby: it had nothing to do with your capacity. Andrew did it on principle, just as he did every perverse and wicked thing on principle. When my father remonstrated, Andrew actually told him to his face that history tells us of only two successful institutions: one the Undershaft firm, and the other the Roman Empire under the Antonines.

That was because the Antonine emperors all adopted their successors. Such rubbish! The Stevenages are as good as the Antonines, I hope: and you are a Stevenage. But that was Andrew all over. There you have the man! Always clever and unanswerable when he was defending nonsense and wickedness: always awkward and sullen when he had to behave sensibly and decently!

STEPHEN   Then it was on my account that your home life was broken up, mother. I am sorry.

LADY BRITOMART   Well, dear, there were other differences. I really cannot bear an immoral man. I am not a Pharisee, I hope; and I should not have minded his merely doing wrong things: we are none of us perfect. But your father didnt exactly do wrong things: he said them and thought them: that was what was so dreadful. He really had a sort of religion of wrongness. Just as one doesnt mind men practising immorality so long as they own that they are in the wrong by preaching morality; so I couldnt forgive Andrew for preaching immorality while he practised morality. You would all have grown up without principles, without any knowledge of right and wrong, if he had been in the house. You know, my dear, your father was a very attractive man in some ways. Children did not dislike him; and he took advantage of it to put the wickedest ideas into their heads, and make them quite unmanageable. I did not dislike him myself: very far from it; but nothing can bridge over moral disagreement.

STEPHEN   All this simply bewilders me, mother. People may differ about matters of opinion, or even about religion; but how can they differ about right and wrong? Right is right; and wrong is wrong; and if a man cannot distinguish them properly, he is either a fool or a rascal: thats all.

LADY BRITOMART   (*touched*)   Thats my own boy (*she pats his cheek*)! Your father never could answer that: he used to laugh and get out of it under cover of some affectionate nonsense. And now that you understand the situation, what do you advise me to do?

STEPHEN   Well, what can you do?

LADY BRITOMART   I must get the money somehow.

STEPHEN   We cannot take money from him. I had rather go and live in some cheap place like Bedford Square or even Hampstead than take a farthing of his money.

LADY BRITOMART   But after all, Stephen, our present income comes from Andrew.

STEPHEN   (*shocked*)   I never knew that.

LADY BRITOMART   Well, you surely didnt suppose your grandfather had anything to give me. The Stevenages could not do everything for you. We gave you social position. Andrew had to contribute something. He had a very good bargain, I think.

STEPHEN (*bitterly*)   We are utterly dependent on him and his cannons, then?

LADY BRITOMART   Certainly not: the money is settled. But he provided it. So you see it is not a question of taking money from him or not: it is simply a question of how much. I dont want any more for myself.

STEPHEN   Nor do I.

LADY BRITOMART   But Sarah does; and Barbara does. That is, Charles Lomax and Adolphus Cusins will cost them more. So I must put my pride in my pocket and ask for it, I suppose. That is your advice, Stephen, is it not?

STEPHEN   No.

LADY BRITOMART (*sharply*)   Stephen!

STEPHEN   Of course if you are determined—

LADY BRITOMART   I am not determined: I ask your advice; and I am waiting for it. I will not have all the responsibility thrown on my shoulders.

STEPHEN (*obstinately*)   I would die sooner than ask him for another penny.

LADY BRITOMART (*resignedly*)   You mean that *I* must ask him. Very well, Stephen: it shall be as you wish. You will be glad to know that your grandfather concurs. But he thinks I ought to ask Andrew to come here and see the girls. After all, he must have some natural affection for them.

STEPHEN   Ask him here!!!

LADY BRITOMART   Do not repeat my words, Stephen. Where else can I ask him?

STEPHEN   I never expected you to ask him at all.

LADY BRITOMART   Now dont tease, Stephen. Come! you see that it is necessary that he should pay us a visit, dont you?

STEPHEN (*reluctantly*)   I suppose so, if the girls cannot do without his money.

LADY BRITOMART   Thank you, Stephen: I knew you would give me the right advice when it was properly explained to you. I have asked your father to come this evening. (STEPHEN *bounds from his seat.*) Dont jump, Stephen: it fidgets me.

STEPHEN (*in utter consternation*)   Do you mean to say that my father is coming here tonight—that he may be here at any moment?

LADY BRITOMART (*looking at her watch*)   I said nine. (*He gasps. She rises.*) Ring the bell, please. (STEPHEN *goes to the smaller writing table; presses a button on it; and sits at it with his elbows on the table and his head in his hands, outwitted and over-whelmed.*) It is ten minutes to nine yet; and I have to prepare the girls. I asked Charles Lomax and Adolphus to dinner on purpose that they might be here. Andrew had better see them in case he should cherish any delusion as to their being capable of supporting their wives. (*The butler enters:* LADY BRITOMART *goes behind the settee to speak to him.*) Morrison: go up to the drawing room and tell everybody to come down here at once. (MORRISON *withdraws.* LADY BRITOMART *turns to* STEPHEN.) Now remember, Stephen: I shall need all your countenance and authority. (*He rises and tries to recover some vestige of these attributes.*) Give me a chair, dear. (*He pushes a chair forward from the wall to where she stands, near the smaller writing table. She sits down; and he goes to the armchair, into which he throws himself.*) I dont know how Barbara will take it. Ever since they made her a major in the Salvation Army she has developed a propensity to have her own way and order people about which quite cows me sometimes. It's not ladylike: I'm sure I dont know where she picked it up. Anyhow, Barbara shant bully me but still it's just as well that your father should be here before she has time to refuse to meet him or make a fuss. Dont look nervous, Stephen: it will only encourage Barbara to make difficulties. *I* am nervous enough, goodness knows; but I dont shew it.

SARAH *and* BARBARA *come in with their respective young men,* CHARLES LOMAX *and* ADOLPHUS CUSINS. SARAH *is slender, bored, and mundane.* BARBARA *is robuster, jollier, much more energetic.* SARAH *is fashionably dressed:* BARBARA *is in Salvation Army uniform.* LOMAX, *a young man about town, is like many other young men about town. He is afflicted with a frivolous sense of humor which plunges him at the most inopportune moments into paroxysms of imperfectly suppressed laughter.* CUSINS *is a spectacled student, slight, thin haired, and sweet voiced, with a more complex form of* LOMAX's *complaint. His sense of humor is intellectual and subtle, and is complicated by an appalling temper. The lifelong struggle of a benevolent temperament and a high conscience against impulses of inhuman ridicule and fierce impatience has set up a chronic strain which has visibly wrecked his constitution. He is a most implacable, determined, tenacious, intolerant person who by mere force of character presents himself as—and indeed actually is—considerate, gentle, explanatory, even mild and apologetic, capable possibly of murder, but not of cruelty or coarseness. By the operation of some instinct which is not merciful enough to blind him with the illusions of love, he is obstinately bent on marrying* BARBARA. LOMAX *likes* SARAH *and thinks it will be rather a lark to marry her. Consequently he has not attempted to resist* LADY BRITOMART's *arrangements to that end.*

All four look as if they had been having a good deal of fun in the drawing room. The girls enter first, leaving the swains outside. SARAH *comes to the settee.* BARBARA *comes in after her and stops at the door.*

BARBARA   Are Cholly and Dolly to come in?

LADY BRITOMART (*forcibly*)   Barbara: I will not have Charles called Cholly: the vulgarity of it positively makes me ill.

BARBARA   It's all right, mother: Cholly is quite correct nowadays. Are they to come in?

LADY BRITOMART   Yes, if they will behave themselves.

BARBARA (*through the door*)   Come in, Dolly; and behave yourself.

BARBARA *comes to her mother's writing table.* CUSINS *enters smiling, and wanders towards* LADY BRITOMART.

SARAH (*calling*)   Come in, Cholly. (LOMAX *enters, controlling his features very imperfectly, and places himself vaguely between* SARAH *and* BARBARA.)

LADY BRITOMART (*peremptorily*)   Sit down, all of you. (*They sit.* CUSINS *crosses to the window and seats himself there.* LOMAX *takes a chair.* BARBARA *sits at the writing table and* SARAH *on the settee.*) I dont in the least know what you are laughing at, Adolphus. I am surprised at you, though I expected nothing better from Charles Lomax.

CUSINS (*in a remarkably gentle voice*)   Barbara has been trying to teach me the West Ham Salvation March.

LADY BRITOMART   I see nothing to laugh at in that; nor should you if you are really converted.

CUSINS (*sweetly*)   You were not present. It was really funny, I believe.

LOMAX   Ripping.

LADY BRITOMART   Be quiet, Charles. Now listen to me, children. Your father is coming here this evening.

General stupefaction. LOMAX, SARAH, *and* BARBARA *rise:* SARAH *scared, and* BARBARA *amused and expectant.*

LOMAX (*remonstrating*)   Oh I say!

LADY BRITOMART   You are not called on to say anything, Charles.

SARAH   Are you serious, mother?

LADY BRITOMART   Of course I am serious. It is on your account, Sarah, and also on Charles's. (*Silence,* SARAH *sits, with a shrug.* CHARLES *looks painfully unworthy.*) I hope you are not going to object, Barbara.

BARBARA   I! why should I? My father has a soul to be saved like everybody else. He's quite welcome as far as I am concerned. (*She sits on the table, and softly whistles "Onward, Christian Soldiers".*)

LOMAX (*still remonstrant*) But really, dont you know! Oh I say!

LADY BRITOMART (*frigidly*) What do you wish to convey, Charles?

LOMAX Well, you must admit that this is a bit thick.

LADY BRITOMART (*turning with ominous suavity to* CUSINS). Adolphus: you are a professor of Greek. Can you translate Charles Lomax's remarks into reputable English for us?

CUSINS (*cautiously*) If I may say so, Lady Brit, I think Charles has rather happily expressed what we feel. Homer, speaking of Autolycus, uses the same phrase. πυκινὸν δόμον ἐλθεῖν means a bit thick.

LOMAX (*handsomely*) Not that I mind, you know, if Sarah dont. (*He sits.*)

LADY BRITOMART (*crushingly*) Thank you. Have I your permission, Adolphus, to invite my own husband to my own house?

CUSINS (*gallantly*) You have my unhesitating support in everything you do.

LADY BRITOMART Tush! Sarah: have you nothing to say?

SARAH Do you mean that he is coming regularly to live here?

LADY BRITOMART Certainly not. The spare room is ready for him if he likes to stay for a day or two and see a little more of you; but there are limits.

SARAH Well, he cant eat us, I suppose. *I* dont mind.

LOMAX (*chuckling*) I wonder how the old man will take it.

LADY BRITOMART Much as the old woman will, no doubt, Charles.

LOMAX (*abashed*) I didnt mean—at least—

LADY BRITOMART You didnt think, Charles. You never do; and the result is, you never mean anything. And now please attend to me, children. Your father will be quite a stranger to us.

LOMAX I suppose he hasnt seen Sarah since she was a little kid.

LADY BRITOMART Not since she was a little kid, Charles, as you express it with that elegance of diction and refinement of thought that seem never to desert you. Accordingly—er—(*impatiently*) Now I have forgotten what I was going to say. That comes of your provoking me to be sarcastic, Charles. Adolphus: will you kindly tell me where I was.

CUSINS (*sweetly*) You were saying that as Mr Undershaft has not seen his children since they were babies, he will form his opinion of the way you have brought them up from their behavior tonight, and that therefore you wish us all to be particularly careful to conduct ourselves well, especially Charles.

LADY BRITOMART (*with emphatic approval*) Precisely.

LOMAX Look here, Dolly: Lady Brit didnt say that.

LADY BRITOMART (*vehemently*)   I did, Charles. Adolphus's recollection is perfectly correct. It is most important that you should be good; and I do beg you for once not to pair off into opposite corners and giggle and whisper while I am speaking to your father.

BARBARA   All right, mother. We'll do you credit. (*She comes off the table, and sits in her chair with ladylike elegance.*)

LADY BRITOMART   Remember, Charles, that Sarah will want to feel proud of you instead of ashamed of you.

LOMAX   Oh I say! theres nothing to be exactly proud of, dont you know.

LADY BRITOMART   Well, try and look as if there was.

MORRISON, *pale and dismayed, breaks into the room in unconcealed disorder.*

MORRISON   Might I speak a word to you, my lady?

LADY BRITOMART   Nonsense! Shew him up.

MORRISON   Yes, my lady. (*He goes.*)

LOMAX   Does Morrison know who it is?

LADY BRITOMART   Of course. Morrison has always been with us.

LOMAX   It must be a regular corker for him, dont you know.

LADY BRITOMART   Is this a moment to get on my nerves, Charles, with your outrageous expressions?

LOMAX   But this is something out of the ordinary, really—

MORRISON (*at the door*)   The—er—Mr Undershaft. (*He retreats in confusion.*)

ANDREW UNDERSHAFT *comes in. All rise.* LADY BRITOMART *meets him in the middle of the room behind the settee.*

ANDREW *is, on the surface, a stoutish, easygoing elderly man, with kindly patient manners, and an engaging simplicity of character. But he has a watchful, deliberate, waiting, listening face, and formidable reserves of power, both bodily and mental, in his capacious chest and long head. His gentleness is partly that of a strong man who has learnt by experience that his natural grip hurts ordinary people unless he handles them very carefully, and partly the mellowness of age and success. He is also a little shy in his present very delicate situation.*

LADY BRITOMART   Good evening, Andrew.

UNDERSHAFT   How d'ye do, my dear.

LADY BRITOMART   You look a good deal older.

UNDERSHAFT (*apologetically*)   I am somewhat older. (*Taking her hand with a touch of courtship.*) Time has stood still with you.

LADY BRITOMART (*throwing away his hand*)   Rubbish! This is your family.

UNDERSHAFT (*surprised*)   Is it so large? I am sorry to say my memory is failing very badly in some things. (*He offers his hand with paternal kindness to* LOMAX.)

LOMAX (*jerkily shaking his hand*)   Ahdedoo.

UNDERSHAFT   I can see you are my eldest. I am very glad to meet you again, my boy.

LOMAX (*remonstrating*)   No, but look here dont you know— (*Overcome.*) Oh I say!

LADY BRITOMART (*recovering from momentary speechlessness*)   Andrew: do you mean to say that you dont remember how many children you have?

UNDERSHAFT   Well, I am afraid I—. They have grown so much— er. Am I making any ridiculous mistake? I may as well confess: I recollect only one son. But so many things have happened since, of course—er—

LADY BRITOMART (*decisively*)   Andrew: you are talking nonsense. Of course you have only one son.

UNDERSHAFT   Perhaps you will be good enough to introduce me, my dear.

LADY BRITOMART   That is Charles Lomax, who is engaged to Sarah.

UNDERSHAFT   My dear sir, I beg your pardon.

LOMAX   Notatall. Delighted, I assure you.

LADY BRITOMART   This is Stephen.

UNDERSHAFT (*bowing*)   Happy to make your acquaintance, Mr Stephen. Then (*going to* CUSINS) you must be my son. (*Taking* CUSINS' *hands in his.*) How are you, my young friend? (*To* LADY BRITOMART.) He is very like you, my love.

CUSINS   You flatter me, Mr Undershaft. My name is Cusins: engaged to Barbara. (*Very explicitly.*) That is Major Barbara Undershaft, of the Salvation Army. This is Sarah, your second daughter. This is Stephen Undershaft, your son.

UNDERSHAFT   My dear Stephen, I beg your pardon.

STEPHEN   Not at all.

UNDERSHAFT   Mr. Cusins: I am much indebted to you for explaining so precisely. (*Turning to* SARAH.) Barbara, my dear—

SARAH (*prompting him*)   Sarah.

UNDERSHAFT   Sarah, of course. (*They shake hands. He goes over to* BARBARA.) Barbara—I am right this time, I hope?

BARBARA   Quite right. (*They shake hands.*)

LADY BRITOMART (*resuming command*)   Sit down, all of you. Sit down, Andrew. (*She comes forward and sits on the settee.* CUSINS *also brings his chair forward on her left.* BARBARA *and* STEPHEN *resume their seats.* LOMAX *gives his chair to* SARAH *and goes for another.*)

UNDERSHAFT   Thank you, my love.

LOMAX (*conversationally, as he brings a chair forward between the writing table and the settee, and offers it to* UNDERSHAFT) Takes you some time to find out exactly where you are, dont it?

UNDERSHAFT (*accepting the chair, but remaining standing*) That is not what embarrasses me, Mr Lomax. My difficulty is that if I play the part of a father, I shall produce the effect of an intrusive stranger; and if I play the part of a discreet stranger, I may appear a callous father.

LADY BRITOMART There is no need for you to play any part at all, Andrew. You had much better be sincere and natural.

UNDERSHAFT (*submissively*) Yes, my dear: I daresay that will be best. (*He sits down comfortably.*) Well, here I am. Now what can I do for you all?

LADY BRITOMART You need not do anything, Andrew. You are one of the family. You can sit with us and enjoy yourself.

A painfully conscious pause. BARBARA *makes a face at* LOMAX, *whose too long suppressed mirth immediately explodes in agonized neighings.*

LADY BRITOMART (*outraged*) Charles Lomax: if you can behave yourself, behave yourself. If not, leave the room.

LOMAX I'm awfully sorry, Lady Brit; but really you know, upon my soul! (*He sits on the settee between* LADY BRITOMART *and* UNDERSHAFT, *quite overcome.*)

BARBARA Why dont you laugh if you want to, Cholly? It's good for your inside.

LADY BRITOMART Barbara: you have had the education of a lady. Please let your father see that; and dont talk like a street girl.

UNDERSHAFT Never mind me, my dear. As you know, I am not a gentleman; and I was never educated.

LOMAX (*encouragingly*) Nobody'd know it, I assure you. You look all right, you know.

CUSINS Let me advise you to study Greek, Mr Undershaft. Greek scholars are privileged men. Few of them know Greek; and none of them know anything else; but their position is unchallengeable. Other languages are the qualifications of waiters and commercial travelers: Greek is to a man of position what the hallmark is to silver.

BARBARA Dolly: dont be insincere. Cholly: fetch your concertina and play something for us.

LOMAX (*jumps up eagerly, but checks himself to remark doubtfully to* UNDERSHAFT) Perhaps that sort of thing isnt in your line, eh?

UNDERSHAFT I am particularly fond of music.

LOMAX (*delighted*) Are you? Then I'll get it. (*He goes upstairs for the instrument.*)

UNDERSHAFT   Do you play, Barbara?

BARBARA   Only the tambourine. But Cholly's teaching me the concertina.

UNDERSHAFT   Is Cholly also a member of the Salvation Army?

BARBARA   No: he says it's bad form to be a dissenter. But I dont despair of Cholly. I made him come yesterday to a meeting at the dock gates, and take the collection in his hat.

UNDERSHAFT   (*looks whimsically at his wife*) *!!*

LADY BRITOMART   It is not my doing, Andrew. Barbara is old enough to take her own way. She has no father to advise her.

BARBARA   Oh yes she has. There are no orphans in the Salvation Army.

UNDERSHAFT   Your father there has a great many children and plenty of experience, eh?

BARBARA   (*looking at him with quick interest and nodding*)   Just so. How did you come to understand that? (LOMAX *is heard at the door trying the concertina.*)

LADY BRITOMART   Come in, Charles. Play us something at once.

LOMAX   Righto! (*He sits down in his former place, and preludes.*)

UNDERSHAFT   One moment, Mr Lomax. I am rather interested in the Salvation Army. Its motto might be my own: Blood and Fire.

LOMAX   (*shocked*)   But not your sort of blood and fire, you know.

UNDERSHAFT   My sort of blood cleanses: my sort of fire purifies.

BARBARA   So do ours. Come down tomorrow to my shelter—the West Ham shelter—and see what we're doing. We're going to march to a great meeting in the Assembly Hall at Mile End. Come and see the shelter and then march with us: it will do you a lot of good. Can you play anything?

UNDERSHAFT   In my youth I earned pennies, and even shillings occasionally, in the streets and in public house parlors by my natural talent for stepdancing. Later on, I became a member of the Undershaft orchestral society, and performed passably on the tenor trombone.

LOMAX   (*scandalized—putting down the concertina*)   Oh I say!

BARBARA   Many a sinner has played himself into heaven on the trombone, thanks to the Army.

LOMAX   (*to* BARBARA, *still rather shocked*)   Yes, but what about the cannon business, dont you know? (*To* UNDERSHAFT.) Getting into heaven is not exactly in your line, is it?

LADY BRITOMART   Charles!!!

LOMAX   Well; but it stands to reason, dont it? The cannon business may be necessary and all that: we cant get on without cannons; but it isnt right, you know. On the other hand, there may be a certain amount of tosh about the Salvation Army—I belong to the Established Church myself—but still you cant deny that it's religion; and you cant go against religion, can you? At least unless youre downright immoral, dont you know.

UNDERSHAFT   You hardly appreciate my position, Mr Lomax—

LOMAX (*hastily*)   I'm not saying anything against you personally—

UNDERSHAFT   Quite so, quite so. But consider for a moment. Here I am, a profiteer in mutilation and murder. I find myself in a specially amiable humor just now because, this morning, down at the foundry, we blew twenty-seven dummy soldiers into fragments with a gun which formerly destroyed only thirteen.

LOMAX (*leniently*)   Well, the more destructive war becomes, the sooner it will be abolished, eh?

UNDERSHAFT   Not at all. The more destructive war becomes the more fascinating we find it. No, Mr Lomax: I am obliged to you for making the usual excuse for my trade; but I am not ashamed of it. I am not one of those men who keep their morals and their business in watertight compartments. All the spare money my trade rivals spend on hospitals, cathedrals, and other receptacles for conscience money, I devote to experiments and researches in improved methods of destroying life and property. I have always done so; and I always shall. Therefore your Christmas card moralities of peace on earth and goodwill among men are of no use to me. Your Christianity, which enjoins you to resist not evil, and to turn the other cheek, would make me a bankrupt. My morality—my religion—must have a place for cannons and torpedoes in it.

STEPHEN (*coldly—almost sullenly*)   You speak as if there were half a dozen moralities and religions to choose from, instead of one true morality and one true religion.

UNDERSHAFT   For me there is only one true morality; but it might not fit you, as you do not manufacture aerial battleships. There is only one true morality for every man; but every man has not the same true morality.

LOMAX (*overtaxed*)   Would you mind saying that again? I didnt quite follow it.

CUSINS   It's quite simple. As Euripides says, one man's meat is another man's poison morally as well as physically.

UNDERSHAFT   Precisely.

LOMAX   Oh, that! Yes, yes, yes. True. True.

STEPHEN   In other words, some men are honest and some are scoundrels.

BARBARA   Bosh! There are no scoundrels.

UNDERSHAFT   Indeed? Are there any good men?

BARBARA   No. Not one. There are neither good men nor scoundrels: there are just children of one Father; and the sooner they stop calling one another names the better. You neednt talk to me: I know them. Ive had scores of them through my hands: scoundrels, criminals, infidels, philanthropists, missionaries, county councillors, all sorts. Theyre all just the same sort of sinner; and theres the same salvation ready for them all.

UNDERSHAFT   May I ask have you ever saved a maker of cannons?

BARBARA   No. Will you let me try?

UNDERSHAFT   Well, I will make a bargain with you. If I go to see you tomorrow in your Salvation Shelter, will you come the day after to see me in my cannon works?

BARBARA   Take care. It may end in your giving up the cannons for the sake of the Salvation Army.

UNDERSHAFT   Are you sure it will not end in your giving up the Salvation Army for the sake of the cannons?

BARBARA   I will take my chance of that.

UNDERSHAFT   And I will take my chance of the other. (*They shake hands on it.*) Where is your shelter?

BARBARA   In West Ham. At the sign of the cross. Ask anybody in Canning Town. Where are your works?

UNDERSHAFT   In Perivale St Andrews. At the sign of the sword. Ask anybody in Europe.

LOMAX   Hadnt I better play something?

BARBARA   Yes. Give us Onward, Christian Soldiers.

LOMAX   Well, thats rather a strong order to begin with, dont you know. Suppose I sing Thourt passing hence, my brother. It's much the same tune.

BARBARA   It's too melancholy. You get saved, Cholly; and youll pass hence, my brother, without making such a fuss about it.

LADY BRITOMART   Really, Barbara, you go on as if religion were a pleasant subject. Do have some sense of propriety.

UNDERSHAFT   I do not find it an unpleasant subject, my dear. It is the only one that capable people really care for.

LADY BRITOMART (*looking at her watch*)   Well, if you are determined to have it, I insist on having it in a proper and respectable way. Charles: ring for prayers.

General amazement. STEPHEN *rises in dismay.*

LOMAX (*rising*)   Oh I say!

UNDERSHAFT (*rising*)   I am afraid I must be going.

LADY BRITOMART   You cannot go now, Andrew: it would be most improper. Sit down. What will the servants think?

UNDERSHAFT My dear: I have conscientious scruples. May I suggest a compromise? If Barbara will conduct a little service in the drawing room, with Mr Lomax as organist, I will attend it willingly. I will even take part, if a trombone can be procured.

LADY BRITOMART Dont mock, Andrew.

UNDERSHAFT (*shocked—to* BARBARA) You dont think I am mocking, my love, I hope.

BARBARA No, of course not; and it wouldnt matter if you were: half the Army came to their first meeting for a lark. (*Rising.*) Come along. (*She throws her arm round her father and sweeps him out, calling to the others from the threshold.*) Come, Dolly. Come, Cholly.

LADY BRITOMART I will not be disobeyed by everybody. Adolphus: sit down. (*He does not.*) Charles: you may go. You are not fit for prayers: you cannot keep your countenance.

LOMAX Oh I say! (*He goes out.*)

LADY BRITOMART (*continuing*) But you, Adolphus, can behave yourself if you choose to. I insist on your staying.

CUSINS My dear Lady Brit: there are things in the family prayer book that I couldnt bear to hear you say.

LADY BRITOMART What things, pray?

CUSINS Well, you would have to say before all the servants that we have done things we ought not to have done, and left undone things we ought to have done, and that there is no health in us. I cannot bear to hear you doing yourself such an injustice, and Barbara such an injustice. As for myself, I flatly deny it: I have done my best. I shouldnt dare to marry Barbara—I couldnt look you in the face—if it were true. So I must go to the drawing room.

LADY BRITOMART (*offended*) Well, go. (*He starts for the door.*) And remember this, Adolphus (*he turns to listen*): I have a very strong suspicion that you went to the Salvation Army to worship Barbara and nothing else. And I quite appreciate the very clever way in which you systematically humbug me. I have found you out. Take care Barbara doesnt. Thats all.

CUSINS (*with unruffled sweetness*) Dont tell on me. (*He steals out.*)

LADY BRITOMART Sarah: if you want to go, go. Anything's better than to sit there as if you wished you were a thousand miles away.

SARAH (*languidly*) Very well, mamma. (*She goes.*)

LADY BRITOMART, *with a sudden flounce, gives way to a little gust of tears.*

STEPHEN (*going to her*) Mother: whats the matter?

LADY BRITOMART (*swishing away her tears with her handkerchief*)

Nothing. Foolishness. You can go with him, too, if you like, and leave me with the servants.

STEPHEN   Oh, you mustnt think that, mother. I—I dont like him.

LADY BRITOMART   The others do. That is the injustice of a woman's lot. A woman has to bring up her children; and that means to restrain them, to deny them things they want, to set them tasks, to punish them when they do wrong, to do all the unpleasant things. And then the father, who has nothing to do but pet them and spoil them, comes in when all her work is done and steals their affection from her.

STEPHEN   He has not stolen our affection from you. It is only curiosity.

LADY BRITOMART   (*violently*)   I wont be consoled, Stephen. There is nothing the matter with me. (*She rises and goes towards the door.*)

STEPHEN   Where are you going, mother?

LADY BRITOMART   To the drawing room, of course. (*She goes out. Onward, Christian Soldiers, on the concertina, with tambourine accompaniment, is heard when the door opens.*) Are you coming, Stephen?

STEPHEN   No. Certainly not. (*She goes. He sits down on the settee, with compressed lips and an expression of strong dislike.*)

ACT II

The yard of the West Ham shelter of the Salvation Army is a cold place on a January morning. The building itself, an old warehouse, is newly whitewashed. Its gabled end projects into the yard in the middle, with a door on the ground floor, and another in the loft above it without any balcony or ladder, but with a pulley rigged over it for hoisting sacks. Those who come from this central gable end into the yard have the gateway leading to the street on their left, with a stone horse-trough just beyond it, and, on the right, a penthouse shielding a table from the weather. There are forms at the table; and on them are seated a man and a woman, both much down on their luck, finishing a meal of bread (one thick slice each, with margarine and golden syrup) and diluted milk.

The man, a workman out of employment, is young, agile, a talker, a poser, sharp enough to be capable of anything in reason except honesty or altruistic considerations of any kind. The woman is a commonplace old bundle of poverty and hard-worn humanity. She looks sixty and probably is forty-five. If they were rich people, gloved and muffed and well wrapped up in furs and overcoats, they would be numbed and miserable; for it is a grindingly cold raw January day; and a glance at the background of grimy warehouses and leaden sky visible over the whitewashed walls of the yard would drive any idle rich person straight to the Mediterranean. But these two, being no more troubled with visions of the Mediterranean than of the moon, and being compelled to keep more of their clothes in the pawnshop, and less on their persons, in winter than in summer, are not depressed by the cold: rather are they stung into vivacity, to which their meal has just now given an almost jolly turn. The man takes a pull at his mug, and then gets up and moves about the yard with his hands deep in his pockets, occasionally breaking into a stepdance.

THE WOMAN   Feel better arter your meal, sir?

THE MAN   No. Call that a meal! Good enough for you, praps, but wot is it to me, an intelligent workin man.

THE WOMAN   Workin man! Wot are you?

THE MAN   Painter.

THE WOMAN (*sceptically*)   Yus, I dessay.

THE MAN   Yus, you dessay! I know. Every loafer that cant do nothink calls isself a painter. Well, I'm a real painter: grainer, finisher, thirty-eight bob a week when I can get it.

THE WOMAN   Then why dont you go and get it?

THE MAN   I'll tell you why. Fust: I'm intelligent—fffff! it's rotten cold here (*he dances a step or two*)—yes: intelligent beyond the station o life into which it has pleased the capitalists to call me; and they dont like a man that sees through em. Second, an intelligent bein needs a doo share of appiness; so I drink somethink cruel when I get the chawnce. Third, I stand by my class and do as little as I can so's to leave arf the job for me fellow workers. Fourth, I'm fly enough to know wots inside the law and wots outside it; and inside it I do as the capitalists do: pinch wot I can lay me ands on. In a proper state of society I am sober, industrious and honest: in Rome, so to speak, I do as the Romans do. Wots the consequence? When trade is bad—and it's rotten bad just now—and the employers az to sack arf their men, they generally start on me.

THE WOMAN   Whats your name?

THE MAN   Price. Bronterre O'Brien Price. Usually called Snobby Price, for short.

THE WOMAN   Snobby's a carpenter, aint it? You said you was a painter.

PRICE   Not that kind of snob, but the genteel sort. I'm too uppish, owing to my intelligence, and my father being a Chartist and a reading, thinking man: a stationer, too. I'm none of your common hewers of wood and drawers of water; and dont you forget it. (*He returns to his seat at the table, and takes up his mug.*) Wots your name?

THE WOMAN   Rummy Mitchens, sir.

PRICE (*quaffing the remains of his milk to her*) Your elth, Miss Mitchens.

RUMMY (*correcting him*) Missis Mitchens.

PRICE Wot! Oh Rummy, Rummy! Respectable married woman, Rummy, gittin rescued by the Salvation Army by pretendin to be a bad un. Same old game!

RUMMY What am I to do? I cant starve. Them Salvation lasses is dear good girls; but the better you are, the worse they likes to think you were before they rescued you. Why shouldnt they av a bit o credit, poor loves? theyre worn to rags by their work. And where would they get the money to rescue us if we was to let on we're no worse than other people? You know what ladies and gentlemen are.

PRICE Thievin swine! Wish I ad their job, Rummy, all the same. Wot does Rummy stand for? Pet name praps?

RUMMY Short for Romola.

PRICE For wot!?

RUMMY Romola. It was out of a new book. Somebody me mother wanted me to grow up like.

PRICE We're companions in misfortune, Rummy. Both on us got names that nobody cawnt pronounce. Consequently I'm Snobby and youre Rummy because Bill and Sally wasnt good enough for our parents. Such is life!

RUMMY Who saved you, Mr Price? Was it Major Barbara?

PRICE No: I come here on my own. I'm going to be Bronterre O'Brien Price, the converted painter. I know wot they like. I'll tell em how I blasphemed and gambled and wopped my poor old mother—

RUMMY (*shocked*) Used you to beat your mother?

PRICE Not likely. She used to beat me. No matter: you come and listen to the converted painter, and youll hear how she was a pious woman that taught me me prayers at er knee, an how I used to come home drunk and drag her out o bed be er snow white airs, an lam into er with the poker.

RUMMY Thats whats so unfair to us women. Your confessions is just as big lies as ours: you dont tell what you really done no more than us; but you men can tell your lies right out at the meetins and be made much of for it, while the sort o confessions we az to make az to be whispered to one lady at a time. It aint right, spite of all their piety.

PRICE Right! Do you spose the Army'd be allowed if it went and did right? Not much. It combs our air and makes us good little blokes to be robbed and put upon. But I'll play the game as good as any of em. I'll see somebody struck by lightnin, or hear a voice sayin "Snobby Price: where will you spend eternity?" I'll av a time of it, I tell you.

RUMMY   You wont be let drink, though.

PRICE   I'll take it out in gorspellin, then. I dont want to drink if I can get fun enough any other way.

JENNY HILL, *a pale, overwrought, pretty Salvation lass of 18, comes in through the yard gate, leading* PETER SHIRLEY, *a half hardened, half worn-out elderly man, weak with hunger.*

JENNY   (*supporting him*)   Come! pluck up. I'll get you something to eat. Youll be all right then.

PRICE   (*rising and hurrying officiously to take the old man off* JENNY's *hands*)   Poor old man! Cheer up, brother: youll find rest and peace and appiness ere. Hurry up with the food, miss: e's fair done. (*Jenny hurries into the shelter.*) Ere, buck up, daddy! she's fetchin y'a thick slice of breadn treacle, an a mug o skyblue. (*He seats him at the corner of the table.*)

RUMMY   (*gaily*)   Keep up your old art! Never say die!

SHIRLEY   I'm not an old man. I'm only 46. I'm as good as ever I was. The grey patch come in my hair before I was thirty. All it wants is three pennorth o hair dye: am I to be turned on the streets to starve for it? Holy God! I've worked ten to twelve hours a day since I was thirteen, and paid my way all through; and now am I to be thrown into the gutter and my job given to a young man that can do it no better than me because Ive black hair that goes white at the first change?

PRICE   (*cheerfully*)   No good jawrin about it. Youre ony a jumped-up, jerked-off, orspittle-turned-out incurable of an ole workin man: who cares about you? Eh? Make the thievin swine give you a meal: theyve stole many a one from you. Get a bit o your own back. (JENNY *returns with the usual meal.*) There you are, brother. Awsk a blessin an tuck that into you.

SHIRLEY   (*looking at it ravenously but not touching it, and crying like a child*)   I never took anything before.

JENNY   (*petting him*)   Come, come! the Lord sends it to you: he wasn't above taking bread from his friends; and why should you be? Besides, when we find you a job you can pay us for it if you like.

SHIRLEY   (*eagerly*)   Yes, yes: thats true. I can pay you back: it's only a loan. (*Shivering.*) Oh Lord! oh Lord! (*He turns to the table and attacks the meal ravenously.*)

JENNY   Well, Rummy, are you more comfortable now?

RUMMY   God bless you, lovey! youve fed my body and saved my soul, havent you? (JENNY, *touched, kisses her.*) Sit down and rest a bit: you must be ready to drop.

JENNY   Ive been going hard since morning. But theres more work than we can do. I mustnt stop.

RUMMY   Try a prayer for just two minutes. Youll work all the better after.

JENNY (*her eyes lighting up*)   Oh isnt it wonderful how a few minutes prayer revives you! I was quite lightheaded at twelve o'clock, I was so tired; but Major Barbara just sent me to pray for five minutes; and I was able to go on as if I had only just begun. (*To* PRICE.) Did you have a piece of bread?

PRICE (*with unction*)   Yes, miss; but Ive got the piece that I value more; and thats the peace that passeth hall hannerstennin.

RUMMY (*fervently*)   Glory Hallelujah!

BILL WALKER, *a rough customer of about 25, appears at the yard gate and looks malevolently at* JENNY.

JENNY   That makes me so happy. When you say that, I feel wicked for loitering here. I must get to work again.

She is hurrying to the shelter, when the new-comer moves quickly up to the door and intercepts her. His manner is so threatening that she retreats as he comes at her truculently, driving her down the yard.

BILL   Aw knaow you. Youre the one that took awy maw girl. Youre the one that set er agen me. Well, I'm gowin to ev er aht. Not that Aw care a carse for er or you: see? Bat Aw'll let er knaow; and Aw'll let you knaow. Aw'm gowing to give her a doin thatll teach er to cat awy from me. Nah in wiv you and tell er to cam aht afore Aw cam in and kick er aht. Tell er Bill Walker wants er. She'll knaow wot thet means; and if she keeps me witin itll be worse. You stop to jawr beck at me: and Aw'll stawt on you: d'ye eah? Theres your wy. In you gow. (*He takes her by the arm and slings her towards the door of the shelter. She falls on her hand and knee.* RUMMY *helps her up again.*)

PRICE (*rising, and venturing irresolutely towards* BILL)   Easy there, mate. She aint doin you no arm.

BILL   Oo are you callin mite? (*Standing over him threateningly.*) Youre gowin to stend ap for er, aw yer? Put ap your ends.

RUMMY (*running indignantly to him to scold him*)   Oh, you great brute—(*He instantly swings his left hand back against her face. She screams and reels back to the trough, where she sits down, covering her bruised face with her hands and rocking herself and moaning with pain.*)

JENNY (*going to her*)   Oh, God forgive you! How could you strike an old woman like that?

BILL (*seizing her by the hair so violently that she also screams, and tearing her away from the old woman*)   You Gawd forgimme again an Aw'll Gawd forgive you one on the jawr thetll stop you pryin for a week. (*Holding her and turning fiercely on* PRICE.) Ev you ennything to sy agen it?

PRICE (*intimidated*)   No, matey: she aint anything to do with me.

BILL   Good job for you! Aw'd pat two meals into you and fawt you with one finger arter, you stawved cur. (*To* JENNY.) Nah are you gowin to fetch aht Mog Ebbijem; or em Aw to knock your fice off you and fetch her meself?

JENNY (*writhing in his grasp*)   Oh please someone go in and tell Major Barbara—(*she screams again as he wrenches her head down; and* PRICE *and* RUMMY *flee into the shelter*).

BILL   You want to gow in and tell your Mijor of me, do you?

JENNY   Oh please dont drag my hair. Let me go.

BILL   Do you or downt you? (*She stifles a scream.*) Yus or nao?

JENNY   God give me strength—

BILL (*striking her with his fist in the face*)   Gow an shaow her thet, and tell her if she wants one lawk it to cam and interfere with me. (*JENNY, crying with pain, goes into the shed. He goes to the form and addresses the old man.*) Eah: finish your mess; an git aht o mah wy.

SHIRLEY (*springing up and facing him fiercely, with the mug in his hand*)   You take a liberty with me, and I'll smash you over the face with the mug and cut your eye out. Aint you satisfied— young whelps like you—with takin the bread out o the mouths of your elders that have brought you up and slaved for you, but you must come shovin and cheekin and bullyin in here, where the bread o charity is sickenin in our stummicks?

BILL (*contemptuously, but backing a little*)   Wot good are you, you aold palsy mag? Wot good are you?

SHIRLEY   As good as you and better. I'll do a day's work agen you or any fat young soaker of your age. Go and take my job at Horrockses, where I worked for ten year. They want young men there: they cant afford to keep men over forty-five. They're very sorry—give you a character and happy to help you to get anything suited to your years—sure a steady man wont be long out of a job. Well, let em try you. Theyll find the differ. What do you know? Not as much as how to beeyave yourself—layin your dirty fist across the mouth of a respectable woman!

BILL   Downt provowk me to ly it acrost yours: d'ye eah?

SHIRLEY (*with blighting contempt*)   Yes: you like an old man to hit, dont you, when youve finished with the women. I ain't seen you hit a young one yet.

BILL (*stung*) You loy, you aold soupkitchener, you. There was a yang menn eah. Did Aw offer to itt him or did Aw not?

SHIRLEY Was he starvin or was he not? Was he a man or only a crossed-eyed thief an a loafer? Would you hit my son-in-law's brother?

BILL Oo's ee?

SHIRLEY Todger Fairmile o Balls Pond. Him that won £20 off the Japanese wrastler at the music hall by standin out 17 minutes 4 seconds agen him.

BILL (*sullenly*) Aw'm nao music awl wrastler. Ken he box?

SHIRLEY Yes: an you cant.

BILL Wot! Aw cawnt, cawnt Aw? Wots thet you sy (*threatening him*)?

SHIRLEY (*not budging an inch*) Will you box Todger Fairmile if I put him on to you? Say the word.

BILL (*subsiding with a slouch*) Aw'll stend ap to enny menn alawv, if he was ten Todger Fairmawls. But Aw dont set ap to be a perfeshnal.

SHIRLEY (*looking down on him with unfathomable disdain*) You box! Slap an old woman with the back o your hand! You hadnt even the sense to hit her where the magistrate couldnt see the mark of it, you silly young lump of conceit and ignorance. Hit a girl in the jaw and ony make her cry! If Todger Fairmile's done it, she wouldnt a got up inside o ten minutes, no more than you would if he got on to you. Yah! I'd set about you myself if I had a week's feedin in me instead o two months' starvation. (*He turns his back on him and sits down moodily at the table.*)

BILL (*following him and stooping over him to drive the taunt in*) You loy! youve the bread and treacle in you that you cam eah to beg.

SHIRLEY (*bursting into tears*) Oh God! it's true: I'm only an old pauper on the scrap heap. (*Furiously.*) But youll come to it yourself; and then youll know. Youll come to it sooner than a teetotaller like me, fillin yourself with gin at this hour o the mornin!

BILL Aw'm nao gin drinker, you oald lawr; but wen Aw want to give my girl a bloomin good awdin Aw lawk to ev a bit o devil in me: see? An eah Aw emm, talkin to a rotten aold blawter like you sted o givin her wot for. (*Working himself into a rage.*) Aw'm gowin in there to fetch her aht. (*He makes vengefully for the shelter door.*)

SHIRLEY Youre goin to the station on a stretcher, more likely; and theyll take the gin and the devil out of you there when they get you inside. You mind what youre about: the major here is the Earl o Stevenage's granddaughter.

BILL (*checked*)   Garn!

SHIRLEY   Youll see.

BILL (*his resolution oozing*)   Well, Aw aint dan nathin to er.

SHIRLEY   Spose she said you did! who'd believe you?

BILL (*very uneasy, skulking back to the corner of the penthouse*) Gawd! theres no jastice in this cantry. To think wot them people can do! Aw'm as good as er.

SHIRLEY   Tell her so. It's just what a fool like you would do.

BARBARA, *brisk and businesslike, comes from the shelter with a note book, and addresses herself to* SHIRLEY. BILL, *cowed, sits down in the corner on a form, and turns his back on them.*

BARBARA   Good morning.

SHIRLEY (*standing up and taking off his hat*)   Good morning, miss.

BARBARA   Sit down: make yourself at home. (*He hesitates; but she puts a friendly hand on his shoulder and makes him obey.*) Now then! since youve made friends with us, we want to know all about you. Names and addresses and trades.

SHIRLEY   Peter Shirley. Fitter. Chucked out two months ago because I was too old.

BARBARA (*not at all surprised*)   Youd pass still. Why didnt you dye your hair?

SHIRLEY   I did. Me age come out at a coroner's inquest on me daughter.

BARBARA   Steady?

SHIRLEY   Teetotaller. Never out of a job before. Good worker. And sent to the knackers like an old horse!

BARBARA   No matter: if you did your part God will do his.

SHIRLEY (*suddenly stubborn*)   My religion's no concern of anybody but myself.

BARBARA (*guessing*)   I know. Secularist?

SHIRLEY (*hotly*)   Did I offer to deny it?

BARBARA   Why should you? My own father's a Secularist, I think. Our Father—yours and mine—fulfils himself in many ways; and I daresay he knew what he was about when he made a Secularist of you. So buck up, Peter! we can always find a job for a steady man like you. (SHIRLEY, *disarmed and a little bewildered, touches his hat. She turns from him to* BILL.) Whats your name?

BILL (*insolently*)   Wots thet to you?

BARBARA (*calmly making a note*)   Afraid to give his name. Any trade?

BILL   Oo's afride to give is nime? (*Doggedly, with a sense of heroically defying the House of Lords in the person of Lord Stevenage.*) If you want to bring a chawge agen me, bring it. (*She waits, unruffled.*) Moy nime's Bill Walker.

BARBARA (*as if the name were familiar: trying to remember how*) Bill Walker? (*Recollecting.*) Oh, I know: youre the man that Jenny Hill was praying for inside just now. (*She enters his name in her note book.*)

BILL   Oo's Jenny Ill? And wot call as she to pry for me?

BARBARA   I dont know. Perhaps it was you that cut her lip.

BILL (*defiantly*)   Yus, it was me that cat her lip. Aw aint afride o you.

BARBARA   How could you be, since youre not afraid of God? Youre a brave man, Mr Walker. It takes some pluck to do our work here; but none of us dare lift our hand against a girl like that, for fear of her father in heaven.

BILL (*sullenly*)   I want nan o your kentin jawr. I spowse you think Aw cam eah to beg from you, like this demmiged lot eah. Not me. Aw downt want your bread and scripe and ketlep. Aw dont belive in your Gawd, no more than you do yourself.

BARBARA (*sunnily apologetic and ladylike, as on a new footing with him*). Oh, I beg your pardon for putting your name down, Mr Walker. I didn't understand. I'll strike it out.

BILL (*taking this as a slight, and deeply wounded by it*)   Eah! you let maw nime alown. Aint it good enaff to be in your book?

BARBARA (*considering*)   Well, you see, theres no use putting down your name unless I can do something for you, is there? Whats your trade?

BILL (*still smarting*)   Thets nao concern o yours.

BARBARA   Just so. (*Very businesslike.*) I'll put you down as (*writing*) the man who—struck—poor little Jenny Hill—in the mouth.

BILL (*rising threateningly*)   See eah. Awve ed enaff o this.

BARBARA (*quite sunny and fearless*)   What did you come to us for?

BILL   Aw cam for maw gel, see? Aw cam to tike her aht o this and to brike er jawr for er.

BARBARA (*complacently*)   You see I was right about your trade. (BILL, *on the point of retorting furiously, finds himself, to his great shame and terror, in danger of crying instead. He sits down again suddenly.*)   Whats her name?

BILL (*dogged*)   Er nime's Mog Ebbijem: thets wot her nime is.

BARBARA   Mog Habbijam! Oh, she's gone to Canning Town, to our barracks there.

BILL (*fortified by his resentment of* MOG's *perfidy*)   Is she? (*Vindictively*). Then Aw'm gowin to Kennintahn arter her. (*He crosses to the gate; hesitates; finally comes back at* BARBARA.) Are you loyin to me to git shat o me?

BARBARA   I dont want to get shut of you. I want to keep you here and save your soul. Youd better stay: youre going to have a bad time today, Bill.

BILL   Oo's gowin to give it to me? You, preps?

BARBARA   Someone you dont believe in. But youll be glad afterwards.

BILL   (*slinking off*)   Aw'll gow to Kennintahn to be aht o reach o your tangue. (*Suddenly turning on her with intense malice.*) And if Aw downt fawnd Mog there, Aw'll cam beck and do two years for you, selp me Gawd if Aw downt!

BARBARA   (*a shade kindlier, if possible*)   It's no use, Bill. She's got another bloke.

BILL   Wot!

BARBARA   One of her own converts. He fell in love with her when he saw her with her soul saved, and her face clean, and her hair washed.

BILL   (*surprised*)   Wottud she wash it for, the carroty slat? It's red.

BARBARA   It's quite lovely now, because she wears a new look in her eyes with it. It's a pity youre too late. The new bloke has put your nose out of joint, Bill.

BILL   Aw'll put his nowse aht o joint for him. Not that Aw care a carse for er, mawnd thet. But Aw'll teach her to drop me as if Aw was dirt. And Aw'll teach him to meddle with maw Judy. Wots iz bleedin nime?

BARBARA   Sergeant Todger Fairmile.

SHIRLEY   (*rising with grim joy*)   I'll go with him, miss. I want to see them two meet. I'll take him to the infirmary when it's over.

BILL   (*to* SHIRLEY, *with undissembled misgiving*)   Is thet im you was speakin on?

SHIRLEY   Thats him.

BILL   Im that wrastled in the music awl?

SHIRLEY   The competitions at the National Sportin Club was worth nigh a hundred a year to him. He's gev em up now for religion; so he's a bit fresh for want of the exercise he was accustomed to. He'll be glad to see you. Come along.

BILL   Wots is wight?

SHIRLEY   Thirteen four. (BILL's *last hope expires.*)

BARBARA   Go and talk to him, Bill. He'll convert you.

SHIRLEY   He'll convert your head into a mashed potato.

BILL   (*sullenly*)   Aw aint afride of im. Aw aint afride of ennybody. Bat e can lick me. She's dan me. (*He sits down moodily on the edge of the horse trough.*)

SHIRLEY You aint going. I thought not. (*He resumes his seat.*)

BARBARA (*calling*) Jenny!

JENNY (*appearing at the shelter door with a plaster on the corner of her mouth*) Yes, Major.

BARBARA Send Rummy Mitchens out to clear away here.

JENNY I think she's afraid.

BARBARA (*her resemblance to her mother flashing out for a moment*) Nonsense! she must do as she's told.

JENNY (*calling into the shelter*) Rummy: the Major says you must come.

JENNY *comes to* BARBARA, *purposely keeping on the side next* BILL, *lest he should suppose that she shrank from him or bore malice.*

BARBARA Poor little Jenny! Are you tired? (*Looking at the wounded cheek.*) Does it hurt?

JENNY No: it's all right now. It was nothing.

BARBARA (*critically*) It was as hard as he could hit, I expect. Poor Bill! You dont feel angry with him, do you?

JENNY Oh no, no, no: indeed I dont, Major, bless his poor heart! (BARBARA *kisses her; and she runs away merrily into the shelter.* BILL *writhes with an agonizing return of his new and alarming symptoms, but says nothing.* RUMMY MITCHENS *comes from the shelter.*)

BARBARA (*going to meet* RUMMY) Now Rummy, bustle. Take in those mugs and plates to be washed; and throw the crumbs about for the birds.

RUMMY *takes the three plates and mugs; but* SHIRLEY *takes back his mug from her, as there is still some milk left in it.*

RUMMY There aint any crumbs. This aint a time to waste good bread on birds.

PRICE (*appearing at the shelter door*) Gentleman come to see the shelter, Major. Says he's your father.

BARBARA All right. Coming. (SNOBBY *goes back into the shelter, followed by* BARBARA.)

RUMMY (*stealing across to* BILL *and addressing him in a subdued voice, but with intense conviction*) I'd av the lor of you, you flat eared pignosed potwalloper, if she'd let me. Youre no gentleman, to hit a lady in the face. (BILL, *with greater things moving in him, takes no notice.*)

SHIRLEY (*following her*) Here! in with you and dont get yourself into more trouble by talking.

RUMMY (*with hauteur*)   I aint ad the pleasure o being hintroduced to you, as I can remember. (*She goes into the shelter with the plates.*)

SHIRLEY   Thats the—

BILL (*savagely*)   Downt you talk to me, d'ye eah? You lea me alown, or Aw'll do you a mischief. Aw'm not dirt under your feet, ennywy.

SHIRLEY (*calmly*)   Dont you be afeerd. You aint such prime company that you need expect to be sought after. (*He is about to go into the shelter when* BARBARA *comes out, with* UNDERSHAFT *on her right.*)

BARBARA   Oh, there you are, Mr Shirley! (*Between them.*) This is my father: I told you he was a Secularist, didn't I? Perhaps youll be able to comfort one another.

UNDERSHAFT (*startled*)   A Secularist! Not the least in the world: on the contrary, a confirmed mystic.

BARBARA   Sorry, I'm sure. By the way, papa, what is your religion? in case I have to introduce you again.

UNDERSHAFT   My religion? Well, my dear, I am a Millionaire. That is my religion.

BARBARA   Then I'm afraid you and Mr Shirley wont be able to comfort one another after all. Youre not a Millionaire, are you, Peter?

SHIRLEY   No; and proud of it.

UNDERSHAFT (*gravely*)   Poverty, my friend, is not a thing to be proud of.

SHIRLEY (*angrily*)   Who made your millions for you? Me and my like. Whats kep us poor? Keepin you rich. I wouldnt have your conscience, not for all your income.

UNDERSHAFT   I wouldnt have your income, not for all your conscience, Mr Shirley. (*He goes to the penthouse and sits down on a form.*)

BARBARA (*stopping* SHIRLEY *adroitly as he is about to retort*)   You wouldnt think he was my father, would you, Peter? Will you go into the shelter and lend the lasses a hand for a while: we're worked off our feet.

SHIRLEY (*bitterly*)   Yes: I'm in their debt for a meal, aint I?

BARBARA   Oh, not because youre in their debt, but for love of them, Peter, for love of them. (*He cannot understand, and is rather scandalized.*) There! dont stare at me. In with you; and give that conscience of yours a holiday (*bustling him into the shelter*).

SHIRLEY (*as he goes in*)   Ah! it's a pity you never was trained to use your reason, miss. Youd have been a very taking lecturer on Secularism.

BARBARA *turns to her father.*

UNDERSHAFT   Never mind me, my dear. Go about your work; and let me watch it for a while.

BARBARA   All right.

UNDERSHAFT   For instance, whats the matter with that outpatient over there?

BARBARA *(looking at* BILL, *whose attitude has never changed, and whose expression of brooding wrath has deepened)*   Oh, we shall cure him in no time. Just watch. *(She goes over to* BILL *and waits. He glances up at her and casts his eyes down again, uneasy, but grimmer than ever.)* It would be nice to just stamp on Mog Habbijam's face, wouldnt it, Bill?

BILL *(starting up from the trough in consternation)*   It's a loy: Aw never said so. *(She shakes her head.)* Oo taold you wot was in moy mawnd?

BARBARA   Only your new friend.

BILL   Wot new friend?

BARBARA   The devil, Bill. When he gets round people they get miserable, just like you.

BILL *(with a heartbreaking attempt at devil-may-care cheerfulness)*   Aw aint miserable. *(He sits down again, and stretches his legs in an attempt to seem indifferent.)*

BARBARA   Well, if youre happy, why dont you look happy, as we do?

BILL *(his legs curling back in spite of him)*   Aw'm eppy enaff, Aw tell you. Woy cawnt you lea me alown? Wot ev I dan to you? Aw aint smashed your fice, ev Aw?

BARBARA *(softly: wooing his soul)*   It's not me thats getting at you, Bill.

BILL   Oo else is it?

BARBARA   Somebody that doesnt intend you to smash women's faces, I suppose. Somebody or something that wants to make a man of you.

BILL *(blustering)*   Mike a menn o me! Aint Aw a menn? eh? Oo sez Aw'm not a menn?

BARBARA   Theres a man in you somewhere, I suppose. But why did he let you hit poor little Jenny Hill? That wasnt very manly of him, was it?

BILL *(tormented)*   Ev dan wiv it, Aw tell you. Chack it. Aw'm sick o your Jenny Ill and er silly little fice.

BARBARA   Then why do you keep thinking about it? Why does it keep coming up against you in your mind? Youre not getting converted, are you?

BILL (*with conviction*) Not ME. Not lawkly.

BARBARA Thats right, Bill. Hold out against it. Put out your strength. Dont lets get you cheap. Todger Fairmile said he wrestled for three nights against his salvation harder than he ever wrestled with the Jap at the music hall. He gave in to the Jap when his arm was going to break. But he didnt give in to his salvation until his heart was going to break. Perhaps youll escape that. You havnt any heart, have you?

BILL Wot d'ye mean? Woy aint Aw got a awt the sime as ennybody else?

BARBARA A man with a heart wouldnt have bashed poor little Jenny's face, would he?

BILL (*almost crying*) Ow, will you lea me alown? Ev Aw ever offered to meddle with you, that you cam neggin and provowkin me lawk this? (*He writhes convulsively from his eyes to his toes.*)

BARBARA (*with a steady soothing hand on his arm and a gentle voice that never lets him go*) It's your soul thats hurting you, Bill, and not me. Weve been through it all ourselves. Come with us, Bill. (*He looks wildly round.*) To brave manhood on earth and eternal glory in heaven. (*He is on the point of breaking down.*) Come. (*A drum is heard in the shelter; and* BILL, *with a gasp, escapes from the spell as* BARBARA *turns quickly.* ADOLPHUS *enters from the shelter with a big drum.*) Oh! there you are, Dolly. Let me introduce a new friend of mine, Mr Bill Walker. This is my bloke, Bill: Mr Cusins. (CUSINS *salutes with his drumstick.*)

BILL Gowin to merry im?

BARBARA Yes.

BILL (*fervently*) Gawd elp im! Gaw-aw-aw-awd elp im!

BARBARA Why? Do you think he wont be happy with me?

BILL Awve aony ed to stend it for a mawnin: e'll ev to stend it for a lawftawm.

CUSINS That is a frightful reflection, Mr Walker. But I cant tear myself away from her.

BILL Well, Aw ken. (*To* BARBARA.) Eah do you knaow where Aw'm gowin to, and wot Aw'm gowin to do?

BARBARA Yes: youre going to heaven; and youre coming back here before the week's out to tell me so.

BILL You loy. Aw'm gowin to Kennintahn, to spit in Todger Fairmawl's eye. Aw beshed Jenny Ill's fice; an nar Aw'll git me aown fice beshed and cam bec and shaow it to er. Ee'll itt me ardern Aw itt her. Thatll mike us square. (*To* ADOLPHUS.) Is thet fair or is it not? Youre a genlmn: you oughter knaow.

BARBARA Two black eyes wont make one white one, Bill.

BILL Aw didnt awst you. Cawnt you never keep your mahth shat? Oy awst the genlmn.

CUSINS (*reflectively*) Yes: I think youre right, Mr Walker. Yes: I should do it. It's curious: it's exactly what an ancient Greek would have done.

BARBARA But what good will it do?

CUSINS Well, it will give Mr Fairmile some exercise; and it will satisfy Mr Walker's soul.

BILL Rot! there aint nao sach a thing as a saoul. Ah kin you tell wevver Awve a saoul or not? You never seen it.

BARBARA Ive seen it hurting you when you went against it.

BILL (*with compressed aggravation*) If you was maw gel and took the word awt o me mahth lawk thet, Aw'd give you sathink youd feel urtin, Aw would. (*To* ADOLPHUS.) You tike maw tip, mite. Stop er jawr or youll doy afoah your tawm (*With intense expression.*) Wore aht: thets wot youll be: wore aht. (*He goes away through the gate.*)

CUSINS (*looking after him*) I wonder!

BARBARA Dolly! (*indignant, in her mother's manner*).

CUSINS Yes, my dear, it's very wearing to be in love with you. If it lasts, I quite think I shall die young.

BARBARA Should you mind?

CUSINS Not at all. (*He is suddenly softened, and kisses her over the drum, evidently not for the first time, as people cannot kiss over a big drum without practice.* UNDERSHAFT *coughs.*)

BARBARA It's all right, papa, weve not forgotten you. Dolly: explain the place to papa: I havnt time. (*She goes busily into the shelter.*)

UNDERSHAFT *and* ADOLPHUS *now have the yard to themselves.* UNDERSHAFT, *seated on a form, and still keenly attentive, looks hard at* ADOLPHUS. *Adolphus looks hard at him.*

UNDERSHAFT I fancy you guess something of what is in my mind, Mr Cusins. (CUSINS *flourishes his drumsticks as if in the act of beating a lively rataplan, but makes no sound.*) Exactly so. But suppose Barbara finds you out!

CUSINS You know, I do not admit that I am imposing on Barbara. I am quite genuinely interested in the views of the Salvation Army. The fact is, I am a sort of collector of religions; and the curious thing is that I find I can believe them all. By the way, have you any religion?

UNDERSHAFT Yes.

CUSINS Anything out of the common?

UNDERSHAFT   Only that there are two things necessary to Salvation.

CUSINS (*disappointed, but polite*)   Ah, the Church Catechism. Charles Lomax also belongs to the Established Church.

UNDERSHAFT   The two things are—

CUSINS   Baptism and—

UNDERSHAFT   No. Money and gunpowder.

CUSINS (*surprised, but interested*)   That is the general opinion of our governing classes. The novelty is in hearing any man confess it.

UNDERSHAFT   Just so.

CUSINS   Excuse me: is there any place in your religion for honor, justice, truth, love, mercy and so forth?

UNDERSHAFT   Yes: they are the graces and luxuries of a rich, strong, and safe life.

CUSINS   Suppose one is forced to choose between them and money or gunpowder?

UNDERSHAFT   Choose money and gunpowder; for without enough of both you cannot afford the others.

CUSINS   That is your religion?

UNDERSHAFT   Yes.

The cadence of this reply makes a full close in the conversation. CUSINS *twists his face dubiously and contemplates* UNDERSHAFT. UNDERSHAFT *contemplates him.*

CUSINS   Barbara wont stand that. You will have to choose between your religion and Barbara.

UNDERSHAFT   So will you, my friend. She will find out that that drum of yours is hollow.

CUSINS   Father Undershaft: you are mistaken: I am a sincere Salvationist. You do not understand the Salvation Army. It is the army of joy, of love, of courage: it has banished the fear and remorse and despair of the old hell-ridden evangelical sects: it marches to fight the devil with trumpet and drum, with music and dancing, with banner and palm, as becomes a sally from heaven by its happy garrison. It picks the waster out of the public house and makes a man of him: it finds a worm wriggling in a back kitchen, and lo! a woman! Men and woman of rank too, sons and daughters of the Highest. It takes the poor professor of Greek, the most artificial and self-suppressed of human creatures, from his meal of roots, and lets loose the rhapsodist in him; reveals the true worship of Dionysos to him; sends him down the public street drumming dithyrambs (*he plays a thundering flourish on the drum*).

UNDERSHAFT You will alarm the shelter.

CUSINS Oh, they are accustomed to these sudden ecstasies. However, if the drum worries you—(*he pockets the drumsticks; unhooks the drum and stands it on the ground opposite the gateway*).

UNDERSHAFT Thank you.

CUSINS You remember what Euripides says about your money and gunpowder?

UNDERSHAFT No.

CUSINS (*declaiming*)

>   One and another
>   In money and guns may outpass his brother;
>   And men in their millions float and flow
>   And seethe with a million hopes as leaven;
>   And they win their will; or they miss their will;
>   And their hopes are dead or are pined for still;
>   But who'er can know
>   As the long days go
>   That to live is happy, has found his heaven.

My translation: what do you think of it?

UNDERSHAFT I think, my friend, that if you wish to know, as the long days go, that to live is happy, you must first acquire money enough for a decent life, and power enough to be your own master.

CUSINS You are damnably discouraging. (*He resumes his declamation.*)

>   Is it so hard a thing to see
>   That the spirit of God—whate'er it be—
>   The law that abides and changes not, ages long,
>   The Eternal and Nature-born: these things be strong?
>   What else is Wisdom? What of Man's endeavor,
>   Of God's high grace so lovely and so great?
>   To stand from fear set free? to breathe and wait?
>   To hold a hand uplifted over Fate?
>   And shall not Barbara be loved for ever?

UNDERSHAFT Euripides mentions Barbara, does he?

CUSINS It is a fair translation. The word means Loveliness.

UNDERSHAFT May I ask—as Barbara's father—how much a year she is to be loved for ever on?

CUSINS As for Barbara's father, that is more your affair than mine. I can feed her by teaching Greek: that is about all.

UNDERSHAFT Do you consider it a good match for her?

CUSINS (*with polite obstinacy*) Mr Undershaft: I am in many ways a weak, timid, ineffectual person; and my health is far from satisfactory. But whenever I feel that I must have anything, I get it, sooner or later. I feel that way about Barbara. I dont like marriage: I feel intensely afraid of it; and I dont know what I shall do with Barbara or what she will do with me. But I feel that I and nobody else must marry her. Please regard that as settled.— Not that I wish to be arbitrary; but why should I waste your time in discussing what is inevitable?

UNDERSHAFT   You mean that you will stick at nothing: not even the conversion of the Salvation Army to the worship of Dionysos.

CUSINS   The business of the Salvation Army is to save, not to wrangle about the name of the pathfinder. Dionysos or another: what does it matter?

UNDERSHAFT   (*rising and approaching him*)   Professor Cusins: you are a young man after my own heart.

CUSINS   Mr Undershaft: you are, as far as I am able to gather, a most infernal old rascal; but you appeal very strongly to my sense of ironic humor.

UNDERSHAFT *mutely offers his hand. They shake.*

UNDERSHAFT   (*suddenly concentrating himself*)   And now to business.

CUSINS   Pardon me. We are discussing religion. Why go back to such an uninteresting and unimportant subject as business?

UNDERSHAFT   Religion is our business at present, because it is through religion alone that we can win Barbara.

CUSINS   Have you, too, fallen in love with Barbara?

UNDERSHAFT   Yes, with a father's love.

CUSINS   A father's love for a grown-up daughter is the most dangerous of all infatuations. I apologize for mentioning my own pale, coy, mistrustful fancy in the same breath with it.

UNDERSHAFT   Keep to the point. We have to win her; and we are neither of us Methodists.

CUSINS   That doesnt matter. The power Barbara wields here—the power that wields Barbara herself—is not Calvinism, not Presbyterianism, not Methodism—

UNDERSHAFT   Not Greek Paganism either, eh?

CUSINS   I admit that. Barbara is quite original in her religion.

UNDERSHAFT   (*triumphantly*)   Aha! Barbara Undershaft would be. Her inspiration comes from within herself.

CUSINS   How do you suppose it got there?

UNDERSHAFT   (*in towering excitement*)   It is the Undershaft inheritance. I shall hand on my torch to my daughter. She shall make my converts and preach my gospel—

CUSINS   What! Money and gunpowder!

UNDERSHAFT Yes, money and gunpowder. Freedom and power. Command of life and command of death.

CUSINS (*urbanely: trying to bring him down to earth*) This is extremely interesting, Mr Undershaft. Of course you know that you are mad.

UNDERSHAFT (*with redoubled force*) And you?

CUSINS Oh, mad as a hatter. You are welcome to my secret since I have discovered yours. But I am astonished. Can a madman make cannons?

UNDERSHAFT Would anyone else than a madman make them? And now (*with surging energy*) question for question. Can a sane man translate Euripides?

CUSINS No.

UNDERSHAFT (*seizing him by the shoulder*) Can a sane woman make a man of a waster or a woman of a worm?

CUSINS (*reeling before the storm*) Father Colossus—Mammoth Millionaire—

UNDERSHAFT (*pressing him*) Are there two mad people or three in this Salvation shelter today?

CUSINS You mean Barbara is as mad as we are?

UNDERSHAFT (*pushing him lightly off and resuming his equanimity suddenly and completely*) Pooh, Professor! let us call things by their proper names. I am a millionaire; you are a poet: Barbara is a savior of souls. What have we three to do with the common mob of slaves and idolators? (*He sits down again with a shrug of contempt for the mob.*)

CUSINS Take care! Barbara is in love with the common people. So am I. Have you never felt the romance of that love?

UNDERSHAFT (*cold and sardonic*) Have you ever been in love with Poverty, like St Francis? Have you ever been in love with Dirt, like St Simeon! Have you ever been in love with disease and suffering, like our nurses and philanthropists? Such passions are not virtues, but the most unnatural of all the vices. This love of the common people may please an earl's granddaughter and a university professor; but I have been a common man and a poor man; and it has no romance for me. Leave it to the poor to pretend that poverty is a blessing: leave it to the coward to make a religion of his cowardice by preaching humility: we know better than that. We three must stand together above the common people: how else can we help their children to climb up beside us? Barbara must belong to us, not to the Salvation Army.

CUSINS Well, I can only say that if you think you will get her away from the Salvation Army by talking to her as you have been talking to me, you dont know Barbara.

UNDERSHAFT My friend: I never ask for what I can buy.

CUSINS (*in a white fury*)   Do I understand you to imply that you can buy Barbara?

UNDERSHAFT   No; but I can buy the Salvation Army.

CUSINS   Quite impossible.

UNDERSHAFT   You shall see. All religious organizations exist by selling themselves to the rich.

CUSINS   Not the Army. That is the Church of the poor.

UNDERSHAFT   All the more reason for buying it.

CUSINS   I dont think you quite know what the Army does for the poor.

UNDERSHAFT   Oh yes I do. It draws their teeth: that is enough for me as a man of business.

CUSINS   Nonsense! It makes them sober—

UNDERSHAFT   I prefer sober workmen. The profits are larger.

CUSINS   —honest—

UNDERSHAFT   Honest workmen are the most economical.

CUSINS—attached to their homes—

UNDERSHAFT   So much the better: they will put up with anything sooner than change their shop.

CUSINS   —happy—

UNDERSHAFT   An invaluable safeguard against revolution.

CUSINS   —unselfish—

UNDERSHAFT   Indifferent to their own interests, which suits me exactly.

CUSINS   —with their thoughts on heavenly things—

UNDERSHAFT (*rising*)   And not on Trade Unionism nor Socialism. Excellent.

CUSINS (*revolted*)   You really are an infernal old rascal.

UNDERSHAFT (*indicating* PETER SHIRLEY, *who has just come from the shelter and strolled dejectedly down the yard between them*)   And this is an honest man!

SHIRLEY   Yes; and what av I got by it? (*He passes on bitterly and sits on the form, in the corner of the penthouse.*)

SNOBBY PRICE, *beaming sanctimoniously, and* JENNY HILL, *with a tambourine full of coppers, come from the shelter and go to the drum, on which* JENNY *begins to count the money.*

UNDERSHAFT (*replying to* SHIRLEY)   Oh, your employers must have got a good deal by it from first to last. (*He sits on the table, with one foot on the side form,* CUSINS, *overwhelmed, sits down on the same form nearer the shelter.* BARBARA *comes from the shelter to the middle of the yard. She is excited and a little overwrought.*)

BARBARA   Weve just had a splendid experience meeting at the other
gate in Cripps's lane. Ive hardly ever seen them so much moved
as they were by your confession, Mr Price.

PRICE   I could almost be glad of my past wickedness if I could believe that it would elp to keep hathers stright.

BARBARA   So it will, Snobby. How much, Jenny?

JENNY   Four and tenpence, Major.

BARBARA   Oh Snobby, if you had given your poor mother just one
more kick, we should have got the whole five shillings!

PRICE   If she heard you say that, miss, she'd be sorry I didnt. But
I'm glad. Oh what a joy it will be to her when she hears I'm
saved!

UNDERSHAFT   Shall I contribute the odd twopence, Barbara? The
millionaire's mite, eh? (*He takes a couple of pennies from his
pocket.*)

BARBARA   How did you make that twopence?

UNDERSHAFT   As usual. By selling cannons, torpedoes, submarines,
and my new patent Grand Duke hand grenade.

BARBARA   Put it back in your pocket. You cant buy your salvation
here for twopence: you must work it out.

UNDERSHAFT   Is twopence not enough? I can afford a little more,
if you press me.

BARBARA   Two million millions would not be enough. There is bad
blood on your hands; and nothing but good blood can cleanse
them. Money is no use. Take it away. (*She turns to* CUSINS.)
Dolly: you must write another letter for me to the papers. (*He
makes a wry face.*) Yes: I know you dont like it; but it must be
done. The starvation this winter is beating us: everybody is un-
employed. The General says we must close this shelter if we cant
get more money. I force the collections at the meetings until I am
ashamed: dont I, Snobby?

PRICE   It's a fair treat to see you work it, miss. The way you got
them up from three-and-six to four-and-ten with that hymn,
penny by penny and verse by verse, was a caution. Not a Cheap
Jack on Mile End Waste could touch you at it.

BARBARA   Yes; but I wish we could do without it. I am getting at
last to think more of the collection than of the people's souls. And
what are those hatfuls of pence and halfpence? We want thousands! tens of thousands! hundreds of thousands! I want to convert people, not to be always begging for the Army in a way I'd
die sooner than beg for myself.

UNDERSHAFT (*in profound irony*)   Genuine unselfishness is capable
of anything, my dear.

BARBARA (*unsuspectingly, as she turns away to take the money from the drum and put it in a cash bag she carries*) Yes, isnt it? (UNDERSHAFT *looks sardonically at* CUSINS.)

CUSINS (*aside to* UNDERSHAFT) Mephistopheles! Machiavelli!

BARBARA (*tears coming into her eyes as she ties the bag and pockets it*) How are we to feed them? I cant talk religion to a man with bodily hunger in his eyes. (*Almost breaking down.*) It's frightful.

JENNY (*running to her*) Major, dear—

BARBARA (*rebounding*) No: dont comfort me. It will be all right. We shall get the money.

UNDERSHAFT How?

JENNY By praying for it, of course. Mrs Baines says she prayed for it last night; and she has never prayed for it in vain: never once. (*She goes to the gate and looks out into the street.*)

BARBARA (*who has dried her eyes and regained her composure*) By the way, dad, Mrs Baines has come to march with us to our big meeting this afternoon and she is very anxious to meet you, for some reason or other. Perhaps she'll convert you.

UNDERSHAFT I shall be delighted, my dear.

JENNY (*at the gate: excitedly*) Major! Major! here's that man back again.

BARBARA What man?

JENNY The man that hit me. Oh, I hope he's coming back to join us.

BILL WALKER, *with frost on his jacket, comes through the gate, his hands deep in his pockets and his chin sunk between his shoulders, like a cleaned-out gambler. He halts between* BARBARA *and the drum.*

BARBARA Hullo, Bill! Back already!

BILL (*nagging at her*) Bin talkin ever sence, ev you?

BARBARA Pretty nearly. Well, has Todger paid you out for poor Jenny's jaw?

BILL Nao e aint.

BARBARA I thought your jacket looked a bit snowy.

BILL Sao it is snaowy. You want to knaow where the snaow cam from, downt you?

BARBARA Yes.

BILL Well, it cam from orf the grahnd in Pawkinses Corner in Kennintahn. It got rabbed orf be maw shaoulders: see?

BARBARA Pity you didnt rub some off with your knees, Bill! That would have done you a lot of good.

BILL (*with sour mirthless humor*) Aw was sivin anather menn's knees at the tawm. E was kneelin on moy ed, e was.

JENNY Who was kneeling on your head?

BILL Todger was. E was pryin for me: pryin camfortable wiv me as a cawpet. Sow was Mog. Sao was the aol bloomin meeting. Mog she sez "Ow Lawd brike is stabborn sperrit; bat downt urt is dear art." Thet was wot she said. "Downt urt is dear art"! An er blowk—thirteen stun four!—kneelin wiv all is wight on me. Fanny, aint it?

JENNY Oh no. We're so sorry, Mr Walker.

BARBARA (*enjoying it frankly*) Nonsense! of course it's funny. Served you right, Bill! You must have done something to him first.

BILL (*doggedly*) Aw did wot Aw said Aw'd do. Aw spit in is eye. E looks ap at the skoy and sez, "Ow that Aw should be fahnd worthy to be spit upon for the gospel's sike!" e sez; an Mog sez "Glaory Allelloolier!"; and then e called me Braddher, an dahned me as if Aw was a kid and he was me mather worshin me a Setterda nawt. Aw ednt jast nao shaow wiv im at all. Arf the street pryed; an the tather arf larfed fit to split theirselves. (*To* BARBARA.) There are you settisfawd nah?

BARBARA (*her eyes dancing*) Wish I'd been there, Bill.

BILL Yus: youd a got in a hextra bit o talk on me, wouldnt you?

JENNY I'm so sorry, Mr Walker.

BILL (*fiercely*) Downt you gow being sorry for me: youve no call. Listen eah. Aw browk your jawr.

JENNY No, it didnt hurt me: indeed it didnt, except for a moment. It was only that I was frightened.

BILL Aw downt want to be forgive be you, or be ennybody. Wot Aw did Aw'll py for. Aw trawd to gat me aown jawr browk to settisfaw you—

JENNY (*distressed*) Oh no—

BILL (*impatiently*) Tell y' Aw did: cawnt you listen to wots being taold you? All Aw got be it was being mide a sawt of in the pablic street for me pines. Well, if Aw cawnt settisfaw you one wy, Aw ken anather. Listen eah! Aw ed two quid sived agen the frost; an Awve a pahnd of it left. A mite o mawn last week ed words with the judy e's gowing to merry. E give er wot-for; an e's bin fawned fifteen bob. E ed a rawt to itt er cause they was gowin to be merrid; but Aw ednt nao rawt to itt you; sao put anather fawv bob on an call it a pahnd's worth. (*He produces a sovereign.*) Eahs the manney. Tike it, and lets ev no more o your forgivin an prying and your Mijor jawrin me. Let wot Aw dan be dan an pide for; and let there be a end of it.

JENNY Oh, I couldn't take it, Mr Walker. But if you would give a shilling or two to poor Rummy Mitchens! you really did hurt her; and she's old.

BILL (*contemptuously*)   Not lawkly. Aw'd give her anather as soon
as look at er. Let her ev the lawr o me as she threatened! She
aint forgiven me: not mach. Wot Aw dan to er is not on me
mawnd—wot she (*indicating* BARBARA) mawt call on me conscience—no more than stickin a pig. It's this Christian gime o
yours that Aw wownt ev plyed agen me: this bloomin forgivin an
neggin an jawrin that mikes a menn thet sore that iz lawf's a
burdn to im. Aw wownt ev it, Aw tell you; sao tike your manney and stop thraowin your silly beshed fice hap agen me.

JENNY   Major: may I take a little of it for the Army?

BARBARA   No: the Army is not to be bought. We want your soul,
Bill; and we'll take nothing less.

BILL (*bitterly*)   Aw knaow. Me an maw few shillins is not good
enaff for you. Youre a earl's grendorter, you are. Nathink less
than a andered pahnd for you.

UNDERSHAFT   Come, Barbara! you could do a great deal of good
with a hundred pounds. If you will set this gentleman's mind at
ease by taking his pound, I will give the other ninety-nine.

BILL, *dazed by such opulence, instinctively touches his cap.*

BARBARA   Oh, youre too extravagant, papa. Bill offers twenty pieces
of silver. All you need offer is the other ten. That will make the
standard price to buy anybody who's for sale. I'm not; and the
Army's not. (*To* BILL.) Youll never have another quiet moment,
Bill, until you come around to us. You cant stand out against your
salvation.

BILL (*sullenly*)   Aw cawnt stend aht agen music awl wrastlers and
awtful tangued women. Awve offered to py. Aw can do no more.
Tike it or leave it. There it is. (*He throws the sovereign on the
drum, and sits down on the horse trough. The coin fascinates
SNOBBY PRICE, who takes an early opportunity of dropping his cap
on it.*)

MRS BAINES *comes from the shelter. She is dressed as a Salvation Army
Commissioner. She is an earnest looking woman of about 40, with a
caressing, urgent voice, and an appealing manner.*

BARBARA   This is my father, Mrs Baines. (UNDERSHAFT *comes from
the table, taking his hat off with marked civility.*) Try what you
can do with him. He wont listen to me, because he remembers
what a fool I was when I was a baby. (*She leaves them together
and chats with* JENNY.)

MRS BAINES   Have you been shewn over the shelter, Mr Undershaft? You know the work we're doing, of course.

UNDERSHAFT (*very civilly*)   The whole nation knows it, Mrs
Baines.

MRS BAINES No, sir: the whole nation does not know it, or we should not be crippled as we are for want of money to carry our work through the length and breadth of the land. Let me tell you that there would have been rioting this winter in London but for us.

UNDERSHAFT You really think so?

MRS BAINES I know it. I remember 1886, when you rich gentlemen hardened your hearts against the cry of the poor. They broke the windows of your clubs in Pall Mall.

UNDERSHAFT (*gleaming with approval of their method*) And the Mansion House Fund went up next day from thirty thousand pounds to seventy-nine thousand! I remember quite well.

MRS BAINES Well, wont you help me to get at the people? They wont break windows then. Come here, Price. Let me shew you to this gentleman (PRICE *comes to be inspected*). Do you remember the window breaking?

PRICE My ole father thought it was the revolution, maam.

MRS BAINES Would you break windows now?

PRICE Oh no, maam. The windows of eaven av bin opened to me. I know now that the rich man is a sinner like myself.

RUMMY (*appearing above at the loft door*) Snobby Price!

SNOBBY Wot is it?

RUMMY Your mother's askin for you at the other gate in Cripps's Lane. She's heard about your confession (PRICE *turns pale*.)

MRS BAINES Go, Mr Price; and pray with her.

JENNY You can go through the shelter, Snobby.

PRICE (*to* MRS BAINES) I couldnt face her now, maam, with all the weight of my sins fresh on me. Tell her she'll find her son at ome, waitin for her in prayer. (*He skulks off through the gate, incidentally stealing the sovereign on his way out by picking up his cap from the drum.*)

MRS BAINES (*with swimming eyes*) You see how we take the anger and the bitterness against you out of their hearts, Mr Undershaft.

UNDERSHAFT It is certainly most convenient and gratifying to all large employers of labor, Mrs Baines.

MRS BAINES Barbara: Jenny: I have good news: most wonderful news. (JENNY *runs to her.*) My prayers have been answered. I told you they would, Jenny, didnt I?

JENNY Yes, yes.

BARBARA (*moving nearer to the drum*) Have we got money enough to keep the shelter open?

MRS BAINES I hope we shall have enough to keep all the shelters open. Lord Saxmundham has promised us five thousand pounds—

BARBARA Hooray!

JENNY Glory!

MRS BAINES —if—

BARBARA "If!" If what?

MRS BAINES —if five other gentlemen will give a thousand each to make it up to ten thousand.

BARBARA Who is Lord Saxmundham? I never heard of him.

UNDERSHAFT (*who has pricked up his ears at the peer's name, and is now watching* BARBARA *curiously*) A new creation, my dear. You have heard of Sir Horace Bodger?

BARBARA Bodger! Do you mean the distiller? Bodger's whisky!

UNDERSHAFT That is the man. He is one of the greatest of our public benefactors. He restored the cathedral at Hakington. They made him a baronet for that. He gave half a million to the funds of his party: they made him a baron for that.

SHIRLEY What will they give him for the five thousand?

UNDERSHAFT There is nothing left to give him. So the five thousand, I should think, is to save his soul.

MRS BAINES Heaven grant it may! Oh Mr Undershaft, you have some very rich friends. Cant you help us towards the other five thousand? We are going to hold a great meeting this afternoon at the Assembly Hall in the Mile End Road. If I could only announce that one gentleman had come forward to support Lord Saxmundham, others would follow. Dont you know somebody? couldnt you? wouldnt you? (*her eyes fill with tears*) oh, think of those poor people, Mr Undershaft: think of how much it means to them, and how little to a great man like you.

UNDERSHAFT (*sardonically gallant*) Mrs Baines: you are irresistible. I cant disappoint you; and I cant deny myself the satisfaction of making Bodger pay up. You shall have your five thousand pounds.

MRS BAINES Thank God!

UNDERSHAFT You dont thank me?

MRS BAINES Oh sir, dont try to be cynical: dont be ashamed of being a good man. The Lord will bless you abundantly; and our prayers will be like a strong fortification round you all the days of your life. (*With a touch of caution.*) You will let me have the cheque to shew at the meeting, wont you? Jenny: go in and fetch a pen and ink. (JENNY *runs to the shelter door.*)

UNDERSHAFT Do not disturb Miss Hill: I have a fountain pen. (JENNY *halts. He sits at the table and writes the cheque.* CUSINS *rises to make room for him. They all watch him silently.*)

BILL (*cynically, aside to* BARBARA, *his voice and accent horribly debased*) Wot prawce selvytion nah?

BARBARA Stop. (UNDERSHAFT *stops writing: they all turn to her in surprise.*) Mrs Baines: are you really going to take this money?

MRS BAINES (*astonished*) Why not, dear?

BARBARA   Why not! Do you know what my father is? Have you forgotten that Lord Saxmundham is Bodger the whisky man? Do
you remember how we implored the County Council to stop him
from writing Bodger's Whisky in letters of fire against the sky; so
that the poor drink-ruined creatures on the Embankment could
not wake up from their snatches of sleep without being reminded
of their deadly thirst by that wicked sky sign? Do you know that
the worst thing I have had to fight here is not the devil, but
Bodger, Bodger, Bodger, with his whisky, his distilleries, and his
tied houses? Are you going to make our shelter another tied house
for him, and ask me to keep it?

BILL   Rotten dranken whisky it is too.

MRS BAINES   Dear Barbara: Lord Saxmundham has a soul to be
saved like any of us. If heaven had found the way to make a good
use of his money, are we to set ourselves up against the answer
to our prayers?

BARBARA   I know he has a soul to be saved. Let him come down
here; and I'll do my best to help him to his salvation. But he
wants to send his cheque down to buy us, and go on being as
wicked as ever.

UNDERSHAFT   (*with a reasonableness which* CUSINS *alone perceives
to be ironical*)   My dear Barbara: alcohol is a very necessary
article. It heals the sick—

BARBARA   It does nothing of the sort.

UNDERSHAFT   Well, it assists the doctor: that is perhaps a less questionable way of putting it. It makes life bearable to millions of
people who could not endure their existence if they were quite
sober. It enables Parliament to do things at eleven at night that
no sane person would do at eleven in the morning. Is it Bodger's
fault that this inestimable gift is deplorably abused by less than
one per cent of the poor? (*He turns again to the table; signs the
cheque; and crosses it.*)

MRS BAINES   Barbara: will there be less drinking or more if all
those poor souls we are saving come tomorrow and find the doors
of our shelters shut in their faces? Lord Saxmundham gives us
the money to stop drinking—to take his own business from him.

CUSINS   (*impishly*)   Pure self-sacrifice on Bodger's part, clearly!
Bless dear Bodger! (BARBARA *almost breaks down as* ADOLPHUS,
too, fails her.)

UNDERSHAFT   (*tearing out the cheque and pocketing the book as he
rises and goes past* CUSINS *to* MRS BAINES)   I also, Mrs Baines,
may claim a little disinterestedness. Think of my business! think
of the widows and orphans! the men and lads torn to pieces with
shrapnel and poisoned with lyddite! (MRS BAINES *shrinks; but
he goes on remorselessly*) the oceans of blood, not one drop of

which is shed in a really just cause! the ravaged crops! the peaceful peasants forced, women and men, to till their fields under the fire of opposing armies on pain of starvation! the bad blood of the fierce little cowards at home who egg on others to fight for the gratification of their national vanity! All this makes money for me: I am never richer, never busier than when the papers are full of it. Well, it is your work to preach peace on earth and good will to men. (MRS BAINES's *face lights up again.*) Every convert you make is a vote against war. (*Her lips move in prayer.*) Yet I give you this money to help you to hasten my own commercial ruin. (*He gives her the cheque.*)

CUSINS (*mounting the form in an ecstasy of mischief*) The millennium will be inaugurated by the unselfishness of Undershaft and Bodger. Oh be joyful! (*He takes the drumsticks from his pocket and flourishes them.*)

MRS BAINES (*taking the cheque*) The longer I live the more proof I see that there is an Infinite Goodness that turns everything to the work of salvation sooner or later. Who would have thought that any good could have come out of war and drink? And yet their profits are brought today to the feet of salvation to do its blessed work. (*She is affected to tears.*)

JENNY (*running to* MRS BAINES *and throwing her arms round her*) Oh dear! how blessed, how glorious it all is!

CUSINS (*in a convulsion of irony*) Let us seize this unspeakable moment. Let us march to the great meeting at once. Excuse me just an instant. (*He rushes into the shelter.* JENNY *takes her tambourine from the drum head.*)

MRS BAINES Mr Undershaft: have you ever seen a thousand people fall on their knees with one impulse and pray? Come with us to the meeting. Barbara shall tell them that the Army is saved, and saved through you.

CUSINS (*returning impetuously from the shelter with a flag and a trombone, and coming between* MRS BAINES *and* UNDERSHAFT) You shall carry the flag down the first street, Mrs Baines (*he gives her the flag*). Mr Undershaft is a gifted trombonist: he shall intone an Olympian diapason to the West Ham Salvation March. (*Aside to* UNDERSHAFT, *as he forces the trombone on him.*) Blow, Machiavelli, blow.

UNDERSHAFT (*aside to him, as he takes the trombone*) The Trumpet in Zion! (CUSINS *rushes to the drum, which he takes up and puts on.* UNDERSHAFT *continues, aloud.*) I will do my best. I could vamp a bass if I knew the tune.

CUSINS It is a wedding chorus from one of Donizetti's operas; but we have converted it. We convert everything to good here, including Bodger. You remember the chorus. 'For thee immense rejoicing—immenso giubilo—immenso giubilo.' (*With drum obbligato.*) Rum tum ti tum tum, tum tum ti ta—

BARBARA Dolly: you are breaking my heart.

CUSINS What is a broken heart more or less here? Dionysos Undershaft has descended. I am possessed.

MRS BAINES Come, Barbara: I must have my dear Major to carry the flag with me.

JENNY Yes, yes, Major darling.

CUSINS (*snatches the tambourine out of* JENNY's *hand and mutely offers it to* BARBARA.)

BARBARA (*coming forward a little as she puts the offer behind her with a shudder, whilst* CUSINS *recklessly tosses the tambourine back to* JENNY *and goes to the gate*) I cant come.

JENNY Not come!

MRS BAINES (*with tears in her eyes*) Barbara: do you think I am wrong to take the money?

BARBARA (*impulsively going to her and kissing her*) No, no: God help you, dear, you must: you are saving the Army. Go; and may you have a great meeting!

JENNY But arnt you coming?

BARBARA No. (*She begins taking off the silver S brooch from her collar.*)

MRS BAINES Barbara: what are you doing?

JENNY Why are you taking your badge off? You cant be going to leave us, Major.

BARBARA (*quietly*) Father: come here.

UNDERSHAFT (*coming to her*) My dear! (*Seeing that she is going to pin the badge on his collar, he retreats to the penthouse in some alarm.*)

BARBARA (*following him*) Don't be frightened. (*She pins the badge on and steps back towards the table, shewing him to the others.*) There! It's not much for £5000, is it?

MRS BAINES Barbara: if you wont come and pray with us, promise me you will pray for us.

BARBARA I cant pray now. Perhaps I shall never pray again.

MRS BAINES Barbara!

JENNY Major!

BARBARA (*almost delirious*) I cant bear any more. Quick march!

CUSINS (*calling to the procession in the street outside*) Off we go. Play up, there! Immenso giubilo. (*He gives the time with his drum; and the band strikes up the march, which rapidly becomes more distant as the procession moves briskly away.*)

MRS BAINES I must go, dear. Youre overworked: you will be all

right tomorrow. We'll never lose you. Now Jenny: step out with
the old flag. Blood and Fire! (*She marches out through the gate
with her flag.*)

JENNY   Glory Hallelujah! (*Flourishing her tambourine and marching.*)

UNDERSHAFT (*to* CUSINS, *as he marches out past him easing the
slide of his trombone*) "My ducats and my daughter"!

CUSINS (*following him out*)   Money and gunpowder!

BARBARA   Drunkenness and Murder! My God: why hast thou forsaken me?

*She sinks on the form with her face buried in her hands. The march
passes away into silence.* BILL WALKER *steals across to her.*

BILL (*taunting*)   Wot prawce selvytion nah?

SHIRLEY   Don't you hit her when she's down.

BILL   She it me wen aw wiz dahn. Waw shouldnt Aw git a bit o
me aown beck?

BARBARA (*raising her head*)   I didnt take your money, Bill. (*She
crosses the yard to the gate and turns her back on the two men
to hide her face from them.*)

BILL (*sneering after her*)   Naow, it warnt enaff for you. (*Turning
to the drum, he misses the money.*)   Ellow! If you aint took it
sammun else ez. Weres it gorn? Bly me if Jenny Ill didnt tike it
arter all!

RUMMY (*screaming at him from the loft*)   You lie, you dirty black-
guard! Snobby Price pinched it off the drum when he took up
his cap. I was up here all the time an see im do it.

BILL   Wot! Stowl may manney! Waw didnt you call thief on him,
you silly aold macker you?

RUMMY   To serve you aht for ittin me acrost the fice. It's cost
y'pahnd, that az. (*Raising a pæn of squalid triumph.*) I done
you. I'm even with you. Uve ad it aht o y—(BILL *snatches up*
SHIRLEY'S *mug and hurls it at her. She slams the loft door and
vanishes. The mug smashes against the door and falls in fragments.*)

BILL (*beginning to chuckle*)   Tell us, aol menn, wot o'clock this
mawnin was it wen im as they call Snobby Prawce was sived?

BARBARA (*turning to him more composedly, and with unspoiled
sweetness*)   About half past twelve, Bill. And he pinched your
pound at a quarter to two. *I* know. Well, you cant afford to lose
it. I'll send it to you.

BILL (*his voice and accent suddenly improving*)   Not if Aw wiz to
stawve for it. Aw aint to be bought.

SHIRLEY   Aint you? Youd sell yourself to the devil for a pint o beer; only there aint no devil to make the offer.

BILL   (*unashamed*)   Sao Aw would, mite, and often ev, cheerful. But she cawnt baw me. (*Approaching* BARBARA.) You wanted maw soul, did you? Well, you aint got it.

BARBARA   I nearly got it, Bill. But weve sold it back to you for ten thousand pounds.

SHIRLEY   And dear at the money!

BARBARA   No, Peter: it was worth more than money.

BILL   (*salvationproof*)   It's nao good: you cawnt get rahnd me nah. Aw downt blieve in it; and Awve seen tody that Aw was rawt. (*Going.*) Sao long, aol soupkitchener! Ta, ta, Mijor Earl's Grendorter! (*Turning at the gate.*) Wot prawce selvytion nah? Snobby Prawce! Ha! ha!

BARBARA   (*offering her hand*)   Goodbye, Bill.

BILL   (*taken aback, half plucks his cap off; then shoves it on again defiantly*)   Get aht. (BARBARA *drops her hand, discouraged. He has a twinge of remorse.*) But thets aw rawt, you knaow. Nathink pasnl. Naow mellice. Sao long, Judy. (*He goes.*)

BARBARA   No malice. So long, Bill.

SHIRLEY   (*shaking his head*)   You make too much of him, miss, in your innocence.

BARBARA   (*going to him*)   Peter: I'm like you now. Cleaned out, and lost my job.

SHIRLEY   Youve youth an hope. Thats two better than me.

BARBARA   I'll get you a job, Peter. Thats hope for you: the youth will have to be enough for me. (*She counts her money.*) I have just enough left for two teas at Lockharts, a Rowton doss for you, and my tram and bus home. (*He frowns and rises with offended pride. She takes his arm.*) Dont be proud, Peter: it's sharing between friends. And promise me youll talk to me and not let me cry. (*She draws him towards the gate.*)

SHIRLEY   Well, I'm not accustomed to talk to the like of you—

BARBARA   (*urgently*)   Yes, yes: you must talk to me. Tell me about Tom Paine's books and Bradlaugh's lectures. Come along.

SHIRLEY   Ah, if you would only read Tom Paine in the proper spirit, miss! (*They go out through the gate together.*)

ACT III

Next day after lunch LADY BRITOMART *is writing in the library in Wilton Crescent.* SARAH *is reading in the armchair near the window.* BARBARA, *in ordinary fashionable dress, pale and brooding, is on the settee.* CHARLES

LOMAX *enters. He starts on seeing* BARBARA *fashionably attired and in low spirits.*

LOMAX   Youve left off your uniform!

BARBARA *says nothing; but an expression of pain passes over her face.*

LADY BRITOMART (*warning him in low tones to be careful*)   Charles!

LOMAX (*much concerned, coming behind the settee and bending sympathetically over* BARBARA)   I'm awfully sorry, Barbara. You know I helped you all I could with the concertina and so forth. (*Momentously.*) Still, I have never shut my eyes to the fact that there is a certain amount of tosh about the Salvation Army. Now the claims of the Church of England—

LADY BRITOMART   Thats enough, Charles. Speak of something suited to your mental capacity.

LOMAX   But surely the Church of England is suited to all our capacities.

BARBARA (*pressing his hand*)   Thank you for your sympathy, Cholly. Now go and spoon with Sarah.

LOMAX (*dragging a chair from the writing table and seating himself affectionately by* SARAH'S *side*)   How is my ownest today?

SARAH   I wish you wouldnt tell Cholly to do things, Barbara. He always comes straight and does them. Cholly: we're going to the works this afternoon.

LOMAX   What works?

SARAH   The cannon works.

LOMAX   What? your governor's shop!

SARAH   Yes.

LOMAX   Oh I say!

CUSINS *enters in poor condition. He also starts visibly when he sees* BARBARA *without her uniform.*

BARBARA   I expected you this morning, Dolly. Didnt you guess that?

CUSINS (*sitting down beside her*)   I'm sorry. I have only just breakfasted.

SARAH   But weve just finished lunch.

BARBARA   Have you had one of your bad nights?

CUSINS   No: I had rather a good night: in fact, one of the most remarkable nights I have ever passed.

BARBARA   The meeting?

CUSINS   No: after the meeting.

LADY BRITOMART   You should have gone to bed after the meeting. What were you doing?

CUSINS   Drinking.

LADY BRITOMART ⎫ Adolphus!
SARAH ⎪ Dolly!
BARBARA ⎬ Dolly!
LOMAX ⎭ Oh I say!

LADY BRITOMART What were you drinking, may I ask?

CUSINS A most devilish kind of Spanish burgundy, warranted free from added alcohol: a Temperance burgundy in fact. Its richness in natural alcohol made any addition superfluous.

BARBARA Are you joking, Dolly?

CUSINS (*patiently*) No. I have been making a night of it with the nominal head of this household: that is all.

LADY BRITOMART Andrew made you drunk!

CUSINS No: he only provided the wine. I think it was Dionysos who made me drunk. (*To* BARBARA.) I told you I was possessed.

LADY BRITOMART Youre not sober yet. Go home to bed at once.

CUSINS I have never before ventured to reproach you, Lady Brit; but how could you marry the Prince of Darkness?

LADY BRITOMART It was much more excusable to marry him than to get drunk with him. That is a new accomplishment of Andrew's, by the way. He usent to drink.

CUSINS He doesnt now. He only sat there and completed the wreck of my moral basis, the rout of my convictions, the purchase of my soul. He cares for you, Barbara. That is what makes him so dangerous to me.

BARBARA That has nothing to do with it, Dolly. There are larger loves and diviner dreams than the fireside ones. You know that, dont you?

CUSINS Yes: that is our understanding. I know it. I hold to it. Unless he can win me on that holier ground he may amuse me for a while; but he can get no deeper hold, strong as he is.

BARBARA Keep to that; and the end will be right. Now tell me what happened at the meeting?

CUSINS It was an amazing meeting. Mrs Baines almost died of emotion. Jenny Hill simply gibbered with hysteria. The Prince of Darkness played his trombone like a madman: its brazen roarings were like the laughter of the damned. 117 conversions took place then and there. They prayed with the most touching sincerity and gratitude for Bodger, and for the anonymous donor of the £5000. Your father would not let his name be given.

LOMAX That was rather fine of the old man, you know. Most chaps would have wanted the advertisement.

CUSINS He said all the charitable institutions would be down on him like kites on a battle-field if he gave his name.

LADY BRITOMART   Thats Andrew all over. He never does a proper thing without giving an improper reason for it.

CUSINS   He convinced me that I have all my life been doing improper things for proper reasons.

LADY BRITOMART   Adolphus: now that Barbara has left the Salvation Army, you had better leave it too. I will not have you playing that drum in the streets.

CUSINS   Your orders are already obeyed, Lady Brit.

BARBARA   Dolly: were you ever really in earnest about it? Would you have joined if you had never seen me?

CUSINS (*disingenuously*)   Well—er—well, possibly, as a collector of religions—

LOMAX (*cunningly*)   Not as a drummer, though, you know. You are a very clearheaded brainy chap, Dolly; and it must have been apparent to you that there is a certain amount of tosh about—

LADY BRITOMART   Charles: if you must drivel, drivel like a grown-up man and not like a schoolboy.

LOMAX (*out of countenance*)   Well, drivel is drivel, dont you know, whatever a man's age.

LADY BRITOMART   In good society in England, Charles, men drivel at all ages by repeating silly formulas with an air of wisdom. Schoolboys make their own formulas out of slang, like you. When they reach your age, and get political private secretaryships and things of that sort, they drop slang and get their formulas out of the Spectator or The Times. You had better confine yourself to The Times. You will find that there is a certain amount of tosh about The Times; but at least its language is reputable.

LOMAX (*overwhelmed*)   You are so awfully strong-minded, Lady Brit—

LADY BRITOMART   Rubbish! (MORRISON *comes in.*) What is it?

MORRISON   If you please, my lady, Mr Undershaft has just drove up to the door.

LADY BRITOMART   Well, let him in (MORRISON *hesitates.*) Whats the matter with you?

MORRISON   Shall I announce him, my lady; or is he at home here, so to speak, my lady?

LADY BRITOMART   Announce him.

MORRISON   Thank you, my lady. You wont mind my asking, I hope. The occasion is in a manner of speaking new to me.

LADY BRITOMART   Quite right. Go and let him in.

MORRISON   Thank you, my lady. (*He withdraws.*)

LADY BRITOMART   Children: go and get ready. (SARAH *and* BARBARA *go upstairs for their out-of-door wraps.*) Charles: go and tell Stephen to come down here in five minutes: you will find him in the drawing room. (CHARLES *goes.*) Adolphus: tell them to send round the carriage in about fifteen minutes. (ADOLPHUS *goes.*)

MORRISON (*at the door*) Mr Undershaft.

UNDERSHAFT *comes in.* MORRISON *goes out.*

UNDERSHAFT Alone! How fortunate!

LADY BRITOMART (*rising*) Dont be sentimental, Andrew. Sit down. (*She sits on the settee: he sits beside her, on her left. She comes to the point before he has time to breath.*) Sarah must have £800 a year until Charles Lomax comes into his property. Barbara will need more, and need it permanently, because Adolphus hasnt any property.

UNDERSHAFT (*resignedly*) Yes, my dear: I will see to it. Anything else? for yourself, for instance?

LADY BRITOMART I want to talk to you about Stephen.

UNDERSHAFT (*rather wearily*) Dont, my dear. Stephen doesnt interest me.

LADY BRITOMART He does interest me. He is our son.

UNDERSHAFT Do you really think so? He has induced us to bring him into the world; but he chose his parents very incongruously, I think. I see nothing of myself in him, and less of you.

LADY BRITOMART Andrew: Stephen is an excellent son, and a most steady, capable, highminded young man. You are simply trying to find an excuse for disinheriting him.

UNDERSHAFT My dear Biddy: the Undershaft tradition disinherits him. It would be dishonest of me to leave the cannon foundry to my son.

LADY BRITOMART It would be most unnatural and improper of you to leave it to anyone else, Andrew. Do you suppose this wicked and immoral tradition can be kept up for ever? Do you pretend that Stephen could not carry on the foundry just as well as all the other sons of the big business houses?

UNDERSHAFT Yes: he could learn the office routine without understanding the business, like all the other sons; and the firm would go by its own momentum until the real Undershaft—probably an Italian or a German—would invent a new method and cut him out.

LADY BRITOMART There is nothing that any Italian or German could do that Stephen could not do. And Stephen at least has breeding.

UNDERSHAFT The son of a foundling! Nonsense!

LADY BRITOMART My son, Andrew! And even you may have good blood in your veins for all you know.

UNDERSHAFT   True. Probably I have. That is another argument in favour of a foundling.

LADY BRITOMART   Andrew: dont be aggravating. And dont be wicked. At present you are both.

UNDERSHAFT   This conversation is part of the Undershaft tradition, Biddy. Every Undershaft's wife has treated him to it ever since the house was founded. It is mere waste of breath. If the tradition be ever broken it will be for an abler man than Stephen.

LADY BRITOMART (*pouting*)   Then go away.

UNDERSHAFT (*deprecatory*)   Go away!

LADY BRITOMART   Yes: go away. If you will do nothing for Stephen, you are not wanted here. Go to your foundling, whoever he is; and look after him.

UNDERSHAFT   The fact is, Biddy—

LADY BRITOMART   Dont call me Biddy. I dont call you Andy.

UNDERSHAFT   I will not call my wife Britomart: it is not good sense. Seriously, my love, the Undershaft tradition has landed me in a difficulty. I am getting on in years; and my partner Lazarus has at last made a stand and insisted that the succession must be settled one way or the other; and of course he is quite right. You see, I havent found a fit successor yet.

LADY BRITOMART (*obstinately*)   There is Stephen.

UNDERSHAFT   Thats just it: all the foundlings I can find are exactly like Stephen.

LADY BRITOMART   Andrew!!

UNDERSHAFT   I want a man with no relations and no schooling: that is, a man who would be out of the running altogether if he were not a strong man. And I cant find him. Every blessed foundling nowadays is snapped up in his infancy by Barnardo homes, or School Board officers, or Boards of Guardians; and if he shews the least ability he is fastened on by schoolmasters; trained to win scholarships like a racehorse; crammed with secondhand ideas; drilled and disciplined in docility and what they call good taste; and lamed for life so that he is fit for nothing but teaching. If you want to keep the foundry in the family, you had better find an eligible foundling and marry him to Barbara.

LADY BRITOMART   Ah! Barbara! Your Pet! You would sacrifice Stephen to Barbara.

UNDERSHAFT   Cheerfully. And you, my dear, would boil Barbara to make soup for Stephen.

LADY BRITOMART   Andrew: this is not a question of our likings and dislikings: it is a question of duty. It is your duty to make Stephen your successor.

UNDERSHAFT   Just as much as it is your duty to submit to your husband. Come, Biddy! these tricks of the governing class are of no use with me. I am one of the governing class myself; and it is waste of time giving tracts to a missionary. I have the power in this matter; and I am not to be hum-bugged into using it for your purposes.

LADY BRITOMART Andrew: you can talk my head off; but you cant change wrong into right. And your tie is all on one side. Put it straight.

UNDERSHAFT (*disconcerted*) It won't stay unless it's pinned (*he fumbles at it with childish grimaces*)—

STEPHEN *comes in.*

STEPHEN (*at the door*) I beg your pardon (*about to retire*).

LADY BRITOMART No: come in, Stephen. (*Stephen comes forward to his mother's writing table.*)

UNDERSHAFT (*not very cordially*) Good afternoon.

STEPHEN (*Coldly*) Good afternoon.

UNDERSHAFT (*to* LADY BRITOMART) He knows all about the tradition, I suppose?

LADY BRITOMART Yes. (*To* STEPHEN.) It is what I told you last night, Stephen.

UNDERSHAFT (*sulkily*) I understand you want to come into the cannon business.

STEPHEN *I* go into trade! Certainly not.

UNDERSHAFT (*opening his eyes, greatly eased in mind and manner*) Oh! in that case—

LADY BRITOMART Cannons are not trade, Stephen. They are enterprise.

STEPHEN I have no intention of becoming a man of business in any sense. I have no capacity for business and no taste for it. I intend to devote myself to politics.

UNDERSHAFT (*rising*) My dear boy: this is an immense relief to me. And I trust it may prove an equally good thing for the country. I was afraid you would consider yourself disparaged and slighted. (*He moves towards* STEPHEN *as if to shake hands with him.*)

LADY BRITOMART (*rising and interposing*) Stephen: I cannot allow you to throw away an enormous property like this.

STEPHEN (*stiffly*) Mother: there must be an end of treating me as a child, if you please. (LADY BRITOMART *recoils, deeply wounded by his tone.*) Until last night I did not take your attitude seriously, because I did not think you meant it seriously. But I find now that you left me in the dark as to matters which you should have explained to me years ago. I am extremely hurt and offended. Any further discussion of my intentions had better take place with my father, as between one man and another.

LADY BRITOMART Stephen! (*She sits down again, her eyes filling with tears.*)

UNDERSHAFT (*with grave compassion*) You see, my dear, it is only the big men who can be treated as children.

STEPHEN I am sorry, mother, that you have forced me—

UNDERSHAFT (*stopping him*) Yes, yes, yes, yes: thats all right, Stephen. She wont interfere with you any more: your independence is achieved: you have won your latchkey. Dont rub it in; and above all, dont apologize. (*He resumes his seat.*) Now what about your future, as between one man and another—I beg your pardon, Biddy: as between two men and a woman.

LADY BRITOMART (*who has pulled herself together strongly*) I quite understand, Stephen. By all means go your own way if you feel strong enough. (STEPHEN *sits down magisterially in the chair at the writing table with an air of affirming his majority.*)

UNDERSHAFT It is settled that you do not ask for the succession to the cannon business.

STEPHEN I hope it is settled that I repudiate the cannon business.

UNDERSHAFT Come, come! dont be so devilishly sulky: it's boyish. Freedom should be generous. Besides, I owe you a fair start in life in exchange for disinheriting you. You cant become prime minister all at once. Havent you a turn for something? What about literature, art, and so forth?

STEPHEN I have nothing of the artist about me, either in faculty or character, thank Heaven!

UNDERSHAFT A philosopher, perhaps? Eh?

STEPHEN I make no such ridiculous pretension.

UNDERSHAFT Just so. Well, there is the army, the navy, the Church, the Bar. The Bar requires some ability. What about the Bar?

STEPHEN I have not studied law. And I am afraid I have not the necessary push—I believe that is the name barristers give to their vulgarity—for success in pleading.

UNDERSHAFT Rather a difficult case, Stephen. Hardly anything left but the stage, is there? (STEPHEN *makes an impatient movement.*) Well, come! is there anything you know or care for?

STEPHEN (*rising and looking at him steadily*) I know the difference between right and wrong.

UNDERSHAFT (*hugely tickled*) You dont say so! What! no capacity for business, no knowledge of law, no sympathy with art, no pretension to philosophy; only a simple knowledge of the secret that has puzzled all the philosophers, baffled all the lawyers, muddled all the men of business, and ruined most of the artists: the secret of right and wrong. Why, man, youre a genius, a master of masters, a god! At twenty-four, too!

STEPHEN (*keeping his temper with difficulty*) You are pleased to be facetious. I pretend to nothing more than any honorable English gentleman claims as his birthright (*he sits down angrily*).

UNDERSHAFT Oh, thats everybody's birthright. Look at poor little Jenny Hill, the Salvation lassie! she would think you were laughing at her if you asked her to stand up in the street and teach grammar or geography or mathematics or even drawing room dancing; but it never occurs to her to doubt that she can teach morals and religion. You are all alike, you respectable people. You cant tell me the bursting strain of a ten-inch gun, which is a very simple matter; but you all think you can tell me the bursting strain of a man under temptation. You darent handle high explosives; but youre all ready to handle honesty and truth and justice and the whole duty of man, and kill one another at that game. What a country! What a world!

LADY BRITOMART (*uneasily*) What do you think he had better do, Andrew?

UNDERSHAFT Oh, just what he wants to do. He knows nothing and he thinks he knows everything. That points clearly to a political career. Get him a private secretaryship to someone who can get him an Under Secretaryship; and then leave him alone. He will find his natural and proper place in the end on the Treasury Bench.

STEPHEN (*springing up again*) I am sorry, sir, that you force me to forget the respect due to you as my father. I am an Englishman and I will not hear the Government of my country insulted. (*He thrusts his hands in his pockets, and walks angrily across to the window.*)

UNDERSHAFT (*with a touch of brutality*) The government of your country! *I* am the government of your country: I, and Lazarus. Do you suppose that you and half a dozen amateurs like you, sitting in a row in that foolish gabble shop, can govern Undershaft and Lazarus? No, my friend: you will do what pays us. You will make war when it suits us, and keep peace when it doesnt. You will find out that trade requires certain measures when we have decided on those measures. When I want anything to keep my dividends up, you will discover that my want is a national need. When other people want something to keep my dividends down, you will call out the police and military. And in return you shall have the support and applause of my newspapers, and the delight of imagining that you are a great statesman. Government of your country! Be off with you, my boy, and play with your caucuses and leading articles and historic parties and great leaders and burning questions and the rest of your toys. *I* am going back to my counting-house to pay the piper and call the tune.

STEPHEN (*actually smiling, and putting his hand on his father's shoulder with indulgent patronage*) Really, my dear father, it is impossible to be angry with you. You dont know how absurd all this sounds to me. You are very properly proud of having been industrious enough to make money; and it is greatly to your credit that you have made so much of it. But it has kept you in circles where you are valued for your money and deferred to for it, instead of in the doubtless very old-fashioned and behind-the-times public school and university where I formed my habits of mind. It is natural for you to think that money governs England; but you must allow me to think I know better.

UNDERSHAFT And what does govern England, pray?

STEPHEN Character, father, character.

UNDERSHAFT Whose character? Yours or mine?

STEPHEN Neither yours nor mine, father, but the best elements in the English national character.

UNDERSHAFT Stephen: Ive found your profession for you. Youre a born journalist. I'll start you with a high-toned weekly review. There!

Before STEPHEN *can reply* SARAH, BARBARA, LOMAX, *and* CUSINS *come in ready for walking.* BARBARA *crosses the room to the window and looks out.* CUSINS *drifts amiably to the armchair.* LOMAX *remains near the door, whilst* SARAH *comes to her mother.*

STEPHEN *goes to the smaller writing table and busies himself with his letters.*

SARAH Go and get ready, mamma: the carriage is waiting. (LADY BRITOMART *leaves the room.*)

UNDERSHAFT (*to* SARAH) Good day, my dear. Good afternoon, Mr Lomax.

LOMAX (*vaguely*) Ahdedoo.

UNDERSHAFT (*to* CUSINS) Quite well after last night, Euripides, eh?

CUSINS As well as can be expected.

UNDERSHAFT Thats right. (*To* BARBARA.) So you are coming to see my death and devastation factory, Barbara?

BARBARA (*at the window*) You came yesterday to see my salvation factory. I promised you a return visit.

LOMAX (*coming forward between* SARAH *and* UNDERSHAFT) Youll find it awfully interesting. Ive been through the Woolwich Arsenal and it gives you a ripping feeling of security, you know, to think of the lot of beggars we could kill if it came to fighting. (*To* UNDERSHAFT, *with sudden solemnity.*) Still, it must be rather an awful reflection for you, from the religious point of view as it were. Youre getting on, you know, and all that.

SARAH   You dont mind Cholly's imbecility, papa, do you?

LOMAX (*much taken aback*)   Oh I say!

UNDERSHAFT   Mr Lomax looks at the matter in a very proper spirit, my dear.

LOMAX   Just so. Thats all I meant, I assure you.

SARAH   Are you coming, Stephen?

STEPHEN   Well, I am rather busy—er—(*Magnanimously.*) Oh well, yes: I'll come. That is, if there is room for me.

UNDERSHAFT   I can take two with me in a little motor I am experimenting with for field use. You wont mind its being rather unfashionable. It's not painted yet; but it's bullet proof.

LOMAX (*appalled at the prospect of confronting Wilton Crescent in an unpainted motor*)   Oh I say!

SARAH   The carriage for me, thank you. Barbara doesnt mind what she's seen in.

LOMAX   I say, Dolly, old chap: do you really mind the car being a guy? Because of course if you do I'll go in it. Still—

CUSINS   I prefer it.

LOMAX   Thanks awfully, old man. Come, my ownest. (*He hurries out to secure his seat in the carriage.* SARAH *follows him.*)

CUSINS (*moodily walking across to* LADY BRITOMART's *writing table*)   Why are we two coming to this Works Department of Hell? that is what I ask myself.

BARBARA   I have always thought of it as a sort of pit where lost creatures with blackened faces stirred up smoky fires and were driven and tormented by my father. Is it like that, dad?

UNDERSHAFT (*scandalized*)   My dear! It is a spotlessly clean and beautiful hillside town.

CUSINS   With a Methodist chapel? Oh do say theres a Methodist chapel.

UNDERSHAFT   There are two: a Primitive one and a sophisticated one. There is even an Ethical Society; but it is not much patronized, as my men are all strongly religious. In the High Explosives Sheds they object to the presence of Agnostics as unsafe.

CUSINS   And yet they dont object to you!

BARBARA   Do they obey all your orders?

UNDERSHAFT   I never give them any orders. When I speak to one of them it is "Well, Jones, is the baby doing well? and has Mrs

Jones made a good recovery?" "Nicely, thank you, sir." And thats all.

CUSINS But Jones has to be kept in order. How do you maintain discipline among your men?

UNDERSHAFT I dont. They do. You see, the one thing Jones wont stand is any rebellion from the man under him, or any assertion of social equality between the wife of the man with 4 shillings a week less than himself, and Mrs Jones! Of course they all rebel against me, theoretically. Practically, every man of them keeps the man just below him in his place. I never meddle with them. I never bully them. I dont even bully Lazarus. I say that certain things are to be done; but I dont order anybody to do them. I dont say, mind you, that there is no ordering about and snubbing and even bullying. The men snub the boys and order them about; the carmen snub the sweepers; the artisans snub the unskilled laborers; the foremen drive and bully both the laborers and artisans; the assistant engineers find fault with the foremen; the chief engineers drop on the assistants; the departmental managers worry the chiefs; and the clerks have tall hats and hymnbooks and keep up the social tone by refusing to associate on equal terms with anybody. The result is a colossal profit, which comes to me.

CUSINS (*revolted*) You really are a—well, what I was saying yesterday.

BARBARA What was he saying yesterday?

UNDERSHAFT Never mind, my dear. He thinks I have made you unhappy. Have I?

BARBARA Do you think I can be happy in this vulgar silly dress? I! who have worn the uniform. Do you understand what you have done to me? Yesterday I had a man's soul in my hand. I set him in the way of life with his face to salvation. But when we took your money he turned back to drunkenness and derision. (*With intense conviction.*) I will never forgive you that. If I had a child, and you destroyed its body with your explosives—if you murdered Dolly with your horrible guns—I could forgive you if my forgiveness would open the gates of heaven to you. But to take a human soul from me, and turn it into the soul of a wolf! that is worse than any murder.

UNDERSHAFT Does my daughter despair so easily? Can you strike a man to the heart and leave no mark on him?

BARBARA (*her face lighting up*) Oh, you are right: he can never be lost now: where was my faith?

CUSINS Oh, clever clever devil!

BARBARA You may be a devil; but God speaks through you sometimes. (*She takes her father's hands and kisses them.*) You have given me back my happiness: I feel it deep down now, though my spirit is troubled.

UNDERSHAFT   You have learnt something. That always feels at first as if you had lost something.

BARBARA   Well, take me to the factory of death; and let me learn something more. There must be some truth or other behind all this frightful irony. Come, Dolly. (*She goes out.*)

CUSINS   My guardian angel! (*To* UNDERSHAFT.) Avaunt! (*He follows* BARBARA.)

STEPHEN (*quietly, at the writing table*)   You must not mind Cusins, father. He is a very amiable good fellow; but he is a Greek scholar and naturally a little eccentric.

UNDERSHAFT   Ah, quite so. Thank you, Stephen. Thank you. (*He goes out.*)

STEPHEN *smiles patronizingly; buttons his coat responsibly; and crosses the room to the door.* LADY BRITOMART, *dressed for out-of-doors, opens it before he reaches it. She looks round for the others; looks at* STEPHEN *and turns to go without a word.*

STEPHEN (*embarrassed*)   Mother—

LADY BRITOMART   Dont be apologetic, Stephen. And dont forget that you have outgrown your mother. (*She goes out.*)

Perivale St Andrews lies between two Middlesex hills, half climbing the northern one. It is an almost smokeless town of white walls, roofs of narrow green slates or red tiles, tall trees, domes, campaniles, and slender chimney shafts, beautifully situated and beautiful in itself. The best view of it is obtained from the crest of a slope about half a mile to the east, where the high explosives are dealt with. The foundry lies hidden in the depths between, the tops of its chimneys sprouting like huge skittles into the middle distance. Across the crest runs an emplacement of concrete, with a firestep, and a parapet which suggests a fortification, because there is a huge cannon of the obsolete Woolwich Infant pattern peering across it at the town. The cannon is mounted on an experimental gun carriage: possibly the original model of the UNDERSHAFT *disappearing rampart gun alluded to by* STEPHEN. *The firestep, being a convenient place to sit, is furnished here and there with straw disc cushions; and at one place there is the additional luxury of a fur rug.*

BARBARA *is standing on the firestep, looking over the parapet towards the town. On her right is the cannon; on her left the end of a shed raised on piles, with a ladder of three or four steps up to the door, which opens outwards and has a little wooden landing at the threshold, with a fire bucket in the corner of the landing. Several dummy soldiers more or less mutilated, with straw protruding from their gashes, have been shoved out of the way under the landing. A few others are nearly upright against the shed; and one has fallen forward and lies, like a grotesque corpse, on the emplacement. The parapet stops short of the shed, leaving a gap which is the beginning of the path down the hill through the foundry to the town. The rug is on the firestep near this gap. Down on the emplacement behind the cannon is a trolley carrying a huge conical bombshell with a red band painted on it. Further to the right is the door of an office, which, like the sheds, is of the lightest possible construction.*

CUSINS *arrives by the path from the town.*

BARBARA Well?

CUSINS Not a ray of hope. Everything perfect! wonderful! real! It only needs a cathedral to be a heavenly city instead of a hellish one.

BARBARA Have you found out whether they have done anything for old Peter Shirley?

CUSINS They have found him a job as gatekeeper and timekeeper. He's frightfully miserable. He calls the time-keeping brainwork, and says he isnt used to it; and his gate lodge is so splendid that he's ashamed to use the rooms, and skulks in the scullery.

BARBARA Poor Peter!

STEPHEN *arrives from the town. He carries a fieldglass.*

STEPHEN (*enthusiastically*) Have you two seen the place? Why did you leave us?

CUSINS I wanted to see everything I was not intended to see; and Barbara wanted to make the men talk.

STEPHEN Have you found anything discreditable?

CUSINS No. They call him Dandy Andy and are proud of his being a cunning old rascal; but it's all horribly, frightfully, immorally, unanswerably perfect.

SARAH *arrives.*

SARAH Heavens! what a place! (*She crosses to the trolley.*) Did you see the nursing home? (*She sits down on the shell.*)

STEPHEN Did you see the libraries and schools?

SARAH Did you see the ball room and the banqueting chamber in the Town Hall!?

STEPHEN Have you gone into the insurance fund, the pension fund, the building society, the various applications of cooperation!?

UNDERSHAFT *comes from the office, with a sheaf of telegrams in his hand.*

UNDERSHAFT Well, have you seen everything? I'm sorry I was called away. (*Indicating the telegrams.*) Good news from Manchuria.

STEPHEN Another Japanese victory?

UNDERSHAFT Oh, I dont know. Which side wins does not concern us here. No: the good news is that the aerial battleship is a tremendous success. At the first trial it has wiped out a fort with three hundred soldiers in it.

CUSINS (*from the platform*) Dummy soldiers?

UNDERSHAFT (*striding across to* STEPHEN *and kicking the prostrate dummy brutally out of his way*) No: the real thing.

CUSINS *and* BARBARA *exchange glances. Then* CUSINS *sits on the step and buries his face in his hands.* BARBARA *gravely lays her hand on his shoulder. He looks up at her in whimsical desperation.*

UNDERSHAFT Well, Stephen, what do you think of the place?

STEPHEN Oh, magnificent. A perfect triumph of modern industry. Frankly, my dear father, I have been a fool: I had no idea of what it all meant: of the wonderful forethought, the power of organization, the administrative capacity, the financial genius, the colossal capital it represents. I have been repeating to myself as I came through your streets "Peace hath her victories no less renowned than War." I have only one misgiving about it all.

UNDERSHAFT Out with it.

STEPHEN Well, I cannot help thinking that all this provision for every want of your workmen may sap their independence and weaken their sense of responsibility. And greatly as we enjoyed our tea at that splendid restaurant—how they gave us all that luxury and cake and jam and cream for threepence I really cannot imagine!—still you must remember that restaurants break up home life. Look at the continent, for instance! Are you sure so much pampering is really good for the men's characters?

UNDERSHAFT Well you see, my dear boy, when you are organizing civilization you have to make up your mind whether trouble and anxiety are good things or not. If you decide that they are, then, I take it, you simply dont organize civilization; and there you are, with trouble and anxiety enough to make us all angels! But if you decide the other way, you may as well go through with it. However, Stephen, our characters are safe here. A sufficient dose of anxiety is always provided by the fact that we may be blown to smithereens at any moment.

SARAH By the way, papa, where do you make the explosives?

UNDERSHAFT In separate little sheds like that one. When one of them blows up, it costs very little, and only the people quite close to it are killed.

STEPHEN, *who is quite close to it, looks at it rather scaredly, and moves away quickly to the cannon. At the same moment the door of the shed is thrown abruptly open; and a foreman in overalls and list slippers comes out on the little landing and holds the door for* LOMAX, *who appears in the doorway.*

LOMAX (*with studied coolness*) My good fellow: you neednt get into a state of nerves. Nothing's going to happen to you; and I suppose it wouldnt be the end of the world if anything did. A little bit of British pluck is what you want, old chap. (*He descends and strolls across to* SARAH.)

UNDERSHAFT (*to the foreman*) Anything wrong, Bilton?

BILTON (*with ironic calm*) Gentleman walked into the high explosives shed and lit a cigaret, sir: thats all.

UNDERSHAFT Ah, quite so. (*Going over to* LOMAX.) Do you happen to remember what you did with the match?

LOMAX Oh come! I'm not a fool. I took jolly good care to blow it out before I chucked it away.

BILTON The top of it was red hot inside, sir.

LOMAX Well, suppose it was! I didnt chuck it into any of your messes.

UNDERSHAFT Think no more of it, Mr. Lomax. By the way, would you mind lending me your matches.

LOMAX (*offering his box*) Certainly.

UNDERSHAFT Thanks. (*He pockets the matches.*)

LOMAX (*lecturing to the company generally*) You know, these high explosives dont go off like gunpowder, except when theyre in a gun. When theyre spread loose, you can put a match to them without the least risk: they just burn quietly like a bit of paper. (*Warming to the scientific interest of the subject.*) Did you know that, Undershaft? Have you ever tried?

UNDERSHAFT Not on a large scale, Mr Lomax. Bilton will give you a sample of guncotton when you are leaving if you ask him. You can experiment with it at home. (BILTON *looks puzzled.*)

SARAH Bilton will do nothing of the sort, papa. I suppose it's your business to blow up the Russians and Japs; but you might really stop short of blowing up poor Cholly. (BILTON *gives it up and retires into the shed.*)

LOMAX My ownest, there is no danger. (*He sits beside her on the shell.*)

LADY BRITOMART *arrives from the town with a bouquet.*

LADY BRITOMART (*impetuously*) Andrew: you shouldnt have let me see this place.

UNDERSHAFT Why, my dear?

LADY BRITOMART Never mind why: you shouldnt have: thats all. To think of all that (*indicating the town*) being yours! and that you have kept it to yourself all these years!

UNDERSHAFT It does not belong to me. I belong to it. It is the Undershaft inheritance.

LADY BRITOMART It is not. Your ridiculous cannons and that noisy banking foundry may be the Undershaft inheritance; but all that plate and linen, all that furniture and those houses and orchards and gardens belong to us. They belong to me: they are not a man's business. I wont give them up. You must be out of your senses to throw them all away; and if you persist in such folly, I will call in a doctor.

UNDERSHAFT (*stooping to smell the bouquet*) Where did you get the flowers, my dear?

LADY BRITOMART Your men presented them to me in your William Morris Labor Church.

CUSINS Oh! It needed only that. A Labor Church! (*He mounts the firestep distractedly, and leans with his elbows on the parapet, turning his back to them.*)

LADY BRITOMART Yes, with Morris's words in mosaic letters ten feet high around the dome. NO MAN IS GOOD ENOUGH TO BE ANOTHER MAN'S MASTER. The cynicism of it!

UNDERSHAFT It shocked the men at first, I am afraid. But now they take no more notice of it than of the ten commandments in church.

LADY BRITOMART Andrew: you are trying to put me off the subject of the inheritance by profane jokes. Well, you shant. I dont ask it any longer for Stephen: he has inherited far too much of your perversity to be fit for it. But Barbara has rights as well as Stephen. Why should not Adolphus succeed to the inheritance? I could manage the town for him and he can look after the cannons, if they are really necessary.

UNDERSHAFT I should ask nothing better if Adophus were a foundling. He is exactly the sort of new blood that is wanted in English business. But he's not a foundling; and theres an end of it. (*He makes for the office door.*)

CUSINS (*turning to them*) Not quite. (*They all turn and stare at him.*) I think—Mind! I am not committing myself in any way as to my future course—but I think the foundling difficulty can be got over. (*He jumps down to the emplacement.*)

UNDERSHAFT (*coming back to him*) What do you mean?

CUSINS Well, I have something to say which is in the nature of a confession.

SARAH
LADY BRITOMART
BARBARA   } Confession!
STEPHEN

LOMAX Oh I say!

CUSINS Yes, a confession. Listen, all. Until I met Barbara I thought myself in the main an honorable, truthful man, because I wanted the approval of my conscience more than I wanted anything else. But the moment I saw Barbara, I wanted her far more than the approval of my conscience.

LADY BRITOMART Adolphus!

CUSINS It is true. You accused me yourself, Lady Brit, of joining the Army to worship Barbara; and so I did. She bought my soul like a flower at a street corner; but she bought it for herself.

UNDERSHAFT What! Not for Dionysos or another?

CUSINS Dionysos and all the others are in herself. I adored what was divine in her, and was therefore a true worshipper. But I was romantic about her too. I thought she was a woman of the people, and that a marriage with a professor of Greek would be far beyond the wildest social ambitions of her rank.

LADY BRITOMART Adolphus!!

LOMAX Oh I say!!!

CUSINS When I learnt the horrible truth—

LADY BRITOMART What do you mean by the horrible truth, pray?

CUSINS That she was enormously rich; that her grandfather was an earl; that her father was the Prince of Darkness—

UNDERSHAFT Chut!

CUSINS —and that I was only an adventurer trying to catch a rich wife, then I stooped to deceive her about my birth.

BARBARA (*rising*) Dolly!

LADY BRITOMART Your birth! Now Adolphus, dont dare to make up a wicked story for the sake of these wretched cannons. Remember: I have seen photographs of your parents; and the Agent General for South Western Australia knows them personally and has assured me that they are most respectable married people.

CUSINS So they are in Australia; but here they are outcasts. Their marriage is legal in Australia, but not in England. My mother is my father's deceased wife's sister; and in this island I am consequently a foundling. (*Sensation.*)

BARBARA Silly! (*She climbs to the cannon, and leans, listening, in the angle it makes with the parapet.*)

CUSINS Is the subterfuge good enough, Machiavelli?

UNDERSHAFT (*thoughtfully*) Biddy: this may be a way out of the difficulty.

LADY BRITOMART Stuff! A man cant make cannons any the better for being his own cousin instead of his proper self (*she sits down on the rug with a bounce that expresses her downright contempt for their casuistry*).

UNDERSHAFT (*to* CUSINS) You are an educated man. That is against the tradition.

CUSINS Once in ten thousand times it happens that the schoolboy is a born master of what they try to teach him. Greek has not destroyed my mind: it has nourished it. Besides, I did not learn it at an English public school.

UNDERSHAFT Hm! Well, I cannot afford to be too particular: you have cornered the foundling market. Let it pass. You are eligible, Euripides: you are eligible.

BARBARA Dolly: yesterday morning, when Stephen told us all about the tradition, you became very silent, and you have been strange and excited ever since. Were you thinking of your birth then?

CUSINS When the finger of Destiny suddenly points at a man in the middle of his breakfast, it makes him thoughtful.

UNDERSHAFT Aha! You have had your eye on the business, my young friend, have you?

CUSINS Take care! There is an abyss of moral horror between me and your accursed aerial battleships.

UNDERSHAFT Never mind the abyss for the present. Let us settle the practical details and leave your final decision open. You know that you will have to change your name. Do you object to that?

CUSINS Would any man named Adolphus—any man called Dolly! —object to be called something else?

UNDERSHAFT Good. Now, as to money! I propose to treat you handsomely from the beginning. You shall start at a thousand a year.

CUSINS (*with sudden heat, his spectacles twinkling with mischief*) A thousand! You dare offer a miserable thousand to the son-in-law of a millionaire! No, by Heavens, Machiavelli! you shall not cheat me. You cannot do without me; and I can do without you. I must have two thousand five hundred a year for two years. At the end of that time, if I am a failure, I go. But if I am a success, and stay on, you must give me the other five thousand.

UNDERSHAFT What other five thousand?

CUSINS To make the two years up to five thousand a year. The two thousand five hundred is only half pay in case I should turn out a failure. The third year I must have ten per cent on the profits.

UNDERSHAFT (*taken aback*) Ten per cent! Why, man, do you know what my profits are?

CUSINS   Enormous, I hope: otherwise I shall require twenty-five per cent.

UNDERSHAFT   But, Mr Cusins, this is a serious matter of business. You are not bringing any capital into the concern.

CUSINS   What! no capital! Is my mastery of Greek no capital? Is my access to the subtlest thought, the loftiest poetry yet attained by humanity, no capital? My character! my intellect! my life! my career! what Barbara calls my soul! are these no capital? Say another word; and I double my salary.

UNDERSHAFT   Be reasonable—

CUSINS   (*peremptorily*)   Mr Undershaft: you have my terms. Take them or leave them.

UNDERSHAFT   (*recovering himself*)   Very well, I note your terms; and I offer you half.

CUSINS   (*disgusted*)   Half!

UNDERSHAFT   (*firmly*)   Half.

CUSINS   You call yourself a gentleman; and you offer me half!!

UNDERSHAFT   I do not call myself a gentleman; but I offer you half.

CUSINS   This to your future partner! your successor! your son-in-law!

BARBARA   You are selling your own soul, Dolly, not mine. Leave me out of the bargain, please.

UNDERSHAFT   Come! I will go a step further for Barbara's sake. I will give you three fifths; but that is my last word.

CUSINS   Done!

LOMAX   Done in the eye! Why, *I* get only eight hundred, you know.

CUSINS   By the way, Mac, I am a classical scholar not an arithmetical one. Is three fifths more than half or less?

UNDERSHAFT   More, of course.

CUSINS   I would have taken two hundred and fifty. How you can succeed in business when you are willing to pay all that money to a University don who is obviously not worth a junior clerk's wages!—well! What will Lazarus say?

UNDERSHAFT   Lazarus is a gentle romantic Jew who cares for nothing but string quartets and stalls at fashionable theatres. He will be blamed for your rapacity in money matters, poor fellow! as he has hitherto been blamed for mine. You are a shark of the first order, Euripides. So much the better for the firm!

BARBARA   Is the bargain closed, Dolly? Does your soul belong to him now?

CUSINS   No: the price is settled: that is all. The real tug of war is still to come. What about the moral question?

LADY BRITOMART   There is no moral question in the matter at all, Adolphus. You must simply sell cannons and weapons to people whose cause is right and just, and refuse them to foreigners and criminals.

UNDERSHAFT (*determinedly*) No: none of that. You must keep the true faith of an Armorer, or you dont come in here.

CUSINS What on earth is the true faith of an Armorer?

UNDERSHAFT To give arms to all men who offer an honest price for them, without respect of persons or principles: to aristocrat and republican, to Nihilist and Tsar, to Capitalist and Socialist, to Protestant and Catholic, to burglar and policeman, to black man, white man and yellow man, to all sorts and conditions, all nationalities, all faiths, all follies, all causes and all crimes. The first Undershaft wrote up in his shop IF GOD GAVE THE HAND, LET NOT MAN WITHHOLD THE SWORD. The second wrote up ALL HAVE THE RIGHT TO FIGHT: NONE HAVE THE RIGHT TO JUDGE. The third wrote up TO MAN THE WEAPON: TO HEAVEN THE VICTORY. The fourth had no literary turn; so he did not write up anything; but he sold cannons to Napoleon under the nose of George the Third. The fifth wrote up PEACE SHALL NOT PREVAIL SAVE WITH A SWORD IN HER HAND. The sixth, my master, was the best of all. He wrote up NOTHING IS EVER DONE IN THIS WORLD UNTIL MEN ARE PREPARED TO KILL ONE ANOTHER IF IT IS NOT DONE. After that, there was nothing left for the seventh to say. So he wrote up, simply, UNASHAMED.

CUSINS My good Machiavelli. I shall certainly write something up on the wall; only, as I shall write it in Greek, you wont be able to read it. But as to your Armorer's faith, if I take my neck out of the noose of my own morality I am not going to put it into the noose of yours. I shall sell cannons to whom I please and refuse them to whom I please. So there!

UNDERSHAFT From the moment when you become Andrew Undershaft, you will never do as you please again. Dont come here lusting for power, young man.

CUSINS If power were my aim I should not come here for it. You have no power.

UNDERSHAFT None of my own, certainly.

CUSINS I have more power than you, more will. You do not drive this place: it drives you. And what drives the place?

UNDERSHAFT (*enigmatically*) A will of which I am a part.

BARBARA (*startled*) Father! Do you know what you are saying; or are you laying a snare for my soul?

CUSINS Dont listen to his metaphysics, Barbara. The place is driven by the most rascally part of society, the money hunters, the pleasure hunters, the military promotion hunters; and he is their slave.

UNDERSHAFT Not necessarily. Remember the Armorer's Faith. I
will take an order from a good man as cheerfully as from a bad
one. If you good people prefer preaching and shirking to buying
my weapons and fighting the rascals, dont blame me. I can make
cannons: I cannot make courage and conviction. Bah! you tire
me, Euripides, with your morality mongering. Ask Barbara: she
understands. (*He suddenly reaches up and takes* BARBARA's *hands,
looking powerfully into her eyes.*) Tell him, my love, what power
really means.

BARBARA (*hypnotized*) Before I joined the Salvation Army, I was
in my own power and the consequence was that I never knew
what to do with myself. When I joined it, I had not time enough
for all the things I had to do.

UNDERSHAFT (*approvingly*) Just so. And why was that, do you
suppose?

BARBARA Yesterday I should have said, because I was in the power
of God. (*She resumes her self-possession, withdrawing her hands
from his with a power equal to his own.*) But you came and
shewed me that I was in the power of Bodger and Undershaft.
Today I feel—oh! how can I put it into words? Sarah: do you
remember the earthquake at Cannes, when we were little children?—how little the surprise of the first shock mattered compared to the dread and horror of waiting for the second? That is
how I feel in this place today. I stood on the rock I thought eternal; and without a word of warning it reeled and crumbled under
me. I was safe with an infinite wisdom watching me, an army
marching to Salvation with me; and in a moment, at a stroke of
your pen in a cheque book, I stood alone; and the heavens were
empty. That was the first shock of the earthquake: I am waiting
for the second.

UNDERSHAFT Come, come, my daughter! dont make too much of
your little tinpot tragedy. What do we do here when we spend
years of work and thought and thousands of pounds of solid cash
on a new gun or an aerial battleship that turns out just a hairs-
breadth wrong after all? Scrap it. Scrap it without wasting another hour or another pound on it. Well, you have made for
yourself something that you call a morality or a religion or what
not. It doesnt fit the facts. Well, scrap it. Scrap it and get one
that does fit. That is what is wrong with the world at present. It
scraps its obsolete steam engines and dynamos; but it wont scrap
its old prejudices and its old moralities and its old religions and
its old political constitutions. Whats the result? In machinery it
does very well; but in morals and religion and politics it is working at a loss that brings it nearer bankruptcy every year. Dont

persist in that folly. If your old religion broke down yesterday, get a newer and a better one for tomorrow.

BARBARA   Oh how gladly I would take a better one to my soul! But you offer me a worse one. (*Turning on him with sudden vehemence.*) Justify yourself: shew me some light through the darkness of this dreadful place, with its beautifully clean workshops, and respectable workmen, and model homes.

UNDERSHAFT   Cleanliness and respectability do not need justification, Barbara: they justify themselves. I see no darkness here, no dreadfulness. In your Salvation shelter I saw poverty, misery, cold and hunger. You gave them bread and treacle and dreams of heaven. I give from thirty shillings a week to twelve thousand a year. They find their own dreams but I look after the drainage.

BARBARA   And their souls?

UNDERSHAFT   I save their souls just as I saved yours.

BARBARA   (*revolted*)   You saved my soul! What do you mean?

UNDERSHAFT   I fed you and clothed you and housed you. I took care that you should have money enough to live handsomely— more than enough; so that you could be wasteful, careless, generous. That saved your soul from the seven deadly sins.

BARBARA   (*bewildered*)   The seven deadly sins!

UNDERSHAFT   Yes, the deadly seven. (*Counting on his fingers.*) Food, clothing, firing, rent, taxes, respectability and children. Nothing can lift those seven millstones from Man's neck but money and the spirit cannot soar until the millstones are lifted. I lifted them from your spirit. I enabled Barbara to become Major Barbara; and I saved her from the crime of poverty.

CUSINS   Do you call poverty a crime?

UNDERSHAFT   The worst of crimes. All the other crimes are virtues beside it: all the other dishonors are chivalry itself by comparison. Poverty blights whole cities; spreads horrible pestilences; strikes dead the very souls of all who come within sight, sound, or smell of it. What you call crime is nothing: a murder here and a theft there, a blow now and a curse then: what do they matter? they are only the accidents and illnesses of life: there are not fifty genuine professional criminals in London. But there are millions of poor people, abject people, dirty people, ill fed, ill clothed people. They poison us morally and physically: they kill the happiness of society: they force us to do away with our own liberties and to organize unnatural cruelties for fear they should rise against us and drag us down into their abyss. Only fools fear crime: we all fear poverty. Pah! (*turning on* BARBARA) you talk of your half-saved ruffian in West Ham: you accuse me of dragging his soul back to perdition. Well, bring him to me here; and

I will drag his soul back again to salvation for you. Not by words and dreams; but by thirty-eight shillings a week, a sound house in a handsome street and a permanent job. In three weeks he will have a fancy waistcoat; in three months a tall hat and a chapel sitting; before the end of the year he will shake hands with a duchess at a Primrose League meeting, and join the Conservative Party.

BARBARA   And will he be the better for that?

UNDERSHAFT   You know he will. Dont be a hypocrite, Barbara. He will be better fed, better housed, better clothed, better behaved; and his children will be pounds heavier and bigger. That will be better than an American cloth mattress in a shelter, chopping firewood, eating bread and treacle, and being forced to kneel down from time to time to thank heaven for it: knee drill, I think you call it. It is cheap work converting starving men with a Bible in one hand and a slice of bread in the other. I will undertake to convert West Ham to Mahometanism on the same terms. Try your hand on my men: their souls are hungry because their bodies are full.

BARBARA   And leave the east end to starve?

UNDERSHAFT   (*his energetic tone dropping into one of bitter and brooding remembrance*)   *I* was an east ender. I moralized and starved until one day I swore that I would be a full-fed free man at all costs; that nothing should stop me except a bullet, neither reason nor morals nor the lives of other men. I said "Thou shalt starve ere I starve"; and with that word I became free and great. I was a dangerous man until I had my will: now I am a useful, beneficent, kindly person. That is the history of most self-made millionaires, I fancy. When it is the history of every Englishman we shall have an England worth living in.

LADY BRITOMART   Stop making speeches, Andrew. This is not the place for them.

UNDERSHAFT   (*punctured*)   My dear: I have no other means of conveying my ideas.

LADY BRITOMART   Your ideas are nonsense. You got on because you were selfish and unscrupulous.

UNDERSHAFT   Not at all. I had the strongest scruples about poverty and starvation. Your moralists are quite unscrupulous about both: they make virtues of them. I had rather be a thief than a pauper. I had rather be a murderer than a slave. I dont want to be either; but if you force the alternative on me, then, by Heaven, I'll choose the braver and more moral one. I hate poverty and slavery worse than any other crimes whatsoever. And let me tell you this.

Poverty and slavery have stood up for centuries to your sermons and leading articles: they will not stand up to my machine guns. Dont preach at them: dont reason with them. Kill them.

BARBARA   Killing. Is that your remedy for everything?

UNDERSHAFT   It is the final test of conviction, the only lever strong enough to overturn a social system, the only way of saying Must. Let six hundred and seventy fools loose in the streets; and three policemen can scatter them. But huddle them together in a certain house in Westminster; and let them go through certain ceremonies and call themselves certain names until at last they get the courage to kill; and your six hundred and seventy fools become a government. Your pious mob fills up ballot papers and imagines it is governing its masters; but the ballot paper that really governs is the paper that has a bullet wrapped up in it.

CUSINS   That is perhaps why, like most intelligent people, I never vote.

UNDERSHAFT   Vote! Bah! When you vote, you only change the names of the cabinet. When you shoot, you pull down governments, inaugurate new epochs, abolish old orders and set up new. Is that historically true. Mr Learned Man, or is it not?

CUSINS   It is historically true. I loathe having to admit it. I repudiate your sentiments. I abhor your nature. I defy you in every possible way. Still, it is true. But it ought not to be true.

UNDERSHAFT   Ought! ought! ought! ought! ought! Are you going to spend your life saying ought, like the rest of our moralists? Turn your oughts into shalls, man. Come and make explosives with me. Whatever can blow men up can blow society up. The history of the world is the history of those who had courage enough to embrace this truth. Have you the courage to embrace it, Barbara?

LADY BRITOMART   Barbara: I positively forbid you to listen to your father's abominable wickedness. And you, Adolphus, ought to know better than to go about saying that wrong things are true. What does it matter whether they are true if they are wrong?

UNDERSHAFT   What does it matter whether they are wrong if they are true?

LADY BRITOMART (*rising*)   Children: come home instantly. Andrew: I am exceedingly sorry I allowed you to call on us. You are wickeder than ever. Come at once.

BARBARA (*shaking her head*)   It's no use running away from wicked people, mamma.

LADY BRITOMART   It is every use. It shews your disapprobation of them.

BARBARA   It does not save them.

LADY BRITOMART   I can see that you are going to disobey me. Sarah: are you coming home or are you not?

SARAH   I daresay it's very wicked of papa to make cannons; but I dont think I shall cut him on that account.

LOMAX (*pouring oil on the troubled waters*)   The fact is, you know, there is a certain amount of tosh about this notion of wickedness. It doesnt work. You must look at facts. Not that I would say a word in favor of anything wrong; but then, you see, all sorts of chaps are always doing all sorts of things; and we have to fit them in somehow, dont you know. What I mean is that you cant go cutting everybody; and thats about what it comes to. (*Their rapt attention to his eloquence makes him nervous.*) Perhaps I dont make myself clear.

LADY BRITOMART   You are lucidity itself, Charles. Because Andrew is successful and has plenty of money to give to Sarah, you will flatter him and encourage him in his wickedness.

LOMAX (*unruffled*)   Well, where the carcase is, there will the eagles be gathered, dont you know. (*To* UNDERSHAFT.) Eh? What?

UNDERSHAFT   Precisely. By the way, may I call you Charles?

LOMAX   Delighted. Cholly is the usual ticket.

UNDERSHAFT (*to* LADY BRITOMART)   Biddy—

LADY BRITOMART (*violently*)   Dont dare call me Biddy. Charles Lomax: you are a fool. Adolphus Cusins: you are a Jesuit. Stephen: you are a prig. Barbara: you are a lunatic. Andrew: you are a vulgar tradesman. Now you all know my opinion; and my conscience is clear, at all events (*she sits down with a vehemence that the rug fortunately softens*).

UNDERSHAFT   My dear: you are the incarnation of morality. (*She snorts.*) Your conscience is clear and your duty done when you have called everybody names. Come, Euripides! it is getting late; and we all want to get home. Make up your mind.

CUSINS   Understand this, you old demon—

LADY BRITOMART   Adolphus!

UNDERSHAFT   Let him alone, Biddy. Proceed, Euripides.

CUSINS   You have me in a horrible dilemma. I want Barbara.

UNDERSHAFT   Like all young men, you greatly exaggerate the difference between one young woman and another.

BARBARA   Quite true, Dolly.

CUSINS   I also want to avoid being a rascal.

UNDERSHAFT (*with biting contempt*)   You lust for personal righteousness, for self-approval, for what you call a good conscience, for what Barbara calls salvation, for what I call patronizing people who are not so lucky as yourself.

CUSINS   I do not: all the poet in me recoils from being a good man. But there are things in me that I must reckon with. Pity—

UNDERSHAFT   Pity! The scavenger of misery.

CUSINS   Well, love.

UNDERSHAFT   I know. You love the needy and the outcast: you love the oppressed races, the negro, the Indian ryot, the underdog everywhere. Do you love the Japanese? Do you love the French? Do you love the English?

CUSINS   No. Every true Englishman detests the English. We are the wickedest nation on earth; and our success is a moral horror.

UNDERSHAFT   That is what comes of your gospel of love, is it?

CUSINS   May I not love even my father-in-law?

UNDERSHAFT   Who wants your love, man? By what right do you take the liberty of offering it to me? I will have your due heed and respect, or I will kill you. But your love! Damn your impertinence!

CUSINS   (*grinning*)   I may not be able to control my affections, Mac.

UNDERSHAFT   You are fencing, Euripides. You are weakening: your grip is slipping. Come! try your last weapon. Pity and love have broken in your hand: forgiveness is still left.

CUSINS   No: forgiveness is a beggar's refuge. I am with you there: we must pay our debts.

UNDERSHAFT   Well said. Come! you will suit me. Remember the words of Plato.

CUSINS   (*starting*)   Plato! You dare quote Plato to me!

UNDERSHAFT   Plato says, my friend, that society cannot be saved until either the Professors of Greek take to making gunpowder, or else the makers of gunpowder become Professors of Greek.

CUSINS   Oh, tempter, cunning tempter!

UNDERSHAFT   Come! choose, man, choose.

CUSINS   But perhaps Barbara will not marry me if I make the wrong choice.

BARBARA   Perhaps not.

CUSINS   (*desperately perplexed*)   You hear!

BARBARA   Father: do you love nobody?

UNDERSHAFT   I love my best friend.

LADY BRITOMART   And who is that, pray?

UNDERSHAFT   My bravest enemy. That is the man who keeps me up to the mark.

CUSINS   You know, the creature is really a sort of poet in his way. Suppose he is a great man, after all!

UNDERSHAFT   Suppose you stop talking and make up your mind, my young friend.

CUSINS   But you are driving me against my nature. I hate war.

UNDERSHAFT   Hatred is the coward's revenge for being intimidated. Dare you make war on war? Here are the means: my friend Mr Lomax is sitting on them.

LOMAX (*springing up*)   Oh I say! You dont mean that this thing is loaded, do you? My ownest: come off it.

SARAH (*sitting placidly on the shell*)   If I am to be blown up, the more thoroughly it is done the better. Dont fuss, Cholly.

LOMAX (*to* UNDERSHAFT, *strongly remonstrant*)   Your own daughter, you know!

UNDERSHAFT   So I see. (*To* CUSINS.) Well, my friend, may we expect you here at six tomorrow morning?

CUSINS (*firmly*)   Not on any account. I will see the whole establishment blown up with its own dynamite before I will get up at five. My hours are healthy, rational hours: eleven to five.

UNDERSHAFT   Come when you please: before a week you will come at six and stay until I turn you out for the sake of your health. (*Calling.*) Bilton! (*He turns to* LADY BRITOMART, *who rises.*) My dear: let us leave these two young people to themselves for a moment. (BILTON *comes from the shed.*) I am going to take you through the guncotton shed.

BILTON (*barring the way*)   You cant take anything explosive in here, sir.

LADY BRITOMART   What do you mean? Are you alluding to me?

BILTON (*unmoved*)   No, maam. Mr Undershaft has the other gentleman's matches in his pocket.

LADY BRITOMART (*abruptly*)   Oh! I beg your pardon! (*She goes into the shed.*)

UNDERSHAFT   Quite right, Bilton, quite right: here you are. (*He gives* BILTON *the box of matches.*) Come, Stephen. Come, Charles. Bring Sarah. (*He passes into the shed.*)

BILTON *opens the box and deliberately drops the matches into the firebucket.*

LOMAX   Oh! I say. (BILTON *stolidly hands him the empty box.*) Infernal nonsense! Pure scientific ignorance! (*He goes in.*)

SARAH   Am I all right, Bilton?

BILTON   Youll have to put on list slippers, miss: thats all. Weve got em inside. (*She goes in.*)

STEPHEN (*very seriously to* CUSINS)   Dolly, old fellow, think. Think before you decide. Do you feel that you are a sufficiently practical man? It is a huge undertaking, an enormous responsibility. All this mass of business will be Greek to you.

CUSINS   Oh, I think it will be much less difficult than Greek.

STEPHEN Well, I just want to say this before I leave you to yourselves. Dont let anything I have said about right and wrong prejudice you against this great chance in life. I have satisfied myself
that the business is one of the highest character and a credit to
our country. (*Emotionally.*) I am very proud of my father. I—
(*Unable to proceed, he presses* CUSINS' *hand and goes hastily
into the shed, followed by* BILTON.)

BARBARA *and* CUSINS, *left alone together, look at one another silently.*

CUSINS Barbara: I am going to accept this offer.

BARBARA I thought you would.

CUSINS You understand, dont you, that I had to decide without
consulting you. If I had thrown the burden of the choice on you,
you would sooner or later have despised me for it.

BARBARA Yes: I did not want you to sell your soul for me any more
than for this inheritance.

CUSINS It is not the sale of my soul that troubles me: I have sold
it too often to care about that. I have sold it for a professorship. I
have sold it for an income. I have sold it to escape being imprisoned for refusing to pay taxes for hangmen's ropes and unjust
wars and things that I abhor. What is all human conduct but the
daily and hourly sale of our souls for trifles? What I am now selling it for is neither money nor position nor comfort, but for reality and for power.

BARBARA You know that you will have no power, and that he has
none.

CUSINS I know. It is not for myself alone. I want to make power
for the world.

BARBARA I want to make power for the world too; but it must be
spiritual power.

CUSINS I think all power is spiritual: these cannons will not go off
by themselves. I have tried to make spiritual power by teaching
Greek. But the world can never be really touched by a dead language and a dead civilization. The people must have power; and
the people cannot have Greek. Now the power that is made here
can be wielded by all men.

BARBARA Power to burn women's houses down and kill their sons
and tear their husbands to pieces.

CUSINS You cannot have power for good without having power
for evil too. Even mother's milk nourishes murderers as well as
heroes. This power which only tears men's bodies to pieces has
never been so horribly abused as the intellectual power, the imaginative power, the poetic, religious power that can enslave men's
souls. As a teacher of Greek I gave the intellectual man weapons

against the common man. I now want to give the common man weapons against the intellectual man. I love the common people. I want to arm them against the lawyers, the doctors, the priests, the literary men, the professors, the artists, and the politicians, who, once in authority, are more disastrous and tyrannical than all the fools, rascals, and impostors. I want a power simple enough for common men to use, yet strong enough to force the intellectual oligarchy to use its genius for the general good.

BARBARA Is there no higher power than that (*pointing to the shell*)?

CUSINS Yes; but that power can destroy the higher powers just as a tiger can destroy a man: therefore Man must master that power first. I admitted this when the Turks and Greeks were last at war. My best pupil went out to fight for Hellas. My parting gift to him was not a copy of Plato's Republic, but a revolver and a hundred Undershaft cartridges. The blood of every Turk he shot—if he shot any—is on my head as well as on Undershaft's. That act committed me to this place for ever. Your father's challenge has beaten me. Dare I make war on war? I must. I will. And now, is it all over between us?

BARBARA (*touched by his evident dread of her answer*) Silly baby Dolly! How could it be!

CUSINS (*overjoyed*) Then you—you—you—Oh for my drum! (*He flourishes imaginary drumsticks.*)

BARBARA (*angered by his levity*) Take care, Dolly, take care. Oh, if only I could get away from you and from father and from it all! if I could have the wings of a dove and fly away to heaven!

CUSINS And leave me!

BARBARA Yes, you, and all the other naughty mischievous children of men. But I cant. I was happy in the Salvation Army for a moment. I escaped from the world into a paradise of enthusiasm and prayer and soul saving; but the moment our money ran short, it all came back to Bodger: it was he who saved our people: he, and the Prince of Darkness, my papa. Undershaft and Bodger: their hands stretch everywhere: when we feed a starving fellow creature, it is with their bread, because there is no other bread; when we tend the sick, it is in the hospitals they endow; if we turn from the churches they build, we must kneel on the stones of the streets they pave. As long as that lasts, there is no getting away from them. Turning our backs on Bodger and Undershaft is turning our backs on life.

CUSINS I thought you were determined to turn your back on the wicked side of life.

BARBARA There is no wicked side: life is all one. And I never wanted to shirk my share in whatever evil must be endured, whether it be sin or suffering. I wish I could cure you of middle-class ideas, Dolly.

CUSINS (*gasping*) Middle cl—! A snub! A social snub to me from the daughter of a foundling!

BARBARA That is why I have no class, Dolly: I come straight out of the heart of the whole people. If I were middle-class I should turn my back on my father's business; and we should both live in an artistic drawing room, with you reading the reviews in one corner, and I in the other at the piano, playing Schumann: both very superior persons, and neither of us a bit of use. Sooner than that, I would sweep out the guncotton shed, or be one of Bodger's barmaids. Do you know what would have happened if you had refused papa's offer?

CUSINS I wonder!

BARBARA I should have given you up and married the man who accepted it. After all, my dear old mother has more sense than any of you. I felt like her when I saw this place—felt that I must have it—that never, never, never could I let it go; only she thought it was the houses and the kitchen ranges and the linen and china, when it was really all the human souls to be saved: not weak souls in starved bodies, sobbing with gratitude for a scrap of bread and treacle, but fullfed, quarrelsome, snobbish, uppish creatures, all standing on their little rights and dignities, and thinking that my father ought to be greatly obliged to them for making so much money for him—and so he ought. That is where salvation is really wanted. My father shall never throw it in my teeth again that my converts were bribed with bread. (*She is transfigured.*) I have got rid of the bribe of bread. I have got rid of the bribe of heaven. Let God's work be done for its own sake: the work he had to create us to do because it cannot be done except by living men and women. When I die, let him be in my debt, not I in his; and let me forgive him as becomes a woman of my rank.

CUSINS Then the way of life lies through the factory of death?

BARBARA Yes, through the raising of hell to heaven and of man to God, through the unveiling of an eternal light in the Valley of The Shadow. (*Seizing him with both hands.*) Oh, did you think my courage would never come back? did you believe that I was a deserter? that I, who have stood in the streets, and taken my people to my heart, and talked of the holiest and greatest things with them, could ever turn back and chatter foolishly to fashionable people about nothing in a drawing room? Never, never, never, never: Major Barbara will die with the colors. Oh! and

I have my dear little Dolly boy still; and he has found me my place and my work. Glory Hallelujah! (*She kisses him.*)

CUSINS My dearest: consider my delicate health. I cannot stand as much happiness as you can.

BARBARA Yes: it is not easy work being in love with me, is it? But it's good for you. (*She runs to the shed, and calls, childlike.*) Mamma! Mamma! (BILTON *comes out of the shed, followed by* UNDERSHAFT.) I want Mamma.

UNDERSHAFT She is taking off her list slippers, dear. (*He passes on to* CUSINS.) Well? What does she say?

CUSINS She has gone right up into the skies.

LADY BRITOMART (*coming from the shed and stopping on the steps, obstructing* SARAH, *who follows with* LOMAX. BARBARA *clutches like a baby at her mother's skirt*) Barbara: when will you learn to be independent and to act and think for yourself? I know, as well as possible what that cry of "Mamma, Mamma," means. Always running to me!

SARAH (*touching* LADY BRITOMART's *ribs with her finger tips and imitating a bicycle horn*) Pip! pip!

LADY BRITOMART (*highly indignant*) How dare you say Pip! pip! to me, Sarah? You are both very naughty children. What do you want, Barbara?

BARBARA I want a house in the village to live in with Dolly. (*Dragging at the skirt.*) Come and tell me which one to take.

UNDERSHAFT (*to* CUSINS) Six o'clock tomorrow morning, Euripides.

SIX CHARACTERS IN SEARCH OF AN AUTHOR (1921)

LUIGI PIRANDELLO (1867–1936)

If you like Chinese puzzles; if you find it fun to be tortured and left high and dry by philosophical dilemmas that cannot be resolved; if you find it exciting to be pulled in all directions at once down several roads to nowhere, then you will be absorbed by the works of Nobel Prize winner, Luigi Pirandello.

When you see a Pirandello play you must surrender yourself to some pure theatricality, but not in the sense of frenzied stage action or technical displays. You will be constantly teased by being asked to make choices between the illusion of what you are seeing and the reality, while being denied at the same time any possible ability of doing so. It is an off-again-on-again world, in which absolute facts disintegrate into thin air, and the truth, always hovering overhead, remains permanently, tantalizingly elusive.

Pirandello has sometimes been considered as the first of the "absurdists," those dramatists identified in the 1950s as the ones who saw life as a maze of contradictions, wrong turns, dead ends, making of existence itself an experience in ridiculous absurdity. Certainly this exceptional Italian dramatist broke some interesting ground which the absurdists eventually cultivated, for he raises fundamental questions in existential terms, common to the absurdists, about who and what we are and how we appear to ourselves and to others. Everything that Pirandello presents is frighteningly, convincingly real, even though it borders on fantasy. It is very often hilariously funny, but it is terrifying. It is, to be sure, monumentally absurd.

In *Six Characters* Pirandello puts us squarely into the make-believe of the theatre in his play within a play, choosing as home base for his story the one place that demands the surrender of our ability to rationalize, where we must absolutely suspend our disbelief. His illusion is set in a world designed for illusion, where "real" men and women play at being what they are not. But suppose, says Pirandello, that there is a further basic "reality" that is beyond "real" actors and "real" theatre. Suppose there is an absolute, unchanging, continuing reality that is art, the reality lived by the characters who have sprung from the mind of the artist, but who have achieved such immediate reality that they must be abandoned. And suppose they turn up in the world of make-believe that "real" men create for themselves in the theatre, where they find that their own version of "reality" is incapable of imitation and interpretation, existing in an absolute that is known only to themselves and incomprehensible to "real" men and women. What then?

By the time you have finished *Six Characters* you will hope to have found the answers to what constitutes illusion and what makes up reality, but you will be totally frustrated. "Reality" will have abandoned you, even as the author has abandoned his characters. You will encounter the problem of the simultaneity of time, watching the six characters exist in linear time, on the stage of the theatre where they have so pitifully, desperately, come for help, but you will recognize that they also exist in a continuous circle of time that is always beginning, never ending, circling back on itself constantly and instantly. The six are doomed to be what they are and nothing more, nothing less. They have no way out; they must act their scene unchanging and forever. They are, in reality, far more *real* than those of us who live in a world of our own illusions, our own perspectives always different from all others.

Who, then, is really alive? Who suffers and dies? The six characters do it, all at once, all the time. It is a desperate, finite, unalterable, and utterly absurd existence, but who dares deny it? Who dares complete the story? Who dares tell these characters that they are only figments of imagination? Whose imagination? Try to figure it out, says Pirandello. Just try.

Six Characters in Search of an Author

PIRANDELLO

English version by Edward Storer

CHARACTERS
OF THE COMEDY IN THE MAKING:

THE FATHER	MADAME PACE
THE MOTHER	THE BOY ⎱ *(These two do not speak)*
THE STEPDAUGHTER	THE CHILD ⎰
THE SON	

ACTORS
OF THE COMPANY:

THE MANAGER	OTHER ACTORS AND ACTRESSES
LEADING LADY	PROPERTY MAN
LEADING MAN	PROMPTER
SECOND LADY LEAD	MACHINIST
L'INGÉNUE	MANAGER'S SECRETARY
JUVENILE LEAD	DOORKEEPER
	SCENE-SHIFTERS

DAYTIME: *The Stage of a Theatre.*

N.B. *The Comedy is without acts or scenes. The performance is interrupted once, without the curtain being lowered, when* THE MANAGER *and the chief characters withdraw to arrange the scenario. A second interruption of the action takes place when, by mistake, the stage hands let the curtain down.*

ACT I

The spectators will find the curtain raised and the stage as it usually is during the daytime. It will be half dark, and empty, so that from the beginning the public may have the impression of an impromptu performance.

PROMPTER's *box and a small table and chair for* THE MANAGER.
Two other small tables and several chairs scattered about as during rehearsals.

The ACTORS *and* ACTRESSES *of the company enter from the back of the stage:*

First one, then another, then two together: nine or ten in all. They are about to rehearse a Pirandello play: Mixing It Up. *Some of the company move off towards their dressing rooms. The* PROMPTER, *who has the "book" under his arm, is waiting for* THE MANAGER *in order to begin the rehearsal.*

The ACTORS *and* ACTRESSES, *some standing, some sitting, chat and smoke. One perhaps reads a paper; another cons his part.*

Finally, THE MANAGER *enters and goes to the table prepared for him. His* SECRETARY *brings him his mail, through which he glances. The* PROMPTER *takes his seat, turns on a light, and opens the "book."*

THE MANAGER (*Throwing a letter down on the table*)   I can't see. (*To* PROPERTY MAN) Let's have a little light, please!

PROPERTY MAN   Yes sir, yes, at once. (*A light comes down on to the stage*)

THE MANAGER (*Clapping his hands*)   Come along! Come along! Second act of *Mixing It Up.* (*Sits down*)

(*The* ACTORS *and* ACTRESSES *go from the front of the stage to the wings, all except the three who are to begin the rehearsal*)

PROMPTER (*Reading the "book"*)   "Leo Gala's house. A curious room serving as dining-room and study."

THE MANAGER (*To* PROPERTY MAN)   Fix up the old red room.

PROPERTY MAN (*Noting it down*)   Red set. All right!

PROMPTER (*Continuing to read from the "book"*)   "Table already laid and writing desk with books and papers. Bookshelves. Exit rear to Leo's bedroom. Exit left to kitchen. Principal exit to right."

THE MANAGER (*Energetically*)   Well, you understand: The principal exit over there; here, the kitchen. (*Turning to* ACTOR *who is to play the part of Socrates*) You make your entrances and exits here. (*To* PROPERTY MAN) The baize doors at the rear, and curtains.

PROPERTY MAN (*Noting it down*)   Right-o!

PROMPTER (*Reading as before*)   "When the curtain rises, Leo Gala, dressed in cook's cap and apron is busy beating an egg in a cup. Philip, also dressed as a cook, is beating another egg. Guido Venanzi is seated and listening."

LEADING MAN (*To* MANAGER)   Excuse me, but must I absolutely wear a cook's cap?

THE MANAGER (*Annoyed*)   I imagine so. It says so there anyway. (*Pointing to the "book"*)

LEADING MAN   But it's ridiculous!

THE MANAGER   Ridiculous? Ridiculous? Is it my fault if France won't send us any more good comedies, and we are reduced to putting on Pirandello's works where nobody understands anything, and where the author plays the fool with us all? (*The* ACTORS *grin.* THE MANAGER *goes to* LEADING MAN *and shouts*) Yes sir, you put on the cook's cap and beat eggs. Do you suppose that with all this egg-beating business you are on an ordinary stage? Get that out of your head. You represent the shell of the eggs you are beating! (*Laughter and comments among the* ACTORS) Silence! and listen to my explanations, please! (*To* LEADING MAN) "The empty form of reason without the fullness of instinct, which is blind"—You stand for reason, your wife is instinct. It's a mixing up of the parts, according to which you who act your own part become the puppet of yourself. Do you understand?

LEADING MAN   I'm hanged if I do.

THE MANAGER   Neither do I. But let's get on with it. It's sure to be a glorious failure anyway. (*Confidentially*) But I say, please face three-quarters. Otherwise, what with the abstruseness of the dialogue, and the public that won't be able to hear you, the whole thing will go to hell. Come on! come on!

PROMPTER   Pardon sir, may I get into my box? There's a bit of a draught.

THE MANAGER   Yes, yes, of course!

At this point, the DOORKEEPER *has entered from the stage door and advances towards* THE MANAGER's *table, taking off his braided cap. During this maneuver, the* SIX CHARACTERS *enter, and stop by the door at back of stage, so that when the* DOORKEEPER *is about to announce their coming to* THE MANAGER, *they are already on the stage. A tenuous light surrounds them, almost as if irradiated by them—the faint breath of their fantastic reality.*

This light will disappear when they come forward towards the ACTORS. *They preserve, however, something of the dream lightness in which they seem almost suspended; but this does not detract from the essential reality of their forms and expressions.*

He who is known as THE FATHER *is a man of about 50: hair, reddish in color, thin at the temples; he is not bald, however; thick moustaches, falling over his still fresh mouth, which often opens in an empty and uncertain smile. He is fattish, pale; with an especially wide forehead. He has blue, oval-shaped eyes, very clear and piercing. Wears light trousers and a dark jacket. He is alternatively mellifluous and violent in his manner.*

THE MOTHER *seems crushed and terrified as if by an intolerable weight* of shame and abasement. *She is dressed in modest black and wears a thick widow's veil of crêpe. When she lifts this, she reveals a wax-like face. She always keeps her eyes downcast.*

THE STEPDAUGHTER *is dashing, almost impudent, beautiful. She wears mourning too, but with great elegance. She shows contempt for the timid half-frightened manner of the wretched* BOY (*14 years old, and also dressed in black*); *on the other hand, she displays a lively tenderness for her little sister,* THE CHILD (*about four*), *who is dressed in white, with a black silk sash at the waist.*

THE SON (*22*) *tall, severe in his attitude of contempt for* THE FATHER, *supercilious and indifferent to* THE MOTHER. *He looks as if he had come on the stage against his will.*

DOORKEEPER (*Cap in hand*) Excuse me, sir. . . .

THE MANAGER (*Rudely*) Eh? What is it?

DOORKEEPER (*Timidly*) These people are asking for you, sir.

THE MANAGER (*Furious*) I am rehearsing, and you know perfectly well no one's allowed to come in during rehearsals! (*Turning to the* CHARACTERS) Who are you, please? What do you want?

THE FATHER (*Coming forward a little, followed by the others, who seem embarrassed*) As a matter of fact . . . we have come here in search of an author. . . .

THE MANAGER (*Half angry, half amazed*) An author? What author?

THE FATHER Any author, sir.

THE MANAGER But there's no author here. We are not rehearsing a new piece.

THE STEPDAUGHTER (*Vivaciously*) So much the better, so much the better! We can be your new piece.

AN ACTOR (*Coming forward from the others*) Oh, do you hear that?

THE FATHER (*To* STEPDAUGHTER) Yes, but if the author isn't here . . . (*To* MANAGER) . . . unless you would be willing. . . .

THE MANAGER You are trying to be funny.

THE FATHER No, for Heaven's sake, what are you saying? We bring you a drama, sir.

THE STEPDAUGHTER We may be your fortune.

THE MANAGER Will you oblige me by going away? We haven't time to waste with mad people.

THE FATHER (*Mellifluously*) Oh sir, you know well that life is full of infinite absurdities, which, strangely enough, do not even need to appear plausible, since they are true.

THE MANAGER What the devil is he talking about?

THE FATHER I say that to reverse the ordinary process may well be considered a madness: that is, to create credible situations, in order that they may appear true. But permit me to observe that if this be madness, it is the sole *raison d'être* of your profession, gentlemen. (*The* ACTORS *look hurt and perplexed*)

THE MANAGER (*Getting up and looking at him*)   So our profession seems to you one worthy of madmen then?

THE FATHER   Well, to make seem true that which isn't true ... without any need ... for a joke as it were ... Isn't that your mission, gentlemen: to give life to fantastic characters on the stage?

THE MANAGER (*Interpreting the rising anger of the* COMPANY)   But I would beg you to believe, my dear sir, that the profession of the comedian is a noble one. If today, as things go, the playwrights give us stupid comedies to play and puppets to represent instead of men, remember we are proud to have given life to immortal works here on these very boards! (*The* ACTORS, *satisfied, applaud their* MANAGER)

THE FATHER (*Interrupting furiously*)   Exactly, perfectly, to living beings more alive than those who breathe and wear clothes: being less real perhaps, but truer! I agree with you entirely. (*The* ACTORS *look at one another in amazement*)

THE MANAGER   But what do you mean? Before, you said ...

THE FATHER   No, excuse me, I meant it for you, sir, who were crying out that you had no time to lose with madmen, while no one better than yourself knows that nature uses the instrument of human fantasy in order to pursue her high creative purpose.

THE MANAGER   Very well—but where does all this take us?

THE FATHER   Nowhere! It is merely to show you that one is born to life in many forms, in many shapes, as tree, or as stone, as water, as butterfly, or as woman. So one may also be born a character in a play.

THE MANAGER (*With feigned comic dismay*)   So you and these other friends of yours have been born characters?

THE FATHER   Exactly, and alive as you see! (MANAGER *and* ACTORS *burst out laughing*)

THE FATHER (*Hurt*)   I am sorry you laugh, because we carry in us a drama, as you can guess from this woman here, veiled in black.

THE MANAGER (*Losing patience at last and almost indignant*)   Oh, chuck it! Get away please! Clear out of here! (*To* PROPERTY MAN) For Heaven's sake, turn them out!

THE FATHER (*Resisting*)   No, no, look here, we. ...

THE MANAGER (*Roaring*)   We come here to work, you know.

LEADING MAN   One cannot let oneself be made such a fool of.

THE FATHER (*Determined, coming forward*)   I marvel at your incredulity, gentlemen. Are you not accustomed to see the characters created by an author spring to life in yourselves and face each other? Just because there is no "book" (*Pointing to the* PROMPT-ER's *box*) which contains us, you refuse to believe. . . .

THE STEPDAUGHTER (*Advances towards* MANAGER, *smiling and co-quettish*)   Believe me, we are really six most interesting charac-ters, sir; side-tracked however.

THE FATHER   Yes, that is the word! (*To* MANAGER *all at once*)   In the sense, that is, that the author who created us alive no longer wished, or was no longer able, materially to put us into a work of art. And this was a real crime, sir; because he who has had the luck to be born a character can laugh even at death. He cannot die. The man, the writer, the instrument of the creation will die, but his creation does not die. And to live for ever, it does not need to have extraordinary gifts or to be able to work wonders. Who was Sancho Panza? Who was Don Abbondio? Yet they live eternally because—live germs as they were—they had the fortune to find a fecundating matrix, a fantasy which could raise and nourish them: make them live for ever!

THE MANAGER   That is quite all right. But what do you want here, all of you?

THE FATHER   We want to live.

THE MANAGER (*Ironically*)   For Eternity?

THE FATHER   No, sir, only for a moment . . . in you.

AN ACTOR   Just listen to him!

LEADING LADY   They want to live, in us! . . .

JUVENILE LEAD (*Pointing to the* STEPDAUGHTER)   I've no objection, as far as that one is concerned!

THE FATHER   Look here! Look here! The comedy has to be made. (*To the* MANAGER)   But if you and your actors are willing, we can soon concert it among ourselves.

THE MANAGER (*Annoyed*)   But what do you want to concert? We don't go in for concerts here. Here we play dramas and comedies!

THE FATHER   Exactly! That is just why we have come to you.

THE MANAGER   And where is the "book"?

THE FATHER. It is in us! (*The* ACTORS *laugh*) The drama is in us, and we are the drama. We are impatient to play it. Our inner passion drives us on to this.

THE STEPDAUGHTER (*Disdainful, alluring, treacherous, full of im-pudence*)   My passion, sir! Ah, if you only knew! My passion for him! (*Points to the* FATHER *and makes a pretence of embrac-ing him. Then she breaks out into a loud laugh*)

THE FATHER (*Angrily*)   Behave yourself! And please don't laugh in that fashion.

THE STEPDAUGHTER   With your permission, gentlemen, I, who am a two months' orphan, will show you how I can dance and sing. (*Sings and then dances* Prenez garde à Tchou-Tchin-Tchou)

Les chinois sont un peuple malin,
De Shanghaî à Pékin,
Ils ont mis des écriteaux partout:
Prenez garde à Tchou-Tchin-Tchou.

ACTORS and ACTRESSES   Bravo! Well done! Tip-top!

THE MANAGER   Silence! This isn't a café concert, you know! (*Turning to the* FATHER *in consternation*) Is she mad?

THE FATHER   Mad? No, she's worse than mad.

THE STEPDAUGHTER (*To* MANAGER)   Worse? Worse? Listen! Stage this drama for us at once! Then you will see that at a certain moment I . . . when this little darling here . . . (*Takes the* CHILD *by the hand and leads her to the* MANAGER) Isn't she a dear? (*Takes her up and kisses her*) Darling! Darling! (*Puts her down again and adds feelingly*) Well, when God suddenly takes this dear little child away from that poor mother there; and this imbecile here (*seizing hold of the* BOY *roughly and pushing him forward*) does the stupidest things, like the fool he is, you will see me run away. Yes, gentlemen, I shall be off. But the moment hasn't arrived yet. After what has taken place between him and me (*indicates the* FATHER *with a horrible wink*) I can't remain any longer in this society, to have to witness the anguish of this mother here for that fool . . . (*Indicates the* SON) Look at him! Look at him! See how indifferent, how frigid he is, because he is the legitimate son. He despises me, despises him (*pointing to the* BOY), despises this baby here; because . . . we are bastards. (*Goes to the* MOTHER *and embraces her*) And he doesn't want to recognize her as his mother—she who is the common mother of us all. He looks down upon her as if she were only the mother of us three bastards. Wretch! (*She says all this very rapidly, excitedly. At the word "bastards" she raises her voice, and almost spits out the final "Wretch!"*)

THE MOTHER (*To the* MANAGER, *in anguish*)   In the name of these two little children, I beg you . . . (*She grows faint and is about to fall*) Oh God!

THE FATHER (*Coming forward to support her as do some of the* ACTORS)   Quick, a chair, a chair for this poor widow!

THE ACTORS   Is it true? Has she really fainted?

THE MANAGER   Quick, a chair! Here!

(*One of the* ACTORS *brings a chair, the others proffer assistance. The* MOTHER *tries to prevent the* FATHER *from lifting the veil which covers her face*)

THE FATHER   Look at her! Look at her!

THE MOTHER   No, stop; stop it please!

THE FATHER (*Raising her veil*)   Let them see you!

THE MOTHER (*Rising and covering her face with her hands, in desperation*)   I beg you, sir, to prevent this man from carrying out his plan which is loathsome to me.

THE MANAGER (*Dumbfounded*)   I don't understand at all. What is the situation? Is this lady your wife? (*To the* FATHER)

THE FATHER   Yes, gentlemen: my wife!

THE MANAGER   But how can she be a widow if you are alive? (*The* ACTORS *find relief for their astonishment in a loud laugh*)

THE FATHER   Don't laugh! Don't laugh like that, for Heaven's sake. Her drama lies just here in this: she has had a lover, a man who ought to be here.

THE MOTHER (*With a cry*)   No! No!

THE STEPDAUGHTER   Fortunately for her, he is dead. Two months ago as I said. We are mourning, as you see.

THE FATHER   He isn't here you see, not because he is dead. He isn't here—look at her a moment and you will understand—because her drama isn't a drama of the love of two men for whom she was incapable of feeling anything except possibly a little gratitude—gratitude not for me but for the other. She isn't a woman, she is a mother, and her drama—powerful, sir, I assure you— lies, as a matter of fact, all in these four children she has had by two men.

THE MOTHER   I had them? Have you got the courage to say that I wanted them? (*To the* COMPANY) It was his doing. It was he who gave me that other man, who forced me to go away with him.

THE STEPDAUGHTER   It isn't true.

THE MOTHER (*Startled*)   Not true, isn't it?

THE STEPDAUGHTER   No, it isn't true, it just isn't true.

THE MOTHER   And what can you know about it?

THE STEPDAUGHTER   It isn't true. Don't believe it. (*To* MANAGER) Do you know why she says so? For that fellow there. (*Indicates the* SON) She tortures herself, destroys herself on account of the neglect of that son there; and she wants him to believe that if she abandoned him when he was only two years old, it was because he (*indicates the* FATHER) made her do so.

THE MOTHER (*Vigorously*)   He forced me to it, and I call God to witness it. (*To the* MANAGER) Ask him (*indicates the* FATHER) if it isn't true. Let him speak. You (*to* DAUGHTER) are not in a position to know anything about it.

THE STEPDAUGHTER   I know you lived in peace and happiness with my father while he lived. Can you deny it?

THE MOTHER   No, I don't deny it . . .

THE STEPDAUGHTER   He was always full of affection and kindness for you. (*To the* BOY, *angrily*) It's true, isn't it? Tell them! Why don't you speak, you little fool?

THE MOTHER   Leave the poor boy alone. Why do you want to make me appear ungrateful, daughter? I don't want to offend your father. I have answered him that I didn't abandon my house and my son through any fault of mine, nor from any wilful passion.

THE FATHER   It is true. It was my doing.

LEADING MAN (*To the* COMPANY)   What a spectacle!

LEADING LADY   We are the audience this time.

JUVENILE LEAD   For once, in a way.

THE MANAGER (*Beginning to get really interested*)   Let's hear them out. Listen!

THE SON   Oh yes, you're going to hear a fine bit now. He will talk to you of the Demon of Experiment.

THE FATHER   You are a cynical imbecile. I've told you so already a hundred times. (*To the* MANAGER) He tries to make fun of me on account of this expression which I have found to excuse myself with.

THE SON (*With disgust*)   Yes, phrases! phrases!

THE FATHER   Phrases! Isn't everyone consoled when faced with a trouble or fact he doesn't understand, by a word, some simple word, which tells us nothing and yet calms us?

THE STEPDAUGHTER   Even in the case of remorse. In fact, especially then.

THE FATHER   Remorse? No, that isn't true. I've done more than use words to quieten the remorse in me.

THE STEPDAUGHTER   Yes, there was a bit of money too. Yes, yes, a bit of money. There were the hundred lire he was about to offer me in payment, gentlemen. . . . (*Sensation of horror among the* ACTORS)

THE SON (*To the* STEPDAUGHTER)   This is vile.

THE STEPDAUGHTER   Vile? There they were in a pale blue envelope on a little mahogany table in the back of Madame Pace's shop. You know Madame Pace—one of those ladies who attract poor girls of good family into their ateliers, under the pretext of their selling *robes et manteaux.*

THE SON   And he thinks he has bought the right to tyrannize over us all with those hundred lire he was going to pay; but which, fortunately—note this, gentlemen—he had no chance of paying.

THE STEPDAUGHTER   It was a near thing, though, you know! (*Laughs ironically*)

THE MOTHER (*Protesting*)   Shame, my daughter, shame!

THE STEPDAUGHTER   Shame indeed! This is my revenge! I am dying to live that scene.... The room ... I see it ... Here is the window with the mantles exposed, there the divan, the looking-glass, a screen, there in front of the window the little mahogany table with the blue envelope containing one hundred lire. I see it. I see it. I could take hold of it... But you, gentlemen, you ought to turn your backs now: I am almost nude, you know. But I don't blush: I leave that to him. (*Indicating* FATHER)

THE MANAGER   I don't understand this at all.

THE FATHER   Naturally enough. I would ask you, sir, to exercise your authority a little here, and let me speak before you believe all she is trying to blame me with. Let me explain.

THE STEPDAUGHTER   Ah yes, explain it in your own way.

THE FATHER   But don't you see that the whole trouble lies here. In words, words. Each one of us has within him a whole world of things, each man of us his own special world. And how can we ever come to an understanding if I put in the words I utter the sense and value of things as I see them; while you who listen to me must inevitably translate them according to the conception of things each one of you has within himself. We think we understand each other, but we never really do. Look here! This woman (*indicating the* MOTHER) takes all my pity for her as a specially ferocious form of cruelty.

THE MOTHER   But you drove me away.

THE FATHER   Do you hear her? I drove her away! She believes I really sent her away.

THE MOTHER   You know how to talk, and I don't; but, believe me sir (*To* MANAGER), after he had married me ... who knows why? ... I was a poor insignificant woman....

THE FATHER   But, good Heaven! it was just for your humility that I married you. I loved this simplicity in you. (*He stops when he sees she makes signs to contradict him, opens his arms wide in sign of desperation, seeing how hopeless it is to make himself understood*) You see she denies it. Her mental deafness, believe me, is phenomenal, the limit (*touches his forehead*): deaf, deaf, mentally deaf! She had plenty of feeling. Oh yes, a good heart for the children; but the brain—deaf, to the point of desperation—!

THE STEPDAUGHTER Yes, but ask him how his intelligence has helped us.

THE FATHER If we could see all the evil that may spring from good, what should we do? (*At this point the* LEADING LADY *who is biting her lips with rage at seeing the* LEADING MAN *flirting with the* STEPDAUGHTER, *comes forward and says to the* MANAGER)

LEADING LADY Excuse me, but are we going to rehearse today?

MANAGER Of course, of course; but let's hear them out.

JUVENILE LEAD This is something quite new.

L'INGÉNUE Most interesting!

LEADING LADY Yes, for the people who like that kind of thing. (*Casts a glance at* LEADING MAN)

THE MANAGER (*To* FATHER) You must please explain yourself quite clearly. (*Sits down*)

THE FATHER Very well then: listen! I had in my service a poor man, a clerk, a secretary of mine, full of devotion, who became friends with her. (*Indicating the* MOTHER) They understood one another, were kindred souls in fact, without, however, the least suspicion of any evil existing. They were incapable even of thinking of it.

THE STEPDAUGHTER So he thought of it—for them!

THE FATHER That's not true. I meant to do good to them—and to myself, I confess, at the same time. Things had come to the point that I could not say a word to either of them without their making a mute appeal, one to the other, with their eyes. I could see them silently asking each other how I was to be kept in countenance, how I was to be kept quiet. And this, believe me, was just about enough of itself to keep me in a constant rage, to exasperate me beyond measure.

THE MANAGER And why didn't you send him away then—this secretary of yours?

THE FATHER Precisely what I did, sir. And then I had to watch this poor woman drifting forlornly about the house like an animal without a master, like an animal one has taken in out of pity.

THE MOTHER Ah, yes! . . .

THE FATHER (*Suddenly turning to the* MOTHER) It's true about the son anyway, isn't it?

THE MOTHER He took my son away from me first of all.

THE FATHER But not from cruelty. I did it so that he should grow up healthy and strong by living in the country.

THE STEPDAUGHTER (*Pointing to him ironically*) As one can see.

THE FATHER (*Quickly*) Is it my fault if he has grown up like this? I sent him to a wet nurse in the country, a peasant, as *she* did not seem to me strong enough, though she is of humble origin. That was, anyway, the reason I married her. Unpleasant all this may be, but how can it be helped? My mistake possibly, but there we are! All my life I have had these confounded aspirations towards a certain moral sanity. (*At this point the* STEP-DAUGHTER *bursts out into a noisy laugh*) Oh, stop it! Stop it! I can't stand it.

THE MANAGER   Yes, please stop it, for Heaven's sake.

THE STEPDAUGHTER   But imagine moral sanity from him, if you please—the client of certain ateliers like that of Madame Pace!

THE FATHER   Fool! That is the proof that I am a man! This seeming contradiction, gentlemen, is the strongest proof that I stand here a live man before you. Why, it is just for this very incongruity in my nature that I have had to suffer what I have. I could not live by the side of that woman (*indicating the* MOTHER) any longer; but not so much for the boredom she inspired me with as for the pity I felt for her.

THE MOTHER   And so he turned me out—.

THE FATHER   —well provided for! Yes, I sent her to that man, gentlemen . . . to let her go free of me.

THE MOTHER   And to free himself.

THE FATHER   Yes, I admit it. It was also a liberation for me. But great evil has come of it. I meant well when I did it; and I did it more for her sake than mine. I swear it. (*Crosses his arms on his chest; then turns suddenly to the* MOTHER) Did I ever lose sight of you until that other man carried you off to another town, like the angry fool he was? And on account of my pure interest in you . . . my pure interest, I repeat, that had no base motive in it . . . I watched with the tenderest concern the new family that grew up around her. She can bear witness to this. (*Points to the* STEPDAUGHTER)

THE STEPDAUGHTER   Oh yes, that's true enough. When I was a kiddie, so so high, you know, with plaits over my shoulders and knickers longer than my skirts, I used to see him waiting outside the school for me to come out. He came to see how I was growing up.

THE FATHER   This is infamous, shameful!

THE STEPDAUGHTER   No. Why?

THE FATHER   Infamous! Infamous! (*Then excitedly to* MANAGER, *explaining*) After she (*indicating* MOTHER) went away, my house seemed suddenly empty. She was my incubus, but she filled my house. I was like a dazed fly alone in the empty rooms. This boy here (*indicating the* SON) was educated away from home, and when he came back, he seemed to me to be no more mine. With no mother to stand between him and me, he grew up entirely for himself, on his own, apart, with no tie of intellect or affection binding him to me. And then—strange but true—I was driven, by curiosity at first and then by some tender sentiment, towards her family, which had come into being through my will. The thought of her began gradually to fill up the emptiness I felt all around me. I wanted to know if she were happy in living out the simple daily duties of life. I wanted to think of her as fortunate and happy because far away from the complicated torments of my spirit. And so, to have proof of this, I used to watch that child coming out of school.

THE STEPDAUGHTER   Yes, yes. True. He used to follow me in the street and smiled at me, waved his hand, like this. I would look at him with interest, wondering who he might be. I told my mother, who guessed at once. (*The* MOTHER *agrees with a nod*) Then she didn't want to send me to school for some days; and when I finally went back, there he was again—looking so ridiculous—with a paper parcel in his hands. He came close to me, caressed me, and drew out a fine straw hat from the parcel, with a bouquet of flowers—all for me!

THE MANAGER   A bit discursive this, you know!

THE SON (*Contemptuously*)   Literature! Literature!

THE FATHER   Literature indeed! This is life, this is passion!

THE MANAGER   It may be, but it won't act.

THE FATHER   I agree. This is only the part leading up. I don't suggest this should be staged. She (*pointing to the* STEPDAUGHTER), as you see, is no longer the flapper with plaits down her back—.

THE STEPDAUGHTER   —and the knickers showing below the skirt!

THE FATHER   The drama is coming now, sir; something new, complex, most interesting.

THE STEPDAUGHTER   As soon as my father died....

THE FATHER   —there was absolute misery for them. They came back here, unknown to me. Through her stupidity! (*Pointing to the* MOTHER) It is true she can barely write her own name; but she could anyhow have got her daughter to write to me that they were in need....

THE MOTHER   And how was I to divine all this sentiment in him?

THE FATHER   That is exactly your mistake, never to have guessed any of my sentiments.

THE MOTHER   After so many years apart, and all that had happened....

THE FATHER   Was it my fault if that fellow carried you away? It happened quite suddenly; for after he had obtained some job or other, I could find no trace of them; and so, not unnaturally, my interest in them dwindled. But the drama culminated unforeseen and violent on their return, when I was impelled by my miserable flesh that still lives. . . . Ah! what misery, what wretchedness is that of the man who is alone and disdains debasing *liaisons!* Not old enough to do without women, and not young enough to go and look for one without shame. Misery? It's worse than misery; it's a horror; for no woman can any longer give him love; and when a man feels this. . . . One ought to do without, you say? Yes, yes, I know. Each of us when he appears before his fellows is clothed in a certain dignity. But every man knows what unconfessable things pass within the secrecy of his own heart. One gives way to the temptation, only to rise from it again, afterwards, with a great eagerness to restablish one's dignity, as if it were a tombstone to place on the grave of one's shame, and a monument to hide and sign the memory of our weaknesses. Everybody's in the same case. Some folks haven't the courage to say certain things, that's all!

THE STEPDAUGHTER   All appear to have the courage to do them though.

THE FATHER   Yes, but in secret. Therefore, you want more courage to say these things. Let a man but speak these things out, and folks at once label him a cynic. But it isn't true. He is like all the others, better indeed, because he isn't afraid to reveal with the light of the intelligence the red shame of human bestiality on which most men close their eyes so as not to see it. Woman—for example, look at her case! She turns tantalizing inviting glances on you. You seize her. No sooner does she feel herself in your grasp than she closes her eyes. It is the sign of her mission, the sign by which she says to man: "Blind yourself, for I am blind."

THE STEPDAUGHTER   Sometimes she can close them no more: when she no longer feels the need of hiding her shame to herself, but dry-eyed and dispassionately, sees only that of the man who has blinded himself without love. Oh, all these intellectual complications make me sick, disgust me—all this philosophy that uncovers the beast in man, and then seeks to save him, excuse him . . . I can't stand it, sir. When a man seeks to "simplify" life bestially, throwing aside every relic of humanity, every chaste aspiration, every pure feeling, all sense of ideality, duty, modesty, shame . . . then nothing is more revolting and nauseous than a certain kind of remorse—crocodiles' tears, that's what it is.

THE MANAGER   Let's come to the point. This is only discussion.

THE FATHER   Very good, sir! But a fact is like a sack which won't stand up when it is empty. In order that it may stand up, one has to put into it the reason and sentiment which have caused it to exist. I couldn't possibly know that after the death of that man, they had decided to return here, that they were in misery, and that she (*pointing to the* MOTHER) had gone to work as a modiste, and at a shop of the type of that of Madame Pace.

THE STEPDAUGHTER A real high-class modiste, you must know, gentlemen. In appearance, she works for the leaders of the best society; but she arranges matters so that these elegant ladies serve her purpose . . . without prejudice to other ladies who are . . . well . . . only so so.

THE MOTHER You will believe me, gentlemen, that it never entered my mind that the old hag offered me work because she had her eye on my daughter.

THE STEPDAUGHTER Poor mamma! Do you know, sir, what that woman did when I brought her back the work my mother had finished? She would point out to me that I had torn one of my frocks, and she would give it back to my mother to mend. It was I who paid for it, always I; while this poor creature here believed she was sacrificing herself for me and these two children here, sitting up at night sewing Madame Pace's robes.

THE MANAGER And one day you met there. . . .

THE STEPDAUGHTER Him, him. Yes, sir, an old client. There's a scene for you to play! Superb!

THE FATHER She, the Mother arrived just then. . . .

THE STEPDAUGHTER (*Treacherously*) Almost in time!

THE FATHER (*Crying out*) No, in time! in time! Fortunately I recognized her . . . in time. And I took them back home with me to my house. You can imagine now her position and mine: she, as you see her; and I who cannot look her in the face.

THE STEPDAUGHTER Absurd! How can I possibly be expected— after that—to be a modest young miss, a fit person to go with his confounded aspirations for "a solid moral sanity"?

THE FATHER For the drama lies all in this—in the conscience that I have, that each one of us has. We believe this conscience to be a single thing, but it is many-sided. There is one for this person, and another for that. Diverse consciences. So we have this illusion of being one person for all, of having a personality that is unique in all our acts. But it isn't true. We perceive this when, tragically perhaps, in something we do, we are, as it were, suspended, caught up in the air on a kind of hook. Then we perceive that all of us was not in that act, and that it would be an atrocious injustice to judge us by that action alone, as if all our existence were summed up in that one deed. Now do you understand the perfidy of this girl? She surprised me in a place where she ought not to have known me, just as I could not exist for her; and she now seeks to attach to me a reality such as I could never suppose

I should have to assume for her in a shameful and fleeting moment of my life. I feel this above all else. And the drama, you will see, acquires a tremendous value from this point. Then there is the position of the others . . . his . . . (*Indicating the* SON)

THE SON (*Shrugging his shoulders scornfully*) Leave me alone! I don't come into this.

THE FATHER What? You don't come into this?

THE SON I've got nothing to do with it, and don't want to have; because you know well enough I wasn't made to be mixed up in all this with the rest of you.

THE STEPDAUGHTER We are only vulgar folk! He is the fine gentleman. You may have noticed, Mr. Manager, that I fix him now and again with a look of scorn while he lowers his eyes—for he knows the evil he has done me.

THE SON (*Scarcely looking at her*) I?

THE STEPDAUGHTER You! you! I owe my life on the streets to you. Did you or did you not deny us, with your behavior, I won't say the intimacy of home, but even that mere hospitality which makes guests feel at their ease? We were intruders who had come to disturb the kingdom of your legitimacy. I should like to have you witness, Mr. Manager, certain scenes between him and me. He says I have tyrannized over everyone. But it was just his behavior which made me insist on the reason for which I had come into the house—this reason he calls "vile"—into his house, with my mother, who is his mother too. And I came as mistress of the house.

THE SON It's easy for them to put me always in the wrong. But imagine, gentlemen, the position of a son, whose fate it is to see arrive one day at his home a young woman of impudent bearing, a young woman who inquires for his father, with whom who knows what business she has. This young man has then to witness her return bolder than ever, accompanied by that child there. He is obliged to watch her treat his father in an equivocal and confidential manner. She asks money of him in a way that lets one suppose he must give it her, *must,* do you understand, because he has every obligation to do so.

THE FATHER But I have, as a matter of fact, this obligation. I owe it to your mother.

THE SON How should I know? When had I ever seen or heard of her? One day there arrive with her (*indicating* STEPDAUGHTER) that lad and this baby here. I am told: "This is *your* mother too, you know." I divine from her manner (*indicating* STEPDAUGHTER *again*) why it is they have come home. I had rather not say what

I feel and think about it. I shouldn't even care to confess to myself. No action can therefore be hoped for from me in this affair.
Believe me, Mr. Manager, I am an "unrealized" character, dramatically speaking; and I find myself not at all at ease in their
company. Leave me out of it, I beg you.

THE FATHER   What? It is just because you are so that...

THE SON   How do you know what I am like? When did you ever
bother your head about me?

THE FATHER   I admit it. I admit it. But isn't that a situation in itself? This aloofness of yours which is so cruel to me and to your
mother, who returns home and sees you almost for the first time
grown up, who doesn't recognize you but knows you are her
son... (*Pointing out the* MOTHER *to the* MANAGER) See, she's
crying!

THE STEPDAUGHTER (*Angrily, stamping her foot*)   Like a fool!

THE FATHER (*Indicating* STEPDAUGHTER)   She can't stand him, you
know. (*Then referring again to the* SON) He says he doesn't
come into the affair, whereas he is really the hinge of the whole
action. Look at that lad who is always clinging to his mother,
frightened and humiliated. It is on account of this fellow here.
Possibly his situation is the most painful of all. He feels himself a
stranger more than the others. The poor little chap feels mortified, humiliated at being brought into a home out of charity as it
were. (*In confidence*)— He is the image of his father. Hardly
talks at all. Humble and quiet.

THE MANAGER   Oh, we'll cut him out. You've no notion what a
nuisance boys are on the stage...

THE FATHER   He disappears soon, you know. And the baby too.
She is the first to vanish from the scene. The drama consists
finally in this: when that mother re-enters my house, her family
born outside of it, and shall we say superimposed on the original,
ends with the death of the little girl, the tragedy of the boy and
the flight of the elder daughter. It cannot go on, because it is
foreign to its surroundings. So after much torment, we three remain: I, the mother, that son. Then, owing to the disappearance
of that extraneous family, we too find ourselves strange to one
another. We find we are living in an atmosphere of mortal desolation which is the revenge, as he (*indicating* SON) scornfully
said of the Demon of Experiment, that unfortunately hides in me.
Thus, sir, you see when faith is lacking, it becomes impossible to
create certain states of happiness, for we lack the necessary humility. Vaingloriously, we try to substitute ourselves for this faith,
creating thus for the rest of the world a reality which we believe

after their fashion, while, actually, it doesn't exist. For each one of us has his own reality to be respected before God, even when it is harmful to one's very self.

THE MANAGER There is something in what you say. I assure you all this interests me very much. I begin to think there's the stuff for a drama in all this, and not a bad drama either.

THE STEPDAUGHTER (*Coming forward*) When you've got a character like me.

THE FATHER (*Shutting her up, all excited to learn the decision of the* MANAGER) You be quiet!

THE MANAGER (*Reflecting, heedless of interruption*) It's new... hem... yes...

THE FATHER Absolutely new!

THE MANAGER You've got a nerve though, I must say, to come here and fling it at me like this...

THE FATHER You will understand, sir, born as we are for the stage...

THE MANAGER Are you amateur actors then?

THE FATHER No, I say born for the stage, because...

THE MANAGER Oh, nonsense. You're an old hand, you know.

THE FATHER No sir, no. We act that rôle for which we have been cast, that rôle which we are given in life. And in my own case, passion itself, as usually happens, becomes a trifle theatrical when it is exalted.

THE MANAGER Well, well, that will do. But you see, without an author... I could give you the address of an author if you like...

THE FATHER No, no. Look here! You must be the author.

THE MANAGER I? What are you talking about?

THE FATHER Yes, you, you! Why not?

THE MANAGER Because I have never been an author: that's why.

THE FATHER Then why not turn author now? Everybody does it. You don't want any special qualities. Your task is made much easier by the fact that we are all here alive before you...

THE MANAGER It won't do.

THE FATHER What? When you see us live our drama...

THE MANAGER Yes, that's all right. But you want someone to write it.

THE FATHER No, no. Someone to take it down, possibly, while we play it, scene by scene! It will be enough to sketch it out at first, and then try it over.

THE MANAGER Well... I am almost tempted. It's a bit of an idea. One might have a shot at it.

THE FATHER Of course. You'll see what scenes will come out of it. I can give you one, at once...

THE MANAGER By Jove, it tempts me. I'd like to have a go at it. Let's try it out. Come with me to my office. (*Turning to the* ACTORS) You are at liberty for a bit, but don't stop out of the theatre for long. In a quarter of an hour, twenty minutes, all back here again! (*To the* FATHER) We'll see what can be done. Who knows if we don't get something really extraordinary out of it?

THE FATHER There's no doubt about it. They (*indicating the* CHARACTERS) had better come with us too, hadn't they?

THE MANAGER Yes, yes. Come on! come on! (*Moves away and then turning to the* ACTORS) Be punctual, please! (MANAGER *and the* SIX CHARACTERS *cross the stage and go off. The other* ACTORS *remain, looking at one another in astonishment*)

LEADING MAN Is he serious? What the devil does he want to do?

JUVENILE LEAD This is rank madness.

THIRD ACTOR Does he expect to knock up a drama in five minutes?

JUVENILE LEAD Like the improvisers!

LEADING LADY If he thinks I'm going to take part in a joke like this . . .

JUVENILE LEAD I'm out of it anyway.

FOURTH ACTOR I should like to know who they are. (*Aludes to* CHARACTERS)

THIRD ACTOR What do you suppose? Madmen or rascals!

JUVENILE LEAD And he takes them seriously!

L'INGÉNUE Vanity! He fancies himself as an author now.

LEADING MAN It's absolutely unheard of. If the stage has come to this . . . well I'm . . .

FIFTH ACTOR It's rather a joke.

THIRD ACTOR Well, we'll see what's going to happen next.

(*Thus talking, the* ACTORS *leave the stage; some going out by the little door at the back; others retiring to their dressing-rooms.*
The curtain remains up.
The action of the play is suspended for twenty minutes)

ACT II

The stage call-bells ring to warn the company that the play is about to begin again.

THE STEPDAUGHTER *comes out of the* MANAGER's *office along with the* CHILD *and the* BOY. *As she comes out of the office, she cries:* Nonsense! Nonsense! Do it yourselves! I'm not going to mix myself up in this mess. (*Turning to the* CHILD *and coming quickly with her on to the stage*) Come on, Rosetta, let's run!

(*The* Boy *follows them slowly, remaining a little behind and seeming perplexed*)

THE STEPDAUGHTER (*Stops, bends over the* CHILD *and takes the latter's face between her hands*) My little darling! You're frightened, aren't you? You don't know where we are, do you? (*Pretending to reply to a question of the* CHILD) What is the stage? It's a place, baby, you know, where people play at being serious, a place where they act comedies. We've got to act a comedy now, dead serious, you know; and you're in it also, little one. (*Embraces her, pressing the little head to her breast, and rocking the* CHILD *for a moment*) Oh darling, darling, what a horrid comedy you've got to play! What a wretched part they've found for you! A garden ... a fountain ... look ... just suppose, kiddie, it's here. Where, you say? Why, right here in the middle. It's all pretence you know. That's the trouble, my pet: it's all make-believe here. It's better to imagine it though, because if they fix it up for you, it'll only be painted cardboard, painted cardboard for the rockery, the water, the plants ... Ah, but I think a baby like this one would sooner have a make-believe fountain than a real one, so she could play with it. What a joke it'll be for the others! But for you, alas! not quite such a joke: you who are real, baby dear, and really play by a real fountain that is big and green and beautiful, with ever so many bamboos around it that are reflected in the water, and a whole lot of little ducks swimming about ... No, Rosetta, no, your mother doesn't bother about you on account of that wretch of a son there. I'm in the devil of a temper, and as for that lad ... (*Seizes* BOY *by the arm to force him to take one of his hands out of his pockets*) What have you got there? What are you hiding? (*Pulls his hand out of his pocket, looks into it and catches the glint of a revolver*) Ah, where did you get this?

(*The* BOY, *very pale in the face, looks at her, but does not answer*)

Idiot! If I'd been in your place, instead of killing myself, I'd have shot one of those two, or both of them: father and son.

(*The* FATHER *enters from the office, all excited from his work. The* MANAGER *follows him*)

THE FATHER Come on, come on, dear! Come here for a minute! We've arranged everything. It's all fixed up.

THE MANAGER (*Also excited*) If you please, young lady, there are one or two points to settle still. Will you come along?

THE STEPDAUGHTER (*Following him towards the office*) Ouff! what's the good, if you've arranged everything.

(*The* FATHER, MANAGER *and* STEPDAUGHTER *go back into the office again* [*off*] *for a moment. At the same time, the* SON, *followed by the* MOTHER, *comes out*)

THE SON (*Looking at the three entering office*)   Oh this is fine, fine! And to think I can't even get away!

(*The* MOTHER *attempts to look at him, but lowers her eyes immediately when he turns away from her. She then sits down. The* BOY *and the* CHILD *approach her. She casts a glance again at the* SON, *and speaks with humble tones, trying to draw him into conversation*)

THE MOTHER   And isn't my punishment the worst of all? (*Then seeing from the* SON's *manner that he will not bother himself about her*) My God! Why are you so cruel? Isn't it enough for one person to support all this torment? Must you then insist on others seeing it also?

THE SON (*Half to himself, meaning the* MOTHER *to hear, however*) And they want to put it on the stage! If there was at least a reason for it! He thinks he has got at the meaning of it all. Just as if each one of us in every circumstance of life couldn't find his own explanation of it! (*Pauses*) He complains he was discovered in a place where he ought not to have been seen, in a moment of his life which ought to have remained hidden and kept out of the reach of that convention which he has to maintain for other people. And what about my case? Haven't I had to reveal what no son ought ever to reveal: how father and mother live and are man and wife for themselves quite apart from that idea of father and mother which we give them? When this idea is revealed, our life is then linked at one point only to that man and that woman; and as such it should shame them, shouldn't it?

(*The* MOTHER *hides her face in her hands. From the dressing-rooms and the little door at the back of the stage the* ACTORS *and* STAGE MAN-AGER *return, followed by the* PROPERTY MAN, *and the* PROMPTER. *At the same moment, the* MANAGER *comes out of his office, accompanied by the* FATHER *and the* STEPDAUGHTER)

THE MANAGER   Come on, come on, ladies and gentlemen! Heh! you there, machinist!

MACHINIST   Yes sir?

THE MANAGER   Fix up the white parlor with the floral decorations. Two wings and a drop with a door will do. Hurry up!

(*The* MACHINIST *runs off at once to prepare the scene, and arranges it while the* MANAGER *talks with the* STAGE MANAGER, *the* PROPERTY MAN, *and the* PROMPTER *on matters of detail*)

THE MANAGER (*To* PROPERTY MAN)   Just have a look, and see if there isn't a sofa or divan in the wardrobe...

PROPERTY MAN   There's the green one.

THE STEPDAUGHTER   No, no! Green won't do. It was yellow, ornamented with flowers—very large! and most comfortable!

PROPERTY MAN   There isn't one like that.

THE MANAGER   It doesn't matter. Use the one we've got.

THE STEPDAUGHTER   Doesn't matter? It's most important!

THE MANAGER   We're only trying it now. Please don't interfere. (*To* PROPERTY MAN) See if we've got a shop window—long and narrowish.

THE STEPDAUGHTER   And the little table! The little mahogany table for the pale blue envelope!

PROPERTY MAN (*To* MANAGER)   There's that little gilt one.

THE MANAGER   That'll do fine.

THE FATHER   A mirror.

THE STEPDAUGHTER   And the screen! We must have a screen. Otherwise how can I manage?

PROPERTY MAN   That's all right, Miss. We've got any amount of them.

THE MANAGER (*To the* STEPDAUGHTER)   We want some clothes pegs too, don't we?

THE STEPDAUGHTER   Yes, several, several!

THE MANAGER   See how many we've got and bring them all.

PROPERTY MAN   All right!

(*The* PROPERTY MAN *hurries off to obey his orders. While he is putting the things in their places, the* MANAGER *talks to the* PROMPTER *and then with the* CHARACTERS *and the* ACTORS)

THE MANAGER (*To* PROMPTER)   Take your seat. Look here: this is the outline of the scenes, act by act. (*Hands him some sheets of paper*) And now I'm going to ask you to do something out of the ordinary.

PROMPTER   Take it down in shorthand?

THE MANAGER (*Pleasantly surprised*)   Exactly! Can you do shorthand?

PROMPTER   Yes, a little.

THE MANAGER   Good! (*Turning to a stage hand*) Go and get some paper from my office, plenty, as much as you can find.

(*The* STAGE HAND *goes off, and soon returns with a handful of paper which he gives to the* PROMPTER)

THE MANAGER (*To* PROMPTER)   You follow the scenes as we play them, and try and get the points down, at any rate the most important ones. (*Then addressing the* ACTORS) Clear the stage, ladies and gentlemen! Come over here (*Pointing to the Left*) and listen attentively.

LEADING LADY   But, excuse me, we . . .

THE MANAGER (*Guessing her thought*) Don't worry! You won't have to improvise.

LEADING MAN   What have we to do then?

THE MANAGER   Nothing. For the moment you just watch and listen. Everybody will get his part written out afterwards. At present we're going to try the thing as best we can. They're going to act now.

THE FATHER (*As if fallen from the clouds into the confusion of the stage*) We? What do you mean, if you please, by a rehearsal?

THE MANAGER   A rehearsal for them. (*Points to the* ACTORS)

THE FATHER   But since we are the characters . . .

THE MANAGER   All right: "characters" then, if you insist on calling yourselves such. But here, my dear sir, the characters don't act. Here the actors do the acting. The characters are there, in the "book"—(*Pointing towards* PROMPTER'S *box*) when there is a "book"!

THE FATHER   I won't contradict you; but excuse me, the actors aren't the characters. They want to be, they pretend to be, don't they? Now if these gentlemen here are fortunate enough to have us alive before them . . .

THE MANAGER   Oh this is grand! You want to come before the public yourselves then?

THE FATHER   As we are . . .

THE MANAGER   I can assure you it would be a magnificent spectacle!

LEADING MAN   What's the use of us here anyway then?

THE MANAGER   You're not going to pretend that you can act? It makes me laugh! (*The* ACTORS *laugh*) There, you see, they are laughing at the notion. But, by the way, I must cast the parts. That won't be difficult. They cast themselves. (*To the* SECOND LADY LEAD) You play the Mother. (*To the* FATHER) We must find her a name.

THE FATHER   Amalia, sir.

THE MANAGER   But that is the real name of your wife. We don't want to call her by her real name.

THE FATHER   Why ever not, if it is her name? . . . Still, perhaps, if that lady must . . . (*Makes a slight motion of the hand to indicate the* SECOND LADY LEAD) I see this woman here (*means the*

MOTHER) as Amalia. But do as you like. (*Gets more and more confused*) I don't know what to say to you. Already, I begin to hear my own words ring false, as if they had another sound . . .

THE MANAGER Don't you worry about it. It'll be our job to find the right tones. And as for her name, if you want her Amalia, Amalia it shall be; and if you don't like it, we'll find another! For the moment though, we'll call the characters in this way (*to* JUVENILE LEAD) You are the Son; (*to the* LEADING LADY) You naturally are the Stepdaughter . . .

THE STEPDAUGHTER (*Excitedly*) What? what? I, that woman there? (*Bursts out laughing*)

THE MANAGER (*Angry*) What is there to laugh at?

LEADING LADY (*Indignant*) Nobody has ever dared to laugh at me. I insist on being treated with respect; otherwise I go away.

THE STEPDAUGHTER No, no, excuse me . . . I am not laughing at you . . .

THE MANAGER (*To* STEPDAUGHTER) You ought to feel honored to be played by . . .

LEADING LADY (*At once, contemptuously*) "That woman there" . . .

THE STEPDAUGHTER But I wasn't speaking of you, you know. I was speaking of myself—whom I can't see at all in you! That is all. I don't know . . . but . . . you . . . aren't in the least like me . . .

THE FATHER True. Here's the point. Look here, sir, our temperaments, our souls. . .

THE MANAGER Temperament, soul, be hanged. Do you suppose the spirit of the piece is in you? Nothing of the kind!

THE FATHER What, haven't we our own temperaments, our own souls?

THE MANAGER Not at all. Your soul or whatever you like to call it takes shape here. The actors give body and form to it, voice and gesture. And my actors—I may tell you—have given expression to much more lofty material than this little drama of yours, which may or may not hold up on the stage. But if it does, the merit of it, believe me, will be due to my actors.

THE FATHER I don't dare contradict you, sir; but, believe me, it is a terrible suffering for us who are as we are, with these bodies of ours, these features to see . . .

THE MANAGER (*Cutting him short and out of patience*) Good heavens! The make-up will remedy all that, man, the make-up . . .

THE FATHER Maybe. But the voice, the gestures . . .

THE MANAGER Now, look here! On the stage, you as yourself, cannot exist. The actor here acts you, and that's an end to it!

THE FATHER I understand. And now I think I see why our author

who conceived us as we are, all alive, didn't want to put us on
the stage after all. I haven't the least desire to offend your actors.
Far from it! But when I think that I am to be acted by . . . I
don't know by whom . . .

LEADING MAN (*On his dignity*) By me, if you've no objection!

THE FATHER (*Humbly, mellifluously*) Honored, I assure you, sir.
(*Bows*) Still, I must say that try as this gentleman may, with all
his good will and wonderful art, to absorb me into himself . . .

LEADING MAN Oh chuck it! "Wonderful art!" Withdraw that,
please!

THE FATHER The performance he will give, even doing his best
with make-up to look like me . . .

LEADING MAN It will certainly be a bit difficult! (*The* ACTORS
laugh)

THE FATHER Exactly! It will be difficult to act me as I really am.
The effect will be rather—apart from the make-up—according as
to how he supposes I am, as he senses me—if he does sense me
—and not as I inside of myself feel myself to be. It seems to me
then that account should be taken of this by everyone whose duty
it may become to criticize us . . .

THE MANAGER Heavens! The man's starting to think about the
critics now! Let them say what they like. It's up to us to put on
the play if we can. (*Looking around*) Come on! come on! Is the
stage set? (*To the* ACTORS *and* CHARACTERS) Stand back—stand
back! Let me see, and don't let's lose any more time! (*To the*
STEPDAUGHTER) Is it all right as it is now?

THE STEPDAUGHTER Well, to tell the truth, I don't recognize the
scene.

THE MANAGER My dear lady, you can't possibly suppose that we
can construct that shop of Madame Pace piece by piece here?
(*To the* FATHER) You said a white room with flowered wall
paper, didn't you?

THE FATHER Yes.

THE MANAGER Well then. We've got the furniture right, more or
less. Bring that little table a bit further forward. (*The* STAGE
HANDS *obey the order. To* PROPERTY MAN) You go and find an
envelope, if possible, a pale blue one; and give it to that gentleman. (*Indicates* FATHER)

PROPERTY MAN An ordinary envelope?

MANAGER *and* FATHER Yes, yes, an ordinary envelope.

PROPERTY MAN At once, sir. (*Exit*)

THE MANAGER Ready, everyone! First scene—the Young Lady.
(*The* LEADING LADY *comes forward*) No, no, you must wait. I

meant her. (*Indicating the* STEPDAUGHTER) You just watch—

THE STEPDAUGHTER (*Adding at once*)   How I shall play it, how I shall live it! . . .

LEADING LADY (*Offended*)   I shall live it also, you may be sure, as soon as I begin!

THE MANAGER (*With his hands to his head*)   Ladies and gentlemen, if you please! No more useless discussions! Scene I: the young lady with Madame Pace: Oh! (*Looks around as if lost*) And this Madame Pace, where is she?

THE FATHER   She isn't with us, sir.

THE MANAGER   Then what the devil's to be done?

THE FATHER   But she is alive too.

THE MANAGER   Yes, but where is she?

THE FATHER   One minute. Let me speak! (*Turning to the* AC-TRESSES) If these ladies would be so good as to give me their hats for a moment . . .

THE ACTRESSES (*Half surprised, half laughing, in chorus*)   What? Why?

Our hats?

What does he say?

THE MANAGER   What are you going to do with the ladies' hats? (*The* ACTORS *laugh*)

THE FATHER   Oh nothing. I just want to put them on these pegs for a moment. And one of the ladies will be so kind as to take off her mantle . . .

THE ACTORS   Oh, what d'you think of that? Only the mantle? He must be mad.

SOME ACTRESSES   But why? Mantles as well?

THE FATHER   To hang them up here for a moment. Please be so kind, will you?

THE ACTRESSES (*Taking off their hats, one or two also their cloaks, and going to hang them on the racks*)   After all, why not? There you are!

This is really funny.

We've got to put them on show.

THE FATHER   Exactly; just like that, on show.

THE MANAGER   May we know why?

THE FATHER   I'll tell you. Who knows if, by arranging the stage for her, she does not come here herself, attracted by the very articles of her trade? (*Inviting the* ACTORS *to look towards the exit at back of stage*) Look! Look!

(*The door at the back of stage opens and* MADAME PACE *enters and takes a few steps forward. She is a fat, oldish woman with puffy oxy-*

genated hair. She is rouged and powdered, dressed with a comical ele-
gance in black silk. Round her waist is a long silver chain from which
hangs a pair of scissors. The STEPDAUGHTER *runs over to her at once*
amid the stupor of the ACTORS)

THE STEPDAUGHTER (*Turning towards her*)   There she is! There
she is!

THE FATHER (*Radiant*)   It's she! I said so, didn't I? There she is!

THE MANAGER (*Conquering his surprise, and then becoming indig-*
nant)   What sort of a trick is this?

LEADING MAN (*Almost at the same time*)   What's going to happen
next?

JUVENILE LEAD   Where does *she* come from?

L'INGÉNUE   They've been holding her in reserve, I guess.

LEADING LADY   A vulgar trick!

THE FATHER (*Dominating the protests*)   Excuse me, all of you!
Why are you so anxious to destroy in the name of a vulgar, commonplace sense of truth, this reality which comes to birth attracted and formed by the magic of the stage itself, which has
indeed more right to live here than you, since it is much truer
than you—if you don't mind my saying so? Which is the actress
among you who is to play Madame Pace? Well, here is Madame
Pace herself. And you will allow, I fancy, that the actress who
acts her will be less true than this woman here, who is herself in
person. You see my daughter recognized her and went over to her
at once. Now you're going to witness the scene!

(*But the scene between the* STEPDAUGHTER *and* MADAME PACE *has*
already begun despite the protest of the ACTORS *and the reply of the*
FATHER. *It has begun quietly, naturally, in a manner impossible for the*
stage. So when the ACTORS, *called to attention by the* FATHER, *turn*
round and see MADAME PACE, *who has placed one hand under the*
STEPDAUGHTER'S *chin to raise her head, they observe her at first with*
great attention, but hearing her speak in an unintelligible manner their
interest begins to wane)

THE MANAGER   Well? well?

LEADING MAN   What does she say?

LEADING LADY   One can't hear a word.

JUVENILE LEAD   Louder! Louder please!

THE STEPDAUGHTER (*Leaving* MADAME PACE, *who smiles a Sphinx-*
like smile, and advancing towards the ACTORS)   Louder? Louder?
What are you talking about? These aren't matters which can be
shouted at the top of one's voice. If I have spoken them out loud,
it was to shame him and have my revenge. (*Indicates* FATHER)
But for Madame it's quite a different matter.

THE MANAGER   Indeed? indeed? But here, you know, people have got to make themselves heard, my dear. Even we who are on the stage can't hear you. What will it be when the public's in the theater? And anyway, you can very well speak up now among yourselves, since we shan't be present to listen to you as we are now. You've got to pretend to be alone in a room at the back of a shop where no one can hear you.

(*The* STEPDAUGHTER *coquettishly and with a touch of malice makes a sign of disagreement two or three times with her finger*)

THE MANAGER   What do you mean by no?

THE STEPDAUGHTER   (*Sotto voce, mysteriously*)   There's someone who will hear us if she (*indicating* MADAME PACE) speaks out loud.

THE MANAGER   (*In consternation*)   What? Have you got someone else to spring on us now? (*The* ACTORS *burst out laughing*)

THE FATHER   No, no sir. She is alluding to me. I've got to be here —there behind that door, in waiting; and Madame Pace knows it. In fact, if you will allow me, I'll go there at once, so I can be quite ready. (*Moves away*)

THE MANAGER   (*Stopping him*)   No! wait! wait! We must observe the conventions of the theater. Before you are ready...

THE STEPDAUGHTER   (*Interrupting him*)   No, get on with it at once! I'm just dying, I tell you, to act this scene. If he's ready, I'm more than ready.

THE MANAGER   (*Shouting*)   But, my dear young lady, first of all, we must have the scene between you and this lady... (*Indicates* MADAME PACE) Do you understand?...

THE STEPDAUGHTER   Good Heavens! She's been telling me what you know already: that Mamma's work is badly done again, that the material's ruined; and that if I want her to continue to help us in our misery I must be patient...

MADAME PACE   (*Coming forward with an air of great importance*) Yes indeed, sir, I no wanta take advantage of her, I no wanta be hard...

(*Note:* MADAME PACE *is supposed to talk in a jargon half Italian, half English*)

THE MANAGER   (*Alarmed*)   What? What? she talks like that? (*The* ACTORS *burst out laughing again*)

THE STEPDAUGHTER   (*Also laughing*)   Yes, yes, that's the way she talks, half English, half Italian! Most comical it is!

MADAME PACE   Itta seem not verra polite gentlemen laugha atta me eef I trya best speaka English.

THE MANAGER *Diamine!* Of course! Of course! Let her talk like that! Just what we want. Talk just like that, Madame, if you please! The effect will be certain. Exactly what was wanted to put a little comic relief into the crudity of the situation. Of course she talks like that! Magnificent!

THE STEPDAUGHTER Magnificent? Certainly! When certain suggestions are made to one in language of that kind, the effect is certain, since it seems almost a joke. One feels inclined to laugh when one hears her talk about an "old signore" "who wanta talka nicely with you." Nice old signore, eh, Madame?

MADAME PACE Not so old, my dear, not so old! And even if you no lika him, he won't make any scandal!

THE MOTHER (*Jumping up amid the amazement and consternation of the* ACTORS *who had not been noticing her. They move to restrain her*) You old devil! You murderess!

THE STEPDAUGHTER (*Running over to calm her* MOTHER) Calm yourself, mother, calm yourself! Please don't . . .

THE FATHER (*Going to her also at the same time*) Calm yourself! Don't get excited! Sit down now!

THE MOTHER Well then, take that woman away out of my sight!

THE STEPDAUGHTER (*To* MANAGER) It is impossible for my mother to remain here.

THE FATHER (*To* MANAGER) They can't be here together. And for this reason, you see: that woman there was not with us when we came . . . If they are on together, the whole thing is given away inevitably, as you see.

THE MANAGER It doesn't matter. This is only a first rough sketch —just to get an idea of the various points of the scene, even confusedly . . . (*Turning to the* MOTHER *and leading her to her chair*) Come along, my dear lady, sit down now, and let's get on with the scene . . .

(*Meanwhile, the* STEPDAUGHTER, *coming forward again, turns to* MADAME PACE)

THE STEPDAUGHTER Come on, Madame, come on!

MADAME PACE (*Offended*) No, no, *grazie*. I not do anything witha your mother present.

THE STEPDAUGHTER Nonsense! Introduce this "old signore" who wants to talk nicely to me. (*Addressing the company imperiously*) We've got to do this scene one way or another, haven't we? Come on! (*To* MADAME PACE) You can go!

MADAME PACE Ah yes! I go'way! I go'way! Certainly! (*Exits furious*)

THE STEPDAUGHTER (*To the* FATHER) Now you make your entry.

No, you needn't go over there. Come here. Let's suppose you've already come in. Like that, yes! I'm here with bowed head, modest-like. Come on! Out with your voice! Say "Good morning, Miss" in that peculiar tone, that special tone . . .

THE MANAGER   Excuse me, but are you the Manager, or am I? (*To the* FATHER, *who looks undecided and perplexed*) Get on with it, man! Go down there to the back of the stage. You needn't go off. Then come right forward here.

(*The* FATHER *does as he is told, looking troubled and perplexed at first. But as soon as he begins to move, the reality of the action affects him, and he begins to smile and to be more natural. The* ACTORS *watch intently*)

THE MANAGER   (*Sotto voce, quickly to the* PROMPTER *in his box*) Ready! ready? Get ready to write now.

THE FATHER   (*Coming forward and speaking in a different tone*) Good afternoon, Miss!

THE STEPDAUGHTER   (*Head bowed down slightly, with restrained disgust*)   Good afternoon!

THE FATHER   (*Looks under her hat which partly covers her face. Perceiving she is very young, he makes an exclamation, partly of surprise, partly of fear lest he compromise himself in a risky adventure*)   Ah . . . but . . . ah . . . I say . . . this is not the first time that you have come here, is it?

THE STEPDAUGHTER   (*Modestly*)   No sir.

THE FATHER   You've been here before, eh? (*Then seeing her nod agreement*) More than once? (*Waits for her to answer, looks under her hat, smiles, and then says*) Well then, there's no need to be so shy, is there? May I take off your hat?

THE STEPDAUGHTER   (*Anticipating him and with veiled disgust*) No sir . . . I'll do it myself. (*Takes it off quickly*)

(*The* MOTHER, *who watches the progress of the scene with the* SON *and the other two* CHILDREN *who cling to her, is on thorns; and follows with varying expressions of sorrow, indignation, anxiety, and horror the words and actions of the other two. From time to time she hides her face in her hands and sobs*)

THE MOTHER   Oh, my God, my God!

THE FATHER   (*Playing his part with a touch of gallantry*)   Give it to me! I'll put it down. (*Takes hat from her hands*) But a dear little head like yours ought to have a smarter hat. Come and help me choose one from the stock, won't you?

L'INGÉNUE   (*Interrupting*)   I say . . . those are our hats, you know.

THE MANAGER (*Furious*)   Silence! silence! Don't try and be funny, if you please . . . We're playing the scene now, I'd have you notice. (*To the* STEPDAUGHTER) Begin again, please!

THE STEPDAUGHTER (*Continuing*)   No thank you, sir.

THE FATHER   Oh, come now. Don't talk like that. You must take it. I shall be upset if you don't. There are some lovely little hats here; and then—Madame will be pleased. She expects it, anyway, you know.

THE STEPDAUGHTER   No, no! I couldn't wear it!

THE FATHER   Oh, you're thinking about what they'd say at home if they saw you come in with a new hat? My dear girl, there's always a way round these little matters, you know.

THE STEPDAUGHTER (*All keyed up*)   No, it's not that. I couldn't wear it because I am . . . as you see . . . you might have noticed . . . (*Showing her black dress*)

THE FATHER   . . . in mourning! Of course: I beg your pardon: I'm frightfully sorry . . .

THE STEPDAUGHTER (*Forcing herself to conquer her indignation and nausea*)   Stop! Stop! It's I who must thank you. There's no need for you to feel mortified or specially sorry. Don't think any more of what I've said. (*Tries to smile*) I must forget that I am dressed so . . .

THE MANAGER (*Interrupting and turning to the* PROMPTER)   Stop a minute! Stop! Don't write that down. Cut out that last bit. (*Then to the* FATHER *and* STEPDAUGHTER) Fine! it's going fine! (*To the* FATHER *only*) And now you can go on as we arranged. (*To the* ACTORS) Pretty good that scene, where he offers her the hat, eh?

THE STEPDAUGHTER   The best's coming now. Why can't we go on?

THE MANAGER   Have a little patience! (*To the* ACTORS) Of course, it must be treated rather lightly.

LEADING MAN   Still, with a bit of go in it!

LEADING LADY   Of course! It's easy enough! (*To* LEADING MAN) Shall you and I try it now?

LEADING MAN   Why, yes! I'll prepare my entrance. (*Exit in order to make his entrance*)

THE MANAGER (*To* LEADING LADY)   See here! The scene between you and Madame Pace is finished. I'll have it written out properly after. You remain here . . . oh, where are you going?

LEADING LADY   One minute. I want to put my hat on again. (*Goes over to hatrack and puts her hat on her head*).

THE MANAGER   Good! You stay here with your head bowed down a bit.

THE STEPDAUGHTER   But she isn't dressed in black.

LEADING LADY   But I shall be, and much more effectively than you.

THE MANAGER (*To* STEPDAUGHTER)   Be quiet please, and watch! You'll be able to learn something. (*Clapping his hands*) Come on! come on! Entrance, please!

(*The door at rear of stage opens, and the* LEADING MAN *enters with the lively manner of an old gallant. The rendering of the scene by the* ACTORS *from the very first words is seen to be quite a different thing, though it has not in any way the air of a parody. Naturally, the* STEP-DAUGHTER *and the* FATHER, *not being able to recognize themselves in the* LEADING LADY *and the* LEADING MAN, *who deliver their words in different tones and with a different psychology, express, sometimes with smiles, sometimes with gestures, the impression they receive*)

LEADING MAN   Good afternoon, Miss . . .

THE FATHER (*At once unable to contain himself*)   No! no!

(*The* STEPDAUGHTER, *noticing the way the* LEADING MAN *enters, bursts out laughing*)

THE MANAGER (*Furious*)   Silence! And you, please, just stop that laughing. If we go on like this, we shall never finish.

THE STEPDAUGHTER   Forgive me, sir, but it's natural enough. This lady (*indicating* LEADING LADY) stands there still; but if she is supposed to be me, I can assure you that if I heard anyone say "Good afternoon" in that manner and in that tone, I should burst out laughing as I did.

THE FATHER   Yes, yes, the manner, the tone . . .

THE MANAGER   Nonsense! Rubbish! Stand aside and let me see the action.

LEADING MAN   If I've got to represent an old fellow who's coming into a house of an equivocal character . . .

THE MANAGER   Don't listen to them, for Heaven's sake! Do it again! It goes fine. (*Waiting for the* ACTORS *to begin again*) Well?

LEADING MAN   Good afternoon, Miss.

LEADING LADY   Good afternoon.

LEADING MAN (*Imitating the gesture of the* FATHER *when he looked under the hat, and then expressing quite clearly first satisfaction and then fear*)   Ah, but . . . I say . . . this is not the first time that you have come here, is it?

THE MANAGER   Good, but not quite so heavily. Like this. (*Acts himself*) "This isn't the first time that you have come here" . . . (*To* LEADING LADY) And you say: "No, sir."

LEADING LADY   No, sir.

LEADING MAN   You've been here before, more than once.

THE MANAGER   No, no, stop! Let her nod "yes" first. "You've been here before, eh?" (*The* LEADING LADY *lifts up her head slightly and closes her eyes as though in disgust. Then she inclines her head twice*)

THE STEPDAUGHTER (*Unable to contain herself*)   Oh my God! (*Puts a hand to her mouth to prevent herself from laughing*)

THE MANAGER (*Turning round*)   What's the matter?

THE STEPDAUGHTER   Nothing, nothing!

THE MANAGER (*To* LEADING MAN)   Go on!

LEADING MAN   You've been here before, eh? Well then, there's no need to be so shy, is there? May I take off your hat?

(*The* LEADING MAN *says this last speech in such a tone and with such gestures that the* STEPDAUGHTER, *though she has her hand to her mouth, cannot keep from laughing*)

LEADING LADY (*Indignant*)   I'm not going to stop here to be made a fool of by that woman there.

LEADING MAN   Neither am I! I'm through with it!

THE MANAGER (*Shouting to* STEPDAUGHTER)   Silence! for once and all, I tell you!

THE STEPDAUGHTER   Forgive me! forgive me!

THE MANAGER   You haven't any manners: that's what it is! You go too far.

THE FATHER (*Endeavoring to intervene*)   Yes, it's true, but excuse her . . .

THE MANAGER   Excuse what? It's absolutely disgusting.

THE FATHER   Yes, sir, but believe me, it has such a strange effect when . . .

THE MANAGER   Strange? Why strange? Where is it strange?

THE FATHER   No, sir; I admire your actors—this gentleman here, this lady; but they are certainly not us!

THE MANAGER   I should hope not. Evidently they cannot be you, if they are actors.

THE FATHER   Just so: actors! Both of them act our parts exceedingly well. But, believe me, it produces quite a different effect on us. They want to be us, but they aren't, all the same.

THE MANAGER   What is it then anyway?

THE FATHER   Something that is . . . that is theirs—and no longer ours . . .

THE MANAGER   But naturally, inevitably. I've told you so already.

THE FATHER   Yes, I understand . . . I understand . . .

THE MANAGER   Well then, let's have no more of it! (*Turning to the* ACTORS)   We'll have the rehearsals by ourselves, afterwards, in the ordinary way. I never could stand rehearsing with the author present. He's never satisfied! (*Turning to* FATHER *and* STEP-DAUGHTER) Come on! Let's get on with it again; and try and see if you can't keep from laughing.

THE STEPDAUGHTER　Oh, I shan't laugh any more. There's a nice little bit coming from me now: you'll see.

THE MANAGER　Well then: when she says "Don't think any more of what I've said. I must forget, etc.," you (*addressing the* FATHER) come in sharp with "I understand, I understand"; and then you ask her . . .

THE STEPDAUGHTER (*Interrupting*)　What?

THE MANAGER　Why she is in mourning.

THE STEPDAUGHTER　Not at all! See here: when I told him that it was useless for me to be thinking about my wearing mourning, do you know how he answered me? "Ah well," he said, "then let's take off this little frock."

THE MANAGER　Great! Just what we want, to make a riot in the theater!

THE STEPDAUGHTER　But its the truth!

THE MANAGER　What does that matter? Acting is our business here. Truth up to a certain point, but no further.

THE STEPDAUGHTER　What do you want to do then?

THE MANAGER　You'll see, you'll see! Leave it to me.

THE STEPDAUGHTER　No sir! What you want to do is to piece together a little romantic sentimental scene out of my disgust, out of all the reasons, each more cruel and viler than the other, why I am what I am. He is to ask me why I'm in mourning; and I'm to answer with tears in my eyes, that it is just two months since papa died. No sir, no! He's got to say to me; as he did say: "Well, let's take off this little dress at once." And I; with my two months' mourning in my heart, went there behind that screen, and with these fingers tingling with shame . . .

THE MANAGER (*Running his hands through his hair*)　For Heaven's sake! What are you saying?

THE STEPDAUGHTER (*Crying out excitedly*)　The truth! The truth!

THE MANAGER　It may be. I don't deny it, and I can understand all your horror; but you must surely see that you can't have this kind of thing on the stage. It won't go.

THE STEPDAUGHTER　Not possible, eh? Very well! I'm much obliged to you—but I'm off!

THE MANAGER　Now be reasonable! Don't lose your temper!

THE STEPDAUGHTER　I won't stop here! I won't! I can see you've fixed it all up with him in your office. All this talk about what is possible for the stage . . . I understand! He wants to get at his complicated "cerebral drama," to have his famous remorses and torments acted; but I want to act my part, *my part!*

THE MANAGER (*Annoyed, shaking his shoulders*) Ah! Just *your* part! But, if you will pardon me, there are other parts than yours: his (*indicating the* FATHER) and hers! (*Indicating the* MOTHER) On the stage you can't have a character becoming too prominent and overshadowing all the others. The thing is to pack them all into a neat little framework and then act what is actable. I am aware of the fact that everyone has his own interior life which he wants very much to put forward. But the difficulty lies in this fact: to set out just so much as is necessary for the stage, taking the other characters into consideration, and at the same time hint at the unrevealed interior life of each. I am willing to admit, my dear young lady, that from your point of view it would be a fine idea if each character could tell the public all his troubles in a nice monologue or a regular one-hour lecture. (*Good-humoredly*) You must restrain yourself, my dear, and in your own interest, too; because this fury of yours, this exaggerated disgust you show, may make a bad impression, you know. After you have confessed to me that there were others before him at Madame Pace's and more than once . . .

THE STEPDAUGHTER (*Bowing her head, impressed*) It's true. But remember those others mean him for me all the same.

THE MANAGER (*Not understanding*) What? The others? What do you mean?

THE STEPDAUGHTER For one who has gone wrong, sir, he who was responsible for the first fault is responsible for all that follow. He is responsible for my faults, was, even before I was born. Look at him, and see if it isn't true!

THE MANAGER Well, well! And does the weight of so much responsibility seem nothing to you? Give him a chance to act it, to get it over!

THE STEPDAUGHTER How? How can he act all his "noble remorses," all his "moral torments," if you want to spare him the horror of being discovered one day—after he had asked her what he did ask her—in the arms of her, that already fallen woman, that child, sir, that child he used to watch come out of school? (*She is moved*)

(*The* MOTHER *at this point is overcome with emotion, and breaks out into a fit of crying.*
All are touched. A long pause)

THE STEPDAUGHTER (*As soon as the* MOTHER *becomes a little quieter, adds resolutely and gravely*)   At present, we are unknown to the public. Tomorrow, you will act us as you wish, treating us in your own manner. But do you really want to see drama, do you want to see it flash out as it really did?

THE MANAGER   Of course! That's just what I do want, so I can use as much of it as is possible.

THE STEPDAUGHTER   Well then, ask that Mother there to leave us.

THE MOTHER (*Changing her low plaint into a sharp cry*)   No! No! Don't permit it, sir, don't permit it!

THE MANAGER   But it's only to try it.

THE MOTHER   I can't bear it. I can't.

THE MANAGER   But since it has happened already . . . I don't understand!

THE MOTHER   It's taking place now. It happens all the time. My torment isn't a pretended one. I live and feel every minute of my torture. Those two children there—have you heard them speak? They can't speak any more. They cling to me to keep my torment actual and vivid for me. But for themselves, they do not exist, they aren't any more. And she (*indicating* STEPDAUGHTER) has run away, she has left me, and is lost. If I now see her here before me, it is only to renew for me the tortures I have suffered for her too.

THE FATHER   The eternal moment! She (*indicating the* STEP-DAUGHTER) is here to catch me, fix me, and hold me eternally in the stocks for that one fleeting and shameful moment of my life. She can't give it up! And you sir, cannot either fairly spare me it.

THE MANAGER   I never said I didn't want to act it. It will form, as a matter of fact, the nucleus of the whole first act right up to her surprise. (*Indicating the* MOTHER)

THE FATHER   Just so! This is my punishment: the passion in all of us that must culminate in her final cry.

THE STEPDAUGHTER   I can hear it still in my ears. It's driven me mad, that cry—You can put me on as you like; it doesn't matter. Fully dressed, if you like—provided I have at least the arm bare; because, standing like this (*she goes close to the* FATHER *and leans her head on his breast*) with my head so, and my arms round his neck, I saw a vein pulsing in my arm here; and then, as if that live vein had awakened disgust in me, I closed my eyes like this, and let my head sink on his breast. (*Turning to the* MOTHER) Cry out, mother! Cry out! (*Buries head in* FATHER's *breast, and with her shoulders raised as if to prevent her hearing the cry, adds in tones of intense emotion*) Cry out as you did then!

THE MOTHER (*Coming forward to separate them*)   No! My daughter, my daughter! (*And after having pulled her away from him*)

You brute! you brute! She is my daughter! Don't you see she's my daughter?

THE MANAGER (*Walking backwards towards footlights*)   Fine! fine! Damned good! And then, of course—curtain!

THE FATHER (*Going towards him excitedly*)   Yes, of course, because that's the way it really happened.

THE MANAGER (*Convinced and pleased*)   Oh, yes, no doubt about it. Curtain here, curtain!

(*At the reiterated cry of the* MANAGER, *the* MACHINIST *lets the curtain down, leaving the* MANAGER *and the* FATHER *in front of it before the footlights*)

THE MANAGER   The darned idiot! I said "curtain" to show the act should end there, and he goes and lets it down in earnest. (*To the* FATHER, *while he pulls the curtain back to go onto the stage again*) Yes, yes, it's all right. Effect certain! That's the right ending. I'll guarantee the first act, at any rate.

ACT III

When the curtain goes up again, it is seen that the stage hands have shifted the bit of scenery used in the last part, and have rigged up instead at the back of the stage a drop, with some trees, and one or two wings. A portion of a fountain basin is visible. THE MOTHER *is sitting on the* Right *with the two children by her side.* THE SON *is on the same side, but away from the others. He seems bored, angry, and full of shame.* THE FATHER *and* THE STEPDAUGHTER *are also seated towards the* Right *front. On the other side* (Left) *are the* ACTORS, *much in the positions they occupied before the curtain was lowered. Only* THE MANAGER *is standing up in the middle of the stage, with his hand closed over his mouth, in the act of meditating.*

THE MANAGER (*Shaking his shoulders after a brief pause*)   Ah yes: the second act! Leave it to me, leave it all to me as we arranged, and you'll see! It'll go fine!

THE STEPDAUGHTER   Our entry into his house (*indicates* FATHER) in spite of him . . . (*indicates the* SON)

THE MANAGER (*Out of patience*)   Leave it to me, I tell you!

THE STEPDAUGHTER   Do let it be clear, at any rate, that it is in spite of my wishes.

THE MOTHER (*From her corner, shaking her head*)   For all the good that's come of it . . .

THE STEPDAUGHTER (*Turning towards her quickly*)   It doesn't matter. The more harm done us, the more remorse for him.

THE MANAGER (*Impatiently*) I understand! Good Heavens! I understand! I'm taking it into account.

THE MOTHER (*Supplicatingly*) I beg you, sir, to let it appear quite plain that for conscience' sake I did try in every way . . .

THE STEPDAUGHTER (*Interrupting indignantly and continuing for the* MOTHER). . . . to pacify me, to dissuade me from spiting him. (*To* MANAGER) Do as she wants: satisfy her, because it is true! I enjoy it immensely. Anyhow, as you can see, the meeker she is, the more she tries to get at his heart, the more distant and aloof does he become.

THE MANAGER Are we going to begin this second act or not?

THE STEPDAUGHTER I'm not going to talk any more now. But I must tell you this: you can't have the whole action take place in the garden, as you suggest. It isn't possible!

THE MANAGER Why not?

THE STEPDAUGHTER Because he (*indicates the* SON *again*) is always shut up alone in his room. And then there's all the part of that poor dazed-looking boy there which takes place indoors.

THE MANAGER Maybe! On the other hand, you will understand— we can't change scenes three or four times in one act.

LEADING MAN They used to once.

THE MANAGER Yes, when the public was up to the level of that child there.

LEADING LADY It makes the illusion easier.

THE FATHER (*Irritated*) The illusion! For Heaven's sake, don't say illusion. Please don't use that word, which is particularly painful for us.

THE MANAGER (*Astounded*) And why, if you please?

THE FATHER It's painful, cruel, really cruel; and you ought to understand that.

THE MANAGER But why? What ought we to say then? The illusion, I tell you, sir, which we've got to create for the audience . . .

LEADING MAN With our acting.

THE MANAGER The illusion of a reality.

THE FATHER I understand; but you, perhaps, do not understand us. Forgive me! You see . . . here for you and your actors, the thing is only—and rightly so . . . a kind of game . . .

LEADING LADY (*Interrupting indignantly*) A game! We're not children here, if you please! We are serious actors.

THE FATHER I don't deny it. What I mean is the game, or play, of your art, which has to give, as the gentleman says, a perfect illusion of reality.

THE MANAGER Precisely——!

THE FATHER   Now, if you consider the fact that we (*indicates himself and the other five* CHARACTERS), as we are, have no other reality outside of this illusion . . .

THE MANAGER   (*Astonished, looking at his* ACTORS, *who are also amazed*)   And what does that mean?

THE FATHER   (*After watching them for a moment with a wan smile*) As I say, sir, that which is a game of art for you is our sole reality. (*Brief pause. He goes a step or two nearer the* MANAGER *and adds*) But not only for us, you know, by the way. Just you think it over well. (*Looks him in the eyes*) Can you tell me who you are?

THE MANAGER   (*Perplexed, half smiling*)   What? Who am I? I am myself.

THE FATHER   And if I were to tell you that that isn't true, because you are I? . . .

THE MANAGER   I should say you were mad——! (*The* ACTORS *laugh*)

THE FATHER   You're quite right to laugh: because we are all making believe here. (*To* MANAGER) And you can therefore object that it's only for a joke that that gentleman there (*indicates the* LEADING MAN), who naturally is himself, has to be me, who am on the contrary myself—this thing you see here. You see I've caught you in a trap! (*The* ACTORS *laugh*)

THE MANAGER   (*Annoyed*)   But we've had all this over once before. Do you want to begin again?

THE FATHER   No, no! that wasn't my meaning! In fact, I should like to request you to abandon this game of art (*Looking at the* LEADING LADY *as if anticipating her*) which you are accustomed to play here with your actors, and to ask you seriously once again: who are you?

THE MANAGER   (*Astonished and irritated, turning to his* ACTORS) If this fellow here hasn't got a nerve! A man who calls himself a character comes and asks me who I am!

THE FATHER   (*With dignity, but not offended*)   A character, sir, may always ask a man who he is. Because a character has really a life of his own, marked with his especial characteristics; for which reason he is always "somebody." But a man—I'm not speaking of you now—may very well be "nobody."

THE MANAGER   Yes, but you are asking these questions of me, the boss, the manager! Do you understand?

THE FATHER   But only in order to know if you, as you really are now, see yourself as you once were with all the illusions that were yours then, with all the things both inside and outside of you as they seemed to you—as they were then indeed for you. Well, sir, if you think of all those illusions that mean nothing to you now, of all those things which don't even *seem* to you to exist any more, while once they *were* for you, don't you feel that—I won't say these boards—but the very earth under your feet is sinking away from you when you reflect that in the same way this *you* as you feel it today—all this present reality of yours—is fated to seem a mere illusion to you tomorrow?

THE MANAGER (*Without having understood much, but astonished by the specious argument*) Well, well! And where does all this take us anyway?

THE FATHER Oh, nowhere! It's only to show you that if we (*indicating the* CHARACTERS) have no other reality beyond illusion, you too must not count overmuch on your reality as you feel it today, since, like that of yesterday, it may prove an illusion for you tomorrow.

THE MANAGER (*Determining to make fun of him*) Ah, excellent! Then you'll be saying next that you, with this comedy of yours that you brought here to act, are truer and more real than I am.

THE FATHER (*With the greatest seriousness*) But of course; without doubt!

THE MANAGER Ah, really?

THE FATHER Why, I thought you'd understand that from the beginning.

THE MANAGER More real than I?

THE FATHER If your reality can change from one day to another . . .

THE MANAGER But everyone knows it can change. It is always changing, the same as anyone else's.

THE FATHER (*With a cry*) No, sir, not ours! Look here! That is the very difference! Our reality doesn't change: it can't change! It can't be other than what it is, because it is already fixed for ever. It's terrible. Ours is an immutable reality which should make you shudder when you approach us if you are really conscious of the fact that your reality is a mere transitory and fleeting illusion, taking this form today and that tomorrow, according to the conditions, according to your will, your sentiments, which in turn are controlled by an intellect that shows them to you today in one manner and tomorrow . . . who knows how? . . . Illusions of reality represented in this fatuous comedy of life that never ends, nor can ever end! Because if tomorrow it were to end . . . then why, all would be finished.

THE MANAGER Oh for God's sake, will you *at least* finish with this philosophizing and let us try and shape this comedy which you yourself have brought me here? You argue and philosophize a bit too much, my dear sir. You know you seem to me almost, almost ... (*Stops and looks him over from head to foot*) Ah, by the way, I think you introduced yourself to me as a—what shall ... we say —a "character," created by an author who did not afterwards care to make a drama of his own creations.

THE FATHER   It is the simple truth, sir.

THE MANAGER   Nonsense! Cut that out, please! None of us believes it, because it isn't a thing, as you must recognize yourself, which one can believe seriously. If you want to know, it seems to me you are trying to imitate the manner of a certain author whom I heartily detest—I warn you—although I have unfortunately bound myself to put on one of his works. As a matter of fact, I was just starting to rehearse it, when you arrived. (*Turning to the* AC-TORS) And this is what we've gained—out of the frying-pan into the fire!

THE FATHER   I don't know to what author you may be alluding, but believe me I feel what I think; and I seem to be philosophizing only for those who do not think what they feel, because they blind themselves with their own sentiment. I know that for many people this self-blinding seems much more "human"; but the contrary is really true. For man never reasons so much and becomes so introspective as when he suffers; since he is anxious to get at the cause of his sufferings, to learn who has produced them, and whether it is just or unjust that he should have to bear them. On the other hand, when he is happy, he takes his happiness as it comes and doesn't analyze it, just as if happiness were his right. The animals suffer without reasoning about their sufferings. But take the case of a man who suffers and begins to reason about it. Oh no! it can't be allowed! Let him suffer like an animal, and then—ah yes, he is "human!"

THE MANAGER   Look here! Look here! You're off again, philosophizing worse than ever.

THE FATHER   Because I suffer, sir! I'm not philosophizing: I'm crying aloud the reason of my sufferings.

THE MANAGER (*Makes brusque movement as he is taken with a new idea*)   I should like to know if anyone has ever heard of a character who gets right out of his part and perorates and speechifies as you do. Have you ever heard of a case? I haven't.

THE FATHER   You have never met such a case, sir, because authors, as a rule, hide the labor of their creations. When the characters are really alive before their author, the latter does nothing but follow them in their action, in their words, in the situations which they suggest to him; and he has to will them the way they will themselves—for there's trouble if he doesn't. When a character is born, he acquires at once such an independence, even of his own author, that he can be imagined by everybody even in many other situations where the author never dreamed of placing him; and so he acquires for himself a meaning which the author never thought of giving him.

THE MANAGER   Yes, yes, I know this.

THE FATHER   What is there then to marvel at in us? Imagine such a misfortune for characters as I have described to you: to be born of an author's fantasy, and be denied life by him; and then answer me if these characters left alive, and yet without life, weren't right in doing what they did do and are doing now, after they have attempted everything in their power to persuade him to give them their stage life. We've all tried him in turn, I, she (*indicating the* STEPDAUGHTER) *and she.* (*Indicating the* MOTHER)

THE STEPDAUGHTER   It's true. I too have sought to tempt him, many, many times, when he had been sitting at his writing table, feeling a bit melancholy, at the twilight hour. He would sit in his armchair too lazy to switch on the light, and all the shadows that crept into his room were full of our presence coming to tempt him. (*As if she saw herself still there by the writing table, and was annoyed by the presence of the* ACTORS) Oh, if you would only go away, go away and leave us alone—mother here with that son of hers—I with that Child—that Boy there always alone —and then I with him—(*just hints at the* FATHER)—and then I alone, alone . . . in those shadows! (*Makes a sudden movement as if in the vision she has of herself illuminating those shadows she wanted to seize hold of herself*) Ah! my life! my life! Oh, what scenes we proposed to him—and I tempted him more than any of the others!

THE FATHER   Maybe. But perhaps it was your fault that he refused to give us life: because you were too insistent, too troublesome.

THE STEPDAUGHTER   Nonsense! Didn't he make me so himself? (*Goes close to the* MANAGER *to tell him as if in confidence*) In my opinion he abandoned us in a fit of depression, of disgust for the ordinary theater as the public knows it and likes it.

THE SON   Exactly what it was, sir; exactly that!

THE FATHER   Not at all! Don't believe it for a minute. Listen to me! You'll be doing quite right to modify, as you suggest, the excesses both of this girl here, who wants to do too much, and of this young man, who won't do anything at all.

THE SON   No, nothing!

THE MANAGER   You too get over the mark occasionally, my dear sir, if I may say so.

THE FATHER   I? When? Where?

THE MANAGER   Always! Continuously! Then there's this insistence of yours in trying to make us believe you are a character. And then too, you must really argue and philosophize less, you know, much less.

THE FATHER   Well, if you want to take away from me the possibility of representing the torment of my spirit which never gives me peace, you will be suppressing me: that's all. Every true man, sir, who is a little above the level of the beasts and plants does not live for the sake of living, without knowing how to live; but he lives so as to give a meaning and a value of his own to life. For me this is *everything*. I cannot give up this, just to represent a mere fact as she (*indicating the* STEPDAUGHTER) wants. It's all very well for her, since her "vendetta" lies in the "fact." I'm not going to do it. It destroys my *raison d'être*.

THE MANAGER   Your *raison d'être*! Oh, we're going ahead fine! First she starts off, and then you jump in. At this rate, we'll never finish.

THE FATHER   Now, don't be offended! Have it your own way—provided, however, that within the limits of the parts you assign us each one's sacrifice isn't too great.

THE MANAGER   You've got to understand that you can't go on arguing at your own pleasure. Drama is action, sir, action and not confounded philosophy.

THE FATHER   All right. I'll do just as much arguing and philosophizing as everybody does when he is considering his own torments.

THE MANAGER   If the drama permits! But for Heaven's sake, man, let's get along and come to the scene.

THE STEPDAUGHTER   It seems to me we've got too much action with our coming into his house. (*Indicating* FATHER) You said, before, you couldn't change the scene every five minutes.

THE MANAGER   Of course not. What we've got to do is to combine and group up all the facts in one simultaneous, close-knit action. We can't have it as you want, with your little brother wandering like a ghost from room to room, hiding behind doors and meditating a project which—what did you say it did to him?

THE STEPDAUGHTER   Consumes him, sir, wastes him away!

THE MANAGER   Well, it may be. And then at the same time, you want the little girl there to be playing in the garden . . . one in the house, and the other in the garden: isn't that it?

THE STEPDAUGHTER   Yes, in the sun, in the sun! That is my only pleasure: to see her happy and careless in the garden after the misery and squalor of the horrible room where we all four slept together. And I had to sleep with her—I, do you understand?—

with my vile contaminated body next to hers; with her folding me fast in her loving little arms. In the garden, whenever she spied me, she would run to take me by the hand. She didn't care for the big flowers, only the little ones; and she loved to show me them and pet me.

THE MANAGER Well then, we'll have it in the garden. Everything shall happen in the garden; and we'll group the other scenes there. (*Calls a* STAGE HAND) Here, a back-cloth with trees and something to do as a fountain basin. (*Turning round to look at the back of the stage*) Ah, you've fixed it up. Good! (*To* STEPDAUGHTER) This is just to give an idea, of course. The Boy, instead of hiding behind the doors, will wander about here in the garden, hiding behind the trees. But it's going to be rather difficult to find a child to do that scene with you where she shows you the flowers. (*Turning to the* BOY) Come forward a little, will you please? Let's try it now! Come along! come along! (*Then seeing him come shyly forward, full of fear and looking lost*) It's a nice business, this lad here. What's the matter with him? We'll have to give him a word or two to say. (*Goes close to him, puts a hand on his shoulders, and leads him behind one of the trees*) Come on! come on! Let me see you a little! Hide here ... yes, like that. Try and show your head just a little as if you were looking for someone... (*Goes back to observe the effect, when the* BOY *at once goes through the action*) Excellent! fine! (*Turning to* STEPDAUGHTER) Suppose the little girl there were to surprise him as he looks round, and run over to him, so we could give him a word or two to say?

THE STEPDAUGHTER It's useless to hope he will speak, as long as that fellow there is here ... (*Indicates the* SON) You must send him away first.

THE SON (*Jumping up*) Delighted! delighted! I don't ask for anything better. (*Begins to move away*)

THE MANAGER (*At once stopping him*) No! No! Where are you going? Wait a bit!

(*The* MOTHER *gets up, alarmed and terrified at the thought that he is really about to go away. Instinctively she lifts her arms to prevent him, without, however, leaving her seat*)

THE SON (*To* MANAGER, *who stops him*) I've got nothing to do with this affair. Let me go please! Let me go!

THE MANAGER What do you mean by saying you've got nothing to do with this?

THE STEPDAUGHTER (*Calmly, with irony*) Don't bother to stop him: he won't go away.

THE FATHER   He has to act the terrible scene in the garden with his mother.

THE SON (*Suddenly resolute and with dignity*)   I shall act nothing at all. I've said so from the very beginning. (*To the* MANAGER) Let me go!

THE STEPDAUGHTER (*Going over to the* MANAGER) Allow me? (*Puts down the* MANAGER's *arm which is restraining the* SON) Well, go away then, if you want to! (*The* SON *looks at her with contempt and hatred. She laughs and says*) You see, he can't, he can't go away! He is obliged to stay here, indissolubly bound to the chain. If I, who fly off when that happens which has to happen, because I can't bear him—if I am still here and support that face and expression of his, you can well imagine that he is unable to move. He has to remain here, has to stop with that nice father of his, and that mother whose only son he is. (*Turning to the* MOTHER) Come on, mother, come along! (*Turning to* MANAGER *to indicate her*) You see, she was getting up to keep him back. (*To the* MOTHER, *beckoning her with her hand*) Come on! come on! (*Then to* MANAGER) You can imagine how little she wants to show these actors of yours what she really feels; but so eager is she to get near him that . . . There, you see? She is willing to act her part. (*And in fact, the* MOTHER *approaches him; and as soon as the* STEPDAUGHTER *has finished speaking, opens her arms to signify that she consents*)

THE SON (*Suddenly*) No! No! If I can't go away, then I'll stop here; but I repeat: I act nothing!

THE FATHER (*To* MANAGER *excitedly*)   You can force him, sir.

THE SON   Nobody can force me.

THE FATHER   I can.

THE STEPDAUGHTER   Wait a minute, wait . . . First of all, the baby has to go to the fountain . . . (*Runs to take the* CHILD *and leads her to the fountain*)

THE MANAGER   Yes, yes of course; that's it. Both at the same time.

(*The* SECOND LADY LEAD *and the* JUVENILE LEAD *at this point separate themselves from the group of* ACTORS. *One watches the* MOTHER *attentively; the other moves about studying the movements and manner of the* SON *whom he will have to act*)

THE SON (*To* MANAGER)   What do you mean by both at the same time? It isn't right. There was no scene between me and her. (*Indicates the* MOTHER) Ask her how it was!

THE MOTHER   Yes, it's true. I had come into his room . . .

THE SON   Into my room, do you understand? Nothing to do with the garden.

THE MANAGER It doesn't matter. Haven't I told you we've got to group the action?

THE SON (*Observing the* JUVENILE LEAD *studying him*) What do you want?

JUVENILE LEAD Nothing! I was just looking at you.

THE SON (*Turning towards the* SECOND LADY LEAD) Ah! she's at it too: to re-act her part! (*Indicating the* MOTHER)

THE MANAGER Exactly! And it seems to me that you ought to be grateful to them for their interest.

THE SON Yes, but haven't you yet perceived that it isn't possible to live in front of a mirror which not only freezes us with the image of ourselves, but throws our likeness back at us with a horrible grimace?

THE FATHER That is true, absolutely true. You must see that.

THE MANAGER (*To* SECOND LADY LEAD *and* JUVENILE LEAD) He's right! Move away from them!

THE SON Do as you like. I'm out of this!

THE MANAGER Be quiet, you, will you? And let me hear your mother! (*To* MOTHER) You were saying you had entered . . .

THE MOTHER Yes, into his room, because I couldn't stand it any longer. I went to empty my heart to him of all the anguish that tortures me . . . But as soon as he saw me come in . . .

THE SON Nothing happened! There was no scene. I went away, that's all! I don't care for scenes!

THE MOTHER It's true, true. That's how it was.

THE MANAGER Well now, we've got to do this bit between you and him. It's indispensable.

THE MOTHER I'm ready . . . when you are ready. If you could only find a chance for me to tell him what I feel here in my heart.

THE FATHER (*Going to* SON *in a great rage*) You'll do this for your mother, for your mother, do you understand?

THE SON (*Quite determined*) I do nothing!

THE FATHER (*Taking hold of him and shaking him*) For God's sake, do as I tell you! Don't you hear your mother asking you for a favor? Haven't you even got the guts to be a son?

THE SON (*Taking hold of the* FATHER) No! No! And for God's sake stop it, or else . . . (*General agitation. The* MOTHER, *frightened, tries to separate them*)

THE MOTHER (*Pleading*) Please! please!

THE FATHER (*Not leaving hold of the* SON) You've got to obey, do you hear?

THE SON (*Almost crying from rage*) What does it mean, this madness you've got? (*They separate*) Have you no decency, that you insist on showing everyone our shame? I won't do it! I won't!

And I stand for the will of our author in this. He didn't want to put us on the stage, after all!

THE MANAGER   Man alive! You came here . . .

THE SON (*Indicating* FATHER)   *He* did! I didn't!

THE MANAGER   Aren't you here now?

THE SON   It was his wish, and he dragged us along with him. He's told you not only the things that did happen, but also things that have never happened at all.

THE MANAGER   Well, tell me then what did happen. You went out of your room without saying a word?

THE SON   Without a word, so as to avoid a scene!

THE MANAGER   And then what did you do?

THE SON   Nothing . . . walking in the garden . . . (*Hesitates for a moment with expression of gloom*)

THE MANAGER (*Coming closer to him, interested by his extraordinary reserve*)   Well, well . . . walking in the garden . . .

THE SON (*Exasperated*)   Why on earth do you insist? It's horrible! (*The* MOTHER *trembles, sobs, and looks towards the fountain*)

THE MANAGER (*Slowly observing the glance and turning towards the* SON *with increasing apprehension*)   The baby?

THE SON   There in the fountain . . .

THE FATHER (*Pointing with tender pity to the* MOTHER)   She was following him at the moment . . .

THE MANAGER (*To the* SON, *anxiously*)   And then you . . .

THE SON   I ran over to her; I was jumping in to drag her out when I saw something that froze my blood . . . the boy there, standing stock still, with eyes like a madman's, watching his little drowned sister, in the fountain! (*The* STEPDAUGHTER *bends over the fountain to hide the* CHILD. *She sobs*) Then . . . (*A revolver shot rings out behind the trees where the* BOY *is hidden*)

THE MOTHER (*With a cry of terror runs over in that direction together with several of the* ACTORS *amid general confusion*)   My son! My son! (*Then amid the cries and exclamations one hears her voice*) Help! Help!

THE MANAGER (*Pushing the* ACTORS *aside while they lift up the* BOY *and carry him off*)   Is he really wounded?

SOME ACTORS   He's dead, dead!

OTHER ACTORS   No, no, it's only make-believe, it's only pretence!

THE FATHER (*With a terrible cry*)   Pretence? Reality, sir, reality!

THE MANAGER   Pretence? Reality? To hell with it all! Never in my life has such a thing happened to me. I've lost a whole day over these people, a whole day!

Curtain

DESIRE UNDER THE ELMS (1924)

EUGENE O'NEILL (1888–1953)

Eugene O'Neill has survived as America's greatest dramatist, but it was not always certain he would do so. Hailed in the 1920s and 1930s as the hewer of new ways, he produced a body of astonishingly good and frightfully bad plays between the two great wars, demonstrating a theatrical talent of unequalled skill and intensity while also displaying some incredibly inept artistic talent. Both in quality of what he did and in his thematic and stylistic approach, O'Neill baffled, confused, and infuriated his public, but he always attracted them. Like Shaw, who called him a "banshee Shakespeare," O'Neill eventually attained the ability to make audiences and actors do his bidding in stupendous feats of endurance in the presentation of the multi-act five-hour and longer marathons which capped the first half of his career prior to his long "retirement" before and during the Second War.

Welcomed as America's first great realist, O'Neill became almost at once our first great expressionist. Seen as the improvisor who would alter the basic concepts of contemporary theatre, he endures as probably the greatest writer of modern naturalistic tragedy. When he lived, his plays were front-page news. Those who liked him would often turn ecstatic; those who did not were known to try to close down his plays as dangerous and immoral obscenities. When he died he had so completely disappeared from public awareness that his funeral passed all but unnoticed, his plays seldom staged. The posthumous production of his later works, now accepted as his best, have returned O'Neill as a dramatic artist of world importance and of permanently high artistic stature.

Very early in his career O'Neill affirmed that he was not interested in the relationship of man to man but of man to God. This did not assume any particular religion or creed, but it was truly a classic tragic concept. *Desire Under the Elms* is O'Neill's first tragedy in the classic sense, although an earlier tragedy, his first commercial success called *Beyond the Horizon* (1920), had shown his very serious artistic bent. *Desire* is not Greek in the literal sense of neo-classic imitation, even though it follows the outline of the classic myth of Queen Phaedra and her incestuous passion for her stepson, Hippolytus. The closer imitation of the Greek was to come later in O'Neill's adaptation of *The Oresteia* in *Mourning Becomes Electra* in 1931, transferring the legend to Civil War New England. *Desire Under the Elms* makes use not of the fates, but of the natural environment, and instead of gods imposing curses it uses elemental passions beyond control of the protagonists. There is a primitive force in evidence, seen in the rock-hard unyielding land under the control of an equally hard unyielding god. The characters are at the mercy of what they are—ignorant, earthy, unlettered, performing with animal lust in the satisfaction of natural urges. They are trapped by what they are as much as is Oedipus, and their escape is equally impossible.

There is great size and stature here. Old Cabot is a huge man, able to challenge his demanding god, yet remaining an absolute child of nature who can find solace among the dumb beasts in the barn. The attraction between Eben and Abbie, first calculated for personal gain, then out of control as a natural force, passes through the walls of the house to create a sinister atmosphere that even old Cabot senses but cannot understand. In the end, the realization of what they have done and the recognition of their fate, which must be shared, compel Eben and Abbie to face the inevitable catastrophe. Ephraim can return to his cows, but destruction is total for the adulterous semi-incestuous lovers who have succumbed to, but at the same time conquered, the elemental forces of their downfall.

Desire Under the Elms　　　　　O'NEILL

CHARACTERS

EPHRAIM CABOT
SIMEON ⎫
PETER　⎬ *his sons*
EBEN　 ⎭
ABBIE PUTNAM

YOUNG GIRL, TWO FARMERS, THE FIDDLER, THE SHERIFF, OTHER FOLK
from the neighboring farms

*The action of the entire play takes place in, and immediately outside of,
the* CABOT *farmhouse in New England, in the year 1850. The south end
of the house faces front to a stone wall with a wooden gate at center
opening on a country road. The house is in good condition but in need of
paint. Its walls are a sickly grayish, the green of the shutters faded. Two
enormous elms are on each side of the house. They bend their trailing
branches down over the roof. They appear to protect and at the same
time subdue. There is a sinister maternity in their aspect, a crushing,
jealous absorption. They have developed from their intimate contact with
the life of man in the house an appalling humaneness. They brood op-
pressively over the house. They are like exhausted women resting their
sagging breasts and hands and hair on its roof, and when it rains their
tears trickle down monotonously and rot on the shingles.*

　　*There is a path running from the gate around the right corner of the
house to the front door. A narrow porch is on this side. The end wall
facing us has two windows in its upper story, two larger ones on the floor
below. The two upper are those of the father's bedroom and that of the
brothers. On the left, ground floor, is the kitchen—on the right, the parlor,
the shades of which are always drawn down.*

PART I

Scene 1

*Exterior of the farmhouse. It is sunset of a day at the beginning of summer
in the year 1850. There is no wind and everything is still. The sky above*

the roof is suffused with deep colors, the green of the elms glows, but the house is in shadow, seeming pale and washed out by contrast.

A door opens and EBEN CABOT *comes to the end of the porch and stands looking down the road to the right. He has a large bell in his hand and this he swings mechanically, awakening a deafening clangor. Then he puts his hands on his hips and stares up at the sky. He sighs with a puzzled awe and blurts out with halting appreciation.*

EBEN   God! Purty! (*His eyes fall and he stares about him frowningly. He is twenty-five, tall and sinewy. His face is well-formed, good-looking, but its expression is resentful and defensive. His defiant, dark eyes remind one of a wild animal's in captivity. Each day is a cage in which he finds himself trapped but inwardly unsubdued. There is a fierce repressed vitality about him. He has black hair, mustache, a thin curly trace of beard. He is dressed in rough farm clothes.*

He spits on the ground with intense disgust, turns and goes back into the house.

SIMEON *and* PETER *come in from their work in the fields. They are tall men, much older than their half-brother [*SIMEON *is thirty-nine and* PETER *thirty-seven], built on a squarer, simpler model, fleshier in body, more bovine and homelier in face, shrewder and more practical. Their shoulders stoop a bit from years of farm work. They clump heavily along in their clumsy thick-soled boots caked with earth. Their clothes, their faces, hands, bare arms and throats are earth-stained. They smell of earth. They stand together for a moment in front of the house and, as if with the one impulse, stare dumbly up at the sky, leaning on their hoes. Their faces have a compressed, unresigned expression. As they look upward, this softens.*)

SIMEON (*grudgingly*)   Purty.

PETER   Ay-eh.

SIMEON (*suddenly*)   Eighteen year ago.

PETER   What?

SIMEON   Jenn. My woman. She died.

PETER   I'd fergot.

SIMEON   I rec'lect—now an' agin. Makes it lonesome. She'd hair long's a hoss' tail—an' yaller like gold!

PETER   Waal—she's gone. (*This with indifferent finality—then after a pause*) They's gold in the West, Sim.

SIMEON (*still under the influence of sunset—vaguely*)   In the sky?

PETER   Waal—in a manner o' speakin'—thar's the promise. (*growing excited*) Gold in the sky—in the West—Golden Gate—Californi-a!—Goldest West!—fields o' gold!

SIMEON (*excited in his turn*)   Fortunes layin' just atop o' the ground waitin' t' be picked! Solomon's mines, they says! (*For a moment they continue looking up at the sky—then their eyes drop.*)

PETER (*with sardonic bitterness*)   Here—it's stones atop o' the ground—stones atop o' stones—makin' stone walls—year atop o' year—him 'n' yew 'n' me 'n' then Eben—makin' stone walls fur him to fence us in!

SIMEON   We've wuked. Give our strength. Give our years. Plowed 'em under in the ground—(*he stamps rebelliously*)—rottin'—makin' soil for his crops! (*a pause*) Waal—the farm pays good for hereabouts.

PETER   If we plowed in Californi-a, they'd be lumps o' gold in the furrow!

SIMEON   Californi-a's t'other side o' earth, a'most. We got t' calc'-late—

PETER (*after a pause*)   'Twould be hard fur me, too, to give up what we've 'arned here by our sweat. (*A pause,* EBEN *sticks his head out of the dining-room window, listening.*)

SIMEON   Ay-eh. (*a pause*)   Mebbe—he'll die soon.

PETER (*doubtfully*)   Mebbe.

SIMEON   Mebbe—fur all we knows—he's dead now.

PETER   Ye'd need proof.

SIMEON   He's been gone two months—with no word.

PETER   Left us in the fields an evenin' like this. Hitched up an' druv off into the West. That's plum onnateral. He hain't never been off this farm 'ceptin' t' the village in thirty year or more, not since he married Eben's maw. (*A pause. Shrewdly*) I calc'late we might git him declared crazy by the court.

SIMEON   He skinnned 'em too slick. He got the best o' all on 'em. They'd never b'lieve him crazy. (*a pause*) We got t' wait—till he's under ground.

EBEN (*with a sardonic chuckle*)   Honor thy father! (*They turn, startled, and stare at him. He grins, then scowls.*) I pray he's died. (*They stare at him. He continues matter-of-factly*) Supper's ready.

SIMEON *and* PETER (*together*)   Ay-eh.

EBEN (*gazing up at the sky*)   Sun's downin' purty.

SIMEON *and* PETER (*together*)   Ay-eh. They's gold in the West.

EBEN   Ay-eh. (*pointing*) Yonder atop o' the hill pasture, ye mean?

SIMEON *and* PETER (*together*)   In Californi-a!

EBEN   Hunh? (*Stares at them indifferently for a second, then drawls*) Waal—supper's gittin' cold. (*He turns back into kitchen.*)

SIMEON (*startled—smacks his lips*)   I air hungry!

PETER (*sniffing*)   I smells bacon!

SIMEON (*with hungry appreciation*) Bacon's good!

PETER (*in same tone*) Bacon's bacon! (*They turn, shouldering each other, their bodies bumping and rubbing together as they hurry clumsily to their food, like two friendly oxen toward their evening meal. They disappear around the right corner of house and can be heard entering the door.*)

Scene 2

The color fades from the sky. Twilight begins. The interior of the kitchen is now visible. A pine table is at center, a cookstove in the right rear corner, four rough wooden chairs, a tallow candle on the table. In the middle of the rear wall is fastened a big advertising poster with a ship in full sail and the word "California" in big letters. Kitchen utensils hang from nails. Everything is neat and in order but the atmosphere is of a men's camp kitchen rather than that of a home.

Places for three are laid. EBEN takes boiled potatoes and bacon from the stove and puts them on the table, also a loaf of bread and a crock of water. SIMEON and PETER shoulder in, slump down in their chairs without a word. EBEN joins them. The three eat in silence for a moment, the two elder as naturally unrestrained as beasts of the field, EBEN picking at his food without appetite, glancing at them with a tolerant dislike.

SIMEON (*suddenly turns to* EBEN) Looky here! Ye'd oughtn't t' said that, Eben.

PETER 'Twa'n't righteous.

EBEN What?

SIMEON Ye prayed he'd died.

EBEN Waal—don't yew pray it? (*a pause*)

PETER He's our Paw.

EBEN (*violently*) Not mine!

SIMEON (*dryly*) Ye'd not let no one else say that about yer Maw! Ha! (*He gives one abrupt sardonic guffaw.* PETER *grins.*)

EBEN (*very pale*) I meant—I hain't his'n—I hain't like him—he hain't me!

PETER (*dryly*) Wait till ye've growed his age!

EBEN (*intensely*) I'm Maw—every drop o' blood! (*A pause. They stare at him with indifferent curiosity.*)

PETER (*reminiscently*) She was good t' Sim 'n' me. A good step-maw's scurse.

SIMEON She was good t' everyone.

EBEN (*greatly moved, gets to his feet and makes an awkward bow to each of them—stammering*) I be thankful t' ye. I'm her—her heir. (*He sits down in confusion.*)

PETER (*after a pause—judicially*) She was good even t' him.

EBEN (*fiercely*) An' fur thanks he killed her!

SIMEON (*after a pause*)   No one never kills nobody. It's allus some-thin'. That's the murderer.

EBEN   Didn't he slave Maw t' death?

PETER   He's slaved himself t' death. He's slaved Sim 'n' me 'n' yew t' death—on'y none o' us hain't died—yit.

SIMEON   It's somethin'—drivin' him—t' drive us!

EBEN (*vengefully*)   Waal—I hold him t' jedgment! (*then scorn-fully*) Somethin'! What's somethin'?

SIMEON   Dunno.

EBEN (*sardonically*)   What's drivin' yew to Californi-a, mebbe? (*They look at him in surprise.*) Oh, I've heerd ye! (*then, after a pause*) But ye'll never go t' the gold fields!

PETER (*assertively*)   Mebbe!

EBEN   Whar'll ye git the money?

PETER   We kin walk. It's an a'mighty ways—Californi-a—but if yew was t' put all the steps we've walked on this farm end t' end we'd be in the moon!

EBEN   The Injuns'll skulp ye on the plains.

SIMEON (*with grim humor*)   We'll mebbe make 'em pay a hair fur a hair!

EBEN (*decisively*)   But t'ain't that. Ye won't never go because ye'll wait here fur yer share o' the farm, thinkin' allus he'll die soon.

SIMEON (*after a pause*)   We've a right.

PETER   Two-thirds belongs t'us.

EBEN (*jumping to his feet*)   Ye've no right! She wa'n't yewr Maw! It was her farm! Didn't he steal it from her? She's dead. It's my farm.

SIMEON (*sardonically*)   Tell that t' Paw—when he comes! I'll bet ye a dollar he'll laugh—fur once in his life. Ha! (*He laughs him-self in one single mirthless bark.*)

PETER (*amused in turn, echoes his brother*)   Ha!

SIMEON (*after a pause*)   What've ye got held agin us, Eben? Year arter year it's skulked in yer eye—somethin'.

PETER   Ay-eh.

EBEN   Ay-eh. They's somethin'. (*suddenly exploding*) Why didn't ye never stand between him 'n' my Maw when he was slavin' her to her grave—t' pay her back fur the kindness she done t' yew? (*There is a long pause. They stare at him in surprise.*)

SIMEON   Waal—the stock'd got t' be watered.

PETER   'R they was woodin' t' do.

SIMEON   'R plowin'.

PETER   'R hayin'.

SIMEON   'R spreadin' manure.

PETER   'R weedin'.

SIMEON   'R prunin'.

PETER   'R milkin'.

EBEN (*breaking in harshly*) An' makin' walls—stone atop o' stone
—makin' walls till yer heart's a stone ye heft up out o' the way
o' growth onto a stone wall t' wall in yer heart!

SIMEON (*matter-of-factly*) We never had no time t' meddle.

PETER (*to* EBEN) Yew was fifteen afore yer Maw died—an' big
fur yer age. Why didn't ye never do nothin'?

EBEN (*harshly*) They was chores t' do, wa'n't they? (*a pause—
then slowly*) It was on'y arter she died I come to think o' it. Me
cookin'—doin' her work—that made me know her, suffer her suf-
ferin'—she'd come back t' help—come back t' bile potatoes—
come back t' fry bacon—come back t' bake biscuits—come back
all cramped up t' shake the fire, an' carry ashes, her eyes weepin'
an' bloody with smoke an' cinders same's they used t' be. She still
comes back—stands by the stove thar in the evenin'—she can't
find it nateral sleepin' an' restin' in peace. She can't git used t'
bein' free—even in her grave.

SIMEON   She never complained none.

EBEN   She'd got too tired. She'd got too used t' being' too tired.
That was what he done. (*with vengeful passion*) An' sooner'r
later, I'll meddle. I'll say the thin's I didn't say then t' him! I'll
yell 'em at the top o' my lungs. I'll see t' it my Maw gits some
rest an' sleep in her grave! (*He sits down again, relapsing into a
brooding silence. They look at him with a queer indifferent curiosity.*)

PETER (*after a pause*) Whar in tarnation d'ye s'pose he went, Sim?

SIMEON   Dunno. He druv off in the buggy, all spick an' span, with
the mare all breshed an' shiny, druv off clackin' his tongue an'
wavin' his whip. I remember it right well. I was finishin' plowin',
it was spring an' May an' sunset, an' gold in the West, an' he
druv off into it. I yells "Whar ye goin', Paw?" an' he hauls up by
the stone wall a jiffy. His old snake's eyes was glitterin' in the sun
like he'd been drinkin' a jugful an' he says with a mule's grin:
"Don't ye run away till I come back!"

PETER   Wonder if he knowed we was wantin' fur Californi-a?

SIMEON   Mebbe. I didn't say nothin' and he says, lookin' kinder
queer an' sick: "I been hearin' the hens cluckin' an' the roosters
crowin' all the durn day. I been listenin' t' the cows lowin' an'
everythin' else kickin' up till I can't stand it no more. It's spring
an' I'm feelin' damned," he says. "Damned like an old bare hickory tree fit on'y fur burnin'," he says. An' then I calc'late I
must've looked a mite hopeful, fur he adds real spry and vicious:

"But don't git no fool idee I'm dead. I've sworn t' live a hundred an' I'll do it, if on'y t' spite yer sinful greed! An' now I'm ridin' out t' learn God's message t' me in the spring, like the prophets done. An' yew git back t' yer plowin'," he says. An' he druv off singin' a hymn. I thought he was drunk—'r I'd stopped him goin'.

EBEN (*scornfully*) No, ye wouldn't! Ye're scared o' him. He's stronger—inside—than both o' ye put together!

PETER (*sardonically*) An' yew—be yew Samson?

EBEN I'm gittin' stronger. I kin feel it growin' in me—growin' an' growin'—till it'll bust out—! (*He gets up and puts on his coat and a hat. They watch him, gradually breaking into grins.* EBEN *avoids their eyes sheepishly.*) I'm goin' out fur a spell—up the road.

PETER T' the village?

SIMEON T' see Minnie?

EBEN (*defiantly*) Ay-eh!

PETER (*jeeringly*) The Scarlet Woman!

SIMEON Lust—that's what's growin' in ye!

EBEN Waal—she's purty!

PETER She's been purty fur twenty year!

SIMEON A new coat o' paint'll make a heifer out of forty.

EBEN She hain't forty!

PETER If she hain't, she's teeterin' on the edge.

EBEN (*desperately*) What d'yew know—

PETER All they is . . . Sim knew her—an' then me arter—

SIMEON An' Paw kin tell yew somethin' too! He was fust!

EBEN D'ye mean t' say he . . . ?

SIMEON (*with a grin*) Ay-eh! We air his heirs in everythin'!

EBEN (*intensely*) That's more to it! That grows on it! It'll bust soon! (*then violently*) I'll go smash my fist in her face! (*He pulls open the door in rear violently.*)

SIMEON (*with a wink at* PETER—*drawlingly*) Mebbe—but the night's wa'm—purty—by the time ye git thar mebbe ye'll kiss her instead!

PETER Sart'n he will! (*They both roar with coarse laughter.* EBEN *rushes out and slams the door—then the outside front door— comes around the corner of the house and stands still by the gate, staring up at the sky.*)

SIMEON (*looking after him*) Like his Paw.

PETER Dead spit an' image!

SIMEON Dog'll eat dog!

PETER Ay-eh. (*Pause. With yearning*) Mebbe a year from now we'll be in Californi-a.

SIMEON   Ay-eh. (*A pause. Both yawn.*) Let's git t'bed. (*He blows out the candle. They go out door in rear.* EBEN *stretches his arms up to the sky—rebelliously.*)

EBEN   Waal—thar's a star, an' somewhar's they's him, an' here's me, an' thar's Min up the road—in the same night. What if I does kiss her? She's like t'night, she's soft 'n' wa'm, her eyes kin wink like a star, her mouth's wa'm, her arms're wa'm, she smells like a wa'm plowed field, she's purty ... Ay-eh! By God A'mighty she's purty, an' I don't give a damn how many sins she's sinned afore mine or who she's sinned 'em with, my sin's as purty as any one on 'em! (*He strides off down the road to the left.*)

Scene 3

It is the pitch darkness just before dawn. EBEN *comes in from the left and goes around to the porch, feeling his way, chuckling bitterly and cursing half-aloud to himself.*

EBEN   The cussed old miser! (*He can be heard going in the front door. There is a pause as he goes upstairs, then a loud knock on the bedroom door of the brothers.*) Wake up!

SIMEON (*startedly*)   Who's thar?

EBEN (*pushing open the door and coming in, a lighted candle in his hand. The bedroom of the brothers is revealed. Its ceiling is the sloping roof. They can stand upright only close to the center dividing wall of the upstairs.* SIMEON *and* PETER *are in a double bed, front.* EBEN'S *cot is to the rear.* EBEN *has a mixture of silly grin and vicious scowl on his face*)   I be!

PETER (*angrily*)   What in hell's-fire ... ?

EBEN   I got news fur ye! Ha! (*He gives one abrupt sardonic guffaw.*)

SIMEON (*angrily*)   Couldn't ye hold it 'til we'd got our sleep?

EBEN   It's nigh sunup. (*then explosively*) He's gone an' married agen!

SIMEON *and* PETER (*explosively*)   Paw?

EBEN   Got himself hitched to a female 'bout thirty-five—an' purty, they says ...

SIMEON (*aghast*)   It's a durn lie!

PETER   Who says?

SIMEON   They been stringin' ye!

EBEN   Think I'm a dunce, do ye? The hull village says. The preacher from New Dover, he brung the news—told it t'our preacher—New Dover, that's whar the old loon got himself hitched—that's whar the woman lived—

PETER (*no longer doubting—stunned*)   Waal ... !

SIMEON (*the same*) Waal...!

EBEN (*sitting down on a bed—with vicious hatred*) Ain't he a devil out o' hell? It's jest t' spite us—the damned old mule!

PETER (*after a pause*) Everythin'll go t' her now.

SIMEON Ay-eh. (*A pause—dully*) Waal—if it's done—

PETER It's done us. (*pause—then persuasively*) They's gold in the fields o' Californi-a, Sim. No good a-stayin' here now.

SIMEON Jest what I was a-thinkin'. (*then with decision*) S'well fust's last! Let's light out and git this mornin'.

PETER Suits me.

EBEN Ye must like walkin'.

SIMEON (*sardonically*) If ye'd grow wings on us we'd fly thar!

EBEN Ye'd like ridin' better—on a boat, wouldn't ye? (*Fumbles in his pocket and takes out a crumpled sheet of foolscap.*) Waal, if ye sign this ye kin ride on a boat. I've had it writ out an' ready in case ye'd ever go. It says fur three hundred dollars t' each ye agree yewr shares o' the farm is sold t' me. (*They look suspiciously at the paper. A pause.*)

SIMEON (*wonderingly*) But if he's hitched agen—

PETER An' whar'd yew git that sum o' money, anyways?

EBEN (*cunningly*) I know whar it's hid. I been waitin'—Maw told me. She knew whar it lay fur years, but she was waitin'... It's her'n—the money he hoarded from her farm an' hid from Maw. It's my money by rights now.

PETER Whar's it hid?

EBEN (*cunningly*) Whar yew won't never find it without me. Maw spied on him—'r she'd never knowed. (*A pause. They look at him suspiciously, and he at them.*) Waal, is it fa'r trade?

SIMEON Dunno.

PETER Dunno.

SIMEON (*looking at window*) Sky's grayin'.

PETER Ye better start the fire, Eben.

SIMEON An' fix some vittles.

EBEN Ay-eh. (*Then with a forced jocular heartiness*) I'll git ye a good one. If ye're startin' t' hoof it t' Californi-a ye'll need somethin' that'll stick t' yer ribs. (*He turns to the door, adding meaningly*) But ye kin ride on a boat if ye'll swap. (*He stops at the door and pauses. They stare at him.*)

SIMEON (*suspiciously*) Whar was ye all night?

EBEN (*defiantly*) Up t' Min's. (*then slowly*) Walkin' thar, fust I felt 's if I'd kiss her; then I got a-thinkin' on' what ye'd said o' him an' her an' I says, I'll bust her nose fur that! Then I got t' the village an' heerd the news an' I got madder'n hell an' run all the way t' Min's not knowin' what I'd do—(*He pauses—then*

sheepishly but more defiantly) Waal—when I seen her, I didn't
hit her—nor I didn't kiss her nuther—I begun t' beller like a calf
an' cuss at the same time, I was so durn mad—an' she got scared
—an' I jest grabbed holt an' tuk her! (*Proudly*) Yes, sirree! I tuk
her. She may've been his'n—an' your'n, too—but she's mine now!
SIMEON (*dryly*)   In love, air yew?
EBEN (*with lofty scorn*)   Love! I don't take no stock in sech slop!
PETER (*winking at* SIMEON)   Mebbe Eben's aimin' t' marry, too.
SIMEON   Min'd make a true faithful he'pmeet! (*They snicker.*)
EBEN   What do I care fur her—'ceptin' she's round an' wa'm? The
p'int is she was his'n—an' now she belongs t' me! (*He goes to the
door—then turns—rebelliously.*) An' Min hain't sech a bad un.
They's worse'n Min in the world, I'll bet ye! Wait'll we see this
cow the Old Man's hitched t'! She'll beat Min, I got a notion!
(*He starts to go out.*)
SIMEON (*suddenly*)   Mebbe ye'll try t' make her your'n, too?
PETER   Ha! (*He gives a sardonic laugh of relish at this idea.*)
EBEN (*spitting with disgust*)   Her—here—sleepin' with him—
stealin' my Maw's farm! I'd as soon pet a skunk 'r kiss a snake!
(*He goes out. The two stare after him suspiciously. A pause. They
listen to his steps receding.*)
PETER   He's startin' the fire.
SIMEON   I'd like t' ride t' Californi-a—but—
PETER   Min might o' put some scheme in his head.
SIMEON   Mebbe it's all a lie 'bout Paw marryin'. We'd best wait
an' see the bride.
PETER   An' don't sign nothin' till we does!
SIMEON   Nor till we've tested it's good money! (*then with a grin*)
But if Paw's hitched we'd be sellin' Eben somethin' we'd never git
nohow!
PETER   We'll wait an' see. (*then with sudden vindictive anger*) An'
till he comes, let's yew 'n' me not wuk a lick, let Eben tend to
thin's if he's a mind t', let's us jest sleep an' eat an' drink likker,
an' let the hull damned farm go t' blazes!
SIMEON (*excitedly*)   By God, we've 'arned a rest! We'll play rich
fur a change. I hain't a-going to stir outa bed till breakfast's
ready.
PETER   An' on the table!
SIMEON (*after a pause—thoughtfully*)   What d'ye calc'late she'll be
like—our new Maw? Like Eben thinks?
PETER   More'n likely.
SIMEON (*vindictively*)   Waal—I hope she's a she-devil that'll make
him wish he was dead an' livin' in the pit o' hell fur comfort!
PETER (*fervently*)   Amen!

SIMEON (*imitating his father's voice*)   "I'm ridin' out t' learn God's message t' me in the spring like the prophets done," he says. I'll bet right then an' thar he knew plumb well he was goin' whorin', the stinkin' old hypocrite!

Scene 4

Same as SCENE 2—*shows the interior of the kitchen with a lighted candle on table. It is gray dawn outside.* SIMEON *and* PETER *are just finishing their breakfast.* EBEN *sits before his plate of untouched food, brooding frowningly.*

PETER (*glancing at him rather irritably*)   Lookin' glum don't help none.

SIMEON (*sarcastically*)   Sorrowin' over his lust o' the flesh!

PETER (*with a grin*)   Was she yer fust?

EBEN (*angrily*)   None o' yer business. (*a pause*) I was thinkin' o' him. I got a notion he's gittin' near—I kin feel him comin' on like yew kin feel malaria chill afore it takes ye.

PETER   It's too early yet.

SIMEON   Dunno. He'd like t' catch us nappin'—jest t' have somethin' t' hoss us 'round over.

PETER (*mechanically gets to his feet.* SIMEON *does the same*)   Waal —let's git t' wuk. (*They both plod mechanically toward the door before they realize. Then they stop short.*)

SIMEON (*grinning*)   Ye're a cussed fool, Pete—and I be wuss! Let him see we hain't wukin'! We don't give a durn!

PETER (*as they go back to the table*)   Not a damned durn! It'll serve t' show him we're done with him. (*They sit down again.* EBEN *stares from one to the other with surprise.*)

SIMEON (*grins at him*)   We're aimin' t' start bein' lilies o' the field.

PETER   Nary a toil 'r spin 'r lick o' wuk do we put in!

SIMEON   Ye're sole owner—till he comes—that's what ye wanted. Waal, ye got t' be sole hand, too.

PETER   The cows air bellerin'. Ye better hustle at the milkin'.

EBEN (*with excited joy*)   Ye mean ye'll sign the paper?

SIMEON (*dryly*)   Mebbe.

PETER   Mebbe.

SIMEON   We're considerin'. (*peremptorily*) Ye better git t' wuk.

EBEN (*with queer excitement*)   It's Maw's farm agen! It's my farm! Them's my cows! I'll milk my durn fingers off fur cows o' mine! (*He goes out door in rear, they stare after him indifferently.*)

SIMEON   Like his Paw.

PETER   Dead spit 'n' image!

SIMEON Waal—let dog eat dog! (EBEN *comes out of front door and around the corner of the house. The sky is beginning to grow flushed with sunrise.* EBEN *stops by the gate and stares around him with glowing, possessive eyes. He takes in the whole farm with his embracing glance of desire.*)

EBEN It's purty! It's damned purty! It's mine! (*He suddenly throws his head back boldly and glares with hard, defiant eyes at the sky.*) Mine, d'ye hear? Mine! (*He turns and walks quickly off left, rear, toward the barn. The two brothers light their pipes.*)

SIMEON (*putting his muddy boots up on the table, tilting back his chair, and puffing defiantly*) Waal—this air solid comfort—fur once.

PETER Ay-eh. (*He follows suit. A pause. Unconsciously they both sigh.*)

SIMEON (*suddenly*) He never was much o' a hand at milkin', Eben wa'n't.

PETER (*with a snort*) His hands air like hoofs! (*a pause*)

SIMEON Reach down the jug thar! Let's take a swaller. I'm feelin' kind o' low.

PETER Good idee! (*He does so—gets two glasses—they pour out drinks of whisky.*) Here's t' the gold in Californi-a!

SIMEON An' luck t' find it! (*They drink—puff resolutely—sigh—take their feet down from the table.*)

PETER Likker don't pear t' sot right.

SIMEON We hain't used t' it this early. (*A pause. They become very restless.*)

PETER Gittin' close in this kitchen.

SIMEON (*with immense relief*) Let's git a breath o' air. (*They arise briskly and go out rear—appear around house and stop by the gate. They stare up at the sky with a numbed appreciation.*)

PETER Purty!

SIMEON Ay-eh. Gold's t' the East now.

PETER Sun's startin' with us fur the Golden West.

SIMEON (*staring around the farm, his compressed face tightened, unable to conceal his emotion*) Waal—it's our last mornin'—mebbe.

PETER (*the same*) Ay-eh.

SIMEON (*stamps his foot on the earth and addresses it desperately*) Waal—ye've thirty year o' me buried in ye—spread out over ye—blood an' bone an' sweat—rotted away—fertilizin' ye—richin' yer soul—prime manure, by God, that's what I been t' ye!

PETER Ay-eh! An' me!

SIMEON An' yew, Peter. (*He sighs—then spits.*) Waal—no use'n cryin' over spilt milk.

PETER They's gold in the West—an' freedom, mebbe. We been slaves t' stone walls here.

SIMEON (*defiantly*) We hain't nobody's slaves from this out—nor nothin's slaves nuther. (*a pause—restlessly*) Speakin' o' milk, wonder how Eben's managin'?

PETER I s'pose he's managin'.

SIMEON Mebbe we'd ought t' help—this once.

PETER Mebbe. The cows knows us.

SIMEON An' likes us. They don't know him much.

PETER An' the hosses, an' pigs, an' chickens. They don't know him much.

SIMEON They knows us like brothers—an' likes us! (*proudly*) Hain't we raised 'em t' be fust-rate, number one prize stock?

PETER We hain't—not no more.

SIMEON (*dully*) I was fergittin'. (*then resignedly*) Waal, let's go help Eben a spell an' git waked up.

PETER Suits me. (*They are starting off down left, rear, for the barn when* EBEN *appears from there hurrying toward them, his face excited.*)

EBEN (*breathlessly*) Waal—har they be! The old mule an' the bride! I seen 'em from the barn down below at the turnin'.

PETER How could ye tell that far?

EBEN Hain't I as far-sight as he's near-sight? Don't I know the mare 'n' buggy, an' two people settin' in it? Who else . . . ? An' I tell ye I kin feel 'em a-comin', too! (*He squirms as if he had the itch.*)

PETER (*beginning to be angry*) Waal—let him do his own un-hitchin'!

SIMEON (*angry in his turn*) Let's hustle in an' git our bundles an' be a-goin' as he's a-comin'. I don't want never t' step inside the door agen arter he's back. (*They both start back around the corner of the house.* EBEN *follows them.*)

EBEN (*anxiously*) Will ye sign it afore ye go?

PETER Let's see the color o' the old skinflint's money an' we'll sign. (*They disappear left. The two brothers clump upstairs to get their bundles.* EBEN *appears in the kitchen, runs to the window, peers out, comes back and pulls up a strip of flooring in under stove, takes out a canvas bag and puts it on table, then sets the floor-board back in place. The two brothers appear a moment after. They carry old carpet bags.*)

EBEN (*puts his hand on bag guardingly*) Have ye signed?

SIMEON (*shows paper in his hand*) Ay-eh. (*greedily*) Be that the money?

EBEN (*opens bag and pours out pile of twenty-dollar gold pieces*)

Twenty-dollar pieces—thirty on 'em. Count 'em. (PETER *does so, arranging them in stacks of five, biting one or two to test them.*)

PETER   Six hundred. (*He puts them in bag and puts it inside his shirt carefully.*)

SIMEON (*handing paper to* EBEN)   Har ye be.

EBEN (*after a glance, folds it carefully and hides it under his shirt— gratefully*)   Thank yew.

PETER   Thank yew fur the ride.

SIMEON   We'll send ye a lump o' gold fur Christmas. (*A pause.* EBEN *stares at them and they at him.*)

PETER (*awkwardly*)   Waal—we're a-goin'.

SIMEON   Comin' out t' the yard?

EBEN   No. I'm waitin' in here a spell. (*Another silence. The brothers edge awkwardly to door in rear—then turn and stand.*)

SIMEON   Waal—good-by.

PETER   Good-by.

EBEN   Good-by. (*They go out. He sits down at the table, faces the stove and pulls out the paper. He looks from it to the stove. His face, lighted up by the shaft of sunlight from the window, has an expression of trance. His lips move. The two brothers come out to the gate.*)

PETER (*looking off toward barn*)   Thar he be—unhitchin'.

SIMEON (*with a chuckle*)   I'll bet ye he's riled!

PETER   An' thar she be.

SIMEON   Let's wait 'n' see what our new Maw looks like.

PETER (*with a grin*)   An' give him our partin' cuss!

SIMEON (*grinning*)   I feel like raisin' fun. I feel light in my head an' feet.

PETER   Me, too. I feel like laffin' till I'd split up the middle.

SIMEON   Reckon it's the likker?

PETER   No. My feet feel itchin' t' walk an' walk—an' jump high over thin's—an' . . . .

SIMEON   Dance? (*a pause*)

PETER (*puzzled*)   It's plumb onnateral.

SIMEON (*a light coming over his face*)   I calc'late it's 'cause school's out. It's holiday. Fur once we're free!

PETER (*dazedly*)   Free?

SIMEON   The halter's broke—the harness is busted—the fence bars is down—the stone walls air crumblin' an' tumblin'! We'll be kickin' up an' tearin' away down the road!

PETER (*drawing a deep breath—oratorically*)   Anybody that wants this stinkin' old rock-pile of a farm kin hev it. 'Tain't our'n, no sirree!

SIMEON (*takes the gate off its hinges and puts it under his arm*) We harby 'bolishes shet gates an' open gates, an' all gates, by thunder!

PETER   We'll take it with us fur luck an' let 'er sail free down some river.

SIMEON (*as a sound of voices comes from left, rear*) Har they comes! (*The two brothers congeal into two stiff, grim-visaged statues.* EPHRAIM CABOT *and* ABBIE PUTNAM *come in.* CABOT *is seventy-five, tall and gaunt, with great, wiry, concentrated power, but stoop-shouldered from toil. His face is as hard as if it were hewn out of a boulder, yet there is a weakness in it, a pretty pride in its own narrow strength. His eyes are small, close together, and extremely near-sighted, blinking continually in the effort to focus on objects, their stare having a straining, ingrowing quality. He is dressed in his dismal black Sunday suit.* ABBIE *is thirty-five, buxom, full of vitality. Her round face is pretty but marred by its rather gross sensuality. There is strength and obstinacy in her jaw, a hard determination in her eyes, and about her whole personality the same unsettled, untamed, desperate quality which is so apparent in* EBEN.)

CABOT (*as they enter—a queer strangled emotion in his dry cracking voice*) Har we be t' hum, Abbie.

ABBIE (*with lust for the word*) Hum! (*Her eyes gloating on the house without seeming to see the two stiff figures at the gate.*) It's purty—purty! I can't b'lieve it's r'ally mine.

CABOT (*sharply*) Yewr'n? Mine! (*He stares at her penetratingly. She stares back. He adds relentingly.*) Our'n—mebbe! It was lonesome too long. I was growin' old in the spring. A hum's got t' hev a woman.

ABBIE (*her voice taking possession*) A woman's got t' hev a hum!

CABOT (*nodding uncertainly*) Ay-eh. (*then irritably*) Whar be they? Ain't thar nobody about—'r wukin'—'r nothin'?

ABBIE (*sees the brothers. She returns their stare of cold appraising contempt with interest—slowly*) Thar's two men loafin' at the gate an' starin' at me like a couple o' strayed hogs.

CABOT (*straining his eyes*) I kin see 'em—but I can't make out. . . .

SIMEON   It's Simeon.

PETER   It's Peter.

CABOT (*exploding*) Why hain't ye wukin'?

SIMEON (*dryly*) We're waitin' t' welcome ye hum—yew an' the bride!

CABOT (*confusedly*) Huh? Waal—this be yer new Maw, boys. (*She stares at them and they at her.*)

SIMEON (*turns away and spits contemptuously*) I see her!

PETER (*spits also*) An' I see her!

ABBIE (*with the conqueror's conscious superiority*) I'll go in an' look at *my* house. (*She goes slowly around to porch.*)

SIMEON (*with a snort*) *Her* house!

PETER (*calls after her*) Ye'll find Eben inside. Ye better not tell him it's *yewr* house.

ABBIE (*mouthing the name*) Eben. (*then quietly*) I'll tell Eben.

CABOT (*with a contemptuous sneer*) Ye needn't heed Eben. Eben's a dumb fool—like his Maw—soft an' simple!

SIMEON (*with his sardonic burst of laughter*) Ha! Eben's a chip o' yew—spit 'n' image—hard 'n' bitter's a hickory tree! Dog'll eat dog. He'll eat ye yet, old man!

CABOT (*commandingly*) Ye git t' wuk!

SIMEON (*as* ABBIE *disappears in house—winks at* PETER *and says tauntingly*) So that thar's our new Maw, be it? Whar in hell did ye dig her up? (*He and* PETER *laugh.*)

PETER Ha! Ye'd better turn her in the pen with the other sows. (*They laugh uproariously, slapping their thighs.*)

CABOT (*so amazed at their effrontery that he stutters in confusion*) Simeon! Peter! What's come over ye? Air ye drunk?

SIMEON We're free, old man—free o' yew an' the hull damned farm! (*They grow more and more hilarious and excited.*)

PETER An' we're startin' out fur the gold fields o' Californi-a!

SIMEON Ye kin take this place an' burn it!

PETER An' bury it—fur all we cares!

SIMEON We're free, old man! (*He cuts a caper.*)

PETER Free! (*He gives a kick in the air.*)

SIMEON (*in a frenzy*) Whoop!

PETER Whoop! (*They do an absurd Indian war dance about the old man who is petrified between rage and the fear that they are insane.*)

SIMEON We're free as Injuns! Lucky we don't sculp ye!

PETER An' burn yer barn an' kill the stock!

SIMEON An' rape yer new woman! Whoop! (*He and* PETER *stop their dance, holding their sides, rocking with wild laughter.*)

CABOT (*edging away*) Lust fur gold—fur the sinful, easy gold o' Californi-a! It's made ye mad!

SIMEON (*tauntingly*) Wouldn't ye like us to send ye back some sinful gold, ye old sinner?

PETER They's gold besides what's in Californi-a! (*He retreats back beyond the vision of the old man and takes the bag of money and flaunts it in the air above his head, laughing.*)

SIMEON And sinfuller, too!

PETER We'll be voyagin' on the sea! Whoop! (*He leaps up and down.*)

SIMEON Livin' free! Whoop! (*He leaps in turn.*)

CABOT (*suddenly roaring with rage*) My cuss on ye!

SIMEON Take our'n in trade fur it! Whoop!

CABOT I'll hev ye both chained up in the asylum!

PETER Ye old skinflint! Good-by!

SIMEON Ye old blood sucker! Good-by!

CABOT Go afore I . . . !

PETER Whoop! (*He picks a stone from the road.* SIMEON *does the same.*)

SIMEON Maw'll be in the parlor.

PETER Ay-eh! One! Two!

CABOT (*frightened*) What air ye . . . ?

PETER Three! (*They both throw, the stones hitting the parlor window with a crash of glass, tearing the shade.*)

SIMEON Whoop!

PETER Whoop!

CABOT (*in a fury now, rushing toward them*) If I kin lay hands on ye—I'll break yer bones fur ye! (*But they beat a capering retreat before him,* SIMEON *with the gate still under his arm.* CABOT *comes back, panting with impotent rage. Their voices as they go off take up the song of the gold-seekers to the old tune of "Oh, Susannah!"*)

> "I jumped aboard the Liza ship,
> And traveled on the sea,
> And every time I thought of home
> I wished it wasn't me!
> Oh! Californi-a,
> That's the land fur me!
> I'm off to Californi-a!
> With my wash bowl on my knee."

(*In the meantime, the window of the upper bedroom on right is raised and* ABBIE *sticks her head out. She looks down at* CABOT— *with a sigh of relief.*)

ABBIE Waal—that's the last o' them two, hain't it? (*He doesn't answer. Then in possessive tones*) This here's a nice bedroom, Ephraim. It's a r'al nice bed. Is it my room, Ephraim?

CABOT (*grimly—without looking up*) Our'n! (*She cannot control a grimace of aversion and pulls back her head slowly and shuts the window. A sudden horrible thought seems to enter* CABOT's *head.*) They been up to somethin'! Mebbe—mebbe they've pizened the stock—'r somethin'! (*He almost runs off down toward the barn. A moment later the kitchen door is slowly pushed open and* ABBIE *enters. For a moment she stands looking at* EBEN. *He does not notice her at first. Her eyes take him in penetratingly with a calculating appraisal of his strength as against hers. But under this her desire is dimly awakened by his youth and good looks. Suddenly he becomes conscious of her presence and looks up. Their eyes meet. He leaps to his feet, glowering at her speechlessly.*)

ABBIE (*in her most seductive tones which she uses all through this scene*) Be you—Eben? I'm Abbie—(*She laughs.*) I mean, I'm yer new Maw.

EBEN (*viciously*) No, damn ye!

ABBIE (*as if she hadn't heard—with a queer smile*) Yer Paw's spoke a lot o' yew. . . .

EBEN Ha!

ABBIE Ye mustn't mind him. He's an old man. (*A long pause. They stare at each other.*) I don't want t' pretend playin' Maw t' ye, Eben. (*admiringly*) Ye're too big an' too strong fur that. I want t' be frens with ye. Mebbe with me fur a fren ye'd find ye'd like livin' here better. I kin make it easy fur ye with him, mebbe. (*with a scornful sense of power*) I calc'late I kin git him t' do most anythin' fur me.

EBEN (*with bitter scorn*) Ha! (*They stare again,* EBEN *obscurely moved, physically attracted to her—in forced stilted tones*) Yew kin go t' the devil!

ABBIE (*calmly*) If cussin' me does ye good, cuss all ye've a mind t'. I'm all prepared t' have ye agin me—at fust. I don't blame ye nuther. I'd feel the same at any stranger comin' t' take my Maw's place. (*He shudders. She is watching him carefully.*) Yew must've cared a lot fur yewr Maw, didn't ye? My Maw died afore I'd growed. I don't remember her none. (*A pause.*) But yew won't hate me long, Eben. I'm not the wust in the world—an' yew an' me've got a lot in common. I kin tell that by lookin' at ye. Waal —I've had a hard life, too—oceans o' trouble an' nuthin' but wuk fur reward. I was a orphan early an' had t' wuk fur others in other folks' hums. Then I married an' he turned out a drunken spreer an' so he had to wuk fur others an' me too agen in other folks' hums, an' the baby died, an' my husband got sick an' died too, an' I was glad sayin' now I'm free fur once, on'y I diskivered right away all I was free fur was t' wuk agen in other folks' hums, doin' other folks' wuk till I'd most give up hope o' ever doin' my own wuk in my own hum, an' then your Paw come. . . . (CABOT *appears returning from the barn. He comes to the gate and looks down the road the brothers have gone. A faint strain of their retreating voices is heard: "Oh, Californi-a! That's the place for me." He stands glowering, his fist clenched, his face grim with rage.*)

EBEN (*fighting against his growing attraction and sympathy—harshly*) An' bought yew—like a harlot! (*She is stung and flushes angrily. She has been sincerely moved by the recital of her troubles. He adds furiously*) An' the price he's payin' ye—this farm —was my Maw's, damn ye!—an' mine now!

ABBIE (*with a cool laugh of confidence*) Yewr'n? We'll see 'bout that! (*then strongly*) Waal—what if I did need a hum? What else'd I marry an old man like him fur?

EBEN (*maliciously*) I'll tell him ye said that!

ABBIE (*smiling*) I'll say ye're lyin' a-purpose—an' he'll drive ye off the place!

EBEN Ye devil!

ABBIE (*defying him*) This be my farm—this be my hum—this be my kitchen—!

EBEN (*furiously, as if he were going to attack her*) Shut up, damn ye!

ABBIE (*walks up to him—a queer coarse expression of desire in her face and body—slowly*) An' upstairs—that be my bedroom— an' my bed! (*He stares into her eyes, terribly confused and torn. She adds softly*) I hain't bad nor mean—'ceptin' fur an enemy —but I got t' fight fur what's due me out o' life, if I ever 'spect t' git it. (*Then putting her hand on his arm—seductively*) Let's yew 'n' me be frens, Eben.

EBEN (*stupidly—as if hypnotized*) Ay-eh. (*Then furiously flinging off her arm*) No, ye durned old witch! I hate ye! (*He rushes out the door.*)

ABBIE (*looks after him smiling satisfiedly—then half to herself, mouthing the word*) Eben's nice. (*She looks at the table, proudly.*) I'll wash up *my* dishes now. (EBEN *appears outside, slamming the door behind him. He comes around corner, stops on seeing his father, and stands staring at him with hate.*)

CABOT (*raising his arms to heaven in the fury he can no longer control*) Lord God o' Hosts, smite the undutiful sons with Thy wust cuss!

EBEN (*breaking in violently*) Yew 'n' yewr God! Allus cussin' folks —allus naggin' 'em!

CABOT (*oblivious to him—summoningly*) God o' the old! God o' the lonesome!

EBEN (*mockingly*) Naggin' His sheep t' sin! T' hell with yewr God! (CABOT *turns. He and* EBEN *glower at each other.*)

CABOT (*harshly*) So it's yew. I might've knowed it. (*shaking his finger threateningly at him*) Blasphemin' fool! (*then quickly*) Why hain't ye t' wuk?

EBEN Why hain't yew? They've went. I can't wuk it all alone.

CABOT (*contemptuously*) Nor noways! I'm wuth ten o' ye yit, old's I be! Ye'll never be more'n half a man! (*then, matter-of-factly*) Waal—let's git t' the barn. (*They go. A last faint note of the "Californi-a" song is heard from the distance.* ABBIE *is washing her dishes.*)

PART II

Scene 1

The exterior of the farmhouse, as in PART I—*a hot Sunday afternoon two months later.* ABBIE, *dressed in her best, is discovered sitting in a rocker at the end of the porch. She rocks listlessly, enervated by the heat, staring in front of her with bored, half-closed eyes.*

EBEN *sticks his head out of his bedroom window. He looks around furtively and tries to see—or hear—if anyone is on the porch, but although he has been careful to make no noise,* ABBIE *has sensed his movement. She stops rocking, her face grows animated and eager, she waits attentively.* EBEN *seems to feel her presence, he scowls back his thoughts of her and spits with exaggerated disdain—then withdraws back into the room.* ABBIE *waits, holding her breath as she listens with passionate eagerness for every sound within the house.*

EBEN *comes out. Their eyes meet. His falter, he is confused, he turns away and slams the door resentfully. At this gesture,* ABBIE *laughs tantalizingly, amused but at the same time piqued and irritated. He scowls, strides off the porch to the path and starts to walk past her to the road with a grand swagger of ignoring her existence. He is dressed in his store suit, spruced up, his face shines from soap and water.* ABBIE *leans forward on her chair, her eyes hard and angry now, and, as he passes her, gives a sneering, taunting chuckle.*

EBEN (*stung—turns on her furiously*) What air yew cacklin' 'bout?

ABBIE (*triumphant*) Yew!

EBEN What about me?

ABBIE Ye look all slicked up like a prize bull.

EBEN (*with a sneer*) Waal—ye hain't so durned purty yerself, be ye? (*They stare into each other's eyes, his held by hers in spite of himself, hers glowingly possessive. Their physical attraction becomes a palpable force quivering in the hot air.*)

ABBIE (*softly*) Ye don't mean that, Eben. Ye may think ye mean it, mebbe, but ye don't. Ye can't. It's agin nature, Eben. Ye been fightin' yer nature ever since the day I come—tryin' t' tell yerself I hain't purty t'ye. (*She laughs a low humid laugh without taking her eyes from his. A pause—her body squirms desirously —she murmurs languorously.*) Hain't the sun strong an' hot? Ye kin feel it burnin' into the earth—Nature—makin' thin's grow— bigger 'n' bigger—burnin' inside ye—makin' ye want t' grow— into somethin' else—till ye're jined with it—an' it's your'n—but it owns ye, too—an' makes ye grow bigger—like a tree—like them elums— (*She laughs again softly, holding his eyes. He takes a step toward her, compelled against his will.*) Nature'll beat ye, Eben. Ye might's well own up t' it fust 's last.

EBEN (*trying to break from her spell—confusedly*) If Paw'd hear ye goin' on.... (*resentfully*) But ye've made such a damned idjit out o' the old devil ... ! (ABBIE *laughs.*)

ABBIE   Waal—hain't it easier fur yew with him changed softer?

EBEN (*defiantly*)   No. I'm fightin' him—fightin' yew—fightin' fur Maw's right t' her hum! (*This breaks her spell for him. He glowers at her.*) An' I'm onto ye. Ye hain't foolin' me a mite. Ye're aimin' t' swaller up everythin' an' make it your'n. Waal, you'll find I'm a heap sight bigger hunk nor yew kin chew! (*He turns from her with a sneer.*)

ABBIE (*trying to regain her ascendancy—seductively*)   Eben!

EBEN   Leave me be! (*He starts to walk away.*)

ABBIE (*more commandingly*)   Eben!

EBEN (*stops—resentfully*)   What d'ye want?

ABBIE (*trying to conceal a growing excitement*)   Whar air ye goin'?

EBEN (*with malicious nonchalance*)   Oh—up the road a spell.

ABBIE   T' the village?

EBEN (*airly*)   Mebbe.

ABBIE (*excitedly*)   T' see that Min, I s'pose?

EBEN   Mebbe.

ABBIE (*weakly*)   What d'ye want t' waste time on her fur?

EBEN (*revenging himself now—grinning at her*)   Ye can't beat Nature, didn't ye say? (*He laughs and again starts to walk away.*)

ABBIE (*bursting out*)   An ugly old hake!

EBEN (*with a tantalizing sneer*)   She's purtier'n yew be!

ABBIE   That every wuthless drunk in the country has....

EBEN (*tauntingly*)   Mebbe—but she's better'n yew. She owns up fa'r 'n' squar' t' her doin's.

ABBIE (*furiously*)   Don't ye dare compare....

EBEN   She don't go sneakin' an' stealin'—what's mine.

ABBIE (*savagely seizing on his weak point*)   Your'n? Yew mean— my farm?

EBEN   I mean the farm yew sold yerself fur like any other old whore—my farm!

ABBIE (*stung—fiercely*)   Ye'll never live t' see the day when even a stinkin' weed on it 'll belong t' ye! (*then in a scream*) Git out o' my sight! Go on t' yer slut—disgracin' yer Paw 'n' me! I'll git yer Paw t' horsewhip ye off the place if I want t'! Ye're only livin' here 'cause I tolerate ye! Git along! I hate the sight o' ye! (*She stops, panting and glaring at him.*)

EBEN (*returning her glance in kind*)   An' I hate the sight o' yew! (*He turns and strides off up the road. She follows his retreating figure with concentrated hate. Old* CABOT *appears coming up from the barn. The hard, grim expression of his face has changed. He seems in some queer way softened, mellowed. His eyes have taken on a strange, incongruous dreamy quality. Yet there is no hint of physical weakness about him—rather he looks more robust and younger.* ABBIE *sees him and turns away quickly with unconcealed aversion. He comes slowly up to her.*)

CABOT (*mildly*)   War yew an' Eben quarrelin' agen?

ABBIE (*shortly*)   No.

CABOT   Ye was talkin' a'mighty loud. (*He sits down on the edge of porch.*)

ABBIE (*snappishly*)   If ye heerd us they hain't no need askin' questions.

CABOT   I didn't hear what ye said.

ABBIE (*relieved*)   Waal—it wa'n't nothin' t' speak on.

CABOT (*after a pause*)   Eben's queer.

ABBIE (*bitterly*)   He's the dead spit 'n' image o' yew!

CABOT (*queerly interested*)   D'ye think so, Abbie? (*After a pause, ruminatingly*) Me 'n' Eben's allus fit 'n' fit. I never could b'ar him noways. He's so thunderin' soft—like his Maw.

ABBIE (*scornfully*)   Ay-eh! 'Bout as soft as yew be!

CABOT (*as if he hadn't heard*)   Mebbe I been too hard on him.

ABBIE (*jeeringly*)   Waal—ye're gittin' soft now—soft as slop! That's what Eben was sayin'.

CABOT (*his face instantly grim and ominous*)   Eben was sayin'? Waal, he'd best not do nothin' t' try me 'r he'll soon diskiver.... (*A pause. She keeps her face turned away. His gradually softens. He stares up at the sky.*) Purty, hain't it?

ABBIE (*crossly*)   I don't see nothin' purty.

CABOT   The sky. Feels like a wa'm field up thar.

ABBIE (*sarcastically*)   Air yew aimin' t' buy up over the farm too? (*She snickers contemptuously.*)

CABOT (*strangely*)   I'd like t' own my place up thar. (*a pause*) I'm gittin' old, Abbie. I'm gittin' ripe on the bough. (*A pause. She stares at him mystified. He goes on.*) It's allus lonesome cold in the house—even when it's bilin' hot outside. Hain't yew noticed?

ABBIE No.

CABOT It's wa'm down t' the barn—nice smellin' an' warm—with the cows. (*a pause*) Cows is queer.

ABBIE Like yew?

CABOT Like Eben. (*a pause*) I'm gittin' t' feel resigned t' Eben— jest as I got t' feel 'bout his Maw. I'm gittin' t' learn to b'ar his softness—jest like her'n. I calc'late I c'd a'most take t' him—if he wa'n't sech a dumb fool! (*a pause*) I s'pose it's old age a-creepin' in my bones.

ABBIE (*indifferently*) Waal—ye hain't dead yet.

CABOT (*roused*) No, I hain't, yew bet—not by a hell of a sight— I'm sound 'n' tough as hickory! (*then moodily*) But arter three score and ten the Lord warns ye t' prepare. (*a pause*) That's why Eben's come in my head. Now that his cussed sinful brothers is gone their path t' hell, they's no one left but Eben.

ABBIE (*resentfully*) They's me, hain't they? (*Agitatedly*) What's all this sudden likin' ye tuk to Eben? Why don't ye say nothin' 'bout me? Hain't I yer lawful wife?

CABOT (*simply*) Ay-eh. Ye be. (*A pause—he stares at her desirously—his eyes grow avid—then with a sudden movement he seizes her hands and squeezes them, declaiming in a queer camp meeting preacher's tempo*) Yew air my Rose o' Sharon! Behold, yew air fair; yer eyes air doves; yer lips air like scarlet; yer two breasts air like two fawns; yer navel be like a round goblet; yer belly be like a heap o' wheat.... (*He covers her hand with kisses. She does not seem to notice. She stares before her with hard angry eyes.*)

ABBIE (*jerking her hands away—harshly*) So ye're plannin' t' leave the farm t' Eben, air ye?

CABOT (*dazedly*) Leave ...? '(*then with resentful obstinacy*) I hain't a-givin' it t' no one!

ABBIE (*remorselessly*) Ye can't take it with ye.

CABOT (*thinks a moment—then reluctantly*) No, I calc'late not. (*after a pause—with a strange passion*) But if I could, I would, by the Etarnal! 'R if I could, in my dyin' hour, I'd set it afire an' watch it burn—this house an' every ear o' corn an' every tree down t' the last blade o' hay! I'd sit an' know it was all a-dying with me an' no one else'd ever own what was mine, what I'd made out o' nothin' with my own sweat 'n' blood! (*a pause— then he adds with a queer affection*) 'Ceptin' the cows. Them I'd turn free.

ABBIE (*harshly*) An' me?

CABOT (*with a queer smile*) Ye'd be turned free, too.

ABBIE (*furiously*) So that's the thanks I git fur marryin' ye—t' have ye change kind to Eben who hates ye, an' talk o' turnin' me out in the road.

CABOT (*hastily*) Abbie! Ye know I wa'n't. . . .

ABBIE (*vengefully*) Just let me tell ye a thing or two 'bout Eben! Whar's he gone? T' see that harlot, Min! I tried fur t' stop him. Disgracin' yew an' me—on the Sabbath, too!

CABOT (*rather guiltily*) He's a sinner—nateral-born. It's lust eatin' his heart.

ABBIE (*enraged beyond endurance—wildly vindictive*) An' his lust fur me! Kin ye find excuses fur that?

CABOT (*stares at her—after a dead pause*) Lust—fur yew?

ABBIE (*defiantly*) He was tryin' t' make love t' me—when ye heerd us quarrelin'.

CABOT (*stares at her—then a terrible expression of rage comes over his face—he springs to his feet shaking all over*) By the A'mighty God—I'll end him!

ABBIE (*frightened now for* EBEN) No! Don't ye!

CABOT (*violently*) I'll git the shotgun an' blow his soft brains t' the top o' them elums!

ABBIE (*throwing her arms around him*) No, Ephraim!

CABOT (*pushing her away violently*) I will, by God!

ABBIE (*in a quieting tone*) Listen, Ephraim. 'Twa'n't nothin' bad —on'y a boy's foolin'—'twa'n't meant serious—jest jokin' an' teasin'. . . .

CABOT Then why did ye say—lust?

ABBIE It must hev sounded wusser'n I meant. An' I was mad at thinkin'—ye'd leave him the farm.

CABOT (*quieter but still grim and cruel*) Waal then, I'll horsewhip him off the place if that much'll content ye.

ABBIE (*reaching out and taking his hand*) No. Don't think o' me! Ye mustn't drive him off. 'Tain't sensible. Who'll ye get to help ye on the farm? They's no one hereabouts.

CABOT (*considers this—then nodding his appreciation*) Ye got a head on ye. (*then irritably*) Waal, let them stay. (*He sits down on the edge of the porch. She sits beside him. He murmurs contemptuously*) I oughtn't t' git riled so—at that 'ere fool calf. (*a pause*) But har's the p'int. What son o' mine'll keep on here t' the farm—when the Lord does call me? Simeon an' Peter air gone t' hell—an' Eben's follerin' 'em.

ABBIE They's me.

CABOT Ye're on'y a woman.

ABBIE I'm yewr wife.

CABOT   That hain't me. A son is me—my blood—mine. Mine ought t' git mine. An' then it's still mine—even though I be six foot under. D'ye see?

ABBIE   (*giving him a look of hatred*)   Ay-eh. I see. (*She becomes very thoughtful, her face growing shrewd, her eyes studying* CABOT *craftily.*)

CABOT   I'm gittin' old—ripe on the bough. (*then with a sudden forced reassurance*) Not but what I hain't a hard nut t' crack even yet—an' fur many a year t' come! By the Etarnal, I kin break most o' the young fellers' backs at any kind o' work any day o' the year!

ABBIE   (*suddenly*)   Mebbe the Lord'll give *us* a son.

CABOT   (*turns and stares at her eagerly*)   Ye mean—a son—t' me 'n' yew?

ABBIE   (*with a cajoling smile*)   Ye're a strong man yet, hain't ye? 'Tain't noways impossible, be it? We know that. Why d'ye stare so? Hain't ye never thought o' that afore? I been thinkin' o' it all along. Ay-eh—an' I been prayin' it'd happen, too.

CABOT   (*his face growing full of joyous pride and a sort of religious ecstasy*)   Ye been prayin', Abbie?—fur a son?—t' us?

ABBIE   Ay-eh. (*with a grim resolution*) I want a son now.

CABOT   (*excitedly clutching both of her hands in his*)   It'd be the blessin' o' God, Abbie—the blessin' o' God A'mighty on me—in my old age—in my lonesomeness! They hain't nothin' I wouldn't do fur ye then, Abbie. Ye'd hev on'y ask it—anythin' ye'd a mind t'!

ABBIE   (*interrupting*)   Would ye will the farm t' me then—t' me an' it ... ?

CABOT   (*vehemently*)   I'd do anythin' ye axed, I tell ye! I swar it! May I be everlastin' damned t' hell if I wouldn't! (*He sinks to his knees pulling her down with him. He trembles all over with the fervor of his hopes.*) Pray t' the Lord agen, Abbie. It's the Sabbath! I'll jine ye! Two prayers air better nor one. "An' God hearkened unto Rachel"! An' God hearkened unto Abbie! Pray, Abbie! Pray fur him to hearken! (*He bows his head, mumbling. She pretends to do likewise but gives him a side glance of scorn and triumph.*)

Scene 2

*About eight in the evening. The interior of the two bedrooms on the top floor is shown—*EBEN *is sitting on the side of his bed in the room on the left. On account of the heat he has taken off everything but his undershirt and pants. His feet are bare. He faces front, brooding moodily, his chin propped on his hands, a desperate expression on his face.*

In the other room CABOT *and* ABBIE *are sitting side by side on the edge of their bed, an old four-poster with feather mattress. He is in his night shirt, she in her nightdress. He is still in the queer, excited mood into which the notion of a son has thrown him. Both rooms are lighted dimly and flickeringly by tallow candles.*

CABOT   The farm needs a son.

ABBIE   I need a son.

CABOT   Ay-eh. Sometimes ye air the farm an' sometimes the farm be yew. That's why I clove t' ye in my lonesomeness. (*A pause. He pounds his knee with his fist.*) Me an' the farm has got t' beget a son!

ABBIE   Ye'd best go t' sleep. Ye're gittin' thin's all mixed.

CABOT   (*with an impatient gesture*) No, I hain't. My mind's clear's a bell. Ye don't know me, that's it. (*He stares hopelessly at the floor.*)

ABBIE   (*indifferently*)   Mebbe. (*In the next room* EBEN *gets up and paces up and down distractedly.* ABBIE *hears him. Her eyes fasten on the intervening wall with concentrated attention.* EBEN *stops and stares. Their hot glances seem to meet through the wall. Unconsciously he stretches out his arms for her and she half rises. Then aware, he mutters a curse at himself and flings himself face downward on the bed, his clenched fists above his head, his face buried in the pillow.* ABBIE *relaxes with a faint sigh but her eyes remain fixed on the wall; she listens with all her attention for some movement from* EBEN.)

CABOT   (*suddenly raises his head and looks at her—scornfully*)   Will ye ever know me—'r will any man 'r woman? (*Shaking his head*) No. I calc'late 't wa'n't t' be. (*He turns away.* ABBIE *looks at the wall. Then, evidently unable to keep silent about his thoughts, without looking at his wife, he puts out his hand and clutches her knee. She starts violently, looks at him, sees he is not watching her, concentrates again on the wall and pays no attention to what he says.*) Listen, Abbie. When I come here fifty odd year ago—I was jest twenty an' the strongest an' hardest ye ever seen—ten times as strong an' fifty times as hard as Eben. Waal—this place was nothin' but fields o' stones. Folks laughed when I tuk it. They couldn't know what I knowed. When he kin make corn sprout out o' stones, God's livin' in yew! They wa'n't strong enuf fur that! They reckoned God was easy. They laughed. They don't laugh no more. Some died hereabouts. Some went West an' died. They're all under ground—fur follerin' arter an easy God. God hain't easy. (*He shakes his head slowly.*) An' I growed hard. Folks kept allus sayin' he's a hard man like 'twas sinful t' be hard, so's at last I said back at 'em: Waal then, by thunder, ye'll git me hard an' see how ye like it! (*Then suddenly*) But I give in t' weakness once. 'Twas arter I'd been here two year. I got weak—despairful—they was so many stones. They was a party leavin', givin' up, goin' West. I jined 'em. We tracked on 'n' on. We come t' broad medders, plains, whar the soil was black an' rich as gold. Nary a stone. Easy. Ye'd on'y to plow an' sow an' then set an' smoke yer pipe an' watch thin's grow. I could o' been a rich man—but somethin' in me fit me an' fit me—the voice o' God sayin': "This hain't wuth nothin' t' Me. Get ye back t' hum!" I got afeerd o' that voice an' I lit out back t' hum here, leavin' my claim an' crops t' whoever'd a mind t' take 'em. Ay-eh. I actolly give up what was rightful mine! God's hard, not easy! God's in the stones! Build my church on a rock—out o' stones an' I'll be in them! That's what He meant t' Peter! (*He sighs heavily —a pause*) Stones. I picked 'em up an' piled 'em into walls. Ye kin read the years o' my life in them walls, every day a hefted stone, climbin' over the hills up and down, fencin' in the fields that was mine, whar I'd made thin's grow out o' nothin'—like the will o' God, like the servant o' His hand. It wa'n't easy. It was hard an' He made me hard fur it. (*He pauses.*) All the time I kept gittin' lonesomer. I tuk a wife. She bore Simeon an' Peter. She was a good woman. She wuked hard. We was married twenty year. She never knowed me. She helped but she never knowed what she was helpin'. I was allus lonesome. She died. After that it wa'n't so lonesome fur a spell. (*a pause*) I lost count o' the years. I had no time t' fool away countin' 'em. Sim an' Peter helped. The farm growed. It was all mine! When I thought o' that I didn't feel lonesome. (*a pause*) But ye can't hitch yer mind t' one thin' day an' night. I tuk another wife—Eben's Maw. Her folks was contestin' me at law over my deeds t' the farm—my farm! That's why Eben keeps a'talkin' his fool talk o' this bein' his Maw's farm. She bore Eben. She was purty—but soft. She tried t' be hard. She couldn't. She never knowed me nor nothin'. It was lonesomer 'n hell with her. After a matter o' sixteen odd years, she died. (*a pause*) I lived with the boys. They hated me 'cause I was hard. I hated them 'cause they was soft. They coveted the farm without knowin' what it meant. It made me bitter 'n wormwood. It aged me—them coveting what I'd made fur mine. Then this spring the call come—the voice o' God cryin' in my wilderness, in my lonesomeness—t' go out an' seek an' find! (*Turning to her with strange passion*) I sought ye an' I found ye! Yew air my Rose o' Sharon! Yer eyes air like.... (*She has turned a *blank face, resentful eyes to his. He stares at her for a moment—then harshly*) Air ye any the wiser fur all I've told ye?

ABBIE (*confusedly*)   Mebbe.

CABOT (*pushing her away from him—angrily*)   Ye don't know nothin'—nor never will. If ye don't hev a son t' redeem ye . . . (*this in a tone of cold threat*)

ABBIE (*resentfully*)   I've prayed, hain't I?

CABOT (*bitterly*)   Pray agen—fur understandin'!

ABBIE (*a veiled threat in her tone*)   Ye'll have a son out o' me, I promise ye.

CABOT   How kin ye promise?

ABBIE   I got second-sight mebbe. I kin foretell. (*She gives a queer smile.*)

CABOT   I believe ye have. Ye give me the chills sometimes. (*He shivers.*) It's cold in this house. It's oneasy. They's thin's pokin' about in the dark—in the corners. (*He pulls on his trousers, tucking in his night shirt, and pulls on his boots.*)

ABBIE (*surprised*)   Whar air ye goin'?

CABOT (*queerly*)   Down whar it's restful—whar it's warm—down t' the barn. (*bitterly*) I kin talk t' the cows. They know. They know the farm an' me. They'll give me peace. (*He turns to go out the door.*)

ABBIE (*a bit frightenedly*)   Air ye ailin' tonight, Ephraim?

CABOT   Growin'. Growin' ripe on the bough. (*He turns and goes, his boots clumping down the stairs. EBEN sits up with a start, listening. ABBIE is conscious of his movement and stares at the wall. CABOT comes out of the house around the corner and stands by the gate, blinking at the sky. He stretches up his hands in a tortured gesture*) God A'mighty, call from the dark! (*He listens as if expecting an answer. Then his arms drop, he shakes his head and plods off toward the barn. EBEN and ABBIE stare at each other through the wall. EBEN sighs heavily and ABBIE echoes it. Both become terribly nervous, uneasy. Finally ABBIE gets up and listens, her ear to the wall. He acts as if he saw every move she was making, he becomes resolutely still. She seems driven into a decision—goes out the door in rear determinedly. His eyes follow her. Then as the door of his room is opened softly, he turns away, waits in an attitude of strained fixity. ABBIE stands for a second staring at him, her eyes burning with desire. Then with a little cry she runs over and throws her arms about his neck, she pulls his head back and covers his mouth with kisses. At first, he submits dumbly; then he puts his arms about her neck and returns her kisses, but finally, suddenly aware of his hatred, he hurls her*

*away from him, springing to his feet. They stand speechless and
breathless, panting like two animals.*)

ABBIE (*at last—painfully*) Ye shouldn't, Eben—ye shouldn't—I'd
make ye happy!

EBEN (*harshly*) I don't want t' be happy—from yew!

ABBIE (*helplessly*) Ye do, Eben! Ye do! Why d'ye lie?

EBEN (*viciously*) I don't take t'ye, I tell ye! I hate the sight o' ye!

ABBIE (*with an uncertain troubled laugh*) Waal, I kissed ye anyways—an' ye kissed back—yer lips was burnin'—ye can't lie
'bout that! (*intensely*) If ye don't care, why did ye kiss me back
—why was yer lips burnin'?

EBEN (*wiping his mouth*) It was like pizen on 'em (*then tauntingly*) When I kissed ye back, mebbe I thought 'twas someone
else.

ABBIE (*wildly*) Min?

EBEN Mebbe.

ABBIE (*torturedly*) Did ye go t' see her? Did ye r'ally go? I thought
ye mightn't. Is that why ye throwed me off jest now?

EBEN (*sneeringly*) What if it be?

ABBIE (*raging*) Then ye're a dog, Eben Cabot!

EBEN (*threateningly*) Ye can't talk that way t' me!

ABBIE (*with a shrill laugh*) Can't I? Did ye think I was in love
with ye—a weak thin' like yew? Not much! I on'y wanted ye
fur a purpose o' my own—an' I'll hev ye fur it yet 'cause I'm
stronger'n yew be!

EBEN (*resentfully*) I knowed well it was on'y part o' yer plan t'
swaller everythin'!

ABBIE (*taughtingly*) Mebbe!

EBEN (*furious*) Git out o' my room!

ABBIE This air my room an' ye're on'y hired help!

EBEN (*threateningly*) Git out afore I murder ye!

ABBIE (*quite confident now*) I hain't a mite afeerd. Ye want me,
don't ye? Yes, ye do! An' yer Paw's son'll never kill what he
wants! Look at yer eyes! They's lust fur me in 'em, burnin' 'em
up! Look at yer lips now! They're tremblin' an' longin' t' kiss me,
an' yer teeth t'bite! (*He is watching her now with a horrible fascination. She laughs a crazy triumphant laugh.*) I'm a-goin' t'
make all o' this hum my hum! They's one room hain't mine yet,
but it's a-goin' t' be tonight. I'm a-goin' down now an' light up!
(*She makes him a mocking bow.*) Won't ye come courtin' me in
the best parlor, Mister Cabot?

EBEN (*staring at her—horribly confused—dully*) Don't ye dare! It
hain't been opened since Maw died an' was laid out thar! Don't

ye ... ! (*But her eyes are fixed on his so burningly that his will seems to wither before hers. He stands swaying toward her help-lessly.*)

ABBIE (*holding his eyes and putting all her will into her words as she backs out the door*)   I'll expect ye afore long, Eben.

EBEN (*stares after her for a while, walking toward the door. A light appears in the parlor window. He murmurs*)   In the parlor? (*This seems to arouse connotations for he comes back and puts on his white shirt, collar, half ties the tie mechanically, puts on coat, takes his hat, stands barefooted looking about him in bewilder-ment, mutters wonderingly*)   Maw! Whar air yew? (*Then goes slowly toward the door in rear.*)

Scene 3

A few minutes later. The interior of the parlor is shown. A grim, repressed room like a tomb in which the family has been interred alive. ABBIE sits on the edge of the horsehair sofa. She has lighted all the candles and the room is revealed in all its preserved ugliness. A change has come over the woman. She looks awed and frightened now, ready to run away.

The door is opened and EBEN appears. His face wears an expression of obsessed confusion. He stands staring at her, his arms hanging disjoint-edly from his shoulders, his feet bare, his hat in his hand.

ABBIE (*after a pause—with a nervous, formal politeness*)   Won't ye set?

EBEN (*dully*)   Ay-eh. (*Mechanically he places his hat carefully on the floor near the door and sits stiffly beside her on the edge of the sofa. A pause. They both remain rigid, looking straight ahead with eyes full of fear.*)

ABBIE   When I fust came in—in the dark—they seemed somethin' here.

EBEN (*simply*)   Maw.

ABBIE   I kin still feel—somethin'. . . .

EBEN   It's Maw.

ABBIE   At fust I was feered o' it. I wanted t' yell an' run. Now—since yew come—seems like it's growin' soft an' kind t' me. (*Ad-dressing the air—queerly*)   Thank yew.

EBEN   Maw allus loved me.

ABBIE   Mebbe it knows I love yew too. Mebbe that makes it kind t' me.

EBEN (*dully*)   I dunno. I should think she'd hate ye.

ABBIE (*with certainty*)   No. I kin feel it don't—not no more.

EBEN   Hate yer fur stealin' her place—here in her hum—settin' in her parlor whar she was laid— (*He suddenly stops, staring stu-pidly before him.*)

ABBIE   What is it, Eben?

EBEN   (*in a whisper*)   Seems like Maw didn't want me t' remind ye.

ABBIE   (*excitedly*)   I knowed, Eben! It's kind t' me! It don't b'ar me no grudges fur what I never knowed an' couldn't help!

EBEN   Maw b'ars him a grudge.

ABBIE   Waal, so does all o' us.

EBEN   Ay-eh. (*with passion*)   I does, by God!

ABBIE   (*taking one of his hands in hers and patting it*)   Thar! Don't git riled thinkin' o' him. Think o' yer Maw who's kind t' us. Tell me about yer Maw, Eben.

EBEN   They hain't nothin' much. She was kind. She was good.

ABBIE   (*putting one arm over his shoulder. He does not seem to notice—passionately*)   I'll be kind an' good t' ye!

EBEN   Sometimes she used t' sing fur me.

ABBIE   I'll sing fur ye!

EBEN   This was her hum. This was her farm.

ABBIE   This is my hum! This is my farm!

EBEN   He married her t' steal 'em. She was soft an' easy. He couldn't 'preciate her.

ABBIE   He can't 'preciate me!

EBEN   He murdered her with his hardness.

ABBIE   He's murderin' me!

EBEN   She died. (*a pause*) Sometimes she used to sing fur me. (*He bursts into a fit of sobbing.*)

ABBIE   (*both arms around him—with wild passion*)   I'll sing fur ye! I'll die fur ye! (*In spite of her overwhelming desire for him, there is a sincere maternal love in her manner and voice—a horribly frank mixture of lust and mother love.*) Don't cry, Eben! I'll take yer Maw's place! I'll be everythin' she was t' ye! Let me kiss ye, Eben! (*She pulls his head around. He makes a bewildered pretense of resistance. She is tender.*) Don't be afeered! I'll kiss ye pure, Eben—same 's if I was a Maw t' ye—an' ye kin kiss me back 's if yew was my son—my boy—sayin' goodnight t' me! Kiss me, Eben. (*They kiss in restrained fashion. Then suddenly wild passion overcomes her. She kisses him lustfully again and again and he flings his arms about her and returns her kisses. Suddenly, as in the bedroom, he frees himself from her violently and springs to his feet. He is trembling all over, in a strange state of terror. ABBIE strains her arms toward him with fierce pleading.*) Don't ye leave me, Eben! Can't ye see it hain't enuf—lovin' ye like a Maw —can't ye see it's got t' be that an' more—much more—a hundred times more—fur me t' be happy—fur yew t' be happy?

EBEN   (*to the presence he feels in the room*)   Maw! Maw! What d'ye want? What air ye tellin' me?

ABBIE She's tellin' ye t' love me. She knows I love ye an' I'll be good t' ye. Can't ye feel it? Don't ye know? She's tellin' ye t' love me, Eben!

EBEN Ah-eh. I feel—mebbe she—but—I can't figger out—why—when ye've stole her place—here in her hum—in the parlor whar she was—

ABBIE (*fiercely*) She knows I love ye!

EBEN (*his face suddenly lighting up with a fierce triumphant grin*) I see it! I sees why. It's her vengeance on him—so's she kin rest quiet in her grave!

ABBIE (*wildly*) Vengeance o' God on the hull o' us! What d'we give a durn? I love ye, Eben! God knows I love ye! (*She stretches out her arms for him.*)

EBEN (*throws himself on his knees beside the sofa and grabs her in his arms—releasing all his pent-up passion*) An' I love yew, Abbie!—now I kin say it! I been dyin' fur want o' ye—every hour since ye come! I love ye! (*Their lips meet in a fierce, bruising kiss.*)

Scene 4

Exterior of the farmhouse. It is just dawn. The front door at right is opened.

EBEN *comes out and walks around to the gate. He is dressed in his working clothes. He seems changed. His face wears a bold and confident expression, he is grinning to himself with evident satisfaction. As he gets near the gate, the window of the parlor is heard opening and the shutters are flung back and* ABBIE *sticks her head out. Her hair tumbles over her shoulders in disarray, her face is flushed, she looks at* EBEN *with tender, languorous eyes and calls softly.*

ABBIE Eben. (*As he turns—playfully*) Jest one more kiss afore ye go. I'm goin' to miss ye fearful all day.

EBEN An' me yew, ye kin bet! (*He goes to her. They kiss several times. He draws away, laughingly.*) Thar. That's enuf, hain't it? Ye won't hev none left fur next time.

ABBIE I got a million o' 'em left fur yew! (*then a bit anxiously*) D'ye r'ally love me, Eben?

EBEN (*emphatically*) I like ye better'n any gal I ever knowed! That's gospel!

ABBIE Likin' hain't lovin'.

EBEN Waal then—I love ye. Now air yew satisfied?

ABBIE Ay-eh, I be. (*She smiles at him adoringly.*)

EBEN I better git t' the barn. The old critter's liable t' suspicion an' come sneakin' up.

ABBIE (*with a confident laugh*) Let him! I kin allus pull the wool over his eyes. I'm goin' t' leave the shutters open and let in the sun 'n' air. This room's been dead long enuf. Now it's goin' t' be my room!

EBEN (*frowning*) Ay-eh.

ABBIE We made it our'n last night, didn't we? We give it life— our lovin' did. (*a pause*)

EBEN (*with a strange look*) Maw's gone back t' her grave. She kin sleep now.

ABBIE May she rest in peace! (*then tenderly rebuking*) Ye oughtn't t' talk o' sad thin's—this mornin'.

EBEN It jest come up in my mind o' itself.

ABBIE Don't let it. (*He doesn't answer. She yawns.*) Waal, I'm a-goin' t' steal a wink o' sleep. I'll tell the Old Man I hain't feelin' pert. Let him git his own vittles.

EBEN I see him comin' from the barn. Ye better look smart an' git upstairs.

ABBIE Ay-eh. Good-by. Don't fergit me. (*She throws him a kiss. He grins—then squares his shoulders and awaits his father confidently.* CABOT *walks slowly up from the left, staring up at the sky with a vague face.*)

EBEN (*jovially*) Mornin', Paw. Star-gazin' in daylight?

CABOT Purty, hain't it?

EBEN (*looking around him possessively*) It's a durned purty farm.

CABOT I mean the sky.

EBEN (*grinning*) How d'ye know? Them eyes o' your'n can't see that fur. (*This tickles his humor and he slaps his thigh and laughs.*) Ho-ho! That's a good un!

CABOT (*grimly sarcastic*) Ye're feelin' right chipper, hain't ye? Whar'd ye steal the likker?

EBEN (*good-naturedly*) 'Taint likker. Jest life. (*Suddenly holding out his hand—soberly*) Yew 'n' me is quits. Let's shake hands.

CABOT (*suspiciously*) What's come over ye?

EBEN Then don't. Mebbe it's jest as well. (*a moment's pause*) What's come over me? (*queerly*) Didn't ye feel her passin'— goin' back t' her grave?

CABOT (*dully*) Who?

EBEN Maw. She kin rest now an' sleep content. She's quit with ye.

CABOT (*confusedly*) I rested. I slept good—down with the cows. They know how t' sleep. They're teachin' me.

EBEN (*suddenly jovial again*) Good fur the cows! Waal—ye better git t' work.

CABOT (*grimly amused*) Air yew bossin' me, ye calf?

EBEN (*beginning to laugh*) Ah-eh! I'm bossin' yew! Ha-ha-ha! see how ye like it! Ha-ha-ha! I'm the prize rooster o' this roost. Ha-ha-ha! (*He goes off toward the barn laughing.*)

CABOT (*looks after him with scornful pity*) Soft-headed. Like his Maw. Dead spit 'n' image. No hope in him! (*He spits with contemptuous disgust.*) A born fool! (*Then matter-of-factly*) Waal —I'm gittin' peckish. (*He goes toward door.*)

PART III

Scene 1

A night in late spring the following year. The kitchen and the two bedrooms upstairs are shown. The two bedrooms are dimly lighted by a tallow candle in each. EBEN *is sitting on the side of the bed in his room, his chin propped on his fists, his face a study of the struggle he is making to understand his conflicting emotions. The noisy laughter and music from below where a kitchen dance is in progress annoy and distract him. He scowls at the floor. In the next room a cradle stands beside the double bed.*

In the kitchen all is festivity. The stove has been taken down to give more room to the dancers. The chairs, with wooden benches added, have been pushed back against the walls. On these are seated, squeezed in tight against one another, farmers and their wives and their young folks of both sexes from the neighboring farms. They are all chattering and laughing loudly. They evidently have some secret joke in common. There is no end of winking, of nudging, of meaning nods of the head toward CABOT *who, in a state of extreme hilarious excitement increased by the amount he has drunk, is standing near the rear door where there is a small keg of whisky and serving drinks to all the men. In the left corner, front, dividing the attention with her husband,* ABBIE *is sitting in a rocking chair, a shawl wrapped about her shoulders. She is very pale, her face is thin and drawn, her eyes are fixed anxiously on the open door in rear as if waiting for someone.*

The MUSICIAN *is tuning up his fiddle, seated in the far right corner. He is a lanky young fellow with a long, weak face. His pale eyes blink incessantly and he grins about him slyly with a greedy malice.*

ABBIE (*suddenly turning to a young girl on her right*) Whar's Eben?

YOUNG GIRL (*eying her scornfully*) I dunno, Mrs. Cabot. I hain't seen Eben in ages. (*meaningly*) Seems like he's spent most o' his time t' hum since yew come.

ABBIE (*vaguely*) I tuk his Maw's place.

YOUNG GIRL Ay-eh. So I've heerd. (*She turns away to retail this bit of gossip to her mother sitting next to her.* ABBIE *turns to her left to a big stoutish middle-aged man whose flushed face and staring eyes show the amount of "likker" he has consumed.*)

ABBIE Ye hain't seen Eben, hev ye?

MAN No, I hain't. (*then he adds with a wink*) If yew hain't, who would?

ABBIE He's the best dancer in the county. He'd ought t' come an' dance.

MAN (*with a wink*) Mebbe he's doin' the dutiful an' walkin' the kid t' sleep. It's a boy, hain't it?

ABBIE (*nodding vaguely*) Ay-eh—born two weeks back—purty's a picter.

MAN They all is—t' their Maws. (*then in a whisper, with a nudge and a leer*) Listen, Abbie—if ye ever git tired o' Eben, remember me! Don't fergit now! (*He looks at her uncomprehending face for a second—then grunts disgustedly.*) Waal—guess I'll likker agin. (*He goes over and joins* CABOT *who is arguing noisily with an old farmer over cows. They all drink.*)

ABBIE (*this time appealing to nobody in particular*) Wonder what Eben's a-doin'? (*Her remark is repeated down the line with many a guffaw and titter until it reaches the fiddler. He fastens his blinking eyes on* ABBIE.)

FIDDLER (*raising his voice*) Bet I kin tell ye, Abbie, what Eben's doin'! He's down t' the church offerin' up prayers o' thanksgivin'. (*They all titter expectantly.*)

MAN What fur? (*Another titter.*)

FIDDLER 'Cause unto him a—(*He hesitates just long enough.*)— brother is born! (*A roar of laughter. They all look from* ABBIE *to* CABOT. *She is oblivious, staring at the door.* CABOT, *although he hasn't heard the words, is irritated by the laughter and steps forward, glaring about him. There is an immediate silence.*)

CABOT What're ye all bleatin' about—like a flock o' goats? Why don't ye dance, damn ye? I axed ye here t' dance—t' eat, drink an' be merry—an' thar ye set cacklin' like a lot o' wet hens with the pip! Ye've swilled my likker an' guzzled my vittles like hogs, hain't ye? Then dance fur me, can't ye? That's fa'r an' squar', hain't it? (*A grumble of resentment goes around but they are all evidently in too much awe of him to express it openly.*)

FIDDLER (*slyly*) We're waitin' fur Eben. (*a suppressed laugh*)

CABOT (*with a fierce exultation*) T'hell with Eben! Eben's done fur now! I got a new son! (*his mood switching with drunken suddenness*) But ye needn't t' laugh at Eben, none o' ye! He's my blood, if he be a dumb fool. He's better nor any o' yew! He kin do a day's work a'most up t' what I kin—an' that'd put any o' yew pore critters t' shame!

FIDDLER An' he kin do a good night's work, too! (*a roar of laughter*)

CABOT   Laugh, ye damn fools! Ye're right jist the same, Fiddler. He kin work day an' night too, like I kin, if need be!

OLD FARMER *(from behind the keg where he is weaving drunkenly back and forth—with great simplicity)* They hain't many t' touch ye, Ephraim—a son at seventy-six. That's a hard man fur ye! I be on'y sixty-eight an' I couldn't do it. *(a roar of laughter in which* CABOT *joins uproariously)*

CABOT *(slapping him on the back)* I'm sorry fur ye, Hi. I'd never suspicion sech weakness from a boy like yew!

OLD FARMER   An' I never reckoned yew had it in ye nuther, Ephraim. *(There is another laugh.)*

CABOT *(suddenly grim)* I got a lot in me—a hell of a lot—folks don't know on. *(turning to the* FIDDLER*)* Fiddle 'er up, durn ye! Give 'em somethin' t' dance t'! What air ye, an ornament? Hain't this a celebration? Then grease yer elbow an' go it!

FIDDLER *(seizes a drink which the* OLD FARMER *holds out to him and downs it)* Here goes! *(He starts to fiddle "Lady of the Lake." Four young fellows and four girls form in two lines and dance a square dance. The* FIDDLER *shouts directions for the different movements, keeping his words in the rhythm of the music and interspersing them with jocular personal remarks to the dancers themselves. The people seated along the walls stamp their feet and clap their hands in unison.* CABOT *is especially active in this respect. Only* ABBIE *remains apathetic, staring at the door as if she were alone in a silent room.)*

FIDDLER   Swing your partner t' the right! That's it, Jim! Give her a b'ar hug! Her Maw hain't lookin'. *(laughter)* Change partners! That suits ye, don't it, Essie, now ye got Reub afore ye? Look at her redden up, will ye! Waal, life is short an' so's love, as the feller says. *(laughter)*

CABOT *(excitedly, stamping his foot)* Go it, boys! Go it, gals!

FIDDLER *(with a wink at the others)* Ye're the spryest seventy-six ever I sees, Ephraim! Now if ye'd on'y good eye-sight . . . ! *(Suppressed laughter. He gives* CABOT *no chance to retort but roars)* Promenade! Ye're walkin' like a bride down the aisle, Sarah! Waal, while they's life they's allus hope, I've heerd tell. Swing your partner to the left! Gosh A'mighty, look at Johnny Cook high-steppin'! They hain't goin' t'be much strength left fur howin' in the corn lot t'morrow. *(laughter)*

CABOT   Go it! Go it! *(Then suddenly, unable to restrain himself any longer, he prances into the midst of the dancers, scattering them, waving his arms about wildly.)* Ye're all hoofs! Git out o' my road! Give me room! I'll show ye dancin'. Ye're all too soft!

(*He pushes them roughly away. They crowd back toward the walls, muttering, looking at him resentfully.*)

FIDDLER (*jeeringly*) Go it, Ephraim! Go it! (*He starts "Pop Goes the Weasel," increasing the tempo with every verse until at the end he is fiddling crazily as fast as he can go.*)

CABOT (*starts to dance, which he does very well and with tremendous vigor. Then he begins to improvise, cuts incredibly grotesque capers, leaping up and cracking his heels together, prancing around in a circle with body bent in an Indian war dance, then suddenly straightening up and kicking as high as he can with both legs. He is like a monkey on a string. And all the while he intersperses his antics with shouts and derisive comments*) Whoop! Here's dancin' fur ye! Whoop! See that! Seventy-six, if I'm a day! Hard as iron yet! Beatin' the young 'uns like I allus done! Look at me! I'd invite ye t' dance on my hundredth birthday on'y ye'll all be dead by then. Ye're a sickly generation! Yer hearts air pink, not red! Yer veins is full o' mud an' water! I be the on'y man in the county! Whoop! See that! I'm a Injun! I've killed Injuns in the West afore ye was born—an' skulped 'em too! They's a arrer wound on my backside I c'd show ye! The hull tribe chased me. I outrun 'em all—with the arrer stuck in me! An' I tuk vengeance on 'em. Ten eyes fur an eye, that was my motter! Whoop! Look at me! I kin kick the ceilin' off the room! Whoop!

FIDDLER (*stops playing—exhaustedly*) God A'mighty, I got enuf. Ye got the devil's strength in ye.

CABOT (*delightedly*) Did I beat yew, too? Wa'al, ye played smart. Hev a swig. (*He pours whisky for himself and* FIDDLER. *They drink. The others watch* CABOT *silently with cold, hostile eyes. There is a dead pause. The* FIDDLER *rests.* CABOT *leans against the keg, panting, glaring around him confusedly. In the room above,* EBEN *gets to his feet and tiptoes out the door in rear, appearing a moment later in the other bedroom. He moves silently, even frightenedly, toward the cradle and stands there looking down at the baby. His face is as vague as his reactions are confused, but there is a trace of tenderness, of interested discovery. At the same moment that he reaches the cradle,* ABBIE *seems to sense something. She gets up weakly and goes to* CABOT.)

ABBIE I'm goin' up t' the baby.

CABOT (*with real solicitude*) Air ye able fur the stairs? D'ye want me t' help ye, Abbie?

ABBIE No. I'm able. I'll be down agen soon.

CABOT Don't ye git wore out! He needs ye, remember—our son

does! (*He grins affectionately, patting her on the back. She shrinks from his touch.*)

ABBIE (*dully*) Don't—tech me. I'm goin'—up. (*She goes.* CABOT *looks after her. A whisper goes around the room.* CABOT *turns. It ceases. He wipes his forehead streaming with sweat. He is breathing pantingly.*)

CABOT I'm a-goin' out t' git fresh air. I'm feelin' a mite dizzy. Fiddle up thar! Dance, all o' ye! Here's likker fur them as wants it. Enjoy yerselves. I'll be back. (*He goes, closing the door behind him.*)

FIDDLER (*sarcastically*) Don't hurry none on our account! (*A suppressed laugh. He imitates* ABBIE.) Whar's Eben? (*more laughter*)

A WOMAN (*loudly*) What's happened in this house is plain as the nose on yer face! (ABBIE *appears in the doorway upstairs and stands looking in surprise and adoration at* EBEN *who does not see her.*)

A MAN Ssshh! He's li'ble t' be listenin' at the door. That'd be like him. (*Their voices die to an intensive whispering. Their faces are concentrated on this gossip. A noise as of dead leaves in the wind comes from the room.* CABOT *has come out from the porch and stands by the gate, leaning on it, staring at the sky blinkingly.* ABBIE *comes across the room silently.* EBEN *does not notice her until quite near.*)

EBEN (*starting*) Abbie!

ABBIE Ssshh! (*She throws her arms around him. They kiss—then bend over the cradle together.*) Ain't he purty?—dead spit 'n' image o' yew!

EBEN (*pleased*) Air he? I can't tell none.

ABBIE E-zactly like!

EBEN (*frowningly*) I don't like this. I don't like lettin' on what's mine's his'n. I been doin' that all my life. I'm gittin' t' the end o' b'arin' it!

ABBIE (*putting her finger on his lips*) We're doin' the best we kin. We got t' wait. Somethin's bound t' happen. (*She puts her arms around him.*) I got t' go back.

EBEN I'm goin' out. I can't b'ar it with the fiddle playin' an' the laughin'.

ABBIE Don't git feelin' low. I love ye, Eben. Kiss me. (*He kisses her. They remain in each other's arms.*)

CABOT (*at the gate, confusedly*) Even the music can't drive it out —somethin'. Ye kin feel it droppin' off the elums, climbin' up the roof, sneakin' down the chimney, pokin' in the corners! They's no peace in houses, they's no rest livin' with folks. Somethin's always livin' with ye. (*with a deep sigh*) I'll go t' the barn an' rest a spell. (*He goes wearily toward the barn.*)

FIDDLER (*tuning up*) Let's celebrate the old skunk gittin' fooled! We kin have some fun now he's went. (*He starts to fiddle "Turkey in the Straw." There is real merriment now. The young folks get up to dance.*)

Scene 2

A half hour later—exterior.

EBEN *is standing by the gate looking up at the sky, an expression of dumb pain bewildered by itself on his face.* CABOT *appears, returning from the barn, walking wearily, his eyes on the ground. He sees* EBEN *and his whole mood immediately changes. He becomes excited, a cruel, triumphant grin comes to his lips, he strides up and slaps* EBEN *on the back. From within comes the whining of the fiddle and the noise of stamping feet and laughing voices.*

CABOT So har ye be!

EBEN (*startled, stares at him with hatred for a moment—then dully*) Ay-eh.

CABOT (*surveying him jeeringly*) Why hain't ye been in t' dance? They was all axin' fur ye.

EBEN Let 'em ax!

CABOT They's a hull pasel o' purty gals.

EBEN T' hell with 'em!

CABOT Ye'd ought t' be marryin' one o' 'em soon.

EBEN I hain't marryin' no one.

CABOT Ye might 'arn a share o' a farm that way.

EBEN (*with a sneer*) Like yew did, ye mean? I hain't that kind.

CABOT (*stung*) Ye lie! 'Twas yer Maw's folks aimed t' steal my farm from me.

EBEN Other folks don't say so. (*after a pause—defiantly*) An' I got a farm, anyways!

CABOT (*derisively*) Whar?

EBEN (*stamps a foot on the ground*) Har!

CABOT (*throws his head back and laughs coarsely*) Ho-ho! Ye hev, hev ye? Waal, that's a good un!

EBEN (*controlling himself—grimly*) Ye'll see!

CABOT (*stares at him suspiciously, trying to make him out—a pause —then with scornful confidence*) Ay-eh. I'll see. So'll ye. It's ye that's blind—blind as a mole underground. (EBEN *suddenly laughs, one short sardonic bark: "Ha." A pause.* CABOT *peers at him with renewed suspicion.*) Whar air ye hawin' 'bout? (EBEN *turns away without answering.* CABOT *grows angry.*) God

A'mighty, yew air a dumb dunce! They's nothin' in that thick skull o' your'n but noise—like a empty keg it be! (EBEN *doesn't seem to hear*—CABOT's *rage grows.*) Yewr farm! God A'mighty! If ye wa'n't a born donkey ye'd know ye'll never own stick nor stone on it, specially now arter him bein' born. It's his'n, I tell ye —his'n arter I die—but I'll live a hundred jest t' fool ye all—an' he'll be growed then—yewr age a'most! (EBEN *laughs again his sardonic "Ha." This drives* CABOT *into a fury.*) Ha? Ye think ye kin git 'round that someways, do ye? Waal, it'll be her'n, too— Abbie's—ye won't git 'round her—she knows yer tricks—she'll be too much fur ye—she wants the farm her'n—she was afeerd o' ye—she told me ye was sneakin' 'round tryin' t' make love t' her t' git her on yer side ... ye ... ye mad fool, ye! (*He raises his clenched fists threateningly.*)

EBEN (*is confronting him choking with rage*) Ye lie, ye old skunk! Abbie never said no sech thing!

CABOT (*suddenly triumphant when he sees how shaken* EBEN *is*) She did. An' I says, I'll blow his brains t' the top o' them elums— an' she says no, that hain't sense, who'll ye git t'help ye on the farm in his place—an' then she says yew'n me ought t' have a son—I know we kin, she says—an' I says, if we do, ye kin have anythin' I've got ye've a mind t'. An' she says, I wants Eben cut off so's this farm'll be mine when ye die! (*with terrible gloating*) An' that's what's happened, hain't it? An' the farm's her'n! An' the dust o' the road—that's you'rn! Ha! Now who's hawin'?

EBEN (*has been listening, petrified with grief and rage—suddenly laughs wildly and brokenly*) Ha-ha-ha! So that's her sneakin' game—all along!—like I suspicioned at fust—t' swaller it all— an' me, too ... ! (*madly*) I'll murder her! (*He springs toward the porch but* CABOT *is quicker and gets in between.*)

CABOT No, ye don't!

EBEN Git out o' my road! (*He tries to throw* CABOT *aside. They grapple in what becomes immediately a murderous struggle. The old man's concentrated strength is too much for* EBEN. CABOT *gets one hand on his throat and presses him back across the stone wall. At the same moment,* ABBIE *comes out on the porch. With a stifled cry she runs toward them.*)

ABBIE Eben! Ephraim! (*She tugs at the hand on* EBEN's *throat.*) Let go, Ephraim! Ye're chokin' him!

CABOT (*removes his hand and flings* EBEN *sideways full length on the grass, gasping and choking. With a cry,* ABBIE *kneels beside him, trying to take his head on her lap, but he pushes her away.* CABOT *stands looking down with fierce triumph*) Ye needn't t've fret, Abbie, I wa'n't aimin' t' kill him. He hain't wuth hangin' fur

—not by a hell of a sight! (*more and more triumphantly*) Seventy-six an' him not thirty yit—an' look whar he be fur thinkin' his Paw was easy! No, by God, I hain't easy! An' him upstairs, I'll raise him t' be like me! (*He turns to leave them.*) I'm goin' in an' dance!—sing an' celebrate! (*He walks to the porch—then turns with a great grin.*) I don't calc'late it's left in him, but if he gits pesky, Abbie, ye jest sing out. I'll come a-runnin' an' by the Etarnal, I'll put him across my knee an' birch him! Ha-ha-ha! (*He goes into the house laughing. A moment later his loud "whoop" is heard.*)

ABBIE (*tenderly*) Eben. Air ye hurt? (*She tries to kiss him but he pushes her violently away and struggles to a sitting position.*)

EBEN (*gaspingly*) T'hell—with ye!

ABBIE (*not believing her ears*) It's me, Eben—Abbie—don't ye know me?

EBEN (*glowering at her with hatred*) Ay-eh—I know ye—now! (*He suddenly breaks down, sobbing weakly.*)

ABBIE (*fearfully*) Eben—what's happened t' ye—why did ye look at me 's if ye hated me?

EBEN (*violently, between sobs and gasps*) I do hate ye! Ye're a whore—a damn trickin' whore!

ABBIE (*shrinking back horrified*) Eben! Ye don't know what ye're sayin'!

EBEN (*scrambling to his feet and following her—accusingly*) Ye're nothin' but a stinkin' passel o' lies! Ye've been lyin' t' me every word ye spoke, day an' night, since we fust—done it. Ye've kept sayin' ye loved me. . . .

ABBIE (*frantically*) I do love ye! (*She takes his hand but he flings hers away.*)

EBEN (*unheeding*) Ye've made a fool o' me—a sick, dumb fool—a-purpose! Ye've been on'y playin' yer sneakin', stealin' game all along—gittin' me t' lie with ye so's ye'd hev a son he'd think was his'n, an' makin' him promise he'd give ye the farm and let me eat dust, if ye did git him a son! (*staring at her with anguished, bewildered eyes*) They must be a devil livin' in ye! 'Tain't human t' be as bad as that be!

ABBIE (*stunned—dully*) He told yew . . . ?

EBEN Hain't it true? It hain't no good in yew lyin'.

ABBIE (*pleadingly*) Eben, listen—ye must listen—it was long ago —afore we done nothin'—yew was scornin' me—goin' t' see Min —when I was lovin' ye—an' I said it t' him t' git vengeance on ye!

EBEN (*unheedingly. With tortured passion*) I wish ye was dead! I wish I was dead along with ye afore this come! (*ragingly*) But

I'll git my vengeance too! I'll pray Maw t' come back t' help me
—t' put her cuss on yew an' him!

ABBIE (*brokenly*)   Don't ye, Eben! Don't ye! (*She throws herself
on her knees before him, weeping.*) I didn't mean t' do bad t'ye!
Fergive me, won't ye?

EBEN (*not seeming to hear her—fiercely*)   I'll git squar' with the
old skunk—an' yew! I'll tell him the truth 'bout the son he's so
proud o'! Then I'll leave ye here t' pizen each other—with Maw
comin' out o' her grave at nights—an' I'll go t' the gold fields
o' Californi-a whar Sim an' Peter be!

ABBIE (*terrified*)   Ye won't—leave me? Ye can't!

EBEN (*with fierce determination*)   I'm a-goin', I tell ye! I'll git
rich thar an' come back an' fight him fur the farm he stole—an'
I'll kick ye both out in the road—t' beg an' sleep in the woods—
an' yer son along with ye—t' starve an' die! (*He is hysterical at
the end.*)

ABBIE (*with a shudder—humbly*)   He's yewr son, too, Eben.

EBEN (*torturedly*)   I wish he never was born! I wish he'd die this
minit! I wish I'd never sot eyes on him! It's him—yew havin' him
—a-purpose t' steal—that's changed everythin'!

ABBIE (*gently*)   Did ye believe I loved ye—afore he come?

EBEN   Ay-eh—like a dumb ox!

ABBIE   An' ye don't believe no more?

EBEN   B'lieve a lyin' thief! Ha!

ABBIE (*shudders—then humbly*)   An did ye r'ally love me afore?

EBEN (*brokenly*)   Ay-eh—an' ye was trickin' me!

ABBIE   An' ye don't love me now!

EBEN (*violently*)   I hate ye, I tell ye!

ABBIE   An' ye're truly goin' West—goin' t' leave me—all account o'
him being born?

EBEN   I'm a-goin' in the mornin'—or may God strike me t' hell!

ABBIE (*after a pause—with a dreadful cold intensity—slowly*)   If
that's what his comin's done t' me—killin' yewr love—takin' yew
away—my on'y joy—the on'y joy I've ever knowed—like heaven
t' me—purtier'n heaven—then I hate him, too, even if I be his
Maw!

EBEN (*bitterly*)   Lies! Ye love him! He'll steal the farm fur ye!
(*brokenly*)   But 'tain't the farm so much—not no more—it's yew
foolin' me—gittin' me t' love ye—lyin' yew loved me—jest t' git
a son t' steal!

ABBIE (*distractedly*)   He won't steal! I'd kill him fust! I do love
ye! I'll prove t' ye . . . !

EBEN (*harshly*)   'Tain't no use lyin' no more. I'm deaf t' ye! (*He
turns away.*) I hain't seein' ye agen. Good-by!

ABBIE (*pale with anguish*)   Hain't ye even goin' t' kiss me—not once—arter all we loved?

EBEN (*in a hard voice*)   I hain't wantin' t' kiss ye never agen! I'm wantin' t' forgit I ever sot eyes on ye!

ABBIE   Eben!—ye mustn't—wait a spell—I want t' tell ye. . . .

EBEN   I'm a-goin' in t' git drunk. I'm a-goin' t' dance.

ABBIE (*clinging to his arm—with passionate earnestness*)   If I could make it—'s if he'd never come up between us—if I could prove t' ye I wa'n't schemin' t' steal from ye—so's everythin' could be jest the same with us, lovin' each other jest the same, kissin' an' happy the same's we've been happy afore he come— if I could do it—ye'd love me agen, wouldn't ye? Ye'd kiss me agen? Ye wouldn't never leave me, would ye?

EBEN (*moved*)   I calc'late not. (*Then shaking her hand off his arm —with a bitter smile*) But ye hain't God, be ye?

ABBIE (*exultantly*)   Remember ye've promised! (*Then with strange intensity*) Mebbe I kin take back one thin' God does!

EBEN (*peering at her*)   Ye're gittin' cracked, hain't ye? (*Then going towards door*) I'm a-goin' t' dance.

ABBIE (*calls after him intensely*)   I'll prove t' ye! I'll prove I love ye better'n. . . . (*He goes in the door, not seeming to hear. She remains standing where she is, looking after him—then she finishes desperately*) Better'n everythin' else in the world!

Scene 3

Just before dawn in the morning—shows the kitchen and CABOT's *bedroom.*

In the kitchen, by the light of a tallow candle on the table, EBEN *is sitting, his chin propped on his hands, his drawn face blank and expressionless. His carpetbag is on the floor beside him. In the bedroom, dimly lighted by a small whale-oil lamp,* CABOT *lies asleep.* ABBIE *is bending over the cradle, listening, her face full of terror yet with an undercurrent of desperate triumph. Suddenly, she breaks down and sobs, appears about to throw herself on her knees beside the cradle; but the old man turns restlessly, groaning in his sleep, and she controls herself, and shrinking away from the cradle with a gesture of horror, backs swiftly toward the door in rear and goes out. A moment later she comes into the kitchen and, running to* EBEN, *flings her arms about his neck and kisses him wildly. He hardens himself, he remains unmoved and cold, he keeps his eyes straight ahead.*

ABBIE (*hysterically*)   I done it, Eben! I told ye I'd do it! I've proved I love ye—better'n everythin'—so's ye can't never doubt me no more!

EBEN (*dully*)   Whatever ye done, it hain't no good now..

ABBIE (*wildly*)   Don't ye say that! Kiss me, Eben, won't ye? I need ye t' kiss me arter what I done! I need ye t' say ye love me!

EBEN (*kisses her without emotion—dully*)   That's fur good-by. I'm a-goin' soon.

ABBIE   No! No! Ye won't go—not now!

EBEN (*going on with his own thoughts*)   I been a-thinkin'—an' I hain't goin' t' tell Paw nothin'. I'll leave Maw t' take vengeance on ye. If I told him, the old skunk'd jest be stinkin' mean enuf to take it out on that baby. (*His voice showing emotion in spite of him*) An' I don't want nothin' bad t' happen t' him. He hain't t' blame fur yew. (*He adds with a certain queer pride*) An' he looks like me! An' by God, he's mine! An' some day I'll be a-comin' back an' . . . !

ABBIE (*too absorbed in her own thoughts to listen to him—pleadingly*)   They's no cause fur ye t' go now—they's no sense—it's all the same's it was—they's nothin' come b'tween us now—arter what I done!

EBEN (*something in her voice arouses him. He stares at her a bit frightenedly*)   Ye look mad, Abbie. What did ye do?

ABBIE   I—I killed him, Eben.

EBEN (*amazed*)   Ye killed him?

ABBIE (*dully*)   Ay-eh.

EBEN (*recovering from his astonishment—savagely*)   An' serves him right! But we got t' do somethin' quick t' make it look s'if the old skunk'd killed himself when he was drunk. We kin prove by 'em all how drunk he got.

ABBIE (*wildly*)   No! No! Not him! (*Laughing distractedly*) But that's what I ought t' done, hain't it? I oughter killed him instead! Why didn't ye tell me?

EBEN (*appalled*)   Instead? What d'ye mean?

ABBIE   Not him.

EBEN (*his face grown ghastly*)   Not—not that baby!

ABBIE (*dully*)   Ay-eh!

EBEN (*falls to his knees as if he'd been struck—his voice trembling with horror*)   Oh, God A'mighty! A'mighty God! Maw, whar was ye, why didn't ye stop her?

ABBIE (*simply*)   She went back t' her grave that night we fust done it, remember? I hain't felt her about since. (*A pause. EBEN hides his head in his hands, trembling all over as if he had the ague. She goes on dully*) I left the piller over his little face. Then he killed himself. He stopped breathin'. (*She begins to weep softly.*)

EBEN (*rage beginning to mingle with grief*)   He looked like me. He was mine, damn ye!

ABBIE (*slowly and brokenly*)   I didn't want t' do it. I hated myself fur doin' it. I loved him. He was so purty—dead spit 'n' image o' yew. But I loved yew more—an' yew was goin' away—far off whar I'd never see ye agen, never kiss ye, never feel ye pressed agin me agen—an' ye said ye hated me fur havin' him—ye said ye hated him an' wished he was dead—ye said if it hadn't been fur him comin' it'd be the same's afore between us.

EBEN (*unable to endure this, springs to his feet in a fury, threatening her, his twitching fingers seeming to reach out for her throat*) Ye lie! I never said—I never dreamed ye'd—I'd cut off my head afore I'd hurt his finger!

ABBIE (*piteously, sinking on her knees*) Eben, don't ye look at me like that—hatin' me—not after what I done fur ye—fur us—so's we could be happy agen—

EBEN (*furiously now*) Shut up, or I'll kill ye! I see yer game now —the same old sneakin' trick—ye're aimin' t' blame me fur the murder ye done!

ABBIE (*moaning—putting her hands over her ears*) Don't ye, Eben! Don't ye! (*She grasps his legs.*)

EBEN (*his mood suddenly changing to horror, shrinks away from her*) Don't ye tech me! Ye're pizen! How could ye—t' murder a pore little critter— Ye must've swapped yer soul t' hell! (*suddenly raging*) Ha! I kin see why ye done it! Not the lies ye jest told—but 'cause ye wanted t' steal agen—steal the last thin' ye'd left me—my part o' him—no, the hull o' him—ye saw he looked like me—ye knowed he was all mine—an' ye couldn't b'ar it—I know ye! Ye killed him fur bein' mine! (*All this has driven him almost insane. He makes a rush past her for the door—then turns —shaking both fists at her, violently.*) But I'll take vengeance now! I'll git the Sheriff! I'll tell him everythin'! Then I'll sing "I'm off to Californi-a!" an' go—gold—Golden Gate—gold sun —fields o' gold in the West! (*This last he half shouts, half croons incoherently, suddenly breaking off passionately.*) I'm a-goin' fur the Sheriff t' come an' git ye! I want ye tuk away, locked up from me! I can't stand t'luk at ye! Murderer an' thief 'r not, ye still tempt me! I'll give ye up t' the Sheriff! (*He turns and runs out, around the corner of house, panting and sobbing, and breaks into a swerving sprint down the road.*)

ABBIE (*struggling to her feet, runs to the door, calling after him*) I love ye, Eben! I love ye! (*She stops at the door weakly, swaying, about to fall.*) I don't care what ye do—if ye'll on'y love me agen—(*She falls limply to the floor in a faint.*)

Scene 4

About an hour later. Same as SCENE 3. *Shows the kitchen and* CABOT's *bedroom. It is after dawn. The sky is brilliant with the sunrise.*

In the kitchen, ABBIE *sits at the table, her body limp and exhausted, her head bowed down over her arms, her face hidden. Upstairs,* CABOT *is still asleep but awakens with a start. He looks toward the window and gives a snort of surprise and irritation—throws back the covers and begins hurriedly pulling on his clothes. Without looking behind him, he begins talking to* ABBIE *whom he supposes beside him.*

CABOT   Thunder 'n' lightnin', Abbie! I hain't slept this late in fifty year! Looks 's if the sun was full riz a'most. Must've been the dancin' an' likker. Must be gittin' old. I hope Eben's t' wuk. Ye might've tuk the trouble t' rouse me, Abbie. (*He turns—sees no one there—surprised.*) Waal—whar air she? Gittin' vittles, I calc'late. (*He tiptoes to the cradle and peers down—proudly*) Mornin', sonny. Purty's a picter! Sleepin' sound. He don't beller all night like most o' 'em. (*He goes quietly out the door in rear —a few moments later enters kitchen—sees* ABBIE—*with satisfaction*) So thar ye be. Ye got any vittles cooked?

ABBIE   (*without moving*)   No.

CABOT   (*coming to her, almost sympathetically*)   Ye feelin' sick?

ABBIE   No.

CABOT   (*pats her on shoulder. She shudders*)   Ye'd best lie down a spell. (*half jocularly*) Yer son'll be needin' ye soon. He'd ought t' wake up with a gnashin' appetite, the sound way he's sleepin'.

ABBIE   (*shudders—then in a dead voice*)   He ain't never goin' to wake up.

CABOT   (*jokingly*)   Takes after me this mornin'. I ain't slept so late in . . .

ABBIE   He's dead.

CABOT   (*stares at her—bewilderedly*)   What . . .

ABBIE   I killed him.

CABOT   (*stepping back from her—aghast*)   Air ye drunk—'r crazy —'r . . . !

ABBIE   (*suddenly lifts her head and turns on him—wildly*)   I killed him, I tell ye! I smothered him. Go up an' see if ye don't b'lieve me! (CABOT *stares at her a second, then bolts out the rear door, can be heard bounding up the stairs, and rushes into the bedroom and over to the cradle.* ABBIE *has sunk back lifelessly into her former position.* CABOT *puts his hand down on the body in the crib. An expression of fear and horror comes over his face.*)

CABOT   (*shrinking away—tremblingly*)   God A'mighty! God A'mighty. (*He stumbles out the door—in a short while returns to the kitchen—comes to* ABBIE, *the stunned expression still on his face—hoarsely*) Why did ye do it? Why? (*As she doesn't answer, he grabs her violently by the shoulder and shakes her.*) I ax ye why ye done it! Ye'd better tell me 'r . . . !

ABBIE (*gives him a furious push which sends him staggering back and springs to her feet—with wild rage and hatred*) Don't ye dare tech me! What right hev ye t' question me 'bout him? He wa'n't yewr son! Think I'd have a son by yew? I'd die fust! I hate the sight o' ye an' allus did! It's yew I should've murdered, if I'd had good sense! I hate ye! I love Eben. I did from the fust. An' he was Eben's son—mine an' Eben's—not your'n!

CABOT (*stands looking at her dazedly—a pause—finding his words with an effort—dully*) That was it—what I felt—pokin' round the corners—while ye lied—holdin' herself from me—sayin' ye'd a'ready conceived—(*He lapses into crushed silence—then with a strange emotion*) He's dead, sart'n. I felt his heart. Pore little critter! (*He blinks back one tear, wiping his sleeve across his nose.*)

ABBIE (*hysterically*) Don't ye! Don't ye! (*She sobs unrestrainedly.*)

CABOT (*with a concentrated effort that stiffens his body into a rigid line and hardens his face into a stony mask—through his teeth to himself*) I got t' be—like a stone—a rock o' jedgment! (*A pause. He gets complete control over himself—harshly*) If he was Eben's, I be glad he air gone! An' mebbe I suspicioned it all along. I felt they was somethin' onnateral—somewhars—the house got so lonesome—an' cold—drivin' me down t' the barn—t' the beasts o' the field.... Ay-eh. I must've suspicioned—somethin'. Ye didn't fool me—not altogether, leastways—I'm too old a bird —growin' ripe on the bough.... (*He becomes aware he is wandering, straightens again, looks at* ABBIE *with a cruel grin.*) So ye'd liked t' hev murdered me 'stead o' him, would ye? Waal, I'll live to a hundred! I'll live t' see ye hung! I'll deliver ye up t' the jedgment o' God an' the law! I'll git the Sheriff now. (*Starts for the door.*)

ABBIE (*dully*) Ye needn't. Eben's gone fur him.

CABOT (*amazed*) Eben—gone fur the Sheriff?

ABBIE Ay-eh.

CABOT T' inform agen ye?

ABBIE Ay-eh.

CABOT (*considers this—a pause—then in a hard voice*) Waal, I'm thankful fur him savin' me the trouble. I'll git t' wuk. (*He goes to the door—then turns—in a voice full of strange emotion*) He'd ought t' been my son, Abbie. Ye'd ought t' loved me. I'm a man. If ye'd loved me, I'd never told no Sheriff on ye no matter what ye did, if they was t' brile me alive!

ABBIE (*defensively*) They's more to it nor yew know, makes him tell.

CABOT (*dryly*) Fur yewr sake, I hope they be. (*He goes out—*

*comes around to the gate—stares up at the sky. His control re-
laxes. For a moment he is old and weary. He murmurs despairingly*) God A'mighty, I be lonesomer'n ever! (*He hears running
footsteps from the left, immediately is himself again.* EBEN *runs
in, panting exhaustedly, wild-eyed and mad looking. He lurches
through the gate.* CABOT *grabs him by the shoulder.* EBEN *stares
at him dumbly.*) Did ye tell the Sheriff?

EBEN (*nodding stupidly*) Ay-eh.

CABOT (*gives him a push away that sends him sprawling—laughing
with withering contempt*) Good fur ye! A prime chip o' yer
Maw ye be! (*He goes toward the barn, laughing harshly.* EBEN
scrambles to his feet. Suddenly CABOT *turns—grimly threatening*)
Git off this farm when the Sheriff takes her—or, by God, he'll
have t' come back an' git me fur murder, too! (*He stalks off.*
EBEN *does not appear to have heard him. He runs to the door
and comes into the kitchen.* ABBIE *looks up with a cry of anguished joy.* EBEN *stumbles over and throws himself on his knees
beside her—sobbing brokenly.*)

EBEN Fergive me!

ABBIE (*happily*) Eben! (*She kisses him and pulls his head over
against her breast.*)

EBEN I love ye! Fergive me!

ABBIE (*ecstatically*) I'd fergive ye all the sins in hell fur sayin'
that! (*She kisses his head, pressing it to her with a fierce passion
of possession.*)

EBEN (*brokenly*) But I told the Sheriff. He's comin' fur ye!

ABBIE I kin b'ar what happens t' me—now!

EBEN I woke him up. I told him. He says, wait 'til I git dressed. I
was waiting. I got to thinkin' o' yew. I got to thinkin' how I'd loved
ye. It hurt like somethin' was bustin' in my chest an' head. I got
t' cryin'. I knowed sudden I loved ye yet, an' allus would love ye!

ABBIE (*caressing his hair—tenderly*) My boy, hain't ye?

EBEN I begun t' run back. I cut across the fields an' through the
woods. I thought ye might have time t' run away—with me—
an' . . .

ABBIE (*shaking her head*) I got t' take my punishment—t' pay fur
my sin.

EBEN Then I want t' share it with ye.

ABBIE Ye didn't do nothin'.

EBEN I put it in yer head. I wisht he was dead! I as much as urged
ye t' do it!

ABBIE No. It was me alone!

EBEN I'm as guilty as yew be! He was the child o' our sin.

ABBIE (*lifting her head as if defying God*) I don't repent that sin! I hain't askin' God t' fergive that!

EBEN Nor me—but it led up t' the other—an' the murder ye did, ye did 'count o' me—an' it's my murder, too, I'll tell the Sheriff —an' if ye deny it, I'll say we planned it t'gether—an' they'll all b'lieve me, fur they suspicion everythin' we've done, an' it'll seem likely an' true to 'em. An' it is true—way down. I did help ye— somehow.

ABBIE (*laying her head on his—sobbing*) No! I don't want ye t' suffer!

EBEN I got t' pay fur my part o' the sin! An' I'd suffer wuss leavin' ye, goin' West, thinkin' o' ye day an' night, bein' out when yew was in—(*lowering his voice*)—'r bein' alive when yew was dead. (*a pause*) I want t' share with ye, Abbie—prison 'r death 'r hell 'r anythin'! (*He looks into her eyes and forces a trembling smile.*) If I'm sharin' with ye, I won't feel lonesome, leastways.

ABBIE (*weakly*) Eben! I won't let ye! I can't let ye!

EBEN (*kissing her—tenderly*) Ye can't he'p yerself. I got ye beat fur once!

ABBIE (*forcing a smile—adoringly*) I hain't beat—s'long's I got ye!

EBEN (*hears the sound of feet outside*) Ssshh! Listen! They've come t' take us!

ABBIE No, it's him. Don't give him no chance to fight ye, Eben. Don't say nothin'—no matter what he says. An' I won't neither. (*It is* CABOT. *He comes up from the barn in a great state of excitement and strides into the house and then into the kitchen.* EBEN *is kneeling beside* ABBIE, *his arm around her, hers around him. They stare straight ahead.*)

CABOT (*stares at them, his face hard. A long pause—vindictively*) Ye make a slick pair o' murderin' turtle doves! Ye'd ought t' be both hung on the same limb an' left thar t' swing in the breeze an' rot—a warnin' t' old fools like me t' b'ar their lonesomeness alone —an' fur young fools like ye t' hobble their lust. (*A pause. The excitement returns to his face, his eyes snap, he looks a bit crazy.*) I couldn't work today. I couldn't take no interest. T' hell with the farm! I'm leavin' it! I've turned the cows an' other stock loose! I've druv 'em into the woods whar they kin be free! By freein' 'em, I'm freein' myself! I'm quittin' here today! I'll set fire t' house an' barn an' watch 'em burn, an' I'll leave yer Maw t' haunt the ashes, an' I'll will the fields back t' God, so that nothin' human kin never touch 'em! I'll be a-goin' to Californi-a—t' jine Simeon an' Peter—true sons o' mine if they be dumb fools—an' the Cabots'll find Solomon's Mines t'gether! (*He suddenly cuts a mad caper.*) Whoop! What was the song they sung? "Oh, Cali-forni-a! That's the land fur me." (*He sings this—then gets on his knees by the floorboard under which the money was hid.*) An' I'll sail thar on one o' the finest clippers I kin find! I've got the money! Pity ye didn't know whar this was hidden so's ye could steal... (*He has pulled up the board. He stares—feels—stares again. A pause of dead silence. He slowly turns, slumping into a sitting position on the floor, his eyes like those of a dead fish, his face the sickly green of an attack of nausea. He swallows pain-fully several times—forces a weak smile at last.*) So—ye did steal it!

EBEN (*emotionlessly*)   I swapped it t' Sim an' Peter fur their share o' the farm—t' pay their passage t' Californi-a.

CABOT (*with one sardonic*)   Ha! (*He begins to recover. Gets slowly to his feet—strangly*) I calc'late God give it to 'em—not yew! God's hard, not easy! Mebbe they's easy gold in the West but it hain't God's gold. It hain't fur me. I kin hear His voice warnin' me agen t' be hard an' stay on my farm. I kin see his hand usin' Eben t' steal t' keep me from weakness. I kin feel I be in the palm o' His hand, His fingers guidin' me. (*A pause—then he mutters sadly*) It's a-goin' t' be lonesomer now than ever it war afore—an' I'm gittin' old, Lord—ripe on the bough.... (*Then stiffen-ing*) Waal—what d'ye want? God's lonesome, hain't He? God's hard an' lonesome! (*A pause. The* SHERIFF *with two men comes up the road from the left. They move cautiously to the door. The* SHERIFF *knocks on it with the butt of his pistol.*)

SHERIFF   Open in the name o' the law! (*They start.*)

CABOT   They've come fur ye. (*He goes to the rear door.*) Come in, Jim! (*The three men enter.* CABOT *meets them in doorway.*) Jest a minit, Jim. I got 'em safe here. (*The* SHERIFF *nods. He and his companions remain in the doorway.*)

EBEN (*suddenly calls*)   I lied this mornin', Jim. I helped her to do it. Ye kin take me, too.

ABBIE (*brokenly*)   No!

CABOT   Take 'em both. (*He comes forward—stares at* EBEN *with a trace of grudging admiration*) Purty good—fur yew! Waal, I got t' round up the stock. Good-by.

EBEN   Good-by.

ABBIE   Good-by. (*CABOT turns and strides past the men—comes out and around the corner of the house, his shoulders squared, his face stony, and stalks grimly toward the barn. In the meantime the* SHERIFF *and men have come into the room.*)

SHERIFF (*embarrassedly*)   Waal—we'd best start.

ABBIE   Wait. (*Turns to* EBEN)   I love ye, Eben.

EBEN   I love ye, Abbie. (*They kiss. The three men grin and shuffle embarrassedly.* EBEN *takes* ABBIE's *hand. They go out the door in rear, the men following, and come from the house, walking hand in hand to the gate.* EBEN *stops there and points to the sunrise sky.*) Sun's a-rizin'. Purty, hain't it?

ABBIE   Ay-eh. (*They both stand for a moment looking up raptly in attitudes strangely aloof and devout.*)

SHERIFF   (*looking around at the farm enviously—to his companion*) It's a jim-dandy farm, no denyin'. Wished I owned it!

MOTHER COURAGE (1939)

BERTOLT BRECHT (1898–1956)

Through the concerted effort of a single admirer, Eric Bentley, whose translations of and critical essays about Bertolt Brecht form a large and important library, this fascinating German dramatist has gradually earned a place as one of the geniuses of modern Western theatre. At times, during his residence in this country at the height of McCarthy witchhunts, he was the subject of ignorant suspicion and fear as an avowed Communist. Then, as a resident of East Germany until his death, he did not receive wide recognition as a major theatre artist until the decade of the 1960s. Only the phenomenally successful *Threepenny Opera,* that raucous raunchy adaptation of John Gay's *The Beggar's Opera* of 1728, originally done in collaboration with musician Kurt Weill in 1928 but not produced in New York until the 1950s, kept his name alive.

Brecht made no bones about his political orientation. He consciously alienated people at all levels of society as well as government, and the theatre which he envisioned and for which he fashioned his plays he defined as the "theatre of alienation," admitting to agitation along clearly political lines. His view was one of attack, more than winning his audiences to his side, and while doing so he made it clear that he was using every effort to remind the audience that it is in the theatre, witnessing a show. He dubbed his style "epic," and tried his best to keep his viewer from any form of empathic identification. He saw governments and society in general as run by exploitive camp followers and gangsters, or petty unscrupulous incompetents. He expressed this view by throwing at his audiences every technical device of the theatre in sound effects, slides, films, and all manner of jolting interruptions specifically designed to destroy illusion and to heighten the theatrical effect.

One of Brecht's main problems, however, as you will see from a study of *Mother Courage,* is that, for all of his attempts to keep his audiences at a considerable aesthetic distance, he frequently succeeded in spite of himself in creating tremendously sympathetic dramatic figures. In *The Good Woman of Setzuan* (1938–1940) his heroine Shen Te, a prostitute turned shopkeeper, suffers endlessly at the hands of exploitive neighbors and cheap "friends," appealing in the end to a trio of shabby gods who tell her to keep the faith and then leave her helpless. Grusha, the kitchen maid of *The Caucasian Chalk Circle* (1944–1945), fleeing her pursuers Eliza-like, refugee infant and all, evokes great pity. Much the same occurs in *Saint Joan of the Stockyards* (1929–1930) and *Galileo* (1938–1939). Try as he might to present as an object of disgust and rejection the scroungy, ugly, selfish old hag of a peddler who is his protagonist in *Mother Courage,* he fails.

Mother Courage with her wagon, her doomed children falling one by one, has become a great modern dramatic heroine. Though designed as an object of ridicule, a horrible example of those who would capitalize upon the misery of others and take their pickings from the frightfulness of war, she becomes, nonetheless, an object of genuine compassionate pity. Alone, almost helpless, still determined, she hitches herself to her cart and walks up the aisle to her next encampment, a powerful, unyielding, and nearly tragic figure.

Mother Courage, as so much of Brecht, is almost opera. The songs and routines and the gloomy unrelieved tales he likes to tell have a distinctive operatic quality. It is all pure *theatre,* designed to be seen and vividly experienced. Epic theatre, or theatre of alienation, or whatever you call it may not have wide appeal, but when he is good, Brecht is very very good, his present fame justly deserved.

Mother Courage

BRECHT

English version by Eric Bentley

CHARACTERS

MOTHER COURAGE
EILIF ⎫
SWISS CHEESE ⎭ *her sons*
KATTRIN, *her daughter*
RECRUITING OFFICER
SERGEANT
COOK
COMMANDER
CHAPLAIN
ORDNANCE OFFICER
SERGEANT
YVETTE POTTIER
ONE EYE
SOLDIER
COLONEL
CLERK

OLDER SOLDIER
YOUNGER SOLDIER
FIRST SOLDIER
PEASANT
SECOND SOLDIER
PEASANT WOMAN
SOLDIER, *singing*
OLD WOMAN
YOUNG MAN
SOLDIER
LIEUTENANT
OLD PEASANT
FIRST SOLDIER
PEASANT WOMAN
SECOND SOLDIER
YOUNG PEASANT

THE TIME: 1624–1636
THE PLACE: *Sweden, Poland, Germany*

PROLOGUE:
THE SONG OF MOTHER COURAGE

The wagon of a vivandière.

MOTHER COURAGE *sits on the wagon with her daughter* KATTRIN. *Her sons,* EILIF *and* SWISS CHEESE, *pull the wagon and join in the refrains of the song.* KATTRIN *plays a harmonica.*

> Here's Mother Courage and her wagon!
>   Hey, Captain, let them come and buy!
> Beer by the keg! Wine by the flagon!

Let your men drink before they die!
Sabers and swords are hard to swallow:
First you must give them beer to drink.
Then they can face what is to follow—
But let 'em swim before they sink!
Christians, awake! The winter's gone!
The snows depart, the dead sleep on.
And though you may not long survive,
Get out of bed and look alive!

Your men will march till they are dead, sir,
But cannot fight unless they eat.
The blood they spill for you is red, sir,
What fires that blood is my red meat.
For meat and soup and jam and jelly
In this old cart of mine are found:
So fill the hole up in your belly
Before you fill one underground.
Christians, awake! The winter's gone!
The snows depart, the dead sleep on.
And though you may not long survive,
Get out of bed and look alive!

SCENE 1

Spring, 1624. In Dalarna, the Swedish King Gustavus is recruiting for the campaign in Poland. The canteen woman ANNA FIERLING, *commonly known as* MOTHER COURAGE, *loses a son.*

Highway outside a town. A TOP SERGEANT *and a* RECRUITING OFFICER *stand shivering.*

RECRUITING OFFICER How the hell can you line up a squadron in *this* place? You know what I keep thinking about, Sergeant? Suicide. I'm supposed to slap four platoons together by the twelfth —four platoons the Chief's asking for! And they're so friendly around here, I'm scared to sleep nights. Suppose I do get my hands on some character and squint at him so I don't notice he's chicken-breasted and has varicose veins. I get him drunk and relaxed, he signs on the dotted line. I pay for the drinks, he steps outside for a minute. I get a hunch I should follow him to the door, and am I right! Off he's shot like a louse from a scratch. You can't take a man's word any more, Sergeant. There's no loyalty left in the world, no trust, no faith, no sense of honor. I'm losing my confidence in mankind, Sergeant.

SERGEANT   What they could use around here is a good war. What else can you expect with peace running wild all over the place? You know what the trouble with peace is? No organization. And when do you get organization? In a war. Peace is one big waste of equipment. Anything goes, no one gives a damn. See the way they eat? Cheese on rye, bacon on the cheese? Disgusting! How many horses they got in this town? How many young men? Nobody knows! They haven't bothered to count 'em! That's peace for you!!! I been places where they haven't had a war in seventy years and you know what? The people can't remember their own names! They don't know who they are! It takes a war to fix that. In a war, everyone registers, everyone's name's on a list. Their shoes are stacked, their corn's in the bag, you count it all up— cattle, men, *et cetera*—and you take it away! That's the story: no organization, no war!

RECRUITING OFFICER   It's the God's truth.

SERGEANT   Course, a war's like every real good deal: hard to get going. But when it's on the road, it's a pisser—everybody's scared off peace—like a crap-shooter that keeps fading to cover his loss. Course, *until* it gets going, they're just as scared off war—afraid to try anything new.

RECRUITING OFFICER   Look, a wagon! Two women and a couple of young punks. Stop 'em, Sergeant. And if there's nothing doing this time, you won't catch *me* freezing my ass in the April wind.

MOTHER COURAGE *enters on her wagon and with her children as in the prologue.*

MOTHER COURAGE   Good day to you, Sergeant.

SERGEANT   (*barring the way*)   Good day! Who d'you think you are?

MOTHER COURAGE   Tradespeople.

(*She prepares to go.*)

SERGEANT   Halt! Where are you from, riffraff?

EILIF   Second Protestant Regiment!

SERGEANT   Where are your papers?

MOTHER COURAGE   Papers?

SWISS CHEESE   But this is Mother Courage!

SERGEANT   Never heard of her. Where'd she get a name like that?

MOTHER COURAGE   In Riga.

EILIF AND SWISS CHEESE   (*reciting together*)   They call her Mother Courage because she drove through the bombardment of Riga with fifty loaves of bread in her wagon!

MOTHER COURAGE   They were going moldy, I couldn't help myself.

SERGEANT   No funny business! Where are your papers?

MOTHER COURAGE *rummages among papers in a tin box and clambers down from her wagon.*

MOTHER COURAGE   Here, Sergeant! Here's a whole Bible—I got it in Altötting to wrap my cucumbers in. Here's a map of Moravia —God knows if I'll ever get there. And here's a document saying my horse hasn't got hoof and mouth disease—too bad he died on us, he cost fifteen guilders, thank God I didn't pay it. Is that enough paper?

SERGEANT   Are you making a pass at me? Well, you got another guess coming. You must have a license and you know it.

MOTHER COURAGE   Show a little respect for a lady and don't go telling these grown children of mine I'm making a pass at you. What would I want with you? My license in the Second Protestant Regiment is an honest face—even if *you* wouldn't know how to read it.

RECRUITING OFFICER   Sergeant, we have a case of insubordination on our hands. (*To her:*) Do you know what we need in the army? (MOTHER COURAGE *starts to answer.*) Discipline!

MOTHER COURAGE   I was going to say sausages.

SERGEANT   Name?

MOTHER COURAGE   Anna Fierling.

SERGEANT   So you're all Fierlings.

MOTHER COURAGE   I was talking about me.

SERGEANT   And I was talking about your children.

MOTHER COURAGE   Must they all have the same name? This boy, for instance, I call him Eilif Noyocki—he got the name from his father who told me he was called Koyocki. Or was it Moyocki? Anyhow, the lad remembers him to this day. Only the man he remembers is someone else, a Frenchman with a pointed beard. But he certainly has his father's brains—that man could whip the pants off a farmer's behind before he could turn around. So we all have our own names.

SERGEANT   You're all called something different?

MOTHER COURAGE   Are you pretending you don't get it?

SERGEANT (*pointing at* SWISS CHEESE)   He's a Chinese, I suppose.

MOTHER COURAGE   Wrong again. A Swiss.

SERGEANT   After the Frenchman?

MOTHER COURAGE   Frenchman? What Frenchman? Don't confuse the issue, Sergeant, or we'll be here all day. He's a Swiss, but he happens to be called Feyos, a name that has nothing to do with his father, who was called something else—a military engineer, if you please, and a drunkard.

SWISS CHEESE *nods, beaming; even* KATTRIN *smiles.*

SERGEANT   Then how come his name's Feyos?

MOTHER COURAGE   Oh, Sergeant, you have no imagination. *Of course* he's called Feyos: When he came, I was with a Hungarian. He didn't mind. He had a floating kidney, though he never touched a drop. He was a very *honest* man. The boy takes after him.

SERGEANT   But that wasn't his father!

MOTHER COURAGE   I said: he took after him. I call him Swiss Cheese. And that is my daughter Kattrin Haupt, she's half German.

SERGEANT   A nice family, I must say!

MOTHER COURAGE   And we've seen the whole wide world together —this wagon-load and me.

SERGEANT (*writing*)   We'll need all that in writing.

RECRUITING OFFICER (*to* EILIF)   So you two are the oxen for the wagon? Do they ever let you out of harness?

EILIF   Mother! May I smack him in the puss?

MOTHER COURAGE   You stay where you are. And now, gentlemen, how about a pair of pistols? Or a belt? Sergeant? Yours is worn clean through.

SERGEANT   It's something else *I'm* looking for. These lads of yours are straight as birch-trees. What are such fine specimens doing out of the army?

MOTHER COURAGE (*quickly*)   The soldier's life is not for sons of mine!

RECRUITING OFFICER   Why not? It means money. It means fame. Peddling shoes is woman's work. (*To* EILIF:) Step this way and let's see if that's muscle or chicken fat.

MOTHER COURAGE   It's chicken fat. Give him a good hard look, and he'll fall right over.

RECRUITING OFFICER   Well, I hope he doesn't fall on me, that's all.

(*He tries to hustle* EILIF *away.*)

MOTHER COURAGE   Let him alone! He's not for you!

RECRUITING OFFICER   He called my face a puss. That is an insult. The two of us will now go settle the affair on the field of honor.

EILIF   Don't worry, Mother, I can handle him.

MOTHER COURAGE   Stay here. You're never happy till you're in a fight. (*To the* OFFICER:) He has a knife in his boot and he knows how to use it.

RECRUITING OFFICER   I'll draw it out of him like a milk tooth. (*To* EILIF:) Come on, young fellow!

MOTHER COURAGE   Officer, I'll report you to the Colonel, and he'll throw you in jail. His lieutenant is courting my daughter.

SERGEANT (*to* OFFICER)   Go easy. (*To* MOTHER COURAGE:) What have you got against the service, wasn't his own father a soldier? Didn't you say he died a soldier's death?

MOTHER COURAGE   He's dead all right. But this one's just a baby. You'll lead him like a lamb to the slaughter. I know you. You'll get five guilders for him.

RECRUITING OFFICER (*to* EILIF)   First thing you know, you'll have a new cap and high boots, how about it?

EILIF   Not from you, thanks.

MOTHER COURAGE   "Let's you and me go fishing," said the angler to the worm. (*To* SWISS CHEESE:) Run and tell everybody they're trying to steal your brother! (*She draws a knife.*) Yes, just you try, and I'll cut you down like dogs! We sell cloth, we sell ham, we are peaceful people!

SERGEANT   You're peaceful all right: your knife proves that. Now tell me, how can we have a war without soldiers?

MOTHER COURAGE   Do they have to be mine?

SERGEANT   So that's the trouble! The war should swallow the pits and spit out the peach, huh? Tsk, tsk, tsk: call yourself Mother Courage and then get scared of the war, your breadwinner? Your sons aren't scared, I know that much.

EILIF   No war can scare me.

SERGEANT   Of course not! Take me. The soldier's life hasn't done *me* any harm, has it? I enlisted at seventeen.

MOTHER COURAGE   You haven't reached seventy.

SERGEANT   I will, though.

MOTHER COURAGE   Above ground?

SERGEANT   Are you trying to rile me, telling me I'll die?

MOTHER COURAGE   Suppose it's the truth? Suppose I see it's your fate? Suppose I *know* you're just a corpse on furlough?

SWISS CHEESE   She can look into the future. Everyone says so.

RECRUITING OFFICER   Then by all means look into the Sergeant's future. It might amuse him.

SERGEANT   I don't believe in that stuff.

MOTHER COURAGE (*obeying the* OFFICER)   Helmet! (SERGEANT *gives her his helmet.*)

SERGEANT   Anything for a laugh.

MOTHER COURAGE *takes a sheet of parchment and tears it in two.*

MOTHER COURAGE   Eilif, Swiss Cheese, Kattrin! So shall we all be torn asunder if we let ourselves get too deep into this war! (*To the* SERGEANT:) I'll give you the bargain rate, and do it for free. Watch! Death is black, so I draw a black cross.

SWISS CHEESE (*pointing to the second piece of parchment*) And the other she leaves blank, see?

MOTHER COURAGE I fold them, put them in the helmet, and mix 'em up, the way we're all mixed up from our mother's womb on. Now draw!

RECRUITING OFFICER (*to* EILIF) I don't take just anybody. I'm choosy. And you've got guts, I like that.

SERGEANT (*after hesitating, fishes around in the helmet*) It's a lot of crap!

SWISS CHEESE (*watching over his shoulder*) The black cross! Oh, his number's up!

SERGEANT (*hoarsely*) You cheated me!

MOTHER COURAGE You cheated yourself the day you enlisted. And now we must drive on. There isn't a war every day in the week.

SERGEANT Hell, you're not getting away with this! We're taking that bastard of yours with *us!*

EILIF I'd like that, mother.

MOTHER COURAGE Quiet—you Finnish devil, you!

EILIF And Swiss Cheese wants to be a soldier, too.

MOTHER COURAGE That's news to me. I see I'll have to draw lots for all three of you. (*She goes to one side to do this.*)

RECRUITING OFFICER (*to* EILIF) People've been saying the Swedish soldier is religious. That kind of loose talk has hurt us a lot. One verse of a hymn every Sunday—and then only if you have a voice . . .

MOTHER COURAGE *returns with the slips and puts them in the* SERGEANT'S *helmet.*

MOTHER COURAGE So they'd desert their old mother, would they, the rascals? They take to war like a cat to cream! Well, there's yours, Eilif, my boy! (*As* EILIF *takes the slip, she snatches it and holds it up.*) See? A cross!

RECRUITING OFFICER (*to* EILIF) If you're going to wet your pants, I'll try your kid brother.

MOTHER COURAGE Take yours, Swiss Cheese. You should be a bet-ter bet—you're my *good* boy. (SWISS CHEESE *draws.*) Don't tell me it's a cross? Is there no saving you either? Just look, Sergeant —a black cross!

SERGEANT What I don't see is why *I* got one: I always stay well in the rear. (*To the* OFFICER:) It can't be a trick: it gets her own children.

MOTHER COURAGE (*to* KATTRIN) Now all I have left is you. You're a cross in yourself but you have a kind heart. (*She holds the helmet up but takes the slip herself.*) Oh dear, there must be some mistake! Don't be too kind, Kattrin, don't be too kind—there's a black cross in your path! So now you all know: be careful! Be very careful! (MOTHER COURAGE *climbs on her wagon, preparing to leave.*)

RECRUITING OFFICER (*to* SERGEANT) Do something!

SERGEANT I don't feel too good.

RECRUITING OFFICER Try doing business with her! (*In a loud voice:*) That belt, Sergeant, you could at least take a look at it! Hey, you, the Sergeant will take the belt!

MOTHER COURAGE Half a guilder. Worth four times the price.

SERGEANT It's not even a new one. But there's too much wind here. I'll go look at it behind the wagon.

MOTHER COURAGE It doesn't seem windy to me.

SERGEANT Maybe it's worth a half guilder at that. There's silver on it.

MOTHER COURAGE (*now following him eagerly behind the wagon*) A solid six ounces worth!

RECRUITING OFFICER (*to* EILIF) I can let you have some cash in advance, how about it?

EILIF *hesitates.* MOTHER COURAGE *is behind the wagon.*

MOTHER COURAGE Half a guilder then. Quick.

SERGEANT I still don't see why *I* had to draw a cross. As I told you, I always stay in the rear—it's the only place that's safe. You've ruined my afternoon, Mother Courage.

MOTHER COURAGE You mustn't take on so. Here. Take a shot of brandy. (*He does.*) And go right on staying in the rear. Half a guilder.

The RECRUITING OFFICER *has taken* EILIF *by the arm and drawn him away.*

RECRUITING OFFICER Ten guilders in advance, and you're a soldier of the king! The women'll be crazy about you, and you can smack me in the puss because I insulted you!

They leave. KATTRIN *makes harsh noises.*

MOTHER COURAGE Coming, Kattrin, coming! The Sergeant's just paying his bill. (*She bites the half guilder.*) All money is suspect, Sergeant, but your half guilder is good. Let's go. Where's Eilif?

SWISS CHEESE Gone with the recruiting officer.

Pause.

MOTHER COURAGE   Oh, you simpleton! (*To* KATTRIN:) You can't speak. You *couldn't* tell me.

SERGEANT   That's life, Mother Courage. Take a shot yourself.

MOTHER COURAGE   You must help your brother now, Kattrin.

Brother and sister get into harness together and pull the wagon. They all move off.

SERGEANT (*looking after them*)
   When a war gives you all you earn
   One day it may claim something in return!

SCENE 2

In the years 1625 and 1626 MOTHER COURAGE *journeys through Poland in the baggage train of the Swedish Army. She meets her brave son again before Wallhof Castle. Of the successful sale of a capon and great days for the brave son.*

The tent of the Swedish Commander, and the kitchen next to it. Sound of cannon. In the kitchen: MOTHER COURAGE *and the* COOK. *The* COOK *has a Dutch accent.*

COOK   Sixty hellers—for that paltry piece of poultry?

MOTHER COURAGE   Paltry poultry? He's the fattest fowl you ever saw. I could get sixty hellers for him—this Commander can *eat!*

COOK   They're ten hellers a dozen on every street corner.

MOTHER COURAGE   A capon like that on every street corner? With a siege going on and people all skin and bones? Maybe you can find a field rat some place. I said maybe, because we're all out of them too. All right, then, in a siege, my price for this giant capon is fifty hellers.

COOK   *We're* doing the besieging, it's the other side that's "in a siege"!

MOTHER COURAGE   A fat lot of difference that makes—we don't have a thing to eat either. Look at the farmers round here. They haven't a thing.

COOK   Sure they have. They hide it.

MOTHER COURAGE   They haven't a thing! They're ruined. They're so hungry they dig up roots to eat. I could boil that leather belt of yours and make their mouths water with it. And I'm supposed to let a capon go for forty hellers?

COOK   Thirty. I said thirty hellers.

MOTHER COURAGE   I know *your* problem. If you don't find something to eat and quick, the Commander will cut your fat head off!

COOK   Look! Here's a piece of beef. I am about to roast it. I give you one more chance.

MOTHER COURAGE   Roast it. Go ahead. It's only twelve months old.

COOK   Twelve hours old! Why, only yesterday it was a cow—I saw it running around!

MOTHER COURAGE   Then it must have started stinking before it died.

COOK   I'll cook it five hours if I have to.

MOTHER COURAGE   Put plenty of pepper in.

The Swedish COMMANDER, *the* CHAPLAIN, *and* EILIF *enter the tent. The* COMMANDER *claps* EILIF *on the shoulder.*

COMMANDER   In your Commander's tent you go, Eilif, my son, sit at my right hand! Well done, good and faithful servant—you've played the hero in God's own war and you'll get a gold bracelet out of it yet if I have any say in the matter! We come to save their souls and what do they do, the filthy, irreligious sons of bitches? Try to hide their cattle from us—meanwhile stuffing beef into their priests at both ends! But you showed 'em—so here's a can of red wine for you. We'll drink together. (*They do so.*) The chaplain gets the dregs, he's so pious. And now, my hearty, what would you like for dinner?

EILIF   How about a slice of meat?

COOK   Nothing to eat—so he brings company to eat it.

MOTHER COURAGE   Sh!

COMMANDER   Cook! Meat!!

EILIF   Tires you out, skinning peasants. Gives you an appetite.

MOTHER COURAGE   Dear God, it's my Eilif!

COOK   Who?

MOTHER COURAGE   My eldest. It's two years since I saw him. He must be *high* in favor—the Commander inviting him to dinner! And what do you have to eat? Nothing. The Commander's guest wants meat! Take my advice: buy the capon. The price is one hundred hellers.

The COMMANDER *has sat down with* EILIF *and the* CHAPLAIN.

COMMANDER (*roaring*)   Dinner, you pig! Or I'll have your head!

COOK   This is blackmail. Give me the damn thing!

MOTHER COURAGE   A paltry piece of poultry like this?

COOK   You were right. Give it here. It's highway robbery, fifty hellers.

MOTHER COURAGE   One hundred hellers. No price is too high for the Commander's guest of honor.

COOK Well, you might at least pluck the wretched thing till I have a fire going.

MOTHER COURAGE *sits down to pluck the capon.*

MOTHER COURAGE I can't wait to see his face when he sees me.

COMMANDER Another glass, my son! It's my favorite Falernian. There's only one keg left but it's worth it to meet a soldier that still believes in God! Our chaplain here only preaches. He hasn't a clue how things get done. So now, Eilif my boy, tell us how you fixed the peasants and grabbed the twenty bullocks.

EILIF It was like this. I found out the peasants had hidden the oxen in a certain wood. The people from the town were to pick them up there. So I let them go for their oxen in peace—they should know better than me where they are, I said to myself. Meanwhile I made my men crazy for meat. Their rations were short already. I made sure they got shorter. Finally, their mouths would water at the sound of *any* word beginning with M—like mother.

COMMANDER Smart kid!

EILIF Not bad. The rest was a snap. Only the peasants had clubs— and outnumbered us three to one. They made a murderous attack on us. Four of them drove me into a clump of trees, knocked my sword from my hand, and screamed: Surrender! What now? I said to myself, they'll make mincemeat of me.

COMMANDER So what did you do?

EILIF I laughed.

COMMANDER You what?

EILIF I laughed. And so we got to talking. I came right down to business and said: "Twenty guilders an ox is too much, I bid fifteen." Like I wanted to buy. That foxed 'em. So while they were scratching their heads, I reached for my good sword and cut 'em to ribbons. Necessity knows no law, huh?

COMMANDER What do *you* say, keeper of souls?

CHAPLAIN Strictly speaking, that saying is not in the Bible. Our Lord made five hundred loaves out of five so that no necessity should arise. So when he told men to love their neighbors, their bellies were full. Things have changed since his day.

COMMANDER (*laughing*) Things have changed! Some wine for those wise words, you old Pharisee! Eilif my boy, you cut them to ribbons in a great cause! As for our fellows, "they were hungry and you gave them to eat!" You don't know how I value a brave soldier like you. (*He points to the map.*) Let's take a look at our position. It isn't all it might be, is it?

MOTHER COURAGE He must be a very bad commander, this fellow.

COOK Just a greedy one. Why bad?

MOTHER COURAGE He says he needs *brave* soldiers. If his plan of campaign was any good, wouldn't plain ordinary soldiers do? Bravery! In a good country, such virtues wouldn't be needed. We could all be cowards and relax.

COMMANDER I bet your father was a soldier.

EILIF A very great soldier. My mother warned me about it. In a little song.

COMMANDER Sing it! (*Roaring:*) Bring that meat!

EILIF It's called The Fishwife and the Soldier.

THE FISHWIFE AND THE SOLDIER

To a soldier lad comes an old fishwife
   And this old fishwife, says she:
A gun will shoot, a knife will knife,
   You will drown if you fall in the sea.
Keep away from the ice if you want my advice,
   Says the old fishwife, says she.
The soldier laughs and loads his gun
Then grabs his knife and starts to run:
   It's the life of a hero for me!
From the north to the south I shall march through the land
With a knife at my side and a gun in my hand!
   Says the soldier lad, says he.

When the lad defies the fishwife's cries
   The old fishwife, says she:
The young are young, the old are wise,
   You will drown if you fall in the sea.
Don't ignore what I say or you'll rue it one day!
   Says the old fishwife, says she.
But gun in hand and knife at side
The soldier steps into the tide:
   It's the life of a hero for me!
When the new moon is shining on shingle roofs white
We are all coming back, go and pray for that night!
   Says the soldier lad, says he.

And the fishwife old does what she's told:
   Down upon her knees drops she.
When the smoke is gone, the air is cold,
   Your heroic deeds won't warm me!

See the smoke, how it goes! May God scatter his foes!
  Down upon her knees drops she.
But gun in hand and knife at side
The lad is swept out by the tide:
  He floats with the ice to the sea.
And the new moon is shining on shingle roofs white
But the lad and his laughter are lost in the night:
  He floats with the ice to the sea.

The third stanza has been sung by Mother Courage, *somewhat to the* Commander's *surprise.*

COMMANDER   What goes on in my kitchen? The liberties they take nowadays!

Eilif *has now left the tent for the kitchen. He embraces his mother.*

EILIF   You! Mother! Where are the others?

MOTHER COURAGE (*still in his arms*)   Happy as ducks in a pond. Swiss Cheese is paymaster with the Second Protestant Regiment.

EILIF   Paymaster, eh?

MOTHER COURAGE   At least he isn't in the fighting.

EILIF   Your feet holding up?

MOTHER COURAGE   I have a bit of trouble getting my shoes on in the morning.

COMMANDER (*also in the kitchen by now*)   So! You're his mother? I hope you have more sons for me like this young fellow?

EILIF   If I'm not the lucky one! To be the Commander's guest—while you sit listening in the kitchen!

MOTHER COURAGE   I heard you all right. (*She gives him a clout on the ear.*)

EILIF (*grinning*)   Because I took the oxen?

MOTHER COURAGE   No. Because you didn't surrender when the four peasants tried to make mincemeat of you! Didn't I teach you to take care of yourself, you Finnish devil, you?

SCENE 3

Three years pass, and Mother Courage, *with parts of a Finnish regiment, is taken prisoner. Her daughter is saved, her wagon likewise, but her honest son dies.*

A camp. The regimental flag is flying from a pole. Afternoon. Mother Courage's *clothes-line is tied to the wagon at one end, to a cannon at the other. She and* Kattrin *are folding the wash on the cannon. At the same time she is bargaining with an* Ordnance Officer *over a bag of bullets.* Swiss Cheese, *wearing his Paymaster's uniform, looks on.* Yvette Pot-

TIER, *a very good-looking young person, is sewing at a colored hat, a glass of brandy before her. Her red boots are nearby; she is in stocking feet.*

ORDNANCE OFFICER   I'm letting you have the bullets for two guilders. Dirt cheap. 'Cause I need the money. The Colonel's been drinking for three days and we're out of liquor.

MOTHER COURAGE   They're army property. If they find them here, I'll be court-martialled. You sell your bullets, you bastards, and send your men out to fight with nothing to shoot with.

ORDNANCE OFFICER   If you scratch my back, I'll scratch yours.

MOTHER COURAGE   I won't touch army stuff. Not at that price.

ORDNANCE OFFICER   You can resell 'em for five guilders, maybe eight—to the Ordnance Officer of the 4th Regiment. All you have to do is give him a receipt for twelve. He hasn't a bullet left.

MOTHER COURAGE   Why don't you do it yourself?

ORDNANCE OFFICER   I don't trust him: we're friends.

MOTHER COURAGE   (*taking the bag, to* KATTRIN)   Take it round the back and pay him a guilder and a half. (*As the* OFFICER *starts to protest:*) A guilder and a half! (KATTRIN *drags the bag away, the* OFFICER *follows. To* SWISS CHEESE:) Here's your underwear. Take care of it. It's October, autumn may come at any time. I don't say it must, but it may. Nothing *must* come, not even the seasons. Only your books *must* balance. Do your books balance, Mr. Paymaster?

SWISS CHEESE   Yes, Mother.

MOTHER COURAGE   Don't forget they made you paymaster because you're honest and so simple you'd never think of running off with the cash. Don't lose that underwear.

SWISS CHEESE   No, Mother. I'll put it under the mattress.

ORDNANCE OFFICER   I'll go with you, Paymaster.

MOTHER COURAGE   Don't teach him any finagling.

The ORDNANCE OFFICER *and* SWISS CHEESE *leave.*

YVETTE   (*waving to the* OFFICER)   You might at least say good-bye!

MOTHER COURAGE   (*to* YVETTE)   I don't like that: he's no company for my Swiss Cheese. But the war's not making a bad start: if I look ahead and make no mistakes, business will be good. (*Noticing the brandy:*) Don't you know you shouldn't drink in the morning—with your sickness and all?

YVETTE   Who says I'm sick? That's a libel!

MOTHER COURAGE   They all say so.

YVETTE   Then they're all liars! I'm desperate, Mother Courage. They avoid me like a stinking fish. Because of those lies! So what am I fixing this hat for? (*She throws it down.*) That's why I drink in the morning. It gives you crow's feet, so what? The whole regiment knows me. I should have stayed home when my first was unfaithful. But pride isn't for the likes of us. You eat dirt or down you go.

MOTHER COURAGE   Don't start in again about your friend Peter Piper and How It All Happened—in front of my innocent daughter.

YVETTE   She's the one that *should* hear it. So she'll get hardened against love.

MOTHER COURAGE   That's something no one ever gets hardened against.

YVETTE   He was an army cook, blond, Dutch, and thin. Kattrin, beware of thin men! I didn't. I didn't even know he'd had another girl before me and she called him Peter Piper because he never took his pipe out of his mouth even in bed—it meant so little to him. (*She sings:*)

THE CAMP FOLLOWER'S SONG

Scarce seventeen was I when
   The foe came to our land
And laid aside his saber
   And took me by the hand.
      And we performed by day
      The sacred rite of May
      And we performed by night
      Another sacred rite.
      The regiment, well exercised,
      Presented arms, then stood at ease,
      Then took us off behind the trees
      Where we fraternized.

Each of us had her foe and
   A cook fell to my lot.
I hated him by daylight
   But in the dark did not.
      So we perform by day
      The sacred rite of May
      And we perform by night
      That other sacred rite.
      The regiment, well exercised,
      Presents its arms, then stands at ease,
      Then takes us off behind the trees
      Where we fraternize.

Ecstasy filled my heart, O
My love seemed heaven-born!
Yet why were people saying
It was not love but scorn ?
The springtime's soft amour
Through summer may endure
But swiftly comes the fall
And winter ends it all.
December came. All of the men
Filed past the trees where once we hid
Then quickly marched away and did
Not come back again.

YVETTE   I made the mistake of running after him. I never found him. It's ten years ago now. (YVETTE *goes behind the wagon.*)

MOTHER COURAGE   You're leaving your hat.

YVETTE   For the birds.

MOTHER COURAGE   Let that be a lesson to you, Kattrin: never start anything with a soldier. Love does seem heaven-born, so watch out: they tell you they worship the ground under your feet— did you wash 'em yesterday, while we're on the subject?—then, if you don't look out, you're their slave for life.

The CHAPLAIN *comes in with the* COOK.

CHAPLAIN   Mother Courage, I bring a message from your son Eilif. The cook came with me—you've made an impression on him.

COOK   Oh, I thought I'd get a little whiff of the breeze.

MOTHER COURAGE   You're welcome to it, but what does Eilif want? I don't have any money!

CHAPLAIN   My message is for his brother, the paymaster.

MOTHER COURAGE   He's not here. He's not anywhere. Look, he is not his brother's paymaster: I won't have him led into temptation! (*She takes money from a purse.*) Give him this. But it's a sin—he's speculating in mother love.

COOK   Maybe not for long. How d'you know he'll come back alive? You're hard, you women. A glass of brandy wouldn't cost you much. But no, you say, no—and six feet under goes your man.

CHAPLAIN   My dear Cook, you talk as if dying for one's beliefs were a misfortune—it is the highest privilege! This is not just any war, remember, it is a religious war, and therefore pleasing unto God.

COOK   I see that. In one sense it's a war because of all the cheating, plunder, rape, and so forth, but it's different from all other wars because it's a religious war and therefore pleasing unto God. At that it does make you thirsty.

CHAPLAIN (*to* MOTHER COURAGE) He says you've bewitched him. He says he dreams about you.

COOK (*lighting his pipe*) Innocent dreams! I dream of a fair lady dispensing brandy! Stop embarrassing me! The stories you were telling on the way over still have me blushing.

MOTHER COURAGE I must get you two something to drink, or you'll be making improper advances out of sheer boredom.

CHAPLAIN That is indeed a temptation—said the Court Chaplain, as he gave way to it. And who is this captivating young person?

MOTHER COURAGE (*looking at* KATTRIN) That is not a captivating young person. That is a respectable young person. (*And she goes with* COOK *and* CHAPLAIN *behind the wagon.*)

MOTHER COURAGE The trouble with Poland is the Poles. It's true our Swedish king moved in on them with his army—but instead of maintaining the peace the Poles would keep interfering. So their blood is on their own heads, *I* say.

CHAPLAIN Anyway, since the German Kaiser had enslaved them, King Gustavus had no alternative but to liberate them!

COOK Just what *I* always say. Your health, Mother Courage, your brandy is first-rate, I'm never mistaken in a face. This war is a religious war.

KATTRIN *watches them go behind the wagon, leaves the washing, picks up the hat, sits, takes up the red boots. The* COOK *sings:*

LUTHER'S HYMN

A mighty fortress is our God
A bulwark never failing.
Our helper He, amid the flood
Of mortal ills prevailing.
For still our ancient Foe
Doth seek to work us woe.
His craft and power are great
And armed with cruel hate
On earth is not his equal.

COOK And King Gustavus liberated Poland from the Germans. Who could deny it? Then his appetite grew with eating, and he liberated *Germany* from the Germans. Made quite a profit on the deal, I'm told.

CHAPLAIN That is a calumny! The Swedish king puts religion first!

MOTHER COURAGE What's more, you eat his bread.

COOK I don't eat his bread: I bake his bread.

MOTHER COURAGE He'll never be conquered, that man, and you

know why? We all back him up—the little fellows like you and
me. Oh yes, to hear the big fellows talk, they're fighting for their
beliefs and so on, but if you look into it, you find they're not that
silly: they do want to make a profit on the deal. So you and I
back them up!

COOK   Surely.

CHAPLAIN   (*pointing to flag, to* COOK)   And as a Dutchman you'd
do well to look which flag is flying here!

MOTHER COURAGE   To our Protestant flag!

COOK   A toast!

And now KATTRIN *has begun to strut about with hat and boots on. Suddenly: cannon and shots. Drums.* MOTHER COURAGE, *the* COOK, *and the*
CHAPLAIN *rush round to the front of the wagon, the two last with glasses
in their hands. The* ORDNANCE OFFICER *and a* SOLDIER *come running for
the cannon. They try to push it.*

MOTHER COURAGE   Hey, let me get my wash off that gun!

ORDNANCE OFFICER   Surprise attack! The Catholics! We don't know
if we can get away!   (*To the* SOLDIER:)   Bring that gun!   (*He runs
off.*)

COOK   Good God! I must go to the commander. Mother Courage,
I'll be back soon—for a short conversation.   (*He rushes off.*)

MOTHER COURAGE   Hey, you're leaving your pipe!

COOK   (*off*)   Keep it for me, I'll need it!

MOTHER COURAGE   This *would* happen just when we were making
money.

CHAPLAIN   "Blessed are the peacemakers!" A good slogan for wartime. Well, I must be going too. Yes, if the enemy's so close, it
can be dangerous. I wish I had a cloak.

MOTHER COURAGE   I'm lending no cloaks. Not even to save a life.
I've had experience in that line.

CHAPLAIN   But I'm in special danger—because of my religion!

MOTHER COURAGE   (*bringing him a cloak*)   It's against my better
judgment. Now run!

CHAPLAIN   Thank you, you're very generous, but on second thought
I better stay put. If I run, I might attract attention.

THE SOLDIER *is still struggling with the cannon.*

MOTHER COURAGE   Let it alone, you idiot, who's going to pay you
for this? *You'll* pay—with your life. Let me keep it for you.

SOLDIER   (*running off*)   You're my witness: I tried!

MOTHER COURAGE   I'll swear to that.   (*And now she sees* KATTRIN
with the hat and boots.)   Yvette's hat! Take it off this minute!
Are you crazy—with the enemy coming?   (*She tears it off her*

head.) They'll make a whore of you when they see it! And she has the boots on, too, straight from Babylon, I'll soon fix that. (*She pulls at the boots.*) Chaplain, help me with these boots, I'll be right back. (*She runs to the wagon.*)

YVETTE *enters, powdering her face.*

YVETTE   What's this—the Catholics are coming? Where's my hat? Who's been trampling on it? I can't run around in that, what will they think of me? And I've no mirror. (*Coming very close to the* CHAPLAIN:) How do I look? Too much powder?
CHAPLAIN   No—er—just right.
YVETTE   And where are my red boots? (KATTRIN *is hiding her feet under her skirt.*) I left them here! Must I go barefoot? It's a scandal.

Exit YVETTE. SWISS CHEESE *comes running on with a cash-box. Enter* MOTHER COURAGE, *her hands smeared with ashes.*

MOTHER COURAGE (*to* SWISS CHEESE)   What have you got there?
SWISS CHEESE   The regimental cash-box.
MOTHER COURAGE   Throw it away! Your paymastering days are over!
SWISS CHEESE   But they trusted me with it! (*He goes to one side.*)
MOTHER COURAGE (*to the* CHAPLAIN)   Take your pastor's coat off, or they'll recognize you, cloak or no cloak. (*She is rubbing ashes into* KATTRIN's *face.*) Keep still! A little dirt, and you're safe. When a soldier sees a clean face, there's one more whore in the world. That does it. Now stop trembling. Nothing can happen now. (*To* SWISS CHEESE:) Where've you put that cash-box?
SWISS CHEESE   I thought I'd just leave it in the wagon.
MOTHER COURAGE   In my wagon?! Why, they'll hang all three of us!
SWISS CHEESE   Somewhere else then. Maybe I'll run away some place.
MOTHER COURAGE   It's too late for that.
CHAPLAIN (*still changing his clothes*)   For Heaven's sake, that Protestant flag!
MOTHER COURAGE (*taking the flag down*)   I've had it twenty-five years. I don't notice it any more.

The sound of cannon grows. Blackout. Three days later. Morning. The cannon is gone. MOTHER COURAGE, KATTRIN, *the* CHAPLAIN, *and* SWISS CHEESE *sit eating anxiously.*

SWISS CHEESE   This is the third day I've sat doing nothing. The sergeant has always been patient with me, but by this time he must be asking himself: Now where is Swiss Cheese with that cash-box?

MOTHER COURAGE   Be glad they're not on the trail.

CHAPLAIN   What about me? I can't even hold service here. It is written: "Out of the abundance of the heart the tongue speaketh" —but woe is me if *my* tongue speaketh!

MOTHER COURAGE   So here you sit—one with his religion, the other with his cash-box! I don't know which is more dangerous.

CHAPLAIN   We're in God's hands now.

MOTHER COURAGE   Oh, I hope we're not as desperate as *that!* But it *is* hard to sleep at night. It'd be easier if you weren't here, Swiss Cheese. All the same I've not done badly.

CHAPLAIN   The milk is good. As for the quantity, we may have to reduce our Swedish appetites somewhat. We are defeated.

MOTHER COURAGE   Who's defeated? There've been cases where a defeat is a victory for the little fellows, it's only their honor that's lost, nothing serious. At that, either victory or defeat can be a costly business. The best thing, *I* say, is for politics to kind of get stuck in the mud. (*To* SWISS CHEESE:) Eat!

SWISS CHEESE   I don't like it. How will the sergeant pay the men?

MOTHER COURAGE   Soldiers in flight don't get paid.

SWISS CHEESE   Then they should refuse to flee! No pay, no flight!

MOTHER COURAGE   Swiss Cheese, I've brought you up honest because you're not very bright, but don't overdo it! And now I'm going with the Chaplain to buy a Catholic flag and some meat. (*She disappears into the wagon.*)

CHAPLAIN   She's worried about the cash-box.

SWISS CHEESE   I can get rid of it.

CHAPLAIN   You may be seen. They have spies everywhere. Yesterday one jumped out of the very hole I was relieving myself in. I was so scared I almost broke into a prayer—think how *that* would have given me away! He was a little brute with a patch over one eye.

MOTHER COURAGE *clambers out of the wagon with a basket.*

MOTHER COURAGE (*to* KATTRIN, *holding up the red boots*) You shameless little hussy! She went and snitched them—because you called her a captivating young person. (*She puts them in the basket. To* KATTRIN:) Stealing Yvette's boots! She at least gets paid for it, you just *enjoy* strutting like a peacock! Save your proud ways for peacetime!

CHAPLAIN   I don't find her proud.

MOTHER COURAGE   I like her when people say, I never even noticed her. I like her when she's a stone in Dalarna, where there's nothing but stones. (*To* Swiss Cheese:) Leave the cash-box where it is, and look after your sister, she needs it. You two are more trouble than a bag of fleas.

Mother Courage *and the* Chaplain *leave.* Kattrin *clears the dishes away.*

swiss cheese   Not many days more when you can sit in the sun in your shirtsleeves. (Kattrin *points to a tree.*) Yes, the leaves are yellow already. (*With gestures,* Kattrin *asks if he wants a drink.*) No, I'm not drinking, I'm thinking. (*Pause.*) Mother says she can't sleep, so I *should* take the cash-box away. I have a place for it: the mole-hole by the river. I can pick it up there—late to-night maybe—and take it to the sergeant. How far can they have fled in three days? The sergeant's eyes'll pop! "You've disappointed me most pleasantly, Swiss Cheese," he'll say, "I trust you with the cash-box, and *you* bring it back!" Yes, Kattrin, I *will* have a glass now.

When Kattrin *gets behind the wagon, two men confront her. One is a* Sergeant; *the other doffs his hat and flourishes it in a showy greeting; he has a patch over one eye.*

one eye   Morning, young lady! Have you seen a staff officer from the Second Protestant Regiment?

Kattrin *is terrified and runs away, spilling her brandy. The two men look at each other, see* Swiss Cheese, *and withdraw.*

swiss cheese (*starting up*)   You're spilling it, can't you see where you're going? I don't understand you. Anyway, I must be leaving. That's what I've decided on. (*He stands up. She tries to make him understand the danger he is in. He pushes her away.*) I know you mean well, poor thing, you just can't get it out. And don't worry about the brandy. I'll live to drink so much brandy —what's one glass? (*He takes the cash-box out of the wagon and puts it under his coat.*) I'll be right back, but don't hold me up, or I'll have to scold you. Yes, I know you're trying to help!

He kisses her as she tries to hold him back, and pulls himself free. Exit Swiss Cheese. Kattrin *is now desperate. She runs up and down, making little sounds.* Mother Courage *and the* Chaplain *return.* Kattrin *rushes at her mother.*

mother courage   What is it, what is it, control yourself! Have they done something to you? Where's Swiss Cheese? (*To the* Chaplain:) And don't you stand around—get that Catholic flag up!

She takes the flag from her basket. The Chaplain *runs it up the pole.*

CHAPLAIN   God bless our Catholic flag!

MOTHER COURAGE   Now calm down, Kattrin, and tell me all about it. What? That little rascal has taken the cash-box away? Oh, he's going to get a good whipping! Now take your time, don't try to talk, use your hands. I don't like that howling—what will the Chaplain think? A man with one eye? Here?

CHAPLAIN   That fellow is an informer. They've captured Swiss Cheese?

KATTRIN *shakes her head, then shrugs her shoulders. Voices off.* ONE EYE *and the same* SERGEANT *bring in* SWISS CHEESE.

SWISS CHEESE   Let me go! I've nothing on me. You're breaking my shoulder. I am innocent!

SERGEANT   This is where he comes from. These are his friends.

MOTHER COURAGE   Us? Since when?

SWISS CHEESE   I was just getting my lunch here. I paid ten hellers for it. Maybe you saw me on that bench. The food was too salty.

MOTHER COURAGE   That's true. He got his lunch here. And it was too salty.

SERGEANT   Are you pretending you don't know him?

MOTHER COURAGE   I can't know all of them.

CHAPLAIN   He sat there like a law-abiding citizen and never opened his mouth except to eat. Which is necessary.

SERGEANT   Who d'you think you are?

MOTHER COURAGE   He's my bartender. And you must be thirsty. I'll bring you some brandy.

SERGEANT   No liquor while on duty. (*To* SWISS CHEESE:) You were carrying something. You must have hidden it. We saw the bulge in your shirt.

MOTHER COURAGE   Are you sure it was him?

SWISS CHEESE   I think you mean another fellow. There *was* a fellow with something under his shirt. I saw him.

MOTHER COURAGE   I think so too. It's a misunderstanding. Could happen to anyone. Oh, I know what people are like. I'm Mother Courage and I can tell you this: he looks honest.

SERGEANT   We want the regimental cash-box. And we know the looks of the fellow that's been taking care of it. It's you!

SWISS CHEESE   No! No, it's not!

SERGEANT   If you don't shell out, you're dead, see!

MOTHER COURAGE   Oh, he'd give it to you to save his life, he's not that stupid! Speak up, my boy, the sergeant's giving you one last chance!

SWISS CHEESE   What if I don't have it?

SERGEANT We'll get it out of you.

ONE EYE *and the* SERGEANT *lead him off.*

MOTHER COURAGE (*shouting after them*) He'll tell you! He's not *that* stupid! And don't you break his shoulder!

She runs a little way after them. Blackout. The same evening. The CHAPLAIN *and* KATTRIN *are waiting.*

MOTHER COURAGE (*entering*) It's a matter of life and death. But the sergeant will still listen to us. Only he mustn't know it's our Swiss Cheese—or they'll say we helped him. It's just a matter of money. But where can *we* get money? Wasn't Yvette here? I just talked with her. She's picked up a Colonel, and she says he might buy her a canteen business.

CHAPLAIN You'd sell the wagon, everything?

MOTHER COURAGE Where else would I get the money for the sergeant?

CHAPLAIN What are you going to live off?

MOTHER COURAGE That's just it.

Enter YVETTE *with a hoary old* COLONEL. *She embraces* MOTHER COURAGE.

YVETTE Dear Mrs. Fierling, we meet again! (*Whispering:*) He didn't say no. (*Loud:*) This is my friend, my ... business adviser. I heard you might want to sell your wagon.

MOTHER COURAGE I want to pawn it, not sell it. And nothing hasty. You don't find another wagon like this in a hurry.

YVETTE In that case, I'm not sure I'd be interested. What do *you* think, my dear?

COLONEL I agree with you, honey bun.

MOTHER COURAGE It's only for pawn.

YVETTE But I thought you *had* to have the money?

MOTHER COURAGE I do have to. But I'd rather run my feet off looking for another offer than just sell. We live off that wagon.

COLONEL Take it! Take it!

YVETTE My friend thinks I might take it. (*Turning to him:*) But you think we should buy it outright, don't you?

COLONEL Oh, I do, bunny, I do!

MOTHER COURAGE Then you must find one that's for sale.

YVETTE Yes! We can travel around looking for one! I love going around looking. Especially with you, Poldy!

COLONEL Really? Do you?

YVETTE Oh, I love it. I could take weeks of it!

COLONEL Really? Could you?

YVETTE   If you get the money, when would you pay it back?

MOTHER COURAGE   In two weeks. Maybe one.

YVETTE   I can't make up my mind. Poldy, chéri, advise me! (*Aside to him:*) She'll have to sell, don't worry. That lieutenant—the blond one—remember?—he'll lend me the money. He's crazy about me. He says I remind him of someone. What do you advise?

COLONEL   Oh, I have to warn you against *him:* he's no good, he'll only exploit the situation. I told you, bunny, I told you I'd buy you something? Didn't I tell you that?

YVETTE   I can't let you.

COLONEL   Oh, please, please!

YVETTE   Well, if you think the lieutenant might exploit the situation?

COLONEL   I do think so.

YVETTE   So you advise me to go ahead?

COLONEL   I do, bunny, I do!

YVETTE   (*returning to* MOTHER COURAGE)   My friend says all right: two hundred guilders. And I need a receipt saying the wagon would be mine in two weeks. With everything in it. I'll look it all over right now. The two hundred can wait. (*To the* COLONEL:) You go on ahead to the camp. I'll follow.

COLONEL   (*helping her up the steps of the wagon*)   I'll help you up. Come soon, honey bun. (*Exit* COLONEL.)

MOTHER COURAGE   Yvette, Yvette!

YVETTE   There aren't many shoes left.

MOTHER COURAGE   Yvette, this is no time for an inventory, yours or not yours. You promised to talk to the sergeant about Swiss Cheese. There isn't a minute to lose. He's up for court martial one hour from now.

YVETTE   I want to check through these shirts.

MOTHER COURAGE *drags her down the steps by the skirt.*

MOTHER COURAGE   You hyena! Swiss Cheese's life is at stake! And don't say where the money comes from. Pretend he's your sweetheart, or we'll all get it in the neck for helping him.

YVETTE   I arranged to meet One Eye in the bushes. He must be there by now.

CHAPLAIN   And don't give him the whole two hundred. A hundred and fifty should do the trick.

MOTHER COURAGE   You keep your nose out of this! I'm not doing you out of *your* porridge. Now run, and no haggling! Remember his life's at stake! (*She pushes* YVETTE *off.*)

CHAPLAIN All I meant was: what are we going to live on?

MOTHER COURAGE I'm counting on that cash-box. At the very least, Swiss Cheese'll get paid out of it.

CHAPLAIN But d'you think Yvette can manage this?

MOTHER COURAGE It's in her interest—if I don't pay their two hundred, she won't get the wagon. And she knows the score: she won't have this colonel on the string forever. Kattrin, go clean the knives! And don't you just stand around: wash those glasses: there'll be fifty cavalrymen here tonight . . . I think they'll let us have him. They're not wolves, they're human and after money. God is merciful and men are bribable—that's how His will is done on earth, I don't know about Heaven.

YVETTE (*entering*) They'll do it for two hundred if you make it snappy. He confessed he'd had the cash-box, they put the thumb screws on him, but he threw it in the river when he saw them coming at him. Shall I go get the money from my colonel?

MOTHER COURAGE The cash-box in the river? How'll I ever get my two hundred back?

YVETTE You were expecting to get it from the cash-box? I *would* have been sunk. Mother Courage, if you want your Swiss Cheese, you'll have to pay. Or shall I let the whole thing drop—so you can keep your wagon?

MOTHER COURAGE Now I *can't* pay two hundred. I must hold on to something. Go say I'll pay one hundred twenty or the deal's off. Even at that I lose the wagon.

YVETTE One Eye's in a hurry. Looks over his shoulder the whole time. Hadn't I better just give them the two hundred?

MOTHER COURAGE I have her to think of. She's twenty-five and still no husband. I know what I'm doing. One hundred twenty or no deal.

YVETTE You know best.

YVETTE *runs off. After walking up and down abstractedly,* MOTHER COURAGE *sits down to help* KATTRIN *with the knives.*

MOTHER COURAGE I *will* pay two hundred if I have to. With eighty guilders we could pack a hamper and begin over. It won't be the end of the world.

CHAPLAIN The Bible says: the Lord will provide.

MOTHER COURAGE (*to* KATTRIN) You must rub them dry.

YVETTE (*re-enters*) They won't do it. I warned you. He said the drums would roll any second now—and that's the sign they've reached a verdict. I offered one hundred fifty. He didn't even shrug his shoulders.

MOTHER COURAGE Tell him I'll pay two hundred. Run! (YVETTE *runs,* MOTHER COURAGE *sits, the* CHAPLAIN *has finished the glasses.*) I believe—I haggled too long.

In the distance: a roll of drums. The CHAPLAIN *stands up and walks away.* MOTHER COURAGE *remains seated. It grows dark; it gets light again.* MOTHER COURAGE *has not moved.*

YVETTE (*re-enters, pale*) You've done it—with your haggling. You can keep your wagon now. He got eleven bullets in him. I don't know why I still bother about you, you don't deserve it, but I just happened to hear they don't think the cash-box is really in the river. They think it's here. And they think you were in with him. I think they're going to bring his body, to see if you give yourself away when you see him. You'd better not know him or we're in for it. And I should tell you straight: they're right behind me. Shall I keep Kattrin out of this? (MOTHER COURAGE *shakes her head.*) Does she know? Maybe she didn't hear the drums or didn't understand.

MOTHER COURAGE She knows. Bring her.

YVETTE *brings* KATTRIN *who stands by her mother, who takes her hand. Two men come on with a stretcher. There is a sheet over it, and something underneath. Beside them, the* SERGEANT. *They put the stretcher down.*

SERGEANT There's a man here we don't know the name of, but he has to be registered to keep the records straight. He bought a meal from you. Look at him. See if you know him. (*He draws back the sheet.*) You know him? (MOTHER COURAGE *shakes her head.*) What? You never saw him before he bought that meal? (MOTHER COURAGE *shakes her head.*) Lift him up. Throw him on the garbage dump. He has no one that knows him.

They carry him off.

SCENE 4

MOTHER COURAGE *sings the Song of the Great Capitulation.*

Outside an officer's tent. MOTHER COURAGE *waits. A* REGIMENTAL CLERK *looks out of the tent.*

REGIMENTAL CLERK You want to speak to the captain? I know you. You had a Protestant paymaster with you. He was hiding out. Better make no complaint here.

MOTHER COURAGE   But I'm innocent and if I give up it'll look like I have a bad conscience. They cut my wagon to ribbons with their sabers, and then claimed a fine of five thalers—for nothing, for less than nothing!

REGIMENTAL CLERK (*quietly*)   For your own good: keep your mouth shut. We haven't many canteens, so we let you stay in business, especially if you've a bad conscience and have to pay a fine now and then.

MOTHER COURAGE   I'm going to lodge a complaint.

REGIMENTAL CLERK   As you wish. Wait here till the captain is free.

The CLERK *retires into the tent. A* YOUNG SOLDIER *comes storming in.*

YOUNG SOLDIER   Screw the captain! Where is the son of a bitch? Grabbing my reward, spending it on brandy for his whores! I'll rip his belly open!

OLDER SOLDIER (*following him*)   Shut your hole, you'll only wind up in the stocks!

YOUNG SOLDIER   I was the only one in the squad who swam the river and *he* grabs the money. I can't even buy me a beer. Come out, you thief, I'll make lamb chops out of you!

OLDER SOLDIER   Holy Christ, he'll destroy himself.

YOUNG SOLDIER (*pulling himself free of the older man*)   Let me go or I'll cut you down too!

OLDER SOLDIER   Saved the colonel's horse and didn't get the reward. He's young. He hasn't been at it long.

MOTHER COURAGE   Let him go. He doesn't have to be chained like a dog. Very reasonable to want a reward. Why else should he go to the trouble?

YOUNG SOLDIER   He's in there pouring it down. I done something special: I want the reward!

MOTHER COURAGE   Young man, don't scream at *me,* I have my own problems.

YOUNG SOLDIER   He's whoring on my money and I'm hungry! I'll murder him!

MOTHER COURAGE   You're hungry. You're angry. I understand.

YOUNG SOLDIER   Talking'll get you nowhere. I won't stand for injustice!

MOTHER COURAGE   How long? How long won't you stand for injustice? One hour? Or two? It's a misery to sit in the stocks: especially if you leave it till then to realize you do stand for injustice.

YOUNG SOLDIER   I don't know why I listen to you. Screw that captain!

MOTHER COURAGE You listen because you know I'm right. Your rage has calmed down already. It was a short one, and you'd need a long one.

YOUNG SOLDIER Are you trying to tell me I shouldn't ask for the money?

MOTHER COURAGE Just the opposite. I only say your rage won't last, you'll get nowhere with it. If your rage was a long one, I'd say: go ahead, slice him up. But what's the use—if you don't slice him up? What's the use if you stand there with your tail between your legs?

OLDER SOLDIER You're quite right: he's crazy.

YOUNG SOLDIER All right, we'll see whether I slice him up or not. (*He draws his sword.*) When he comes out, I slice him up.

CLERK (*looking out again*) The captain will be right out. (*A military order:*) Be seated!

The YOUNG SOLDIER *sits.*

MOTHER COURAGE What did I tell you? Oh, they know us inside out. "Be seated!" And we sit. *I'm* no better. Let me tell you about the great capitulation.

THE GREAT CAPITULATION

Long, long ago, a green beginner
    I thought myself a special case.
(None of your ordinary, run of the mill girls, with my looks and my talent and my love of the Higher Things.)
I picked a hair out of my dinner
    And put the waiter in his place.
(All or nothing. Anyway, never the second best. I am the master of my fate. I'll take no orders from no one.)
Then a little bird whispers!
      The bird says: "Wait a year or so
      And marching with the band you'll go
      Keeping in step, now fast, now slow,
      And piping out your little spiel.
      Then one day the battalions wheel!
      And you go down upon your knees
      To God Almighty if you please!"

My friend, before that year was over
    I'd learned to drink their cup of tea.
(Two children round your neck and the price of bread and what all!)

When they were through with me, moreover,
  They had me where they wanted me.
(You must get in with people. If you scratch my back, I'll
scratch yours. Don't stick your neck out!)
Then a little bird whispers!
    The bird says: "Scarce a year or so
    And marching with the band she'd go
    Keeping in step, now fast, now slow,
    And piping out her little spiel.
    Then one day the battalions wheel!
    And she goes down upon her knees
    To God Almighty if you please!"

Our plans are big, our hopes colossal.
  We hitch our wagon to a star.
(Where there's a will, there's a way. You can't hold a good
man down.)
"We can lift mountains," says the apostle.
  And yet: how heavy one cigar!
(You must cut your coat according to your cloth.)
That little bird whispers!
    The bird says: "Wait a year or so
    And marching with the band we go
    Keeping in step, now fast, now slow,
    And piping out our little spiel.
    Then one day the battalions wheel!
    And we go down upon our knees
    To God Almighty if you please!"

MOTHER COURAGE So stay here with your sword drawn, if your
  anger is big enough. If it isn't, you'd better go.
YOUNG SOLDIER Aw, shove it! (*He stumbles off, the* OLDER SOL-
  DIER *following him.*)
REGIMENTAL CLERK (*again sticking his head out*) The captain is
  free now. You can lodge your complaint.
MOTHER COURAGE I've thought better of it. I'm not complaining.

She leaves. The CLERK *looks after her, shaking his head.*

SCENE 5

*Two years have passed. The war covers wider and wider territory. Always
on the move, the little wagon crosses Poland, Moravia, Bavaria, Italy, and
again Bavaria. 1631. General Tilly's victory at Leipzig costs* MOTHER
COURAGE *four shirts.*

The wagon stands in a war-ruined village. Victory march in the distance. Two Soldiers *are being served at a counter by* Kattrin *and* Mother Courage. *One of them has a woman's fur coat about his shoulders.*

mother courage   What, you can't pay? No money, no schnapps! If they can play victory marches, they should pay their men.

first soldier   I want my schnapps! I arrived too late for plunder. The Chief allowed just one hour to plunder the town. He's not inhuman, he says—so I guess they bought him off.

chaplain   (*staggering in*)   There are people in the farmhouse. A whole family. Help me, someone! I need linen.

The Second Soldier *goes with him.* Kattrin, *becoming excited, tries to get her mother to bring linen out of the wagon.*

mother courage   I have none. I sold all my bandages to the regiment. I'm not tearing up my officer's shirts for these people.

chaplain   (*over his shoulder*)   I said: I need linen!

Mother Courage *stops* Kattrin *from entering the wagon.*

mother courage   Not on your life! They have nothing and they pay nothing.

The Chaplain *carries in a* Woman.

chaplain   Why did you stay there—in the line of fire?

woman   (*faintly*)   Our farm . . .

mother courage   Think they'd ever let go of anything? And now *I'm* supposed to pay. Well, I won't!

first soldier   They're Protestants. Why do they have to be Protestants?

mother courage   Protestant, Catholic, what do they care? It's their farm they're thinking of.

second soldier   Anyway, they're not Protestants. They're Catholics.

first soldier   I guess our cannon don't know the difference.

The Chaplain *brings in a* Peasant.

peasant   My arm's shot.

chaplain   Where's that linen?

mother courage   I can't give you any. With all I have to pay out in taxes, duties, bribes . . . (Kattrin *picks up a board and threatens her mother with it, making gurgling sounds.*) Are you out of your mind? Put that board down this minute! I'm giving nothing! (*The* Chaplain *lifts her bodily off the wagon steps, then brings the shirts from the wagon, and tears them in strips.*) My shirts! My officer's shirts!

From the house, the cry of a child in pain.

PEASANT   The child's still in the house.

KATTRIN *runs into the house.*

MOTHER COURAGE   Hey, grab Kattrin, the roof may fall in!
CHAPLAIN   I'm not going back in there.
MOTHER COURAGE   My officer's shirts, half a guilder apiece. I'm
ruined! (KATTRIN *comes out with a baby in her arms. To her:*)
Never happy till you're dragging babies around! Give it to its
mother at once!

KATTRIN *is humming a lullaby to the child.*

CHAPLAIN (*bandaging*)   The blood comes through.
MOTHER COURAGE   And, in all this, she's happy as a lark! Stop that
music! I don't need music to tell me what victory's like. (*The*
FIRST SOLDIER *tries to make off with the bottle he's been drinking from.*) Come back, you! If you want another victory, you'll
have to pay for it.
FIRST SOLDIER   But I'm broke.

MOTHER COURAGE *tears the fur coat off his back.*

MOTHER COURAGE   Then leave this. It's stolen goods anyhow.

KATTRIN *rocks the child and raises it high above her head.*

SCENE 6

*The Catholic General Tilly is killed before the city of Ingolstadt and
is buried in state.* MOTHER COURAGE *gives her views of heroes, and the*
CHAPLAIN *sings a song about the duration of the war.* KATTRIN *gets the
red boots at last. The year is 1632.*

*The interior of a canteen tent. The inside part of the counter is seen
at the rear. Funeral march in the distance. The* CHAPLAIN *and the* REGI-
MENTAL CLERK *are playing checkers.* MOTHER COURAGE *and* KATTRIN
are taking inventory.

CHAPLAIN   The funeral procession is just starting out.
MOTHER COURAGE   Pity about the Chief—twenty-two pairs, socks
—getting killed that way. They say it was an accident. There was
a fog over the fields that morning, and the fog was to blame.
He'd been telling his men to fight to the death, and was just riding back to safety when he lost his way in the fog, went forward
instead of back, found himself in the thick of the battle, and ran
right smack into a bullet. (*A whistle from the counter. She goes*

over to attend to a soldier.) It's a disgrace—the way you're all skipping your Commander's funeral.

REGIMENTAL CLERK They shouldn't have handed out the money before the funeral. Now the men are getting drunk instead of going to it.

CHAPLAIN (*to the* REGIMENTAL CLERK) Don't you have to be there?

REGIMENTAL CLERK I stayed away because of the rain.

MOTHER COURAGE It's different for you. The rain might spoil your uniform.

Another SOLDIER *comes to the counter. He sings:*

BATTLE HYMN

One schnapps, mine host, be quick, make haste!
A soldier's got no time to waste:
He must be shooting, shooting, shooting,
His Kaiser's enemies uprooting!

SOLDIER A brandy.

Two breasts, my girl, be quick, make haste,
A soldier's got no time to waste:
He must be hating, hating, hating,
He cannot keep his Kaiser waiting!

SOLDIER Make it a double, this is a holiday.

MOTHER COURAGE Money first. No, you can't come inside, not with those boots on. Only officers are allowed in here, rain or no rain.

CHAPLAIN (*as the funeral music resumes*) Now they're filing past the body.

MOTHER COURAGE I feel sorry for a commander like that—when maybe he had something big in mind, something they'd talk about in times to come, something they'd raise a statue to him for, the conquest of the whole world, for example—Lord, the worms have got into these biscuits!—he works his hands to the bone and then the common riffraff don't support him because all they care about is a jug of beer or a bit of company. Am I right?

CHAPLAIN You're right, Mother Courage. Till you come to the riffraff. You underestimate them. Take those fellows outside right now, drinking their brandy in the rain, why, they'd fight for a hundred years, one war after another—if necessary, two at a time.

MOTHER COURAGE Seventeen leather belts.—Then you don't think the war might end?

CHAPLAIN Because a commander's dead? Don't be childish. Heroes are cheap. There are plenty of others where he came from.

MOTHER COURAGE I wasn't asking just for the sake of argument. I was wondering if I should buy up a lot of supplies. They happen to be cheap right now. But if the war's going to end, I might just as well forget it.

CHAPLAIN There are people who think the war's about to end, but I say: you can't be sure it will *ever* end. Oh, it may have to pause occasionally, for breath, as it were. It can even meet with an accident—nothing on this earth is perfect—one can't think of everything—a little oversight and a war may be in the hole and someone's got to pull it out again. That someone is the King or the Emperor or the Pope. But they're such friends in need, this war hasn't got much to worry about: it can look forward to a prosperous future.

MOTHER COURAGE If I was sure you're right . . .

CHAPLAIN Think it out for yourself. How *could* the war end?

REGIMENTAL CLERK I'm from Bohemia. I'd like to get home once in a while. So I'm hoping for peace.

CHAPLAIN Peace?

REGIMENTAL CLERK Yes, peace! How can we live without it?

CHAPLAIN We don't have to. There's peace even in war. War satisfies all needs—even those of peace. I know a song about that. (*He sings:*)

THE ARMY CHAPLAIN'S SONG

Does war, my friend, stop you from drinking?
    Does it not give you bread to chew?
To my old-fashioned way of thinking
    That much at least a war can do.

And even in the thick of slaughter
    A soldier feels the amorous itch
And many a buxom farmer's daughter
    Has lost her virtue in a ditch.

REGIMENTAL CLERK Maybe. But when shall I get another good night's sleep?

CHAPLAIN That also has been care of.

Somehow we find the bread and brandy
    And finding women is a snap.
And when there is a gutter handy
    We catch a twenty-minute nap.

As for the sleep that lasts forever
  Though it will come in any case
In war more Christian souls than ever
  Reach their eternal resting place.

REGIMENTAL CLERK   And when everyone's dead, the war won't stop
  even then, I suppose?
CHAPLAIN   Let me finish.

What won't a soldier do in wartime
  His savage lust to satisfy!
But after all, 'twas said aforetime:
  Be fruitful, lads, and multiply!

If you ignore this high injunction,
  The war will have to stop, my friend:
Perform your biologic function
  And then the war need never end!

REGIMENTAL CLERK   You admit the war *could* stop.
CHAPLAIN   Tsk, tsk, tsk. You don't know where God lives. Listen!

Peacemakers shall the earth inherit:
  We bless those men of simple worth.
Warmakers have still greater merit:
  They *have* inherited the earth.

I'll tell you, my good sir, what peace is:
  The hole when all the cheese is gone.
And what is war? This is my thesis:
  It's what the world is founded on.

War is like love: it'll always find a way. Why *should* it end?

MOTHER COURAGE   Then I *will* buy those supplies. I'll take your
  word for it. (KATTRIN, *who has been staring at the* CHAPLAIN,
  *suddenly bangs a basket of glasses down on the ground and runs
  out.* MOTHER COURAGE *laughs.*) She'll go right on waiting for
  peace. I promised her she'll get a husband when peace comes.
  (*She follows* KATTRIN.)
REGIMENTAL CLERK (*standing up*)   You were singing. I win.

MOTHER COURAGE *brings* KATTRIN *back.*

MOTHER COURAGE   Be sensible, the war'll go on a bit longer, and
  we'll make a bit more money—then peace'll be all the nicer.

Now you go into the town, it's not ten minutes' walk, and bring the things from the Golden Lion. Just the special things for your trousseau: the rest we can pick up later in the wagon. The Clerk will go with you, you'll be quite safe. Do a good job, and don't lose anything, think of your trousseau! (KATTRIN *ties a kerchief round her head and leaves with the* CLERK.) Now you can chop me a bit of firewood.

The CHAPLAIN *takes his coat off and prepares to chop wood.*

CHAPLAIN   Properly speaking, I am a pastor of souls, not a wood-cutter.

MOTHER COURAGE   But I don't have a soul, and I do need wood.

CHAPLAIN   What's that little pipe you've got there?

MOTHER COURAGE   Just a pipe.

CHAPLAIN   I think it's a very particular pipe.

MOTHER COURAGE   Oh?

CHAPLAIN   The cook's pipe in fact. Our Swedish Commander's cook.

MOTHER COURAGE   If you know, why beat about the bush?

CHAPLAIN   I wondered if *you* knew. It was possible you just rummaged among your belongings and just lit on . . . some pipe.

MOTHER COURAGE   How d' you know that's not it?

CHAPLAIN   It isn't! You did know! (*He brings the axe down on the block.*)

MOTHER COURAGE   What if I did?

CHAPLAIN   Mother Courage, it is my duty to warn you. You are unlikely to see the gentleman again, but that's a blessing. Mother Courage, he did not strike me as trustworthy.

MOTHER COURAGE   Really? He was such a nice man.

CHAPLAIN   Well! So that's what you call a nice man! I do not. (*Again the axe falls.*) Far be it from me to wish him ill, but I cannot, cannot describe him as nice. No, he's a Don Juan, a cunning Don Juan. Just look at that pipe if you don't believe me—it tells all!

MOTHER COURAGE   I see nothing special about this pipe. It's been used, of course . . .

CHAPLAIN   It's been practically bitten through! Oho, he's a wild man! That is the pipe of a wild man! (*The axe falls more violently than ever.*)

MOTHER COURAGE   Now it's my chopping block that's bitten through!

CHAPLAIN   I told you the care of souls was my field. In physical labor my God-given talents find no adequate expression. You haven't heard me preach. Why, I can put such spirit into a regiment with a single sermon that the enemy's a mere flock of sheep to them and their own lives are no more than a smelly old pair of shoes to be instantly thrown away at the thought of final victory! God has given me the gift of tongues! I can preach you out of your senses!

MOTHER COURAGE But I need my senses. What would I do without them?

CHAPLAIN Mother Courage, I have often thought that—under a veil of blunt speech—you conceal a heart. You are human, you need warmth.

MOTHER COURAGE The best way of warming this tent is to chop plenty of firewood.

CHAPLAIN Seriously, my dear Courage, I sometimes ask myself how it would be if our relationship should be somewhat more firmly cemented. I mean: now the wild wind of war has whirled us so strangely together.

MOTHER COURAGE The cement's pretty firm already. I cook your meals. And you lend a hand—at chopping firewood, for instance.

The CHAPLAIN *flourishes the axe as he approaches her.*

CHAPLAIN Oh, you know what I mean by a closer relationship. Let your heart speak!

MOTHER COURAGE Don't come at me like that with your axe! That'd be *too* close a relationship!

CHAPLAIN This is no laughing matter. I have given it careful thought.

MOTHER COURAGE My dear Chaplain, be sensible, I do like you. All I want is for me and mine to get by in this war. Now chop the firewood and we'll be warm in the evenings. What's that? (MOTHER COURAGE *stands up.* KATTRIN *enters with a nasty wound above her eye. She is letting everything fall, parcels, leather goods, a drum, etc.*) What happened? Were you attacked? On the way back? It's not serious, only a flesh wound. I'll bandage it up, and you'll be better within a week. Didn't the clerk walk you back? That's because you're a good girl, he thought they'd leave you alone. The wound isn't deep. It will never show. There! (*She has finished the bandage.*) Now I have a little present for you. (*She fishes Yvette's red boots out of a bag.*) See? You always wanted them—now you have them. Put them on before I change my mind. It will never show. Look, the boots have kept well, I cleaned them good before I put them away.

But KATTRIN *leaves the boots alone, and creeps into the wagon.*

CHAPLAIN   I hope she won't be disfigured.

MOTHER COURAGE   There'll be quite a scar. She needn't wait for peace now.

CHAPLAIN   She didn't let them get any of the things.

MOTHER COURAGE   I wish I knew what goes on inside her head. She stayed out all night once—once in all the years. I never did get out of her what happened. (*She picks up the things that* KATTRIN *spilled and angrily sorts them out.*)   And this is war! A nice source of income, I must say!

Cannon.

CHAPLAIN   They're lowering the Commander in his grave. A historic moment!

MOTHER COURAGE   It's historic to me all right. She's finished. How would she ever get a husband now? And she's crazy for children. Even her dumbness comes from the war. A soldier stuck something in her mouth when she was little. I'll never see Swiss Cheese again, and where my Eilif is the Good Lord knows. Curse the war!

SCENE 7

A highway. The CHAPLAIN *and* KATTRIN *are pulling the wagon. It is dirty and neglected, though new goods are hung around it.*

MOTHER COURAGE   (*walking beside the wagon, a flask at her waist*) I won't have my war all spoiled for me! Destroys the weak, does it? Well, what does peace do for 'em? Huh? (*She sings The Song of Mother Courage:*)

> So cheer up, boys, the rose is fading!
>   When victory comes you may be dead!
> A war is just the same as trading:
>   But not with cheese—with steel and lead!
>   Christians, awake! The winter's gone!
>   The snows depart, the dead sleep on.
>   And though you may not long survive
>   Get out of bed and look alive!

SCENE 8

In the same year, the Protestant king falls in the battle of Lützen. The peace threatens MOTHER COURAGE *with ruin. Her brave son performs one heroic deed too many and comes to a shameful end.*

A camp. Summer morning. In front of the wagon, an OLD WOMAN *and her* SON. *The* SON *drags a large bag of bedding.* MOTHER COURAGE *is inside the wagon.*

MOTHER COURAGE Must you come at the crack of dawn?

YOUNG MAN We've been walking all night. Twenty miles. We have to get back today.

MOTHER COURAGE What do I want with bed feathers? Take them to the town!

YOUNG MAN At least wait till you see them.

OLD WOMAN Nothing doing here either. Let's go.

YOUNG MAN And let 'em sign away the roof over our heads for taxes? Maybe she'll pay three guilders if you throw in that bracelet. (*Bells start ringing.*) Hear that, Mother?

VOICE FROM A DISTANCE It's peace! The King of Sweden got killed!

MOTHER COURAGE *sticks her head out of the wagon. She hasn't done her hair yet.*

MOTHER COURAGE Bells? Bells in the middle of the week?

The CHAPLAIN *crawls out from under the wagon.*

CHAPLAIN What's that they're shouting?

YOUNG MAN It's peace.

CHAPLAIN Peace?!

MOTHER COURAGE Don't tell me peace has broken out—I've gone and bought all these supplies!

CHAPLAIN (*shouting*) Is it peace?

VOICE Yes! The war stopped three weeks ago!

CHAPLAIN (*To* MOTHER COURAGE) Why else would they ring the bells?

VOICE A big crowd of Lutherans just arrived—they brought the news.

YOUNG MAN It's peace, Mother. (*The* OLD WOMAN *collapses.*) What's the matter?

MOTHER COURAGE (*back in the wagon*) Kattrin, it's peace! Put on your black dress, we're going to church, we owe it to Swiss Cheese.

YOUNG MAN The war's over. (*The* OLD WOMAN *gets up, dazed.*) I'll get the harness shop going again now. Everything will be all right. Father will get his bed back. Can you walk? (*To the* CHAPLAIN:) It was the news. She didn't believe there'd ever be peace again. Father always said there would. We'll be going home.

They leave.

MOTHER COURAGE (*from the wagon*) Give them a schnapps!

CHAPLAIN Too late: they've gone! And who may this be coming over from the camp? If it isn't our Swedish Commander's cook?!

The COOK *comes on, bedraggled, carrying a bundle.*

CHAPLAIN Mother Courage, a visitor!

MOTHER COURAGE *clambers out of the wagon.*

COOK I promised to come back, remember? For a short conversation? I didn't forget your brandy, Mrs. Fierling.

MOTHER COURAGE The Commander's cook! After all these years! Where's Eilif?

COOK Isn't he here yet? He went on ahead yesterday. He was on his way here.

CHAPLAIN I'll be putting my pastor's clothes back on. (*He goes behind the wagon.*)

MOTHER COURAGE Kattrin, Eilif's coming! Bring a glass of brandy for the cook! (*But* KATTRIN *doesn't.*) Oh, pull your hair over your face and forget it, the cook's no stranger! (*To him:*) She won't come out. Peace is nothing to her. It took too long to get here. Here's your schnapps. (*She has got it herself. They sit.*)

COOK Dear old peace!

MOTHER COURAGE Dear old peace has broken my neck. On the chaplain's advice I went and bought a lot of supplies. Now everybody's leaving, and I'm holding the baby.

COOK How could you listen to a windbag like the chaplain? If I'd had the time I'd have warned you against him. But the Catholics were too quick for me. Since when did he become the big wheel around here?

MOTHER COURAGE He's been doing the dishes and helping me with the wagon.

COOK And telling you a few of his jokes? He has a most unhealthy attitude to women. He's completely unsound.

MOTHER COURAGE And you're completely sound?

COOK And I am completely sound. Your health!

MOTHER COURAGE Sound! Only one person around here was ever sound, and I never had to slave as I did then. He sold the blankets off the children's beds in autumn. You aren't recommending yourself to me if you claim to be sound.

COOK Ah well, here we sit, drinking your famous brandy while the bells of peace do ring!

MOTHER COURAGE I don't see where they're going to find all this pay that's in arrears. Were you people paid?

COOK (*hesitating*) Not exactly. That's why we disbanded. Why stay? I said to myself. Why not look up a couple of friends? So here I am.

MOTHER COURAGE   In other words: you're broke.

COOK   (*annoyed by the bells*)   I wish they'd stop that racket! I'd like to set myself up in some business.

The CHAPLAIN *enters in his pastor's coat again.*

CHAPLAIN   Pretty good, eh? Just a few moth holes.

COOK   I have a bone to pick with you. You advised a lady to buy superfluous goods on the pretext that the war would never end.

CHAPLAIN   And what business is that of yours?

COOK   It's unprincipled behavior! How dare you interfere with the conduct of other people's businesses?

CHAPLAIN   Who's interfering now, I'd like to know? (*To* MOTHER COURAGE:) I was far from suspecting you had to account to *this* gentleman for everything!

MOTHER COURAGE   Now don't get excited. The cook's giving his personal opinion. You can hardly deny your war was a flop.

CHAPLAIN   You are a hyena of the battlefield! You are taking the name of peace in vain!

MOTHER COURAGE   I'm a what, did you say?

CHAPLAIN   A hyena!

COOK   Who insults my girl friend, insults me!

CHAPLAIN   *Your* intentions are only too transparent! (*To* MOTHER COURAGE:) But when I see *you* take peace between finger and thumb like a snotty old handkerchief, the humanity in me rebels! You want war, do you? Well, don't you forget the proverb: who sups with the devil must use a long spoon!

MOTHER COURAGE   Remember what one fox said to another that was caught in a trap? "If you stay there, you're just asking for trouble." I'm not in love with war, Mr. Army Chaplain, and when it comes to calling people hyenas, you and I part company!

CHAPLAIN   Then why all this grumbling about the peace? Is it just for the junk in your wagon?

MOTHER COURAGE   My goods are not junk. I live off them.

CHAPLAIN   You live off war. Exactly!

COOK   As a grown man, you should know better than to run around advising people. (*To* MOTHER COURAGE:) In your situation you should get rid of certain goods at once—before prices sink to zero.

MOTHER COURAGE   That's good advice. I think I'll take it. (*She climbs on to her wagon.*)

COOK   One up for me. Anyway, Chaplain, cockfights are unbecoming to your cloth!

CHAPLAIN   If you don't shut your mouth, I'll murder you, cloth or no cloth!

Enter YVETTE, *wearing black, leaning on a stick. She is much older, fatter, and heavily powdered. Behind her, a* VALET.

YVETTE   Hullo everybody! Is this the Mother Courage establishment?

CHAPLAIN   Quite right. And with whom have we the pleasure?

YVETTE   I am Madam Colonel Starhemberg, good people. Where's Mother Courage?

CHAPLAIN (*calling to the wagon*)   Madam Colonel Starhemberg to speak with you!

MOTHER COURAGE   Coming!

YVETTE (*calling*)   It's me—Yvette!

MOTHER COURAGE   Yvette!

YVETTE   I've come to see how you're getting on! (*The* COOK *turns round in horror.*) Peter!

COOK   Yvette!

YVETTE   Of all things. How did *you* get here?

COOK   On a cart.

CHAPLAIN   Well! You know each other? Intimately?

YVETTE   I'll say! You're fat.

COOK   For that matter, you're no beanpole.

YVETTE   It's good we've met. Now I can tell you what I think of you, tramp.

CHAPLAIN   Do that. Tell him exactly what you think of him. But wait till Mother Courage comes out.

COOK   Now don't make a scene.

MOTHER COURAGE *comes out, laden with goods.*

MOTHER COURAGE   Yvette! (*They embrace.*) But why are you in mourning?

YVETTE   Doesn't it suit me? My husband, the colonel, died several years ago.

MOTHER COURAGE   The old fellow that nearly bought my wagon?

YVETTE   Nah, not him. His older brother.

MOTHER COURAGE   Good to see one person that got somewhere in this war.

CHAPLAIN   You promised to give us your opinion of this gentleman.

COOK   Now, Yvette, don't make a stink!

MOTHER COURAGE   He's a friend of mine, Yvette.

YVETTE   He's Peter Piper, that's what.

COOK   Cut the nicknames!

MOTHER COURAGE Peter Piper? The one that turned the girls' heads? I'll have to sit down. And I've been keeping your pipe for you.

CHAPLAIN And smoking it.

YVETTE Lucky I can warn you against him. He's a bad lot. You won't find a worse on the whole coast of Flanders. He got more girls in trouble than . . .

COOK That's a long time ago. It's not true any more.

YVETTE Stand up when you talk to a lady! How I loved that man, and all the time he was having a little bowlegged brunette. He got her in trouble, too, of course.

COOK I seem to have brought *you* luck.

YVETTE Speak when you're spoken to, you hoary ruin! And take care, Mother Courage, this type is dangerous even in decay!

MOTHER COURAGE (*to* YVETTE) Come with me. I must get rid of this stuff before the prices fall.

YVETTE (*to* COOK) Miserable cur!

MOTHER COURAGE Maybe you can help me at army headquarters —with your contacts.

YVETTE Damnable whore hunter!

MOTHER COURAGE Kattrin, church is all off, I'm going to market!

YVETTE Inveterate seducer!

MOTHER COURAGE (*still to* KATTRIN) When Eilif comes, give him something to drink!

YVETTE I've put an end to your tricks, Peter Piper, and one day, in a better life than this, the Lord God will reward me! (*She sniffs.*) Come, Mother Courage!

The two leave. Pause.

CHAPLAIN As our text this morning, let us take the saying: the mills of God grind slowly. And you complain of my jokes!

COOK I'll be frank with you: I was hoping for a good hot dinner. And now she'll be getting a wrong picture of me. I think I should leave before she comes back.

CHAPLAIN I think so too.

COOK Chaplain, peace makes me sick! It's the lot of mankind to perish by fire and sword! Oh, how I wish I was roasting a great fat capon for the Commander—with mustard sauce and those little yellow carrots . . .

CHAPLAIN Red cabbage. With capon: red cabbage.

COOK You're right. But he always wanted yellow carrots.

CHAPLAIN He never understood anything.

COOK You always put plenty away.

CHAPLAIN Under protest.

COOK   Anyway, you must admit, those were the days.

CHAPLAIN   Yes, that I might admit.

COOK   And now you've called her a hyena, you haven't much future here either . . . What are you staring at?

CHAPLAIN   Why, it's Eilif! (EILIF *enters followed by two soldiers with halberds. His hands are fettered. He is white as chalk.*) What happened?

EILIF   Where's my mother?

CHAPLAIN   Gone to the town.

EILIF   They said she was here. I was allowed a last visit.

COOK (*to the soldiers*)   Where are you taking him?

SOLDIER   For a ride.

The other SOLDIER *makes the gesture of throat cutting.*

CHAPLAIN   What has he done?

SOLDIER   He broke in on a peasant. The wife is dead.

CHAPLAIN   Eilif, how could you?

EILIF   It's no different. It's what I did before.

COOK   That was in wartime.

EILIF   Shut your mouth. Can I sit down till she comes?

SOLDIER   No.

CHAPLAIN   It's true. In wartime they honored him for it. He sat at the Commander's right hand. It was bravery. Couldn't we speak with the provost?

SOLDIER   What's the use? Stealing cattle from a peasant, what's brave about that?

COOK   It was just dumb.

EILIF   If I'd been dumb, I'd have starved, smarty.

COOK   So you were bright—and paid for it.

CHAPLAIN   We must bring Kattrin out.

EILIF   Let her alone. Just give me some brandy.

SOLDIER   No.

CHAPLAIN   What shall we tell your mother?

EILIF   Tell her it was no different. Tell her it was the same. Aw, tell her nothing.

The SOLDIERS *lead him away.*

CHAPLAIN   I'll come with you!

EILIF   I don't need any priest.

CHAPLAIN   You don't know—yet. (*He follows them.*)

COOK   I'll have to tell her, she'll expect to see him.

CHAPLAIN   Tell her he'll be back.

He leaves. The COOK *shakes his head, finally approaches the wagon.*

COOK　Hi! Won't you come out? I'm the cook! Have you got anything to eat in there? (*He looks in.*) She's got a blanket over her head.

Cannon. Re-enter MOTHER COURAGE, *breathless, still carrying her goods.*

MOTHER COURAGE　The peace is over! The war's on again—has been for three days! I didn't get rid of this stuff after all, thank God! The shooting has started in the town already. We must get away. Pack, Kattrin! What's on *your* mind?

COOK　Nothing.

MOTHER COURAGE　But there is. I see it in your face.

COOK　Eilif was here. Only he had to go away again.

MOTHER COURAGE　He was here? Then we'll see him on the march. I'll be with our side this time. How'd he look?

COOK　The same.

MOTHER COURAGE　He'll *never* change. And the war won't get *him,* he's bright. Help me with the packing. (*She starts it.*) Is Eilif in good with the captain? Did he tell you about his heroic deeds?

COOK　He's done one of them over again.

MOTHER COURAGE　Tell me about it later. (KATTRIN *appears.*) Kattrin, the peace is over. We're on the move again. (*To the* COOK:) What *is* eating you?

COOK　I'll enlist.

MOTHER COURAGE　Where's the Chaplain?

COOK　In the town. With Eilif.

MOTHER COURAGE　Stay with us a while, Cook, I need a bit of help.

COOK　This Yvette matter . . .

MOTHER COURAGE　Hasn't done you any harm in my eyes. Just the opposite. Where there's smoke, there's fire. You'll come?

COOK　I may as well.

MOTHER COURAGE　The twelfth regiment is under way. (THE COOK *gets into harness with* KATTRIN.) Maybe I'll see Eilif before the day is out! Let's go! (*She sings, and the* COOK *joins in the refrain, The Song of Mother Courage:*)

> Up hill, down dale, past dome and steeple,
>   My wagon always moves ahead.
> The war can care for all its people
>   So long as there is steel and lead.
> Though steel and lead are stout supporters
>   A war needs human beings too.
> Report today to your headquarters!
>   If it's to last, this war needs you!
>   Christians, awake! The winter's gone!

The snow departs, the dead sleep on.
And though you may not long survive
Get out of bed and look alive!

SCENE 9

The religious war has lasted sixteen years, and Germany has lost half its inhabitants. Those who are spared in battle die by plague. Over once-blooming countryside hunger rages. Towns are burned down. Wolves prowl the empty streets. In the autumn of 1634 we find MOTHER COURAGE *in the Fitchtelgebirge not far from the road the Swedish Army is taking. Winter has come early and is severe. Business is bad. Only begging remains. The* COOK *receives a letter from Utrecht and is sent packing.*

In front of a half-ruined parsonage. Early winter. A grey morning. Gusts of wind. MOTHER COURAGE *and the* COOK *at the wagon in rags.*

COOK   There are no lights. No one is up.

MOTHER COURAGE   But it's a parsonage. The parson'll have to leave his feather bed to go ring the bells. Then he'll have himself some hot soup.

COOK   Where'll he find it? The whole village is starving.

MOTHER COURAGE   Why don't we sing him something?

COOK   Anna, I've had enough. A letter came from Utrecht, did I tell you? My mother died of cholera. The inn is mine. Look!

(He hands her the letter. She glances through it.)

MOTHER COURAGE   I'm tired of this wandering life. I feel like a butcher's dog, taking meat to the customers and getting none for myself.

COOK   The world's coming to an end.

MOTHER COURAGE   Sometimes I dream of driving through hell with this wagon—and selling brimstone. Or I see myself driving through heaven handing out supplies to wandering souls! If only we could find a place where there's no shooting, me and my children—what's left of 'em—we might rest up a while.

COOK   Why don't we open this inn together? With you or without you, I'm leaving for Utrecht today. Think it over.

MOTHER COURAGE   I must tell Kattrin. Kattrin! (KATTRIN *comes out of the wagon.*) Listen. We're thinking of going to Utrecht, the cook and me. His mother's left him an inn. We'd be sure of our dinner. And you'd have a bed of your own. What about it?

COOK   Anna, I must speak to you alone.

MOTHER COURAGE   Go back in, Kattrin.

KATTRIN *does so.*

COOK   There's a misunderstanding. I hoped I wouldn't have to come right out with it—but if you're bringing her, it's all off.

KATTRIN *is listening—her head sticking out at the back of the wagon.*

MOTHER COURAGE   You want me to leave Kattrin behind?

COOK   There's no room. The inn isn't a place with three counters. If the two of us stand on our hind legs we can earn a living, but three's too many. Let Kattrin keep your wagon.

MOTHER COURAGE   I was thinking she might find a husband in Utrecht.

COOK   At her age? With that scar?

MOTHER COURAGE   Not so loud!

COOK   The customers wouldn't like it!

MOTHER COURAGE   Not so loud, I said!

COOK   There's a light in the parsonage. We'd better sing. Worthy Master Parson, and all within, we shall now sing the song of Solomon, Holy Saint Martin, and other good men who came to a bad end, so you can see we're good folk too, and have a hard time getting by, especially in winter. (*He sings.* MOTHER COURAGE *joins him in the refrains.*)

THE SONG OF THE WISE AND GOOD

You've heard of wise old Solomon
   You know his history.
He thought so little of this earth
He cursed the hour of his birth
   Declaring: all is vanity.
How very wise was Solomon!
   But ere night came and day did go
This fact was clear to everyone:
   It was his wisdom that had brought him low.
(Better for you if you have none.)

For the virtues are dangerous in this world, you're better off without, you have a nice life—some good hot soup included. We're told to be unselfish and share what we have, but what if we have nothing? Unselfishness is a very rare virtue, it simply doesn't pay.

Unselfish Martin could not bear
   His fellow creatures' woes.
   He met a beggar in the snows
And gave him half his cloak to wear:
   So both of them fell down and froze.

What an unselfish paragon!
    But ere night came and day did go
This fact was clear to everyone:
    It was unselfishness that brought him low.
(Better for you if you have none.)

That's how it is! We're good, we don't steal, we don't kill, we don't burn the house down, and so, as the song says, we sink lower and lower and there isn't a plate of soup going.

God's Ten Commandments we have kept
    And acted as we should.
    It has not done us any good.
O you who sit beside a fire
    Please help us now: our need is dire!
Strict godliness we've always shown.
    But ere night came and day did go
This fact was clear to everyone:
    It was our godliness that brought us low.
(Better for you if you have none.)

VOICE (*from above*)   You there! Come up! There's some hot soup for you!
MOTHER COURAGE   I couldn't swallow a thing. Was that your last word?
COOK   The inn isn't big enough. We better go up.
MOTHER COURAGE   I'll get Kattrin.
COOK   If there are three of us the parson won't like it. Stick something in your pocket for her.

The COOK *and* MOTHER COURAGE *enter the parsonage.* KATTRIN *climbs out of the wagon with a bundle. Making sure the others have gone, she lays out on a wagon wheel a skirt of her mother's and a pair of the* COOK's *pants. She has just finished, and picked her bundle up, when* MOTHER COURAGE *comes down with soup for her.*

MOTHER COURAGE   Kattrin! Where do you think you're going? (*She examines the bundle.*) Ah! So you were listening! I told him: nothing doing—he can have his lousy inn. (*Now she sees the skirt and pants.*) Oh, you stupid girl! Now what if I'd seen that, and you'd been gone! (KATTRIN *tries to leave. Her mother holds her.*) And don't imagine I sent him packing on your account. It was the wagon. They can't part me from my wagon. Now we'll put the cook's things here where he'll find 'em, that silly man. You and I are leaving. (*She climbs up on the wagon and throws the rest of the* COOK's *few things down on to the pants.*) There! He's fired! The last man I'll ever take into *this* business! Get into harness, Kattrin. This winter will pass like all the others.

The two women harness themselves to the wagon and start out. A gust of wind. When they have disappeared, the COOK *re-enters, still chewing. He sees his things.*

SCENE 10

On the highway. MOTHER COURAGE *and* KATTRIN *are pulling the wagon. They come to a prosperous farmhouse. Someone inside is singing.*

THE SONG OF SHELTER

In March a tree we planted
To make the garden gay.
In June we were enchanted:
A lovely rose was blooming
The balmy air perfuming!
Blest of the gods are they
Who have a garden gay!
In June we were enchanted.

When snow falls helter-skelter
And loudly blows the storm
Our farmhouse gives us shelter.
The winter's in a hurry
But we've no cause to worry.
Cosy are we and warm
Though loudly blows the storm:
Our farmhouse gives us shelter.

MOTHER COURAGE *and* KATTRIN *have stopped to listen. They start out again.*

SCENE 11

January, 1636. Catholic troops threaten the Protestant town of Halle. The stones begin to talk. MOTHER COURAGE *loses her daughter and journeys onward alone. The war is not yet near its end.*

The wagon, very far gone now, stands near a farmhouse with a straw roof. It is night. Out of the wood comes a LIEUTENANT *and* THREE SOLDIERS *in full armor.*

LIEUTENANT   And there mustn't be a sound. If anyone yells, cut him down.

FIRST SOLDIER   But we'll have to knock—if we want a guide.

LIEUTENANT   Knocking's a natural noise, it's all right, could be a cow hitting the wall of the cowshed.

The SOLDIERS *knock at the farmhouse door. An* OLD PEASANT WOMAN *opens. A hand is clapped over her mouth. Two* SOLDIERS *enter.*

PEASANT'S VOICE   What is it? (*The soldiers bring out an* OLD PEASANT *and his* SON.)

LIEUTENANT (*pointing to the wagon on which* KATTRIN *has appeared*)   There's another. (*A* SOLDIER *pulls her out.*) Is this everybody?

OLD PEASANT   That's our son.

PEASANT WOMAN   And that's a girl that can't talk. Her mother's in town buying up stocks because the shopkeepers are running away and selling cheap.

OLD PEASANT   They're canteen people.

LIEUTENANT   I'm warning you. Keep quiet. One sound and you'll have a sword in your ribs. I need someone to show us the path to the town. (*Points to the* YOUNG PEASANT:) You! Come here!

YOUNG PEASANT   I don't know any path!

SECOND SOLDIER (*grinning*)   He don't know any path!

YOUNG PEASANT   I don't help Catholics.

LIEUTENANT (*to* SECOND SOLDIER)   Show him your sword.

YOUNG PEASANT (*forced to his knees, a sword at his throat*)   I'd rather die!

SECOND SOLDIER (*again mimicking*)   He'd rather die!

FIRST SOLDIER   We'll soon fix this. (*Walks over to the cowshed.*) Two cows and a bull. Listen, you. If you aren't going to be reasonable, I'll saber your cattle.

YOUNG PEASANT   Not the cattle!

PEASANT WOMAN (*weeping*)   Spare the cattle, Captain, or we'll starve!

LIEUTENANT   If he must be stubborn.

FIRST SOLDIER   I think I'll start with the bull.

YOUNG PEASANT (*to his father*)   Do I have to? (*The* OLD PEASANT *nods.*) I'll do it.

PEASANT WOMAN   Thank you, thank you, Captain, for sparing us, for ever and ever, Amen.

The OLD PEASANT *stops her going on thanking him.*

FIRST SOLDIER   I knew the bull came first all right!

Led by the YOUNG PEASANT, *the* LIEUTENANT *and the* SOLDIERS *go on their way.*

OLD PEASANT   What goes on? Nothing good, I guess.

PEASANT WOMAN   Maybe they're just scouts. What are you doing?

OLD PEASANT   (*setting a ladder against the roof and climbing up*)
I'm seeing if they're alone. (*On the roof:*) Things are moving
—all over. I can see armor. And a cannon. There must be more
than a regiment. God have mercy on the town and its people!

PEASANT WOMAN   Are there lights in the town?

OLD PEASANT   No, they're all asleep. (*He climbs down.*) It's an
attack. They'll all be slaughtered in their beds.

PEASANT WOMAN   The watchman'll give warning.

OLD PEASANT   They must have killed the watchman in the tower
on the hill or he'd have sounded his horn before this.

PEASANT WOMAN   If there were more of us . . .

OLD PEASANT   But being that we're alone with that cripple . . .

PEASANT WOMAN   There's nothing we can do, is there?

OLD PEASANT   Nothing.

PEASANT WOMAN   We can't get to the town in the dark.

OLD PEASANT   The whole hillside's swarming with men.

PEASANT WOMAN   We could give a sign?

OLD PEASANT   And be cut down for it?

PEASANT WOMAN   No, there's nothing we can do. (*To* KATTRIN:)
Pray, poor thing, pray! There's nothing we can do to stop this
bloodshed, so even if you can't talk, at least pray! *He* hears, if
no one else does. (*All kneel,* KATTRIN *behind.*) Our
Father, which art in Heaven, hear our prayer, let not the town
perish with all that lie therein asleep and fearing nothing. Wake
them, that they rise and go to the walls and see the foe that comes
with fire and sword in the night down the hill and across the
fields. God protect our mother and make the watchman not sleep
but wake ere it's too late. And save our son-in-law too, O God,
he's there with his four children, let them not perish, they're innocent, they know nothing, one of them's not two years old, the
eldest is seven. (KATTRIN *rises, troubled.*) Heavenly Father, hear
us, only Thou canst help us or we die, for we are weak and have
no sword nor nothing; we cannot trust our own strength but only
Thine, O Lord; we are in Thy hands, our cattle, our farm, and
the town too, we're all in Thy hands, and the foe is nigh unto
the walls with all his power. (KATTRIN, *unperceived, has crept off
to the wagon, has taken something out of it, put it under her skirt,
and has climbed up the ladder to the roof.*) Be mindful of the
children in danger, especially the little ones, be mindful of the
old folk who cannot move, and of all Christian souls, O Lord.

OLD PEASANT   And forgive us our trespasses as we forgive them
that trespass against us. Amen.

Sitting on the roof, KATTRIN *takes a drum from under her skirt, and starts to beat it.*

PEASANT WOMAN   Heavens, what's she doing?

OLD PEASANT   She's out of her mind!

PEASANT WOMAN   Get her down, quick! (*The* OLD PEASANT *runs to the ladder but* KATTRIN *pulls it up on the roof.*) She'll get us in trouble.

OLD PEASANT   Stop it this minute, you silly cripple!

PEASANT WOMAN   The soldiers'll come!

OLD PEASANT (*looking for stones*)   I'll stone you!

PEASANT WOMAN   Have you no pity, don't you have a heart? We have relations there too, four grandchildren. If they find us now, it's the end, they'll stab us to death! (KATTRIN *is staring into the far distance, toward the town. She goes on drumming. To the* PEASANT:) I told you not to let that sort into the farm. What do *they* care if we lose our cattle?

LIEUTENANT (*running back with soldiers and* YOUNG PEASANT) I'll cut you all to bits!

PEASANT WOMAN   We're innocent, sir, we couldn't stop her!

LIEUTENANT   Where's the ladder?

OLD PEASANT   On the roof.

LIEUTENANT (*calling*)   Throw down the drum. I order you! (*To* PEASANTS:) You're all in this, but you won't live to tell the tale.

OLD PEASANT   They've been cutting down fir trees around here. If we get a good long trunk we can knock her off the roof . . .

FIRST SOLDIER (*to the* LIEUTENANT)   May I make a suggestion? (*He whispers something to the* LIEUTENANT, *who nods. To* KATTRIN:) Listen, you! We'll do you a favor. Everyone in that town is gonna get killed. Come down, go with us to the town, show us your mother and we'll spare her.

KATTRIN *replies with more drumming.*

LIEUTENANT (*pushing him away*)   She doesn't trust you, no wonder with your face. (*He calls up to* KATTRIN:) Hey, you! Suppose I give you my word? I'm an officer, my word's my bond! (KATTRIN *again replies with drumming—harder this time.*) Nothing is sacred to her.

FIRST SOLDIER   They'll sure as hell hear it in the town.

LIEUTENANT   We must make another noise. Louder than that drum. What can we make a noise with?

FIRST SOLDIER   We mustn't make a noise!

LIEUTENANT   A harmless noise, fool, a peacetime noise!

OLD PEASANT   I could start chopping wood.

LIEUTENANT That's it! (*The* PEASANT *brings his axe and chops away.*) Chop! Chop harder! Chop for your life! It's not enough. (*To* FIRST SOLDIER:) You chop too!

OLD PEASANT I've only one axe.

LIEUTENANT We must set fire to the farm. Smoke her out.

OLD PEASANT That's no good, Captain, when they see fire from the town, they'll know everything.

KATTRIN *is laughing now and drumming harder than ever.*

LIEUTENANT Laughing at us, is she? I'll settle *her* hash if it's the last thing I do. Bring me a musket!

Two SOLDIERS *off.*

PEASANT WOMAN I have it, Captain. That's their wagon over there, Captain. If we smash that, she'll stop. It's all they have, Captain.

LIEUTENANT (*to the* YOUNG PEASANT) Smash it! (*Calling:*) If you don't stop that noise, we'll smash up your wagon!

The YOUNG PEASANT *deals the wagon a couple of feeble blows with a board.*

PEASANT WOMAN (*to* KATTRIN) Stop, you little beast!

KATTRIN *stares at the wagon and pauses. Noises of distress come out of her. She goes on drumming.*

LIEUTENANT Where are those sonsofbitches with that gun?

FIRST SOLDIER They can't have heard anything in the town or we'd hear their cannon.

LIEUTENANT (*calling*) They don't hear you. And now we're going to shoot. I'll give you one more chance: throw down that drum!

YOUNG PEASANT (*dropping the board, screaming to* KATTRIN:) Don't stop now! Go on, go on, go on!

The SOLDIER *knocks him down and stabs him.* KATTRIN *starts crying but goes on drumming.*

PEASANT WOMAN You're killing him!

The SOLDIERS *arrive with the gun.*

LIEUTENANT Set it up! (*Calling while the gun is set up on forks:*) Once for all: stop that drumming! (*Still crying,* KATTRIN *is drumming as hard as she can.*) Fire!

The SOLDIERS *fire.* KATTRIN *is hit. She gives the drum another feeble beat or two, then collapses.*

LIEUTENANT So that ends the noise.

But the last beats of the drum are lost in the din of cannon from the town. Mingled with the thunder of cannon, alarm-bells are heard in the distance.

FIRST SOLDIER   She made it.

SCENE 12

Toward morning. The drums and pipes of troops on the march, receding. In front of the wagon MOTHER COURAGE *sits by* KATTRIN's *body. The* THREE PEASANTS *of the last scene are standing near.*

PEASANT WOMAN   The regiments have all left. No, there's still one to go.

OLD PEASANT (*to* MOTHER COURAGE)   You must latch on to it. You'll never get by alone. Hurry!

MOTHER COURAGE   Maybe she's asleep. (*She sings:*)

> Lullay, lullay, what's that in the hay?
> The neighbor's kids cry but mine are gay.
> The neighbor's kids are dressed in dirt:
> Your silks were cut from an angel's skirt.
> They are all starving: you have a cake;
> If it's too stale, you need but speak.
> Lullay, lullay, what's rustling there?
> One lad fell in Poland. The other is—where?

MOTHER COURAGE   You shouldn't have told her about the children.

OLD PEASANT   If you hadn't gone off to get your cut, maybe it wouldn't have happened.

MOTHER COURAGE   I'm glad she can sleep.

PEASANT WOMAN   She's not asleep, it's time you realized, she's through.

OLD PEASANT   You must get away. There are wolves in these parts. And the bandits are worse.

MOTHER COURAGE (*stands up*)   That's right.

OLD PEASANT   Have you no one left?

MOTHER COURAGE   Yes, my son Eilif.

OLD PEASANT   Find him then, leave *her* to us.

PEASANT WOMAN   We'll give her a proper burial, you needn't worry.

MOTHER COURAGE   Here's a little money for the expenses. (*She harnesses herself to the wagon.*) I hope I can pull the wagon by myself. Yes, I'll manage. There's not much in it now. (*The last regiment is heard passing.*) Hey! Take me with you!

The men are heard singing The Song of Mother Courage:

> Dangers, surprises, devastations—
> The war takes hold and will not quit.
> But though it last three generations
> We shall get nothing out of it.
> Starvation, filth, and cold enslave us.
> The army robs us of our pay.
> Only a miracle can save us
> And miracles have had their day.
>> Christians, awake! The winter's gone!
>> The snows depart, the dead sleep on.
>> And though you may not long survive
>> Get out of bed and look alive!

THE GLASS MENAGERIE (1944)

TENNESSEE WILLIAMS (1911–   )

Thomas Lanier Williams, nicknamed "Tennessee" for reasons not altogether clear, drifter in and out of jobs, in and out of colleges, abysmally unsuccessful writer of an abysmally unsuccessful play called *Battle of Angels* almost literally driven out of Boston in 1940, shy, introverted, but determined to become a writer, broke sharply upon the scene in 1944 when the successful Chicago premiere of *The Glass Menagerie* was followed quickly by equal success and critical acclaim in New York. Four years later one of the great modern American dramatic masterpieces, *A Streetcar Named Desire,* made Marlon Brando an instant star and virtual household word, and raised Tennessee Williams to membership in an elite group of post-war American dramatic artists of international reputation. O'Neill, Arthur Miller, of late Edward Albee, and Tennessee Williams still remain the best we're ever had.

Williams' dramatic technique relies all too often on overworked themes of decadence in the South, particularly among women, strutting young studs, horribly violent deaths and mutilations, and a look at the world and its inhabitants as in one way or another depraved. An effective picture of this world is summarized in the almost purely expressionistic *Camino Real,* an artistic failure of 1953, now regarded as one of Williams' major works. Even at that, Williams has been able to compose a substantial body of superior dramatic literature which has rightfully earned his far-reaching artistic reputation. His first commercial success, the charmingly appealing *The Glass Menagerie*, remains among his best efforts.

The Glass Menagerie has the surface qualities of realistic drama with its petty little people and their struggle for meaning and dignity in a shoddy world, but Williams has actually written one of the few truly *impressionistic* plays. The style suggests the quality of a painting by Pizzaro, or Monet, or, in music, of Debussy. There is a tremendous amount of mood, a sense of viewing through a glass, perhaps darkly, certainly hazily, and hearing from afar a life experience from a single vantage point. The actions are meant to be seen in the memory of the storyteller who colors it as he sees fit, reveals it as he wishes, creating for us his deeply personal impression of the way it was. We watch the play in certain sequences through a theatrical gauze, and the filminess is thus further heightened. We listen to the chorus figure, Tom, as he steps in and out of his reminiscences at will. It is a prolonged impression, a lengthy look, full of nostalgia, resentment, some hate, certainly regrets, and a lot of love.

Is *The Glass Menagerie* a tragedy? Probably not. It is a drama of compassion, and tragic only in the most pathetic sense, often much too fragile—like Laura's tiny animals—to achieve the necessary strength. There is, of course, an inevitability and sense of unavoidable catastrophe, and there is no way out. These people possess their individual flaws, but we see them with too much conscious emotion for tragedy. The tears raised on Laura's behalf become too sentimental. Amanda may be understandable as the frantic mother seeking a modicum of gentility among the ruins, but she is too much the smothering monster stage mother. Tom is certainly no tragic protagonist in his detachment.

Still, *The Glass Menagerie* is a forceful play. Williams wants us to understand and to pity these three lost creatures, driven into themselves, each by the others, to a final disintegration of the spirit. In *The Glass Menagerie* all survive, yet all die, making the play, perhaps, simply a tragedy of life itself.

The Glass Menagerie

CHARACTERS

AMANDA WINGFIELD, *the mother.*

A little woman of great but confused vitality clinging frantically to another time and place. Her characterization must be carefully created, not copied from type. She is not paranoiac, but her life is paranoia. There is much to admire in AMANDA, *and as much to love and pity as there is to laugh at. Certainly she has endurance and a kind of heroism, and though her foolishness makes her unwittingly cruel at times, there is tenderness in her slight person.*

LAURA WINGFIELD, *her daughter.*

AMANDA, *having failed to establish contact with reality, continues to live vitally in her illusions, but* LAURA'S *situation is even graver. A childhood illness has left her crippled, one leg slightly shorter than the other, and held in a brace. This defect need not be more than suggested on the stage. Stemming from this,* LAURA'S *separation increases till she is like a piece of her own glass collection, too exquisitely fragile to move from the shelf.*

TOM WINGFIELD, *her son, and the narrator of the play.*

A poet with a job in a warehouse. His nature is not remorseless, but to escape from a trap he has to act without pity.

JIM O'CONNOR, *the gentleman caller.*

A nice, ordinary, young man.

SCENE: *An alley in St. Louis.*
PART I: *Preparation for a Gentleman Caller.*
PART II: *The Gentleman Calls.*
TIME: *Now and the Past.*

SCENE I

The Wingfield apartment is in the rear of the building, one of those vast hive-like conglomerations of cellular living-units that flower as warty growths in overcrowded urban centers of lower middle-class population and are symptomatic of the impulse of this largest and fundamentally enslaved section of American society to avoid fluidity and differentiation and to exist and function as one interfused mass of automatism.

The apartment faces an alley and is entered by a fire-escape, a structure whose name is a touch of accidental poetic truth, for all of these huge buildings are always burning with the slow and implacable fires of human desperation. The fire-escape is included in the set—that is, the landing of it and steps descending from it.

The scene is memory and is therefore nonrealistic. Memory takes a lot of poetic license. It omits some details; others are exaggerated, according to the emotional value of the articles it touches, for memory is seated predominantly in the heart. The interior is therefore rather dim and poetic.

At the rise of the curtain, the audience is faced with the dark, grim rear wall of the Wingfield tenement. This building, which runs parallel to the footlights, is flanked on both sides by dark, narrow alleys which run into murky canyons of tangled clotheslines, garbage cans and the sinister lattice-work of neighboring fire-escapes. It is up and down these side alleys that exterior entrances and exits are made, during the play. At the end of TOM's *opening commentary, the dark tenement wall slowly reveals (by means of a transparency) the interior of the ground floor Wingfield apartment.*

Downstage is the living room, which also serves as a sleeping room for LAURA, *the sofa unfolding to make her bed. Upstage, center, and divided by a wide arch or second proscenium with transparent faded portieres (or second curtain), is the dining room. In an old-fashioned what-not in the living room are seen scores of transparent glass animals. A blown-up photograph of the father hangs on the wall of the living room, facing the audience, to the left of the archway. It is the face of a very handsome young man in a doughboy's First World War cap. He is gallantly smiling, ineluctably smiling, as if to say, "I will be smiling forever."*

The audience hears and sees the opening scene in the dining room through both the transparent fourth wall of the building and the transparent gauze portieres of the dining-room arch. It is during this revealing scene that the fourth wall slowly ascends, out of sight. This transparent exterior wall is not brought down again until the very end of the play, during TOM's *final speech.*

The narrator is an undisguised convention of the play. He takes whatever license with dramatic convention as is convenient to his purposes.

TOM *enters dressed as a merchant sailor from alley, stage left, and strolls across the front of the stage to the fire-escape. There he stops and lights a cigarette. He addresses the audience.*

TOM   Yes, I have tricks in my pocket, I have things up my sleeve. But I am the opposite of a stage magician. He gives you illusion that has the appearance of truth. I give you truth in the pleasant disguise of illusion. To begin with, I turn back time. I reverse it to that quaint period, the thirties, when the huge middle class of America was matriculating in a school for the blind. Their eyes had failed them, or they had failed their eyes, and so they were having their fingers pressed forcibly down on the fiery Braille alphabet of a dissolving economy. In Spain there was revolution.

Here there was only shouting and confusion. In Spain there was Guernica. Here there were disturbances of labor, sometimes pretty violent, in otherwise peaceful cities such as Chicago, Cleveland, Saint Louis. . . . This is the social background of the play.

(MUSIC.)

The play is memory. Being a memory play, it is dimly lighted, it is sentimental, it is not realistic. In memory everything seems to happen to music. That explains the fiddle in the wings. I am the narrator of the play, and also a character in it. The other characters are my mother, Amanda, my sister, Laura, and a gentleman caller who appears in the final scenes. He is the most realistic character in the play, being an emissary from a world of reality that we were somehow set apart from. But since I have a poet's weakness for symbols, I am using this character also as a symbol; he is the long delayed but always expected something that we live for. There is a fifth character in the play who doesn't appear except in this larger-than-life photograph over the mantel. This is our father who left us a long time ago. He was a telephone man who fell in love with long distances; he gave up his job with the telephone company and skipped the light fantastic out of town . . . The last we heard of him was a picture post-card from Mazatlan, on the Pacific coast of Mexico, containing a message of two words—"Hello—Goodbye!" and an address. I think the rest of the play will explain itself. . . .

Amanda's voice becomes audible through the portieres.

(LEGEND ON SCREEN: "OÙ SONT LES NEIGES.")

He divides the portieres and enters the upstage area.
AMANDA *and* LAURA *are seated at a drop-leaf table. Eating is indicated by gestures without food or utensils.* AMANDA *faces the audience.* TOM *and* LAURA *are seated in profile.*
The interior has lit up softly and through the scrim we see AMANDA *and* LAURA *seated at the table in the upstage area.*

AMANDA *(calling)*   Tom?
TOM   Yes, Mother.
AMANDA   We can't say grace until you come to the table!
TOM   Coming, Mother. (*He bows slightly and withdraws, reappearing a few moments later in his place at the table.*)
AMANDA *(to her son)*   Honey, don't *push* with your *fingers*. If you have to push with something, the thing to push with is a crust of bread. And chew—chew! Animals have sections in their stomachs which enable them to digest food without mastication, but human

beings are supposed to chew their food before they swallow it down. Eat food leisurely, son, and really enjoy it. A well-cooked meal has lots of delicate flavors that have to be held in the mouth for appreciation. So chew your food and give your salivary glands a chance to function!

TOM *deliberately lays his imaginary fork down and pushes his chair back from the table.*

TOM   I haven't enjoyed one bite of this dinner because of your constant directions on how to eat it. It's you that makes me rush through meals with your hawk-like attention to every bite I take. Sickening—spoils my appetite—all this discussion of animals' secretion—salivary glands—mastication!

AMANDA *(lightly)* Temperament like a Metropolitan star! *(He rises and crosses downstage.)* You're not excused from the table.

TOM   I am getting a cigarette.

AMANDA   You smoke too much.

LAURA *rises.*

LAURA   I'll bring in the blanc mange.

He remains standing with his cigarette by the portieres during the following.

AMANDA *(rising)* No, sister, no, sister—you be the lady this time and I'll be the darky.

LAURA   I'm already up.

AMANDA   Resume your seat, little sister—I want you to stay fresh and pretty—for gentlemen callers!

LAURA   I'm not expecting any gentlemen callers.

AMANDA *(crossing out to kitchenette. Airily)* Sometimes they come when they are least expected! Why, I remember one Sunday afternoon in Blue Mountain—*(Enters kitchenette.)*

TOM   I know what's coming!

LAURA   Yes. But let her tell it.

TOM   Again?

LAURA   She loves to tell it.

AMANDA *returns with bowl of dessert.*

AMANDA   One Sunday afternoon in Blue Mountain—your mother received—*seventeen!*—gentlemen callers! Why, sometimes there weren't chairs enough to accommodate them all. We had to send the nigger over to bring in folding chairs from the parish house.

TOM *(remaining at portieres)* How did you entertain those gentlemen callers?

AMANDA   I understood the art of conversation!

TOM   I bet you could talk.

AMANDA   Girls in those days *knew* how to talk, I can tell you.

TOM   Yes?

(IMAGE: AMANDA AS A GIRL ON A PORCH GREETING CALLERS.)

AMANDA   They knew how to entertain their gentlemen callers. It wasn't enough for a girl to be possessed of a pretty face and a graceful figure—although I wasn't slighted in either respect. She also needed to have a nimble wit and a tongue to meet all occasions.

TOM   What did you talk about?

AMANDA   Things of importance going on in the world! Never anything coarse or common or vulgar. (*She addresses* TOM *as though he were seated in the vacant chair at the table though he remains by portieres. He plays this scene as though he held the book.*) My callers were gentlemen—all! Among my callers were some of the most prominent young planters of the Mississippi Delta—planters and sons of planters!

TOM *motions for music and a spot of light on* AMANDA. *Her eyes lift, her face glows, her voice becomes rich and elegiac.*

(SCREEN LEGEND: "OÙ SONT LES NEIGES.")

There was young Champ Laughlin who later became vice-president of the Delta Planters Bank. Hadley Stevenson who was drowned in Moon Lake and left his widow one hundred and fifty thousand in Government bonds. There were the Cutrere brothers, Wesley and Bates. Bates was one of my bright particular beaux! He got in a quarrel with that wild Wainright boy. They shot it out on the floor of Moon Lake Casino. Bates was shot through the stomach. Died in the ambulance on his way to Memphis. His widow was also well-provided for, came into eight or ten thousand acres, that's all. She married him on the rebound—never loved her—carried my picture on him the night he died! And there was that boy that every girl in the Delta had set her cap for! That beautiful, brilliant young Fitzhugh boy from Green County!

TOM   What did he leave his widow?

AMANDA   He never married! Gracious, you talk as though all of my old admirers had turned up their toes to the daisies!

TOM   Isn't this the first you mentioned that still survives?

AMANDA   That Fitzhugh boy went North and made a fortune—came to be known as the Wolf of Wall Street! He had the Midas touch, whatever he touched turned to gold! And I could have been Mrs. Duncan J. Fitzhugh, mind you! But—I picked your *father!*

LAURA (*rising*) Mother, let me clear the table.

AMANDA No, dear, you go in front and study your typewriter chart. Or practice your shorthand a little. Stay fresh and pretty—It's almost time for our gentlemen callers to start arriving. (*She flounces girlishly toward the kitchenette.*) How many do you suppose we're going to entertain this afternoon?

TOM *throws down the paper and jumps up with a groan.*

LAURA (*alone in the dining room*) I don't believe we're going to receive any, Mother.

AMANDA (*reappearing, airily*) What? No one—not one? You must be joking! (LAURA *nervously echoes her laugh. She slips in a fugitive manner through the half-open portieres and draws them gently behind her. A shaft of very clear light is thrown on her face against the faded tapestry of the curtains.* MUSIC: "THE GLASS MENAGERIE" UNDER FAINTLY. *Lightly.*) Not one gentleman caller? It can't be true! There must be a flood, there must have been a tornado!

LAURA It isn't a flood, it's not a tornado, Mother. I'm just not popular like you were in Blue Mountain.... (TOM *utters another groan.* LAURA *glances at him with a faint, apologetic smile. Her voice catching a little.*) Mother's afraid I'm going to be an old maid.

(THE SCENE DIMS OUT WITH "GLASS MENAGERIE" MUSIC.)

SCENE II

"Laura, Haven't You Ever Liked Some Boy?"

On the dark stage the screen is lighted with the image of blue roses. Gradually LAURA's *figure becomes apparent and the screen goes out. The music subsides.*

LAURA *is seated in the delicate ivory chair at the small clawfoot table.*

She wears a dress of soft violet material for a kimono—her hair tied back from her forehead with a ribbon.

She is washing and polishing her collection of glass.

AMANDA *appears on the fire-escape steps. At the sound of her ascent,* LAURA *catches her breath, thrusts the bowl of ornaments away and seats herself stiffly before the diagram of the typewriter keyboard as though it held her spellbound. Something has happened to* AMANDA. *It is written in her face as she climbs to the landing: a look that is grim and hopeless and a little absurd.*

She has on one of those cheap or imitation velvety-looking cloth coats

with imitation fur collar. Her hat is five or six years old, one of those dreadful cloche hats that were worn in the late twenties and she is clasping an enormous black patent-leather pocket-book with nickel clasp and initials. This is her full-dress outfit, the one she usually wears to the D.A.R.
Before entering she looks through the door.
She purses her lips, opens her eyes wide, rolls them upward, and shakes her head.
Then she slowly lets herself in the door. Seeing her mother's expression LAURA *touches her lips with a nervous gesture.*

LAURA   Hello, Mother, I was—(*She makes a nervous gesture toward the chart on the wall.* AMANDA *leans against the shut door and stares at* LAURA *with a martyred look.*)

AMANDA   Deception? Deception? (*She slowly removes her hat and gloves, continuing the swift suffering stare. She lets the hat and gloves fall on the floor—a bit of acting.*)

LAURA   (*shakily*)   How was the D.A.R. meeting? (AMANDA *slowly opens her purse and removes a dainty white handkerchief which she shakes out delicately and delicately touches to her lips and nostrils.*) Didn't you go to the D.A.R. meeting, Mother?

AMANDA   (*faintly, almost inaudibly*)   —No.—No. (*Then more forcibly.*) I did not have the strength—to go to the D.A.R. In fact, I did not have the courage! I wanted to find a hole in the ground and hide myself in it forever! (*She crosses slowly to the wall and removes the diagram of the typewriter keyboard. She holds it in front of her for a second, staring at it sweetly and sorrowfully— then bites her lips and tears it in two pieces.*)

LAURA   (*faintly*)   Why did you do that, Mother? (AMANDA *repeats the same procedure with the chart of the Gregg Alphabet.*) Why are you—

AMANDA   Why? Why? How old are you, Laura?

LAURA   Mother, you know my age.

AMANDA   I thought that you were an adult; it seems that I was mistaken. (*She crosses slowly to the sofa and sinks down and stares at* LAURA.)

LAURA   Please don't stare at me, Mother.

AMANDA *closes her eyes and lowers her head. Count ten.*

AMANDA   What are we going to do, what is going to become of us, what is the future?

Count ten.

LAURA   Has something happened, Mother? (AMANDA *draws a long breath and takes out the handkerchief again. Dabbing process.*) Mother, has—something happened?

AMANDA I'll be all right in a minute. I'm just bewildered—(*Count five.*)—by life. . . .

LAURA Mother, I wish that you would tell me what's happened.

AMANDA As you know, I was supposed to be inducted into my office at the D.A.R. this afternoon. (IMAGE: A SWARM OF TYPEWRITERS.) But I stopped off at Rubicam's Business College to speak to your teachers about your having a cold and ask them what progress they thought you were making down there.

LAURA Oh. . . .

AMANDA I went to the typing instructor and introduced myself as your mother. She didn't know who you were. Wingfield, she said. We don't have any such student enrolled at the school! I assured her she did, that you had been going to classes since early in January. "I wonder," she said, "if you could be talking about that terribly shy little girl who dropped out of school after only a few days' attendance?" "No," I said, "Laura, my daughter, has been going to school every day for the past six weeks!" "Excuse me," she said. She took the attendance book out and there was your name, unmistakably printed, and all the dates you were absent until they decided that you had dropped out of school. I still said, "No, there must have been some mistake! There must have been some mix-up in the records!" And she said, "No—I remember her perfectly now. Her hand shook so that she couldn't hit the right keys! The first time we gave a speed-test, she broke down completely—was sick at the stomach and almost had to be carried into the wash-room! After that morning she never showed up any more. We phoned the house but never got any answer—while I was working at Famous and Barr, I suppose, demonstrating those —Oh!" I felt so weak I could barely keep on my feet! I had to sit down while they got me a glass of water! Fifty dollars' tuition, all of our plans—my hopes and ambitions for you—just gone up the spout, just gone up the spout like that. (LAURA *draws a long breath and gets awkwardly to her feet. She crosses to the victrola and winds it up.*) What are you doing?

LAURA Oh! (*She releases the handle and returns to her seat.*)

AMANDA Laura, where have you been going when you've gone out pretending that you were going to business college?

LAURA I've just been going out walking.

AMANDA That's not true.

LAURA It is. I just went walking.

AMANDA Walking? Walking? In winter? Deliberately courting pneumonia in that light coat? Where did you walk to, Laura?

LAURA All sorts of places—mostly in the park.

AMANDA Even after you'd started catching that cold?

LAURA It was the lesser of two evils, Mother. (IMAGE: WINTER
SCENE IN PARK.) I couldn't go back up. I—threw up—on the
floor!

AMANDA From half past seven till after five every day you mean
to tell me you walked around in the park, because you wanted to
make me think that you were still going to Rubicam's Business
College?

LAURA It wasn't as bad as it sounds. I went inside places to get
warmed up.

AMANDA Inside where?

LAURA I went in the art museum and the bird-houses at the Zoo.
I visited the penguins every day! Sometimes I did without lunch
and went to the movies. Lately I've been spending most of my
afternoons in the Jewel-box, that big glass house where they raise
the tropical flowers.

AMANDA You did all this to deceive me, just for the deception?
(LAURA *looks down.*) Why?

LAURA Mother, when you're disappointed, you get that awful suffering look on your face, like the picture of Jesus' mother in the
museum!

AMANDA Hush!

LAURA I couldn't face it.

Pause. A whisper of strings.

(LEGEND: "THE CRUST OF HUMILITY.")

AMANDA (*hopelessly fingering the huge pocketbook*) So what are
we going to do the rest of our lives? Stay home and watch the
parades go by? Amuse ourselves with the glass menagerie, darling?
Eternally play those worn-out phonograph records your father
left as a painful reminder of him? We won't have a business career—we've given that up because it gave us nervous indigestion!
(*Laughs wearily.*) What is there left but dependency all our lives?
I know so well what becomes of unmarried women who aren't
prepared to occupy a position. I've seen such pitiful cases in the
South—barely tolerated spinsters living upon the grudging patronage of sister's husband or brother's wife!—stuck away in some little mouse-trap of a room—encouraged by one in-law to visit another—little birdlike women without any nest—eating the crust
of humility all their life! Is that the future that we've mapped
out for ourselves? I swear it's the only alternative I can think of!
It isn't a very pleasant alternative, is it? Of course—some girls
do marry. (LAURA *twists her hands nervously.*) Haven't you ever
liked some boy?

LAURA   Yes. I liked one once. (*Rises.*) I came across his picture a
while ago.

AMANDA (*with some interest*)   He gave you his picture?

LAURA   No, it's in the year-book.

AMANDA (*disappointed*)   Oh—a high-school boy.

(SCREEN IMAGE: JIM AS A HIGH-SCHOOL HERO BEARING A SILVER CUP.)

LAURA   Yes. His name was Jim. (LAURA *lifts the heavy annual from
the claw-foot table.*) Here he is in *The Pirates of Penzance.*

AMANDA (*absently*)   The what?

LAURA   The operetta the senior class put on. He had a wonderful
voice and we sat across the aisle from each other Mondays, Wednesdays and Fridays in the Aud. Here he is with the silver cup for
debating! See his grin?

AMANDA (*absently*)   He must have had a jolly disposition.

LAURA   He used to call me—Blue Roses.

(IMAGE: BLUE ROSES.)

AMANDA   Why did he call you such a name as that?

LAURA   When I had that attack of pleurosis—he asked me what was
the matter when I came back. I said pleurosis—he thought that I
said Blue Roses! So that's what he always called me after that.
Whenever he saw me, he'd holler, "Hello, Blue Roses!" I didn't
care for the girl that he went out with. Emily Meisenbach. Emily
was the best-dressed girl at Soldan. She never struck me, though,
as being sincere . . . It says in the Personal Section—they're engaged. That's—six years ago! They must be married by now.

AMANDA   Girls that aren't cut out for business careers usually wind
up married to some nice man. (*Gets up with a spark of revival.*)
Sister, that's what you'll do!

LAURA *utters a startled, doubtful laugh. She reaches quickly for a piece
of glass.*

LAURA   But, Mother—

AMANDA   Yes? (*Crossing to photograph.*)

LAURA (*in a tone of frightened apology*)   I'm—crippled!

(IMAGE: SCREEN.)

AMANDA   Nonsense! Laura, I've told you never, never to use that
word. Why, you're not crippled, you just have a little defect—
hardly noticeable, even! When people have some slight disadvan-
tage like that, they cultivate other things to make up for it—
develop charm—and vivacity—and—*charm!* That's all you have

to do! (*She turns again to the photograph.*) One thing your father had *plenty of*—was *charm!*

Tom *motions to the fiddle in the wings.*

(THE SCENE FADES OUT WITH MUSIC.)

SCENE III

(LEGEND ON SCREEN: "AFTER THE FIASCO—")

Tom *speaks from the fire-escape landing.*

TOM   After the fiasco at Rubicam's Business College, the idea of getting a gentleman caller for Laura began to play a more important part in Mother's calculations. It became an obsession. Like some archetype of the universal unconscious, the image of the gentleman caller haunted our small apartment.... (IMAGE: YOUNG MAN AT DOOR WITH FLOWERS.)   An evening at home rarely passed without some allusion to this image, this spectre, this hope.... Even when he wasn't mentioned, his presence hung in Mother's preoccupied look and in my sister's frightened, apologetic manner—hung like a sentence passed upon the Wingfields! Mother was a woman of action as well as words. She began to take logical steps in the planned direction. Late that winter and in the early spring—realizing that extra money would be needed to properly feather the nest and plume the bird—she conducted a vigorous campaign on the telephone, roping in subscribers to one of those magazines for matrons called *The Home-maker's Companion,* the type of journal that features the serialized sublimations of ladies of letters who think in terms of delicate cup-like breasts, slim, tapering waists, rich, creamy thighs, eyes like woodsmoke in autumn, fingers that soothe and caress like strains of music, bodies as powerful as Etruscan sculpture.

(SCREEN IMAGE: GLAMOR MAGAZINE COVER.)

AMANDA *enters with phone on long extension cord. She is spotted in the dim stage.*

AMANDA   Ida Scott? This is Amanda Wingfield! We *missed* you at the D.A.R. last Monday! I said to myself: She's probably suffering with that sinus condition! How is that sinus condition? Horrors! Heaven have mercy!—You're a Christian martyr, yes, that's what you are, a Christian martyr! Well, I just now happened to notice that your subscription to the *Companion*'s about to expire!

Yes, it expires with the next issue, honey!—just when that wonderful new serial by Bessie Mae Hopper is getting off to such an exciting start. Oh, honey, it's something that you can't miss! You remember how *Gone With the Wind* took everybody by storm? You simply couldn't go out if you hadn't read it. All everybody *talked* was Scarlett O'Hara. Well, this is a book that critics already compare to *Gone With the Wind*. It's the *Gone With the Wind* of the post-World War generation!—What?—Burning?—Oh, honey, don't let them burn, go take a look in the oven and I'll hold the wire! Heavens—I think she's hung up!

(DIM OUT.)

(LEGEND ON SCREEN: "YOU THINK I'M IN LOVE WITH CONTINENTAL SHOEMAKERS?")

Before the stage is lighted, the violent voices of TOM *and* AMANDA *are heard.*

They are quarreling behind the portieres. In front of them stands LAURA *with clenched hands and panicky expression.*

A clear pool of light on her figure throughout this scene.

TOM What in Christ's name am I—

AMANDA (*shrilly*) Don't you use that—

TOM Supposed to do!

AMANDA Expression! Not in my—

TOM Ohhh!

AMANDA Presence! Have you gone out of your senses?

TOM I have, that's true, *driven* out!

AMANDA What is the matter with you, you—big—big—IDIOT!

TOM Look—I've got *no thing*, no single thing—

AMANDA Lower your voice!

TOM In my life here that I can call my OWN! Everything is—

AMANDA Stop that shouting!

TOM Yesterday you confiscated my books! You had the nerve to—

AMANDA I took that horrible novel back to the library—yes! That hideous book by that insane Mr. Lawrence. (TOM *laughs wildly.*) I cannot control the output of diseased minds or people who cater to them—(TOM *laughs still more wildly.*) BUT I WON'T ALLOW SUCH FILTH BROUGHT INTO MY HOUSE! No, no, no, no, no!

TOM House, house! Who pays rent on it, who makes a slave of himself to—

AMANDA (*fairly screeching*) Don't you DARE to—

TOM No, no, *I* mustn't say things! *I've* got to just—

AMANDA Let me tell you—

TOM   I don't want to hear any more! (*He tears the portieres open. The upstage area is lit with a turgid smoky red glow.*)

AMANDA's *hair is in metal curlers and she wears a very old bathrobe, much too large for her slight figure, a relic of the faithless Mr. Wingfield.*
   An upright typewriter and a wild disarray of manuscripts is on the drop-leaf table. The quarrel was probably precipitated by AMANDA's *interruption of his creative labor. A chair lying overthrown on the floor.*
   Their gesticulating shadows are cast on the ceiling by the fiery glow.

AMANDA   You *will* hear more, you—

TOM   No, I won't hear more, I'm going out!

AMANDA   You come right back in—

TOM   Out, out out! Because I'm—

AMANDA   Come back here, Tom Wingfield! I'm not through talking to you!

TOM   Oh, go—

LAURA   (*desperately*)   —Tom!

AMANDA   You're going to listen, and no more insolence from you! I'm at the end of my patience! (*He comes back toward her.*)

TOM   What do you think I'm at? Aren't I supposed to have any patience to reach the end of, Mother? I know, I know. It seems unimportant to you, what I'm *doing*—what I *want* to do—having a little *difference* between them! You don't think that—

AMANDA   I think you've been doing things that you're ashamed of. That's why you act like this. I don't believe that you go every night to the movies. Nobody goes to the movies night after night. Nobody in their right minds goes to the movies as often as you pretend to. People don't go to the movies at nearly midnight, and movies don't let out at two A.M. Come in stumbling. Muttering to yourself like a maniac! You get three hours sleep and then go to work. Oh, I can picture the way you're doing down there. Moping, doping, because you're in no condition.

TOM   (*wildly*)   No, I'm in no condition!

AMANDA   What right have you got to jeopardize your job? Jeopardize the security of us all? How do you think we'd manage if you were—

TOM   Listen! You think I'm crazy *about* the *warehouse?* (*He bends fiercely toward her slight figure.*) You think I'm in love with the Continental Shoemakers? You think I want to spend fifty-five years down there in that—*celotex interior!* with—*fluorescent—tubes!* Look! I'd rather somebody picked up a crowbar and battered out my brains—than go back mornings! I *go!* Every time you come in yelling that God damn *"Rise and Shine!" "Rise and*

Shine!" I say to myself "How *lucky dead* people are!" But I get
up. I *go!* For sixty-five dollars a month I give up all that I dream
of doing and being *ever!* And you say self—*self's* all I ever think
of. Why, listen, if self is what I thought of, Mother, I'd be where
he is—GONE! (*Pointing to father's picture.*) As far as the system
of transportation reaches! (*He starts past her. She grabs his arm.*)
Don't grab me, Mother!

AMANDA　Where are you going?

TOM　I'm going to the *movies!*

AMANDA　I don't believe that lie!

TOM (*crouching toward her, overtowering her tiny figure. She backs
away, gasping*)　I'm going to opium dens! Yes, opium dens, dens
of vice and criminals' hang-outs, Mother. I've joined the Hogan
gang, I'm a hired assassin, I carry a tommy-gun in a violin case!
I run a string of cat-houses in the Valley! They call me Killer,
Killer Wingfield, I'm leading a double-life, a simple, honest warehouse worker by day, by night, a dynamic *czar* of the *underworld,
Mother.* I go to gambling casinos, I spin away fortunes on the
roulette table! I wear a patch over one eye and a false mustache,
sometimes I put on green whiskers. On those occasions they call
me—*El Diablo!* Oh, I could tell you things to make you sleepless!
My enemies plan to dynamite this place. They're going to blow us
all sky-high some night! I'll be glad, very happy, and so will you!
You'll go up, up on a broomstick, over Blue Mountain with seventeen gentlemen callers! You ugly—babbling old—*witch.* . . . (*He
goes through a series of violent, clumsy movements, seizing his
overcoat, lunging to the door, pulling it fiercely open. The women
watch him, aghast. His arm catches in the sleeve of the coat as he
struggles to pull it on. For a moment he is pinioned by the bulky
garment. With an outraged groan he tears the coat off again,
splitting the shoulders of it, and hurls it across the room. It strikes
against the shelf of* LAURA's *glass collection, there is a tinkle of
shattering glass.* LAURA *cries out as if wounded.*)

(MUSIC LEGEND: "THE GLASS MENAGERIE.")

LAURA (*shrilly*)　My glass!—menagerie. . . . (*She covers her face
and turns away.*)

But AMANDA *is still stunned and stupefied by the "ugly witch" so that she
barely notices this occurrence. Now she recovers her speech.*

AMANDA (*in an awful voice*)　I won't speak to you—until you apologize! (*She crosses through portieres and draws them together
behind her.* TOM *is left with* LAURA. LAURA *clings weakly to the*

mantel with her face averted. TOM *stares at her stupidly for a moment. Then he crosses to shelf. Drops awkwardly to his knees to collect the fallen glass, glancing at* LAURA *as if he would speak but couldn't.*

"The Glass Menagerie" steals in as

(THE SCENE DIMS OUT.)

SCENE IV

The interior is dark. Faint light in the alley.

A deep-voiced bell in a church is tolling the hour of five as the scene commences.

TOM *appears at the top of the alley. After each solemn boom of the bell in the tower, he shakes a little noise-maker or rattle as if to express the tiny spasm of man in contrast to the sustained power and dignity of the Almighty. This and the unsteadiness of his advance make it evident that he has been drinking.*

As he climbs the few steps to the fire-escape landing light steals up inside. LAURA *appears in night-dress, observing* TOM's *empty bed in the front room.*

TOM *fishes in his pockets for the door-key, removing a motley assortment of articles in the search, including a perfect shower of movie-ticket stubs and an empty bottle. At last he finds the key, but just as he is about to insert it, it slips from his fingers. He strikes a match and crouches below the door.*

TOM (*bitterly*)   One crack—and it falls through!

LAURA *opens the door.*

LAURA   Tom! Tom, what are you doing?

TOM   Looking for a door-key.

LAURA   Where have you been all this time?

TOM   I have been to the movies.

LAURA   All this time at the movies?

TOM   There was a very long program. There was a Garbo picture and a Mickey Mouse and a travelogue and a newsreel and a preview of coming attractions. And there was an organ solo and a collection for the milk-fund—simultaneously—which ended up in a terrible fight between a fat lady and an usher!

LAURA (*innocently*)   Did you have to stay through everything?

TOM   Of course! And, oh, I forgot! There was a big stage show! The headliner on this stage show was Malvolio the Magician. He performed wonderful tricks, many of them, such as pouring water back and forth between pitchers. First it turned to wine and then it turned to beer and then it turned to whiskey. I know it was whiskey it finally turned into because he needed somebody to come up out of the audience to help him, and I came up—both shows! It was Kentucky Straight Bourbon. A very generous fellow, he gave souvenirs. (*He pulls from his back pocket a shimmering rainbow-colored scarf.*) He gave me this. This is his magic scarf. You can have it, Laura. You wave it over a canary cage and you get a bowl of gold-fish. You wave it over the gold-fish bowl and they fly away canaries. . . . But the wonderfullest trick of all was the coffin trick. We nailed him into a coffin and he got out of the coffin without removing one nail. (*He has come inside.*) There is a trick that would come in handy for me—get me out of this 2 by 4 situation! (*Flops onto bed and starts removing shoes.*)

LAURA   Tom—Shhh!

TOM   What you shushing me for?

LAURA   You'll wake up Mother.

TOM   Goody, goody! Pay 'er back for all those "Rise an' Shines." (*Lies down, groaning.*) You know it don't take much intelligence to get yourself into a nailed-up coffin, Laura. But who in hell ever got himself out of one without removing one nail?

As if in answer, the father's grinning photograph lights up.

(SCENE DIMS OUT.)

Immediately following: The church bell is heard striking six. At the sixth stroke the alarm clock goes off in AMANDA's *room, and after a few moments we hear her calling: "Rise and Shine! Rise and Shine! Laura, go tell your brother to rise and shine!"*

TOM   (*Sitting up slowly*)   I'll rise—but I won't shine.

The light increases.

AMANDA   Laura, tell your brother his coffee is ready.

LAURA *slips into front room.*

LAURA   Tom! it's nearly seven. Don't make Mother nervous. (*He stares at her stupidly. Beseechingly.*) Tom, speak to Mother this morning. Make up with her, apologize, speak to her!

TOM   She won't to me. It's her that started not speaking.

LAURA   If you just say you're sorry she'll start speaking.

TOM   Her not speaking—is that such a tragedy?

LAURA   Please—please!

AMANDA   (*calling from kitchenette*)   Laura, are you going to do what I asked you to do, or do I have to get dressed and go out myself?

LAURA   Going, going—soon as I get on my coat! (*She pulls on a shapeless felt hat with nervous, jerky movement, pleadingly glancing at* TOM. *Rushes awkwardly for coat. The coat is one of* AMANDA'*s, inaccurately made-over, the sleeves too short for* LAURA.) Butter and what else?

AMANDA (*entering upstage*)   Just butter. Tell them to charge it.

LAURA   Mother, they make such faces when I do that.

AMANDA   Sticks and stones may break my bones, but the expression on Mr. Garfinkel's face won't harm us! Tell your brother his coffee is getting cold.

LAURA (*at door*)   Do what I asked you, will you, will you, Tom?

He looks sullenly away.

AMANDA   Laura, go now or just don't go at all!

LAURA (*rushing out*)   Going—going! (*A second later she cries out.* TOM *springs up and crosses to the door.* AMANDA *rushes anxiously in.* TOM *opens the door.*)

TOM   Laura?

LAURA   I'm all right. I slipped, but I'm all right.

AMANDA (*peering anxiously after her*)   If anyone breaks a leg on those fire-escape steps, the landlord ought to be sued for every cent he possesses! (*She shuts door. Remembers she isn't speaking and returns to other room.*)

As TOM *enters listlessly for his coffee, she turns her back to him and stands rigidly facing the window on the gloomy gray vault of the areaway. Its light on her face with its aged but childish features is cruelly sharp, satirical as a Daumier print.*

(MUSIC UNDER: "AVE MARIA.")

TOM *glances sheepishly but sullenly at her averted figure and slumps at the table. The coffee is scalding hot; he sips it and gasps and spits it back in the cup. At his gasp,* AMANDA *catches her breath and half turns. Then catches herself and turns back to window.*

TOM *blows on his coffee, glancing sidewise at his mother. She clears her throat.* TOM *clears his. He starts to rise. Sinks back down again, scratches his head, clears his throat again.* AMANDA *coughs.* TOM *raises his cup in both hands to blow on it, his eyes staring over the rim of it at his mother for several moments. Then he slowly sets the cup down and awkwardly and hesitantly rises from the chair.*

TOM (*hoarsely*)   Mother. I—I apologize. Mother. (AMANDA *draws a quick, shuddering breath. Her face works grotesquely. She breaks into childlike tears.*) I'm sorry for what I said, for everything that I said, I didn't mean it.

AMANDA (*sobbingly*) My devotion has made me a witch and so I make myself hateful to my children!

TOM No, you *don't*.

AMANDA I worry so much, don't sleep, it makes me nervous!

TOM (*gently*) I understand that.

AMANDA I've had to put up a solitary battle all these years. But you're my right-hand bower! Don't fall down, don't fail!

TOM (*gently*) I try, Mother.

AMANDA (*with great enthusiasm*) Try and you will SUCCEED! (*The notion makes her breathless.*) Why, you—you're just *full* of natural endowments! Both of my children—they're *unusual* children! Don't you think I know it? I'm so—*proud!* Happy and—feel I've —so much to be thankful for but—Promise me one thing, son!

TOM What, Mother?

AMANDA Promise, son, you'll—never be a drunkard!

TOM (*turns to her grinning*) I will never be a drunkard, Mother.

AMANDA That's what frightened me so, that you'd be drinking! Eat a bowl of Purina!

TOM Just coffee, Mother.

AMANDA Shredded wheat biscuit?

TOM No. No, Mother, just coffee.

AMANDA You can't put in a day's work on an empty stomach. You've got ten minutes—don't gulp! Drinking too-hot liquids makes cancer of the stomach. . . . Put cream in.

TOM No, thank you.

AMANDA To cool it.

TOM No! No, thank you, I want it black.

AMANDA I know, but it's not good for you. We have to do all that we can to build ourselves up. In these trying times we live in, all that we have to cling to is—each other. . . . That's why it's so important to—Tom, I—I sent out your sister so I could discuss something with you. If you hadn't spoken I would have spoken to you. (*Sits down.*)

TOM (*gently*) What is it, Mother, that you want to discuss?

AMANDA Laura!

TOM *puts his cup down slowly.*

(LEGEND ON SCREEN: "LAURA.")

(MUSIC: "THE GLASS MENAGERIE.")

TOM —Oh.—Laura . . .

AMANDA (*touching his sleeve*) You know how Laura is. So quiet but—still water runs deep! She notices things and I think she—

broods about them. (TOM *looks up.*) A few days ago I came in and she was crying.

TOM What about?

AMANDA You.

TOM Me?

AMANDA She has an idea that you're not happy here.

TOM What gave her that idea?

AMANDA What gives her any idea? However, you do act strangely. I—I'm not criticizing, understand *that!* I know your ambitions do not lie in the warehouse, that like everybody in the whole wide world—you've had to—make sacrifices, but—Tom—Tom —life's not easy, it calls for—Spartan endurance! There's so many things in my heart that I cannot describe to you! I've never told you but I—*loved* your father. . . .

TOM (*gently*) I know that, Mother.

AMANDA And you—when I see you taking after his ways! Staying out late—and—well, you *had* been drinking the night you were in that—terrifying condition! Laura says that you hate the apartment and that you go out nights to get away from it! Is that true, Tom?

TOM No. You say there's so much in your heart that you can't describe to me. That's true of me, too. There's so much in my heart that I can't describe to *you!* So let's respect each other's—

AMANDA But, why—*why,* Tom—are you always so *restless?* Where do you go to, nights?

TOM I—go to the movies.

AMANDA Why do you go to the movies so much, Tom?

TOM I go to the movies because—I like adventure. Adventure is something I don't have much of at work, so I go to the movies.

AMANDA But, Tom, you go to the movies *entirely* too *much!*

TOM I like a lot of adventure.

AMANDA *looks baffled, then hurt. As the familiar inquisition resumes he becomes hard and impatient again.* AMANDA *slips back into her querulous attitude toward him.*

(IMAGE ON SCREEN: SAILING VESSEL WITH JOLLY ROGER.)

AMANDA Most young men find adventure in their careers.

TOM Then most young men are not employed in a warehouse.

AMANDA The world is full of young men employed in warehouses and offices and factories.

TOM Do all of them find adventure in their careers?

AMANDA They do or they do without it! Not everybody has a craze for adventure.

TOM Man is by instinct a lover, a hunter, a fighter, and none of those instincts are given much play at the warehouse!

AMANDA Man is by instinct! Don't quote instinct to me! Instinct is something that people have got away from! It belongs to animals! Christian adults don't want it!

TOM What do Christian adults want, then, Mother?

AMANDA Superior things! Thinks of the mind and the spirit! Only animals have to satisfy instincts! Surely your aims are somewhat higher than theirs! Than monkeys—pigs—

TOM I reckon they're not.

AMANDA You're joking. However, that isn't what I wanted to discuss.

TOM (*rising*) I haven't much time.

AMANDA (*pushing his shoulders*) Sit down.

TOM You want me to punch in red at the warehouse, Mother?

AMANDA You have five minutes. I want to talk about Laura.

(LEGEND: "PLANS AND PROVISIONS.")

TOM All right! What about Laura?

AMANDA We have to be making plans and provisions for her. She's older than you, two years, and nothing has happened. She just drifts along doing nothing. It frightens me terribly how she just drifts along.

TOM I guess she's the type that people call home girls.

AMANDA There's no such type, and if there is, it's a pity! That is unless the home is hers, with a husband!

TOM What?

AMANDA Oh, I can see the handwriting on the wall as plain as I see the nose in front of my face! It's terrifying! More and more you remind me of your father! He was out all hours without explanation—Then *left! Goodbye!* And me with a bag to hold. I saw that letter you got from the Merchant Marine. I know what you're dreaming of. I'm not standing here blindfolded. Very well, then. Then *do* it! But not till there's somebody to take your place.

TOM What do you mean?

AMANDA I mean that as soon as Laura has got somebody to take care of her, married, a home of her own, independent—why, then you'll be free to go wherever you please, on land, on sea, whichever way the wind blows! But until that time you've got to look out for your sister. I don't say me because I'm old and don't matter! I say for your sister because she's young and dependent. I put her in business college—a dismal failure! Frightened her so it made her sick to her stomach. I took her over to the Young People's League at the church. Another fiasco. She spoke to nobody,

nobody spoke to her. Now all she does is fool with those pieces of glass and play those worn-out records. What kind of a life is that for a girl to lead?

TOM   What can I do about it?

AMANDA   Overcome selfishness! Self, self, self is all that you ever think of! (TOM *springs up and crosses to get his coat. It is ugly and bulky. He pulls on a cap with earmuffs.*) Where is your muffler? Put your wool muffler on! (*He snatches it angrily from the closet and tosses it around his neck and pulls both ends tight.*) Tom! I haven't said what I had in mind to ask you.

TOM   I'm too late to—

AMANDA   (*catching his arm—very importunately. Then shyly*). Down at the warehouse, aren't there some—nice young men?

TOM   No!

AMANDA   There *must* be—*some* . . .

TOM   Mother—

Gesture.

AMANDA   Find out one that's clean-living—doesn't drink and—ask him out for sister!

TOM   What?

AMANDA   For *sister!* To *meet!* Get *acquainted!*

TOM   (*stamping to door*)   Oh, my go-osh!

AMANDA   Will you? (*He opens door. Imploringly.*) Will you? (*He starts down.*) Will you? *Will* you, dear?

TOM   (*calling back*)   YES!

AMANDA *closes the door hesitantly and with a troubled but faintly hopeful expression.*

(SCREEN IMAGE: GLAMOR MAGAZINE COVER.)

Spot AMANDA *at phone.*

AMANDA   Ella Cartwright? This is Amanda Wingfield! How are you, honey? How is that kidney condition? (*Count five.*) *Horrors!* (*Count five.*) You're a Christian martyr, yes, honey, that's what you are, a Christian martyr! Well, I just happened to notice in my little red book that your subscription to the *Companion* has just run out! I knew that you wouldn't want to miss out on the wonderful serial starting in this new issue. It's by Bessie Mae Hopper, the first thing she's written since *Honeymoon for Three.* Wasn't that a strange and interesting story? Well, this one is even lovelier, I believe. It has a sophisticated society background. It's all about the horsey set on Long Island!

(FADE OUT.)

SCENE V

(LEGEND ON SCREEN: "ANNUNCIATION.")

Fade with music.

It is early dusk of a spring evening. Supper has just been finished in the Wingfield apartment. AMANDA *and* LAURA *in light colored dresses are removing dishes from the table, in the upstage area, which is shadowy, their movements formalized almost as a dance or ritual, their moving forms as pale and silent as moths.*

Tom, in white shirt and trousers, rises from the table and crosses toward the fire-escape.

AMANDA (*as he passes her*)   Son, will you do me a favor?

TOM   What?

AMANDA   Comb your hair! You look so pretty when your hair is combed! (TOM *slouches on sofa with evening paper. Enormous caption "Franco Triumphs.*") There is only one respect in which I would like you to emulate your father.

TOM   What respect is that?

AMANDA   The care he always took of his appearance. He never allowed himself to look untidy. (*He throws down the paper and crosses to fire-escape.*) Where are you going?

TOM   I'm going out to smoke.

AMANDA   You smoke too much. A pack a day at fifteen cents a pack. How much would that amount to in a month? Thirty times fifteen is how much, Tom? Figure it out and you will be astounded at what you could save. Enough to give you a night-school course in accounting at Washington U! Just think what a wonderful thing that would be for you, son!

TOM *is unmoved by the thought.*

TOM   I'd rather smoke. (*He steps out on landing, letting the screen door slam.*)

AMANDA (*sharply*)   I know! That's the tragedy of it.... (*Alone, she turns to look at her husband's picture.*)

(DANCE MUSIC: "ALL THE WORLD IS WAITING FOR THE SUNRISE!")

TOM (*to the audience*)   Across the alley from us was the Paradise Dance Hall. On evenings in spring the windows and doors were open and the music came outdoors. Sometimes the lights were turned out except for a large glass sphere that hung from the ceiling. It would turn slowly about and filter the dusk with delicate rainbow colors. Then the orchestra played a waltz or a tango, something that had a slow and sensuous rhythm. Couples would come outside, to the relative privacy of the alley. You could see them kissing behind ash-pits and telephone poles. This was the compensation for lives that passed like mine, without any change or adventure. Adventure and change were imminent in this year. They were waiting around the corner for all these kids. Suspended in the mist over Berchtesgaden, caught in the folds of Chamberlain's umbrella—In Spain there was Guernica! But here there was only hot swing music and liquor, dance halls, bars, and movies, and sex that hung in the gloom like a chandelier and flooded the world with brief, deceptive rainbows. . . . All the world was waiting for bombardments!

AMANDA *turns from the picture and comes outside.*

AMANDA (*sighing*) A fire-escape landing's a poor excuse for a porch. (*She spreads a newspaper on a step and sits down, gracefully and demurely as if she were settling into a swing on a Mississippi veranda.*) What are you looking at?

TOM The moon.

AMANDA Is there a moon this evening?

TOM It's rising over Garfinkel's Delicatessen.

AMANDA So it is! A little silver slipper of a moon. Have you made a wish on it yet?

TOM Um-hum.

AMANDA What did you wish for?

TOM That's a secret.

AMANDA A secret, huh? Well, I won't tell mine either. I will be just as mysterious as you.

TOM I bet I can guess what yours is.

AMANDA Is my head so transparent?

TOM You're not a sphinx.

AMANDA No, I don't have secrets. I'll tell you what I wished for on the moon. Success and happiness for my precious children! I wish for that whenever there's a moon, and when there isn't a moon, I wish for it, too.

TOM I thought perhaps you wished for a gentleman caller.

AMANDA Why do you say that?

TOM Don't you remember asking me to fetch one?

AMANDA I remember suggesting that it would be nice for your sister if you brought home some nice young man from the warehouse. I think I've made that suggestion more than once.

TOM Yes, you have made it repeatedly.

AMANDA Well?

TOM   We are going to have one.

AMANDA   *What?*

TOM   A gentleman caller!

(THE ANNUNCIATION IS CELEBRATED WITH MUSIC.)

AMANDA *rises.*

(IMAGE ON SCREEN: CALLER WITH BOUQUET.)

AMANDA   You mean you have asked some nice young man to come over?

TOM   Yep. I've asked him to dinner.

AMANDA   You really did?

TOM   I did!

AMANDA   You did, and did he—*accept?*

TOM   He did!

AMANDA   Well, well—well, well! That's—lovely!

TOM   I thought that you would be pleased.

AMANDA   It's definite, then?

TOM   Very definite.

AMANDA   Soon?

TOM   Very soon.

AMANDA   For heaven's sake, stop putting on and tell me some things, will you?

TOM   What things do you want me to tell you?

AMANDA   *Naturally* I would like to know when he's *coming!*

TOM   He's coming tomorrow.

AMANDA   *Tomorrow?*

TOM   Yep. Tomorrow.

AMANDA   But, Tom!

TOM   Yes, Mother?

AMANDA   Tomorrow gives me no time!

TOM   Time for what?

AMANDA   Preparations! Why didn't you phone me at once, as soon as you asked him, the minute that he accepted? Then, don't you see, I could have been getting ready!

TOM   You don't have to make any fuss.

AMANDA   Oh, Tom, Tom, Tom, of course I have to make a fuss! I want things nice, not sloppy! Not thrown together. I'll certainly have to do some fast thinking, won't I?

TOM   I don't see why you have to think at all.

AMANDA   You just don't know. We can't have a gentleman caller in a pig-sty! All my wedding silver has to be polished, the monogrammed table linen ought to be laundered! The windows have to be washed and fresh curtains put up. And how about clothes? We have to *wear* something, don't we?

TOM   Mother, this boy is no one to make a fuss over!

AMANDA   Do you realize he's the first young man we've introduced to your sister? It's terrible, dreadful, disgraceful that poor little sister has never received a single gentleman caller! Tom, come inside! (*She opens the screen door.*)

TOM   What for?

AMANDA   I want to ask you some things.

TOM   If you're going to make such a fuss, I'll call it off, I'll tell him not to come.

AMANDA   You certainly won't do anything of the kind. Nothing offends people worse than broken engagements. It simply means I'll have to work like a Turk! We won't be brilliant, but we'll pass inspection. Come on inside. (TOM *follows, groaning.*) Sit down.

TOM   Any particular place you would like me to sit?

AMANDA   Thank heavens I've got that new sofa! I'm also making payments on a floor lamp I'll have sent out! And put the chintz covers on, they'll brighten things up! Of course I'd hoped to have these walls re-papered. . . . What is the young man's name?

TOM   His name is O'Connor.

AMANDA   That, of course, means fish—tomorrow is Friday! I'll have that salmon loaf—with Durkee's dressing! What does he do? He works at the warehouse?

TOM   Of course! How else would I—

AMANDA   Tom, he—doesn't drink?

TOM   Why do you ask me that?

AMANDA   Your father *did!*

TOM   Don't get started on that!

AMANDA   He *does* drink, then?

TOM   Not that I know of!

AMANDA   Make sure, be certain! The last thing I want for my daughter's a boy who drinks!

TOM   Aren't you being a little premature? Mr. O'Connor has not yet appeared on the scene!

AMANDA   But will tomorrow. To meet your sister, and what do I know about his character? Nothing! Old maids are better off than wives of drunkards!

TOM   Oh, my God!

AMANDA   Be still!

TOM (*leaning forward to whisper*)   Lots of fellows meet girls whom they don't marry!

AMANDA   Oh, talk sensibly, Tom—and don't be sarcastic! (*She has gotten a hairbrush.*)

TOM   What are you doing?

AMANDA   I'm brushing that cow-lick down! What is this young man's position at the warehouse?

TOM   (*submitting grimly to the brush and the interrogation*)   This young man's position is that of a shipping clerk, Mother.

AMANDA   Sounds to me like a fairly responsible job, the sort of a job *you* would be in if you just had more *get-up*. What is his salary? Have you got any idea?

TOM   I would judge it to be approximately eighty-five dollars a month.

AMANDA   Well—not princely, but—

TOM   Twenty more than I make.

AMANDA   Yes, how well I know! But for a family man, eighty-five dollars a month is not much more than you can just get by on. . . .

TOM   Yes, but Mr. O'Connor is not a family man.

AMANDA   He might be, mightn't he? Some time in the future?

TOM   I see. Plans and provisions.

AMANDA   You are the only young man that I know of who ignores the fact that the future becomes the present, the present the past, and the past turns into everlasting regret if you don't plan for it!

TOM   I will think that over and see what I can make of it.

AMANDA   Don't be supercilious with your mother! Tell me some more about this—what do you call him?

TOM   James D. O'Connor. The D. is for Delaney.

AMANDA   Irish on *both* sides! *Gracious!* And doesn't drink?

TOM   Shall I call him up and ask him right this minute?

AMANDA   The only way to find out about those things is to make discreet inquiries at the proper moment. When I was a girl in Blue Mountain and it was suspected that a young man drank, the girl whose attentions he had been receiving, if any girl *was,* would sometimes speak to the minister of his church, or rather her father would if her father was living, and sort of feel him out on the young man's character. That is the way such things are discreetly handled to keep a young woman from making a tragic mistake!

TOM   Then how did you happen to make a tragic mistake?

AMANDA   That innocent look of your father's had everyone fooled! He *smiled*—the world was *enchanted!* No girl can do worse than put herself at the mercy of a handsome appearance! I hope that Mr. O'Connor is not too good-looking.

TOM   No, he's not too good-looking. He's covered with freckles and hasn't too much of a nose.

AMANDA   He's not right-down homely, though?

TOM Not right-down homely. Just medium homely. I'd say.

AMANDA Character's what to look for in a man.

TOM That's what I've always said, Mother.

AMANDA You've never said anything of the kind and I suspect you would never give it a thought.

TOM Don't be suspicious of me.

AMANDA At least I hope he's the type that's up and coming.

TOM I think he really goes in for self-improvement.

AMANDA What reason have you to think so?

TOM He goes to night school.

AMANDA (*beaming*) Splendid! What does he do, I mean study?

TOM Radio engineering and public speaking!

AMANDA Then he has visions of being advanced in the world! Any young man who studies public speaking is aiming to have an executive job some day! And radio engineering? A thing for the future! Both of these facts are very illuminating. Those are the sort of things that a mother should know concerning any young man who comes to call on her daughter. Seriously or—not.

TOM One little warning. He doesn't know about Laura. I didn't let on that we had dark ulterior motives. I just said, why don't you come have dinner with us? He said okay and that was the whole conversation.

AMANDA I bet it was! You're eloquent as an oyster. However, he'll know about Laura when he gets here. When he sees how lovely and sweet and pretty she is, he'll thank his lucky stars he was asked to dinner.

TOM Mother, you mustn't expect too much of Laura.

AMANDA What do you mean?

TOM Laura seems all those things to you and me because she's ours and we love her. We don't even notice she's crippled any more.

AMANDA Don't say crippled! You know that I never allow that word to be used!

TOM But face facts, Mother. She is and—that's not all—

AMANDA What do you mean "not all"?

TOM Laura is very different from other girls.

AMANDA I think the difference is all to her advantage.

TOM Not quite all—in the eyes of others—strangers—she's terribly shy and lives in a world of her own and those things make her seem a little peculiar to people outside the house.

AMANDA Don't say peculiar.

TOM Face the facts. She is.

(THE DANCE-HALL MUSIC CHANGES TO A TANGO THAT HAS A MINOR AND SOMEWHAT OMINOUS TONE.)

AMANDA In what way is she peculiar—may I ask?

TOM (*gently*) She lives in a world of her own—a world of—little glass ornaments, Mother. . . . (*Gets up.* AMANDA *remains holding brush, looking at him, troubled.*) She plays old phonograph records and—that's about all—(*He glances at himself in the mirror and crosses to door.*)

AMANDA (*sharply*) Where are you going?

TOM I'm going to the movies. (*Out screen door.*)

AMANDA Not to the movies, every night to the movies! (*Follows quickly to screen door.*) I don't believe you always go to the movies! (*He is gone.* AMANDA *looks worriedly after him for a moment. Then vitality and optimism return and she turns from the door. Crossing to portieres.*) Laura! Laura! (LAURA *answers from kitchenette.*)

LAURA Yes, Mother.

AMANDA Let those dishes go and come in front! (LAURA *appears with dish towel. Gaily.*) Laura, come here and make a wish on the moon!

LAURA (*entering*) Moon—moon?

AMANDA A little silver slipper of a moon. Look over your left shoulder, Laura, and make a wish! (LAURA *looks faintly puzzled as if called out of sleep.* AMANDA *seizes her shoulders and turns her at an angle by the door.*) No! Now, darling, *wish!*

LAURA What shall I wish for, Mother?

AMANDA (*her voice trembling and her eyes suddenly filling with tears*) Happiness! Good Fortune!

The violin rises and the stage dims out.

SCENE VI

(IMAGE: HIGH SCHOOL HERO.)

TOM And so the following evening I brought Jim home to dinner. I had known Jim slightly in high school. In high school Jim was a hero. He had tremendous Irish good nature and vitality with the scrubbed and polished look of white chinaware. He seemed to move in a continual spotlight. He was a star in basketball, captain of the debating club, president of the senior class and the glee club and he sang the male lead in the annual light operas. He was always running or bounding, never just walking. He seemed always at the point of defeating the law of gravity. He was shooting with such velocity through his adolescence that you would logically expect him to arrive at nothing short of the White House by the time he was thirty. But Jim apparently ran into more interference after his graduation from Soldan. His speed had definitely slowed. Six years after he left high school he was holding a job that wasn't much better than mine.

(IMAGE: CLERK.)

He was the only one at the warehouse with whom I was on friendly terms. I was valuable to him as someone who could remember his former glory, who had seen him win basketball games and the silver cup in debating. He knew of my secret practice of retiring to a cabinet of the washroom to work on poems when business was slack in the warehouse. He called me Shakespeare. And while the other boys in the warehouse regarded me with suspicious hostility, Jim took a humorous attitude toward me. Gradually his attitude affected the others, their hostility wore off and they also began to smile at me as people smile at an oddly fashioned dog who trots across their path at some distance.

I knew that Jim and Laura had known each other at Soldan, and I had heard Laura speak admiringly of his voice. I didn't know if Jim remembered her or not. In high school Laura had been as unobtrusive as Jim had been astonishing. If he did remember Laura, it was not as my sister, for when I asked him to dinner, he grinned and said, "You know, Shakespeare, I never thought of you as having folks!"

He was about to discover that I did. . . .

(LIGHT UP STAGE.)

(LEGEND ON SCREEN: "THE ACCENT OF A COMING FOOT.")

Friday evening. It is about five o'clock of a late spring evening which comes "scattering poems in the sky."

A delicate lemony light is in the Wingfield apartment.

AMANDA has worked like a Turk in preparation for the gentleman caller. The results are astonishing. The new floor lamp with its rose-silk shade is in place, a colored paper lantern conceals the broken light fixture in the ceiling, new billowing white curtains are at the windows, chintz covers are on chairs and sofa, a pair of new sofa pillows make their initial appearance.

Open boxes and tissue paper are scattered on the floor.

LAURA stands in the middle with lifted arms while AMANDA crouches before her, adjusting the hem of the new dress, devout and ritualistic. The dress is colored and designed by memory. The arrangement of LAURA's hair is changed; it is softer and more becoming. A fragile, unearthly prettiness has come out in LAURA: she is like a piece of translucent glass touched by light, given a momentary radiance, not actual, not lasting.

AMANDA (*impatiently*)   Why are you trembling?

LAURA   Mother, you've made me so nervous!

AMANDA   How have I made you nervous?

LAURA   By all this fuss! You make it seem so important!

AMANDA   I don't understand you, Laura. You couldn't be satisfied with just sitting home, and yet whenever I try to arrange something for you, you seem to resist it. (*She gets up.*) Now take a look at yourself. No, wait! Wait just a moment—I have an idea!

LAURA   What is it now?

AMANDA *produces two powder puffs which she wraps in handkerchiefs and stuffs in* LAURA'S *bosom.*

LAURA   Mother, what are you doing?

AMANDA   They call them "Gay Deceivers"!

LAURA   I won't wear them!

AMANDA   You will!

LAURA   Why should I?

AMANDA   Because, to be painfully honest, your chest is flat.

LAURA   You make it seem like we were setting a trap.

AMANDA   All pretty girls are a trap, a pretty trap, and men expect them to be. (LEGEND: "A PRETTY TRAP.") Now look at yourself, young lady. This is the prettiest you will ever be! I've got to fix myself now! You're going to be surprised by your mother's appearance! (*She crosses through portieres, humming gaily.*)

LAURA *moves slowly to the long mirror and stares solemnly at herself.*
A wind blows the white curtains inward in a slow, graceful motion and with a faint, sorrowful sighing.

AMANDA (*off stage*)   It isn't dark enough yet. (*She turns slowly before the mirror with a troubled look.*)

(LEGEND ON SCREEN: "THIS IS MY SISTER: CELEBRATE HER WITH STRINGS!" MUSIC.)

AMANDA (*laughing, off*)   I'm going to show you something. I'm going to make a spectacular appearance!

LAURA   What is it, mother?

AMANDA   Possess your soul in patience—you will see! Something I've resurrected from that old trunk! Styles haven't changed so terribly much after all.... (*She parts the portieres.*) Now just look at your mother! (*She wears a girlish frock of yellowed voile with a blue silk sash. She carries a bunch of jonquils—the legend of her youth is nearly revived. Feverishly.*) This is the dress in which I led the cotillion. Won the cakewalk twice at Sunset Hill, wore one spring to the Governor's ball in Jackson! See how I sashayed around the ballroom, Laura? (*She raises her skirt and does a mincing step around the room.*) I wore it on Sundays for my gentlemen callers! I had it on the day I met your father—I had malaria fever all that spring. The change of climate from East Tennessee to the Delta—weakened resistance—I had a little temperature all the time—not enough to be serious—just enough to make me restless and giddy! Invitations poured in—parties all over the Delta!—"Stay in bed," said Mother, "you have fever!" —but I just wouldn't.—I took quinine but kept on going, going! —Evenings, dances!—Afternoons, long, long rides! Picnics— lovely!—So lovely, that country in May.—All lacy with dogwood, literally flooded with jonquils!—That was the spring I had the craze for jonquils. Jonquils became an absolute obsession. Mother said, "Honey, there's no more room for jonquils." And still I kept bringing in more jonquils. Whenever, wherever I saw them, I'd say, "Stop! Stop! I see jonquils!" I made the young men help me gather the jonquils! It was a joke, Amanda and her jonquils! Finally there were no more vases to hold them, every available space was filled with jonquils. No vases to hold them? All right, I'll hold them myself! And then I—(*She stops in front of the picture. *MUSIC.) met your father! Malaria fever and jonquils and then—this—boy.... (*She switches on the rose-colored lamp.*) I hope they get here before it starts to rain. (*She crosses upstage and places the jonquils in bowl on table.*) I gave your brother a little extra change so he and Mr. O'Connor could take the service car home.

LAURA (*with altered look*) What did you say his name was?
AMANDA O'Connor.
LAURA What is his first name?
AMANDA I don't remember. Oh, yes, I do. It was—Jim!

LAURA *sways slightly and catches hold of a chair.*

(LEGEND ON SCREEN: "NOT JIM!")

LAURA (*faintly*) Not—Jim!
AMANDA Yes, that was it, it was Jim! I've never known a Jim that wasn't nice!

(MUSIC: OMINOUS.)

LAURA Are you sure his name is Jim O'Connor?
AMANDA Yes. Why?
LAURA Is he the one that Tom used to know in high school?
AMANDA He didn't say so. I think he just got to know him at the warehouse.
LAURA There was a Jim O'Connor we both knew in high school—

(*Then, with effort.*) If that is the one that Tom is bringing to dinner—you'll have to excuse me, I won't come to the table.

AMANDA   What sort of nonsense is this?

LAURA   You asked me once if I'd ever liked a boy. Don't you remember I showed you this boy's picture?

AMANDA   You mean the boy you showed me in the year book?

LAURA   Yes, that boy.

AMANDA   Laura, Laura, were you in love with that boy?

LAURA   I don't know, Mother. All I know is I couldn't sit at the table if it was him!

AMANDA   It won't be him! It isn't the least bit likely. But whether it is or not, you will come to the table. You will not be excused.

LAURA   I'll have to be, Mother.

AMANDA   I don't intend to humor your silliness, Laura. I've had too much from you and your brother, both! So just sit down and compose yourself till they come. Tom has forgotten his key so you'll have to let them in, when they arrive.

LAURA   (*panicky*)   Oh, Mother—*you* answer the door!

AMANDA   (*lightly*)   I'll be in the kitchen—busy!

LAURA   Oh, Mother, please answer the door, don't make me do it!

AMANDA   (*crossing into kitchenette*)   I've got to fixe the dressing for the salmon. Fuss, fuss—silliness!—over a gentleman caller!

Door swings shut. LAURA *is left alone.*

(LEGEND: "TERROR!")

She utters a low moan and turns off the lamp—sits stiffly on the edge of the sofa, knotting her fingers together.

(LEGEND ON SCREEN: "THE OPENING OF A DOOR!")

TOM *and* JIM *appear on the fire-escape steps and climb to landing. Hearing their approach,* LAURA *rises with a panicky gesture. She retreats to the portieres.*

    The doorbell. LAURA *catches her breath and touches her throat. Low drums.*

AMANDA   (*calling*)   Laura, sweetheart! The door!

LAURA *stares at it without moving.*

JIM   I think we just beat the rain.

TOM   Uh-huh. (*He rings again, nervously.* JIM *whistles and fishes for a cigarette.*)

AMANDA   (*very, very gaily*)   Laura, that is your brother and Mr. O'Connor! Will you let them in, darling?

LAURA *crosses toward kitchenette door.*

LAURA (*breathlessly*)   Mother—you go to the door!

AMANDA *steps out of kitchenette and stares furiously at* LAURA. *She points imperiously at the door.*

LAURA   Please, please!

AMANDA (*in a fierce whisper*)   What is the matter with you, you silly thing?

LAURA (*desperately*)   Please, you answer it, *please!*

AMANDA   I told you I wasn't going to humor you, Laura. Why have you chosen this moment to lose your mind?

LAURA   Please, please, please, you go!

AMANDA   You'll have to go to the door because I can't!

LAURA (*despairingly*)   I can't either!

AMANDA   Why?

LAURA   I'm *sick!*

AMANDA   I'm sick, too—of your nonsense! Why can't you and your brother be normal people? Fantastic whims and behavior! (TOM *gives a long ring.*) Preposterous goings on! Can you give me one reason—(*Calls out lyrically.*) COMING! JUST ONE SECOND!—why should you be afraid to open a door? Now you answer it, Laura!

LAURA   Oh, oh, oh ... (*She returns through the portieres. Darts to the victrola and winds it frantically and turns it on.*)

AMANDA   Laura Wingfield, you march right to that door!

LAURA   Yes—yes, Mother!

A faraway, scratchy rendition of "Dardanella" softens the air and gives her strength to move through it. She slips to the door and draws it cautiously open.

   TOM *enters with the caller,* JIM O'CONNOR.

TOM   Laura, this is Jim. Jim, this is my sister, Laura.

JIM (*stepping inside*)   I didn't know that Shakespeare had a sister!

LAURA (*retreating stiff and trembling from the door*)   How—how do you do?

JIM (*heartily extending his hand*)   Okay!

LAURA *touches it hesitantly with hers.*

JIM   Your hand's *cold*, Laura!

LAURA   Yes, well—I've been playing the victrola. . . .

JIM   Must have been playing classical music on it! You ought to play a little hot swing music to warm you up!

LAURA   Excuse me—I haven't finished playing the victrola. . . .

She turns awkwardly and hurries into the front room. She pauses a second by the victrola. Then catches her breath and darts through the portieres like a frightened deer.

JIM (*grinning*)   What was the matter?

TOM   Oh—with Laura? Laura is—terribly shy.

JIM   Shy, huh? It's unusual to meet a shy girl nowadays. I don't believe you ever mentioned you had a sister.

TOM   Well, now you know. I have one. Here is the *Post Dispatch.* You want a piece of it?

JIM   Uh-huh.

TOM   What piece? The comics?

JIM   Sports! (*Glances at it.*) Ole Dizzy Dean is on his bad behavior.

TOM (*disinterest*)   Yeah? (*Lights cigarette and crosses back to fire-escape door.*)

JIM   Where are *you* going?

TOM   I'm going out on the terrace.

JIM (*goes after him*)   You know, Shakespeare—I'm going to sell you a bill of goods!

TOM   What goods?

JIM   A course I'm taking.

TOM   Huh?

JIM   In public speaking! You and me, we're not the warehouse type.

TOM   Thanks—that's good news. But what has public speaking got to do with it?

JIM   It fits you for—executive positions!

TOM   Awww.

JIM   I tell you it's done a helluva lot for me.

(IMAGE: EXECUTIVE AT DESK.)

TOM   In what respect?

JIM   In every! Ask yourself what is the difference between you an' me and men in the office down front? Brains?—No!—Ability?—No! Then what? Just one little thing—

TOM   What is that one little thing?

JIM   Primarily it amounts to—social poise! Being able to square up to people and hold your own on any social level!

AMANDA (*off stage*)   Tom?

TOM   Yes, Mother?

AMANDA   Is that you and Mr. O'Connor?

TOM   Yes, Mother.

AMANDA   Well, you just make yourselves comfortable in there.

TOM   Yes, Mother.

AMANDA   Ask Mr. O'Connor if he would like to wash his hands.

JIM   Aw—no—no—thank you—I took care of that at the warehouse. Tom—

TOM Yes?

JIM Mr. Mendoza was speaking to me about you.

TOM Favorably?

JIM What do you think?

TOM Well—

JIM You're going to be out of a job if you don't wake up.

TOM I am waking up—

JIM You show no signs.

TOM The signs are interior.

(IMAGE ON SCREEN: THE SAILING VESSEL WITH JOLLY ROGER AGAIN.)

TOM I'm planning to change. (*He leans over the rail speaking with quiet exhilaration. The incandescent marquees and signs of the first-run movie houses light his face from across the alley. He looks like a voyager.*) I'm right at the point of committing myself to a future that doesn't include the warehouse and Mr. Mendoza or even a night-school course in public speaking.

JIM What are you gassing about?

TOM I'm tired of the movies.

JIM Movies!

TOM Yes, movies! Look at them—(*A wave toward the marvels of Grand Avenue.*) All of those glamorous people—having adventures—hogging it all, gobbling the whole thing up! You know what happens? People go to the *movies* instead of *moving!* Hollywood characters are supposed to have all the adventures for everybody in America, while everybody in America sits in a dark room and watches them have them! Yes, until there's a war. That's when adventure becomes available to the masses! *Everyone's* dish, not only Gable's! Then the people in the dark room come out of the dark room to have some adventures themselves— Goody, goody!—It's our turn now, to go to the South Sea Island —to make a safari—to be exotic, far-off!—But I'm not patient. I don't want to wait till then. I'm tired of the *movies* and I am *about* to move!

JIM (*incredulously*) Move?

TOM Yes.

JIM When?

TOM Soon!

JIM Where? Where?

(THEME THREE MUSIC SEEMS TO ANSWER THE QUESTION, WHILE TOM THINKS IT OVER. HE SEARCHES AMONG HIS POCKETS.)

TOM I'm starting to boil inside. I know I seem dreamy, but inside —well, I'm boiling! Whenever I pick up a shoe, I shudder a little thinking how short life is and what I am doing!—Whatever that means. I know it doesn't mean shoes—except as something to wear on a traveler's feet! (*Finds paper.*) Look—

JIM   What?

TOM   I'm a member.

JIM (*reading*)   The Union of Merchant Seamen.

TOM   I paid my dues this month, instead of the light bill.

JIM   You will regret it when they turn the lights off.

TOM   I won't be here.

JIM   How about your mother?

TOM   I'm like my father. The bastard son of a bastard! See how he grins? And he's been absent going on sixteen years!

JIM   You're just talking, you drip. How does your mother feel about it?

TOM   Shhh!—Here comes Mother! Mother is not acquainted with my plans!

AMANDA (*enters portieres*)   Where are you all?

TOM   On the terrace, Mother.

They start inside. She advances to them. TOM *is distinctly shocked at her appearance. Even* JIM *blinks a little. He is making his first contact with girlish Southern vivacity and in spite of the night-school course in public speaking is somewhat thrown off the beam by the unexpected outlay of social charm.*

Certain responses are attempted by JIM *but are swept aside by* AMANDA's *gay laughter and chatter.* TOM *is embarrassed but after the first shock* JIM *reacts very warmly. Grins and chuckles, is altogether won over.*

(IMAGE: AMANDA AS A GIRL.)

AMANDA (*coyly smiling, shaking her girlish ringlets*)   Well, well, well, so this is Mr. O'Connor. Introductions entirely unnecessary. I've heard so much about you from my boy. I finally said to him, Tom—good gracious!—why don't you bring this paragon to supper? I'd like to meet this nice young man at the warehouse!— Instead of just hearing him sing your praises so much! I don't know why my son is so stand-offish—that's not Southern behavior! Let's sit down and—I think we could stand a little more air in here! Tom, leave the door open. I felt a nice fresh breeze a moment ago. Where has it gone? Mmm, so warm already! And not quite summer, even. We're going to burn up when summer really gets started. However, we're having—we're having a very light supper. I think light things are better fo' this time of year. The same as light clothes are. Light clothes an' light food are what warm weather calls fo'. You know our blood gets so thick during th' winter—it takes a while fo' us to *adjust* ou'selves!—

when the season changes . . . It's come so quick this year. I wasn't prepared. All of a sudden—heavens! Already summer!—I ran to the trunk an' pulled out this light dress—Terribly old! Historical almost! But feels so good—so good an' co-ol, y'know. . . .

TOM   Mother—

AMANDA   Yes, honey?

TOM   How about—supper?

AMANDA   Honey, you go ask Sister if supper is ready! You know that Sister is in full charge of supper! Tell her you hungry boys are waiting for it. (*To* JIM.) Have you met Laura?

JIM   She—

AMANDA   Let you in? Oh, good, you've met already! It's rare for a girl as sweet an' pretty as Laura to be domestic! But Laura is, thank heavens, not only pretty but also very domestic. I'm not at all. I never was a bit. I never could make a thing but angel-food cake. Well, in the South we had so many servants. Gone, gone, gone. All vestige of gracious living! Gone completely! I wasn't prepared for what the future brought me. All of my gentlemen callers were sons of planters and so of course I assumed that I would be married to one and raise my family on a large piece of land with plenty of servants. But man proposes—and woman accepts the proposal!—To vary that old, old saying a little bit—I married no planter! I married a man who worked for the telephone company!—That gallantly smiling gentleman over there! (*Points to the picture.*) A telephone man who—fell in love with long-distance!—Now he travels and I don't even know where!— But what am I going on for about my—tribulations? Tell me yours—I hope you don't have any! Tom?

TOM (*returning*)   Yes, Mother?

AMANDA   Is supper nearly ready?

TOM   It looks to me like supper is on the table.

AMANDA   Let me look—(*She rises prettily and looks through portieres.*) Oh, lovely!—But where is Sister?

TOM   Laura is not feeling well and she says that she thinks she'd better not come to the table.

AMANDA   What?—Nonsense!—Laura? Oh, Laura!

LAURA (*off stage, faintly*)   Yes, Mother.

AMANDA   You really must come to the table. We won't be seated until you come to the table! Come in, Mr. O'Connor. You sit over there and I'll—Laura? Laura Wingfield! You're keeping us waiting, honey! We can't say grace until you come to the table!

The back door is pushed weakly open and LAURA *comes in. She is obviously quite faint, her lips trembling, her eyes wide and staring. She moves unsteadily toward the table.*

(LEGEND: "TERROR!")

Outside a summer storm is coming abruptly. The white curtains billow inward at the windows and there is a sorrowful murmur and deep blue dusk.

LAURA *suddenly stumbles—she catches at a chair with a faint moan.*

TOM   Laura!

AMANDA   Laura! (*There is a clap of thunder.*) (LEGEND: "AH!") (*Despairingly.*) Why, Laura, you *are* sick, darling! Tom, help your sister into the living room, dear! Sit in the living room, Laura —rest on the sofa. Well! (*To the gentleman caller.*) Standing over the hot stove made her ill!—I told her that it was just too warm this evening, but—(TOM *comes back in.* LAURA *is on the sofa.*) Is Laura all right now?

TOM   Yes.

AMANDA   What *is* that? Rain? A nice cool rain has come up! (*She gives the gentleman caller a frightened look.*) I think we may— have grace—now . . . (TOM *looks at her stupidly.*) Tom, honey— you say grace!

TOM   Oh . . . "For these and all thy mercies—" (*They bow their heads,* AMANDA *stealing a nervous glance at* JIM. *In the living room* LAURA, *stretched on the sofa, clenches her hand to her lips, to hold back a shuddering sob.*) God's Holy Name be praised—

(THE SCENE DIMS OUT.)

SCENE VII

(LEGEND: "A SOUVENIR.")

Half an hour later. Dinner is just being finished in the upstage area which is concealed by the drawn portieres.

As the curtain rises LAURA *is still huddled upon the sofa, her feet drawn under her, her head resting on a pale blue pillow, her eyes wide and mysteriously watchful. The new floor lamp with its shade of rose-colored silk gives a soft, becoming light to her face, bringing out the fragile, unearthly prettiness which usually escapes attention. There is a steady murmur of rain, but it is slackening and stops soon after the scene begins; the air outside becomes pale and luminous as the moon breaks out.*

A moment after the curtain rises, the lights in both rooms flicker and go out.

JIM   Hey, there, Mr. Light Bulb!

AMANDA *laughs nervously.*

(LEGEND: "SUSPENSION OF A PUBLIC SERVICE.")

AMANDA   Where was Moses when the lights went out? Ha-ha. Do
you know the answer to that one, Mr. O'Connor?

JIM   No, Ma'am, what's the answer?

AMANDA   In the dark! (JIM *laughs appreciably.*) Everybody sit still.
I'll light the candles. Isn't it lucky we have them on the table?
Where's a match? Which of you gentlemen can provide a match?

JIM   Here.

AMANDA   Thank you, sir.

JIM   Not at all, Ma'am!

AMANDA   I guess the fuse has burnt out. Mr. O'Connor, can you
tell a burnt-out fuse? I know I can't and Tom is a total loss when
it comes to mechanics. (SOUND: GETTING UP: VOICES RECEDE A
LITTLE TO KITCHENETTE.) Oh, be careful you don't bump into
something. We don't want our gentleman caller to break his neck.
Now wouldn't that be a fine howdy-do?

JIM   Ha-ha! Where is the fuse-box?

AMANDA   Right here next to the stove. Can you see anything?

JIM   Just a minute.

AMANDA   Isn't electricity a mysterious thing? Wasn't it Benjamin
Franklin who tied a key to a kite? We live in such a mysterious
universe, don't we? Some people say that science clears up all the
mysteries for us. In my opinion it only creates more! Have you
found it yet?

JIM   No, Ma'am. All these fuses look okay to me.

AMANDA   Tom!

TOM   Yes, Mother?

AMANDA   That light bill I gave you several days ago. The one I told
you we got the notices about?

TOM   Oh.—Yeah.

(LEGEND: "HA!")

AMANDA   You didn't neglect to pay it by any chance?

TOM   Why, I—

AMANDA   Didn't! I might have known it!

JIM   Shakespeare probably wrote a poem on that light bill, Mrs.
Wingfield.

AMANDA   I might have known better than to trust him with it!
There's such a high price for negligence in this world!

JIM   Maybe the poem will win a ten-dollar prize.

AMANDA   We'll just have to spend the remainder of the evening in
the nineteenth century, before Mr. Edison made the Mazda lamp!

JIM   Candlelight is my favorite kind of light.

AMANDA   That shows you're romantic! But that's no excuse for

TOM. Well, we got through dinner. Very considerate of them to let us get through dinner before they plunged us into everlasting darkness, wasn't it, Mr. O'Connor?

JIM Ha-ha!

AMANDA Tom, as a penalty for your carelessness you can help me with the dishes.

JIM Let me give you a hand.

AMANDA Indeed you will not!

JIM I ought to be good for something.

AMANDA Good for something? (*Her tone is rhapsodic.*) *You?* Why, Mr. O'Connor, nobody, *nobody's* given me this much entertainment in years—as you have!

JIM Aw, now, Mrs. Wingfield!

AMANDA I'm not exaggerating, not one bit! But Sister is all by her lonesome. You go keep her company in the parlor! I'll give you this lovely old candelabrum that used to be on the altar at the church of the Heavenly Rest. It was melted a little out of shape when the church burnt down. Lightning struck it one spring. Gypsy Jones was holding a revival at the time and he intimated that the church was destroyed because the Episcopalians gave card parties.

JIM Ha-ha.

AMANDA And how about coaxing Sister to drink a little wine? I think it would be good for her! Can you carry both at once?

JIM Sure. I'm Superman!

AMANDA Now, Thomas, get into this apron!

The door of kitchenette swings closed on AMANDA's *gay laughter; the flickering light approaches the portieres.*

LAURA *sits up nervously as he enters. Her speech at first is low and breathless from the almost intolerable strain of being alone with a stranger.*

(THE LEGEND: "I DON'T SUPPOSE YOU REMEMBER ME AT ALL!")

In her first speeches in this scene, before JIM's *warmth overcomes her paralyzing shyness,* LAURA's *voice is thin and breathless as though she has just run up a steep flight of stairs.*

JIM's *attitude is gently humorous. In playing this scene it should be stressed that while the incident is apparently unimportant, it is to* LAURA *the climax of her secret life.*

JIM Hello, there, Laura.

LAURA (*faintly*) Hello (*She clears her throat.*)

JIM How are you feeling now? Better?

LAURA Yes. Yes, thank you.

JIM This is for you. A little dandelion wine. (*He extends it toward her with extravagant gallantry.*)

LAURA   Thank you.

JIM   Drink it—but don't get drunk! (*He laughs heartily.* LAURA *takes the glass uncertainly; laughs shyly.*) Where shall I set the candles?

LAURA   Oh—oh, anywhere . . .

JIM   How about here on the floor? Any objections?

LAURA   No.

JIM   I'l spread a newspaper under to catch the drippings. I like to sit on the floor. Mind if I do?

LAURA   Oh, no.

JIM   Give me a pillow?

LAURA   What?

JIM   A pillow!

LAURA   Oh . . . (*Hands him one quickly.*)

JIM   How about you? Don't you like to sit on the floor?

LAURA   Oh—yes.

JIM   Why don't you, then?

LAURA   I—will.

JIM   Take a pillow! (LAURA *does. Sits on the other side of the candelabrum.* JIM *crosses his legs and smiles engagingly at her.*) I can't hardly see you sitting way over there.

LAURA   I can—see you.

JIM   I know, but that's not fair, I'm in the limelight. (LAURA *moves her pillow closer.*) Good! Now I can see you! Comfortable?

LAURA   Yes.

JIM   So am I. Comfortable as a cow. Will you have some gum?

LAURA   No, thank you.

JIM   I think that I will indulge, with your permission. (*Musingly unwraps it and holds it up.*) Think of the fortune made by the guy that invented the first piece of chewing gum. Amazing, huh? The Wrigley Building is one of the sights of Chicago.—I saw it summer before last when I went up to the Century of Progress. Did you take in the Century of Progress?

LAURA   No, I didn't.

JIM   Well, it was quite a wonderful exposition. What impressed me most was the Hall of Science. Gives you an idea of what the future will be in America, even more wonderful than the present time is! (*Pause. Smiling at her.*) Your brother tells me you're shy. Is that right, Laura?

LAURA   I—don't know.

JIM   I judge you to be an old-fashioned type of girl. Well, I think that's a pretty good type to be. Hope you don't think I'm being too personal—do you?

LAURA   (*hastily, out of embarrassment*)   I believe I *will* take a piece of gum, if you—don't mind. (*Clearing her throat.*) Mr. O'Connor, have you—kept up with your singing?

JIM Singing? Me?

LAURA Yes. I remember what a beautiful voice you had.

JIM When did you hear me sing?

(VOICE OFF STAGE IN THE PAUSE.)

VOICE (*off stage*)

> O blow, ye winds, heigh-ho,
> A-roving I will go!
> I'm off to my love
> With a boxing glove—
> Ten thousand miles away!

JIM You say you've heard me sing?

LAURA Oh, yes! Yes, very often . . . I—don't suppose you remember me—at all?

JIM (*smiling doubtfully*) You know I have an idea I've seen you before. I had that idea soon as you opened the door. It seemed almost like I was about to remember your name. But the name that I started to call you—wasn't a name! And so I stopped myself before I said it.

LAURA Wasn't it—Blue Roses?

JIM (*springs up, grinning*) Blue Roses! My gosh, yes—Blue Roses! That's what I had on my tongue when you opened the door! Isn't it funny what tricks your memory plays? I didn't connect you with the high school somehow or other. But that's where it was; it was high school. I didn't even know you were Shakespeare's sister! Gosh, I'm sorry.

LAURA I didn't expect you to. You—barely knew me!

JIM But we did have a speaking acquaintance, huh?

LAURA Yes, we—spoke to each other.

JIM When did you recognize me?

LAURA Oh, right away!

JIM Soon as I came in the door?

LAURA When I heard your name I thought it was probably you. I knew that Tom used to know you a little in high school. So when you came in the door—Well, then I was—sure.

JIM Why didn't you *say* something, then?

LAURA (*breathlessly*) I didn't know what to say, I was—too surprised!

JIM For goodness' sakes! You know, this sure is funny!

LAURA Yes! Yes, isn't it, though . . .

JIM Didn't we have a class in something together?

LAURA Yes, we did.

JIM What class was that?

LAURA It was—singing—Chorus!

JIM Aw!

LAURA I sat across the aisle from you in the Aud.

JIM Aw.

LAURA Mondays, Wednesdays and Fridays.

JIM Now I remember—you always came in late.

LAURA Yes, it was so hard for me, getting upstairs. I had that brace on my leg—it clumped so loud!

JIM I never heard any clumping.

LAURA (*wincing at the recollection*) To me it sounded like—thunder!

JIM Well, well, well. I never even noticed.

LAURA And everybody was seated before I came in. I had to walk in front of all those people. My seat was in the back row. I had to go clumping all the way up the aisle with everyone watching!

JIM You shouldn't have been self-conscious.

LAURA I know, but I was. It was always such a relief when the singing started.

JIM Aw, yes. I've placed you now! I used to call you Blue Roses. How was it that I got started calling you that?

LAURA I was out of school a little while with pleurosis. When I came back you asked me what was the matter. I said I had pleurosis—you thought I said Blue Roses. That's what you always called me after that!

JIM I hope you didn't mind.

LAURA Oh, no—I liked it. You see, I wasn't acquainted with many —people. . . .

JIM As I remember you sort of stuck by yourself.

LAURA I—I—never had much luck at—making friends.

JIM I don't see why you wouldn't.

LAURA Well, I—started out badly.

JIM You mean being—

LAURA Yes, it sort of—stood between me—

JIM You shouldn't have let it!

LAURA I know, but it did, and—

JIM You were shy with people!

LAURA I tried not to be but never could—

JIM Overcome it?

LAURA No, I—I never could!

JIM I guess being shy is something you have to work out of kind of gradually.

LAURA (*sorrowfully*) Yes—I guess it—

JIM   Takes time!

LAURA   Yes—

JIM   People are not so dreadful when you know them. That's what you have to remember! And everybody has problems, not just you, but practically everybody has got some problems. You think of yourself as having the only problems, as being the only one who is disappointed. But just look around you and you will see lots of people as disappointed as you are. For instance, I hoped when I was going to high school that I would be further along at this time, six years later, than I am now—You remember that wonderful write-up I had in *The Torch?*

LAURA   Yes! (*She rises and crosses to table.*)

JIM   It said I was bound to succeed in anything I went into! (LAURA *returns with the annual.*) Holy Jeez! *The Torch!* (*He accepts it reverently. They smile across it with mutual wonder.* LAURA *crouches beside him and they begin to turn through it.* LAURA'S *shyness is dissolving in his warmth.*)

LAURA   Here you are in *Pirates of Penzance!*

JIM   (*wistfully*)   I sang the baritone lead in that operetta.

LAURA   (*rapidly*)   So—*beautifully!*

JIM   (*protesting*)   Aw—

LAURA   Yes, yes—beautifully—beautifully!

JIM   You heard me?

LAURA   All three times!

JIM   No!

LAURA   Yes!

JIM   All three performances?

LAURA   (*looking down*)   Yes.

JIM   Why?

LAURA   I—wanted to ask you to—autograph my program.

JIM   Why didn't you ask me to.

LAURA   You were always surrounded by your own friends so much that I never had a chance to.

JIM   You should have just—

LAURA   Well, I—thought you might think I was—

JIM   Thought I might think you was—what?

LAURA   Oh—

JIM   (*with reflective relish*)   I was beleaguered by females in those days.

LAURA   You were terribly popular!

JIM   Yeah—

LAURA   You had such a—friendly way—

JIM   I was spoiled in high school.

LAURA   Everybody—liked you!

JIM   Including you?

LAURA   I—yes, I—I did, too—(*She gently closes the book in her lap.*)

JIM   Well, well, well!—Give me that program, Laura. (*She hands it to him. He signs it with a flourish.*) There you are—better late than never!

LAURA   Oh, I—what a—surprise!

JIM   My signature isn't worth very much right now. But some day —maybe—it will increase in value! Being disappointed is one thing and being discouraged is something else. I am disappointed but I am not discouraged. I'm twenty-three years old. How old are you?

LAURA   I'll be twenty-four in June.

JIM   That's not old age!

LAURA   No, but—

JIM   You finished high school?

LAURA   (*with difficulty*)   I didn't go back.

JIM   You mean you dropped out?

LAURA   I made bad grades in my final examinations. (*She rises and replaces the book and the program. Her voice strained.*) How is—Emily Meisenbach getting along?

JIM   Oh, that kraut-head!

LAURA   Why do you call her that?

JIM   That's what she was.

LAURA   You're not still—going with her?

JIM   I never see her.

LAURA   It said in the Personal Section that you were—engaged!

JIM   I know, but I wasn't impressed by that—propaganda!

LAURA   It wasn't—the truth?

JIM   Only in Emily's optimistic opinion!

LAURA   Oh—

(LEGEND: "WHAT HAVE YOU DONE SINCE HIGH SCHOOL?")

JIM *lights a cigarette and leans indolently back on his elbows smiling at* LAURA *with a warmth and charm which lights her inwardly with altar candles. She remains by the table and turns in her hands a piece of glass to cover her tumult.*

JIM   (*after several reflective puffs on a cigarette*)   What have you done since high school? (*She seems not to hear him.*) Huh? (LAURA *looks up.*) I said what have you done since high school, Laura?

LAURA   Nothing much.

JIM   You must have been doing something these six long years.

LAURA   Yes.

JIM Well, then, such as what?

LAURA I took a business course at business college—

JIM How did that work out?

LAURA Well, not very—well—I had to drop out, it gave me—indigestion—

JIM *laughs gently.*

JIM What are you doing now?

LAURA I don't do anything—much. Oh, please don't think I sit around doing nothing! My glass collection takes up a good deal of my time. Glass is something you have to take good care of.

JIM What did you say—about glass?

LAURA Collection I said—I have one—(*She clears her throat and turns away again, acutely shy.*)

JIM (*abruptly*) You know what I judge to be the trouble with you? Inferiority complex! Know what that is? That's what they call it when someone low-rates himself! I understand it because I had it, too. Although my case was not so aggravated as yours seems to be. I had it until I took up public speaking, developed my voice, and learned that I had an aptitude for science. Before that time I never thought of myself as being outstanding in any way whatsoever! Now I've never made a regular study of it, but I have a friend who says I can analyze people better than doctors that make a profession of it. I don't claim that to be necessarily true, but I can sure guess a person's psychology, Laura! (*Takes out his gum.*) Excuse me, Laura. I always take it out when the flavor is gone. I'll use this scrap of paper to wrap it in. I know how it is to get it stuck on a shoe. Yep—that's what I judge to be your principal trouble. A lack of confidence in yourself as a person. You don't have the proper amount of faith in yourself. I'm basing that fact on a number of your remarks and also on certain observations I've made. For instance that clumping you thought was so awful in high school. You say that you even dreaded to walk into class. You see what you did? You dropped out of school, you gave up an education because of a clump, which as far as I know was practically non-existent! A little physical defect is what you have. Hardly noticeable even! Magnified thousands of times by imagination! You know what my strong advice to you is? Think of yourself as *superior* in some way!

LAURA In what way would I think?

JIM Why, man alive, Laura! Just look about you a little. What do you see? A world full of common people! All of 'em born and all of 'em going to die! Which of them has one-tenth of your good points! Or mine! Or anyone else's, as far as that goes—Gosh!

Everybody excels in some one thing. Some in many! (*Unconsciously glances at himself in the mirror.*) All you've got to do is discover in *what!* Take me, for instance. (*He adjusts his tie at the mirror.*) My interest happens to lie in electro-dynamics. I'm taking a course in radio engineering at night school, Laura, on top of a fairly responsible job at the warehouse. I'm taking that course and studying public speaking.

LAURA   Ohhhh.

JIM   Because I believe in the future of television! (*Turning back to her.*) I wish to be ready to go up right along with it. Therefore I'm planning to get in on the ground floor. In fact, I've already made the right connections and all that remains is for the industry itself to get under way! Full steam—(*His eyes are starry.*) Knowledge—Zzzzzp! Money—Zzzzzzp!—Power! That's the cycle democracy is built on! (*His attitude is convincingly dynamic.* LAURA *stares at him, even her shyness eclipsed in her absolute wonder. He suddenly grins.*) I guess you think I think a lot of myself!

LAURA   No—o-o-o, I—

JIM   Now how about you? Isn't there something you take more interest in than anything else?

LAURA   Well, I do—as I said—have my—glass collection—

A peal of girlish laughter from the kitchen.

JIM   I'm not right sure I know what you're talking about. What kind of glass is it?

LAURA   Little articles of it, they're ornaments mostly! Most of them are little animals made out of glass, the tiniest little animals in the world. Mother calls them a glass menagerie! Here's an example of one, if you'd like to see it! This one is one of the oldest. It's nearly thirteen. (*He stretches out his hand.*) (MUSIC: "THE GLASS MENAGERIE.") Oh, be careful—if you breathe, it breaks!

JIM   I'd better not take it. I'm pretty clumsy with things.

LAURA   Go on, I trust you with him! (*Places it in his palm.*) There now—you're holding him gently! Hold him over the light, he loves the light! You see how the light shines through him?

JIM   It sure does shine!

LAURA   I shouldn't be partial, but he is my favorite one.

JIM   What kind of a thing is this one supposed to be?

LAURA   Haven't you noticed the single horn on his forehead?

JIM   A unicorn, huh?

LAURA   Mmm-hmmm!

JIM   Unicorns, aren't they extinct in the modern world?

LAURA   I know!

JIM   Poor little fellow, he must feel sort of lonesome.

LAURA (*smiling*)   Well, if he does he doesn't complain about it. He stays on a shelf with some horses that don't have horns and all of them seem to get along nicely together.

JIM   How do you know?

LAURA (*lightly*)   I haven't heard any arguments among them!

JIM (*grinning*)   No arguments, huh? Well, that's a pretty good sign! Where shall I set him?

LAURA   Put him on the table. They all like a change of scenery once in a while!

JIM (*stretching*)   Well, well, well, well—Look how big my shadow is when I stretch!

LAURA   Oh, oh, yes—it stretches across the ceiling!

JIM (*crossing to door*)   I think it's stopped raining. (*Opens fire-escape door.*) Where does the music come from?

LAURA   From the Paradise Dance Hall across the alley.

JIM   How about cutting the rug a little, Miss Wingfield?

LAURA   Oh, I—

JIM   Or is your program filled up? Let me have a look at it. *Grasps imaginary card.*) Why, every dance is taken! I'll just have to scratch some out. (WALTZ MUSIC: "LA GOLONDRINA.") Ahhh, a waltz! (*He executes some sweeping turns by himself, then holds his arms toward* LAURA.)

LAURA (*breathlessly*)   I—can't dance!

JIM   There you go, that inferiority stuff!

LAURA   I've never danced in my life!

JIM   Come on, try!

LAURA   Oh, but I'd step on you!

JIM   I'm not made out of glass.

LAURA   How—how—how do we start?

JIM   Just leave it to me. You hold your arms out a little.

LAURA   Like this?

JIM   A little bit higher. Right. Now don't tighten up, that's the main thing about it—relax.

LAURA (*laughing breathlessly*)   It's hard not to.

JIM   Okay.

LAURA   I'm afraid you can't budge me.

JIM   What do you bet I can't? (*He swings her into motion.*)

LAURA   Goodness, yes, you can!

JIM   Let yourself go, now, Laura, just let yourself go.

LAURA   I'm—

JIM   Come on!

LAURA   Trying!

JIM   Not so stiff—Easy does it!

LAURA   I know but I'm—

JIM   Loosen th' backbone! There now, that's a lot better.

LAURA   Am I?

JIM   Lots, lots better! (*He moves her about the room in a clumsy waltz.*)

LAURA   Oh, my!

JIM   Ha-ha!

LAURA   Goodness, yes you can!

JIM   Ha-ha-ha! (*They suddenly bump into the table.* JIM *stops.*) What did we hit on?

LAURA   Table.

JIM   Did something fall off it? I think—

LAURA   Yes.

JIM   I hope that it wasn't the little glass horse with the horn!

LAURA   Yes.

JIM   Aw, aw, aw. Is it broken?

LAURA   Now it is just like all the other horses.

JIM   It's lost its—

LAURA   Horn! It doesn't matter. Maybe it's a blessing in disguise.

JIM   You'll never forgive me. I bet that that was your favorite piece of glass.

LAURA   I don't have favorites much. It's no tragedy, Freckles. Glass breaks so easily. No matter how careful you are. The traffic jars the shelves and things fall off them.

JIM   Still I'm awfully sorry that I was the cause.

LAURA   (*smiling*)   I'll just imagine he had an operation. The horn was removed to make him feel less—freakish! (*They both laugh.*) Now he will feel more at home with the other horses, the ones that don't have horns . . .

JIM   Ha-ha, that's very funny! (*Suddenly serious.*) I'm glad to see that you have a sense of humor. You know—you're—well—very different! Surprisingly different from anyone else I know! (*His voice becomes soft and hesitant with a genuine feeling.*) Do you mind me telling you that? (LAURA *is abashed beyond speech.*) You make me feel sort of—I don't know how to put it! I'm usually pretty good at expressing things, but—This is something that I don't know how to say! (LAURA *touches her throat and clears it—turns the broken unicorn in her hands.*) (*Even softer.*) Has anyone ever told you that you were pretty? (PAUSE: MUSIC.) (LAURA *looks up slowly, with wonder, and shakes her head.*) Well, you are! In a very different way from anyone else. And all the nicer because of the difference, too. (*His voice becomes low and husky.* LAURA *turns away, nearly faint with the novelty of her emotions.*) I wish that you were my sister. I'd teach you to have some confidence in yourself. The different people are not like other people, but being different is nothing to be ashamed of. Because other people are not such wonderful people. They're one hundred times one thousand. You're one times one! They walk all over the earth. You just stay here. They're common as—weeds, but—you—well, you're—*Blue Roses!*

(IMAGE ON SCREEN: BLUE ROSES.)

(MUSIC CHANGES.)

LAURA   But blue is wrong for—roses . . .

JIM   It's right for you—You're—pretty!

LAURA   In what respect am I pretty?

JIM   In all respects—believe me! Your eyes—your hair—are pretty! Your hands are pretty! (*He catches hold of her hand.*) You think I'm making this up because I'm invited to dinner and have to be nice. Oh, I could do that! I could put on an act for you, Laura, and say lots of things without being very sincere. But this time I am. I'm talking to you sincerely. I happened to notice you had this inferiority complex that keeps you from feeling comfortable with people. Somebody needs to build your confidence up and make you proud instead of shy and turning away and—blushing —Somebody ought to—Ought to—*kiss* you, Laura! (*His hand slips slowly up her arm to her shoulder.*) (MUSIC SWELLS TUMULTUOUSLY.) (*He suddenly turns her about and kisses her on the lips. When he releases her* LAURA *sinks on the sofa with a bright, dazed look.* JIM *backs away and fishes in his pocket for a cigarette.*) (LEGEND ON SCREEN: "SOUVENIR.") Stumble-john! (*He lights the cigarette, avoiding her look. There is a peal of girlish laughter from* AMANDA *in the kitchen.* LAURA *slowly raises and opens her hand. It still contains the little broken glass animal. She looks at it with a tender, bewildered expression.*) Stumble-john! I shouldn't have done that—That was way off the beam. You don't smoke, do you? (*She looks up, smiling, not hearing the question. He sits beside her a little gingerly. She looks at him speechlessly —waiting. He coughs decorously and moves a little farther aside as he considers the situation and senses her feelings, dimly, with perturbation. Gently.*) Would you—care for a—mint? (*She doesn't seem to hear him but her look grows brighter even.*) Peppermint—Life Saver? My pocket's a regular drug store—wherever I go . . . (*He pops a mint in his mouth. Then gulps and decides to make a clean breast of it. He speaks slowly and gingerly.*) Laura, you know, if I had a sister like you, I'd do the same thing as Tom. I'd bring out fellows—introduce her to them. The right type of boys of a type to—appreciate her. Only—well—he made a mistake about me. Maybe I've got no call to be saying this. That may not have been the idea in having me over. But what if it was? There's nothing wrong about that. The only trouble is that in my case—I'm not in a situation to—do the right thing. I can't take down your number and say I'll phone. I can't call up next week and—ask for a date. I thought I had better explain the situation in case you misunderstood it and—hurt your feelings. . . . (*Pause. Slowly, very slowly,* LAURA's *look changes, her eyes returning slowly from his to the ornament in her palm.*)

AMANDA *utters another gay laugh in the kitchen.*

LAURA (*faintly*)   You—won't—call again?

JIM   No, Laura, I can't. (*He rises from the sofa.*) As I was just explaining, I've—got strings on me, Laura, I've—been going steady! I go out all the time with a girl named Betty. She's a home-girl like you, and Catholic, and Irish, and in a great many ways we—get along fine. I met her last summer on a moonlight boat trip up the river to Alton, on the *Majestic*. Well—right away from the start it was—love! (LEGEND: LOVE!) (LAURA *sways slightly forward and grips the arm of the sofa. He fails to notice, now enrapt in his own comfortable being.*) Being in love has made a new man of me! (*Leaning stiffly forward, clutching the arm of the sofa,* LAURA *struggles visibly with her storm. But* JIM *is oblivious, she is a long way off.*) The power of love is really pretty tremendous! Love is something that—changes the whole world, Laura! (*The storm abates a little and* LAURA *leans back. He notices her again.*) It happened that Betty's aunt took sick, she got a wire and had to go to Centralia. So Tom—when he asked me to dinner—I naturally just accepted the invitation, not knowing that you—that he—that I—(*He stops awkwardly.*) Huh—I'm a stumble-john! (*He flops back on the sofa. The holy candles in the altar of* LAURA's *face have been snuffed out! There is a look of almost infinite desolation.* JIM *glances at her uneasily.*) I wish that you would—say something. (*She bites her lip which was trembling and then bravely smiles. She opens her hand again on the broken glass ornament. Then she gently takes his hand and raises it level with her own. She carefully places the unicorn in the palm of his hand, then pushes his fingers closed upon it.*) What are you—doing that for? You want me to have him?—Laura? (*She nods.*) What for?

LAURA   A—souvenir . . .

She rises unsteadily and crouches beside the victrola to wind it up.

(LEGEND ON SCREEN: "THINGS HAVE A WAY OF TURNING OUT SO BADLY.")

(OR IMAGE: "GENTLEMAN CALLER WAVING GOODBYE!—GAILY.")

At this moment AMANDA *rushes brightly back in the front room. She bears a pitcher of fruit punch in an old-fashioned cut-glass pitcher and a plate of macaroons. The plate has a gold border and poppies painted on it.*

AMANDA Well, well, well! Isn't the air delightful after the shower? I've made you children a little liquid refreshment. (*Turns gaily to the gentleman caller.*) Jim, do you know that song about lemonade?

> "Lemonade, lemonade
> Made in the shade and stirred with a spade—
> Good enough for any old maid!"

JIM (*uneasily*) Ha-ha! No—I never heard it.

AMANDA Why, Laura! You look so serious!

JIM We were having a serious conversation.

AMANDA Good! Now you're better acquainted!

JIM (*uncertainly*) Ha-ha! Yes.

AMANDA You modern young people are much more serious-minded than my generation. I was so gay as a girl!

JIM You haven't changed, Mrs. Wingfield.

AMANDA Tonight I'm rejuvenated! The gaiety of the occasion, Mr. O'Connor! (*She tosses her head with a peal of laughter. Spills lemonade.*) Oooo! I'm baptizing myself!

JIM Here—let me—

AMANDA (*setting the pitcher down*) There now. I discovered we had some maraschino cherries. I dumped them in, juice and all!

JIM You shouldn't have gone to that trouble, Mrs. Wingfield.

AMANDA Trouble, trouble? Why it was loads of fun! Didn't you hear me cutting up in the kitchen? I bet your ears were burning! I told Tom how outdone with him I was for keeping you to himself so long a time! He should have brought you over much, much sooner! Well, now that you've found your way, I want you to be a very frequent caller! Not just occasional but all the time. Oh, we're going to have a lot of gay times together! I see them coming! Mmm, just breathe that air! So fresh, and the moon's so pretty! I'll skip back out—I know where my place is when young folks are having a—serious conversation!

JIM Oh, don't go out, Mrs. Wingfield. The fact of the matter is I've got to be going.

AMANDA   Going, now? You're joking! Why, it's only the shank of the evening, Mr. O'Connor!

JIM   Well, you know how it is.

AMANDA   You mean you're a young workingman and have to keep workingmen's hours. We'll let you off early tonight. But only on the condition that next time you stay later. What's the best night for you? Isn't Saturday night the best night for you workingmen?

JIM   I have a couple of time-clocks to punch, Mrs. Wingfield. One at morning, another one at night!

AMANDA   My, but you *are* ambitious! You work at night, too?

JIM   No, Ma'am, not work but—Betty! (*He crosses deliberately to pick up his hat. The band at the Paradise Dance Hall goes into a tender waltz.*)

AMANDA   Betty? Betty? Who's—Betty! (*There is an ominous cracking sound in the sky.*)

JIM   Oh, just a girl. The girl I go steady with! (*He smiles charmingly. The sky falls.*)

(LEGEND: "THE SKY FALLS.")

AMANDA   (*a long-drawn exhalation*)   Ohhhh . . . Is it a serious romance, Mr. O'Connor?

JIM   We're going to be married the second Sunday in June.

AMANDA   Ohhhh—how nice! Tom didn't mention that you were engaged to be married.

JIM   The cat's not out of the bag at the warehouse yet. You know how they are. They call you Romeo and stuff like that. (*He stops at the oval mirror to put on his hat. He carefully shapes the brim and the crown to give a discreetly dashing effect.*) It's been a wonderful evening, Mrs. Wingfield. I guess this is what they mean by Southern hospitality.

AMANDA   It really wasn't anything at all.

JIM   I hope it don't seem like I'm rushing off. But I promised Betty I'd pick her up at the Wabash depot, an' by the time I get my jalopy down there her train'll be in. Some women are pretty upset if you keep 'em waiting.

AMANDA   Yes, I know—The tyranny of women! (*Extends her hand.*) Goodbye, Mr. O'Connor. I wish you luck—and happiness —and success! All three of them, and so does Laura!—Don't you, Laura?

LAURA   Yes!

JIM   (*taking her hand*)   Good-bye, Laura. I'm certainly going to treasure that souvenir. And don't you forget the good advice I gave you. (*Raises his voice to a cheery shout.*) So long, Shakespeare! Thanks again, ladies—Good night!

He grins and ducks jauntily out.

Still bravely grimacing, AMANDA *closes the door on the gentleman caller. Then she turns back to the room with a puzzled expression. She and* LAURA *don't dare to face each other.* LAURA *crouches beside the victrola to wind it.*

AMANDA (*faintly*) Things have a way of turning out so badly. I don't believe that I would play the victrola. Well, well—well— Our gentleman caller was engaged to be married! Tom!

TOM (*from back*) Yes, Mother?

AMANDA Come in here a minute. I want to tell you something awfully funny.

TOM (*enters with a macaroon and a glass of the lemonade*) Has the gentleman caller gotten away already?

AMANDA The gentleman caller has made an early departure. What a wonderful joke you played on us!

TOM How do you mean?

AMANDA You didn't mention that he was engaged to be married.

TOM Jim? Engaged?

AMANDA That's what he just informed us.

TOM I'll be jiggered! I didn't know about that.

AMANDA That seems very peculiar.

TOM What's peculiar about it?

AMANDA Didn't you call him your best friend down at the warehouse?

TOM He is, but how did I know?

AMANDA It seems extremely peculiar that you wouldn't know your best friend was going to be married!

TOM The warehouse is where I work, not where I know things about people!

AMANDA You don't know things anywhere! You live in a dream; you manufacture illusions! (*He crosses to door.*) Where are you going?

TOM I'm going to the movies.

AMANDA That's right, now that you've had us make such fools of ourselves. The effort, the preparations, all the expense! The new floor lamp, the rug, the clothes for Laura! All for what? To entertain some other girl's fiancé! Go to the movies, go! Don't think about us, a mother deserted, an unmarried sister who's crippled and has no job! Don't let anything interfere with your selfish pleasure! Just go, go, go—to the movies!

TOM All right, I will! The more you shout about my selfishness to me the quicker I'll go, and I won't go to the movies!

AMANDA Go, then! Then go to the moon—you selfish dreamer!

Tom *smashes his glass on the floor. He plunges out on the fire-escape, slamming the door,* Laura *screams—cut off by the door.*

Dance-hall music up. Tom *goes to the rail and grips it desperately, lifting his face in the chill white moonlight penetrating the narrow abyss of the alley.*

(LEGEND ON SCREEN: "AND SO GOOD-BYE . . .")

Tom's *closing speech is timed with the interior pantomime. The interior scene is played as though viewed through soundproof glass.* Amanda *appears to be making a comforting speech to* Laura *who is huddled upon the sofa. Now that we cannot hear the mother's speech, her silliness is gone and she has dignity and tragic beauty.* Laura's *dark hair hides her face until at the end of the speech she lifts it to smile at her mother.* Amanda's *gestures are slow and graceful, almost dancelike, as she comforts the daughter. At the end of her speech she glances a moment at the father's picture—then withdraws through the portieres. At close of* Tom's *speech,* Laura *blows out the candles, ending the play.*

tom   I didn't go to the moon, I went much further—for time is the longest distance between two places—Not long after that I was fired for writing a poem on the lid of a shoe-box. I left Saint Louis. I descended the steps of this fire-escape for a last time and followed, from then on, in my father's footsteps, attempting to find in motion what was lost in space—I traveled around a great deal. The cities swept about me like dead leaves, leaves that were brightly colored but torn away from the branches. I would have stopped, but I was pursued by something. It always came upon me unawares, taking me altogether by surprise. Perhaps it was a familiar bit of music. Perhaps it was only a piece of transparent glass—Perhaps I am walking along a street at night, in some strange city, before I have found companions. I pass the lighted window of a shop where perfume is sold. The window is filled with pieces of colored glass, tiny transparent bottles in delicate colors, like bits of a shattered rainbow. Then all at once my sister touches my shoulder. I turn around and look into her eyes . . . Oh, Laura, Laura, I tried to leave you behind me, but I am more faithful than I intended to be! I reach for a cigarette, I cross the street, I run into the movies or a bar, I buy a drink, I speak to the nearest stranger—anything that can blow your candles out! (Laura *bends over the candles.*)—for nowadays the world is lit by lightning! Blow out your candles, Laura—and so good-bye. . . .

She blows the candles out.

(THE SCENE DISSOLVES.)

DEATH OF A SALESMAN (1949)

ARTHUR MILLER (1915–   )

If, among the four great modern American dramatists, the final reputation of Eugene O'Neill rests upon *Long Day's Journey Into Night*, produced posthumously in 1955, of Tennessee Williams upon *A Streetcar Named Desire*, and of Edward Albee upon *Who's Afraid of Virginia Woolf* (1962), so will the ultimate judgment of Arthur Miller probably rest upon *Death of a Salesman*.

Death of a Salesman was the theatre sensation of the immediate post-Second War years. *All My Sons* (1947) and *The Crucible* (1953) could well have earned Arthur Miller a distinguished place in American drama, but *Salesman* clearly surpasses them in its portrait of the broken drummer, Willy Loman. If O'Neill was the dramatic artist pursuing the relationship of man to God, Miller is certainly the one who devotes his full energies to exploring the relationship of man to man, particularly father to son, most explicitly and devastatingly in Willy and his family. The father-son love-hate combat predominates in *All My Sons, A View from the Bridge* (1955) and *The Price* (1968), but *Salesman* gives it its most powerful thrust.

Because Willy has quite rightfully been viewed as a kind of universal figure from American business folklore, his play has too often been regarded as the great *American* tragedy, a brutal indictment of "the system," which makes and breaks the best it has, chews it up, spits it out, and leaves it helpless without a sign of appreciation. It builds giant cities that suffocate and drown the little men in their cottages in shadows that prevent the flowering of the fruits of the earth. It turns good men into burned-out shells. There, but for the Grace of God, go all of us, and God Help Willy Loman.

Death of a Salesman is not, however, a modern tragedy. Society has not destroyed Willy Loman. Willy Loman has destroyed himself. More precisely, he has destroyed an image of himself in his own imagination of what society is and what the business world expects of him. Nowhere are we permitted to see Willy Loman except through his own eyes. He says he was a great salesman. There is not a shred of evidence. Why has the old refrigerator had to last so many years, the old car so many miles? Willy insists that there are great rewards for what he does and he seems at one time to have reaped them. But we see nothing of substance to support his claims. Willy is a sham, through and through, living on what he thinks he is and what he thinks is right, while all along the young Bernard next door gives the lie to Willy's theories of how to raise a family and how to perform in society. The fact that Bernard can argue before the Supreme Court is incomprehensible to the Willy who could see no purpose in the scholarly bookishness of his next door neighbor's son. And Willy never really sees that Charlie is the one who has succeeded, and who has the money to keep Willy alive. How come Willy doesn't have it?

Brother Ben is shown only as Willy sees him. Was he the whiz-kid that Willy makes him out? Or was he as false as Willy? To the very end Willy never realizes what he has done. All that he has discovered is that, despite his shabby sleaziness and the ruin he has brought, Biff loves him. Indeed!

Willy's suicide is not the positive act of tragedy. It is the act of one who still thinks in terms of self-redemption, of being able to "make it up" to those he has done wrong. True, Willy is a man, and maybe he should have some attention paid. But Willy is a very little man in all ways, and while we weep for him and may be deeply moved, he remains with feet of very sticky clay, firmly fastened to the ground, far from the heights demanded of tragedy.

Death of a Salesman

Certain Private Conversations in Two Acts and a Requiem

CHARACTERS

WILLY LOMAN
LINDA
BIFF
HAPPY
BERNARD
THE WOMAN
CHARLEY
UNCLE BEN
HOWARD WAGNER
JENNY
STANLEY
MISS FORSYTHE
LETTA

The action takes place in WILLY LOMAN'S *house and yard and in various places he visits in the New York and Boston of today.*

Throughout the play, in the stage directions, left and right mean stage left and stage right.

ACT ONE

An Overture

A melody is heard, played upon a flute. It is small and fine, telling of grass and trees and the horizon. The curtain rises.

Before us is the Salesman's house. We are aware of towering, angular shapes behind it, surrounding it on all sides. Only the blue light of the sky falls upon the house and forestage; the surrounding area shows an angry glow of orange. As more light appears, we see a solid vault of apartment houses around the small, fragile-seeming home. An air of the dream clings to the place, a dream rising out of reality. The kitchen at center seems actual enough, for there is a kitchen table with three chairs, and a refrig-

erator. But no other fixtures are seen. At the back of the kitchen there is a draped entrance, which leads to the living room. To the right of the kitchen, on a level raised two feet, is a bedroom furnished only with a brass bedstead and a straight chair. On a shelf over the bed a silver athletic trophy stands. A window opens onto the apartment house at the side.

Behind the kitchen, on a level raised six and a half feet, is the boys' bedroom, at present barely visible. Two beds are dimly seen, and at the back of the room a dormer window. (This bedroom is above the unseen living room.) At the left a stairway curves up to it from the kitchen.

The entire setting is wholly or, in some places, partially transparent. The roof-line of the house is one-dimensional; under and over it we see the apartment buildings. Before the house lies an apron, curving beyond the forestage into the orchestra. This forward area serves as the back yard as well as the locale of all WILLY'S *imaginings and of his city scenes. Whenever the action is in the present the actors observe the imaginary wall-lines, entering the house only through its door at the left. But in the scenes of the past these boundaries are broken, and characters enter or leave a room by stepping "through" a wall onto the forestage.*

From the right, WILLY LOMAN, *the Salesman, enters, carrying two large sample cases. The flute plays on. He hears but is not aware of it. He is past sixty years of age, dressed quietly. Even as he crosses the stage to the doorway of the house, his exhaustion is apparent. He unlocks the door, comes into the kitchen, and thankfully lets his burden down, feeling the soreness of his palms. A word-sigh escapes his lips—it might be "Oh, boy, oh, boy." He closes the door, then carries his cases out into the living room, through the draped kitchen doorway.*

LINDA, *his wife, has stirred in her bed at the right. She gets out and puts on a robe, listening. Most often jovial, she has developed an iron repression of her exceptions to* WILLY'S *behavior—she more than loves him, she admires him, as though his mercurial nature, his temper, his massive dreams and little cruelties, served her only as sharp reminders of the turbulent longings within him, longings which she shares but lacks the temperament to utter and follow to their end.*

LINDA (*hearing* WILLY *outside the bedroom, calls with some trepidation*) Willy!

WILLY It's all right. I came back.

LINDA Why? What happened? (*Slight pause*) Did something happen, Willy?

WILLY No, nothing happened.

LINDA You didn't smash the car, did you?

WILLY (*with casual irritation*) I said nothing happened. Didn't you hear me?

LINDA Don't you feel well?

WILLY I'm tired to the death. (*The flute has faded away. He sits on the bed beside her, a little numb*) I couldn't make it. I just couldn't make it, Linda.

LINDA (*very carefully, delicately*)   Where were you all day? You look terrible.

WILLY   I got as far as a little above Yonkers. I stopped for a cup of coffee. Maybe it was the coffee.

LINDA   What?

WILLY (*after a pause*)   I suddenly couldn't drive any more. The car kept going off onto the shoulder, y'know?

LINDA (*helpfully*)   Oh. Maybe it was the steering again. I don't think Angelo knows the Studebaker.

WILLY   No, it's me, it's me. Suddenly I realize I'm goin' sixty miles an hour and I don't remember the last five minutes. I'm—I can't seem to—keep my mind to it.

LINDA   Maybe it's your glasses. You never went for your new glasses.

WILLY   No, I see everything. I came back ten miles an hour. It took me nearly four hours from Yonkers.

LINDA (*resigned*)   Well, you'll just have to take a rest, Willy, you can't continue this way.

WILLY   I just got back from Florida.

LINDA   But you didn't rest your mind. Your mind is overactive, and the mind is what counts, dear.

WILLY   I'll start out in the morning. Maybe I'll feel better in the morning. (*She is taking off his shoes*) These goddam arch supports are killing me.

LINDA   Take an aspirin. Should I get you an aspirin? It'll soothe you.

WILLY (*with wonder*)   I was driving along, you understand? And I was fine. I was even observing the scenery. You can imagine, me looking at scenery, on the road every week of my life. But it's so beautiful up there, Linda, the trees are so thick, and the sun is warm. I opened the windshield and just let the warm air bathe over me. And then all of a sudden I'm goin' off the road! I'm tellin' ya, I absolutely forgot I was driving. If I'd've gone the other way over the white line I might've killed somebody. So I went on again—and five minutes later I'm dreamin' again, and I nearly—(*He presses two fingers against his eyes*) I have such thoughts, I have such strange thoughts.

LINDA   Willy, dear. Talk to them again. There's no reason why you can't work in New York.

WILLY   They don't need me in New York. I'm the New England man. I'm vital in New England.

LINDA   But you're sixty years old. They can't expect you to keep traveling every week.

WILLY   I'll have to send a wire to Portland. I'm supposed to see

Brown and Morrison tomorrow morning at ten o'clock to show the line. Goddammit, I could sell them! (*He starts putting on his jacket*)

LINDA (*taking the jacket from him*) Why don't you go down to the place tomorrow and tell Howard you've simply got to work in New York? You're too accommodating, dear.

WILLY If old man Wagner was alive I'd a been in charge of New York now! That man was a prince, he was a masterful man. But that boy of his, that Howard, he don't appreciate. When I went north the first time, the Wagner Company didn't know where New England was!

LINDA Why don't you tell those things to Howard, dear?

WILLY (*encouraged*) I will, I definitely will. Is there any cheese?

LINDA I'll make you a sandwich.

WILLY No, go to sleep. I'll take some milk. I'll be up right away. The boys in?

LINDA They're sleeping. Happy took Biff on a date tonight.

WILLY (*interested*) That so?

LINDA It was so nice to see them shaving together, one behind the other, in the bathroom. And going out together. You notice? The whole house smells of shaving lotion.

WILLY Figure it out. Work a lifetime to pay off a house. You finally own it, and there's nobody to live in it.

LINDA Well, dear, life is a casting off. It's always that way.

WILLY No, no, some people—some people accomplish something. Did Biff say anything after I went this morning?

LINDA You shouldn't have criticized him, Willy, especially after he just got off the train. You mustn't lose your temper with him.

WILLY When the hell did I lose my temper? I simply asked him if he was making any money. Is that a criticism?

LINDA But, dear, how could he make any money?

WILLY (*worried and angered*) There's such an undercurrent in him. He became a moody man. Did he apologize when I left this morning?

LINDA He was crestfallen, Willy. You know how he admires you. I think if he finds himself, then you'll both be happier and not fight any more.

WILLY How can he find himself on a farm? Is that a life? A farm-hand? In the beginning, when he was young, I thought, well, a young man, it's good for him to tramp around, take a lot of different jobs. But it's more than ten years now and he has yet to make thirty-five dollars a week!

LINDA He's finding himself, Willy.

WILLY Not finding yourself at the age of thirty-four is a disgrace!

LINDA   Shh!

WILLY   The trouble is he's lazy, goddammit!

LINDA   Willy, please!

WILLY   Biff is a lazy bum!

LINDA   They're sleeping. Get something to eat. Go on down.

WILLY   Why did he come home? I would like to know what brought him home.

LINDA   I don't know. I think he's still lost, Willy. I think he's very lost.

WILLY   Biff Loman is lost. In the greatest country in the world a young man with such—personal attractiveness, gets lost. And such a hard worker. There's one thing about Biff—he's not lazy.

LINDA   Never.

WILLY   (*with pity and resolve*)   I'll see him in the morning; I'll have a nice talk with him. I'll get him a job selling. He could be big in no time. My God! Remember how they used to follow him around in high school? When he smiled at one of them their faces lit up. When he walked down the street . . . (*He loses himself in reminiscences*)

LINDA   (*trying to bring him out of it*)   Willy, dear, I got a new kind of American-type cheese today. It's whipped.

WILLY   Why do you get American when I like Swiss?

LINDA   I just thought you'd like a change—

WILLY   I don't want a change! I want Swiss cheese. Why am I always being contradicted?

LINDA   (*with a covering laugh*)   I thought it would be a surprise.

WILLY   Why don't you open a window in here, for God's sake?

LINDA   (*with infinite patience*)   They're all open, dear.

WILLY   The way they boxed us in here. Bricks and windows, windows and bricks.

LINDA   We should've bought the land next door.

WILLY   The street is lined with cars. There's not a breath of fresh air in the neighborhood. The grass don't grow any more, you can't raise a carrot in the back yard. They should've had a law against apartment houses. Remember those two beautiful elm trees out there? When I and Biff hung the swing between them?

LINDA   Yeah, like being a million miles from the city.

WILLY   They should've arrested the builder for cutting those down. They massacred the neighborhood. (*Lost*) More and more I think of those days, Linda. This time of year it was lilac and wisteria. And then the peonies would come out, and the daffodils. What fragrance in this room!

LINDA   Well, after all, people had to move somewhere.

WILLY   No, there's more people now.

LINDA   I don't think there's more people. I think—

WILLY   There's more people! That's what's ruining this country!
Population is getting out of control. The competition is maddening! Smell the stink from that apartment house! And another one
on the other side . . . How can they whip cheese?

On WILLY'S *last line,* BIFF *and* HAPPY *raise themselves up in their beds,
listening.*

LINDA   Go down, try it. And be quiet.

WILLY   (*turning to* LINDA, *guiltily*)   You're not worried about me,
are you, sweetheart?

BIFF   What's the matter?

HAPPY   Listen!

LINDA   You've got too much on the ball to worry about.

WILLY   You're my foundation and my support, Linda.

LINDA   Just try to relax, dear. You make mountains out of mole-
hills.

WILLY   I won't fight with him any more. If he wants to go back
to Texas, let him go.

LINDA   He'll find his way.

WILLY   Sure. Certain men just don't get started till later in life.
Like Thomas Edison, I think. Or B. F. Goodrich. One of them
was deaf. (*He starts for the bedroom doorway*) I'll put my
money on Biff.

LINDA   And Willy—if it's warm Sunday we'll drive in the country.
And we'll open the windshield, and take lunch.

WILLY   No, the windshields don't open on the new cars.

LINDA   But you opened it today.

WILLY   Me? I didn't. (*He stops*) Now isn't that peculiar! Isn't
that a remarkable—(*He breaks off in amazement and fright as
the flute is heard distantly*)

LINDA   What, darling?

WILLY   That is the most remarkable thing.

LINDA   What, dear?

WILLY   I was thinking of the Chevvy. (*Slight pause*) Nineteen
twenty-eight . . . when I had that red Chevvy—(*Breaks off*) That
funny? I coulda sworn I was driving that Chevvy today.

LINDA   Well, that's nothing. Something must've reminded you.

WILLY   Remarkable. Ts. Remember those days? The way Biff used
to simonize that car? The dealer refused to believe there was
eighty thousand miles on it. (*He shakes his head*) Heh! (*To*
LINDA) Close your eyes, I'll be right up. (*He walks out of the
bedroom*)

HAPPY   (*to* BIFF)   Jesus, maybe he smashed up the car again!

LINDA (*calling after* WILLY) Be careful on the stairs, dear! The cheese is on the middle shelf! (*She turns, goes over to the bed, takes his jacket, and goes out of the bedroom*)

Light has risen on the boys' room. Unseen, WILLY *is heard talking to himself, "Eighty thousand miles," and a little laugh.* BIFF *gets out of bed, comes downstage a bit, and stands attentively.* BIFF *is two years older than his brother* HAPPY, *well built, but in these days bears a worn air and seems less self-assured. He has succeeded less, and his dreams are stronger and less acceptable than* HAPPY's. HAPPY *is tall, powerfully made. Sexuality is like a visible color on him, or a scent that many women have discovered. He, like his brother, is lost, but in a different way, for he has never allowed himself to turn his face toward defeat and is thus more confused and hard-skinned, although seemingly more content.*

HAPPY (*getting out of bed*) He's going to get his license taken away if he keeps that up. I'm getting nervous about him, y'know, Biff?

BIFF His eyes are going.

HAPPY No, I've driven with him. He sees all right. He just doesn't keep his mind on it. I drove into the city with him last week. He stops at a green light and then it turns red and he goes. (*He laughs*)

BIFF Maybe he's color-blind.

HAPPY Pop? Why he's got the finest eye for color in the business. You know that.

BIFF (*sitting down on his bed*) I'm going to sleep.

HAPPY You're not still sour on Dad, are you, Biff?

BIFF He's all right, I guess.

WILLY (*underneath them, in the living-room*) Yes, sir, eighty thousand miles—eighty-two thousand!

BIFF You smoking?

HAPPY (*holding out a pack of cigarettes*) Want one?

BIFF (*taking a cigarette*) I can never sleep when I smell it.

WILLY What a simonizing job, heh!

HAPPY (*with deep sentiment*) Funny, Biff, y'now? Us sleeping in here again? The old beds. (*He pats his bed affectionately*) All the talk that went across those two beds, huh? Our whole lives.

BIFF Yeah. Lotta dreams and plans.

HAPPY (*with a deep and masculine laugh*) About five hundred women would like to know what was said in this room.

They share a soft laugh.

BIFF Remember that big Betsy something—what the hell was her name—over on Bushwick Avenue?

HAPPY (*combing his hair*) With the collie dog!

BIFF   That's the one. I got you in there, remember?

HAPPY   Yeah, that was my first time—I think. Boy, there was a pig! (*They laugh, almost crudely*) You taught me everything I know about women. Don't forget that.

BIFF   I bet you forgot how bashful you used to be. Especially with girls.

HAPPY   Oh, I still am, Biff.

BIFF   Oh, go on.

HAPPY   I just control it, that's all. I think I got less bashful and you got more so. What happened, Biff? Where's the old humor, the old confidence? (*He shakes* BIFF's *knee.* BIFF *gets up and moves restlessly about the room*) What's the matter?

BIFF   Why does Dad mock me all the time?

HAPPY   He's not mocking you, he—

BIFF   Everything I say there's a twist of mockery on his face. I can't get near him.

HAPPY   He just wants you to make good, that's all. I wanted to talk to you about Dad for a long time, Biff. Something's—happening to him. He—talks to himself.

BIFF   I noticed that this morning. But he always mumbled.

HAPPY   But not so noticeable. It got so embarrassing I sent him to Florida. And you know something? Most of the time he's talking to you.

BIFF   What's he say about me?

HAPPY   I can't make it out.

BIFF   What's he say about me?

HAPPY   I think the fact that you're not settled, that you're still kind of up in the air . . .

BIFF   There's one or two other things depressing him, Happy.

HAPPY   What do you mean?

BIFF   Never mind. Just don't lay it all to me.

HAPPY   But I think if you just got started—I mean—is there any future for you out there?

BIFF   I tell ya, Hap, I don't know what the future is. I don't know —what I'm supposed to want.

HAPPY   What do you mean?

BIFF   Well, I spent six or seven years after high school trying to work myself up. Shipping clerk, salesman, business of one kind or another. And it's a measly manner of existence. To get on that subway on the hot mornings in summer. To devote your whole life to keeping stock, or making phone calls, or selling or buying. To suffer fifty weeks of the year for the sake of a two-week vacation, when all you really desire is to be outdoors, with your shirt

off. And always to have to get ahead of the next fella. And still—
that's how you build a future.

HAPPY   Well, you really enjoy it on a farm? Are you content out
there?

BIFF   (*with rising agitation*)   Hap, I've had twenty or thirty different kinds of jobs since I left home before the war, and it always
turns out the same. I just realized it lately. In Nebraska when I
herded cattle, and the Dakotas, and Arizona, and now in Texas.
It's why I came home now, I guess, because I realized it. This
farm I work on, it's spring there now, see? And they've got about
fifteen new colts. There's nothing more inspiring or—beautiful
than the sight of a mare and a new colt. And it's cool there now,
see? Texas is cool now, and it's spring. And whenever spring
comes to where I am, I suddenly get the feeling, my God, I'm
not gettin' anywhere! What the hell am I doing, playing around
with horses, twenty-eight dollars a week! I'm thirty-four years old,
I oughta be makin' my future. That's when I come running home.
And now, I get here, and I don't know what to do with myself.
(*After a pause*) I've always made a point of not wasting my life,
and everytime I come back here I know that all I've done is to
waste my life.

HAPPY   You're a poet, you know that, Biff? You're a—you're an
idealist!

BIFF   No, I'm mixed up very bad. Maybe I oughta get married.
Maybe I oughta get stuck into something. Maybe that's my trouble. I'm like a boy. I'm not married, I'm not in business, I just
—I'm like a boy. Are you content, Hap? You're a success, aren't
you? Are you content?

HAPPY   Hell, no!

BIFF   Why? You're making money, aren't you?

HAPPY   (*moving about with energy, expressiveness*)   All I can do
now is wait for the merchandise manager to die. And suppose I
get to be merchandise manager? He's a good friend of mine, and
he just built a terrific estate on Long Island. And he lived there
about two months and sold it, and now he's building another
one. He can't enjoy it once it's finished. And I know that's just
what I would do. I don't know what the hell I'm workin' for.
Sometimes I sit in my apartment—all alone. And I think of the
rent I'm paying. And it's crazy. But then, it's what I always
wanted. My own apartment, a car, and plenty of women. And
still, goddammit. I'm lonely.

BIFF   (*with enthusiasm*)   Listen, why don't you come out West with
me?

HAPPY   You and I, heh?

BIFF   Sure, maybe we could buy a ranch. Raise cattle, use our muscles. Men built like we are should be working out in the open.

HAPPY   (*avidly*)   The Loman Brothers, heh?

BIFF   (*with vast affection*)   Sure, we'd be known all over the counties!

HAPPY   (*enthralled*)   That's what I dream about, Biff. Sometimes I want to just rip my clothes off in the middle of the store and outbox that goddam merchandise manager. I mean I can outbox, outrun, and outlift anybody in that store, and I have to take orders from those common, petty sons-of-bitches till I can't stand it any more.

BIFF   I'm tellin' you, kid, if you were with me I'd be happy out there.

HAPPY   (*enthused*)   See, Biff, everybody around me is so false that I'm constantly lowering my ideals . . .

BIFF   Baby, together we'd stand up for one another, we'd have someone to trust.

HAPPY   If I were around you—

BIFF   Hap, the trouble is we weren't brought up to grub for money. I don't know how to do it.

HAPPY   Neither can I!

BIFF   Then let's go!

HAPPY   The only thing is—what can you make out there?

BIFF   But look at your friend. Builds an estate and then hasn't the peace of mind to live in it.

HAPPY   Yeah, but when he walks into the store the waves part in front of him. That's fifty-two thousand dollars a year coming through the revolving door, and I got more in my pinky finger than he's got in his head.

BIFF   Yeah, but you just said—

HAPPY   I gotta show some of those pompous, self-important executives over there that Hap Loman can make the grade. I want to walk into the store the way he walks in. Then I'll go with you, Biff. We'll be together yet, I swear. But take those two we had tonight. Now weren't they gorgeous creatures?

BIFF   Yeah, yeah, most gorgeous I've had in years.

HAPPY   I get that any time I want, Biff. Whenever I feel disgusted. The only trouble is, it gets like bowling or something. I just keep knockin' them over and it doesn't mean anything. You still run around a lot?

BIFF   Naa. I'd like to find a girl—steady, somebody with substance.

HAPPY   That's what I long for.

BIFF Go on! You'd never come home.

HAPPY I would! Somebody with character, with resistance! Like Mom, y'know? You're gonna call me a bastard when I tell you this. That girl Charlotte I was with tonight is engaged to be married in five weeks. (*He tries on his new hat*)

BIFF No kiddin'!

HAPPY Sure, the guy's in line for the vice-presidency of the store. I don't know what gets into me, maybe I just have an over-developed sense of competition or something, but I went and ruined her, and furthermore I can't get rid of her. And he's the third executive I've done that to. Isn't that a crummy character-istic? And to top it all, I go to their weddings! (*Indignantly, but laughing*) Like I'm not supposed to take bribes. Manufacturers offer me a hundred-dollar bill now and then to throw an order their way. You know how honest I am, but it's like this girl, see. I hate myself for it. Because I don't want the girl, and, still, I take it and—I love it!

BIFF Let's go to sleep.

HAPPY I guess we didn't settle anything, heh?

BIFF I just got one idea that I think I'm going to try.

HAPPY What's that?

BIFF Remember Bill Oliver?

HAPPY Sure, Oliver is very big now. You want to work for him again?

BIFF No, but when I quit he said something to me. He put his arm on my shoulder, and he said, "Biff, if you ever need any-thing, come to me."

HAPPY I remember that. That sounds good.

BIFF I think I'll go to see him. If I could get ten thousand or even seven or eight thousand dollars I could buy a beautiful ranch.

HAPPY I bet he'd back you. 'Cause he thought highly of you, Biff. I mean, they all do. You're well liked, Biff. That's why I say to come back here, and we both have the apartment. And I'm tellin' you, Biff, any babe you want . . .

BIFF No, with a ranch I could do the work I like and still be some-thing. I just wonder though. I wonder if Oliver still thinks I stole that carton of basketballs.

HAPPY Oh, he probably forgot that long ago. It's almost ten years. You're too sensitive. Anyway, he didn't really fire you.

BIFF Well, I think he was going to. I think that's why I quit. I was never sure whether he knew or not. I know he thought the world of me, though. I was the only one he'd let lock up the place.

WILLY (*below*) You gonna wash the engine, Biff?
HAPPY Shh!

BIFF *looks at* HAPPY, *who is gazing down, listening.* WILLY *is mumbling in the parlor.*

HAPPY You hear that?

They listen. WILLY *laughs warmly.*

BIFF (*growing angry*) Doesn't he know Mom can hear that?
WILLY Don't get your sweater dirty, Biff!

A look of pain crosses BIFF's *face.*

HAPPY Isn't that terrible? Don't leave again, will you? You'll find a job here. You gotta stick around. I don't know what to do about him, it's getting embarrassing.
WILLY What a simonizing job!
BIFF Mom's hearing that!
WILLY No kiddin', Biff, you got a date? Wonderful!
HAPPY Go on to sleep. But talk to him in the morning, will you?
BIFF (*reluctantly getting into bed*) With her in the house. Brother!
HAPPY (*getting into bed*) I wish you'd have a good talk with him.

The light on their room begins to fade.

BIFF (*to himself in bed*) That selfish, stupid . . .
HAPPY Sh . . . Sleep, Biff.

Their light is out. Well before they have finished speaking, WILLY's *form is dimly seen below in the darkened kitchen. He opens the refrigerator, searches in there, and takes out a bottle of milk. The apartment houses are fading out, and the entire house and surroundings become covered with leaves. Music insinuates itself as the leaves appear.*

WILLY Just wanna be careful with those girls, Biff, that's all. Don't make any promises. No promises of any kind. Because a girl, y'know, they always believe what you tell 'em, and you're very young, Biff, you're too young to be talking seriously to girls.

Light rises on the kitchen. WILLY, *talking, shuts the refrigerator door and comes downstage to the kitchen table. He pours milk into a glass. He is totally immersed in himself, smiling faintly.*

WILLY Too young entirely, Biff. You want to watch your schooling first. Then when you're all set, there'll be plenty of girls for a boy like you. (*He smiles broadly at a kitchen chair*) That so? The girls pay for you? (*He laughs*) Boy, you must really be makin' a hit.

WILLY *is gradually addressing—physically—a point offstage, speaking through the wall of the kitchen, and his voice has been rising in volume to that of a normal conversation.*

WILLY   I been wondering why you polish the car so careful. Ha! Don't leave the hubcaps, boys. Get the chamois to the hubcaps. Happy, use newspaper on the windows, it's the easiest thing. Show him how to do it, Biff! You see, Happy? Pad it up, use it like a pad. That's it, that's it, good work. You're doin' all right, Hap. (*He pauses, then nods in approbation for a few seconds, then looks upward*) Biff, first thing we gotta do when we get time is clip that big branch over the house. Afraid it's gonna fall in a storm and hit the roof. Tell you what. We get a rope and sling her around, and then we climb up there with a couple of saws and take her down. Soon as you finish the car, boys, I wanna see ya. I got a surprise for you, boys.

BIFF   (*offstage*)   Whatta ya got, Dad?

WILLY   No, you finish first. Never leave a job till you're finished— remember that. (*Looking toward the "big trees"*) Biff, up in Albany I saw a beautiful hammock. I think I'll buy it next trip, and we'll hang it right between those two elms. Wouldn't that be something? Just swingin' there under those branches. Boy, that would be . . .

Young BIFF *and Young* HAPPY *appear from the direction* WILLY *was addressing.* HAPPY *carries rags and a pail of water.* BIFF, *wearing a sweater with a block "S," carries a football.*

BIFF   (*pointing in the direction of the car offstage*)   How's that, Pop, professional?

WILLY   Terrific. Terrific job, boys. Good work, Biff.

HAPPY   Where's the surprise, Pop?

WILLY   In the back seat of the car.

HAPPY   Boy! (*He runs off*)

BIFF   What is it, Dad? Tell me, what'd you buy?

WILLY   (*laughing, cuffs him*)   Never mind, something I want you to have.

BIFF   (*turns and starts off*)   What is it, Hap?

HAPPY   (*offstage*)   It's a punching bag!

BIFF   Oh, Pop!

WILLY   It's got Gene Tunney's signature on it!

HAPPY *runs onstage with a punching bag.*

BIFF   Gee, how'd you know we wanted a punching bag?

WILLY   Well, it's the finest thing for the timing.

HAPPY (*lies down on his back and pedals with his feet*)   I'm losing weight, you notice, Pop?

WILLY (*to* HAPPY)   Jumping rope is good too.

BIFF   Did you see the new football I got?

WILLY (*examining the ball*)   Where'd you get a new ball?

BIFF   The coach told me to practice my passing.

WILLY   That so? And he gave you the ball, heh?

BIFF   Well, I borrowed it from the locker room. (*He laughs confidentially*)

WILLY (*laughing with him at the theft*)   I want you to return that.

HAPPY   I told you he wouldn't like it!

BIFF (*angrily*)   Well, I'm bringing it back!

WILLY (*stopping the incipient argument, to* HAPPY)   Sure, he's gotta practice with a regulation ball, doesn't he? (*To* BIFF) Coach'll probably congratulate you on your initiative!

BIFF   Oh, he keeps congratulating my initiative all the time, Pop.

WILLY   That's because he likes you. If somebody else took that ball there'd be an uproar. So what's the report, boys, what's the report?

BIFF   Where'd you go this time, Dad? Gee we were lonesome for you.

WILLY (*pleased, puts an arm around each boy and they come down to the apron*)   Lonesome, heh?

BIFF   Missed you every minute.

WILLY   Don't say? Tell you a secret, boys. Don't breathe it to a soul. Someday I'll have my own business, and I'll never have to leave home any more.

HAPPY   Like Uncle Charley, heh?

WILLY   Bigger than Uncle Charley! Because Charley is not—liked. He's liked, but he's not—well liked.

BIFF   Where'd you go this time, Dad?

WILLY   Well, I got on the road, and I went north to Providence. Met the Mayor.

BIFF   The Mayor of Providence!

WILLY   He was sitting in the hotel lobby.

BIFF   What'd he say?

WILLY   He said, "Morning!" And I said, "You got a fine city here, Mayor." And then he had coffee with me. And then I went to Waterbury. Waterbury is a fine city. Big clock city, the famous Waterbury clock. Sold a nice bill there. And then Boston—Boston is the cradle of the Revolution. A fine city. And a couple of other towns in Mass., and on to Portland and Bangor and straight home!

BIFF   Gee, I'd love to go with you sometime, Dad.

WILLY   Soon as summer comes.

HAPPY   Promise?

WILLY   You and Hap and I, and I'll show you all the towns. America is full of beautiful towns and fine, upstanding people. And they know me, boys, they know me up and down New England. The finest people. And when I bring you fellas up, there'll be open sesame for all of us, 'cause one thing, boys: I have friends. I can park my car in any street in New England, and the cops protect it like their own. This summer, heh?

BIFF and HAPPY (*together*)   Yeah! You bet!

WILLY   We'll take our bathing suits.

HAPPY   We'll carry your bags, Pop!

WILLY   Oh, won't that be something! Me comin' into the Boston stores with you boys carryin' my bags. What a sensation!

BIFF *is prancing around, practicing passing the ball.*

WILLY   You nervous, Biff, about the game?

BIFF   Not if you're gonna be there.

WILLY   What do they say about you in school, now that they made you captain?

HAPPY   There's a crowd of girls behind him everytime the classes change.

BIFF (*taking* WILLY's *hand*)   This Saturday, Pop, this Saturday— just for you, I'm going to break through for a touchdown.

HAPPY   You're supposed to pass.

BIFF   I'm takin' one play for Pop. You watch me, Pop, and when I take off my helmet, that means I'm breakin' out. Then you watch me crash through that line!

WILLY (*kisses* BIFF)   Oh, wait'll I tell this in Boston!

BERNARD *enters in knickers. He is younger than* BIFF, *earnest and loyal, a worried boy.*

BERNARD   Biff, where are you? You're supposed to study with me today.

WILLY   Hey, looka Bernard. What're you lookin' so anemic about, Bernard?

BERNARD   He's gotta study, Uncle Willy. He's got Regents next week.

HAPPY (*tauntingly, spinning* BERNARD *around*)   Let's box, Bernard!

BERNARD   Biff! (*He gets away from* HAPPY) Listen, Biff, I heard Mr. Birnbaum say that if you don't start studyin' math he's gonna flunk you, and you won't graduate. I heard him!

WILLY   You better study with him, Biff. Go ahead now.

BERNARD   I heard him!

BIFF   Oh, Pop, you didn't see my sneakers! (*He holds up a foot for* WILLY *to look at*)

WILLY   Hey, that's a beautiful job of printing!

BERNARD (*wiping his glasses*)   Just because he printed University of Virginia on his sneakers doesn't mean they've got to graduate him, Uncle Willy!

WILLY (*angrily*)   What're you talking about? With scholarships to three universities they're gonna flunk him?

BERNARD   But I heard Mr. Birnbaum say—

WILLY   Don't be a pest, Bernard! (*To his boys*) What an anemic!

BERNARD   Okay, I'm waiting for you in my house, Biff.

BERNARD *goes off. The* LOMANS *laugh.*

WILLY   Bernard is not well liked, is he?

BIFF   He's liked, but he's not well liked.

HAPPY   That's right, Pop.

WILLY   That's just what I mean. Bernard can get the best marks in school, y'understand, but when he gets out in the business world, y'understand, you are going to be five times ahead of him. That's why I thank Almighty God you're both built like Adonises. Because the man who makes an appearance in the business world, the man who creates personal interest, is the man who gets ahead. Be liked and you will never want. You take me, for instance. I never have to wait in line to see a buyer. "Willy Loman is here!" That's all they have to know, and I go right through.

BIFF   Did you knock them dead, Pop?

WILLY   Knocked 'em cold in Providence, slaughtered 'em in Boston.

HAPPY (*on his back, pedaling again*)   I'm losing weight, you notice, Pop?

LINDA *enters, as of old, a ribbon in her hair, carrying a basket of washing.*

LINDA (*with youthful energy*)   Hello, dear!

WILLY   Sweetheart!

LINDA   How'd the Chevvy run?

WILLY   Chevrolet, Linda, is the greatest car ever built. (*To the boys*) Since when do you let your mother carry wash up the stairs?

BIFF   Grab hold there, boy!

HAPPY   Where to, Mom?

LINDA   Hang them up on the line. And you better go down to your friends, Biff. The cellar is full of boys. They don't know what to do with themselves.

BIFF Ah, when Pop comes home they can wait!

WILLY (*laughs appreciatively*) You better go down and tell them what to do, Biff.

BIFF I think I'll have them sweep out the furnace room.

WILLY Good work, Biff.

BIFF (*goes through wall-line of kitchen to doorway at back and calls down*) Fellas! Everybody sweep out the furnace room! I'll be right down!

VOICES All right! Okay, Biff.

BIFF George and Sam and Frank, come out back! We're hangin' up the wash! Come on, Hap, on the double! (*He and* HAPPY *carry out the basket*)

LINDA The way they obey him!

WILLY Well, that's training, the training. I'm tellin' you, I was sellin' thousands and thousands, but I had to come home.

LINDA Oh, the whole block'll be at that game. Did you sell anything?

WILLY I did five hundred gross in Providence and seven hundred gross in Boston.

LINDA No! Wait a minute, I've got a pencil. (*She pulls pencil and paper out of her apron pocket*) That makes your commission . . . Two hundred—my God! Two hundred and twelve dollars!

WILLY Well, I didn't figure it yet, but . . .

LINDA How much did you do?

WILLY Well, I—I did—about a hundred and eighty gross in Providence. Well, no—it came to—roughly two hundred gross on the whole trip.

LINDA (*without hesitation*) Two hundred gross. That's . . . (*She figures*)

WILLY The trouble was that three of the stores were half closed for inventory in Boston. Otherwise I woulda broke records.

LINDA Well, it makes seventy dollars and some pennies. That's very good.

WILLY What do we owe?

LINDA Well, on the first there's sixteen dollars on the refrigerator—

WILLY Why sixteen?

LINDA Well, the fan belt broke, so it was a dollar eighty.

WILLY But it's brand new.

LINDA Well, the man said that's the way it is. Till they work themselves in, y'know.

They move through the wall-line into the kitchen.

WILLY I hope we didn't get stuck on that machine.

LINDA They got the biggest ads of any of them!

WILLY   I know, it's a fine machine. What else?

LINDA   Well, there's nine-sixty for the washing machine. And for the vacuum cleaner there's three and a half due on the fifteenth. Then the roof, you got twenty-one dollars remaining.

WILLY   It don't leak, does it?

LINDA   No, they did a wonderful job. Then you owe Frank for the carburetor.

WILLY   I'm not going to pay that man! That goddam Chevrolet, they ought to prohibit the manufacture of that car!

LINDA   Well, you owe him three and a half. And odds and ends, comes to around a hundred and twenty dollars by the fifteenth.

WILLY   A hundred and twenty dollars! My God, if business don't pick up I don't know what I'm gonna do!

LINDA   Well, next week you'll do better.

WILLY   Oh, I'll knock 'em dead next week. I'll go to Hartford. I'm very well liked in Hartford. You know, the trouble is, Linda, people don't seem to take to me.

They move onto the forestage.

LINDA   Oh, don't be foolish.

WILLY   I know it when I walk in. They seem to laugh at me.

LINDA   Why? Why would they laugh at you? Don't talk that way, Willy.

WILLY *moves to the edge of the stage.* LINDA *goes into the kitchen and starts to darn stockings.*

WILLY   I don't know the reason for it, but they just pass me by. I'm not noticed.

LINDA   But you're doing wonderful, dear. You're making seventy to a hundred dollars a week.

WILLY   But I gotta be at it ten, twelve hours a day. Other men— I don't know—they do it easier. I don't know why—I can't stop myself—I talk too much. A man oughta come in with a few words. One thing about Charley. He's a man of few words, and they respect him.

LINDA   You don't talk too much, you're just lively.

WILLY *(smiling)* Well, I figure, what the hell, life is short, a couple of jokes. *(To himself)* I joke too much! *(The smile goes)*

LINDA   Why? You're—

WILLY   I'm fat. I'm very—foolish to look at, Linda. I didn't tell you, but Christmas time I happened to be calling on F. H. Stewarts, and a salesman I know, as I was going in to see the buyer I heard him say something about—walrus. And I—I cracked him right across the face. I won't take that. I simply will not take that. But they do laugh at me. I know that.

LINDA Darling . . .

WILLY I gotta overcome it. I know I gotta overcome it. I'm not dressing to advantage, maybe.

LINDA Willy, darling, you're the handsomest man in the world—

WILLY Oh, no, Linda.

LINDA To me you are. (*Slight pause*) The handsomest.

From the darkness is heard the laughter of a woman. WILLY *doesn't turn to it, but it continues through* LINDA'*s lines.*

LINDA And the boys, Willy. Few men are idolized by their children the way you are.

Music is heard as behind a scrim, to the left of the house. THE WOMAN, *dimly seen, is dressing.*

WILLY (*with great feeling*) You're the best there is, Linda, you're a pal, you know that? On the road—on the road I want to grab you sometimes and just kiss the life outa you.

The laughter is loud now, and he moves into a brightening area at the left, where THE WOMAN *has come from behind the scrim and is standing, putting on her hat, looking into a "mirror" and laughing.*

WILLY 'Cause I get so lonely—especially when business is bad and there's nobody to talk to. I get the feeling that I'll never sell anything again, that I won't make a living for you, or a business, a business for the boys. (*He talks through* THE WOMAN'*s subsiding laughter;* THE WOMAN *primps at the "mirror."*) There's so much I want to make for—

THE WOMAN Me? You didn't make me, Willy. I picked you.

WILLY (*pleased*) You picked me?

THE WOMAN (*who is quite proper-looking,* WILLY'*s age*) I did. I've been sitting at that desk watching all the salesmen go by, day in, day out. But you've got such a sense of humor, and we do have such a good time together, don't we?

WILLY Sure, sure. (*He takes her in his arms*) Why do you have to go now?

THE WOMAN It's two o'clock . . .

WILLY No, come on in! (*He pulls her*)

THE WOMAN . . . my sisters'll be scandalized. When'll you be back?

WILLY Oh, two weeks about. Will you come up again?

THE WOMAN Sure thing. You do make me laugh. It's good for me. (*She squeezes his arm, kisses him*) And I think you're a wonderful man.

WILLY You picked me, heh?

THE WOMAN Sure. Because you're so sweet. And such a kidder.

WILLY Well, I'll see you next time I'm in Boston.

THE WOMAN I'll put you right through to the buyers.

WILLY (*slapping her bottom*) Right. Well, bottoms up!

THE WOMAN (*slaps him gently and laughs*) You just kill me, Willy. (*He suddenly grabs her and kisses her roughly*) You kill me. And thanks for the stockings. I love a lot of stockings. Well, good night.

WILLY Good night. And keep your pores open!

THE WOMAN Oh, Willy!

THE WOMAN *bursts out laughing, and* LINDA's *laughter blends in.* THE WOMAN *disappears into the dark. Now the area at the kitchen table brightens.* LINDA *is sitting where she was at the kitchen table, but now is mending a pair of her silk stockings.*

LINDA You are, Willy. The handsomest man. You've got no reason to feel that—

WILLY (*coming out of* THE WOMAN's *dimming area and going over to* LINDA) I'll make it all up to you, Linda, I'll—

LINDA There's nothing to make up, dear. You're doing fine, better than—

WILLY (*noticing her mending*) What's that?

LINDA Just mending my stockings. They're so expensive—

WILLY (*angrily, taking them from her*) I won't have you mending stockings in this house! Now throw them out!

LINDA *puts the stockings in her pocket.*

BERNARD (*entering on the run*) Where is he? If he doesn't study!

WILLY (*moving to the forestage, with great agitation*) You'll give him the answers!

BERNARD I do, but I can't on a Regents! That's a state exam! They're liable to arrest me!

WILLY Where is he? I'll whip him, I'll whip him!

LINDA And he'd better give back that football, Willy, it's not nice.

WILLY Biff! Where is he? Why is he taking everything?

LINDA He's too rough with the girls, Willy. All the mothers are afraid of him!

WILLY I'll whip him!

BERNARD He's driving the car without a license!

THE WOMAN's *laugh is heard.*

WILLY Shut up!

LINDA All the mothers—

WILLY Shut up!

BERNARD (*backing quietly away and out*) Mr. Birnbaum says he's stuck up.

WILLY Get outa here!

BERNARD If he doesn't buckle down he'll flunk math! (*He goes off*)

LINDA He's right, Willy, you've gotta—

WILLY (*exploding at her*) There's nothing the matter with him! You want him to be a worm like Bernard? He's got spirit, personality . . .

As he speaks, LINDA, *almost in tears, exits into the living room.* WILLY *is alone in the kitchen, wilting and staring. The leaves are gone. It is night again, and the apartment houses look down from behind.*

WILLY Loaded with it. Loaded! What is he stealing? He's giving it back, isn't he? Why is he stealing? What did I tell him? I never in my life told him anything but decent things.

HAPPY *in pajamas has come down the stairs;* WILLY *suddenly becomes aware of* HAPPY's *presence.*

HAPPY Let's go now, come on.

WILLY (*sitting down at the kitchen table*) Huh! Why did she have to wax the floors herself? Everytime she waxes the floors she keels over. She knows that!

HAPPY Shh! Take it easy. What brought you back tonight?

WILLY I got an awful scare. Nearly hit a kid in Yonkers. God! Why didn't I go to Alaska with my brother Ben that time! Ben! That man was a genius, that man was success incarnate! What a mistake! He begged me to go.

HAPPY Well, there's no use in—

WILLY You guys! There was a man started with the clothes on his back and ended up with diamond mines!

HAPPY Boy, someday I'd like to know how he did it.

WILLY What's the mystery? The man knew what he wanted and went out and got it! Walked into a jungle, and comes out, the age of twenty-one, and he's rich! The world is an oyster, but you don't crack it open on a mattress!

HAPPY Pop, I told you I'm gonna retire you for life.

WILLY You'll retire me for life on seventy goddam dollars a week? And your women and your car and your apartment, and you'll retire me for life! Christ's sake, I couldn't get past Yonkers today! Where are you guys, where are you? The woods are burning! I can't drive a car!

CHARLEY *has appeared in the doorway. He is a large man, slow of speech, laconic, immovable. In all he says, despite what he says, there is pity, and, now, trepidation. He has a robe over pajamas, slippers on his feet. He enters the kitchen.*

CHARLEY   Everything all right?

HAPPY   Yeah, Charley, everything's . . .

WILLY   What's the matter?

CHARLEY   I heard some noise. I thought something happened. Can't we do something about the walls? You sneeze in here, and in my house hats blow off.

HAPPY   Let's go to bed, Dad. Come on.

CHARLEY *signals to* HAPPY *to go.*

WILLY   You go ahead, I'm not tired at the moment.

HAPPY   (*to* WILLY)   Take it easy, huh? (*He exits*)

WILLY   What're you doin' up?

CHARLEY   (*sitting down at the kitchen table opposite* WILLY)   Couldn't sleep good. I had a heartburn.

WILLY   Well, you don't know how to eat.

CHARLEY   I eat with my mouth.

WILLY   No, you're ignorant. You gotta know about vitamins and things like that.

CHARLEY   Come on, let's shoot. Tire you out a little.

WILLY   (*hesitantly*)   All right. You got cards?

CHARLEY   (*taking a deck from his pocket*)   Yeah, I got them. Someplace. What is it with those vitamins?

WILLY   (*dealing*)   They build up your bones. Chemistry.

CHARLEY   Yeah, but there's no bones in a heartburn.

WILLY   What are you talkin' about? Do you know the first thing about it?

CHARLEY   Don't get insulted.

WILLY   Don't talk about something you don't know anything about.

They are playing. Pause.

CHARLEY   What're you doin' home?

WILLY   A little trouble with the car.

CHARLEY   Oh. (*Pause*) I'd like to take a trip to California.

WILLY   Don't say.

CHARLEY   You want a job?

WILLY   I got a job, I told you that. (*After a slight pause*) What the hell are you offering me a job for?

CHARLEY   Don't get insulted.

WILLY   Don't insult me.

CHARLEY   I don't see no sense in it. You don't have to go on this way.

WILLY   I got a good job. (*Slight pause*) What do you keep comin'
in here for?

CHARLEY   You want me to go?

WILLY (*after a pause, withering*)   I can't understand it. He's going
back to Texas again. What the hell is that?

CHARLEY   Let him go.

WILLY   I got nothin' to give him, Charley. I'm clean, I'm clean.

CHARLEY   He won't starve. None a them starve. Forget about him.

WILLY   Then what have I got to remember?

CHARLEY   You take it too hard. To hell with it. When a deposit
bottle is broken you don't get your nickel back.

WILLY   That's easy enough for you to say.

CHARLEY   That ain't easy for me to say.

WILLY   Did you see the ceiling I put up in the living-room?

CHARLEY   Yeah, that's a piece of work. To put up a ceiling is a
mystery to me. How do you do it?

WILLY   What's the difference?

CHARLEY   Well, talk about it.

WILLY   You gonna put up a ceiling?

CHARLEY   How could I put up a ceiling?

WILLY   Then what the hell are you bothering me for?

CHARLEY   You're insulted again.

WILLY   A man who can't handle tools is not a man. You're disgusting.

CHARLEY   Don't call me disgusting, Willy.

UNCLE BEN, *carrying a valise and an umbrella, enters the forestage from
around the right corner of the house. He is a stolid man, in his sixties,
with a mustache and an authoritative air. He is utterly certain of his destiny, and there is an aura of far places about him. He enters exactly as*
WILLY *speaks.*

WILLY   I'm getting awfully tired, Ben.

BEN's *music is heard.* BEN *looks around at everything.*

CHARLEY   Good, keep playing; you'll sleep better. Did you call me
Ben?

BEN *looks at his watch.*

WILLY   That's funny. For a second there you reminded me of my
brother Ben.

BEN   I only have a few minutes. (*He strolls, inspecting the place.*
WILLY *and* CHARLEY *continue playing*)

CHARLEY   You never heard from him again, heh? Since that time?

WILLY   Didn't Linda tell you? Couple of weeks ago we got a letter
from his wife in Africa. He died.

CHARLEY That so.

BEN (*chuckling*) So this is Brooklyn, eh?

CHARLEY Maybe you're in for some of his money.

WILLY Naa, he had seven sons. There's just one opportunity I had with that man . . .

BEN I must make a train, William. There are several properties I'm looking at in Alaska.

WILLY Sure, sure! If I'd gone with him to Alaska that time, everything would've been totally different.

CHARLEY Go on, you'd froze to death up there.

WILLY What're you talking about?

BEN Opportunity is tremendous in Alaska, William. Surprised you're not up there.

WILLY Sure, tremendous.

CHARLEY Heh?

WILLY There was the only man I ever met who knew the answers.

CHARLEY Who?

BEN How are you all?

WILLY (*taking a pot, smiling*) Fine, fine.

CHARLEY Pretty sharp tonight.

BEN Is Mother living with you?

WILLY No, she died a long time ago.

CHARLEY Who?

BEN That's too bad. Fine specimen of a lady, Mother.

WILLY (*to* CHARLEY) Heh?

BEN I'd hoped to see the old girl.

CHARLEY Who died?

BEN Heard anything from Father, have you?

WILLY (*unnerved*) What do you mean, who died?

CHARLEY (*taking a pot*) What're you talkin' about?

BEN (*looking at his watch*) William, it's half-past eight!

WILLY (*as though to dispel his confusion he angrily stops* CHARLEY'S *hand*) That's my build!

CHARLEY I put the ace—

WILLY If you don't know how to play the game I'm not gonna throw my money away on you!

CHARLEY (*rising*) It was my ace, for God's sake!

WILLY I'm through, I'm through!

BEN When did Mother die?

WILLY Long ago. Since the beginning you never knew how to play cards.

CHARLEY (*picks up the cards and goes to the door*) All right! Next time I'll bring a deck with five aces.

WILLY   I don't play that kind of game!

CHARLEY   (*turning to him*)   You ought to be ashamed of yourself!

WILLY   Yeah?

CHARLEY   Yeah! (*He goes out*)

WILLY   (*slamming the door after him*)   Ignoramus!

BEN   (*as* WILLY *comes toward him through the wall-line of the kitchen*)   So you're William.

WILLY   (*shaking* BEN's *hand*)   Ben! I've been waiting for you so long! What's the answer? How did you do it?

BEN   Oh, there's a story in that.

LINDA *enters the forestage, as of old, carrying the wash basket.*

LINDA   Is this Ben?

BEN   (*gallantly*)   How do you do, my dear.

LINDA   Where've you been all these years? Willy's always wondered why you—

WILLY   (*pulling* BEN *away from her impatiently*)   Where is Dad? Didn't you follow him? How did you get started?

BEN   Well, I don't know how much you remember.

WILLY   Well, I was just a baby, of course, only three or four years old—

BEN   Three years and eleven months.

WILLY   What a memory, Ben!

BEN   I have many enterprises, William, and I have never kept books.

WILLY   I remember I was sitting under the wagon in—was it Nebraska?

BEN   It was South Dakota, and I gave you a bunch of wild flowers.

WILLY   I remember you walking away down some open road.

BEN   (*laughing*)   I was going to find Father in Alaska.

WILLY   Where is he?

BEN   At that age I had a very faulty view of geography, William. I discovered after a few days that I was heading due south, so instead of Alaska, I ended up in Africa.

LINDA   Africa!

WILLY   The Gold Coast!

BEN   Principally diamond mines.

LINDA   Diamond mines!

BEN   Yes, my dear. But I've only a few minutes—

WILLY   No! Boys! Boys! (*Young* BIFF *and* HAPPY *appear*)   Listen to this. This is your Uncle Ben, a great man! Tell my boys, Ben!

BEN   Why, boys, when I was seventeen I walked into the jungle, and when I was twenty-one I walked out. (*He laughs*)   And by God I was rich.

WILLY (*to the boys*) You see what I been talking about? The greatest things can happen!

BEN (*glancing at his watch*) I have an appointment in Ketchikan Tuesday week.

WILLY No, Ben! Please tell about Dad. I want my boys to hear. I want them to know the kind of stock they spring from. All I remember is a man with a big beard, and I was in Mamma's lap, sitting around a fire, and some kind of high music.

BEN His flute. He played the flute.

WILLY Sure, the flute, that's right!

New music is heard, a high, rollicking tune.

BEN Father was a very great and a very wild-hearted man. We would start in Boston, and he'd toss the whole family into the wagon, and then he'd drive the team right across the country; through Ohio, and Indiana, Michigan, Illinois, and all the Western states. And we'd stop in the towns and sell the flutes that he'd made on the way. Great inventor, Father. With one gadget he made more in a week than a man like you could make in a lifetime.

WILLY That's just the way I'm bringing them up, Ben—rugged, well liked, all-around.

BEN Yeah? (*To* BIFF) Hit that, boy—hard as you can. (*He pounds his stomach*)

BIFF Oh, no, sir!

BEN (*taking boxing stance*) Come on, get to me! (*He laughs*)

WILLY Go to it, Biff! Go ahead, show him!

BIFF Okay! (*He cocks his fists and starts in*)

LINDA (*to* WILLY) Why must he fight, dear?

BEN (*sparring with* BIFF) Good boy! Good boy!

WILLY How's that, Ben, heh?

HAPPY Give him the left, Biff!

LINDA Why are you fighting?

BEN Good boy! (*Suddenly comes in, trips* BIFF, *and stands over him, the point of his umbrella poised over* BIFF's *eye*)

LINDA Look out, Biff!

BIFF Gee!

BEN (*patting* BIFF's *knee*) Never fight fair with a stranger, boy. You'll never get out of the jungle that way. (*Taking* LINDA's *hand and bowing*) It was an honor and a pleasure to meet you, Linda.

LINDA (*withdrawing her hand coldly, frightened*) Have a nice—trip.

BEN (*to* WILLY) And good luck with your—what do you do?

WILLY   Selling.

BEN   Yes. Well . . . (*He raises his hand in farewell to all*)

WILLY   No, Ben, I don't want you to think . . . (*He takes* BEN's *arm to show him*) It's Brooklyn, I know, but we hunt too.

BEN   Really, now.

WILLY   Oh, sure, there's snakes and rabbits and—that's why I moved out here. Why, Biff can fell any one of these trees in no time! Boys! Go right over to where they're building the apartment house and get some sand. We're gonna rebuild the entire front stoop right now! Watch this, Ben!

BIFF   Yes, sir! On the double, Hap!

HAPPY   (*as he and* BIFF *run off*)   I lost weight, Pop, you notice?

CHARLEY *enters in knickers, even before the boys are gone.*

CHARLEY   Listen, if they steal any more from that building the watchman'll put the cops on them!

LINDA (*to* WILLY)   Don't let Biff . . .

BEN *laughs lustily.*

WILLY   You shoulda seen the lumber they brought home last week. At least a dozen six-by-tens worth all kinds a money.

CHARLEY   Listen, if that watchman—

WILLY   I gave them hell, understand. But I got a couple of fearless characters there.

CHARLEY   Willy, the jails are full of fearless characters.

BEN (*clapping* WILLY *on the back, with a laugh at* CHARLEY)   And the stock exchange, friend!

WILLY (*joining in* BEN's *laughter*)   Where are the rest of your pants?

CHARLEY   My wife bought them.

WILLY   Now all you need is a golf club and you can go upstairs and go to sleep. (*To* BEN) Great athlete! Between him and his son Bernard they can't hammer a nail!

BERNARD (*rushing in*)   The watchman's chasing Biff!

WILLY (*angrily*)   Shut up! He's not stealing anything!

LINDA (*alarmed, hurrying off left*)   Where is he? Biff, dear! (*She exits*)

WILLY (*moving toward the left, away from* BEN)   There's nothing wrong. What's the matter with you?

BEN   Nervy boy. Good!

WILLY (*laughing*)   Oh, nerves of iron, that Biff!

CHARLEY   Don't know what it is. My New England man comes back and he's bleedin', they murdered him up there.

WILLY   It's contacts, Charley, I got important contacts!

CHARLEY (*sarcastically*)   Glad to hear it, Willy. Come in later, we'll shoot a little casino. I'll take some of your Portland money. (*He laughs at* WILLY *and exits*)

WILLY (*turning to* BEN)   Business is bad, it's murderous. But not for me, of course.

BEN   I'll stop by on my way back to Africa.

WILLY (*longingly*)   Can't you stay a few days? You're just what I need, Ben, because I—I have a fine position here, but I—well, Dad left when I was such a baby and I never had a chance to talk to him and I still feel—kind of temporary about myself.

BEN   I'll be late for my train.

They are at opposite ends of the stage.

WILLY   Ben, my boys—can't we talk? They'd go into the jaws of hell for me, see, but I—

BEN   William, you're being first-rate with your boys. Outstanding, manly chaps!

WILLY (*hanging on to his words*)   Oh, Ben, that's good to hear! Because sometimes I'm afraid that I'm not teaching them the right kind of— Ben, how should I teach them?

BEN (*giving great weight to each word, and with a certain vicious audacity*)   William, when I walked into the jungle, I was seventeen. When I walked out I was twenty-one. And, by God, I was rich! (*He goes off into darkness around the right corner of the house*)

WILLY   . . . was rich! That's just the spirit I want to imbue them with! To walk into a jungle! I was right! I was right! I was right!

BEN *is gone, but* WILLY *is still speaking to him as* LINDA, *in nightgown and robe, enters the kitchen, glances around for* WILLY, *then goes to the door of the house, looks out and sees him. Comes down to his left. He looks at her.*

LINDA   Willy, dear? Willy?

WILLY   I was right!

LINDA   Did you have some cheese? (*He can't answer*) It's very late, darling. Come to bed, heh?

WILLY (*looking straight up*)   Gotta break your neck to see a star in this yard.

LINDA   You coming in?

WILLY   Whatever happened to that diamond watch fob? Remember? When Ben came from Africa that time? Didn't he give me a watch fob with a diamond in it?

LINDA You pawned it, dear. Twelve, thirteen years ago. For Biff's radio correspondence course.

WILLY Gee, that was a beautiful thing. I'll take a walk.

LINDA But you're in your slippers.

WILLY (*starting to go around the house at the left*) I was right! I was! (*Half to* LINDA, *as he goes, shaking his head*) What a man! There was a man worth talking to I was right!

LINDA (*calling after* WILLY) But in your slippers, Willy!

WILLY *is almost gone when* BIFF, *in his pajamas, comes down the stairs and enters the kitchen.*

BIFF What is he doing out there?

LINDA Sh!

BIFF God Almighty, Mom, how long has he been doing this?

LINDA Don't, he'll hear you.

BIFF What the hell is the matter with him?

LINDA It'll pass by morning.

BIFF Shouldn't we do anything?

LINDA Oh, my dear, you should do a lot of things, but there's nothing to do, so go to sleep.

HAPPY *comes down the stairs and sits on the steps.*

HAPPY I never heard him so loud, Mom.

LINDA Well, come around more often; you'll hear him. (*She sits down at the table and mends the lining of* WILLY's *jacket*)

BIFF Why didn't you ever write me about this, Mom?

LINDA How would I write to you? For over three months you had no address.

BIFF I was on the move. But you know I thought of you all the time. You know that, don't you, pal?

LINDA I know, dear, I know. But he likes to have a letter. Just to know that there's still a possibility for better things.

BIFF He's not like this all the time, is he?

LINDA It's when you come home he's always the worst.

BIFF When I come home?

LINDA When you write you're coming, he's all smiles, and talks about the future, and—he's just wonderful. And then the closer you seem to come, the more shaky he gets, and then, by the time you get here, he's arguing, and he seems angry at you. I think it's just that maybe he can't bring himself to—to open up to you. Why are you so hateful to each other? Why is that?

BIFF (*evasively*) I'm not hateful, Mom.

LINDA But you no sooner come in the door than you're fighting!

BIFF I don't know why. I mean to change. I'm tryin', Mom, you understand?

LINDA Are you home to stay now?

BIFF I don't know. I want to look around, see what's doin'.

LINDA Biff, you can't look around all your life, can you?

BIFF I just can't take hold, Mom. I can't take hold of some kind of a life.

LINDA Biff, a man is not a bird, to come and go with the springtime.

BIFF Your hair... (*He touches her hair*) Your hair got so gray.

LINDA Oh, it's been gray since you were in high school. I just stopped dyeing it, that's all.

BIFF Dye it again, will ya? I don't want my pal looking old. (*He smiles*)

LINDA You're such a boy! You think you can go away for a year and... You've got to get it into your head now that one day you'll knock on this door and there'll be strange people here—

BIFF What are you talking about? You're not even sixty, Mom.

LINDA But what about your father?

BIFF (*lamely*) Well, I meant him too.

HAPPY He admires Pop.

LINDA Biff, dear, if you don't have any feeling for him, then you can't have any feeling for me.

BIFF Sure I can, Mom.

LINDA No. You can't just come to see me, because I love him. (*With a threat, but only a threat, of tears*) He's the dearest man in the world to me, and I won't have anyone making him feel unwanted and low and blue. You've got to make up your mind now, darling, there's no leeway any more. Either he's your father and you pay him that respect, or else you're not to come here. I know he's not easy to get along with—nobody knows that better than me—but...

WILLY (*from the left, with a laugh*) Hey, hey, Biffo!

BIFF (*starting to go out after* WILLY) What the hell is the matter with him? (HAPPY *stops him*)

LINDA Don't—don't go near him!

BIFF Stop making excuses for him! He always, always wiped the floor with you. Never had an ounce of respect for you.

HAPPY He's always had respect for—

BIFF What the hell do you know about it?

HAPPY (*surlily*) Just don't call him crazy!

BIFF He's got no character—Charley wouldn't do this. Not in his own house—spewing out that vomit from his mind.

HAPPY Charley never had to cope with what he's got to.

BIFF People are worse off than Willy Loman. Believe me, I've seen them!

LINDA Then make Charley your father, Biff. You can't do that, can you? I don't say he's a great man. Willy Loman never made a lot of money. His name was never in the paper. He's not the finest character that ever lived. But he's a human being, and a terrible thing is happening to him. So attention must be paid. He's not to be allowed to fall into his grave like an old dog. Attention, attention must be finally paid to such a person. You called him crazy—

BIFF I didn't mean—

LINDA No, a lot of people think he's lost his—balance. But you don't have to be very smart to know what his trouble is. The man is exhausted.

HAPPY Sure!

LINDA A small man can be just as exhausted as a great man. He works for a company thirty-six years this March, opens up unheard-of territories to their trademark, and now in his old age they take his salary away.

HAPPY (*indignantly*) I didn't know that, Mom.

LINDA You never asked, my dear! Now that you get your spending money someplace else you don't trouble your mind with him.

HAPPY But I gave you money last—

LINDA Christmas time, fifty dollars! To fix the hot water it cost ninety-seven fifty! For five weeks he's been on straight commission, like a beginner, an unknown!

BIFF Those ungrateful bastards!

LINDA Are they any worse than his sons? When he brought them business, when he was young, they were glad to see him. But now his old friends, the old buyers that loved him so and always found some order to hand him in a pinch—they're all dead, retired. He used to be able to make six, seven calls a day in Boston. Now he takes his valises out of the car and puts them back and takes them out again and he's exhausted. Instead of walking he talks now. He drives seven hundred miles, and when he gets there no one knows him any more, no one welcomes him. And what goes through a man's mind, driving seven hundred miles home without having earned a cent? Why shouldn't he talk to himself? Why? When he has to go to Charley and borrow fifty dollars a week and pretend to me that it's his pay? How long can that go on? How long? You see what I'm sitting here and waiting for? And you tell me he has no character? The man who never worked a day but for your benefit? When does he get the medal for that? Is this his reward—to turn around at the age of sixty-three and find his sons, who he loved better than his life, one a philandering bum—

HAPPY   Mom!

LINDA   That's all you are, my baby! (*To* BIFF) And you! What happened to the love you had for him? You were such pals! How you used to talk to him on the phone every night! How lonely he was till he could come home to you!

BIFF   All right, Mom. I'll live here in my room, and I'll get a job. I'll keep away from him, that's all.

LINDA   No, Biff. You can't stay here and fight all the time.

BIFF   He threw me out of this house, remember that.

LINDA   Why did he do that? I never knew why.

`BIFF   Because I know he's a fake and he doesn't like anybody around who knows!

LINDA   Why a fake? In what way? What do you mean?

BIFF   Just don't lay it all at my feet. It's between me and him— that's all I have to say. I'll chip in from now on. He'll settle for half my pay check. He'll be all right. I'm going to bed. (*He starts for the stairs*)

LINDA   He won't be all right.

BIFF   (*turning on the stairs, furiously*)   I hate this city and I'll stay here. Now what do you want?

LINDA   He's dying, Biff.

HAPPY *turns quickly to her, shocked.*

BIFF   (*after a pause*)   Why is he dying?

LINDA   He's been trying to kill himself.

BIFF   (*with great horror*)   How?

LINDA   I live from day to day.

BIFF   What're you talking about?

LINDA   Remember I wrote you that he smashed up the car again? In February?

BIFF   Well?

LINDA   The insurance inspector came. He said that they have evidence. That all these accidents in the last year—weren't—weren't —accidents.

HAPPY   How can they tell that? That's a lie.

LINDA   It seems there's a woman . . . (*She takes a breath as . . .*)

⎰BIFF (*sharply but contained*)   What woman?
⎱LINDA (*simultaneously*)   . . . and this woman . . .

LINDA   What?

BIFF   Nothing. Go ahead.

LINDA   What did you say?

BIFF   Nothing. I just said what woman?

HAPPY   What about her?

LINDA   Well, it seems she was walking down the road and saw his car. She says that he wasn't driving fast at all, and that he didn't skid. She says he came to that little bridge, and then deliberately smashed into the railing, and it was only the shallowness of the water that saved him.

BIFF   Oh, no, he probably just fell asleep again.

LINDA   I don't think he fell asleep.

BIFF   Why not?

LINDA   Last month . . . (*With great difficulty*) Oh, boys, it's so hard to say a thing like this! He's just a big stupid man to you, but I tell you there's more good in him than in many other people. (*She chokes, wipes her eyes*) I was looking for a fuse. The lights blew out, and I went down the cellar. And behind the fuse box —it happened to fall out—was length of rubber pipe—just short.

HAPPY   No kidding?

LINDA   There's a little attachment on the end of it. I knew right away. And sure enough, on the bottom of the water heater there's a new little nipple on the gas pipe.

HAPPY   (*angrily*)   That—jerk.

BIFF   Did you have it taken off?

LINDA   I'm—I'm ashamed to. How can I mention it to him? Every day I go down and take away that little rubber pipe. But, when he comes home, I put it back where it was. How can I insult him that way? I don't know what to do. I live from day to day, boys. I tell you, I know every thought in his mind. It sounds so old-fashioned and silly, but I tell you he put his whole life into you and you've turned your backs on him. (*She is bent over in the chair, weeping, her face in her hands*) Biff, I swear to God! Biff, his life is in your hands!

HAPPY   (*to* BIFF)   How do you like that damned fool!

BIFF   (*kissing her*)   All right, pal, all right. It's all settled now. I've been remiss. I know that, Mom. But now I'll stay, and I swear to you, I'll apply myself. (*Kneeling in front of her, in a fever of self-reproach*) It's just—you see, Mom, I don't fit in business. Not that I won't try. I'll try, and I'll make good.

HAPPY   Sure you will. The trouble with you in business was you never tried to please people.

BIFF   I know, I—

HAPPY   Like when you worked for Harrison's. Bob Harrison said you were tops, and then you go and do some damn fool thing like whistling whole songs in the elevator like a comedian.

BIFF (*against* HAPPY) So what? I like to whistle sometimes.

HAPPY You don't raise a guy to a responsible job who whistles in the elevator!

LINDA Well, don't argue about it now.

HAPPY Like when you'd go off and swim in the middle of the day instead of taking the line around.

BIFF (*his resentment rising*) Well, don't you run off? You take off sometimes, don't you? On a nice summer day?

HAPPY Yeah, but I cover myself!

LINDA Boys!

HAPPY If I'm going to take a fade the boss can call any number where I'm supposed to be and they'll swear to him that I just left. I'll tell you something that I hate to say, Biff, but in the business world some of them think you're crazy.

BIFF (*angered*) Screw the business world!

HAPPY All right, screw it! Great, but cover yourself!

LINDA Hap, Hap!

BIFF I don't care what they think! They've laughed at Dad for years, and you know why? Because we don't belong in this nuthouse of a city! We should be mixing cement on some open plain, or—or carpenters. A carpenter is allowed to whistle!

WILLY *walks in from the entrance of the house, at left.*

WILLY Even your grandfather was better than a carpenter. (*Pause. They watch him*) You never grew up. Bernard does not whistle in the elevator, I assure you.

BIFF (*as though to laugh* WILLY *out of it*) Yeah, but you do, Pop.

WILLY I never in my life whistled in an elevator! And who in the business world thinks I'm crazy?

BIFF I didn't mean it like that, Pop. Now don't make a whole thing out of it, will ya?

WILLY Go back to the West! Be a carpenter, a cowboy, enjoy yourself!

LINDA Willy, he was just saying—

WILLY I heard what he said!

HAPPY (*trying to quiet* WILLY) Hey, Pop, come on now . . .

WILLY (*continuing over* HAPPY's *line*) They laugh at me, heh? Go to Filene's, go to the Hub, go to Slattery's, Boston. Call out the name Willy Loman and see what happens! Big shot!

BIFF All right, Pop.

WILLY Big!

BIFF All right!

WILLY Why do you always insult me?

BIFF I didn't say a word. (*To* LINDA) Did I say a word?

LINDA He didn't say anything, Willy.

WILLY (*going to the doorway of the living-room*) All right, good night, good night.

LINDA Willy, dear, he just decided . . .

WILLY (*to* BIFF) If you get tired hanging around tomorrow, paint the ceiling I put up in the living-room.

BIFF I'm leaving early tomorrow.

HAPPY He's going to see Bill Oliver, Pop.

WILLY (*interestedly*) Oliver? For what?

BIFF (*with reserve, but trying, trying*) He always said he'd stake me. I'd like to go into business, so maybe I can take him up on it.

LINDA Isn't that wonderful?

WILLY Don't interrupt. What's wonderful about it? There's fifty men in the City of New York who'd stake him. (*To* BIFF) Sporting goods?

BIFF I guess so. I know something about it and—

WILLY He knows something about it! You know sporting goods better than Spalding, for God's sake! How much is he giving you?

BIFF I don't know, I didn't even see him yet, but—

WILLY Then what're you talkin' about?

BIFF (*getting angry*) Well, all I said was I'm gonna see him, that's all!

WILLY (*turning away*) Ah, you're counting your chickens again.

BIFF (*starting left for the stairs*) Oh, Jesus, I'm going to sleep!

WILLY (*calling after him*) Don't curse in this house!

BIFF (*turning*) Since when did you get so clean?

HAPPY (*trying to stop them*) Wait a . . .

WILLY Don't use that language to me! I won't have it!

HAPPY (*grabbing* BIFF, *shouts*) Wait a minute! I got an idea. I got a feasible idea. Come here, Biff, let's talk this over now, let's talk some sense here. When I was down in Florida last time, I thought of a great idea to sell sporting goods. It just came back to me. You and I, Biff—we have a line, the Loman Line. We train a couple of weeks, and put on a couple of exhibitions, see?

WILLY That's an idea!

HAPPY Wait! We form two basketball teams, see? Two water-polo teams. We play each other. It's a million dollars' worth of publicity. Two brothers, see? The Loman Brothers. Displays in the Royal Palms—all the hotels. And banners over the ring and the basketball court: "Loman Brothers." Baby, we could sell sporting goods!

WILLY That is a one-million-dollar idea!

LINDA Marvelous!

BIFF I'm in great shape as far as that's concerned.

HAPPY And the beauty of it is, Biff, it wouldn't be like a business. We'd be out playin' ball again . . .

BIFF (*enthused*) Yeah, that's . . .

WILLY Million-dollar . . .

HAPPY And you wouldn't get fed up with it, Biff. It'd be the family again. There'd be the old honor, and comradeship, and if you wanted to go off for a swim or somethin'—well, you'd do it! Without some smart cooky gettin' up ahead of you!

WILLY Lick the world! You guys together could absolutely lick the civilized world.

BIFF I'll see Oliver tomorrow. Hap, if we could work that out . . .

LINDA Maybe things are beginning to—

WILLY (*wildly enthused, to* LINDA) Stop interrupting! (*To* BIFF) But don't wear sport jacket and slacks when you see Oliver.

BIFF No, I'll—

WILLY A business suit, and talk as little as possible, and don't crack any jokes.

BIFF He did like me. Always liked me.

LINDA He loved you!

WILLY (*to* LINDA) Will you stop! (*To* BIFF) Walk in very serious. You are not applying for a boy's job. Money is to pass. Be quiet, fine, and serious. Everybody likes a kidder, but nobody lends him money.

HAPPY I'll try to get some myself, Biff. I'm sure I can.

WILLY I see great things for you kids, I think your troubles are over. But remember, start big and you'll end big. Ask for fifteen. How much you gonna ask for?

BIFF Gee, I don't know—

WILLY And don't say "Gee." "Gee" is a boy's word. A man walking in for fifteen thousand dollars does not say "Gee!"

BIFF Ten, I think, would be top though.

WILLY Don't be so modest. You always started too low. Walk in with a big laugh. Don't look worried. Start off with a couple of your good stories to lighten things up. It's not what you say, it's how you say it—because personality always wins the day.

LINDA Oliver always thought the highest of him—

WILLY Will you let me talk?

BIFF Don't yell at her, Pop, will ya?

WILLY (*angrily*) I was talking, wasn't I?

BIFF I don't like you yelling at her all the time, and I'm tellin' you, that's all.

WILLY What're you, takin' over this house?

LINDA Willy—

WILLY (*turning on her*) Don't take his side all the time, goddammit!

BIFF (*furiously*) Stop yelling at her!

WILLY (*suddenly pulling on his cheek, beaten down, guilt ridden*) Give my best to Bill Oliver—he may remember me. (*He exits through the living-room doorway*)

LINDA (*her voice subdued*) What'd you have to start that for? (BIFF *turns away*) You see how sweet he was as soon as you talked hopefully? (*She goes over to* BIFF) Come up and say good night to him. Don't let him go to bed that way.

HAPPY Come on, Biff, let's buck him up.

LINDA Please, dear. Just say good night. It takes so little to make him happy. Come. (*She goes through the living-room doorway, calling upstairs from within the living-room*) Your pajamas are hanging in the bathroom, Willy!

HAPPY (*looking toward where* LINDA *went out*) What a woman! They broke the mold when they made her. You know that, Biff?

BIFF He's off salary. My God, working on commission!

HAPPY Well, let's face it: he's no hot-shot selling man. Except that sometimes, you have to admit, he's a sweet personality.

BIFF (*deciding*) Lend me ten bucks, will ya? I want to buy some new ties.

HAPPY I'll take you to a place I know. Beautiful stuff. Wear one of my striped shirts tomorrow.

BIFF She got gray. Mom got awful old. Gee, I'm gonna go in to Oliver tomorrow and knock him for a—

HAPPY Come on up. Tell that to Dad. Let's give him a whirl. Come on.

BIFF (*steamed up*) You know, with ten thousand bucks, boy!

HAPPY (*as they go into the living-room*) That's the talk, Biff, that's the first time I've heard the old confidence out of you! (*From within the living-room, fading off*) You're gonna live with me, kid, and any babe you want just say the word . . .

The last lines are hardly heard. They are mounting the stairs to their parents' bedroom.

LINDA (*entering her bedroom and addressing* WILLY, *who is in the bathroom. She is straightening the bed for him*) Can you do anything about the shower? It drips.

WILLY (*from the bathroom*) All of a sudden everything falls to pieces! Goddam plumbing, oughta be sued, those people. I hardly finished putting it in and the thing . . . (*His words rumble off*)

LINDA I'm just wondering if Oliver will remember him. You think he might?

WILLY (*coming out of the bathroom in his pajamas*)   Remember him? What's the matter with you, you crazy? If he'd've stayed with Oliver he'd be on top by now! Wait'll Oliver gets a look at him. You don't know the average caliber any more. The average young man today—(*he is getting into bed*)—is got a caliber of zero. Greatest thing in the world for him was to bum around.

BIFF *and* HAPPY *enter the bedroom. Slight pause.*

WILLY (*stops short, looking at* BIFF)   Glad to hear it, boy.

HAPPY   He wanted to say good night to you, sport.

WILLY (*to* BIFF)   Yeah. Knock him dead, boy. What'd you want to tell me?

BIFF   Just take it easy, Pop. Good night. (*He turns to go*)

WILLY (*unable to resist*)   And if anything falls off the desk while you're talking to him—like a package or something—don't you pick it up. They have office boys for that.

LINDA   I'll make a big breakfast—

WILLY   Will you let me finish? (*To* BIFF) Tell him you were in the business in the West. Not farm work.

BIFF   All right, Dad.

LINDA   I think everything—

WILLY (*going right through her speech*)   And don't undersell yourself. No less than fifteen thousand dollars.

BIFF (*unable to bear him*)   Okay. Good night, Mom. (*He starts moving*)

WILLY   Because you got a greatness in you, Biff, remember that. You got all kinds a greatness . . . (*He lies back, exhausted.* BIFF *walks out*)

LINDA (*calling after* BIFF)   Sleep well, darling!

HAPPY   I'm gonna get married, Mom. I wanted to tell you.

LINDA   Go to sleep, dear.

HAPPY (*going*)   I just wanted to tell you.

WILLY   Keep up the good work. (HAPPY *exits*) God . . . remember that Ebbets Field game? The championship of the city?

LINDA   Just rest. Should I sing to you?

WILLY   Yeah. Sing to me. (LINDA *hums a soft lullaby*) When that team came out—he was the tallest, remember?

LINDA   Oh, yes. And in gold.

BIFF *enters the darkened kitchen, takes a cigarette, and leaves the house. He comes downstage into a golden pool of light. He smokes, staring at the night.*

WILLY   Like a young god. Hercules—something like that. And the sun, the sun all around him. Remember how he waved to me?

Right up from the field, with the representatives of three colleges standing by? And the buyers I brought, and the cheers when he came out—Loman, Loman, Loman! God almighty, he'll be great yet. A star like that, magnificent, can never really fade away!

The light on WILLY *is fading. The gas heater begins to glow through the kitchen wall, near the stairs, a blue flame beneath red coils.*

LINDA (*timidly*) Willy dear, what has he got against you?

WILLY I'm so tired. Don't talk any more.

BIFF *slowly returns to the kitchen. He stops, stares toward the heater.*

LINDA Will you ask Howard to let you work in New York?

WILLY First thing in the morning. Everything'll be all right.

BIFF *reaches behind the heater and draws out a length of rubber tubing. He is horrified and turns his head toward* WILLY'S *room, still dimly lit, from which the strains of* LINDA'S *desperate but monotonous humming rise.*

WILLY (*staring through the window into the moonlight*) Gee, look at the moon moving between the buildings!

BIFF *wraps the tubing around his hand and quickly goes up the stairs.*

Curtain

ACT TWO

Music is heard, gay and bright. The curtain rises as the music fades away. WILLY, *in shirt sleeves, is sitting at the kitchen table, sipping coffee, his hat in his lap.* LINDA *is filling his cup when she can.*

WILLY Wonderful coffee. Meal in itself.

LINDA Can I make you some eggs?

WILLY No. Take a breath.

LINDA You look so rested, dear.

WILLY I slept like a dead one. First time in months. Imagine, sleeping till ten on a Tuesday morning. Boys left nice and early, heh?

LINDA They were out of here by eight o'clock.

WILLY Good work!

LINDA It was so thrilling to see them leaving together. I can't get over the shaving lotion in this house!

WILLY (*smiling*) Mmm—

LINDA Biff was very changed this morning. His whole attitude seemed to be hopeful. He couldn't wait to get downtown to see Oliver.

WILLY He's heading for a change. There's no question, there simply are certain men that take longer to get—solidified. How did he dress?

LINDA His blue suit. He's so handsome in that suit. He could be a—anything in that suit!

WILLY *gets up from the table.* LINDA *holds his jacket for him.*

WILLY There's no question, no question at all. Gee, on the way home tonight I'd like to buy some seeds.

LINDA (*laughing*) That'd be wonderful. But not enough sun gets back there. Nothing'll grow any more.

WILLY You wait, kid, before it's all over we're gonna get a little place out in the country, and I'll raise some vegetables, a couple of chickens . . .

LINDA You'll do it yet, dear.

WILLY *walks out of his jacket.* LINDA *follows him.*

WILLY And they'll get married, and come for a weekend. I'd build a little guest house. 'Cause I got so many fine tools, all I'd need would be a little lumber and some peace of mind.

LINDA (*joyfully*) I sewed the lining . . .

WILLY I could build two guest houses, so they'd both come. Did he decide how much he's going to ask Oliver for?

LINDA (*getting him into the jacket*) He didn't mention it, but I imagine ten or fifteen thousand. You going to talk to Howard today?

WILLY Yeah. I'll put it to him straight and simple. He'll just have to take me off the road.

LINDA And Willy, don't forget to ask for a little advance, because we've got the insurance premium. It's the grace period now.

WILLY That's a hundred . . . ?

LINDA A hundred and eight, sixty-eight. Because we're a little short again.

WILLY Why are we short?

LINDA Well, you had the motor job on the car . . .

WILLY That goddam Studebaker!

LINDA And you got one more payment on the refrigerator . . .

WILLY But it just broke again!

LINDA Well, it's old, dear.

WILLY I told you we should've bought a well-advertised machine. Charley bought a General Electric and it's twenty years old and it's still good, that son-of-a-bitch.

LINDA But, Willy—

WILLY   Whoever heard of a Hastings refrigerator? Once in my life I would like to own something outright before it's broken! I'm always in a race with the junkyard! I just finished paying for the car and it's on its last legs. The refrigerator consumes belts like a goddam maniac. They time those things. They time them so when you finally paid for them, they're used up.

LINDA   (*buttoning up his jacket as he unbuttons it*)   All told, about two hundred dollars would carry us, dear. But that includes the last payment on the mortgage. After this payment, Willy, the house belongs to us.

WILLY   It's twenty-five years!

LINDA   Biff was nine years old when we bought it.

WILLY   Well, that's a great thing. To weather a twenty-five year mortgage is—

LINDA   It's an accomplishment.

WILLY   All the cement, the lumber, the reconstruction I put in this house! There ain't a crack to be found in it any more.

LINDA   Well, it served its purpose.

WILLY   What purpose? Some stranger'll come along, move in, and that's that. If only Biff would take this house, and raise a family . . . (*He starts to go*) Good-by, I'm late.

LINDA   (*suddenly remembering*)   Oh, I forgot! You're supposed to meet them for dinner.

WILLY   Me?

LINDA   At Frank's Chop House on Forty-eighth near Sixth Avenue.

WILLY   Is that so! How about you?

LINDA   No, just the three of you. They're gonna blow you to a big meal!

WILLY   Don't say! Who thought of that?

LINDA   Biff came to me this morning, Willy, and he said, "Tell Dad, we want to blow him to a big meal." Be there six o'clock. You and your two boys are going to have dinner.

WILLY   Gee whiz! That's really somethin'. I'm gonna knock Howard for a loop, kid. I'll get an advance, and I'll come home with a New York job. Goddammit, now I'm gonna do it!

LINDA   Oh, that's the spirit, Willy!

WILLY   I will never get behind a wheel the rest of my life!

LINDA   It's changing, Willy, I can feel it changing!

WILLY   Beyond a question. G'by, I'm late. (*He starts to go again*)

LINDA   (*calling after him as she runs to the kitchen table for a hand-kerchief*)   You got your glasses?

WILLY   (*feels for them, then comes back in*)   Yeah, yeah, got my glasses.

LINDA (*giving him the handkerchief*)   And a handkerchief.

WILLY   Yeah, handkerchief.

LINDA   And your saccharine?

WILLY   Yeah, my saccharine.

LINDA   Be careful on the subway stairs.

She kisses him, and a silk stocking is seen hanging from her hand. WILLY *notices it.*

WILLY   Will you stop mending stockings? At least while I'm in the house. It gets me nervous. I can't tell you. Please.

LINDA *hides the stocking in her hand as she follows* WILLY *across the fore-stage in front of the house.*

LINDA   Remember, Frank's Chop House.

WILLY (*passing the apron*)   Maybe beets would grow out there.

LINDA (*laughing*)   But you tried so many times.

WILLY   Yeah. Well, don't work hard today. (*He disappears around the right corner of the house*)

LINDA   Be careful!

As WILLY *vanishes,* LINDA *waves to him. Suddenly the phone rings. She runs across the stage and into the kitchen and lifts it.*

LINDA   Hello? Oh, Biff! I'm so glad you called, I just . . . Yes, sure, I just told him. Yes, he'll be there for dinner at six o'clock, I didn't forget. Listen, I was just dying to tell you. You know that little rubber pipe I told you about? That he connected to the gas heater? I finally decided to go down the cellar this morning and take it away and destroy it. But it's gone! Imagine? He took it away himself, it isn't there! (*She listens*) When? Oh, then you took it. Oh—nothing, it's just that I'd hoped he'd taken it away himself. Oh, I'm not worried, darling, because this morning he left in such high spirits, it was like the old days! I'm not afraid any more. Did Mr. Oliver see you? . . . Well, you wait there then. And make a nice impression on him, darling. Just don't perspire too much before you see him. And have a nice time with Dad. He may have big news too! . . . That's right, a New York job. And be sweet to him tonight, dear. Be loving to him. Because he's only a little boat looking for a harbor. (*She is trembling with sorrow and joy*) Oh, that's wonderful, Biff, you'll save his life. Thanks, darling. Just put your arm around him when he comes into the restaurant. Give him a smile. That's the boy . . . Good-by, dear. . . . You got your comb? . . . That's fine. Good-by, Biff dear.

In the middle of her speech, HOWARD WAGNER, *thirty-six, wheels on a small typewriter table on which is a wire-recording machine and proceeds to plug it in. This is on the left forestage. Light slowly fades on* LINDA *as it rises on* HOWARD. HOWARD *is intent on threading the machine and only glances over his shoulder as* WILLY *appears.*

WILLY   Pst! Pst!

HOWARD   Hello, Willy, come in.

WILLY   Like to have a little talk with you, Howard.

HOWARD   Sorry to keep you waiting. I'll be with you in a minute.

WILLY   What's that, Howard?

HOWARD   Didn't you ever see one of these? Wire recorder.

WILLY   Oh. Can we talk a minute?

HOWARD   Records things. Just got delivery yesterday. Been driving me crazy, the most terrific machine I ever saw in my life.
I was up all night with it.

WILLY   What do you do with it?

HOWARD   I bought it for dictation, but you can do anything with
it. Listen to this. I had it home last night. Listen to what I picked
up. The first one is my daughter. Get this. (*He flicks the switch
and "Roll out the Barrel" is heard being whistled*) Listen to that
kid whistle.

WILLY   That is lifelike, isn't it?

HOWARD   Seven years old. Get that tone.

WILLY   Ts, ts. Like to ask a little favor if you . . .

The whistling breaks off, and the voice of HOWARD's *daughter is heard.*

HIS DAUGHTER   "Now you, Daddy."

HOWARD   She's crazy for me! (*Again the same song is whistled*)
That's me! Ha! (*He winks*)

WILLY   You're very good!

The whistling breaks off again. The machine runs silent for a moment.

HOWARD   Sh! Get this now, this is my son.

HIS SON   "The capital of Alabama is Montgomery; the capital of
Arizona is Phoenix; the capital of Arkansas is Little Rock; the
capital of California is Sacramento . . ." (*and on, and on*)

HOWARD   (*holding up five fingers*)   Five years old, Willy!

WILLY   He'll make an announcer some day!

HIS SON   (*continuing*)   "The capital . . ."

HOWARD   Get that—alphabetical order! (*The machine breaks off
suddenly*) Wait a minute. The maid kicked the plug out.

WILLY   It certainly is a—

HOWARD   Sh, for God's sake!

HIS SON   "It's nine o'clock, Bulova watch time. So I have to go to
sleep."

WILLY   That really is—

HOWARD   Wait a minute! The next is my wife.

They wait.

HOWARD's VOICE   "Go on, say something." (*Pause*) "Well, you gonna talk?"

HIS WIFE   "I can't think of anything."

HOWARD's VOICE   "Well, talk—it's turning."

HIS WIFE (*shyly, beaten*)   "Hello." (*Silence*) "Oh, Howard, I can't talk into this . . ."

HOWARD (*snapping the machine off*)   That was my wife.

WILLY   That is a wonderful machine. Can we—

HOWARD   I tell you, Willy, I'm gonna take my camera, and my bandsaw, and all my hobbies, and out they go. This is the most fascinating relaxation I ever found.

WILLY   I think I'll get one myself.

HOWARD   Sure, they're only a hundred and a half. You can't do without it. Supposing you wanna hear Jack Benny, see? But you can't be at home at that hour. So you tell the maid to turn the radio on when Jack Benny comes on, and this automatically goes on with the radio . . .

WILLY   And when you come home you . . .

HOWARD   You can come home twelve o'clock, one o'clock, any time you like, and you get yourself a Coke and sit yourself down, throw the switch, and there's Jack Benny's program in the middle of the night!

WILLY   I'm definitely going to get one. Because lots of time I'm on the road, and I think to myself, what I must be missing on the radio!

HOWARD   Don't you have a radio in the car?

WILLY   Well, yeah, but who ever thinks of turning it on?

HOWARD   Say, aren't you supposed to be in Boston?

WILLY   That's what I want to talk to you about, Howard. You got a minute? (*He draws a chair in from the wing*)

HOWARD   What happened? What're you doing here?

WILLY   Well . . .

HOWARD   You didn't crack up again, did you?

WILLY   Oh, no. No . . .

HOWARD   Geez, you had me worried there for a minute. What's the trouble?

WILLY   Well, tell you the truth, Howard. I've come to the decision that I'd rather not travel any more.

HOWARD   Not travel! Well, what'll you do?

WILLY   Remember, Christmas time, when you had the party here? You said you'd try to think of some spot for me here in town.

HOWARD   With us?

WILLY   Well, sure.

HOWARD   Oh, yeah, yeah. I remember. Well, I couldn't think of anything for you, Willy.

WILLY   I tell ya, Howard. The kids are all grown up, y'know. I don't need much any more. If I could take home—well, sixty-five dollars a week, I could swing it.

HOWARD   Yeah, but Willy, see I—

WILLY   I tell ya why, Howard. Speaking frankly and between the two of us, y'know—I'm just a little tired.

HOWARD   Oh, I could understand that, Willy. But you're a road man, Willy, and we do a road business. We've only got a half-dozen salesmen on the floor here.

WILLY   God knows, Howard, I never asked a favor of any man. But I was with the firm when your father used to carry you in here in his arms.

HOWARD   I know that, Willy, but—

WILLY   Your father came to me the day you were born **and** asked me what I thought of the name of Howard, may he rest in peace.

HOWARD   I appreciate that, Willy, but there just is no spot here for you. If I had a spot I'd slam you right in, but I just don't have a single solitary spot.

He looks for his lighter. WILLY *has picked it up and gives it to him. Pause.*

WILLY   (*with increasing anger*)   Howard, all I need to set my table is fifty dollars a week.

HOWARD   But where am I going to put you, kid?

WILLY   Look, it isn't a question of whether I can sell merchandise, is it?

HOWARD   No, but it's a business, kid, and everybody's gotta pull his own weight.

WILLY   (*desperately*)   Just let me tell you a story, Howard—

HOWARD   'Cause you gotta admit, business is business.

WILLY   (*angrily*)   Business is definitely business, but just listen for a minute. You don't understand this. When I was a boy—eighteen, nineteen—I was already on the road. And there was a question in my mind as to whether selling had a future for me. Because in those days I had a yearning to go to Alaska. See, there were three gold strikes in one month in Alaska, and I felt like going out. Just for the ride, you might say.

HOWARD   (*barely interested*)   Don't say.

WILLY   Oh, yeah, my father lived many years in Alaska. He was an adventurous man. We've got quite a little streak of self-reliance in our family. I thought I'd go out with my older brother and try to locate him, and maybe settle in the North with the old man. And I was almost decided to go, when I met a sales-man in the Parker House. His name was Dave Singleman. And he was eighty-four years old, and he'd drummed merchandise in thirty-one states. And old Dave, he'd go up to his room, y'under-stand, put on his green velvet slippers—I'll never forget—and pick up his phone and call the buyers, and without ever leaving his room, at the age of eighty-four, he made his living. And when I saw that, I realized that selling was the greatest career a man could want. 'Cause what could be more satisfying than to be able to go, at the age of eighty-four, into twenty or thirty different cities, and pick up a phone, and be remembered and loved and helped by so many different people? Do you know? when he died —and by the way he died the death of a salesman, in his green velvet slippers in the smoker of the New York, New Haven and Hartford, going into Boston—when he died, hundreds of sales-men and buyers were at his funeral. Things were sad on a lotta trains for months after that. (*He stands up.* HOWARD *has not looked at him*) In those days there was personality in it, Howard. There was respect, and comradeship, and gratitude in it. Today, it's all cut and dried, and there's no chance for bringing friend-ship to bear—or personality. You see what I mean? They don't know me any more.

HOWARD   (*moving away, to the right*)   That's just the thing, Willy.

WILLY   If I had forty dollars a week—that's all I'd need. Forty dollars, Howard.

HOWARD   Kid, I can't take blood from a stone, I—

WILLY   (*desperation is on him now*)   Howard, the year Al Smith was nominated, your father came to me and—

HOWARD   (*starting to go off*)   I've got to see some people, kid.

WILLY   (*stopping him*)   I'm talking about your father! There were promises made across this desk! You mustn't tell me you've got people to see—I put thirty-four years into this firm, Howard, and now I can't pay my insurance! You can't eat the orange and throw the peel away—a man is not a piece of fruit! (*After a pause*) Now pay attention. Your father—in 1928 I had a big year. I averaged a hundred and seventy dollars a week in com-missions.

HOWARD   (*impatiently*)   Now, Willy, you never averaged—

WILLY   (*banging his hand on the desk*)   I averaged a hundred and seventy dollars a week in the year of 1928! And your father came to me—or rather, I was in the office here—it was right over this desk—and he put his hand on my shoulder—

HOWARD (*getting up*)   You'll have to excuse me, Willy, I gotta see some people. Pull yourself together. (*Going out*) I'll be back in a little while.

On HOWARD'S *exit, the light on his chair grows very bright and strange.*

WILLY   Pull myself together! What the hell did I say to him? My God, I was yelling at him! How could I! (WILLY *breaks off, staring at the light, which occupies the chair, animating it. He approaches this chair, standing across the desk from it*) Frank, Frank, don't you remember what you told me that time? How you put your hand on my shoulder, and Frank . . .

He leans on the desk and as he speaks the dead man's name he accidentally switches on the recorder, and instantly

HOWARD'S SON   ". . . of New York is Albany. The capital of Ohio is Cincinnati, the capital of Rhode Island is . . ." (*The recitation continues*)

WILLY (*leaping away with fright, shouting*)   Ha! Howard! Howard! Howard!

HOWARD (*rushing in*)   What happened?

WILLY (*pointing at the machine, which continues nasally, childishly, with the capital cities*)   Shut it off! Shut it off!

HOWARD (*pulling the plug out*)   Look, Willy . . .

WILLY (*pressing his hands to his eyes*)   I gotta get myself some coffee. I'll get some coffee . . .

WILLY *starts to walk out.* HOWARD *stops him.*

HOWARD (*rolling up the cord*)   Willy, look . . .

WILLY   I'll go to Boston.

HOWARD   Willy, you can't go to Boston for us.

WILLY   Why can't I go?

HOWARD   I don't want you to represent us. I've been meaning to tell you for a long time now.

WILLY   Howard, are you firing me?

HOWARD   I think you need a good long rest, Willy.

WILLY   Howard—

HOWARD   And when you feel better, come back, and we'll see if we can work something out.

WILLY   But I gotta earn money, Howard. I'm in no position to—

HOWARD   Where are your sons? Why don't your sons give you a hand?

WILLY   They're working on a very big deal.

HOWARD   This is no time for false pride, Willy. You go to your sons and you tell them that you're tired. You've got two great boys, haven't you?

WILLY   Oh, no question, no question, but in the meantime...

HOWARD   Then that's that, heh?

WILLY   All right, I'll go to Boston tomorrow.

HOWARD   No, no.

WILLY   I can't throw myself on my sons. I'm not a cripple!

HOWARD   Look, kid, I'm busy this morning.

WILLY   (*grasping* HOWARD's *arm*)   Howard, you've got to let me go to Boston!

HOWARD   (*hard, keeping himself under control*)   I've got a line of people to see this morning. Sit down, take five minutes, and pull yourself together, and then go home, will ya? I need the office, Willy. (*He starts to go, turns, remembering the recorder, starts to push off the table holding the recorder*) Oh, yeah. Whenever you can this week, stop by and drop off the samples. You'll feel better, Willy, and then come back and we'll talk. Pull yourself together, kid, there's people outside.

HOWARD *exits, pushing the table off left.* WILLY *stares into space, exhausted. Now the music is heard—*BEN's *music—first distantly, then closer, closer. As* WILLY *speaks,* BEN *enters from the right. He carries valise and umbrella.*

WILLY   Oh, Ben, how did you do it? What is the answer? Did you wind up the Alaska deal already?

BEN   Doesn't take much time if you know what you're doing. Just a short business trip. Boarding ship in an hour. Wanted to say good-by.

WILLY   Ben, I've got to talk to you.

BEN   (*glancing at his watch*)   Haven't the time, William.

WILLY   (*crossing the apron to* BEN)   Ben, nothing's working out. I don't know what to do.

BEN   Now, look here, William. I've bought timberland in Alaska and I need a man to look after things for me.

WILLY   God, timberland! Me and my boys in those grand outdoors!

BEN   You've a new continent at your doorstep, William. Get out of these cities, they're full of talk and time payments and courts of law. Screw on your fists and you can fight for a fortune up there.

WILLY   Yes, yes! Linda, Linda!

LINDA *enters as of old, with the wash.*

LINDA   Oh, you're back?

BEN   I haven't much time.

WILLY   No, wait! Linda, he's got a proposition for me in Alaska.

LINDA   But you've got—(*To* BEN) He's got a beautiful job here.

WILLY   But in Alaska, kid, I could—

LINDA   You're doing well enough, Willy!

BEN   (*to* LINDA)   Enough for what, my dear?

LINDA   (*frightened of* BEN *and angry at him*)   Don't say those things to him! Enough to be happy right here, right now. (*To* WILLY, *while* BEN *laughs*) Why must everybody conquer the world? You're well liked, and the boys love you, and someday— (*to* BEN)—why, old man Wagner told him just the other day that if he keeps it up he'll be a member of the firm, didn't he, Willy?

WILLY   Sure, sure. I am building something with this firm, Ben, and if a man is building something he must be on the right track, mustn't he?

BEN   What are you building? Lay your hand on it. Where is it?

WILLY   (*hesitantly*)   That's true, Linda, there's nothing.

LINDA   Why? (*To* BEN) There's a man eighty-four years old—

WILLY   That's right, Ben, that's right. When I look at that man I say, what is there to worry about?

BEN   Bah!

WILLY   It's true, Ben. All he has to do is go into any city, pick up the phone, and he's making his living and you know why?

BEN   (*picking up his valise*)   I've got to go.

WILLY   (*holding* BEN *back*)   Look at this boy!

BIFF, *in his high school sweater, enters carrying suitcase.* HAPPY *carries* BIFF's *shoulder guards, gold helmet, and football pants.*

WILLY   Without a penny to his name, three great universities are begging for him, and from there the sky's the limit, because it's not what you do, Ben. It's who you know and the smile on your face! It's contacts, Ben, contacts! The whole wealth of Alaska passes over the lunch table at the Commodore Hotel, and that's the wonder, the wonder of this country, that a man can end with diamonds here on the basis of being liked! (*He turns to* BIFF) And that's why when you get out on that field today it's important. Because thousands of people will be rooting for you and loving you. (*To* BEN, *who has again begun to leave*) And Ben! when he walks into a business office his name will sound out like a bell and all the doors will open to him! I've seen it, Ben, I've seen it a thousand times! You can't feel it with your hand like timber, but it's there!

BEN   Good-by, William.

WILLY Ben, am I right? Don't you think I'm right? I value your advice.

BEN There's a new continent at your doorstep, William. You could walk out rich. Rich! (*He is gone*)

WILLY We'll do it here, Ben! You hear me? We're gonna do it here!

Young BERNARD *rushes in. The gay music of the Boys is heard.*

BERNARD Oh, gee, I was afraid you left already!

WILLY Why? What time is it?

BERNARD It's half-past one!

WILLY Well, come on, everybody! Ebbets Field next stop! Where's the pennants? (*He rushes through the wall-line of the kitchen and out into the living-room*)

LINDA (*to* BIFF) Did you pack fresh underwear?

BIFF (*who has been limbering up*) I want to go!

BERNARD Biff, I'm carrying your helmet, ain't I?

HAPPY No, I'm carrying the helmet.

BERNARD Oh, Biff, you promised me.

HAPPY I'm carrying the helmet.

BERNARD How am I going to get in the locker room?

LINDA Let him carry the shoulder guards. (*She puts her coat and hat on in the kitchen*)

BERNARD Can I, Biff? 'Cause I told everybody I'm going to be in the locker room.

HAPPY In Ebbets Field it's the clubhouse.

BERNARD I meant the clubhouse. Biff!

HAPPY Biff!

BIFF (*grandly, after a slight pause*) Let him carry the shoulder guards.

HAPPY (*as he gives* BERNARD *the shoulder guards*) Stay close to us now.

WILLY *rushes in with the pennants.*

WILLY (*handing them out*) Everybody wave when Biff comes out on the field. (HAPPY *and* BERNARD *run off*) You set now, boy?

The music has died away.

BIFF Ready to go, Pop. Every muscle is ready.

WILLY (*at the edge of the apron*) You realize what this means?

BIFF That's right, Pop.

WILLY (*feeling* BIFF'S *muscles*) You're comin' home this afternoon captain of the All-Scholastic Championship Team of the City of New York.

BIFF I got it, Pop. And remember, pal, when I take off my helmet, that touchdown is for you.

WILLY Let's go! (*He is starting out, with his arm around* BIFF, *when* CHARLEY *enters, as of old, in knickers*) I got no room for you, Charley.

CHARLEY Room? For what?

WILLY In the car.

CHARLEY You goin' for a ride? I wanted to shoot some casino.

WILLY (*furiously*) Casino! (*Incredulously*) Don't you realize what today is?

LINDA Oh, he knows, Willy. He's just kidding you.

WILLY That's nothing to kid about!

CHARLEY No, Linda, what's goin' on?

LINDA He's playing in Ebbets Field.

CHARLEY Baseball in this weather?

WILLY Don't talk to him. Come on, come on! (*He is pushing them out*)

CHARLEY Wait a minute, didn't you hear the news?

WILLY What?

CHARLEY Don't you listen to the radio? Ebbets Field just blew up.

WILLY You go to hell! (CHARLEY *laughs*) (*Pushing them out*) Come on, come on! We're late.

CHARLEY (*as they go*) Knock a homer, Biff, knock a homer!

WILLY (*the last to leave, turning to* CHARLEY) I don't think that was funny, Charley. This is the greatest day of his life.

CHARLEY Willy, when are you going to grow up?

WILLY Yeah, heh? When this game is over, Charley, you'll be laughing out of the other side of your face. They'll be calling him another Red Grange. Twenty-five thousand a year.

CHARLEY (*kidding*) Is that so?

WILLY Yeah, that's so.

CHARLEY Well, then, I'm sorry. Willy. But tell me something.

WILLY What?

CHARLEY Who is Red Grange?

WILLY Put up your hands. Goddam you, put up your hands!

CHARLEY, *chuckling, shakes his head and walks away, around the left corner of the stage.* WILLY *follows him. The music rises to a mocking frenzy.*

WILLY Who the hell do you think you are, better than everybody else? You don't know everything, you big, ignorant, stupid . . . Put up your hands!

Light rises, on the right side of the forestage, on a small table in the reception room of CHARLEY's *office. Traffic sounds are heard.* BERNARD, *now mature, sits whistling to himself. A pair of tennis rackets and an overnight bag are on the floor beside him.*

WILLY (*offstage*)   What are you walking away for? Don't walk away! If you're going to say something say it to my face! I know you laugh at me behind my back. You'll laugh out of the other side of your goddam face after this game. Touchdown! Touchdown! Eighty thousand people! Touchdown! Right between the goal posts.

BERNARD *is a quiet, earnest, but self-assured young man.* WILLY's *voice is coming from right upstage now.* BERNARD *lowers his feet off the table and listens.* JENNY, *his father's secretary, enters.*

JENNY (*distressed*)   Say, Bernard, will you go out in the hall?
BERNARD   What is that noise? Who is it?
JENNY   Mr. Loman. He just got off the elevator.
BERNARD (*getting up*)   Who's he arguing with?
JENNY   Nobody. There's nobody with him. I can't deal with him any more, and your father gets all upset everytime he comes. I've got a lot of typing to do, and your father's waiting to sign it. Will you see him?
WILLY (*entering*)   Touchdown! Touch—(*He sees* JENNY) Jenny, Jenny, good to see you. How're ya? Working'? Or still honest?
JENNY   Fine. How've you been feeling?
WILLY   Not much any more, Jenny. Ha, ha! (*He is surprised to see the rackets*)
BERNARD   Hello, Uncle Willy.
WILLY (*almost shocked*)   Bernard! Well, look who's here! (*He comes quickly, guiltily, to* BERNARD *and warmly shakes his hand*)
BERNARD   How are you? Good to see you.
WILLY   What are you doing here?
BERNARD   Oh, just stopped by to see Pop. Get off my feet till my train leaves. I'm going to Washington in a few minutes.
WILLY   Is he in?
BERNARD   Yes, he's in his office with the accountant. Sit down.
WILLY (*sitting down*)   What're you going to do in Washington?
BERNARD   Oh, just a case I've got there, Willy.
WILLY   That so? (*Indicating the rackets*) You going to play tennis there?
BERNARD   I'm staying with a friend who's got a court.
WILLY   Don't say. His own tennis court. Must be fine people, I bet.
BERNARD   They are, very nice. Dad tells me Biff's in town.
WILLY (*with a big smile*)   Yeah, Biff's in. Working on a very big deal, Bernard.

BERNARD   What's Biff doing?

WILLY   Well, he's been doing very big things in the West. But he decided to establish himself here. Very big. We've having dinner. Did I hear your wife had a boy?

BERNARD   That's right. Our second.

WILLY   Two boys! What do you know!

BERNARD   What kind of a deal has Biff got?

WILLY   Well, Bill Oliver—very big sporting-goods man—he wants Biff very badly. Called him in from the West. Long distance, carte blanche, special deliveries. Your friends have their own private tennis court?

BERNARD   You still with the old firm, Willy?

WILLY   (*after a pause*)   I'm—I'm overjoyed to see how you made the grade, Bernard, overjoyed. It's an encouraging thing to see a young man really—really— Looks very good for Biff—very— (*He breaks off, then*) Bernard—(*He is so full of emotion, he breaks off again*)

BERNARD   What is it, Willy?

WILLY   (*small and alone*)   What—what's the secret?

BERNARD   What secret?

WILLY   How—how did you? Why didn't he ever catch on?

BERNARD   I wouldn't know that, Willy.

WILLY   (*confidentially, desperately*)   You were his friend, his boyhood friend. There's something I don't understand about it. His life ended after that Ebbets Field game. From the age of seventeen nothing good ever happened to him.

BERNARD   He never trained himself for anything.

WILLY   But he did, he did. After high school he took so many correspondence courses. Radio mechanics; television; God knows what, and never made the slightest mark.

BERNARD   (*taking off his glasses*)   Willy, do you want to talk candidly?

WILLY   (*rising, faces* BERNARD)   I regard you as a very brilliant man, Bernard. I value your advice.

BERNARD   Oh, the hell with the advice, Willy. I couldn't advise you. There's just one thing I've always wanted to ask you. When he was supposed to graduate, and the math teacher flunked him—

WILLY   Oh, that son-of-a-bitch ruined his life.

BERNARD   Yeah, but, Willy, all he had to do was go to summer school and make up that subject.

WILLY   That's right, that's right.

BERNARD   Did you tell him not to go to summer school?

WILLY   Me? I begged him to go. I ordered him to go!

BERNARD Then why wouldn't he go?

WILLY Why? Why! Bernard, that question has been trailing me like a ghost for the last fifteen years. He flunked the subject, and laid down and died like a hammer hit him!

BERNARD Take it easy, kid.

WILLY Let me talk to you—I got nobody to talk to. Bernard, Bernard, was it my fault? Y'see? It keeps going around in my mind, maybe I did something to him. I got nothing to give him.

BERNARD Don't take it so hard.

WILLY Why did he lay down? What is the story there? You were his friend!

BERNARD Willy, I remember, it was June, and our grades came out. And he'd flunked math.

WILLY That son-of-a-bitch!

BERNARD No, it wasn't right then. Biff just got very angry, I remember, and he was ready to enroll in summer school.

WILLY *(surprised)* He was?

BERNARD He wasn't beaten by it at all. But then, Willy, he disappeared from the block for almost a month. And I got the idea that he'd gone up to New England to see you. Did he have a talk with you then?

WILLY *stares in silence.*

BERNARD Willy?

WILLY *(with a strong edge of resentment in his voice)* Yeah, he came to Boston. What about it?

BERNARD Well, just that when he came back—I'll never forget this, it always mystifies me. Because I'd thought so well of Biff, even though he'd always taken advantage of me. I loved him, Willy, y'know? And he came back after that month and took his sneakers—remember those sneakers with "University of Virginia" printed on them? He was so proud of those, wore them every day. And he took them down in the cellar, and burned them up in the furnace. We had a fist fight. It lasted at least half an hour. Just the two of us, punching each other down the cellar, and crying right through it. I've often thought of how strange it was that I knew he'd given up his life. What happened in Boston, Willy?

WILLY *looks at him as at an intruder.*

BERNARD I just bring it up because you asked me.

WILLY *(angrily)* Nothing. What do you mean, "What happened?" What's that got to do with anything?

BERNARD Well, don't get sore.

WILLY What are you trying to do, blame it on me? If a boy lays down is that my fault?

BERNARD Now, Willy, don't get—

WILLY Well, don't—don't talk to me that way! What does that mean, "What happened?"

CHARLEY *enters. He is in his vest, and he carries a bottle of bourbon.*

CHARLEY Hey, you're going to miss that train. (*He waves the bottle*)

BERNARD Yeah, I'm going. (*He takes the bottle*) Thanks, Pop. (*He picks up his rackets and bag*) Good-by, Willy, and don't worry about it. You know, "If at first you don't succeed . . ."

WILLY Yes, I believe in that.

BERNARD But sometimes, Willy, it's better for a man just to walk away.

WILLY Walk away?

BERNARD That's right.

WILLY But if you can't walk away?

BERNARD (*after a slight pause*) I guess that's when it's tough. (*Extending his hand*) Good-by, Willy.

WILLY (*shaking* BERNARD's *hand*) Good-by, boy.

CHARLEY (*an arm on* BERNARD's *shoulder*) How do you like this kid? Gonna argue a case in front of the Supreme Court.

BERNARD (*protesting*) Pop!

WILLY (*genuinely shocked, pained, and happy*) No! The Supreme Court!

BERNARD I gotta run. 'By, Dad!

CHARLEY Knock 'em dead, Bernard!

BERNARD *goes off.*

WILLY (*as* CHARLEY *takes out his wallet*) The Supreme Court! And he didn't even mention it!

CHARLEY (*counting out money on the desk*) He don't have to— he's gonna do it.

WILLY And you never told him what to do, did you? You never took any interest in him.

CHARLEY My salvation is that I never took any interest in anything. There's some money—fifty dollars. I got an accountant inside.

WILLY Charley, look . . . (*With difficulty*) I got my insurance to pay. If you can manage it—I need a hundred and ten dollars.

CHARLEY *doesn't reply for a moment; merely stops moving.*

WILLY   I'd draw it from my bank but Linda would know, and
I . . .

CHARLEY   Sit down, Willy.

WILLY   (*moving toward the chair*)   I'm keeping an account of
everything, remember. I'll pay every penny back. (*He sits*)

CHARLEY   Now listen to me, Willy.

WILLY   I want you to know I appreciate . . .

CHARLEY   (*sitting down on the table*)   Willy, what're you doin'?
What the hell is goin' on in your head?

WILLY   Why? I'm simply . . .

CHARLEY   I offered you a job. You can make fifty dollars a week.
And I won't send you on the road.

WILLY   I've got a job.

CHARLEY   Without pay? What kind of a job is a job without pay?
(*He rises*)   Now, look, kid, enough is enough. I'm no genius but
I know when I'm being insulted.

WILLY   Insulted!

CHARLEY   Why don't you want to work for me?

WILLY   What's the matter with you? I've got a job.

CHARLEY   Then what're you walkin' in here every week for?

WILLY   (*getting up*)   Well, if you don't want me to walk in here—

CHARLEY   I am offering you a job.

WILLY   I don't want your goddam job!

CHARLEY   When the hell are you going to grow up?

WILLY   (*furiously*)   You big ignoramus, if you say that to me again
I'll rap you one! I don't care how big you are! (*He's ready to
fight*)

Pause.

CHARLEY   (*kindly, going to him*)   How much do you need, Willy?

WILLY   Charley, I'm strapped. I'm strapped. I don't know what to
do. I was just fired.

CHARLEY   Howard fired you?

WILLY   That snotnose. Imagine that? I named him. I named him
Howard.

CHARLEY   Willy, when're you gonna realize that them things don't
mean anything? You named him Howard, but you can't sell that.
The only thing you got in this world is what you can sell. And
the funny thing is that you're a salesman, and you don't know
that.

WILLY   I've always tried to think otherwise, I guess. I always felt
that if a man was impressive, and well liked, that nothing—

CHARLEY   Why must everybody like you? Who liked J. P. Morgan?

Was he impressive? In a Turkish bath he'd look like a butcher. But with his pockets on he was very well liked. Now listen, Willy, I know you don't like me, and nobody can say I'm in love with you, but I'll give you a job because—just for the hell of it, put it that way. Now what do you say?

WILLY   I—I just can't work for you, Charley.

CHARLEY   What're you, jealous of me?

WILLY   I can't work for you, that's all, don't ask me why.

CHARLEY   (*angered, takes out more bills*)   You been jealous of me all your life, you damned fool! Here, pay your insurance. (*He puts the money in* WILLY's *hand*)

WILLY   I'm keeping strict accounts.

CHARLEY   I've got some work to do. Take care of yourself. And pay your insurance.

WILLY   (*moving to the right*)   Funny, y'know? After all the highways, and the trains, and the appointments, and the years, you end up worth more dead than alive.

CHARLEY   Willy, nobody's worth nothin' dead. (*After a slight pause*)   Did you hear what I said?

WILLY *stands still, dreaming.*

CHARLEY   Willy!

WILLY   Apologize to Bernard for me when you see him. I didn't mean to argue with him. He's a fine boy. They're all fine boys, and they'll end up big—all of them. Someday they'll all play tennis together. Wish me luck, Charley. He saw Bill Oliver today.

CHARLEY   Good luck.

WILLY   (*on the verge of tears*)   Charley, you're the only friend I got. Isn't that a remarkable thing? (*He goes out*)

CHARLEY   Jesus!

CHARLEY *stares after him a moment and follows. All light blacks out. Suddenly raucous music is heard, and a red glow rises behind the screen at right.* STANLEY, *a young waiter, appears, carrying a table, followed by* HAPPY, *who is carrying two chairs.*

STANLEY   (*putting the table down*)   That's all right, Mr. Loman, I can handle it myself. (*He turns and takes the chairs from* HAPPY *and places them at the table*)

HAPPY   (*glancing around*)   Oh, this is better.

STANLEY   Sure, in the front there you're in the middle of all kinds a noise. Whenever you got a party, Mr. Loman, you just tell me and I'll put you back here. Y'know, there's a lotta people they don't like it private, because when they go out they like to see a lotta action around them because they're sick and tired to stay in the house by theirself. But I know you, you ain't from Hackensack. You know what I mean?

HAPPY (*sitting down*)   So how's it coming, Stanley?

STANLEY   Ah, it's a dog's life. I only wish during the war they'd a took me in the Army. I coulda been dead by now.

HAPPY   My brother's back, Stanley.

STANLEY   Oh, he come back, heh? From the Far West.

HAPPY   Yeah, big cattle man, my brother, so treat him right. And my father's coming too.

STANLEY   Oh, your father too!

HAPPY   You got a couple of nice lobsters?

STANLEY   Hundred per cent, big.

HAPPY   I want them with the claws.

STANLEY   Don't worry, I don't give you no mice. (HAPPY *laughs*) How about some wine? It'll put a head on the meal.

HAPPY   No. You remember, Stanley, that recipe I brought you from overseas? With the champagne in it?

STANLEY   Oh, yeah, sure. I still got it tacked up yet in the kitchen. But that'll have to cost a buck apiece anyways.

HAPPY   That's all right.

STANLEY   What'd you, hit a number or somethin'?

HAPPY   No, it's a little celebration. My brother is—I think he pulled off a big deal today. I think we're going into business together.

STANLEY   Great! That's the best for you. Because a family business, you know what I mean?—that's the best.

HAPPY   That's what I think.

STANLEY   'Cause what's the difference? Somebody steals? It's in the family. Know what I mean? (*Sotto voce*) Like this bartender here. The boss is goin' crazy what kinda leak he's got in the cash register. You put it in but it don't come out.

HAPPY (*raising his head*)   Sh!

STANLEY   What?

HAPPY   You notice I wasn't lookin' right or left, was I?

STANLEY   No.

HAPPY   And my eyes are closed.

STANLEY   So what's the—?

HAPPY   Strudel's comin'.

STANLEY (*catching on, looks around*)   Ah, no, there's no—

He breaks off as a furred, lavishly dressed girl enters and sits at the next table. Both follow her with their eyes.

STANLEY   Geez, how'd ya know?

HAPPY   I got radar or something. (*Staring directly at her profile*) Oooooooo . . . Stanley.

STANLEY   I think that's for you, Mr. Loman.

HAPPY   Look at that mouth. Oh, God. And the binoculars.

STANLEY   Geez, you got a life, Mr. Loman.

HAPPY   Wait on her.

STANLEY   (*going to the* GIRL's *table*)   Would you like a menu, ma'am?

GIRL   I'm expecting someone, but I'd like a—

HAPPY   Why don't you bring her—excuse me, miss, do you mind? I sell champagne, and I'd like you to try my brand. Bring her a champagne, Stanley.

GIRL   That's awfully nice of you.

HAPPY   Don't mention it. It's all company money. (*He laughs*)

GIRL   That's a charming product to be selling, isn't it?

HAPPY   Oh, gets to be like everything else. Selling is selling, y'know.

GIRL   I suppose.

HAPPY   You don't happen to sell, do you?

GIRL   No, I don't sell.

HAPPY   Would you object to a compliment from a stranger? You ought to be on a magazine cover.

GIRL   (*looking at him a little archly*)   I have been.

STANLEY *comes in with a glass of champagne.*

HAPPY   What'd I say before, Stanley? You see? She's a cover girl.

STANLEY   Oh, I could see, I could see.

HAPPY   (*to the* GIRL)   What magazine?

GIRL   Oh, a lot of them. (*She takes the drink*) Thank you.

HAPPY   You know what they say in France, don't you? "Champagne is the drink of the complexion"—Hya, Biff!

BIFF *has entered and sits with* HAPPY.

BIFF   Hello, kid. Sorry I'm late.

HAPPY   I just got here. Uh, Miss—?

GIRL   Forsythe.

HAPPY   Miss Forsythe, this is my brother.

BIFF   Is Dad here?

HAPPY   His name is Biff. You might've heard of him. Great football player.

GIRL   Really? What team?

HAPPY   Are you familiar with football?

GIRL   No, I'm afraid I'm not.

HAPPY   Biff is quarterback with the New York Giants.

GIRL   Well, that is nice, isn't it? (*She drinks*)

HAPPY   Good health.

GIRL   I'm happy to meet you.

HAPPY   That's my name. Hap. It's really Harold, but at West Point they called me Happy.

GIRL (*now really impressed*)   Oh, I see. How do you do? (*She turns her profile*)

BIFF   Isn't Dad coming?

HAPPY   You want her?

BIFF   Oh, I could never make that.

HAPPY   I remember the time that idea would never come into your head. Where's the old confidence, Biff?

BIFF   I just saw Oliver—

HAPPY   Wait a minute. I've got to see that old confidence again. Do you want her? She's on call.

BIFF   Oh, no. (*He turns to look at the* GIRL)

HAPPY   I'm telling you. Watch this. (*Turning to the* GIRL) Honey? (*She turns to him*) Are you busy?

GIRL   Well, I am . . . but I could make a phone call.

HAPPY   Do that, will you, honey? And see if you can get a friend. We'll be here for a while. Biff is one of the greatest football players in the country.

GIRL (*standing up*)   Well, I'm certainly happy to meet you.

HAPPY   Come back soon.

GIRL   I'll try.

HAPPY   Don't try, honey, try hard.

The GIRL *exits.* STANLEY *follows, shaking his head in bewildered admiration.*

HAPPY   Isn't that a shame now? A beautiful girl like that? That's why I can't get married. There's not a good woman in a thousand. New York is loaded with them, kid!

BIFF   Hap, look—

HAPPY   I told you she was on call!

BIFF (*strangely unnerved*)   Cut it out, will ya? I want to say something to you.

HAPPY   Did you see Oliver?

BIFF   I saw him all right. Now look, I want to tell Dad a couple of things and I want you to help me.

HAPPY   What? Is he going to back you?

BIFF   Are you crazy? You're out of your goddam head, you know that?

HAPPY   Why? What happened?

BIFF   (*breathlessly*)   I did a terrible thing today, Hap. It's been the strangest day I ever went through. I'm all numb, I swear.

HAPPY   You mean he wouldn't see you?

BIFF   Well, I waited six hours for him, see? All day. Kept sending my name in. Even tried to date his secretary so she'd get me to him, but no soap.

HAPPY   Because you're not showin' the old confidence, Biff. He remembered you, didn't he?

BIFF   (*stopping* HAPPY *with a gesture*)   Finally, about five o'clock, he comes out. Didn't remember who I was or anything. I felt like such an idiot, Hap.

HAPPY   Did you tell him my Florida idea?

BIFF   He walked away. I saw him for one minute. I got so mad I could've torn the walls down! How the hell did I ever get the idea I was a salesman there? I even believed myself that I'd been a salesman for him! And then he gave me one look and— I realized what a ridiculous lie my whole life has been! We've been talking in a dream of fifteen years. I was a shipping clerk.

HAPPY   What'd you do?

BIFF   (*with great tension and wonder*)   Well, he left, see. And the secretary went out. I was all alone in the waiting-room. I don't know what came over me, Hap. The next thing I know I'm in his office—paneled walls, everything. I can't explain it. I—Hap, I took his fountain pen.

HAPPY   Geez, did he catch you?

BIFF   I ran out. I ran down all eleven flights. I ran and ran and ran.

HAPPY   That was an awful dumb—what'd you do that for?

BIFF   (*agonized*)   I don't know, I just—wanted to take something, I don't know. You gotta help me, Hap. I'm gonna tell Pop.

HAPPY   You crazy? What for?

BIFF   Hap, he's got to understand that I'm not the man somebody lends that kind of money to. He thinks I've been spiting him all these years and it's eating him up.

HAPPY   That's just it. You tell him something nice.

BIFF   I can't.

HAPPY   Say you got a lunch date with Oliver tomorrow.

BIFF   So what do I do tomorrow?

HAPPY   You leave the house tomorrow and come back at night and say Oliver is thinking it over. And he thinks it over for a couple of weeks, and gradually it fades away and nobody's the worse.

BIFF But it'll go on forever!

HAPPY Dad is never so happy as when he's looking forward to something!

WILLY *enters.*

HAPPY Hello, scout!

WILLY Gee, I haven't been here in years!

STANLEY *has followed* WILLY *in and sets a chair for him.* STANLEY *starts off but* HAPPY *stops him.*

HAPPY Stanley!

STANLEY *stands by, waiting for an order.*

BIFF *(going to* WILLY *with guilt, as to an invalid)* Sit down, Pop. You want a drink?

WILLY Sure, I don't mind.

BIFF Let's get a load on.

WILLY You look worried.

BIFF N-no. *(To* STANLEY*)* Scotch all around. Make it doubles.

STANLEY Doubles, right. *(He goes)*

WILLY You had a couple already, didn't you?

BIFF Just a couple, yeah.

WILLY Well, what happened, boy? *(Nodding affirmatively, with a smile)* Everything go all right?

BIFF *(takes a breath, then reaches out and grasps* WILLY's *hand)* Pal . . . *(He is smiling bravely, and* WILLY *is smiling too)* I had an experience today.

HAPPY Terrific, Pop.

WILLY That so? What happened?

BIFF *(high, slightly alcoholic, above the earth)* I'm going to tell you everything from first to last. It's been a strange day. *(Silence. He looks around, composes himself as best he can, but his breath keeps breaking the rhythm of his voice)* I had to wait quite a while for him, and—

WILLY Oliver?

BIFF Yeah, Oliver. All day, as a matter of cold fact. And a lot of —instances—facts, Pop, facts about my life came back to me. Who was it, Pop? Who ever said I was a salesman with Oliver?

WILLY Well, you were.

BIFF No, Dad, I was a shipping clerk.

WILLY But you were practically—

BIFF *(with determination)* Dad, I don't know who said it first, but I was never a salesman for Bill Oliver.

WILLY What're you talking about?

BIFF   Let's hold on to the facts tonight, Pop. We're not going to get anywhere bullin' around. I was a shipping clerk.

WILLY   (*angrily*)   All right, now listen to me—

BIFF   Why don't you let me finish?

WILLY   I'm not interested in stories about the past or any crap of that kind because the woods are burning, boys, you understand? There's a big blaze going on all around. I was fired today.

BIFF   (*shocked*)   How could you be?

WILLY   I was fired, and I'm looking for a little good news to tell your mother, because the woman has waited and the woman has suffered. The gift of it is that I haven't got a story left in my head, Biff. So don't give me a lecture about facts and aspects. I am not interested. Now what've you got to say to me?

STANLEY *enters with three drinks. They wait until he leaves.*

WILLY   Did you see Oliver?

BIFF   Jesus, Dad!

WILLY   You mean you didn't go up there?

HAPPY   Sure he went up there.

BIFF   I did. I—saw him. How could they fire you?

WILLY   (*on the edge of his chair*)   What kind of a welcome did he give you?

BIFF   He won't even let you work on commission?

WILLY   I'm out! (*Driving*)   So tell me, he gave you a warm welcome?

HAPPY   Sure, Pop, sure!

BIFF   (*driven*)   Well, it was kind of—

WILLY   I was wondering if he'd remember you. (*To* HAPPY) Imagine, man doesn't see him for ten, twelve years and gives him that kind of a welcome!

HAPPY   Damn right!

BIFF   (*trying to return to the offensive*)   Pop, look—

WILLY   You know why he remembered you, don't you? Because you impressed him in those days.

BIFF   Let's talk quietly and get this down to the facts, huh?

WILLY   (*as though* BIFF *had been interrupting*)   Well, what happened? It's great news, Biff. Did he take you into his office or'd you talk in the waiting-room?

BIFF   Well, he came in, see, and—

WILLY   (*with a big smile*)   What'd he say? Betcha he threw his arm around you.

BIFF   Well, he kinda—

WILLY   He's a fine man. (*To* HAPPY) Very hard man to see, y'know.

HAPPY (*agreeing*)   Oh, I know.

WILLY (*to* BIFF)   Is that where you had the drinks?

BIFF   Yeah, he gave me a couple of—no, no!

HAPPY (*cutting in*)   He told him my Florida idea.

WILLY   Don't interrupt. (*To* BIFF) How'd he react to the Florida idea?

BIFF   Dad, will you give me a minute to explain?

WILLY   I've been waiting for you to explain since I sat down here! What happened? He took you into his office and what?

BIFF   Well—I talked. And—and he listened, see.

WILLY   Famous for the way he listens, y'know. What was his answer?

BIFF   His answer was—(*He breaks off, suddenly angry*) Dad, you're not letting me tell you what I want to tell you!

WILLY (*accusing, angered*)   You didn't see him, did you?

BIFF   I did see him!

WILLY   What'd you insult him or something? You insulted him, didn't you?

BIFF   Listen, will you let me out of it, will you just let me out of it!

HAPPY   What the hell!

WILLY   Tell me what happened!

BIFF (*to* HAPPY)   I can't talk to him!

A single trumpet note jars the ear. The light of green leaves stains the house, which holds the air of night and a dream. Young BERNARD *enters and knocks on the door of the house.*

YOUNG BERNARD (*frantically*)   Mrs. Loman, Mrs. Loman!

HAPPY   Tell him what happened!

BIFF (*to* HAPPY)   Shut up and leave me alone!

WILLY   No, no! You had to go and flunk math!

BIFF   What math? What're you talking about?

YOUNG BERNARD   Mrs. Loman, Mrs. Loman!

LINDA *appears in the house, as of old.*

WILLY (*wildly*)   Math, math, math!

BIFF   Take it easy, Pop!

YOUNG BERNARD   Mrs. Loman!

WILLY (*furiously*)   If you hadn't flunked you'd've been set by now!

BIFF   Now, look, I'm gonna tell you what happened, and you're going to listen to me.

YOUNG BERNARD   Mrs. Loman!

BIFF   I waited six hours—

HAPPY   What the hell are you saying?

BIFF   I kept sending in my name but he wouldn't see me. So finally he ... (*He continues unheard as light fades low on the restaurant*)

YOUNG BERNARD   Biff flunked math!

LINDA   No!

YOUNG BERNARD   Birnbaum flunked him! They won't graduate him!

LINDA   But they have to. He's gotta go to the university. Where is he? Biff! Biff!

YOUNG BERNARD   No, he left. He went to Grand Central.

LINDA   Grand— You mean he went to Boston!

YOUNG BERNARD   Is Uncle Willy in Boston?

LINDA   Oh, maybe Willy can talk to the teacher. Oh, the poor, poor boy!

Light on house area snaps out.

BIFF   (*at the table, now audible, holding up a gold fountain pen*) ... so I'm washed up with Oliver, you understand? Are you listening to me?

WILLY   (*at a loss*)   Yeah, sure. If you hadn't flunked—

BIFF   Flunked what? What're you talking about?

WILLY   Don't blame everything on me! I didn't flunk math—you did! What pen?

HAPPY   That was awful dumb, Biff, a pen like that is worth—

WILLY   (*seeing the pen for the first time*)   You took Oliver's pen?

BIFF   (*weakening*)   Dad, I just explained it to you.

WILLY   You stole Bill Oliver's fountain pen!

BIFF   I didn't exactly steal it! That's just what I've been explaining to you!

HAPPY   He had it in his hand and just then Oliver walked in, so he got nervous and stuck it in his pocket!

WILLY   My God, Biff!

BIFF   I never intended to do it, Dad!

OPERATOR'S VOICE   Standish Arms, good evening!

WILLY   (*shouting*)   I'm not in my room!

BIFF   (*frightened*)   Dad, what's the matter? (*He and HAPPY stand up*)

OPERATOR   Ringing Mr. Loman for you!

WILLY   I'm not there, stop it!

BIFF   (*horrified, gets down on one knee before WILLY*)   Dad, I'll make good, I'll make good. (*WILLY tries to get to his feet. BIFF holds him down*) Sit down now.

WILLY   No, you're no good, you're no good for anything.

BIFF   I am, Dad, I'll find something else, you understand? Now don't worry about anything. (*He holds up* WILLY's *face*) Talk to me, Dad.

OPERATOR   Mr. Loman does not answer. Shall I page him?

WILLY   (*attempting to stand, as though to rush and silence the Operator*)   No, no, no!

HAPPY   He'll strike something, Pop.

WILLY   No, no . . .

BIFF   (*desperately, standing over* WILLY)   Pop, listen! Listen to me! I'm telling you something good. Oliver talked to his partner about the Florida idea. You listening? He—he talked to his partner, and he came to me . . . I'm going to be all right, you hear? Dad, listen to me, he said it was just a question of the amount!

WILLY   Then you . . . got it?

HAPPY   He's gonna be terrific, Pop!

WILLY   (*trying to stand*)   Then you got it, haven't you? You got it! You got it!

BIFF   (*agonized, holds* WILLY *down*)   No, no. Look, Pop. I'm supposed to have lunch with them tomorrow. I'm just telling you this so you'll know that I can still make an impression, Pop. And I'll make good somewhere, but I can't go tomorrow, see?

WILLY   Why not? You simply—

BIFF   But the pen, Pop!

WILLY   You give it to him and tell him it was an oversight!

HAPPY   Sure, have lunch tomorrow!

BIFF   I can't say that—

WILLY   You were doing a crossword puzzle and accidentally used his pen!

BIFF   Listen, kid, I took those balls years ago, now I walk in with his fountain pen? That clinches it, don't you see? I can't face him like that! I'll try elsewhere.

PAGE's VOICE   Paging Mr. Loman!

WILLY   Don't you want to be anything?

BIFF   Pop, how can I go back?

WILLY   You don't want to be anything, is that what's behind it?

BIFF   (*now angry at* WILLY *for not crediting his sympathy*)   Don't take it that way! You think it was easy walking into that office after what I'd done to him? A team of horses couldn't have dragged me back to Bill Oliver!

WILLY   Then why'd you go?

BIFF   Why did I go? Why did I go! Look at you! Look at what's become of you!

Off left, THE WOMAN *laughs.*

WILLY   Biff, you're going to go to that lunch tomorrow, or—
BIFF   I can't go. I've got no appointment!
HAPPY   Biff, for ...!
WILLY   Are you spiting me?
BIFF   Don't take it that way! Goddammit!
WILLY   (*strikes* BIFF *and falters away from the table*)   You rotten little louse! Are you spiting me?
THE WOMAN   Someone's at the door, Willy!
BIFF   I'm no good, can't you see what I am?
HAPPY   (*separating them*)   Hey, you're in a restaurant! Now cut it out, both of you! (*The girls enter*) Hello, girls, sit down.

THE WOMAN *laughs, off left.*

MISS FORSYTHE   I guess we might as well. This is Letta.
THE WOMAN   Willy, are you going to wake up?
BIFF   (*ignoring* WILLY)   How're ya, miss, sit down. What do you drink?
MISS FORSYTHE   Letta might not be able to stay long.
LETTA   I gotta get up very early tomorrow. I got jury duty. I'm so excited! Were you fellows ever on a jury?
BIFF   No, but I been in front of them! (*The girls laugh*)   This is my father.
LETTA   Isn't he cute? Sit down with us, Pop.
HAPPY   Sit him down, Biff!
BIFF   (*going to him*)   Come on, slugger, drink us under the table. To hell with it! Come on, sit down, pal.

On BIFF's *last insistence,* WILLY *is about to sit.*

THE WOMAN   (*now urgently*)   Willy, are you going to answer the door!

THE WOMAN's *call pulls* WILLY *back. He starts right, befuddled.*

BIFF   Hey, where are you going?
WILLY   Open the door.
BIFF   The door?
WILLY   The washroom ... the door ... where's the door?
BIFF   (*leading* WILLY *to the left*)   Just go straight down.

WILLY *moves left.*

THE WOMAN   Willy, Willy, are you going to get up, get up, get up, get up?

WILLY *exits left.*

LETTA I think it's sweet you bring your daddy along.

MISS FORSYTHE Oh, he isn't really your father!

BIFF (*at left, turning to her resentfully*) Miss Forsythe, you've just seen a prince walk by. A fine, troubled prince. A hard-working, unappreciated prince. A pal, you understand? A good companion. Always for his boys.

LETTA That's so sweet.

HAPPY Well, girls, what's the program? We're wasting time. Come on, Biff. Gather round. Where would you like to go?

BIFF Why don't you do something for him?

HAPPY Me!

BIFF Don't you give a damn for him, Hap?

HAPPY What're you talking about? I'm the one who—

BIFF I sense it, you don't give a good goddam about him. (*He takes the rolled-up hose from his pocket and puts it on the table in front of* HAPPY) Look what I found in the cellar, for Christ's sake. How can you bear to let it go on?

HAPPY Me? Who goes away? Who runs off and—

BIFF Yeah, but he doesn't mean anything to you. You could help him—I can't! Don't you understand what I'm talking about? He's going to kill himself, don't you know that?

HAPPY Don't I know it! Me!

BIFF Hap, help him! Jesus . . . help him . . . Help me, help me, I can't bear to look at his face! (*Ready to weep, he hurries out, up right*)

HAPPY (*starting after him*) Where are you going?

MISS FORSYTHE What's he so mad about?

HAPPY Come on, girls, we'll catch up with him.

MISS FORSYTHE (*as* HAPPY *pushes her out*) Say, I don't like that temper of his!

HAPPY He's just a little overstrung, he'll be all right!

WILLY (*off left, as* THE WOMAN *laughs*) Don't answer! Don't answer!

LETTA Don't you want to tell your father—

HAPPY No, that's not my father. He's just a guy. Come on, we'll catch Biff, and, honey, we're going to paint this town! Stanley, where's the check! Hey, Stanley!

They exit. STANLEY *looks toward left.*

STANLEY (*calling to* HAPPY *indignantly*) Mr. Loman! Mr. Loman!

STANLEY *picks up a chair and follows them off. Knocking is heard off left.*

The Woman enters, laughing. Willy follows her. She is in a black slip; he is buttoning his shirt. Raw, sensuous music accompanies their speech.

WILLY   Will you stop laughing? Will you stop?

THE WOMAN   Aren't you going to answer the door? He'll wake the whole hotel.

WILLY   I'm not expecting anybody.

THE WOMAN   Whyn't you have another drink, honey, and stop being so damn self-centered?

WILLY   I'm so lonely.

THE WOMAN   You know you ruined me, Willy? From now on, whenever you come to the office, I'll see that you go right through to the buyers. No waiting at my desk any more, Willy. You ruined me.

WILLY   That's nice of you to say that.

THE WOMAN   Gee, you are self-centered! Why so sad? You are the saddest, self-centeredest soul I ever did see-saw. (*She laughs. He kisses her*) Come on inside, drummer boy. It's silly to be dressing in the middle of the night. (*As knocking is heard*) Aren't you going to answer the door?

WILLY   They're knocking on the wrong door.

THE WOMAN   But I felt the knocking. And he heard us talking in here. Maybe the hotel's on fire!

WILLY   (*his terror rising*)   It's a mistake.

THE WOMAN   Then tell him to go away!

WILLY   There's nobody there.

THE WOMAN   It's getting on my nerves, Willy. There's somebody standing out there and it's getting on my nerves!

WILLY   (*pushing her away from him*)   All right, stay in the bathroom here, and don't come out. I think there's a law in Massachusetts about it, so don't come out. It may be that new room clerk. He looked very mean. So don't come out. It's a mistake, there no fire.

The knocking is heard again. He takes a few steps away from her, and she vanishes into the wing. The light follows him, and now he is facing Young Biff, who carries a suitcase. Biff steps toward him. The music is gone.

BIFF   Why didn't you answer?

WILLY   Biff! What are you doing in Boston?

BIFF   Why didn't you answer? I've been knocking for five minutes, I called you on the phone—

WILLY   I just heard you. I was in the bathroom and had the door shut. Did anything happen home?

BIFF   Dad—I let you down.

WILLY   What do you mean?

BIFF   Dad . . .

WILLY   Biffo, what's this about? (*Putting his arm around* BIFF)
Come on, let's go downstairs and get you a malted.

BIFF   Dad, I flunked math.

WILLY   Not for the term?

BIFF   The term. I haven't got enough credits to graduate.

WILLY   You mean to say Bernard wouldn't give you the answers?

BIFF   He did, he tried, but I only got a sixty-one.

WILLY   And they wouldn't give you four points?

BIFF   Birnbaum refused absolutely. I begged him, Pop, but he
won't give me those points. You gotta talk to him before they
close the school. Because if he saw the kind of man you are, and
you just talked to him in your way, I'm sure he'd come through
for me. The class came right before practice, see, and I didn't go
enough. Would you talk to him? He'd like you, Pop. You know
the way you could talk.

WILLY   You're on. We'll drive right back.

BIFF   Oh, Dad, good work! I'm sure he'll change it for you!

WILLY   Go downstairs and tell the clerk I'm checkin' out. Go right
down.

BIFF   Yes, sir! See, the reason he hates me, Pop—one day he was
late for class so I got up at the blackboard and imitated him. I
crossed my eyes and talked with a lithp.

WILLY   (*laughing*)   You did? The kids like it?

BIFF   They nearly died laughing!

WILLY   Yeah? What'd you do?

BIFF   The thquare root of thixty twee is . . . (WILLY *bursts out
laughing;* BIFF *joins him*) And in the middle of it he walked in!

WILLY *laughs and* THE WOMAN *joins in offstage.*

WILLY   (*without hesitation*)   Hurry downstairs and—

BIFF   Somebody in there?

WILLY   No, that was next door.

THE WOMAN *laughs offstage.*

BIFF   Somebody got in your bathroom!

WILLY   No, it's the next room, there's a party—

THE WOMAN   (*enters, laughing. She lisps this*)   Can I come in?
There's something in the bathtub, Willy, and it's moving!

WILLY *looks at* BIFF, *who is staring open-mouthed and horrified at* THE
WOMAN.

WILLY   Ah—you better go back to your room. They must be finished painting by now. They're painting her room so I let her
take a shower here. Go back, go back ... (*He pushes her*)

THE WOMAN (*resisting*)   But I've got to get dressed, Willy, I
can't—

WILLY   Get out of here! Go back, go back ... (*Suddenly striving
for the ordinary*) This is Miss Francis, Biff, she's a buyer. They're
painting her room. Go back, Miss Francis, go back ...

THE WOMAN   But my clothes, I can't go out naked in the hall!

WILLY (*pushing her offstage*)   Get outa here! Go back, go back!

BIFF *slowly sits down on his suitcase as the argument continues offstage.*

THE WOMAN   Where's my stockings? You promised me stockings,
Willy!

WILLY   I have no stockings here!

THE WOMAN   You had two boxes of size nine sheers for me, and I
want them!

WILLY   Here, for God's sake, will you get outa here!

THE WOMAN (*enters holding a box of stockings*)   I just hope there's
nobody in the hall. That's all I hope. (*To* BIFF) Are you football
or baseball?

BIFF   Football.

THE WOMAN (*angry, humiliated*)   That's me too. G'night. (*She
snatches her clothes from* WILLY, *and walks out*)

WILLY (*after a pause*)   Well, better get going. I want to get to the
school first thing in the morning. Get my suits out of the closet.
I'll get my valise. (BIFF *doesn't move*) What's the matter? (BIFF
remains motionless, tears falling) She's a buyer. Buys for J. H.
Simmons. She lives down the hall—they're painting. You don't
imagine—(*He breaks off. After a pause*) Now listen, pal, she's
just a buyer. She sees merchandise in her room and they have to
keep it looking just so ... (*Pause. Assuming command*) All right,
get my suits. (BIFF *doesn't move*) Now stop crying and do as I
say. I gave you an order. Biff, I gave you an order! Is that what
you do when I give you an order? How dare you cry! (*Putting
his arm around* BIFF) Now look, Biff, when you grow up you'll
understand about these things. You mustn't—you mustn't over-
emphasize a thing like this. I'll see Birnbaum first thing in the
morning.

BIFF   Never mind.

WILLY (*getting down beside* BIFF)   Never mind! He's going to give
you those points. I'll see to it.

BIFF   He wouldn't listen to you.

WILLY He certainly will listen to me. You need those points for the U. of Virginia.

BIFF I'm not going there.

WILLY Heh? If I can't get him to change that mark you'll make it up in summer school. You've got all summer to—

BIFF (*his weeping breaking from him*) Dad . . .

WILLY (*infected by it*) Oh, my boy . . .

BIFF Dad . . .

WILLY She's nothing to me, Biff. I was lonely, I was terribly lonely.

BIFF You—you gave her Mama's stockings! (*His tears break through and he rises to go*)

WILLY (*grabbing for* BIFF) I gave you an order!

BIFF Don't touch me, you—liar!

WILLY Apologize for that!

BIFF You fake! You phony little fake! You fake! (*Overcome, he turns quickly and weeping fully goes out with his suitcase.* WILLY *is left on the floor on his knees*)

WILLY I gave you an order! Biff, come back here or I'll beat you! Come back here! I'll whip you!

STANLEY *comes quickly in from the right and stands in front of* WILLY.

WILLY (*shouts at* STANLEY) I gave you an order . . .

STANLEY Hey, let's pick it up, pick it up, Mr. Loman. (*He helps* WILLY *to his feet*) Your boys left with the chippies. They said they'll see you home.

A second WAITER *watches some distance away.*

WILLY But we were supposed to have dinner together.

Music is heard, WILLY's *theme.*

STANLEY Can you make it?

WILLY I'll—sure, I can make it. (*Suddenly concerned about his clothes*) Do I—I look all right?

STANLEY Sure, you look all right. (*He flicks a speck off* WILLY's *lapel*)

WILLY Here—here's a dollar.

STANLEY Oh, your son paid me. It's all right.

WILLY (*putting it in* STANLEY's *hand*) No, take it. You're a good boy.

STANLEY Oh, no, you don't have to . . .

WILLY Here—here's some more, I don't need it any more. (*After a slight pause*) Tell me—is there a seed store in the neighborhood?

STANLEY   Seeds? You mean like to plant?

As WILLY *turns,* STANLEY *slips the money back into his jacket pocket.*

WILLY   Yes. Carrots, peas...

STANLEY   Well, there's hardware stores on Sixth Avenue, but it may be too late now.

WILLY (*anxiously*)   Oh, I'd better hurry. I've got to get some seeds. (*He starts off to the right*) I've got to get some seeds, right away. Nothing's planted. I don't have a thing in the ground.

WILLY *hurries out as the light goes down.* STANLEY *moves over to the right after him, watches him off. The other* WAITER *has been staring at* WILLY.

STANLEY (*to the* WAITER)   Well, whatta you looking at?

The WAITER *picks up the chairs and moves off right.* STANLEY *takes the table and follows him. The light fades on this area. There is a long pause, the sound of the flute coming over. The light gradually rises on the kitchen, which is empty.* HAPPY *appears at the door of the house, followed by* BIFF. HAPPY *is carrying a large bunch of long-stemmed roses. He enters the kitchen, looks around for* LINDA. *Not seeing her, he turns to* BIFF, *who is just outside the house door, and makes a gesture with his hands, indicating "Not here, I guess." He looks into the living-room and freezes. Inside,* LINDA, *unseen, is seated,* WILLY's *coat on her lap. She rises ominously and quietly and moves toward* HAPPY, *who backs up into the kitchen, afraid.*

HAPPY   Hey, what're you doing up? (LINDA *says nothing but moves toward him implacably*) Where's Pop? (*He keeps backing to the right, and now* LINDA *is in full view in the doorway to the living-room*) Is he sleeping?

LINDA   Where were you?

HAPPY (*trying to laugh it off*)   We met two girls, Mom, very fine types. Here, we brought you some flowers. (*Offering them to her*) Put them in your room, Ma.

She knocks them to the floor at BIFF's *feet. He has now come inside and closed the door behind him. She stares at* BIFF, *silent.*

HAPPY   Now what'd you do that for? Mom, I want you to have some flowers—

LINDA (*cutting* HAPPY *off, violently to* BIFF)   Don't you care whether he lives or dies?

HAPPY (*going to the stairs*)   Come upstairs, Biff.

BIFF (*with a flare of disgust, to* HAPPY)   Go away from me! (*To* LINDA) What do you mean, lives or dies? Nobody's dying around here, pal.

LINDA   Get out of my sight! Get out of here!

BIFF   I wanna see the boss.

LINDA   You're not going near him!

BIFF   Where is he? (*He moves into the living-room and* LINDA *follows*)

LINDA   (*shouting after* BIFF)   You invite him for dinner. He looks forward to it all day—(BIFF *appears in his parents' bedroom, looks around, and exits*)—and then you desert him there. There's no stranger you'd do that to!

HAPPY   Why? He had a swell time with us. Listen, when I— (LINDA *comes back into the kitchen*)—desert him I hope I don't outlive the day!

LINDA   Get out of here!

HAPPY   Now look, Mom . . .

LINDA   Did you have to go to women tonight? You and your lousy rotten whores!

BIFF *re-enters the kitchen.*

HAPPY   Mom, all we did was follow Biff around trying to cheer him up! (*To* BIFF) Boy, what a night you gave me!

LINDA   Get out of here, both of you, and don't come back! I don't want you tormenting him any more. Go on now, get your things together! (*To* BIFF) You can sleep in his apartment. (*She starts to pick up the flowers and stops herself*) Pick up this stuff, I'm not your maid any more. Pick it up, you bum, you!

HAPPY *turns his back to her in refusal.* BIFF *slowly moves over and gets down on his knees, picking up the flowers.*

LINDA   You're a pair of animals! Not one, not another living soul would have had the cruelty to walk out on that man in a restaurant!

BIFF   (*not looking at her*)   Is that what he said?

LINDA   He didn't have to say anything. He was so humiliated he nearly limped when he came in.

HAPPY   But, Mom, he had a great time with us—

BIFF   (*cutting him off violently*)   Shut up!

Without another word, HAPPY *goes upstairs.*

LINDA   You! You didn't even go in to see if he was all right!

BIFF   (*still on the floor in front of* LINDA, *the flowers in his hand; with self-loathing*)   No. Didn't. Didn't do a damned thing. How do you like that, heh? Left him babbling in a toilet.

LINDA   You louse. You . . .

BIFF   Now you hit it on the nose! (*He gets up, throws the flowers in the wastebasket*) The scum of the earth, and you're looking at him!

LINDA   Get out of here!

BIFF   I gotta talk to the boss, Mom. Where is he?

LINDA   You're not going near him. Get out of this house!

BIFF   (*with absolute assurance, determination*)   No. We're gonna have an abrupt conversation, him and me.

LINDA   You're not talking to him!

Hammering is heard from outside the house, off right. BIFF *turns toward the noise.*

LINDA   (*suddenly pleading*)   Will you please leave him alone?

BIFF   What's he doing out there?

LINDA   He's planting the garden!

BIFF   (*quietly*)   Now? Oh, my God!

BIFF *moves outside,* LINDA *following. The light dies down on them and comes up on the center of the apron as* WILLY *walks into it. He is carrying a flashlight, a hoe, and a handful of seed packets. He raps the top of the hoe sharply to fix it firmly, and then moves to the left, measuring off the distance with his foot. He holds the flashlight to look at the seed packets, reading off the instructions. He is in the blue of night.*

WILLY   Carrots . . . quarter-inch apart. Rows . . . one-foot rows. (*He measures it off*) One foot. (*He puts down a package and measures off*) Beets. (*He puts down another package and measures again*) Lettuce. (*He reads the package, puts it down*) One foot— (*He breaks off as* BEN *appears at the right and moves slowly down to him*) What a proposition, ts, ts. Terrific, terrific. 'Cause she's suffered, Ben, the woman has suffered. You understand me? A man can't go out the way he came in, Ben, a man has got to add up to something. You can't, you can't—(BEN *moves toward him as though to interrupt*) You gotta consider, now. Don't answer so quick. Remember, it's a guaranteed twenty-thousand-dollar proposition. Now look, Ben, I want you to go through the ins and outs of this thing with me. I've got nobody to talk to, Ben, and the woman has suffered, you hear me?

BEN   (*standing still, considering*)   What's the proposition?

WILLY   It's twenty thousand dollars on the barrelhead. Guaranteed, gilt-edged, you understand?

BEN   You don't want to make a fool of yourself. They might not honor the policy.

WILLY   How can they dare refuse? Didn't I work like a coolie to

meet every premium on the nose? And now they don't pay off?
Impossible!

BEN It's called a cowardly thing, William.

WILLY Why? Does it take more guts to stand here the rest of my
life ringing up a zero?

BEN (*yielding*) That's a point, William. (*He moves, thinking,
turns*) And twenty thousand—that *is* something one can feel with
the hand, it is there.

WILLY (*now assured, with rising power*) Oh, Ben, that's the whole
beauty of it! I see it like a diamond, shining in the dark, hard
and rough, that I can pick up and touch in my hand. Not like—
like an appointment! This would not be another damned-fool appointment, Ben, and it changes all the aspects. Because he thinks
I'm nothing, see, and so he spites me. But the funeral— (*Straightening up*) Ben, that funeral will be massive! They'll come from
Maine, Massachusetts, Vermont, New Hampshire! All the old-
timers with the strange license plates—that boy will be thunderstruck, Ben, because he never realized—I am known! Rhode
Island, New York, New Jersey—I am known, Ben, and he'll see
it with his eyes once and for all. He'll see what I am, Ben! He's
in for a shock, that boy!

BEN (*coming down to the edge of the garden*) He'll call you a
coward.

WILLY (*suddenly fearful*) No, that would be terrible.

BEN Yes. And a damned fool.

WILLY No, no, he mustn't, I won't have that! (*He is broken and
desperate*)

BEN He'll hate you, William.

The gay music of the Boys is heard.

WILLY Oh, Ben, how do we get back to all the great times? Used
to be so full of light, and comradeship, the sleigh-riding in winter, and the ruddiness on his cheeks. And always some kind of
good news coming up, always something nice coming up ahead.
And never even let me carry the valises in the house, and simonizing, simonizing that little red car! Why, why can't I give him
something and not have him hate me?

BEN Let me think about it. (*He glances at his watch*) I still have
a little time. Remarkable proposition, but you've got to be sure
you're not making a fool of yourself.

BEN *drifts off upstage and goes out of sight.* BIFF *comes down from the
left.*

WILLY (*suddenly conscious of* BIFF, *turns and looks up at him, then begins picking up the packages of seeds in confusion*)   Where the hell is that seed? (*Indignantly*) You can't see nothing out here! They boxed in the whole goddam neighborhood!

BIFF   There are people all around here. Don't you realize that?

WILLY   I'm busy. Don't bother me.

BIFF   (*taking the hoe from* WILLY)   I'm saying good-by to you, Pop. (WILLY *looks at him, silent, unable to move*) I'm not coming back any more.

WILLY   You're not going to see Oliver tomorrow?

BIFF   I've got no appointment, Dad.

WILLY   He put his arm around you, and you've got no appointment?

BIFF   Pop, get this now, will you? Everytime I've left it's been a fight that sent me out of here. Today I realized something about myself and I tried to explain it to you and I—I think I'm just not smart enough to make any sense out of it for you. To hell with whose fault it is or anything like that. (*He takes* WILLY's *arm*) Let's just wrap it up, heh? Come on in, we'll tell Mom. (*He gently tries to pull* WILLY *to left*)

WILLY   (*frozen, immobile, with guilt in his voice*)   No, I don't want to see her.

BIFF   Come on! (*He pulls again, and* WILLY *tries to pull away*)

WILLY   (*highly nervous*)   No, no, I don't want to see her.

BIFF   (*tries to look into* WILLY's *face, as if to find the answer there*)   Why don't you want to see her?

WILLY   (*more harshly now*)   Don't bother me, will you?

BIFF   What do you mean, you don't want to see her? You don't want them calling you yellow, do you? This isn't your fault; it's me, I'm a bum. Now come inside! (WILLY *strains to get away*) Did you hear what I said to you?

WILLY *pulls away and quickly goes by himself into the house.* BIFF *follows.*

LINDA   (*to* WILLY)   Did you plant, dear?

BIFF   (*at the door, to* LINDA)   All right, we had it out. I'm going and I'm not writing any more.

LINDA   (*going to* WILLY *in the kitchen*)   I think that's the best way, dear. 'Cause there's no use drawing it out, you'll just never get along.

WILLY *doesn't respond.*

BIFF   People ask where I am and what I'm doing, you don't know, and you don't care. That way it'll be off your mind and you can start brightening up again. All right? That clears it, doesn't it?

(WILLY *is silent, and* BIFF *goes to him*) You gonna wish me luck, scout? (*He extends his hand*) What do you say?

LINDA Shake his hand, Willy.

WILLY (*turning to her, seething with hurt*) There's no necessity to mention the pen at all, y'know.

BIFF (*gently*) I've got no appointment, Dad.

WILLY (*erupting fiercely*) He put his arm around . . . ?

BIFF Dad, you're never going to see what I am, so what's the use of arguing? If I strike oil I'll send you a check. Meantime forget I'm alive.

WILLY (*to* LINDA) Spite, see?

BIFF Shake hands, Dad.

WILLY Not my hand.

BIFF I was hoping not to go this way.

WILLY Well, this is the way you're going. Good-by.

BIFF *looks at him a moment, then turns sharply and goes to the stairs.*

WILLY (*stops him with*) May you rot in hell if you leave this house!

BIFF (*turning*) Exactly what is it that you want from me?

WILLY I want you to know, on the train, in the mountains, in the valleys, wherever you go, that you cut down your life for spite!

BIFF No, no.

WILLY Spite, spite, is the word of your undoing! And when you're down and out, remember what did it. When you're rotting somewhere beside the railroad tracks, remember, and don't you dare blame it on me!

BIFF I'm not blaming it on you!

WILLY I won't take the rap for this, you hear?

HAPPY *comes down the stairs and stands on the bottom step, watching.*

BIFF That's just what I'm telling you!

WILLY (*sinking into a chair at the table, with full accusation*) You're trying to put a knife in me—don't think I don't know what you're doing!

BIFF All right, phony! Then let's lay it on the line. (*He whips the rubber tube out of his pocket and puts it on the table*)

HAPPY You crazy—

LINDA Biff! (*She moves to grab the hose, but* BIFF *holds it down with his hand*)

BIFF Leave it there! Don't move it!

WILLY (*not looking at it*) What is that?

BIFF You know goddam well what that is.

WILLY (*caged, wanting to escape*) I never saw that.

BIFF You saw it. The mice didn't bring it into the cellar! What is this supposed to do, make a hero out of you? This supposed to make me sorry for you?

WILLY Never heard of it.

BIFF There'll be no pity for you, you hear it? No pity!

WILLY (*to* LINDA) You hear the spite!

BIFF No, you're going to hear the truth—what you are and what I am!

LINDA Stop it!

WILLY Spite!

HAPPY (*coming down toward* BIFF) You cut it now!

BIFF (*to* HAPPY) The man don't know who we are! The man is gonna know! (*To* WILLY) We never told the truth for ten minutes in this house!

HAPPY We always told the truth!

BIFF (*turning on him*) You big blow, are you the assistant buyer? You're one of the two assistants to the assistant, aren't you?

HAPPY Well, I'm practically—

BIFF You're practically full of it! We all are! And I'm through with it. (*To* WILLY) Now hear this, Willy, this is me.

WILLY I know you!

BIFF You know why I had no address for three months? I stole a suit in Kansas City and I was in jail. (*To* LINDA, *who is sobbing*) Stop crying. I'm through with it.

LINDA *turns away from them, her hands covering her face.*

WILLY I suppose that's my fault!

BIFF I stole myself out of every good job since high school!

WILLY And whose fault is that?

BIFF And I never got anywhere because you blew me so full of hot air I could never stand taking orders from anybody! That's whose fault it is!

WILLY I hear that!

LINDA Don't, Biff!

BIFF It's goddam time you heard that! I had to be boss big shot in two weeks, and I'm through with it!

WILLY Then hang yourself! For spite, hang yourself!

BIFF No! Nobody's hanging himself, Willy! I ran down eleven flights with a pen in my hand today. And suddenly I stopped, you hear me? And in the middle of that office building, do you hear this? I stopped in the middle of that building and I saw—the sky. I saw the things that I love in this world. The work and the food and time to sit and smoke. And I looked at the pen and said to myself, what the hell am I grabbing this for? Why am I trying to become what I don't want to be? What am I doing in an office, making a contemptuous, begging fool of myself, when all I want is out there, waiting for me the minute I say I know who I am! Why can't I say that, Willy? (*He tries to make* WILLY *face him, but* WILLY *pulls away and moves to the left*)

WILLY (*with hatred, threateningly*) The door of your life is wide open!

BIFF Pop! I'm a dime a dozen, and so are you!

WILLY (*turning on him now in an uncontrolled outburst*) I am not a dime a dozen! I am Willy Loman, and you are Biff Loman!

BIFF *starts for* WILLY, *but is blocked by* HAPPY. *In his fury,* BIFF *seems on the verge of attacking his* FATHER.

BIFF I am not a leader of men, Willy, and neither are you. You were never anything but a hard-working drummer who landed in the ash can like all the rest of them! I'm one dollar an hour, Willy! I tried seven states and couldn't raise it. A buck an hour! Do you gather my meaning? I'm not bringing home any prizes any more, and you're going to stop waiting for me to bring them home!

WILLY (*directly to* BIFF) You vengeful, spiteful mut!

BIFF *breaks from* HAPPY. WILLY, *in fright, starts up the stairs.* BIFF *grabs him.*

BIFF (*at the peak of his fury*) Pop, I'm nothing! I'm nothing, Pop. Can't you understand that? There's no spite in it any more. I'm just what I am, that's all.

BIFF's *fury has spent itself, and he breaks down, sobbing, holding on to* WILLY, *who dumbly fumbles for* BIFF's *face.*

WILLY (*astonished*) What're you doing? What're you doing? (*To* LINDA) Why is he crying?

BIFF (*crying, broken*) Will you let me go, for Christ's sake? Will you take that phony dream and burn it before something happens? (*Struggling to contain himself, he pulls away and moves to the stairs*) I'll go in the morning. Put him—put him to bed. (*Exhausted,* BIFF *moves up the stairs to his room*)

WILLY (*after a long pause, astonished, elevated*) Isn't that—isn't that remarkable? Biff—he likes me!

LINDA He loves you, Willy!

HAPPY (*deeply moved*) Always did, Pop.

WILLY Oh, Biff! (*Staring wildly*) He cried! Cried to me. (*He is choking with his love, and now cries out his promise*) That boy —that boy is going to be magnificent!

BEN *appears in the light just outside the kitchen.*

BEN   Yes, outstanding, with twenty thousand behind him.

LINDA (*sensing the racing of his mind, fearfully, carefully*)   Now come to bed, Willy. It's all settled now.

WILLY (*finding it difficult not to rush out of the house*)   Yes, we'll sleep. Come on. Go to sleep, Hap.

BEN   And it does take a great kind of a man to crack the jungle.

In accents of dread, BEN'S *idyllic music starts up.*

HAPPY (*his arm around* LINDA)   I'm getting married, Pop, don't forget it. I'm changing everything. I'm gonna run that department before the year is up. You'll see, Mom. (*He kisses her*)

BEN   The jungle is dark but full of diamonds, Willy.

WILLY *turns, moves, listening to* BEN.

LINDA   Be good. You're both good boys, just act that way, that's all.

HAPPY   'Night, Pop. (*He goes upstairs*)

LINDA (*to* WILLY)   Come, dear.

BEN (*with greater force*)   One must go in to fetch a diamond out.

WILLY (*to* LINDA, *as he moves slowly along the edge of the kitchen, toward the door*)   I just want to get settled down, Linda. Let me sit alone for a little.

LINDA (*almost uttering her fear*)   I want you upstairs.

WILLY (*taking her in his arms*)   In a few minutes, Linda. I couldn't sleep right now. Go on, you look awful tired. (*He kisses her*)

BEN   Not like an appointment at all. A diamond is rough and hard to the touch.

WILLY   Go on now. I'll be right up.

LINDA   I think this is the only way, Willy.

WILLY   Sure, it's the best thing.

BEN   Best thing!

WILLY   The only way. Everything is gonna be—go on, kid, get to bed. You look so tired.

LINDA   Come right up.

WILLY   Two minutes.

LINDA *goes into the living-room, then reappears in her bedroom.* WILLY *moves just outside the kitchen door.*

WILLY   Loves me. (*Wonderingly*)   Always loved me. Isn't that a remarkable thing? Ben, he'll worship me for it!

BEN (*with promise*)   It's dark there, but full of diamonds.

WILLY Can you imagine that magnificence with twenty thousand dollars in his pocket?

LINDA (*calling from her room*) Willy! Come up!

WILLY (*calling into the kitchen*) Yes! Yes. Coming! It's very smart, you realize that, don't you, sweetheart? Even Ben sees it. I gotta go, baby. 'By! 'By! (*Going over to* BEN, *almost dancing*) Imagine? When the mail comes he'll be ahead of Bernard again!

BEN A perfect proposition all around.

WILLY Did you see how he cried to me? Oh, if I could kiss him, Ben!

BEN Time, William, time!

WILLY Oh, Ben, I always knew one way or another we were gonna make it, Biff and I!

BEN (*looking at his watch*) The boat. We'll be late. (*He moves slowly off into the darkness*)

WILLY (*elegiacally, turning to the house*) Now when you kick off, boy, I want a seventy-yard boot, and get right down the field under the ball, and when you hit, hit low and hit hard, because it's important, boy. (*He swings around and faces the audience*) There's all kinds of important people in the stands, and the first thing you know ... (*Suddenly realizing he is alone*) Ben! Ben, where do I ... ? (*He makes a sudden movement of search*) Ben, how do I ... ?

LINDA (*calling*) Willy, you coming up?

WILLY (*uttering a gasp of fear, whirling about as if to quiet her*) Sh! (*He turns around as if to find his way; sounds, faces, voices, seem to be swarming in upon him and he flicks at them, crying*) Sh! Sh! (*Suddenly music, faint and high, stops him. It rises in intensity, almost to an unbearable scream. He goes up and down on his toes, and rushes off around the house*) Shhh!

LINDA Willy?

There is no answer. LINDA *waits.* BIFF *gets up off his bed. He is still in his clothes.* HAPPY *sits up.* BIFF *stands listening.*

LINDA (*with real fear*) Willy, answer me! Willy!

There is the sound of a car starting and moving away at full speed.

LINDA No!

BIFF (*rushing down the stairs*) Pop!

As the car speeds off, the music crashes down in a frenzy of sound, which becomes the soft pulsation of a single cello string. BIFF *slowly returns to his bedroom. He and* HAPPY *gravely don their jackets.* LINDA *slowly walks out of her room. The music has developed into a dead march. The leaves of day are appearing over everything.* CHARLEY *and* BERNARD, *somberly dressed, appear and knock on the kitchen door.* BIFF *and* HAPPY *slowly descend the stairs to the kitchen as* CHARLEY *and* BERNARD *enter. All stop a moment when* LINDA, *in clothes of mourning, bearing a little bunch of roses, comes through the draped doorway into the kitchen. She goes to* CHARLEY *and takes his arm. Now all move toward the audience, through the wall-line of the kitchen. At the limit of the apron,* LINDA *lays down the flowers, kneels, and sits back on her heels. All stare down at the grave.*

REQUIEM

CHARLEY   It's getting dark, Linda.

LINDA *doesn't react. She stares at the grave.*

BIFF   How about it, Mom? Better get some rest, heh? They'll be closing the gate soon.

LINDA *makes no move. Pause.*

HAPPY *(deeply angered)*   He had no right to do that. There was no necessity for it. We would've helped him.

CHARLEY *(grunting)*   Hmmm.

BIFF   Come along, Mom.

LINDA   Why didn't anybody come?

CHARLEY   It was a very nice funeral.

LINDA   But where are all the people he knew? Maybe they blame him.

CHARLEY   Naa. It's a rough world, Linda. They wouldn't blame him.

LINDA   I can't understand it. At this time especially. First time in thirty-five years we were just about free and clear. He only needed a little salary. He was even finished with the dentist.

CHARLEY   No man only needs a little salary.

LINDA   I can't understand it.

BIFF   There were a lot of nice days. When he'd come home from a trip; or on Sundays, making the stoop; finishing the cellar; putting on the new porch; when he built the extra bathroom; and put up the garage. You know something, Charley, there's more of him in that front stoop than in all the sales he ever made.

CHARLEY   Yeah. He was a happy man with a batch of cement.

LINDA   He was so wonderful with his hands.

BIFF   He had the wrong dreams. All, all, wrong.

HAPPY *(almost ready to fight* BIFF)   Don't say that!

BIFF   He never knew who he was.

CHARLEY *(stopping* HAPPY's *movement and reply. To* BIFF)   No-body dast blame this man. You don't understand: Willy was a salesman. And for a salesman, there is no rock bottom to the life. He don't put a bolt to a nut, he don't tell you the law or give you medicine. He's a man way out there in the blue, riding on a smile and a shoeshine. And when they start not smiling back—that's an earthquake. And then you get yourself a couple of spots on your hat, and you're finished. Nobody dast blame this man. A salesman is got to dream, boy. It comes with the territory.

BIFF Charley, the man didn't know who he was.

HAPPY (*infuriated*) Don't say that!

BIFF Why don't you come with me, Happy?

HAPPY I'm not licked that easily. I'm staying right in this city, and I'm gonna beat this racket! (*He looks at* BIFF, *his chin set*) The Loman Brothers!

BIFF I know who I am, kid.

HAPPY All right, boy. I'm gonna show you and everybody else that Willy Loman did not die in vain. He had a good dream. It's the only dream you can have—to come out number-one man. He fought it out here, and this is where I'm gonna win it for him.

BIFF (*with a hopeless glance at* HAPPY, *bends toward his mother*) Let's go, Mom.

LINDA I'll be with you in a minute. Go on, Charley. (*He hesitates*) I want to, just for a minute. I never had a chance to say good-by.

CHARLEY *moves away, followed by* HAPPY. BIFF *remains a slight distance up and left of* LINDA. *She sits there, summoning herself. The flute begins, not far away, playing behind her speech.*

LINDA Forgive me, dear. I can't cry. I don't know what it is, but I can't cry. I don't understand it. Why did you ever do that? Help me, Willy, I can't cry. It seems to me that you're just on another trip. I keep expecting you. Willy, dear, I can't cry. Why did you do it? I search and search and I search, and I can't understand it, Willy. I made the last payment on the house today. Today, dear. And there'll be nobody home. (*A sob rises in her throat*) We're free and clear. (*Sobbing more fully, released*) We're free. (BIFF *comes slowly toward her*) We're free . . . We're free . . .

BIFF *lifts her to her feet and moves out up right with her in his arms.* LINDA *sobs quietly.* BERNARD *and* CHARLEY *come together and follow them, followed by* HAPPY. *Only the music of the flute is left on the darkening stage as over the house the hard towers of the apartment buildings rise into sharp focus, and*

The Curtain Falls

THE DUMB WAITER (1957)

HAROLD PINTER (1930–   )

In his 1961 volume about contemporary drama British critic and
theatrical producer Martin Esslin coined a new phrase in the title
of his book which has stuck as a definition of a particular dramatic
style, *The Theatre of the Absurd.* Esslin's lengthy discussions of Ro-
manian Eugene Ionesco, Irish Samuel Beckett, French Jean Genet,
American Edward Albee, and British Harold Pinter include a substantial body of plays under the "absurd" rubric, and ever since
there has been debate as to precisely what the absurd is, and
whether or not all of the major and minor writers assigned by Esslin
to the genre really belong there.

Generally speaking the absurd assumes a fundamental ridiculous-
ness in the fact of being alive. Man knows, above all other creatures, that he will die and that whatever he accomplishes in his
instant of eternity is an exercise in futility. He waits endlessly for
he knows not what; he hopes endlessly for something significant to
happen, deprived of that hope, but never abandoning it. There are
unseen and uncomprehended forces at work somewhere in the dim
background, but nobody knows quite what they are or where they
come from. It is a dark and dismal view, but it is often riotously
funny. It looks at the maddening quirks of "nature" or whatever it
is that rules mankind, and it shows the often idiotic bumblings of
human creatures desperately trying to find out what is happening,
but unable to do so. The world won't stand still; things grow and
diminish not only in size, but in shape and numbers, without rea-

son. A gibberish called language seems meant for communication, but all too often that very language prevents it.

The plays of Harold Pinter, still an active dramatist, fit comfortably within Esslin's tradition of the absurd, but they also have about them an individuality of their own. Their speciality is an air of sinister suspense and undefined lurking horrors in a world almost entirely out of rational control. Tenements, suburban homes, shabby seaside hostelries are invaded by mysterious characters, mostly human but with an air of something unnatural, arriving out of nowhere, sometimes remaining unseen, who force themselves upon their hosts, control their lives, kill and kidnap on occasion, and remain forever unidentified.

In *The Dumb Waiter* Ben and Gus feel most of these Pinteresque effects. They are hoods of some kind, hit-men in the hire of some Mr. Big, amusing characters in themselves, but nothing to admire. They are obviously extremely efficient at what they do. They have now been called upon to do it again. They have made their rendezvous, but with whom? The cellar kitchen and lavatory are the depths of something. Hell? Purgatory? Or just an old basement kitchen? Who is upstairs? What prompts the senseless maddening instructions that come clattering down the dumb waiter? These men are conditioned to obey orders. Their frantic attempt to meet the idiotic requests is excruciatingly funny. It is also terribly frightening. Who is pulling the ropes, literally and figuratively? Do they know who's down below? Do they care?

The sinister forces, be they god, devil, society, or nothingness, send down the final directive. Specifics for the hit have arrived. Now the captive servers of the dumb waiter suddenly see their own horrifying involvement. What happened in the hallway? Why did it happen? As in Pirandello, who is to determine truth, reality, illusion? But Pirandello lets you have all the facts, while proving to you that facts mean nothing in determining ultimate truths. In Pinter, nobody knows the facts. Not even the audience. And most certainly, not even Pinter.

The Dumb Waiter
PINTER

SCENE: *A basement room. Two beds, flat against the back wall. A serving hatch, closed, between the beds. A door to the kitchen and lavatory, left. A door to a passage, right.*

BEN *is lying on a bed, left, reading a paper.* GUS *is sitting on a bed, right, tying his shoelaces, with difficulty. Both are dressed in shirts, trousers and braces.*
Silence.
GUS *ties his laces, rises, yawns and begins to walk slowly to the door, left. He stops, looks down, and shakes his foot.*
BEN *lowers his paper and watches him.* GUS *kneels and unties his shoe-lace and slowly takes off the shoe. He looks inside it and brings out a flattened matchbox. He shakes it and examines it. Their eyes meet.* BEN *rattles his paper and reads.* GUS *puts the matchbox in his pocket and bends down to put on his shoe. He ties his lace, with difficulty.* BEN *lowers his paper and watches him.* GUS *walks to the door, left, stops, and shakes the other foot. He kneels, unties his shoe-lace, and slowly takes off the shoe. He looks inside it and brings out a flattened cigarette packet. He shakes it and examines it. Their eyes meet.* BEN *rattles his paper and reads.* GUS *puts the packet in his pocket, bends down, puts on his shoe and ties the lace.*
He wanders off, left.
BEN *slams the paper down on the bed and glares after him. He picks up the paper and lies on his back, reading.*
Silence.
A lavatory chain is pulled twice off, left, but the lavatory does not flush.
Silence.
GUS *re-enters, left, and halts at the door, scratching his head.*
BEN *slams down the paper.*

BEN   Kaw!

He picks up the paper.

What about this? Listen to this!

He refers to the paper.

A man of eighty-seven wanted to cross the road. But there was a lot of traffic, see? He couldn't see how he was going to squeeze through. So he crawled under a lorry.
GUS   He what?

BEN   He crawled under a lorry. A stationary lorry.
GUS   No?
BEN   The lorry started and ran over him.
GUS   Go on!
BEN   That's what it says here.
GUS   Get away.
BEN   It's enough to make you want to puke, isn't it?
GUS   Who advised him to do a thing like that?
BEN   A man of eighty-seven crawling under a lorry!
GUS   It's unbelievable.
BEN   It's down here in black and white.
GUS   Incredible.

Silence.
GUS *shakes his head and exits.* BEN *lies back and reads.*
The lavatory chain is pulled once off left, but the lavatory does not flush.
BEN *whistles at an item in the paper.*
GUS *re-enters.*

   I want to ask you something.
BEN   What are you doing out there?
GUS   Well, I was just—
BEN   What about the tea?
GUS   I'm just going to make it.
BEN   Well, go on, make it.
GUS   Yes, I will. (*He sits in a chair. Ruminatively.*) He's laid on
   some very nice crockery this time, I'll say that. It's sort of striped.
   There's a white stripe.

BEN *reads.*

   It's very nice. I'll say that.

BEN *turns the page.*

   You know, sort of round the cup. Round the rim. All the rest of
   it's black, you see. Then the saucer's black, except for right in the
   middle, where the cup goes, where it's white.

BEN *reads.*

   Then the plates are the same, you see. Only they've got a black
   stripe—the plates—right across the middle. Yes, I'm quite taken
   with the crockery.
BEN   (*still reading*)   What do you want plates for? You're not going to eat.
GUS   I've brought a few biscuits.

BEN Well, you'd better eat them quick.

GUS I always bring a few biscuits. Or a pie. You know I can't drink tea without anything to eat.

BEN Well, make the tea then, will you? Time's getting on.

Gus *brings out the flattened cigarette packet and examines it.*

GUS You got any cigarettes? I think I've run out.

He throws the packet high up and leans forward to catch it.

I hope it won't be a long job, this one.

Aiming carefully, he flips the packet under his bed.

Oh, I wanted to ask you something.

BEN (*slamming his paper down*)   Kaw!

GUS What's that?

BEN A child of eight killed a cat!

GUS Get away.

BEN It's a fact. What about that, eh? A child of eight killing a cat!

GUS How did he do it?

BEN It was a girl.

GUS How did she do it?

BEN She—

He picks up the paper and studies it.

It doesn't say.

GUS Why not?

BEN Wait a minute. It just says—Her brother, aged eleven, viewed the incident from the toolshed.

GUS Go on!

BEN That's bloody ridiculous.

Pause.

GUS I bet he did it.

BEN Who?

GUS The brother.

BEN I think you're right.

Pause.

(*Slamming down the paper.*) What about that, eh? A kid of eleven killing a cat and blaming it on his little sister of eight! It's enough to—

He breaks off in disgust and seizes the paper. Gus *rises.*

GUS   What time is he getting in touch?

BEN *reads.*

What time is he getting in touch?

BEN   What's the matter with you? It could be any time. Any time.

GUS (*moves to the foot of* BEN's *bed*)   Well, I was going to ask you something.

BEN   What?

GUS   Have you noticed the time that tank takes to fill?

BEN   What tank?

GUS   In the lavatory.

BEN   No. Does it?

GUS   Terrible.

BEN   Well, what about it?

GUS   What do you think's the matter with it?

BEN   Nothing.

GUS   Nothing?

BEN   It's got a deficient ballcock, that's all.

GUS   A deficient what?

BEN   Ballcock.

GUS   No? Really?

BEN   That's what I should say.

GUS   Go on! That didn't occur to me.

GUS *wanders to his bed and presses the mattress.*

I didn't have a very restful sleep today, did you? It's not much of a bed. I could have done with another blanket too. (*He catches sight of a picture on the wall.*) Hello, what's this? (*Peering at it.*) "The First Eleven." Cricketers. You seen this, Ben?

BEN (*reading*)   What?

GUS   The first eleven.

BEN   What?

GUS   There's a photo here of the first eleven.

BEN   What first eleven?

GUS (*studying the photo*)   It doesn't say.

BEN   What about that tea?

GUS   They all look a bit old to me.

GUS *wanders downstage, looks out front, then all about the room.*

I wouldn't like to live in this dump. I wouldn't mind if you had a window, you could see what it looked like outside.

BEN   What do you want a window for?

GUS   Well, I like to have a bit of a view, Ben. It whiles away the time.

He walks about the room.

I mean, you come into a place when it's still dark, you come into a room you've never seen before, you sleep all day, you do your job, and then you go away in the night again.

Pause.

I like to get a look at the scenery. You never get the chance in this job.

BEN   You get your holidays, don't you?

GUS   Only a fortnight.

BEN   (*lowering the paper*)   You kill me. Anyone would think you're working every day. How often do we do a job? Once a week? What are you complaining about?

GUS   Yes, but we've got to be on tap though, haven't we? You can't move out of the house in case a call comes.

BEN   You know what your trouble is?

GUS   What?

BEN   You haven't got any interests.

GUS   I've got interests.

BEN   What? Tell me one of your interests.

Pause.

GUS   I've got interests.

BEN   Look at me. What have I got?

GUS   I don't know. What?

BEN   I've got my woodwork. I've got my model boats. Have you ever seen me idle? I'm never idle. I know how to occupy my time, to its best advantage. Then when a call comes, I'm ready.

GUS   Don't you ever get a bit fed up?

BEN   Fed up? What with?

Silence.

BEN *reads.* GUS *feels in the pocket of his jacket, which hangs on the bed.*

GUS   You got any cigarettes? I've run out.

The lavatory flushes off left.

There she goes.

GUS *sits on his bed.*

No, I mean, I say the crockery's good. It is. It's very nice. But that's about all I can say for this place. It's worse than the last one. Remember that last place we were in? Last time, where was it? At least there was a wireless there. No, honest. He doesn't seem to bother much about our comfort these days.

BEN   When are you going to stop jabbering?

GUS   You'd get rheumatism in a place like this, if you stay long.

BEN   We're not staying long. Make the tea, will you? We'll be on the job in a minute.

Gus picks up a small bag by his bed and brings out a packet of tea. He examines it and looks up.

GUS   Eh, I've been meaning to ask you.

BEN   What the hell is it now?

GUS   Why did you stop the car this morning, in the middle of that road?

BEN   (*lowering the paper*)   I thought you were asleep.

GUS   I was, but I woke up when you stopped. You did stop, didn't you?

Pause.

In the middle of that road. It was still dark, don't you remember? I looked out. It was all misty. I thought perhaps you wanted to kip, but you were sitting up dead straight, like you were waiting for something.

BEN   I wasn't waiting for anything.

GUS   I must have fallen asleep again. What was all that about then? Why did you stop?

BEN   (*picking up the paper*)   We were too early.

GUS   Early? (*He rises.*) What do you mean? We got the call, didn't we, saying we were to start right away. We did. We shoved out on the dot. So how could we be too early?

BEN   (*quietly*)   Who took the call, me or you?

GUS   You.

BEN   We were too early.

GUS   Too early for what?

Pause.

You mean someone had to get out before we got in?

He examines the bedclothes.

I thought these sheets didn't look too bright. I thought they ponged a bit. I was too tired to notice when I got in this morning. Eh, that's taking a bit of a liberty, isn't it? I don't want to share my bed-sheets. I told you things were going down the drain. I mean, we've always had clean sheets laid on up till now. I've noticed it.

BEN   How do you know those sheets weren't clean?

GUS   What do you mean?

BEN   How do you know they weren't clean? You've spent the whole day in them, haven't you?

GUS   What, you mean it might be my pong? (*He sniffs sheets.*) Yes. (*He sits slowly on bed.*) It could be my pong, I suppose. It's difficult to tell. I don't really know what I pong like, that's the trouble.

BEN   (*referring to the paper*)   Kaw!

GUS   Eh, Ben.

BEN   Kaw!

GUS   Ben.

BEN   What?

GUS   What town are we in? I've forgotten.

BEN   I've told you. Birmingham.

GUS   Go on!

He looks with interest about the room.

That's in the Midlands. The second biggest city in Great Britain. I'd never have guessed.

He snaps his fingers.

Eh, it's Friday today, isn't it? It'll be Saturday tomorrow.

BEN   What about it?

GUS   (*excited*)   We could go and watch the Villa.

BEN   They're playing away.

GUS   No, are they? Caarr! What a pity.

BEN   Anyway, there's no time. We've got to get straight back.

GUS   Well, we have done in the past, haven't we? Stayed over and watched a game, haven't we? For a bit of relaxation.

BEN   Things have tightened up, mate. They've tightened up.

Gus chuckles to himself.

GUS   I saw the Villa get beat in a cup tie once. Who was it against now? White shirts. It was one-all at half-time. I'll never forget it. Their opponents won by a penalty. Talk about drama. Yes, it was a disputed penalty. Disputed. They got beat two–one, anyway, because of it. You were there yourself.

BEN   Not me.

GUS   Yes, you were there. Don't you remember that disputed penalty?

BEN   No.

GUS   He went down just inside the area. Then they said he was just acting. I didn't think the other bloke touched him myself. But the referee had the ball on the spot.

BEN   Didn't touch him! What are you talking about? He laid him out flat!

GUS   Not the Villa. The Villa don't play that sort of game.

BEN   Get out of it.

Pause.

GUS   Eh, that must have been here, in Birmingham.

BEN   What must?

GUS   The Villa. That must have been here.

BEN   They were playing away.

GUS   Because you know who the other team was? It was the Spurs. It was Tottenham Hotspur.

BEN   Well, what about it?

GUS   We've never done a job in Tottenham.

BEN   How do you know?

GUS   I'd remember Tottenham.

BEN *turns on his bed to look at him.*

BEN   Don't make me laugh, will you?

BEN *turns back and reads.* GUS *yawns and speaks through his yawn.*

GUS   When's he going to get in touch?

Pause.

Yes, I'd like to see another football match. I've always been an ardent football fan. Here, what about coming to see the Spurs to-morrow?

BEN *(tonelessly)*   They're playing away.

GUS   Who are?

BEN   The Spurs.

GUS   Then they might be playing here.

BEN   Don't be silly.

GUS   If they're playing away they might be playing here. They might be playing the Villa.

BEN *(tonelessly)*   But the Villa are playing away.

Pause. An envelope slides under the door, right. GUS *sees it. He stands, looking at it.*

GUS   Ben.

BEN   Away. They're all playing away.

GUS   Ben, look here.

BEN   What?

GUS   Look.

BEN *turns his head and sees the envelope. He stands.*

BEN   What's that?
GUS   I don't know.
BEN   Where did it come from?
GUS   Under the door.
BEN   Well, what is it?
GUS   I don't know.

They stare at it.

BEN   Pick it up.
GUS   What do you mean?
BEN   Pick it up!

GUS *slowly moves towards it, bends and picks it up.*

What is it?
GUS   An envelope.
BEN   Is there anything on it?
GUS   No.
BEN   Is it sealed?
GUS   Yes.
BEN   Open it.
GUS   What?
BEN   Open it!

GUS *opens it and looks inside.*

What's in it?

GUS *empties twelve matches into his hand.*

GUS   Matches.
BEN   Matches?
GUS   Yes.
BEN   Show it to me.

GUS *passes the envelope.* BEN *examines it.*

Nothing on it. Not a word.
GUS   That's funny, isn't it?
BEN   It came under the door?
GUS   Must have done.
BEN   Well, go on.
GUS   Go on where?
BEN   Open the door and see if you can catch anyone outside.
GUS   Who, me?

BEN Go on!

Gus *stares at him, puts the matches in his pocket, goes to his bed and brings a revolver from under the pillow. He goes to the door, opens it, looks out and shuts it.*

GUS No one.

He replaces the revolver.

BEN What did you see?
GUS Nothing.
BEN They must have been pretty quick.

Gus *takes the matches from pocket and looks at them.*

GUS Well, they'll come in handy.
BEN Yes.
GUS Won't they?
BEN Yes, you're always running out, aren't you?
GUS All the time.
BEN Well, they'll come in handy then.
GUS Yes.
BEN Won't they?
GUS Yes, I could do with them. I could do with them too.
BEN You could, eh?
GUS Yes.
BEN Why?
GUS We haven't got any.
BEN Well, you've got some now, haven't you?
GUS I can light the kettle now.
BEN Yes, you're always cadging matches. How many have you got there?
GUS About a dozen.
BEN Well, don't lose them. Red too. You don't even need a box.

Gus *probes his ear with a match.*

(*Slapping his hand*). Don't waste them! Go on, go and light it.
GUS Eh?
BEN Go and light it.
GUS Light what?
BEN The kettle.
GUS You mean the gas.
BEN Who does?
GUS You do.
BEN (*his eyes narrowing*) What do you mean, I mean the gas?
GUS Well, that's what you mean, don't you? The gas.

BEN (*powerfully*)   If I say go and light the kettle I mean go and light the kettle.

GUS   How can you light a kettle?

BEN   It's a figure of speech! Light the kettle. It's a figure of speech!

GUS   I've never heard it.

BEN   Light the kettle! It's common usage!

GUS   I think you've got it wrong.

BEN (*menacing*)   What do you mean?

GUS   They say put on the kettle.

BEN (*taut*)   Who says?

They stare at each other, breathing hard.

(*Deliberately.*)   I have never in all my life heard anyone say put on the kettle.

GUS   I bet my mother used to say it.

BEN   Your mother? When did you last see your mother?

GUS   I don't know, about—

BEN   Well, what are you talking about your mother for?

They stare.

Gus, I'm not trying to be unreasonable. I'm just trying to point out something to you.

GUS   Yes, but—

BEN   Who's the senior partner here, me or you?

GUS   You.

BEN   I'm only looking after your interests, Gus. You've got to learn, mate.

GUS   Yes, but I've near heard—

BEN (*vehemently*)   Nobody says light the gas! What does the gas light?

GUS   What does the gas—?

BEN (*grabbing him with two hands by the throat, at arm's length*)   THE KETTLE, YOU FOOL!

Gus *takes the hands from his throat.*

GUS   All right, all right.

Pause.

BEN   Well, what are you waiting for?

GUS   I want to see if they light.

BEN   What?

GUS   The matches.

He takes out the flattened box and tries to strike.

No.

He throws the box under the bed.
Ben stares at him.
Gus raises his foot.

Shall I try it on here?

Ben stares. Gus strikes a match on his shoe. It lights.

Here we are.
BEN (*wearily*)   Put on the bloody kettle, for Christ's sake.

Ben goes to his bed, but, realizing what he has said, stops and half turns.
They look at each other. Gus slowly exits, left, Ben slams his paper down
on the bed and sits on it, head in hands.

GUS (*entering*)   It's going.
BEN   What?
GUS   The stove.

Gus goes to his bed and sits.

I wonder who it'll be tonight.

Silence.

Eh, I've been wanting to ask you something.
BEN (*putting his legs on the bed*)   Oh, for Christ's sake.
GUS   No. I was going to ask you something.

He rises and sits on Ben's bed.

BEN   What are you sitting on my bed for?

Gus sits.

What's the matter with you? You're always asking me questions.
What's the matter with you?
GUS   Nothing.
BEN   You never used to ask me so many damn questions. What's
come over you?
GUS   No, I was just wondering.
BEN   Stop wondering. You've got a job to do. Why don't you just
do it and shut up?
GUS   That's what I was wondering about.
BEN   What?
GUS   The job.
BEN   What job?
GUS (*tentatively*)   I thought perhaps you might know something.

Ben looks at him.

I thought perhaps you—I mean—have you got any idea—who it's going to be tonight?

BEN   Who what's going to be?

They look at each other.

GUS *(at length)*   Who it's going to be.

Silence.

BEN   Are you feeling all right?
GUS   Sure.
BEN   Go and make the tea.
GUS   Yes, sure.

GUS *exits, left,* BEN *looks after him. He then takes his revolver from under the pillow and checks it for ammunition.* GUS *re-enters.*

The gas has gone out.

BEN   Well, what about it?
GUS   There's a meter.
BEN   I haven't got any money.
GUS   Nor have I.
BEN   You'll have to wait.
GUS   What for?
BEN   For Wilson.
GUS   He might not come. He might just send a message. He doesn't always come.
BEN   Well, you'll have to do without it, won't you?
GUS   Blimey.
BEN   You'll have a cup of tea afterwards. What's the matter with you?
GUS   I like to have one before.

BEN *holds the revolver up to the light and polishes it.*

BEN   You'd better get ready anyway.
GUS   Well, I don't know, that's a bit much, you know, for my money.

He picks up a packet of tea from the bed and throws it into the bag.

I hope he's got a shilling, anyway, if he comes. He's entitled to have. After all, it's his place, he could have seen there was enough gas for a cup of tea.

BEN   What do you mean, it's his place?
GUS   Well, isn't it?
BEN   He's probably only rented it. It doesn't have to be his place.

GUS   I know it's his place. I bet the whole house is. He's not even laying on any gas now either.

GUS *sits on his bed.*

It's his place all right. Look at all the other places. You go to this address, there's a key there, there's a teapot, there's never a soul in sight—(*He pauses.*) Eh, nobody ever hears a thing, have you ever thought of that? We never get any complaints, do we, too much noise or anything like that? You never see a soul, do you?—except the bloke who comes. You ever noticed that? I wonder if the walls are sound-proof. (*He touches the wall above his bed.*) Can't tell. All you do is wait, eh? Half the time he doesn't even bother to put in an appearance, Wilson.

BEN   Why should he? He's a busy man.

GUS   (*thoughtfully*)   I find him hard to talk to, Wilson. Do you know that, Ben?

BEN   Scrub round it, will you?

Pause.

GUS   There are a number of things I want to ask him. But I can never get round to it, when I see him.

Pause.

I've been thinking about the last one.

BEN   What last one?

GUS   That girl.

BEN *grabs the paper, which he reads.*

(*Rising, looking down at* BEN). How many times have you read that paper?

BEN *slams the paper down and rises.*

BEN   (*angrily*)   What do you mean?

GUS   I was just wondering how many times you'd—

BEN   What are you doing, criticizing me?

GUS   No, I was just—

BEN   You'll get a swipe round your earhole if you don't watch your step.

GUS   Now look here, Ben—

BEN   I'm not looking anywhere! (*He addresses the room.*) How many times have I—! A bloody liberty!

GUS   I didn't mean that.

BEN   You just get on with it, mate. Get on with it, that's all.

BEN *gets back on the bed.*

GUS   I was just thinking about that girl, that's all.

GUS *sits on his bed.*

>She wasn't much to look at, I know, but still. It was a mess though, wasn't it? What a mess. Honest, I can't remember a mess like that one. They don't seem to hold together like men, women. A looser texture, like. Didn't she spread, eh? She didn't half spread. Kaw! But I've been meaning to ask you.

BEN *sits up and clenches his eyes.*

>Who clears up after we've gone? I'm curious about that. Who does the clearing up? Maybe they don't clear up. Maybe they just leave them there, eh? What do you think? How many jobs have we done? Blimey, I can't count them. What if they never clear anything up after we've gone.

BEN   (*pityingly*)   You mutt. Do you think we're the only branch of this organization? Have a bit of common. They got departments for everything.

GUS   What cleaners and all?

BEN   You birk!

GUS   No, it was that girl made me start to think—

There is a loud clatter and racket in the bulge of wall between the beds, of something descending. They grab their revolvers, jump up and face the wall. The noise comes to a stop. Silence. They look at each other. BEN gestures sharply towards the wall. GUS approaches the wall slowly. He bangs it with his revolver. It is hollow. BEN moves to the head of his bed, his revolver cocked. GUS puts his revolver on his bed and pats along the bottom of the centre panel. He finds a rim. He lifts the panel. Disclosed is a serving-hatch, a "dumb waiter." A wide box is held by pulleys. GUS peers into the box. He brings out a piece of paper.

BEN   What is it?

GUS   You have a look at it.

BEN   Read it.

GUS   (*reading*)   Two braised steak and chips. Two sago puddings. Two teas without sugar.

BEN   Let me see that. (*He takes the paper.*)

GUS   (*to himself*)   Two teas without sugar.

BEN   Mmnn.

GUS   What do you think of that?

BEN   Well—

The box goes up. BEN levels his revolver.

GUS Give us a chance! They're in a hurry, aren't they?

BEN *re-reads the note.* GUS *looks over his shoulder.*

That's a bit—that's a bit funny, isn't it?

BEN (*quickly*) No. It's not funny. It probably used to be a café here, that's all. Upstairs. These places change hands very quickly.

GUS A café?

BEN Yes.

GUS What, you mean this was the kitchen, down here?

BEN Yes, they change hands overnight, these places. Go into liquidation. The people who run it, you know, they don't find it a going concern, they move out.

GUS You mean the people who ran this place didn't find it a going concern and moved out?

BEN Sure.

GUS WELL, WHO'S GOT IT NOW?

Silence.

BEN What do you mean, who's got it now?

GUS Who's got it now? If they moved out, who moved in?

BEN Well, that all depends—

The box descends with a clatter and bang. BEN *levels his revolver.* GUS *goes to the box and brings out a piece of paper.*

GUS (*reading*) Soup of the day. Liver and onions. Jam tart.

A pause. GUS *looks at* BEN. BEN *takes the note and reads it. He walks slowly to the hatch.* GUS *follows.* BEN *looks into the hatch but not up it.* GUS *puts his hand on* BEN'S *shoulder.* BEN *throws it off.* GUS *puts his finger to his mouth. He leans on the hatch and swiftly looks up it.* BEN *flings him away in alarm.* BEN *looks at the note. He throws his revolver on the bed and speaks with decision.*

BEN We'd better send something up.

GUS Eh?

BEN We'd better send something up.

GUS Oh! Yes. Yes. Maybe you're right.

They are both relieved at the decision.

BEN (*purposefully*) Quick! What have you got in that bag?

GUS Not much.

GUS *goes to the hatch and shouts up it.*

Wait a minute!

BEN Don't do that!

GUS *examines the contents of the bag and brings them out, one by one.*

GUS   Biscuits. A bar of chocolate. Half a pint of milk.

BEN   That all?

GUS   Packet of tea.

BEN   Good.

GUS   We can't send the tea. That's all the tea we've got.

BEN   Well, there's no gas. You can't do anything with it, can you?

GUS   Maybe they can send us down a bob.

BEN   What else is there?

GUS   (*reaching into bag*)   One Eccles cake.

BEN   One Eccles cake?

GUS   Yes.

BEN   You never told me you had an Eccles cake.

GUS   Didn't I?

BEN   Why only one? Didn't you bring one for me?

GUS   I didn't think you'd be keen.

BEN   Well, you can't send up one Eccles cake, anyway.

GUS   Why not?

BEN   Fetch one of those plates.

GUS   All right.

GUS *goes towards the door, left, and stops.*

Do you mean I can keep the Eccles cake then?

BEN   Keep it?

GUS   Well, they don't know we've got it, do they?

BEN   That's not the point.

GUS   Can't I keep it?

BEN   No, you can't. Get the plate.

GUS *exits, left.* BEN *looks in the bag. He brings out a packet of crisps. Enter* GUS *with a plate.*

(*Accusingly, holding up the crisps*)   Where did these come from?

GUS   What?

BEN   Where did these crisps come from?

GUS   Where did you find them?

BEN   (*hitting him on the shoulder*)   You're playing a dirty game, my lad!

GUS   I only eat those with beer!

BEN   Well, where were you going to get the beer?

GUS   I was saving them till I did.

BEN   I'll remember this. Put everything on the plate.

They pile everything on to the plate. The box goes up without the plate.

Wait a minute!

They stand.

GUS   It's gone up.
BEN   It's all your stupid fault, playing about!
GUS   What do we do now?
BEN   We'll have to wait till it comes down.

BEN *puts the plate on the bed, puts on his shoulder holster, and starts to put on his tie.*

You'd better get ready.

GUS *goes to his bed, puts on his tie, and starts to fix his holster.*

GUS   Hey, Ben.
BEN   What?
GUS   What's going on here?

Pause.

BEN   What do you mean?
GUS   How can this be a café?
BEN   It used to be a café.
GUS   Have you seen the gas stove?
BEN   What about it?
GUS   It's only got three rings.
BEN   So what?
GUS   Well, you couldn't cook much on three rings, not for a busy place like this.
BEN   (*irritably*)   That's why the service is slow!

BEN *puts on his waistcoat.*

GUS   Yes, but what happens when we're not here? What do they do then? All these menus coming down and nothing going up. It might have been going on like this for years.

BEN *brushes his jacket.*

What happens when we go?

BEN *puts on his jacket.*

They can't do much business.

The box descends. They turn about. GUS *goes to the hatch and brings out a note.*

GUS   (*reading*)   Macaroni Pastitsio. Ormitha Macarounada.
BEN   What was that?
GUS   Macaroni Pastitsio. Ormitha Macarounada.

BEN   Greek dishes.

GUS   No.

BEN   That's right.

GUS   That's pretty high class.

BEN   Quick before it goes up.

GUS *puts the plate in the box.*

GUS   (*calling up the hatch*)   Three McVitie and Price! One Lyons Red Label! One Smith's Crisps! One Eccles cake! One Fruit and Nut!

BEN   Cadbury's.

GUS   (*up the hatch*)   Cadbury's!

BEN   (*handing the milk*)   One bottle of milk.

GUS   (*up the hatch*)   One bottle of milk! Half a pint! (*He looks at the label.*) Express Dairy! (*He puts the bottle in the box.*)

The box goes up.

Just did it.

BEN   You shouldn't shout like that.

GUS   Why not?

BEN   It isn't done.

BEN *goes to his bed.*

Well, that should be all right, anyway, for the time being.

GUS   You think so, eh?

BEN   Get dressed, will you? It'll be any minute now.

GUS *puts on his waistcoat.* BEN *lies down and looks up at the ceiling.*

GUS   This is some place. No tea and no biscuits.

BEN   Eating makes you lazy, mate. You're getting lazy, you know that? You don't want to get slack on your job.

GUS   Who me?

BEN   Slack, mate, slack.

GUS   Who me? Slack?

BEN   Have you checked your gun? You haven't even checked your gun. It looks disgraceful, anyway. Why don't you ever polish it?

GUS *rubs his revolver on the sheet.* BEN *takes out a pocket mirror and straightens his tie.*

GUS   I wonder where the cook is. They must have had a few, to cope with that. Maybe they had a few more gas stoves. Eh! Maybe there's another kitchen along the passage.

BEN   Of course there is! Do you know what it takes to make an Ormitha Macarounada?

GUS   No, what?

BEN   An Ormitha—! Buck your ideas up, will you?

GUS   Takes a few cooks, eh?

GUS *puts his revolver in its holster.*

The sooner we're out of this place the better.

He puts on his jacket.

Why doesn't he get in touch? I feel like I've been here years. (*He takes his revolver out of its holster to check the ammunition.*) We've never let him down though, have we? We've never let him down. I was thinking only the other day, Ben. We're reliable, aren't we?

He puts his revolver back in its holster.

Still, I'll be glad when it's over tonight.

He brushes his jacket.

I hope the bloke's not going to get excited tonight, or anything. I'm feeling a bit off. I've got a splitting headache.

Silence.
The box descends. BEN *jumps up.*
GUS *collects the note.*

(*Reading.*) One Bamboo Shoots, Water Chestnuts and Chicken. One Char Siu and Beansprouts.

BEN   Beansprouts?

GUS   Yes.

BEN   Blimey.

GUS   I wouldn't know where to begin.

He looks back at the box. The packet of tea is inside it. He picks it up.

They've sent back the tea.

BEN (*anxious*)   What'd they do that for?

GUS   Maybe it isn't tea-time.

The box goes up. Silence.

BEN (*throwing the tea on the bed, and speaking urgently*)   Look here. We'd better tell them.

GUS   Tell them what?

BEN   That we can't do it, we haven't got it.

GUS   All right then.

BEN   Lend us your pencil. We'll write a note.

Gus, *turning for a pencil, suddenly discovers the speaking-tube, which hangs on the right wall of the hatch facing his bed.*

GUS   What's this?
BEN   What?
GUS   This.
BEN   (*examining it*)   This? It's a speaking-tube.
GUS   How long has that been there?
BEN   Just the job. We should have used it before, instead of shouting up there.
GUS   Funny I never noticed it before.
BEN   Well, come on.
GUS   What do you do?
BEN   See that? That's a whistle.
GUS   What, this?
BEN   Yes, take it out. Pull it out.

Gus *does so.*

That's it.
GUS   What do we do now?
BEN   Blow into it.
GUS   Blow?
BEN   It whistles up there if you blow. Then they know you want to speak. Blow.

Gus *blows. Silence.*

GUS   (*tube at mouth*)   I can't hear a thing.
BEN   Now you speak! Speak into it!

Gus *looks at* BEN, *then speaks into the tube.*

GUS   The larder's bare!
BEN   Give me that!

He grabs the tube and puts it to his mouth.

(*Speaking with great deference.*) Good evening. I'm sorry to— bother you, but we just thought we'd better let you know that we haven't got anything left. We sent up all we had. There's no more food down here.

He brings the tube slowly to his ear.

What?

To mouth.

What?

To ear. He listens. To mouth.

No, all we had we sent up.

To ear. He listens. To mouth.

Oh, I'm very sorry to hear that.

To ear. He listens. To GUS.

The Eccles cake was stale.

He listens. To GUS.

The chocolate was melted.

He listens. To GUS.

The milk was sour.
GUS   What about the crisps?
BEN   (*listening*)   The biscuits were mouldy.

He glares at GUS. *Tube to mouth.*

Well, we're very sorry about that.

Tube to ear.

What?

To mouth.

What?

To ear.

Yes. Yes.

To mouth.

Yes certainly. Certainly. Right away.

To ear. The voice has ceased. He hangs up the tube.

(*Excitedly*).   Did you hear that?
GUS   What?
BEN   You know what he said? Light the kettle! Not put on the
kettle! Not light the gas! But light the kettle!
GUS   How can we light the kettle?
BEN   What do you mean?
GUS   There's no gas.
BEN   (*clapping hand to head*)   Now what do we do?
GUS   What did he want us to light the kettle for?
BEN   For tea. He wanted a cup of tea.

GUS   *He* wanted a cup of tea! What about me? I've been wanting a cup of tea all night!

BEN   (*despairingly*)   What do we do now?

GUS   What are we supposed to drink?

BEN *sits on his bed, staring.*

What about us?

BEN *sits.*

I'm thirsty too. I'm starving. And he wants a cup of tea. That beats the band, that does.

BEN *lets his head sink on to his chest.*

I could do with a bit of sustenance myself. What about you? You look as if you could do with something too.

GUS *sits on his bed.*

We send him up all we've got and he's not satisfied. No, honest, it's enough to make the cat laugh. Why did you send him up all that stuff? (*Thoughtfully.*) Why did I send it up?

Pause.

Who knows what he's got upstairs? He's probably got a salad bowl. They must have something up there. They won't get much from down here. You notice they didn't ask for any salads? They've probably got a salad bowl up there. Cold meat, radishes, cucumbers. Watercress. Roll mops.

Pause.

Hardboiled eggs.

Pause.

The lot. They've probably got a crate of beer too. Probably eating my crisps with a pint of beer now. Didn't have anything to say about those crisps, did he? They do all right, don't worry about that. You don't think they're just going to sit there and wait for stuff to come up from down here, do you? That'll get them nowhere.

Pause.

They do all right.

Pause.

And he wants a cup of tea.

Pause.

That's past a joke, in my opinion.

He looks over at BEN, *rises, and goes to him.*

What's the matter with you? You don't look too bright. I feel like an Alka-Seltzer myself.

BEN *sits up.*

BEN (*in a low voice*)   Time's getting on.
GUS   I know. I don't like doing a job on an empty stomach.
BEN (*wearily*)   Be quiet a minute. Let me give you your instructions.
GUS   What for? We always do it the same way, don't we?
BEN   Let me give you your instructions.

GUS *sighs and sits next to* BEN *on the bed. The instructions are stated and repeated automatically.*

When we get the call, you go over and stand behind the door.
GUS   Stand behind the door.
BEN   If there's a knock on the door you don't answer it.
GUS   If there's a knock on the door I don't answer it.
BEN   But there won't be a knock on the door.
GUS   So I won't answer it.
BEN   When the bloke comes in—
GUS   When the bloke comes in—
BEN   Shut the door behind him.
GUS   Shut the door behind him.
BEN   Without divulging your presence.
GUS   Without divulging my presence.
BEN   He'll see me and come towards me.
GUS   He'll see you and come towards you.
BEN   He won't see you.
GUS (*absently*)   Eh?
BEN   He won't see you.
GUS   He won't see me.
BEN   But he'll see me.
GUS   He'll see you.
BEN   He won't know you're there.
GUS   He won't know you're there.
BEN   He won't know *you're* there.
GUS   He won't know I'm there.
BEN   I take out my gun.
GUS   You take out your gun.

BEN He stops in his tracks.

GUS He stops in his tracks.

BEN If he turns round—

GUS If he turns round—

BEN You're there.

GUS I'm here.

BEN *frowns and presses his forehead.*

You've missed something out.

BEN I know. What?

GUS I haven't taken my gun out, according to you.

BEN You take your gun out—

GUS After I've closed the door.

BEN After you've closed the door.

GUS You've never missed that out before, you know that?

BEN When he sees you behind him—

GUS Me behind him—

BEN And me in front of him—

GUS And you in front of him—

BEN He'll feel uncertain—

GUS Uneasy.

BEN He won't know what to do.

GUS So what will he do?

BEN He'll look at me and he'll look at you.

GUS We won't say a word.

BEN We'll look at him.

GUS He won't say a word.

BEN He'll look at us.

GUS And we'll look at him.

BEN Nobody says a word.

Pause.

GUS What do we do if it's a girl?

BEN We do the same.

GUS Exactly the same?

BEN Exactly.

Pause.

GUS We don't do anything different?

BEN We do exactly the same.

GUS Oh.

GUS *rises, and shivers.*

Excuse me.

He exits through the door on the left. BEN *remains sitting on the bed, still. The lavatory chain is pulled once off left, but the lavatory does not flush. Silence.*

GUS *re-enters and stops inside the door, deep in thought. He looks at* BEN, *then walks slowly across to his own bed. He is troubled. He stands, thinking. He turns and looks at* BEN. *He moves a few paces towards him.*

(*Slowly in a low, tense voice.*) Why did he send us matches if he knew there was no gas?

Silence.

BEN *stares in front of him.* GUS *crosses to the left side of* BEN, *to the foot of his bed, to get to his other ear.*

Ben. Why did he send us matches if he knew there was no gas?

BEN *looks up.*

Why did he do that?

BEN   Who?

GUS   Who sent us those matches?

BEN   What are you talking about?

GUS *stares down at him.*

GUS (*thickly*)   Who is it upstairs?

BEN (*nervously*)   What's one thing to do with another?

GUS   Who is it, though?

BEN   What's one thing to do with another?

BEN *fumbles for his paper on the bed.*

GUS   I asked you a question.

BEN   Enough!

GUS (*with growing agitation*)   I asked you before. Who moved in? I asked you. You said the people who had it before moved out. Well, who moved in?

BEN (*hunched*)   Shut up.

GUS   I told you, didn't I?

BEN (*standing*)   Shut up!

GUS (*feverishly*)   I told you before who owned this place, didn't I? I told you.

BEN *hits him viciously on the shoulder.*

I told you who ran this place, didn't I?

BEN *hits him viciously on the shoulder.*

(*Violently.*) Well, what's he playing all these games for? That's what I want to know. What's he doing it for?

BEN What games?

GUS (*passionately, advancing*) What's he doing it for? We've been through our tests, haven't we? We got right through our tests, years ago, didn't we? We took them together, don't you remember, didn't we? We've proved ourselves before now, haven't we? We've always done our job. What's he doing all this for? What's the idea? What's he playing these games for?

The box in the shaft comes down behind them. The noise is this time accompanied by a shrill whistle, as it falls. GUS *rushes to the hatch and seizes the note.*

(*Reading.*) Scampi!

He crumples the note, picks up the tube, takes out the whistle, blows and speaks.

WE'VE GOT NOTHING LEFT! NOTHING! DO YOU UNDERSTAND?

BEN *seizes the tube and flings* GUS *away. He follows* GUS *and slaps him hard, back-handed, across the chest.*

BEN Stop it! You maniac!

GUS But you heard!

BEN (*savagely*) That's enough! I'm warning you!

Silence.
BEN *hangs the tube. He goes to his bed and lies down. He picks up his paper and reads.*
Silence.
The box goes up.
They turn quickly, their eyes meet. BEN *turns to his paper.*
Slowly GUS *goes back to his bed, and sits.*
Silence.
The hatch falls back into place.
They turn quickly, their eyes meet. BEN *turns back to his paper.*
Silence.
BEN *throws his paper down.*

BEN Kaw!

He picks up the paper and looks at it.

Listen to this!

Pause.

What about that, eh?

Pause.

Kaw!

Pause.

Have you ever heard such a thing?

GUS (*dully*) Go on!

BEN It's true.

GUS Get away.

BEN It's down here in black and white.

GUS (*very low*) Is that a fact?

BEN Can you imagine it.

GUS It's unbelievable.

BEN It's enough to make you want to puke, isn't it?

GUS (*almost inaudible*) Incredible.

BEN *shakes his head. He puts the paper down and rises. He fixes the revolver in his holster.*
GUS *stands up. He goes towards the door on the left.*

BEN Where are you going?

GUS I'm going to have a glass of water.

He exits. BEN *brushes dust off his clothes and shoes. The whistle in the speaking-tube blows. He goes to it, takes the whistle out and puts the tube to his ear. He listens. He puts it to his mouth.*

BEN Yes.

To ear. He listens. To mouth.

Straight away. Right.

To ear. He listens. To mouth.

Sure we're ready.

To ear. He listens. To mouth.

Understood. Repeat. He has arrived and will be coming in straight away. The normal method to be employed. Understood.

To ear. He listens. To mouth.

Sure we're ready.

To ear. He listens. To mouth.

Right.

He hangs the tube up.

Gus!

He takes out a comb and combs his hair, adjusts his jacket to diminish the bulge of the revolver. The lavatory flushes off left. BEN *goes quickly to the door, left.*

Gus!

The door right opens sharply. BEN *turns, his revolver levelled at the door.*
GUS *stumbles in.*
He is stripped of his jacket, waistcoat, tie, holster and revolver.
He stops, body stooping, his arms at his sides.
He raises his head and looks at BEN.
A long silence.
They stare at each other.

Curtain

SELECT BIBLIOGRAPHY

This is a highly selective bibliography designed to provide a list of basic references. No play anthologies are included. A number of these books are now out of print, but nearly every one can be found in standard library collections, and all of them are very pertinent to the study of dramatic literature. Many will have further bibliographies for additional reference.

Classical Drama

EPPS, PRESTON H. *The Poetics of Aristotle*. Chapel Hill, Univ. of N. C. Press, 1970.
There are many versions of *The Poetics*. This is a convenient and very readable one.

HAMILTON, EDITH. *The Greek Way*. New York, The New American Library, reprinted from Little, Brown edition, Boston, 1942.

HAMILTON, EDITH. *Mythology*, New York. The New American Library, 1953, reprinted from Little, Brown edition, Boston, 1942.
These are not about drama as such but are basic texts for the study of the Greek view of themselves, the gods, and tragedy. They are also fascinating reading.

KITTO, H. D. F. *Greek Tragedy*. Garden City, N. Y., Doubleday, 1954.

KOTT, JAN. *The Eating of the Gods: An Interpretation of Greek Tragedy*, New York, Vintage Books, Random House, 1974.

NORWOOD, GILBERT. *Greek Comedy*. New York, Hill & Wang Dramabook, 1963.

NORWOOD, GILBERT, *Greek Tragedy*. New York, Hill & Wang Dramabook, 1960.

Medieval Drama

NICOLL, ALLARDYCE. *Masks, Mimes, and Miracles*. New York, Cooper Square Publishers, 1963.
There is no better book than this, fully illustrated, to use in the study of the medieval drama and theatre.

Shakespeare

The books are, of course, legion. One of the most recent, which is fairly brief and very helpful in studying the theatre of the time is:

SMITH, WARREN D. *Shakespeare's Playhouse Practice*. Hanover, N. H., Univ. Press of New England, 1975.

The Restoration Drama

While it includes only Molière as an example of the high comedy technique so popular in the 17th century, the best book on the whole approach to the Restoration-18th Century Comedies of Manners, or Social Comedies, is:

KRUTCH, JOSEPH WOOD. *Comedy and Conscience after the Restoration*. New York, Columbia University Press, 1949.

The Modern Theatre and Drama

The following represent general histories which include discussions from the latter part of the 19th century until the present day. Single volumes on individual writers are so numerous, what with research anthologies, books of interpretation, and collections of various essays, that to list any of them would be impractical.

BROCKETT, OSCAR G., and ROBERT R. FINDLAY. *Century of Innovation: A History of European and American Theatre and Drama Since 1870*. Englewood Cliffs, N. J., Prentice-Hall, 1973.

DRIVER, TOM F. *Romantic Quest and Modern Query: A History of the Modern Theatre*. New York, Dell Publishing Co., 1970.

FREEDLEY, GEORGE, and JOHN A. REEVES. *A History of the Theatre*. New York, Crown Publishers, 1955.

GASSNER, JOHN. *Masters of the Drama*. New York, Dover, 1954.

KRUTCH, JOSEPH WOOD. *The American Drama Since 1918*. New York, George Braziller, 1957.

MACGOWAN, KENNETH, and WILLIAM MELNITZ. *The Living State: A History of the World Theater*. Englewood Cliffs, N. J., Prentice-Hall, 1955.

NICOLL, ALLARDYCE. *World Drama*. New York, Harcourt Brace, 1949.

VALENCY, MAURICE. *The Flower and the Castle: An Introduction to Modern Drama*. New York, Macmillan, 1963.

WILSON, GARFF B. *Three Hundred Years of American Drama and Theatre*. Englewood Cliffs, N. J., Prentice-Hall, 1973.

The Twayne's Author Series and the Prentice-Hall Twentieth Century Views and Twentieth Century Interpretations Series contain many books about specific authors and specific plays.

INDEX

Absurdism, 28, 871
Accretive plot, 13
Action
  falling, 14
  rising, 13
  unity of, 275
Aesthetic distance, 11
Agon, 12
Alienation, theatre of, 671
Antagonist, 13
Anticlimax, 14
Argument, 12
Aristotle, 4, 5, 12, 13, 18, 20
Attack, point of, 13
Audience, 9

Bergson, Henri, 22

Catastrophe, 14
Catharsis, 18
Character, 5
Classic style, 23
Climactic plot, 13
Climax, 14
Closet drama, 7
Coleridge, Samuel Taylor, 10
Comedy
  defined, 20
  drawing room, 21
  high, 21
  low, 21
  of manners, 21
  New Greek, 276
  Old Greek, 77
  of sensibility, 21
  social, 21
  "straight," 21
  tragi-comedy, 16

Complications, 13
Conclusion, 14
Conflict, 13
Cycles, 125

Denouement, 14
Detached point of view, 20
Dionysus, Festival of, 16, 77
Director, 8
Drama
  closet, 7
  defined, 3
  literate, 7
  Medieval, 125
  type of, 3
Dramatic literature, 7
Dramatist, 3
Drame, 20
Drawing room comedy, 21

Elizabethan style, 22
Empathy, 10
Ensemble acting, 436
Epic style, 671
Exposition, 13
Expressionism, 27

Fable, 4
Falling action, 14
Farce, 21
Festival of Dionysus, 16, 77
Flaw, tragic, 19
Form, 13
French Renaissance style, 275

Genre, middle, 20

Greek comedy
  New, 276
  Old, 77

High comedy, 21
Historical play, 15
House of Thebes, 31
Hubris, 19

Idea, 3
Impressionism, 28
Indicant, 5
Irony, 19

Literate drama, 7
Liturgical drama, 125
Low comedy, 21

Manners, comedy of, 21
Martyr, 17
Medieval drama, 125
Melodrama, 19
Middle genre, 20
Miracle play, 125
Mise-en-scène, 8
Mystery play, 125

Nativity play, 126
Naturalism, 26
Naturalistic style, 26
Neo-classical revival, 275
New Comedy, 276

Obligatory scene, 14
Old Comedy, 77
Oresteia, The, 31, 618

Parabasis, 77
Pastoral, 15
Phallus, 77
Pity, 18
Place, unity of, 275
Play
  defined, 3
  Nativity, 126
  "well made," 14
Playwright, 3
Plot
  accretive, 13
  climactic, 13
  defined, 4
Poetics, The, 4, 20
Point of attack, 13
Protagonist, 13, 17
Purgation, 18

Realism, 25
Realistic style, 25
Restoration style, 22
Rising action, 13
Romantic style, 23

Sensibility, comedy of, 21
Social comedy, 21
Spectacle, 8
Story, 4
"Straight" comedy, 21
"Straight" drama, 20
Structure, 13
Style
  classic, 23
  defined, 3, 22
  Elizabethan, 22
  epic, 671
  French Renaissance, 275
  naturalistic, 26
  realistic, 25
  Restoration, 22
  romantic, 23

Stylization
 absurdism, 28
 defined, 27
 expressionism, 27
 impressionism, 28
 "suspension of disbelief," 10

Terror, 18
Theatre
 of the absurd, 871
 of alienation, 671
 defined, 7
Thebes, House of, 31
Theme, 3
Three Unities, 275

Time
 limits of, 4
 unity of, 275
Tragedy, 16
Tragi-comedy, 16
Tragic flaw, 19
Tragic protagonist, 17
Tropes, 125
Type of drama, 3

Unities, Three, 275

Wakefield Cycle, 126
"Well-made" play, 14